ÉCRITS

BY JACQUES LACAN

Television

Feminine Sexuality

The Seminar of Jacques Lacan, edited by Jacques-Alain Miller

Book I, Freud's Papers on Technique, 1953–1954

Book II, The Ego in Freud's Theory and in the Technique of Psychoanalysis, 1954–1955

Book III, The Psychoses, 1955–1956

Book VII, The Ethics of Psychoanalysis, 1959–1960

Book XI, The Four Fundamental Concepts of Psychoanalysis, 1964

Book XX, On Feminine Sexuality, the Limits of Love and Knowledge, 1972–1973 (Encore)

JACQUES LACAN

ÉCRITS

THE FIRST COMPLETE EDITION IN ENGLISH

TRANSLATED BY

BRUCE FINK

IN COLLABORATION WITH

HÉLOÏSE FINK

AND

RUSSELL GRIGG

W. W. NORTON & COMPANY

New York • London

Printed in the United States of America

For information about permission to reproduce selections from this book, write to Permissions, W. W. Norton & Company, Inc., 500 Fifth Avenue, New York, NY 10110

Manufacturing by LSC Harrisonburg
Book design by Rhea Braunstein
Production manager: Julia Druskin

Library of Congress Cataloging-in-Publication Data

Lacan, Jacques, 1901–
[Ecrits. English]
Ecrits : the first complete edition in English / Jacques Lacan ; translated by Bruce Fink in collaboration with Héloïse Fink and Russell Grigg.
p. cm.
Includes bibliographical references and index.
ISBN 0-393-06115-9 (hardcover)
1. Psychoanalysis. I. Fink, Bruce, 1956– II. Title.
BF173.L14213 2005
150.19'5—dc22

2005014598

ISBN-13: 978-0-393-32925-4 pbk.
ISBN-10: 0-393-32925-9 pbk.

W. W. Norton & Company, Inc., 500 Fifth Avenue, New York, N.Y. 10110
www.wwnorton.com

W. W. Norton & Company Ltd., 15 Carlisle Street, London W1D 3BS

5 6 7 8 9 0

Table of Contents

III

IV

V

Acknowledgments

My work on this translation received support from several quarters: from Jacques-Alain Miller, the general editor of Lacan's work in France and head of the École de la Cause Freudienne, who approved the project back in 1994; from the National Endowment for the Humanities, which committed $90,000 over the course of three years to prepare this new translation; from the Society for the Humanities at Cornell University, where I was a fellow during the 1997–1998 academic year and released from my usual teaching and administrative responsibilities; and last but far from least, from Duquesne University, where I teach, which provided financial backing for several years of the project and generously reduced my teaching load on a number of occasions. At Duquesne I would especially like to thank Drs. Russell Walsh, Constance Ramirez, Andrea Lex, William Fischer, and the late Michael Weber for their unfailing efforts on my behalf.

Translator's Note

The translation provided here includes all 35 of the texts published in the complete French edition of Lacan's *Écrits* (Paris: Éditions du Seuil, 1966), only nine of which were included in *Écrits: A Selection* (New York and London: Norton, 2002). About half of these texts have never come out in English before, and the translation supplied here for each text is entirely new.

Given the degree to which Lacan's texts have been—and will continue to be, I suspect—subjected to close readings, I have been careful to respect his terminology as much as possible. I have translated here with the notion that the repetition of terms from one sentence to the next, from one paragraph to the next, and from one text to the next, may be springboards for future interpretations and have attempted to either repeat them identically in the translation or at least provide the French in brackets or endnotes so that the repetition is not lost.

All paragraph breaks here correspond to Lacan's, and the original French pagination is included in the margins to facilitate comparison with the French text, referred to throughout as "*Écrits* 1966." The footnotes included at the end of each text are Lacan's, several of which were added in the smaller two-volume edition published in the Points collection by Seuil in 1970 and 1971 as *Écrits I* and *Écrits II*, referred to throughout simply as "Points." Words or phrases followed by an asterisk (*) are given by Lacan in English in the French original. Translator's interpolations are always placed in square brackets and translator's notes are included at the back of the book, keyed to the marginal French pagination.

Although the texts are placed in chronological order for the most part, they were written for very different occasions and audiences and need not be read in any specific order (indeed, I'd recommend starting with "Seminar on 'The Purloined Letter,'" "The Situation of Psychoanalysis in 1956," or "Function and Field"). It might be helpful to keep in mind that the first few pages of many of the texts are far more difficult than what follows, and that the persistent reader is usually well rewarded (the last few pages are often quite dense as well!). Should the English sometimes strike the reader as obscure, I can only point to the difficulty of the French original and indicate that I have already removed as many obscurities as I could at this time.

Collaborators

Héloïse Fink was a constant collaborator throughout this project, hashing out difficult formulations and constructions with me day in and day out, comparing the French and English line by line, and researching obscure terms and expressions. She helped me avoid myriad pitfalls, and together we explored the ways in which two languages encounter and miss each other.

Russell Grigg, psychoanalyst and professor of philosophy at Deakin University in Australia, provided innumerable corrections, alternative readings, and recommendations concerning style on the basis of his close comparison of the French and English texts. He made a very substantial contribution to the finished product.

A number of other people helped me struggle with Lacan's texts on a more occasional basis. Jacques-Alain Miller graciously devoted a couple of afternoons to helping me with some of Lacan's more difficult formulations and responded to further questions in writing; Dany Nobus commented extensively on the entire translation, providing myriad corrections, small and large, and hundreds of references; Slavoj Zizek advised me on a number of Hegelian references; Richard Klein (Cornell University) supplied insight into several passages; Henry Sullivan (University of Missouri-Columbia) provided useful comments on "The Mirror Stage"; Stacey E. Levine (Duquesne University) checked the mathematical footnote in "Position of the Unconscious"; Marc Silver collaborated on a draft of "Logical Time" that we published in 1988 and made valuable suggestions regarding "Function and Field"; Mario Beira gave helpful feedback on "Direction of the Treatment"; Yael Goldman, Matt Baldwin, Naoki Nishikawa, Dan Collins, Rong-Bang Peng, Slawomir Maslon, and Thomas Svolos provided a number of references; Cristina Laurita went through the manuscript with a fine-tooth comb; and Anette Schwarz and Suzanne Stewart assisted me with several Latin phrases. Margot Backas at the National Endowment for the Humanities and Susan Buck-Morss at Cornell University supported this project in more ways than one.

I have also looked to several published sources for help with references, including Anthony Wilden's early translation of Lacan's "The Function and Field of Speech and Language in Psychoanalysis" in *The Language of the Self* (Baltimore: Johns Hopkins University Press, 1975), William Richardson and John Muller's *Lacan and Language* (New York: International Universities Press, 1982) and their edited collection *The Purloined Poe* (Baltimore: The Johns Hopkins University Press, 1988), James Swenson's translation of "Kant with Sade" in *October* 51 (1989), and Alan Sheridan's 1977 version of *Écrits: A Selection*. The first four provide far more notes than I could include here and readers may find their additional notes helpful. I have checked the notes I have borrowed for further corroboration and my judgment will sometimes be seen to differ from theirs.

Despite input from several collaborators and consultation of varied sources (my favorites being the recent *Robert: Dictionnaire historique de la langue française* and the voluminous *Trésor de la langue française*), numerous errors no doubt remain. Lacan's incredibly broad background and in-depth knowledge of psychiatry, psychoanalysis, philosophy, mathematics, and literature are such that I have surely misunderstood specialized terminology, overlooked references to specific authors, and just generally misinterpreted the French—Lord knows it's easy enough to do given Lacan's singular style! Readers who believe they have found mistakes of whatever kind are encouraged to send comments to me via the publisher. I consider this translation a work in progress, and hope to improve on the texts here in future editions. A small number of typos found in the 2002 version of *Écrits: A Selection* have been fixed here, and a few footnotes to the texts included in it have been corrected and several other footnotes have been added.

Bruce Fink

Abbreviations Used in the Text

GW	*Gesammelte Werke* (Sigmund Freud)
IJP	*International Journal of Psycho-Analysis*
IPA	International Psycho-Analytical Association
PQ	*Psychoanalytic Quarterly*
PUF	Presses Universitaires de France
RFP	*Revue Française de Psychanalyse*
SE	*Standard Edition of the Complete Psychological Works of Sigmund Freud*

ÉCRITS

I

Overture to this Collection

9

"The style is the man himself," people repeat without seeing any harm in it, and without worrying about the fact that man is no longer so sure a reference point. Besides, the image of the cloth that adorned Buffon while he wrote is there to keep us inattentive.

A re-edition of *Voyage à Montbard* (published posthumously in the year IX by the Solvet press), penned by Hérault de Séchelles—the title alters that of the edition published in 1785, *Visite à Buffon*—gives us pause for thought. Not simply because one finds in it another style, which prefigures the best of our buffoonish reporting, but because it resituates the saying itself in a context of impertinence in which the host is in no wise outdone by his guest.

For the man discussed in the adage—which was already classic by that time [1785], having been extracted from Buffon's discourse to the Academy—proves, in Séchelles' portrait, to be a fantasy of the great man, Buffon turning it into a scenario that involves his whole household. There is nothing natural here; Voltaire generalizes maliciously on this point, as we recall.

Shall we adopt the formulation—the style is the man—if we simply add to it: the man one addresses?

This would be simply to comply with the principle I have proposed: that in language our message comes to us from the Other, and—to state the rest of the principle—in an inverted form. (Let me remind you that this principle applied to its own enunciation since, although I proposed it, it received its finest formulation from another, an eminent interlocutor.)

But if man were reduced to being nothing but the echoing locus of our discourse, wouldn't the question then come back to us, "What is the point of addressing our discourse to him?"

That is the question posed to me by the new reader, this reader being the reason that has been put forward to convince me to publish a collection of my writings.

I am offering this reader an easy entryway into my style by opening this collection with "The Purloined Letter," even though that means taking it out of chronological order.

10 It will be up to this reader to give the letter in question, beyond those to whom it was one day addressed, the very thing he will find as its concluding word: its destination. Namely, Poe's message deciphered and returning from him, the reader, so that in reading this message he realizes that he is no more feigned than the truth is when it inhabits fiction.

This "purloining of the letter" [*vol de la lettre*] will be said to be the parody of my discourse, whether one confines one's attention to the etymology of "parody," which indicates an accompaniment and implies the precedence of the trajectory that is parodied, or, in returning to the usual meaning of the term, one sees the shadow of the intellectual master dispelled in it in order to obtain the effect that I prefer to it.

The title of the poem "The Rape of the Lock"* [*le vol de la boucle*] is evoked here in which Pope, thanks to parody, ravishes—from the epic, in his case—the secret feature of its derisory stakes.

Our task brings back this charming lock, in the topological sense of the term [*boucle* also means loop]: a knot whose trajectory closes on the basis of its inverted redoubling—namely, such as I have recently formulated it as sustaining the subject's structure.

It is here that my students would be right to recognize the "already" for which they sometimes content themselves with less well-founded homologies.

For I decipher here in Poe's fiction, which is so powerful in the mathematical sense of the term, the division in which the subject is verified in the fact that an object traverses him without them interpenetrating in any respect, this division being at the crux of what emerges at the end of this collection that goes by the name of object *a* (to be read: little *a*).

It is the object that (cor)responds to the question about style that I am raising right at the outset. In the place man marked for Buffon, I call for the falling away [*chute*] of this object, which is revealing due to the fact that the fall isolates this object, both as the cause of desire in which the subject disappears and as sustaining the subject between truth and knowledge. With this itinerary, of which these writings are the milestones, and this style, which the audience to whom they were addressed required, I want to lead the reader to a consequence in which he must pay the price with elbow grease.

October 1966

11

Seminar on "The Purloined Letter"

Und wenn es uns glückt,
Und wenn es sich schickt,
So sind es Gedanken.

My research has led me to the realization that repetition automatism (*Wiederholungszwang*) has its basis in what I have called the *insistence* of the signifying chain. I have isolated this notion as a correlate of the *ex-sistence* (that is, of the eccentric place) in which we must necessarily locate the subject of the unconscious, if we are to take Freud's discovery seriously. As we know, it is in the experience inaugurated by psychoanalysis that we can grasp by what oblique imaginary means the *symbolic* takes hold in even the deepest recesses of the human organism.

The teaching of this seminar is designed to maintain that imaginary effects, far from representing the core of analytic experience, give us nothing of any consistency unless they are related to the symbolic chain that binds and orients them.

I am, of course, aware of the importance of imaginary impregnations (*Prägung*) in the partializations of the symbolic alternative that give the signifying chain its appearance. Nevertheless, I posit that it is the law specific to this chain which governs the psychoanalytic effects that are determinant for the subject—effects such as foreclosure (*Verwerfung*), repression (*Verdrängung*), and negation (*Verneinung*) itself—and I add with the appropriate emphasis that these effects follow the displacement (*Entstellung*) of the signifier so faithfully that imaginary factors, despite their inertia, figure only as shadows and reflections therein.

But this emphasis would be lavished in vain if it merely served, in your view, to abstract a general form from phenomena whose particularity in analytic experience would remain the core thing to you and whose original composite nature could be broken down only through artifice.

12 This is why I have decided to illustrate for you today a truth which may be drawn from the moment in Freud's thought we have been studying—namely, that it is the symbolic order which is constitutive for the subject—by demonstrating in a story the major determination the subject receives from the itinerary of a signifier.

It is this truth, let us note, that makes the very existence of fiction possible. Thus a fable is as appropriate as any other story for shedding light on it—provided we are willing to put the fable's coherence to the test. With this proviso, a fable even has the advantage of manifesting symbolic necessity all more purely in that we might be inclined to believe it is governed by the arbitrary.

This is why, without looking any further, I have taken my example from the very story in which we find the dialectic of the game of "even or odd," from which we very recently gleaned something of importance. It is probably no accident that this story proved propitious for the continuation of a line of research which had already relied upon it.

As you know, I am referring to the tale Baudelaire translated into French as "La lettre volée." In it we must immediately distinguish between a drama and its narration as well as the conditions of that narration.

We quickly perceive, moreover, what makes these components necessary and realize that their composer could not have created them unintentionally.

For the narration effectively doubles the drama with a commentary without which no *mise-en-scène* would be possible. Let us say that the action would remain, strictly speaking, invisible to the audience—aside from the fact that the dialogue would be expressly and by dramatic necessity devoid of whatever meaning it might have for a listener. In other words, nothing of the drama could appear, either in the framing of the images or the sampling of the sounds, without the oblique light shed, so to speak, on each scene by the narration from the point of view that one of the actors had while playing his role in it.

There are two such scenes, the first of which I shall immediately designate as the primal scene, and by no means inattentively, since the second may be considered its repetition in the sense of the latter term that I have been articulating in this very seminar.

13 The primal scene is thus performed, we are told, in the royal boudoir, such that we suspect that the "personage of most exalted station," also referred to as the "illustrious personage," who is alone there when she receives a letter, is the Queen. This sense is confirmed by the awkward situation she is put in "by the entrance of the other exalted personage," of whom we have already

been told prior to this account that, were he to come to know of the letter in question, it would jeopardize for the lady nothing less than her "honor and peace." Any doubt that he is in fact the King is promptly dissipated in the course of the scene which begins with the entrance of Minister D—. For at that moment the Queen can do no better than to take advantage of the King's inattentiveness by leaving the letter on the table turned face down, "address uppermost." This does not, however, escape the Minister's lynx eye, nor does he fail to notice the Queen's distress and thus to fathom her secret. From then on everything proceeds like clockwork. After dealing with the business of the day with his customary speed and intelligence, the Minister draws from his pocket a letter similar in appearance to the one before his eyes and, after pretending to read it, places it next to the other. A bit more conversation to pull the wool over the royal eyes, whereupon he picks up the embarrassing letter without flinching and decamps, while the Queen, on whom none of his maneuver has been lost, remains unable to intervene for fear of attracting the attention of her royal spouse, who is standing at her elbow at that very moment.

An ideal spectator might have noticed nothing of this operation in which no one batted an eye, and whose *quotient* is that the Minister has filched from the Queen her letter and, even more important, that the Queen knows that he now has it, and by no means innocently.

A *remainder* that no analyst will neglect, trained as he is to remember everything having to do with the signifier even if he does not always know what to do with it: the letter, left on hand by the Minister, which the Queen is now free to crumple up.

Second scene: in the Minister's office at the Ministerial hotel. We know from the account the Prefect of Police has given Dupin, whose genius for solving enigmas Poe mentions here for the second time, that the police have searched the hotel and its surroundings from top to bottom for the last three months, returning there as often as the Minister's regular absences at night allow them
14 to. In vain, however, although anyone can deduce from the situation that the Minister keeps the letter within easy reach.

Dupin calls on the Minister. The latter greets him with a show of nonchalance, affecting in his conversation romantic ennui. Meanwhile Dupin, who is not taken in by this feigning, inspects the premises, his eyes protected by green spectacles. When his gaze alights upon a very chafed letter—which seems to have been abandoned in a compartment of a wretched, eye-catching, trumpery card-rack of pasteboard, hanging right smack in the middle of the mantelpiece—he already knows that he has found what he was looking for.

His conviction is reinforced by the very details which seem designed to contradict the description he has been given of the stolen letter, with the exception of the size, which fits.

Whereupon he has but to take his leave, after having "forgotten" his snuffbox on the table, in order to return the following day to reclaim it—armed with a facsimile of the letter in its present state. When an incident out in the street, prepared for the right moment, draws the Minister to the window, Dupin seizes the opportunity to snatch, in his turn, the letter while replacing it with an imitation [*semblant*], and need but maintain the appearances of a normal exit thereafter.

Here too all has transpired, if not without any sound, at least without any din. The quotient of the operation is that the Minister no longer has the letter, but he knows nothing of it and is far from suspecting that it is Dupin who ravished it from him. Moreover, what he is left with here is far from insignificant for what follows. I shall return later to what led Dupin to jot something down on his factitious letter. In any case, when the Minister tries to make use of it, he will be able to read the following words, whose source, Dupin tells us, is Crébillon's *Atrée,* written so that he may recognize Dupin's hand:

Un dessein si funeste
S'il n'est digne d'Atrée, est digne de Thyeste.

Need I emphasize the resemblance between these two actions? Yes, for the similarity I have in mind is not made up of the simple union of traits chosen only in order to prepare [*appareiller*] their difference. And it would not suffice to retain the traits of resemblance at the expense of the others for any truth whatsoever to result therefrom. It is, rather, the intersubjectivity by which the two actions are motivated that I wish to highlight, as well as the three terms 15
with which that intersubjectivity structures them.

These terms derive their privileged status from the fact that they correspond both to the three logical moments through which decision is precipitated and to the three places which this decision assigns to the subjects that it separates out.

This decision is reached in the moment of a glance [*regard*].[1] For the maneuvers that follow, however stealthily that moment is prolonged in them, add nothing to it, no more than their deferral of the opportunity in the second scene disrupts the unity of that moment.

This glance presupposes two others, which it assembles to provide a view of the opening left in their fallacious complementarity, anticipating there the plunder afforded by that uncovering. Thus three moments, ordering three glances, sustained by three subjects, incarnated in each case by different people.

The first is based on a glance that sees nothing: the King and then the police.

The second is based on a glance which sees that the first sees nothing and deceives itself into thereby believing to be covered what it hides: the Queen and then the Minister.

The third is based on a glance which sees that the first two glances leave what must be hidden uncovered to whomever would seize it: the Minister and finally Dupin.

In order to get you to grasp in its unity the intersubjective complex thus described, I would willingly seek patronage for it in the technique legendarily attributed to the ostrich [*autruche*] when it seeks shelter from danger. For this technique might finally be qualified as political, distributed as it is here among three partners, the second believing himself invisible because the first has his head stuck in the sand, all the while letting the third calmly pluck his rear. We need but enrich its proverbial denomination by a letter, producing *la politique de l'autruiche*, for this technique in itself to finally take on a new everlasting meaning.

Having thus established the intersubjective module of the action that repeats, we must now indicate in it a *repetition automatism* in the sense that interests us in Freud's work.

16 The fact that we have here a plurality of subjects can, of course, in no way constitute an objection to those who are long accustomed to the perspectives summarized by my formulation: *the unconscious is the Other's discourse*. I will not remind you now what the notion of the *inmixing of subjects*, recently introduced in my reanalysis of the dream of Irma's injection, adds here.

What interests me today is the way in which the subjects, owing to their displacement, relay each other in the course of the intersubjective repetition.

We shall see that their displacement is determined by the place that a pure signifier—the purloined letter—comes to occupy in their trio. This is what will confirm for us that it is repetition automatism.

It does not, however, seem superfluous, before pursuing this line of inquiry, to ask whether the aim of the tale and the interest we take in it—inasmuch as they coincide—do not lie elsewhere.

Can we consider the fact that the tale is told to us as a mystery story to be a simple "rationalization," as we say in our crude jargon?

In truth, we would be justified in considering this to be highly dubious, noting as we do that everything about a crime or offense that creates such a mystery—its nature and motives, instruments and execution, the procedure used to discover its author, and the means employed to convict him for it—is carefully eliminated here at the beginning of each episode.

Indeed, the act of deceit is as clearly known from the outset as the plotting of the culprit and its effects on his victim. The problem, as it is exposed to us, is limited to the search for the deceitfully acquired object, for the purposes of restitution; and it seems quite intentional that the solution is already known when it is explained to us. Is that how we are kept in suspense? However much credit we may give the conventions of a genre for arousing a specific interest in the reader, we should not forget that the "Dupin tale"—this being the second to come out—is a prototype, and that since it receives its genre only from the first, it is a little too early for the author to play on a convention.

It would, however, be equally excessive to reduce the whole thing to a fable 17
whose moral would be that, in order to shelter from inquisitive eyes correspondence whose secrecy is sometimes necessary to conjugal peace, it suffices to leave the letters lying around on one's table, even if one turns them signifying face down. For that would be a lure which, personally, I would never recommend anyone try, lest he be disappointed at having trusted in it.

Is there then no other mystery here than incompetence resulting in failure on the part of the Prefect of Police? Is there not a certain discordance on Dupin's part, which we are loath to admit, between the assuredly penetrating remarks (which are not, however, always absolutely relevant when generalized) with which he introduces us to his method and the way in which he in fact intervenes?

Were we to pursue a bit further our sense that we are being hoodwinked, we might soon begin to wonder whether—from the inaugural scene, which only the rank of the protagonists saves from degenerating into vaudeville, to the descent into ridicule that seems to await the Minister at the story's conclusion—it is not, indeed, the fact that everyone is duped which gives us such pleasure here.

I would be all the more inclined to think so in that, along with my readers, I would find anew here the definition I once gave, somewhere in passing, of the modern hero, "represented by ridiculous feats in situations of confusion."[2]

But are we ourselves not taken with the imposing bearing of the amateur detective, prototype of a new kind of braggart, as yet safe from the insipidity of our contemporary superman*?

That was a joke, yet it makes us note, by way of contrast, so perfect a verisimilitude in this tale that it may be said that truth here reveals its fictional ordering.

For this is certainly the pathway along which the reasons for this verisimilitude lead us. Entering first into its procedure, we perceive, in effect, a new

drama that I would call complementary to the first, since the first was what is
18 termed a silent drama whereas the interest of the second plays on the properties of discourse.[3]

Indeed, while it is obvious that each of the two scenes of the real drama is narrated in the course of a different dialogue, one must be provided with certain notions brought out in my teaching to realize that this is not done simply to make the exposition more pleasing, but that the dialogues themselves, in the opposite use they make of the virtues of speech, take on a tension that makes them into a different drama, one which my terminology will distinguish from the first as sustaining itself in the symbolic order.

The first dialogue—between the Prefect of Police and Dupin—is played out as if it were between a deaf man and one who hears. That is, it represents the veritable complexity of what is ordinarily simplified, with the most confused of results, in the notion of communication.

This example demonstrates how communication can give the impression, at which theorists too often stop, of conveying in its transmission but one meaning, as though the highly significant commentary into which he who hears integrates it could be considered neutralized because it is unperceived by he who does not hear.

The fact remains that if we only retain the dialogue's meaning as a report, its verisimilitude appears to depend on a guarantee of accuracy. But the report then turns out to be more fruitful than it seems, provided we demonstrate its procedure, as we shall see by confining our attention to the recounting of the first scene.

For the double and even triple subjective filter through which that scene comes to us—a narration by Dupin's close friend (whom I will refer to henceforth as the story's general narrator) of the account by which the Prefect reveals to Dupin the version the Queen gave him of it—is not merely the consequence of a fortuitous arrangement.

If, indeed, the extremity to which the original narrator is reduced precludes
19 her altering any of the events, we would be wrong to believe that the Prefect is authorized to lend her his voice here only owing to the lack of imagination for which he holds, as it were, the patent.

The fact that the message is retransmitted in this way assures us of something that is absolutely not self-evident: that the message truly belongs to the dimension of language.

Those who are here are familiar with my remarks on the subject, specifically those illustrated by the counterexample of the supposed language of bees, in which a linguist[4] can see nothing more than a signaling of the location of objects—in other words, an imaginary function that is simply more differentiated than the others.

Let me emphasize here that such a form of communication is not absent in man, however evanescent the natural pregivenness [*donné naturel*] of objects may be for him due to the disintegration they undergo through his use of symbols.

Something equivalent may, in effect, be grasped in the communion established between two people in their hatred directed at a common object, with the proviso that this can never occur except in the case of one single object, an object defined by the characteristics of (the) being that each of the two refuses to accept.

But such communication is not transmittable in symbolic form. It can only be sustained in relation to this object. This is why it can bring together an indefinite number of subjects in a common “ideal”; the communication of one subject with another within the group thus constituted will nonetheless remain irreducibly mediated by an ineffable relation.

This excursion is not merely a reminder here of principles distantly addressed to those who tax me with neglecting nonverbal communication; in determining the scope of what discourse repeats, it prepares the question of what symptoms repeat.

Thus the indirect relating [of the first scene] clarifies the dimension of language, and the general narrator, by redoubling it, “hypothetically” adds nothing to it. But this is not at all true of his role in the second dialogue.

For the latter is opposed to the first like the poles in language that I have 20
distinguished elsewhere and that are opposed to each other like word to speech.

Which is to say that we shift here from the field of accuracy to the register of truth. Now this register—I dare think I need not go back over this—is situated somewhere else altogether: at the very foundation of intersubjectivity. It is situated where the subject can grasp nothing but the very subjectivity that constitutes an Other as an absolute. I shall confine my attention, in order to indicate its place here, to evoking the dialogue which seems to me to warrant its attribution as a Jewish joke due to the nakedness with which the relation between the signifier and speech appears in the entreaty which brings it to a head: “Why are you lying to me?” one character exclaims exasperatedly, “Yes, why are you lying to me by saying you’re going to Cracow in order to make me believe you’re going to Lemberg, when in reality you *are* going to Cracow?”

A similar question might be raised in our minds by the torrent of aporias, eristic enigmas, paradoxes, and even quips presented to us as an introduction to Dupin’s method if the fact that they were confided to us by a would-be disciple did not add some virtue to them, owing to the act of delegation. Such is the unmistakable prestige of legacies: the witness' faithfulness is the wool pulled over the eyes of those who might criticize his testimony.

What could be more convincing, moreover, than the gesture of turning one's cards face up on the table? It is so convincing that we are momentarily persuaded that the prestidigitator has in fact demonstrated, as he promised he would, how his trick was performed, whereas he has only performed it anew in a purer form; this moment makes us appreciate the supremacy of the signifier in the subject.

This is how Dupin operates when he starts with the story of the child prodigy who takes in all his classmates at the game of even or odd with his trick of identifying with his opponent, concerning which I have shown that he cannot reach the first level of its mental elaboration—namely, the notion of intersubjective alternation—without immediately being tripped up by the stop of its recurrence.[5]

This does not stop us from being treated—in order to dazzle us—to the
21 names of La Rochefoucauld, La Bruyère, Machiavelli, and Campanella, whose reputations now seem trivial compared to the child's prowess.

And then to Chamfort, whose maxim that "the odds are that every idea embraced by the public, every accepted convention, is foolish, since it suits the greatest number" will indubitably satisfy all those who think they escape its law, that is, precisely, the greatest number. The fact that Dupin taxes the French with dishonesty when they apply the word "analysis" to algebra has little chance of threatening our pride when, moreover, the freeing of that term for other ends implies nothing that should stop a psychoanalyst from considering himself in a position to assert his rights to it. And off he goes making philological remarks which should positively delight lovers of Latin; when he recalls without deigning to say any more about it that " '*ambitus*' [doesn't imply] 'ambition,' '*religio*' 'religion,' '*homines honesti*' a set of *honorable* men," who among you would not take pleasure in remembering . . . what these words mean to assiduous readers of Cicero and Lucretius? No doubt Poe is having a good time . . .

But a suspicion dawns on us: isn't this display of erudition designed to make us hear the magic words of our drama?[6] Isn't the prestidigitator repeating his trick before our eyes, without deluding us into thinking that he is divulging his secret to us this time, but taking his gamble even further by really shedding light on it for us without us seeing a thing? That would be the height of the illusionist's art: to have one of his fictional beings *truly fool us*.

And isn't it such effects which justify our harmless way of referring to many imaginary heroes as real personages?

Thus, when we are open to hearing the way in which Martin Heidegger uncovers for us in the word *alethes* the play of truth, we merely rediscover a secret to which truth has always initiated her lovers, and through which they have learned that it is in hiding that she offers herself to them *most truly*.

Thus, even if Dupin's comments did not defy us so blatantly to lend cre- 22
dence to them [*y fier*], we would still have to make this attempt against the opposite temptation.

Let us thus detect his track [*dépistons sa foulée*] where it throws us off track [*dépiste*].[7] And first of all in the criticism by which he explains the Prefect's lack of success. We already saw it surface in those furtive gibes the Prefect, in the first conversation with Dupin, paid no mind, finding in them only a pretext for hilarity. The fact that it is, as Dupin insinuates, because a problem is too simple, indeed too self-evident, that it may appear obscure, will never have any more impact on him than a somewhat vigorous rub of the ribcage.

Everything is done to make us believe he is an imbecile. This is powerfully articulated in the claim that he and his henchmen will never conceive of anything beyond what an ordinary rascal might imagine for hiding an object—that is, precisely the all-too-well-known series of extraordinary hiding places, running the gamut from hidden desk drawers to removable tabletops, from the unstitched upholstery of chairs to their hollowed-out legs, and from the back side of the quicksilvering of mirrors to the thickness of book bindings.

This gives way to making fun of the Prefect's error when he deduces that because the Minister is a poet, he is only one remove from a fool, an error, it is argued, that simply consists, although this is hardly negligible, in a *non distributio medii*, since it is far from following from the fact that all fools are poets.

Yes indeed. But we ourselves are left to err regarding what constitutes the poet's superiority in the art of concealment—even if he turns out to be a mathematician to boot—since we suddenly lose whatever momentum we had when we are dragged into a thicket of unprovoked arguments directed against the reasoning of mathematicians, who have never, to my knowledge, showed such devotion to their formulas as to identify them with reasoning reason. At least,
let me bear witness to the fact that, unlike what seems to be Poe's experience, 23
I occasionally hazard such serious mischief (virtual blasphemy, according to Poe) before my friend Riguet—whose presence here guarantees you that my incursions into combinatorial analysis do not lead us astray—as to question whether perhaps "$x^2 + px$ is *not* altogether equal to q," without ever (here I refute Poe) having to fend off any unexpected attack.

Isn't so much intelligence being expended then simply to divert our attention from what had been indicated earlier as given, namely, that the police have looked *everywhere*? We were to understand this—regarding the field in which the police, not without reason, assumed the letter must be found—in the sense of an exhaustion of space, which is no doubt theoretical but which we are expected to take literally if the story is to have its piquancy. The division of the entire surface into numbered "compartments," which was the principle governing the operation, is presented to us as so accurate that "the fiftieth part of a line," it is said, could not escape the probing of the investigators. Are we not then within our rights to ask how it happened that the letter was not found *anywhere*, or rather to observe that nothing we are told about a higher-caliber conception of concealment ultimately explains how the letter managed to escape detection, since the field exhaustively combed did in fact contain it, as Dupin's discovery eventually proved?

Must the letter then, of all objects, have been endowed with the property of "nullibiety," to use a term which the well-known *Roget's Thesaurus* picks up from the semiological utopia of Bishop Wilkins?[8]

It is evident ("a little *too* self-evident")[9] that the letter has, in effect, relations with location [*le lieu*] for which no French word has the entire import of the English adjective "odd." *Bizarre*, by which Baudelaire regularly translates it into French, is only approximate. Let us say that these relations are *singuliers* (singular), for they are the very same ones that the signifier maintains with location.

24 You realize that my intention is not to turn them into "subtle" relations, that my aim is not to confuse letter with spirit [*esprit*], even when we receive the former by pneumatic dispatch, and that I readily admit that one kills if the other gives life, insofar as the signifier—you are perhaps beginning to catch my drift—materializes the instance of death. But whereas it is first of all the materiality of the signifier that I have emphasized, that materiality is *singular* in many ways, the first of which is not to allow of partition. Cut a letter into small pieces, and it remains the letter that it is—and this in a completely different sense than *Gestalttheorie* can account for with the latent vitalism in its notion of the whole.[10]

Language hands down its sentence to those who know how to hear it: through the use of the article employed as a partitive particle. Indeed, it is here that spirit—if spirit be living signification—seems, no less singularly, to allow for quantification more than the letter does. To begin with, through the very signification that allows us to say, "this discourse full *of* meaning" [*plein* de *signification*], just as it allows us to recognize *some* intentionality [de *l'intention*] in an act, to deplore that there is no longer *any* love [*plus* d'*amour*], to store up hatred [de la *haine*] and expend devotion [du *dévouement*], and to note that so much infatuation [*tant* d'*infatuation*] can be reconciled with the fact that there will always be plenty *of* ass [de la *cuisse*] to go around and brawling among men [du *rififi chez les hommes*].

But as for the letter itself, whether we take it in the sense of a typographical element, of an epistle, or of what constitutes a man of letters, we commonly say that what people say must be understood *à la lettre* (to the letter or literally), that *a letter* is being held for you at the post office, or even that you are well versed in *letters*—never that there is (some amount of) *letter* [de la lettre] anywhere, whatever the context, even to designate late mail.

For the signifier is a unique unit of being which, by its very nature, is the symbol of but an absence. This is why we cannot say of the purloined letter that, like other objects, it must be *or* not be somewhere but rather that, unlike them, it will be *and* will not be where it is wherever it goes.

Let us, in fact, look more closely at what happens to the police. We are spared none of the details concerning the procedures used in searching the space subjected to their investigation: from the division of that space into vol- 25
umes from which the slightest bulk cannot escape detection, to needles probing soft cushions, and, given that they cannot simply sound the hard wood [for cavities], to an examination with a microscope to detect gimlet-dust from any holes drilled in it, and even the slightest gaping in the joints [of the furniture]. As their network tightens to the point that, not satisfied with shaking the pages of books, the police take to counting them, don't we see space itself shed its leaves like the letter?

But the seekers have such an immutable notion of reality [*réel*] that they fail to notice that their search tends to transform it into its object—a trait by which they might be able to distinguish that object from all others.

This would no doubt be too much to ask them, not because of their lack of insight but rather because of ours. For their imbecility is of neither the individual nor the corporate variety; its source is subjective. It is the imbecility of the realist who does not pause to observe that nothing, however deep into the bowels of the world a hand may shove it, will ever be hidden there, since another hand can retrieve it, and that what is hidden is never but what is *not in its place* [manque à sa place], as a call slip says of a volume mislaid in a library. And even if the book were on an adjacent shelf or in the next slot, it would be hidden there, however visible it may seem there. For it can *literally* [à la lettre] be said that something is not in its place only of what can change places—that is, of the symbolic. For the real, whatever upheaval we subject it to, is always and in every case in its place; it carries its place stuck to the sole of its shoe, there being nothing that can exile it from it.

Now, to return to our policemen, how could they have grasped the letter

when they took it from the place where it was hidden? What were they turning over with their fingers but something that *did not fit* the description they had been given of it? "A letter, a litter": in Joyce's circle, they played on the homophony of the two words in English.[11] The seeming scrap of waste paper [*déchet*] the police were handling at that moment did not reveal its other nature
26 by being only half torn in two. A different cipher on a seal [*cachet*] of another color and the distinctive mark [*cachet*] of a different handwriting in the superscription served as the most inviolable of hiding places [*cachettes*] here. And if they stopped at the reverse side of the letter, on which, as we know, the recipient's address was written at that time, it was because the letter had for them no other side but this reverse side.

What might they have detected on the basis of its obverse? Its message, as it is often said, an answer pleasing to our amateur cybernetic streak? . . . But does it not occur to us that this message has already reached its addressee and has even been left behind along with the insignificant scrap of paper, which now represents it no less well than the original note?

If we could say that a letter has fulfilled its destiny after having served its function, the ceremony of returning letters would be a less commonly accepted way to bring to a close the extinguishing of the fires of Cupid's festivities. The signifier is not functional. And the mobilization of the elegant society, whose frolics we are following, would have no meaning if the letter limited itself to having but one. Announcing that meaning to a squad of cops would hardly be an adequate means of keeping it secret.

We could even admit that the letter has an entirely different (if not a more consuming) meaning to the Queen than the one it offers up to the Minister's ken. The sequence of events would not be appreciably affected, not even if the letter were strictly incomprehensible to a reader not in the know.

For the letter is certainly not incomprehensible to everybody, since, as the Prefect emphatically assures us, eliciting everyone's mockery, "the disclosure of the document to a third person, who shall be nameless" (his name leaping to mind like a pig's tail twixt the teeth of Father Ubu) "would bring in question the honor of a personage of most exalted station"—indeed, the illustrious personage's very "honor and peace [would be] so jeopardized."

Hence it would be dangerous to let circulate not only the meaning but also the text of the message, and it would be all the more dangerous the more harmless it might appear to be, since the risks of an unwitting indiscretion by one of the letter's trustees would thus be increased.

Nothing then can save the police's position, and nothing would be changed
27 by making them more "cultured." *Scripta manent:* in vain would they learn from a deluxe-edition humanism the proverbial lesson which the words *verba*

volant conclude. Would that it were the case that writings remain, as is true, rather, of spoken words [*paroles*]: for the indelible debt of those words at least enriches our acts with its transfers.

Writings scatter to the four winds the blank checks of a mad charge of the cavalry. And were there no loose sheets, there would be no purloined letters.

But what of it? For there to be purloined letters, we wonder, to whom does a letter belong? I stressed a moment ago the oddity implicit in returning a letter to the person who had formerly let ardently fly its pledge. And we generally deem unworthy the method of such premature publications, as the one by which the Knight of Eon put several of his correspondents in a rather pitiful position.

Might a letter to which the sender retains certain rights then not belong altogether to the person to whom it is addressed? Or might it be that the latter was never the true addressee?

What will enlighten us is what may at first obscure the matter—namely, the fact that the story tells us virtually nothing about the sender or about the contents of the letter. We are merely informed that the Minister immediately recognized the hand that wrote the Queen's address on it and it is only incidentally mentioned, in a discussion of the camouflaging of the letter by the Minister, that the original cipher is that of the Duke of S—. As for the letter's import, we know only the dangers it would bring with it were it to fall into the hands of a certain third party, and that its possession has allowed the Minister to wield, "for political purposes, to a very dangerous extent," the power it assures him over the person concerned. But this tells us nothing about the message it carries.

Love letter or conspiratorial letter, informant's letter or directive, demanding letter or letter of distress, we can rest assured of but one thing: the Queen cannot let her lord and master know of it.

Now these terms, far from allowing for the disparaging tone they have in bourgeois comedy, take on an eminent meaning since they designate her sov- 28
ereign, to whom she is bound by pledge of loyalty, and doubly so, since her role as spouse does not relieve her of her duties as a subject, but rather elevates her to the role of guardian of the power that royalty by law incarnates, which is called legitimacy.

Thus, whatever action the Queen has decided to take regarding the letter, the fact remains that this letter is the symbol of a pact and that, even if its addressee does not assume responsibility for this pact, the existence of the letter situates her in a symbolic chain foreign to the one which constitutes her loyalty. Its incompatibility with her loyalty is proven by the fact that possession of the letter is impossible to bring forward publicly as legitimate, and that in order to have this possession respected, the Queen can only invoke her right to privacy, whose privilege is based on the very honor that this possession violates.

For she who incarnates the graceful figure of sovereignty cannot welcome even a private communication without power being concerned, and she cannot lay claim to secrecy in relation to the sovereign without her actions becoming clandestine.

Hence, the responsibility of the letter's author takes a back seat to that of its holder: for the offense to majesty is compounded by *high treason*.

I say the "holder" and not the "owner." For it becomes clear thus that the addressee's ownership of the letter is no less questionable than that of anyone else into whose hands it may fall, since nothing concerning the existence of the letter can fall back into place without the person whose prerogatives it infringes on having pronounced judgment on it.

However, none of this implies that, even though the letter's secrecy is indefensible, it would in any way be honorable to denounce that secret. *Honesti homines*, decent people, cannot get off the hook so easily. There is more than one *religio*, and sacred ties shall not cease to pull us in opposite directions any time soon. As for *ambitus*, a detour, as we see, is not always inspired by ambition. For although I am taking a detour here, I have not stolen [*volé*] it—that's the word for it—since, to be quite frank, I have adopted the title Baudelaire gave the story only in order to stress, not the signifier's "conventional" nature,
29 as it is incorrectly put, but rather its priority over the signified. Despite his devotion, Baudelaire nevertheless betrayed Poe by translating his title "The Purloined Letter" as "La lettre volée" (the stolen letter), the English title containing a word rare enough for us to find it easier to define its etymology than its usage.

To *purloin*, says the Oxford English Dictionary, is an Anglo-French word—that is, it is composed of the prefix *pur-*, found in *purpose*, *purchase*, and *purport*, and of the Old French word *loing*, *loinger*, *longé*. We recognize in the first element the Latin *pro-*, as opposed to *ante*, insofar as it presupposes a back in front of which it stands, possibly to guarantee it or even to stand in as its guarantor (whereas *ante* goes forth to meet what comes to meet it). As for the second, the Old French word *loigner* is a verb that attributes place *au loing* (or *longé*), which does not mean *au loin* (far off), but *au long de* (alongside). To purloin is thus *mettre de côté* (to set aside) or, to resort to a colloquialism which plays off the two meanings, *mettre à gauche* (to put to the left side [literally] and to tuck away).

Our detour is thus validated by the very object which leads us into it: for we are quite simply dealing with a *letter* which has been *detoured*, one whose trajectory has been *prolonged* (this is literally the English word in the title), or, to resort to the language of the post office, a letter *en souffrance* (awaiting delivery or unclaimed).

Here then, the letter's singularity, reduced to its simplest expression, is "simple and odd," as we are told on the very first page of the story; and the letter is, as the title indicates, the *true subject* of the tale. Since it can be made to take a detour, it must have a trajectory *which is proper to it*—a feature in which its impact as a signifier is apparent here. For we have learned to conceive of the signifier as sustaining itself only in a displacement comparable to that found in electronic news strips or in the rotating memories of our machines-that-think-like-men,[12] this because of the alternating operation at its core that requires it to leave its place, if only to return to it by a circular path.

This is what happens in repetition automatism. What Freud teaches us in the 30
text I have been commenting on is that the subject follows the channels of the symbolic. But what is illustrated here is more gripping still: It is not only the subject, but the subjects, caught in their intersubjectivity, who line up—in other words, they are our ostriches, to whom we thus return here, and who, more docile than sheep, model their very being on the moment of the signifying chain that runs through them.

If what Freud discovered, and rediscovers ever more abruptly, has a meaning, it is that the signifier's displacement determines subjects' acts, destiny, refusals, blindnesses, success, and fate, regardless of their innate gifts and instruction, and irregardless of their character or sex; and that everything pertaining to the psychological pregiven follows willy-nilly the signifier's train, like weapons and baggage.

Here we are, in fact, once again at the crossroads at which we had left our drama and its round with the question of the way in which the subjects relay each other in it. My apologue is designed to show that it is the letter and its detour which governs their entrances and roles. While the letter may be *en souffrance*, they are the ones who shall suffer from it. By passing beneath its shadow, they become its reflection. By coming into the letter's possession—an admirably ambiguous bit of language—its meaning possesses them.

This is what is demonstrated to us by the hero of the drama that is recounted to us here, when the very situation his daring triumphantly crafted the first time around repeats itself. If he now succumbs to it, it is because he has shifted to the second position in the triad where he was initially in the third position and was simultaneously the thief—this by virtue of the object of his theft.

For if, now as before, the point is to protect the letter from inquisitive eyes, he cannot help but employ the same technique he himself already foiled: that of leaving it out in the open. And we may legitimately doubt that he thus knows what he is doing when we see him suddenly captivated by a dyadic relationship, in which we find all the features of a mimetic lure or of an animal playing dead, and caught in the trap of the typically imaginary situation of seeing
31 that he is not seen, leading him to misconstrue the real situation in which he is seen not seeing. And what does he fail to see? The very symbolic situation which he himself was so able to see, and in which he is now seen seeing himself not being seen.

The Minister acts like a man who realizes that the police's search is his own defense, since we are told he deliberately gives the police total access to his hotel by his absences; he nevertheless overlooks the fact that he has no defense against anything beyond that form of search.

This is the very *autruicherie*—if I may be allowed to multiply my monster by layering—he himself crafted, but it cannot be by some imbecility that he now comes to be its dupe.

For in playing the game of the one who hides, he is obliged to don the role of the Queen, including even the attributes of woman and shadow, so propitious for the act of concealment.

I do not mean to reduce the veteran couple of Yin and Yang to the primal opposition of dark and light. For its precise handling involves what is blinding in a flash of light, no less than the shimmering that shadows exploit in order not to release their prey.

Here the sign and being, marvelously disjoint, reveal which wins out when they are opposed. A man who is man enough to brave, and even scorn, a woman's dreaded ire suffers the curse of the sign of which he has dispossessed her so greatly as to undergo metamorphosis.

For this sign is clearly that of woman, because she brings out her very being therein by founding it outside the law, which ever contains her—due to the effect of origins—in a position as signifier, nay, as fetish. In order to be worthy of the power of this sign she need but remain immobile in its shadow, managing thereby, moreover, like the Queen, to simulate mastery of nonaction that the Minister's "lynx eye" alone was able to see through.

The man is now thus in this ravished sign's possession, and this possession is harmful in that it can be maintained only thanks to the very honor it defies, and it is accursed for inciting him who maintains it to punishment or crime, both of which breach his vassalage to the Law.

There must be a very odd *noli me tangere* in this sign for its possession to,

like the Socratic stingray, make its man so numb that he falls into what 32
unequivocally appears in his case to be a state of inaction.

For in remarking, as the narrator does already in the first meeting, that the letter's power departs when used, we perceive that this remark concerns only its use for ends of power—and simultaneously that the Minister will be forced to use it in this way.

For him to be unable to rid himself of it, the Minister must not know what else to do with the letter. For this use places him in so total a dependence on the letter as such, that in the long run this use no longer concerns the letter at all.

I mean that, for this use to truly concern the letter, the Minister—who, after all, would be authorized to do so by his service to the King, his master—could present respectful reproaches to the Queen, even if he had to ensure their desired effects by appropriate guarantees; or he could initiate a suit against the author of the letter (the fact that its author remains on the sidelines reveals the extent to which guilt and blame are not at stake here, but rather the sign of contradiction and scandal constituted by the letter, in the sense in which the Gospel says that the sign must come regardless of the misfortune of he who serves as its bearer); or he could even submit the letter as an exhibit in a case to the "third personage" who is qualified to decide whether he will institute a Chambre Ardente for the Queen or bring disgrace upon the Minister.

We will not know why the Minister does not use the letter in any of these ways, and it is fitting that we do not, since the effect of this non-use alone concerns us; all we need to know is that the manner in which the letter was acquired would pose no obstacle to any of them.

For it is clear that while the Minister will be forced to make use of the letter in a non-significant way, its use for ends of power can only be potential, since it cannot become actual [*passer à l'acte*] without immediately vanishing. Hence the letter exists as a means of power only through the final summons of the pure signifier—either by prolonging its detour, making it reach he whom it may concern through an extra transit (that is, through another betrayal whose repercussions the letter's gravity makes it difficult to prevent), or by destroying the letter, which would be the only sure way, as Dupin proffers at the out- 33
set, to be done with what is destined by nature to signify the canceling out [*annulation*] of what it signifies.

The ascendancy which the Minister derives from the situation is thus not drawn from the letter but, whether he knows it or not, from the personage it constitutes for him. The Prefect's remarks thus present him as someone "who dares all things," which is commented upon significantly: "those unbecoming as well as those becoming a man," words whose thrust escapes Baudelaire when he translates: "ce qui est indigne d'un homme aussi bien que ce qui est digne de lui" (those unbecoming a man as well as those becoming him). For in its original form, the appraisal is far more appropriate to what concerns a woman.

This allows us to see the imaginary import of the personage, that is, the narcissistic relationship in which the Minister is engaged, this time certainly without knowing it. It is also indicated right on the second page of the English text by one of the narrator's remarks, whose form is worth savoring: the Minister's ascendancy, we are told, "would depend upon the robber's knowledge of the loser's knowledge of the robber." Words whose importance the author underscores by having Dupin repeat them word for word right after the Prefect's account of the scene of the theft of the letter, when the conversation resumes. Here again we might say that Baudelaire is imprecise in his language in having one ask and the other confirm in the following terms: "Le voleur sait-il? . . ." (Does the robber know?), then: "Le voleur sait . . ." (The robber knows). What? "que la personne volée connaît son voleur" (that the loser knows her robber).

For what matters to the robber is not only that the said person know who robbed her, but that she know what kind of robber she is dealing with; the fact is that she believes him capable of anything, which should be understood as follows: she confers upon him a position that no one can really assume, because it is imaginary, that of absolute master.

In truth, it is a position of absolute weakness, but not for the person we lead to believe in it. The proof is not merely that the Queen takes the audacious step of calling upon the police. For the police merely conform to their displacement to the next slot in the array constituted by the initial triad, accepting the very blindness that is required to occupy that place: "No more
34 sagacious agent could, I suppose," Dupin notes ironically, "be desired, or even imagined." No, if the Queen has taken this step, it is less because she has been "driven to despair," as we are told, than because she takes on the burden [*charge*] of an impatience that should rather be attributed to a specular mirage.

For the Minister has a hard time confining himself to the inaction which is presently his lot. The Minister, in point of fact, is "not *altogether* a fool." This remark is made by the Prefect, whose every word is golden: it is true that the gold of his words flows only for Dupin and does not stop flowing until it reaches the fifty thousand francs' worth it will cost him by the metal standard of the day, though not without leaving him a tidy profit. The Minister then is not *altogether* a fool in his foolish stagnation, and this is why he must behave according to the mode of neurosis. Like the man who withdrew to an island to forget—to forget what? he forgot—so the Minister, by not making use of the letter, comes to forget it. This is expressed by the persistence of his conduct. But the letter, no more than the neurotic's unconscious, does not forget him. It forgets him so little that it transforms him more and more in the image of her who offered it up to his discovery, and that he now will surrender it, following her example, to a similar discovery.

The features of this transformation are noted, and in a form characteristic enough in their apparent gratuitousness that they might legitimately be compared to the return of the repressed.

Thus we first learn that the Minister in turn has *turned* the letter *over*, not, of course, as in the Queen's hasty gesture, but more assiduously, as one turns a garment inside out. This is, in effect, how he must proceed, according to the methods of the day for folding and sealing a letter, in order to free the virgin space in which to write a new address.[13]

This address becomes his own. Whether it be in his handwriting or 35
another's, it appears in a diminutive female script, and, the seal changing from the red of passion to the black of its mirrors, he stamps his own cipher upon it. The oddity of a letter marked with the cipher of its addressee is all the more worth noting as an invention because, although it is powerfully articulated in the text, it is not even mentioned thereafter by Dupin in the discussion he devotes to his identification of the letter.

Whether this omission is intentional or involuntary, it is surprising in the organization of a creation whose meticulous rigor is evident. But in either case it is significant that the letter which the Minister addresses to himself, ultimately, is a letter from a woman: as though this were a phase he had to go through owing to one of the signifier's natural affinities.

And everything—from the aura of nonchalance, that goes as far as an affectation of listlessness, to the display of an ennui verging on disgust in his conversation, to the ambiance that the author of the "Philosophy of Furniture"[14] knows how to elicit from virtually impalpable details (like that of the musical instrument on the table)—seems to conspire to make a personage, whose every remark has surrounded him with the most virile of traits, exude the oddest *odor di femina* when he appears.

Dupin does not fail to emphasize that this is indeed an artifice, describing behind the spurious appearance the vigilance of a beast of prey ready to spring. But how could we find a more beautiful image of the fact that this is the very effect of the unconscious, in the precise sense in which I teach that the unconscious is the fact that man is inhabited by the signifier, than the one Poe himself forges to help us understand Dupin's feat? For, to do so, Poe refers to those toponymic inscriptions which a map, in order not to be silent, superimposes on its outline, and which may become the object of "a game of puzzles" in which one has to find the name chosen by another player. He then notes that the name most likely to foil a novice will be one which the eye often overlooks, but which provides, in large letters spaced out widely across the field of the map, the name of an entire country . . .

36 Just so does the purloined letter, like an immense female body, sprawl across the space of the Minister's office when Dupin enters it. But just so does he already expect to find it there, having only to undress that huge body, with his eyes veiled by green spectacles.

This is why, without any need (nor any opportunity either, for obvious reasons) to listen in at Professor Freud's door, he goes straight to the spot where lies and lodges what that body is designed to hide, in some lovely middle toward which one's gaze slips, nay, to the very place seducers call Sant'Angelo's Castle in their innocent illusion of being able to control the City from the castle. Lo! Between the jambs of the fireplace, there is the object already in reach of the hand the ravisher has but to extend . . . Whether he seizes it above the mantelpiece, as Baudelaire translates it, or beneath it, as in the original text, is a question that may be abandoned without harm to inferences emanating from the kitchen.[15]

Now if the effectiveness of symbols stopped there, would it mean that the symbolic debt is extinguished there too? If we could believe so, we would be advised of the contrary by two episodes which we must be all the more careful not to dismiss as accessory in that they seem, at first blush, to be at odds with the rest of the work.

First of all, there is the business of Dupin's remuneration, which, far from being one last game, has been present from the outset in the rather offhanded question Dupin asks the Prefect about the amount of the reward promised him, and whose enormousness the Prefect, however reticent he may be about citing the exact figure, does not dream of hiding from him, even returning to the subject later in mentioning its having been doubled.

The fact that Dupin was previously presented to us as a virtual pauper taking refuge in ethereal pursuits ought rather to lead us to reflect on the deal he cuts for delivery of the letter, promptly assured as it is by the checkbook he produces. I do not regard it as negligible that the direct hint* by which he broaches the matter is a "story attributed to the personage, as famous as he was eccentric," Baudelaire tells us, of an English doctor named Abernethy;
37 this doctor replied to a rich miser, who was hoping to sponge a free medical opinion off him, not to take medicine, but rather to take advice.

Are we not, in fact, justified in feeling implicated when Dupin is perhaps about to withdraw from the letter's symbolic circuit—we who make ourselves the emissaries of all the purloined letters which, at least for a while, remain *en souffrance* with us in the transference? And is it not the responsibility their transference entails that we neutralize by equating it with the signifier that most thoroughly annihilates every signification—namely, money?

But that's not all here. The profit Dupin so blithely extracts from this feat, assuming its purpose is to allow him to withdraw his ante from the game before it is too late, merely renders all the more paradoxical, even shocking, the rebuke and underhanded blow he suddenly permits himself to deal the Minister, whose insolent prestige would, after all, seem to have been sufficiently deflated by the trick Dupin has just played on him.

I have already quoted the atrocious lines Dupin claims he could not stop himself from dedicating, in his counterfeit letter, to the moment at which the Minister, flying off the handle at the Queen's inevitable acts of defiance, will think of bringing her down and will fling himself into the abyss—*facilis descensus Averni*,[16] he says, waxing sententious—adding that the Minister will not fail to recognize his handwriting. Leaving behind a merciless opprobrium, at the cost of no peril to himself, would seem to be a triumph without glory over a figure who is not without merit, and the resentment Dupin invokes, stemming from "an evil turn" done him in Vienna (at the Congress?), merely adds an extra touch of darkness to it.

Let us consider this explosion of feeling more closely, however, and more specifically the moment at which it occurs in an act whose success depends on so cool a head.

It comes just after the moment at which it may be said that Dupin already holds the letter as securely as if he had seized it, the decisive act of identifying the letter having been accomplished, even though he is not yet in a position to rid himself of it.

He is thus clearly a participant in the intersubjective triad and, as such, finds himself in the median position previously occupied by the Queen and the Minister. In showing himself to be superior here, will he simultaneously reveal to 38
us the author's intentions?

While he has succeeded in putting the letter back on its proper course, it has yet to be made to reach its address. And that address is the place previously occupied by the King, since it is there that it must fall back into the order based on the Law.

As we have seen, neither the King nor the police who replaced Him in that position were capable of reading the letter because that *place entailed blindness*.

Rex et augur—the legendary archaism of the words seems to resound only to make us realize how derisive it is to call upon a man to live up to them. And history's figures have hardly encouraged us to do so for some time now. It is not natural for man to bear the weight of the highest of signifiers all alone. And the place he comes to occupy when he dons it may be equally apt to become the symbol of the most enormous imbecility.[17]

Let us say that the King here is invested—thanks to the amphibology natural to the sacred—with the imbecility that is based precisely on the Subject.

This is what will give meaning to the personages who succeed him in his place. Not that the police can be regarded as constitutionally illiterate, and we are aware of the role played by pikes planted around the university in the birth of the State. But the police who exercise their functions here are plainly marked by liberal forms, that is, by forms imposed on them by masters who are not very interested in enduring their indiscreet tendencies. This is why words are not minced, at times, regarding what is expected of them: "*Sutor ne ultra crepidam*, just take care of your crooks. We'll even give you the scientific means with which to do so. That will help you not to think of truths you'd be better off leaving in the dark."[18]

We know that the relief that results from such sensible principles shall have lasted but a morning's time in history, and that everywhere the march of des-
39 tiny is already bringing back, after a just aspiration to the reign of freedom, an interest in those who trouble it with their crimes, an interest that occasionally goes so far as to forge its own evidence. It may even be observed that this practice, which has always been accepted as long as it was engaged in only for the benefit of the greatest number, is in fact authenticated through public confessions of its forgeries by the very people who might well object to it: the most recent manifestation of the preeminence of the signifier over the subject.

The fact remains that police files have always been treated with a certain reserve, a reserve which goes well beyond the circle of historians, for some odd reason.

Dupin's intended delivery of the letter to the Prefect of Police will diminish the magnitude of this evanescent credit. What now remains of the signifier when, having already been relieved of its message for the Queen, its text is invalidated as soon as it leaves the Minister's hands?

The only thing left for it to do is to answer this very question: what remains of a signifier when it no longer has any signification? This is the very question asked of it by the person Dupin now finds in the place marked by blindness.

For this is clearly the question that has led the Minister there, assuming he is the gambler we are told he is, as his act suffices to indicate. For the gambler's passion is no other than the question asked of the signifier, which is figured by the *automaton* of chance.

"What are you, figure of the dice I roll in your chance encounter (*tyche*)[19] with my fortune? Nothing, if not the presence of death that makes human life into a reprieve obtained from morning to morning in the name of significations of which your sign is the shepherd's crook. Thus did Scheherazade for a thousand and one nights, and thus have I done for eighteen months, experiencing the ascendancy of this sign at the cost of a dizzying series of loaded tosses in the game of even or odd."

This is why Dupin, *from the place where he is* [*il est*], cannot help but feel rage of a manifestly feminine nature at he who questions in this manner. The high- 40
caliber image, in which the poet's inventiveness and the mathematician's rigor were married to the impassivity of the dandy and the elegance of the cheat, suddenly becomes, for the very person who gave us a taste of it, the true *monstrum horrendum*, to borrow his own words, "an unprincipled man of genius."

It is here that the origin of the horror shows itself, and he who experiences it has no need to declare himself, most unexpectedly at that, "a partisan of the lady" in order to reveal it to us: ladies, as we know, detest it when principles are called into question, for their charms owe much to the mystery of the signifier.

This is why Dupin will at last turn toward us the dumbfounding [*médusante*] face of this signifier of which no one but the Queen has been able to read anything but the other face. The commonplace practice of supplying a quotation is fitting for the oracle that this face bears in its grimace, as is the fact that it is borrowed from tragedy:

Un destin si funeste,
S'il n'est digne d'Atrée, est digne de Thyeste.

Such is the signifier's answer, beyond all significations: "You believe you are taking action when I am the one making you stir at the bidding of the bonds with which I weave your desires. Thus do the latter grow in strength and multiply in objects, bringing you back to the fragmentation of your rent childhood. That will be your feast until the return of the stone guest whom I shall be for you since you call me forth."

To return to a more temperate tone, let us say—as goes the joke with which some of you who followed me to the Congress in Zurich last year and I rendered homage to the local password—that the signifier's answer to whomever questions it is: "Eat your Dasein."

Is that then what awaits the Minister at his appointment with fate? Dupin assures us that it is, but we have also learned not to be overly credulous of his diversions.

The audacious creature is, of course, reduced here to the state of imbecilic

blindness in which man finds himself in relation to the wall-like letters that dictate his destiny. But, in summoning him to confront them, what effect can we expect the sole provocations of the Queen to have on a man like him? Love or
41 hatred. The one is blind and will make him lay down his arms. The other is lucid, but will awaken his suspicions. But provided he is truly the gambler we are told he is, he will consult his cards one final time before laying them on the table and, upon seeing his hand, will leave the table in time to avoid disgrace.

Is that all, and must we believe we have deciphered Dupin's true strategy beyond the imaginary tricks with which he was obliged to deceive us? Yes, no doubt, for if "any point requiring reflection," as Dupin states at the start, is examined "to better purpose in the dark," we may now easily read its solution in broad daylight. It was already contained in and easy to bring out of the title of our tale, according to the very formulation of intersubjective communication that I have long since offered up to your discernment, in which the sender, as I tell you, receives from the receiver his own message in an inverted form. This is why what the "purloined letter," nay, the "letter *en souffrance*," means is that a letter always arrives at its destination.

Guitrancourt and San Casciano, mid-May to mid-August 1956

Presentation of the Suite

To anyone wanting to get a feel for my seminar from this text, I hardly ever recommended it without advising him that this text had to serve to introduce him to the introduction that preceded it and that will follow it here.

This introduction was designed for others who were leaving, having gotten a feel for my seminar.

This advice usually was not followed, a taste for obstacles being the ornament of persevering in being.

I am only concerning myself here with the reader's economy [of effort] to return to the topic of whom my discourse is addressed to and to indicate what can no longer be denied: my writings have their place within an adventure which is that of the psychoanalyst, assuming psychoanalysis goes so far as to call him into question.

42 The detours of this adventure, and even its accidents, have led me to a teaching position.

Whence an intimate reference which, by first looking over this introduction, will be grasped in the reminder of exercises done as a group.

For the preceding text merely refines on the grace of one of those exercises.

One would thus make poor use of the introduction that follows were one to consider it difficult: That would be to transfer to the object that it presents what is related only to its aim, insofar as that aim is training.

The four pages that are a conundrum here for certain people were thus not intended to be confusing. I have reworked them slightly to remove any pretext one might come up with for ignoring what they say.

Which is that the remembering [*mémoration*] at stake in the unconscious—and I mean the Freudian unconscious—is not related to the register that is assumed to be that of memory, insofar as memory is taken to be a property of a living being.

To sharpen our focus on what this negative reference involves, I say that what has been imagined in order to account for this effect of living matter is not rendered any more acceptable to me by the resignation it suggests.

Whereas it is quite obvious that, in doing without this subjection, we can find in the ordered chains of a formal language the entire appearance of remembering, and quite especially of the kind required by Freud's discovery.

I will therefore go so far as to say that the burden of proof rests, rather, with those who argue that the constitutive order of the symbolic does not suffice to explain everything here.

For the time being, the links of this order are the only ones that can be *suspected to suffice* to account for Freud's notion of the indestructibility of what his unconscious preserves.

(I refer the reader to Freud's text on the *Wunderblock* which, on this point and many others as well, goes far beyond the trivial meaning attributed to it by inattentive readers.)

The program traced out for us is hence to figure out how a formal language determines the subject.

But the interest of such a program is not simple, since it assumes that a subject will not fulfill it except by contributing something of his own to it.

A psychoanalyst can but indicate his interest in it, which is precisely as great as the obstacle he finds in it.

Those who share this interest agree and even the others would admit 43
it, if they were appropriately questioned: we have here an aspect of subjective conversion that gave rise to a dramatic reaction in my companions, and the imputation of "intellectualization" expressed by others, with which they would like to thwart me, clearly shows what it protects when seen in this light.

Probably no one made a more praiseworthy effort in these pages than someone close to me who, in the end, saw fit only to denounce in them the hypostasis that troubled his Kantianism.

But the Kantian brush itself needs its alkali.

It is helpful here to introduce my objector, and even others who were less relevant, because of what they do each time—in explaining to themselves their everyday subject, their patient, as they say, or even explaining themselves to him—they employ magical thinking.

Let them enter through that door themselves; it is, in effect, the same step the first objector made to take from me the chalice of the hypostasis, whereas he had just filled the cup with his own hand.

For, with my αs, βs, γs, and δs, I do not claim to extract from the real more than I have presupposed in its given—in other words, nothing here—but simply to demonstrate that they already bring with them a syntax by simply turning this real into chance [*hasard*].

Regarding which I propose that the effects of repetition that Freud calls "automatism" come from nowhere else.

But, people object, my αs, βs, γs, and δs *are not* without a subject remembering them. This is precisely what I am calling into question here: what is repeated is a product, not of nothing from the real (which people believe they have to presuppose in it), but precisely of *what was not* [*ce qui n'était pas*].

Note that it then becomes less astonishing that what is repeated insists so much in order to get itself noticed.

The least of my "patients" in analysis attests to this, and in words that confirm all the better my doctrine since they are the same words that led me to it—as those whom I train know, having often heard my very terms anticipated in the hot-off-the-presses text of an analytic session.

Now, what I want to achieve is that the patient [*malade*] be heard in the proper manner at the moment at which he speaks. For it would be strange for one to listen only for the idea of what leads him astray at the moment at which he is simply prey to truth.

44 This is helpful in taking the psychologist's assurance down a notch—in other words, the pedantry that invented the "level of aspiration," for example, expressly, no doubt, to indicate his own therein as an unsurpassable upper limit.

It must not be thought that the philosopher with fine university credentials is the blackboard [*planche*] that can accommodate this divertissement.

It is here that, by echoing old School debates, my discussion discovers the intellectual's debt, but it is also a question of the infatuation that must be removed.

Caught in the act of unduly imputing to me a transgression of the Kantian critique, the subject, who was well-meaning in mentioning my text, is not Father Ubu and does not persist.

But he has little taste for adventure left. He wants to sit down. It is a corporal antinomy to the analyst's profession. How can one remain seated when one has placed oneself in the situation of no longer having to answer a subject's question in any way than by lying him down first? It is obvious that remaining standing is no less uncomfortable.

This is why the question of the transmission of psychoanalytic experience begins here, when the didactic aim is implied in it, negotiating a knowledge.

The impact of a market structure is not null in the field of truth, but it is scabrous there.

Introduction

The class of my seminar that I have written up to present here was given on April 26, 1955. It represents a moment in the commentary that I devoted to *Beyond the Pleasure Principle* for the whole of that academic year.

It is well known that many people who authorize themselves the title of psychoanalyst do not hesitate to reject this text by Freud as superfluous and even risky speculation, and we can gauge—on the basis of the antinomy *par excellence* constituted by the notion of the "death instinct" with which it concludes—to what extent it can be unthinkable, if you will allow me the term, to most of them.

It is nevertheless difficult to consider this text—which serves as a prelude 45
to the new topography represented by the terms "ego," "id," and "superego," which have become as prevalent in the work of theorists as in the popular mind—to be an excursion, much less a faux pas, in Freudian doctrine.

This simple apprehension is confirmed when we fathom the motivations that link the abovementioned speculation with the theoretical revision of which it turns out to be constitutive.

When we do so, we are left with no doubt but that the current use of these terms is bastardized and even ass-backwards; this can be clearly seen in the fact that the theorist and the man on the street use them identically. Which is, no doubt, what justifies the remark made by certain epigones to the effect that they find in these terms the means by which to bring the experience of psychoanalysis back into the fold of what they call general psychology.

Let me simply provide a few markers along our path.

Repetition automatism (*Wiederholungszwang*)—although the notion is presented in the book in question here as designed to respond to certain paradoxes in clinical work, like the dreams found in traumatic neurosis and the negative therapeutic reaction—cannot be conceived of as an add-on to the doctrinal edifice, even if it is viewed as a crowning addition.

For it is his inaugural discovery that Freud reaffirms in it: namely, the conception of memory implied by his "unconscious." The new facts provide him with an occasion to restructure that conception in a more rigorous manner by giving it a generalized form, but also to reopen his problematic to combat the decline, which one could sense already at that time, seen in the fact that people were taking its effects as a simple pregiven.

What is revamped here was already articulated in the "Project,"[20] in which Freud's divination traced the avenues his research would force him to go down: the Ψ system, a predecessor of the unconscious, manifests its originality therein, in that it is unable to satisfy itself except by *refinding an object that has been fundamentally lost*.

46 This is how Freud situates himself right from the outset in the opposition Kierkegaard taught us about, regarding whether the notion of existence is founded upon reminiscence or repetition. If Kierkegaard admirably discerns in that opposition the difference between Antiquity's conception of man and the modern conception of man, it appears that Freud makes the latter take its decisive step by ravishing the necessity included in this repetition from the human agent identified with consciousness. Since this repetition is symbolic repetition, it turns out that the symbol's order can no longer be conceived of there as constituted by man but must rather be conceived of as constituting him.

This is why I felt obliged to give my audience practice in the notion of remembering implied by Freud's work: I did this due to the all-too-well-founded consideration that by leaving it implicit, the very basics of analysis remain fuzzy.

It is because Freud does not compromise regarding the original quality of his experience that we see him constrained to evoke therein an element that governs it from beyond life—an element he calls the death instinct.

The indication that Freud gives here to those who call themselves his followers can only scandalize people in whom the sleep of reason is sustained by the monsters it produces, to borrow Goya's pithy formulation.

For, in order to remain at his usual level of rigor, Freud only delivers his notion to us accompanied by an example that dazzlingly exposes the fundamental formalization which this notion designates.

This game, in which the child practices making an object (which is, moreover, indifferent by its very nature) disappear from his sight, only to bring it back, and then obliterate it anew, while he modulates this alternation with distinctive syllables—this game, as I was saying, manifests in its radical traits the determination that the human animal receives from the symbolic order.

Man literally devotes his time to deploying the structural alternative in which presence and absence each find their jumping-off point [*prennent . . . leur appel*]. It is at the moment of their essential conjunction and, so to speak, at the zero point of desire that the human object comes under the sway of the grip which, canceling out its natural property, submits it henceforth to the symbol's conditions.

In fact, we have here nothing more than an illuminating insight into the entrance of the individual into an order whose mass supports him and welcomes 47
him in the form of language, and superimposes determination by the signifier onto determination by the signified in both diachrony and synchrony.

One can grasp in its very emergence the overdetermination that is the only kind of overdetermination at stake in Freud's apperception of the symbolic function.

Simply connoting with (+) and (–) a series playing on the sole fundamental alternative of presence and absence allows us to demonstrate how the strictest symbolic determinations accommodate a succession of [coin] tosses whose reality is strictly distributed "by chance" [*au hasard*].

Indeed, it suffices to symbolize, in the diachrony of such a series, groups of three which conclude with each toss[21] by defining them synchronically—for example, through the symmetry of constancy (+ + + and – – –), noted as 1, or of alternation (+ – + and – + –), noted as 3, the notation 2 being reserved for the dissymmetry revealed by the odd [*impair*][22] in the form of a group of two similar signs either preceded or followed by the opposite sign (+ – –, – + +, + + –, and – – +)—for possibilities and impossibilities of succession to appear in the new series constituted by these notations that the following network summarizes. This network at the same time manifests the concentric symmetry implicit in the triad—which is, let it be noted, the very structure of concern in the question continually raised anew[23] by anthropologists whether the dualism found in symbolic organizations is of a fundamental or apparent character.

Here is the network: 48

1–3 NETWORK

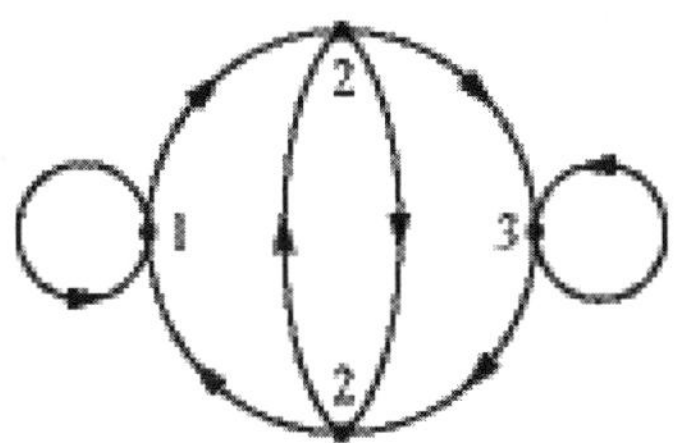

In the series of the symbols 1, 2, and 3, one can observe, for example, that for as long as a uniform succession of 2s, which began after a 1, lasts, the series *will remember* the even or odd rank of each of these 2s, since this rank is responsible for the fact that this sequence can only be broken by a 1 after an even number of 2s or by a 3 after an odd number of 2s.

Thus, right from the primordial symbol's first composition with itself—and I will indicate that I have not proposed this composition as I have arbitrarily—a structure, as transparent as it may still remain to its givens, brings out the essential link between memory and law.

But we will see simultaneously how the symbolic determination becomes more opaque, at the same time as the nature of the signifier is revealed, simply by recombining the elements of our syntax, in skipping a term in order to apply a quadratic relation to this binary.

Let us thus posit that if the binary, 1 and 3, in the group (1 2 3), for example, joins with their symbols a symmetry to a symmetry (1—1, 3—3, 1—3, or 3—1), it shall be noted α. A dissymmetry joined to a dissymmetry (2—2 alone) shall be noted γ. But, unlike our first symbolization, the crossed conjunctions will have two signs, β and δ, at their disposal, β noting the conjunction of symmetry with dissymmetry (1—2 and 3—2), and δ noting the conjunction of dissymmetry with symmetry (2—1 and 2—3).

49 Note that, although this convention restores a strict equality of combinatorial chances among four symbols, α, β, γ, and δ (as opposed to the combinatorial ambiguity that equated the chance of the symbol 2 with the chances of the two other symbols [1 and 3] in the preceding convention), the new syntax, in governing the succession of αs, βs, γs, and δs, determines absolutely dissymmetrical distribution possibilities between α and γ, on the one hand, and β and δ, on the other.

Indeed, recognizing that any one of these terms can immediately follow any of the others, and can also be found at Time 4 starting with any one of them [at Time 1], it turns out, on the other hand, that Time 3—in other words, the constitutive time of the binary—is subject to a law of exclusion which is such that, starting with an α or a δ [at Time 1], one can only obtain an α or a β [at Time 3], and that starting with a γ or a β [at Time 1], one can only obtain a γ or δ [at Time 3]. This can be written in the following form:

A Δ DISTRIBUTION

$$\frac{\alpha, \delta}{\gamma, \beta} \longrightarrow \alpha, \beta, \gamma, \delta \longrightarrow \frac{\alpha, \beta}{\gamma, \delta}$$

Time 1	Time 2	Time 3

The symbols that are compatible from Time 1 to Time 3 line up here with each other in the different horizontal tiers that divide them in the distribution, whereas any one of them can be selected at Time 2.

The fact that the link that has appeared here is nothing less than the simplest formalization of exchange is what confirms for us its anthropological interest. I will merely indicate at this level its constitutive value for a primordial subjectivity, the notion of which I will situate later.

Given its orientation, this link is in fact reciprocal; in other words, it is not reversible but it is retroactive. Thus by determining which term is to appear at Time 4, the one at Time 2 will not be indifferent.

It can be demonstrated that by setting the first and fourth terms of a series, there will always be a letter whose possibility will be excluded from the two intermediary terms, and that there are two other letters, one of which will always be excluded from the first of these intermediary terms, the other from 50
the second. These letters are distributed in Tables Ω and O below.[24]

TABLE Ω

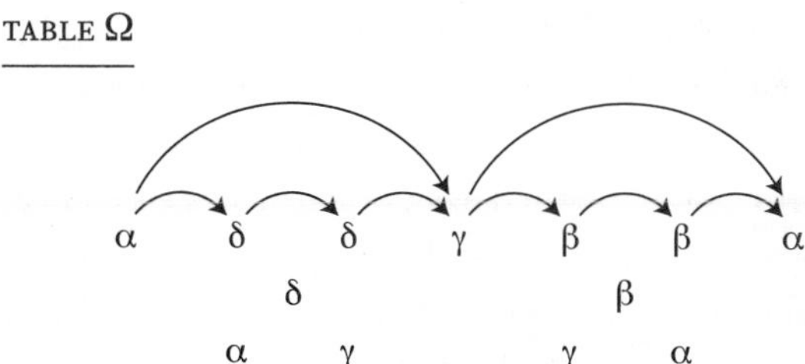

TABLE O

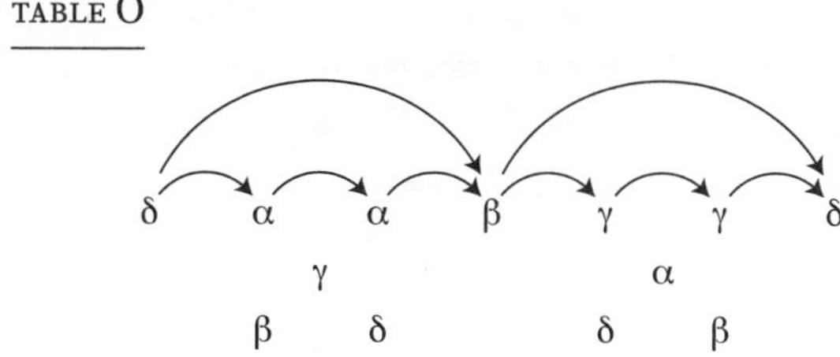

In these tables, the first line allows us to situate between the two tables the combination sought out from Time 1 to Time 4, the letter in the second line being the letter that this combination excludes from the two times in their interval [Times 2 and 3]; the two letters in the third line are, from left to right, those which are excluded from Time 2 and Time 3, respectively.

This could illustrate a rudimentary subjective trajectory, by showing that it is grounded in the actuality which has the future anterior in its present. The fact that, in the interval of this past that it is already insofar as it projects, a hole opens up that is constituted by a certain *caput mortuum* of the signifier (which is set here at three-quarters of the possible combinations in which it must situate itself),[25] suffices to make it depend on absence, obliging it to repeat its contour.

At the outset, subjectivity has no relation to the real, but rather to a syntax which is engendered by the signifying mark there.

The construction of the network of αs, βs, γs, and δs has the property (or insufficiency) of suggesting how the real, the imaginary, and the symbolic form in three tiers, although only the symbolic can intrinsically play there as representing the first two strata.

It is by meditating as it were naively on the small number of steps required
51 for syntax to triumph that it is worthwhile taking the time to explore the chain ordered here along the same lines as the chain that interested Poincaré and Markov.

Thus we notice that if, in our chain, one can encounter two βs that follow each other without the interposition of a δ, it is always either directly (ββ) or after the interposition of an indeterminate number of αγ couples (for example, βαγα . . . γβ), but that after the second β, no new β can appear in the chain before the appearance of a δ. Nevertheless, the above-defined succession of two βs cannot recur without a second δ being added to the first in a link [*liaison*] equivalent (apart from a reversal of the αγ couple into γα) to the link imposed on the two βs—namely, without the interposition of a β.

The immediate consequence of which is the dissymmetry that I announced earlier in probability of appearance for the different symbols of the chain.

Whereas the αs and γs can, in fact, through a felicitous random [*du hasard*] series, each repeat separately so as to overrun the entire chain, it is impossible for β and δ, even with the most favorable luck, to increase their percentage if not in strictly equal proportions (within one term), which limits to 50% the maximum possible frequency of each of them.

The probability of the combination represented by the βs and the δs being equivalent to that presupposed by the αs and the γs—and the real outcome of the tosses being, moreover, left strictly to chance—we see separate out from the real a symbolic determination which, as faithful as it may be in recording any partiality of the real, merely produces all the more clearly the disparities that it brings with it.

This disparity can also be seen by simply considering the structural contrast between Tables Ω and O, that is, the direct or crossed way in which the grouping (and order) of the exclusions is subordinated by reproducing it in the order of the extremes, depending on the table to which the latter belongs.

This is why, in the series of four letters, the two intermediary and extreme couples can be identical if the latter is written in the order provided in Table O (such as αααα, ααββ, ββγγ, ββδδ, γγγγ, γγδδ, δδαα, and δδββ, which are possible); they cannot be identical if the latter are written in the order of Table Ω (ββββ, ββαα, γγββ, γγαα, δδδδ, δδγγ, ααδδ, and ααγγ, which are impossible).

Remarks whose recreational character must not lead us astray. 52

For there is no other link [*lien*] than that of this symbolic determination in which the signifying overdetermination, the notion of which Freud brings us, can be situated, and which was never able to be conceived of as a *real* overdetermination by a mind like his—everything contradicting the idea that he abandoned himself to this conceptual aberration in which philosophers and physicians find it all too easy to calm their religious excitations.

This position regarding the autonomy of the symbolic is the only position that allows us to clarify the theory and practice of free association in psychoanalysis. For relating its mainspring to symbolic determination and to its laws is altogether different from relating it to the scholastic presuppositions of an imaginary inertia that prop it up in associationism, whether philosophical or pseudophilosophical, before claiming to be experimental. Having abandoned its examination, psychoanalysts find here yet another jumping-off point for the psychologizing confusion into which they constantly fall, some of them deliberately.

In fact, only examples of preservation (whose suspension is indefinite) based on the exigencies of the symbolic chain, such as the examples that I have just provided, allow us to conceptualize where the indestructible persistence of unconscious desire is situated, that persistence, however paradoxical it may seem in Freud's doctrine, nevertheless being one of the features of it that is the most strongly asserted by Freud.

This characteristic is, in any case, incommensurate with certain effects recognized in authentically experimental psychology and which, regardless of the delays or time lags to which they are subject, eventually weaken and die out like every vital response.

This is precisely the question to which Freud returns once again in *Beyond the Pleasure Principle*, in order to indicate that the *insistence* which I take to be the essential characteristic of the phenomena of *repetition automatism*, seems to him to be explainable only by something prevital and transbiological. This conclusion may be surprising, but it is Freud's, speaking about what he was the first to have spoken about. And one must be deaf not to hear it. Coming from his pen, as it does, it will not be thought to involve recourse to spiritualism: for it is the structure of determination that is in question here. The matter that it displaces in its effects extends far beyond the matter of cerebral 53 organization, to the vicissitudes of which certain among them are entrusted, but others remain no less active and structured as symbolic even though they are materialized differently.

Thus, if man comes to think about the symbolic order, it is because he is first caught in it in his being. The illusion that he has formed this order through his consciousness stems from the fact that it is through the pathway of a specific gap in his imaginary relationship with his semblable that he has been able to enter into this order as a subject. But he has only been able to make this entrance by passing through the radical defile of speech, a genetic moment of which we have seen in a child's game, but which, in its complete form, is reproduced each time the subject addresses the Other as absolute, that is, as the Other who can annul him himself, just as he can act accordingly with the Other, that is, by making himself into an object in order to deceive the Other. This dialectic of intersubjectivity, the necessary usage of which I have demonstrated in the course of the past three years of my seminar at Saint Anne Hospital, from the theory of transference to the structure of paranoia, readily finds support in the following schema:

L SCHEMA

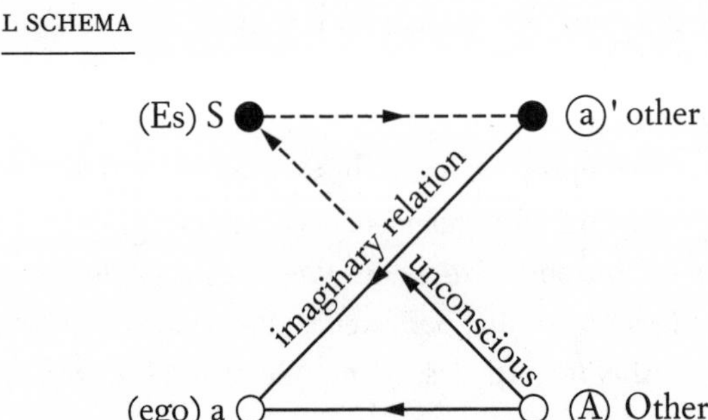

This schema is by now familiar to my students. The two middle terms here [*a* and *a'*] represent the couple involved in reciprocal imaginary objectification that I have brought out in "The Mirror Stage."

The specular relationship with the other—by which I at first wanted, in fact, to return the theory of narcissism, so crucial to Freud's work, to its dominant position in the function of the ego—can only reduce to its effective subordination the whole fantasmatization brought to light by analytic experience by interposing itself, as the schema expresses it, between this shy of [*en-deça*]

54 the Subject and this beyond [*au-delà*] of the Other, where speech in effect inserts it, insofar as the existences that are grounded in speech are entirely at the mercy of its faith [*foi*].

It is by having confused these two couples that the legatees of a praxis and a teaching that as decisively settled the question as Freud's did regarding the fundamentally narcissistic nature of all being in love (*Verliebtheit*) were able to so utterly deify the chimera of so-called genital love as to attribute to it the virtue of "oblativity," a notion that gave rise to so many therapeutic mistakes.

But by simply eliminating any and all reference to the symbolic poles of intersubjectivity in order to reduce analytic treatment to a utopian rectification of the imaginary couple, we have now arrived at a form of practice in which, under the banner of "object relations," what any man of good faith can only react to with a feeling of abjection is consummated.

This is what justifies the true gymnastics of the intersubjective register constituted by some of the exercises over which my seminar may have seemed to tarry.

The similarity between the relationship among the terms of the L schema and the relationship that unites the four times distinguished above (in the oriented series in which we see the first finished form of a symbolic chain) cannot fail to strike one as soon as one considers the connection between them.

Parenthesis of Parentheses (Added in 1966)

I will express here my perplexity at the fact that none of the people who took it upon themselves to decipher the ordering to which my chain lent itself, thought of writing in the form of parentheses the structure thereof that I had nevertheless clearly enunciated.

A parenthesis enclosing one or several other parentheses—that is, (( )) or (( ) ( ) . . . ( ))—is equivalent to the above-analyzed distribution of βs and δs, in which it is easy to see that the redoubled parenthesis is fundamental.

I will call the latter "quotes."

I intend to use this redoubled parenthesis to cover the structure of the subject (that is, the S in my L schema), insofar as it implies a redoubling, 55
or rather the sort of division that involves a lining [*doublure*] function.

I have already placed in this lining the direct or inverse alternation of $\alpha\gamma\alpha\gamma$ . . . pairs, on the condition that the number of signs be even or zero.

Between the inside parentheses, an alternation of $\gamma\alpha\gamma\alpha$ . . . γ signs, the number of signs being zero or odd.

On the other hand, inside the parentheses, as many γs as one would like, starting with zero.

Outside of the quotes we find, on the contrary, any series of αs, which includes none, one, or several parentheses stuffed with $\alpha\gamma\alpha\gamma$ . . . α signs, the number of signs being zero or odd.

If we replace the αs and the γs by 1s and 0s, we can write the so-called L chain in a form that seems to me to be more "telling" [*parlante*].

L Chain: (10...(00...0) 0101...0 (00...0)...01) 11111...(1010...1) 111 . . . etc.

"Telling" in the sense that a reading of it will be facilitated at the cost of a supplementary convention which accords it with the L schema.

This convention is to give the 0s between parentheses the value of moments of silence, a value of scansion being left to the 0s in the alternations, a convention justified by the fact that they are not homogeneous, as we shall see below.

What is inside the quotes can then represent the structure of the S (Es) in my L schema, symbolizing the subject supposedly completed by the Freudian *Es*, the subject of the psychoanalytic session, for example. The *Es* then appears there in the form given to it by Freud, insofar as he distinguishes it from the unconscious—namely, as logistically disjoint and subjectively silent (the silence of the drives).

It is then the alternation of the 01s that represents the imaginary grill (aa′) of the L schema.

It remains for me to define the privilege of the alternation characteristic of the between-two of the quotes (01 pairs)—that is, obviously, of the status of a and a′ in themselves.[26]

What is outside of the quotes will represent the field of the Other (A in the L schema). Repetition dominates there in the form of the 1, the unary
56 trait, representing (as a complement to the preceding convention) the times marked by the symbolic as such.

The subject S receives his message in an inverted form from there as well (interpretation).

Isolated from this chain, the parenthesis including (10 . . . 01) represents the ego of the psychological *cogito*—that is, of the false *cogito*—which can just as well prop up perversion pure and simple.[27]

The only remainder required by this attempt is the formalism of a certain remembering [*mémoration*] related to the symbolic chain, whose law one could easily formulate with respect to the L chain.

(This law is essentially defined by the relay constituted, in the alternation of 0s and 1s, by the surmounting [*franchissement*] of one or several parenthetical signs and of which signs.)

What must be kept in mind here is the rapidity with which a formalization is obtained that is suggestive both of a remembering that is primordial in the subject and of a structuration in which it is notable that stable disparities can be distinguished therein (indeed, the same dissymmetrical structure persists if, for example, we reverse all the quotes).[28]

This is but an exercise, but it fulfills my intent to inscribe therein the sort of contour where what I have called the signifier's *caput mortuum* takes on its causal aspect.

This effect is as manifest when grasped here as in the fiction of "The Purloined Letter."

The essence of the latter is that the letter was able to have its effects on 57
the inside—on the tale's actors, including the narrator—just as much as on the outside—on us, its readers, and also on its author—without anyone ever having had to worry about what it meant. This is the usual fate of everything that is written.

But at present we are only at the point of erecting an arch on which a bridge will be built in years to come.[29]

This is why, in order to demonstrate to my audience what distinguishes true intersubjectivity from the dyadic relationship implied by the notion of "projection," I had already used the reasoning approvingly recounted by Poe himself in the story that will be the subject of the present seminar, as the reasoning that guided a supposedly prodigal child in helping him win more often than he should have otherwise in the game of even or odd.

In following this reasoning—which is childish, that's the word for it, but 58
which still manages to seduce certain people in other locales—we must grasp the point at which the lure therein appears.

Here the subject is the one who is questioned: he has to guess whether the number of objects that his opponent hides in his hand is even or odd.

After a round won or lost by me, the boy essentially tells us, I know that if my opponent is a simpleton, "his amount of cunning" will not exceed the change from even to odd, but if he is "a simpleton a degree above the first," it will cross his mind that I will think of that myself and hence that it makes sense for him to play even again.

The child thus relied upon the objectification of the higher or lower number of his opponent's cerebral folds in order to achieve his success. A point of view whose link with imaginary identification is immediately indicated by the fact that it is through an internal imitation of his opponent's attitudes and mimicry that he claims to arrive at the proper assessment of his object.

But what then of the next level, when my opponent, having recognized that I am intelligent enough to follow him in this move, will manifest his own intelligence in realizing that it is by acting like an idiot that he has his best chance of deceiving me? There is no other valid time of the reasoning in this moment, precisely because it can but repeat thereafter in an indefinite oscillation.

And apart from the case of pure imbecility, in which the reasoning seemed to be objectively grounded, the child cannot but think that his opponent will arrive at the obstacle of this third time since he granted him the second, by which he himself is considered by his opponent to be a subject who objectifies him, for *it is true that he may be this subject;* hence we see him caught with him in the impasse implied by every purely dyadic intersubjectivity, which is that of having no recourse against an absolute Other.

Let us note in passing the vanishing role played by intelligence in the constitution of the second time in which the dialectic detaches itself from the contingencies of the pregiven; let us note, too, that I need but impute intelligence to my opponent for its function to be useless since, from that point on, it collapses back into these contingencies.

59 I will not say, however, that the path of imaginary identification with the opponent at the instant of each of these rounds is a path that is sealed off in advance; I will say that it excludes the properly symbolic process which appears as soon as this identification occurs, not with the opponent, but with his reasoning as articulated by this identification (this difference is, moreover, enunciated in Poe's text). The fact proves, moreover, that such a purely imaginary identification generally fails.

Hence each player, if he reasons, can only resort to something beyond the dyadic relationship—in other words, to some law which presides over the succession of the rounds of the game.

This is so true that if I am the one who selects the number to be guessed—that is, if I am the active subject—I will at each instant attempt to convince my opponent that there is a law which presides over a certain regularity in my selection, in order to pull the ground of his understanding out from under him as often as possible by breaking that law.

The more this approach manages to free itself from real regularities that are sketched out *in spite of myself*, the more successful it will effectively be, which is why someone who participated in one of the trials of this game that I did not hesitate to turn into in-class exercises, admitted that, at a moment at which he had the feeling, whether justified or not, of being too often found out, he freed himself from it by basing himself on the conventionally transposed succession of letters in a verse by Mallarmé for the series of rounds that he thereafter proposed to his opponent.

But had the game lasted as long as the entire poem and if, by some miracle, the opponent had been able to recognize it, the latter would then have won every round.

This is what allowed me to say that if the unconscious exists, in Freud's sense of the term—I mean if we understand the implications of the lesson that he draws from the experiences of the psychopathology of everyday life, for example—it is not unthinkable that a modern calculating machine, by detecting the sentence that, unbeknown to him and in the long term, modulates a subject's choices, could manage to win beyond any usual proportions in the game of even and odd.

This is a pure paradox, no doubt, but in it is expressed the fact that it is not
because it lacks the supposed virtue of human consciousness that we refuse to
call the machine to which we would attribute such fabulous performances a
"thinking machine," but simply because it would think no more than the ordi- 60
nary man does, without that making him any less prey to the summonses
[*appels*] of the signifier.

Thus the possibility suggested here was of interest insofar as it conveyed to me the effect of distress and even anxiety that certain participants felt and were willing to share with me.

A reaction about which one can wax ironic, coming as it does from analysts whose entire technique relies upon the unconscious determination that is granted in that technique to so-called free association, and who can find clearly spelled out in the text by Freud that I just mentioned that a number is never chosen at random.

But it is a legitimate reaction if one considers that nothing has taught them to leave behind everyday opinion by distinguishing what it neglects: namely, the nature of Freudian overdetermination—in other words, the nature of symbolic determination such as I promote it here.

If this overdetermination had to be considered real—as my example suggested to them, because, like everyone else, they confused the machine's calculations with its mechanism[30]—then, indeed, their anxiety would be justified, for in a gesture more sinister than that of touching the ax, I would be the one who brings it down on "the laws of chance." Being good determinists, those who found this gesture so moving rightly felt that if we changed these laws, there would no longer be any conceivable law at all.

But these laws are precisely those of symbolic determination. For it is clear that they predate any real observation of randomness [*hasard*], as is clear from the fact that we judge whether an object is apt or not to be used to obtain a series (always symbolic, in this case) of random throws according to its obedience to these laws—for example, whether or not a coin, or this object admirably known as a "die" [*dé*], qualifies for this function.

Once this practical training was over, I had to illustrate in a concrete man- 61
ner the dominance that I assert the signifier has over the subject. If it is a truth,

then it can be found everywhere, and we should be able to start with anything within range of our tap and make it flow like wine in Auerbach's tavern.

This is why I took the very tale from which I had extracted the dubious reasoning about the game of even or odd, without seeing anything more in that tale at first. I found something useful in it that my notion of symbolic determination would have already prohibited me from considering to be simply accidental [*hasard*], even if it had not turned out, in the course of my examination, that Poe—as a fine precursor of research into combinatorial strategy which is in the process of revamping the order of the sciences—had been guided in his fiction by the same aim [*dessein*] as mine. At least I can say that what I brought out in my exposé of it touched my audience enough for it to be at their request that I am publishing a version of it here.

In reworking it in accordance with the requirements of writing [*l'écrit*], which are different from those of speech, I could not help but present the further development I have provided since that time of certain notions it introduced.

This is why the emphasis, with which I have increasingly promoted the notion of signifier in the symbol, occurred retroactively here. To obscure its traits through a sort of historical feint would have seemed, I believe, artificial to my students. I can only hope that the fact that I spared myself this task will not disappoint their memory of it.

Notes

1. The necessary reference here may be found in my essay, "Logical Time and the Assertion of Anticipated Certainty," in *Écrits* 1966, 197–213.

2. See "The Function and Field of Speech and Language in Psychoanalysis," in *Écrits* 1966, 244.

3. To completely understand what follows one must reread the short and readily available text of "The Purloined Letter."

4. See Émile Benveniste, "Communication animale et langage humain," *Diogène* I, and my Rome Report ["The Function and Field of Speech and Language"], *Écrits* 1966, 297. [In English, see Émile Benveniste, *Problems in General Linguistics*, trans. M. Meek (Coral Gables: University of Miami Press, 1971), 49–54.]

5. See *Écrits* 1966, 58.

6. [Added in 1968:] I had at first added a note on the meaning these three [Latin] words would provide by way of commentary on this story, if the structure did not suffice, although it aspires to do so.

I am eliminating that indication, which was overly imperfect, because in rereading my text for this reprinting someone has confirmed to me that, after the era of those who are selling me out (even today, December 9, 1968), another era is coming in which people read my work to explicate it further.

The latter shall take place elsewhere than on this page.

7. I would like to pose again to Benveniste the question of the antithetical meaning of certain words, whether primal or not, after the masterful correction he made to the erroneous path Freud took in studying the question on philological ground (see *La Psychanalyse* 1 [1956]: 5–16). For I think that the question remains unanswered once the instance of the signifier has been rigorously formulated. Bloch and Von Wartburg date back to 1875

the first appearance of the signification of the verb *dépister* as I used it the second time in this sentence. [In English, see Émile Benveniste, *Problems in General Linguistics*, 65–75. See also Freud's article "The Antithetical Meaning of Primal Words," *SE* XI, 155–61.]

8. The very utopia to which Jorge Luis Borges, in his work which harmonizes so well with the phylum of my subject matter, has accorded an importance which others reduce to its proper proportions. See *Les Temps Modernes* 113–14 (June–July 1955): 2135–36 and 118 (October 1955): 574–75.

9. Poe's emphasis.

10. This is so true that philosophers, in those hackneyed examples with which they argue on the basis of the one and the many, will not put to the same purposes a simple sheet of white paper ripped down the middle and a broken circle, or even a shattered vase, not to mention a cut worm.

11. See *Our Exagmination Round His Factification for Incamination of "Work in Progress"* (Paris: Shakespeare & Co., 12 rue de l'Odéon, 1929).

12. See *Écrits* 1966, 59.

13. I felt obliged at this point to demonstrate the procedure to the audience using a letter from that period which concerned Chateaubriand and his search for a secretary. I was amused to find that Chateaubriand had completed the first version of his memoirs (recently published in its original form) in the very month of November 1841 in which "The Purloined Letter" appeared in *Chambers' Journal*. Will Chateaubriand's devotion to the power he decries, and the honor which that devotion does him ("the gift" had not yet been invented), place him in the category to which we will later see the Minister assigned: among men of genius with or without principles?

14. Poe is the author of an essay by this title.

15. [Added in 1966:] And even from the cook herself.

16. Virgil's line reads: *facilis descensus Averno*. ["The descent to Hades is easy"; see Virgil's *Aeneid*, book 6, line 126.]

17. Let us recall the witty distich attributed before his fall to the most recent person to have rejoined Candide's meeting in Venice. "*Il n'est plus aujourd'hui que cinq rois sur la terre, / Les quatre rois des cartes et le roi d'Angleterre.*" (There are only five kings left on earth today: / The four kings of cards and the King of England.)

18. This statement was openly made by a noble Lord speaking to the Upper House in which his dignity earned him a seat.

19. I am referring to the fundamental opposition Aristotle makes between these two terms [*automaton* and *tyche*] in the conceptual analysis of chance he provides in his *Physics*. Many discussions would be clarified if it were not overlooked.

20. I am referring here to the *Entwurf einer Psychologie* ["Project for a Scientific Psychology"] written in 1895 which, unlike the famous letters to Fliess (with which it was included [in *The Origins of Psychoanalysis*] since it was addressed to him), was not censored by its editors. Certain mistakes found in the German edition, owing to the misreading of the handwritten manuscript, even indicate how little attention was paid to its meaning. It is clear in this passage that I am merely punctuating a position that was developed in my seminar.

21. [Added in 1966:] For greater clarity, let me illustrate this notation using the following random [*hasard*] series:

+	+	+	−	+	+	−	−	+	−	
		1	2	3	2	2	2	2	3	etc.

22. This dissymmetry is truly the one that unites the usages of the English word that, as far as I know, has no equivalent in any other language: "odd." The French usage of the word "*impair*" to designate an aberration of conduct shows us something of a sketch thereof; but the word "*disparate*" itself proves inadequate here.

23. See the revitalizing reprising of it by Claude Lévi-Strauss in his article "Les organisations dualistes existent-elles?" in *Bijdragen tot de taal-, land- en Volkenkunde*, Deel 112, 2 (Gravenhage, 1956), 99–128. This article can be found in French in a collection of works by Claude Lévi-Strauss published as *Anthropologie structurale* (Paris: Plon, 1958). [In English,

see "Do Dual Organizations Exist?" in *Structural Anthropology*, trans. C. Jacobson and B. G. Schoepf (New York: Basic Books, 1963).]

24. These two letters correspond to the dextrogyrate and levogyrate nature of a figuration that situates the excluded terms in quadrants.

25. [Added in 1966:] If one does not take into account the order of the letters, this *caput mortuum* is only 7/16.

26. This is why I have since introduced a more appropriate topology.

27. See the Abbot of Choisy, whose famous memoirs can be translated as: *I think, when I am* the one who dresses like a woman.

28. Let me add here the network of the αs, βs, γs, and δs, which is constituted by a transformation of the 1–3 Network. As all mathematicians know, it is obtained by transforming the segments of the first network into the cuts of the second and by marking the oriented paths joining these cuts. It is as follows (I am placing it next to the first for greater clarity):

1–3 NETWORK

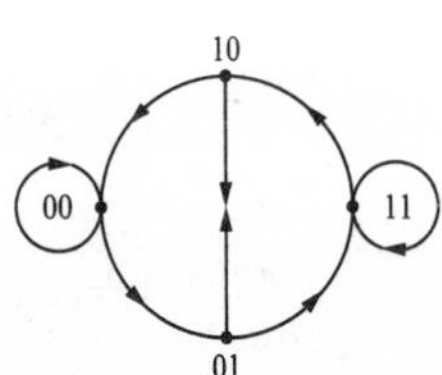

α, β, γ, δ NETWORK

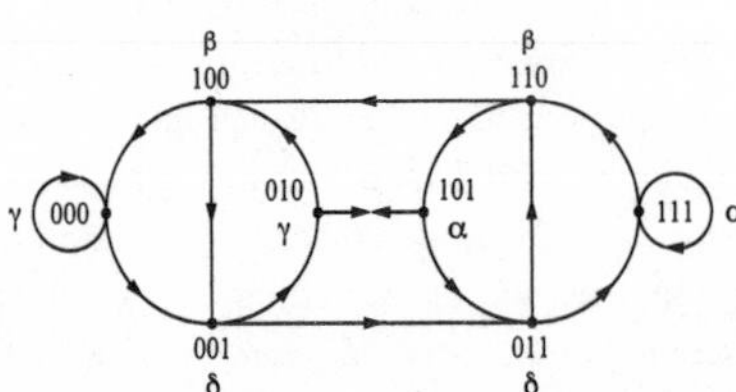

Here I propose the convention upon which the letters are based:

1.1 = α
0.0 = γ
1.0 = β
0.1 = δ

(One can see here why I said that there are two types of 0 in my L chain, for there are those 0s that correspond to γ = 000 and those 0s that correspond to γ = 010.)

29. [Added in 1966:] The text written in 1955 resumes here. The introduction of a structural approach to the field in psychoanalytic theory through such exercises was, in fact, followed by important developments in my teaching. Concepts related to subjectivization progressed hand-in-hand with a reference to the *analysis situs* in which I claim to materialize the subjective process.

30. It was in order to dispel this illusion that I closed that year's seminar with a lecture on "Psychoanalysis and Cybernetics" [Seminar II, chapter 23], which disappointed many because I barely spoke in it of anything other than binary numeration, the arithmetic triangle, and even of the simple gate, defined by the fact that it must be open or closed—in short, because it seemed that I had not gone very far beyond the Pascalian stage of the question.

II

On My Antecedents

In taking a step back now to present the work that marked my entry into psychoanalysis, I will remind the reader by what doorway this entry occurred.

As a physician and a psychiatrist, I had introduced, under the heading of "paranoiac knowledge," several end results of the method of clinical exhaustion that my doctoral thesis in medicine exemplified.[1]

Rather than mention the group (Évolution Psychiatrique) that was willing to publish my exposition of these results, or even mention their echo in the surrealist environment in which a former link was reestablished on the basis of a new relay, including Salvador Dalí's "critical paranoia" and René Crevel's *Le Clavecin de Diderot*—my offspring can be found in the first issues of the journal *Minotaure*[2]—I will indicate the origin of my interest in it.

It stems from the work of Gatian de Clérambault, my only master in psychiatry.

His notion of "mental automatism," with its metaphorical, mechanistic ideology, which is assuredly open to criticism, seems to me, in its attempt to come to grips with the [patient's] subjective text, closer to what can be constructed on the basis of a structural analysis than any other clinical approach in French psychiatry.

I was sensitive to the hint of a promise that I perceived in it due to the contrast between it and the decline that could be seen in a semiology that was ever more bogged down in assumptions related to rationality.

66 Clérambault achieved, through the quality of his gaze and the biases of his thought, a sort of recurrence of what has recently been described for us in a figure that dates back to the birth of the clinic.[3]

Clérambault was very familiar with the French tradition, but it was Kraepelin, whose clinical genius was of a higher caliber, who trained him.

Oddly enough, but necessarily, I believe, I was thereby led to Freud.

For faithfulness to the symptom's formal envelope, which is the true clinical trace for which I acquired a taste, led me to the limit at which it swings back in creative effects. In the case included in my dissertation (the case of Aimée), there were literary effects—of high enough quality to have been collected, under the (reverent) heading of involuntary poetry, by Éluard.

The function of ideals presented itself to me here in a series of reduplications that led me to the notion of a structure, which was more instructive than the account the clinicians in Toulouse would have provided, for they would have lowered its price by situating it in the register of passion.

Moreover, the sort of gust effect that, in my subject, blew down the screen known as a delusion as soon as her hand touched, in a serious act of aggression, one of the images in her theater—who was doubly fictitious for her since she was also a star in reality—redoubled the conjugation of her poetic space with a gulf-like scansion.

This brought me closer to the stage machinery of acting out [*passage à l'acte*] and, if only by confining myself to the all-purpose word "self-punishment" that Berlin-style criminology offered me through the mouthpieces of Alexander and Staub, I was led to Freud.

The way in which a knowledge [*connaissance*] is specified on the basis of its stereotypy, and also of its discharges, providing evidence of another function, [seemed to me to] lead to an enrichment which no academicism, even that of the avant-garde, could have turned away.

Perhaps it will be understood that by crossing the doorstep of psychoanalysis, I immediately recognized in its practice knowledge-related biases that are far more interesting, since they are those that must be eliminated in its fundamental listening.

67 I had not awaited that moment to meditate upon the fantasies through which the idea of the ego is apprehended, and if I presented the "mirror stage" in 1936,[4] when I had yet to be granted the customary title of analyst, at the first International Congress at which I had my first taste of an association that was to give me plenty of others, I was not lacking in merit for doing so. For its invention brought me to the very heart of a resistance

in theory and technique which, constituting an ever more blatant problem thereafter, was, it must be admitted, far from being perceived by the milieu I started out in.

I have thought it well to first offer the reader a short article, which was written around the same time as that presentation.

My students occasionally delude themselves into thinking that they have found "already there" in my writings what my teaching has only brought out since then. Is it not enough that what is there did not bar the way to what came later? Let the reference to language that is sketched out here be seen as the fruit of the only imprudence that has never failed me: that of trusting in nothing but the experience of the subject who is the only material of analytic work.

My title, "Beyond . . . ," did not hesitate to paraphrase the other *Beyond* that Freud assigns to his pleasure principle in 1920. Which leads us to wonder: Did Freud throw off the yoke thanks to which he maintained this principle by pairing it with the reality principle?

In his *Beyond*, Freud makes room for the fact that the pleasure principle —to which he has, in sum, given a new meaning by instating its signifying articulation of repetition in the circuit of reality, in the form of the primary process—takes on a still newer meaning by helping force open its traditional barrier related to a jouissance, a jouissance that is pinpointed at that time in masochism, and even opens onto [the question of] the death drive.

What happens, under such conditions, to this intertwining by which the identity of thoughts that stem from the unconscious offers its woof to the
secondary process, by permitting reality to become established *to the* plea- 68
sure principle's *satisfaction*?

That is the question with which the reversed reprisal of the Freudian project, by which I have recently characterized my project, could be announced.

While we have the beginnings of it here, it could go no further. Let us simply say that it does not exaggerate the scope of psychoanalytic action [*l'acte psychanalytique*] when it assumes that the latter transcends the secondary process to attain a reality that is not produced in it, even if it dispels the illusion that reduced the identity of thoughts to the thought of their identity.

Although everyone agrees, in fact (even those who are dumb enough not to realize that they agree), that the primary process encounters nothing real except the impossible, which in the Freudian perspective remains the best definition that can be given of reality [*réel*], the point is to know more about what Else [*d'Autre*] it encounters so that we can concern ourselves with it.

Thus it is not to be duped by an effect of perspective to see here the first delineation of the imaginary, whose letters, associated with those of the symbolic and the real, will decorate much later (just before my Rome discourse) the pots—that are forever empty, since they are all so symbolic—in which I will prepare the theriac with which to resolve the confusions of analytic cogitation.

There is nothing here that is not justified by my attempt to refute the misguided idea that there must be something, anything whatsoever, in the subject that corresponds to a reality [*réel*] system—or even, as people in other circles say, to a characteristic function of reality. It is to this very mirage that a theory of the ego is currently devoted which, in basing itself on the return Freud assures this agency in his *Group Psychology and the Analysis of the Ego*, goes astray since that text includes nothing but the theory of identification.

The aforementioned theory [ego psychology] fails to refer to the necessary antecedent to *Group Psychology*, which served as its basis: the article entitled "On Narcissism." It was, of course, published in 1914, a year in which the attention of the analytic community was stretched a bit thin.

There is nothing here, in any case, which allows us to consider unequivocal the reality that people invoke by combining in it the two terms, *Wirklichkeit* and *Realität*, that Freud distinguishes in this article, the second being especially reserved for psychical reality.

69 Whence derives the value, which is *wirklich*, operative, of the wedge that I drive in here by putting back in its place the deceptive truism that identicalness to oneself, which is presumed to exist in the ego's usual sense [of itself], has something to do with a supposed instance of reality [*réel*].

If Freud reminds us of the relationship between the ego and the perception-consciousness system, it is only to indicate that our reflective tradition—we would be wrong to think that it has had no social impact insofar as it has served as a basis for political forms of personal status—has tested its standards of truth in this system.

But it is in order to call these standards of truth into question that Freud links the ego, on the basis of a twofold reference, to one's own body—that is narcissism—and to the complexity of the three orders of identification.

The mirror stage establishes the watershed between the imaginary and the symbolic in the moment of capture by an historic inertia, responsibility for which is borne by everything that alleges to be psychology, even if it is by pathways that claim to release it from that responsibility.

This is why I did not give my article on the reality principle the sequel it announced, which was to assail Gestalt theory and phenomenology.

Instead, I constantly emphasized a moment in analytic practice which is not one of history but of configuring insight*, which I designated as a stage, even if it emerged as a phase.

Must this phase be reduced to a biological crisis? The dynamic of this phase, as I outline it, is based on diachronic effects: the delayed coordination of the nervous system related to man's prematurity at birth, and the formal anticipation of its resolution.

But to presume the existence of a harmony that is contradicted by many facts of ethology is tantamount to dupery.

It masks the crux of a function of lack with the question of the place that this function can assume in a causal chain. Now, far from imagining eliminating it from it, I currently consider such a function to be the very origin of causalist noesis, which goes so far as to mistake it for its crossing into reality [*passage au réel*].

But to consider it effective due to its imaginary discordance is to still leave too much room for the presumption of birth.

This function involves a more critical lack, its cover being the secret to 70
the subject's jubilation.

Here we can see that any dwelling [*attardement*] on the genesis of the ego shares in the vanity of what it judges. Which seems self-evident if we think about it: Can any step in the imaginary go beyond the imaginary's limits if it does not stem from another order?

This is nevertheless what psychoanalysis clearly promises, and it would remain mythical were analysis to retreat to the same level as the imaginary.

To pinpoint it in the mirror stage, we first have to know how to read in it the paradigm of the properly imaginary definition that is given of metonymy: the part for the whole. For let us not forget that my concept envelops the so-called partial images—the only ones that warrant the term "archaic"—found in the analytic experience of fantasy; I group those images together under the heading of images of the fragmented body, and they are confirmed by the assertion of fantasies of the so-called paranoid phase in the phenomenology of Kleinian experience.

What is involved in the triumph of assuming [*assomption*] the image of one's body in the mirror is the most evanescent of objects, since it only appears there in the margins: the exchange of gazes, which is manifest in the fact that the child turns back toward the person who is assisting the child in some way, if only by being present during the game.

Let me add to this something that a movie, which was made by people with no knowledge of my conceptions, showed us when it captured on film a little girl looking at herself naked in the mirror: with an awkward gesture, her hand quickly encountered the phallic lack.

Regardless of what covers the image, nevertheless, the latter merely centers a power that is deceptive insofar as it diverts alienation—which already situates desire in the Other's field—toward the totalitarian rivalry which prevails due to the fact that the semblable exercises a dyadic fascination on him: that "one or the other" is the depressive return of the second phase in Melanie Klein's work; it is the figure of Hegelian murder.

Let me add here, by way of an apologue with which to summarize the early misrecognition that takes root here, the use of the inversion produced in planar symmetry [right-left reversal]. It could only take on value through a more in-depth discussion of spatial orientation, which philosophy has not been more interested in, surprisingly enough, since Kant, holding his glove at the end of his hand, based an aesthetics on it—an aesthetics that is nevertheless just as simple to turn inside out as the glove itself is.

But this is already to situate the experience at a point that does not allow
71 one to delude oneself regarding the link with the ability to see. Even a blind man is a subject here because he knows he is an object of other people's gazes. But the problem lies elsewhere and its articulation is as theoretical as that of Molyneux's problem:[5] we would have to know what the ego would be in a world where no one knows anything about planar symmetry.

Lastly, let me remind you of the reference points of specular knowledge [*connaissance*] based on a semiology that runs the gamut from the most subtle depersonalization to the hallucination of one's double. They are known to have no intrinsic diagnostic value as concerns the structure of the subject (the psychotic, among others). It is more important to note, however, that they do not constitute a more consistent reference point for fantasy in psychoanalytic treatment.

I thus find myself situating these texts in a future perfect: they will have anticipated my insertion of the unconscious into language. In seeing them spread out over the years that were not very full, aren't I exposing myself to the reproach of having given into dwelling on the past [*attardement*]?

Apart from the fact that I certainly had to gain a following in our field of practice, I will plead that I could do no better during that time than prepare my audience.

Present generations of psychiatrists will find it hard to imagine that, at the time that I was doing my residency, there were only three of us who got involved in psychoanalysis; and without being ungrateful to the group of people involved in *Évolution Psychiatrique*, I will say that although it was to their credit that psychoanalysis saw the light of day [in France], psychoanalysis was not radically called into question by them. The intrusion of worldly matters did not increase either their solidarity or their information to this end.

In fact, no teaching other than a routine fast-track existed prior to 1951 when I began mine in a private capacity.

While the quantity of recruits, from which an effect of quality is engendered, completely changed after the war, perhaps the standing-room-only
crowd that came to hear me speak about "Training Analysis" will serve as 72
a reminder that I played an important role therein.

Up until then, however, the major institution that offered me the opportunity to give several public lectures was the *Collège Philosophique*, where, at Jean Wahl's invitation, the intellectual fevers of the time faced off.[6]

Allow me to add that this note owes what is biographical in it only to my desire to enlighten the reader.

Notes

1. My thesis was published as *De la psychose paranoïaque dans ses rapports avec la personnalité* (Paris: Le François, 1932). It was based on 30 cases, although its method required that it include a monograph: the case of Aimée. This fact explains the gallant assessment of it, by a luminary, found on page 536.

2. They include "Le problème du style" ("The Problem of Style") and "Motifs du crime paranoïaque" ("Motives of Paranoiac Crime"); the latter article was devoted to the Papin sisters and was left out of a recent discussion of this subject by a contemporary.

3. See Michel Foucault's *Naissance de la clinique* (Paris: PUF, 1964) [*The Birth of the Clinic* (New York: Pantheon, 1973)].

4. It was at the Congress in Marienbad (August 3, 1936) that my first pivotal intervention in psychoanalytic theory took place. The reader will find an ironic reference to it on pages 184–85 of this collection, along with a reference to the volume of the *Encyclopédie française* that attests to the date of the theses it contained (1938). I, in fact, neglected to send the write-up of my talk to those who prepared the report on the Congress.

5. See the article by Alain Grosrichard, "Une expérience psychologique au XVIIIe siècle," *Cahiers Pour l'Analyse* II (May 1966), which would also allow us to further explore the question of the subject from the fiction of the philosophically inclined blind man to the fiction of the blind philosopher.

6. One of the talks I gave there was on the "Individual Myth of the Neurotic," the beginning of a duly structuralist reference (see the first text by Claude Lévi-Strauss on myth). The mimeographed text of the talk, which came out without being corrected by me, will testify to its existence for a later reprisal. [The text, originally printed in French in 1953, appeared in English as "The Neurotic's Individual Myth," trans. M. N. Evans, *PQ* XLVIII, 3 (1979): 405–25.]

Beyond the "Reality Principle"

THE SECOND GENERATION OF FREUD'S SCHOOL CAN DEFINE ITS DEBT AND ITS DUTY IN TERMS OF A FUNDAMENTAL PRINCIPLE OF HIS DOCTRINE: THE REALITY PRINCIPLE.

For the psychiatrist or psychologist of the 1930s, initiation into psychoanalytic method no longer involves a conversion that constitutes a break in one's intellectual development, a conversion that thus attests less to a carefully thought out choice of an avenue of research than to the outburst of secret affective strife. The appealing features that analysis once offered to the detours of *compensation*—the ethical seduction of devotion to a controversial cause, combined with the economic seduction of a form of speculation running counter to established values—are not missed. The new psychology not only fully accepts psychoanalysis; by constantly corroborating it by research in disciplines that begin from other starting points, it demonstrates the value of psychoanalysis' pioneering work. Psychoanalysis is thus, one could say, approached from a normal angle of incidence by what I will call—without commenting on the arbitrary nature of such a formulation—the second generation of analysts. It is this angle of incidence that I would like to define here in order to indicate the path by which it is reflected back.

PART I. PSYCHOLOGY WAS CONSTITUTED AS A SCIENCE WHEN THE RELATIVITY OF ITS OBJECT WAS POSITED BY FREUD, EVEN THOUGH IT WAS RESTRICTED TO FACTS CONCERNING DESIRE.

Critique of Associationism

The Freudian revolution, like any revolution, derives its meaning from its context, that is, from the form of psychology that dominated at the time it occurred. Now, any judgment about that form of psychology presupposes an exegesis of the documents in which it is propounded. I will establish the frame 74
of this article by asking the reader to credit me here, at least provisionally, with having done this basic work, so that I can provide what seems to me to be an essential moment of critique. For while I consider it legitimate to privilege the historical method in studying facts of consciousness, I do not use it as a pretext to elude the intrinsic critique that questions their value. Such a critique, grounded in the secondary order conferred upon these facts in history by the element of reflection they involve, remains immanent in the data recognized by the method—in our case, in the expressed forms of the doctrine and the technique—assuming the method simply requires each of the forms in question to be what it purports to be. This will allow us to see why the late nineteenth century form of psychology that claimed to be scientific and forced itself even on its adversaries, thanks both to its apparatus of objectivity and its profession of materialism, simply failed to be positive, excluding from the outset both objectivity and materialism.

Indeed, one might say that this form of psychology was based on a so-called associationist conception of the psyche, not so much because it formulated this conception into a theory, but because it received a series of postulates from this conception—as though they were commonsense data—that determined its very way of situating problems. Of course, we see right from the outset that the framework with which it classified the phenomena into sensations, perceptions, images, beliefs, logical operations, judgments, and so on, was borrowed unchanged from scholastic psychology, which had itself borrowed it from centuries of philosophy. We must thus realize that this framework, far from having been created for an objective conception of psychical reality, was merely the product of a sort of conceptual decline in which the vicissitudes of a specific effort that impels man to seek a *guarantee of truth* for his own knowledge were retraced—a guarantee which, as we can see, is transcendent by its position and therefore remains transcendent in its form, even when philoso-

phers deny its existence. What hint of transcendence do the concepts that are relics of such research themselves retain? To answer this question would involve defining what associationism introduces that is not positive into the very constitution of the object of psychology. We will see how difficult it is
75 to sort out at this level, in recalling that contemporary psychology preserves many of these concepts and that the purification of principles is what occurs last in every science.

But question begging blossoms in the general economy of problems that characterizes the stage of a theory at any particular moment in time. Thus considered as a whole, which is facilitated by our ability to view it with hindsight, associationism will strikingly reveal to us its metaphysical implications. In order to oppose it simply to a conception that is more or less judiciously defined in the theoretical foundations of various contemporary schools by the term "function of reality," let us say that associationist theory is dominated by the "function of truth."

Associationism is based on two concepts: the first, the "engram," is mechanistic; the second, the "associative link" of the mental phenomenon, is fallaciously considered to be given by experience. The first is a research formulation, and a rather flexible one at that, designed to designate the psychophysical element; it merely introduces the hypothesis, which is nevertheless fundamental, of the passive production of this element. It is notable that the associationist school added a postulate, that of the atomistic nature of this element. It is, in fact, this postulate that limited the vision of its adherents to the point of making them "overlook" experimental facts in which the subject's activity in organizing the *form* is manifest, facts which are, moreover, so compatible with a materialist interpretation that their inventors later conceptualized them from a materialist vantage point.

The second of these concepts, that of the *associative link*, is based on the experience of the living being's reactions. It is extended, however, to mental phenomena without the question begging implied in it being in any way critiqued, question begging that this concept borrows precisely from the psychical pregiven, in particular, the question begging which assumes that the mental form of *similarity* is given, even though it is in itself so difficult to analyze. The very pregivenness of the phenomenon that is purportedly explained here is thus smuggled into the explanatory concept. All this involves veritable conceptual sleight of hand (whose innocence does not excuse its crudeness) which, as Janet stressed, in functioning as a veritable intellectual flaw
76 characteristic of a school, truly becomes a master key used at every turning

point in the theory. Needless to say, one can thereby totally ignore the need for the kind of analysis known as "phenomenological analysis"—which no doubt requires subtlety but whose absence renders null and void any explanation in psychology.

We must thus wonder about the meaning of these failings in the development of a discipline that claims to be objective. Is it due to materialism, as a certain critic maintained without meeting with any objection? Or worse still, is objectivity itself impossible to attain in psychology?

People will denounce the theoretical flaw here once they recognize that the problem of knowledge is posed in associationism's structure from a philosophical perspective. This is certainly the traditional position on this problem which, having been inherited, in its first disguise, from Locke's so-called empiricist formulations, is found anew in two of the doctrine's fundamental concepts—namely, in the ambiguity of a critique which, (1) with the thesis "nihil est in intellectu quod non prius fuerit in sensu," reduces reality's action to its point of contact with *pure sensation*, that mythical entity, in other words, reduces it to being nothing but the blind spot of knowledge, since nothing is recognized there, and which (2) imposes all the more strongly, whether this is made explicit or not in "nisi intellectus ipse," as the dialectical antinomy of an incomplete thesis, the primacy of pure mind, insofar as it constitutes the *true moment* of knowledge, through the essential decree of identification, recognizing the object at the same time that it asserts it.

This is the source of the atomistic conception of the engram from which the blindnesses of the doctrine with respect to experience stem, while the *associative link*, through its uncriticized implications, brings with it a fundamentally idealist theory of knowledge phenomena.

This last point, which is obviously paradoxical in a doctrine whose pretensions are those of a naive materialism, clearly appears as soon as one attempts to formulate it in a slightly systematic manner, that is, in a manner that subjects it to the coherence of its concepts. Taine's attempt, which is that of a popularizer, but still consistent, is precious to us in this regard. We see in it a construction on the basis of knowledge phenomena, the objective of which is to reduce the higher activities to complexes of elementary reactions; it is reduced thereby to 77
seeking differential criteria of elementary reactions in the control of the higher activities. In order to fully grasp this paradox, consider the striking definition he gives of perception as a "veridical hallucination."

The dynamism of concepts borrowed from a transcendental dialectic is thus such that associationist psychology, in attempting to base itself on that dialectic, fails to constitute its object in positive terms, failing all the more fatally in that it receives those concepts emptied of the reflection they bring with them. Indeed, once the phenomena are defined in that form of psychology as a function of their *truth*, they are submitted in their very conception to a classification on the basis of value. Such a hierarchy not only vitiates, as we have seen, the objective study of the phenomena as regards their import in knowledge itself, but by subordinating all of the psychical pregiven to its perspective, it also skews the analysis thereof and impoverishes its meaning.

By assimilating the phenomenon of hallucination with the sensory order, associationist psychology thus merely reproduces the absolutely mythical import that the philosophical tradition attributes to this phenomenon in the standard question regarding the error of the senses. The fascination characteristic of this theoretically scandalous role no doubt explains the true misrecognitions in the analysis of the phenomenon that allow for the perpetuation of a position regarding the problem that is so erroneous, yet still tenaciously held to by many a clinician.

Let us now consider the problems of the *image*. The latter, which is no doubt the most important phenomenon in psychology due to the wealth of concrete data we have about it, is also important due to the complexity of its function, a complexity that one cannot attempt to encompass with a single term, unless it is with that of "information function." The various acceptations of this term that, running from the ordinary to the archaic, target the notion regarding an event, the stamp of an impression or the organization by an idea, express rather well, in fact, the roles of the image as the intuitive form of the object, the plastic form of the engram, and the generative form of development. This extraordinary phenomenon—the problems of which run from mental phenomenology to biology and the action of which echoes from the conditions of the mind to the organic determinisms of a perhaps unsuspected depth—is reduced in asso-
78 ciationism to its function as an *illusion*. The image, being viewed, according to the spirit of the theory, as a *weakened* sensation insofar as it attests less *surely* to reality, is considered to be the echo and shadow of sensation, and is consequently identified with its trace, the engram. The conception of the mind as a "polypary of images," which is essential to associationism, has been criticized above all for asserting a purely metaphysical mechanism; it has less often been pointed out that its essential absurdity lies in the intellectualist impoverishment that it imposes upon images.

In fact, a very large number of psychical phenomena are considered to signify nothing, according to the conceptions of this school. These phenomena thus supposedly cannot be included within the framework of an authentic psychology, which has to take into account the fact that a certain intentionality is phenomenologically inherent in its object. In associationism, this is equivalent to considering them to be insignificant, in other words, to rejecting them either to the nothingness of neglect or to the emptiness of "epiphenomena."

Such a conception thus creates two categories of psychical phenomena: those phenomena that fit into some level of the operations of rational knowledge, and all the others, including feelings, beliefs, delusions, assents, intuitions, and dreams. The former necessitated an *associationist* analysis of the psyche; the latter must be explained by some determinism that is foreign to their "appearance" and that is said to be "organic" insofar as it reduces them to being either the prop of a physical object or related to a biological end.

Psychical phenomena are thus granted no reality of their own: those that do not belong to "true" reality have only an illusory reality. This true reality is constituted by the system of references that are valid in already established sciences—in other words, mechanisms that are considered tangible in the physical sciences, to which may be added the motivations considered utilitarian in the natural sciences. The role of psychology is merely to reduce psychical phenomena to this system and to *verify* the system by determining through it the very phenomena that constitute our knowledge of it. It is insofar as this psychology is a function of this truth that it is not a science.

The Truth of Psychology and the Psychology of Truth 79

Let me try to make my point clear. I am not playing at being paradoxical by claiming that science need know nothing about truth. But I am not forgetting that truth is a value that (cor)responds to the uncertainty with which man's lived experience is phenomenologically marked or that the search for truth historically motivates, under the heading of the spiritual, the mystic's flights and the moralist's rules, the ascetic's progress and the mystagogue's finds alike.

This search, by imposing on an entire culture the preeminence of truth in testimony, created a moral attitude that was and remains for science a condition of its existence. But truth in its specific value remains foreign to the order of science: science can be proud of its alliances with truth; it can adopt the phenomenon and value of truth as its object; but it cannot in any way identify truth as its own end.

If there seems to be something artificial about this, one should dwell an instant on the lived criteria of truth and wonder what, in the dizzying relativisms that contemporary physics and mathematics have arrived at, subsists of the most concrete of these criteria: Where are *certainty*, that proof of mystical knowledge, *self-evidence*, the foundation of philosophical speculation, and *noncontradiction* itself, the more modest requirement of the empirical/rationalist construction?

To consider an example that is more within the reach of our judgment, can we say that scientists wonder if the rainbow is *true*? All that matters to them is that this phenomenon be communicable in some language (the condition of the *intellectual order*), that it be reportable in some form (the condition of the *experimental order*), and that it be possible to insert into the chain of symbolic identifications with which their science unifies the diversity of its own object (the condition of the *rational order*).

It must be admitted that physicomathematical theory at the end of the nineteenth century was still based on foundations that were intuitive enough that one could consider those foundations, which have since been eliminated, responsible for the prodigious fecundity of that theory and thus see in them
80 the omnipotence implied in the idea of truth. Furthermore, the practical successes of this science conferred upon it a brilliant prestige for the masses which is not unrelated to the phenomenon of self-evidence. Science thus found itself in a good position to serve as the ultimate object of the passion for truth, leading everyman to bow to the new idol called "scientism" and leading "scholars" ["*clerc*"] to the eternal pedantry that mutilates what they are able to grasp of reality, because they do not realize how much their truth is relative to the walls of their tower. This is the mutilation committed by associationist psychologists because they are only interested in the act of knowing, that is, in their own activity as scientists; the fact that it is speculative does not make it have any the less cruel consequences for living beings and for human beings.

Indeed, a similar point of view forces upon the physician an astonishing contempt for psychical reality, the scandalous nature of which, perpetuated in our times by the maintenance of an entirely academic approach to training, is expressed both in the biased nature of observation and in hybrid conceptions like that of "pithiatism." But because it was in the physician, that is, in the practitioner par excellence of inner life, that this point of view appeared in the most flagrant manner as a systematic negation, the negation of this very point of view also had to come from a physician. I am not referring to the purely critical negation that flourished, around that same time, in speculation about the "immediate data of consciousness," but rather to a negation that was efficient in that it asserted itself in the form of a new positivity. Freud took this fruitful step no doubt because, as he indicates in his autobiography, he was made to do so by his concern with healing, that is, by an activity in which we must recognize the very intelligence of human reality insofar as it attempts to transform that reality, as opposed to those who enjoy relegating this activity to the subordinate rank of an "art."

Freud's Revolutionary Method 81

The first sign of an attitude of submission to reality in Freud's work was the recognition that, since the majority of psychical phenomena in man are apparently related to a social relations function, there is no reason to exclude the pathway which provides the most usual access to it: the subject's own account of these phenomena.

We may well wonder, moreover, on what the physician of that time based the ostracism with which he greeted the patient's account on grounds of principle, if it was not his annoyance at seeing that his own biases were so ordinary as to be shared by everyone else. Indeed, it is the attitude shared by an entire culture which guided the abstraction that I analyzed earlier as that of the learned: to the patient and the physician alike, psychology is the field of the "imaginary," in the sense of the illusory. Consequently, the symptom, which has a *real* signification, cannot be psychological except "in appearance," and it is distinguished from the ordinary register of psychical life by some discordant feature in which its "serious" character manifests itself.

Freud understood that it was this very choice that made the patient's account worthless. If we wish to recognize a reality that is proper to psychical reactions, we must not begin by choosing among them; we must begin by no longer choosing. In order to gauge their efficacy, we must respect their succession. Certainly, there is no question of restoring the chain of those reactions through the narrative, but the very moment in which the account is given can constitute a significant fragment of the chain, on condition that we demand that the patient provide the entire text and that we free him from the chains of the narrative.

This is the way in which what we may call "analytic experience" is constituted: its first condition is formulated in a *law of non-omission*, which promotes everything that "is self-explanatory," the everyday and the ordinary, to the status of interesting that is usually reserved for the remarkable; but it is incomplete without the second condition, the *law of non-systematization*, which, positing incoherence as a condition of analytic experience, presumes significant all the dross of mental life—not only the representations in which 82
scholastic psychology sees only nonmeaning (dream scenarios, presentiments, daydreams, and confused or lucid delusions), but also the phenomena that are not even granted a civil status in it, so to speak, since they are altogether negative (slips of the tongue and bungled actions). Let us note that these two laws, or better, rules of analytic experience, the first of which was isolated by Pichon, appear in Freud's work in the form of a single rule that

he formulated, in accordance with the concept prevailing at the time, as the *law of free association.*

A Phenomenological Description of Psychoanalytic Experience

It is analytic experience itself that constitutes the element of therapeutic technique, but the doctor may propose, if he has some theoretical sense, to define what it contributes to observation. He will then have many an opportunity to marvel, if that is indeed the form of astonishment that corresponds in research to the appearance of a relationship that is so simple that it seems to evade thought's grasp.

The pregiven of this experience is, first, some language, a language—in other words, a sign. How complex is the problem of what it signifies, when the psychologist relates it to the subject of knowledge, that is, to the subject's thought? What relationship is there between the latter and language? Is the subject's thought but a language, albeit a secret one, or is it but the expression of a pure, unformulated thought? Where can we find the measure that is common to the two terms of this problem, that is, the unity of which language is the sign? Is it contained in words: names, verbs, or even adverbs? In the density of their history? Why not in the mechanisms that form them phonetically? How can we choose in this maze into which we are dragged by philosophers and linguists, psychophysicists and physiologists? How can we choose a reference which, the more elementary we posit it to be, the more mythical it seems to us?

But the psychoanalyst, in order not to detach analytic experience from the language of the situation that it implies, the situation of the interlocutor, comes upon the simple fact that language, prior to signifying something, signifies to
83 someone. It is simply because the analyst is there listening that the man who speaks addresses him, and since he forces his discourse not to want to say anything [*ne rien vouloir dire*], he becomes what this man *wants to tell him*. What the man says may, in fact, "have no meaning," but what he says *to the analyst* conceals one anyway. It is in the impulse to respond that the listener senses this; and it is by suspending this impulse to respond that the analyst understands the meaning of the discourse. He then recognizes in it an intention, one of the intentions that represent a certain tension in social relations: a demanding intention, a punitive intention, a propitiatory intention, a demonstrative intention, or a purely aggressive intention. Having thus understood this intention, let us observe how language transmits it. It does so in two ways about which analysis teaches us a great deal: it is expressed, but not understood by the subject, in what his discourse relates about his lived experience, and this

is true as long as the subject assumes the moral anonymity of expression (this is the form of symbolism); it is conceptualized, but denied by the subject, in what his discourse asserts about his lived experience, and this is true as long as the subject systematizes his conception (this is the form of negation). In analytic experience, intention thus turns out to be unconscious insofar as it is expressed and conscious insofar as it is repressed [*réprimée*]. And language, being approached via its function of social expression, reveals both its significant unity in intention and its constitutive ambiguity as subjective expression, admitting something that contradicts thought or using thought to lie. Let us note in passing that these relations, which analytic experience offers up here to phenomenological exploration, provide a wealth of directives to all theories of "consciousness," especially morbid consciousness, since their incomplete recognition renders the majority of these theories useless.

But let us pursue our outline of analytic experience. The listener is thus situated in it as an *interlocutor*. The subject solicits him to assume this role, implicitly at first, but soon explicitly. Remaining silent nevertheless, and hiding everything including even his facial expressions (which are, moreover, barely noticed in him), the psychoanalyst patiently refuses to play this role. Is there not a threshold at which such an attitude must bring the subject's monologue to a halt? If the subject continues, it is by virtue of the law of analytic experience; but is he still addressing the listener who is truly present or is he instead addressing some other now, someone who is imagi- 84
nary but realer still: the phantom of a memory, witness of his solitude, statue of his duty, or messenger of his fate?

In his very reaction to the listener's refusal [to assume the role of interlocutor], the subject reveals the *image* he has replaced him with. He communicates to the analyst the outline of this *image* through his imploring, imprecations, insinuations, provocations, and ruses, through the fluctuations of the intention that he directs at the analyst and that the latter motionlessly but not impassively takes note of. Nevertheless, as these intentions become more explicit in his discourse, they interweave with the accounts with which the subject supports them, gives them consistency, and gives them a rest. In this discourse, he formulates what he suffers from and what he wants to overcome through his analysis, he confides his secret failures and his successful designs, he judges his own character and his relations with other people. He thus informs the analyst about the entirety of his behavior, and the analyst, who witnesses a moment of that behavior, finds in it a basis for its critique. After such a critique, this behavior shows the analyst that the very *image* that he sees emerge from the subject's current behavior is actually involved in all of his behavior. But the analyst's discoveries do not stop there, for as the subject's demands take the form of pleas, his testimony broadens through its appeals to the witness. These are pure narratives that appear "outside the subject" that the subject now throws into the stream of his discourse: unintended events and fragments of the memories that constitute his history, and, among the most disjointed, those that surface from his childhood. But we see that among these, the analyst stumbles anew upon the very *image* that, by playing the game as he does, he has awakened in the subject, the trace of which he found impressed upon himself by the subject. He certainly knew that this image was of human essence, since it provokes passion and oppresses, but it hid its characteristics from his gaze, like he himself does from the patient's. He discovers these characteristics in a family portrait that includes the image of the father or of the mother, of the all-powerful adult—tender or terrible, kindly or punishing—the image of a brother, a rival sibling, a reflection of the subject himself or of one of his companions.

But the very image that the subject makes present through his behavior, and that is constantly reproduced in it, *is ignored by him*, in both senses of the word: he does not know that this image explains what he repeats in his behav-
85 ior, whether he considers it to be his own or not; and he refuses to realize [*méconnaît*] the importance of this image when he evokes the memory it represents.

Now, while the analyst completes the task of recognizing this image, the subject, through the debate that he carries on, completes the process of imposing its role on the analyst. The analyst derives the power he will have at his disposal in his action on the subject from this position.

In effect, the analyst then acts in such a way that the subject becomes aware of the unity of the *image* that is refracted in him into disparate effects, depending on whether he plays it out, incarnates it, or knows it. I will not describe here how the analyst proceeds in his intervention. He operates on the two registers of intellectual elucidation through *interpretation* and handling affect through the *transference*. But to establish the times at which he does so is a matter for *technique*, which defines them as a function of the subject's reactions; adjusting the speed at which he does so is a matter of *tact*, thanks to which the analyst is informed about the rhythm of these reactions.

Let us simply say that, as the subject pursues his analysis and the lived process in which the image is reconstituted, his behavior stops mimicking the image's suggestion, his memories reassume their real density, and the analyst sees his own power decline, having been rendered useless by the demise of the symptoms and the completion of the personality.

Discussion of the Objective Value of the Experience

Such is the phenomenological description that can be given of what happens in the series of experiences that form a psychoanalysis. Some might say that it is the work of an illusionist were the result not precisely to dispel an illusion. Its therapeutic action, on the contrary, must be essentially defined as a twofold movement through which the *image*, which is at first diffuse and broken, is progressively assimilated with reality, in order to be progressively dissimilated from reality, that is, restored to its proper reality. This action attests to the efficacy of this reality.

But if it is not an illusory kind of work, then it must be a simple technique, some will say, and as an experience it is highly unsuitable for scientific observation since it is based on conditions that are diametrically opposed to objectivity. For have I not just described this experience as a constant *interaction* 86
between the observer and the object? It is, in effect, in the very movement that the subject gives it through his intention that the observer is informed of this intention—I have even stressed the primordial nature of this pathway. Inversely, through the assimilation that it fosters between himself and the image, it subverts from the outset the function of this image in the subject. Of course, he only identifies the image in the very progress of this subversion—I have not tried to dissimulate the constitutive nature of this process.

The absence of a fixed reference in the system that is observed and the use, for the purposes of observation, of the very subjective movement that is eliminated everywhere else as a source of error, are challenges, it seems, to a sound method.

Let me also indicate the challenge to proper usage that can be seen here. In the very case study [*observation*] that he provides us, can the observer hide his personal stake in the game? The intuitions of his finds are elsewhere referred to as delusions and we find it hard to discern from what experiences the insistence of his perspicacity proceeds. No doubt, the pathways by which truth is discovered are unsoundable, and there have even been mathematicians who have admitted to having seen the truth in dreams or having stumbled upon it by accident. Nevertheless, propriety requires one to present one's discovery as having proceeded from a process that conforms more closely to the purity of the idea. Science, like Caesar's wife, must be above suspicion.

In any case, the scientist's good reputation has been assured for quite some time now. Nature can no longer reveal itself in any sort of human form and every step forward in science has effaced from nature an anthropomorphic trait.

While I think I can speak ironically about what these objections betray by way of emotional resistance, I do not think I can dispense with responding to their ideological import. Without going too far afield on epistemological questions, I will posit first that physical science, as purified as it may seem in its modern progress from any intuitive category, nevertheless betrays, indeed all the more strikingly, the structure of the intelligence that constructed it. If someone like
87 Meyerson could show that physical science is subjected in all its processes to the form of intellectual *identification* (a form that is so constitutive of human knowledge that he finds it anew through reflection in ordinary thought processes), and if the phenomenon of light (to provide here the standard of reference and the atom of action) manifests a relationship to the human sensorium that is more obscure here, don't these points—ideal points by which physics is related to man, but which are the poles around which physics revolves—demonstrate the most unsettling homologies to the pivotal roles assigned to human knowledge, as I mentioned earlier, by a tradition of reflection that does not resort to experimentation?

Be that as it may, the anthropomorphism that has been eliminated by physics in the notion of *force*, for example, is an anthropomorphism that is not noetic but psychological, for it is essentially the projection of human *intention*. To require a similar elimination in an anthropology that is in the process of being born and to impose such an elimination upon its most distant goals, would be to misrecognize its object and to authentically manifest an anthropocentrism of another order, that of knowledge.

Indeed, man has relations with nature that are specified, on the one hand, by the properties of *identificatory* thought, and on the other hand, by the use of instruments or artificial tools. His relations with his semblable proceed along pathways that are far more direct: I am not designating language here, or the elementary social institutions that are marked with artificiality in their structure, regardless of their genesis. I am thinking, rather, of emotional communication, which is essential to social groups and manifests itself immediately enough in the fact that man exploits his semblable, recognizes himself in this semblable, and is attached to this semblable by the indelible psychical link that perpetuates the truly specific vital misery of his first years of life.

These relations can be contrasted with the relations that constitute knowledge, in the narrow sense of the term, as *relations of connaturality*: I mean to evoke with this term their homology to more immediate, global, and adapted forms that characterize, on the whole, animals' psychical relations with their natural environment and by which such psychical relations are distinguished from psychical relations in man. I shall return to the value of the teachings of
88 animal psychology. In any case, man's idea of a world that is united to him

through a harmonious relationship allows us to divine its basis in the anthropomorphism of the myth of *nature*. As the effort is achieved that animates this idea, the reality of this basis is revealed in the ever vaster subversion of nature implied by the *hominization* of the planet: the "nature" of man is its relationship to man.

The Object of Psychology Is Defined in Essentially Relativistic Terms

It is in the specific reality of *interpersonal relations* that a psychology can define its own object and its method of investigation. The concepts implied by this object and this method are not subjective, but *relativistic*. Although they are anthropomorphic in their foundations, these concepts can develop into general forms of psychology, assuming their abovementioned extension to animal psychology proves valid.

Furthermore, the objective value of a form of research is demonstrated like the reality of motion is demonstrated: by the efficacy of its progress. What best confirms the excellence of the pathway that Freud defined by which to approach the phenomenon, with a purity that distinguished him from all other psychologists, is the prodigious advance that gave him a lead on all others in psychological reality.

I will demonstrate this in part two of this article. I will simultaneously show the felicitous use he was able to make of the notion of the *image*. And if, with the term "imago," he did not fully extract it from the confused state of everyday intuition, he nevertheless masterfully exploited its concrete importance, preserving the entirety of its *informational* function in intuition, memory, and development.

He demonstrated this function in discovering through analytic experience the process of *identification*. The latter is quite different from the process of *imitation*, which is distinguished by its partial and groping form of approximation; *identification* contrasts with imitation not simply as the *global* assimilation of a structure but as the *virtual assimilation of development* implied by 89
that structure in a still undifferentiated state.

We thus know that a child perceives certain affective situations—for example, the particular bond between two individuals in a group—with far more immediate perspicacity than an adult. An adult, despite his greater psychical differentiation, is in fact inhibited both in human knowledge and in the conduct of his relationships by conventional categories that censor them. But the absence of these categories serves a child less in permitting him to better perceive the signs than the primal structure of his psyche serves him in immediately imbuing him with the essential meaning of the situation. But this is not the whole of his advantage: along with the significant impression, it also brings with it the germ, which it will develop in all its richness, of the social *interaction* that is expressed in it.

This is why a man's character can include an *identification* with a parental feature that disappeared before the time of his earliest memories. What is transmitted by the psychical pathway are traits that give the individual the particular form of his human relations, in other words, his *personality*. But what man's behavior thus reflects are not simply these traits, which nevertheless are often among the most hidden, but the current situation in which the parent, who was the object of the identification, found himself when the identification occurred—for example, in a situation of conflict or of inferiority in the married couple.

The result of this process is that man's individual behavior bears the mark of a certain number of typical psychical relations in which a certain social structure is expressed, at the very least the *constellation* within that structure that especially dominates the first years of his childhood.

These fundamental psychical relations have been revealed in analytic experience and defined by analytic theory with the term "complexes." We should see in this term the most concrete, fruitful concept that has been contributed to the study of human behavior, as opposed to the concept of instinct which, up until the former's introduction, had proven to be as inadequate in this field as it was sterile. Although analytic doctrine has, in fact, related complexes to instincts, it seems that the theory is better clarified by the former than it is supported by the latter.

90 It is through the pathway of the *complex* that the images that inform the broadest units of behavior are instated in the psyche, images with which the subject identifies one after the other in order to act out, as sole actor, the drama of their conflicts. This comedy, which is situated by the genius of the species under the sign of laughter and tears, is a commedia dell'arte in that each individual improvises it and makes it mediocre or highly expressive depending on his gifts, of course, but also depending on a paradoxical law that seems to show the psychical fecundity of all vital insufficiency. It is a commedia dell'arte in the sense that it is performed in accordance with a typical framework and traditional roles. One can recognize in it the very characters that have typified folklore, stories, and theater for children and adults—the ogre, the bogeyman, the miser, and the noble father—that complexes express in more scholarly terms. We will see the figure of harlequin in an image to which the second part of this article will lead us.

After having highlighted Freud's phenomenologically acquired knowledge, I now turn to a critique of his metapsychology. It begins, precisely, with the introduction of the notion of "libido." Freudian psychology, propelling its induction with an audacity that verges on recklessness, claims to move from interpersonal relations, isolating them as determined by our culture, to the biological function that is taken to be their substratum; it locates this function in *sexual desire*.

We must nevertheless distinguish between two different uses of the term "libido," which are constantly confounded in analytic theory: libido as an *energetic concept*, regulating the equivalence of phenomena, and libido as a *substantialist hypothesis*, relating the phenomena to matter.

I refer to the *hypothesis* as *substantialist*, and not as materialist, because recourse to the idea of matter is but a naïve, outmoded form of authentic materialism. In any case, it is the metabolism of the sexual function in man that Freud designates as the basis of the infinitely varied "sublimations" manifested in his behavior.

I will not debate this hypothesis here, because it seems to me to lie outside 91
of psychology's proper field. I will nevertheless emphasize that it is based on a clinical discovery of essential value: a correlation that constantly manifests itself between the exercise, type, and anomalies of the sexual function, on the one hand, and a large number of psychical forms and "symptoms," on the other hand. Let me add here that the mechanisms by which the hypothesis is developed, which are very different from those of associationism, lead to facts that can be observationally verified.

In effect, if the libido theory posits, for example, that childhood sexuality goes through an anal stage of organization and grants erotic value to the excretory function and the excremental object alike, this interest can be observed in the child exactly where the theory says it should be.

As an *energetic concept*, on the contrary, libido is merely the symbolic notation for the equivalence between the dynamisms invested by images in behavior. It is the very condition of *symbolic identification* and the essential entity of the rational order, without which no science could be constituted. With this notation, the efficacy of images—although it cannot yet be tied to a unit of measurement, but is already provided with a positive or negative sign—can be expressed through the equilibrium that the images establish and, in some sense, by balancing a *pair of scales*.

The notion of *libido* in this usage is no longer metapsychological: it is the instrument of psychology's progress toward positive knowledge. The combination, for example, of the notion of libidinal cathexis with a structure as concretely defined as that of the "superego," represents—regarding both the ideal definition of *moral conscience* and the functional abstraction of so-called reactions of *opposition* and *imitation*—progress that can only be compared to that provided in the physical sciences by the relationship "weight divided by volume" when it replaced the quantitative categories heavy and light.

The elements of a *positive* determination were thus introduced between psychical realities that a *relativistic* definition has allowed us to objectify. This determination is dynamic or relative to the *facts regarding desire*.

It was possible in this way to establish a scale for the constitution of man's
92 objects of interest, and especially for those, which are prodigiously diverse, that remain an enigma, if psychology in theory posits reality such as knowledge constitutes it: anomalies of emotion and drive, idiosyncrasies of attraction and repulsion, phobias and panic attacks, nostalgias and irrational wills; personal curiosities, selective collecting, inventions of knowledge, and job vocations.

On the other hand, a classification of what one might call the "imaginary posts" that constitute the *personality* was defined, posts which are distributed and in which the images mentioned above as informing development—the *id*, the *ego*, and the archaic and secondary instances of the *superego*—are composed according to their types.

Two questions arise here: how is the *reality* to which man's knowledge is universally attuned constituted by these images, these objects of interest? And how is the *I* constituted, in which the subject recognizes himself, by his typical identifications?

Freud answers these two questions by again moving onto metapsychological ground. He posits a "reality principle" whose role in his theory I propose to critique. But before doing so, I must first examine what has been provided by the studies that have been contributing to the new psychological science, alongside Freud's discipline, regarding the *reality of the image* and *forms of knowledge*. These will constitute the two parts of my second article.

Marienbad and Noirmoutier, August–October 1936

The Mirror Stage as Formative of the *I* Function as Revealed in Psychoanalytic Experience 93

Delivered on July 17, 1949, in Zurich at the Sixteenth International Congress of Psychoanalysis

The conception of the mirror stage I introduced at our last congress thirteen years ago, having since been more or less adopted by the French group, seems worth bringing to your attention once again—especially today, given the light it sheds on the *I* function in the experience psychoanalysis provides us of it. It should be noted that this experience sets us at odds with any philosophy directly stemming from the *cogito*.

Some of you may recall the behavioral characteristic I begin with that is explained by a fact of comparative psychology: the human child, at an age when he is for a short while, but for a while nevertheless, outdone by the chimpanzee in instrumental intelligence, can already recognize his own image as such in a mirror. This recognition is indicated by the illuminative mimicry of the *Aha-Erlebnis*, which Köhler considers to express situational apperception, an essential moment in the act of intelligence.

Indeed, this act, far from exhausting itself, as in the case of a monkey, in eventually acquired control over the uselessness of the image, immediately gives rise in a child to a series of gestures in which he playfully experiences the relationship between the movements made in the image and the reflected environment, and between this virtual complex and the reality it duplicates—namely, the child's own body, and the persons and even things around him.

This event can take place, as we know from Baldwin's work, from the age of six months on; its repetition has often given me pause to reflect upon the
striking spectacle of a nursling in front of a mirror who has not yet mastered 94

walking, or even standing, but who—though held tightly by some prop, human or artificial (what, in France, we call a *trotte-bébé* [a sort of walker])—overcomes, in a flutter of jubilant activity, the constraints of his prop in order to adopt a slightly leaning-forward position and take in an instantaneous view of the image in order to fix it in his mind.

In my view, this activity has a specific meaning up to the age of eighteen months, and reveals both a libidinal dynamism that has hitherto remained problematic and an ontological structure of the human world that fits in with my reflections on paranoiac knowledge.

It suffices to understand the mirror stage in this context *as an identification*, in the full sense analysis gives to the term: namely, the transformation that takes place in the subject when he assumes [*assume*] an image—an image that is seemingly predestined to have an effect at this phase, as witnessed by the use in analytic theory of antiquity's term, "imago."

The jubilant assumption [*assomption*] of his specular image by the kind of being—still trapped in his motor impotence and nursling dependence—the little man is at the *infans* stage thus seems to me to manifest in an exemplary situation the symbolic matrix in which the *I* is precipitated in a primordial form, prior to being objectified in the dialectic of identification with the other, and before language restores to it, in the universal, its function as subject.

This form would, moreover, have to be called the "ideal-I"[1]—if we wanted to translate it into a familiar register—in the sense that it will also be the rootstock of secondary identifications, this latter term subsuming the libidinal normalization functions. But the important point is that this form situates the agency known as the ego, prior to its social determination, in a fictional direction that will forever remain irreducible for any single individual or, rather, that will only asymptotically approach the subject's becoming, no matter how successful the dialectical syntheses by which he must resolve, as *I*, his discordance with his own reality.

For the total form of his body, by which the subject anticipates the matu-
95 ration of his power in a mirage, is given to him only as a gestalt, that is, in an exteriority in which, to be sure, this form is more constitutive than constituted, but in which, above all, it appears to him as the contour of his stature that freezes it and in a symmetry that reverses it, in opposition to the turbulent movements with which the subject feels he animates it. Through these two aspects of its appearance, this gestalt—whose power [*prégnance*] should be considered linked to the species, though its motor style is as yet unrecognizable—symbolizes the *I*'s mental permanence, at the same time as it prefigures its alienating destination. This gestalt is also replete with the correspondences that unite the *I* with the statue onto which man projects himself, the phantoms

that dominate him, and the automaton with which the world of his own making tends to achieve fruition in an ambiguous relation.

Indeed, for imagos—whose veiled faces we analysts see emerge in our daily experience and in the penumbra of symbolic effectiveness[2]—the specular image seems to be the threshold of the visible world, if we take into account the mirrored disposition of the *imago of one's own body* in hallucinations and dreams, whether it involves one's individual features, or even one's infirmities or object projections; or if we take note of the role of the mirror apparatus in the appearance of *doubles*, in which psychical realities manifest themselves that are, moreover, heterogeneous.

The fact that a gestalt may have formative effects on an organism is attested to by a biological experiment that is so far removed from the idea of psychical causality that it cannot bring itself to formulate itself in such terms. The experiment nevertheless acknowledges that it is a necessary condition for the maturation of the female pigeon's gonad that the pigeon see another member of its species, regardless of its sex; this condition is so utterly sufficient that the same effect may be obtained by merely placing a mirror's reflective field near the individual. Similarly, in the case of the migratory locust, the shift within a family line from the solitary to the gregarious form can be brought about by exposing an individual, at a certain stage of its development, to the exclusively visual action of an image akin to its own, provided the movements of this image sufficiently resemble those characteristic of its species. Such facts fall within a realm of homeomorphic identification that is itself subsumed 96
within the question of the meaning of beauty as formative and erogenous.

But mimetic facts, understood as heteromorphic identification, are of just as much interest to us insofar as they raise the question of the signification of space for living organisms—psychological concepts hardly seeming less appropriate for shedding light here than the ridiculous attempts made to reduce these facts to the supposedly supreme law of adaptation. We need but recall how Roger Caillois (still young and fresh from his break with the sociological school at which he trained) illuminated the subject when, with the term "legendary psychasthenia," he subsumed morphological mimicry within the derealizing effect of an obsession with space.

As I myself have shown, human knowledge is more independent than animal knowledge from the force field of desire because of the social dialectic that structures human knowledge as paranoiac;[3] but what limits it is the "scant reality" surrealistic unsatisfaction denounces therein. These reflections lead me to recognize in the spatial capture manifested by the mirror stage, the effect in man, even prior to this social dialectic, of an organic inadequacy of his natural reality—assuming we can give some meaning to the word "nature."

The function of the mirror stage thus turns out, in my view, to be a particular case of the function of imagos, which is to establish a relationship between an organism and its reality—or, as they say, between the *Innenwelt* and the *Umwelt*.

In man, however, this relationship to nature is altered by a certain dehiscence at the very heart of the organism, a primordial Discord betrayed by the signs of malaise and motor uncoordination of the neonatal months. The objective notions of the anatomical incompleteness of the pyramidal tracts and of certain humoral residues of the maternal organism in the newborn confirm my view that we find in man a veritable *specific prematurity of birth*.

97 Let us note in passing that this fact is recognized as such by embryologists, under the heading "fetalization," as determining the superiority of the so-called higher centers of the central nervous system, and especially of the cerebral cortex which psychosurgical operations will lead us to regard as the intra-organic mirror.

This development is experienced as a temporal dialectic that decisively projects the individual's formation into history: the mirror stage is a drama whose internal pressure pushes precipitously from insufficiency to anticipation—and, for the subject caught up in the lure of spatial identification, turns out fantasies that proceed from a fragmented image of the body to what I will call an "orthopedic" form of its totality—and to the finally donned armor of an alienating identity that will mark his entire mental development with its rigid structure. Thus, the shattering of the *Innenwelt* to *Umwelt* circle gives rise to an inexhaustible squaring of the ego's audits.

This fragmented body—another expression I have gotten accepted into the French school's system of theoretical references—is regularly manifested in dreams when the movement of an analysis reaches a certain level of aggressive disintegration of the individual. It then appears in the form of disconnected limbs or of organs exoscopically represented, growing wings and taking up arms for internal persecutions that the visionary Hieronymus Bosch fixed for all time in painting, in their ascent in the fifteenth century to the imaginary zenith of modern man. But this form turns out to be tangible even at the organic level, in the lines of "fragilization" that define the hysteric's fantasmatic anatomy, which is manifested in schizoid and spasmodic symptoms.

Correlatively, the *I* formation is symbolized in dreams by a fortified camp, or even a stadium—distributing, between the arena within its walls and its outer border of gravel-pits and marshes, two opposed fields of battle where the subject bogs down in his quest for the proud, remote inner castle whose form (sometimes juxtaposed in the same scenario) strikingly symbolizes the id. Similarly, though here in the mental sphere, we find fortified structures constructed, the

metaphors for which arise spontaneously, as if deriving from the subject's very
symptoms, to designate the mechanisms of obsessive neurosis: inversion, iso- 98
lation, reduplication, undoing what has been done, and displacement.

But were I to build on these subjective data alone—were I to so much as free them from the experiential condition that makes me view them as based on a language technique—my theoretical efforts would remain exposed to the charge of lapsing into the unthinkable, that of an absolute subject. This is why I have sought, in the present hypothesis grounded in a confluence of objective data, a *method of symbolic reduction* as my guiding grid.

It establishes a genetic order in *ego defenses*, in accordance with the wish formulated by Anna Freud in the first part of her major book, and situates (as against a frequently expressed prejudice) hysterical repression and its returns at a more archaic stage than obsessive inversion and its isolating processes, situating the latter as prior to the paranoiac alienation that dates back to the time at which the specular *I* turns into the social *I*.

This moment at which the mirror stage comes to an end inaugurates, through identification with the imago of one's semblable and the drama of primordial jealousy (so well brought out by the Charlotte Bühler school in cases of transitivism in children), the dialectic that will henceforth link the *I* to socially elaborated situations.

It is this moment that decisively tips the whole of human knowledge [*savoir*] into being mediated by the other's desire, constitutes its objects in an abstract equivalence due to competition from other people, and turns the *I* into an apparatus to which every instinctual pressure constitutes a danger, even if it corresponds to a natural maturation process. The very normalization of this maturation is henceforth dependent in man on cultural intervention, as is exemplified by the fact that sexual object choice is dependent upon the Oedipus complex.

In light of my conception, the term "primary narcissism," by which analytic doctrine designates the libidinal investment characteristic of this moment, reveals in those who invented it a profound awareness of semantic latencies. But it also sheds light on the dynamic opposition between this libido and sexual libido, an opposition they tried to define when they invoked destructive and even death instincts in order to explain the obvious relationship between narcissistic libido and the alienating *I* function, and the aggressiveness deriving therefrom in all relations with others, even in relations involving aid of the most good-Samaritan variety.

The fact is that they encountered that existential negativity whose reality
is so vigorously proclaimed by the contemporary philosophy of being and 99
nothingness.

Unfortunately, this philosophy grasps that negativity only within the limits of a self*-sufficiency of consciousness, which, being one of its premises, ties the illusion of autonomy in which it puts its faith to the ego's constitutive misrecognitions. While it draws considerably on borrowings from psychoanalytic experience, this intellectual exercise culminates in the pretense of grounding an existential psychoanalysis.

At the end of a society's historical enterprise to no longer recognize that it has any but a utilitarian function, and given the individual's anxiety faced with the concentration-camp form of the social link whose appearance seems to crown this effort, existentialism can be judged on the basis of the justifications it provides for the subjective impasses that do, indeed, result therefrom: a freedom that is never so authentically affirmed as when it is within the walls of a prison; a demand for commitment that expresses the inability of pure consciousness to overcome any situation; a voyeuristic-sadistic idealization of sexual relationships; a personality that achieves self-realization only in suicide; and a consciousness of the other that can only be satisfied by Hegelian murder.

These notions are opposed by the whole of analytic experience, insofar as it teaches us not to regard the ego as centered on the *perception-consciousness system* or as organized by the "reality principle"—the expression of a scientific bias most hostile to the dialectic of knowledge—but, rather, to take as our point of departure the *function of misrecognition* that characterizes the ego in all the defensive structures so forcefully articulated by Anna Freud. For, while *Verneinung* [negation] represents the blatant form of that function, its effects remain largely latent as long as they are not illuminated by some reflected light at the level of fate where the id manifests itself.

The inertia characteristic of the *I* formations can thus be understood as providing the broadest definition of neurosis, just as the subject's capture by his situation gives us the most general formulation of madness—the kind found within the asylum walls as well as the kind that deafens the world with its sound and fury.

The sufferings of neurosis and psychosis provide us schooling in the passions of the soul, just as the balance arm of the psychoanalytic scales—when we calculate the angle of its threat to entire communities—provides us with
100 an amortization rate for the passions of the city.

At this intersection of nature and culture, so obstinately scrutinized by the anthropology of our times, psychoanalysis alone recognizes the knot of imaginary servitude that love must always untie anew or sever.

For such a task we can find no promise in altruistic feeling, we who lay bare the aggressiveness that underlies the activities of the philanthropist, the idealist, the pedagogue, and even the reformer.

In the subject to subject recourse we preserve, psychoanalysis can accompany the patient to the ecstatic limit of the *"Thou art that,"* where the cipher of his mortal destiny is revealed to him, but it is not in our sole power as practitioners to bring him to the point where the true journey begins.

Notes

1. I have let stand the peculiar translation I adopted in this article for Freud's *Ideal Ich* [*je-idéal*], without further comment except to say that I have not maintained it since.

2. See Claude Lévi-Strauss' essay, entitled "L'efficacité symbolique," in *Revue de l'histoire des religions* CXXXV, 1 (1949): 5–27.

3. See, on this point, the texts that follow, pages 111 and 180 [*Écrits* 1966].

101

Aggressiveness in Psychoanalysis

Theoretical paper presented in Brussels in mid-May 1948 at the Eleventh Congress of French-Speaking Psychoanalysts

The preceding paper presented to you the use I make of the notion of aggressiveness in clinical work and therapy.[1] That notion must now be put to the test before you to determine whether or not we can wrest a concept from it that may lay claim to scientific usefulness—in other words, a concept that can objectify facts that are of a comparable order in reality or, more categorically, that can establish a dimension of analytic experience in which these objectified facts may be regarded as variables.

All of us here at this gathering share an experience based on a technique and a system of concepts to which we are faithful, as much because the system was developed by the man who opened up all of that experience's pathways to us, as because it bears the living mark of its stages of development. In other words, contrary to the dogmatism with which we are taxed, we know that this system remains open as regards both its completion and a number of its articulations.

These hiatuses seem to come together in the enigmatic signification Freud expressed with the term "death instinct"—attesting, rather like the figure of the Sphinx, to the aporia this great mind encountered in the most profound attempt to date to formulate one of man's experiences in the biological register.

This aporia lies at the heart of the notion of aggressiveness, whose role in the psychical economy we appreciate better every day.

That is why the question of the metapsychological nature of the deadly tendencies is constantly being raised by our theoretically inclined colleagues, not without contradiction, and often, it must be admitted, in a rather formalistic way.

I would simply like to proffer a few remarks or theses inspired by my years 102
of reflection upon this veritable aporia in psychoanalytic doctrine, and by the sense I have—after reading numerous works—of our responsibility for the current evolution of laboratory psychology and psychotherapy. I am referring, on the one hand, to so-called "behaviorist" research that seems to me to owe its best results (insignificant as they sometimes appear compared to the sizable theoretical apparatus with which they are framed) to the often implicit use it makes of categories psychoanalysis has contributed to psychology; and, on the other hand, to the kind of treatment, given to both adults and children, that might be placed under the heading of "psychodrama," which looks to abreaction for its therapeutic power—trying to exhaust it at the level of role playing—and to which classical psychoanalysis has, once again, contributed the actual guiding notions.

Thesis I: *Aggressiveness manifests itself in an experience that is subjective in its very constitution.*

It is, in fact, useful to reconsider the phenomenon of psychoanalytic experience. In trying to get at the basics, reflection upon this is often omitted.

It can be said that psychoanalytic action develops in and through verbal communication, that is, in a dialectical grasping of meaning. Thus it presupposes a subject who manifests himself verbally in addressing another subject.

It cannot be objected to us that this latter subjectivity must be null and void, according to the ideal physics lives up to—eliminating it by using recording devices, though it cannot avoid responsibility for human error in reading the results.

Only a subject can understand a meaning; conversely, every meaning phenomenon implies a subject. In analysis, a subject presents himself as capable of being understood and is, in effect; introspection and supposedly projective intuition are not the *a priori* vitiations that psychology, taking its first steps along the path of science, believed to be irreducible. This would be to create an impasse out of moments that are abstractly isolated from a dialogue,
whereas one should instead trust in its movement: it was to Freud's credit that 103
he assumed the risks involved before overcoming them by means of a rigorous technique.

Can his results ground a positive science? Yes, if the experience can be verified by everyone. Now this experience, constituted between two subjects, one of whom plays in the dialogue the role of ideal impersonality (a point that will require explanation later), may, once completed—its only conditions having to do with the capability of this subject, which is something that may be required in all specialized research—be begun anew by the second subject with a third. This apparently initiatory path is simply transmission by recurrence, which should surprise no one since it stems from the very bipolar structure of all subjectivity. Only the speed at which the experience spreads is affected thereby; and while it may be debated whether the experience is restricted to the region in which a specific culture reigns—although no sound anthropology can raise objections on that score—all the indicators suggest that its results can be relativized sufficiently to become generalizable, thus satisfying the humanitarian postulate inseparable from the spirit of science.

Thesis II: *Aggressiveness presents itself in analysis as an aggressive intention and as an image of corporal dislocation, and it is in such forms that it proves to be effective.*

Analytic experience allows us to experience intentional pressure. We read it in the symbolic meaning of symptoms—once the subject sheds the defenses by which he disconnects them from their relations with his everyday life and history—in the implicit finality of his behavior and his refusals, in his bungled actions, in the avowal of his favorite fantasies, and in the rebuses of his dream life.

We can almost measure it in the demanding tone that sometimes permeates his whole discourse, in his pauses, hesitations, inflections, and slips of the tongue, in the inaccuracies of his narrative, irregularities in his application of the fundamental rule, late arrivals at sessions, calculated absences, and often in his recriminations, reproaches, fantasmatic fears, angry emotional reactions, and displays designed to intimidate. Actual acts of violence are as rare as might
104 be expected given the predicament that led the patient to the doctor, and its transformation, accepted by the patient, into a convention of dialogue.

The specific effect of this aggressive intention is plain to see. We regularly observe it in the formative action of an individual on those who are dependent upon him: intentional aggressiveness gnaws away, undermines, and disintegrates; it castrates; it leads to death. "And I thought you were impotent!" growled a mother with a tiger's cry, to her son, who, not without great difficulty, had confessed to her his homosexual tendencies. One could see that her permanent aggressiveness as a virile woman had taken its toll. It has always been impossible, in such cases, for us to divert the blows of the analytic enterprise itself.

This aggressiveness is, of course, exercised within real constraints. But we know from experience that it is no less effective when conveyed by one's mien [*expressivité*]: a harsh parent intimidates by his mere presence, and the image of the Punisher scarcely needs to be brandished for the child to form such an image. Its effects are more far-reaching than any physical punishment.

After the repeated failures encountered by classical psychology in its attempts to account for the mental phenomena known as "images"—a term whose expressive value is confirmed by all its semantic acceptations—psychoanalysis proved itself capable of accounting for the concrete reality they represent. That was because it began with their formative function in the subject, and revealed that if common images make for certain individual differences in tendencies, they do so as variations of the matrices that other specific images—which in my vocabulary correspond to antiquity's term "imago"—constitute for the "instincts" themselves.

Among the latter images are some that represent the elective vectors of aggressive intentions, which they provide with an efficacy that might be called magical. These are the images of castration, emasculation, mutilation, dismemberment, dislocation, evisceration, devouring, and bursting open of the body—in short, the imagos that I personally have grouped together under the heading "imagos of the fragmented body," a heading that certainly seems to be structural.

There is a specific relationship here between man and his own body that is also more generally manifested in a series of social practices: from tattooing, incision, and circumcision rituals in primitive societies to what might be called 105
the procrustean arbitrariness of fashion, in that it contradicts, in advanced societies, respect for the natural forms of the human body, the idea of which is a latecomer to culture.

One need but listen to the stories and games made up by two to five year olds, alone or together, to know that pulling off heads and cutting open bellies are spontaneous themes of their imagination, which the experience of a busted-up doll merely fulfills.

One must leaf through a book of Hieronymus Bosch's work, including views of whole works as well as details, to see an atlas of all the aggressive images that torment mankind. The prevalence that psychoanalysis has discovered among them of images based on a primitive autoscopy of the oral organs and organs derived from the cloaca is what gives rise to the shapes of the demons in Bosch's work. Even the ogee of the *angustiae* of birth can be found in the gates to the abyss through which they thrust the damned; and even narcissistic structure may be glimpsed in the glass spheres in which the exhausted partners of the "Garden of Earthly Delights" are held captive.

These phantasmagorias crop up constantly in dreams, especially when an analysis appears to reflect off the backdrop of the most archaic fixations. I will mention here a dream recounted by one of my patients, whose aggressive drives manifested themselves in obsessive fantasies. In the dream he saw himself in a car, with the woman with whom he was having a rather difficult love-affair, being pursued by a flying fish whose balloon-like body was so transparent that one could see the horizontal level of liquid it contained: an image of vesical persecution of great anatomical clarity.

These are all basic aspects of a gestalt that is characteristic of aggression in man and that is tied to both the symbolic character and cruel refinement of the weapons he builds, at least at the artisanal stage of his industry. The imaginary function of this gestalt will be clarified in what follows.

Let us note here that to attempt a behaviorist reduction of the analytic process—to which a concern with rigor, quite unjustified in my view, might impel some of us—is to deprive the imaginary function of its most important subjective facts, to which favorite fantasies bear witness in consciousness and
106 which have enabled us to conceptualize the imago, which plays a formative role in identification.

Thesis III: *The mainsprings of aggressiveness determine the rationale for analytic technique.*

Dialogue in itself seems to involve a renunciation of aggressiveness; from Socrates onward, philosophy has always placed its hope in dialogue to make reason triumph. And yet ever since Thrasymachus made his mad outburst at the beginning of that great dialogue, *The Republic*, verbal dialectic has all too often proved a failure.

I have emphasized that the analyst cures through dialogue, curing cases of madness that are just as serious. What virtue, then, did Freud add to dialogue?

The rule proposed to the patient in analysis allows him to advance in an intentionality that is blind to any other purpose than that of freeing him from suffering or ignorance of whose very limits he is unaware.

His voice alone will be heard for a period of time whose duration depends on the analyst's discretion. In particular, it will soon become apparent to him, indeed confirmed, that the analyst refrains from responding at the level of giving advice or making plans. This constraint seems to run counter to the desired end and so must be justified by some profound motive.

What, then, lies behind the analyst's attitude, sitting there as he does across from him? The concern to provide the dialogue with a participant who is as devoid as possible of individual characteristics. We efface ourselves, we leave the field in which the interest, sympathy, and reactions a speaker seeks to find on his interlocutor's face might be seen, we avoid all manifestations of our personal tastes, we conceal whatever might betray them, we depersonalize ourselves and strive to represent to the other an ideal of impassability.

We are not simply expressing thereby the apathy we have had to bring about in ourselves to be equal to the task of understanding our subject, nor are we striving to make our interpretative interventions take on the oracular quality they must possess against this backdrop of inertia.

We wish to avoid the trap hidden in the appeal, marked by faith's eternal 107
pathos, the patient addresses to us. It harbors a secret within itself: "Take upon yourself," he tells us, "the suffering that weighs so heavily on my shoulders; but I can see that you are far too content, composed, and comfortable to be worthy of bearing it."

What appears here as the arrogant affirmation of one's suffering will show its face—and sometimes at a moment decisive enough to give rise to the kind of "negative therapeutic reaction" that attracted Freud's attention—in the form of the resistance of *amour-propre*, to use the term in all the depth given it by La Rochefoucauld, which is often expressed thus: "I can't bear the thought of being freed by anyone but myself."

Of course, due to a more unfathomable heartfelt exigency, the patient expects us to share in his pain. But we take our cue from his hostile reaction, which already made Freud wary of any temptation to play the prophet. Only saints are sufficiently detached from the deepest of our shared passions to avoid the aggressive repercussions of charity.

As for presenting our own virtues and merits as examples, the only person I have ever known to resort to that was some big boss, thoroughly imbued with the idea, as austere as it was innocent, of his own apostolic value; I still recall the fury he unleashed.

In any case, such reactions should hardly surprise us analysts, we who expose the aggressive motives behind all so-called philanthropic activity.

We must, nevertheless, bring out the subject's aggressiveness toward us, because, as we know, aggressive intentions form the negative transference that is the inaugural knot of the analytic drama.

This phenomenon represents the patient's imaginary transference onto us of one of the more or less archaic imagos, which degrades, diverts, or inhibits the cycle of a certain behavior by an effect of symbolic subduction, which has excluded a certain function or body part from the ego's control by an accident of repression, and which has given its form to this or that agency of the personality through an act of identification.

It can be seen that the most incidental pretext is enough to arouse an aggres-
108 sive intention that reactualizes the imago—which has remained permanent at
the level of symbolic overdetermination that we call the subject's unconscious—along with its intentional correlate.

Such a mechanism often proves to be extremely simple in hysteria: in the case of a girl afflicted with astasia-abasia, which for months had resisted the most varied forms of therapeutic suggestion, I was immediately identified with a constellation of the most unpleasant features that the object of a passion formed for her, a passion marked, moreover, by a fairly strong delusional tone. The underlying imago was that of her father, and it was enough for me to remark that she had not had his support (a lack which I knew had dominated her biography in a highly fanciful manner) for her to be cured of her symptom, without, it might be said, her having understood anything or her morbid passion having in any way been affected.

Such knots are, as we know, more difficult to untie in obsessive neurosis, precisely because of the well-known fact that its structure is particularly designed to camouflage, displace, deny, divide, and muffle aggressive intentions; it does so by a defensive decomposition that is so similar in its principles to that illustrated by the stepping and staggering technique that a number of my patients have themselves employed military fortification metaphors to describe themselves.

As to the role of aggressive intention in phobia, it is, as it were, manifest.

Thus it is not inadvisable to reactivate such an intention in psychoanalysis.

What we try to avoid in our technique is to allow the patient's aggressive intention to find support in a current idea about us that is well enough developed for it to become organized in such reactions as opposition, negation, ostentation, and lying that our experience has shown to be characteristic modes of the agency known as the ego in dialogue.

I am characterizing this agency here, not by the theoretical construction
Freud gives of it in his metapsychology—that is, as the "perception-consciousness" system—but by what he recognized as the ego's most constant
109 phenomenological essence in analytic experience, namely, *Verneinung* [nega-
tion], urging us to detect its presence in the most general index of an inversion owing to a prior judgment.

In short, by "ego" I designate [1] the nucleus given to consciousness—though it is opaque to reflection—that is marked by all the ambiguities which, from self-indulgence to bad faith, structure the human subject's lived experience of the passions; [2] the "I" that, while exposing its facticity to existential criticism, opposes its irreducible inertia of pretenses and misrecognition to the concrete problematic of the subject's realization.

Far from attacking it head on, the analytic maieutic takes a detour that amounts, in the end, to inducing in the subject a guided paranoia. Indeed, one aspect of analytic action is to bring about the projection of what Melanie Klein calls "bad internal objects," which is a paranoiac mechanism certainly, but in this context it is highly systematized, in some sense filtered, and properly checked.

This is the aspect of our praxis that corresponds to the category of space, provided we include in it the imaginary space in which the dimension of symptoms develops, which structures them like excluded islets, inert scotomas, or parasitic autonomisms in the person's functioning.

Corresponding to the other dimension, the temporal, is anxiety and its impact, whether patent as in the phenomenon of flight or inhibition, or latent as when it only appears with the imago that arouses it.

Again, let me repeat, this imago reveals itself only to the extent that our attitude offers the subject the pure mirror of a smooth surface.

To understand what I'm saying here, imagine what would happen if a patient saw in his analyst an exact replica of himself. Everyone senses that the patient's excess of aggressive tension would prove such an obstacle to the manifestation of transference that its useful effect could only be brought about very slowly—and this is what happens in certain training analyses. If we imagine it, in the extreme case, experienced in the uncanny form characteristic of the apprehensions of one's *double*, the situation would trigger uncontrollable anxiety.

THESIS IV: *Aggressiveness is the tendency correlated with a mode of identification I call narcissistic, which determines the formal structure of man's ego and of the register of entities characteristic of his world.* 110

The subjective experience of analysis immediately inscribes its results in concrete psychology. Let me simply indicate here what it contributes to the psychology of the emotions when it demonstrates the meaning common to states as diverse as fantasmatic fear, anger, active sorrow, and psychasthenic fatigue.

To shift now from the subjectivity of intention to the notion of a tendency to aggress is to make a leap from the phenomenology of our experience to metapsychology.

But this leap manifests nothing more than a requirement of our thought which, in order now to objectify the register of aggressive reactions, and given our inability to seriate it according to its quantitative variations, must include it in a formula of equivalence. That is what we do with the notion of "libido."

The aggressive tendency proves to be fundamental in a certain series of significant personality states, namely, the paranoid and paranoiac psychoses.

In my work I have emphasized that there is a correlation—due to their strictly parallel seriation—between the quality of aggressive reaction to be expected from a particular form of paranoia and the stage of mental genesis represented by the delusion that is symptomatic of that form. The correlation appears even more profound when the aggressive act dissolves the delusional construction; I have shown this in the case of a curable form, self-punishing paranoia.

Thus aggressive reactions form a continuous series, from the violent, unmotivated outburst of the act, through the whole range of belligerent forms, to the cold war of interpretative demonstrations. This series parallels another, that of imputations of harm, the explanations for which—without mentioning the obscure *kakon* to which the paranoiac attributes his discordance with all living things—run the gamut from poison (borrowed from the register of a highly primitive organicism), to evil spells (magic), influence
111 (telepathy), physical intrusion (lesions), diversion of intent (abuse), theft of secrets (dispossession), violation of privacy (profanation), injury (legal action), spying and intimidation (persecution), defamation and character assassination (prestige), and damages and exploitation (claims).

I have shown that in each case this series—in which we find all the successive envelopes of the person's biological and social status—is based on an original organization of ego and object forms that are also structurally affected thereby, even down to the spatial and temporal categories in which the ego and the object are constituted. The latter are experienced as events in a perspective of mirages, as affections with something stereotypical about them that suspends their dialectical movement.

Janet, who so admirably demonstrated the signification of feelings of persecution as phenomenological moments of social behaviors, did not explore their common characteristic, which is precisely that they are constituted by stagnation in one of these moments, similar in strangeness to the faces of actors when a film is suddenly stopped in mid-frame.

Now, this formal stagnation is akin to the most general structure of human knowledge, which constitutes the ego and objects as having the attributes of permanence, identity, and substance—in short, as entities or "things" that are very different from the gestalts that experience enables us to isolate in the mobility of the field constructed according to the lines of animal desire.

Indeed, this formal fixation, which introduces a certain difference of level, a certain discordance between man as organism and his *Umwelt*, is the very condition that indefinitely extends his world and his power, by giving his objects their instrumental polyvalence and symbolic polyphony, as well as their potential as weaponry.

What I have called paranoiac knowledge is therefore shown to correspond in its more or less archaic forms to certain critical moments that punctuate the history of man's mental genesis, each representing a stage of objectifying identification.

We can glimpse its stages in children by simple observation, in which Charlotte Bühler, Elsa Köhler, and, following in their footsteps, the Chicago School
have revealed several levels of significant manifestations, though only ana- 112
lytic experience can give them their exact value by making it possible to reintegrate subjective relations in them.

The first level shows us that the very young child's experience of itself—insofar as it is related to the child's semblable—develops on the basis of a situation that is experienced as undifferentiated. Thus, around the age of eight months, in confrontations between children—which, if they are to be fruitful, must be between children whose difference in age is no more than two and a half months—we see gestures of fictitious actions by which one subject renews the other's imperfect gesture by confusing their distinct application, and synchronies of spectacular capture that are all the more remarkable as they precede the complete coordination of the motor systems they involve.

Thus the aggressiveness that is manifested in the retaliations of slaps and blows cannot be regarded solely as a playful manifestation of the exercise of strength and their employment in getting to know the body. It must be understood within a broader realm of coordination: one that will subordinate the functions of tonic postures and vegetative tension to a social relativity, whose prevalence in the expressive constitution of human emotions has been remarkably well emphasized by Wallon.

Furthermore, I believed I myself could highlight the fact that, on such occasions, the child anticipates at the mental level the conquest of his own body's functional unity, which is still incomplete at the level of volitional motricity at that point in time.

What we have here is a first capture by the image in which the first moment of the dialectic of identifications is sketched out. It is linked to a gestalt phenomenon, the child's very early perception of the human form, a form which, as we know, holds the child's interest right from the first months of life and, in the case of the human face, right from the tenth day. But what demonstrates the phenomenon of recognition, implying subjectivity, are the signs of triumphant jubilation and the playful self-discovery that characterize the child's encounter with his mirror image starting in the sixth month. This behavior

113 contrasts sharply with the indifference shown by the very animals that perceive this image—the chimpanzee, for example—once they have tested its vanity as an object; and it is even more noteworthy as it occurs at an age when the child lags behind the chimpanzee in instrumental intelligence, only catching up with the latter at eleven months of age.

What I have called the "mirror stage" is of interest because it manifests the affective dynamism by which the subject primordially identifies with the visual gestalt of his own body. In comparison with the still very profound lack of coordination in his own motor functioning, that gestalt is an ideal unity, a salutary imago. Its value is heightened by all the early distress resulting from the child's intra-organic and relational discordance during the first six months of life, when he bears the neurological and humoral signs of a physiological prematurity at birth.

It is this capture by the imago of the human form—rather than *Einfühlung*, the absence of which is abundantly clear in early childhood—that dominates the whole dialectic of the child's behavior in the presence of his semblable between six months and two and a half years of age. Throughout this period, one finds emotional reactions and articulated evidence of a normal transitivism. A child who beats another child says that he himself was beaten; a child who sees another child fall, cries. Similarly, it is by identifying with the other that he experiences the whole range of bearing and display reactions—whose structural ambivalence is clearly revealed in his behaviors, the slave identifying with the despot, the actor with the spectator, the seduced with the seducer.

There is a sort of structural crossroads here to which we must accommodate our thinking if we are to understand the nature of aggressiveness in man and its relation to the formalism of his ego and objects. It is in this erotic relationship, in which the human individual fixates on an image that alienates him from himself, that we find the energy and the form from which the organization of the passions that he will call his ego originates.

Indeed, this form crystallizes in the subject's inner conflictual tension, which leads to the awakening of his desire for the object of the other's desire: here the primordial confluence precipitates into aggressive competition, from which develops the triad of other people, ego, and object. Spangling the space of spectacular communion, this triad is inscribed there according to its own
114 formalism, and it so completely dominates the affect of *Einfühlung* that a child at that age may not recognize the people he knows best if they appear in completely different surroundings.

But if the ego seems to be marked, right from the outset, by this aggressive relativity—which minds starved for objectivity might equate with an animal's emotional erections when it is distracted by a desire in the course of its experimental conditioning—how can we escape the conclusion that each great instinctual metamorphosis, punctuating the individual's life, throws its delimitation back into question, composed as it is of the conjunction of the subject's history with the unthinkable innateness of his desire?

This is why man's ego is never reducible to his lived identity, except at a limit that even the greatest geniuses have never been able to approach; and why, in the depressive disruptions constituted by reversals experienced due to a sense of inferiority, the ego essentially engenders deadly negations that freeze it in its formalism. "What happens to me has nothing to do with what I am. There's nothing about you that is worthwhile."

Thus the two moments, when the subject negates himself and when he accuses the other, become indistinguishable; and we see here the paranoiac structure of the ego that finds its analog in the fundamental negations highlighted by Freud in the three delusions: jealousy, erotomania, and interpretation. It is the very delusion of the misanthropic beautiful soul, casting out onto the world the disorder that constitutes his being.

Subjective experience must be fully accredited if we are to recognize the central knot of ambivalent aggressiveness, which at the present stage of our culture is given to us in the dominant form of *resentment*, including even its most archaic aspects in the child. Thus, Saint Augustine, because he lived at a similar time, without having to suffer from a "behaviorist" resistance—in the sense in which I use the term—foreshadowed psychoanalysis by giving us an exemplary image of such behavior in the following terms: *"Vidi ego et expertus sum zelantem parvulum: nondum loquebatur et intuebatur pallidus amaro aspectu conlactaneum suum"* ("I myself have seen and known an infant to be jealous even though it could not speak. It became pale, and cast bitter looks on its foster-brother"). Thus Augustine forever ties the situation of spectacular absorption (the child observed), the emotional reaction (pale), and the reactivation of images of primordial frustration (with an envenomed look)— 115
which are the psychical and somatic coordinates of the earliest aggressiveness—to the infant (preverbal) stage of early childhood.

Only Melanie Klein, studying children on the verge of language, dared to project subjective experience into that earlier period; observation, nevertheless, enables us to affirm its role there in the simple fact, for example, that a child who does not yet speak reacts differently to punishment than to brutality.

Through Klein we have become aware of the function of the imaginary primordial enclosure formed by the imago of the mother's body; through her we have the mapping, drawn by children's own hands, of the mother's inner empire, and the historical atlas of the internal divisions in which the imagos of the father and siblings—whether real or virtual—and the subject's own voracious aggression dispute their deleterious hold over her sacred regions. We have also become aware of the persistence in the subject of the shadow of "bad internal objects," related to some accidental "association" (to use a term concerning which we should emphasize the organic meaning analytic experience gives it, as opposed to the abstract meaning it retains from Humean ideology). Hence we can understand by what structural means re-evoking certain imaginary *personae* and reproducing certain situational inferiorities may *disconcert* the adult's voluntary functions in the most rigorously predictable way—namely, by their fragmenting impact on the imago involved in the earliest identification.

By showing us the primordial nature of the "depressive position," the extremely archaic subjectivization of a *kakon*, Melanie Klein pushes back the limits within which we can see the subjective function of identification at work, and she especially enables us to situate the first superego formation as extremely early.

But it is important to delimit the orbit within which the following relations, some of which have yet to be elucidated, are situated in our theoretical work—guilt tension, oral harmfulness, hypochondriacal fixation, not to mention primordial masochism which I am excluding from my remarks here—in order to isolate the notion of an aggressiveness linked to the narcissistic relationship
116 and to the structures of systematic misrecognition and objectification that characterize ego formation.

A specific satisfaction, based on the integration of an original organic chaos [*désarroi*], corresponds to the *Urbild* of this formation, alienating as it may be due to its function of rendering foreign. This satisfaction must be conceived of in the dimension of a vital dehiscence constitutive of man and makes unthinkable the idea of an environment that is preformed for him; it is a "negative" libido that enables the Heraclitean notion of Discord—which the Ephesian held to be prior to harmony—to shine once more.

Thus, there is no need to look any further to find the source of the energy the ego borrows to put in the service of the "reality principle," a question Freud raises regarding repression.

This energy indubitably comes from "narcissistic passion"—provided one conceives of the ego according to the subjective notion I am proposing here as consonant with the register of analytic experience. The theoretical difficulties encountered by Freud seem, in fact, to stem from the mirage of objectification, inherited from classical psychology, constituted by the idea of the "perception-consciousness" system, in which the existence of everything the ego neglects, scotomizes, and misrecognizes in the sensations that make it react to reality, and of everything it doesn't know, exhausts, and ties down in the meanings it receives from language, suddenly seems to be overlooked—a surprising oversight on the part of the man who succeeded in forcing open the borders of the unconscious with the power of his dialectic.

Just as the superego's insane oppression lies at the root of the well-founded imperatives of moral conscience, mad passion—specific to man, stamping his image on reality—is the obscure foundation of the will's rational mediations.

The notion of aggressiveness as a tension correlated with narcissistic structure in the subject's becoming allows us to encompass in a very simply formulated function all sorts of accidents and atypicalities in that becoming.

I shall indicate here how I conceive of its dialectical link with the function of the Oedipus complex. In its normal form, its function is that of sublimation, which precisely designates an identificatory reshaping of the subject 117
and—as Freud wrote when he felt the need for a "topographical" coordination of psychical dynamisms—a *secondary identification* by introjection of the imago of the parent of the same sex.

The energy for that identification is provided by the first biological surge of genital libido. But it is clear that the structural effect of identification with a rival is not self-evident, except at the level of fable, and can only be conceptualized if the way is paved for it by a primary identification that structures the subject as rivaling with himself. In fact, a note of biological impotence is met with again here—as is the effect of anticipation characteristic of the human psyche's genesis—in the fixation of an imaginary "ideal," which, as analysis has shown, determines whether or not the "instinct" conforms to the individual's physiological sex. A point, let it be said in passing, whose anthropological import cannot be too highly stressed. But what interests me here is what I shall refer to as the "pacifying" function of the ego-ideal: the connection between its libidinal normativeness and a cultural normativeness, bound up since the dawn of history with the imago of the father. Here, obviously, lies the import that Freud's work, *Totem and Taboo*, still has, despite the mythical circularity that vitiates it, insofar as from a mythological event—the killing of the father—it derives the subjective dimension that gives this event its meaning: guilt.

Indeed, Freud shows us that the need for a form of participation, which neutralizes the conflict inscribed after killing him in the situation of rivalry among the brothers, is the basis for identification with the paternal totem. Oedipal identification is thus the identification by which the subject transcends the aggressiveness constitutive of the first subjective individuation. I have stressed elsewhere that it constitutes a step in the establishment of the distance by which, with feelings akin to respect, a whole affective assumption of one's fellow man is brought about.

Only the anti-dialectical mentality of a culture which, dominated as it is by objectifying ends, tends to reduce all subjective activity to the ego's being, can justify Von den Steinen's astonishment when confronted by a Bororo who said,
118 "I'm an ara." All the "primitive mind" sociologists scurry about trying to fathom this profession of identity, which is no more surprising upon reflection than declaring, "I'm a doctor" or "I'm a citizen of the French Republic," and certainly presents fewer logical difficulties than claiming, "I'm a man," which at most can mean no more than, "I'm like the person who, in recognizing him to be a man, I constitute as someone who can recognize me as a man." In the final analysis, these various formulations can be understood only in reference to the truth of "I is an other," less dazzling to the poet's intuition than it is obvious from the psychoanalyst's viewpoint.

Who, if not us, will call back into question the objective status of this "I," which a historical evolution peculiar to our culture tends to confuse with the subject? The specific impact of this anomaly on every level of language deserves to be displayed, and first and foremost as regards the first person as grammatical subject in our languages [*langues*]—the "I love" that hypostasizes a tendency in a subject who denies it. An impossible mirage in linguistic forms, among which the most ancient are to be found, and in which the subject appears fundamentally in the position of a determinative or instrumental of the action.

Let us not pursue here the critique of all the abuses of the *cogito ergo sum*, recalling instead that, in analytic experience, the ego represents the center of all resistances to the treatment of symptoms.

It was inevitable that analysis, after emphasizing the reintegration of tendencies excluded by the ego—those tendencies underlying the symptoms it tackled at first, most of which were related to *failed* Oedipal identification—should eventually discover the "moral" dimension of the problem.

Parallel to that, what came to the fore were, on the one hand, the role played by the aggressive tendencies in the structure of symptoms and personality and, on the other, all sorts of "uplifting" conceptions of the liberated libido, one of the first of which can be attributed to French psychoanalysts under the heading of "oblativity."

It is, in fact, clear that genital libido operates by blindly going beyond the individual for the sake of the species and that its sublimating effects in the Oedipal crisis are at the root of the whole process of man's cultural subordination.
119 Nevertheless, one cannot overemphasize the irreducible character of narcis-

sistic structure and the ambiguity of a notion that tends to misrecognize the constancy of aggressive tension in all moral life that involves subjection to this structure: for no amount of oblativity could free altruism from it. This is why La Rochefoucauld could formulate his maxim, in which his rigor concurs with the fundamental theme of his thought, on the incompatibility between marriage and delight.

We would be allowing the cutting edge of analytic experience to become dull if we deluded ourselves, if not our patients, into believing in some sort of pre-established harmony that would free social conformity—made possible by the reduction of symptoms—of its tendency to induce aggressiveness in the subject.

Theoreticians in the Middle Ages showed a rather different kind of penetration when they debated whether love could be understood in terms of a "physical" theory or an "ecstatic" theory, both of which involved the reabsorption of man's ego, the one by its reintegration into a universal good, the other by the subject's effusion toward an object devoid of alterity.

In all of an individual's genetic phases and at every degree of a person's human accomplishment, we find this narcissistic moment in the subject in a before in which he must come to terms with a libidinal frustration and in an after in which he transcends himself in a normative sublimation.

This conception allows us to understand the aggressiveness involved in the effects of all the subject's regressions, aborted undertakings, and refusals of typical development, especially at the level of sexual realization—and more precisely within each of the great phases that the libidinal metamorphoses bring about in human life, whose major function analysis has demonstrated: weaning, the Oedipal stage, puberty, maturity, and motherhood, not to mention the involutional climacteric. I have often said that the emphasis initially placed in psychoanalytic doctrine on the Oedipal conflict's aggressive retortions in the subject corresponded to the fact that the effects of the complex were first glimpsed in *failed attempts* to resolve it.

There is no need to emphasize that a coherent theory of the narcissistic
phase clarifies the ambivalence peculiar to the "partial drives" of scotophilia, 120
sadomasochism, and homosexuality, as well as the stereotypical, ceremonial formalism of the aggressiveness that is manifested in them. I am talking here about the often barely "realized" apprehension of other people in the practice of certain of these perversions, their subjective value actually being very different from that ascribed to them in the otherwise very striking existential reconstructions Sartre provided.

I should also like to mention in passing that the decisive function I ascribe to the imago of one's own body in the determination of the narcissistic phase enables us to understand the clinical relation between congenital anomalies of functional lateralization (left-handedness) and all forms of inversion of sexual and cultural normalization. This reminds us of the role attributed to gymnastics in the "beautiful and good" ideal of education among the Ancient Greeks and leads us to the social thesis with which I will conclude.

THESIS V: *This notion of aggressiveness as one of the intentional coordinates of the human ego, especially as regards the category of space, allows us to conceive of its role in modern neurosis and in the malaise in civilization.*

Here I want to merely sketch out a perspective regarding the verdicts analytic experience allows us to come to in the present social order. The preeminence of aggressiveness in our civilization would already be sufficiently demonstrated by the fact that it is usually confused in everyday morality with the virtue of strength. Quite rightly understood as indicative of ego development, aggressiveness is regarded as indispensable in social practice and is so widely accepted in our mores that, in order to appreciate its cultural peculiarity, one must become imbued with the meaning and efficient virtues of a practice like that of *yang* in the public and private morality of the Chinese.

Were it not superfluous, the prestige of the idea of the struggle for life would be sufficiently attested to by the success of a theory that was able to make us endorse a notion of selection based solely on the animal's conquest of space
121 as a valid explanation for the developments of life. Indeed, Darwin's success seems to derive from the fact that he projected the predations of Victorian society and the economic euphoria that sanctioned for that society the social devastation it initiated on a planetary scale, and that he justified its predations with the image of a laissez-faire system in which the strongest predators compete for their natural prey.

Before Darwin, however, Hegel had provided the definitive theory of the specific function of aggressiveness in human ontology, seeming to prophesy the iron law of our own time. From the conflict between Master and Slave, he deduced the entire subjective and objective progress of our history, revealing in its crises the syntheses represented by the highest forms of the status of the person in the West, from the Stoic to the Christian, and even to the future citizen of the Universal State.

Here the natural individual is regarded as nil, since the human subject is nothing, in effect, before the absolute Master that death is for him. The satisfaction of human desire is possible only when mediated by the other's desire and labor. While it is the recognition of man by man that is at stake in the conflict between Master and Slave, this recognition is based on a radical negation of natural values, whether expressed in the master's sterile tyranny or in work's productive tyranny.

The support this profound doctrine lent to the slave's constructive Spartacism, recreated by the barbarity of the Darwinian century, is well known.

The relativization of our sociology by the scientific collection of the cultural forms we are destroying in the world—and the analyses, bearing truly psychoanalytic marks, in which Plato's wisdom shows us the dialectic common to the passions of the soul and of the city—can enlighten us as to the reason for this barbarity. Namely, to employ the jargon that corresponds to our approaches to man's subjective needs, the increasing absence of all the saturations of the superego and ego-ideal that occur in all kinds of organic forms in traditional societies, forms that extend from the rituals of everyday intimacy to the periodical festivals in which the community manifests itself. We no longer know them except in their most obviously degraded guises. Furthermore, in abolishing the cosmic polarity of the male and female principles, our society is experiencing the full psychological impact of the modern phe- 122
nomenon known as the "battle of the sexes." Ours is an immense community, midway between a "democratic" anarchy of the passions and their hopeless leveling out by the "great winged drone" of narcissistic tyranny; it is clear that the promotion of the ego in our existence is leading, in conformity with the utilitarian conception of man that reinforces it, to an ever greater realization of man as an individual, in other words, in an isolation of the soul that is ever more akin to its original dereliction.

Correlatively, it seems—I mean for reasons whose historical contingency is based on a necessity that certain of my considerations make it possible to perceive—we are engaged in a technological enterprise on the scale of the entire species. The question is whether the conflict between Master and Slave will find its solution in the service of the machine, for which a psychotechnics, that is already yielding a rich harvest of ever more precise applications, will strive to provide race-car drivers and guards for regulating power stations.

The notion of the role of spatial symmetry in man's narcissistic structure is essential in laying the groundwork for a psychological analysis of space, whose place I can merely indicate here. Animal psychology has shown us that the individual's relation to a particular spatial field is socially mapped in certain species, in a way that raises it to the category of subjective membership. I would say that it is the subjective possibility of the mirror projection of such a field into the other's field that gives human space its originally "geometrical" structure, a structure I would willingly characterize as *kaleidoscopic*.

Such, at least, is the space in which the imagery of the ego develops, and which intersects the objective space of reality. But does it provide us a secure

basis? Already in the *Lebensraum* ("living space") in which human competition grows ever keener, an observer of our species from outer space would conclude we possess needs to escape with very odd results. But doesn't conceptual extension, to which we believed we had reduced reality [*réel*], later seem to refuse to lend its support to the physicist's thinking? Having extended
123 our grasp to the farthest reaches of matter, won't this "realized" space—which makes the great imaginary spaces in which the free games of the ancient sages roamed seem illusory to us—thus vanish in turn in a roar of the universal ground?

Whatever the case may be, we know how our adaptation to these exigencies proceeds, and that war is increasingly proving to be the inevitable and necessary midwife of all our organizational progress. The adaptation of adversaries, opposed in their social systems, certainly seems to be progressing toward a confluence of forms, but one may well wonder whether it is motivated by agreement as to their necessity, or by the kind of identification Dante, in the *Inferno*, depicts in the image of a deadly kiss.

Moreover, it doesn't seem that the human individual, as the material for such a struggle, is absolutely flawless. And the detection of "bad internal objects," responsible for reactions (that may prove extremely costly in terms of equipment) of inhibition and headlong flight—which we have recently learned to use in the selection of shock, fighter, parachute, and commando troops—proves that war, after having taught us a great deal about the genesis of the neuroses, is perhaps proving too demanding in its need for ever more neutral subjects to serve an aggression in which feeling is undesirable.

Nevertheless, we have a few psychological truths to contribute here too: namely, the extent to which the ego's supposed "instinct of self-preservation" willingly gives way before the temptation to dominate space, and above all the extent to which the fear of death, the "absolute Master"—presumed to exist in consciousness by a whole philosophical tradition from Hegel onward—is psychologically subordinate to the narcissistic fear of harm to one's own body.

I do not think it was futile to have highlighted the relation between the spatial dimension and a subjective tension, which—in the malaise of civilization—intersects with the tension of anxiety, approached so humanely by Freud, and which develops in the temporal dimension. I would willingly shed light on the latter, too, using the contemporary significations of two philosophies that would seem to correspond to the philosophies I just mentioned: that of Bergson, owing to its naturalistic inadequacy, and that of Kierkegaard owing to its dialectical signification.

Only at the intersection of these two tensions should one envisage the
124 assumption by man of his original fracturing, by which it might be said that at

every instant he constitutes his world by committing suicide, and the psychological experience of which Freud had the audacity to formulate as the "death instinct," however paradoxical its expression in biological terms may be.

In the "emancipated" man of modern society, this fracturing reveals that his formidable crack goes right to the very depths of his being. It is a self-punishing neurosis, with hysterical/hypochondriacal symptoms of its functional inhibitions, psychasthenic forms of its derealizations of other people and of the world, and its social consequences of failure and crime. It is this touching victim, this innocent escapee who has thrown off the shackles that condemn modern man to the most formidable social hell, whom we take in when he comes to us; it is this being of nothingness for whom, in our daily task, we clear anew the path to his meaning in a discreet fraternity—a fraternity to which we never measure up.

Note

1. Apart from the first line, this text is reproduced here in its original form.

125

A Theoretical Introduction to the Functions of Psychoanalysis in Criminology

Presentation Given at the Thirteenth Conference of French-Speaking Psychoanalysts (May 29, 1950)

Written in Collaboration with Michel Cénac

I. On the Motor Force of Truth in the Human Sciences

While theory in the physical sciences has never really escaped from the requirement of internal coherence that is the very motor force of knowledge, the human sciences, being embodied as behaviors in the very reality of their object, cannot elude the question of the meaning of these behaviors or ensure that the answer to this question need not be in terms of truth.

The fact that human reality implies a process of revelation leads certain people to think of history as a dialectic inscribed in matter; it is a truth that no "behaviorist"* ritual engaged in by the subject to protect his object can castrate of its creative and deadly tip, and it makes scientists themselves, who are devoted to "pure" knowledge, primarily responsible.

No one knows this better than psychoanalysts who, in their understanding of what their subjects confide to them, as in their handling of the behaviors that are conditioned by analytic technique, work on the basis of a form of revelation whose truth conditions its efficacy.

Now isn't the search for truth what constitutes the object of criminology in the judicial realm and also what unifies its two facets: the truth of the crime, which is the facet that concerns the police, and the truth of the criminal, the anthropological facet?

The question we will address today is: What can the technique that guides the analyst's dialogue with the subject and the psychological notions that ana-

lytic experience has defined contribute to this search for truth? We are less
interested in indicating analysis' contribution to the study of delinquency, 126
which was discussed in the other presentations here, than in laying out its legitimate limits, and are certainly not interested in propagating the letter of analytic doctrine without concern for method, but rather in rethinking it, as we are advised to constantly do, in relation to a new object.

II. On the Sociological Reality of Crime and Law and on the Relation of Psychoanalysis to their Dialectical Foundation

Neither crime nor criminals are objects that can be conceptualized apart from their sociological context.

The statement that the "law makes the sin" remains true outside the eschatological perspective of Grace in which Saint Paul formulated it.

It is scientifically verified by the observation that there is no society that does not include positive law, whether traditional or written, common law or civil law. Nor is there any society in which we do not find all the degrees of transgression of the law that define crime.

Supposed "unconscious," "forced," "intuitive" obedience by primitive man to the group's rules is an ethnological conception deriving from an imaginary insistence that has cast a shadow on many other conceptions of "origins," but it is just as mythical as they are.

Every society, lastly, manifests the relationship between crime and law by punishments whose infliction, regardless of the forms it takes, requires subjective assent. Whether the criminal himself actually inflicts the punishment that the law requires as the price to be paid for his crime—as in the case of incest between matrilineal cousins on the Trobriand Islands, whose outcome Malinowski recounts in his book, *Crime and Custom in Savage Society*, which is essential on this subject (and regardless of the various psychological motives for this act or even the vindictive oscillations that the curses of he who commits suicide can engender in the group)—or whether the sanction stipulated by a code of criminal law includes a procedure involving widely varied social systems, subjective assent is necessary to the very signification of the punishment.

The beliefs by which this punishment is explained in the individual, and the
institutions by which the punishment is inflicted in the group, allow us to define 127
in any given society what we call "responsibility" in our own society.

But the responsible entity is not always equivalent. Let us say that if, originally, it is the society as a whole (a society is always self-contained in theory, as ethnologists have emphasized) that is considered to be destabilized by the action of one of its members and that must be set right, this member is held individually responsible to so small an extent that the law often requires satisfaction at the expense either of one of his partisans or of the whole of an "ingroup"* that he is part of.

It sometimes even happens that a society considers itself to be so impaired in its structure that it takes steps to exclude its ills in the form of a scapegoat, or even to regenerate itself by resorting to something external. We see here a collective or mystical responsibility, of which our own mores contain traces, assuming this form of responsibility is not staging a return for opposite reasons.

But even in cases in which the punishment strikes only the individual perpetrator of a crime, he is not [in all cases] held responsible with respect to the same function or, as it were, the same image of himself. This is evident when we reflect upon the difference between a person who has to answer for his acts before a judge who represents the Holy Office and a person who does so before a judge who presides over the People's Court.

It is here that psychoanalysis, with the agencies that it distinguishes in the modern individual, can shed light on vacillations in the contemporary notion of responsibility and the related advent of an objectification of crime that it can collaborate on.

While psychoanalysis cannot, since its experience is limited to the individual, claim to grasp the totality of any sociological object or even the whole set of forces currently operating in our society, the fact remains that it discovered in analytic experience relational tensions that seem to play a basic role in all societies, as if the discontent in civilization went so far as to lay bare the very meeting point of nature and culture. We can extend analysis' equations to certain human sciences that can utilize them—especially, as we shall see, to criminology—provided we perform the correct transformation.

Let us add that if reliance on the subject's confession, which is one of the keys to criminological truth, and reintegration of the subject into the social
128 community, which is one of the goals of its application, seem to find an especially favorable form in analytic dialogue, it is above all because this dialogue, which can be continued until it reaches the most radical significations, intersects with the universal—the universal that is included in language and that, far from being eliminable from anthropology, constitutes its very foundation and goal. For psychoanalysis is merely an extension of anthropology in its technique that explores in the individual the import of the dialectic which scands our society's creations and in which Saint Paul's statement finds anew its absolute truth.

To he who would ask where our remarks are heading, we would respond, at the risk, willingly accepted, of eliminating the clinician's smugness [*suffi-*

sance] and preventionistic pharisaism from them, by referring him to one of Plato's dialogues that recount the deeds of the hero of dialectic, especially to the *Gorgias*, whose subtitle, which invokes rhetoric and is well designed to dissuade our uncultivated contemporaries from studying it, harbors a veritable treatise on the motives of the Just and the Unjust.

In the *Gorgias*, Socrates refutes infatuation with the Master, which is incarnated in a free man of Athens, whose limits are marked by the reality of the Slave. This form marks the shift to the free man of Wisdom, by admitting the absolute nature of Justice, he being trained in it solely by virtue of language in the Interlocutor's maieutic. Thus Socrates—by making the Master perceive the dialectic (which is bottomless like the Danaïds' vessel) of man's passions for power and recognize the law of his own political being in the City's injustice—brings him to bow before the eternal myths that express the meaning of punishment, as a way of making amends for the individual and of setting an example for the group, while he himself, in the name of the same universal, accepts his own destiny and submits in advance to the insanely harsh verdict of the City that makes him a man.

It is worth recalling the historical moment at which a tradition was born that conditioned the appearance of all our sciences and that Freud firmly rooted his work in when he proffered with poignant confidence: "The voice of the intellect is a soft one, but it does not rest till it has gained a hearing." We think we hear in this a muffled echo of Socrates' own voice addressing Callicles, when he opines that "Philosophy always says the same thing."

III. On Crime as Expressing the Symbolism of the Superego as a 129
Psychopathological Agency: Although Psychoanalysis Unrealizes [Irréalise] *Crime, It Does Not Dehumanize the Criminal*

While we cannot even grasp the concrete reality of crime without relating it to a symbolism whose actual forms combine harmoniously in society, but which is inscribed in the radical structures that language unconsciously transmits, psychoanalytic experience has demonstrated just how extensively, to what formerly unknown limits, this first symbolism reverberates in individuals, in their physiology as well as in their conduct, by studying its pathogenic effects.

Thus it was by starting with one of the relational significations that the psychology of "intellectual syntheses," in its reconstruction of individual functions, had located at the earliest possible stage, that Freud inaugurated a form of psychology that has bizarrely been called "depth psychology," no doubt because of the utterly superficial scope of what it replaced.

Psychoanalysis boldly designated these pathogenic effects, whose meaning it was discovering, by the feeling that corresponded to them in lived experience: guilt.

Nothing can better demonstrate the importance of the Freudian revolution than the use (technical or everyday, implicit or rigorous, avowed or surreptitious) that has been made, in psychology, of this now truly ubiquitous category, which was thoroughly neglected before—nothing if not the strange attempt by certain people to reduce guilt to "genetic" or "objective" forms, supposedly guaranteed by a kind of "behaviorist" experimentalism that would have been exhausted long ago had it actually forced itself not to read in human actions the significations that specify them as human.

We are also beholden to Freud for having brought the notion of the first *situation* into psychology so that it could prosper there, in the course of time—not as an abstract confrontation sketching out a relationship, but as a dramatic crisis that is resolved in a structure—this first situation being that of crime in
130 its two most abhorrent forms, incest and parricide, whose shadow engenders all the pathogenesis of the Oedipus complex.

We can understand why Freud, the physician, having received in the field of psychology such a significant contribution from the social realm, was tempted to return the favor, and why he wanted to demonstrate the origin of universal Law in the primal crime in *Totem and Taboo* in 1912. Whatever criticism his method in that book might be open to, what was essential was his recognition that man began with law and crime, after Freud the clinician had shown that their significations sustained everything right down to the very form of the individual—not only in his value to the other but in his erection for himself.

This is how the concept of the superego came into being, first based on the effects of unconscious censorship explaining previously identified psychopathological structures, soon shedding light on the anomalies of everyday life, and finally being correlated with the simultaneous discovery of an immense morbidity and of its psychogenic roots: character neurosis, failure mechanisms, sexual impotence, and "der gehemmte Mensch."

The modern face of man was thus revealed and it contrasted strangely with the prophecies of late nineteenth-century thinkers; it seemed pathetic when compared with both the illusions nourished by libertarians and the moralists' worries inspired by man's emancipation from religious beliefs and the weakening of his traditional ties. To the concupiscence gleaming in old man Karamazov's eyes when he questioned his son—"God is dead, thus all is permitted"—modern man, the very one who dreams of the nihilistic suicide of Dostoevsky's hero or forces himself to blow up Nietzsche's inflatable superman, replies with all his ills and all his deeds: "God is dead, nothing is permitted anymore."

These ills and deeds all bear the signification of self-punishment. Will it thus be necessary to see all criminals as self-punishing? For, according to the legislator's icy humor, no one is supposed to be ignorant of the law, and thus everyone can foresee its repercussions and must be considered to be seeking out its blows.

This ironic remark, by obliging us to define what psychoanalysis recognizes as crimes and offenses [*délits*] emanating from the superego, should allow us to formulate a critique of the scope of this notion in anthropology.

Consider the remarkable first observations with which Franz Alexander and 131
Hugo Staub brought psychoanalysis into criminology. Their content is convincing, whether it concerns "the attempted homicide by a neurotic," or the odd thefts by a medical student (who did not stop until he was imprisoned by the Berlin police and who, rather than earn the diploma to which his knowledge and real gifts gave him the right, preferred to exercise them by breaking the law), or even "the man obsessed with car trips." Consider anew Marie Bonaparte's analysis of "The Case of Mrs. Lefebvre." Here the morbid structure of the crime and offenses is obvious—the forced way in which the crimes were carried out, the stereotypy seen in their repetition, the provocative style of the defense and the confession, the incomprehensibility of the motives—all of this confirms "coercion by a force that the subject was unable to resist," and the judges in all these cases came to this same conclusion.

These behaviors become perfectly clear, however, in light of an Oedipal interpretation. But what makes them morbid is their symbolic character. Their psychopathological structure is not found in the criminal situation that they express, but in their *unreal* mode of expression.

To fully explain this, let us contrast these behaviors with something that is a constant element in the annals of armies and that derives its full import from the very broad and yet narrow range of asocial elements in our population from which we have, for over a century, recruited defenders of our homeland and even of our social order. We are referring to the propensity found in military units, on the day of glory that places them in contact with the enemy civilian population, to rape one or more women in the presence of a male who is preferably old and has first been rendered powerless. There is nothing to indicate that the individuals who engage in such an act morally differ—either before or afterward, as sons or husbands, fathers or citizens—from anyone else. This simple act might well be described as a random news item [*fait . . . divers*] owing to the diverse quantity of credence it is lent depending on its source—and even, strictly speaking, as a divertissement owing to the material that this diversity offers up to propaganda.

We say that it is a real crime, even though it is committed in a precisely 132

Oedipal form, and the perpetrators would be justly punished for it if the heroic conditions under which it is considered to have been carried out did not most often place responsibility for it on the group to which the individuals belong.

Let us thus concur with Marcel Mauss' clear formulations, which his recent death has brought once again to our attention: The structures of society are symbolic; individuals, insofar as they are normal, use them in real behaviors; insofar as they are mentally ill [*psychopathe*], they express them by symbolic behaviors.

But it is obvious that the symbolism thus expressed can only be fragmented; at most, one can assert that this symbolism signals the breaking point the individual occupies in the network of social aggregations. Psychopathological manifestations can reveal the structure of the fault line, but this structure can only be viewed as one element in the exploration of the whole.

This is why we must rigorously distinguish psychoanalytic theory from the ever renewed fallacious attempts to base notions such as "modal personality," "national character," or "collective superego" on analytic theory. One can certainly see the appeal that a theory that so palpably reveals human reality has for pioneers in less clearly objective fields. Have we not heard a well-intentioned cleric boast of his plan to apply the data of psychoanalysis to Christian symbolism? To cut short such untoward extrapolations, we need but continually relate anew the theory to experience.

This symbolism, which was already recognized in the first order of delinquency that psychoanalysis had isolated as psychopathological, should allow us to indicate, in extension as well as in comprehension, the social signification of "Oedipalism," and to critique the scope of the notion of the superego for all of the human sciences.

Most, if not all, of the psychopathological effects in which the tensions stemming from Oedipalism are revealed, along with the historical coordinates that imposed these effects on Freud's investigative genius, lead us to believe that these effects express a dehiscence of the family unit at the heart of society. This
133 conception—which is justified by the ever greater reduction of this unit to its conjugal form and by the ever more exclusive formative role it consequently plays in the child's first identifications and early discipline—explains why the family unit's power to captivate the individual has waxed as the family's social power has waned.

To illustrate this, let us simply mention the fact that in a matrilineal society such as that of the Zuni or the Hopi Indians, responsibility for the care of an infant from the moment of its birth on falls by law to the father's sister. This inscribes the infant from the outset in a double system of parental relations that are enriched at each stage of its life by a growing complexity of hierarchized relationships.

The problem of comparing the advantages that a supposed matriarchal family organization might have over the classical triangle of Oedipal structure in forming a superego that is bearable to the individual is thus outdated. Experience has clearly shown that this triangle is merely the reduction, produced by an historical evolution, to the natural group of a formation in which the authority reserved for the father—the only remaining trait of its original structure—proves in effect to be ever more unstable, nay obsolete; the psychopathological impact of this situation must be related both to the tenuousness of the group relations that it provides the individual with and to the ever greater ambivalence of this structure.

This conception is confirmed by the notion of latent delinquency to which Aichhorn was led in applying analytic experience to the youth he was in charge of owing to special jurisdiction. It is well known that Kate Friedlander developed a genetic conception of latent delinquency under the heading of "neurotic character," and also that the best informed critics, from August Aichhorn himself to Edward Glover, seem to have been astonished by the theory's inability to distinguish the structure of this character as "criminogenic" from the structure of neurosis in which tensions remain latent in symptoms.

The perspective we are presenting here allows us to see that "neurotic character" is the reflection in individual behavior of the isolation of the fam- 134
ily unit, the asocial position of which is always found in such cases, whereas neurosis expresses instead the family unit's structural anomalies. What requires explanation is thus less a criminal acting out by a subject trapped in what Daniel Lagache has quite correctly characterized as imaginary behavior, than the processes by which neurotics partially adapt to reality [*réel*]: these are, as we know, the auto-plastic mutilations that can be recognized at the origin of symptoms.

This sociological reference—"neurotic character"—agrees, moreover, with Kate Friedlander's account of its genesis, if it is correct to summarize the latter as the repetition, across the subject's biography, of drive frustrations that are seemingly arrested by short-circuiting the Oedipal situation, without ever again being engaged in a structural development.

Psychoanalysis, in its understanding of crimes caused by the superego, thus has the effect of *unrealizing* them. It agrees, in this respect, with a dim recognition that has long forced itself on the best of those responsible for law enforcement.

The vacillations that were seen throughout the nineteenth century in social conscience regarding society's right to punish were thus characteristic. Penologists, sure of themselves and even implacable as soon as a utilitarian motivation appeared—so much so that English practice at that time considered misdemeanors (even if they only involved petty theft) that occasioned homicide to be equivalent to the premeditation that defines first degree murder (see Alimena's *La premeditazione*)—hesitated when faced with crimes in which instincts surfaced whose nature escaped the utilitarian register within which someone like Bentham developed his ideas.

A first response was provided by Lombroso in the early days of criminology; he viewed these instincts as atavistic and took criminals to be survivors of an archaic form of the species that could be biologically isolated. One can say of this response that it betrayed, above all, a far realer philosophical regression in its author and that its success can only be explained by the satisfactions that the euphoria of the dominant class then demanded, both for its intellectual comfort and its guilty conscience.

135 The calamities of World War I having invalidated its claims, Lombroso's theory was relegated to the slag heap of history, and simple respect for the conditions proper to every human science—conditions we thought necessary to recall in our introduction—forced itself even on the study of criminals.

Healy's *The Individual Delinquent* is an important landmark in the return to principles, stating as it does, first of all, the principle that this study must be monographic. The concrete results of psychoanalysis constitute another landmark, which is as decisive owing to the doctrinal confirmation that they bring this principle as by the importance of the facts that are brought out.

Psychoanalysis simultaneously resolves a dilemma in criminological theory: in unrealizing crime, it does not dehumanize the criminal.

Moreover, by means of transference, psychoanalysis grants us access to the imaginary world of the criminal, which can open the door to reality [*réel*] for him.

Let us note here the spontaneous manifestation of transference in the criminal's behavior, in particular the transference that tends to develop with the criminal's judge, proof of which it would be easy to collect. Let us cite, for their sheer beauty, the remarks confided by a certain Frank to the psychiatrist Gilbert who was charged with the favorable presentation of the defendants at the Nuremberg trials. This pathetic Machiavelli, neurotic enough for fascism's insane regime to entrust him with its great works, felt remorse stir his soul at the dignified appearance of his judges, especially that of the English judge who he said was "so elegant."

The results obtained with "major" criminals by Melitta Schmideberg, while their publication is thwarted by the same obstacle we encounter regarding all of our cases, would deserve to be followed up in their catamnesis.

Be that as it may, the cases that clearly fall under Oedipalism should be entrusted to the analyst without any of the limitations that can hinder his action.

How can we not completely put analysis to the test when penology's claims are so poorly justified that the popular mind balks at enforcing them even when faced with *real* crimes? This is seen in the famous case in America that Grotjahn reported on in his article in *Searchlights on Delinquency*, where, to the 136
delight of the public, we see the jury acquit the defendants, even though all the charges seemed to have overwhelmed them during the probation of first degree murder, disguised as an accident at sea, of the parents of one of them.

Let us complete these considerations by enumerating the theoretical consequences that follow from this in the use of the notion of the superego. The superego must, in our view, be taken as an individual manifestation that is tied to the social conditions of Oedipalism. This is why the criminal tensions included in the family situation become pathogenic only in societies in which the family situation is disintegrating.

In this sense, the superego reveals tension, just as illness sometimes sheds light on a physiological function.

But analytic experience of the effects of the superego and direct observation of children in light of this experience indicate that the superego appears at so early a stage that it seems to form contemporaneously with the ego, if not before it.

Melanie Klein asserts that the categories Good and Bad are operative in the infant stage of behavior; this view raises a knotty problem—that of retroactively inserting significations into a stage at which language has yet to appear. We know how her method—using, despite all objections, Oedipal tensions in her extremely early interpretations of small children's intentions—simply cut the knot, provoking passionate debates about her theories in the process.

The fact remains that the imaginary persistence of good and bad primordial objects in avoidance behaviors, which can bring adults into conflict with their responsibilities, leads us to conceptualize the superego as a psychological agency that has a generic signification in man. There is, nevertheless, nothing idealist about this notion; it is inscribed in the reality of the physiological misery that is characteristic of the first months of man's life, which one of us has emphasized, and it expresses man's dependence, which is, in effect, generic, on the human milieu.

The fact that this dependence may seem to be signifying in individuals at an incredibly early stage of their development is not something psychoanalysts need back away from.

If our experience of psychopathology has brought us to the meeting point 137
of nature and culture, we have discovered an obscure agency there, a blind

and tyrannical agency, which seems to be the antinomy, at the individual's biological pole, of the ideal of pure Duty that Kant posited as a counterweight to the incorruptible order of the star-spangled heavens.

Ever ready to emerge from the chaos of social categories to recreate the morbid universe of wrongdoing, to borrow Hesnard's lovely expression, this agency is nevertheless graspable only in the psychopathological state—that is, in the individual.

Thus no form of the superego can be inferred from the individual to a given society. And the only form of collective superego that one can conceive of would require a complete molecular disintegration of society. It is true that the enthusiasm with which an entire generation of young people sacrificed itself to the ideals of nothingness allows us to glimpse its possible realization on the horizon of mass social phenomena that would then presuppose that it occur on a universal scale.

IV. On Crime in Relation to the Criminal's Reality: If Psychoanalysis Provides Its Measure, It [Also] Indicates Its Fundamental Social Mainspring

Responsibility—that is, punishment—is an essential characteristic of the idea of man that prevails in a given society.

A civilization whose ideals are ever more utilitarian, since it is caught up in the accelerated movement of production, can no longer understand anything about the expiatory signification of punishment. While it may consider punishment useful as a warning to others, it tends to assimilate it into its correctional goal. And this goal imperceptibly changes objects. The ideals of humanism dissolve into the utilitarianism of the group. And since the group that lays down the law is, for social reasons, not at all sure that the foundations of its power are just, it relies on a humanitarianism in which are expressed both the revolt of the exploited and the guilty conscience of the exploiters, to whom the notion of punishment has become equally unbearable. An ideological antinomy reflects, here as elsewhere, a social malaise. It is now seeking the solution to that malaise in a scientific approach to the problem, that is, in a psychi-
138 atric analysis of the criminal to which—in the final analysis of all the measures for preventing crime and guarding against recidivism—what can be called a sanitary conception of penology must be related.

This conception assumes that the relations between law and violence and the power of a universal police have been resolved. Indeed, we saw this conception reigning proudly in Nuremberg, and although the sanitary effect of those trials remains doubtful regarding the suppression of the social ills that it claimed to repress, psychiatrists had to be included for reasons of "humanity," these reasons more closely resembling respect for the human object than the notion of our fellowman.

A parallel evolution in the probation of crime corresponds, in fact, to the evolution in the meaning of punishment.

Beginning in religious societies with the ordeal and the test of sworn oath, in which the guilty party is identified by means of belief or offers up his fate to God's judgment, probation demands ever more of the individual's involvement in confession as his juridical personality is progressively specified. This is why the entire humanist evolution of Law in Europe—which began with the rediscovery of Roman Law at the University of Bologna and extended to the entire appropriation [*captation*] of justice by royal jurists and the universalization of the notion of the Law of Nations [*Droit des gens*]—is strictly correlative, in time and space, to the spread of torture that also began in Bologna as a means in the probation of a crime. This is a fact whose import people apparently still have not gauged.

For the contempt for conscience that is manifest in the widespread reappearance of this practice as a means of oppression hides from us what faith in man it presupposes as a means of enforcing justice.

If the juridical practice of torture was abandoned precisely when our society began promulgating Human Rights, which were ideologically founded in the abstraction of man's natural being, it was not because of an improvement in mores, which would be difficult to sustain given the historical perspective we have on nineteenth century social reality. Rather, it was because this new man, abstracted from his social consistency, *was no longer believable* in either sense of the term. That is, since he was no longer subject to sinning [*peccable*], one could lend credence neither to his existence as a criminal nor to his 139
confession. From then on, it was necessary to know his motivations, along with his motives for committing the crime, and these motivations and motives had to be comprehensible—comprehensible to everyone. As Tarde, one of the best minds among those who tried to solve the crisis in "penal philosophy," formulated it (with a sociological rectitude for which he deserves to be remembered, not forgotten as he is), two conditions are required for the subject to be fully responsible: social similarity and personal identity.

This opened the door of the praetorium to psychologists, and the fact that they only rarely appear there in person simply proves the social insolvency of their function.

From that moment on, the "situation of the accused," to borrow Roger Grenier's expression, could no longer be described as anything but the meeting place of irreconcilable truths, as is apparent when listening to the most trivial trials in criminal court at which an expert is called on to testify. There is an obvious incommensurability between the emotions the prosecution and the defense refer to in their debate (because they are the emotions understood by the jury), on the one hand, and the objective notions that the expert brings, on the other hand—notions that he does not manage to get across, poor dialectician that he is, since he is unable to nail them down in a conclusion of *non compos mentis* [*irresponsabilité*].

This incommensurability can be seen in the minds of the experts themselves, for it interferes with their function in the resentment they manifest regardless of their duty. Consider the case of the expert called before the Court to testify who refused to conduct anything but a physical examination of an indicted man who manifestly was mentally healthy. The expert hid behind the Code of Law, arguing that he did not have to conclude whether the act imputed to the subject by a police investigation had occurred or not, whereas a psychiatric evaluation explicitly informed him that a simple psychiatric exam would demonstrate with certainty that the act in question merely looked like a crime; since it figured in the subject's obsession as a repetitive gesture, it could not constitute a criminal act of exhibitionism in the enclosed but monitored space where it occurred.

Expert witnesses are, however, granted almost discretionary power over the severity of the sentence [in France], provided they make use of the extension added by law for their use in Article 64 of the Code.

140 But while this sole article cannot help them explain the coercive nature of the force that led to the subject's act, it at least allows them to seek to discover *who* suffered its coercion.

But only psychoanalysts can answer such a question, in that only they have a dialectical experience of the subject.

Let us note that one of the first things to which this experience taught them to attribute psychical autonomy—namely, what analysis has progressively theorized as representing the ego as an agency—is also what subjects in the analytic dialogue admit to be part of themselves or, more precisely, that part of their actions and intentions that they admit to. Freud recognized the form of this admission that is most characteristic of the function it represents: *Verneinung*, that is, negation.

We could trace out here a whole semiology of cultural forms through which subjectivity is communicated. We could begin with the intellectual restriction characteristic of Christian humanism, the codified usage of which the Jesuits, those admirable moralists, have so often been reproached for. We could continue with the "ketman," a sort of exercise for protecting against truth, which Gobineau, in his penetrating account of social life in the Middle East, indicates is widespread. From there we could move on to Yang, a ceremony of refusals that Chinese politeness lays out as steps in the recognition of other people. This would allow us to see that the most characteristic form of expression of the subject in Western society is the assertion of one's innocence. We could thus posit that sincerity is the first obstacle encountered by the dialectic in the search for true intentions, the first goal of speech apparently being to disguise them.

But this is merely the tip of a structure that is found anew at every stage in the genesis of the ego, and it shows that the dialectic provides the unconscious law of even the earliest formations of the system [*appareil*] of adaptation, thus confirming Hegel's gnoseology which formulates the law that generates reality through the unfolding of thesis, antithesis, and synthesis. It is certainly piquant to see Marxists wrestling to discover imperceptible traces of this unfolding in the progression of the essentially idealist notions that constitute mathematics, and overlooking it precisely where it is most likely to appear: in the only psychology that clearly deals with the concrete, even if its theory does 141
not acknowledge being guided by this unfolding.

It is all the more significant to recognize the latter in the succession of crises—weaning, intrusion, Oedipus, puberty, and adolescence—each of which produces a new synthesis of the ego systems [*appareils*] in a form that is ever more alienating for the drives that are frustrated therein, and ever less ideal for the drives that are normalized thereby. This form is produced by what is perhaps the most fundamental psychical phenomenon that psychoanalysis has discovered: identification, whose formative power is confirmed even in biology. Each of the periods of so-called drive latency (the corresponding series of which is completed by the one that Fritz Wittels discovered in the adolescent ego) is characterized by the domination of a typical structure of objects of desire.

One of us has described the infant's identification with his specular image as the most significant model, as well as the earliest moment, of the fundamentally alienating relationship in which man's being is dialectically constituted.

He has also demonstrated that each identification gives rise to an aggressiveness which cannot be adequately explained by drive frustration—except in the commonsense manner dear to Franz Alexander—but which expresses the discordance that is produced by the alienation. This phenomenon can be exemplified by the grimacing form of it found in experiments in which animals are exposed to an increasingly ambiguous stimulus—for example, one that gradually changes from an ellipse to a circle—when the animals have been conditioned to respond to the two different stimuli in opposite ways.

This tension manifests the dialectical negativity inscribed in the very forms in which the life forces are taken up in man, and we can say that Freud showed his genius when, with the term "death instinct," he recognized this tension as an "ego drive."

Indeed, every form of the ego embodies this negativity, and we can say that if Clotho, Lachesis, and Atropos share the wardship of our fate, it is in concert that they spin the thread of our identity.

Aggressive tension thus becomes part of the drive, whenever the drive is frustrated because the "other's" noncorrespondence [to one's wishes] aborts
142 the resolving identification, and this produces a type of object that becomes criminogenic by interrupting the dialectical formation of one's ego.

One of us has attempted to show the functional role and the correlation with delusion of this object's structure in two extreme forms of paranoiac homicide, the case of "Aimée" and that of the Papin sisters. The latter provides proof that only the analyst can demonstrate that a criminal is alienated from reality in a case in which popular opinion is deluded into believing that the crime was simply a response to its social context.

These are also the object structures that Anna Freud, Kate Friedlander, and John Bowlby found, in their work as analysts, in acts of theft committed by juvenile delinquents, structures that differed depending on whether these acts manifested the symbolism of a gift of excrement or an Oedipal demand, the frustration of nourishing presence or that of phallic masturbation. What these analysts call the educative portion of their work with the subject is guided by the notion that each object structure corresponds to a type of reality that determines his actions.

This education is, rather, a living dialectic, in accordance with which the educators, through their non-action, relegate the aggressions characteristic of the ego to becoming bound [*se lier*] for the subject as he becomes alienated in his relations with the other, so that they can then unbind [*délier*] these aggressions using classical analysis' typical techniques.

The ingenuity and patience that we admire in the initiatives of a pioneer like Aichhorn certainly do not make us forget that the form of these techniques must always be renewed in order to overcome the *resistances* that the "aggressive group" cannot help but deploy against every recognized form of practice.

Such a conception of the action of "setting straight" is diametrically opposed to everything that can be inspired by a psychology that calls itself genetic. The latter merely measures children's degressive aptitudes in response to questions that are posed to them in the purely abstract register of adult mental categories, and it can be overturned by the simple apprehension of the primordial fact that children, right from their very first manifestations of language, use syntax and particles with a level of sophistication that the postulates of intellectual "genesis" would allow them to reach only at the height of a metaphysician's career.

And since genetic psychology claims to reach the child's reality in this idi- 143
otic manner, let us say that it is the pedants who should be warned that they will have to realize their mistake when the words, "Long live death," proffered by mouths that know not what they say, make the pedants see that the burning dialectic circulates in the flesh along with the blood.

This conception also specifies the sort of expert opinion that analysts can give on the reality of a crime in basing themselves on the study of what we can call the ego's negativistic techniques—whether they be suffered by a person who becomes a criminal because of a one-time opportunity or are directed by the hardened criminal—namely, the basal inanition [*inanisation*] of spatial and temporal perspectives that are necessitated by the intimidating prediction in which the so-called "hedonistic" theory of penology naively trusts; the progressive subduction of interests in the field of object temptation; the shrinking of the field of consciousness in tandem with a somnambulistic apprehension of the immediate situation in carrying out the criminal act; and the structural coordination of the act with fantasies from which the author is absent—ideal annulment or imaginary creations—to which are attached, according to an unconscious spontaneity, the negations, alibis, and simulations by which the alienated reality that characterizes the subject is sustained.

We wish to say here that this entire chain does not ordinarily have the *arbitrary* organization of a deliberate behavior, and that the structural anomalies that analysts can note in it will serve them as so many landmarks on the path to truth. Thus analysts will attach more meaning to the often paradoxical traces by which the author of the crime identifies himself, which signify less errors of imperfect execution of the act than failures of an all too real "everyday psychopathology."

Anal identifications, which analysis has discovered at the origins of the ego, give meaning to what forensic medicine designates in police jargon by the name of "calling card." The often flagrant "signature" left by the criminal can indicate at what moment of ego identification the repression [*répression*] occurred thanks to which one can say that the subject cannot answer for his crime, and thanks to which he remains attached to that repression in his negation.

A recently published case by Boutonier shows us the mainspring of a criminal's awakening to the realization of what condemned him, which goes as far as the mirror phenomenon itself.

To overcome these repressions, should we resort to one of those narcosis 144
procedures so oddly brought into the news by the alarms they set off in the virtuous defenders of the inviolability of consciousness?

No one can find his way along this path better than the psychoanalyst—first, because, contrary to the confused mythology in the name of which the ignorant expect narcosis to "lift the censorship," the psychoanalyst knows the precise meaning of the repressions that define the limits of ego synthesis.

Therefore, if he already knows that when the analysis restores the repressed unconscious to consciousness, it is less the content of its revelation than the mainspring of its reconquest that constitutes the efficacy of the treatment—and this is true *a fortiori* for the unconscious determinations that prop up the very affirmation of the ego—the analyst also knows that reality, whether it concerns the subject's motivation or (as is sometimes the case) his very action, can appear only through the progress of a dialogue that the narcotic twilight can but render inconsistent. Here, as elsewhere, truth is not a pregiven that one can grasp in its inertia, but rather a dialectic in motion.

Let us not, then, seek the reality of the crime or of the criminal by means of narcosis. The vaticinations that narcosis provokes, which are disconcerting to the investigator, are dangerous to the subject for whom they can constitute the "fertile moment" of a delusion if he has even the slightest hint of a psychotic structure.

Narcosis, like torture, has its limits: it cannot make the subject confess to something he does not know.

Zacchias' *Quaestiones medico-legales* informs us that questions were raised about the unity of the personality and the possible breaks in it that illness can bring about already in the seventeenth century. In response to these questions, psychoanalysis provides the apparatus for examination that still covers a field linking nature and culture—namely, that of personal synthesis, in its twofold relation of formal identification, which begins with the gaps in neurological dissociations (from epileptic fits to organically-based amnesias), and of alienating assimilation, which begins with the tensions in group relations.

Here the psychoanalyst can indicate to the sociologist the criminogenic func-
145 tions characteristic of a society which, requiring an extremely complex and extensive vertical integration of social collaboration for the purpose of production, proposes to the subjects it employs for this purpose individual ideals that tend to boil down to an ever more horizontal plane of assimilation.

This formulation designates a process whose dialectical aspect can be summarized by noting that, in a civilization in which the ideal of individualism has been raised to a previously unknown power, individuals find themselves tending toward a state in which they will think, feel, act, and love things exactly at the same times, and in strictly equivalent portions of space, as everyone else.

Now, the fundamental notion of an aggressiveness that is correlative to every alienating identification allows us to perceive that, in the phenomena of social assimilation, there must be a limit, based on a certain quantitative scale, at which standardized aggressive tensions are precipitated at points where the mass breaks apart and becomes polarized.

We know, moreover, that these phenomena have already, from the vantage point of output alone, attracted the attention of exploiters of labor power who are not all talk and no action, justifying the price paid by the Western Electric Company in Hawthorne, Illinois, for a sustained study of the effects of group relations on the most desirable psychical attitudes in employees.

The following are objects of study regarding which analytic theory can offer statisticians the correct coordinates on the basis of which to begin measuring things: a complete separation between the vital group, constituted by the subject and his family, and the functional group in which the vital group's means of subsistence must be found (a fact that we can sufficiently illustrate by saying that it makes Monsieur Verdoux seem plausible); an anarchy of desire-eliciting images that is all the greater as they seem to gravitate ever more around scopophilic satisfactions that are homogenized in the social mass; and an ever greater involvement of the fundamental passions for power, possession, and prestige in social ideals.

Thus even the politician and the philosopher will find something useful here. They will note, in a certain democratic society whose mores are extending their domination around the globe, (1) the appearance of a form of crim- 146
inality that so riddles the social body now that it is assuming legalized forms in it; (2) the inclusion of the criminal's psychological type into the set of types comprising the record-holder, the philanthropist, and the star, and even his reduction to the general type of the wage slave; and (3) crime's social signification reduced to its use in advertising.

These structures—in which an extreme social assimilation of the individual is correlated with an aggressive tension whose relative impunity in the State is quite palpable to someone from a different culture (as was, for example, the young Sun Yat-sen)—seem to be reversed when, according to a formal process already described by Plato, tyranny succeeds democracy and carries out the cardinal act of addition on individuals, who are reduced to their ordinal numbers, which is soon followed by the other three fundamental operations of arithmetic.

This is why, in totalitarian societies, while the leaders' "objective guilt" leads them to be treated as criminal and responsible, the relative effacement of these notions, which is signaled by the sanitary conception of penology, bears fruit for everyone else. The concentration camp is opened and, in determining who will fill it, rebellious intentions are less decisive qualifications than a certain quantitative relationship between the social mass and the banished mass.

This relationship will no doubt be calculable in terms of the mechanics developed by so-called "group psychology," and will allow us to determine the irrational constant that must correspond to the aggressiveness characteristic of the individual's fundamental alienation.

The progress by which man creates himself in his own image is thus revealed in the city's very injustice, which is always incomprehensible to the "intellectual" who is subjugated by the "law of the heart."

V. On the Non-existence of "Criminal Instincts": Psychoanalysis Stops Short at the Objectification of the Id and Proclaims the Autonomy of an Irreducibly Subjective Experience

Assuming now that psychoanalysis illuminates, as we have claimed, the psychological objectification of crime and criminals, doesn't it also have something to say about their innate factors?

147 Let us note first the critique to which it is necessary to submit the confused idea that many decent people endorse: that crime involves an eruption of "instincts" that breaks down the "barrier" constituted by the moral forces of intimidation. This is a difficult illusion to dispel, owing to the satisfaction it gives even to the serious-minded by depicting the criminal as well guarded; the tutelary policeman, who is characteristic of our society, here takes on a reassuring ubiquity.

But if instinct does, in fact, signify man's indisputable animal nature, it is not at all clear why this animal nature should be less docile when it is embodied in a reasonable being. The form of the adage, *homo homini lupus*, deceives us as to its meaning, and Baltasar Gracián, in a chapter of his *Criticón* (*The Critick*), constructs a fable in which he shows what the moralist tradition means when it says that man's ferocity toward his semblable exceeds everything animals are capable of, and that carnivores themselves recoil in horror at the threat man poses to nature as a whole.

But this very cruelty implies humanity. It targets a semblable, even in [cases in which the cruelty more directly targets] a being from another species. Nothing has sounded more deeply than psychoanalysis the equivalence [of self and other] in lived experience to which we are alerted by Love's moving appeal—it is yourself that you are striking—and by the Mind's icy deduction: it is in the fight to the death for pure prestige that man wins recognition from man.

If, in another sense, one uses "instincts" to mean atavistic behaviors whose violence might have been necessitated by the law of the primitive jungle, which some physiopathologic lapse supposedly releases, like morbid impulses, from the lower level in which they are bottled up, one can wonder why impulses to shovel, plant, cook, and even bury the dead have not surfaced since man has been man.

Psychoanalysis certainly includes a theory of instincts, a highly elaborate one at that, which is the first verifiable theory of man that has ever been proffered. But psychoanalysis shows us the instincts caught up in a metamorphism in which the formulation of their organ, direction, and object is a Jeannot knife with infinitely exchangeable parts. The *Triebe* (drives) that are identified in this theory simply constitute a system of energetic equivalences 148
to which we relate psychical exchanges, not insofar as they become subordinate to some entirely set behavior, whether natural or learned, but insofar as they symbolize, nay dialectically incorporate [*intègrent*], the functions of the organs in which these natural exchanges appear—that is, the oral, anal, and genito-urinary orifices.

These drives thus appear to us only through highly complex links; we cannot prejudge their original intensity on the basis of their sheer deflection. It is meaningless to speak of an excess of libido.

If there is a notion that can be derived from a great number of individuals who—due both to their past history and the "constitutional" impression people receive from contact with them and from their appearance—inspire in us the idea of "criminal tendencies," it is rather that of a shortage than of an excess of vitality. Their hypogenitality is often clear and their personal climate radiates libidinal coldness.

While many subjects seek and find sexual stimulation in their misdemeanors, exhibitions, thefts, bill dodging, and anonymous slander, and even in their crimes of murderous passion, this stimulation (whatever the status of the mechanisms that cause it, whether anxiety, sadism, or its association with a particular situation) cannot be viewed as the effect of an overflowing of instincts.

Assuredly, there is a high correlation between many perversions and the subjects who are sent for criminological examinations, but this correlation can only be evaluated psychoanalytically as a function of fixation on an object, developmental stagnation, the impact of ego structure, and neurotic repressions in each individual case.

More concrete is the notion with which psychoanalytic experience completes the psychical topography of the individual, that of the id, which is also much more difficult to grasp than the others.

To make the id the sum total of the subject's innate dispositions is a purely abstract definition devoid of use value.

A situational constant, which is fundamental in what psychoanalytic theory calls repetition automatisms, appears to be related to it (after subtracting the effects of the repressed and of ego identifications) and can be relevant to recidivism.

149 Of course, the id also refers to the fateful choices evident in marriage, profession, and friendship that often appear in a crime as a revelation of the faces of destiny.

The subject's "tendencies" do not fail, moreover, to manifest slippage in relation to their level of satisfaction. The question of the effects that a certain index of criminal satisfaction can have there should be raised.

But we are perhaps at the limits of our dialectical action here, and the truth that we are able to recognize in it with the subject cannot be reduced to scientific objectification.

On the basis of the confession we hear from the neurotic or pervert of the ineffable jouissance he finds in losing himself in the fascinating image, we can gauge the power of a hedonism that introduces us to the ambiguous relations between reality and pleasure. If, in referring to these two grand principles, we are tracing out the direction of normative development, how can we not but be struck by the importance of fantasmatic functions in the grounds for this progression, and by how captive human life remains to the narcissistic illusion with which it weaves, as we know, life's "realest" coordinates? And, on the other hand, isn't everything already weighed out next to the cradle in the incommensurable scales of Strife and Love?

Beyond these antinomies, which lead us to the threshold of wisdom, there is no absolute crime; and, despite the police action extended by our civilization to the whole world, there are still religious associations that are bound together by a practice of crime—crime in which their members know how to find anew the superhuman presences that ensure destruction in order to keep the Universe in balance.

For our part, if we can—within the limits that we have endeavored to define as those to which our social ideals reduce the comprehension of crime and which condition its criminological objectification—contribute a more rigorous truth, let us not forget that we owe it to a privileged function: the subject-to-subject practice that inscribes our duties in the order of eternal brotherhood. Its rule is also the rule of every action that is permitted to us.

Presentation on Psychical Causality 151

This presentation was given on September 28th, 1946, at the psychiatric conference held in Bonneval that was organized by Henri Ey on the topic of psychogenesis. A collection of the presentations made at the conference and of the discussion that followed them was published by Desclée de Brouwer in a volume entitled *Le Problème de la psychogenèse des névroses et des psychoses* ("The Problem of the Psychogenesis of the Neuroses and Psychoses"). My presentation served to open the meeting.

1. Critique of an Organicist Theory of Madness, Henri Ey's Organo-Dynamism

Having been invited by our host, three years ago already, to explain my views on psychical causality to you, my task here will be twofold. I have been asked to formulate a radical position concerning this topic—a position that people assume to be mine, and indeed it is. In addition, I must do so in the context of a debate that has reached a degree of development to which I have by no means contributed. I hope to meet your expectations by directly addressing both facets of this task, although no one can demand that I do so thoroughly here.

For several years I avoided all opportunities to express my views. The humiliation of our times, faced with the enemies of humankind, dissuaded me from doing so. Like Fontenelle, I gave myself over to the fantasy of having my hand filled with truths all the better to hold on to them. I confess that it is a ridiculous fantasy, marking, as it does, the limitations of a being who is on the verge of bearing witness. Must we view it as a failure on my part to live up to what the course of the world demands of me, when I was asked anew to speak at the very moment when even the least clairvoyant could see that the infatua- 152
tion with power had, once again, merely served the ruse of Reason? I'll let you be the judge of how my research may suffer from this.

At least I do not think I am failing to live up to the requirements of truth in rejoicing at the fact that my research can be defended here in the courteous forms of verbal debate.

This is why I will first respectfully bow before the enterprise of thinking and teaching that makes for honor in one's lifetime and is the foundation of one's lifework; if I remind my friend Henri Ey that, by endorsing the same initial theoretical positions, we entered the ring together on the same side, it is not simply in order to express surprise at the fact that we find ourselves on such opposite sides today.

In fact, ever since Ey published his fine work, "*Essai d'application des principes de Jackson à une conception dynamique de la neuropsychiatrie*" ("An Attempt to Apply Jackson's Principles to a Dynamic Conception of Neuropsychiatry"), written in collaboration with Julien Rouart, in the journal *Encéphale* in 1936, I noted—and my copy attests to this—everything that linked his views, and would link them ever more closely, to a doctrine of mental problems that I consider incomplete and false, a doctrine which, in psychiatry, is known as "organicism."

Strictly speaking, Ey's organo-dynamism can legitimately be included in this doctrine simply because it cannot relate the genesis of mental problems as such—whether functional or lesional in their nature, global or partial in their manifestations, and as dynamic as they may be in their mainspring—to anything but the play of systems constituted in the material substance [*l'étendue*] located within the body's integument. The crucial point, in my view, is that this play, no matter how energetic and integrating one conceives it to be, always rests in the final analysis on molecular interaction of the *partes-extra-partes*, material-substance type that classical physics is based on—that is, in a way which allows one to express this interaction as a relation between function and variable, this relation constituting its determinism.

Organicism is being enriched with conceptions that range from mechanistic to dynamistic and even Gestaltist ones. The conception that Ey borrows from Jackson certainly lends itself to this enriching, to which his own discussion of it has contributed—showing that Ey's conception does not exceed the limits I have just defined. This is what, from my point of view, makes the difference between his position and that of my master, Clérambault, or of
153 Guiraud negligible—and I should note that the position adopted by the latter two authors has proven to be of the least negligible psychiatric value, and we shall see in what sense further on.

In any case, Ey cannot repudiate the frame within which I am confining him. Since this frame is based on a Cartesian reference—which he has certainly recognized and whose meaning I would ask him to reconsider—it designates nothing but recourse to the (self-)evidence of physical reality, which is of importance to him, as it is to all of us, ever since Descartes based it on the notion of material substance [*l'étendue*]. "Energetic functions," to adopt Ey's terminology, can be integrated into this just as much as "instrumental functions" can,[1] for he writes "that it is not only possible but necessary to search for the chemical and anatomical conditions" of the "specific cerebral process that produces mental illness"; he also mentions "lesions that weaken the energetic processes which are necessary for the deployment of the psychical functions."

This is self-evident, in any case, and I am merely laying out in an introductory manner here the border that I intend to place between our views.

Having said that, I will first present a critique of Ey's organo-dynamism. I will do so, not in order to say that his conception does not stand up, for our presence here today provides ample proof of the contrary, but in order to demonstrate—in the authentic explanation of it that this conception owes as much to the intellectual rigor of its author as to the dialectical quality of your debates—that it does not possess the characteristics of a true idea.

It may perhaps surprise some of you that I am disregarding the philosophical taboo that has overhung the notion of truth in scientific epistemology ever since the so-called pragmatist speculative theses were disseminated in it. You will see that the question of truth conditions the phenomenon of madness in 154
its very essence, and that by trying to avoid this question, one castrates this phenomenon of the signification by virtue of which I think I can show you that it is tied to man's very being.

As for the critical use that I will make of it in a moment, I will stay close to Descartes by positing the notion of truth in the famous form Spinoza gave it: "*Idea vera debet cum suo ideato convenire.* A true idea must" (the emphasis falls on the word "must," meaning that this is its own necessity) "agree with its object."

Ey's doctrine evinces the exact opposite feature, in that, as it develops, it increasingly contradicts its original, permanent problem.

This problem—and it is to Ey's keen merit that he sensed its import and took responsibility for it—is the one found in the titles of his most recent publications: the problem of the limits of neurology and psychiatry. This problem would certainly have no more importance here than in any other medical specialty, if it did not concern the originality of the object of our experience—namely, madness. I sincerely praise Ey for obstinately maintaining this term, given all the suspicions it can arouse, due to its antiquated stench of the sacred, in those who would like to reduce it in some way to the *omnitudo realitatis.*

Plainly speaking, is there nothing that distinguishes the insane [*l'aliéné*] from other patients apart from the fact that the first are locked up in asylums, whereas the others are hospitalized? Is the originality of our object related to practice, social practice? or to reason, scientific reason?

It was clear that Ey could not but distance himself from such reason once he went looking for it in Jackson's conceptions. No matter how remarkable they were for their time, owing to their all-encompassing requirements regarding the organism's relational functions, their principle and goal were to reduce neurological and psychiatric problems to one and the same scale of dissolutions. And, in fact, this is what happened. No matter how subtle the corrective that Ey brought to this conception, his students, Hécaen, Follin, and Bonnafé, easily proved to him that it does not allow us to essentially distinguish aphasia from dementia, functional pain from hypochondria, hallucinosis from hallucinations, or even certain forms of agnosia from certain delusions.

I myself would ask Ey to explain, for example, the famous patient discussed
155 by Gelb and Goldstein, whose study has been examined from other angles by Bénary and by Hochheimer. This patient, afflicted with an occipital lesion that destroyed both calcarine sulci, presented (1) psychical blindness accompanied by selective problems with all categorial symbolism, such as abolishment of pointing behavior, in contrast with the preservation of grasping behavior; (2) extreme agnostic troubles that must be conceived of as an asymbolia of the entire perceptual field; and (3) a deficit in the apprehension of significance as such, manifested in (a) an inability to understand analogies directly at the intellectual level, whereas he was able to refind them in verbal symmetry; (b) an odd "blindness to the intuition of number" (as Hochheimer puts it), which did not stop him, however, from performing mechanical operations on numbers; and (c) an absorption in his present circumstances, which rendered him incapable of entertaining anything fictional, and thus of any abstract reasoning, *a fortiori* barring all access to speculation.

This is truly an extreme, across-the-board dissolution, which, let it be noted in passing, goes right to the very core of the patient's sexual behavior, where the immediacy of the sexual project is reflected in the brevity of the act, and even in the fact that its interruption is met by him with indifference.

Don't we see here a negative dissolution problem that is simultaneously global and apical, whereas the gap between the patient's organic condition and his clinical picture is seen clearly enough in the contrast between the localization of the lesion in the zone of visual projection and the extension of the symptom to the entire sphere of symbolism?

Would Ey tell me that what distinguishes this patient with an obviously neurological problem from a psychotic is the fact that the remaining personality fails to react to the negative problem? I would answer that this is not at all the case. For this patient, beyond the routine professional activity that he

has kept up, expresses, for instance, nostalgia for the religious and political speculations that he cannot engage in anymore. In medical tests, he manages to reach certain objectives, which he no longer understands, in a roundabout manner by mechanically though deliberately getting a "handle" on them via behaviors that have remained possible for him. Even more striking than the way he manages to limit his agnosia of somatic functions, in order to recover
some pointing activity, is the way he feels around in his stock of language in 156
order to overcome some of his agnostic deficits. Still more moving is his collaboration with his physician in the analysis of his problems, as when he comes up with certain words (for example, *Anhaltspunkte*, handles) with which to name certain of his artifices.

Here then is what I would ask Ey: How can he distinguish this patient from a madman? If he cannot give me an answer in his system, it will be up to me to give him one in my own.

And if he answers with "noetic problems" of "functional dissolutions," I will ask him how the latter differ from what he calls "global dissolutions."

In fact, in Ey's theory it is clearly the personality's reaction that is specific to psychosis, regardless of his reservations about it. This is where his theory reveals both its contradiction and its weakness, because as he ever more systematically misunderstands all forms of psychogenesis—so much so that he admits that he can no longer even understand what psychogenesis means[2]—we see him increasingly weigh down his exposés with ever more complicated "structural" descriptions of psychical activity, in which the same internal contradiction appears anew in a still more paralyzing form. As I will show by quoting him.

In order to criticize psychogenesis, we see Ey reduce it to the forms of an idea that can be refuted all the more easily because one addresses only those forms provided by the idea's adversaries. Let me enumerate these forms with him: emotional shock, conceived of in terms of its physiological effects; reactional factors, viewed from a constitutionalist perspective; unconscious traumatic effects, insofar as they are abandoned, according to him, by even those who support the idea; and, lastly, pathogenic suggestion, insofar "as the staunchest organicists and neurologists—no need to mention their names here—leave themselves this escape hatch and admit as exceptional evidence a psychogenesis that they thoroughly reject from the rest of pathology."

I have omitted only one term from the series, the theory of regression in the unconscious, which is included among the most serious [forms of the idea of psychogenesis], no doubt because it can, at least apparently, be reduced "to
an attack on the ego which, once again, is indistinguishable, in the final analy- 157
sis, from the notion of functional dissolution." I have cited this phrase, which

is repeated in a hundred different ways in Ey's work, because it will help me point out the radical flaw in his conception of psychopathology.

The forms I have just enumerated sum up, Ey tells us, the "facts that are invoked" (his words exactly) to demonstrate the existence of psychogenesis. It is just as easy for Ey to remark that these facts "demonstrate anything but that" as it is for me to note that adopting such a facile position allows him to avoid running any risks.

Why is it that, in inquiring into the doctrinal tendencies to which, in the absence of facts, we would have to attribute "a [notion of] psychogenesis that is hardly compatible with the psychopathological facts," he immediately thinks he has to show they derive from Descartes, by attributing to the latter an absolute dualism between the organic realm and the psychical realm? I myself have always thought—and, in the talks we had in our younger days, Ey seemed to realize this too—that Descartes' dualism is, rather, that of extension [*l'étendue*] and thought. One is surprised, on the contrary, that Ey seeks no support from an author for whom thought can err only insofar as confused ideas, which are determined by the body's passions, have found admittance into it.

Perhaps, indeed, it is better for Ey not to base anything on such an ally, in whom I seem to have such confidence. But, for God's sake, after having trotted out for us Cartesian psychogeneticists of the caliber of Babinski, André-Thomas, and Lhermitte, he should at least avoid identifying "the fundamental Cartesian intuition" with a psychophysiological parallelism that is worthier of Taine than of Spinoza. Such a straying from the sources might make us think that Jackson's influence is still more pernicious than it at first seemed.

Having vilified the dualism he imputes to Descartes, Ey introduces us directly—through a "theory of psychical life that is incompatible with the idea that there can be a psychogenesis of mental problems"—to his own dualism, which finds complete expression in this final sentence, the tone of which is quite singularly passionate: "mental illnesses are insults and obstacles to freedom; they are not caused by free, that is, purely psychogenic, activity."

Ey's dualism seems all the more serious to me in that it points to an untenable equivocation in his thinking. Indeed, I suspect that his entire analysis of
158 psychical activity hinges on a play on words: that between his free play and his freedom [*son libre jeu et sa liberté*]. Let us add to it the key provided by the word "deployment."

Like Goldstein, Ey posits that "integration is being." Hence he must include in this integration not only the psychical realm, but the entire movement of the mind; he in fact incorporates everything down to existential problems into it, running the gamut from syntheses to structures and from forms to phenomena. I even thought, God forgive me, I noticed that he used the expression "dialectical hierarchism"; the conceptual coupling of these two terms would, I believe, have made even the late Pichon himself wonder—Pichon, whose reputation will not be besmirched if I say that, to him, Hegel's very alphabet remained a dead letter.

Ey's moves are certainly spry, but we cannot follow them for long because we realize that the reality of psychical life is crushed in the noose—which is always similar and in fact always the same—that tightens all the more surely around our friend's thought the more he tries to free himself from it, denying him access to both the truth of the psyche and that of madness by a telling necessity.

Indeed, when Ey begins to define this oh so marvelous psychical activity as "our personal adaptation to reality," I start to feel that I have such sure views about the world that all my undertakings must be those of a clairvoyant prince. What could I possibly be incapable of accomplishing in the lofty realms where I reign? Nothing is impossible for man, says the Vaudois peasant with his inimitable accent: if ever there is something he cannot do, he drops it. Should Ey carry me with his art of "psychical trajectory" into the "psychical field," and invite me to pause for a moment to consider with him "the trajectory in the field," I will persist in my happiness, because of my satisfaction at recognizing formulations that are akin to ones I myself once provided—in the exordium to my doctoral thesis on the paranoiac psychoses, when I tried to define the phenomenon of personality—momentarily overlooking the fact that we are not aiming at the same ends.

Of course, I wince a tad when I read that "for dualism" (still Cartesian, I presume) "the mind is a mind without existence," remembering as I do that the first judgment of certainty that Descartes bases on the consciousness that thinking has of itself is a pure judgment of existence: *cogito ergo sum*. I also get
concerned when I come across the assertion that "according to materialism, 159
the mind is an epiphenomenon," recalling as I do that form of materialism in which the mind immanent in matter is realized by the latter's very movement.

But when, moving on to Ey's lecture on the notion of nervous disorders,[3] I come upon "this level characterized by the creation of a properly psychical causality," and I learn that "the reality of the ego is concentrated there" and that through it,

> the structural duality of psychical life is consummated, a life of relations between the world and the ego, which is animated by the whole dialectical movement of the mind that is always striving—both in the order of action and in the theoretical order—to reduce this antinomy without

> ever managing to do so, or at the very least trying to reconcile and harmonize the demands made by objects, other people, the body, the Unconscious, and the conscious Subject,

then I wake up and protest: the free play of my psychical activity by no means implies that I strive with such difficulty. For there is no antinomy whatsoever between the objects I perceive and my body, whose perception is constituted by a quite natural harmony with those objects. My unconscious leads me quite blithely to annoyances that I would hardly dream of attributing to it, at least not until I begin to concern myself with it through the refined means of psychoanalysis. And none of this stops me from behaving toward other people with irrefragable egoism, in the most sublime unconsciousness of my conscious Subject. For as long as I do not try to reach the intoxicating sphere of oblativity that is so dear to French psychoanalysts, my naïve experience does not set me the task of dealing with what La Rochefoucauld, in his perverse genius, detected in the fabric of all human sentiments, even that of love: pride [*amour-propre*].

All this "psychical activity" thus truly seems like a dream to me. Can this be the dream of a physician who has heard that hybrid chain unfurl in his ears thousands of times—that chain which is made of fate and inertia, throws of the dice and astonishment, false successes and missed encounters, and which makes up the usual script of a human life?

No, it is rather the dream of an automaton maker, the likes of whom Ey and
160 I used to make fun of in the past, Ey nicely quipping that hidden in every organicist conception of the psyche one always finds "the little man within the man" who is busy ensuring that the machine responds.

What, dear Ey, are drops in the level of consciousness, hypnoid states, and physiological dissolutions, if not the fact that the little man within the man has a headache—that is, an ache in the other little man that he himself, no doubt, has in his head, and so on *ad infinitum*? Polyxena's age-old argument still holds, no matter how one takes man's being to be given, whether in its essence as an Idea, or in its existence as an organism.

I am no longer dreaming now, but what I read next is that,

> projected into a still more mental reality, the world of ideal values—that are no longer integrated, but infinitely integrating—is constituted: beliefs, ideals, vital programs, and the values of logical judgment and moral conscience.

I see quite clearly here that there are, indeed, beliefs and ideals that become linked in the same psyche to vital programs, which are just as repugnant to logical judgment as they are to moral conscience, in order to produce a fascist, or more simply an imbecile or a rascal. I conclude that the integrated form of these ideals implies no psychical culmination for them and that their integrating action bears no relation to their value—and thus that there must be a mistake here too.

I certainly do not intend, gentlemen, to belittle the scope of your debates or the results you have reached. I would soon embarrass myself were I to underestimate the difficulty of the issues involved. By mobilizing Gestalt theory, behaviorism, and structural and phenomenological terms in order to put organo-dynamism to the test, you have relied on scientific resources that I seem to neglect in resorting to principles that are perhaps a bit too certain and to an irony that is no doubt a bit risqué. This is because it seemed to me that I could better help you untie the noose that I mentioned earlier by reducing the number of terms in the scales. But for this to be completely successful in the minds of those whom the noose holds fast, perhaps it should have been Socrates himself who came to speak to you here, or rather perhaps I should simply listen to you in silence.

For the authentic dialectic in which you situate your terms and which gives 161
your young Academy its style suffices to guarantee the rigor of your progress. I rely on this dialectic myself and feel far more at ease in it than in the idolatrous reverence for words seen to reign elsewhere, especially in psychoanalysts' inner circles. But beware the echo your words may have outside the confines of the realm for which you intended them.

The use of speech requires far more vigilance in human science than anywhere else, because speech engages the very being of its object there.

Every uncertain attitude toward truth inevitably ends up diverting our terms from their meaning and such abuse is never innocent.

You publish—I apologize for bringing up a personal experience—an article entitled "Beyond the Reality Principle," in which you take on nothing less than the status of the psychological object, trying first to lay out a phenomenology of the psychoanalytic relationship as it is experienced between doctor and patient. But what you hear back from your colleagues is considerations about the "relativity of reality," which make you rue the day you ever chose such a title.

It was, as I know, with such misgivings that Politzer, the great thinker, decided not to provide the theoretical expression with which he would have left his indelible mark, in order to devote himself to an activity that was to take him away from us definitively. When, following in his footsteps, we demand that concrete psychology be established as a science, let us not lose sight of the fact that we are still only at the stage of formal pleas. I mean that we have not yet been able to posit even the slightest law that accounts for the efficacy of our actions.

This is so true that, when we begin to glimpse the operative meaning of the traces left by prehistoric man on the walls of his caves, the idea may occur to us that we really know less than him about what I will very intentionally call psychical matter. Since we cannot, like Deucalion, make men from stones, let us be careful not to transform words into stones.

It would already be very nice if by a simple mental ploy we were able to see the concept of the object taking form, on which a scientific psychology
162 could be based. It is the definition of such a concept that I have always declared to be necessary, that I have announced as forthcoming, and that—thanks to the problem you have presented me—I will try to pursue today, exposing myself in turn to your criticism.

2. The Essential Causality of Madness

What could be more suited to this end than to start out from the situation in which we find ourselves, gathered together, as we are here, to discuss the causality of madness? Now, why this privilege? Is a madman more interesting to us than Gelb and Goldstein's case whom I mentioned earlier in broad strokes? The latter reveals—not only to the neurologist but also to the philosopher, and no doubt to the philosopher more so than to the neurologist—a structure that is constitutive of human knowledge, namely, the support that thought's symbolism finds in visual perception, and that I will call, following Husserl, a *Fundierung*, a foundational relationship.

What other human value could lie in madness?

When I defended my thesis on *Paranoiac Psychosis as Related to Personality*, one of my professors asked me to indicate what, in a nutshell, I had proposed to do in it: "In short, sir," I began, "we cannot forget that madness is a phenomenon of thought . . ." I am not suggesting that this sufficed to summarize my perspective, but the firm gesture with which he interrupted me was tantamount to a call for modesty: "Yeah! So what?" it meant, "Let's be serious. Are you going to thumb your nose at us? Let us not dishonor this solemn moment. *Num dignus eris intrare in nostro docto corpore cum isto voce: pensare!*" I was nevertheless granted my Ph.D. and offered the kind of encouragement that it is appropriate to give to impulsive minds.

Now, fourteen years later, I have the opportunity to summarize my perspective for you. As you can see, at this rate the definition of the object of psychology will not get very far between now and the time I part company with the enlightened intellects [*lumières*] that illuminate our world—unless

you take the torch from my hands, so please take it! At least I hope that, by
now, the course of things has given these enlightened intellects themselves a 163
hard enough time that none of them can still find in Bergson's work the expanding synthesis that satisfied the "intellectual needs" of a generation, or anything other than a rather curious collection of exercises in metaphysical ventriloquism.

Before we try to extract anything from the facts, we would do well, indeed, to recognize the very conditions of meaning that make them into facts for us. This is why I think that it would not be superfluous to call for a return to Descartes.

While Descartes does not look deeply into the phenomenon of madness in his *Meditations*, I at least consider it telling that he encounters it in his very first steps, taken with unforgettable jubilance, on the pathway to truth.

> But on what grounds could one deny that these hands and this entire body are mine? Unless perhaps I were to liken myself to the insane, whose brains are impaired by such an unrelenting vapor of black bile that they steadfastly insist that they are kings when they are utter paupers, or that they are arrayed in purple robes when they are naked, or that they have heads made of clay, or that they are gourds, or that they are made of glass. But such people are mad, and I would appear no less mad, were I to take their behavior as an example for myself.

He then moves on, whereas we will see that he could have delved more deeply into the phenomenon of madness, and it might well have been fruitful for him to do so.

Let us then reconsider together this phenomenon according to Descartes' method. Not in the fashion of the revered professor who cut short the explanatory effusions not only of his students—but who even considered those of hallucinating patients to be so scandalous that he would interrupt them by saying: "What are you telling me, my friend? None of that is true. Come now!" From such an intervention we can at least draw a spark of meaning: truth is "involved." But at what point? Regarding the meaning of the word, we assuredly cannot trust any more in the mind of the doctor than in that of the patient.

Instead, let us follow Ey who, like Descartes in his simple sentence, and at the time that probably was not accidental, highlights the essential mainspring of belief in his early works.

Ey admirably realized that belief, with its ambiguity in human beings and
its excess and inadequacy for knowledge [*connaissance*]—since it is less than 164

knowing [*savoir*], but perhaps more, for to assert is to make a commitment, but it is not the same as being sure—cannot be eliminated from the phenomenon of hallucination and of delusion.

However, phenomenological analysis demands that we not skip any steps, and precipitation is fatal to it. I will maintain that the figure only appears if we appropriately focus our thinking. Here Ey—in order to avoid the mistake, for which he reproaches mechanists, of becoming delusional along with the patient—makes the opposite mistake by all too quickly including a value judgment in the phenomenon; the abovementioned comic example, appropriately savored by him, should have warned him that this would simultaneously destroy any chance of understanding it. With some kind of dizzying mental move, he reduces the notion of belief, which he had right before his eyes, to that of error, which absorbs it like one drop of water absorbing another drop that is made to abut it. Hence, the whole operation backfires. Once the phenomenon is fixed in place, it becomes an object of judgment and, soon thereafter, an object *tout court*.

As he asks himself in his book, *Hallucinations et Délire* ("Hallucinations and Delusion"),[4] "Where would error, and delusion too, lie if patients did not make mistakes! Everything in their assertions and their judgment reveals their errors (interpretations, illusions, etc.) to us" (170). And further on, while setting out the two "attitudes that are possible" toward hallucination, he defines his own:

> Hallucination should be viewed as a mistake that must be admitted and explained as such without letting oneself be carried away by its mirage. And yet its mirage necessarily leads one, if one is not careful, to ground it in actual phenomena and thus to construct neurological hypotheses that are useless, at best, because they do not reach what lies at the heart of the symptom itself: error and delusion (176).

How then could we be anything but astonished when, despite the fact that he is well aware of the temptation to base the "mirage of hallucination conceived of as an abnormal sensation" on a neurological hypothesis, he hurriedly bases what he calls "the fundamental error" of delusion on a similar hypothesis? Or when—although he is rightly loath (page 168) to make of hallucination, qua abnormal sensation, "an object situated in the sulci of the brain"—he
165 does not hesitate to locate the phenomenon of delusional belief, considered as a deficit phenomenon, in the brain himself?

No matter how lofty the tradition within which his work is situated, it is nonetheless here then that he took the wrong path. He might have avoided this by pausing before taking the leap that the very notion of truth ordained him to take. For while there can be no progress possible in knowledge unless this notion is behind it, it is part of the human condition, as we shall see, to ever risk going astray in following our best impulses.

We could say that error is a deficit, in the sense this word has on a balance sheet, but the same does not go for belief, even if it deceives us. For belief can go awry even at the height of our intellectual powers, as Ey himself proves here.

What then is (the phenomenon of) delusional belief? I say that it is misrecognition, with everything this term brings with it by way of an essential antinomy. For to misrecognize presupposes recognition, as is seen in systematic misrecognition, in which case we must certainly admit that what is denied is in some way recognized.

Regarding the relationship between the phenomenon and the subject, Ey stresses—and one can never stress enough what is self-evident—that an hallucination is an error that is "kneaded from the dough of the subject's personality and shaped by his own activity." Aside from the reservations I have about the use of the words "dough" and "activity," it seems clear to me that the subject does not recognize his productions as his own when he has ideas of influence or feels that an automatism is at work. This is why we all agree that a madman is a madman. But isn't the remarkable thing, rather, that he should know anything about them at all? And isn't the point to figure out what he knows about himself here without recognizing himself in it?

Regarding the reality that the subject attributes to these phenomena, what is far more decisive than the sensorial quality he experiences in them, or the belief he attaches to them, is the fact that all of them—no matter which ones (whether hallucinations, interpretations, or intuitions) and no matter how foreignly and strangely he experiences them—target him personally: they split him, talk back to him, echo him, and read in him, just as he identifies them, questions them, provokes them, and deciphers them. And when all means of expressing them fail him, his perplexity still manifests to us a questioning gap in him: which is to say that madness is experienced entirely within the regis- 166
ter of meaning.

The interest that madness thus kindles in us owing to its pathos provides a first answer to the question I raised about the human value of the phenomenon of madness. And its metaphysical import is revealed in the fact that it is inseparable from the problem of signification for being in general—that is, the problem of language for man.

Indeed, no linguist or philosopher could any longer defend a theory of language as a system of signs that would double the system of realities, realities defined by the common assent of healthy minds in healthy bodies. I cannot think of anyone other than Charles Blondel who seems to believe this—see his book, *La conscience morbide* ("Morbid Consciousness"), which is certainly the most narrow-minded lucubration ever produced on either madness or language. He runs up against the problem of the ineffable, as if language did not posit this without the help of madness.

Man's language, the instrument of his lies, is thoroughly ridden with the problem of truth:

- whether it betrays the truth insofar as it is an expression of (a) his organic heredity in the phonology of the *flatus vocis*; (b) the "passions of his body" in the Cartesian sense, that is, of his soul, in the changes in his emotions; (c) and the culture and history that constitute his humanity, in the semantic system that formed him as a child;
- or it manifests this truth as an intention, by eternally asking how what expresses the lie of his particularity can manage to formulate the universality of his truth.

The whole history of philosophy is inscribed in this question, from Plato's aporias of essence to Pascal's abysses of existence, and on to the radical ambiguity Heidegger points to in it, insofar as truth signifies revelation.

The word is not a sign, but a nodal point [*noeud*] of signification. When I say the word "curtain" [*rideau*], for example, it is not merely to designate by convention an object whose use can be varied in a thousand ways depending on the intentions of the artisan, shopkeeper, painter, or Gestalt psychologist—whether as labor, exchange value, colorful physiognomy, or spatial structure. Metaphorically, it is a curtain of rain [*rideau d'arbres*]; forging plays on words,
167 it is when I am being curt and sweet or can curr tangentially with the best of them [*les rides et les ris de l'eau*], and my friend Curt Ans off [*Leiris dominant*] these glossological games better than I do. By decree, it is the limit of my domain or, on occasion, a screen for my meditation in a room I share with someone else. Miraculously, it is the space that opens onto infinity, the unknown at the threshold, or the solitary walker's morning departure. Apprehensively, it is the flutter that betrays Agrippina's presence at the Roman Empire's Council, or Madame de Chasteller's gaze out the window as Lucien Leuwen passes by. Mistakenly, it is Polonius that I stab, shouting, "How now! a rat?" As an interjection, during the tragedy's intermission, it is my cry of impatience or the sign of my boredom: "Curtain!" It is, finally, an image of meaning *qua* meaning, which must be unveiled if it is to reveal itself.

In this sense, being's attitudes are justified and exposed in language, and among those attitudes "common sense" clearly manifests "the most commonly seen thing in the world," but not to the extent that it is recognized by those for whom Descartes is too easy on this point.

This is why, in an anthropology that takes the register of culture in man to include, as is fitting, the register of nature, one could concretely define psychology as the domain of nonsense [*l'insensé*], in other words, of everything that forms a knot in discourse—as is clearly indicated by the "words" of passion.

Let us follow this path in order to study the significations of madness, as we are certainly invited to by the original forms that language takes on in it: all the verbal allusions, cabalistic relationships, homonymic play, and puns that captivated the likes of Guiraud.[5] And, I might add, by the singular accent whose resonance we must know how to hear in a word so as to detect a delusion; the transfiguration of a term in an ineffable intention; the fixation [*figement*] of an idea in a semanteme (which tends to degenerate into a sign here specifically); the lexical hybrids; the verbal cancer constituted by neologisms; the bogging down of syntax; the duplicity of enunciation; but also the coherence that amounts to a logic, the characteristic, running from the unity
of a style to repetitive terms, that marks each form of delusion—the madman 168
communicates with us through all of this, whether in speech or writing.

It is here that the structures of the madman's knowledge must reveal themselves to us. And it is odd, though probably not coincidental, that it was mechanists like Clérambault and Guiraud who outlined them best. As false as the theory in which these authors included them may be, it made them remarkably attuned to an essential phenomenon of such structures: the kind of "anatomy" that manifests itself in them. Clérambault's constant reference in his analysis to what he calls, with a slightly Diafoirus-like term, "the ideogenic," is nothing but a search for the limits of signification. Employing a method involving nothing but comprehension, he paradoxically manages to display the magnificent range of structures that runs the gamut from the so-called *"postulates"* of the delusions of passion to the so-called *basal* phenomena of *mental automatism*.

This is why I think that he has done more than anyone else to support the hypothesis of the psychogenesis of madness; in any case, you will see what I mean by this shortly.

Clérambault was my only master in the observation of patients, after the very subtle and delectable Trénel, whom I made the mistake of abandoning too soon, in order to seek a position in the consecrated spheres of professorial ignorance.

I claim to have followed his method in the analysis of the case of paranoiac psychosis discussed in my thesis; I demonstrated the psychogenic structure of the case and designated its clinical entity with the more or less valid term of "self-punishing paranoia."

This patient had caught my interest because of the impassioned signification of her written productions, whose literary value struck many writers, from Fargue and dear Crevel, both of whom read them before anyone else, to Joë Bousquet, who immediately and admirably commented on them,[6] to Éluard, who more recently published some of them in a collection of "involuntary" poetry.[7] It is now well known that the name, Aimée, with which I disguised her identity, is that of the central figure in her fictional creation.

If I assemble here the results of the analysis I did of her case, it is because I believe that a phenomenology of madness, which is complete in its terms, can already be seen to emerge from it.

169 The structural points that prove to be essential in this analysis can be formulated as follows:

(a) The succession of female persecutors in her history repeated almost without variation the personification of a maleficent ideal, and her need to aggressively strike out at this ideal kept growing.

However, not only did she constantly seek to curry both favor and abuse from the people to whom she had access in reality who incarnated this stereotype, but in her behavior she tended to carry out, without recognizing it, the very evildoing she denounced in them: vanity, coldness, and abandonment of one's natural duties.

(b) She presented herself, on the contrary, as upholding the completely opposite ideal of purity and devotion, which made her a victim of the schemes of the being she detested.

(c) We also note a neutralization of the sexual category with which she identified. This neutralization—which was confessed in her writings and taken at least as far as sexual ambiguity, and perhaps as far as imagined homosexuality—is coherent with the Platonic nature of the classical erotomania she manifested toward several male personifications, and with the prevalence of female friends in her real life.

(d) The latter was characterized by an indecisive struggle to achieve an ordinary existence, all the while maintaining ideals that I will call Bovary-like, without intending anything disparaging by the term.

Her older sister's progressive intervention in her life then little by little enucleated her completely from her place as wife and mother.

(e) This intervention effectively released her from her familial duties.

But as this "liberated" her, her delusional phenomena were triggered and took shape, reaching their apex when, with the help of their very impact, she found herself completely independent.

(f) These phenomena appeared in a series of spurts that I designated as *fertile moments* of the delusion, a term that some researchers have been willing to adopt.

Part of the resistance I encountered to people understanding the "*elementary*" nature of these moments in a thesis on the psychogenesis [of paranoia] 170
would, it seems to me, be mitigated now due to the more profound work on the subject that I did subsequently—as I will show shortly, to the extent to which I can do so while providing a balanced presentation.

(g) It should be noted that, although the patient seemed to suffer from the fact that her child was taken away from her by her sister—who even struck *me* as bad news in the one meeting I had with her—she refused to consider her sister as hostile or even harmful to herself, on this account or any other.

Instead, with a murderous intent she stabbed the person with whom she had most recently identified her female persecutors. The effect of this act—once she realized the high price she would have to pay for it in prison—was the implosion of the beliefs and fantasies involved in her delusion.

I tried thus to delineate the psychosis in relation to all of her earlier life events, her intentions, whether admitted or not, and, lastly, the motives, whether perceived by her or not, that emerged from the situation contemporaneous with her delusion—in other words, in relation to her personality (as the title of my thesis indicates).

This seems to me to bring out the general structure of misrecognition, right from the outset. Still, this must be understood correctly.

Assuredly, one can say that the madman believes he is different [*autre*] than he is. Descartes said as much in his sentence about those who believe "that they are arrayed in gold and purple robes," where he conformed to the most anecdotal of all stories about madmen; this also seemed to satisfy the authority on the matter who wrote that the phenomenon of *bovarism*, adapted to the degree of his sympathy for his patients, was the key to understanding paranoia.

However, apart from the fact that Jules de Gaultier's theory concerns one of most normal relations of human personality—namely, its ideals—it should be noted that if a man who thinks he is a king is mad, a king who thinks he is a king is no less so.

This is proven by the example of Louis II of Bavaria and a few other royal personages, as well as by everyone's "common sense," in the name of which
we justifiably demand that people put in such situations "play their parts well," 171
but are uncomfortable with the idea that they really "believe in them," even if this involves a lofty view of their duty to incarnate a function in the world

order, through which they assume rather well the figure of chosen victims.

The turning point here lies in the mediacy or immediacy of the identification and, to be quite explicit, in the subject's infatuation.

To make myself clear, I will evoke the likable figure of the young dandy, born to a well-to-do family, who, as they say, "hasn't a clue," especially about what he owes to this good fortune. Common sense is in the habit of characterizing him as either a "happy fool" or as a "little moron," depending on the case. *Il "se croit,"* as we say in French (he "thinks he's really something"): the genius of the language puts the emphasis here where it should go, that is, not on the inapplicability of an attribute, but on a verbal mode. For, all in all, the subject thinks he is [*se croit*] what he is—a lucky little devil—but common sense secretly wishes him a hitch that will show him that he is not one as much as he thinks he is. Don't think that I am being witty, certainly not with the quality of wit that shows in the saying that Napoleon was someone who thought he was Napoleon. Because Napoleon did not think he was Napoleon at all, since he knew full well by what means Bonaparte had produced Napoleon and how Napoleon, like Malebranche's God, sustained his existence at every moment. If he ever thought he was Napoleon, it was at the moment that Jupiter had decided to bring him down; once fallen, he spent his spare time lying to Las Cases in as many pages as you could want, so that posterity would think that he had thought he was Napoleon—a necessary condition for convincing posterity that he had truly been Napoleon.

Do not think that I am getting off on a tangent here in a talk designed to go right to the heart of the dialectic of being—because the essential misrecognition involved in madness is situated at just such a point, as my patient made perfectly clear.

This misrecognition can be seen in the revolt through which the madman seeks to impose the law of his heart onto what seems to him to be the havoc [*désordre*] of the world. This is an "insane" enterprise—but not because it suggests a failure to adapt to life, which is the kind of thing people often say in
172 our circles, whereas the slightest reflection on our experience proves the dishonorable inanity of such a viewpoint. It is an insane enterprise, rather, in that the subject does not recognize in this havoc the very manifestation of his actual being, or that what he experiences as the law of his heart is but the inverted and virtual image of that same being. He thus doubly misrecognizes it, precisely so as to split its actuality from its virtuality. Now, he can escape this actuality only via this virtuality. His being is thus caught in a circle, unless he breaks it through some form of violence by which, in lashing out at what he takes to be the havoc, he ends up harming himself because of the social repercussions of his actions.

This is the general formulation of madness as we find it in Hegel's work[8]—just because I felt it necessary to illustrate it for you does not mean that I am innovating here. It is the general formulation of madness in the sense that it can be seen to apply in particular to any one of the phases in which the dialectical development of human beings more or less occurs in each person's destiny; and in the sense that it always appears in this development as a moment of stasis, for being succumbs to stasis in an ideal identification that characterizes this moment in a particular person's destiny.

This identification, the unmediated and "infatuated" nature of which I tried to convey a moment ago, turns out to be the relation of being to the very best in it, since this ideal represents that being's freedom.

To put this more gallantly, I could demonstrate it to you with the example Hegel recalled to mind in presenting this analysis in his *Phenomenology of Spirit*[9]—that is, if I recall correctly, in 1806, while he was awaiting (let this be noted in passing to be added to a file I just opened) the approach of the *Weltseele*, the World Soul, which he saw in Napoleon—with the precise aim of revealing to Napoleon what Napoleon had the honor of thus incarnating, even 173
though he seemed profoundly unaware of it. The example I am talking about is the character Karl Moor, the hero in Schiller's *Robbers*, who is well known to every German.

More familiar to us and, also, more amusing in my book, is Molière's Alceste [from *The Misanthrope*]. But before using it as an example, I must mention that the very fact that he has never ceased to be a problem for our highbrow literati nourished in the "classics," since his first appearance, proves that the things I talk about are not nearly as useless as these highbrow literati would have us believe when they call them pedantic—less, no doubt, to spare themselves the effort of understanding them than to spare themselves the painful conclusions they would have to draw from them for themselves about their society, once they understood them.

It all stems from the fact that Alceste's "beautiful soul" exerts a fascination on the highbrow literati that the latter, "steeped in the classics," cannot resist. Does Molière thus approve of Philinte's high society indulgence? "That's just not possible!" some cry, while others must acknowledge, in the disabused strains of wisdom, that it surely must be the case at the rate things are going.

I believe that the question does not concern Philinte's wisdom, and the solution would perhaps shock these gentlemen, for the fact is that Alceste is mad and that Molière demonstrates that he is—precisely insofar as Alceste, in his beautiful soul, does not recognize that he himself contributes to the havoc he revolts against.

I specify that he is mad, not because he loves a woman who is flirtatious and betrays him—which is something the learned analysts I mentioned earlier would no doubt attribute to his failure to adapt to life—but because he is caught, under Love's banner, by the very feeling that directs this art of mirages at which the beautiful Célimène excels: namely, the narcissism of the idle rich that defines the psychological structure of "high society" [*"monde"*] in all eras, which is doubled here by the other narcissism that is especially manifest in certain eras in the collective idealization of the feeling of being in love.

Célimène, at the mirror's focal point, and her admirers, forming a radiating circumference around her, indulge in the play of these passions [*feux*]. Alceste does too, no less than the others, for if he does not tolerate its lies, it
174 is simply because his narcissism is more demanding. Of course, he expresses it to himself in the form of the law of the heart:

I'd have them be sincere, and never part
With any word that isn't from the heart.

Yes, but when his heart speaks, it makes some strange exclamations. For example, when Philinte asks him, "You think then that she loves you?," Alceste replies, "Heavens, yes! I wouldn't love her did I not think so."

I suspect that Clérambault would have recognized this reply as having more to do with a delusion of passion than with love.

And no matter how widespread the fantasy may be in such passions of the test of the loved object's fall from grace, I find that it has an odd accent in Alceste's case:

I love you more than can be said or thought;
Indeed, I wish you were in such distress
That I might show to all my devotedness.
Yes, I could wish that you were wretchedly poor,
Unloved, uncherished, utterly obscure;
That fate had set you down upon the earth
Without possessions, rank, or gentle birth . . .

With this lovely wish and the taste he has for the song "J'aime mieux ma mie," why doesn't he court a salesgirl at his local flower shop? He would not be able to "show to all" his love for such a girl, and this is the true key to the feeling he expresses here: it is the passion to demonstrate his unicity to everyone, even if only in the form of the isolation of a victim, an isolation in which he finds bitter, jubilatory satisfaction in the final act of the play.

As for the mainspring of his twists and turns, it lies in a mechanism that I would relate not to the *self-punishment* but rather to the *suicidal aggression of narcissism.*

For what infuriates Alceste upon hearing Oronte's sonnet is that he recognizes his own situation in it, depicted all too precisely in its ridiculousness, and 175
the imbecile who is his rival appears to him as his own mirror image. The words of mad fury to which he then gives vent blatantly betray the fact that he seeks to lash out at himself. And whenever one of the repercussions of his words shows him that he has managed to do so, he delights in suffering its effect.

Here we can note an odd defect in Ey's conception: it diverts him from the signification of the delusional act, leaving him to take it as the contingent effect of a lack of control, whereas the problem of this act's signification is constantly brought to our attention by the medical and legal exigencies that are essential to the phenomenology of our experience.

Someone like Guiraud, who is a mechanist, again goes much farther in his article, "Meurtres immotivés" ("Unexplained Murders"),[10] when he attempts to show that it is precisely the *kakon* of his own being that the madman tries to get at in the object he strikes.

Let us take one last look at Alceste who has victimized no one but himself and let us hope he finds what he is looking for, namely:

> *. . . some spot unpeopled and apart*
> *Where I'll be free to have an honest heart.*

I want to examine the word "free" here. For it is not simply by way of derision that the impeccable rigor of classical comedy makes it appear here.

The import of the drama that classical comedy expresses cannot, in effect, be measured by the narrowness of the action in which it takes shape, and—like Descartes' lofty march in the "Secret Note" in which he declares himself to be on the verge of becoming a player on the world scene—it "advances behind a mask."

Instead of Alceste, I could have looked for the play of the law of the heart in the fate that put the old revolutionary of 1917 in the dock at the Moscow trials. But what is demonstrated in the poet's imaginary space is metaphysically comparable to the world's bloodiest events, since it is what causes blood to be spilled in the world.

I am not thus avoiding the social tragedy that dominates our era, but my marionette's acting will show each of us more clearly the risk he is tempted 176
to run whenever freedom is at stake.

For the risk of madness is gauged by the very appeal of the identifications on which man stakes both his truth and his being.

Thus rather than resulting from a contingent fact—the frailties of his organism—madness is the permanent virtuality of a gap opened up in his essence.

And far from being an "insult"[11] to freedom, madness is freedom's most faithful companion, following its every move like a shadow.

Not only can man's being not be understood without madness, but it would not be man's being if it did not bear madness within itself as the limit of his freedom.

It is certainly true—to interrupt this serious talk with something humorous from my youth, which I wrote in a pithy form on the wall in the hospital staff room—that "Not just anyone can go mad" [*"Ne devient pas fou qui veut"*].

But it is also true that not just anyone who wants to can run the risks that enshroud madness.

A weak organism, a deranged imagination, and conflicts beyond one's capacities do not suffice to cause madness. It may well be that a rock-solid body, powerful identifications, and the indulgence of fate, as written in the stars, lead one more surely to find madness seductive.

This conception at least has the immediate benefit of dispelling the problematic emphasis placed in the nineteenth century on the madness of superior individuals—and of putting a stop to the low blows Homais and Bournisien exchanged regarding the madness of saints and freedom fighters.

For while Pinel's work has—thank God!—made us act more humanely toward ordinary madmen, it must be acknowledged that it has not increased our respect for the madness involved in taking supreme risks.

In any case, Homais and Bournisien represent one and the same manifestation of being. Isn't it striking that we laugh only at the first? I defy you to explain this fact otherwise than with the significant distinction I pointed out earlier. Because Homais "believes in it" [*"y croit"*] whereas Bournisien, who
177 is equally stupid but not mad, justifies his belief and, being backed by his hierarchy, maintains a distance between himself and his truth in which he can come to an agreement with Homais, assuming the latter "becomes reasonable" by recognizing the reality of "spiritual needs."

Having thus disarmed both him and his adversary thanks to my understanding of madness, I recover the right to evoke the hallucinatory voices heard by Joan of Arc and what took place on the road to Damascus, without anyone being able to summon me to change the tone of my real voice, or to go into an altered state of consciousness [*état second*] to exercise my judgment.

Having arrived at this point in my talk on the causality of madness, mustn't I be careful so that heaven may keep me from going awry? Mustn't I realize that, after having argued that Henry Ey misrecognizes the causality of madness, and that he is not Napoleon, I am falling into the trap of proposing as ultimate proof thereof that I am the one who understands this causality, in other words, that I am Napoleon?

I don't think, however, that this is my point, because it seems to me that, by being careful to maintain the right human distances that constitute our experience of madness, I have obeyed the law which literally brings the apparent facts of madness into existence. Without this, the physician—like the one I mentioned who replied to the madman that what he said was not true—would rave no less than the madman himself.

And when, for this occasion, I reread the case write-up on which I have relied here, it seemed to me that it bore witness to the fact that, no matter how one judges its results, I maintained for my object the respect she deserved as a human being, as a patient, and as a case.

Lastly, I believe that in relegating the causality of madness to the unsoundable decision of being in which human beings understand or fail to recognize their liberation, in the snare of fate that deceives them about a freedom they have not in the least conquered, I am merely formulating the law of our becoming as it is expressed in Antiquity's formulation: Γένοὶ, οἷος ἐσσὶ.

In order to define psychical causality in this law, I will now try to grasp the mode of form and action that establishes the determinations of this drama, since I think it can be identified scientifically with the concept of "imagos."

3. The Psychical Effects of the Imaginary Mode 178

A subject's history develops in a more or less typical series of *ideal identifications* that represent the purest of psychical phenomena in that they essentially reveal the function of imagos. I do not conceptualize the ego otherwise than as a central system of these formations, a system that one must understand, like these formations, in its imaginary structure and libidinal value.

Thus, without dwelling on those who, even in the sciences, blithely confuse the ego with the subject's being, you can see where I diverge from the most common conception that identifies the ego with the synthesis of the organism's relational functions, a conception which must certainly be called hybrid in that a subjective synthesis is defined in it in objective terms.

One recognizes Ey's position here, as it is expressed in the passage I mentioned earlier where he posits "an attack on the ego which, once again, is indistinguishable, in the final analysis, from the notion of functional dissolution."

Can one reproach him for this conception when the bias of parallelism is so strong that Freud himself remained its prisoner, even though it ran counter to the entire tendency of his research? To have attacked this bias in Freud's time might, moreover, have amounted to preventing oneself from communicating one's ideas to the scientific community.

It is well known that Freud identified the ego with the "perception-consciousness system," which comprises all of the systems by which an organism is adapted to the "reality principle."[12]

If we think about the role played by the notion of error in Ey's conception, we can see the bond that ties the organicist illusion to a realist metapsychology. This does not, however, bring us any closer to a concrete psychology.

Moreover, although the best minds in psychoanalysis avidly demand, if we
179 are to believe them, a theory of the ego, there is little chance that its place will be marked by anything other than a gaping hole as long as they do not resolve to consider obsolete what is clearly obsolete in the work of a peerless master.

For Merleau-Ponty's work[13] decisively demonstrates that any healthy phenomenology, that of perception, for instance, requires us to consider lived experience prior to any objectification and even prior to any reflexive analysis that interweaves objectification and experience. Let me explain what I mean: the slightest visual illusion proves to force itself upon us experientially before detailed, piecemeal observation of the figure corrects it; it is the latter that allows us to objectify the so-called real form. Reflection makes us recognize in this form the a priori category of extension [*l'étendue*], the property of which is precisely to present itself "*partes extra partes*," but it is still the illusion in itself that gives us the gestalt action that is psychology's true object here.

This is why no considerations about ego synthesis can excuse us from considering the phenomenon of synthesis in the subject—namely, everything the subject includes under this term, which is not exactly synthetic, nor even exempt from contradiction, as we learned from Montaigne, and learned even better when Freud designated it as the very locus of *Verneinung*. The latter is the phenomenon by which the subject reveals one of his impulses in his very denial [*dénégation*] of it and at the very moment at which he denies it. Let me emphasize that it is not a disavowal of membership that is at stake here, but a formal negation—in other words, a typical phenomenon of misrecognition, and in the inverted form I have stressed. The most common expression of this form, "Don't think that . . . ," already points to the profound relationship with the other as such that I will bring out in the ego.

Doesn't experience thus show us, upon the slightest inspection, that nothing separates the ego from its ideal forms (*Ich Ideal*, a term with which Freud recovers his rights) and that everything limits it on the side of the being it represents, since almost the entire life of the organism escapes it, not merely insofar as that life is most often ignored, but insofar as the ego need know nothing about it for the most part. 180

As for the genetic psychology of the ego, the results that it has obtained seem all the more valid to me since they are stripped of any postulate of functional integration.

I myself have given proof of this in my study of the phenomena typical of what I call the *fertile moments* of delusion. Carried out according to the phenomenological method that I am promoting here, this study led me to analyses from which my conception of the ego has progressively emerged; this progressive emergence was visible to my audiences at the lectures and classes I gave over the years at conferences organized by the *Évolution Psychiatrique* group, at the Medical School Clinic, and at the Institute of Psychoanalysis. Although for my own reasons those lectures and classes have remained unpublished, they nevertheless publicized my term "paranoiac knowledge," which was designed to hit home.

By including under this heading one of the fundamental structures of these phenomena, I intended to indicate that, if it is not equivalent, it is at least akin to a form of relation to the world that has a very specific import: the reaction recognized by psychiatrists that has been psychologically generalized with the term "transitivism." Now, this reaction—which is never completely eliminated from man's world, in its most idealized forms (for example, in relations of rivalry)—first manifests itself as the matrix of the ego's *Urbild*.

This reaction significantly dominates the primordial phase in which the child becomes aware of his individuality; his language translates this, as you know, into the third person prior to translating it into the first person. Charlotte Bühler,[14] to mention only her, in observing the behavior of a child with its playmate, has recognized this transitivism in the striking form of a child being truly captured by another child's image.

A child can thus, in a complete trance-like state, share in his friend's tumble or attribute to him, without lying, the punch he himself has given his friend.
I will skip the series of these phenomena, which run the gamut from spectac- 181
ular identification to mimetic suggestion and on to the seduction of bearing. All of them are understood by Bühler in the dialectic that goes from jealousy (the jealousy whose instructive value Saint Augustine already glimpsed in a flash) to the first forms of sympathy. They are inscribed in a primordial ambivalence that seems to me, as I am already indicating, to be *mirrored*, in the sense that the subject identifies, in his feeling of Self, with the other's image and that the other's image captivates this feeling in him.

Now this reaction occurs only under one condition: the difference in age between the two children must remain below a certain limit, a limit that cannot exceed one year at the beginning of the phase studied.

We already see here an essential feature of an imago: the observable effects of a form, in the broadest sense of the term, that can only be defined in terms of generic resemblance, thus implying that a certain recognition occurred prior to that.

We know that these effects manifest themselves in relation to the human façe right from the tenth day after birth, that is, right from the appearance of the first visual reactions and prior to any other experience than that of blind sucking.

Thus, and this is an essential point, the first effect of the imago that appears in human beings is that of the subject's *alienation*. It is in the other that the subject first identifies himself and even experiences himself. This phenomenon will seem less surprising if we recall the fundamental social conditions of the human *Umwelt* and if we evoke the intuition that dominates all of Hegel's speculations.

Man's very desire is constituted, he tells us, under the sign of mediation: it is the desire to have one's desire recognized. Its object is a desire, that of other people, in the sense that man has no object that is constituted for his desire without some mediation. This is clear from his earliest needs, in that, for example, his very food must be prepared; and we find this anew in the whole development of his satisfaction, beginning with the conflict between master and slave, through the entire dialectic of labor.

This dialectic, which is that of man's very being, must bring about, through
182 a series of crises, the synthesis of his particularity and his universality, going so far as to universalize this very particularity.

This means that, in the movement that leads man to an ever more adequate consciousness of himself, his freedom becomes bound up with the development of his servitude.

Does the imago then serve to instate a fundamental relationship in being between his reality and his organism? Does man's psychical life show us a similar phenomenon in any other forms?

No experience has contributed more than psychoanalysis to revealing this phenomenon. And the necessity of repetition that psychoanalysis points to as the effect of the [Oedipus] complex—even though analytic doctrine expresses this with the inert and unthinkable notion of the unconscious—is sufficiently eloquent here.

Habit and forgetting are signs of the integration of a psychical relation into the organism; an entire situation, having become both unknown to the subject and as essential as his body to him, is normally manifested in effects that are consistent with the sense he has of his body.

The Oedipus complex turns out, in analytic experience, to be capable not only of provoking, by its atypical impact, all the somatic effects of hysteria, but also of normally constituting the sense of reality.

The father represents a function of both power and temperament simultaneously; an imperative that is no longer blind but "categorical"; and a person who dominates and arbitrates the avid wrenching and jealous ambivalence that were at the core of the child's first relations with its mother and its sibling rival. And he seems all the more to represent this the more he is "on the sidelines" of the first affective apprehensions. The effects of his appearance are expressed in various manners in analytic doctrine, but they obviously appear skewed there by their traumatizing impact, for it was the latter that first allowed these effects to be perceived by analysis. It seems to me that they can be most generally expressed as follows: The new image makes a world of persons "flocculate" in the subject; insofar as they represent centers of autonomy, they completely change the structure of reality for him.

I would not hesitate to say that one could demonstrate that the Oedipal crisis has physiological echoes, and that, however purely psychological its 183
mainspring may be, a certain "dose of Oedipus" can be considered to have the same humoral efficacy as the absorption of a desensitizing medication.

Furthermore, the decisive role of an affective experience of this kind for the constitution of the world of reality as regards the categories of time and space is so obvious that even someone like Bertrand Russell, in his essay *The Analysis of Mind*,[15] with its radically mechanistic inspiration, cannot avoid admitting, in his genetic theory of perception, the function of "feelings of distance" which, with the sense of the concrete that is characteristic of Anglo-Saxons, he relates to the "feeling of respect."

I stressed this significant feature in my doctoral thesis, when I attempted to account for the structure of the "elementary phenomena" of paranoiac psychosis.

Suffice it to say that my examination of these phenomena led me to complete the catalogue of the structures—symbolism, condensation, and others—that Freud had explained as those of the *imaginary mode*, to use my own terminology. I sincerely hope that people will soon stop using the word "unconscious" to designate what manifests itself in consciousness.

I realized (and why don't I ask you to look at my chapter,[16] since it bears witness to the authentic groping involved in my research), in considering the case history of my patient, that it is impossible to situate, through the anamnesis, the exact time and place at which certain intuitions, memory illusions,

convictive resentments, and imaginary objectifications occurred that could only be attributed to the *fertile moment* of the delusion taken as a whole. I will illustrate this by mentioning the column and photograph that my patient remembered, during one of these periods, having been struck by some months before in a certain newspaper, but which she was unable to find when she went through the complete collection of months of its daily papers. I supposed that these phenomena were originally experienced as reminiscences, iterations,
184 series, and mirror games—it being impossible for the subject to situate their very occurrence in objective time and space with any more precision than she could situate her dreams in them.

We are thus nearing a structural analysis of an imaginary space and time as well as the connections between them.

Returning to my notion of paranoiac knowledge, I tried to conceptualize the network structure, the relations of participation, the aligned perspectives, and the palace of mirages that reign in the limbo regions of the world that the Oedipus complex causes to fade into forgetting.

I have often taken a stand against the hazardous manner in which Freud sociologically interpreted the Oedipus complex—that very important discovery about the human mind that we owe to him. I think that the Oedipus complex did not appear with the origin of man (assuming it is not altogether senseless to try to write the history of this complex), but at the threshold of history, of "historical" history, at the limit of "ethnographic" cultures. It can obviously appear only in the patriarchal form of the family as an institution, but it nevertheless has an indisputably liminary value. I am convinced that its function had to be served by initiatory experiences in cultures that excluded it, as ethnology allows us to see even today. And its value in bringing a psychical cycle to a close stems from the fact that it represents the family situation, insofar as the latter, by its institution, marks the intersection of the biological and the social in the cultural.

However, the structure that is characteristic of the human world—insofar as it involves the existence of objects that are independent of the actual field of the tendencies and that can be used both symbolically and instrumentally—appears in man from the very first phases of development. How can we conceive of its psychological genesis?

My construction known as "the mirror stage"—or, as it would be better to say, "the mirror phase"—addresses such a problem.

I duly presented it at the Marienbad Congress in 1936, at least up to the point, coinciding exactly with the fourth stroke of the ten-minute mark, at which I was interrupted by Ernest Jones who was presiding over the congress. He was doing so as president of the London Psycho-Analytical Society, a posi-

tion for which he was no doubt qualified by the fact that I have never encountered a single English colleague of his who didn't have something unpleasant 185
to say about his character. Nevertheless, the members of the Viennese group who were gathered there, like birds right before their impending migration, gave my exposé a rather warm reception. I did not submit my paper for inclusion in the proceedings of the congress; you can find the gist of it in a few lines in my article about the family published in 1938 in the *Encyclopédie Française*, in the volume on "The Life of the Mind."[17]

My aim there was to indicate the connection between a number of fundamental imaginary relations in an exemplary behavior characteristic of a certain phase of development.

This behavior is none other than that of the human infant before its image in the mirror starting at the age of six months, which is so strikingly different from the behavior of a chimpanzee, whose development in the instrumental application of intelligence the infant is far from having reached.

What I have called the triumphant assumption [*assomption*] of the image with the jubilatory mimicry that accompanies it and the playful indulgence in controlling the specular identification, after the briefest experimental verification of the nonexistence of the image behind the mirror, in contrast with the opposite phenomena in the monkey—these seemed to me to manifest one of the facts of identificatory capture by the imago that I was seeking to isolate.

It was very directly related to the image of the human being that I had already encountered in the earliest organization of human knowledge.

This idea has gained ground and has been corroborated by other researchers, among whom I will cite Lhermitte, whose 1939 book published the findings of the work he had devoted for many years to the singularity and autonomy in the psyche of the *image of one's own body*.

An enormous series of subjective phenomena revolve around this image, running the gamut from the amputee's illusion to the hallucination of one's double, including the latter's appearance in dreams and the delusional objectifications that go with it. But what is most important is still its autonomy as the imaginary locus of reference for proprioceptive sensations, that can be 186
found in all kinds of phenomena, of which Aristotle's illusion is only one example.

Gestalt theory and phenomenology also contribute to the file of data related to this image. And all sorts of imaginary mirages of concrete psychology, which are familiar to psychoanalysts, ranging from sexual games to moral ambiguities, remind one of my mirror stage by virtue of the image and the magical power of language. "Hey," one says to oneself, "that reminds me of Lacan's thing, the mirror stage. What exactly did he say about it?"

I have, in fact, taken my conception of the existential meaning of the phenomenon a bit further by understanding it in relation to what I have called man's *prematurity at birth*, in other words, the incompleteness and "delay" in the development of the central nervous system during the first six months of life. These phenomena are well known to anatomists and have, moreover, been obvious, since man's first appearance, in the nursling's lack of motor coordination and balance; the latter is probably not unrelated to the process of "fetalization," which Bolk considered to be the mainspring of the higher development of the encephalic vesicles in man.

It is owing to this delay in development that the early maturation of visual perception takes on the role of functional anticipation. This results, on the one hand, in the marked prevalence of visual structure in recognition of the human form, which begins so early, as I mentioned before. On the other hand, the odds of identifying with this form, if I may say so, receive decisive support from this, which comes to constitute the absolutely essential imaginary knot in man that psychoanalysis—obscurely and despite inextricable doctrinal contradictions—has admirably designated as "narcissism."

Indeed, the relation of the image to the suicidal tendency essentially expressed in the myth of Narcissus lies in this knot. This suicidal tendency—which represents in my opinion what Freud sought to situate in his metapsychology with the terms "death instinct" and "primary masochism"—depends, in my view, on the fact that man's death, long before it is reflected (in a way that is, moreover, always so ambiguous) in his thinking, is experienced by him
187 in the earliest phase of misery that he goes through from *the trauma of birth* until the end of the first six months of *physiological prematurity*, and that echoes later in the *trauma of weaning*.

It is one of the most brilliant features of Freud's intuition regarding the order of the psychical world that he grasped the revelatory value of concealment games that are children's first games.[18] Everyone can see them and yet no one before him had grasped in their iterative character the liberating repetition of all separation and weaning as such that the child assumes [*assume*] in these games.

Thanks to Freud we can think of them as expressing the first vibration of the stationary wave of renunciations that scand the history of psychical development.

At the beginning of this development we see the primordial ego, as essentially alienated, linked to the first sacrifice as essentially suicidal.

In other words, we see here the fundamental structure of madness.

Thus, the earliest dissonance between the ego and being would seem to be the fundamental note that resounds in a whole harmonic scale across the phases of psychical history, the function of which is to resolve it by developing it.

Any resolution of this dissonance through an illusory coincidence of reality with the ideal would resonate all the way to the depths of the imaginary knot of narcissistic, suicidal aggression.

Yet this mirage of appearances, in which the organic conditions of intoxication, for instance, can play their role, requires the ungraspable consent of freedom, as can be seen in the fact that madness is found only in man and only after he reaches "the age of reason"—Pascal's intuition that "a child is not a man" is thus borne out here.

Indeed, the child's first identificatory choices, which are "innocent" choices, determine nothing, apart from the affective [*pathétiques*] "fixations" of neurosis, but the madness by which man thinks he is a man.

This paradoxical formulation nevertheless takes on its full value when we consider that man is far more than his body, even though he can know 188
[*savoir*] nothing more about his being.

Here we see the fundamental illusion to which man is a slave, much more so than to all the "passions of the body" in the Cartesian sense: the passion of being a man. It is, I would say, the passion of the soul *par excellence*, *narcissism*, that imposes its structure on all his desires, even the loftiest ones.

In the encounter between body and mind, the soul appears as what it traditionally is, that is, as the limit of the monad.

When man, seeking to empty himself of all thoughts, advances in the shadowless gleam of imaginary space, abstaining from even awaiting what will emerge from it, a dull mirror shows him a surface in which nothing is reflected.

I think, therefore, that I can designate the imago as the true object of psychology, to the exact same extent that Galileo's notion of the inert mass point served as the foundation of physics.

However, we cannot yet fully grasp the notion, and my entire exposé has had no other goal than to guide you toward its obscure self-evidence.

It seems to me to be correlated with a kind of unextended space—that is, indivisible space, our intuition of which should be clarified by progress in the notion of gestalts—and with a kind of time that is caught between expectation and release, a time of phases and repetition.

A form of causality grounds this notion, which is psychical causality itself: *identification*. The latter is an irreducible phenomenon, and the imago is the form, which is definable in the imaginary spatiotemporal complex, whose function is to bring about the identification that resolves a psychical phase—in other words, a metamorphosis in the individual's relationships with his semblables.

Those who do not wish to understand me might object that I am begging the question and that I am gratuitously positing that the phenomenon is irreducible merely in order to foster a thoroughly metaphysical conception of man.

I will thus address the deaf by offering them facts which will, I think, pique
189 their sense of the visible, since these facts should not appear to be contaminated, in their eyes at least, by either the mind or being: for I will seek them out in the animal kingdom.

It is clear that psychical phenomena must manifest themselves in that kingdom if they have an independent existence, and that what I call the imago must be found there—at least in those animals whose *Umwelt* involves, if not society, at least an aggregation of their fellow creatures, that is, those animals who present, among their specific characteristics, the trait known as "gregariousness." In any case, ten years ago, when I referred to the imago as a "psychical object" and stated that the appearance of Freud's Oedipus complex marked a conceptual watershed, insofar as it contained the promise of a true psychology, I simultaneously indicated in several of my writings that, with the imago, psychology had given us a concept which could be at least as fruitful in biology as many other concepts that are far more uncertain but that have nevertheless gained currency there.

This indication was borne out starting in 1939, and as proof I will simply present two "facts" among others that have by now become quite numerous.

The first is found in a paper by L. Harrison Matthews published in the *Proceedings of the Royal Society* in 1939.[19]

It had long been known that a female pigeon does not ovulate when isolated from other members of its species.

Matthews' experiments demonstrated that ovulation is triggered by a female pigeon's sight of the specific form of a member of its own species, to the exclusion of any other sensory form of perception, and without that member having to be male.

Placed in the same room with individuals of both sexes, but in cages that are fabricated in such a way that the pigeons cannot see each other, although they can easily perceive each other's calls and smells, the females do not ovulate. Conversely, if we allow two pigeons to view each other—even if it is through a glass barrier that suffices to thwart the onset of the mating game, and even when both pigeons are female—ovulation is triggered within a period of time that varies from twelve days (when the separated pigeons include a male and
190 a female) to two months (when the separated pigeons are both female).

But what is more remarkable still is that the mere sight by the animal of its own image in a mirror suffices to trigger ovulation within two and a half months.

Another researcher has noted that the secretion of milk in the male pigeon's crops, which normally occurs when the eggs hatch, does not occur when he cannot see the female brooding the eggs.

A second group of facts is found in a paper by Chauvin, which was published in 1941 in the *Annales de la Société entomologique de France*.[20]

Chauvin's work concerns an insect species with two very different varieties of individuals: a so-called "solitary" type and a so-called "gregarious" one. Chauvin studied the migratory locust, that is, one of the species commonly referred to as grasshoppers, in which the phenomenon of swarming is linked to the appearance of the gregarious type. In this locust, also called *Schistocerca*, the two varieties show profound differences (as in *Locusta* and other similar species) in both their instincts—sexual cycle, voracity, and motor agitation—and their morphology, as can be seen from biometric measures and from the pigmentation that produces their differing characteristic outward appearances.

Limiting ourselves to this last feature, I will indicate that in *Schistocerca*, the solitary type is solid green throughout its development, which includes five larval stages, whereas the gregarious type changes colors depending on its stage and has certain black striations on different parts of its body, one of the most permanent striations being on its hind femur. But I am not exaggerating when I say that, in addition to these highly visible features, the insects differ biologically in every respect.

We find that the appearance of the gregarious type is triggered, in this insect, by perception of the characteristic form of the species during the first larval periods. Two solitary individuals placed together will thus evolve toward the gregarious type. Through a series of experiments—raising them in darkness and isolated sectioning of the palpus, the antennae, and so on—it was possible to locate this perception very precisely in the senses of sight and touch, to the exclusion of smell, hearing, and shared movement. It is not nec- 191
essary for the two individuals that are put together to be in the same larval stage, and they react in the same way to the presence of an adult. The presence of an adult from a similar species, such as *Locusta*, also determines gregariousness, but not the presence of an adult *Gryllus*, which is from a more distant species.

After an in-depth discussion, Chauvin is led to bring in the notion of a specific form and a specific movement, characterized by a certain "style," a formulation that is all the less questionable in his case in that he does not seem to even dream of tying it to the notion of gestalts. I will let him conclude in his own words, which will show how little he is inclined to wax metaphysical: "There clearly must be some sort of recognition here, however rudimentary one assumes it to be. Yet how can we speak of recognition without presupposing a *psychophysiological* mechanism?"[21] Such is the discretion of the physiologist.

But that is not the whole story: gregarious individuals are born from the coupling of two solitary individuals in a proportion that depends on the amount of time they are allowed to spend together. Furthermore, these excitations are such that the proportion of gregarious births rises as the number of couplings after certain intervals rises.

Inversely, suppression of the image's morphogenic action leads to progressive reduction of the number of gregarious individuals among the offspring.

Although the sexual characteristics of gregarious adults depend on conditions that still better manifest the originality of the role of the specific imago in the phenomenon that I have just described, I would do better not to elaborate any further on this topic in a presentation on psychical causality in cases of madness.

I would simply like to highlight here the equally significant fact that, contrary to what Ey allows himself to be led to propose somewhere, there is no parallelism between the anatomical differentiation of the nervous system and the wealth of psychical manifestations, even of intelligence. This is demon-
192 strated by a huge amount of data regarding the behavior of lower animals; consider the crab, for example, whose skill in using mechanical impact to deal with a mussel I have repeatedly praised in my lectures.

In concluding, I hope that this brief discourse on the imago will strike you, not as an ironic challenge, but as a genuine threat to man. For, while our ability to realize that the imago's unquantifiable distance and freedom's minute blade are decisive in madness does not yet allow us to cure it, the time is perhaps not far off when such knowledge will allow us to induce it. While nothing can guarantee that we will not get lost in a free movement toward truth, a little nudge will suffice to ensure that we change truth into madness. Then we will have moved from the domain of metaphysical causality, which one can deride, to that of scientific technique, which is no laughing matter.

Here and there we have seen the beginnings of such an enterprise. The art of the image will soon be able to play off the values of the imago, and some day we will see serial orders of "ideals" that withstand criticism: that is when the label "true guarantee" will take on its full meaning.

Neither the intention nor the enterprise will be new, but their systematic form will be.

In the meantime, I propose to equate the various delusional structures with the therapeutic methods applied to the psychoses, as a function of the principles I have developed here:

- running from the ridiculous attachment to the object demanded, to the cruel tension of hypochondriacal fixation, and on to the suicidal backdrop of the delusion of negation; and
- running from the sedative value of medical explanations, to the disruptive act of inducing epilepsy, and on to analysis' narcissistic *catharsis*.

It sufficed to reflect upon a few "optical illusions" to lay the groundwork for a Gestalt theory that produces results that might seem to be minor miracles. For instance, predicting the following phenomenon: when an arrangement composed of blue-colored sectors is made to spin in front of a screen 193
that is half black and half yellow, the colors remain isolated or combine and you either see the two colors of the screen through a blue swirling or else you see a blue-black and a grey blend together, according to whether you see the arrangement or not, thus depending solely on a thought adjustment.

Judge for yourself, then, what our combinatory faculties could wrest from a theory that refers to the very relationship between being and the world, if this theory became somewhat precise. It should be clear to you that the visual perception of a man raised in a cultural context completely different from our own is a perception that is completely different from our own.

The aspects of the imago—which are more invisible to our eyes (made, as they are, for the signs of the money changer) than what the desert hunter knows how to see the imperceptible trace of, namely, the gazelle's footprint on the rock—will someday be revealed to us.

You have heard me lovingly refer to Descartes and Hegel in order to situate the place of the imago in our research. It is rather fashionable these days to "go beyond" the classical philosophers. I could just as easily have started with the admirable dialogue in the *Parmenides*. For neither Socrates nor Descartes, nor Marx, nor Freud, can be "gone beyond," insofar as they carried out their research with the passion to unveil that has an object: truth.

As one such prince of words wrote—I mean Max Jacob, poet, saint, and novelist, through whose fingers the threads of the ego's* mask seem to slip of their own accord—in *Cornet à dés* ("The Dice Cup"), if I am not mistaken: the truth is always new.

Notes

1. One can read the most recent exposition available of Henri Ey's viewpoints in the brochure that contains the presentation made by J. de Ajuriaguerra and H. Hécaen at the conference held in Bonneval in 1943 (that is, the conference just before this one). Ey added an introduction and a long response of his own to their presentation, which included a critique of his doctrine. See *Rapports de la Neurologie et de la Psychiatrie*, H. Ey, J. de Ajuriaguerra, and

H. Hécaen (Paris: Hermann, 1947), issue number 1018 of the well-known collection "Actualités scientifiques et industrielles" ("Current Scientific and Industrial Developments"). Some of the quotations that follow are borrowed from them; others are found only in typewritten texts thanks to which a highly productive discussion took place that paved the way for the Bonneval conference in 1946.

2. Henri Ey, *Rapports de la Neurologie*, 14.

3. Henri Ey, *Rapports de la Neurologie*, 122. (Cf. Ey's article published in *Évolution Psychiatrique* XII, 1 (1947): 71–104.

4. Henri Ey, *Hallucinations et Délire* (Paris: Alcan, 1934).

5. P. Guiraud, "Les formes verbales de l'interprétation délirante," *Annales médico-psychologiques* LXXIX, 5 (1921): 395–412.

6. In the first issue of the journal entitled *14, rue du Dragon* (Paris: Cahiers d'Art).

7. Paul Éluard, *Poésie involontaire et poésie intentionnelle* (Villeneuve-les-Avignon: Seghers, 1942).

8. See *La Philosophie de l'esprit*, trans. Véra (Paris: Germer Baillière, 1867), and the excellent French translation in two volumes by Jean Hyppolite, *La Phénomenologie de l'esprit* (Paris: Aubier, 1939), which I will return to further on.

9. French readers can no longer ignore this work now that Jean Hyppolite has made it accessible to them, in a way that will satisfy even the most exacting of readers, in his thesis which has just been published (Paris: Aubier, 1946), and once the *Nouvelle Revue Française* publishes the notes from the course that Alexandre Kojève devoted to Hegel's text for five years at the École des Hautes Études.

10. In *Évolution psychiatrique*, 2 (March 1931): 25–34. See also P. Guiraud and B. Cailleux, "Le meurtre immotivé, réaction libératrice de la maladie chez les hébéphrènes," *Annales Médico-psychiatriques* 2 (November 1928): 352–60.

11. See *Écrits* 1966, 157.

12. See Freud's *Das Ich und das Es* [*The Ego and the Id*, *SE* XIX, especially chapter 2].

13. *Phénoménologie de la perception* (Paris: Gallimard, 1945). [*The Phenomenology of Perception*, trans. Colin Smith (New York: Humanities Press, 1962).]

14. Charlotte Bühler, *Soziologische und psychologische Studien über das erste Lebensjahr* (Jena: Fischer, 1927). See also Elsa Köhler, *Die Persönlichkeit des dreijahrigen Kindes* (Leipzig: 1926).

15. Bertrand Russell, *The Analysis of Mind* (New York: Macmillan, 1921).

16. *De la psychose paranoïaque dans ses rapports avec la personnalité* (Paris: Le François, 1932), Part II, Chap. II, 202–15 and also Chap. IV, Section III, b, 300–306.

17. *Encyclopédie Française*, founded by A. de Monzie, vol. VIII, edited by Henri Wallon; see Part 2, Section A, "La famille," especially pages 8·40–6 to 8·40–11.

18. In *Jenseits des Lustprinzips* [*Beyond the Pleasure Principle*, *SE* XVIII, 14–17].

19. See [L. Harrison Matthews, "Visual Stimulation and Ovulation in Pigeons" in] *Proceedings of the Royal Society*, Series B (Biological Sciences), 126 (February 3, 1939): 557–60.

20. R. Chauvin, *Annales de la Société entomologique de France* (1941, third quarter): 133–272.

21. R. Chauvin, *Annales de la Société entomologique de France*, 251 (my italics).

III

Logical Time and the Assertion of Anticipated Certainty 197

A New Sophism

In March 1945, Christian Zervos asked me to contribute, along with a certain number of writers, to the recommencement issue of his journal, *Les Cahiers d'Art*, conceived with the intent of filling the space between the figures on its cover, 1940–1944, dates significant to many people, with the illustrious names in its table of contents.

I submitted this article, knowing full well that this would immediately make it unavailable to most readers.

May it resound with the right note here where I am placing it, between the before and the after, even if it demonstrates that the after was kept waiting [*faisait antichambre*] so that the before could assume its own place [*pût prendre rang*].

A Logical Problem

A prison warden summons three choice prisoners and announces to them the following:

> For reasons I need not make known to you now, gentlemen, I must free one of you. In order to decide which, I will entrust the outcome to a test that you will, I hope, agree to undergo.
>
> There are three of you present. I have here five disks differing only in color: three white and two black. Without letting you know which I will have chosen, I will fasten one of them to each of you between the shoulders, outside, that is, your direct visual field—indirect ways of getting a look at the disk also being excluded by the absence here of any means by which to see your own reflection.
>
> You will then be left at your leisure to consider your companions and their respective disks, without being allowed, of course, to communicate among yourselves the results of your inspection. Your own inter- 198
> est would, in any case, proscribe such communication, for the first to be able to deduce his own color will be the one to benefit from the discharging measure at my disposal.
>
> But his conclusion must be founded upon logical and not simply probabilistic grounds. Keeping this in mind, it is agreed that as soon as one

> of you is ready to formulate such a conclusion, he will pass through this door so that he may be judged individually on the basis of his response.

This having been agreed to, each of our three subjects is adorned with a white disk, no use being made of the black ones, of which there were, let us recall, but two.

How can the subjects solve the problem?

The Perfect Solution

After having contemplated one another for *a certain time*, the three subjects take *a few steps* together, passing side by side through the doorway. Each of them then separately furnishes a similar response which can be expressed as follows:

> I am a white, and here is how I know it. Since my companions were whites, I thought that, had I been a black, each of them would have been able to infer the following: "If I too were a black, the other would have necessarily realized straight away that he was a white and would have left immediately; therefore I am not a black." And both would have left together, convinced they were whites. As they did nothing of the kind, I must be a white like them. At that, I made for the door to make my conclusion known.

All three thus exited simultaneously, armed with the same reasons for concluding.

Sophistic Value of this Solution

Can this solution, which presents itself as the most perfect of which the problem allows, be obtained experimentally? I leave to the initiative of each the task of deciding.

199 Not that I would go so far as to recommend putting it to the test in real life—even though our era's antinomic progress has, it seems, for some time now, been putting such conditions within the reach of an ever greater number. Indeed, I am afraid that although only winners are foreseen here, practice may well diverge considerably from theory. Moreover, I am not one of those recent philosophers for whom confinement within four walls merely helps us attain the ultimate in human freedom.

But when carried out under the innocent conditions of fiction, the experiment will not disappoint those who have not lost all taste for surprise—I guarantee it. It will perhaps turn out to be of some scientific value to the psychologist, at least if we can trust what seemed to me to result from having tried it with various groups of appropriately chosen, qualified intellectuals: a very peculiar misrecognition on the part of these subjects of the reality of other people.

My only interest is in the logical value of the solution presented. I consider it, in effect, to be a remarkable sophism, in the classical sense of the term—that is, a significant example for the resolution of the forms of a logical function at the historical moment at which the problem these forms raise presents itself to philosophical examination. The story's sinister images will certainly prove to be contingent. But to whatever degree my sophism may seem not irrelevant to our times, its bearing their sign in such images is in no way superfluous—which is why I have preserved here the trappings with which it was brought to my attention one evening by an ingenious host.

I will now place myself under the auspices of he who sometimes dons the philosopher's garb, who—ambiguous—is more often to be sought in the comedian's banter, but who is always encountered in the politician's secretive action: the good logician, odious to the world.

Discussion of the Sophism

Every sophism initially presents itself as a logical error, and a first objection to this sophism can be easily formulated. Let us call "A" the real subject who concludes for himself, and "B" and "C" those reflected subjects upon whose 200
conduct A founds his deduction. One might object that since B's conviction is based on C's expectative, the strength of his conviction must logically dissipate when C stops hesitating; and reciprocally for C with respect to B; both must thus remain indecisive. Nothing therefore necessitates their departure in the case that A is a black. Consequently, A cannot deduce that he is a white.

To this it must first be replied that B and C's whole cogitation is *falsely* imputed to them, for the only situation which could motivate it—the fact of seeing a black—is not, in effect, the true situation. What must be discerned here is whether, supposing this situation were the case, it would be *wrong* to impute this logical thought process to them. Now it would be nothing of the kind, for, according to my hypothesis, it is the fact that neither of them *left first* which allows each to believe he is a white, and their hesitating for but one instant would clearly suffice to reconvince each of them beyond the shadow of a doubt that he is a white. For hesitation is logically excluded for whomever sees two blacks. But it is also excluded in reality in this first step of the deduction for, since no one finds himself in the presence of a black and a white, there is no way for anyone to leave on the basis of what can be deduced therefrom.

But the objection presents itself more forcibly at the second stage of A's deduction. For if he has legitimately concluded that he is a white—positing that, had he been a black, the others would not have been long in realizing they were whites and leaving—he must nevertheless abandon his conclusion as soon as he comes to it; for at the very moment at which he is stirred into action by his conclusion, he sees the others setting off with him.

Before responding to this objection, let me carefully lay out anew the logical terms of the problem. "A" designates each of the subjects insofar as he himself is in the hot seat and resolves or fails to resolve to conclude about his own case. "B" and "C" are the two others insofar as they are objects of A's reasoning. But while A can correctly impute to the others a thought process which is in fact false (as I have just shown), he can, nevertheless, only take into account their real behavior.

If A, seeing B and C set off with him, wonders again whether they have not in fact seen that he is black, it suffices for him to stop and newly pose the question in order to answer it. For he sees that they too stop: since each
201 of them is really in the same situation as him, or more aptly stated, *is* A insofar as [he is] real—that is, insofar as he resolves or fails to resolve to conclude about himself—each encounters the same doubt at the same moment as him. Regardless of the reasoning A now imputes to B and C, he will legitimately conclude again that he is a white. For he posits anew that, had he been a black, B and C would have had to *continue*; or at the very least, acknowledging their hesitation—which concurs with the preceding argument (here supported by the facts) that makes them wonder whether they are not blacks themselves—he posits that they would have had to *set off again before him* (it is the fact that he is black that gives their very hesitation its definite import, allowing them to conclude that they are whites). It is because they, seeing that he is in fact white, do nothing of the kind, that he himself takes the initiative; which is to say that they all head for the door together to declare that they are whites.

But one can still object that, having removed in this way the obstacle, we have not for all that refuted the logical objection—for the same objection turns up with the reiteration of the movement, reproducing in each of the subjects the very same doubt and arrest.

Assuredly, but logical progress must have been made in the interim. For this time A can draw but one unequivocal conclusion from the common cessation of movement: had he been a black, B and C *absolutely should not have stopped.* Their hesitating a second time in concluding that they are whites would be ruled out at this point: Indeed, a single hesitation suffices for them to demonstrate to each other that certainly neither of them is a black. Thus, if B and C have halted again, A can only be a white. Which is to say that this time the three subjects are confirmed in a certainty permitting of no further doubt or objection.

Withstanding the test of critical discussion, the sophism thus maintains all the constraining rigor of a logical process, on condition that one integrates therein the value of the two *suspensive scansions*. This test exposes the process of verification in the very act in which each of the subjects manifests that it has led him to his conclusion.

Value of the Suspended Motions in the Process 202

Is it justifiable to integrate into the sophism the two *suspended motions* which have thus made their appearance? In order to decide, we must examine their role in the solution of the logical problem.

In fact, they take on this role only after the conclusion of the logical process, since the act they suspend evinces this very conclusion. One thus cannot object on that basis that they bring into the solution an element external to the logical process itself.

Their role, while crucial to the carrying-out [*pratique*] of the logical process, is not that of experience in the verification of an hypothesis, but rather that of something intrinsic to logical ambiguity.

For at first sight the givens of the problem would seem to break down as follows:

(1) Three combinations of the subjects' characteristic attributes are logically possible: two blacks, one white; one black, two whites; or three whites. Once the first combination is ruled out by what all three subjects see, the question as to which of the other two is the case remains open. Its answer derives from:

(2) the experiential data provided by the suspended motions, which amount to signals by which the subjects communicate to each other—in a mode determined by the conditions of the test—what they are forbidden to exchange in an intentional mode, namely, what each sees of the others' attributes.

But this is not at all the case, as it would give the logical process a spatialized conception—the same spatialized conception that turns up every time the logical process appears to be erroneous, and that constitutes the only objection to the solubility of the problem.

It is precisely because my sophism will not tolerate a spatialized conception that it presents itself as an aporia for the forms of classical logic, whose "eternal" prestige reflects an infirmity which is nonetheless recognized as their own[1]—namely, that these forms never give us anything which cannot already *be seen all at once*.

203 In complete opposition to this, the coming into play as signifiers of the phenomena here contested makes the temporal, not spatial, structure of the logical process prevail. What the *suspended motions* disclose is not what the subjects see, but rather what they have found out positively about *what they do not see*: the appearance of the black disks. What constitutes these suspended motions as signifying is not their direction, but rather their *interruption* [*temps d'arrêt*]. Their crucial value is not that of a binary choice between two inertly[2] juxtaposed combinations—rendered incomplete by the visual exclusion of the third combination—but rather of a verificatory movement instituted by a logical process in which a subject transforms the three possible combinations into three *times of possibility*.

This is also why, while *a single* signal should suffice for the sole choice imposed by the first erroneous interpretation, *two* scansions are necessary to verify the two lapses implied by the second, and only valid, interpretation.

Far from being experiential data external to the logical process, the *suspended motions* are so necessary to it that only experience can make the logical process lack here the synchronicity implied by the suspended motions as produced by a purely logical subject; only experience can make their function in the verification process founder.

The suspended motions represent nothing, in effect, but levels of degrada-
204 tion whose necessity brings out the increasing order of temporal instances that are registered within the logical process so as to be integrated into its conclusion.

This can be seen in the logical determination of the *interruptions* they constitute, this determination—whether logician's objection or subject's doubt—revealing itself at each moment as the subjective unfolding of a temporal instance, or more aptly stated, as the slipping away [*fuite*] of the subject within a formal exigency.

These temporal instances, which are constitutive of the process of the sophism, permit us to recognize a true logical movement in it. This process calls for an examination of the quality of its times.

The Modulation of Time in the Sophism's Movement: The Instant of the Glance, the Time for Comprehending, and the Moment of Concluding

One can isolate in the sophism three *evidential moments* whose logical values prove to be different and of increasing order. To lay out the chronological succession of the three moments would amount once again to spatializing them through a formalism which tends to reduce discourse to an alignment of signs. To show that the instance of time presents itself in a different *mode* in each of these moments would be to preserve their hierarchy, revealing therein a tonal discontinuity that is essential to their value. But to discern in the temporal *modulation* the very function by which each of these moments, in its passage to the next, is resorbed therein, the last moment which absorbs them alone remaining, would be to reconstruct their real succession and truly understand their genesis in the logical movement. That is what I will attempt, starting from as rigorous a formulation as possible of these evidential moments.

(I) Being opposite two blacks, one knows that one is a white.

We have here a *logical exclusion* which gives the movement its basis. The fact that this logical exclusion is anterior to the movement, that is, that we can assume it to be clear to the subjects *with* the givens of the problem—givens which forbid a combination involving three blacks—is independent of the dramatic contingency isolating the preambular statement of these givens. Expressing it in the form *two blacks : one white*, we see the *instantaneousness* of its evidence—its fulguration time, so to speak, being equal to zero.

But its formulation at the outset is already modulated by the subjectiviza- 205
tion, albeit impersonal, which takes form here in the "one knows that . . . ," and by the conjunction of propositions which constitutes less a formal hypothesis than a still indeterminate matrix of such a hypothesis; we can put it in the following consequential form designated by linguists with the terms "protasis" and "apodosis": "Being . . . , *only then* does one know that one is . . ."

An instance of time widens the interval so that the pregiven [*le donné*] of the *protasis*, "opposite two blacks," changes into the given [*la donnée*] of the *apodosis*, "one is a white," *the instant of the glance* being necessary for this to occur. Into the logical equivalence between the two terms, "two blacks : one white," temporal modulation introduces a form which, in the second moment, crystallizes into an authentic hypothesis; for it aims now at the real unknown of the problem, namely, the attribute of which the subject himself is unaware. In this step, the subject encounters the next logical combination, and—being the only one to whom the attribute "black" can be assigned—is able, in the first phase of the logical movement, to formulate thus the following evidence:

(II) Were I a black, the two whites that I see would waste no time realizing that they are whites.

We have here an *intuition* by which the subject *objectifies* something more than the factual givens offered him by the sight of the two whites. A certain time is defined (in the two senses of taking on meaning and finding its limit) by its end, an end that is at once goal and term. For the two whites in the situation of seeing a white and a black, this time is *the time for comprehending*, each of the whites finding the key to his own problem in the inertia of his semblable. The evidence of this moment presupposes the duration of a *time of meditation* that each of the two whites must ascertain in the other, and that the subject manifests in the terms he attributes to their lips, as though they were written on a banderole: "Had I been a black, he would have left without waiting an instant. If he stays to meditate, it is because I am a white."

But how can we measure the limit of this time whose meaning has been thus objectified? The time for comprehending can be reduced to the instant of the glance, but this glance can include in its instant all the time needed for comprehending. The objectivity of this time thus vacillates with its limit. Its mean-
206 ing alone subsists, along with the form it engenders of subjects who are *undefined except by their reciprocity*, and whose action is suspended by mutual causality in a time which gives way due to [*sous*] the very return of the intuition that it has objectified. It is through this temporal modulation that, with the second phase of the logical movement, a path is blazed which leads to the following evidence:

(III) I hasten to declare myself a white, so that these whites, whom I consider in this way, do not precede me in recognizing themselves for what they are.

We have here the *assertion about oneself* through which the subject concludes the logical movement in the making of a *judgment*. The very return of the movement of comprehending, before [*sous*] which the temporal instance that objectively sustains it has vacillated, continues on in the subject in reflection. This instance reemerges for him therein in the subjective mode of a *time of lagging behind* the others in that very movement, logically presenting itself as the urgency of the *moment of concluding*. More strictly speaking, its evidence is revealed in a subjective penumbra as the growing illumination of a fringe at the edge of the eclipse that the objectivity of the *time for comprehending* undergoes due to [*sous*] reflection.

It seems to the subject that the time required for the two whites to understand the situation in which they are faced with a white and a black does not logically differ from the time it took him to understand it himself, since this situation is merely his own hypothesis. But if his hypothesis is correct—if, that is, the two whites actually see a black—they do not have to make an assumption about it, and will thus precede him by the beat [*temps de battement*] he misses in having to formulate this very hypothesis. It is thus the *moment for concluding* that he is a white; should he allow himself to be beaten to this conclusion by his semblables, he *will no longer be able to determine* whether he is a black or not. Having surpassed the *time for comprehending the moment of concluding*, it is *the moment of concluding the time for comprehending*. Otherwise this time would lose its meaning. It is thus not because of some dramatic contingency, the seriousness of the stakes, or the competitiveness of the game, that time presses; it is owing to [*sous*] the urgency of the logical movement that the subject *precipitates* both his judgment and his departure ("precipitates" in the etymological sense of the verb: headlong), establishing the modulation in which temporal tension is reversed in a move to action [*tendance à l'acte*] manifesting to the others that the subject has concluded. But let us stop at this point 207
at which the subject arrives in his assertion at a truth that will be submitted to the test of doubt, but that he will be incapable of verifying unless he first attains it as a certainty. *Temporal tension* culminates here since, as we already know, it is the sequential steps of its release that will scand the test of its logical necessity. What is the logical value of this conclusive assertion? That is what I shall now try to bring out in the logical movement in which this conclusive assertion is verified.

Temporal Tension in the Subjective Assertion and Its Value Manifested in the Demonstration of the Sophism

The logical value of the third evidential moment, that is formulated in the assertion by which the subject concludes his logical movement, seems to me to deserve deeper exploration. It reveals, in effect, a form proper to an *assertive logic*, and we must indicate to which original *relations* this assertive logic can be applied.

Building on the propositional relations of the first two moments, *apodosis* and *hypothesis*, the conjunction manifested here builds up to a *motivation* of the conclusion "*so that there will not be*" (a lagging behind that engenders error), in which the ontological form of anxiety, curiously reflected in the grammatically equivalent expression "*for fear that*" (the lagging behind might engender error), seems to emerge.

This form is undoubtedly related to the logical originality of the subject of the assertion; that is why I characterize it as *subjective assertion*, the logical subject here being but the *personal* form of the knowing subject who can only be expressed by "*I*." Otherwise stated, the judgment which concludes the sophism can only be borne by a subject who has formulated the assertion about himself, and cannot be imputed to him unreservedly by anyone else—unlike the relations of the *impersonal* and *undefined reciprocal* subjects of the first two moments that are essentially transitive, since the personal subject of the logical movement assumes [*assume*] them at each of these moments.

The reference to these two subjects highlights the logical value of the subject of the assertion. The former, expressed in the "*one*" of the "*one knows*
208 *that* . . . ," provides only the general form of the noetic subject: he can as easily be god, table, or washbasin. The latter, expressed in "*the two whites*" who must recognize "*one another*," introduces the form of *the other as such*—that is, as pure reciprocity—since the one can only recognize himself in the other and only discover his own attribute in the equivalence of their characteristic time. The "*I*," subject of the conclusive assertion, is isolated from the other—that is, from the relation of reciprocity—by a logical *beat* [*battement de temps*]. This movement of the logical genesis of the *"I"* through a decanting of its own logical time largely parallels its psychological birth. Just as, let us recall, the psychological *"I"* emerges from an indeterminate specular transitivism, assisted by an awakened jealous tendency, the *"I"* in question here defines itself through a subjectification of *competition* with the other, in the function of logical time. As such, it seems to me to provide the essential logical form (rather than the so-called existential form) of the psychological "*I*."[3]

The essentially subjective ("*assertive*," in my terminology) value of the sophism's conclusion is attested to by how uncertain an observer (for example, the prison warden overseeing the game) would be, faced with the three subjects' simultaneous departure, in trying to decide whether any of them has correctly deduced the attribute he bears. For the subject has seized the moment of concluding that he is a white due to [*sous*] the *subjective* evidence of a lag-time which presses him on towards the exit, but even if he has not seized it, the *objective* evidence constituted by the others' departure leads him to act no differently: he leaves in step with them, convinced, however, that he is a black. All the observer can foresee is that if one of the three declares upon questioning that he is a black, having hastened to follow the other two, he will be the only one to do so in these terms.

The assertive judgment finally manifests itself here in an *act*. Modern

thought has shown that every judgment is essentially an act, and the dramatic contingencies here merely isolate this act in the subjects' departing movement. 209
One could imagine other means of expression for this act of concluding. What makes this act so remarkable in the subjective assertion demonstrated by the sophism is that it anticipates its own certainty owing to the temporal tension with which it is subjectively charged; and that, based on this very anticipation, its certainty is verified in a logical precipitation that is determined by the discharge of this tension—so that in the end the conclusion is no longer grounded on anything but completely objectified temporal instances, and the assertion is desubjectified to the utmost. As is demonstrated by what follows.

First of all, we witness the reappearance of the *objective time* of the initial intuition of the movement which, as though sucked up between the instant of its beginning and the haste of its end, had seemed to burst like a bubble. Owing to the force of doubt, which exfoliates the subjective certainty of the *moment of concluding*, objective time condenses here like a nucleus in the interval of the first *suspended motion*, and manifests to the subject its limit in the *time for comprehending* that, for the two others, the *instant of the glance* has passed and that the *moment of concluding* has returned.

While doubt has, since Descartes' time, been integrated into the value of judgment, it should certainly be noted that—for the form of assertion studied here—the latter's value depends less upon the doubt which suspends the assertion than on the *anticipated certainty* which first introduced it.

But in order to understand the function of this doubt for the subject of the assertion, let us consider the objective value of the first suspension for the observer whose attention we have already drawn to the subjects' overall motion. Although it may have been impossible up until this point to judge what any of them had concluded, we find that each of them manifests uncertainty about his conclusion, but will have it confirmed without fail if it was correct, rectified—perhaps—if it was erroneous.

Indeed, if any one of them is subjectively able to make the first move, but then stops, it is because he begins to doubt whether he has really grasped the *moment of concluding* that he is a white—but he will immediately grasp it anew since he has already experienced it subjectively. If, on the contrary, he let the others precede him and, in so doing, convince him that he is a black, he cannot doubt whether he has grasped the moment of concluding precisely because he has not *subjectively appropriated* it (and in effect he can even find in the others' new initiative logical confirmation of his belief that he differs 210
from them). If he stops, it is because he subordinates his own conclusion so thoroughly to that which manifests the others' conclusion that he immediately suspends his own when they seem to suspend theirs; thus he doubts whether

he is a black until they again show him the way, or he himself discovers it, concluding this time that he is a black or that he is a white—perhaps incorrectly, perhaps correctly—the point remaining impenetrable to everyone other than himself.

But the logical descent continues on towards the second temporal suspension. Each of the subjects, having reappropriated the subjective certainty of the *moment of concluding*, can once again call it into question. It is now sustained, however, by the already accomplished objectification of the *time for comprehending*, and its being called into question lasts but the *instant of the glance*; for the mere fact that this hesitation is not the others' first but rather their second, suffices to put an end to his own hesitation as soon as he perceives theirs, immediately indicating to him as it does that he is certainly not a black.

The subjective time of the *moment of concluding* is at last objectified here. This is proven by the fact that, even if any one of the subjects had not yet grasped it, it would nevertheless force itself upon him now; for this subject who would have concluded the first scansion by following the two others, convinced thereby that he was a black, would now—because of the present second scansion—be constrained to reverse his judgment.

With the termination of the logical assembling of the two suspended motions in the act in which they reach completion, the sophism's assertion of certainty is *desubjectified to the utmost.* As is shown by the fact that according to our observer, assuming he finds the suspended motions to be synchronous for the three subjects, all three of them will indubitably declare themselves white upon questioning.

Lastly, one can point out that at this same moment, if each subject can, when questioned, express, in the *subjective assertion* which has given him a certainty as the sophism's conclusion, the certainty he has finally verified—stating it in these terms:

> I hastened to conclude that I was a white, because otherwise they would
> have preceded me in reciprocally recognizing themselves to be whites
> (and had I given them the time to do so, they would have led me astray,
> 211 which would have been my undoing)

—he can also express this certainty, in its *verification* which has been *desubjectified* to the utmost in the logical movement, in the following terms:

> One must know that one is a white when the others have hesitated twice in leaving.

In its first form, this conclusion can be advanced as veritable by a subject once he has constituted the sophism's logical movement, but can as such only be assumed [*assumé*] personally by him; whereas in its second form, it requires the logical descent verifying the sophism to be consummated by all the subjects, although it remains applicable by any one of them to each of the others. It is not even ruled out that one, but only one, of the subjects might reach this second form without having constituted the sophism's logical movement, having simply followed its verification as manifested by the other two.

The Truth of the Sophism as Temporalized Reference of Oneself to Another: Anticipating Subjective Assertion as the Fundamental Form of a Collective Logic

The truth of the sophism thus only comes to be verified through its *presumption*, so to speak, in the assertion it constitutes. Its truth thus turns out to depend upon a tendency that aims at the truth—a notion that would be a logical paradox were it not reducible to the temporal tension that determines the moment of concluding.

Truth manifests itself in this form as preceding error and advancing solely in the act that engenders its certainty; error, conversely, manifests itself as being confirmed by its inertia and correcting itself only with difficulty by following truth's conquering initiative.

But to what sort of relation does such a logical form correspond? To a form of objectification engendered by the logical form in its movement—namely, the reference of an *"I"* to the common measure of the reciprocal subject, or otherwise stated, of others as such, that is, insofar as they are others for one another. This common measure is provided by a certain *time for comprehending*, which proves to be an essential function of the logical relationship of reciprocity. This reference of the *"I"* to others as such must, in each critical
moment, be temporalized in order to dialectically reduce the *moment of con-* 212
cluding the time for comprehending to last but the *instant of the glance*.

Only the slightest disparity need appear in the logical term "others" for it to become clear how much the truth for all depends upon the rigor of each; that truth—if reached by only some—can engender, if not confirm, error in the others; and, moreover, that if in this race to the truth one is but alone, although not all may get to the truth, still no one can get there but by means of the others.

These forms assuredly find easy application in bridge table and diplomatic strategy, not to mention in the handling of the "complex" in psychoanalytic practice.

Here, however, I would like to indicate their contribution to the logical notion of collectivity.

Tres faciunt collegium, as the adage goes, and the *collectivity* is already integrally represented in the form of the sophism, since the collectivity is defined as a group formed by the reciprocal relations of a definite number of individuals—unlike the *generality*, which is defined as a class abstractly including an indefinite number of individuals.

But it suffices to extend the sophism's proof by recurrence to see that it can be logically applied to an unlimited number of subjects,[4] it being stipulated that the "negative" attribute can only appear in a number equal to the num-
213 ber of subjects minus one.[5] But temporal objectification is more difficult to conceptualize as the collectivity grows, seeming to pose an obstacle to a *collective logic* with which one could complete classical logic.

I will nevertheless show what such a logic would have to furnish, faced with the inadequacy one senses in an assertion such as "I am a man," couched in whatever form of classical logic and derived as the conclusion from whatever premises one likes (for example, "man is a rational animal," etc.).

This assertion assuredly appears closer to its true value when presented as the conclusion of the form here demonstrated of anticipating subjective assertion:

(1) A man knows what is not a man;
(2) Men recognize themselves among themselves as men;
(3) I declare myself to be a man for fear of being convinced by men that I am not a man.

This movement provides the logical form of all "human" assimilation, precisely insofar as it posits itself as assimilative of a barbarism, but it nonetheless reserves the essential determination of the *"I"*. . .[6]

Notes

1. This infirmity applies no less to the minds formed by this tradition, as is evinced by the following note I received from an intellect—who is nevertheless adventurous in other fields—after a soirée at which the discussion of my fruitful sophism had provoked a veritable confusional panic amongst the select intellects of an intimate circle. Despite its opening words, the note bears the traces of a laborious restatement of the problem.

My dear Lacan, a hasty note to direct your attention to a new difficulty: the reasoning admitted yesterday is not truly conclusive, for none of the three possible states—000, 00●, or 0●●—is reducible to any of the others (appearances notwithstanding); only the last is decisive.

Consequence: when A assumes he is black, neither B nor C can leave, for they cannot deduce from their behavior whether they are black or white. For if one of them is black, the other leaves; and if, instead, the first is white, the other leaves anyway, because the first does not do so (and vice versa). If A assumes he is white, B and C cannot leave in this case either. The upshot being that, here too, A cannot deduce the color of his disk from the others' behavior.

My contradictor, in *seeing* the case too clearly, thus remained blind to the fact that it is not the others' departure, but rather their waiting, which determines the subject's judgment. And in order to hastily refute me, he allowed himself to overlook what I am trying to demonstrate here: the function of haste in logic.

2. "Irreducibles," as my contradictor in the previous footnote put it.

3. Thus the "*I*," third form of the subject of enunciation in logic, is here still the "first person," but also the only and last. For the grammatical second person is related to another function of language. As for the grammatical third person, it is only alleged: it is a demonstrative, which is equally applicable to the field of the enunciated and to everything distinguishable therein.

4. Here is the example for four subjects, four white disks, and three black ones:

A thinks that, if he were a black, any one of the others—B, C, or D—could surmise concerning the two others that, if he himself were black, they would waste no time realizing they are whites. Thus one of the others—B, C, or D—would quickly have to conclude that he himself is white, which does not happen. When A realizes that, if they—B, C, and D—see that he is a black, they have the advantage over him of not having to make a supposition about it, he hurries to conclude that he is a white.

But don't they all leave at the same time as him? A, in doubt, stops; and the others do too. But what does it mean if they all stop too? Either they stop because they fall prey to the same doubt as A, and A can thus race off again without worry. Or it is that A is black, and that one of the others (B, C, or D) has been led to wonder whether the departure of the other two does not in fact signify that he is a black, and to surmise that their stopping does not necessarily imply he is white—since either can still wonder for an instant whether he is not a black. Still this allows him [B, C, or D] to posit that they [reading *ils* (they) for *il* (he)] should both start up again before him if he is a black, and to start up again himself from this waiting in vain, assured of being what he is, that is, white. Why do B, C, and D not do it? Well if they do not, then I will, says A. So they all start up again.

Second stop. Assuming I am black, A says to himself, it must now dawn upon one of the others—B, C, or D—that, if he were a black, he could not impute to the other two this further hesitation; therefore he is white. B, C, and D should thus start up again before him [A]. Failing which, A starts up again, and all the others along with him.

Third stop. But all of them should know by now that they are whites if I am truly black, A says to himself. If they stop, then . . .

And the certainty is verified in three *suspensive scansions*.

5. [Added in 1966:] Compare the condition of this minus one in the attribute with the psychoanalytic function of the One-extra [*l'Un-en-plus*] in the subject of psychoanalysis (*Écrits* 1966, 480).

6. [Added in 1966:] The reader who continues on in this collection is advised to return to this reference to the collective, which constitutes the end of the present article, in order to situate what Freud produced in the field of collective psychology (*Massenpsychologie und Ich-Analyse*, 1920 [*Group Psychology and the Analysis of the Ego*]): the collective is nothing but the subject of the individual.

215

Presentation on Transference

Given at the 1951 Congress of
"Romance Language–Speaking Psychoanalysts"

My goal here again was to accustom people's ears to the term "subject." The person who provided me with this opportunity shall remain anonymous, which will spare me the task of mentioning all the passages in which I refer to him in what follows.

Were the question of the part Freud played in the case of Dora to be considered settled here, it would be the net profit of my efforts to reinitiate the study of transference when Daniel Lagache's paper by that name came out, his originality being to account for it by means of the Zeigarnik effect.[1] It was an idea that was designed to please at a time when psychoanalysis seemed to be running out of alibis.

When our colleague, who shall remain nameless, discretely retorted to Lagache that one could equally well find evidence of transference in this effect, I considered the time ripe to speak of psychoanalysis.

I have had to temper my expectations, since I also suggested a good deal here that I articulated later on the subject of transference. (1966)

By commenting that the Zeigarnik effect seems to depend on transference more than it determines it, my colleague, B., introduced what might be called aspects of resistance into this psychotechnical experiment. Their import is to highlight the primacy of the subject-to-subject relationship in all of an individual's reactions, inasmuch as they are human, and the dominance of this rela-
216 tionship in any test of individual dispositions, whether this test be defined by the conditions of a task or a situation.

What must be understood about psychoanalytic experience is that it proceeds entirely in this subject-to-subject relationship, which means that it preserves a dimension that is irreducible to any psychology considered to be the objectification of certain of an individual's properties.

Indeed, what happens in an analysis is that the subject, strictly speaking, is constituted through a discourse to which the mere presence of the psychoanalyst, prior to any intervention he may make, brings the dimension of dialogue.

Whatever irresponsibility, not to say incoherence, the conventions of the fundamental rule of psychoanalysis impose on the principle of this discourse, it is clear that they are merely a hydraulic engineer's artifices (see the case of Dora, p. 15),[2] intended to ensure the crossing of certain dams, and that the course must proceed according to the laws of a kind of gravitation that is peculiar to it, which is called truth. For "truth" is the name of the ideal movement that this discourse introduces into reality. In short, *psychoanalysis is a dialectical experience*, and this notion should prevail when raising the question of the nature of transference.

My sole design here will be to show, by means of an example, the kind of propositions to which this line of argument might lead. But first I will allow myself a few remarks that strike me as urgent for the present guidance of our work of theoretical elaboration, relating, as they do, to the responsibilities thrust upon us by our historical times and the tradition entrusted to our keeping.

Doesn't the fact that a dialectical conception of psychoanalysis has to be presented as an orientation peculiar to *my* way of thinking indicate misrecognition of an immediate given, and even of the commonsensical fact that psychoanalysis relies solely upon words? Must we not recognize, in the privileged attention paid to the function of the nonverbal aspects of behavior in the psychological maneuver, a preference on the part of the analyst for a vantage point from which the subject is no longer anything but an object? If, indeed, such misrecognition is occurring here, we must investigate it according to the meth- 217
ods we would apply in any other such case.

It is well known that I am inclined to think that, at the very moment when psychology, and with it all the human sciences, underwent a profound revamping of perspectives due to conceptions stemming from psychoanalysis (even if it was without their consent or even their knowledge), the opposite movement took place among analysts that I would describe in the following terms:

Whereas Freud assumed responsibility for showing us that there are illnesses that speak (unlike Hesiod, for whom the illnesses sent by Zeus come over men in silence) and for making us hear the truth of what they say, it seems that this truth inspires more fear in the practitioners who perpetuate this technique as its relation to a historical moment and an institutional crisis becomes clearer.

Thus, in any number of forms, ranging from pietism to ideals of the crudest efficiency, running the whole gamut of naturalist propaedeutics, they can be seen seeking refuge under the wing of a psychologism which, in reifying human beings, could lead to crimes next to which those of the physicist's scientism would pale.

For due to the very power of the forces exposed by analysis, nothing less than a new type of alienation of man will come into being, as much through the efforts of a collective belief as through the activity of selecting techniques with all the formative scope of rituals: in short, a *homo psychologicus*, the danger of which I am warning you against.

Will we allow ourselves to be fascinated by the fabrication of *homo psychologicus*? Or can we, by rethinking Freud's work, find anew the authentic meaning of his initiative and the means by which to maintain its salutary value?

Let me stress here, should there be any need to do so, that these questions are in no sense directed at the work of someone like my friend Lagache; the prudence of his method, the scrupulousness of his procedure, and the openness of his conclusions are all exemplary of the distance between our praxis and psychology. I will base my demonstration on the case of Dora, because of
218 what it stood for in the still new experience of transference, being the first case in which Freud recognized that the analyst plays a part.[3]

It is striking that heretofore no one has stressed that the case of Dora is laid out by Freud in the form of a series of dialectical reversals. This is not a mere contrivance for presenting material whose emergence is left up to the patient, as Freud clearly states here. What is involved is a scansion of structures in which truth is transmuted for the subject, structures that affect not only her comprehension of things, but her very position as a subject, her "objects" being a function of that position. This means that the conception of the case history is *identical* to the progress of the subject, that is, to the reality of the treatment.

Now, this is the first time Freud uses the term "transference" as the concept of the obstacle owing to which the analysis broke down. This alone gives the examination I will conduct here of the dialectical relations that constituted the moment of failure its value, at the very least, as a return to the source. I will attempt hereby *to define in terms of pure dialectic the transference* that is said to be negative on the part of the subject as the doing [*opération*] of the analyst who interprets it.

We shall, however, have to review all the phases that led up to this moment, and examine it in terms of the problematic anticipations which, in the facts of the case, indicate where it might have found a successful outcome. Thus we find:

A first development, which is exemplary in that it takes us straight to the level of the assertion of truth. For Dora, having tested Freud to see if he would prove to be as hypocritical as her father, begins her indictment by opening up a file full of memories whose rigor contrasts with the lack of biographical precision characteristic of neurosis: Frau K and her father have been lovers for so many years, and have been hiding it with what are at times ridiculous fictions; but what takes the cake is that Dora is thus offered up defenseless to Herr K's attentions, to which her father turns a blind eye, thus making her the object of an odious exchange.

219 Freud is far too wise to the constancy of the social lie to have been duped

by it, even from the mouth of a man he believes owes him the whole story. He therefore has no difficulty in removing from the patient's mind any imputation of complicity regarding this lie. But at the end of this development he finds himself faced with a question, which is classic in the first stages of treatment: "All of this is factual, being based on reality and not on my own will. What's to be done about it?" To which Freud replies with:

A first dialectical reversal, which in no wise pales next to Hegel's analysis of the claim made by the "beautiful soul" who rises up against the world in the name of the law of the heart: "Look at your own involvement," he tells her, "in the mess [*désordre*] you complain of" (p. 32).[4] What then appears is:

A second development of truth, namely, that it was not on the basis of Dora's mere silence, but of her complicity and even vigilant protection, that the fiction had been able to last which allowed the relationship between the two lovers to continue.

What can be seen here is not simply Dora's participation in Herr K's courtship of which she is the object; new light is shed on her relationship with the other partners of the quadrille by the fact that it is caught up in a subtle circulation of precious gifts, which serves to make up for a deficiency in sexual services. This circulation starts with her father in relation to Frau K, and then comes back to the patient through Herr K's consequent availability, in no way diminishing the lavish generosity which comes to her directly from the first source, by way of parallel gifts—this being the classic manner of making amends by which the bourgeois male manages to combine reparation due his lawful wedded wife with his concern for passing on an inheritance (note that the presence of the figure of the wife is reduced here to this lateral link in the chain of exchanges).

At the same time Dora's Oedipal relation turns out to be grounded in an identification with her father, which is fostered by his sexual impotence and is, moreover, experienced by Dora as identical to his supervalent status as rich; this is betrayed by the unconscious allusion Dora is allowed by the semantics
of the word "rich" [*fortune*] in German: *Vermögen*. Indeed, this identification 220
was apparent in all the conversion symptoms presented by Dora, a large number of which were removed by this discovery.

The following question then arises: In light of this, what is the meaning of the jealousy Dora suddenly shows toward her father's love affair? The fact that this jealousy presents itself in such a *supervalent* form calls for an explanation which goes beyond her [apparent] motives (p. 50).[5] Here takes place:

The second dialectical reversal, which Freud brings about by commenting that, far from the alleged object of jealousy providing her true motive, it conceals an interest in the rival-subject herself, an interest whose nature, since it is quite foreign to ordinary discourse, can only be expressed in it in this inverted form. This gives rise to:

A third development of truth: Dora's fascinated attachment to Frau K ("her adorable white body"), the confessions Dora received—how far they went shall remain unsounded—on the state of Frau K's relations with her husband, and the blatant fact of their exchanges of useful techniques as mutual ambassadors of their desires regarding Dora's father.

Freud glimpsed the question to which this new development was leading.

["]If, therefore, it is being dispossessed by this woman that makes you so bitter, how come you do not resent her for betraying you further by accusing you of intrigue and perversity, imputations which they all now believe when they accuse you of lying? What is the motive for this loyalty which makes you keep for her the deepest secret of your relations?["] (in other words, the sexual initiation, readily discernible in the very accusations made by Frau K). It is this very secret which brings us to:

The third dialectical reversal, the one that would reveal to us the real value of the object that Frau K is for Dora. Frau K is not an individual, but a mystery, the mystery of Dora's own femininity, by which I mean her bodily femininity—as it appears undisguised in the second of the two dreams whose study
221 makes up the second part of the case history, dreams I suggest you reread in order to see how greatly their interpretation is simplified by my commentary.

The boundary post we must go around in order to reverse course one last time already appears within reach. It is the most distant image that Dora retrieves from her early childhood (didn't all the keys always fall into Freud's hands, even in those cases that were broken off like this one?): that of Dora, probably still an infant, sucking her left thumb, while with her right hand she tugs at the ear of her brother, who is her elder by a year and a half (pp. 20 and 47).[6]

What we seem to have here is the imaginary mold in which all the situations orchestrated by Dora during her life came to be cast—a perfect illustration of the theory, yet to appear in Freud's work, of repetition automatisms. We can gauge in it what woman and man signify to her now.

Woman is the object which cannot be dissociated from a primitive oral desire, in which she must nevertheless learn to recognize her own genital nature. (It is surprising that Freud fails to see here that Dora's aphonia during Herr K's absences [p. 36][7] expressed the violent call of the oral erotic drive when Dora was left alone with Frau K, there being no need for him to assume she had seen her father receiving fellatio [p. 44],[8] when everyone knows that cunnilingus is the artifice most commonly adopted by "rich men" [*messieurs fortunés*] when their powers begin to fail them.) In order for her to gain access to this recognition of her femininity, she would have to assume [*assumer*] her own body, failing which she remains open to the functional fragmentation (to refer to the theoretical contribution of the mirror stage) that constitutes conversion symptoms.

Now, her only means for gaining this access was via her earliest imago, which shows us that the only path open to her to the object was via the masculine partner, with whom, because of their difference in age, she was able to identify, in that primordial identification through which the subject recognizes herself as *I* . . .

Hence Dora identified with Herr K, just as she was in the process of iden- 222
tifying with Freud himself (the fact that it was upon waking from her "transference" dream that Dora noticed the smell of smoke associated with the two men is not indicative, as Freud says [p. 67],[9] of some more deeply repressed identification, but rather of the fact that this hallucination corresponded to the twilight stage of the return to the ego). And all her dealings with the two men manifest the aggressiveness in which we see the dimension characteristic of narcissistic alienation.

Thus it is true, as Freud thinks, that the return to a passionate complaint about the father represents a regression when compared with the relations that had begun to develop with Herr K.

But this homage, whose beneficial value for Dora was glimpsed by Freud, could be received by her as a manifestation of desire only if she could accept herself as an object of desire—that is, only once she had exhausted the meaning of what she was looking for in Frau K.

As is true for all women, and for reasons that are at the very crux of the most elementary social exchanges (the very exchanges Dora names as the grounds for her revolt), the problem of her condition is fundamentally that of accepting herself as a man's object of desire, and this is the mystery that motivates Dora's idolization of Frau K. In her long meditation before the Madonna and in her recourse to the role of distant worshipper, this mystery drives Dora toward the solution Christianity has offered for this subjective impasse by making woman the object of a divine desire or a transcendent object of desire, which amounts to the same thing.

If, therefore, in a third dialectical reversal, Freud had directed Dora towards a recognition of what Frau K was for her, by getting her to confess the deepest secrets of their relationship, wouldn't that have contributed to his prestige (I am merely touching on the question of the meaning of positive transference here), opening up the path to her recognition of the virile object? This is not my opinion, but rather Freud's (p. 107).[10]

But the fact that his failure to do so was fatal to the treatment is attributed

by Freud to the action of the transference (pp. 103–7),[11] to his error that makes him put off the interpretation thereof (p. 106),[12] when, as he was able to ascer-
223 tain after the fact, he had only two hours left to sidestep its effects (p. 106).[13]

But each time he proffers this explanation—whose subsequent development in analytic doctrine is well known—a footnote provides recourse to another explanation: his inadequate appreciation of the homosexual tie binding Dora to Frau K.

What does this mean if not that the second reason only struck him truly as the most crucial in 1923, whereas the first bore fruit in his thinking beginning in 1905, the year the Dora case study was published?

Which side should we choose? Surely that of believing both accounts and attempting to grasp what can be deduced from their synthesis.

What we then find is this: Freud admits that for a long time he was unable to face this homosexual tendency (which he nonetheless tells us is so constant in hysterics that its subjective role cannot be overestimated) without falling into a state of distress (p. 107, note)[14] that rendered him incapable of dealing with it satisfactorily.

I would say that this has to be ascribed to a bias, the very same bias that falsifies the conception of the Oedipus complex right from the outset, making him consider the predominance of the paternal figure to be natural, rather than normative—the same bias that is expressed simply in the well-known refrain, "Thread is to needle as girl is to boy."

Freud has felt kindly toward Herr K for a long time, since it was Herr K who brought Dora's father to Freud (p. 18),[15] and this comes out in numerous comments he makes (p. 27, note).[16] After the treatment founders, Freud persists in dreaming of a "victory of love" (p. 99).[17]

Freud admits to his personal investment in Dora, interesting him as she does, at many points in the account. The truth of the matter is that she brings the whole case alive in a way which, vaulting the theoretical digressions, elevates this text, among the psychopathological monographs that constitute a genre in our literature, to the tone of a Princesse de Clèves bound by an infernal gag.

224 It is because he put himself rather too much in Herr K's shoes that Freud did not succeed in moving the Infernal Regions this time around.

Due to his countertransference, Freud harps too often on the love Herr K supposedly inspired in Dora, and it is odd to see how he always interprets Dora's very varied retorts as though they were confessions. The session when he thinks he has reduced her to "no longer contradicting him" (p. 93)[18] and at the end of which he believes he can express his satisfaction to her, Dora in fact concludes on a very different note. "Why, has anything so very remarkable come out?" she says, and it is at the beginning of the next session that she [announces that she is going to] take leave of him.

What thus happened during the scene of the lakeside declaration, the catastrophe which drove Dora to illness, leading everyone to recognize her as ill—this, ironically, being their response to her refusal to continue to serve as a prop for their common infirmity (not all the "gains" of a neurosis work solely to the advantage of the neurotic)?

As in any valid interpretation, we need but stick to the text in order to understand it. Herr K could only get in a few words, decisive though they were: "My wife is nothing to me." His reward for this feat was instantaneous—a hard slap (whose burning after-effects Dora felt long after the treatment had ended in the form of a transitory neuralgia) quipped back to the blunderer, "If she is nothing to you, then what are you to me?"

What then would he be to her, this puppet who had nonetheless just broken the spell she had been living under for years?

The latent pregnancy fantasy that followed this scene does not invalidate my interpretation, since it is well known that it occurs in hysterics precisely as a function of their identification with men.

It is through the very same trap door that Freud disappears, with a still more insidious sliding. Dora leaves with a *Mona Lisa* smile and even when she reappears, Freud is not so naïve as to believe she intends to resume her analysis.

By that time, she has gotten everyone to recognize the truth which, as truthful as it may be, she nevertheless knows does not constitute the final truth; and she has managed through the mere *mana* of her presence to precipitate the 225
unfortunate Herr K under the wheels of a carriage. The subsidence of her symptoms, which had been brought about during the second phase of the treatment, did last, nevertheless. Thus the arrest of the dialectical process resulted in an apparent retreat, but the positions recaptured could only be held by an affirmation of the ego, which can be considered progress.

What then is this transference whose work, Freud states somewhere, goes on *invisibly* behind the progress of the treatment and whose effects, furthermore, are "not susceptible of definite proof" (p. 67)?[19] Can it not be considered here to be an entity altogether related to countertransference, defined as the sum total of the analyst's biases, passions, and difficulties, or even of his inadequate information, at any given moment in the dialectical process? Doesn't Freud himself tell us (p. 105)[20] that Dora might have transferred the paternal figure onto him, had he been foolish enough to believe the version of things her father had presented to him?

In other words, transference is nothing real in the subject if not the appearance, at a moment of stagnation in the analytic dialectic, of the permanent modes according to which she constitutes her objects.

What then does it mean to interpret transference? Nothing but to fill the emptiness of this standstill with a lure. But even though it is deceptive, this lure serves a purpose by setting the whole process in motion anew.

The denial [*dénégation*] with which Dora would have greeted any suggestion by Freud that she was imputing to him the same intentions as those that Herr K had displayed, would not in any way have changed the scope of the suggestion's effects. The very opposition to which it would have given rise would probably, despite Freud, have set Dora off in the right direction: the one that would have led her to the object of her real interest.

And to have set himself up personally as a substitute for Herr K would have spared Freud from overemphasizing the value of Herr K's marriage proposals.

Thus transference does not fall under any mysterious property of affectivity and, even when it reveals itself in an emotional [*émoi*] guise, this guise has a meaning only as a function of the dialectical moment at which it occurs.

But this moment is of no great significance since it normally signals an error
226 on the analyst's part, if only that of wanting what is good for the patient to too great an extent, a danger Freud warned against on many occasions.

Thus analytic neutrality derives its authentic meaning from the position of the pure dialectician who, knowing that all that is real is rational (and vice versa), knows that all that exists, including the evil against which he struggles, is and shall always be equivalent to the level of its particularity, and that the subject only progresses through the integration he arrives at of his position into the universal: technically speaking, through the projection of his past into a discourse in the process of becoming.

The case of Dora is especially relevant for demonstrating this in that, since it involves an hysteric, the screen of the ego is transparent enough for there never to be, as Freud said, a lower threshold between the unconscious and the conscious, or better, between analytic discourse and the *key* [*mot*] to the symptom.

I believe, however, that transference always has the same meaning of indicating the moments where the analyst goes astray and takes anew his bearings, and the same value of reminding us of our role: that of a positive nonaction aiming at the ortho-dramatization of the patient's subjectivity.

Notes

1. In short, this consists of the psychological effect produced by an unfinished task when it leaves a gestalt in abeyance—for instance, that of the generally felt need to resolve a musical phrase.

2. PUF, 8; *SE* VII, 16 [Lacan explains his ref-

erence format in the next footnote].

3. So that the reader can verify the verbatim character of my commentary, wherever I refer to Freud's case study I provide references to the Denoël edition [*Cinq psychanalyses*, translated by Marie Bonaparte and Rudolf Loewenstein (Paris: Denoël & Steele, 1935)] in the text and to the 1954 Presses Universitaires de France edition [*Cinq psychanalyses*, revised by Anne Berman (Paris: PUF, 1954)] in the footnotes. [The translator has added the corresponding references to volume VII of the *Standard Edition*.]

4. PUF, 23–24; *SE* VII, 34–36.

5. PUF, 39; *SE* VII, 54.

6. PUF, 12 and 37; *SE* VII, 21 and 51.

7. PUF, 27; *SE* VII, 39–40.

8. PUF, 33; *SE* VII, 47–48.

9. PUF, 54; *SE* VII, 73–74.

10. PUF, 90 [footnote 1]; *SE* VII, 120, footnote 1.

11. PUF, 86–90; *SE* VII, 115–20.

12. PUF, 89; *SE* VII, 118–19.

13. PUF, 89; *SE* VII, 118–19.

14. PUF, 90 [footnote 1]; *SE* VII, 120, footnote 1.

15. PUF, 11; *SE* VII, 19.

16. PUF, 19 [footnote 1]; *SE* VII, 29, footnote 3.

17. PUF, 82; *SE* VII, 109–10.

18. PUF, 77–78; *SE* VII, 103–5.

19. PUF, 54; *SE* VII, 74.

20. PUF, 88; *SE* VII, 118–19.

IV

On the Subject Who Is Finally in Question

Including a whiff of enthusiasm in a written text utterly ensures that it will become dated, in the regrettable sense of the term. Let us regret this as regards my Rome discourse ["Function and Field of Speech and Language"], which immediately became dated, the circumstances I mentioned in it leading to nothing that attenuated the problem.

In publishing it, I assumed it would be of interest to read, misunderstanding and all.

Even in wishing to be cautious, I will not redouble its original address (to the Congress) with an "address to the reader," when the constant feature—which I mentioned at the outset—of my address to psychoanalysts culminated here in being adapted to a group that called upon me for help.

Instead, my parry [*parade*] will be to redouble its interest, assuming that unveiling what commands it, whether the subject is conscious of this or not, does not divide that interest.

I wish to speak of the subject called into question by this discourse, when putting him back into his place here—from the point where I, for my part, have not failed him—is simply to honor the place where he asked us to meet him.

I will no longer do anything for the reader henceforth—apart from pointing out, a little further on, the aim of my Seminar—but trust in his tête-à-tête with texts that are certainly no easier, but that are intrinsically situable.

Meta, the post that marks the turning point to be approached as closely as possible in a race, is the metaphor I will give him as a viaticum in reminding him of the new [*inédit*] discourse I have been pronouncing every Wednesday of the academic year since that time, whose circulation elsewhere he may possibly attend to (if he does not attend in person).

Regarding the subject who is called into question, training analysis will be my point of departure. As we know, this is the name for a psychoanalysis
230 that one proposes to undertake for the purpose of training—especially as an element in qualifying to practice psychoanalysis.

When a psychoanalysis is specified by such a request [*demande*] [made by a potential analysand to an analyst], the supposedly ordinary parameters of analysis are considered to be modified, and the analyst thinks that he must deal with that.

Accepting to conduct an analysis under such conditions brings with it a responsibility. It is curious to note how that responsibility is displaced onto the guarantees that one derives from it.

For the unexpected baptism received by that which proposes to undertake training, in the form of a "personal psychoanalysis"[1] (as if there were any other form of analysis)—assuming that in it things are brought back to the uninviting point desired—does not seem to me to in any way concern what the proposal leads to in the subject whom we welcome in this way, in sum, neglecting that "personal analysis."

Perhaps we will see more clearly if we purify the said subject of his preoccupations, which can be summarized with the term "propaganda": the ranks of analysts which must be swelled, the faith which must be propagated, and the standard which must be protected.

Let us extract from this the subject who is implied by the request [*demande*] in which he presents himself. The reader will take a step forward if he notes here that the unconscious gives him a poor basis upon which to reduce this subject to what the realm of precision instrumentation designates as "subjective error"—assuming he is prepared to add that psychoanalysis does not have the privilege of a more consistent subject, but must rather allow us to shed light on him in the avenues of other disciplines as well.

This ambitious approach would unduly distract us from acknowledging what we in fact argue on the basis of: namely, the subject whom we qualify (and significantly so) as a patient, which is not the subject as strictly implied by his request [*demande*], but rather the product that we would like to see determined by it.

In other words, we obscure the picture in the very process of painting it. In the name of this patient, our listening too will be patient. It is for his own good that techniques are elaborated so we will know how to measure the aid we provide. The point is to make the psychoanalyst capable of this patience and measurement. But, after all, the uncertainty that remains regarding the very end of analysis has the effect of leaving between the patient and the subject that we append to him only the difference, promised to the second, of repeating the experience [with patients of his own], it even being legitimated that their theoretical equivalence is fully main- 231
tained in the countertransference. How then could training analysis constitute a problem?

I have no negative intention in preparing this balance sheet. I am simply pointing out the way things are—a situation in which we find many opportune remarks, a permanent calling into question of technique, and often odd glows in the enthusiasm of avowing—in short, a richness which can certainly be understood as the fruit of the relativism that is characteristic of our discipline and that provides it with its guarantee.

Even the objection that stems from the total absence of discussion of the end of training analysis can go unheeded given the unquestionable nature of the usual routine.

Only the never broached question of the threshold that must be reached in order for a psychoanalyst to be promoted to the rank of "training analyst" (where the criterion of seniority is derisory) reminds us that it is the subject in question in training analysis who poses a problem and who remains an intact subject there.

Shouldn't we, rather, conceptualize training analysis as the perfect form which sheds light on analysis itself, since it provides a restriction to it?

Such is the reversal that never occurred to anyone before I mentioned it. It seems to force itself upon us, nevertheless. For while psychoanalysis has a specific field, the concern with therapeutic results justifies short-circuits and even tempering modifications within it; but if there is one case in which all such reductions are prohibited, it must be training analysis.

Should someone claim that I am maintaining that the training of analysts is what psychoanalysis is most justified in doing, he would be barking up the wrong tree. For such insolence, were it such, would not implicate psychoanalysts. Rather, it would point to a certain gap in civilization that must be filled, but which is not yet clearly enough discerned for anyone to boast that he has taken it upon himself to do so.

Only a theory that is capable of grounding psychoanalysis in a way that preserves its relationship to science can pave the way for this.

It is obvious that psychoanalysis was born from science. It is inconceivable that it could have arisen from another field.

It is no accident but rather a consequence that in those circles where psychoanalysis distinguishes itself by remaining Freudian, it is considered self-evident that psychoanalysis has no other support than that of science and that there is no possible transition to psychoanalysis from the realm
232 of the esoteric, by which practices that seem to be similar to psychoanalysis are structured.

How then can we account for the obvious misunderstandings that abound in the conceptualizations in vogue in established circles? Regardless of how their creations are slapped together—from the supposed feelings of unity, where, at the height of the treatment the bliss that we are led to believe inaugurates libidinal development is found anew, to the much-ballyhooed miracles obtained by reaching genital maturity, with its sublime ability to join in all regressions—we can recognize in them the mirage which is not even debated: the completeness of the subject. People even formally take such completeness as a goal which should in theory be reachable, even if in practice infirmity—attributable to the technique or to the aftermath of the patient's history—requires that it remain an overly distant ideal.

Such is the crux of the theoretical extravagance, in the strict sense of the term, into which we see that anyone can fall, from the most authentic explorer of the analyst's therapeutic responsibility to the most rigorous examiner of analytic concepts. This can be confirmed regarding the paragon I mentioned first, Ferenczi, in his biological delusion about *amphimixis*; and in the second case, where I was thinking of Jones, it can be gauged in the latter's phenomenological *faux pas*, the *aphanisis* of desire, to which he was led by his need to ensure the equal rights of the sexes with respect to castration—that scandalous fact that can only be accepted by giving up on [the idea of] the subject's completeness.

Next to these illustrious examples, we are less surprised by the profusion of economic recenterings to which each theorist gives himself over, extrapolating from the treatment to development, and even to human history—for example, transferring the fantasy of castration back onto the anal phase, or basing everything on a universal oral neurosis . . . without any assignable limit to his . . . etc. At best it can be taken as evidence of what I will call the naïveté of personal perversion, the thing being understood to give way to some illumination.

I am not referring here to the inanity of the term "personal analysis," about which one can say that all too often what it designates is as inane as the term itself, being sanctioned only by highly practical rearrangements. Whence rearises the question of the benefit this curious fabrication offers.

The practitioner who is not inveterate is probably not insensitive to a 233
reality that has been rendered more nostalgic by rising up to meet him, and he responds in this case to the essential relationship between the veil and his experience with myth-like sketches.

A fact prevents us from qualifying these sketches as myths, for what we see in psychoanalysis are not authentic myths (by which I simply mean those that are found in the field), which never fail to leave visible the subject's decompletion, but folklore-like fragments of these myths, and precisely those that have been used by propaganda religions in their themes of salvation. This fact will be contested by those whose truth is hidden by these themes, who are all too happy to find in them corroboration for their truth on the basis of what they call "hermeneutics."

(A healthy reform of spelling would allow us to give their exploitation of this term the import of a famillionaire practice: that of the faux-filosopher, for example, or of fuzzyosophy, without adding any more dots or i's.)

Their radical vice can be seen in [their approach to] the transmission of knowledge. At best this transmission could be defended by comparing psychoanalysis to those trades in which, for centuries, transmission occurred only in a veiled manner, maintained by the institution of apprenticeship and guild [*compagnonnage*]. A master's in the art and different ranks protect therein the secret of a substantial knowledge. (It is, nevertheless, the liberal arts, which do not practice the arcane, that I will refer to later in evoking the youth of psychoanalysis.)

The comparison does not hold up, no matter how slight it may be. This is so clear that one might say that reality itself is designed in such a way as to reject this comparison, since what it requires is an entirely different position of the subject.

The theory—or rather the hackneyed views that go by this name, the formulations of which are so variable that it sometimes seems that the only thing they have in common is their insipid character—is merely the filling of a locus in which a deficiency can be demonstrated without our even knowing how to formulate it.

I propose an algebra that tries to correspond, in the place thus defined, to what the sort of logic that is known as symbolic does when it establishes the rights of mathematical practice.

I realize full well how much prudence and care are required to do so.

All I can say here is that it is important to preserve the availability of

the experience acquired by the subject—in the characteristic structure of
234 displacement and splitting in which that experience had to be constituted—referring the reader to my actual discussions of this topic.

What I must stress here is that I claim to pave the way for the scientific position of psychoanalysis by analyzing in what way it is already implied at the very heart of the psychoanalytic discovery.

The reform of the subject that is inaugural in psychoanalysis must be related to the reform that occurs at the core of science, the latter involving a certain reprieve from ambiguous questions that one might call questions of truth.

It is difficult not to see that, even before the advent of psychoanalysis, a dimension that might be called that of the symptom was introduced, which was articulated on the basis of the fact that it represents the return of truth as such into the gap of a certain knowledge.

I am not referring to the classical problem of error, but rather to a concrete manifestation that must be appreciated "clinically," in which we find not a failure of representation but a truth of another reference than the one, whether representation or not, whose fine order it manages to disturb . . .

In this sense, one can say that this dimension is highly differentiated in Marx's critique, even if it is not made explicit there. And one can say that a part of the reversal of Hegel that he carries out is constituted by the return (which is a materialist return, precisely insofar as it gives it figure and body) of the question of truth. The latter actually forces itself upon us, I would go so far as to say, not by taking up the thread of the ruse of reason, a subtle form with which Hegel sends it packing, but by upsetting these ruses (read Marx's political writings) which are merely dressed up with reason . . .

I am aware of the precision with which it is fitting to accompany this theme of truth and its detour [*biais*] in knowledge—which is nevertheless the crux, it seems to me, of philosophy as such.

I am only mentioning it in order to point out the leap made by Freud therein.

Freud sets himself apart from the rest by clearly linking the status of the symptom to the status of his own operation, for the Freudian operation is the symptom's proper operation, in the two senses of the term.

Unlike a sign—or smoke which is never found in the absence of fire, a fire that smoke indicates with the possible call to put it out—a symptom can only be interpreted in the signifying order. A signifier has meaning
235 only through its relation to another signifier. The truth of symptoms

resides in this articulation. Symptoms remained somewhat vague when they were understood as representing some irruption of truth. In fact they *are* truth, being made of the same wood from which truth is made, if we posit materialistically that truth is what is instated on the basis of the signifying chain.

I would like to distinguish myself from the level of joking around at which certain theoretical debates ordinarily occur.

I will do so by asking how we are supposed to take what smoke, since that is the classical paradigm, proposes to our gaze when it billows out of crematorium furnaces.

I do not doubt that people will agree that we can take it only in terms of its signifying value; and that even if we were to refuse to be dumbfounded by the criterion here, this smoke would remain for the materialist reduction an element that is less metaphorical than all the smoke that could be stirred up in debating whether what it represents should be broached from a biological or a social standpoint.

By taking one's bearings from the joint between the consequences of language and the desire for knowledge—a joint that the subject is—perhaps the paths will become more passable regarding what has always been known about the distance that separates the subject from his existence as a sexed being, not to mention as a living being.

And, indeed, the construction that I provide of the subject in following the thread of Freudian experience removes none of the personal poignancy from the several displacements and splits he may have to undergo in the course of his training analysis.

If his training analysis registers the resistances he has overcome, it is insofar as they fill the space of defense in which the subject is organized; it is only on the basis of certain structural reference points that one can pinpoint the trajectory he is following, in order to outline its exhaustion.

Similarly, a certain order of construction can be required regarding what must be attained by way of what fundamentally screens the real in the unconscious fantasy.

All of these verification values will not stop castration—which is the key to the subject's radical dodge [*biais*] by which the symptom comes into being—from remaining, even in a training analysis, the enigma that the subject resolves only by avoiding it.

At least if some order—being established in what he has experienced—later gave him responsibility for his statements, he would not try to reduce to the anal phase that aspect of castration that he grasped in the [fundamental] fantasy.

In other words, analytic experience would be protected from sanc-
236 tioning theoretical orientations that are likely to lead to the derailing of its transmission.

The status of training analysis and of the teaching of psychoanalysis must be understood anew to be identical in their scientific openness.

The latter involves, like any other teaching, minimal conditions: a defined relationship to the instrument as an instrument and a certain idea of the question raised by the material. The fact that the two converge here in a question, which is not thereby simplified, nevertheless, will perhaps close this other question with which psychoanalysis redoubles the first, in the form of a question posed to science, by constituting a science by itself which is raised to the second power [*au second degré*].

Should the reader be surprised that I am raising this question so late in the game—and with the same temperament which is such that it required two of the most improbable echoes of my teaching to receive from two college students in the United States the careful (and successful) translation that two of my articles (including "Function and Field") deserved—he should realize that my top priority was that there first be psychoanalysts.

At least I can now be happy that as long as there is still some trace of what I have instituted, there will be *some* psychoanalyst [*du psychanalyste*] who responds to certain subjective emergencies, should qualifying *them* with the definite article be saying too much, or else still desiring too much.

1966

Note

1. A means by which people avoid having to decide at first whether a psychoanalysis will or will not be a training analysis.

The Function and Field of Speech and Language in Psychoanalysis

Paper delivered at the Rome Congress held at the Institute of Psychology at the University of Rome on September 26 and 27, 1953

Preface

> In particular, it should not be forgotten that the division into embryology, anatomy, physiology, psychology, sociology, and clinical work does not exist in nature and that there is only one discipline: a *neurobiology* to which observation obliges us to add the epithet *human* when it concerns us.
>
> —Quotation chosen as an inscription for a psychoanalytic institute in 1952

The talk included here warrants an introduction that provides some context, since it was marked by its context.

The theme of this talk was proposed to me and my contribution was intended to constitute the customary theoretical paper given at the annual meeting that the association representing psychoanalysis in France at that time had held for eighteen years, a venerable tradition known as the "Congress of French-Speaking Psychoanalysts," though for the past two years it had been extended to Romance-language-speaking psychoanalysts (Holland being included out of linguistic tolerance). The Congress was to take place in Rome in September of 1953.

In the meantime, serious disagreements led to a secession within the French group. These disagreements came out on the occasion of the founding of a "psychoanalytic institute." The team that succeeded in imposing its statutes and program on the new institute was then heard to proclaim that it would prevent the person who, along with others, had tried to introduce a different conception of analysis from speaking in Rome, and it employed every means in its power to do so.

238 Yet it did not seem to those who thus founded the new Société Française de Psychanalyse that they had to deprive the majority of the students, who had rallied to their teaching, of the forthcoming event, or even to hold it elsewhere than in the eminent place in which it had been planned to be held.

The generous fellow feeling that had been shown them by the Italian group meant that they could hardly be regarded as unwelcome guests in the Universal City.

For my part, I considered myself assisted—however unequal I might prove to be to the task of speaking about speech—by a certain complicity inscribed in the place itself.

Indeed, I recalled that, well before the glory of the world's loftiest throne had been established, Aulus Gellius, in his *Noctes Atticae*, attributed to the place called *Mons Vaticanus* the etymology *vagire*, which designates the first stammerings of speech.

If, then, my talk was to be nothing more than a newborn's cry, at least it would seize the auspicious moment to revamp the foundations our discipline derives from language.

Moreover, this revamping derived too much meaning from history for me not to break with the traditional style—that places a "paper" somewhere between a compilation and a synthesis—in order to adopt an ironic style suitable to a radical questioning of the foundations of our discipline.

Since my audience was to be the students who expected me to speak, it was above all with them in mind that I composed this talk, and for their sake that I dispensed with the rules, observed by our high priests, requiring one to mime rigor with meticulousness and confuse rule with certainty.

Indeed, in the conflict that led to the present outcome, people had shown such an exorbitant degree of misrecognition regarding the students' autonomy as subjects that the first requirement was to counteract the constant tone that had permitted this excess.

The fact is that a vice came to light that went well beyond the local circumstances that led to the conflict. The very fact that one could claim to regulate the training of psychoanalysts in so authoritarian a fashion raised the question whether the established modes of such training did not paradoxically result in perpetual minimization.

239 The initiatory and highly organized forms which Freud considered to be a guarantee of his doctrine's transmission are certainly justified by the situation of a discipline that can only perpetuate itself by remaining at the level of a complete experience.

But haven't these forms led to a disappointing formalism that discourages initiative by penalizing risk, and turns the reign of the opinion of the learned into a principle of docile prudence in which the authenticity of research is blunted even before it finally dries up?

The extreme complexity of the notions brought into play in our field is such that in no other area does a mind run a greater risk, in laying bare its judgment, of discovering its true measure.

But this ought to result in making it our first, if not only, concern to emancipate theses by elucidating principles.

The severe selection that is, indeed, required cannot be left to the endless postponements of a fastidious cooptation, but should be based on the fecundity of concrete production and the dialectical testing of contradictory claims.

This does not imply that I particularly value divergence. On the contrary, I was surprised to hear, at the London International Congress—where, because we had failed to follow the prescribed forms, we had come as appellants—a personality well disposed toward us deplore the fact that we could not justify our secession on the grounds of some doctrinal disagreement. Does this mean that an association that is supposed to be international has some other goal than that of maintaining the principle of the collective nature of our experience?

It is probably no big secret that it has been eons since this was the case, and it was without creating the slightest scandal that, to the impenetrable Mr. Zilboorg—who, making ours a special case, insisted that no secession should be accepted unless it is based on a scientific dispute—the penetrating Mr. Wälder could reply that, if we were to challenge the principles in which each of us believes his experience is grounded, our walls would very quickly dissolve into the confusion of Babel.

To my way of thinking, if I innovate, I prefer not to make a virtue of it.

In a discipline that owes its scientific value solely to the theoretical concepts Freud hammered out as his experience progressed—concepts which, because they continue to be poorly examined and nevertheless retain the ambiguity of everyday language, benefit from the latter's resonances while incur- 240
ring misunderstanding—it would seem to me to be premature to break with the traditional terminology.

But it seems to me that these terms can only be made clearer if we establish their equivalence to the current language of anthropology, or even to the latest problems in philosophy, fields where psychoanalysis often need but take back its own property.

In any case, I consider it to be an urgent task to isolate, in concepts that are being deadened by routine use, the meaning they recover when we reexamine their history and reflect on their subjective foundations.

That, no doubt, is the teacher's function—the function on which all the others depend—and the one in which the value of experience figures best.

If this function is neglected, the meaning of an action whose effects derive solely from meaning is obliterated, and the rules of analytic technique, being reduced to mere recipes, rob analytic experience of any status as knowledge [*connaissance*] and even of any criterion of reality.

For no one is less demanding than a psychoanalyst when it comes to what gives his actions their status, which he himself is not far from regarding as magical because he doesn't know where to situate them in a conception of his field that he hardly dreams of reconciling with his practice.

The epigraph with which I have adorned this preface is a rather fine example of this.

Doesn't his conception of his field correspond to a conception of analytic training that is like that of a driving school which, not content to claim the unique privilege of issuing drivers' licenses, also imagines that it is in a position to supervise car construction?

Whatever this comparison may be worth, it is just as valid as those which are bandied about in our most serious conventicles and which, because they originated in our discourse to idiots, do not even have the savor of inside jokes, but seem to gain currency nevertheless due to their pompous ineptitude.

They begin with the well-known comparison between the candidate who allows himself to be prematurely dragged into practicing analysis and the surgeon who operates without sterilizing his instruments, and they go on to the comparison that brings tears to one's eyes for those unfortunate students who
241 are torn by their masters' conflicts just like children torn by their parents' divorce.

This late-born comparison seems to me to be inspired by the respect due to those who have, in effect, been subjected to what, toning down my thought, I will call a pressure to teach, which has put them sorely to the test; but on hearing the quavering tones of the masters, one may also wonder whether the limits of childishness have not, without warning, been stretched to the point of foolishness.

Yet the truths contained in these clichés are worthy of more serious examination.

As a method based on truth and demystification of subjective camouflage, does psychoanalysis display an incommensurate ambition to apply its principles to its own corporation—that is, to psychoanalysts' conception of their role in relation to the patient, their place in intellectual society, their relations with their peers, and their educational mission?

Perhaps, by reopening a few windows to the broad daylight of Freud's thought, my paper will allay the anguish some people feel when a symbolic action becomes lost in its own opacity.

Whatever the case may be, in referring to the context of my talk, I am not trying to blame its all too obvious shortcomings on the haste with which it was written, since both its meaning and its form derive from that same haste.

Moreover, in an exemplary sophism involving intersubjective time, I have shown the function of haste in logical precipitation, where truth finds its unsurpassable condition.[1]

Nothing created appears without urgency; nothing in urgency fails to surpass itself in speech.

Nor is there anything that does not become contingent here when the time comes when a man can identify in a single reason the side he takes and the disorder he denounces, in order to understand their coherence in reality [*réel*] and anticipate by his certainty the action that weighs them against each other.

Introduction 242

> We shall determine this while we are still at the aphelion of our matter, for, when we arrive at the perihelion, the heat is liable to make us forget it.
> —Lichtenberg

> "Flesh composed of suns. How can such be?" exclaim the simple ones.
> —R. Browning, *Parleying with Certain People*

Such is the fright that seizes man when he discovers the true face of his power that he turns away from it in the very act—which is his act—of laying it bare. This is true in psychoanalysis. Freud's Promethean discovery was such an act, as his work attests; but that act is no less present in each psychoanalytic experience humbly conducted by any one of the workers trained in his school.

One can trace over the years a growing aversion regarding the functions of speech and the field of language. It is responsible for the "changes in aim and technique" that are acknowledged within the psychoanalytic movement, and whose relation to the general decline in therapeutic effectiveness is nevertheless ambiguous. Indeed, the emphasis on the object's resistance in current psychoanalytic theory and technique must itself be subjected to the dialectic of analysis, which can but recognize in this emphasis the attempt to provide the subject with an alibi.

Let me try to outline the topography of this movement. If we examine the literature that we call our "scientific activity," the current problems of psychoanalysis clearly fall into three categories:

(A) The function of the imaginary, as I shall call it, or, to put it more directly, of fantasies in the technique of psychoanalytic experience and in the constitution of the object at the different stages of psychical development. The impetus in this area has come from the analysis of children and from the favorable field offered to researchers' efforts and temptations by the preverbal structurations approach. This is also where its culmination is now inducing a return by raising the question of what symbolic sanction is to be attributed to fantasies in their interpretation.

243 (B) The concept of libidinal object relations which, by renewing the idea of treatment progress, is quietly altering the way treatment is conducted. The new perspective began here with the extension of psychoanalytic method to the psychoses and with the momentary receptiveness of psychoanalytic technique to data based on a different principle. Psychoanalysis leads here to an existential phenomenology—indeed, to an activism motivated by charity. Here, too, a clear-cut reaction is working in favor of a return to symbolization as the crux of technique.

(C) The importance of countertransference and, correlatively, of analytic training. Here the emphasis has resulted from the difficulties related to the termination of analytic treatment that intersect the difficulties related to the moment at which training analysis ends with the candidate beginning to practice. The same oscillation can be observed here: On the one hand, the analyst's being is said, not without audacity, to be a non-negligible factor in the effects of an analysis and even a factor whose conduct should be brought out into the open at the end of the game; on the other hand, it is put forward no less energetically that a solution can come only from an ever deeper exploration of the unconscious mainspring.

Apart from the pioneering activity these three problems manifest on three different fronts, they have one thing in common with the vitality of the psychoanalytic experience that sustains them. It is the temptation that presents itself to the analyst to abandon the foundation of speech, and this precisely in areas where its use, verging on the ineffable, would seem to require examination more than ever: namely, the child's education by its mother, Samaritan-type aid, and dialectical mastery. The danger becomes great indeed if the analyst also abandons his own language, preferring established languages about whose compensations for ignorance he knows very little.

In truth, we would like to know more about the effects of symbolization in the child, and the officiating mothers in psychoanalysis—even those who give our top committees a matriarchal air—are not exempt from the confusion of tongues by which Ferenczi designated the law of the child/adult relationship.[2]

Our wise men's ideas about the perfect object-relation are based on a rather uncertain conception and, when exposed, they reveal a mediocrity that hardly 244
does credit to the profession.

There can be no doubt that these effects—where the psychoanalyst resembles the type of modern hero represented by ridiculous feats in situations of confusion—could be corrected by an appropriate return to the study of the functions of speech, a field the analyst ought by now to have mastered.

But it seems that this central field of our domain has been left fallow since Freud. Note how he himself refrained from venturing too far into its periphery: He discovered children's libidinal stages by analyzing adults and intervened in little Hans's case only through the mediation of his parents; he deciphered a whole section of the language of the unconscious in paranoid delusion, but used for this purpose only the key text Schreber left behind in the volcanic debris of his spiritual catastrophe. Freud rose, however, to a position of total mastery regarding the dialectic of the work and the tradition of its meaning.

Does this mean that if the place of the master remains empty, it is not so much due to his disappearance as to an increasing obliteration of the meaning of his work? To convince ourselves of this, isn't it enough for us to note what is happening in that place?

A technique is being transmitted there, one that is gloomy in style—indeed, it is reticent in its opacity—and that any attempt to let in critical fresh air seems to upset. It has, in truth, assumed the appearance of a formalism that is taken to such ceremonial lengths that one might well suspect that it bears the same similarity to obsessive neurosis as Freud found so convincingly in the practice, if not the genesis, of religious rites.

When we consider the literature that this activity produces for its own nourishment, the analogy becomes even more marked: the impression is often that of a curious closed circuit in which ignorance of the origin of terms generates problems in reconciling them, and in which the effort to solve these problems reinforces the original ignorance.

In order to home in on the causes of this deterioration of analytic discourse, one may legitimately apply psychoanalytic method to the collectivity that sustains it.

Indeed, to speak of a loss of the meaning of psychoanalytic action is as true and futile as it is to explain a symptom by its meaning as long as the lat- 245
ter is not recognized. But we know that, in the absence of such recognition, analytic action can only be experienced as aggressive at the level at which it is situated; and that, in the absence of the social "resistances" which the psychoanalytic group used to find reassuring, the limits of its tolerance toward its own activity—now "accepted," if not actually approved of—no longer

depend upon anything but the numerical percentage by which its presence in society is measured.

These principles suffice to separate out the symbolic, imaginary, and real conditions that determine the defenses we can recognize in the doctrine—isolation, undoing what has been done, denial, and, in general, misrecognition.

Thus, if the importance of the American group to the psychoanalytic movement is measured by its mass, we can evaluate the conditions one finds there by their weight.

In the symbolic order, first of all, one cannot neglect the importance of the *c* factor which, as I noted at the Congress of Psychiatry in 1950, is a constant that is characteristic of a given cultural milieu: the condition, in this case, of ahistoricism, which is widely recognized as the major feature of "communication" in the United States, and which in my view is diametrically opposed to analytic experience. To this must be added a native mindset, known as behaviorism, which so dominates psychological notions in America that it clearly has now altogether topped Freud's inspiration in psychoanalysis.

As for the other two orders, I leave to those concerned the task of assessing what the mechanisms that manifest themselves in the life of psychoanalytic associations owe to relations of standing within the group and to the effects of their free enterprise felt by the whole of the social body, respectively. I also leave to them the task of determining the credence to be lent to a notion emphasized by one of their most lucid representatives—namely, the convergence that occurs between the alien status of a group dominated by immigrants and the distance it is lured into taking from its roots by the function called for by the aforementioned cultural conditions.

In any case, it seems indisputable that the conception of psychoanalysis in the United States has been inflected toward the adaptation of the individual to the social environment, the search for behavior patterns, and all the objectification implied in the notion of "human relations."* And the indigenous term,
246 "human engineering,"* strongly implies a privileged position of exclusion with respect to the human object.

Indeed, the eclipse in psychoanalysis of the liveliest terms of its experience—the unconscious and sexuality, which will apparently cease before long to even be mentioned—may be attributed to the distance necessary to sustain such a position.

We need not take sides concerning the formalism and small-time shop mentality, both of which have been noted and decried in the analytic group's own official documents. Pharisees and shopkeepers interest us only because of their common essence, which is the source of the difficulties both have with speech, particularly when it comes to "talking shop."*

The fact is that while incommunicability of motives may sustain a "grand master," it does not go hand in hand with true mastery—at least not with the mastery teaching requires. This was realized in the past when, in order to sustain one's preeminence, it was necessary, for form's sake, to give at least one class.

This is why the attachment to traditional technique—which is unfailingly reaffirmed by the same camp—after a consideration of the results of the tests carried out in the frontier fields enumerated above, is not unequivocal; the equivocation can be gauged on the basis of the substitution of the term "classic" for "orthodox" that is used to qualify it. One remains true to propriety because one has nothing to say about the doctrine itself.

For my part, I would assert that the technique cannot be understood, nor therefore correctly applied, if one misunderstands the concepts on which it is based. My task shall be to demonstrate that these concepts take on their full meaning only when oriented in a field of language and ordered in relation to the function of speech.

A point regarding which I should note that in order to handle any Freudian concept, reading Freud cannot be considered superfluous, even for those concepts that go by the same name as everyday notions. This is demonstrated, as I am reminded by the season, by the misadventure of Freud's theory of the instincts when revised by an author somewhat less than alert to what Freud explicitly stated to be its mythical content. Obviously, the author could hardly be aware of it, since he approaches the theory through Marie Bonaparte's work, which he repeatedly cites as if it were equivalent to Freud's text—without the reader being in any way alerted to the fact—relying per- 247
haps, not without reason, on the reader's good taste not to confuse the two, but proving nonetheless that he hasn't the slightest inkling of the secondary text's true level. The upshot being that—moving from reductions to deductions and from inductions to hypotheses—the author, by way of the strict tautology of his false premises, comes to the conclusion that the instincts in question are reducible to the reflex arc. Like the classic image of the pile of plates—whose collapse leaves nothing in the hands of the comedian but two ill-matched fragments—the complex construction that moves from the discovery of the migrations of the libido in the erogenous zones to the metapsychological passage from a generalized pleasure principle to the death instinct becomes the binomial of a passive erotic instinct, modeled on the activity of the lice seekers so dear to the poet, and a destructive instinct, identified simply with motor functioning. A result that merits an honorable mention for the art, intentional or otherwise, of taking the consequences of a misunderstanding to their most rigorous conclusions.

I. Empty Speech and Full Speech in the Psychoanalytic Realization of the Subject

"Put true and stable speech into my mouth and make of me a cautious tongue"
—*The Internal Consolation*, Chapter XLV: That one should not believe everyone and of slight stumbling over words.

Cause toujours.
—Motto of "causalist" thought

Whether it wishes to be an agent of healing, training, or sounding the depths, psychoanalysis has but one medium: the patient's speech. The obviousness of this fact is no excuse for ignoring it. Now all speech calls for a response.

I will show that there is no speech without a response, even if speech meets only with silence, provided it has an auditor, and this is the heart of its function in analysis.

But if the psychoanalyst is not aware that this is how speech functions, he
248 will experience its call [*appel*] all the more strongly; and if emptiness is the first thing to make itself heard in analysis, he will feel it in himself and he will seek a reality beyond speech to fill the emptiness.

This leads the analyst to analyze the subject's behavior in order to find in it what the subject is not saying. Yet for him to get the subject to admit to the latter, he obviously has to talk about it. He thus speaks now, but his speech has become suspicious because it is merely a response to the failure of his silence, when faced with the perceived echo of his own nothingness.

But what, in fact, was the appeal the subject was making beyond the emptiness of his words [*dire*]? It was an appeal to truth at its very core, through which the calls of humbler needs vacillate. But first and from the outset it was the call of emptiness itself, in the ambiguous gap of an attempted seduction of the other by means in which the subject manifests indulgence, and on which he stakes the monument of his narcissism.

"That's introspection all right!" exclaims the bombastic, smug fellow who knows its dangers only too well. He is certainly not the last, he admits, to have tasted its charms, even if he has exhausted its benefits. Too bad he has no more time to waste. For you would hear some fine profundities from him were he to come and lie on your couch!

It is strange that analysts who encounter this sort of person early on in their experience still consider introspection to be of importance in psychoanalysis. For the minute you accept his wager, all the fine things he thought he had been saving up slip his mind. If he forces himself to recount a few, they don't amount to much; but others come to him so unexpectedly that they strike him as idiotic and silence him for quite a while. That's what usually happens.[3]

He then grasps the difference between the mirage of the monologue whose accommodating fancies once animated his bombast, and the forced labor of a discourse that leaves one no way out, on which psychologists (not without humor) and therapists (not without cunning) have bestowed the name "free association."

For it really is work—so much so that some have said it requires an apprenticeship, and have even considered this apprenticeship to constitute its true formative value. But if viewed in this way, what does it train but a skilled worker?

Then what of this work? Let us examine its conditions and fruit in the hope 249
of shedding more light on its aim and benefits.

The aptness of the German word *Durcharbeiten*—equivalent to the English "working through"*—has been recognized in passing. It has been the despair of French translators, despite what the immortal words of a master of French style offered them by way of an exhaustive exercise: "Cent fois sur le métier, remettez . . ."—but how does the work [*l'ouvrage*] progress here?

The theory reminds us of the triad: frustration, aggressiveness, regression. This explanation seems so comprehensible that it may well spare us the effort to comprehend. Intuition is prompt, but we should be all the more suspicious of something obvious when it has become a received idea. Should analysis ever expose its weakness, it would be advisable not to rest content with recourse to "affectivity." This taboo-word of dialectical incapacity will, along with the verb "to intellectualize" (whose pejorative acceptation makes this incapacity meritorious), remain, in the history of the language, the stigmata of our obtuseness regarding the subject.[4]

Let us ask ourselves instead where this frustration comes from. Is it from the analyst's silence? Responding to the subject's empty speech—even and especially in an approving manner—often proves, by its effects, to be far more frustrating than silence. Isn't it, rather, a frustration that is inherent in the subject's very discourse? Doesn't the subject become involved here in an ever greater dispossession of himself as a being, concerning which—by dint of sincere portraits which leave the idea of his being no less incoherent, of rectifications that do not succeed in isolating its essence, of stays and defenses that do not prevent his statue from tottering, of narcissistic embraces that become like a puff of air in animating it—he ends up recognizing that this being has never been anything more than his own construction [*oeuvre*] in the imaginary and that this construction undercuts all certainty in him? For in the work he does to reconstruct it *for another*, he encounters anew the fundamental alienation that made him construct it *like another*, and that has always destined it to be taken away from him *by another*.[5]

This ego,* whose strength our theorists now define by its capacity to bear
250 frustration, is frustration in its very essence.[6] Not frustration of one of the subject's desires, but frustration of an object in which his desire is alienated; and the more developed this object becomes, the more profoundly the subject becomes alienated from his jouissance. It is thus a frustration at one remove, a frustration that the subject—even were he to reduce its form in his discourse to the passivating image by which the subject makes himself an object by displaying himself before the mirror—could not be satisfied with, since even if he achieved the most perfect resemblance to that image, it would still be the other's jouissance that he would have gotten recognized there. Which is why there is no adequate response to this discourse, for the subject regards as contemptuous [*mépris*] any speech that buys into his mistake [*méprise*].

The subject's aggressiveness here has nothing to do with animals' aggressiveness when their desires are frustrated. This explanation, which most seem happy with, masks another that is less agreeable to each and every one of us: the aggressiveness of a slave who responds to being frustrated in his labor with a death wish.

Thus we can see how this aggressiveness may respond to any intervention which, by exposing the imaginary intentions of the subject's discourse, dismantles the object the subject has constructed to satisfy them. This is, in effect, what is referred to as the analysis of resistances, and we can immediately see the danger that lies therein. It is already indicated by the existence of the naive analyst who has never seen any manifestations of aggressiveness except for the aggressive signification of his subjects' fantasies.[7]

251 He is the same one who, not hesitating to plead for a "causalist" analysis that would aim to transform the subject in the present by learned explanations of his past, betrays well enough, even in his very tone, the anxiety he wishes to spare himself—the anxiety of having to think that his patient's freedom may depend on that of his own intervention. If the expedient he seizes upon is beneficial at some point to the subject, it is no more beneficial than a stimulating joke and will not detain me any longer.

Let us focus instead on the *hic et nunc* [here and now] to which some analysts feel we should confine the handling of the analysis. It may indeed be useful, provided the analyst does not detach the imaginary intention he uncovers in it from the symbolic relation in which it is expressed. Nothing must be read into it concerning the subject's ego that cannot be assumed anew by him in the form of the "*I*," that is, in the first person.

"I was this only in order to become what I can be": if this were not the constant culmination of the subject's assumption [*assomption*] of his own mirages, where could we find progress here?

Thus the analyst cannot without danger track down the subject in the intimacy of his gestures, or even in that of his stationary state, unless he reintegrates them as silent parties into the subject's narcissistic discourse—and this has been very clearly noted, even by young practitioners.

The danger here is not of a negative reaction on the subject's part, but rather of his being captured in an objectification—no less imaginary than before—of his stationary state, indeed, of his statue, in a renewed status of his alienation.

The analyst's art must, on the contrary, involve suspending the subject's certainties until their final mirages have been consumed. And it is in the subject's discourse that their dissolution must be punctuated.

Indeed, however empty his discourse may seem, it is so only if taken at face value—the value that justifies Mallarmé's remark, in which he compares the common use of language to the exchange of a coin whose obverse and reverse no longer bear but eroded faces, and which people pass from hand to hand "in silence." This metaphor suffices to remind us that speech, even when almost completely worn out, retains its value as a *tessera*.

Even if it communicates nothing, discourse represents the existence of communication; even if it denies the obvious, it affirms that speech constitutes truth; even if it is destined to deceive, it relies on faith in testimony. 252

Thus the psychoanalyst knows better than anyone else that the point is to figure out [*entendre*] to which "part" of this discourse the significant term is relegated, and this is how he proceeds in the best of cases: he takes the description of an everyday event as a fable addressed as a word to the wise, a long prosopopeia as a direct interjection, and, contrariwise, a simple slip of the tongue as a highly complex statement, and even the rest of a silence as the whole lyrical development it stands in for.

It is, therefore, a propitious punctuation that gives meaning to the subject's discourse. This is why the ending of the session—which current technique makes into an interruption that is determined purely by the clock and, as such, takes no account of the thread of the subject's discourse—plays the part of a scansion which has the full value of an intervention by the analyst that is designed to precipitate concluding moments. Thus we must free the ending from its routine framework and employ it for all the useful aims of analytic technique.

This is how regression can occur, regression being but the bringing into the present in the subject's discourse of the fantasmatic relations discharged by an ego* at each stage in the decomposition of its structure. After all, the regression is not real; even in language it manifests itself only by inflections, turns of phrase, and "stumblings so slight" that even in the extreme case they cannot go beyond the artifice of "baby talk" engaged in by adults. Imputing to regression the reality of a current relation to the object amounts to projecting the subject into an alienating illusion that merely echoes one of the analyst's own alibis.

This is why nothing could be more misleading for the analyst than to seek to guide himself by some supposed "contact" he experiences with the subject's reality. This vacuous buzzword of intuitionist and even phenomenological psychology has become extended in contemporary usage in a way that is thoroughly symptomatic of the ever scarcer effects of speech in the present social context. But its obsessive value becomes flagrant when it is recommended in a relationship which, according to its very rules, excludes all real contact.

Young analysts, who might nevertheless allow themselves to be impressed by the impenetrable gifts such recourse implies, will find no better way of
253 dispelling their illusions than to consider the success of the supervision they themselves receive. The very possibility of that supervision would become problematic from the perspective of contact with the patient's reality [*réel*]. On the contrary, the supervisor manifests a second sight—that's the word for it!—which makes the experience at least as instructive for him as for his supervisee. And the less the supervisee demonstrates such gifts—which are considered by some to be all the more incommunicable the bigger the to-do they themselves make about their secrets regarding technique—the truer this almost becomes.

The reason for this enigma is that the supervisee serves as a filter, or even as a refractor, of the subject's discourse, and in this way a ready-made stereography is presented to the supervisor, bringing out from the start the three or four registers on which the musical score constituted by the subject's discourse can be read.

If the supervisee could be put by the supervisor into a subjective position different from that implied by the sinister term *contrôle* (advantageously replaced, but only in English, by "supervision"*), the greatest benefit he would derive from this exercise would be to learn to put himself in the position of that second subjectivity into which the situation automatically puts the supervisor.

There he would find the authentic path by which to reach what is expressed only very approximately by the classic formulation of the analyst's diffuse, or even absentminded, attention. For it is essential to know what that attention aims at; as all my work shows, it certainly does not aim at an object beyond the subject's speech the way it does for certain analysts who force themselves to never lose sight of that object. If this had to be the path of analysis, then it would surely have recourse to other means—otherwise it would provide the only example of a method that forbade itself the means to its own ends.

The only object that is within the analyst's reach is the imaginary relation that links him to the subject qua ego; and although he cannot eliminate it, he can use it to adjust the receptivity of his ears, which is, according to both physiology and the Gospels, the normal use made of them: having ears *in order not to hear* [*entendre*], in other words, in order to detect what is to be understood [*entendu*]. For he has no other ears, no third or fourth ear designed for what some have tried to describe as a direct transaudition of the unconscious by the unconscious. I shall say what we are to make of this supposed mode of com- 254
munication later.

I have, thus far, approached the function of speech in analysis from its least rewarding angle, that of "empty" speech in which the subject seems to speak in vain about someone who—even if he were such a dead ringer for him that you might confuse them—will never join him in the assumption of his desire. I have pointed out the source of the growing devaluation of speech in both analytic theory and technique, and have had to lift incrementally, as if a heavy mill wheel had fallen on speech, what can only serve as the sails that drive the movement of analysis: namely, individual psychophysiological factors that are, in reality, excluded from its dialectic. To regard the goal of psychoanalysis as to modify their characteristic inertia is to condemn oneself to the fiction of movement, with which a certain trend in psychoanalytic technique seems to be satisfied.

If we turn now to the other end of the spectrum of psychoanalytic experience—its history, casuistry, and treatment process—we shall learn to oppose the value of anamnesis as the index and mainspring of therapeutic progress to the analysis of the *hic et nunc*, hysterical intersubjectivity to obsessive intrasubjectivity, and symbolic interpretation to the analysis of resistance. The realization of full speech begins here.

Let us examine the relation it constitutes.

Let us recall that, shortly after its birth, the method introduced by Breuer and Freud was baptized the "talking cure"* by one of Breuer's patients, Anna O. Let us keep in mind that it was the experience inaugurated with this hysteric that led them to the discovery of the pathogenic event dubbed traumatic.

If this event was recognized as the cause of the symptom, it was because putting the event into words (in the patient's "stories"*) led to the removal of the symptom. Here the term *"prise de conscience"* (conscious realization), borrowed from the psychological theory that was immediately constructed to explain the fact, retains a prestige that merits the healthy distrust I believe is

called for when it comes to explanations that parade as self-evident. The psychological prejudices of Freud's day were opposed to seeing in verbalization
255 as such any other reality than its *flatus vocis*. The fact remains that, in the hypnotic state, verbalization is dissociated from conscious realization, and this alone is enough to require a revision of such a conception of its effects.

But why don't the valiant defenders of the behaviorist *Aufhebung* set an example here, making their point that they do not need to know whether the subject remembers anything whatsoever? She simply recounts the event. For my part, I would say that she verbalizes it, or—to further exploit this term whose resonances in French call to mind a Pandora figure other than the one with the box (in which the term should probably be locked up)—that she forces the event into the Word [*le verbe*] or, more precisely, into the *epos* by which she relates in the present the origins of her person. And she does this in a language that allows her discourse to be understood by her contemporaries and that also presupposes their present discourse. Thus it happens that the recitation of the *epos* may include a discourse of earlier days in its own archaic, even foreign tongue, or may even be carried out in the present with all the vivacity of an actor; but it is like indirect speech, isolated in quotation marks in the thread of the narrative, and, if the speech is performed, it is on a stage implying the presence not only of a chorus, but of spectators as well.

Hypnotic remembering is, no doubt, a reproduction of the past, but it is above all a spoken representation and, as such, implies all sorts of presences. It stands in the same relation to the remembering while awake of what in analysis is curiously called "the material," as drama—in which the original myths of the City State are produced before its assembly of citizens—stands in relation to history, which may well be made up of materials, but in which a nation today learns to read the symbols of a destiny on the march. In Heideggerian language one could say that both types of remembering constitute the subject as *gewesend*—that is, as being the one who has thus been. But in the internal unity of this temporalization, entities [*l'étant*] mark the convergence of the having-beens [*des ayant été*]. In other words, if other encounters are assumed to have occurred since any one of these moments having been, another entity would have issued from it that would cause him to have been altogether differently.

The reason for the ambiguity of hysterical revelation of the past is not so much the vacillation of its content between the imaginary and reality [*réel*], for it is situated in both. Nor is it the fact that it is made up of lies. It is that it
256 presents us with the birth of truth in speech, and thereby brings us up against the reality of what is neither true nor false. At least, that is the most disturbing aspect of the problem.

For it is present speech that bears witness to the truth of this revelation in current reality and grounds it in the name of this reality. Now only speech bears witness in this reality to that portion of the powers of the past that has been thrust aside at each crossroads where an event has chosen.

This is why the condition of continuity in the anamnesis, by which Freud measures the completeness of the cure, has nothing to do with the Bergsonian myth of a restoration of duration in which the authenticity of each instant would be destroyed if it did not recapitulate the modulation of all the preceding instants. To Freud's mind, it is not a question of biological memory, nor of its intuitionist mystification, nor of the paramnesia of the symptom, but of remembering, that is, of history; he rests the scales—in which conjectures about the past make promises about the future oscillate—on the knife-edge of chronological certainties alone. Let's be categorical: in psychoanalytic anamnesis, what is at stake is not reality, but truth, because the effect of full speech is to reorder past contingencies by conferring on them the sense of necessities to come, such as they are constituted by the scant freedom through which the subject makes them present.

The meanders of the research pursued by Freud in his account of the case of the Wolf Man confirm these remarks by deriving their full meaning from them.

Freud demands a total objectification of proof when it comes to dating the primal scene, but he simply presupposes all the resubjectivizations of the event that seem necessary to him to explain its effects at each turning point at which the subject restructures himself—that is, as many restructurings of the event as take place, as he puts it, *nachträglich*, after the fact.[8] What's more, with an audacity bordering on impudence, he declares that he considers it legitimate, in analyzing the processes, to elide the time intervals during which the event 257
remains latent in the subject.[9] That is to say, he annuls the *times for understanding* in favor of the *moments of concluding* which precipitate the subject's meditation toward deciding the meaning to be attached to the early event.

Let it be noted that *time for understanding* and *moment of concluding* are functions I have defined in a purely logical theorem,[10] and are familiar to my students as having proven extremely helpful in the dialectical analysis through which I guide them in the process of a psychoanalysis.

This assumption by the subject of his history, insofar as it is constituted by speech addressed to another, is clearly the basis of the new method Freud called psychoanalysis, not in 1904—as was taught until recently by an authority who, when he finally threw off the cloak of prudent silence, appeared on that day to know nothing of Freud except the titles of his works—but in 1895.[11]

In this analysis of the meaning of his method, I do not deny, any more than Freud himself did, the psychophysiological discontinuity manifested by the states in which hysterical symptoms appear, nor do I deny that these symptoms may be treated by methods—hypnosis or even narcosis—that reproduce the discontinuity of these states. It is simply that I repudiate any reliance on these states—as expressly as Freud forbade himself recourse to them after a certain moment in time—to either explain symptoms or cure them.

For if the originality of the method derives from the means it foregoes, it is because the means that it reserves for itself suffice to constitute a domain whose limits define the relativity of its operations.

Its means are those of speech, insofar as speech confers a meaning on the functions of the individual; its domain is that of concrete discourse qua field of the subject's transindividual reality; and its operations are those of history, insofar as history constitutes the emergence of truth in reality [*réel*].

First, in fact, when a subject begins an analysis, he accepts a position that
258 is more constitutive in itself than all the orders by which he allows himself to be more or less taken in—the position of interlocution—and I see no disadvantage in the fact that this remark may leave the listener dumbfounded [*interloqué*]. For I shall take this opportunity to stress that the subject's act of addressing [*allocution*] brings with it an addressee [*allocutaire*][12]—in other words, that the speaker [*locuteur*][13] is constituted in it as intersubjectivity.

Second, it is on the basis of this interlocution, insofar as it includes the interlocutor's response, that it becomes clear to us why Freud requires restoration of continuity in the subject's motivations. An operational examination of this objective shows us, in effect, that it can only be satisfied in the intersubjective continuity of the discourse in which the subject's history is constituted.

Thus, while the subject may vaticinate about his history under the influence of one or other of those drugs that put consciousness to sleep and have been christened in our day "truth serums"—where the sureness of the misnomer betrays the characteristic irony of language—the simple retransmission of his own recorded discourse, even if pronounced by his doctor, cannot have the same effects as psychoanalytic interlocution because it comes to the subject in an alienated form.

The true basis of the Freudian discovery of the unconscious becomes clear in its position as a third term. This may be simply formulated in the following terms:

The unconscious is that part of concrete discourse qua transindividual, which is not at the subject's disposal in reestablishing the continuity of his conscious discourse.

This disposes of the paradox presented by the concept of the unconscious when it is related to an individual reality. For to reduce this concept to unconscious tendencies is to resolve the paradox only by avoiding analytic experience, which clearly shows that the unconscious is of the same nature as ideational functions, and even of thought. Freud plainly stressed this when, unable to avoid a conjunction of opposing terms in the expression "unconscious thought," he gave it the necessary support with the invocation: *sit venia verbo*. Thus we obey him by casting the blame, in effect, onto the Word, but onto the Word realized in discourse that darts from mouth to mouth, conferring on the act of the subject who receives its message the meaning that makes this act an act of his history and gives it its truth. 259

Hence the objection that the notion of unconscious thought is a contradiction in terms, which is raised by a psychology poorly grounded in its logic, collapses when confronted by the very distinctiveness of the psychoanalytic domain, insofar as this domain reveals the reality of discourse in its autonomy. And the psychoanalyst's *eppur si muove!* has the same impact as Galileo's, which is not that of a fact-based experiment but of an *experimentum mentis*.

The unconscious is the chapter of my history that is marked by a blank or occupied by a lie: it is the censored chapter. But the truth can be refound; most often it has already been written elsewhere. Namely,

- in monuments: this is my body, in other words, the hysterical core of neurosis in which the hysterical symptom manifests the structure of a language, and is deciphered like an inscription which, once recovered, can be destroyed without serious loss;
- in archival documents too: these are my childhood memories, just as impenetrable as such documents are when I do not know their provenance;
- in semantic evolution: this corresponds to the stock of words and acceptations of my own particular vocabulary, as it does to my style of life and my character;
- in traditions, too, and even in the legends which, in a heroicized form, convey my history;
- and, lastly, in its traces that are inevitably preserved in the distortions necessitated by the insertion of the adulterated chapter into the chapters surrounding it, and whose meaning will be re-established by my exegesis.

Students who believe that, in order to understand Freud, reading Freud is preferable to reading Fenichel—and this belief is so rare that I try to foster it in my teaching—will realize, once they set about it, that what I have just said is hardly original, even in its verve; indeed, I have not used a single metaphor that Freud's works do not repeat with the frequency of a *leitmotif*, revealing the very fabric of his work. 260

At every instant of their practice from then on, they will more easily grasp the fact that these metaphors—like negation, whose doubling undoes it—lose their metaphorical dimension, and they will recognize that this is so because they are operating in metaphor's own realm, metaphor being but a synonym for the symbolic displacement brought into play in the symptom.

After that it will be easier for them to evaluate the imaginary displacement that motivates Fenichel's work, by gauging the difference in the solidity and efficacy of technique generated by referring to the supposedly organic stages of individual development and by searching for the particular events of a subject's history. It is precisely the difference that separates authentic historical research from the supposed laws of history, of which it can be said that every age finds its own philosopher to propagate them according to the values prevalent at the time.

This is not to say that there is nothing worth keeping in the different meanings uncovered in the general march of history along the path which runs from Bossuet (Jacques-Bénigne) to Toynbee (Arnold), and which is punctuated by the edifices of Auguste Comte and Karl Marx. Everyone knows, of course, that the laws of history are worth as little for directing research into the recent past as they are for making any reasonable presumptions about tomorrow's events. Besides, they are modest enough to postpone their certainties until the day after tomorrow, and not too prudish either to allow for the adjustments that permit predictions to be made about what happened yesterday.

If, therefore, their role in scientific progress is rather slight, their interest nevertheless lies elsewhere: in their considerable role as ideals. For it leads us to distinguish between what might be called the primary and secondary functions of historicization.

For to say of psychoanalysis and of history that, qua sciences, they are both
261 sciences of the particular, does not mean that the facts they deal with are purely accidental or even factitious, or that their ultimate value comes down to the brute aspect of trauma.

Events are engendered in a primal historicization—in other words, history is already being made on the stage where it will be played out once it has been written down, both in one's heart of hearts and outside.

At one moment in time, a certain riot in the Faubourg Saint-Antoine is experienced by its actors as a victory or defeat of the Parliament or the Court; at another moment, as a victory or defeat of the proletariat or the bourgeoisie. And although it is "the common people," to use Cardinal de Retz's expression, who always pay the price, it is not at all the same historical event—I mean that they do not leave behind the same sort of memory in men's minds.

This is because, with the disappearance of the reality of the Parliament and the Court, the first event will return to its traumatic value, allowing for a progressive and authentic effacement, unless its meaning is expressly revived. Whereas the memory of the second event will remain very much alive even under censorship—just as the amnesia brought on by repression is one of the liveliest forms of memory—as long as there are men who enlist their revolt in the struggle for the proletariat's political ascension, that is, men for whom the keywords of dialectical materialism have meaning.

Thus it would be going too far to say that I am about to carry these remarks over into the field of psychoanalysis, since they are already there, and since the clear distinction they establish between two things that were formerly confused—the technique of deciphering the unconscious and the theory of instincts, or even drives—goes without saying.

What we teach the subject to recognize as his unconscious is his history—in other words, we help him complete the current historicization of the facts that have already determined a certain number of the historical "turning points" in his existence. But if they have played this role, it is already as historical facts, that is, as recognized in a certain sense or censored in a certain order.

Thus, every fixation at a supposed instinctual stage is above all a historical
stigma: a page of shame that one forgets or undoes, or a page of glory that 262
obliges. But what is forgotten is recalled in acts, and the undoing of what has been done contradicts what is said elsewhere, just as obligation perpetuates in symbols the very mirage in which the subject found himself trapped.

To put it succinctly, the instinctual stages are already organized in subjectivity when they are being lived. And to put it clearly, the subjectivity of the child who registers as victories and defeats the epic of the training of his sphincters—enjoying in the process the imaginary sexualization of his cloacal orifices, turning his excremental expulsions into aggressions, his retentions into seductions, and his movements of release into symbols—*is not fundamentally different* from the subjectivity of the psychoanalyst who strives to restore the forms of love that he calls "pregenital" in order to understand them.

In other words, the anal stage is no less purely historical when it is actually experienced than when it is reconceptualized, nor is it less purely grounded in intersubjectivity. But officially recognizing it as a stage in some supposed instinctual maturation immediately leads even the best minds off track, to the point of seeing in it the reproduction in ontogenesis of a stage of the animal phylum that should be sought in ascaris, even in jellyfish—a speculation which, ingenious as it may be when penned by Balint, leads others to the most incoherent musings, or even to the folly that goes looking in protista for the imaginary schema of breaking and entering the body, fear of which is supposed to govern feminine sexuality. Why not look for the image of the ego in shrimp, under the pretext that both acquire a new shell after every molting?

In the 1910s and 1920s, a certain Jaworski constructed a very pretty system in which the "biological level" could be found right up to the very confines of culture, and which actually provided shellfish their historical counterpart at some period of the late Middle Ages, if I remember rightly, due to a flourishing of armor in both; indeed, it left no animal form without some human correspondent, excepting neither mollusks nor vermin.

Analogy is not the same thing as metaphor, and the use that the philosophers of nature have made of it requires the genius of Goethe, but even his example is not encouraging. No course is more repugnant to the spirit of our
263 discipline, and it was by deliberately avoiding analogy that Freud opened up the path appropriate to the interpretation of dreams and, along with it, to the notion of analytic symbolism. Analytic symbolism, I insist, is strictly opposed to analogical thinking—a dubious tradition that still leads some people, even in our own ranks, to consider the latter to go hand in hand with the former.

This is why excessive excursions into the ridiculous must be used for their eye-opening value, since, by opening our eyes to the absurdity of a theory, they direct our attention back to dangers that have nothing theoretical about them.

This mythology of instinctual maturation, built out of bits and pieces selected from Freud's work, actually engenders intellectual problems whose vapor, condensing into nebulous ideals, in return irrigates the original myth with its showers. The best writers spill their ink positing equations that satisfy the requirements of that mysterious "genital love"* (there are notions whose strangeness is better placed in the parenthesis of a borrowed term, and they initial their attempt with an admission of a *non liquet*). No one, however, appears to be shaken up by the malaise this results in; and people see it, rather, as a reason to encourage all the Münchhausens of psychoanalytic normalization to raise themselves up by the hair on their head in the hope of attaining the paradise of full realization of the genital object, indeed of the object itself.

The fact that we analysts are in a good position to know the power of words is no reason to emphasize the insoluble character of their power, or to "bind heavy burdens, hard to bear, and lay them on men's shoulders," as Christ's malediction is expressed to the Pharisees in the text of Saint Matthew.

The poverty of the terms within which we try to contain a subjective problem may thus leave a great deal to be desired to particularly exacting minds, should they compare these terms to those that structured, in their very con-
264 fusion, the ancient quarrels over Nature and Grace.[14] This poverty may thus leave them apprehensive as to the quality of the psychological and sociological effects they can expect from the use of these terms. And it is to be hoped that a better appreciation of the functions of the Logos will dissipate the mysteries of our fantastic charismata.

To confine ourselves to a more lucid tradition, perhaps we can understand the celebrated maxim by La Rochefoucauld—"There are people who would never have fallen in love but for hearing love discussed"—not in the romantic sense of a thoroughly imaginary "realization" of love that would make this remark into a bitter objection, but as an authentic recognition of what love owes to the symbol and of what speech brings with it by way of love.

In any case, one need but consult Freud's work to realize to what a secondary and hypothetical rank he relegates the theory of the instincts. The theory cannot in his eyes stand up for a single instant to the least important particular fact of a history, he insists, and the *genital narcissism* he invokes when summarizing the case of the Wolf Man clearly shows how much he scorns the constituted order of the libidinal stages. Moreover, he evokes instinctual conflict there only to immediately distance himself from it and recognize in the symbolic isolation of the "I am not castrated," in which the subject asserts himself, the compulsive form to which his heterosexual object choice remains riveted, in opposition to the effect of homosexualizing capture undergone by the ego when it was brought back to the imaginary matrix of the primal scene. This is, in truth, the subjective conflict—in which it is only a question of the vicissitudes of subjectivity, so much so that the "I" wins and loses against the "ego" at the whim of religious catechization or indoctrinating *Aufklärung*—a conflict whose effects Freud brought the subject to realize through his help before explaining them to us in the dialectic of the Oedipus complex.

It is in the analysis of such a case that one clearly sees that the realization of perfect love is the fruit not of nature but of grace—that is, the fruit of an intersubjective agreement imposing its harmony on the rent nature on which it is based.

"But what, then, is this subject that you keep drumming into our ears?" some impatient auditor finally exclaims. "Haven't we already learned the lesson from Monsieur de La Palice that everything experienced by the individual is subjective?"

Naïve mouth—whose eulogy I shall spend my final days preparing—open 265
up again to hear me. No need to close your eyes. The subject goes far beyond what is experienced "subjectively" by the individual; he goes exactly as far as the truth he is able to attain—which will perhaps come out of the mouth you have already closed again. Yes, this truth of his history is not all contained in his script, and yet the place is marked there in the painful conflicts he experiences because he knows only his own lines, and even in the pages whose disarray gives him little comfort.

The fact that the subject's unconscious is the other's discourse appears more clearly than anywhere else in the studies Freud devoted to what he called telepathy, as it is manifested in the context of an analytic experience. This is the coincidence between the subject's remarks and facts he cannot have known about, but which are still at work in the connections to another analysis in which the analyst is an interlocutor—a coincidence which is, moreover, most often constituted by an entirely verbal, even homonymic, convergence, or which, if it includes an act, involves an "acting out"* by one of the analyst's other patients or by the patient's child who is also in analysis. It is a case of resonance in the communicating networks of discourse, an exhaustive study of which would shed light on similar facts of everyday life.

The omnipresence of human discourse will perhaps one day be embraced under the open sky of an omnicommunication of its text. This is not to say that human discourse will be any more in tune with it than it is now. But this is the field that our experience polarizes in a relation that is only apparently a two-person relation, for any positioning of its structure in merely dyadic terms is as inadequate to it in theory as it is damaging to its technique.

266 *II. Symbol and Language as Structure and Limit of the Psychoanalytic Field*

> Τήν ἀρχήν ὅ τι καί λαλῶ ὑμῖν
> —Gospel according to Saint John, 8.25

> Do crossword puzzles.
> —Advice to a young psychoanalyst

To take up the thread of my argument again, let me repeat that it is by a reduction of a particular subject's history that psychoanalysis touches on relational gestalts, which analysis extrapolates into regular development; but that neither genetic psychology nor differential psychology, on both of which analysis may shed light, is within its scope, because both require experimental and observational conditions that are related to those of analysis in name alone.

To go even further: What separates out from common experience (which is confused with sense experience only by professional thinkers) as psychology in its crudest form—namely, the wonder that wells up, during some momentary suspension of daily cares, at what pairs off human beings in a disparity that goes beyond that of the grotesques of Leonardo or Goya, or surprise at the resistance of the thickness characteristic of a person's skin to the caress of a hand still moved by the thrill of discovery without yet being blunted by desire—this, one might say, is abolished in an experience that is averse to such caprices and recalcitrant to such mysteries.

A psychoanalysis normally proceeds to its end without revealing to us very much of what is particular to our patient as regards his sensitivity to blows or colors, how quickly he grasps things with his hands or which parts of his body are sensitive, or his ability to retain things or invent, not to mention the vivacity of his tastes.

This paradox is only an apparent one and is not due to any personal failing; if it can be justified by the negative conditions of analytic experience, it simply presses us a little harder to examine that experience in terms of what is positive in it.

For this paradox is not resolved by the efforts of certain people who—like 267
the philosophers Plato mocked for being so driven by their appetite for reality [*réel*] that they went about embracing trees—go so far as to take every episode in which this reality, that slips away, rears its head for the lived reaction of which they prove so fond. For these are the very people who, making their objective what lies beyond language, react to analysis' "Don't touch" rule by a sort of obsession. If they keep going in that direction, I dare say the last word in transference reaction will be sniffing each other. I am not exaggerating in the least: nowadays, a young analyst-in-training, after two or three years of fruitless analysis, can actually hail the long-awaited advent of the object-relation in being smelled by his subject, and can reap as a result of it the *dignus est intrare* of our votes, the guarantors of his abilities.

If psychoanalysis can become a science (for it is not yet one) and if it is not to degenerate in its technique (and perhaps this has already happened), we must rediscover the meaning of its experience.

To this end, we can do no better than return to Freud's work. Claiming to be an expert practitioner does not give an analyst the right to challenge Freud III, because he does not understand him, in the name of a Freud II whom he thinks he understands. And his very ignorance of Freud I is no excuse for considering the five great psychoanalyses as a series of case studies as badly chosen as they are written up, however marvelous he thinks it that the grain of truth hidden within them managed to escape.[15]

We must thus take up Freud's work again starting with the *Traumdeutung* [*The Interpretation of Dreams*] to remind ourselves that a dream has the structure of a sentence or, rather, to keep to the letter of the work, of a rebus—that is, of a form of writing, of which children's dreams are supposed to represent the primordial ideography, and which reproduces, in adults' dreams, the simultaneously phonetic and symbolic use of signifying elements found in the hieroglyphs of ancient Egypt and in the characters still used in China.

But even this is no more than the deciphering of the instrument. What is
important is the version of the text, and that, Freud tells us, is given in the 268
telling of the dream—that is, in its rhetoric. Ellipsis and pleonasm, hyperbaton or syllepsis, regression, repetition, apposition—these are the syntactical

displacements; metaphor, catachresis, antonomasia, allegory, metonymy, and synecdoche—these are the semantic condensations; Freud teaches us to read in them the intentions—whether ostentatious or demonstrative, dissimulating or persuasive, retaliatory or seductive—with which the subject modulates his oneiric discourse.

We know that he laid it down as a rule that the expression of a desire must always be sought in a dream. But let us be sure we understand what he meant by this. If Freud accepts, as the reason for a dream that seems to run counter to his thesis, the very desire to contradict him on the part of a subject whom he had tried to convince of his theory,[16] how could he fail to accept the same reason for himself when the law he arrived at is supposed to have come to him from other people?

In short, nowhere does it appear more clearly that man's desire finds its meaning in the other's desire, not so much because the other holds the keys to the desired object, as because his first object(ive) is to be recognized by the other.

Indeed, we all know from experience that from the moment an analysis becomes engaged in the path of transference—and this is what indicates to us that it has become so engaged—each of the patient's dreams is to be interpreted as a provocation, a latent avowal or diversion, by its relation to the analytic discourse, and that as the analysis progresses, his dreams become ever more reduced to the function of elements in the dialogue taking place in the analysis.

In the case of the psychopathology of everyday life, another field consecrated by another text by Freud, it is clear that every bungled action is a successful, even "well phrased," discourse, and that in slips of the tongue it is the gag that turns against speech, and from just the right quadrant for its word to the wise to be sufficient.

But let us go straight to the part of the book where Freud deals with chance and the beliefs it gives rise to, and especially to the facts regarding which he
269 applies himself to showing the subjective efficacy of associations to numbers that are left to the fate of an unmotivated choice, or even of a random selection. Nowhere do the dominant structures of the psychoanalytic field reveal themselves better than in such a success. Freud's appeal, in passing, to unknown thought processes is nothing more in this case than his last-ditch excuse for the total confidence he placed in symbols, a confidence that wavers as the result of being fulfilled beyond his wildest dreams.

If, for a symptom, whether neurotic or not, to be considered to come under psychoanalytic psychopathology, Freud insists on the minimum of overdetermination constituted by a double meaning—symbol of a defunct conflict beyond its function in a *no less symbolic* present conflict—and if he teaches us to follow the ascending ramification of the symbolic lineage in the text of the patient's free associations, in order to detect the nodal points [*noeuds*] of its structure at the places where its verbal forms intersect, then it is already quite clear that symptoms can be entirely resolved in an analysis of language, because a symptom is itself structured like a language: a symptom is language from which speech must be delivered.

To those who have not studied the nature of language in any depth, the experience of numerical association will immediately show what must be grasped here—namely, the combinatory power that orders its equivocations—and they will recognize in this the very mainspring of the unconscious.

Indeed, if—from the numbers obtained by breaking up the series of digits [*chiffres*] in the chosen number, from their combination by all the operations of arithmetic, and even from the repeated division of the original number by one of the numbers split off from it—the resulting numbers[17] prove symbolic among all the numbers in the subject's own history, it is because they were already latent in the initial choice. And thus if the idea that these very numbers [*chiffres*] determined the subject's fate is refuted as superstitious, we must nevertheless admit that everything analysis reveals to the subject as his unconscious lies in the existing order of their combinations—that is, in the concrete language they represent.

We shall see that philologists and ethnographers reveal enough to us about 270
the combinatory sureness found in the completely unconscious systems with which they deal for them to find nothing surprising in the proposition I am putting forward here.

But should anyone still have reservations about what I am saying, I would appeal once more to the testimony of the man who, having discovered the unconscious, warrants credence when he designates its place; he will not fail us.

For, however little interest has been taken in it—and for good reason—*Jokes and Their Relation to the Unconscious* remains the most unchallengeable of his works because it is the most transparent; in it, the effect of the unconscious is demonstrated in all its subtlety. And the visage it reveals to us is that of wit [*l'esprit*] in the ambiguity conferred on it by language, where the other face of its regalian power is the witticism [*pointe*], by which the whole of its order is annihilated in an instant—the witticism, indeed, in which language's creative activity unveils its absolute gratuitousness, in which its domination of reality [*réel*] is expressed in the challenge of nonmeaning, and in which the humor, in the malicious grace of the free spirit [*esprit libre*], symbolizes a truth that does not say its last word.

We must follow Freud, along the book's admirably compelling detours, on the walk on which he leads us in this chosen garden of bitterest love.

Here everything is substantial, everything is a real gem. The mind [*esprit*] that lives as an exile in the creation whose invisible support he is, knows that he is at every instant the master capable of annihilating it. No matter how disdained the forms of this hidden royalty—haughty or perfidious, dandy-like or debonair—Freud can make their secret luster shine. Stories of the marriage-broker on his rounds in the ghettos of Moravia—that derided Eros figure, like him born of penury and pain—discreetly guiding the avidity of his ill-mannered client, and suddenly ridiculing him with the illuminating nonsense of his reply. "He who lets the truth escape like that," comments Freud, "is in reality happy to throw off the mask."

It is truth, in fact, that throws off the mask in coming out of his mouth, but only so that the joke might take on another and more deceptive mask: the sophistry that is merely a stratagem, the logic that is merely a lure, even comedy that tends merely to dazzle. The joke is always about something else. "A joke [*esprit*] in fact entails such a subjective conditionality [. . .]: a joke is only
271 what I accept as such," continues Freud, who knows what he is talking about.

Nowhere is the individual's intent more evidently surpassed by the subject's find—nowhere is the distinction I make between the individual and the subject so palpable—since not only must there have been something foreign to me in my find for me to take pleasure in it, but some of it must remain foreign for this find to hit home. This takes on its importance due to the necessity, so clearly indicated by Freud, of a joke's third person, who is always presupposed, and to the fact that a joke does not lose its power when told in the form of indirect speech. In short, this points, in the Other's locus, to the amboceptor that is illuminated by the artifice of the joke [*mot*] erupting in its supreme alacrity.

There is only one reason for a joke to fall flat: the platitude of any explanation given of its truth.

Now this relates directly to our problem. The current disdain for studies on the language of symbols—which can be seen simply by glancing at the table of contents of our publications before and after the 1920s—corresponds in our discipline to nothing less than a change of object, whose tendency to align itself with the most undifferentiated level of communication, in order to accommodate the new objectives proposed for psychoanalytic technique, is perhaps responsible for the rather gloomy balance sheet that the most lucid analysts have drawn up of its results.[18]

How, indeed, could speech exhaust the meaning of speech or—to put it better with the Oxford logical positivists, the meaning of meaning*—if not in the act that engenders it? Thus Goethe's reversal of its presence at the origin, "In the beginning was the act," is itself reversed in its turn: it was certainly the Word that was [*était*] in the beginning, and we live in its creation, but it is our mental [*esprit*] action that continues this creation by constantly renewing it. And we can only think back to this action by allowing ourselves to be driven ever further ahead by it.

I shall try it myself only in the knowledge that this is its pathway . . .

No one is supposed to be ignorant of the law; this formulation, provided by 272
the humor in our Code of Laws, nevertheless expresses the truth in which our experience is grounded, and which our experience confirms. No man is actually ignorant of it, because the law of man has been the law of language since the first words of recognition presided over the first gifts—it having taken the detestable Danai, who came and fled by sea, for men to learn to fear deceptive words accompanying faithless gifts. Up until then, these gifts, the act of giving them and the objects given, their transmutation into signs, and even their fabrication, were so closely intertwined with speech for the pacific Argonauts—uniting the islets of their community with the bonds [*noeuds*] of a symbolic commerce—that they were designated by its name.[19]

Is it with these gifts, or with the passwords that give them their salutary nonmeaning, that language begins along with law? For these gifts are already symbols, in the sense that symbol means pact, and they are first and foremost signifiers of the pact they constitute as the signified; this is plainly seen in the fact that the objects of symbolic exchange—vases made to remain empty, shields too heavy to be carried, sheaves that will dry out, lances that are thrust into the ground—are all destined to be useless, if not superfluous by their very abundance.

Is this neutralization by means of the signifier the whole of the nature of language? Were this the case, one would find a first approximation of language among sea swallows, for instance, during display, materialized in the fish they pass each other from beak to beak; ethologists—if we must agree with them in seeing in this the instrument of a stirring into action of the group that is tantamount to a party—would then be altogether justified in recognizing a symbol in this activity.

It can be seen that I do not shrink from seeking the origins of symbolic behavior outside the human sphere. But it is certainly not by the pathway of an elaboration of signs, the pathway Jules H. Masserman,[20] following in the footsteps of so many others, has taken. I shall dwell on it for an instant here,
not only because of the savvy tone with which he outlines his approach, but 273
also because his work has been well received by the editors of our official

journal, who—following a tradition borrowed from employment agencies—never neglect anything that might provide our discipline with "good references."

Think of it—we have here a man who has reproduced neurosis ex-pe-ri-men-tal-ly in a dog tied down on a table, and by what ingenious methods: a bell, the plate of meat that it announces, and the plate of apples that arrives instead; I'll spare you the rest. He will certainly not be one, at least so he assures us, to let himself be taken in by the "extensive ruminations," as he puts it, that philosophers have devoted to the problem of language. Not him, he's going to grab it by the throat.

Can you imagine?—a raccoon can be taught, by a judicious conditioning of his reflexes, to go to his food box when he is presented with a card on which the meal he is to be served is printed. We are not told whether it lists the various prices, but the convincing detail is added that if the service disappoints him, he comes back and tears up the card that promised too much, just as a furious woman might do with the letters of a faithless lover (*sic*).

This is one of the arches supporting the road by which the author leads us from the signal to the symbol. It is a two-way street, and the way back is illustrated by no less imposing structures.

For if, in a human subject, you associate the ringing of a bell with the projection of a bright light into his eyes and then the ringing alone to the order, "contract,"* you will succeed in getting the subject to make his pupils contract just by pronouncing the order himself, then by whispering it, and eventually just by thinking it—in other words, you will obtain a reaction of the nervous system that is called autonomic because it is usually inaccessible to intentional effects. Thus, if we are to believe Masserman, a certain Hudgkins "had created in a group of people a highly individualized configuration of cognate and visceral reactions to the idea-symbol 'contract'—a response which could be traced through their special experiences to an apparently remote but actually basic physiologic source: in this instance, simply the protection of the retina from excessive light." And Masserman concludes: "The
274 significance of such experiments for psycho-somatic and linguistic research hardly needs further elaboration."

For my part, I would have been curious to know whether subjects trained in this way also react to the enunciation of the same term in the expressions "marriage contract,"* "contract bridge,"* and "breach of contract,"* and even when the term is progressively shortened to the articulation of its first syllable alone: contract, contrac, contra, contr... The control test required by strict scientific method would then be supplied all by itself as the French reader muttered this syllable under his breath, even though he would have been subjected to no other conditioning than that of the bright light projected on the problem by Masserman himself. I would then ask this author whether the effects thus observed among conditioned subjects still appeared to so easily do without further elaboration. For either the effects would no longer be produced, thus revealing that they do not even conditionally depend on the semanteme, or they would continue to be produced, raising the question of the semanteme's limits.

In other words, they would cause the distinction between the signifier and the signified, so blithely confounded by the author in the English term "idea-symbol,"* to appear in the very word as instrument. And without needing to examine the reactions of subjects conditioned to react to the command "don't contract," or even to the complete conjugation of the verb "to contract," I could remark to the author that what defines any element whatsoever of a language [*langue*] as belonging to language is that, for all the users of the language [*langue*], this element is distinguished as such in the supposedly constituted set of homologous elements.

Thus, the particular effects of this element of language are linked to the existence of this set, prior to any possible link with any of the subject's particular experiences. And to consider this last link independently of any reference to the first is simply to deny the characteristic function of language to this element.

This reminder of first principles might perhaps save our author from discovering, with an unequaled naïveté, the verbatim correspondence of the grammatical categories of his childhood to relations found in reality.

This monument of naïveté—of a kind which is, moreover, common enough in these matters—would not be worth so much attention if it had not been erected by a psychoanalyst, or rather by someone who, as if by chance, 275
relates everything to it which is produced by a certain tendency in psychoanalysis—under the heading of the theory of the ego or technique of the analysis of defenses—that is diametrically opposed to Freudian experience; he thereby manifests *a contrario* that a sound conception of language is coherent with the preservation of Freudian experience. For Freud's discovery was that of the field of the effects, in man's nature, of his relations to the symbolic order and the fact that their meaning goes all the way back to the most radical instances of symbolization in being. To ignore the symbolic order is to condemn Freud's discovery to forgetting and analytic experience to ruin.

I declare—and this is a declaration that cannot be divorced from the serious intent of my present remarks—that I would prefer to have the raccoon I mentioned earlier sitting in the armchair to which, according to our author, Freud's shyness confined the analyst by placing him behind the couch, rather than a scientist who discourses on language and speech as Masserman does.

For—thanks to Jacques Prévert ("A stone, two houses, three ruins, four ditch diggers, a garden, some flowers, a raccoon")—the raccoon, at least, has definitively entered the poetic bestiary and partakes as such, in its essence, of the symbol's eminent function. But that being resembling us who professes, as Masserman does, a systematic misrecognition of that function, forever banishes himself from everything that can be called into existence by it. Thus, the question of the place to be assigned the said semblable in the classification of natural beings would seem to me to smack of a misplaced humanism, if his discourse, crossed with a technique of speech of which we are the guardians, were not in fact too fertile, even in producing sterile monsters within it. Let it be known therefore, since he also credits himself with braving the reproach of anthropomorphism, that this is the last term I would employ in saying that he makes his own being the measure of all things.

Let us return to our symbolic object, which is itself extremely substantial [*consistant*] in its matter, even if it has lost the weight of use, but whose imponderable meaning will produce displacements of some weight. Is that, then, law and language? Perhaps not yet.

276 For even if there appeared among the sea swallows some kaid of the colony who, by gulping down the symbolic fish from the others' gaping beaks, were to inaugurate the exploitation of swallow by swallow—a fanciful notion I enjoyed developing one day—this would not in any way suffice to reproduce among them that fabulous history, the image of our own, whose winged epic kept us captive on *Penguin Island*; something else would still be needed to create a "swallowized" universe.

This "something else" completes the symbol, making language of it. In order for the symbolic object freed from its usage to become the word freed from the *hic et nunc*, the difference resides not in the sonorous quality of its matter, but in its vanishing being in which the symbol finds the permanence of the concept.

Through the word—which is already a presence made of absence—absence itself comes to be named in an original moment whose perpetual re-creation Freud's genius detected in a child's game. And from this articulated couple of presence and absence—also sufficiently constituted by the drawing in the sand of a simple line and a broken line of the *koua* mantics of China—a language's [*langue*] world of meaning is born, in which the world of things will situate itself.

Through what becomes embodied only by being the trace of a nothingness and whose medium thus cannot be altered, concepts, in preserving the duration of what passes away, engender things.

For it is still not saying enough to say that the concept is the thing itself, which a child can demonstrate against the Scholastics. It is the world of words that creates the world of things—things which at first run together in the *hic et nunc* of the all in the process of becoming—by giving its concrete being to their essence, and its ubiquity to what has always been: κτῆμα ἐς ἀεί.

Man thus speaks, but it is because the symbol has made him man. Even if, in fact, overabundant gifts welcome a stranger who has made himself known to a group, the life of natural groups that constitute a community is subject to the rules of matrimonial alliance—determining the direction in which the exchange of women takes place—and to the mutual services determined by marriage: as the ŠiRonga proverb says, "A relative by marriage is an elephant's hip." Marriage ties are governed by an order of preference whose law concerning kinship names is, like language, imperative for the group in its forms, but unconscious in its structure. Now, in this structure, whose harmony or conflicts govern the restricted or generalized exchange discerned in it by eth- 277
nologists, the startled theoretician refinds the whole logic of combinations; thus the laws of number—that is, of the most highly purified of all symbols—prove to be immanent in the original symbolism. At least, it is the richness of the forms—in which what are known as the elementary structures of kinship develop—that makes those laws legible in the original symbolism. And this suggests that it is perhaps only our unawareness of their permanence that allows us to believe in freedom of choice in the so-called complex structures of marriage ties under whose law we live. If statistics has already allowed us to glimpse that this freedom is not exercised randomly, it is because a subjective logic seems to orient its effects.

This is precisely where the Oedipus complex—insofar as we still acknowledge that it covers the whole field of our experience with its signification—will be said, in my remarks here, to mark the limits our discipline assigns to subjectivity: namely, what the subject can know of his unconscious participation in the movement of the complex structures of marriage ties, by verifying the symbolic effects in his individual existence of the tangential movement toward incest that has manifested itself ever since the advent of a universal community.

The primordial Law is therefore the Law which, in regulating marriage ties, superimposes the reign of culture over the reign of nature, the latter being subject to the law of mating. The prohibition of incest is merely the subjective pivot of that Law, laid bare by the modern tendency to reduce the objects the subject is forbidden to choose to the mother and sisters, full license, moreover, not yet being entirely granted beyond them.

This law, then, reveals itself clearly enough as identical to a language order. For without names for kinship relations, no power can institute the order of preferences and taboos that knot and braid the thread of lineage through the generations. And it is the confusion of generations which, in the Bible as in all traditional laws, is cursed as being the abomination of the Word and the desolation of the sinner.

Indeed, we know the damage a falsified filiation can do, going as far as dissociation of the subject's personality, when those around him conspire to sus-
278 tain the lie. It may be no less when, as a result of a man marrying the mother of the woman with whom he has had a son, the son's brother will be his biological mother's half-brother. But if the son is later adopted—and I have not invented this example—by the sympathizing couple formed by a daughter of his father's previous marriage and her husband, he will find himself once again a half-brother, this time of his foster mother; and one can imagine the complex feelings he will have while awaiting the birth of a child who, in this recurring situation, will be his brother and nephew simultaneously.

So too, the mere time-lag produced in the order of generations by a late-born child of a second marriage, where a young mother finds herself the same age as an older brother from the first marriage, can produce similar effects; as we know, this was true in Freud's own family.

This same function of symbolic identification—allowing primitive man to believe he is the reincarnation of an ancestor with the same name, and even determining an alternating recurrence of characteristics in modern man—thus brings about a dissociation of the Oedipus complex in subjects exposed to such discordances in the paternal relation, in which the constant source of its pathogenic effects must be seen. Indeed, even when it is represented by a single person, the paternal function concentrates in itself both imaginary and real relations that always more or less fail to correspond to the symbolic relation that essentially constitutes it.

It is in the *name of the father* that we must recognize the basis of the symbolic function which, since the dawn of historical time, has identified his person with the figure of the law. This conception allows us to clearly distinguish, in the analysis of a case, the unconscious effects of this function from the narcissistic relations, or even real relations, that the subject has with the image and actions of the person who embodies this function; this results in a mode of comprehension that has repercussions on the very way in which interventions are made by the analyst. Practice has confirmed the fecundity of this conception to me, as well as to the students whom I have introduced to this method. And, both in supervision and case discussions, I have often had occasion to stress the harmful confusion produced by neglecting it.

Thus it is the virtue of the Word that perpetuates the movement of the Great Debt whose economy Rabelais, in a famous metaphor, extended to the stars

themselves. And we shall not be surprised that the chapter in which he anticipates ethnographic discoveries with the macaronic inversion of kinship 279
names, reveals in the Word the substantific divination of the human mystery that I am trying to elucidate here.

Identified with sacred *hau* or omnipresent *mana*, the inviolable Debt is the guarantee that the voyage on which women and goods are sent will bring back to their point of departure, in a never-failing cycle, other women and other goods, all bearing an identical entity: what Lévi-Strauss calls a "zero-symbol," thus reducing the power of Speech to the form of an algebraic sign.

Symbols in fact envelop the life of man with a network so total that they join together those who are going to engender him "by bone and flesh" before he comes into the world; so total that they bring to his birth, along with the gifts of the stars, if not with the gifts of the fairies, the shape of his destiny; so total that they provide the words that will make him faithful or renegade, the law of the acts that will follow him right to the very place where he is not yet and beyond his very death; and so total that through them his end finds its meaning in the last judgment, where the Word absolves his being or condemns it—unless he reaches the subjective realization of being-toward-death.

Servitude and grandeur in which the living being would be annihilated, if desire did not preserve his part in the interferences and pulsations that the cycles of language cause to converge on him, when the confusion of tongues intervenes and the orders thwart each other in the tearing asunder of the universal undertaking.

But for this desire itself to be satisfied in man requires that it be recognized, through the accord of speech or the struggle for prestige, in the symbol or the imaginary.

What is at stake in an analysis is the advent in the subject of the scant reality that this desire sustains in him, with respect to symbolic conflicts and imaginary fixations, as the means of their accord, and our path is the intersubjective experience by which this desire gains recognition.

Thus we see that the problem is that of the relations between speech and language in the subject.

Three paradoxes in these relations present themselves in our domain.

In madness, of whatever nature, we must recognize on the one hand the negative freedom of a kind of speech that has given up trying to gain recognition, which is what we call an obstacle to transference; and, on the other, 280
the singular formation of a delusion which—whether fabular, fantastical, or cosmological, or rather interpretative, demanding, or idealist—objectifies the subject in a language devoid of dialectic.[21]

The absence of speech is manifested in madness by the stereotypes of a discourse in which the subject, one might say, is spoken instead of speaking; we recognize here the symbols of the unconscious in petrified forms that find their place in a natural history of these symbols alongside the embalmed forms in which myths are presented in our collections of them. But it would be wrong to say that the subject assumes these symbols: the resistance to their recognition is no less strong in psychosis than in the neuroses, when the subject is led to recognize them by an attempt at treatment.

Let it be said in passing that it would be worthwhile noting the places in social space that our culture has assigned these subjects, especially as regards their relegation to the social services relating to language, for it is not unlikely that we find here one of the factors that consign such subjects to the effects of the breakdown produced by the symbolic discordances characteristic of the complex structures of civilization.

The second case is represented by the privileged field of psychoanalytic discovery—namely, symptoms, inhibition, and anxiety in the constitutive economy of the different neuroses.

Here speech is driven out of the concrete discourse that orders consciousness, but it finds its medium either in the subject's natural functions—provided a painful organic sensation wedges open the gap between his individual being and his essence, which makes illness what institutes the existence of the subject in the living being[22]—or in the images that, at the border between the *Umwelt* and the *Innenwelt*, organize their relational structuring.

A symptom here is the signifier of a signified that has been repressed from the subject's consciousness. A symbol written in the sand of the flesh and on
281 the veil of Maia, it partakes of language by the semantic ambiguity that I have already highlighted in its constitution.

But it is fully functioning speech, for it includes the other's discourse in the secret of its cipher [*chiffre*].

It was by deciphering this speech that Freud rediscovered the first language of symbols,[23] still alive in the sufferings of civilized man (*Das Unbehagen in der Kultur* [*Civilization and Its Discontents*]).

Hieroglyphics of hysteria, blazons of phobia, and labyrinths of *Zwangsneurose* [obsessive neurosis]; charms of impotence, enigmas of inhibition, and oracles of anxiety; talking arms of character,[24] seals of self-punishment, and disguises of perversion: these are the hermetic elements that our exegesis resolves, the equivocations that our invocation dissolves, and the artifices that our dialectic absolves, by delivering the imprisoned meaning in ways that run the gamut from revealing the palimpsest to providing the solution [*mot*] of the mystery and to pardoning speech.

The third paradox of the relation of language to speech is that of the subject who loses his meaning in the objectifications of discourse. However metaphysical its definition may seem, we cannot ignore its presence in the foreground of our experience. For this is the most profound alienation of the subject in our scientific civilization, and it is this alienation that we encounter first when the subject begins to talk to us about himself. In order to eliminate it entirely, analysis should thus be conducted until it has reached the endpoint of wisdom.

To provide an exemplary formulation of this, I can find no more relevant terrain than the usage of everyday speech, pointing out that the expression *"ce suis-je"* ["it is I"] of Villon's era has become inverted in the expression *"c'est moi"* ["it's me"] of modern man.

The me [*moi*] of modern man, as I have indicated elsewhere, has taken on its form in the dialectical impasse of the beautiful soul who does not recognize his very reason for being in the disorder he denounces in the world.

But a way out of this impasse is offered to the subject where his discourse
rants and raves. Communication can be validly established for him in science's 282
collective undertaking and in the tasks science ordains in our universal civilization; this communication will be effective within the enormous objectification constituted by this science, and it will allow him to forget his subjectivity. He will make an effective contribution to the collective undertaking in his daily work and will be able to occupy his leisure time with all the pleasures of a profuse culture which—providing everything from detective novels to historical memoirs and from educational lectures to the orthopedics of group relations—will give him the wherewithal to forget his own existence and his death, as well as to misrecognize the particular meaning of his life in false communication.

If the subject did not rediscover through regression—often taken as far back as the mirror stage [*stade*]—the inside of a stadium [*stade*] in which his ego contains his imaginary exploits, there would hardly be any assignable limits to the credulity to which he would have to succumb in this situation. Which is what makes our responsibility so formidable when, with the mythical manipulations of our doctrine, we bring him yet another opportunity to become alienated, in the decomposed trinity of the ego,* the superego,* and the id,* for example.

Here it is a wall of language that blocks speech, and the precautions against verbalism that are a theme of the discourse of "normal" men in our culture merely serve to increase its thickness.

There might be some point in measuring its thickness by the statistically determined total pounds of printed paper, miles of record grooves, and hours of radio broadcasts that the said culture produces per capita in sectors A, B, and C of its domain. This would be a fine research topic for our cultural organizations, and it would be seen that the question of language does not remain entirely within the region of the brain in which its use is reflected in the individual.

We are the hollow men
We are the stuffed men
Leaning together
Headpiece filled with straw. Alas!
(and so on.)

283 The resemblance between this situation and the alienation of madness—insofar as the formulation given above is authentic, namely, that the mad subject is spoken rather than speaking—is obviously related to the requirement, presupposed by psychoanalysis, of true speech. If this consequence, which takes the paradoxes that are constitutive of what I am saying here as far as they can go, were to be turned against the common sense of the psychoanalytic perspective, I would readily grant the pertinence of this objection, but only to find my own position confirmed in it—by a dialectical reversal for which there would be no shortage of authorized patrons, beginning with Hegel's critique of "the philosophy of the skull," and stopping only at Pascal's resounding warning, at the dawn of the historical era of the "me" [*"moi"*], formulated in the following terms: "Men are so necessarily mad that it would be another twist of madness not to be mad."

This is not to say, however, that our culture pursues its course in the shadows outside of creative subjectivity. On the contrary, creative subjectivity has not ceased in its struggle to renew here the never-exhausted power of symbols in the human exchange that brings them to light.

To emphasize the small number of subjects who prop up this creation would be to give in to a romantic perspective by comparing things that are not equivalent. The fact is that this subjectivity, regardless of the domain in which it appears—mathematics, politics, religion, or even advertising—continues to animate the movement of humanity as a whole. Looking at it from another, probably no less illusory, angle would lead us to emphasize the opposite trait: the fact that its symbolic character has never been more manifest. The irony of revolutions is that they engender a power that is all the more absolute in its exercise, not because it is more anonymous, as people say, but because it is reduced more completely to the words that signify it. The strength of churches lies more than ever in the language they have been able to maintain—an instance, it should be noted, that Freud left aside in the article in which he sketches out for us what I call the "collective subjectivities" of the Church and the Army.

Psychoanalysis has played a role in the direction of modern subjectivity, and it cannot sustain this role without aligning it with the movement in modern science that elucidates it.

This is the problem of the foundations that must assure our discipline its 284
place among the sciences: a problem of formalization, which, it must be admitted, has gotten off to a very bad start.

For it seems that, possessed anew by the very shortcoming in the medical mind in opposition to which psychoanalysis had to constitute itself, we were trying to jump back on the bandwagon of science—being half a century behind the movement of the sciences—by following medicine's example.

This leads to abstract objectification of our experience on the basis of fictitious, or even simulated, principles of experimental method—in which we find the effect of biases that must first be swept from our field if we wish to cultivate it according to its authentic structure.

As practitioners of the symbolic function, it is surprising that we shy away from delving deeper into it, going so far as to neglect the fact that this function situates us at the heart of the movement that is establishing a new order of the sciences, with a rethinking of anthropology.

This new order simply signifies a return to a notion of true science whose credentials are already inscribed in a tradition that begins with Plato's *Theaetetus*. This notion has degenerated, as we know, in the positivist reversal which, by making the human sciences the crowning glory of the experimental sciences, in fact subordinates them to the latter. This conception results from an erroneous view of the history of science founded on the prestige of a specialized development of experimentation.

Today, however, the conjectural sciences are discovering once again the age-old notion of science, forcing us to revise the classification of the sciences we have inherited from the nineteenth century in a direction clearly indicated by the most lucid thinkers.

One need but follow the concrete evolution of the various disciplines in order to become aware of this.

Linguistics can serve us as a guide here, since that is the vanguard role it is given by contemporary anthropology, and we cannot remain indifferent to it.

The form of mathematicization in which the discovery of the *phoneme* is inscribed, as a function of pairs of oppositions formed by the smallest graspable discriminative semantic elements, leads us to the very foundations that Freud's final doctrine designates as the subjective sources of the symbolic function in a vocalic connotation of presence and absence. 285

And the reduction of any language [*langue*] to a group comprised of a very small number of such phonemic oppositions, initiating an equally rigorous formalization of its highest-level morphemes, puts within our reach a strict approach to our own field.

It is up to us to adopt this approach to discover how it intersects with our own field, just as ethnography, which follows a course parallel to our own, is already doing by deciphering myths according to the synchrony of mythemes.

Isn't it striking that Lévi-Strauss—in suggesting the involvement in myths of language structures and of those social laws that regulate marriage ties and kinship—is already conquering the very terrain in which Freud situates the unconscious?[25]

It is thus impossible not to make a general theory of the symbol the axis of a new classification of the sciences where the sciences of man will reassume their central position as sciences of subjectivity. Let me indicate its core principle, which, of course, does not obviate the need for further elaboration.

The symbolic function presents itself as a twofold movement in the subject: man makes his own action into an object, but only to return its foundational place to it in due time. In this equivocation, operating at every instant, lies the whole progress of a function in which action and knowledge [*connaissance*] alternate.[26]

Here are two examples, one borrowed from the classroom, the other from the very pulse of our time:

- The first is mathematical: in phase one, man objectifies two collections he has counted in the form of two cardinal numbers; in phase two, he manages to add the two collections using these numbers (see the example cited by Kant in the introduction to the transcendental aesthetic, section IV, in the second edition of the *Critique of Pure Reason*);
- The second is historical: in phase one, a man who works at the level of production in our society considers himself to belong to the ranks of the proletariat; in phase two, in the name of belonging to it, he joins in a general strike.

286 If these two examples come from areas which, for us, are the most highly contrasted in the domain of the concrete—the first involving the ever freer play of mathematical law, the second, the brazen face of capitalist exploitation—it is because, although they seem to come from radically different realms, their effects come to constitute our subsistence, precisely by intersecting there in a double reversal: the most subjective science having forged a new reality, and the shadow of the social divide arming itself with a symbol in action.

Here the distinction people make between the exact sciences and those for which there is no reason to refuse the appellation "conjectural" no longer seems to be acceptable—for lack of any grounds for that distinction.[27]

For exactness must be distinguished from truth, and conjecture does not exclude rigor. If experimental science derives its exactness from mathematics, its relation to nature is nonetheless problematic.

Indeed, if our link to nature incites us to wonder poetically whether it is not nature's own movement that we refind in our science, in

> *. . . cette voix*
> *Qui se connaît quand elle sonne*
> *N'être plus la voix de personne*
> *Tant que des ondes et des bois,*

it is clear that our physics is but a mental fabrication in which mathematical symbols serve as instruments.

For experimental science is not so much defined by the quantity to which it is in fact applied, as by the measurement it introduces into reality [*réel*].

This can be seen in relation to the measurement of time without which experimental science would be impossible. Huyghens' clock, which alone gave experimental science its precision, is merely the organ that fulfills Galileo's hypothesis concerning the equal gravitational pull on all bodies—that is, the hypothesis of uniform acceleration that confers its law, since it is the same, on every instance of falling.

It is amusing to point out that the instrument was completed before the
hypothesis could be verified by observation, and that the clock thereby ren- 287
dered the hypothesis useless at the same time as it offered it the instrument it
needed to be rigorous.[28]

But mathematics can symbolize another kind of time, notably the intersubjective time that structures human action, whose formulas are beginning to be provided by game theory, still called strategy, but which it would be better to call "stochastics."

The author of these lines has attempted to demonstrate in the logic of a sophism the temporal mainsprings through which human action, insofar as it is coordinated with the other's action, finds in the scansion of its hesitations the advent of its certainty; and, in the decision that concludes it, gives the other's action—which it now includes—its direction [*sens*] to come, along with its sanction regarding the past.

I demonstrate there that it is the certainty anticipated by the subject in the "time for understanding" which—through the haste that precipitates the "moment of concluding"—determines the other's decision that makes the subject's own movement an error or truth.

This example indicates how the mathematical formalization that inspired

Boolean logic, and even set theory, can bring to the science of human action the structure of intersubjective time that psychoanalytic conjecture needs to ensure its own rigor.

If, moreover, the history of the historian's technique shows that its progress is defined in the ideal of an identification of the historian's subjectivity with the constitutive subjectivity of the primal historicization in which events are humanized, it is clear that psychoanalysis finds its precise scope here: that is, in knowledge [*connaissance*], as realizing this ideal, and in efficacy, as finding its justification here. The example of history also dissipates like a mirage the recourse to the "lived reaction" that obsesses both our technique and our theory, for the fundamental historicity of the events we are concerned with suffices to conceive the possibility of a subjective reproduction of the past in the present.

Furthermore, this example makes us realize how psychoanalytic regression
288 implies the progressive dimension of the subject's history—which Freud rightly considered to be lacking in the Jungian concept of neurotic regression—and we see how analytic experience itself renews this progression by assuring its continuation.

Finally, the reference to linguistics will introduce us to the method which, by distinguishing synchronic from diachronic structurings in language, will enable us to better understand the different value our language takes on in the interpretation of resistances and of transference, and to differentiate the effects characteristic of repression and the structure of the individual myth in obsessive neurosis.

The list of disciplines Freud considered important sister sciences for an ideal Department of Psychoanalysis is well known. Alongside psychiatry and sexology we find "the history of civilization, mythology, the psychology of religions, literary history, and literary criticism."

This whole group of subjects, determining the curriculum for instruction in technique, can be easily accommodated in the epistemological triangle I have described, and would provide an advanced level of instruction in analytic theory and technique with its primer.

For my part, I would be inclined to add: rhetoric, dialectic (in the technical sense this term takes on in Aristotle's *Topics*), grammar, and poetics—the supreme pinnacle of the aesthetics of language—which would include the neglected technique of witticisms.

While these subject headings may sound somewhat old-fashioned to certain people, I would not hesitate to endorse them as a return to our sources.

For psychoanalysis in its early development, intimately linked to the discovery and study of symbols, went so far as to partake in the structure of what

was called "the liberal arts" in the Middle Ages. Deprived, like them, of a true formalization, psychoanalysis became organized, like them, into a body of privileged problems, each one promoted by some felicitous relation of man to his own measure, taking on a charm and a humanity owing to this particularity that in our eyes might well make up for their somewhat recreational appearance. But let us not disdain this appearance in the early developments of psychoanalysis; indeed, it expresses nothing less than the re-creation of human 289
meaning in an arid era of scientism.

These early developments should be all the less disdained since psychoanalysis has hardly raised the bar by setting off along the false pathways of a theorization that runs counter to its dialectical structure.

Psychoanalysis can provide scientific foundations for its theory and technique only by adequately formalizing the essential dimensions of its experience, which—along with the historical theory of the symbol—are intersubjective logic and the temporality of the subject.

III. The Resonances of Interpretation and the Time of the Subject in Psychoanalytic Technique

> Between man and love,
>   There is woman.
> Between man and woman,
>   There is a world.
> Between man and the world,
>   There is a wall.
> —Antoine Tudal, *Paris in the Year 2000*

> *Nam Sibyllam quidem Cumis ego ipse oculis meis vidi in ampulla pendere, et cum illi pueri dicerent:* Σιβύλλα τι θέλεις, *respondebat illa:* ἀποθανείν θέλω.
> —Petronius, *Satyricon*, XLVIII

Bringing psychoanalytic experience back to speech and language as its foundations is of direct concern to its technique. While it is not situated in the ineffable, we see the one-way slippage that has occurred, distancing interpretation from its core. We are thus justified in suspecting that this deviation in psychoanalytic practice explains the new aims to which psychoanalytic theory has become receptive.

If we look at the situation a little more closely, we see that the problems of symbolic interpretation began by intimidating our little group before becoming embarrassing to it. The successes obtained by Freud now astonish people because of the unseemly indoctrination they appear to involve, and the dis- 290
play thereof—so evident in the cases of Dora, the Rat Man, and the Wolf

Man—strikes us as nothing short of scandalous. Indeed, our clever colleagues do not shrink from doubting whether the technique employed in these cases was actually any good.

This disaffection in the psychoanalytic movement stems, in truth, from a confusion of tongues, about which the most representative personality of its present hierarchy made no secret in a recent conversation with me.

It is well worth noting that this confusion grows when each analyst believes he has been assigned the job of discovering in our experience the conditions of a complete objectification, and when the enthusiasm that greets his theoretical attempts is greater the more detached from reality they prove to be.

It is clear that the principles of the analysis of the resistances, as well-founded as they may be, have in practice occasioned an ever greater misrecognition of the subject, because they have not been understood in relation to the intersubjectivity of speech.

If we follow the proceedings of Freud's first seven sessions with the Rat Man, which are reported to us in full, it seems highly improbable that Freud did not recognize the resistances as they arose—arising precisely in the places where our modern practitioners tell us he overlooked them—since it is Freud's own text, after all, that enables the practitioners to pinpoint them. Once again Freud's texts manifest an exhaustion of the subject that amazes us, and no interpretation has thus far exploited all of its resources.

I mean that Freud not only let himself be duped into encouraging his subject to go beyond his initial reticence, but also understood perfectly well the seductive scope of this game in the imaginary. To convince oneself of this, one need but read the description he gives us of the expression on his patient's face during the patient's painful narrative of the purported torture that supplied the theme of his obsession, that of the rat forced into the victim's anus: "His face," Freud tells us, "reflected horror at a jouissance of which he was unaware." The effect in the present of his repeating this narrative did not escape Freud, no more than did the fact that he identified his analyst with the "cruel captain" who forced this narrative to become etched in the subject's memory,
291 nor therefore the import of the theoretical clarifications the subject required as security before going on with what he was saying.

Far from interpreting the resistance here, however, Freud astonishes us by granting the patient's request, to such an extent that he seems to let himself be roped into the subject's game.

But the extremely approximate character of the explanations with which Freud gratifies him, so approximate as to appear crude, is sufficiently instructive: it is clearly not so much a question here of doctrine or indoctrination as of a symbolic gift of speech—ripe with a secret pact, in the context of the imaginary participation which includes it—whose import will be revealed later in the symbolic equivalence the subject establishes in his mind between rats and the florins with which he remunerates the analyst.

We can see therefore that Freud, far from misrecognizing the resistance, uses it as a propitious predisposition for setting in motion the resonances of speech, and he conducts himself, as far as possible, in accordance with the first definition he gave of resistance, by employing it to involve the subject in his message. He later changes tack abruptly when he sees that, as a result of being handled delicately, the resistance is serving to keep the dialogue at the level of a conversation in which the subject tries to continue seducing the analyst by slipping beyond his reach.

But we learn that analysis consists in playing on the multiple staves of the score that speech constitutes in the registers of language—which is where overdetermination comes in, the latter having no meaning except in this order.

And we have simultaneously isolated here the mainspring of Freud's success. In order for the analyst's message to respond to the subject's profound questioning, the subject must understand it as a response that concerns him alone; and the privilege Freud's patients enjoyed, in receiving its good word from the lips of the very man who was its herald, satisfied this demand of theirs.

Let us note in passing that the Rat Man had had a prior taste of it, since he had thumbed through *The Psychopathology of Everyday Life*, which had just come out.

Which doesn't imply that the book is very much better known today, even among analysts, but the popularization of Freud's concepts and their resorption into what I call the wall of language, would deaden the effect of our speech were we to give it the style of Freud's remarks to the Rat Man. 292

The point here is not to imitate him. In order to rediscover the effect of Freud's speech, I won't resort to its terms but rather to the principles that govern it.

These principles are nothing but the dialectic of self-consciousness, as it is realized from Socrates to Hegel, beginning with the ironic assumption that all that is rational is real, only to precipitate into the scientific judgment that all that is real is rational. But Freud's discovery was to demonstrate that this verifying process authentically reaches the subject only by decentering him from self-consciousness, to which he was confined by Hegel's reconstruction of the phenomenology of mind. In other words, this discovery renders still flimsier any search for "conscious realization" which, apart from being a psychological phenomenon, is not inscribed within the conjuncture of the particular moment that alone gives body to the universal, and failing which the latter dissipates into generality.

These remarks define the limits within which it is impossible for our technique to ignore the structuring moments of Hegel's phenomenology: first and foremost, the master/slave dialectic, the dialectic of the beautiful soul and the law of the heart, and generally everything that allows us to understand how the constitution of the object is subordinate to the realization of the subject.

But if there is still something prophetic in Hegel's insistence on the fundamental identity of the particular and the universal, an insistence that reveals the extent of his genius, it is certainly psychoanalysis that provides it with its paradigm by revealing the structure in which this identity is realized as disjunctive of the subject, and without appealing to the future.

Let me simply say that this, in my view, constitutes an objection to any reference to totality in the individual, since the subject introduces division therein, as well as in the collectivity that is the equivalent of the individual. Psychoanalysis is what clearly relegates both the one and the other to the status of mirages.

This would seem to be something that could no longer be forgotten, were it not precisely psychoanalysis that teaches us that it is forgettable—confir-
293 mation of which turns out, by a reversal [*retour*] that is more legitimate than one might think, to come from psychoanalysts themselves, their "new tendencies" representing this forgetting.

Now while Hegel's work is also precisely what we need to confer a meaning on so-called analytic neutrality other than that the analyst is simply in a stupor, this does not mean that we have nothing to learn from the elasticity of the Socratic method or even from the fascinating proceedings of the technique by which Plato presents it to us, were it only by our sensing in Socrates and his desire the unresolved enigma of the psychoanalyst, and by situating in relation to Platonic vision our own relation to truth—in this case, however, in a way that respects the distance separating the reminiscence Plato was led to presume to exist in any advent of the ideas, from the exhaustion of being consummated in Kierkegaardian repetition.[29]

But there is also a historical difference between Socrates' interlocutor and ours that is worth weighing. When Socrates relies on an artisanal form of reason that he can extract just as well from a slave's discourse, it is in order to impress upon authentic masters the necessity of an order that turns their power into justice and the city's magic words [*maîtres-mots*] into truth. But we analysts deal with slaves who think they are masters, and who find in a language—whose mission is universal—support for their servitude in the bonds of its ambiguity. So much so that one might humorously say that our goal is to restore in them the sovereign freedom displayed by Humpty Dumpty when he reminds Alice that he is, after all, master of the signifier, even if he is not master of the signified from which his being derived its shape.

We always come back, then, to our twofold reference to speech and language. In order to free the subject's speech, we introduce him to the language of his desire, that is, to the *primary language* in which—beyond what he tells us of himself—he is already speaking to us unbeknown to himself, first and foremost, in the symbols of his symptom.

It is certainly a language that is at stake in the symbolism brought to light in analysis. This language, corresponding to the playful wish found in one of Lichtenberg's aphorisms, has the universal character of a tongue that would be understood in all other tongues, but at the same time—since it is the language that grabs hold of desire at the very moment it becomes humanized by 294
gaining recognition—it is absolutely particular to the subject.

It is thus a *primary language*, by which I do not mean a primitive language, since Freud—whose merit for having made this total discovery warrants comparison with Champollion's—deciphered it in its entirety in the dreams of our contemporaries. The essential field of this language was rather authoritatively defined by one of the earliest assistants associated with Freud's work, and one of the few to have brought anything new to it: I mean Ernest Jones, the last survivor of those to whom the seven rings of the master were passed and who attests by his presence in the honorary positions of an international association that they are not reserved solely for relic bearers.

In a fundamental article on symbolism,[30] Jones points out on page 102 that, although there are thousands of symbols in the sense in which the term is understood in analysis, all of them refer to one's own body, blood relatives, birth, life, and death.

This truth, recognized *de facto* by Jones, enables us to understand that although the symbol, psychoanalytically speaking, is repressed in the unconscious, it bears in itself no mark of regression or even of immaturity. For it to have its effects in the subject, it is thus enough that it make itself heard, since these effects operate unbeknown to him—as we admit in our everyday experience, when we explain many reactions by normal and neurotic subjects as their response to the symbolic meaning of an act, a relation, or an object.

It is thus indisputable that the analyst can play on the power of symbols by evoking them in a calculated fashion in the semantic resonances of his remarks.

This is surely the path by which a return to the use of symbolic effects can proceed in a renewed technique of interpretation.

We could adopt as a reference here what the Hindu tradition teaches about *dhvani*,[31] defining it as the property of speech by which it conveys what it does
not say. This is illustrated by a little tale whose naïveté, which appears to be 295
required in such examples, proves funny enough to induce us to penetrate to the truth it conceals.

A girl, it is said, is awaiting her lover on the bank of a river when she sees a Brahmin coming along. She approaches him and exclaims in the most amiable tones: "What a lucky day this is for you! The dog whose barking used to frighten you will not be on this river bank again, for it was just devoured by a lion that roams around here . . ."

The absence of the lion may thus have as many effects as his spring—which, were he present, would only come once, according to the proverb relished by Freud.

The *primary* character of symbols in fact makes them similar to those numbers out of which all other numbers are composed; and if they therefore underlie all the semantemes of a language, we shall be able to restore to speech its full evocative value by a discreet search for their interferences, following the course of a metaphor whose symbolic displacement neutralizes the secondary meanings of the terms it associates.

To be taught and to be learned, this technique would require a profound assimilation of the resources of a language [*langue*], especially those that are concretely realized in its poetic texts. It is well known that Freud was steeped in German literature, which, by virtue of an incomparable translation, can be said to include Shakespeare's plays. Every one of his works bears witness to this, and to the continual recourse he had to it, no less in his technique than in his discovery. Not to mention his broad background in the classics, his familiarity with the modern study of folklore, and his keeping abreast of contemporary humanism's conquests in the area of ethnography.

Analytic practitioners should be asked not to consider it futile to follow Freud along this path.

But the tide is against us. It can be gauged by the condescending attention paid to the "wording,"* as if to some novelty; and the English morphology here provides a notion that is still difficult to define with a prop that is sufficiently subtle for people to make a big to-do about it.

296 What this notion covers, however, is hardly encouraging when we see an author[32] amazed at having achieved an entirely different success in the interpretation of one and the same resistance by the use, "without conscious premeditation," he emphasizes, of the term "need for love"* instead of and in the place of "demand for love,"* which he had first put forward, without seeing anything in it (as he himself tells us). While the anecdote is supposed to confirm the interpretation's reference to the "ego psychology"* in the title of the article, it refers instead, it seems, to the analyst's ego psychology,* insofar as this interpretation makes do with such a weak use of English that he can extend his practice of analysis right to the very brink of gibberish.[33]

The fact is that need* and demand* have diametrically opposed meanings for the subject, and to maintain that they can be used interchangeably for even an instant amounts to a radical ignorance of the *summoning* characteristic of speech.

For in its symbolizing function, speech tends toward nothing less than a transformation of the subject to whom it is addressed by means of the link it establishes with the speaker—namely, by bringing about a signifying effect.

This is why we must return once more to the structure of communication in language and definitively dispel the mistaken notion of "language as signs," a source in this realm of confusions about discourse and of errors about speech.

If communication based on language is conceived as a signal by which the sender informs the receiver of something by means of a certain code, there is no reason why we should not lend as much credence and even more to every other kind of sign when the "something" in question concerns the individual: indeed, we are quite right to prefer every mode of expression that verges on natural signs.

It is in this way that the technique of speech has been discredited among us and we find ourselves in search of a gesture, a grimace, a posture adopted, a
face made, a movement, a shudder—nay, a stopping of usual movement—for 297
we are subtle and nothing will stop us from setting our bloodhounds on the scent.

I shall show the inadequacy of the conception of language as signs by the very manifestation that best illustrates it in the animal kingdom, a manifestation which, had it not recently been the object of an authentic discovery, would have to have been invented for this purpose.

It is now generally recognized that, when a bee returns to its hive after gathering nectar, it transmits an indication of the existence of nectar near or far away from the hive to its companions by two sorts of dances. The second is the most remarkable, for the plane in which the bee traces out a figure-eight—a shape that gave it the name "wagging dance"*—and the frequency of the figures executed within a given time, designate, on the one hand, the exact direction to be followed, determined in relation to the sun's inclination (by which bees are able to orient themselves in all kinds of weather, thanks to their sensitivity to polarized light), and, on the other hand, the distance at which the nectar is to be found up to several miles away. The other bees respond to this message by immediately setting off for the place thus designated.

It took some ten years of patient observation for Karl von Frisch to decode this kind of message, for it is certainly a code or signaling system, whose generic character alone forbids us to qualify it as conventional.

But is it a language, for all that? We can say that it is distinguished from language precisely by the fixed correlation between its signs and the reality they signify. For, in a language, signs take on their value from their relations to each other in the lexical distribution of semantemes as much as in the positional, or even flectional, use of morphemes—in sharp contrast to the fixity of the coding used by bees. The diversity of human languages takes on its full value viewed in this light.

Furthermore, while a message of the kind described here determines the action of the "socius," it is never retransmitted by the socius. This means that the message remains frozen in its function as a relay of action, from which no
298 subject detaches it as a symbol of communication itself.[34]

The form in which language expresses itself in and of itself defines subjectivity. Language says: "You will go here, and when you see this, you will turn off there." In other words, it refers to discourse about the other [*discours de l'autre*]. It is enveloped as such in the highest function of speech, inasmuch as speech commits its author by investing its addressee with a new reality, as for example, when a subject seals his fate as a married man by saying "You are my wife."

Indeed, this is the essential form from which all human speech derives more than the form at which it arrives.

Hence the paradox that one of my most acute auditors believed to be an objection to my position when I first began to make my views known on analysis as dialectic; he formulated it as follows: "Human language would then constitute a kind of communication in which the sender receives his own message back from the receiver in an inverted form." I could but adopt this objector's formulation, recognizing in it the stamp of my own thinking; for I maintain that speech always subjectively includes its own reply, that "Thou wouldst not seek Me, if thou hadst not found Me" simply validates the same truth, and that this is why, in the paranoiac refusal of recognition, it is in the form of a negative verbalization that the unavowable feeling eventually emerges in a persecutory "interpretation."

Thus when you congratulate yourself for having met someone who speaks the same language as you, you do not mean that you encounter each other in the discourse of everyman, but that you are united to that person by a particular way of speaking.

The antinomy immanent in the relations between speech and language thus
299 becomes clear. The more functional language becomes, the less suited it is to speech, and when it becomes overly characteristic of me alone, it loses its function as language.

We are aware of the use made in primitive traditions of secret names, with which the subject identifies his own person or his gods so closely that to reveal these names is to lose himself or betray these gods; and what our patients confide in us, as well as our own recollections, teach us that it is not at all rare for children to spontaneously rediscover the virtues of that use.

Finally, the speech value of a language is gauged by the intersubjectivity of the "we" it takes on.

By an inverse antinomy, it can be observed that the more language's role is neutralized as language becomes more like information, the more *redundancies* are attributed to it. This notion of redundancy originated in research that was all the more precise because a vested interest was involved, having been prompted by the economics of long-distance communication and, in particular, by the possibility of transmitting several conversations on a single telephone line simultaneously. It was observed that a substantial portion of the phonetic medium is superfluous for the communication actually sought to be achieved.

This is highly instructive to us,[35] for what is redundant as far as information is concerned is precisely what plays the part of resonance in speech.

For the function of language in speech is not to inform but to evoke.

What I seek in speech is a response from the other. What constitutes me as a subject is my question. In order to be recognized by the other, I proffer what was only in view of what will be. In order to find him, I call him by a name that he must assume or refuse in order to answer me.

I identify myself in language, but only by losing myself in it as an object.
What is realized in my history is neither the past definite as what was, since it 300
is no more, nor even the perfect as what has been in what I am, but the future anterior as what I will have been, given what I am in the process of becoming.

If I now face someone to question him, there is no cybernetic device imaginable that can turn his response into a reaction. The definition of "response" as the second term in the "stimulus-response" circuit is simply a metaphor sustained by the subjectivity attributed to animals, only to be elided thereafter in the physical schema to which the metaphor reduces it. This is what I have called putting a rabbit into a hat so as to pull it out again later. But a reaction is not a response.

If I press an electric button and a light goes on, there is a response only to *my* desire. If in order to obtain the same result I must try a whole system of relays whose correct position is unknown to me, there is a question only in relation to my expectation, and there will not be a question any more once I have learned enough about the system to operate it flawlessly.

But if I call the person to whom I am speaking by whatever name I like, I notify him of the subjective function he must take up in order to reply to me, even if it is to repudiate this function.

The decisive function of my own response thus appears, and this function is not, as people maintain, simply to be received by the subject as approval or rejection of what he is saying, but truly to recognize or abolish him as a subject. Such is the nature of the analyst's *responsibility* every time he intervenes by means of speech.

The problem of the therapeutic effects of inexact interpretation, raised by Edward Glover in a remarkable paper,[36] thus led him to conclusions where the question of exactness fades into the background. For not only is every spoken intervention received by the subject as a function of his structure, but the intervention itself takes on a structuring function due to its form. Indeed, non-analytic psychotherapies, and even utterly ordinary medical "prescriptions," have the precise impact of interventions that could be qualified as
301 obsessive systems of suggestion, as hysterical suggestions of a phobic nature, and even as persecutory supports, each psychotherapy deriving its particular character from the way it sanctions the subject's misrecognition of his own reality.

Speech is in fact a gift of language, and language is not immaterial. It is a subtle body, but body it is. Words are caught up in all the body images that captivate the subject; they may "knock up" the hysteric, be identified with the object of *Penisneid*, represent the urinary flow of urethral ambition, or represent the feces retained in avaricious jouissance.

Furthermore, words themselves can suffer symbolic lesions and accomplish imaginary acts whose victim is the subject. Recall the *Wespe* (wasp), castrated of its initial W to become the S.P. of the Wolf Man's initials, at the moment he carried out the symbolic punishment to which he himself was subjected by Grusha, the wasp.

Recall too the S that constitutes the residue of the hermetic formula into which the Rat Man's conjuratory invocations became condensed after Freud had extracted the anagram of his beloved's name from its cipher, and that, tacked onto the beginning of the final "amen" of his jaculatory prayer, eternally inundated the lady's name with the symbolic ejecta of his impotent desire.

Similarly, an article by Robert Fliess,[37] inspired by Abraham's inaugural remarks, shows us that one's discourse as a whole may become eroticized, following the displacements of erogeneity in the body image, momentarily determined by the analytic relationship.

Discourse then takes on a urethral-phallic, anal-erotic, or even oral-sadistic function. It is noteworthy, moreover, that the author grasps its effect above all in the silences that mark inhibition of the satisfaction the subject derives from it.

In this way speech may become an imaginary or even real object in the subject and, as such, debase in more than one respect the function of language. I shall thus relegate such speech to the parenthesis of the resistance it manifests.

But not in order to exclude it from the analytic relationship, for the latter would then lose everything, including its *raison d'être*. 302

Analysis can have as its goal only the advent of true speech and the subject's realization of his history in its relation to a future.

Maintaining this dialectic is directly opposed to any objectifying orientation of analysis, and highlighting this necessity is of capital importance if we are to see through the aberrations of the new trends in psychoanalysis.

I shall illustrate my point here by once again returning to Freud, and, since I have already begun to make use of it, to the case of the Rat Man.

Freud goes so far as to take liberties with the exactness of the facts when it is a question of getting at the subject's truth. At one point, Freud glimpses the determinant role played by the mother's proposal that he marry her cousin's daughter at the origin of the present phase of his neurosis. Indeed, as I have shown in my seminar, this flashes through Freud's mind owing to his own personal experience. But he does not hesitate to interpret its effect to the subject as that of a prohibition by his dead father against his liaison with his lady-love.

This interpretation is not only factually, but also psychologically, inexact, for the father's castrating activity—which Freud affirms here with an insistence that might be believed systematic—played only a secondary role in this case. But Freud's apperception of the dialectical relationship is so apt that the interpretation he makes at that moment triggers the decisive destruction of the lethal symbols that narcissistically bind the subject both to his dead father and to his idealized lady, their two images being sustained, in an equivalence characteristic of the obsessive, one by the fantasmatic aggressiveness that perpetuates it, the other by the mortifying cult that transforms it into an idol.

Similarly, it is by recognizing the forced subjectivization of the obsessive debt[38]—in the scenario of futile attempts at restitution, a scenario that too perfectly expresses its imaginary terms for the subject to even try to enact it, the 303
pressure to repay the debt being exploited by the subject to the point of delusion—that Freud achieves his goal. This is the goal of bringing the subject to rediscover—in the story of his father's lack of delicacy, his marriage to the subject's mother, the "pretty but penniless girl," his wounded love-life, and his ungrateful forgetting of his beneficent friend—to rediscover in this story, along with the fateful constellation that presided over the subject's very birth, the unfillable gap constituted by the symbolic debt against which his neurosis is a protest.

There is no trace here at all of recourse to the ignoble specter of some sort of early "fear," or even to a masochism that it would be easy enough to brandish, much less to that obsessive buttressing propagated by some analysts in the name of the analysis of the defenses. The resistances themselves, as I have shown elsewhere, are used as long as possible in the direction [*sens*] of the progress of the discourse. And when it is time to put an end to them, we manage to do so by giving in to them.

For this is how the Rat Man is able to insert into his subjectivity its true mediation in a transferential form: the imaginary daughter he gives Freud in order to receive her hand in marriage from him, and who unveils her true face to him in a key dream—that of death gazing at him with its bituminous eyes.

And although it was with this symbolic pact that the ruses of the subject's servitude came to an end, reality did not fail him, it seems, in granting him these nuptial wishes. The footnote added to the case in 1923—which Freud dedicated as an epitaph to this young man who had found in the risks of war "the end that awaited so many worthy young men on whom so many hopes had been founded," thus concluding the case with all the rigor of destiny—elevates it to the beauty of tragedy.

In order to know how to respond to the subject in analysis, the method is to first determine where his ego* is situated—the ego* that Freud himself defined as formed by a verbal nucleus—in other words, to figure out through whom and for whom the subject asks *his question*. As long as this is not known, we risk misconstruing the desire that must be recognized there and the object to whom this desire is addressed.

The hysteric captivates this object in a subtle intrigue and her ego* is in the third person by means of whom the subject enjoys the object who incarnates
304 her question. The obsessive drags into the cage of his narcissism the objects in which his question reverberates in the multiplied alibi of deadly figures and, mastering their high-wire act, addresses his ambiguous homage toward the box in which he himself has his seat, that of the master who cannot be seen [*se voir*].

Trahit sua quemque voluptas; one identifies with the spectacle and the other puts on a show [*donne à voir*].

In the case of the hysterical subject, for whom the term "acting out"* takes on its literal meaning since he acts outside himself, you have to get him to recognize where his action is situated. In the case of the obsessive, you have to get yourself recognized in the spectator, who is invisible from the stage, to whom he is united by the mediation of death.

It is therefore always in the relation between the subject's *ego* and his discourse's *I* that you must understand the meaning of the discourse if you are to unalienate the subject.

But you cannot possibly achieve this if you cleave to the idea that the subject's ego is identical to the presence that is speaking to you.

This error is fostered by the terminology of the topography that is all too tempting to an objectifying cast of mind, allowing it to slide from the ego defined as the perception-consciousness system—that is, as the system of the subject's objectifications—to the ego conceived of as the correlate of an absolute reality and thus, in a singular return of the repressed in psychologistic thought, to once again take the ego as the "reality function" in relation to which Pierre Janet organizes his psychological conceptions.

Such slippage occurred only because it was not realized that, in Freud's work, the ego,* id,* superego* topography is subordinate to the metapsychology whose terms he was propounding at the same time and without which the topography loses its meaning. Analysts thus became involved in a sort of psychological orthopedics that will continue to bear fruit for a long time to come.

Michael Balint has provided a thoroughly penetrating analysis of the interaction between theory and technique in the genesis of a new conception of analysis, and he finds no better term to indicate its result than the watchword he borrows from Rickman: the advent of a "two-body psychology."*

Indeed, it couldn't be better put. Analysis is becoming the relation of two bodies between which a fantasmatic communication is established in which the analyst teaches the subject to apprehend himself as an object. Subjectivity is admitted into analysis only as long as it is bracketed as an illusion, and speech 305
is excluded from a search for lived experience that becomes its supreme aim; but its dialectically necessary result appears in the fact that, since the analyst's subjectivity is freed [*délivrée*] from all restraint, this leaves the subject at the mercy [*livré*] of every summons of the analyst's speech.

Once the intrasubjective topography has become entified, it is in fact realized in the division of labor between the subjects present. This deviant use of Freud's formulation that all that is id* must become ego* appears in a demystified form: the subject, transformed into an *it*, has to conform to an ego* which the analyst has no trouble recognizing as his ally, since it is, in fact, the analyst's own ego.*

It is precisely this process that is expressed in many a theoretical formulation of the splitting* of the ego* in analysis. Half of the subject's ego* crosses over to the other side of the wall that separates the analysand from the analyst, then half of the remaining half, and so on, in an asymptotic progression that never succeeds—regardless of how great the inroads it makes into the opinion the subject will have formed of himself—in crushing his every possibility of reversing the aberrant effects of his analysis.

But how could a subject, who undergoes a type of analysis based on the principle that all his formulations are systems of defense, defend himself against the total disorientation to which this principle consigns the analyst's dialectic?

Freud's interpretation, the dialectical method of which appears so clearly in the case of Dora, does not present these dangers, for when the analyst's biases (that is, his countertransference, a term whose correct use, in my view, cannot be extended beyond the dialectical reasons for his error) have misled him in his intervention, he immediately pays a price for it in the form of a negative transference. For the latter manifests itself with a force that is all the greater the further such an analysis has already led the subject toward an authentic recognition, and what usually results is the breaking off of the analysis.

This is exactly what happened in Dora's case, because of Freud's relentless attempts to make her think Herr K. was the hidden object of her desire; the constitutive biases of Freud's countertransference led him to see in Herr K. the promise of Dora's happiness.

Dora herself was undoubtedly mistaken [*feintée*] about her relationship with
306 Herr K., but she did not feel any the less that Freud was too. Yet when she comes back to see him, after a lapse of fifteen months—in which the fateful cipher of her "time for understanding" is inscribed—we can sense that she begins to feign to have been feigning. The convergence of this feint, raised to the second power, with the aggressive intent Freud attributes to it—not inaccurately, of course, but without recognizing its true mainspring—presents us with a rough idea of the intersubjective complicity that an "analysis of resistances," sure of being within its rights, might have perpetuated between them. There can be little doubt that, with the means now available to us due to the "progress" that has been made in our technique, this human error could have been extended well beyond the point at which it would have become diabolical.

None of this is my own invention, for Freud himself recognized after the fact the preliminary source of his failure in his own misrecognition at that time of the homosexual position of the object aimed at by the hysteric's desire.

The whole process that led to this current trend in psychoanalysis no doubt goes back, first of all, to the analyst's guilty conscience about the miracle his speech performs. He interprets the symbol and, lo and behold, the symptom—which inscribes the symbol in letters of suffering in the subject's flesh—disappears. This thaumaturgy is unbecoming to us. For, after all, we are scientists and magic is not a justifiable practice. So we disclaim responsibility by accusing the patient of magical thinking. Before long we'll be preaching the Gospel according to Lévy-Bruhl to him. But in the meantime—behold—we have become thinkers again, and have re-established the proper distance between ourselves and our patients; for we had, no doubt, a little too quickly abandoned the tradition of respecting that distance, a tradition expressed so nobly in the lines by Pierre Janet in which he spoke of the feeble abilities of the hysteric compared to our own lofty ones. "She understands nothing about science," he confides to us regarding the poor little thing, "and doesn't even imagine how anybody could be interested in it . . . If we consider the absence of control that characterizes hysterics' thinking, rather than allowing ourselves to be scandalized by their lies, which, in any case, are very naive, we should instead be astonished that there are so many honest ones . . ."

Since these lines represent the feelings to which many of those present-day analysts who condescend to speak to the patient "in his own language" have reverted, they may help us understand what has happened in the meantime. For had Freud been capable of endorsing such lines, how could he have heard 307
as he did the truth contained in the little stories told by his first patients, or deciphered a dark delusion like Schreber's to such a great extent as to broaden it to encompass man eternally bound to his symbols?

Is our reason so weak that it cannot see that it is the same in the meditations of scientific discourse and in the first exchange of symbolic objects, and cannot find here the identical measure of its original cunning?

Need I point out what the yardstick of "thought" is worth to practitioners of an experience that associates the job of thought more closely with a mental eroticism than with an equivalent of action?

Must the person who is speaking to you attest that he need not resort to "thought" to understand that, if he is speaking to you at this moment about speech, it is insofar as we have in common a technique of speech which enables you to understand him when he speaks to you about it, and which inclines him to address those who understand nothing of it through you?

Of course, we must be attentive to the unsaid that dwells in the holes in discourse, but the unsaid is not to be understood like knocking coming from the other side of the wall.

If we are to concern ourselves from now on with nothing but such noises, as some analysts pride themselves on doing, it must be admitted that we have not placed ourselves in the most favorable of conditions to decipher their meaning—for how, without jumping to conclusions about their meaning, are we to translate what is not in and of itself language? Led then to call upon the subject, since it is after all to his account that we must transfer this understanding, we shall involve him with us in a wager, a wager that we understand their meaning, and then wait for a return that makes us both winners. As a result, in continuing to perform this shuttling back and forth, he will learn quite simply to beat time himself; it is a form of suggestion which is no worse than any other—in other words, one in which, as in every other form of suggestion, one does not know who starts the ball rolling. The procedure is recognized as being sound enough when it is a question of going to prison.[39]

Halfway to this extreme the question arises: does psychoanalysis remain a dialectical relation in which the analyst's nonaction guides the subject's dis- 308 course toward the realization of his truth, or is it to be reduced to a fantasmatic relation in which "two abysses brush up against each other" without touching, until the whole range of imaginary regressions is exhausted—reduced, that is, to a sort of "bundling"*[40] taken to the extreme as a psychological test?

In fact, this illusion—which impels us to seek the subject's reality beyond the wall of language—is the same one that leads the subject to believe that his truth is already there in us, that we know it in advance. This is also why he is so open to our objectifying interventions.

He, of course, does not have to answer for this subjective error which, whether it is avowed or not in his discourse, is immanent in the fact that he entered analysis and concluded the original pact involved in it. And we can still less neglect the subjectivity of this moment because it reveals the reason for what may be called the constitutive effects of transference, insofar as they are distinguished by an indication of reality from the constituted effects that follow them.[41]

Freud, let us recall, in discussing the feelings people relate to the transference, insisted on the need to discern in them a reality factor. He concluded that it would be taking undue advantage of the subject's docility to try to persuade him in every case that these feelings are a mere transferential repetition of the neurosis. Now, since these real feelings manifest themselves as primary and since our own charm remains a matter of chance, there might seem to be some mystery here.

But this mystery is solved when viewed from the vantage point of the phe-
309 nomenology of the subject, insofar as the subject is constituted in the search for truth. We need but consider the traditional facts—which Buddhists provide us with, although they are not the only ones—to recognize in this form of transference the characteristic error of existence, broken down by Buddhists into the following three headings: love, hate, and ignorance. It is therefore as a counter to the analytic movement that we shall understand their equivalence in what is called a positive transference at the outset—each one being shed light on by the other two in this existential aspect, as long as one does not except the third, which is usually omitted because of its proximity to the subject.

I am alluding here to the invective with which someone called upon me to witness the lack of discretion shown by a certain work (which I have already cited too often) in its insane objectification of the play of the instincts in analysis, someone whose debt to me can be recognized by his use of the term "real" in conformity with mine. It was in the following words that he "unburdened his heart," as they say: "It is high time we put an end to the fraud that tends to perpetrate the belief that anything real whatsoever takes place during treatment." Let us leave aside what has become of him, for alas, if analysis has not cured the dog's oral vice mentioned in the Scriptures, its state is worse than before: it is others' vomit that it laps up.

This sally was not ill directed, since it sought in fact to distinguish between those elementary registers, whose foundations I have since laid, known as the symbolic, the imaginary, and the real—a distinction never previously made in psychoanalysis.

Reality in analytic experience often, in fact, remains veiled in negative forms, but it is not that difficult to situate.

Reality is encountered, for instance, in what we usually condemn as active interventions; but it would be an error to limit its definition in this way.

For it is clear that the analyst's abstention—his refusal to respond—is also an element of reality in analysis. More exactly, the junction between the symbolic and the real lies in this negativity, insofar as it is pure—that is, detached from any particular motive. This follows from the fact that the analyst's non-action is founded on the knowledge affirmed in the principle that all that is
real is rational, and on the resulting motive that it is up to the subject to find 310
anew its measure.

The fact remains that this abstention is not maintained indefinitely; when the subject's question assumes the form of true speech, we sanction it with our response; but I have shown that true speech already contains its own response—thus we are simply doubling his antiphon with our lay. What can this mean except that we do no more than give the subject's speech its dialectical punctuation?

Thus we see the other moment—which I have already pointed out theoretically—in which the symbolic and the real come together: in the function of time. It is worth dwelling for a moment on time's impact on technique.

Time plays a role in analytic technique in several ways.

It presents itself first in the total length of an analysis, and concerns the meaning to be given to the term of the analysis, which is a question that must be addressed prior to examining that of the signs of its end. I shall touch on the problem of setting a time limit to an analysis. But it is already clear that its length can only be expected to be indefinite for the subject.

This is true for two reasons that can only be distinguished from a dialectical perspective:

- The first, which is based on the limits of our field, and which confirms my remarks on the definition of its confines: we cannot predict how long a subject's *time for understanding* will last, insofar as it includes a psychological factor that escapes us by its very nature.

- The second, which is a characteristic of the subject, owing to which setting a time limit to his analysis amounts to a spatializing projection in which he already finds himself alienated from himself: from the moment his truth's due date can be predicted—whatever may become of it in the intervening intersubjectivity—the fact is that the truth is already there; that is, we reestablish in the subject his original mirage insofar as he situates his truth in us and, by sanctioning this mirage with the weight of our authority, we set the analysis off on an aberrant path whose results will be impossible to correct.

311 This is precisely what happened in the famous case of the Wolf Man, and Freud so well understood its exemplary importance that he used the case to support his argument in his article on analysis, finite or indefinite.[42]

Setting in advance a time limit to an analysis, the first form of active intervention, inaugurated (*pro pudor!*) by Freud himself—regardless of the divinatory (in the true sense of the term)[43] sureness the analyst may evince in following Freud's example—will invariably leave the subject alienated from his truth.

We find confirmation of this point in two facts from the Wolf Man case:

In the first place, despite the whole network of proofs demonstrating the historicity of the primal scene, and despite the conviction he displays concerning it—remaining imperturbable to the doubts Freud methodically cast on it in order to test him—the Wolf Man never managed to integrate his recollection of the primal scene into his history.

Secondly, the same patient later demonstrated his alienation in the most categorical way: in a paranoid form.

It is true that another factor comes in here, through which reality intervenes in the analysis—namely, the gift of money whose symbolic value I shall leave aside for another occasion, but whose import is already indicated in what I have said about the link between speech and the gift that constitutes primitive exchange. In this case, the gift of money is reversed by an initiative of Freud's in which—as in the frequency with which he returns to the case—we can recognize his unresolved subjectivization of the problems this case left in abeyance. And no one doubts but that this was a triggering factor of the Wolf
312 Man's psychosis, though without really being able to say why.

Don't we realize, nevertheless, that allowing a subject to be nourished at the expense of the analytic academy in return for the services he rendered to science as a case (for it was in fact through a group collection that the Wolf Man was supported) is also to decisively alienate him from his truth?

The material furnished in the supplementary analysis of the Wolf Man entrusted to Ruth Mack Brunswick illustrates the responsibility of the previous treatment with Freud by demonstrating my remarks on the respective places of speech and language in psychoanalytic mediation.

What's more, it is from the perspective of speech and language that one can grasp how Mack Brunswick took her bearings not at all badly in her delicate position in relation to the transference. (The reader will be reminded of the very "wall" in my metaphor, as it figures in one of the Wolf Man's dreams, the wolves in the key dream displaying their eagerness to get around it . . .) Those who attend my seminar know all this, and others can try their hand at it.[44]

What I want to do is touch on another aspect of the function of time in analytic technique that is currently a matter of much debate. I wish to say something about the length of sessions.

Here again it is a question of an element that manifestly belongs to reality, since it represents our work time, and viewed from this angle it falls within the purview of professional regulations that may be considered predominant.

But its subjective impact is no less important—and, first of all, on the analyst. The taboo surrounding recent discussion of this element is sufficient proof that the analytic group's subjectivity is hardly liberated on this question; and the scrupulous, not to say obsessive, character that observing a standard takes on for some if not most analysts—a standard whose historical and geographical variations nevertheless seem to bother no one—is a clear sign of the existence of a problem that analysts are reluctant to broach because they realize to what extent it would entail questioning the analyst's function.

Secondly, no one can ignore its importance to the subject in analysis. The unconscious, it is said—in a tone that is all the more knowing the less the speaker is capable of justifying what he means—the unconscious needs time to reveal itself. I quite agree. But I ask: how is this time to be measured? By 313
what Alexandre Koyré calls "the universe of precision"? We obviously live in such a universe, but its advent for man is relatively recent, since it goes back precisely to Huyghens' clock—in other words, to 1659—and the discontent of modern man precisely does not indicate that this precision serves him as a liberating factor. Is this time—the time characteristic of the fall of heavy bodies—in some way sacred in the sense that it corresponds to the time of the stars as it was fixed for all eternity by God—who, as Lichtenberg tells us, winds our sundials? Perhaps we could acquire a somewhat better idea of time by comparing the amount of time required for the creation of a symbolic object with the moment of inattention in which we drop it.

Whatever the case may be, if it is problematic to characterize what we do during this time as work, I believe I have made it quite clear that we can characterize what the patient does during this time as work.

But the reality, whatever it may be, of this time consequently takes on a localized value: that of receiving the product of this labor.

We play a recording role by serving a function which is fundamental in any symbolic exchange—that of gathering what *do kamo*, man in his authenticity, calls "the lasting word."

A witness blamed for the subject's sincerity, trustee of the record of his discourse, reference attesting to its accuracy, guarantor of its honesty, keeper of its testament, scrivener of its codicils, the analyst is something of a scribe.

But he remains the master of the truth of which this discourse constitutes the progress. As I have said, it is the analyst above all who punctuates its dialectic. And here he is apprehended as the judge of the value of this discourse. This has two consequences.

The ending of a session cannot but be experienced by the subject as a punctuation of his progress. We know how he calculates the moment of its arrival in order to tie it to his own timetable, or even to his evasive maneuvers, and how he anticipates it by weighing it like a weapon and watching out for it as he would for a place of shelter.

It is a fact, which can be plainly seen in the study of manuscripts of symbolic writings, whether the Bible or the Chinese canonical texts, that the absence
314 of punctuation in them is a source of ambiguity. Punctuation, once inserted, establishes the meaning; changing the punctuation renews or upsets it; and incorrect punctuation distorts it.

The indifference with which ending a session after a fixed number of minutes has elapsed interrupts the subject's moments of haste can be fatal to the conclusion toward which his discourse was rushing headlong, and can even set a misunderstanding in stone, if not furnish a pretext for a retaliatory ruse.

Beginners seem more struck by the effects of this impact than others—which gives one the impression that for others it is just a routine.

The neutrality we manifest in strictly applying the rule that sessions be of a specified length obviously keeps us on the path of non-action.

But this nonaction has a limit, otherwise we would never intervene at all—so why make intervening impossible at this point, thereby privileging it?

The danger that arises if this point takes on an obsessive value for the analyst lies simply in the fact that it lends itself to the subject's connivance, a connivance that is available not only to the obsessive, although it takes on a special force for him, owing precisely to his impression that he is working. The sense of forced labor that envelops everything for this subject, including even his leisure activities, is only too well known.

This sense is sustained by his subjective relation to the master insofar as it is the master's death that he awaits.

Indeed, the obsessive manifests one of the attitudes that Hegel did not develop in his master/slave dialectic. The slave slips away when faced with the risk of death, when the opportunity to acquire mastery is offered to him in a struggle for pure prestige. But since he knows he is mortal, he also knows that the master can die. Hence he can accept to work for the master and give up jouissance in the meantime; and, unsure as to when the master will die, he waits.

This is the intersubjective reason for both the doubt and procrastination that are obsessive character traits.

Meanwhile, all his work is governed by this intention and thus becomes doubly alienating. For not only is the subject's creation [*oeuvre*] taken away from him by another—the constitutive relation of all labor—but the subject's recognition of his own essence in his creation, in which this labor finds its justification, eludes him no less, for he himself "is not in it." He is in the anticipated moment of the master's death, at which time he will begin to live; but in the meantime he identifies with the master as dead and is thus already dead himself.

He nevertheless strives to fool the master by demonstrating his good inten- 315
tions through hard work. This is what the dutiful children of the analytic catechism express in their crude language by saying that the subject's ego* is trying to seduce his superego.*

This intrasubjective formulation is immediately demystified if we understand it in the analytic relationship, where the subject's "working through" is in fact employed to seduce the analyst.

And it is no accident that, once the dialectical progress begins to approach the challenging of the ego's* intentions in our subjects, the fantasy of the analyst's death—often experienced in the form of fear or even of anxiety—never fails to be produced.

And the subject then sets off again in an even more demonstrative elaboration of his "good will."

Can there be any doubt, then, about what happens when the master manifests disdain for the product of such work? The subject's resistance may become completely disconcerted.

From then on, his alibi—hitherto unconscious—begins to unveil itself to him, and we see him passionately seek the why and wherefore of so much effort.

I would not say so much about it if I had not been convinced—in experimenting with what have been called my "short sessions," at a stage in my career that is now over—that I was able to bring to light in a certain male subject fantasies of anal pregnancy, as well as a dream of its resolution by Cesarean section, in a time frame in which I would normally still have been listening to his speculations on Dostoyevsky's artistry.

In any case, I am not here to defend this procedure, but to show that it has a precise dialectical meaning in analytic technique.[45]

And I am not the only one to have remarked that it bears a certain resemblance to the technique known as Zen, which is applied to bring about the subject's revelation in the traditional ascesis of certain Far Eastern schools.

316 Without going to the extremes to which this technique is taken, since they would be contrary to certain of the limitations imposed by our own, a discreet application of its basic principle in analysis seems much more acceptable to me than certain methods of the so-called analysis of the resistances, insofar as such an application does not in itself entail any danger of alienating the subject.

For it shatters discourse only in order to bring forth speech.

Here we are, then, up against the wall—up against the wall of language. We are in our place here, that is, on the same side of the wall as the patient, and it is off this wall—which is the same for him as for us—that we shall try to respond to the echo of his speech.

There is nothing that is anything but outer darkness to us beyond this wall. Does this mean that we thoroughly master the situation? Certainly not, and on this point Freud has bequeathed us his testament regarding the negative therapeutic reaction.

The key to this mystery, it is said, is in the insistence [*instance*] of a primary masochism—in other words, in a pure manifestation of the death instinct whose enigma Freud propounded for us at the height of his career.

We cannot discount it, any more than I can postpone examining it here.

For I note that two different groups join forces in refusing to accept this culminating point of Freud's doctrine: those whose approach to analysis revolves around a conception of the ego* which I have shown to be erroneous, and those who, like Reich, take the principle of seeking an ineffable organic expression beyond speech so far that, like him, in order to free it from its armor, they might symbolize, as he does, the orgasmic induction that, like him, they expect from analysis in the superimposition of the two vermicular forms whose stupefying schema is found in his book, *Character Analysis*.

Once I have demonstrated the profound relationship uniting the notion of the death instinct to problems of speech, we will see that a rigorous logic governing intellectual productions underlies this joining of forces.

As even a moment's reflection shows, the notion of the death instinct involves a basic irony, since its meaning has to be sought in the conjunction
317 of two opposing terms: "instinct" which, in its broadest acceptation, is the law that regulates the successive stages of a behavioral cycle in order to accomplish a life function; and "death" which appears first of all as the destruction of life.

Nevertheless, the definition of life provided by Bichat at the dawn of biology as the set of forces that resist death, and the most modern conception of life—found in Cannon's notion of homeostasis—as the function of a system maintaining its own equilibrium, are there to remind us that life and death come together in a relation of polar opposites at the very heart of phenomena that people associate with life.

Hence the congruence of the contrasting terms of the death instinct with the phenomena of repetition, Freud in fact relating the former to the latter with the term "automatism," would not cause difficulty were it simply a question of a biological notion.

But, as we all know, it is not, which is what makes the problem a stumbling block to so many of us. The fact that numerous analysts balk at the apparent incompatibility of these terms might well be worth our attention, for it manifests a dialectical innocence that would probably be disconcerted by the classical problem posed to semantics in the determinative statement, "a hamlet on the Ganges," by which Hindu aesthetics illustrates the second form of the resonances of language.[46]

This notion of the death instinct must be broached through its resonances in what I will call the poetics of Freud's work—a first avenue for getting at its meaning, and a dimension that is essential for understanding the dialectical repercussion of its origins at the apogee marked by this notion. It should be recalled, for example, that Freud tells us his vocation for medicine came to him during a public reading of Goethe's famous "Hymn to Nature"—that is, in a text that was brought to light by one of Goethe's friends, which the poet, in the twilight of his life, agreed to recognize as a putative child of the most youthful effusions of his pen.

At the other end of Freud's life, we see in the article on analysis considered as finite or indefinite that he explicitly relates his new conception to the conflict of the two principles governing the alternation of all life according to 318
Empedocles of Agrigentum in the fifth century B.C.—that is, in the pre-Socratic era in which nature and mind were not distinguished.

These two facts are a sufficient indication to us that what is at stake here is a myth of the dyad, whose exposition by Plato is, moreover, mentioned in *Beyond the Pleasure Principle*, a myth that can only be understood in the subjectivity of modern man by raising it to the negativity of the judgment in which it is inscribed.

This is to say that, just as the repetition automatism—which is just as completely misunderstood by those who wish to separate its two terms—aims at nothing but the historicizing temporality of the experience of transference, so the death instinct essentially expresses the limit of the subject's historical function. This limit is death—not as the possible end date of the individual's life, nor as the subject's empirical certainty, but, as Heidegger puts it, as that "possibility which is the subject's ownmost, which is unconditional, unsurpassable, certain, and as such indeterminable"—the subject being understood as defined by his historicity.

Indeed, this limit is present at every instant in what is finished in this history. It represents the past in its real form; it is not the physical past whose existence is abolished, nor the epic past as it has become perfected in the work of memory, nor the historical past in which man finds the guarantor of his future, but rather the past which manifests itself in an inverted form in repetition.[47]

This is the dead person [*le mort*] subjectivity takes as its partner in the triad instituted by its mediation in the universal conflict of *Philia*, love, and *Neikos*, strife.

Thus there is no further need to resort to the outdated notion of primary masochism to explain repetitive games in which subjectivity simultaneously masters its dereliction and gives birth to the symbol.

These are occultation games which Freud, in a flash of genius, presented
319 to us so that we might see in them that the moment at which desire is humanized is also that at which the child is born into language.

We can now see that the subject here does not simply master his deprivation by assuming it—he raises his desire to a second power. For his action destroys the object that it causes to appear and disappear by *bringing about* its absence and presence in advance. His action thus negativizes the force field of desire in order to become its own object to itself. And this object, being immediately embodied in the symbolic pair of two elementary exclamations, announces the subject's diachronic integration of the dichotomy of phonemes, whose synchronic structure the existing language offers up for him to assimilate; the child thus begins to become engaged in the system of the concrete discourse of those around him by reproducing more or less approximately in his *Fort!* and *Da!* the terms he receives from them.

Fort! Da! It is already when quite alone that the desire of the human child becomes the desire of another, of an alter ego who dominates him and whose object of desire is henceforth his own affliction.

Should the child now address an imaginary or real partner, he will see that this partner too obeys the negativity of his discourse, and since his call has the effect of making the partner slip away, he will seek to bring about the reversal that brings the partner back to his desire through a banishing summons.

Thus the symbol first manifests itself as the killing of the thing, and this death results in the endless perpetuation of the subject's desire.

The first symbol in which we recognize humanity in its vestiges is the burial, and death as a means can be recognized in every relation in which man is born into the life of his history.

This is the only life that endures and is true, since it is transmitted without being lost in a tradition passed on from subject to subject. It is impossible not to see how loftily this life transcends that inherited by the animal, in which the individual fades into the species, since no memorial distinguishes its ephemeral appearance from the appearance that reproduces it in the invariability of the type. Indeed, apart from the hypothetical mutations of the phylum that must be integrated by a subjectivity that man is still only approaching from the outside, nothing, except the experiments in which man uses it, distinguishes a particular rat from rats in general, a horse from horses, nothing except the amorphous passage from life to death—whereas Empedocles, by
throwing himself into Mount Etna, leaves forever present in the memory of 320
men the symbolic act of his being-toward-death.

Man's freedom is entirely circumscribed within the constitutive triangle of the following: the renunciation he imposes on the other's desire by threatening to kill the other in order to enjoy the fruits of the other's serfdom, the sacrifice of his life that he agrees to for the reasons that give human life its measure, and the suicidal abnegation of the vanquished party that deprives the master of his victory and leaves him to his inhuman solitude.

Of these figures of death, the third is the supreme detour by which the immediate particularity of desire, reconquering its ineffable form, refinds in negation a final triumph. And we must recognize its meaning, for as analysts we deal with it. It is not, in fact, a perversion of instinct, but rather a desperate affirmation of life that is the purest form we can find of the death instinct.

The subject says "No!" to this darting game of intersubjectivity in which desire gains recognition for a moment only to lose itself in a will that is the other's will. The subject patiently withdraws his precarious life from the churning aggregations of the symbol's Eros in order to finally affirm life in a speechless curse.

When we want to get at what was before the serial games of speech in the subject and what is prior to the birth of symbols, we find it in death, from which his existence derives all the meaning it has. Indeed, he asserts himself with respect to others as a death wish; if he identifies with the other, it is by freezing him in the metamorphosis of his essential image, and no being is ever conjured up by him except among the shadows of death.

To say that this mortal meaning reveals in speech a center that is outside of language is more than a metaphor—it manifests a structure. This structure differs from the spatialization of the circumference or sphere with which some people like to schematize the limits of the living being and its environment: it corresponds rather to the relational group that symbolic logic designates topologically as a ring.

If I wanted to give an intuitive representation of it, it seems that I would
321 have to resort not to the two-dimensionality of a zone, but rather to the three-dimensional form of a torus, insofar as a torus' peripheral exteriority and central exteriority constitute but one single region.[48]

This schema represents the endless circularity of the dialectical process that occurs when the subject achieves his solitude, whether in the vital ambiguity of immediate desire or in the full assumption of his being-toward-death.

But we can simultaneously see that the dialectic is not individual, and that the question of the termination of an analysis is that of the moment at which the subject's satisfaction is achievable in the satisfaction of all—that is, of all those it involves in a human undertaking. Of all the undertakings that have been proposed in this century, the psychoanalyst's is perhaps the loftiest, because it mediates in our time between the care-ridden man and the subject of absolute knowledge. This is also why it requires a long subjective ascesis, indeed one that never ends, since the end of training analysis itself is not separable from the subject's engagement in his practice.

Let whoever cannot meet at its horizon the subjectivity of his time give it up then. For how could he who knows nothing of the dialectic that engages him in a symbolic movement with so many lives possibly make his being the axis of those lives? Let him be well acquainted with the whorl into which his era draws him in the ongoing enterprise of Babel, and let him be aware of his function as an interpreter in the strife of languages. As for the darkness of the *mundus* around which the immense tower is coiled, let him leave to mystical vision the task of seeing the putrescent serpent of life rise up there on an everlasting rod.

Allow me to laugh if these remarks are accused of turning the meaning of Freud's work away from the biological foundations he would have wished for it toward the cultural references with which it is rife. I do not wish to preach to you the doctrine of the *b* factor, designating the first, nor of the *c* factor, designating the second. All I have tried to do is remind you of the neglected *a, b, c* structure of language, and to teach you to spell once again the forgotten ABC's of speech.

322 For what recipe would guide you in a technique that is composed of the first and derives its effects from the second, if you did not recognize the field of the one and the function of the other?

Psychoanalytic experience has rediscovered in man the imperative of the Word as the law that has shaped him in its image. It exploits the poetic function of language to give his desire its symbolic mediation. May this experience finally enable you to understand that the whole reality of its effects lies in the gift of speech[49]; for it is through this gift that all reality has come to man and through its ongoing action that he sustains reality.

If the domain defined by this gift of speech must be sufficient for both your action and your knowledge, it will also be sufficient for your devotion. For it offers the latter a privileged field.

When the Devas, the men, and the Asuras were finishing their novitiate with Prajapati, as we read in the first Brahmana of the fifth lesson of the Brihadaranyaka Upanishad, they begged him, "Speak to us."

"*Da*," said Prajapati, god of thunder. "Did you hear me?" And the Devas answered, saying: "Thou hast said to us: *Damyata*, master yourselves"—the sacred text meaning that the powers above are governed by the law of speech.

"*Da*," said Prajapati, god of thunder. "Did you hear me?" And the men answered, saying: "Thou hast said to us: *Datta*, give"—the sacred text meaning that men recognize each other by the gift of speech.

"*Da*," said Prajapati, god of thunder. "Did you hear me?" And the Asuras answered, saying: "Thou hast said to us: *Dayadhvam*, be merciful"—the sacred text meaning that the powers below resound [*résonnent*] [50] to the invocation of speech.

That, continues the text, is what the divine voice conveys in the thunder: Submission, gift, grace. *Da da da*.

For Prajapati replies to all: "You have heard me."

Notes

1. See "Logical Time," *Écrits* 1966, 197–213.

2. Ferenczi, "Confusion of Tongues between the Adult and the Child," *IJP* XXX, 4 (1949): 225–30.

3. (Added in 1966:) The preceding paragraph has been rewritten.

4. (Added in 1966:) Previously I had written: "in psychological matters."

5. (Added in 1966:) The preceding paragraph has been rewritten.

6. This is the crux of a deviation that concerns both practice and theory. For to identify the ego* with the subject's self-discipline is to confuse imaginary isolation with mastery of the instincts; here one is liable to make errors of judgment in the conduct of the treatment—such as trying to strengthen the ego* in many neuroses that are caused by its overly strong structure, which is a dead end. Hasn't my friend Michael Balint written that a strengthening of the ego* should be beneficial to a subject suffering from *ejaculatio praecox* because it would permit him to prolong the suspension of his desire? But how can we think this, when it is precisely to the fact that his desire depends on the imaginary function of the ego* that the subject owes the short-circuiting of the act—which psychoanalytic clinical experience clearly shows to be intimately related to narcissistic identification with the partner.

7. This in the same work I praised at the end of my introduction (added in 1966). It is clear in what follows that aggressiveness is only a side effect of analytic frustration, though it can be reinforced by a certain type of intervention; as such, it is not the reason for the frustration/regression pair.

8. *GW* XII, 71; *Cinq psychanalyses* (Paris:

PUF, 1954), 356, a weak translation of the term.

9. *GW* XII, 72, fn1, the last few lines. The concept of *Nachträglichkeit* is underlined in the footnote. *Cinq psychanalyses*, 356, fn1.

10. See *Écrits* 1966, 204–10.

11. Freud uses the term in an article accessible to even the least demanding of French readers, since it came out in the *Revue Neurologique*, a journal generally found on bookshelves in hospital staff rooms. The blunder exposed here illustrates, among other things, how the said authority I saluted on page 246 [in *Écrits* 1966] measures up to his leadership.*

12. (Added in 1966:) Even if he is speaking to everyone in general and no one in particular [*à la cantonade*]. He addresses that Other (with a capital *O*) whose theoretical basis I have since consolidated, and which demands a certain *epoche* in returning to the term to which I limited myself at that time: that of "intersubjectivity."

13. I am borrowing these terms from the late and sorely missed Édouard Pichon who, both in the directions he gave for the advent of our discipline and in those that guided him in the murky shadows of persons, showed a divination that I can only attribute to his practice of semantics.

14. (Added in 1966:) This reference to the aporia of Christianity announced a more precise one at its Jansenist climax: a reference to Pascal whose wager, still intact, forced me to take up the whole question again in order to get at what it conceals that is inestimable to psychoanalysts—which is still, at this date (June 1966), unrevealed.

15. (Added in 1966:) This remark was made by one of the psychoanalysts most involved in the debate.

16. See *Gegenwunschträume* in the *Traumdeutung*, *GW* II, 156–57 and 163–64; *SE* IV, 151 and 157–58.

17. (Added in 1966:) In order to evaluate the results of these procedures the reader should become thoroughly acquainted with the notes found in Émile Borel's book *Le Hasard* (Paris: F. Alcan, 1914), which I recommended already at that time, on the triviality of the "remarkable" results obtained by beginning in this way with just any number.

18. See C. I. Oberndorf, "Unsatisfactory Results of Psychoanalytic Therapy," *PQ* XIX (1950): 393–407.

19. See, among others, *Do Kamo: Person and Myth in the Melanesian World*, by Maurice Leenhardt [trans. Basia Miller Gulati (Chicago: University of Chicago Press, 1979)], chapters IX and X.

20. Jules H. Masserman, "Language, Behaviour and Dynamic Psychiatry," *IJP* XXV, 1–2 (1944): 1–8.

21. Aphorism of Lichtenberg's: "A madman who imagines himself a prince differs from the prince who is in fact a prince only because the former is a negative prince, while the latter is a negative madman. Considered without their sign, they are alike."

22. To obtain an immediate subjective confirmation of this remark of Hegel's, it is enough to have seen in the recent epidemic a blind rabbit in the middle of a road, lifting the emptiness of its vision changed into a gaze toward the setting sun: it was human to the point of tragedy.

23. The lines before and after this term will show what I mean by it.

24. Reich's error, to which I shall return, caused him to mistake a coat of arms for armor.

25. See Claude Lévi-Strauss, "Language and the Analysis of Social Laws," *American Anthropologist* LIII, 2 (April–June 1951): 155–63.

26. (Added in 1966:) The last four paragraphs have been rewritten.

27. (Added in 1966:) The last two paragraphs have been rewritten.

28. On the Galilean hypothesis and Huyghens' clock, see Alexandre Koyré, "An Experiment in Measurement," *Proceedings of the American Philosophical Society* XCVII, 2 (April 1953): 222–37. (Added in 1966:) The last two paragraphs of my text have been rewritten.

29. (Added in 1966:) I have developed these indications as the opportunity presented itself. Four paragraphs rewritten.

30. "The Theory of Symbolism," *British Journal of Psychology* IX, 2. Reprinted in his *Papers on Psycho-Analysis* (Boston: Beacon, 1961) [the page number given in the text corresponds to this edition]. See [Lacan's article: "À la mémoire d'Ernest Jones: Sur sa théorie

du symbolisme," *La Psychanalyse* V (1960): 1–20] *Écrits* 1966, 697–717.

31. I am referring here to the teaching of Abhinavagupta in the tenth century. See Dr. Kanti Chandra Pandey, "Indian Aesthetics," *Chowkamba Sanskrit Series*, Studies, II (Benares: 1950).

32. Ernst Kris, "Ego Psychology and Interpretation in Psychoanalytic Therapy," *PQ* XX, 1 (1951): 15–29; see the passage quoted on pages 27–28.

33. (Added in 1966:) Paragraph rewritten.

34. This for the use of whoever can still understand it after looking in the Littré for justification of a theory that makes speech into an "action beside," by the translation that it gives of the Greek *parabole* (why not "action toward" instead?)—without having noticed at the same time that, if this word nevertheless designates what it means, it is because of sermonizing usage that, since the tenth century, has reserved "Word" [*verbe*] for the Logos incarnate.

35. Each language has its own form of transmission, and since the legitimacy of such research is founded on its success, nothing stops us from drawing a moral from it. Consider, for example, the maxim I chose as an epigraph for the preface to this paper. [*En particulier, il ne faudra pas oublier que la séparation en embryologie, anatomie, physiologie, psychologie, sociologie, clinique n'existe pas dans la nature et qu'il n'y a qu'une discipline: la* neurobiologie *à laquelle l'observation nous oblige d'ajouter l'épithète d'*humaine *en ce qui nous concerne*.] Since it is so laden with redundancies, its style may strike you as a bit lackluster. But lighten it of them and its audacity will arouse the enthusiasm it deserves. Hear ye: "Parfaupe ouclaspa nannanbryle anaphi ologi psysocline ixispad anlana—égnia kune n'rbiol' ô blijouter têtumaine ennouconç . . ." Here the purity of its message is finally laid bare. Its meaning raises its head here, the owning of being [*l'aveu de l'être*] begins, and our victorious intelligence bequeaths to the future its immortal stamp.

36. "The Therapeutic Effect of Inexact Interpretation: A Contribution to the Theory of Suggestion," *IJP* XII, 4 (1931): 397–411.

37. "Silence and Verbalization: A Supplement to the Theory of the 'Analytic Rule,' " *IJP* XXX, 1 (1949): 21–30.

38. Here equivalent to my mind to the term *Zwangsbefürchtung* [obsessive or compulsive fear or apprehension], which should be broken down into its component elements without losing any of the semantic resources of the German language.

39. (Added in 1966:) Two paragraphs rewritten.

40. This term refers to the custom, of Celtic origin and still practiced by certain Bible sects in America, of allowing a couple engaged to be married, or even a passing guest and the family's daughter, to spend the night together in the same bed, provided that they keep their clothes on. The word derives its meaning from the fact that the girl is usually wrapped up in sheets. (Quincey speaks of it. See also the book by Aurand le Jeune on this practice among the Amish.) Thus the myth of Tristan and Isolde, and even the complex that it represents, now underwrites the analyst in his quest for the soul destined for mystifying nuptials via the extenuation of its instinctual fantasies.

41. (Added in 1966:) What I have since designated as the basis of transference—namely, the "subject-supposed-to-know"—is thus already defined here.

42. This is the correct translation of the two terms that have been rendered, with that unfailing flair for mistranslation I mentioned earlier, by "terminated analysis and interminable analysis."

43. See Aulus Gellius, *Attic Nights*, II, 4: "In a trial, when it is a question of knowing who shall be given the task of presenting the accusation, and when two or more people volunteer for this office, the judgment by which the tribunal names the accuser is called divination . . . This word comes from the fact that since accuser and accused are two correlative terms that cannot continue to exist without each other, and since the type of judgment in question here presents an accused without an accuser, it is necessary to resort to divination in order to find what the trial does not provide, what it leaves still unknown, that is, the accuser."

44. (Added in 1966:) Two paragraphs rewritten.

45. (Added in 1966:) Whether a chipped stone or a cornerstone, my forte is that I haven't given in on this point.

46. This is the form called Laksanalaksana.

47. (Added in 1966:) These four words [*renversé dans la répétition*], in which my latest formulation of repetition is found (1966), have been substituted for an improper recourse to the "eternal return" [*toujours présent dans l'éternel retour*], which was all that I could get across at that time.

48. (Added in 1966:) These are premises of the topology I have been putting into practice over the past five years.

49. It should be clear that it is not a question here of the "gifts" that novices are always supposed not to have, but of a tone that they are, indeed, missing more often than they should be.

50. (Added in 1966:) Ponge writes it as follows: *réson*.

Variations on the Standard Treatment 323

This title, the counterpart of another title promoting the unheard-of heading, "standard treatment," was assigned to me in 1953 as part of a project for which a committee of psychoanalysts was responsible. Selected from various tendencies due to their competence in the area, my friend Henri Ey had delegated to them the general responsibility he himself had received for the volume on therapeutic methods in psychiatry, to be published in the *Encyclopédie médico-chirurgicale*.

I accepted this role in order to investigate the scientific foundation of the said treatment, the only foundation on which the implicit reference to a deviation that such a title offered me could make any sense.

A deviation that was all too palpable, in effect. At least I believe I succeeded in raising a question about it, even though this undoubtedly ran counter to the intentions of its promoters.

Are we to think that the question was resolved by the removal of my article [from subsequent editions of the encyclopedia], quickly explained, by the abovementioned committee, as part of the ordinary updating of this kind of work?

Many people saw it as the sign of a certain precipitation, which would be understandable in this case by the very way in which a certain majority considered itself to be defined by my criticism. (The article was published in 1955.)

A Bat Question: Examining It in the Light of Day

"Variations on the Standard Treatment"—this title constitutes a pleonasm, though not a simple one:[1] based on a contradiction, it is nonetheless lame. Is this twisting due to the fact that it is addressed to a medical audience? Or is it 324
a distortion intrinsic to the question?

This stopping point serves as an entry point into the problem, since it recalls what the public senses: namely, that psychoanalysis is not like any other form of therapeutics. For the term "variations" implies neither the adapting of the treatment to the "variety" of cases, in accordance with empirical or even clinical criteria,[2] nor a reference to the "variables" by which the field of psychoanalysis is distinguished, but rather a concern, which may even be hypersensitive, for purity in the means and ends, which allows us to foresee a more meritorious status than the label presented here.

At stake here is clearly a rigor that is in some sense ethical, without which any treatment, even if it is filled with psychoanalytic knowledge, can only amount to psychotherapy.

This rigor would require a formalization, by which I mean a theoretical formalization, which has hardly been provided to date because it has been confused with a practical formalism—that is, a [set of rules] regarding what is done and what is not done.

This is why it is not inauspicious to start from the "theory of therapeutic criteria" in order to shed light on this situation.

Certainly, the psychoanalyst's lack of concern about the basics required for the use of statistics is only equaled by that still found in medicine. It is, however, more innocent in the analyst's case. For he makes less of assessments as cursory as "improved," "much improved," and "cured," being warned against them by a discipline that knows how to isolate haste in concluding as an element that is in and of itself questionable.

Clearly advised by Freud to closely examine the effects in his experience of the danger sufficiently announced by the term *furor sanandi,* he does not, in the end, wish to appear to be motivated by it.

While he thus views cure as an added benefit [*la guérison comme bénéfice de surcroît*] of psychoanalytic treatment, he is wary of any misuse of the desire to
325 cure. This is so ingrained in him that, when an innovation in technique is based upon this desire, he worries deep inside and even reacts inside the analytic group by raising the automatic question: "Is that still psychoanalysis?"

This point may appear to be tangential to the question at hand. But its import is precisely to encircle this question with a line which, while barely visible from the outside, constitutes the inner supporter of a circle, without the latter ceasing for all that to present himself as if nothing there separated him.

In this silence, which is the privilege of undisputed truths, psychoanalysts find the refuge that makes them impermeable to all criteria other than those of a dynamic, a topography, and an economy that they are incapable of justifying to those outside.

Hence no recognition of psychoanalysis, as either a profession or a science, can occur except by hiding a principle of extraterritoriality which it is as impossible for the psychoanalyst to give up as it is for him not to deny. This obliges him to place all validation of its problems under the heading of dual membership and to arm himself with the postures of inscrutability adopted by the bat in the fable.

All discussion of the present question thus begins with a misunderstanding, which is further heightened when it is backlit by a paradox from the inside.

This paradox is clearly introduced by what all analytic writers express, the most authorized affirming it no less than the others, regarding analysis' therapeutic criteria—namely, that the more stridently we demand a theoretical reference the more these criteria vanish. This is a matter of serious concern, when theory is alleged to give treatment its status. More serious is when, at such times, it suddenly becomes abundantly clear that the most widely accepted terms are utterly useless except as indices of inadequacy or as screens for incompetence.

To appreciate this it suffices to read the papers given at the last Congress of the International Psychoanalytical Association, held in London [on July 27, 1953]. These papers warrant being included in our file—all of them and each of them in its entirety.[3] I will cite a measured assessment from one of them, the one by Edward Glover:

> About twenty years ago, I circulated a questionnaire with the intention 326
> of ascertaining what were the actual technical practices and working standards of analysts in this country [Great Britain]. Full replies were obtained from twenty-four of twenty-nine practising members, from the examination of which it transpired [*sic*] that on only six out of the sixty-three points raised was there complete agreement. Only one of these six points could be regarded as fundamental, viz., the necessity of analysing the transference; the others concerned such lesser matters as the inadvisability of accepting presents, avoidance of the use of technical terms during analysis, avoidance of social contact, abstention from answering questions, objection to preliminary injunctions and, interestingly enough, payment for all nonattendances.[4]

This survey taken long ago derives its value from the quality of the practitioners to whom it was addressed, since they still constituted a small elite at that time. Glover only mentions it here due to the urgency, which has now become public, of what had before been merely a personal need—namely (and this is the title of his article), to define the "Therapeutic Criteria of Psycho-Analysis." The major obstacle to doing so is found, in his view, in fundamental theoretical divergences:

> We need not go afield to find psycho-analytical societies riven by such differences, with extreme groups holding mutually incompatible views, the opposing sections being held in uneasy alliance by "middle groups" whose members, as is the habit of eclectics the world over, compensate themselves for their absence of originality by extracting virtue from their eclecticism, maintaining, either implicitly or explicitly, that, whether or not principles differ, scientific truth lies only in compromise. Despite these eclectic efforts to maintain a united front to the scientific or psychological public, it is obvious that in certain fundamental respects the

327 techniques practised by the opposing groups must be as different as chalk from cheese.[5]

Moreover, the author cited has no illusions about his chances of attenuating these discordances at the plenary Congress he is addressing, due to the lack of any critique of the

> sedulously cultivated assumptions that participants in such discussions hold roughly the same views, speak the same technical language, follow identical systems of diagnosis, prognosis, and selection of cases, [and] practise approximately the same technical procedures [. . .].
>
> *Not one of these assumptions will bear close investigation.*[6]

As it would require ten full pages of this encyclopedia to list merely those articles and books in which the most widely recognized authorities confirm this view, any attempt to resort to philosophy's common sense would be ruled out in seeking some standard against which to measure variations in analytic treatment. The maintenance of standards falls more and more within the ambit of the group's interests, as is seen in the U.S.A. where the analytic group represents a significant power.

What is at stake is thus less a standard* than standing*. What I earlier termed "formalism" is what Glover calls "perfectionism." To realize this, it suffices to underscore how he speaks of it: analysis loses any measure of its "therapeutic applicability"; this ideal leads analysis to criteria of its operation that are "undefined and uncontrolled," and even to a "*mystique* (he uses the French word) which not only baffles investigation but blankets all healthy discussion."[7]

This mystification—which is, in fact, the technical term for any process that hides from the subject the origin of the effects of his own action—is all the more striking in that analysis enjoys favor, a favor which earns its stripes by its duration, only because it is well regarded broadly enough to occupy its putative place. It suffices to have those in human science circles look to psychoanalysis to give them their place, for psychoanalysis to have found its guarantee.

328 Problems result from this that become of public interest in a country like America where the quantity of analysts gives the quality of the group the scope of a sociological factor influencing the collective.

The fact that the milieu considers it necessary for the technique to be coherent with the theory is no more reassuring for all that.

Only a global apprehension of the divergences, which is able to grasp them synchronically, can determine the cause of their discord.

If we attempt to gain such an apprehension, we get the idea of a massive phenomenon of passivity, and even of subjective inertia, whose effects seem to grow with the spreading of the movement.

At least this is what is suggested by the dispersion we observe both in the coordination of concepts and in their comprehension.

Fine texts try to revitalize them and seem to take the hardy approach of arguing on the basis of their antinomies, but it is only to fall into purely fictive syncretisms that do not rule out indifference to false appearances.

People even go so far as to rejoice in the fact that the weakness of invention has not allowed for more damage to the fundamental concepts, those still being the concepts we owe to Freud. The latter's resistance to so many attempts to adulterate them becomes the *a contrario* proof of their consistency.

This is true of transference, which manages to weather the storm of popularizing theory and even popular ideas. It owes this to the Hegelian robustness of its constitution: Indeed, what other concept is there that better brings out its identity with the thing, the analytic thing in this case, cleaving to it with all the ambiguities that constitute its logical time?

This temporal foundation is the one with which Freud inaugurates transference and that I modulate by asking: Is it a return or a memorial? Others dwell on the thing regarding this resolved point by asking: Is it real or dereistic? Lagache[8] raises a question about the concept of transference: Need for repetition or repetition of need?[9]

We see here that the dilemmas in which the practitioner gets bogged down 329
derive from depreciations by which his thinking fails his action. These contradictions captivate us when, extenuated in his theory, they seem to force his pen with some semantic *Ananke* in which the dialectic of his action can be read *ab inferiori*.

Thus an external coherence persists in the deviations of analytic experience that surround its axis, with the same rigor with which the shrapnel of a projectile, in dispersing, maintains its ideal trajectory with the center of gravity of the pyramidal shape it traces out.

The condition of the misunderstanding which, as I noted above, obstructs psychoanalysis' path to recognition thus turns out to be redoubled by a misrecognition internal to its own movement.

It is here that the question of variations—which must arise anew for the analyst after having been presented to the medical public—can find an unforeseen advantage.

This platform is narrow: It is based entirely on the fact that a practice based on intersubjectivity cannot escape the latter's laws when, in seeking to gain recognition, it invokes their effects.

Perhaps the flash will be bright enough to bring out the fact that the hidden extraterritoriality by which psychoanalysis proceeds in order to spread suggests that we treat it in the same way as a tumor by exteriorization.

But we can only do justice to a claim that is rooted in misrecognition by accepting it in its crudest terms.

The question of variations in treatment, taken further still here with the gallant jibe of "standard treatment," incites me to retain here but one criterion, since it is the only one at the disposal of the physician who orients his patient in the treatment. This criterion, which is rarely enunciated since it is considered tautological, can be stated as follows: A psychoanalysis, whether standard or not, is the treatment one expects from a psychoanalyst.

From the Psychoanalyst's Pathway to Its Maintenance, Considered from the Viewpoint of Its Deviation

The remark with which I closed the preceding section is only obvious ironically. Highlighting, as it does, the apparent impasse of the question when taken
330 dogmatically, it reiterates it—if we look at it closely, without omitting the necessary grain of salt—by way of a synthetic a priori judgment, on the basis of which practical reason could no doubt find its bearings.

For if psychoanalysis' pathway is called into question so seriously by its variations that it can no longer recommend itself except on the basis of a standard, such a precarious existence requires that a man maintain this pathway and that he be a real man.

Furthermore, it is in the solicitations to which the real man is exposed by the ambiguity of this pathway that people will try to gauge what he makes of it through its effect on him. For if he pursues his task amid this ambiguity, it is because it does not stop him any more than is common in the majority of human practices. But if the question of the limit to be assigned to these variations remains endemic to this particular practice, it is because no one sees where the ambiguity ends.

Hence it is of little importance that the real man spares himself the effort of defining this endpoint on the basis of authorities who provide support here only by making him mistake one thing for another, or that he makes do by misrecognizing this endpoint in its rigor, avoiding experiencing its limit. In both cases, he is more duped [*joué*] by his action than he performs it [*qu'il ne la joue*], but he finds it all the easier to situate therein the gifts that adapt him to it—without noticing that, in abandoning himself to the bad faith of instituted practice, he degrades it to the level of routines whose secrets are dispensed by clever analysts. Such secrets become unassailable, since they are always subordinated to the same gifts—even if there were none left in the world—that they reserve themselves the right to detect.

He who spares himself the trouble of concerning himself with his mission at such a cost will even consider his decision confirmed by a warning that still resonates from the very voice which formulated the fundamental rules of his practice: not to form too lofty an idea of this mission, still less to become the prophet of some established truth. Hence this precept, by which the master thought he was offering these rules for the understanding, merely lends itself to false humility because, being presented in a negative form, it was misunderstood [*contresens*].

Along the path of true humility, we will not have to look far for the unbearable ambiguity that is proposed to psychoanalysis; it is within everyone's reach. It is revealed in the question of what it means to speak, and one encounters it simply by welcoming [*accueillir*] a discourse. For the very locution in which 331
the French language records [*recueille*] its most naive intention—that of understanding what this discourse "means to say" [*ce qu'il "veut dire"*]—tells us clearly enough that it does not say it. But what this "means to say" means to say is still a double entendre and it is up to the hearer whether it is one or the other: whether it is what the speaker means to say to him by the discourse he addresses to him or what this discourse tells him about the condition of the speaker. Thus not only does the meaning of this discourse reside in he who listens to it, but the reception [*accueil*] he gives it determines *who* says it—namely, whether it is the subject to whom he gives permission and lends credence or the other that his discourse delivers to the listener as constituted.

Now the analyst seizes the listener's discretionary power to raise it to a second power. For apart from the fact that he expressly positions himself as an interpreter of the discourse for himself, and even for the speaking subject, he imposes upon the subject, in the topic of his discourse, the proper opening for the rule he assigns him as fundamental: This discourse must be pursued first without stopping and second without holding anything back, [something the subject might be inclined to do] not only out of a concern for its coherence or internal rationality but also out of shame regarding its *ad hominem* thrust or its unacceptability in polite society. The analyst thus widens the gap that places at his mercy the subject's overdetermination in the ambiguity of constituting speech and constituted discourse, as if he hoped that the extremes would meet up by a revelation that brings them together. But this conjunction cannot occur due to the rarely noticed limits within which supposedly free association remains contained, by which the subject's speech is maintained in syntactic forms that articulate it in discourse in the language employed as understood by the analyst.

Hence the analyst retains complete responsibility, in the weighty sense that I have just defined on the basis of his position as a listener. An ambiguity that is direct, since it is at his own discretion as an interpreter, turns into a secret summons that he cannot dismiss even by remaining silent.

Psychoanalytic authors thus admit to its weight, as obscure as it remains to them. This is seen in all the ways in which their uneasiness can be identified, running the gamut from the awkwardness and even formlessness of their theories of interpretation, to the ever rarer use of interpretation in practice owing
332 to its never properly explained postponement. The vague term "analyzing" all too often makes up for the imprecision that keeps them from using "interpreting," because it has not been updated. This is an effect of the avoidance at work in the practitioner's thinking. The false consistency of the notion of countertransference, its stylishness, and the fanfare it fosters can be explained by the fact that it serves as an alibi: the analyst thereby avoids considering the action that it is incumbent upon him to take in the production of truth.[10]

The question of variations would be clarified by following this effect, diachronically this time, in a *history of variations* of the psychoanalytic movement, in bringing the type of parodic catholicity in which this question takes shape back to its universal root—namely, its introduction into the experience of speech.

Moreover, there is no need to be a genius to realize that the key words that the real man I mentioned uses so sparingly to illustrate his technique are not always the words he conceptualizes the most clearly. Our oracles would turn red were they to all try to explain them at once, and are not unhappy that the shame of their junior colleagues—extending to the most inexperienced by a paradox explained by the training methods currently in favor—spares them any such ordeal.

Analysis of the material, analysis of resistances—it is in these terms that analysts explain both the basic principle of and the ultimate key to their technique, the analysis of the material seeming outdated since the promotion of the analysis of resistances. Nevertheless, since the relevance of the interpretation of a resistance is demonstrated by the production of "new material," the nuances, or even divergences, begin with what is done with this new material. And if we are to interpret it like we did before, we will be justified in wondering whether the term "interpretation" has the same meaning at these two different points in time.

To answer this question, we can look back to around 1920 when the "turning point" (that is the term consecrated in the history of analytic technique) occurred which has since been considered decisive in the pathways of analysis. It was explained at that time by an ebbing in the results analysis was able

to achieve, a finding one could only shed light on heretofore with the recommendation—whether apocryphal or not, in which the master's humor retroactively acquires the status of foresight—that we had better quickly take 333
inventory of the unconscious before it closes back down.

Yet the very term "material" has since denoted the fact that the set of phenomena in which we had hitherto learned to find the symptom's secret—an immense domain annexed by Freud's genius to man's knowledge [*connaissance*] that warrants the true title of "psychoanalytic semantics," including dreams, bungled actions, slips of the tongue, memory disturbances, whims of thought association, and so on—has fallen out of favor in analytic technique.

Prior to this "turning point," it was by deciphering such material that the subject was able to remember his history along with the outlines of the conflict that determined his symptoms. And the value to be granted in technique to the elimination of symptoms was based on how well the order in his history was restored and the gaps in it were filled. The observed elimination of symptoms demonstrated a dynamic in which the unconscious was defined as a clearly constituting subject, since it sustained symptoms in their meaning before it was revealed, and we experienced the unconscious directly, recognizing it in the ruse of disturbances in which the repressed compromises with the censorship—in this respect, let it be noted in passing, neurosis is akin to the most common condition of truth in speech and writing.

If, then, the analyst gave the subject the solution [*mot*] to his symptom, but the symptom persisted, it was because the subject resisted recognizing its meaning; analysts thus concluded that it was this resistance that must, above all, be analyzed. Note that this conclusion still put its faith in interpretation, but it was the particular aspect of the subject in which people sought this resistance that led to the approaching deviation; for it is clear that this notion tends to take the subject to be constitut*ed* in his discourse. Should the deviation go on to seek his resistance outside of this discourse, it will be irremediable. No one will come back to question the constitut*ing* function of interpretation regarding its failure.

This move to give up on the use of speech justifies my saying that psychoanalysis has not since left behind its childhood illness, this term going beyond the commonplace here, with all the propriety it encounters due to this very move—where everything is, in effect, based on the methodological faux pas made by the best-known name in child analysis.

The idea of resistance was not new, however. In 1895, Freud had already 334
recognized its effect in the verbalization of chains of speech in which the subject constitutes his history. Freud did not hesitate to illustrate his conception of this process by representing these chains as encompassing with their array

the pathogenic nucleus around which they bend, in order to indicate that resistance operates in a direction perpendicular to the parallelism of these chains. He even went so far as to posit the mathematical formula that this effect is inversely proportional to the distance between the nucleus and the chain being remembered, allowing us to gauge thereby how closely we have managed to approach it.

It is clear here that while interpretation of the resistance at work in such a chain of speech is different from interpretation of meaning by which the subject passes from one chain to another "deeper" chain, the first form of interpretation nevertheless operates on the very text of that speech, which includes its elusions, distortions, elisions, and even holes and syncopes.

The interpretation of resistance thus introduces the same ambiguity that I analyzed above in the position of the listener, which is taken up again here in the question: *Who* is resisting? "The ego," answered the first doctrine, including therein the personal subject, no doubt, but solely from the undiscriminating angle of its dynamics.

It is here that the new orientation in technique runs headlong at a lure: it answers the question in the same way, neglecting the fact that it puts the blame on an ego whose meaning Freud, its oracle, has just changed; for Freud has just installed the ego in a new topography precisely in order to specify that resistance is not the privilege of the ego alone, but also of the id and the superego.

Nothing else in his last conceptualization will henceforth be truly understood, as can be seen in the fact that the authors of the "turning point" wave are still at the stage of examining the death instinct from every angle, and even of getting bogged down regarding what the subject must properly identify with, the analyst's ego or his superego, without making a single worthwhile step forward, multiplying ever more instead an irresistible misconception.

By reversing the correct choice that determines which subject is welcomed in speech, the symptom's constituting subject is treated as if he were consti-
335 tuted—like material [*en matériel*], as they say—while the ego, as constituted as it may be in resistance, becomes the subject upon whom the analyst henceforth calls as the constituting agency.

The idea that this subject involves the person in his "totality" is a false effect of the new concept, even and especially insofar as it ensures a connection with the organs of the so-called perception-consciousness system. (Doesn't Freud, moreover, make the superego the first guarantor of an experience of reality?)

What is in fact at stake is the return, of the most reactionary and thus of a highly instructive kind, of an ideology that has been given up everywhere else because it is quite simply bankrupt.[11]

Consider the lines with which Anna Freud's book *The Ego and the Mechanisms of Defense* opens:

> There have been periods in the development of psychoanalytic science when the theoretical study of the individual ego was distinctly unpopular. [. . .] Whenever interest was shifted from the deeper to the more superficial psychic strata—whenever, that is to say, research was deflected from the id to the ego—it was felt that here was a beginning of apostasy from psychoanalysis as a whole.

These few lines suffice to allow us to hear, in the anxious sound with which they preluded the advent of a new era, the sinister music with which Euripides inscribed, in *The Phoenician Women*, the mythical link between the character of Antigone and the moment of the Sphinx's repercussion on the hero's action.

Since then it has become commonplace to repeat that we know nothing more about the subject than what his ego is willing to let us know. Otto Fenichel goes so far as to proffer quite simply, as if it were an indisputable truth, that "The understanding of the meaning of words is particularly a concern of the ego."[12]

The next step led to the confusing of resistances with ego defenses.

The idea of defense, put forward by Freud already in 1894 when he first 336
relates neurosis to a widely accepted conception of the function of illness, is taken up again by him in his major work, *Inhibitions, Symptoms and Anxiety*, to indicate that the ego forms on the basis of the same moments as a symptom.

But the semantic use Anna Freud makes of the ego, in the book just mentioned, as the subject of verbs, suffices by itself to display the transgression she consecrates in it; it shows too that, in the thereafter-received deviation, the ego is truly the objectified subject whose defense mechanisms constitute resistance.

Treatment is henceforth conceptualized as an attack, positing in theory the existence of a succession of systems of defense in the subject, which is adequately confirmed by the "cant phrase"—made fun of in passing by Edward Glover—by which one facilely tries to sound important by raising the question on any and every occasion whether one has sufficiently "analyse[d] the aggression."[13] In this way, the simpleton asserts that he has never encountered any transferential effects other than aggression.

It is in this way that Fenichel tries to set things right by a reversal that confuses things still more. For while there may be some value in the order he traces of the operation to be carried out against the subject's defenses, which he considers to be like a fortress—implying that the defenses as a whole merely tend to divert the attack from the one defense which, since it too closely covers what it hides, already gives it away, but also that this latter defense is henceforth the essential stake, so much so that the drive hidden by this defense, when it offers itself up nakedly, must be considered to be the supreme artifice designed to preserve it—the impression of reality that holds our attention in this strategy serves as a prelude to the awakening that is such that where all suspicion of truth disappears, the dialectic reasserts its rights by appearing not to have to be useless in practice, if only by giving it a meaning.

For there is no longer any end to the supposed depths or even any reason to seek them if what such a search discovers is no truer than what covers it
337 over. In forgetting this, analysis degenerates into an immense psychological mess, and what we hear about the way it is practiced by certain analysts merely confirms this impression.

If pretending to pretend is, indeed, a possible moment of the dialectic, the fact remains that the truth the subject confesses in order that we take it to be a lie is not the same as an error on his part. But the maintenance of this distinction is only possible in a dialectic of intersubjectivity in which constituting speech is presupposed in constituted discourse.

Indeed, to flee the area shy of the reason for this discourse, people displace it to the beyond. While the subject's discourse could, possibly and occasionally, be bracketed in the initial perspective of an analysis because it may serve as a lure in or even as an obstruction to the revelation of truth, it is insofar as it serves as a sign that it is now permanently devalued. For it is no longer only that it is stripped of its content in order to dwell instead on its flow, its tone, its interruptions, and even its melody. It seems that any other manifestation of the subject's presence will soon have to be preferred to it: his presentation in his approach and gait, the affectation of his manners, and the way he takes his leave of us. An attitudinal reaction in the session will hold our attention more than a syntactical error and will be examined more in terms of its energy level than its gestural import. An up-welling of emotion and a visceral gurgle will be the sought-for evidence of the mobilization of resistance, and the idiocy of the fanatics of lived experience will go so far as to find the crème de la crème in smelling each other.

But the more we separate the authenticity of the analytic relationship from the discourse in which it is inscribed, what we continue to call its "interpretation" derives ever more exclusively from the analyst's knowledge. This knowledge has, of course, grown considerably in this pathway, but people cannot claim they have, in this way, left behind an intellectualist form of analysis, unless they admit that the communication of this knowledge to the subject acts only as a suggestion to which the criterion of truth remains foreign. Thus

Wilhelm Reich, who clearly defined the conditions of this kind of intervention in his form of *character analysis,* which is rightly considered to be an essen- 338
tial stage in the development of the new technique, admits that he can expect it to have an effect only on the basis of his insistence.[14]

This use of suggestion does not become a veritable interpretation just because it is analyzed as such. Such an analysis merely traces out the relation of one ego to another ego. This can be seen in the usual formulation that the analyst must become an ally of the healthy part of the subject's ego, when it is completed with the theory of the dissociation of the ego in psychoanalysis.[15] If we thus proceed to make a series of bipartitions in the subject's ego by doing this *ad infinitum*, it is clear that his ego is reduced, in the end, to the analyst's ego.

Along this pathway, what does it matter if we proceed according to a formulation in which the return to the scholar's traditional disdain for "morbid thought" is clearly reflected? For by speaking to the patient in "his own language," we still will not render him his own speech.

The ground of the question remains unchanged and is instead confirmed when it is formulated from an entirely different perspective, that of the object-relation, whose recent role in technique we shall see. But when object relations theory refers to an introjection by the subject of the analyst's ego, in the guise of the good object, it makes us wonder what an observant Huron would deduce about the mentality of modern civilized man from this mystical meal, assuming he makes the same strange mistake we make in taking literally the symbolic identifications seen in the kind of thought that we call "primitive."

The fact remains that a theoretician weighing in on the delicate question of the termination of analysis can crudely posit that it implies that the subject has identified with the analyst's ego, insofar as this ego analyzes him.[16]

This formulation, once demystified, signifies nothing if not that in ruling out any foundation of his relationship with the subject in speech, the analyst can communicate nothing to him that the analyst does not already know from his preconceived views or immediate intuition—that is, nothing that is not 339
subject to the organization of the analyst's own ego.

I will momentarily accept this aporia to which analysis is reduced in order to maintain its core in its deviation, and I will raise the question: What must the analyst's ego thus be if it assumes the role of being the measure of truth for all of us and for each subject who puts himself in the analyst's hands?

On the Ego in Analysis and Its End in the Analyst

The term "aporia" with which, at the end of the second section, I summed up the gain made with respect to the impasse in the first chapter, announces that

I intend to confront this gain in the psychoanalyst's common sense—and certainly not take pleasure in the fact that he may be offended by it.

Here again I will proceed by noting that the same things require a different discourse when they are taken up in another context, and will introduce my remarks by recalling that, if this connivance (*Einfühlung*) and assessment (*Abschätzung*)—which Ferenczi (1928, p. 209)[17] will not have come from anywhere but from the preconscious—have prevailed over the notorious "communication of unconsciouses" (considered, not unjustifiably, in an early phase of analysis to be the crux of true interpretation), the current promotion of effects that are placed under the heading of "countertransference"[18] is equally a step backward.

Moreover, the quibbling can only continue given that the ego as an agency is situated as unrelated to its neighbor agencies by those who consider it to represent the subject's collateral [*sûreté*].

We must call upon the first impression the analyst gives, which is certainly not that the ego is his strength, at least when it comes to his own ego and the foundation it can serve as for him.

Isn't that the hitch that requires the analyst to be analyzed, a principle that Ferenczi considers to warrant the title of the second fundamental rule of psychoanalysis? And doesn't the analyst bend under the weight of the judgment
340 that might well be viewed as Freud's last, since it was handed down by him two years before his death: "analysts in their own personalities have not invariably come up to the standard of psychical normality to which they wish to educate their patients."[19] This astonishing verdict, which there is no reason to revise today, means that the analyst cannot take advantage of the excuse that can be used in favor of every elite, which is that it finds its recruits among ordinary mortals.

Since this elite is below average, the most favorable hypothesis is to attribute it to the adverse repercussion of a disturbance [*désarroi*] that originates in the analytic act itself, as the preceding shows.

Ferenczi, the first-generation author who most relevantly raised the question of what is required of the analyst as a person, in particular as regards the end of the treatment, elsewhere mentions the root of the problem.

In his luminous article on psychoanalytic elasticity, he expresses himself as follows:

> I should like to mention, as a problem that has not been considered, that of the metapsychology of the analyst's mental processes during analysis. His cathexes oscillate between identification (analytic object-love) on the one hand and self-control or intellectual activity on the other.

> During the long day's work he can never allow himself the pleasure of giving his narcissism and egoism free play in reality, and he can give free play to them in his fantasy only for brief moments. A strain of this kind scarcely occurs otherwise in life, and I do not doubt that sooner or later it will call for the creation of a special hygiene for the analyst.[20]

Such is the abrupt precondition whose importance derives from the fact that it concerns what the psychoanalyst must first vanquish in himself. For why else would Ferenczi use this to introduce the tempered pathway that he wants to trace for us of the analyst's intervention with the elastic line he tries to define?

The order of subjectivity that the analyst must bring about in himself is the only thing Ferenczi indicates with an arrow at each intersection, and it is monotonously repeated by recommendations that are too varied for us not to try to 341
grasp how they fit together. *Menschenkenntnis* and *Menschenforschung* are two terms he uses whose romantic ancestry, which pushes them toward the art of leading men and the natural history of man, allows us to appreciate what the author hopes to do with them, by way of a sure method and an open market: reduction of one's personal impact; knowledge relegated to a subordinate position; authority that knows not to insist; goodness without indulgence;[21] distrust of the altar of good deeds; the only resistance to be attacked being that of indifference, *Unglauben*, or of refusal, *Ablehnung;* encouraging nasty comments; and true modesty regarding one's knowledge. In all of these rules, isn't it the ego that effaces itself in order to give way to the subject-point of interpretation? Thus these rules can only take effect on the basis of the psychoanalyst's personal analysis, and especially its end.

Where is the end of analysis as far as the ego is concerned? How can we know this if we misrecognize the ego's function in the very action of psychoanalysis? Let us follow the path of a kind of criticism that puts a text to the test of the very principles it defends.

And let us submit the so-called analysis of character to it. Character analysis presents itself as based on the discovery that the subject's personality is structured like a symptom that his personality feels to be foreign; in other words, like a symptom, his personality harbors a meaning, that of a repressed conflict. The material that reveals this conflict is elicited in the second stage, after a preliminary stage of treatment whose goal—as Reich expressly states it in his conception, which has remained a classic in analysis—is to get the subject to take his own personality as a symptom.

This point of view has clearly borne fruit in an objectification of structures, such as the so-called "genital-narcissistic" and "masochistic" characters,

which were previously neglected because they were apparently asymptomatic, not to mention the hysterical and compulsive characters, which were already indicated by their symptoms, whose collection of traits constitutes a precious
342 contribution to psychological knowledge, even if their theorization leaves something to be desired.

It is all the more important to pause at the results of this form of analysis, of which Reich was the master craftsman, in the assessment he gives of them. It amounts to the following: the quantity of change in the subject that legitimates this kind of analysis never even goes so far as to blur the lines that separate the original structures from each other.[22] Hence, the positive effects of the analysis of these structures that are felt by the subject, after the structures have been "symptomatized" through the objectification of their traits, oblige us to more closely indicate their relation to the tensions that the analysis has resolved. The whole theory that Reich provides of it is based on the idea that these structures are a defense by the individual against the orgasmic effusion whose primacy in lived experience can alone ensure its harmony. The extremes this idea led him to are well known—they went so far as to get him ousted by the analytic community. But, in ousting him not unjustifiably, no one ever really knew how to formulate why Reich was wrong.

We have to realize, first, that these structures play only the role of a medium or material, since they persist after the resolution of the tensions that seem to motivate them. This medium or material is, no doubt, ordered like the symbolic material of neurosis, as analysis proves, but it derives its efficacy here from the imaginary function, as it is revealed in the triggering of instinctual behavior; we learn about this from animal ethology, even though ethology itself has been strongly influenced by the concepts of displacement and identification stemming from psychoanalysis.

Thus Reich made only one mistake in his character analysis: what he calls "character armor"* and treats as such is actually but an armorial. The subject, after treatment, still carries the weight of the arms he received from nature, having merely effaced from them the mark of a blazon.

If this confusion was nevertheless possible, it is because the imaginary function—which in animals serves as a guide in their sexual fixation on the congener, in their display rituals by which the reproductive act is triggered, and
343 even in their marking of territory—seems in man to be entirely diverted toward the narcissistic relation on which the ego is based, giving rise to an aggressiveness whose coordinate denotes the signification that I will try to show to be the first and last word of this relation. Reich's error can be explained by his deliberate refusal of the signification that is tied to the death instinct, which was introduced by Freud at the height of his conceptual powers, and which is,

as we know, the touchstone of the mediocrity of analysts, whether they reject it or disfigure it.

Thus character analysis is only able to establish a properly mystifying conception of the subject on the basis of what proves to be a defense in that analysis, if we apply its own principles to it.

To return psychoanalysis to a veridical path, it is worth recalling that analysis managed to go so far in the revelation of man's desires only by following, in the veins of neurosis and the marginal subjectivity of the individual, the structure proper to a desire that thus proves to model it at an unexpected depth—namely, the desire to have his desire recognized. This desire, in which it is literally verified that man's desire is alienated in the other's desire, in effect structures the drives discovered in analysis, in accordance with all the vicissitudes of the logical substitutions in their source, aim [*direction*], and object.[23] But these drives, however far back we go into their history, instead of proving to derive from the need for a natural satisfaction, simply modulate in phases that reproduce all the forms of sexual perversion—that, at least, is the most obvious and best known fact of analytic experience.

But we more easily neglect the dominance found there of the narcissistic relation, that is, of a second alienation by which the internal splitting of his existence and his facticity is inscribed in the subject, along with the complete ambivalence of the position he identifies with in the perverse couple. It is nevertheless in the properly subjective meaning thus highlighted in perversion, far more than in its accession to a widely acknowledged objectification, that lies the step that psychoanalysis made man's knowledge take through its annexation, as the evolution of scientific literature alone demonstrates. 344

Now, the theory of the ego in analysis remains marked by a fundamental misrecognition if we neglect the period of its elaboration in Freud's work running from 1910 to 1920, in which it is entirely inscribed in the structure of the narcissistic relation.

In the early stage of psychoanalysis, the study of the ego never constituted a subject of aversion, as Anna Freud would have it in the above-cited passage. Rather, it is since people came up with the idea of promoting it in analysis that this study truly favors the subversion of psychoanalysis.

The conception of the phenomenon of passionate love [*amour-passion*] as determined by the image of the ideal ego, like the question of its imminent hatred, are the points we must examine from the abovementioned period of Freud's thought if we are to properly understand the relation between the ego and the image of the other—such as it is already made sufficiently clear in his very title, which joins *Group Psychology and the Analysis of the Ego* (1921)[24]—in one of the texts with which Freud inaugurates the last period of his thought, the one in which he completes the definition of the ego in his topography.

But this completion can only be understood by grasping the coordinates of his progress in developing the notions of primary masochism and the death instinct, found in *Beyond the Pleasure Principle* (1920),[25] and in developing the conception of the negating root of objectification, as it is laid out in the short 1925 article on *Verneinung* (negation).[26]

Only by studying Freud's progress in these areas can we explain his growing interest in aggressiveness in transference, in resistance, and even in *Civilization and Its Discontents* (1929),[27] showing that the kind of aggression we imagine to be at the root of the struggle for survival is not what is at stake in them. The notion of aggressiveness corresponds, on the contrary, to the rending of the subject from himself, a rending whose primordial moment comes
345 when the sight of the other's image, apprehended by him as a unified whole, anticipates his sense that he lacks motor coordination, this image retroactively structuring this lack of motor coordination in images of fragmentation. This experience explains both the depressive reaction, as reconstructed by Melanie Klein at the origins of the ego, and the child's jubiliatory assumption of his image in the mirror, the phenomenon of which, characteristic of the period beginning at six to eight months of age, is considered by the author of these lines to manifest in an exemplary manner the properly imaginary nature of the ego's function in the subject, along with the constitution of the ego's ideal *Urbild*.[28]

It is thus at the heart of experiences of bearing and intimidation during the first years of his life that the individual is introduced to the mirage of mastery of his functions, in which his subjectivity will remain split, and whose imaginary formation, naively objectified by psychologists as the ego's synthetic function, manifests instead the condition that introduces him to the alienating master/slave dialectic.

But if these experiences—which can be seen in animals too at many moments in their instinctual cycles, and especially in the preliminary displays of the reproductive cycle, with all the lures and aberrations these experiences involve—in fact open onto this signification in order to durably structure the human subject, it is because they receive this signification from the tension stemming from the impotence proper to the prematurity of birth, by which naturalists characterize the specificity of man's anatomical development—a fact that helps us grasp the dehiscence from natural harmony, required by Hegel to serve as the fruitful illness, life's happy fault, in which man, distinguishing himself from his essence, discovers his existence.

There is, in effect, no other reality behind the new prestige the imaginary

function takes on in man than this touch of death whose mark he receives at birth. For it is clearly the same "death instinct" that is manifested in this function in the animal kingdom, if we stop to consider that (1) by serving in the specific fixation on the congener in the sexual cycle, subjectivity is not dis- 346
tinguished there from the image that captivates it, and that (2) the individual appears there only as the passing representative of this image—that is, only as the passage of this represented image into life. Only to man does this image reveal its mortal signification and, at the same time, that he exists. But this image is only given to him as an image of the other—that is to say, it is ravished from him.

Thus the ego is never but half of the subject; moreover, it is the half he loses in finding that image. We can thus understand why he clings to it and tries to hold on to it in everything that seems to stand in for [*doubler*] it in himself or in the other, and offers him its resemblance, along with its effigy.

Demystifying the meaning of what analytic theory calls "primary identifications," let us say that the subject always imposes on the other—in the radical diversity of relational modes that run the gamut from the invocation of speech to the most immediate sympathy—an imaginary form which bears the seal, or even superimposed seals, of the experiences of impotence by which this form has been shaped in the subject. And this form is no other than the ego.

Thus, to return to the action of analysis, the subject always naïvely tends to concentrate his discourse on the focal point of the imaginary where this form is produced once he is freed, by the condition of the fundamental rule of psychoanalysis, from the threat that a total rejection may be addressed to him. It is the visual power this imaginary form retains from its origins that, in fact, justifies a condition which is rarely explained, even though it is felt to be crucial in variations in technique: the condition that the analyst occupy, in the session, a place that makes him invisible to the subject. For this allows the narcissistic image to be produced all the more purely and the regressive proteanism of its seductions to have freer range.

Now, the analyst undoubtedly knows, on the other hand, that he must not respond to appeals that the subject makes to him in this place, as implicit as they may be; otherwise he will see transference love arise there that nothing, except its artificial production, distinguishes from passionate love, the conditions which produced it thus failing due to their effect, analytic discourse being
reduced to the silence of the evoked presence. The analyst also knows that the 347
more he fails to respond, the more he provokes in the subject the aggression, and even hatred, characteristic of negative transference.

But he knows less well that what he says in his response is less important here than the place from which he responds. For he cannot content himself with the precaution of avoiding entering into the subject's game when the principle of the analysis of resistances orders him to objectify it.

Indeed, by simply targeting the object whose image is the subject's ego, that is, by targeting his character traits, the analyst falls under the sway of the illusions [*prestiges*] of his own ego, no less naively than the subject himself does. And the effect here is not so much to be gauged in the mirages they produce as in the distance they bring about in his object-relation. For it suffices for it to be fixed for the subject to know how to find it there.

The analyst thus enters into the game of a more radical connivance in which the shaping of the subject by the analyst's ego serves merely as an excuse for the analyst's narcissism.

If the truth of this aberration were not openly avowed in the theorization provided for it, whose forms I highlighted above, the proof could be found in the phenomena that one of the analysts the best trained in Ferenczi's school of authenticity so sensitively analyzes as characteristic of the cases that he considers to have been successfully terminated: whether he is describing the narcissistic ardor with which the subject is consumed and which we encourage him to douse in the cold shower of reality, or his oozing of an indescribable emotion at the final leave taking, going so far as to note that the analyst shares his emotion.[29] This is corroborated by the author's disappointed resignation at having to admit that certain beings cannot hope for anything more than to separate from their analysts in hatred.[30]

These results justify a use of transference corresponding to a theory of so-
348 called "primary" love which takes as its model the mutual voracity of the mother/child couple:[31] in all the forms envisioned, we see the purely dyadic conception that has come to govern the analytic relationship.[32]

If the intersubjective relationship in analysis is, indeed, conceptualized as that of a dyad of individuals, it can only be based on the unity of a perpetuated vital dependency, the idea of which altered the Freudian conception of neurosis (abandonment neurosis); and it can only be carried out in the passivation/activation polarity of the subject, the terms of which are expressly considered by Alice Balint to formulate the impasse that makes this theory necessary.[33] Such errors can be considered human inasmuch as they are rendered subtle in connotation by their author.

These errors cannot be corrected without reference to the mediation that speech constitutes between subjects. But this mediation is inconceivable unless one presupposes the presence of a third term in the imaginary relationship itself: mortal reality—the death instinct—which conditions the illusions [*prestiges*] of narcissism, as I showed earlier, and whose effects can be found anew in a brilliant form in the results considered by Balint to be those of an analysis carried to its full term in an ego-to-ego relationship.

In order for the transference relationship to escape these effects, the analyst would have to strip the narcissistic image of his own ego of all the forms of desire by which that image has been constituted, reducing it to the only face that sustains it behind their masks: the face of the absolute master, death.

It is thus clearly here that the analysis of the ego finds its ideal terminus: that in which the subject, having refound the origins of his ego in an imaginary regression, comes, by the progression of remembering, to its end in analysis—namely, the subjectification of his death.

And this is supposed to be the end required of the analyst's ego, about whom
we can say that he must acknowledge the prestige of but one master—death— 349
in order for life, which he must guide through so many vicissitudes, to be his friend. This goal does not seem beyond human grasp—for it does not imply that for him, or for others, death is anything more than an illusion [*prestige*]—and it merely satisfies the requirements of his task, such as someone like Ferenczi had defined it earlier.

This imaginary condition can only be brought about, nevertheless, through an ascesis that is affirmed in a being by following a path along which all objective knowledge is progressively suspended. This is true because, for the subject, the reality of his own death is in no wise an object that can be imagined, and the analyst can know nothing about it, no more than anyone else, except that he is a being destined to die [*promis à la mort*]. Thus, assuming he has eliminated all the illusions [*prestiges*] of his ego in order to accede to "being-toward-death," no other knowledge, whether immediate or constructed, can be preferred by him to be made a power of, assuming it [*il*] is not simply abolished thereby.

Thus he can now respond to the subject from the place he wants to respond from, but he no longer wants anything that determines this place.

Here we find, if we think about it, the reason for the profound oscillatory movement that brings analysis back to an "expectant" practice after each misguided attempt to make it more "active."

The analyst's approach cannot be left up to the indeterminacy of a freedom of indifference, nevertheless. But the usual watchword of benevolent neutrality does not provide a sufficient indication here. For while it subordinates the analyst's pleasure to the subject's own good, it still does not place his knowledge at his disposal.

Which brings us to the following question: What must the analyst know in analysis?

What the Psychoanalyst Must Know: How to Ignore What He Knows

The imaginary condition with which the preceding section culminates must be understood only as an ideal condition. But if we realize that the fact that
350 something belongs to the imaginary does not mean that it is illusory, we can say that being taken to be ideal does not make it any more dereistic. For an ideal point and even a solution that is called "imaginary" in mathematics, because it provides the pivotal point of transformation, the node point of convergence of figures or functions that are entirely determined in reality [*réel*], are clearly constitutive parts of those figures and functions. This is true of the condition involving the analyst's ego in the form of the problem whose challenge I have accepted.

The question now directed at the analyst's knowledge derives its power from the fact that it does not bring with it the answer that the analyst knows what he is doing, since it is the obvious fact that he does not, whether in theory or in technique, which led us to raise the question here.

For, if it is taken for granted that an analysis changes nothing in reality [*réel*] but "changes everything" for the subject, as long as the analyst cannot say what he is doing, the term "magical thinking"—used to designate the naive faith the subject he works with has in his power—only serves as an excuse for his own ignorance.

If, indeed, there are many opportunities to demonstrate how idiotically this term is used both inside and outside of analysis, we will find here, no doubt, the most favorable opportunity for asking the analyst what authorizes him to consider his knowledge to be privileged.

For his imbecilic recourse to the term "lived experience" to qualify the knowledge [*connaissance*] he gains from his own analysis, as if all knowledge [*connaissance*] deriving from an experience were not lived, does not suffice to distinguish his way of thinking from the way of thinking that considers him to be a man "not like the others." Nor can we attribute the vanity of this statement to the "they" [*on*] who repeat it. For if "they" are not justified, in effect, in saying that he is not a man like the others, since "they" recognize in their semblable a man in that "they" can speak to him, "they" are not wrong to mean by this that he is not a man like everyone else in that "they" recognize a man as their equal on the basis of the weight [*portée*] of his words.

Now the analyst is different in that he makes use of a function that is common to all men in a way that is not within everyone's grasp [*portée*] when he *supports* [porte] speech.

351 For that is what he does for the subject's speech, even by simply welcom-

ing it, as I showed earlier, with an attentive silence. For this silence implies [*comporte*] speech, as we see in the expression "to keep silent" which, speaking of the analyst's silence, means not only that he makes no noise but that he keeps quiet *instead of* responding.

We can go no further in this direction without asking: What is speech? And I will do my best to ensure that all the words hit their target [*portent*] here.

Nevertheless, no concept supplies the meaning of speech, not even the concept of concept, for speech is not the meaning of meaning. But speech gives meaning its medium in the symbol that speech incarnates through its act.

It is thus an act and, as such, it presupposes a subject. But it is not enough to say that, in this act, the subject presupposes another subject, for it is rather that he establishes himself here by being the other, but in a paradoxical unity of the one and the other by means of which, as I showed earlier, the one defers to the other in order to become identical to himself.

We can thus say that speech manifests itself as a communication in which the subject, expecting the other to render his message true, proffers his message in an inverted form, *and* in which this message transforms him by announcing that he is the same. As is seen in any promise made [*foi donnée*], in which the declarations "You are my wife" and "You are my master" signify "I am your husband" and "I am your disciple."

Speech thus seems to be an all the more true instance of speech [*une parole*] the less its truth is based on what is known as its "correspondence to the thing": true speech is thus paradoxically opposed to true discourse, their truth being distinguished by the fact that the former constitutes the recognition [*reconnaissance*] by the subjects of their beings insofar as they are invested [*intéressés*] in them, while the latter is constituted by knowledge [*connaissance*] of reality [*réel*], insofar as the subject targets reality in objects. But each of the truths distinguished here is altered when it crosses the path of the other truth.

This is how true discourse, by isolating the givens [*données*] of promises in the giving of one's word [*parole donnée*], makes the latter appear to be lying speech—since it pledges the future which, as they say, belongs to no one—and ambiguous too in that it constantly outstrips the being it concerns in the alienation in which its becoming is constituted.

But true speech, questioning true discourse as to what it signifies, will find 352
that one signification always refers to another signification in true discourse, no thing being able to be shown other than by a sign, and will thus make true discourse seem to be doomed to error.

How, in navigating between the Charybdis and the Scylla of this inter-accusation of speech, could the intermediate discourse—that in which the subject, in his design to get himself recognized, addresses speech to the other while taking into account what he knows of his being as given—avoid being forced into proceeding by way of ruse?

This is, in effect, how discourse proceeds to con-vince, a word that involves strategy in the process of reaching an agreement. And, however little we may have participated in the enterprise of a human institution, or even in merely supporting it, we know that the struggle continues over the terms, even when the things have been agreed to. The prevalence of speech as the middle term is again manifested in this.

This process is carried out while the subject manifests bad faith, steering his discourse between trickery, ambiguity, and error. But this struggle to assure so precarious a peace would not offer itself as the most common field of intersubjectivity if man were not already completely per-suaded by speech, which means that he indulges in it thoroughly.

For it is also true that man, in subordinating his being to the law of recognition, is traversed by the avenues of speech, which is why he is open to every suggestion. But he pauses and loses himself in the discourse of conviction, due to the narcissistic mirages that dominate his ego's relation to the other.

Thus the subject's bad faith, being so constitutive of this intermediary discourse that it is not even absent in his declaration of friendship, redoubles due to the misrecognition in which these mirages are instated. This is what Freud called the unconscious function of the ego in his topography, before he demonstrated its essential form in the discourse of negation (see "Die Verneinung," 1925).

If the analyst is thus subjected to the ideal condition that the mirages of his narcissism must have become transparent to him, it is in order that he be permeable to the other's authentic speech; we must now try to understand how he can recognize the latter through the other's discourse.

353 Of course this intermediate discourse, even qua discourse of trickery and error, does not fail to bear witness to the existence of the kind of speech on which truth is based; for it sustains itself only by attempting to pass itself off as such, and even when it openly presents itself as a lying discourse, it merely affirms all the more strongly the existence of such speech. If we refind, through this phenomenological approach to truth, the key the loss of which leads positivist logicism in search of the "meaning of meaning," doesn't this approach also get us to recognize in truth the concept of concept insofar as it is revealed in speech in action [*acte*]?

This speech, which constitutes the subject in its truth, is nevertheless forever forbidden to him, except in rare moments of his existence when he strives, ever so confusedly, to grasp it in his sworn word [*foi jurée*]; it is forbidden in that he is doomed to misrecognize it by the intermediate discourse. This speech nonetheless speaks wherever it can be read in his being—that is, at all the levels at which it has shaped him. This antinomy is the very antinomy found in the meaning Freud gave to the notion of the unconscious.

But if this speech is nevertheless accessible, it is because no true speech is simply the subject's speech, since true speech always operates by grounding the subject's speech in its mediation by another subject. In that way, this speech is open to the endless chain—which is not, of course, an indefinite chain, since it forms a closed loop—of words [*paroles*] in which the dialectic of recognition is concretely realized in the human community.

It is to the extent that the analyst manages to silence the intermediate discourse in himself, in order to open himself up to the chain of true speech [*paroles*], that he can interpolate his revelatory interpretation.

This can be seen whenever we consider an authentic interpretation in its concrete form. For example, in the analysis classically known as that of the Rat Man, the major turning point comes when Freud comprehends the resentment aroused in the subject by the fact that his mother suggested that his choice of a wife should be dictated in a calculating manner. The fact that the prohibition this advice brought with it for the subject, the prohibition against becoming engaged to the woman he thinks he loves, is associated by Freud with the father's speech, despite obvious facts to the contrary—especially the one, which takes precedence over all the others, that his father is dead—leaves us quite surprised. But it is justified at the level of a deeper truth that Freud seems 354
to have unwittingly divined, which is revealed by the series of associations the subject then goes on to provide. This truth is situated solely in what Freud refers to here as the "word chain"—which, making itself heard both in the neurosis and in the subject's destiny, extends well beyond him as an individual—and consists in the fact that a similar lack of good faith presided over his father's marriage and that this ambiguity itself covered over a breach of trust in money matters which, in causing his father to be discharged from the army, determined the latter's decision whom to marry.

Now this chain, which is not made up of pure events (all of which had, in any case, occurred prior to the subject's birth), but rather of a failure (which was perhaps the most serious because it was the most subtle) to live up to the truth of speech and of an infamy more sullying to his honor—the debt engendered by the failure seeming to have cast its shadow over the whole of his parents' marriage, and the debt engendered by the infamy never having been paid—this chain provides the meaning by which we can understand the simulacrum of redemption that the subject foments to the point of delusion in the course of the great obsessive trance that leads him to ask Freud for help.

Note that this chain is certainly not the whole structure of his obsessive neurosis, but that, in the text of the neurotic's individual myth, it crossbreeds with the web of fantasies in which the shadow of his dead father and the ideal of his lady-love are conjoined in a couple of narcissistic images.

But if Freud's interpretation, by undoing this chain in all its latent import, leads the imaginary web of the neurosis to disintegrate, it is because this chain summons the subject, concerning the symbolic debt that is promulgated in his tribunal, less as its legatee than as its living witness.

For it is important to consider that speech constitutes the subject's being not merely by a symbolic assumption, but that prior to his birth speech determines—through the laws of marriage, by which the human order is distinguished from nature—not only the subject's status but even the birth of his biological being.

Now, it seems that Freud's access to the crucial point of the meaning with which the subject could literally decipher his destiny was made possible by the
355 fact that a similar suggestion of familial prudence had been made to Freud himself, as we know from a fragment of his self-analysis, mentioned in his work, which was unmasked by Bernfeld. Had Freud himself not rejected it on that occasion, perhaps he might have missed the opportunity to recognize it when treating the Rat Man.

The dazzling comprehension Freud demonstrates in such cases is, of course, clouded over often enough by the effects of his own narcissism. Still, owing nothing to an analysis conducted in the usual manner, it allows us to see that, in the lofty heights of his final doctrinal constructions, the paths of being were cleared for him.

While this example makes us realize how important it is to comment upon Freud's work in order to understand analysis, it will serve here only as a springboard for the last stop in our discussion of this question—namely, *the contrast between the objects proposed to the analyst by his experience and the discipline necessary to his training.*

Never having been fully conceptualized, or even approximately formulated, this contrast is nevertheless expressed, as we might well expect of any neglected truth, in the rebelliousness of the facts.

The facts rebel first at the level of analytic experience, where no one gives voice to their rebellion better than Theodor Reik; we can confine our attention here to his sounding of the alarm in his book *Listening with the Third Ear*,[34] the "third ear" designating nothing other, no doubt, than the two at every man's disposal, on the condition that the function the Scriptures claim they do not have be restored to them.

The reader will find there his reasons for opposing the requirement of a

regular succession of levels of imaginary regression, whose principle was stipulated by the analysis of resistances, no less than the more systematic forms of planning* this kind of analysis went on to formulate—while he recalls, with a hundred lively examples, the pathway proper to true interpretation. One cannot, in reading his book, fail to note his recourse, that is unfortunately poorly defined, to divination, if the use of this term can refind its former virtue by evoking the juridical procedure it originally designated (Aulus Gellius, *Attic
Nights, II, 4), reminding us that human destiny depends upon the choice of 356
he who will support speech's accusation in a trial.

We will be no less concerned by the malaise that reigns regarding everything related to the analyst's training. To take but the most recent reverberation, consider the declarations made in December 1952 by Dr. Knight in his presidential address to the American Psychoanalytic Association.[35] Among the factors that tend to "alter the character of analytic training," he points out, alongside the increase in the number of analysts-in-training, "the more structured training" in the institutes that offer training, opposing it to the earlier type of training by a master ("the earlier preceptorship type of training"*) [page 218]. Regarding the recruitment of analytic trainees, he says the following:

> [Formerly] they were primarily introspective individuals, inclined to be studious and thoughtful, and tended to be highly individualistic and to limit their social life to clinical and theoretical discussions with colleagues. They read prodigiously and knew the psychoanalytic literature thoroughly. [. . .] In contrast, perhaps the majority of students of the past decade [. . .] are not so introspective, are inclined to read only the literature that is assigned in institute courses, and wish to get through with the training requirements as rapidly as possible. Their interests are primarily clinical rather than research and theoretical. Their motivation for being analyzed is more to get through this requirement of training. [. . .] The partial capitulation of some institutes [to the pressure arising from their students'] ambitious haste, and from their tendency to be satisfied with a more superficial grasp of theory, has created some of the training problems we now face [218–19].

It is quite clear, in this highly public discourse, how serious the problem is and also how poorly it is understood, if it is understood at all. What is desirable is not that the analysands be more "introspective" but rather that they understand what they are doing; and the remedy is not that the institutes be
less structured, but rather that analysts stop dispensing predigested knowl- 357
edge in them, even if it summarizes the data of analytic experience.

But what we must understand above all is that, whatever the dose of knowledge thus transmitted, it is of no value in training analysts.

For the knowledge accumulated in the course of an analyst's experience concerns the imaginary, which his experience constantly runs up against, so much so that his experience has come to adjust its pace to the systematic exploration of the imaginary in the subject. This experience has thus succeeded in constituting the natural history of the forms of desire's capture and even of the subject's identifications that had never before been cataloged this rigorously in their richness or even approached in terms of their means of action, whether by science or even wisdom, even though their luxuriance and seduction had long been deployed in artists' fanciful imaginings.

But beyond the fact that the imaginary's capture effects are extremely difficult to objectify in a true discourse—creating the major obstacle to true discourse in our daily work, which constantly threatens to make analysis into a bad science, given its continued uncertainty as to their limits in reality [*réel*]—this science, even if we assumed it were correct, is of only deceptive help in the analyst's action, for it concerns only the deposit, not the mainspring.

In this respect, experience privileges neither the so-called "biological" tendency in analytic theory, which of course has nothing biological about it except the terminology, nor the sociological tendency sometimes referred to as "culturalist." The first tendency's ideal of "drive" harmony, based on individualist ethics, cannot, as it is easy to see, yield effects that are any more humanizing than the ideal of conformity to the group with which the second tendency exposes itself to the covetousness of "engineers of the soul." The difference one can see in their results derives only from the distance that separates an autoplastic graft from a member made of the orthopedic device that replaces it—what remains lame, in the first case, with regard to instinctual functioning (what Freud calls the "scar" of neurosis) leaves only an uncertain advantage over the compensatory artifice aimed at by the second's sublimations.

In truth, if analysis borders closely enough on the scientific domains thus
358 evoked that certain of its concepts have been adopted by them, these concepts are not grounded in the experience of those domains, and the attempts analysis makes to get its experience naturalized in science remain in a state of suspension that leads analysis to be highly regarded in science only insofar as it is posited as a problem.

For psychoanalysis is also a practice subordinated by its purpose to what is most particular about the subject. And when Freud emphasizes this, going so far as to say that analytic science must be called back into question in the analysis of each case (see the case of "The Wolf Man," *passim*, the entire discussion of the case unfolding on the basis of this principle), he quite clearly indicates to the analysand the path his training should follow.

Indeed, the analyst cannot follow this path unless he recognizes in his own knowledge the symptom of his own ignorance, in the properly analytic sense that the symptom is the return of the repressed in a compromise [formation] and that repression, here as elsewhere, constitutes the censorship of truth. Ignorance must not, in fact, be understood here as an absence of knowledge but, just as much as love and hate, as a passion for being—for it can, like them, be a path by which being forms.

This is clearly the passion that must give meaning to all of analytic training, as is obvious if one simply allows oneself to see that this passion structures the analytic situation.

People have tried to detect the inner obstacle to training analysis in the psychological attitude of candidacy in which the candidate places himself in relation to the analyst, but they fail to realize that the obstacle lies in its essential foundation, which is the desire to know or the desire for power that motivates the candidate at the core of his decision. Nor have they recognized that this desire must be treated like the neurotic's desire to love, which is the very antinomy of love, according to the wisdom of the ages—unless this is what is aimed at by the best analytic writers when they declare that every training analysis is obliged to analyze the reasons why the candidate chose the career of analyst.[36]

The positive fruit of the revelation of ignorance is nonknowledge, which is not a negation of knowledge but rather its most elaborate form. The candidate's training cannot be completed without some action on the part of the master or masters who train him in this nonknowledge—failing which he will 359
never be anything more than a robotic analyst.

It is here that we understand this closing up of the unconscious whose enigma I pointed out at the major turning point of analytic technique; Freud foresaw, in more than just a quick remark, that this closing up could result some day from the very effects on a social scale of analysis becoming more widespread.[37] Indeed, the unconscious shuts down insofar as the analyst no longer "supports speech [*porte la parole*]," because he already knows or thinks he knows what speech has to say. Thus, if he speaks to the subject, who, moreover, knows as much about it as he does, the latter cannot recognize in what the analyst says the truth *in statu nascendi* of his own particular speech. This also explains the effects, which are often astonishing to us, of the interpretations Freud himself gave: the response he gave the subject was the true speech in which he himself was grounded; for in order to unite two subjects in its truth, speech requires that it be true speech for both of them.

This is why the analyst must aspire to a kind of mastery of his speech that makes it identical to his being. For he does not need to say much in the treatment (so little, indeed, that we might believe there is no need for him to say anything) in order to hear—every time he has, with the help of God, that is, with the help of the subject himself, brought an analysis to its full term—the subject pronounce before him the very words in which he recognizes the law of his own being.

How could he be surprised by this, he whose action, in the solitude in which he must answer for his patient, does not fall solely under the jurisdiction of consciousness [*conscience*], as they say of surgeons, since his technique teaches him that the very speech it reveals concerns an unconscious subject. Thus the analyst must know, better than anyone else, that he can only be himself in his speech.

Isn't this the answer to the question that tormented Ferenczi, namely: In order for the patient's avowal to come to its full term, mustn't the analyst's avowal also be pronounced? Indeed, the analyst's being acts even in his silence, and it is at the low-water level of the truth that sustains him that the subject proffers his speech. But while, in accordance with the law of speech,
360 it is in him qua other that the subject finds his own identity, it is in order to maintain his own being there.

This result is far removed from narcissistic identification, so finely described by Balint (see above), for such identification leaves the subject, in infinite beatitude, more than ever exposed to the obscene and ferocious figure that analysis calls the superego and that must be understood as the gap opened up in the imaginary by any and every rejection (*Verwerfung*) of the commandments of speech.[38]

And there is no doubt but that a training analysis has this effect if the subject finds therein nothing more proper to witness the authenticity of his experience, for example, of having fallen in love with the person who opens the door at his analyst's house, mistaking her for his analyst's wife. A titillating fancy, of course, by its specious conformity, but about which he can hardly brag that he derived his lived knowledge of it from Oedipus, this knowledge being destined, rather, to take this fancy away from him. For, in going no further, he will have experienced nothing more than the myth of Amphitryon, and he will have done so the way Sosia did, that is, without understanding anything about it. How then can we expect that, as subtle as he may have seemed to be in his promises, such a subject will prove to be anything other than a follower whose head is full of idle gossip, when it will be his turn to add his two cents' worth to the question of variations in treatment?

In order to avoid such results, training analysis, about which all analytic authors note that its conditions are never discussed except in a censored form, must not drive its ends and practice ever further into the shadows, as the formalism of the guarantees that people claim to provide of it grows stronger—as Michael Balint declares and demonstrates with the greatest clarity.[39]

Indeed, the sheer quantity of researchers cannot bring quality to psychoanalytic research the way it does in a science that is constituted in objectivity. A hundred mediocre psychoanalysts do not advance analytic knowledge one iota, whereas a physician, being the author of a wonderful book on grammar (you must not imagine that it was some pleasant little product of medical humanism), defended his whole life long a certain style of communication
within a group of analysts against the winds of its discordance and the tide of 361
its servitudes.

The fact is that psychoanalysis, since it progresses essentially in non-knowledge, is tied in the history of science to a state prior to its Aristotelian definition, which is known as dialectic. Freud's work bears witness to this in its references to Plato and even to the pre-Socratics.

But far from being isolated or even isolable, it simultaneously finds its place at the center of the vast conceptual movement which in our time—restructuring so many sciences that are improperly called "social," changing or refinding the meaning of certain sections of the exact science *par excellence*, mathematics, in order to restore the foundations of a science of human action insofar as it is based on conjecture—is reclassifying the body of sciences of intersubjectivity under the name "human sciences."

The analyst will find much to borrow from linguistic research in its most concrete modern developments, with which to shed light on difficult problems posed to him by verbalization in both his practice and doctrine. And we can see, in the most unexpected manner, in the elaboration of the unconscious' most original phenomena—dreams and symptoms—the very figures of the outdated rhetoric, which prove in practice to provide the most subtle specifications of those phenomena.

The modern notion of history will be no less necessary to the analyst if he is to understand the function of history in the subject's individual life.

But it is above all the theory of symbols—revived from its status as a curiosity during what one might call the paleontological age of analysis, when it was classed under the heading of a supposed "depth psychology"—that analysis must restore to its universal function. No study would be better suited to this than the study of whole numbers, whose nonempirical origin cannot be excessively pondered by the analyst. And without going into the fruitful exercises of modern game theory, much less into the highly suggestive formalizations of set theory, the analyst will find sufficient material upon which to base his

362 practice by simply learning to correctly count to four, as the author of these lines is trying to teach people to do (that is, to integrate the function of death into the ternary Oedipal relationship).

My point is not to define the fields of a program of study, but rather to indicate that, in order to situate analysis in the eminent place that those responsible for public education should grant it, its foundations must be laid open to criticism, without which it will degenerate into effects of collective subornation.

It is up to the discipline of analysis itself to avoid these effects in the training of analysts and to thus bring clarity to the question of its variations.

Only then will we be able to understand the extreme discretion with which Freud introduced the very forms of the "standard treatment" that have since become the norm:

> I must however make it clear that what I am asserting is that this technique is the only one suited to my individuality; I do not venture to deny that a physician quite differently constituted might find himself driven to adopt a different attitude to his patients and to the task before him.[40]

For this discretion will then cease to be relegated to the status of a sign of Freud's profound modesty, and will instead be recognized as affirming the truth that analysis cannot find its measure except along the pathways of a learned ignorance.

Notes

1. [Added in 1966:] In 1966 let us say that I consider it to be abject. This assessment, which I cannot help but pronounce, legitimates my rewriting of the first section here in a lighter manner.

2. [Added in 1966:] Except in taking up anew in the structure what specifies our "clinical approach" [*clinique*], in the sense it still maintains from its moment of birth, an originally repressed moment in the physician who extends it, he himself becoming ever more thoroughly the lost child of this moment. See Michel Foucault, *Naissance de la Clinique* (Paris: PUF, 1963) [*The Birth of the Clinic* (New York: Pantheon, 1973)].

3. See *IJP* XXXV, 2 (1954), the entire issue.

4. Edward Glover, "Therapeutic Criteria of Psycho-Analysis," *IJP* XXXV, 2 (1954): 95. [Added in 1966:] A French translation of the whole of this article can be found in the final pages of the collection of this author's work published under the title *Technique de la psychanalyse* (Paris: PUF, 1958). [In English, see *The Technique of Psycho-Analysis* (New York: International Universities Press, 1955)].

5. Glover, "Therapeutic Criteria," 95–96.

6. Glover, "Therapeutic Criteria," 96. Italics in the original.

7. Glover, "Therapeutic Criteria," 96.

8. "Le problème du transfert" ("The Problem of Transference"), *RFP* XVI, 1–2 (1952): 5–115. [A sample of Lagache's work on transference can be found in English in "Some Aspects of Transference," *IJP* XXXIV, 1 (1953): 1–10.]

9. [Added in 1966:] In 1966, Lagache is

someone who keeps up with my teaching without seeing in it that transference is the inmixing of the time of knowing.

While rewritten, this text scrupulously follows the statements I made in 1955.

10. [Added in 1966:] Three paragraphs rewritten.

11. [Added in 1966:] If I have managed with these lines, as with my classes, to lift the reign of boredom that I combat enough for their style of emission to self-correct in being reread here, let me add to them this note: in 1966, I would say that the ego is the theology of free enterprise, and I would designate its patron saints as the triad Fénelon, Guizot, and Victor Cousin.

12. *Problèmes de technique psychanalytique* (Paris: PUF, 1953), 63. [In English, see *Problems of Psychoanalytic Technique* (Albany: Psychoanalytic Quarterly, 1941), 54.]

13. Glover, "Therapeutic Criteria," 97.

14. Wilhelm Reich, "Charakteranalyse" ("Character Analysis"), *Internationale Zeitschrift für Psychoanalyse* XIV, 2 (1928): 180–96. English translation in *The Psycho-analytic Reader* (New York: International Universities Press, 1948). [See also Reich's book *Character Analysis* (New York: Farrar, Straus and Giroux, 1972).]

15. Richard Sterba, "The Fate of the Ego in Analytic Therapy," *IJP* XV, 2–3 (1934): 117–26.

16. W. Hoffer, "Three Psychological Criteria for the Termination of Treatment," *IJP* XXXI, 3 (1950): 194–95.

17. Sandor Ferenczi, "Die Elastizität der psychoanalytischen Technik," *Internationale Zeitschrift für Psychoanalyse* XIV, 2 (1928): 197–209. [In English, see "The Elasticity of Psycho-Analytic Technique," in *The Selected Papers of Sandor Ferenczi, M.D.*, Vol. III, *Final Contributions to the Problems and Methods of Psycho-Analysis* (New York: Basic Books, 1955), 87–101. Note that Lacan renders *Einfühlung* as *connivence* (connivance), not as "empathy" (or "understanding" or "sensitivity") as is usually the case and as it is rendered in the translation of Ferenczi's work cited here. See also the revised translation included in *Sandor Ferenczi: Selected Writings* (London: Penguin, 1999), 255–68.]

18. [Added in 1966:] That is, the analyst's transference.

19. Freud, "Die Endliche und die Unendliche Analyse," *GW* XVI, 93 ["Analysis Terminable and Interminable," *SE* XXIII, 247; Lacan here translates the title of the article as "*L'analyse finie et l'analyse sans fin*," "Finite (or Finished) Analysis and Endless Analysis."]

20. Ferenczi, "Die Elastizität der psychoanalytischen Technik," 207. ["The Elasticity of Psycho-analytic Technique," 98.]

21. [Added in 1966:] Ferenczi never imagined that this might one day serve as a billboard slogan.

22. Reich, "Charakteranalyse," 196 [*The Psycho-analytic Reader*, 123].

23. Freud, "Triebe und Triebschicksale," *GW* X, 210–32. ["Drives and Their Vicissitudes," *SE* XIV, 117–40, especially 122–23.]

24. *GW* XIII, 71–161 [*SE* XVIII, 69–143].

25. *GW* XIII, 1–69 [*SE* XVIII, 7–64].

26. "Die Verneinung," *GW* XIV, 11–15 ["Negation," *SE* XIX, 235–39].

27. *GW* XIV, 421–506 [*SE* XXI, 64–145].

28. Lacan, "Aggressiveness in Psychoanalysis" (1948) and "The Mirror Stage" (1949), in *Écrits* 1966.

29. M. Balint, "On the Termination of Analysis," *IJP* XXXI, 3 (1950): 197.

30. M. Balint, "On Love and Hate," in *Primary Love and Psychoanalytic Technique* (London: Hogarth, 1952), 155. [The article is also found in *IJP* XXXIII (1952): 355–62; see especially 361–62.]

31. A. Balint, "Love for the Mother and Mother-Love," *IJP* XXX, 4 (1949): 251–59. [I have corrected the mistaken attribution of this article to Michael Balint instead of to Alice Balint in the footnotes and text.]

32. M. Balint, "Changing Therapeutic Aims and Techniques in Psycho-Analysis," *IJP* XXXI, 1–2 (1950). See his remarks on the "two-body psychology" on pages 123–24.

33. See the appendix to her abovementioned article, "Love for the Mother."

34. New York: Garden City Books, 1949. [Published in Great Britain as *The Inner Experience of a Psychoanalyst* (London: George Allen & Unwin, 1949).]

35. R. P. Knight, "The Present Status of Organized Psychoanalysis in the United States," *Journal of the American Psychoanalytic Association* I, 2 (1953): 197–221.

36. Maxwell Gitelson, "Therapeutic Problems in the Analysis of the 'Normal' Candidate," *IJP* XXXV, 2 (1954): 174–83.

37. Freud, "Die zukünftigen Chancen der psychoanalytischen Therapie" (1910), *GW* VIII, 104–15 ["The Future Prospects of Psycho-Analytic Therapy," *SE* XI, 141–51].

38. Freud, "Aus der Geschichte einer infantilen Neurose," *GW* XII, 111 ["From the History of an Infantile Neurosis (the Wolf Man)," *SE* XVII, 79–80].

39. M. Balint, "Analytic Training and Training Analysis," *IJP* XXXV, 2 (1954): 157–62.

40. Freud, "Ratschläge für den Arzt bei der psychoanalytischen Behandlung," *GW* VIII, 376 ["Recommendations to Physicians Practising Psycho-Analysis," *SE* XII, 111. Lacan provides his own French translation here].

On a Purpose 363

The two samples of my seminar that follow inspire me to give the reader some idea of the purpose of my teaching.

These texts still bear traces of the violent novelty they brought with them. One can gauge how great a risk I ran at that time by observing that the subjects they deal with have yet to be taken up by others, even though I provided an elaboration of them which I have continued to corroborate through critique and construction.

In rereading these texts, I am happy to see that I highlighted the repression that struck the word "signor," which was recently echoed by a question that was posed to me about the locus where the forgotten term resides—to put it more precisely in the terms of my topology: Is that locus "the dummy" mentioned later in my "Direction of the Treatment" or the Other's discourse as formulated in "Function and Field"?

To this work in progress let me add the personal difficulties that make it hard for someone to grasp a notion like that of *Verwerfung* [foreclosure] when he himself may be characterized by it. This is an everyday tragedy which serves as a reminder that my teaching, although it exposes its theory to everyone, has as its practical stakes the training of psychoanalysts.

How influential is my teaching? Let us approach the question by first considering that the two pieces presented here were published in the first issue, which is now out of print, of the journal *La Psychanalyse*, the room my texts took up in it measuring only imperfectly, by their very excess, the work I put into it.

How can we evaluate what was required, due to the ever composite nature of such an undertaking, on the terrain of an exigency whose status I shall state?

It would not be the whole story to note that such invective earth-moving, were it to stir up dust here, would still be relevant.

364 I would also maintain that the tenor of this journal stopped French circles from sliding down the slippery slope seen in international psychoanalytic congresses. I occasionally receive news from abroad of people's astonishment at its collapse.

It goes without saying that the journal was disavowed in psychoanalytic circles right from its very introduction.

Nothing in it goes beyond or goes against the order of importance that I have recently captured with a pun of my own making: *poubellication*.

The two texts that follow here warrant further consideration since they are representative of the kind of work done in my Seminar, having framed the contribution that Jean Hyppolite, who was one of my auditors at the time, was willing to make at my request in the form of a commentary on Freud's paper entitled "Verneinung" ("Negation").

The reader will find his commentary in an appendix to the present volume, permission for its reproduction having been graciously granted by its author. The latter would like its character as a memorial to be clear, and the reader will see that the efforts made to preserve its character as a set of notes obviate any and all misunderstanding, but also thereby its value for us.

For it was by allowing himself to be led in this way by the letter of Freud's work, up to the spark that it necessitates, without selecting a destination in advance—and by not backing away from the residue, found anew at the end, of its enigmatic point of departure, and even by not considering that he had accounted, at the end of the proceedings, for the astonishment by which he entered into the proceedings—that a tried and true logician brought me the guarantee of what constituted my request, when for the preceding three years already I had been legitimating my work as a *literal commentary* on Freud's work.

The *requirement to read* does not take up as much space in the culture of psychoanalysis as one might think.

There is nothing superstitious in my privileging the letter of Freud's work. It is in circles where liberties are taken with that letter that people render that letter sacred in a way that is altogether compatible with its debasement to routinized use.

Freud's discovery shows the structural reason why the literality of any text, whether proposed as sacred or profane, increases in importance the more it involves a genuine confrontation with truth.

That structural reason is found precisely in what the truth that it bears, that of the unconscious, owes to the letter of language—that is, to what I call "the signifier."

While this incidentally accounts for Freud's quality as a writer, it is 365
above all decisive in interesting psychoanalysts as much as possible in language and in what language determines in the subject.

Herein too lies the motive for the collaborations I obtained for the first issue of my journal *La Psychanalyse*: Martin Heidegger's for his article entitled "Logos"—even if I had to be so audacious as to translate it myself—and Émile Benveniste's for his critique of one of Freud's references, which was eminent in proving to be governed by language at the deepest level of the affective realm.

Therein lay my motive, and not in some vain semblance of dialogue, even and especially philosophical: We need not, in psychoanalysis, broaden people's minds.

All of the illustrious neighboring fields that I brought together at certain moments in lectures designed to further my purpose were destined by the structuralist nature of their own tasks to accentuate that purpose for us. It should be indicated that the exceptional stupidity that put an end to them, taking umbrage at them, had already quashed the undertaking by seeing in it nothing but propaganda.

What thus impels the psychoanalyst to cast his anchor elsewhere? If approaching the repressed is accompanied by resistances that indicate the degree of repression, as Freud tells us, this implies at the very least that there is a close relationship between the two terms. This relationship is borne out here by functioning in the opposite direction.

The truth effect that is delivered up in the unconscious and the symptom requires that knowledge adopt an inflexible discipline in following its contours, for these contours run counter to intuitions that keep it all too comfortably safe.

This truth effect culminates in a veiled irreducibility in which the primacy of the signifier is stamped, and we know from Freud's doctrine that nothing real shares in this more than sex. But the subject's foothold there can only be overdetermined: Desire is the desire to know, aroused by a cause connected with a subject's formation, owing to which this connection is related to sex only through an awkward detour [*biais*]—an expression in which the reader can recognize the topology with which I try to close in on that cause.

This makes it necessary to render present a hole which can no longer be situated in the transcendental nature of knowledge [*connaissance*]—a locus that is, in sum, designed to simply move it back a step—but only in a place which is closer that pressures us to forget it.

This is the place where being, which is so inclined to flee its jouissance
366 that it shows itself in the process, nevertheless does not assume, even in a less permanent way, that it has rightful access to it—a pretension that escapes being comical due only to the anxiety provoked by the experience that deflates it.

Curiously enough, Freud's success can be explained on the basis of this impasse; people capitulate when they understand his success so as not to encounter this impasse, and "his language"—as people say to reduce discourse to the verbal—appears in statements involving a "we" [*on*] that most thoroughly flees the light of day.

Who will be surprised, outside of this "we," that psychoanalysts attribute the same success to Freud when—engaging in a sort of sucking of his thought through the gap that opens up in his thought, which is so much closer in that it takes on, in his practice, the insistence of an indecent intimacy—this gap redoubles analysts' horror by usually forcing them to engage in the morose operation of obstructing it?

This is why no one any longer deals with each delicate joint that Freud borrows from the most subtle aspects of language [*langue*], without pouring into them beforehand the confused images into which the worst translations run headlong.

In short, people read Freud in the same way that they write in psychoanalysis—enough said.

One can thus see that the watchword I adopted, a "return to Freud," has nothing to do with a return to the sources that could, here as elsewhere, signify no more than a regression.

Even if the point were to correct a deviation from Freud that is too obvious not to be apparent at every crossroads, I would merely be making way for an external, albeit salubrious, necessity.

My return to Freud has an entirely different meaning insofar as it is based on the subject's topology, which can only be elucidated through a second twist back [*tour*] on itself. Everything about it must be restated on another side so that what it hones in on can be closed, which is certainly not absolute knowledge but rather the position from which knowledge can reverse truth effects. It is, no doubt, on the basis of a suture that was made at one moment at this joint that what we have absolutely achieved by way of science was assured. Isn't that also enough to tempt us to undertake a new operation where this joint remains gaping in our lives?

This double twist [*tour*], of which I provide the theory, lends itself, in effect, to another seam by offering up a new edge [*bord*]: a seam from which
arises a structure that is far more apt than Antiquity's sphere to answer 367
for what proposes itself to the subject as an inside and an outside.[1]

When Freud, in a famous text, presents Ananke and Logos together, should we believe that he does so because he enjoys the effect created or to restore a firm footing to the rabble [*pied-plat*] by holding out for them the step down to earth?

The formidable power that Freud invokes—awakening us from the sleep in which we weaken it—great Necessity, is no other than that which is exercised *in* the Logos, which he was the first to clarify with the glancing light of his discovery.

It is repetition itself whose face he, as much as Kierkegaard, renews for us in the division of the subject, the fate of scientific man. Let another confusion be dispelled: it bears no relation to Nietzsche's "eternal return."

Repetition is unique in being necessary, and should I be unable to tame the repetition for which I assume responsibility, my index would command it to continue.

1966

Note

1. As I began to establish the very year (1961–1962) that my students concerned themselves with the same relationship (inside-outside) in a more worldly context. Whereby others will benefit from the fact that I returned to it this year (1965–1966).

369 # Introduction to Jean Hyppolite's Commentary on Freud's "Verneinung"

Seminar on Freudian Technique, February 10th, 1954[1]

You have been able to gauge how fruitful my method of returning to Freud's texts proves to be for providing a critical examination of the current use of the fundamental concepts of psychoanalytic technique and especially of the notion of resistance.

The adulteration this latter notion has undergone is all the more serious because of the order that Freud consecrated with his own authority to give pride of place in psychoanalytic technique to the analysis of resistances. For although Freud intended to mark thereby a turning point in psychoanalytic practice, I believe that there is nothing but confusion and misinterpretation in the way in which people justify a technique that misrecognizes nothing less than what it is applied to on the basis of an emergency measure.

The question is that of the meaning that we must restore to the precepts of this technique which, since they will soon be reduced to fixed formulas, have lost the indicative virtue that they can only preserve through an authentic comprehension of the truth of the experience they are designed to guide. Freud, of course, could not but have such a comprehension, like those who immerse themselves in his work. But, as you have had the opportunity to see, this is not
370 the case of those in our discipline who noisily seek refuge behind the primacy of technique—no doubt in order to hide behind the simultaneous harmonizing of their technique with progress in the theory, in the dumbed-down usage of analytic concepts which alone can justify their technique.

One will be quite disappointed if one attempts to look a little more closely at what the analysis of resistances represents in the dominant usage. For what strikes one first in reading the work of the doctrinaires of this perspective is that the dialectical handling of any idea whatsoever is so unthinkable to them that they cannot even recognize it when they are thrown into it—like Monsieur Jourdain was when he spoke in prose without realizing it—by a practice in which dialectic is in fact immanent. Thus they cannot reflect upon it without latching in panic onto the most simplistic or the most grossly imaginative objectifications.

This is why resistance comes to be imagined rather than conceptualized by them according to what it connotes in its average semantic usage[2]—namely, if we examine this usage closely, in the indefinite transitive acceptation. Thanks to which the phrase "the subject resists" is understood as "he resists something." What does he resist? No doubt he resists his tendencies in the way he forces himself to behave as a neurotic subject, and resists avowing them in the justifications he proposes for his behavior to the analyst. But since the tendencies come back in force, and since the analyst's technique had something to do with it, this resistance is presumed to be seriously tried; hence, in order to maintain it, he must work at it and, before we even have the chance to turn around, we have slipped into the rut of the obtuse idea that the patient "is being defensive." For the misinterpretation is only definitively sealed due to its conjunction with another misuse of language, the one that gives the term "defense" the carte blanche it has in medicine, without us realizing—for one does not become a better physician by being a bad psychoanalyst—that there 371
is a misunderstanding in medicine too regarding the notion if we intend to echo its correct meaning in physiopathology. And we betray no less—for one becomes no better instructed in psychoanalysis by being ignorant in medicine—the perfectly well-informed application Freud made of it in his first writings on the pathogenesis of the neuroses.

But, people will ask us, by centering your aim of grasping a confused idea at its lowest point of disintegration, don't you fall into the trap of condemning the patient, not for his acts, but for intentions you attribute to him [*procès de tendance*]? The fact is, I will answer, that nothing stops the users of a technique thus fitted out from sliding down this dangerous slope, for the precepts with which they parry its original confusion do not in any wise remedy its consequences. This is what allows people to proffer the following: that the subject can communicate to us only about his ego and with his ego (here we see the defiant look of common sense that comes home to roost); that it is necessary, in order to get anywhere, to strengthen the ego or at least, they correct themselves, its healthy part (and heads nod in assent at this tomfoolery); that in the use of analytic material we proceed by following blueprints (of which we have, of course, the certified plans in our pocket); that we proceed thusly from the surface to the depths (no putting the cart before the horse); that in order to do so the masters' secret is to analyse the subject's aggressiveness (no attaching a cart which would kill the horse); here, finally, are the dynamics of anxiety and the arcanes of its economy (let no one touch the potential of this sublime mana if he is not an expert in hydraulics). All these precepts, let it be said, and their theoretical trappings shall be ignored here because they are simply macaronic.

In effect, resistance can but be misrecognized in its essence if it is not understood on the basis of the dimensions of the discourse in which it manifests itself in analysis. We encountered them right away in the metaphor with which Freud illustrated his first definition of resistance. I mean the one I commented on some time ago which evokes the staves on which the subject unfolds the chains
372 of his discourse "longitudinally," to use Freud's term, according to a musical score whose "pathogenic nucleus" is the leitmotiv.[3] In the reading of this score, resistance manifests itself "radially"—a term which is opposed to the preceding term ["longitudinally"]—and with a strength proportional to the proximity of the line being deciphered to the line that delivers the central melody by completing it. So much so that this strength, Freud stresses, can serve as a measure of this proximity.

Certain analysts even tried to find in this metaphor an indication of the mechanistic tendency with which Freud's thought is supposedly shackled. This attempt evinces a complete lack of comprehension, as can be seen in the research I have carried out step-by-step into the successive clarifications Freud gave to the notion of resistance, especially in the writing we are now considering in which he gives the clearest formulation of it.

What does Freud tell us, in fact? He reveals to us a phenomenon that structures every revelation of truth in the [psychoanalytic] dialogue. There is the fundamental difficulty that the subject encounters in what he has to say; the most common is the one that Freud demonstrated in repression, namely, the sort of discordance between the signified and the signifier that is brought on by all censorship of social origin. The truth can always, in this case, be communicated between the lines. That is, he who wishes to make the truth known can always adopt the technique indicated by the fact that truth is identical to the symbols that reveal it; in other words, he can always arrive at his ends by deliberately introducing into a text discordances that cryptographically correspond to those imposed by the censorship.

The true subject—that is, the subject of the unconscious—proceeds no differently in the language of his symptoms; that language is not so much deciphered by the analyst as it comes to be more and more solidly addressed to him, for the ever renewed satisfaction of analytic experience. Indeed, this is what analysis recognized in the phenomenon of transference.

What the subject who speaks says, however empty his discourse may at first be, derives its effect from the approximation made in it on the basis of speech in which he tries to fully convert the truth expressed by his symptoms. Let me indicate right away that this formulation is of more general import, as we shall see today, than the phenomenon of repression by which I just introduced it.

Be that as it may, it is insofar as the subject arrives at the limit of what the 373
moment allows his discourse to effectuate by way of speech, that a phenomenon is produced in which, as Freud shows us, resistance is linked to the psychoanalytic dialectic. For this moment and this limit are balanced in the emergence, outside of the subject's discourse, of the trait that can most particularly be addressed to you in what he is in the process of saying. And this juncture is raised to the function of the punctuation of his speech. In order to convey this effect I have used the image that the subject's speech suddenly swings toward the presence of the listener.[4]

This presence, which is the purest relationship the subject can have with a being and which is all the more deeply felt as such since this being is for him less qualified, this presence, momentarily freed to the utmost from the veils that cover it over and elude it in everyday discourse insofar as the latter is constituted as "they" [*on*] discourse precisely for this purpose, this presence is marked in discourse by a suspensive scansion often connoted by a moment of anxiety, as I have shown you in an example from my own experience.

Hence the import of the indication that Freud gave us from his own experience: namely, that when the subject interrupts his discourse you can be sure that a thought is occupying him that is related to the analyst.

You will see this indication most often confirmed if you ask the subject the following question: "What are you thinking about right now that is related to what is around you here and more precisely to me who is listening to you?" Still, the inner satisfaction you may derive from hearing more or less unflattering remarks about your general appearance and your mood that day, about your taste as denoted by your choice of furniture or the way in which you are dressed, does not suffice to justify your initiative if you do not know what you are expecting from these remarks, and the idea—which for many is a received idea—that these remarks give the subject the opportunity to discharge his aggression is utterly idiotic.

As Freud said prior to the elaboration of the new topography, resistance is 374
essentially an ego phenomenon. Let us try to understand here what that means. This will allow us later to understand what we mean by resistance when we relate it to the subject's other agencies.

The phenomenon in question here shows one of the purest forms in which the ego can manifest its function in the dynamic of analysis. This is why it makes us realize that the ego, as it operates in analytic experience, has nothing to do with the supposed unity of the subject's reality that so-called general psychology abstracts as instituted in its "synthetic functions." The ego we are talking about is absolutely impossible to distinguish from the imaginary captures that constitute it from head to toe—in both its genesis and its status, in both its function and its actuality—by an other and for an other. Stated differently, the dialectic that sustains our experience, being situated at the most enveloping level of the subject's efficacy, obliges us to understand the ego entirely in the movement of progressive alienation in which self-consciousness is constituted in Hegel's phenomenology.

This means that if, in the moment we are studying, you are dealing with the subject's ego*, it is because you are at that moment the prop for his alter ego.

I have reminded you that one of our colleagues—who has since been cured of this pruritus of thought which still tormented him at the time when he was cogitating about the cases in which psychoanalysis is indicated as a treatment—was seized by a suspicion of this truth; the miracle of intelligence illuminating his face, he ended his talk regarding these indications by announcing the great news that analysis had to be subordinated to the primary condition that the subject have some sense of the existence of the other.

It is precisely here that the question begins: What is the kind of alterity by which the subject is interested in this existence? For the subject's ego partakes of this very alterity, so much so that if there is something to be known [*une connaissance*] which is truly classificatory for the analyst—and of a kind that can satisfy the requirement of having a preliminary orientation that the new technique proclaims with a tone that is all the more hilarious since it
375 misrecognizes it right to the very core—it is the thing which in each neurotic structure defines the sector that is open to the ego's* alibis.

In short, what we expect from the subject's reply in asking him this stereotypical question, which most often frees him from the silence that serves us as a signal of this privileged moment of resistance, is that he show us *who* is speaking and to *whom*—which is, in fact, one and the same question.

But it remains up to you to get him to understand it by questioning him in the imaginary place where he is situated; this will depend on whether or not you can tie the [unflattering] jibe [he makes at that moment of resistance] to the point in his discourse where his speech ground to a halt.

You will thereby confirm this point as a correct punctuation. And it is here that the analysis of resistances and the analysis of the material, whose opposition it would be ruinous to formally endorse, harmoniously converge. This is a technique in which you are given practical training in supervision.

To those who have nevertheless learned another technique, the systematics of which I know only too well, and who still lend it some credence, I would observe that you of course will not fail to obtain a relevant response by pointing out the subject's aggression toward you and even by showing some modicum of finesse in recognizing therein, by way of contrast, the "need for love." And after thus plying your art, the field of defense's ploys will open up before you. Big deal! Don't we know that where speech gives up, the domain of violence begins, and that violence reigns there already without us even provoking it?

Thus, if you bring war to it, you should at least be aware of its principles and realize that we misrecognize its limits when we do not understand it, as Clausewitz does, as a particular form of human commerce.

We know that it was by recognizing, by the name of total war, its internal dialectic that Clausewitz was able to formulate that war is in command because it is considered to be an extension of political expedients.

This has allowed more advanced practitioners in the modern experience of social warfare, to which he served as a prelude, to formulate the corollary that the first rule to be observed is not to allow the moment at which the adversary becomes other than he was to slip away—which means that we should rapidly divide up the stakes that form the basis of an equitable peace. It has 376
been made amply clear to your generation that this art is unknown to demagogues who can no more detach themselves from abstractions than your ordinary psychoanalyst can. This is why the very wars they win serve only to engender contradictions in which one can rarely perceive the effects that they promised would be achieved thereby.

Hence they throw themselves headlong into the undertaking of humanizing the adversary who has become their responsibility through his defeat—even calling the psychoanalyst to the rescue to collaborate in restoring "human relations,"* a task in which the analyst, given the pace at which he now pursues things, does not hesitate to go astray.

None of this seems irrelevant when we rediscover, at a turning point, Freud's note (in the same text) about which I have already spoken, and this perhaps sheds new light on what Freud means when he says that one must not infer, on the basis of a battle that is waged sometimes for months around an isolated farm, that the farm itself represents the national sanctuary of one of the warring parties, or even that it shelters one of their military industries. In other words, the meaning of a defensive or offensive action is not to be found in the object that is apparently fought over, but rather in the plan it forms a part of, which defines the adversary by his strategy.

The gallows humor evinced in the morosity of the analysis of the defenses would no doubt bear more encouraging fruit for those who trust in it if they simply took their cue from the smallest real struggle, which would teach them that the most effective response to a defense is not to bring to bear upon it the test of strength.

What they in fact do—instead of confining themselves to the dialectical pathways by which psychoanalysis has been elaborated, and lacking the talent necessary to return to the pure and simple use of suggestion—is merely resort to a pedantic form of suggestion, taking advantage of our culture's ambient psychologism. In doing so, they offer up to their contemporaries the spectacle of people who were drawn to their profession by nothing other than the desire to always be able to have the last word, and who, when they encounter a little more difficulty than in other so-called professional [*libérales*] activities,
377 sport the ridiculous face of Purgons, obsessed as they are by the "defense" of whomsoever does not understand why his daughter is mute.

But in so doing they merely enter the dialectic of the ego and the other that constitutes the neurotic's impasse and renders his situation of a piece with the analyst's biased belief [*préjugé*] in his ill will. This is why I sometimes say that there is no other resistance in analysis than that of the analyst. For this biased belief can only give way through a true dialectical conversion, a conversion that must, moreover, be maintained in the analyst by continual use. This is what all the conditions of the training of a psychoanalyst truly come down to.

Without such training this bias [*préjugé*], which has found its most stable formulation in the conception of pithiatism, will remain forever dominant. But other formulations had preceded it and I merely want to infer what Freud thought of it by recalling his feelings about its latest incarnation during his youth. I will extract his testimony about it from Chapter 4 of his great text, *Group Psychology and the Analysis of the Ego*. He speaks there of Bernheim's astonishing *tours de force* with suggestion, which he witnessed in 1899.

> But I can remember even then feeling a muffled hostility to this tyranny of suggestion. When a patient who showed himself unamenable was met with a shout: "What are you doing? *Vous vous contre-suggestionnez!*", I said to myself that this was an evident injustice and an act of violence. For the man certainly had a right to countersuggestions if people were trying to subdue him with suggestions. Later on my resistance took the direction of protesting against the view that suggestion, which

explained everything, was itself to be exempt from explanation. Thinking of it, I repeated the old conundrum:

Christopher bore Christ; Christ bore the whole world;
Say, where did Christopher then put his foot? [*SE* XVIII, 89]

And given that Freud goes on to deplore the fact that the concept of suggestion has drifted in an ever vaguer direction, which does not allow us to 378
foresee the clarification of the phenomenon any time soon, what mightn't he have said about the current usage of the notion of resistance? How could he not have encouraged, at the very least, my efforts to tighten up its use in analytic technique? In any case, my way of reintegrating it into the whole of the dialectical movement of an analysis is perhaps what will allow me to someday provide a formulation of suggestion that will stand up to the criteria of analytic experience.

This is the aim that guides me when I shed light on resistance at the moment of transparency at which it presents itself by its transferential end, to borrow an apt expression from Octave Mannoni.

This is why I shed light on it with examples in which one can see the same dialectical syncope at work.

This led me to highlight the example with which Freud illustrates, almost acrobatically, what he means by the desire in a dream.[5] For while he provides this example in order to cut short the objection that a dream undergoes alteration when it is recollected in the narrative, it appears quite clearly that only the elaboration of the dream interests him insofar as it is carried out in the narrative itself—in other words, the dream has no value for him except as a vector of speech. Hence all the phenomena that he furnishes of forgetting, and even of doubt, which block the narrative must be interpreted as signifiers in this speech. And were there to remain of a dream but a fragment as evanescent as the memory floating in the air of the Cheshire cat who fades away in such a worrisome manner in Alice's eyes, this would simply render more certain that we have here the broken end of what constitutes the dream's transferential tip—in other words, the part of the dream that directly addresses the analyst. Here this occurs by means of the word "channel," the sole vestige remaining of the dream—namely, a smile here too, but this time a woman's impertinent smile, with which she to whom Freud took the trouble to give a taste of his theory of jokes paid homage to it—which is translated by the sentence that concludes the funny story that she associates, at Freud's invitation, to the word "channel": "Du sublime au ridicule il n'y a qu'un pas" ("From the sublime to the ridiculous there is but one step").

Similarly, in the example of the forgetting of names which I just recently 379 examined, it being literally the first that came along, in *The Psychopathology of Everyday Life*,[6] I was able to discern that Freud's inability to find the name Signorelli in the dialogue he carried on with his colleague who was his traveling companion at that time, corresponded to the fact that—by censoring earlier in the conversation with the same gentleman everything that this man's remarks had stirred up in him both by their content and by memories that came in their wake, regarding the relationship of man and doctor to death, the absolute master, *Herr*, *signor*—Freud had literally left in his partner, excised [*retranché*] from himself therefore, the broken half (to be understood in the most material sense of the term) of the sword of speech. For a little while, precisely the time during which he continued to speak with this partner, he could no longer have this term as signifying material at his disposal since it remained attached to the repressed signification—especially since the theme of the work he needed to find anew in Signorelli, the author, namely, the fresco of the Antichrist at Orvieto, simply illustrated the mastery of death in one of the most manifest, albeit apocalyptic, forms.

But can we confine our attention to repression here? I can, of course, assure you that repression is at work here thanks to the overdeterminations Freud himself supplies us with regarding the phenomenon; and we can also confirm here, thanks to the relevance of these circumstances, the import of what I want to convey to you with the formulation, "the unconscious is the Other's discourse."

For the man who breaks the bread of truth with his semblable in the act of speech shares a lie.

But is that the whole story? Could the speech that was excised [*retranchée*] here avoid being extinguished before being-toward-death when speech approached it at a level at which only witticisms are still viable, appearances of seriousness no longer seeming to be anything but hypocritical in responding to its gravity?

Hence death brings the question of what negates [*nie*] discourse, but also the question whether or not it is death that introduces negation into discourse. For the negativity of discourse, insofar as it brings into being that which is
380 not, refers us to the question of what nonbeing, which manifests itself in the symbolic order, owes to the reality of death.

It is in this way that the axis of poles by which a first field of speech was oriented, whose primordial image is the material of the tessera (in which one finds anew the etymology of the symbol), is crossed here by a second dimension which is not repressed but of necessity a lure. This is the dimension from which, alongside nonbeing, the definition of reality arises.

Thus we already see the cement crumble, the cement with which the so-called new technique ordinarily plugs up its cracks by resorting to the relationship to reality [*réel*], without in any way critiquing the notion.

In order to get you to see that such critique is part and parcel of Freud's thought, I didn't think I could do any better than to confide the demonstration to Jean Hyppolite who not only graces this seminar with his kind interest, but who, by his very presence, also in some sense guarantees you that I don't go astray in my dialectic.

I asked him to comment on a text by Freud that is very short, but that, being situated in 1925—in other words, much further along in the development of Freud's thought, since it comes after the main writings on the new topography[7]—brings us right to the heart of the new question raised by our examination of resistance. I am referring to the text on negation [*dénégation*].

Jean Hyppolite, by taking responsibility for this text, is sparing me an exercise in which my competence is far from attaining the level of his own. Let me thank him for having granted my request and let us give him the floor regarding Freud's "Verneinung."[8]

Notes

1. I am providing here the text of one of the meetings of the seminar held at the Saint Anne Hospital University Clinic which was devoted, during the 1953–1954 academic year, to Freud's writings on technique and their relation to current technique. I have added to it a few references, which seemed useful, back to earlier classes, but I was not able to remove the difficulty of access inherent to a piece extracted from an ongoing teaching.

2. This usage, let it be said in passing, certainly includes nonnegligible oscillations regarding the accentuation of its transitivity, depending on the type of alterity to which it is applied. One says, "to resist the evidence"* like to "resist the authority of the Court,"* but, on the other hand, one says, *nicht der Versuchung widerstehen*. Note the range of nuances that can far more easily be displayed in the diversity of the semanteme in German—*widerstehen*; *widerstreben*; *sich sträuben gegen*, *andauern*, *fortbestehen*—whereby *widerstehen* can intentionally correspond more closely to the meaning I am going to isolate as being the properly analytic meaning of resistance.

3. See pages 290–307 of the chapter "Zur Psychotherapie der Hysterie," written by Freud, in *Studien über hysterie*, *GW* I, published in 1895 with Josef Breuer. In English, see *Studies on Hysteria* [*SE* II].

4. One will recognize in this the formulation by which I introduced what is at stake here at the very beginning of my teaching. The subject, as I said then, begins analysis by speaking of himself without speaking to you, or by speaking to you without speaking of himself. When he can speak to you about himself, the analysis will be finished.

5. *GW* II–III, 522, fn1; *SE* V, 517–18, fn2; *Science des rêves*, 427.

6. Indeed, this example opens the book: *GW* IV, 5–12 [*SE* VI, 2–7], *Psychopathologie de la vie quotidienne*, 1–8.

7. I devoted the next year [of my seminar] to a commentary on the writing entitled *Beyond the Pleasure Principle*.

8. Jean Hyppolite's discourse can be found as an appendix to the present volume, beginning on page 879.

381 Response to Jean Hyppolite's Commentary on Freud's "Verneinung"

I hope that the gratitude we all feel for the favor Prof. Hyppolite did for us by providing such an illuminating exposé will justify in your eyes, no less I hope than in his, my insistence in asking him to prepare it.

We see once again here that, in proposing a text by Freud—that is apparently of but the most local interest—to a mind that has the fewest preconceptions about it, even if that mind is certainly not the least practiced, we find in the text the inexhaustible richness of significations that it is destined to offer up to the discipline of commentary. It is not one of those two dimensional texts, which are infinitely flat, as mathematicians say, which have only a fiduciary value in a constituted discourse, but rather a text which carries speech insofar as speech constitutes a new emergence of truth.

While it is fitting to apply to this sort of text all the resources of our exegesis, we do so not simply, as you see in this example, in order to investigate it in relation to he who is its author—a mode of historical or literary criticism whose value as "resistance" must be immediately obvious to a trained psychoanalyst—but rather in order to make it respond to questions that it raises for us, to treat it like true speech in its transferential value, as we should say, assuming we know our own terms.

This, of course, assumes that we interpret it. And is there, in fact, a better critical method than the method that applies to the comprehension of a message the very principles of comprehension that the message itself conveys? This is the most rational means by which to test its authenticity.

For full speech is defined by the fact that it is identical to what it speaks
about. And this text by Freud provides us with an illuminating example by 382
confirming my thesis regarding the transpsychological nature of the psychoanalytic field, as Jean Hyppolite just told you quite directly.

This is why Freud's texts turn out, in the final analysis, to have true training value for the psychoanalyst, making him practiced—which he must be, as I teach explicitly—in a register without which his experience becomes worthless.

For what is at stake is nothing less than whether the analyst is equal to the level of man at which he grabs hold of him, regardless of what he thinks of it, at which he is called upon to respond to him, whether he likes it or not, and for which he assumes responsibility, despite any reservations he may have about doing so. This means that he is not free to let himself off the hook with a hypocritical reference to his medical qualifications and an indeterminate reference to clinical foundations.

For the psychoanalytic New Deal* has more than one face—indeed, it changes faces depending on its interlocutors, such that it has had so many faces for some time now that it has been getting caught in its own alibis, starting to believe them itself, and even to erroneously see itself in them.

Regarding what we have just heard, today I simply want to indicate to you the avenues that it opens up for our most concrete research.

Prof. Hyppolite, in his analysis, has brought us over the high pass, marked by the difference in level in the subject of the symbolic creation of negation with respect to *Bejahung*. This creation of the symbol, as he stressed, must be conceptualized as a mythical moment rather than as a genetic moment. One cannot even relate it to the constitution of the object, since it concerns the relation between the subject and being and not between the subject and the world.

In this short text, as in the whole of his work, Freud thus proves to be very far ahead of his time and not at all lacking compared with the most recent aspects of philosophical reflection. He does not in any way anticipate the modern development of the philosophy of existence. But this philosophy is no more than the parry [*parade*] that reveals in certain people and covers over in others the more or less well understood repercussions of a meditation on being, which goes so far as to contest the whole tradition of our thought, believing it to stem from a primordial confusion of being among beings [*l'être dans l'étant*].

Now, we cannot fail to be struck by what constantly shines through in 383
Freud's work regarding the proximity of these problems, which leads me to believe that his repeated references to pre-Socratic doctrines do not simply bear witness to a discreet use of notes on his reading (which would, moreover, contradict Freud's almost mystifying reluctance to show how immensely cul-

tivated he was), but rather to a properly metaphysical apprehension of what were pressing problems for him.

What Freud designates here as the affective has nothing to do—need we go back over this?—with the use made of this term by backers of the new psychoanalysis; they use it as a psychological *qualitas occulta* in order to designate that "lived experience" whose subtle gold, they claim, is only rendered through the decanting of a high alchemy; yet their quest for it evokes little more than a sniffing that hardly seems promising when we see them panting before its most inane forms.

In this text by Freud, the affective is conceived of as what preserves its effects right down to the discursive structuration on the basis of a primordial symbolization, this structuration (which is also called "intellectual") having been constituted in such a way as to translate in the form of misrecognition what the first symbolization owes to death.

We are thus brought to a sort of intersection of the symbolic with the real that one might call immediate, insofar as it occurs without an imaginary intermediary, but that is mediated—although in a form that goes back on itself [*se renie*]—by what was excluded at the first moment [*temps*] of symbolization.

These formulations are accessible to you, despite their aridity, thanks to everything they condense related to the use of the categories of the symbolic, the imaginary, and the real, which you are kind enough to grant me.

I want to give you an idea of the fertile fields, the key to which is what I earlier called the high pass defined by these categories.

In order to do so, I will extract two examples as premises from two different fields: the first, from what these formulations can clarify about psychopathological structures and simultaneously allow nosography to understand; the second, from what these categories allow us to understand about psychotherapeutic clinical work and simultaneously shed light on for the theory of technique.

384 The first concerns the function of hallucination. We cannot, of course, overestimate the magnitude of the displacement which occurred in the position of this problem by the so-called phenomenological envisioning of the data of hallucination.

But whatever progress has been made here, the problem of hallucination remains just as centered as before on the attributes of consciousness. This is a stumbling block for a theory of thought that sought the guarantee of its certainty in consciousness. As such—at the origin of the hypothesis of this counterfeiting of consciousness that one understands as one can using the term "epiphenomenon"—it is once again and more than ever as a phenomenon of consciousness that hallucination is subjected to phenomenological reduction, [phenomenologists] believing that it yields its meaning to us when we triturate the component forms of its intentionality.

There is no more striking example of such a method than the pages devoted by Maurice Merleau-Ponty to hallucination in his *Phenomenology of Perception.* But the limits to the autonomy of consciousness that he so admirably apprehended there in the phenomenon itself were too subtle to bar the way to the crude simplification of the hallucinatory noesis into which psychoanalysts regularly fall, incorrectly using Freud's notions in their attempt to explain hallucinatory consciousness on the basis of an eruption of the pleasure principle.[1]

It would be all too easy to object to this that the noeme of an hallucination—the hallucination's "content," as we would say in the vernacular—in fact has only the most contingent of relations with any of the subject's satisfactions. Hence the phenomenological preparation of the problem allows us to glimpse that it no longer has any value here other than that of laying out the terms necessary for a true conversion of the question—namely, whether or not the noesis of the phenomenon bears any necessary relationship to its noeme.

It is here that this article, put back on the analyst's reading list, assumes its proper place by pointing out how much more structuralist Freud's thought is 385
than received ideas would have it. For we distort the meaning of the pleasure principle if we neglect the fact that it is never posited all by itself in Freud's theory.

The casting into structural form found in this article, as Prof. Hyppolite just outlined it for you, brings us immediately beyond the conversion that I consider to be necessary, if we know how to understand it. I am going to try to accustom you to this conversion by analyzing an example in which I hope you will sense the promise of a truly scientific reconstitution of the givens of a problem. Together we shall perhaps be the artisans of this reconstitution, insofar as we can find the handholds that have heretofore eluded [theoreticians concerned with] the crucial alternative of experience.

I need go no further to find such an example than to take up the one that fell into our lap last week, by investigating a significant moment in the analysis of the Wolf Man.[2]

I believe that you still recall the hallucination whose trace the subject finds anew when he remembers [a scene from his childhood]. The hallucination appeared erratically in his fifth year, but it comes to him now with the illusion, whose falsity is soon demonstrated, that he has already told Freud about it. Our examination of this phenomenon will be rendered easier by what we already know about its context. For it is not on the basis of an accumulation of facts that light can shine forth, but on the basis of a fact that is well reported with all its correlations, in other words, with the correlations that one forgets precisely because one does not understand the fact—except when a genius intervenes who formulates the enigma precisely (here again) as if he already knew its solution(s).

This context is furnished to us in the obstacles to analysis that this case presented, Freud seeming to proceed here from one surprise to the next. For he did not, of course, have the omniscience that allows our neopractitioners to situate case planning at the crux [*principe*] of the analysis. Indeed, it is in this very case study that he asserts with the greatest force that the crux should be quite the opposite—namely, that he would rather give up the entire stability
386 of his theory than misrecognize the tiniest particularities of a case that might call his theory into question. This means that even if the sum total of analytic experience allows us to isolate some general forms, an analysis proceeds only from the particular to the particular.

The obstacles of the present case, like Freud's surprises—assuming you remember not only what came to light last week but also my commentary on this case in the first year of this seminar[3]—lie at the heart of contemporary concerns: namely, the "intellectualization" of the analytic process, on the one hand, and the maintenance of repression, despite conscious acknowledgment [*prise de conscience*] of the repressed, on the other.

For Freud, in his inflexible inflection of analytic experience, comments here that, although the subject manifested in his behavior that he had access (not without audacity) to genital reality, the latter went unheeded in his unconscious where the "sexual theory" of the anal phase still reigned.

Freud discerns the reason for this phenomenon in the fact that the feminine position, assumed by the subject in the imaginary capture of the primal trauma (namely, the one whose historicity gives the case write-up its major *raison d'être*), makes it impossible for him to accept genital reality without inevitably being threatened with castration.

But what Freud says about the nature of the phenomenon is far more remarkable. It is not a question, he says, of repression (*Verdrängung*), for repression cannot be distinguished from the return of the repressed in which the subject cries out from every pore of his being what he cannot talk about.

Regarding castration, Freud tells us that this subject "did not want to know anything about it in the sense of repression" ("er von ihr nichts wissen wollte im Sinne der Verdrängung").[4] And to designate this process he uses the term *Verwerfung*, for which, on the whole, I would propose the term "excision" [*retranchement*].[5]

Its effect is a symbolic abolition. For, when Freud says, "Er verwarf sie," "he excises" castration (adding, "und blieb auf dem Standpunkt des Verkehrs

im After," "and held to his theory of anal intercourse"), he continues: "thereby 387
one cannot say that any judgment regarding its existence was properly made, but it was as if it had never existed."[6]

Several pages earlier, right after having determined the historical situation of this process in the subject's biography, Freud concluded by distinguishing it expressly from repression in the following terms: "Eine Verdrängung ist etwas anderes als eine Verwerfung."[7] This is presented to us in the following terms in the French translation: "A repression is something other than a judgment which rejects and chooses." I will let you judge what kind of evil spell we must admit has cursed Freud's texts in French—assuming we refuse to believe that the translators made a pact to render them incomprehensible—not to mention the added impact of the complete extinguishing of the liveliness of his style.

The process in question here known as *Verwerfung*, which I do not believe has ever been commented on in a sustained manner in the analytic literature, is situated very precisely in one of the moments that Prof. Hyppolite has just brought out for us in the dialectic of *Verneinung*: *Verwerfung* is exactly what opposes the primal *Bejahung* and constitutes as such what is expelled. You will see proof of this in a sign whose obviousness will surprise you. For it is here that we find ourselves at the point at which I left you last week, a point beyond which it will be much easier for us to go after what we have just learned from Prof. Hyppolite's talk.

I will thus forge on ahead, and the most fervent devotees of the idea of development, if there still are any here, will be unable to object that the phenomenon occurred at too late a date [to constitute a primal scene], since Prof. Hyppolite has admirably shown you that it is mythically speaking that Freud describes it as primal.

Verwerfung thus cut short any manifestation of the symbolic order—that is, it cut short the *Bejahung* that Freud posits as the primary procedure in which
the judgment of attribution finds its root, and which is no other than the pri- 388
mordial condition for something from the real to come to offer itself up to the revelation of being, or, to employ Heidegger's language, to be let-be. For it is clearly to this distant point that Freud brings us, since it is only afterwards that anything whatsoever can be found there as existent [*comme étant*].

Such is the inaugural affirmation, which can no longer recur [*être renouvelée*] except through the veiled forms of unconscious speech, for it is only by the negation of the negation that human discourse allows us to return to it.

But what thus becomes of that which is not let-be in this *Bejahung*? Freud told us right away that what the subject has thus excised (*verworfen*), as I put it, from the opening toward being will not be refound in his history, assuming we designate by the latter term the locus in which the repressed manages to reappear. For I ask you to note how striking the formulation is since there is not the slightest ambiguity in it: the subject *will not want "to know anything about it in the sense of repression."* For, in order for him to be able to know something about it in this sense, it would have had to come in some way to light in the primordial symbolization. But once again, what becomes of it? You can see what becomes of it: *what did not come to light in the symbolic appears in the real.*

For that is how we must understand "Einbeziehung ins Ich," taking into the subject, and "Ausstossung aus dem Ich," expelling from the subject. The latter constitutes the real insofar as it is the domain of that which subsists outside of symbolization. This is why castration—which is excised by the subject here from the very limits of what is possible, but which is also thereby withdrawn from the possibilities of speech—appears in the real, erratically. In other words, it appears in relations of resistance without transference—to extend the metaphor I used earlier, I would say, like a punctuation without a text.

For the real does not wait [*attend*], especially not for the subject, since it expects [*attend*] nothing from speech. But it is there, identical to his existence, a noise in which one can hear anything and everything, ready to submerge with its roar what the "reality principle" constructs there that goes by the name of the "outside world." For if the judgment of existence truly functions as we
389 have understood it in Freud's myth, it is clearly at the expense of a world from which the cunning [*ruse*] of reason has twice collected its share [*part*].

There is no other value to be given, in fact, to the reiteration of the dividing up [*partage*] of the outside and the inside articulated by Freud's sentence: "Es ist, wie man sieht, wieder eine Frage des Aussen und Innen." "It is, we see, once more a question of the outside and the inside." When exactly does this sentence come? First there was the primal expulsion, that is, the real as outside the subject. Then, within representation (*Vorstellung*), constituted by the (imaginary) reproduction of the original perception, there was the discrimination of reality as that aspect of the object of the original perception which is not simply posited as existing by the subject but can be refound (*wiedergefunden*) in a place where he can grab hold of it. It is in this respect alone that the operation, even if it is set in motion by the pleasure principle, escapes the latter's mastery. But in this reality, which the subject must compose according to the well-tempered scale of his objects, the real—as that which is excised from the primordial symbolization—*is already there*. We might even say that it talks all by itself [*cause tout seul*]. The subject can see something of it emerge in the form of a thing which is far from being an object that satisfies him and which involves his present intentionality only in the most incongruous way—this is the hallucination here insofar as it is radically differentiated from the interpretive phenomenon. As we see here in the testimony Freud transcribes as the subject speaks.

The subject tells him that:

> when he was five, he was playing in the garden next to his maid, and was cutting notches into the bark of one of the walnut trees (whose role in his dream we are aware of). Suddenly, he noticed, with a terror which was impossible to express, that he had sectioned his pinkie (right or left? he doesn't know) and that the finger was hanging on by the skin alone. He didn't feel any pain but a great deal of anxiety. He did not have the heart to say anything to the maid who was only a few steps away from him; he let himself fall onto a bench and remained there, incapable of looking at his finger again. In the end, he calmed down, looked carefully at his finger, and—lo and behold!—it was altogether intact.

Let us leave it to Freud to confirm for us—with his usual scrupulous care, employing all the thematic resonances and biographical correlations that he 390
extracts from the subject by the pathway of association—the whole symbolic richness of the hallucinated scenario. But let us not ourselves be fascinated by it.

The correlations of the phenomenon will teach us more, regarding what we are interested in, than the narrative that submits the phenomenon to the conditions of the transmissibility of discourse. The fact that its content lends itself to this so easily, and that it goes so far as to coincide with themes of myth and poetry, certainly raises a question, a question which can be formulated immediately, but which perhaps must be posed anew in a second moment, if only owing to the fact that we know at the outset that the simple solution is not sufficient here.

For a fact is brought out in the narrative of the episode which is not at all necessary for its comprehension, quite the contrary: the fact that the subject felt it impossible to speak about at the time. Let us note that there is a reversal of the difficulty here in relation to the case of the forgetting of a name that we analyzed earlier. In that case the subject no longer had the signifier at his disposal, whereas here he is arrested by the strangeness of the signified—to so great an extent that he cannot communicate the feeling he has, even if only by crying out, whereas the person who is most suited to hear his call, his beloved Nania, is right nearby.

Instead, he doesn't balk [*moufte*], if you'll allow me the term due to its expressive value. What he says about his attitude suggests that it is not simply that he sinks into immobility but that he sinks into a kind of temporal funnel out of which he eventually rises without having been able to count how many times he has wound around during his descent and his reascent, and without his return to the surface of ordinary time having in any way occured in response to an effort on his part.

Strangely enough, we find the feature of terrified mutism in another case, which is almost a carbon copy of this one, a case that is related to Freud by an occasional correspondent of his.[8]

This feature of a temporal abyss proves to have significant correlations.

391 We shall find them in the current forms in which the recollection occurs. You know that the subject, at the moment of undertaking his narrative, at first believed that he had already recounted it, and that this aspect of the phenomenon seemed worth considering separately to Freud, being the subject of one of his writings that is on our syllabus this year.[9]

The very way in which Freud comes to explain this illusion of memory—namely, by the fact that the subject had recounted several times an episode in which his uncle bought him a pocketknife at his request while his sister received a book—is of concern to us only in terms of what it tells us about the function of screen memories.

Another aspect of the movement of the recollection seems to me to converge on an idea that I will propose. It is the correction that the subject adds secondarily, namely, that the walnut tree involved in the narrative—and which is no less familiar to us than to him when he mentions its presence in the anxiety dream, the latter being in some sense the key piece of material in this case—is probably brought in from elsewhere, in particular, from another memory of an hallucination where it is from the tree itself that he makes blood seep.

Doesn't all of this indicate to us, in the recollection's in some sense extratemporal character, something like the seal of origin of what is remembered?

And don't we find in this character something not identical but that we might call complementary to what occurs in the famous sense of déjà vu which, since it constitutes the cross of psychologists, has not been clarified despite the number of explanations it has received, and regarding which it is no accident and not simply out of a taste for erudition that Freud recalls them in the article I was just speaking about?

One might say that the feeling of déjà vu comes to meet the erratic hallucination, that it is the imagiary echo which arises as a response to a point of reality that belongs to the limit where it has been excised from the symbolic.

392 This means that the sense that something is unreal is exactly the same phenomenon as the sense of reality, if we designate by this term the "click" [*déclic*] that signals the resurfacing, which is hard to obtain, of a forgotten memory.

What allows the second to be felt as such is the fact that it is produced inside the symbolic text that constitutes the register of the recollection, whereas the first corresponds to the immemorial forms that appear on the palimpsest of the imaginary when the text, leaving off, lays bare the medium of reminiscence.

To understand it in Freud's theory we need but listen to the latter all the way to the end, for if a representation is of value there only in terms of what it reproduces from the original perception, this recurrence cannot stop at the original perception, except mythically. This observation already led Plato to the eternal idea; today it presides over the rebirth of the archetype. As for me, I will confine myself to remarking that perception takes on its characteristic of reality only through symbolic articulations that interweave it with a whole world.

But the subject has a no less convincing sense if he encounters the symbol that he originally excised from his *Bejahung*. For this symbol does not enter the imaginary, for all that. It constitutes, as Freud tells us, that which truly does not exist; as such, it ek-sists, for nothing exists except against a supposed background of absence. Nothing exists except insofar as it does not exist.

This is what we see in our example. The content of the hallucination, which is so massively symbolic, owes its appearance in the real to the fact that it does not exist for the subject. Everything indicates, indeed, that the subject remains fixated in his unconscious in an imaginary feminine position that evacuates all meaning from his hallucinatory mutilation.

In the symbolic order, the empty spaces are as signifying as the full ones; in reading Freud today, it certainly seems that the first step of the whole of his dialectical movement is constituted by the gap of an emptiness [*la béance d'un vide*].

This is what seems to explain the insistence with which the schizophrenic reiterates this step. In vain, however, since for him all of the symbolic is real.

He is very different in this respect from the paranoiac whose predominant 393
imaginary structures I laid out in my doctoral thesis, that is, the retroaction in a cyclical time that makes the anamnesis of his troubles so difficult, the anamnesis of his elementary phenomena which are merely presignifying and which only attain that ever partial universe we call a delusion after a discursive organization that is long and painful to establish and constitute.[10]

I will go no further today with these indications, which we will have to take up again in a clinical context, because I would like to provide a second example by which to put my thesis today to the test.

This example concerns another mode of interference between the symbolic and the real, not that the subject suffers in this case, but that he acts on. Indeed, this is the mode of reaction that we designate in analytic technique as "acting out,"* without always clearly delimiting its meaning. As we shall see, our considerations today can help us revamp the notion.

The acting out* that we are going to examine, even though it apparently was of as little consequence for the subject as was the hallucination we have just discussed, may be no less demonstrative. If it will not allow us to go as far, it is because the author from whom I am borrowing it does not demonstrate Freud's investigative power and divinatory penetration and because we quickly run out of the material we would need to learn more from it.

This example is recounted by Ernst Kris, an author who is nevertheless quite important because he is part of the triumvirate that has assumed responsibility for giving the New Deal* of ego psychology its in some sense official status, and even passes for its intellectual leader.

He does not give us a more assured formulation of ego psychology, for all that; and the technical precepts that the example he provides in his article, "Ego Psychology and Interpretation in Psychoanalytic Therapy,"[11] is supposed to illustrate lead (in their vacillations, in which we can see the nostalgia of the old-school psychoanalyst) to wishy-washy notions that I will examine at some
394 later date—ever hoping, as I am, that a half-wit will come along who, in his naïveté, will keenly size up this infatuation with normalizing analysis and land Kris the definitive blow without anyone else having to get involved.

In the meantime, let us consider the case that he presents to us in order to shed light on the elegance with which he, one might say, cleared it up, thanks to the principles whose masterful application his decisive intervention demonstrates—these principles being the appeal to the subject's ego, the approach "from the surface," the reference to reality, and all the rest.

We have here a subject for whom Kris is serving as the second psychoanalyst. The subject is seriously thwarted in his profession, an intellectual profession which seems not so far removed from our own. This is couched by Kris in the following terms: although he holds a respected academic position he cannot rise to a higher rank because he is unable to publish his research [page 22]. The obstacle is a compulsion that he feels impels him to take other people's ideas. He is thus obsessed with the idea of plagiarizing and even with plagiarism. Although he derived a pragmatic improvement from his first analysis, at present he is tormented by the constant effort not to take others' ideas, especially those of a brilliant scholar* he knows. In any case, the subject has a study that he is ready to publish.

One fine day he arrives at his session with an air of triumph. He has found proof: he has just come across a book in the library that contains all the ideas in his own book. One might say that he did not know the book since he had merely glanced at it some time ago. Nevertheless, he is a plagiarist in spite of himself. The (woman) analyst with whom he did his first analysis was certainly right when she told him more or less the following, "he who has stolen once will steal again," since at puberty as well he pilfered books and sweets.

It is here that Ernst Kris intervenes with his science and audacity, expecting us to appreciate their great merits, a wish we are likely to only half-satisfy. He asks to see the book from the library. He reads it. He discovers that nothing in it justifies what the subject thinks is in it. It is the subject alone who has attributed to the author everything the subject himself wanted to say.

At this point, Kris tells us, the question "appeared in a new light. The eminent colleague, it transpired, had repeatedly taken the patient's ideas, and embellished and repeated them without acknowledgment" [page 22]. This was 395
what the subject was afraid of taking from him, having failed to recognize his own property therein.

An era of new comprehension begins. Were I to say that it was Kris' big heart that opened its doors, he probably would not agree. He would tell me, with the seriousness proverbially attributed to the Pope, that he followed the grand principle of approaching problems from the surface. Why not add that he approaches them from the outside and even that there is, unbeknown to him, something quixotic in the way he settles a question as delicate as that of plagiarism?

The reversal of intention that Freud has taught us about again earlier today no doubt leads to something, but it does not lead to objectivity. In truth, if we can be sure that it is in no wise useless to alert the beautiful soul, who is revolting against the disorder of his world, to the part he plays therein, the opposite is not at all true: we should not assure someone that he is not in the least bit guilty just because he accuses himself of bad intentions.

It was, nevertheless, a fine opportunity to perceive that if there is at least one bias a psychoanalyst should have jettisoned thanks to psychoanalysis, it is that of "intellectual property." Perhaps this would have made it easier for Kris to take his bearings from the way in which the patient understood that notion himself.

And, since we are crossing the line of a prohibition, which is actually more imaginary than real, in order to allow the analyst to make a judgment on the basis of documentary evidence, why not perceive that we would be adopting an overly abstract perspective were we not to examine the true content of the ideas at issue here, for that content cannot be indifferent?

Furthermore, the impact of the inhibition on his vocation perhaps must not be altogether neglected, even if such effects obviously seem more significant in the success*-oriented context of American culture.

Now, although I have noticed some modicum of restraint in the exposition of the principles of interpretation implied by a form of psychoanalysis that has definitively reverted to ego psychology, we are certainly not spared anything in Kris' commentary on the case.

396 Finding passing comfort in having come across formulations by the honorable Edward Bibring, and considering himself very fortunate to have done so, Kris exposes his method to us as follows:

> [T]here was . . . an initial exploratory (*sic*) period, during which . . . typical patterns of behavior, present and past, [were studied]. Noted first were his critical and admiring attitudes of other people's ideas; then the relation of these to the patient's own ideas and intuitions (page 24).

Please excuse me for following the text step by step. I am doing this so that we will not be left with any doubt as to what the author thinks.

> At this point the comparison between the patient's own productivity and that of others had to be traced in great detail . . . Finally, the distortion of imputing to others his own ideas could be analyzed and the mechanism of "give and take" made conscious.

One of my early and sorely missed teachers, whose every twist and turn in thought I did not follow for all that, long ago designated as "summaryism" ["*bilanisme*"] what Kris describes to us here. We should not, of course, disdain the making conscious of an obsessive symptom, but it is something else altogether to fabricate such a symptom from scratch.

Abstractly posited, this analysis, which is descriptive we are told, still does not strike me as very different from the approach adopted by the patient's first analyst, based on what we are told of it. No mystery is made of the fact that the analyst was Melitta Schmideberg, for Kris cites a passage from a commentary she apparently published of this case:

> A patient who during puberty had occasionally stolen . . . retained later a certain inclination to plagiarism. Since to him activity was connected with stealing, scientific endeavor with plagiarism, etc. [page 23].

I have been unable to check whether this sentence exhausts the part played in the analysis by the author mentioned, some of the psychoanalytic literature having unfortunately become very difficult to find.[12]

But we understand much better the emphasis of the author whose text we do have, when he trumpets his conclusion: "It is now possible to compare the two types of analytic approach" [page 23].

For insofar as he has concretely indicated what his approach consists of, 397
we clearly see that the analysis of the subject's behavior patterns* amounts to inscribing his behavior in the analyst's patterns.

Not that nothing else is stirred up in this analysis. Kris sketches for us a situation involving three people, including the subject's father and grandfather, which is quite attractive in appearance, all the more so in that the father seems to have failed, as sometimes happens, to rise to the level of the grandfather, a distinguished scientist in his homeland. Kris provides a few astute remarks here about the grandfather and the father who was not grand, whereas I might have preferred a few indications about the role of death in this whole game. I don't doubt but that the big [*grand*] and little fish caught on the fishing trips with his father symbolized the classic "comparison," which in our mental world has taken the place held in earlier centuries by other more gallant comparisons. But all that does not seem to me to be approached from the right "end," so to speak.

I will provide no other proof of this than the *corpus delicti* promised in my example, in other words, precisely what Kris produces as the trophy of his victory. He believes that he has arrived at his goal; he shares this with his patient:

> Only the ideas of others were truly interesting, only ideas one could take; hence the taking had to be engineered. At this point of the interpretation I was waiting for the patient's reaction. The patient was silent and the very length of the silence had a special significance. Then, as if reporting a sudden insight, he said: "Every noon, when I leave here, before luncheon, and before returning to my office, I walk through X Street (a street well known for its small but attractive restaurants) and I look at the menus in the windows. In one of the restaurants I usually find my preferred dish—fresh brains."

These are the closing words of Kris' clinical vignette. I can only hope that
my abiding interest in cases in which a mountain is made out of a molehill 398
will convince you to pay attention for another moment as I examine this case more closely.

We have here in every respect an example of an acting out*, which is no doubt small in size, but very well constituted.

The very pleasure this acting out seems to give its midwife surprises me. Does Kris actually believe that the height of his art has managed to give rise to a valid way out for this id*?[13]

I have no doubt but that the subject's confession has its full transferential value, although the author decided, deliberately as he stresses, to spare us any details regarding the link—I am stressing this myself—between "the defenses" (whose breakdown he has just described for us) and "the patient's resistance in analysis" [page 24].

But what can we make of the act itself if not a true emergence of a primordially "excised" oral relation, which no doubt explains the relative failure of his first analysis?

But the fact that it appears in the form of an act which is not at all understood by the subject does not seem to me to be of any benefit to the subject, even if it demonstrates to us what an analysis of the resistances leads to when it consists in attacking the subject's world (that is, his patterns*) in order to reshape it on the model of the analyst's world, in the name of the analysis of defense. I don't doubt but that the patient feels quite good, on the whole, going on a diet of fresh brains in his analysis too. He will thus follow one more pattern*, the one that a large number of theoreticians ascribe quite literally to the process of analysis—namely, the introjection of the analyst's ego. We can only hope that, here too, they are referring to the healthy part of his ego. Kris' ideas about intellectual productivity thus seem to me to receive the Good Housekeeping Seal of Approval for America.

It might seem incidental to ask how he is going to deal with the fresh brains, the real brains, the brains that one fries in black butter, it being recommended to first peel the *pia mater*, which requires a great deal of care. It is not a futile question, however, for suppose that he had discovered in himself a taste for
399 young boys instead, demanding no less refined preparations; wouldn't there ultimately be the same misunderstanding? And wouldn't this acting out*, as we would call it, be just as foreign to the subject?

This means that by approaching the ego's resistance in the subject's defenses, and by asking his world to answer the questions that he himself should answer, one may elicit highly incongruous answers whose reality value, in terms of the subject's drives, is not the reality value that manages to get itself recognized in symptoms. This is what allows us to better understand the examination made by Prof. Hyppolite of the theses Freud contributes in "Die Verneinung."

Notes

1. As an example of this simplistic perspective, one can cite the paper given by Raymond de Saussure at the 1950 Congress of Psychiatry and the all-purpose use he makes there of the frankly new notion, "hallucinated emotion"!

2. *GW* XII, 103–21 ["From the History of

an Infantile Neurosis," chapter 7, "Anal Erotism and the Castration Complex," *SE* XVII, 72–88].

3. Namely, in 1951–1952.

4. *GW* XII, 117 [*SE* XVII, 84].

5. [Added in 1966:] As you know, having since weighed this term more carefully, I have gotten the term "foreclosure" accepted as the translation for it.

6. *GW* XII, 117 [*SE* XVII, 84, reads "He rejected castration, and held to his theory of intercourse by the anus. [. . .] This really involved no judgement upon the question of its existence, but it was the same as if it did not exist"].

7. *GW* XII, 111 [*SE* XVII, 79–80, reads, "A repression is something very different from a condemning judgement"].

8. See "Über fausse reconnaissance ('déjà raconté') während der psychoanalytischen Arbeit" in *GW* X, 116–23, especially the passage quoted on page 122 [*SE* XIII, 201–7, especially 206].

9. That is the article just cited.

10. *De la psychose paranoïaque dans ses rapports avec la personnalité* (Paris: Le François, 1932).

11. The article was published in *PQ* XX, 1 (1951): 15–29 [and reprinted in *Selected Papers of Ernst Kris* (New Haven: Yale University Press, 1975), 237–51].

12. See, if you can find it, Melitta Schmideberg, "Intellektuelle Hemmung und Essstörung," *Zeitschrift für Psychoanalytische Pädagogik* VIII (1934). [In English, see "Intellectual Inhibition and Disturbances in Eating," *IJP* XIX (1938): 17–22.]

13. "Id" being the standard English translation of Freud's *Es*.

401

The Freudian Thing

or the Meaning of the Return to Freud in Psychoanalysis

An expanded version of a lecture given at the Vienna Neuropsychiatric Clinic on November 7, 1955[1]

To Sylvia

Situation in Time and Place of this Exercise

At a time when Vienna, in making itself heard again through the voice of its Opera, is reassuming, in a moving variation, its age-old mission at a crossroads of cultures from which she was able to create harmony, I have come here—not unfittingly, I think—to evoke the fact that this chosen city will remain, this time forever more, associated with a revolution in knowledge of Copernican proportions. I am referring to the fact that Vienna is the eternal site of Freud's discovery and that, owing to this discovery, the veritable center of human beings is no longer at the place ascribed to it by an entire humanist tradition.

Perhaps even prophets whose own countries were not entirely deaf to them must be eclipsed at some point in time, if only after their death. It is appropriate for a foreigner to exercise restraint in evaluating the forces at work in such a phase-effect.

The return to Freud, for which I am assuming here the role of herald, is thus situated elsewhere: where it is amply called for by the symbolic scandal which Dr. Alfred Winterstein, who is here with us today, rightly highlighted when it occurred during his tenure as president of the Vienna Psychoanalytic Society—namely, upon the inauguration of the commemorative plaque marking the house in which Freud pursued his heroic work—the scandal being not that this monument was not dedicated to Freud by his fellow citizens, but that it was not commissioned by the international association of those who live off his patronage.

This failure is symptomatic, for it indicates that he was disowned, not by 402
the land in which, by virtue of his tradition, he was merely a temporary guest, but by the very field he left in our care and by those to whom custody of that field was entrusted—that is, the psychoanalytic movement itself, where things have come to such a pass that to call for a return to Freud is seen as a reversal.

Since the time when the first sound of the Freudian message rang out from the Viennese bell to echo far and wide, many contingent factors have played a part in this story. Its reverberations seemed to be drowned out by the muffled collapses brought about by the first world conflict. Its propagation resumed with the immense human wrenching that fomented the second and was its most powerful vehicle. It was on the waves of hate's tocsin and discord's tumult—the panic-stricken breath of war—that Freud's voice reached us, as we witnessed the Diaspora of those who transmitted it, whose persecution was no coincidence. The shock waves were to reverberate to the very confines of our world, echoing on a continent where it would be untrue to say that history loses its meaning, since it is where history finds its limit. It would even be a mistake to think that history is absent there, since, already several centuries in duration, it weighs all the more heavily there due to the gulf traced out by its all-too-limited horizon. Rather it is where history is denied with a categorical will that gives enterprises their style, that of a cultural ahistoricism characteristic of the United States of North America.

This ahistoricism defines the assimilation required for one to be recognized there, in the society constituted by this culture. It was to its summons that a group of emigrants had to respond; in order to gain recognition, they could only stress their difference, but their function presupposed history at its very core, their discipline being the one that had reconstructed the bridge between modern man and ancient myths. The combination of circumstances was too strong and the opportunity too attractive for them not to give in to the temptation to abandon the core in order to base function on difference. Let us be clear about the nature of this temptation. It was neither that of ease nor that of profit. It is certainly easier to efface the principles of a doctrine than the stigmata of one's origins, and more profitable to subordinate one's function 403
to demand. But to reduce one's function to one's difference in this case is to give in to a mirage that is internal to the function itself, a mirage that grounds the function in this difference. It is to return to the reactionary principle that covers over the duality of he who suffers and he who heals with the opposition between he who knows and he who does not. How could they avoid regard-

ing this opposition as true when it is real and, on that basis, avoid slipping into becoming managers of souls in a social context that demands such offices? The most corrupting of comforts is intellectual comfort, just as the worst corruption is corruption of the best.

Thus Freud's comment to Jung (I have it from Jung's own mouth)—when, having been invited by Clark University, they arrived in view of New York Harbor and of the famous statue illuminating the universe, "They don't realize we're bringing them the plague"—was turned against him as punishment for the hubris whose antiphrasis and darkness do not extinguish its turbid brilliance. To catch its author in her trap, Nemesis had merely to take him at his word. We would be justified in fearing that Nemesis added a first-class ticket home.

Indeed, if something of the sort has happened, we have only ourselves to blame. For Europe seems rather to have faded from the concerns and style—if not the minds—of those who left, along with the repression of their bad memories.

I will not pity you for having been forgotten since it leaves me freer to present to you the project of a return to Freud, as some of us teaching at the Société Française de Psychanalyse conceive of it. We are not seeking to emphasize a return of the repressed here, but want to use the antithesis constituted by the phase that has passed in the psychoanalytic movement since Freud's death to show what psychoanalysis is not, and find with you a way to put back into force what has continued to sustain it, even in its very deviation—namely, the original meaning Freud preserved in it by his mere presence, which I should like to explain here.

How could this meaning escape us when it is attested to in a body of written work of the most lucid and organic kind? And how could it leave us hes-
404 itant when the study of this work shows us that its different stages and changes in direction are governed by Freud's inflexibly effective concern to maintain its original rigor?

His texts prove to be comparable to those that, in other times, human veneration has invested with the highest qualities, in that they withstand the test of the discipline of commentary, whose virtue one rediscovers in making use of it in the traditional way—not simply to situate what someone says in the context of his time, but to gauge whether the answer he gives to the questions he raises has or has not been superseded by the answer one finds in his work to current questions.

Will I be telling you anything new if I say that these texts—to which for the past four years I have devoted a two-hour seminar every Wednesday from November to July, without having taken up more than a quarter of them,

although my commentary is based on the whole set of them—have surprised me and those who attend my seminars as only genuine discoveries can? These discoveries range from concepts that have remained unexploited to clinical details left to be unearthed by our exploration; they demonstrate how far the field investigated by Freud went beyond the avenues he left us by which to gain access to it, and how little his case studies, which sometimes give an impression of exhaustiveness, were subordinated to what he intended to demonstrate. Who, among the experts in disciplines other than psychoanalysis whom I have guided in reading these texts, has not been moved by this research in action—whether it is the research he has us follow in the *Traumdeutung* [*The Interpretation of Dreams*], the case study of the Wolf Man, or *Beyond the Pleasure Principle*? What an exercise for the training of minds, and what a message to lend one's voice to! And what better confirmation could there be of the methodical value of this training and the truth effect this message produces than the fact that the students to whom you transmit them bring you evidence of a transformation, occurring sometimes overnight, in their practice, which becomes simpler or more effective even before it becomes more transparent to them. I cannot provide you with a detailed account of this work in my talk here, for which I am indebted to the kindness of Professor Hoff for the opportunity to give it in this place of noble memory, to the convergence between my views and those of Dr. Arnold for the suggestion to give this talk here, and to my excellent and long-standing relations with Mr. Igor Caruso for knowing how 405
it would be received in Vienna.

But I cannot forget that I owe part of my audience today to the indulgence of Mr. Susini, the director of the French Institute in Vienna. And this is why I must ask myself, coming now as I am to the meaning of the return to Freud that I am professing here, whether I am not running the risk of disappointing this part of my audience because it is less prepared than the specialists may be to understand me.

The Adversary

I am sure of my answer here—"Absolutely not"—assuming that what I am going to say is as it should be. The meaning of a return to Freud is a return to Freud's meaning. And the meaning of what Freud said may be conveyed to anyone because, while addressed to everyone, it concerns each person. One word suffices to make this point: Freud's discovery calls truth into question, and there is no one who is not personally concerned by truth.

It must seem rather odd that I should be flinging this word in your faces—a word of almost ill repute, a word banished from polite society. But isn't it inscribed in the very heart of analytic practice, since this practice is constantly rediscovering the power of truth in ourselves and in our very flesh?

Why, indeed, would the unconscious be more worthy of being recognized than the defenses that oppose it in the subject, so successfully that the defenses seem no less real than it? I am not reviving here the shoddy Nietzschean notion of the lie of life, nor am I marveling at the fact that one believes one believes, nor do I accept that to will something one need but want it badly enough. But I am asking where the peace that ensues in recognizing an unconscious tendency comes from if the latter is not truer than what restrained it in the conflict. For some time now this peace has, moreover, been quickly proving illusory, for psychoanalysts, not content to recognize as unconscious the
406 defenses to be attributed to the ego, have increasingly identified the defense mechanisms—displacement of the object, turning back against the subject, regression of form—with the very dynamic that Freud analyzed in the tendency, which thus seems to persist in the defenses with no more than a change of sign. Haven't people gone too far when they submit that the drive itself may be made conscious by the defense so that the subject won't recognize himself in it?

In order to try to explain these mysteries in a coherent discourse, I am, in spite of myself, using words that reestablish in that discourse the very duality that sustains them. But what I deplore is not that one cannot see the forest of the theory for the trees of the technique employed, but rather that it would take so little to believe that one is in the Bondy Forest, precisely because of the following notion, which is hiding behind each tree—namely, that there must be some trees that are truer than others, or, if you prefer, that not all trees are bandits. Without which, one might wind up asking where the bandits are who are not trees. Does this little, then, which can become everything on occasion, perhaps deserve an explanation? What is this truth without which there is no way of distinguishing the face from the mask, and apart from which there seems to be no other monster than the labyrinth itself? In other words, how are they to be distinguished, in truth, if they are all equally real?

Here the big clodhoppers come forward to slip onto the dove's feet—on which, as we know, truth is borne—and to swallow up the bird occasionally as well: "Our criterion," they cry, "is simply economic, you ideologist. Not all organizations of reality are equally economical." But at the point at which truth has already been brought to bear, the bird escapes unscathed when I ask, "Economical for whom?"

Things have gone too far this time. The adversary snickers: "We get the picture. Monsieur has a philosophical bent. Plato and Hegel will be showing up any minute now. Their stamp suffices. Whatever they endorse should be discarded and, anyway, if, as you said, this concerns everyone, it's of no interest to specialists like us. It can't even be classified in our documentation."

You think I'm joking here. But not at all: I subscribe to it.

If Freud contributed nothing more to the knowledge of man than the verity that there is something veritable, there is no Freudian discovery. Freud sim- 407
ply belongs then to the line of moralists in whom a tradition of humanistic analysis is embodied, a milky way in the heavenly vault of European culture in which Balthazar Gracian and La Rochefoucauld are among the brightest stars, and Nietzsche is a nova as dazzling as it is short-lived. The latest to join them—and spurred on, like them, no doubt by a characteristically Christian concern for the authenticity of the stirrings of the soul—Freud was able to precipitate a whole casuistry into a map of Tendre, in which one couldn't care less about an orientation for the offices for which it was intended. Its objectivity is, in fact, strictly tied to the analytic situation, which, within the four walls that limit its field, can do very well without people knowing which way is north since they confuse north with the long axis of the couch, assumed to point in the direction of the analyst. Psychoanalysis is the science of the mirages that arise within this field. A unique experience, a rather abject one at that, but one that cannot be too highly recommended to those who wish to get to the crux of mankind's forms of madness, for, while revealing itself to be akin to a whole range of alienations, it sheds light on them.

This language is moderate enough—I am not the one who invented it. I have even heard a zealot of supposedly classical psychoanalysis define the latter as an experience whose privilege is strictly tied to the forms that regulate its practice, forms that cannot be altered one iota because, having been obtained by means of a miracle of chance, they provide access to a reality that transcends the phenomena of history, a reality in which a taste for order and a love of beauty, for example, find their permanent ground—namely, the objects of the preoedipal relation, shit and all that other crap.

This position cannot be refuted since its rules are justified by their outcomes, and the latter are taken as proof that the rules are well founded. Yet our questions proliferate anew: How did this prodigious miracle of chance occur? Whence stems this contradiction between the preoedipal mess, to which the analytic relationship can be reduced, according to our modern analysts, and the fact that Freud wasn't satisfied until he had reduced it to the Oedipal position? How can the sort of hothouse auscultation on which this "new-look"* of analytic experience borders be the final stage in a development that appeared at the outset to open up multiple paths among all the fields of creation? Or the same question put the other way round: If the objects discerned 408
in this elective fermentation were thus discovered through some other path-

way than that of experimental psychology, is experimental psychology qualified to rediscover them through its own procedures?

The replies we will receive from the interested parties leave no room for doubt. The motor force of analytic experience, even when explained in their terms, cannot simply be this mirage-like truth that can be reduced to the mirage of truth. It all began with a particular truth, an unveiling, the effect of which is that reality is no longer the same for us as it was before. This is what continues to attach the crazy cacophony of theory to the very heart of worldly things, and to prevent practice from degenerating to the level of the wretched who never manage to leave them behind (it should be understood that I am using the term to exclude cynics).

A truth, if it must be said, is not easy to recognize once it has become received. Not that there aren't any established truths, but they are so easily confused with the reality that surrounds them that no other artifice was for a long time found to distinguish them from it than to mark them with the sign of the spirit and, in order to pay them homage, to regard them as having come from another world. It is not the whole story to attribute to a sort of blindness on man's part the fact that truth is never to him a finer looking girl than when the light, held aloft by his arm as in the proverbial emblem, unexpectedly illuminates her nakedness. And one must play the fool [*la bête*] a bit to feign knowing nothing of what happens next. But stupidity remains characterized by bullheaded frankness when one wonders where one could have been looking for her before, the emblem scarcely helping to indicate the well, an unseemly and even malodorous place, rather than the jewelry box in which every precious form must be preserved intact.

The Thing Speaks of Itself

But now the truth in Freud's mouth takes the said bull [*bête*] by the horns: "To you I am thus the enigma of she who slips away as soon as she appears, you men who try so hard to hide me under the tawdry finery of your proprieties.
409 Still, I admit your embarrassment is sincere, for even when you take it upon yourselves to become my heralds, you acquire no greater worth by wearing my colors than your own clothes, which are like you, phantoms that you are. Where am I going, having passed into you? And where was I prior to that? Will I perhaps tell you someday? But so that you will find me where I am, I will teach you by what sign you can recognize me. Men, listen, I am telling you the secret. I, truth, speak.

"Must I point out that you did not yet know this? Of course, some of you who proclaimed yourselves my lovers, no doubt because of the principle that one is never better served than by oneself in this kind of boasting, had posited—in an ambiguous manner, and not without revealing the clumsiness brought on by the vanity that they were really concerned about—that the errors of philosophy, that is, their own, could subsist only on my subsidies. Yet having embraced these daughters of their thought, they eventually found them as insipid as they were futile, and began associating anew with opinions considered to be vulgar according to the moral standards of the sages of old; the latter knew how to put such opinions—whether narrative, litigious, guileful, or simply mendacious—in their place, but also to seek them out in the home and in the forum, at the forge and at the fair. They then realized that, by not being my parasites, these opinions seemed to be serving me far better, and—who knows?—even to be acting as my militia, the secret agents of my power. Several cases observed in certain games of sudden transformations of error into truth, which seemed to be due only to perseverance, set them on the path of this discovery. The discourse of error—its articulation in action—could bear witness to the truth against the apparent facts themselves. It was then that one of them tried to get the cunning of reason accepted into the rank of objects deemed worthy of study. Unfortunately, he was a professor, and you were only too happy to listen to his teachings with the dunce caps you were made to wear at school and which have since served as ear-trumpets for those of you who are a bit deaf. Remain content, then, with your vague sense of history and leave it to clever people to found the world market in lies, the trade in all-out war, and the new law of self-criticism on the guarantee of my future firm. If reason is as cunning as Hegel said it was, it will do its job without your help.

"But for all that, you haven't rendered what you owe me obsolete or end- 410
lessly postponable. It falls due after yesterday and before tomorrow. And it hardly matters whether you rush ahead to honor or evade it, since it will grab you from behind in both cases. Whether you flee me in deceit or think you can catch me in error, I will catch up with you in the mistake from which you cannot hide. Where the most cunning speech reveals a slight stumbling, it doesn't live up to its perfidy—I am now publicly announcing the fact—and it will be a bit harder after this to act as if nothing is happening, whether in good company or bad. But there is no need to wear yourselves out keeping a closer watch on yourselves. Even if the combined jurisdictions of politeness and politics declared that whatever claims to be associated with me is inadmissible when it presents itself in such an illicit manner, you would not get off so lightly, for the most innocent intention is disconcerted once it can no longer conceal the fact that one's bungled actions are the most successful and that one's failures fulfill one's most secret wishes. In any case, doesn't my escape—first from the dungeon of the fortress in which you think you are most sure to hold me

by situating me not in yourselves, but in being itself—suffice to prove your defeat? I wander about in what you regard as least true by its very nature: in dreams, in the way the most far-fetched witticisms and the most grotesque nonsense* of jokes defy meaning, and in chance—not in its law, but rather in its contingency. And I never more surely proceed to change the face of the world than when I give it the profile of Cleopatra's nose.

"You can therefore reduce the traffic on the roads that you strove so hard to prove radiate from consciousness, and which were the ego's pride and joy, crowned by Fichte with the insignias of its transcendence. The long-term trade in truth no longer involves thought; strangely enough, it now seems to involve things: *rebus*, it is through you that I communicate, as Freud formulates it at the end of the first paragraph of the sixth chapter, devoted to the dreamwork, of his work on dreams and what dreams mean.

"But you must be careful here: the hard time Freud had becoming a pro-
411 fessor will perhaps spare him your neglect, if not your deviation," the prosopopeia continues. "Listen carefully to what he says, and—as he said it of me, the truth that speaks—the best way to grasp it is to take it quite literally. Here, no doubt, things are my signs, but, I repeat, signs of my speech. If Cleopatra's nose changed the world's course, it was because it entered the world's discourse; for in order to change it for the longer or the shorter, it was sufficient, but it was also necessary, that it be a speaking nose.

"But it is your own nose that you must now use, albeit for more natural ends. Let a sense of smell surer than all your categories guide you in the race to which I challenge you. For if the cunning of reason, however disdainful it may have been of you, remained open to your faith, I, truth, will against you be the great Trickster, since I slip in not only via falsehood, but through a crack too narrow to be found at feigning's weakest point and through the dream's inaccessible cloud, through the groundless fascination with mediocrity and the seductive impasse of absurdity. Seek, dogs that you become upon hearing me, bloodhounds that Sophocles preferred to put on the scent of the hermetic traces of Apollo's thief than on Oedipus' bleeding heels, certain as he was of finding the moment of truth with him at the sinister meeting at Colonus. Enter the lists at my call and howl at the sound of my voice. Now that you are already lost, I belie myself, I defy you, I slip away: you say that I am being defensive."

Parade

The return to darkness, which I think must be expected at this moment, is the signal for a "murder party"* that begins with an order forbidding everyone to

leave, since anyone may now be hiding the truth under her dress, or even in her womb, as in the amorous fiction, *The Indiscreet Jewels*. The general question is: Who is speaking? And the question is not an irrelevant one. Unfortunately, the answers given are a bit hasty. First the libido is accused, which leads us in the direction of the jewels; but we must realize that the ego itself—although it fetters the libido, which pines for satisfaction—is sometimes the object of the libido's undertakings. One senses that the ego is about to collapse any minute, when the sound of broken glass informs everyone that it is the large drawing-
room mirror that has sustained the accident, the golem of narcissism, hastily 412
invoked to assist the ego, having thereby made its entrance. The ego is then generally regarded as the assassin, if not the victim, the upshot being that the divine rays of the good President Schreber begin to spread their net over the world, and the Sabbath of the instincts becomes truly complicated.

The comedy, which I shall interrupt here at the beginning of its second act, is less mean-spirited than is usually believed, since—attributing to a drama of knowledge a buffoonery that belongs only to those who act in this drama without understanding it—it restores to such people the authenticity from which they had fallen away ever further.

But if a more serious metaphor befits the protagonist, it is one that would show us in Freud an Actaeon perpetually set upon by dogs that are thrown off the scent right from the outset, dogs that he strives to get back on his tail, without being able to slow the race in which only his passion for the goddess leads him on. It leads him on so far that he cannot stop until he reaches the cave in which the chthonian Diana, in the damp shade that confounds the cave with the emblematic abode of truth, offers to his thirst, along with the smooth surface of death, the quasi-mystical limit of the most rational discourse the world has ever heard, so that we might recognize there the locus in which the symbol substitutes for death in order to take possession of the first budding of life.

As we know, this limit and this locus are still far from being reached by his disciples, when they don't simply refuse to follow him there altogether, and so the Actaeon who is dismembered here is not Freud, but every analyst in proportion to the passion that inflamed him and made him—according to the signification Giordano Bruno drew from this myth in his *Heroic Frenzies*—the prey of the dogs of his own thoughts.

To gauge the extent of this rending we must hear the irrepressible protests that arise from both the best and the worst, when one tries to bring them back to the beginning of the hunt, with the words that truth gave us as a viaticum—"I speak"—adding, "There is no speech without language." Their tumult drowns out what follows.

"Logomachia!" goes the strophe on one side. "What do you make of the

413 preverbal, gestures and facial expressions, tone, melody, mood, and af-fec-tive con-tact?" To which others, no less vehement, give the antistrophe: "Everything is language: language when my heart beats faster as fear strikes and, if my patient faints at the roar of an airplane at its zenith, it is a way of *telling* me the memory she still has of the last bombing." Yes, eagle of thought, and when the plane's shape cuts out your semblance in the night-piercing beam of the searchlight, it is heaven's response.

Yet, in trying out these premises, people did not challenge the use of any of the forms of communication people might resort to in their exploits, neither signals nor images, content nor form, whether man or woman, even if this content were one of sympathy, the virtue of any proper form not being debated.

They began merely to repeat after Freud the key to his discovery: it [*ça*] speaks, precisely where it was least expected—namely, where it suffers. If there ever was a time when, to respond to it, it sufficed to listen to what it was saying (for the answer is already there in hearing it), let us assume that the great ones of the early days, the armchair giants, were struck by the curse that befalls titanic acts of daring, or that their chairs ceased to be conductors of the good word which they were vested to sit before. Be that as it may, since then, there have been more meetings between the psychoanalyst and psychoanalysis in the hope that the Athenian would reach his apex with Athena having emerged fully armed from Freud's head. Shall I tell you of the jealous fate, ever the same, that thwarted these meetings? Behind the mask where each of us was to meet his betrothed—alas! thrice alas! and a cry of horror at the thought of it, another woman having taken her place—he who was there was not him either.

Let us thus calmly return and spell out with the truth what it said of itself. The truth said, "I speak." In order for us to recognize this "I" on the basis of the fact that it speaks, perhaps we should not have jumped on the "I," but should have paused at the facets of the speaking. "There is no speech without language" reminds us that language is an order constituted by laws, about which we could at least learn what they exclude. For example, that language is different from natural expression and that it is not a code either; that language is not the same as information—take a close look at cybernetics and you'll see
414 the difference; and that language is so far from being reducible to a superstructure that materialism itself was alarmed by this heresy—see Stalin's pronouncement on the question.

Should you like to know more about it, read Saussure, and since a bell tower can hide even the sun, let me make it clear that I am not referring to the Saussure of psychoanalytic repute, but to Ferdinand, who may be said to be the founder of modern linguistics.

The Thing's Order

A psychoanalyst should find it easy to grasp the fundamental distinction between signifier and signified, and to begin to familiarize himself with the two networks of nonoverlapping relations they organize.

The first network, that of the signifier, is the synchronic structure of the material of language insofar as each element takes on its precise usage therein by being different from the others; this is the principle of distribution that alone regulates the function of the elements of language [*langue*] at its different levels, from the phonemic pair of oppositions to compound expressions, the task of the most modern research being to isolate the stable forms of the latter.

The second network, that of the signified, is the diachronic set of concretely pronounced discourses, which historically affects the first network, just as the structure of the first governs the pathways of the second. What dominates here is the unity of signification, which turns out to never come down to a pure indication of reality [*réel*], but always refers to another signification. In other words, signification comes about only on the basis of taking things as a whole [*d'ensemble*].

Its mainspring cannot be grasped at the level at which signification usually secures its characteristic redundancy, for it always proves to exceed the things it leaves indeterminate within it.

The signifier alone guarantees the theoretical coherence of the whole as a whole. Its ability to do so is confirmed by the latest development in science, just as, upon reflection, we find it to be implicit in early linguistic experience.

These are the foundations that distinguish language from signs. Dialectic 415
derives new strength from them.

For the remark on which Hegel bases his critique of the beautiful soul—according to which it is said to live (in every sense, even the economic sense of having something to live off of) precisely off the disorder it denounces—escapes being tautological only by maintaining the "tauto-ontic" of the beautiful soul as mediation, unrecognized by itself, of this disorder as primary in being.

However dialectical it may be, this remark cannot shake up the delusion of presumption to which Hegel applied it, remaining caught in the trap offered by the mirage of consciousness to the *I* infatuated with its own feeling, which Hegel turns into the law of the heart.

Of course this "I" in Hegel is defined as a legal being, making it more concrete than the real being from which people formerly thought it could be abstracted—as is clear from the fact that it implies both a civil status and an account status.

But it was left to Freud to make this legal being responsible for the disorder manifest in the most tightly closed field of the real being—namely, in the organism's pseudo-totality.

I explain this possibility by the congenital gap presented by man's real being in his natural relations, and by the reprising, in a sometimes ideographic, but also a phonetic and even grammatical usage, of the imaginary elements that appear to be fragmented in this gap.

But we have no need for this genesis to demonstrate the symptom's signifying structure. Once deciphered, it is plain to see and shows the omnipresence for human beings of the symbolic function stamped on the flesh.

What distinguishes a society grounded in language from an animal society, which even the ethnological standpoint allows us to see—namely, the fact that the exchange that characterizes such a society has other foundations than needs (even if it satisfies them), specifically, what has been called the gift "as total social fact"—can then be taken much further, so far as to constitute an objection to defining this society as a collection of individuals, since the immixing of subjects makes it a group with a very different structure.

This reintroduces the impact of truth as cause from a totally different angle,
416 and requires a reappraisal of the process of causality—the first stage of which would seem to be to recognize the degree to which the heterogeneity of this impact is inherent.[2] It is strange that materialist thought seems to forget that it derived its impetus from this recourse to the heterogeneous. More interest might then be shown in a feature that is much more striking than the resistance to Freud mounted by the pedants—namely, the connivance this resistance encountered in collective consciousness.

If all causality evinces the subject's involvement, it will come as no surprise that every order conflict is attributed to him.

The terms in which I am posing the problem of psychoanalytic intervention make it sufficiently clear, I think, that its ethics are not individualistic.

But its practice in the American sphere has so summarily degenerated into a means of obtaining "success"* and into a mode of demanding "happiness"* that it must be pointed out that this constitutes a repudiation of psychoanalysis, a repudiation that occurs among too many of its adherents due to the pure and simple fact that they have never wanted to know anything about Freud's discovery, and that they will never know anything about it, even in the way implied by repression: for what is at work here is the mechanism of systematic misrecognition insofar as it simulates delusion, even in its group forms.

But had analytic experience been more rigorously linked to the general structure of semantics, in which it has its roots, it would have allowed us to convince [*convaincre*] them before having to vanquish [*vaincre*] them.

For the subject of whom I was just speaking as the legatee of recognized truth is definitely not the ego perceptible in the more or less immediate data of conscious jouissance or the alienation of labor. This de facto distinction is the same distinction found from the beginning to the end of Freud's work: from the Freudian unconscious, insofar as it is separated by a profound gulf from the preconscious functions, to Freud's last will and testament in lecture thirty-one of his *Neue Vorlesungen* [*New Introductory Lectures*], "Wo Es war, soll Ich werden."

A formulation in which signifying structuration clearly prevails.

Let us analyze it. Contrary to the form that the English translation— 417
"Where the id was, there the ego shall be"*—cannot avoid, Freud said neither *das Es*, nor *das Ich*, as was his wont when designating the agencies he had used to organize his new topography for the previous ten years; and, considering the inflexible rigor of his style, this gives a particular emphasis to their use in this sentence. In any case—even without having to confirm, through a detailed examination of Freud's opus, that he in fact wrote *Das Ich und das Es* [*The Ego and the Id*] in order to maintain the fundamental distinction between the true subject of the unconscious and the ego as constituted in its nucleus by a series of alienating identifications—it seems here that it is in the locus *Wo* (Where) *Es* (the subject devoid of any *das* or other objectifying article) *war* (was [*était*]—it is a locus of being that is at stake, and that in this locus), *soll* (it is a duty in the moral sense that is announced here, as is confirmed by the single sentence that follows it, bringing the chapter to a close)[3] *Ich* (I, there must I—just as in French one announced "ce suis-je," "it is I," before saying "c'est moi," "it's me") *werden* (become [*devenir*]—not occur [*survenir*], or even happen [*advenir*], but be born [*venir au jour*] of this very locus insofar as it is a locus of being).

Even though it runs counter to the principles of economy of expression that must dominate a translation, I would thus agree to force the forms of the signifier a little in French in order to bring them into line with the weight of a still refractory signification, which the German tolerates better here; to do so I would play on the homophony between the German *Es* and the first letter of the word "subject." By the same token, I might feel more indulgent, at least momentarily, toward the first French translation that was provided of the word *Es*—namely, *le soi* (the self). The *ça* [the it or the id], which was eventually preferred, not groundlessly, does not seem to me to be much better, since it is rather to the German *das*, in the question, *Was ist das?*, that it corresponds in *das ist* (*c'est* [it is]). The elided *c'* that appears if we stick to the accepted equivalence thus suggests to me the production of a verb, *s'être*, which would express the mode of absolute subjectivity, insofar as Freud truly discovered it in its radical eccentricity: "Where it was" ["*Là où c'était*"], one might say, "Where

(it) was itself" [*là où s'était*], as I would like it to be heard, "it is my duty that
418 I come into being."[4]

You should realize that the point is not to analyze if and how the I [*le je*] and the ego [*le moi*] are distinct and overlap in each particular subject on the basis of a grammatical conception of their functions.

What a linguistic conception, which must shape the analytic worker in his basic initiation, will teach him is to expect the symptom to prove its signifying function, that is, that by which it differs from the natural index commonly designated by the term "symptom" in medicine. And in order to satisfy this methodological requirement, he will oblige himself to recognize its conventional use in the significations brought out by analytic dialogue (a dialogue whose structure I shall try to articulate). But he will maintain that these very significations can be grasped with certainty only in their context, that is, in the sequence constituted for each one of them by the signification that refers back to it and the signification to which it refers in the analytic discourse.

These basic principles can be easily applied in analytic technique and, in elucidating it, they dissipate many of the ambiguities which, being maintained even in the major concepts of transference and resistance, make the use that is made of them in practice exceedingly costly.

Resistance to the Resisters

To consider only resistance, whose use is increasingly confused with that of defense—and all the latter thus implies by way of maneuvers designed to eliminate it, maneuvers whose coercive nature we can no longer ignore—it is worth recalling that the first resistance analysis faces is that of discourse itself, insofar as it is first of all a discourse of opinion, and that all psychological objectification proves to be intimately tied to this discourse. This is, in effect, what
419 motivated the remarkable simultaneity with which the psychoanalytic practice of the burgraves of analysis came to a standstill in the 1920s: for by then they knew both too much and not enough about it to get their patients, who scarcely knew less about it, to recognize the truth.

But the principle adopted at that time of granting primacy to the analysis of resistance hardly led to a favorable development. For the reason that giving top priority to an operation doesn't suffice to make it reach its objective when one is unclear as to what that objective is.

Now the analysis of resistance was designed precisely to reinforce the subject's objectifying position, to so great an extent, indeed, that this directive now permeates the principles that are supposed to be applied in the conduct of a standard treatment.

Far from having to maintain the subject in a state of self-observation, therefore, one must know that by inviting him to adopt such a position one enters a circle of misunderstanding that nothing in the treatment, or even in the analytic literature, will be able to shatter. Any intervention that moves in this direction can thus only be justified by a dialectical aim—namely, to demonstrate that it amounts to an impasse.

But I will go further and say that you cannot both carry out this objectification of the subject yourself and speak to him as you should. And for a reason, which is not simply that you can't, as the English proverb has it, have your cake and eat it too—that is, adopt two different approaches to the same objects whose consequences are mutually exclusive. But for the deeper reason that is expressed in the saying "you can't serve two masters," that is, conform your being to two actions that lead in opposite directions.

For objectification in psychological matters is subject, at its very core, to a law of misrecognition that governs the subject not only as observed, but also as observer. In other words, it is not about him that you must speak to him, for he can do this well enough himself, and in doing so, it is not even to you that he speaks. While it is to him that you must speak, it is literally about something else—that is, about some-thing other than what is at stake when he speaks of himself—which is the thing that speaks to you. Regardless of what he says, this thing will remain forever inaccessible to him if, being speech addressed to you, it cannot elicit its response in you, and if, having heard its message in 420
this inverted form, you cannot, in re-turning it to him, give him the twofold satisfaction of having recognized it and of making him recognize its truth.

Can't we then know the truth that we know in this way? *Adæquatio rei et intellectus*—thus has the concept of truth been defined since there were thinkers who lead us into the pathways of their thought. Intellects like ours will certainly measure up to the thing that speaks to us, nay, that speaks in us; and even when it hides behind a discourse that says nothing merely to make us speak, it would be shocking indeed if the thing did not find someone to speak to.

I hope you will be so lucky; we must speak about it now, and those who put the thing into practice have the floor.

Interlude

But don't expect too much here, for ever since the psychoanalytic thing became an accepted thing and its servants started having their hands manicured, the housecleaning they have been performing makes do with sacrifices to good taste, which, as far as ideas—which psychoanalysts have never had in abundance—are concerned, is certainly convenient: ideas on sale for everyone will make up the balance of what each person is lacking in. We are sufficiently abreast of things to know that *chosisme* is hardly in good taste—which is our way of sidestepping the question.

"Why go off in search of something other than the ego you distinguish, when you forbid us to see it?" it may be objected. "So we objectify it. What's wrong with that?" Here the delicate shoes move stealthily forward to deliver the following kick in the face: "Do you think, then, that the ego can be taken as a thing? We'd never entertain any such notion."

From thirty-five years of cohabitation with the ego under the roof of the second Freudian topography—including ten years of a rather stormy relationship, finally legitimized by the ministry of Miss Anna Freud in a marriage whose social credit has done nothing but grow ever since, so much so that people
421 assure me it will soon request the Church's blessing—in short, from the most sustained work of psychoanalysts, you will draw nothing more than this drawer.

It is true that it is chock-full of old novelties and new antiques, the sheer mass of which is at least entertaining. The ego is a function, the ego is a synthesis, a synthesis of functions, a function of synthesis. It is autonomous! That's a good one! It's the latest fetish introduced into the holy of holies of a practice that is legitimated by the superiority of the superiors. It does the job as well as any other, everyone realizing that it is always the most outmoded, dirty, and repulsive object that best fulfills this function—this function being entirely real. That this object should gain for its inventor the veneration it does where it is in operation is just barely tolerable, but the most amazing thing is that in enlightened circles it has earned him the prestige of having returned psychoanalysis to the fold of the laws of general psychology. It is as if His Excellency the Aga Khan, not content with receiving his weight in gold—which in no way diminishes the esteem in which he is held in cosmopolitan society—were to be awarded the Nobel Prize for, in exchange, distributing to his followers the precise rules for pari-mutuel.

But the latest find is the best: the ego, like everything else we have been handling of late in the human sciences, is an op-er-a-tion-al notion.

At this point I appeal, before those in the audience, to this naive *chosisme* which keeps them sitting so properly in their seats, listening to me despite the barrage of calls to serve, so that they might, with me, agree to put a stop to this op [*stopper c't o-pé*].

In what respect does this op rationally distinguish what one makes of the notion of the ego in analysis from the common usage of any other thing, of this lectern, to take the first thing at hand? It distinguishes them so little that

I am confident I can show that the discourses about them—and that is what is at stake—coincide point for point.

For this lectern, no less than the ego, is dependent on the signifier, namely on the word, which—generalizing its function compared to the pulpit of quarrelsome memory and to the Tronchin table of noble pedigree—is responsible for the fact that it is not merely a tree that has been felled, cut down to size,
and glued back together by a cabinetmaker, for reasons of commerce tied to 422
need-creating fashions that maintain its exchange value, assuming it is not led too quickly to satisfy the least superfluous of those needs by the final use to which wear and tear will eventually reduce it: namely, fuel for the fire.

Moreover, the significations to which the lectern refers are in no way less dignified than those of the ego, and the proof is that they occasionally envelop the ego itself, if it is by the functions Heinz Hartmann attributes to the ego that one of our semblables may become our lectern: namely, maintain a position suitable enough for him to consent to it. An operational function, no doubt, that will allow the said semblable to display within himself all the possible values of this lectern as a thing: from the hefty rent charged for its use that kept and still keeps the standing of the little hunchback of the rue Quincampoix above both the vicissitudes and the very memory of the first great speculative crash of modern times, through all the purposes of everyday convenience, of furnishing a room, of transfer for cash or assignment of interest, to its use—and why not? it has happened before—as firewood.

But that isn't all, for I am willing to lend my voice to the true lectern so that it might deliver a lecture on its existence, which, even though it is instrumental, is individual; on its history, which, however radically alienated it may seem to us, has left all the written traces a historian might require: documents, texts, and bills from suppliers; and on its very destiny, which, though inert, is dramatic, since a lectern is perishable, is engendered by labor, and has a fate subject to chance, obstacles, misadventures, prestige, and even fatalities whose index it becomes; and it is destined to an end of which it need know nothing for it to be the lectern's own, since we all know what it is.

But it would be nothing more than sheer banality if, after this prosopopeia, one of you dreams that he is this lectern, whether or not it is endowed with the gift of speech. And since the interpretation of dreams has become a well known, if not a widespread, practice, there would be no reason to be surprised if—by deciphering the use as a signifier that this lectern has taken on in the rebus in which the dreamer immures his desire, and by analyzing the more or less equivocal reference implied by this use to the significations the lectern's
consciousness has awakened in him, with or without its lecture—we reached 423
what might be called the lectern's "preconscious."

At this point I hear a protest, which I am not sure how to name, even though it is totally predictable: for, in effect, it concerns that which has no name in any language [*langue*], and which, generally manifesting itself in the ambiguous mollifying motion of "the total personality," comprises everything that leads us to be publicly ridiculed in psychiatry for our worthless phenomenology and in society for our stationary "progressivism." The protest is that of the beautiful soul, no doubt, but in forms suited to the wishy-washy being, wry manner, and tenebrous approach of the modern intellectual, whether on the right or left. Indeed, it is in this quarter that the fictional protest of those that disorder causes to proliferate finds its noble alliances. Let us listen rather to the tone of this protest.

The tone is measured but serious: neither the preconscious nor consciousness, we are told, belongs to the lectern, but to we who perceive the desk and give it its meaning—all the more easily, moreover, since we ourselves have made the thing. But even if a more natural being were at stake, we should never thoughtlessly debase in consciousness the high form which, however feeble we may be in the universe, assures us an imprescriptible dignity in it—look up "reed" in the dictionary of spiritualist thought.

I must admit that Freud incites me to be irreverent here by the way in which, in a passing remark somewhere, as if without touching on it, he speaks about the modes of spontaneous provocation that are usual when universal consciousness goes into action. And this relieves me of any constraint about pursuing my paradox.

Is the difference between the lectern and us, as far as consciousness is concerned, so very great then if, in being brought into play between you and me, the lectern can so easily acquire a semblance of consciousness that my sentences could allow us to mistake the one for the other? Being placed with one of us between two parallel mirrors, it will be seen to reflect indefinitely, which means that it will be far more like the person who is looking than we think, since in seeing his image repeated in the same way, he too truly sees himself
424 through another's eyes when he looks at himself, since without the other, his image, he would not see himself seeing himself.

In other words, the ego's privileged status compared to things must be sought elsewhere than in this false recurrence to infinity of the reflection which constitutes the mirage of consciousness, and which, despite its utter uselessness, still titillates those who work with thought enough for them to see in it some supposed progress in interiority, whereas it is a topological phenomenon whose distribution in nature is as sporadic as the dispositions of pure exteriority that condition it, even if it is true that man has helped spread them with such immoderate frequency.

How, moreover, can we separate the term "preconscious" from the affectations of this lectern, or from those which are potentially or actually found in any other thing and which, by adjusting themselves so exactly to my affections, will become conscious along with them?

I am willing to accept that the ego, and not the lectern, is the seat of perceptions, but it thus reflects the essence of the objects it perceives and not its own essence, insofar as consciousness is supposedly its privilege, since these perceptions are, for the most part, unconscious.

It is no accident, moreover, that I have detected the origin of the protest that I must address here in the bastardized forms of phenomenology that cloud the technical analyses of human action, especially those required in medicine. If their cheap material, to borrow a term Jaspers uses in his assessment of psychoanalysis, really is what gives his work its style, and its weight to him as the epitome of the cast-iron spiritual advisor and tin-plate guru, they are not useless—indeed, their use is always the same, namely, to create a diversion.

They are used here, for example, in order to avoid discussing the important point that the lectern does not talk, which the upholders of the false protest want to know nothing about, because my lectern, hearing me grant them the point, would immediately begin to speak.

The other's Discourse 425

"In what way, then, is the ego you treat in analysis better than the lectern that I am?" it would ask them.

"For if its health is defined by its adaptation to a reality that is quite frankly regarded as being measured against the ego, and if you need the alliance of 'the healthy part of the ego' in order to eliminate discordances with reality (in the other part of the ego, no doubt)—which only appear to be discordances due to your principle of regarding the analytic situation as simple and innocuous, and concerning which you won't stop until you have made the subject see them as you see them—isn't it clear that there is no way to discern which is the healthy part of the subject's ego except by its agreement with your point of view? And, since the latter is assumed to be healthy, it becomes the measure of all things. Isn't it similarly clear that there is no other criterion of cure than the complete adoption by the subject of your measure? This is confirmed by the common admission by certain serious authors that the end of analysis is achieved when the subject identifies with the analyst's ego.

"Certainly, the fact that such a view can spread and be accepted so calmly leads one to think that, contrary to the commonly held view that it is easy to impress the naive, it is much easier for the naive to impress others. And the hypocrisy revealed in the declaration—whose repentant tone appears with such curious regularity in this discourse—that we should speak to the subject in 'his own language,' gives one still further pause for thought regarding the depth of this naïveté. We still have to overcome the nausea we feel at the idea it suggests of employing baby talk, without which well informed parents would believe themselves incapable of inculcating their lofty reasons in the poor little guys that have to be made to keep quiet! These are simple attentions people consider necessary because, according to the notion projected by analytic imbecility, neurotics supposedly have weak egos.

"But we are not here to dream between nausea and vertigo. The fact remains that, although I may be a mere lectern in speaking to you, I am the ideal patient; for not so much trouble has to be taken with me—the results are
426 obtained immediately, I am cured in advance. Since the point is simply to replace my discourse with yours, I am a perfect ego, since I have never had any other discourse, and I leave it to you to inform me of the things to which my adjustment controls do not allow you to adapt me directly—namely, of everything other than your eyesight, your height, and the dimensions of your papers."

Not a bad speech for a lectern, I'd say. I must be kidding, of course. In what it said under my command, it did not have its say. For the reason that it itself was a word; it was "me" [*moi*] as grammatical subject. Well, that's one rank achieved, one worth being picked up by the opportunistic soldier in the ditch of an entirely eristic claim, but which also provides us with an illustration of the Freudian motto, which, expressed as "La où était ça, le *je* doit être," would confirm, to our benefit, the feeble character of a translation that substantifies the *Ich*, by giving a "t" to *doit* translating *soll*, and fixes the price of the *Es* according to the rate of the ç. The fact remains that the lectern is not an ego, however eloquent it was, but a means that I have employed in my discourse.

But, after all, if we envision its virtue in analysis, the ego, too, is a means, and they can be compared.

As the lectern so pertinently mentioned, it has the advantage over the ego of not being a means of resistance, and that's precisely why I chose it to prop up my discourse and proportionately mitigate whatever resistance a greater interference of my ego in Freud's words might have given rise to in you—satisfied as I would already be if the resistance you must be left with, despite this effacement, led you to find what I am saying "interesting." It's no accident that this expression, in its euphemistic use, designates what interests us only moderately, and manages to come full circle in its antithesis, by which speculations of universal interest are called "disinterested."

But were what I am saying to come to interest you personally—as they say, filling out an antonomasia with a pleonasm—the lectern would soon be in pieces for us to use as a weapon.

Well, all of that applies to the ego, except that its uses seem to be reversed in their relation to its states. The ego is a means of the speech addressed to you from the subject's unconscious, a weapon for resisting its recognition; it is fragmented when it conveys speech and whole when it serves not to hear it. 427

Indeed, the subject finds the signifying material of his symptoms in the disintegration of the imaginary unity that the ego constitutes. And it is from the sort of interest the ego awakens in him that come the significations that turn his discourse away from it.

Imaginary Passion

This interest in the ego is a passion whose nature was already glimpsed by the traditional moralists, who called it *amour-propre*, but whose dynamics in relation to one's own body image only psychoanalytic investigation could analyze. This passion brings to every relation with this image, constantly represented by my semblable, a signification which interests me so greatly—that is, which makes me so dependent on this image—that it links all the objects of my desires to the other's desire, more closely than to the desire they arouse in me.

I am talking about objects as we expect them to appear in a space structured by vision—that is, objects characteristic of the human world. As to the knowledge on which desire for these objects depends, men are far from confirming the expression that says they see no further than the end of their nose; on the contrary, their misfortune is such that their world begins at the end of their nose, and they can apprehend their desire only by means of the same thing that allows them to see their nose itself: a mirror. But no sooner has this nose been discerned than they fall in love with it, and this is the first signification by which narcissism envelops the forms of desire. It is not the only signification, and the growing importance of aggressiveness in the firmament of analytic concerns would remain obscure if we confined our attention to this one alone.

This is a point I believe I myself have helped elucidate by conceptualizing the so-called dynamics of the "mirror stage" as the consequence of man's generic prematurity at birth, leading at the age indicated to the jubilant iden- 428
tification of the individual who is still an infant with the total form in which this reflection of the nose is integrated—namely, with the image of his body. This operation—which is carried out in an approximate manner that might be off by a nose [*faite à vue de nez*], an apt expression here, in other words,

falling more or less into the same category as the "aha!" that enlightens us about the chimpanzee's intelligence, amazed as we always are to detect the miracle of intelligence on our peers' faces—does not fail to bring deplorable consequences in its wake.

As a witty poet so rightly remarks, the mirror would do well to reflect a little more before sending us back our image. For at this point the subject has not yet seen anything. But let the same capture be reproduced under the nose of one of his semblables—the nose of a notary, for example—and Lord knows where the subject will be led by the nose, given the places such legal professionals are in the habit of sticking theirs. And whatever else we have—hands, feet, heart, mouth, even the eyes—that is so reluctant to follow is threatened by a breaking up of the team, whose announcement through anxiety could only lead to severe measures. Regroup!—an appeal to the power of this image which made the honeymoon with the mirror so jubilant, to the sacred union of right and left that is affirmed in it, as inverted as it may appear to be should the subject prove to be a bit more observant.

But what finer model of this union is there than the very image of the other, that is, of the notary in his function? It is thus that the functions of mastery, improperly called the ego's synthetic functions, institute on the basis of a libidinal alienation the subsequent development—namely, what I formerly termed the "paranoiac principle of human knowledge," according to which man's objects are subjected to a law of imaginary reduplication, evoking ratification by an indefinite series of notaries, which owes nothing to their professional federation.

But the signification that strikes me as decisive in the constitutive alienation of the ego's *Urbild* appears in the relation of exclusion that henceforth structures the dyadic ego-to-ego relationship in the subject. For should the imaginary coaptation of the one to the other bring about a complementary distribution of roles between, for example, the notary and the notarized party, an effect of the ego's precipitated identification with the other in the subject is that this distribution never constitutes even a kinetic harmony, but is instituted on the basis of a permanent "it's you or me" form of war in which the
429 existence of one or the other of the two notaries in each of the subjects is at stake. This situation is symbolized in the "So are you" of the transitivist quarrel, the original form of aggressive communication.

We can see to what the ego's language is reduced: intuitive illumination, recollective command, and the retorting aggressiveness of verbal echo. Let us add to this what the ego receives from the automatic scraps of everyday discourse: rote-learning and delusional refrain, modes of communication perfectly reproduced by objects scarcely more complicated than this lectern, a feed-back* construction for the former, a gramophone record, preferably scratched in the right place, for the latter.

It is, nevertheless, in this register that the systematic analysis of defense is proffered. It is corroborated by semblances of regression. The object-relation provides appearances of it, and this forcing has no other outcome than one of the three allowed by the technique currently in force. Either the impulsive leap into reality [*réel*] through the hoop of fantasy: acting out* in a direction that is ordinarily the opposite of suggestion. Or transitory hypomania due to ejection of the object itself, which is correctly described in the megalomaniacal intoxication which my friend Michael Balint, in an account so veracious as to make him a still better friend, recognizes as the index of the termination of an analysis according to current norms. Or in the sort of somatization constituted by mild hypochondria, discretely theorized under the heading of the doctor/patient relationship.

The dimension of a "two body psychology,"* suggested by Rickman, is the fantasy in which a "two ego analysis"* hides, which is as untenable as it is coherent in its results.

Analytic Action

This is why I teach that there are not only two subjects present in the analytic situation, but two subjects each of whom is provided with two objects, the ego and the other, the latter beginning with a lowercase o. Now, due to the singularities of a dialectical mathematics with which we must familiarize ourselves, their union in the pair of subjects S and A includes only four terms in all, because the relation of exclusion that obtains between *a* and *a′* reduces the two couples thus indicated to a single couple in the juxtaposition of the subjects. 430

In this game for four players, the analyst will act on the significant resistances that weigh down, impede, and divert speech, while himself introducing into the quartet the primordial sign of the exclusion that connotes the either/or of presence or absence which formally brings out death as included in the narcissistic *Bildung*. This sign is lacking, let it be noted in passing, in the algorithmic apparatus of the modern logic that is called symbolic, demonstrating the dialectical inadequacy that renders it still unsuitable for formalizing the human sciences.

This means that the analyst concretely intervenes in the dialectic of analysis by playing dead—by "cadaverizing" his position, as the Chinese say—either by his silence where he is the Other with a capital O, or by canceling out his own resistance where he is the other with a lowercase o. In both cases, and via symbolic and imaginary effects, respectively, he makes death present.

Still, he must recognize and therefore distinguish his action in each of these two registers to know why he is intervening, at what moment the opportunity is presenting itself, and how to act on it.

The primordial condition for this is that the analyst should be thoroughly convinced of the radical difference between the Other to whom his speech should be addressed, and the second other who is the one he sees before him, about whom and by means of whom the first speaks to him in the discourse it pursues before him. For, in this way, the analyst will be able to be the one to whom this discourse is addressed.

The fable of my lectern and the usual practice of the discourse of conviction will show him clearly enough, if he thinks about it, that no word [*discours*]—whatever inertia it may be based on or whatever passion it may appeal to—is ever addressed to anyone except the wise to whom it is sufficient. Even what is known as an *ad hominem* argument is only regarded by the person who uses it as a seduction designed to get the other, in his authenticity, to accept what the person says [*parole*]; this speech constitutes a pact, whether it is made explicit or not, between the two subjects, but it is situated in either case beyond the reasons furnished in the argument.

In general, each person knows that others will remain, like himself, inaccessible to the constraints of reason, failing an a priori acceptance of a rule of
431 debate that cannot function without an explicit or implicit agreement as to what is called its ground [*fonds*], which is almost always tantamount to a prior agreement regarding the stakes. What is called logic or law is never anything more than a body of rules that were laboriously worked out at a moment of history, duly dated and situated by a stamp of origin—whether agora or forum, church, or even political party. Thus I won't expect anything from these rules without the Other's good faith and, as a last resort, will only make use of them, if I see fit or am forced to, in order to beguile bad faith.

The Locus of Speech

The Other is, therefore, the locus in which is constituted the I who speaks along with he who hears, what is said by the one being already the reply, the other deciding, in hearing [*entendre*] it, whether the one has spoken or not.

But, in return, this locus extends as far into the subject as the laws of speech reign there, that is, well beyond the discourse that takes its watchwords from the ego, since Freud discovered its unconscious field and the laws that structure it.

It is not because of some mystery concerning the indestructibility of certain childhood desires that the laws of the unconscious determine analyzable symptoms. The subject's imaginary shaping by his desires—which are more or less fixated or regressed in relation to the object—is too inadequate and partial to provide the key.

The necessary and sufficient reason for the repetitive insistence of these desires in the transference and their permanent remembrance in a signifier that repression has appropriated—that is, in which the repressed returns—is found if one accepts the idea that in these determinations the desire for recognition dominates the desire that is to be recognized, preserving it as such until it is recognized.

Indeed, the laws of remembering and symbolic recognition are different in their essence and manifestation from the laws of imaginary reminiscence—that is, from the echo of feeling or instinctual imprinting *(Prägung)*—even if the elements organized by the former as signifiers are borrowed from the material to which the latter give signification.

To grasp the nature of symbolic memory, it suffices to have studied once, 432
as I had people do in my seminar, the simplest symbolic sequence, that of a linear series of signs connoting the presence/absence alternative, each sign being chosen at random by whatever pure or impure means adopted. If this sequence is then elaborated in the simplest way, isolating three-term sequences to generate a new series, syntactical laws arise that impose on each term of this new series certain exclusions of possibility until the compensations demanded by its antecedents have been satisfied.

Freud's discovery went right to the heart of this determination by the symbolic law, for in the unconscious—which, he insisted, was quite different from everything that had previously been designated by that name—he recognized the instance of the laws on which marriage and kinship are based, establishing the Oedipus complex as its central motivation already in the *Traumdeutung*. This is what now allows me to tell you why the motives of the unconscious are limited to sexual desire, a point on which Freud was quite clear from the outset and from which he never deviated. Indeed, it is essentially on sexual relations [*liaison*]—by regulating them according to the law of preferential marriage alliances and forbidden relations—that the first combinatory for exchanges of women between family lines relies, developing the fundamental commerce and concrete discourse on which human societies are based in an exchange of gratuitous goods and magic words.

The concrete field of individual preservation, on the other hand, through its links with the division not of labor, but of desire and labor—already manifest right from the first transformation that introduced human signification into food and up to the most highly developed forms of the production of consumable goods—sufficiently shows that it is structured in the master/slave

dialectic, in which we can recognize the symbolic emergence of the imaginary struggle to the death that I defined above as the ego's essential structure; it is hardly surprising, then, that this field is exclusively reflected in this structure.
433 In other words, this explains why the other great generic desire, hunger, is not represented, as Freud always maintained, in what the unconscious preserves in order to get it recognized.

Thus Freud's intention, which was quite legible to anyone who didn't confine himself to merely parroting Freud's texts, became increasingly clear when he promoted the topography of the ego; his intention was to restore, in all its rigor, the separation—right down to their unconscious interference—between the field of the ego and that of the unconscious he discovered first, by showing that the former is in a "blocking" position in relation to the latter, the former resisting recognition of the latter through the effect of its own significations in speech.

Here lies the contrast between the significations of guilt, whose discovery in the subject's action dominated the first phase in the history of psychoanalysis, and the significations of the subject's affective frustration, instinctual inadequacy, and imaginary dependence that dominate its current phase.

It isn't going very far to say that the latter significations, whose predominance is now consolidating through a forgetting of the former significations, promise us a preparatory course in general infantilization; for psychoanalysis is already allowing large-scale practices of social mystification to claim legitimacy by appealing to analytic principles.

Symbolic Debt

Will our action go so far, then, as to repress the very truth that it implies in its practice? Will it put this truth back to sleep—a truth that Freud, in the passion of the Rat Man, forever offers up so that we may recognize it, should we increasingly turn our vigilance away from it—namely, that the stone guest who came, in symptoms, to disturb the banquet of his desires was fashioned out of acts of treachery and vain oaths, broken promises and empty words, whose constellation presided over a man's birth?

For the sour grape of speech by which the child received the authentication of the nothingness of existence from a father too early, and the grapes of wrath that responded to the words of false hope with which his mother lured him in feeding him with the milk of her true despair, set his teeth on edge more
434 than if he had been weaned from an imaginary jouissance or even deprived of some real attentions.

Will we escape unscathed from the symbolic game in which the real misdeed pays the price for imaginary temptation? Will we turn our attention away from what becomes of the law when, by virtue of having been intolerable to the subject's loyalty, it is misrecognized by him already when it is still unknown to him, and from what becomes of the imperative when, having presented itself to him through imposture, it is challenged in his heart before being discerned? In other words, will we turn our attention away from the mainsprings that, in the broken link of the symbolic chain, raise from the imaginary the obscene, ferocious figure in which the true signification of the superego must be seen?

It should be understood here that my criticism of a kind of analysis that claims to be an analysis of resistance, and is reduced ever more to the mobilization of the defenses, bears solely on the fact that it is as disoriented in its practice as it is in its principles, and is designed to remind analysts of their legitimate ends.

The maneuvers involving dyadic complicity that this form of analysis forces itself to implement to achieve happiness and success can have value in our eyes only if they reduce the resistance, stemming from the effects of prestige in which the ego asserts itself, to the speech that is owned [*s'avoue*] at a certain moment of analysis, which is the analytic moment.

I believe that it is in the owning [*l'aveu*] of this speech, of which transference is the enigmatic actualization, that analysis must refind its center along with its gravity; and let no one imagine from what I said earlier that I conceptualize this speech as some mystical mode reminiscent of karma. For what is striking in the moving drama of neurosis is the absurd aspects of a disconcerted symbolization whose case of mistaken identity seems more derisory the more one delves into it.

Adœquatio rei et intellectus: the homonymic enigma that can be brought out in the genitive, *rei*—which without even changing accents can be the genitive of the word *reus*, meaning the party to the case in a lawsuit, specifically the accused, and metaphorically he who has incurred a debt—surprises us by providing, in the end, a formulation for this singular correspondence [*adéquation*] that I raised as a question for our intellect and that finds its answer in the symbolic debt for which the subject is responsible as a subject of speech.

The Training of Analysts to Come 435

In taking up anew my analysis of the ways in which speech is able to recover the debt it engenders, I will thus return to the structures of language that are so manifestly recognizable in the earliest discovered mechanisms of the unconscious.

We need but thumb through the pages of Freud's work for it to become abundantly clear that he regarded a history of languages [*langue*] and institutions, and the resonances—whether attested to or not in human memory—of literature and of the significations involved in works of art, as necessary to an understanding of the text of our experience; indeed, Freud himself found his inspiration, ways of thinking, and arsenal of techniques therein. But he also believed it wasn't superfluous to make them a condition for instituting the teaching of psychoanalysis.

The fact that this condition has been neglected, even in the selection of analysts, cannot be unconnected with the results we see around us; it indicates to us that it is only by articulating Freud's requirements in terms of technique that we will be able to satisfy them. It is with an initiation into the methods of the linguist, the historian, and, I would add, the mathematician that we should now be concerned if a new generation of practitioners and researchers is to recover the meaning and motor force of the Freudian experience. This generation will also find in these methods a way to avoid social-psychological objectification, in which the psychoanalyst seeks, in his uncertainty, the substance of what he does, whereas it can provide him with no more than an inadequate abstraction in which his practice gets bogged down and dissolves.

Such reform will require an institutional undertaking, for it can only be sustained by means of constant communication with disciplines that would define themselves as sciences of intersubjectivity, or by the term "conjectural sciences," a term by which I indicate the kind of research that is now changing the implication of the "human sciences."

But such a direction can only be maintained by a true teaching, that is, teaching that constantly subjects itself to what is known as renewal. For the pact
436 instituting analytic experience must take into account the fact that this experience instates the very effects that capture it, diverting it from the subject.

Thus, in exposing magical thinking, people don't see that it is magical thinking and, in fact, an alibi for thoughts about wielding power that are ever ready to bring about their own rejection in an action that is sustained only by its connection with truth.

Freud is referring to this connection with truth when he declares that it is impossible to meet three challenges: to educate, govern, and psychoanalyze. Why are they impossible, if not for the fact that the subject can only be missed in these undertakings, slipping away in the margin Freud reserves for truth?

For in these undertakings truth proves to be complex in its essence, humble in its offices and foreign to reality, refractory to the choice of sex, akin to death and, on the whole, rather inhuman, Diana perhaps . . . Actaeon, too guilty to hunt the goddess, prey in which is caught, O huntsman, the shadow that you become, let the pack go without hastening your step, Diana will recognize the hounds for what they are worth . . .

Notes

1. This text was first published in *L'Évolution psychiatrique* 1 (1956): 225–52.

2. (Added in 1966:) This rewritten paragraph predates a line of thought I have since explored.

3. Namely, "Es ist Kulturarbeit etwa wie die Trockenlegung der Zuydersee." "It is a civilizing task like the drying out of the Zuider Zee."

4. One can but wonder what demon inspired the author of the extant French translation, whoever it was, to render it as "Le moi doit déloger le ça" ("The ego must dislodge the id"). It is true that one can savor in it the tone of an analytic quarter in which people know how to carry out the sort of operation it evokes.

437 # Psychoanalysis and Its Teaching

Talk given at the French Philosophical Society during the session held February 23, 1957

As was customary, the following abstract was distributed to the members of the Society prior to the talk:

Psychoanalysis and What It Teaches Us . . .

I. In the unconscious, which is not so much deep as it is inaccessible to conscious scrutiny, *it speaks*; the notion of a subject within the subject, transcending the subject, has raised questions for philosophers since Freud first wrote *The Interpretation of Dreams*.

II. The fact that symptoms are symbolic is not the whole story. The author demonstrates:

- that their use as signifiers distinguishes them from their natural meaning, thanks to the step of *narcissism*, in which the imaginary separates from the symbolic;
- that the truth of the unconscious must be situated *between the lines*, since a broader metonymy encompasses their metaphors;
- that, with his notion of the *death instinct*, Freud investigates the basis [*suppôt*] of this truth.

III. By challenging the propriety of Freud's investigation, contemporary psychoanalysts

- have arrived at a declared "environmentalism," which contradicts the contingency Freud assigned to the object in the vicissitudes of the tendencies,
- and have returned to the most simplistic form of egocentrism, which suggests a misunderstanding of the dependent status Freud later assigned to the ego.

And yet . . .

438

How to Teach It

IV. The vast literature in which this contradiction and misunderstanding are revealed can serve as useful casuistry by demonstrating where resistance, which is a dupe here of its own course, is situated—namely, in the imaginary effects of the dyadic relation. When shed light on by another source, its fantasies make people take the series [*suite*] of these effects to be consistent.

And this impoverished path tries to legitimate itself on the basis of the following condition of psychoanalysis: that the true work in it is, by its very nature, hidden.

V. But the same is not true of the structure of analysis, which can be formalized in a way that is completely accessible to the scientific community, provided one relies on Freud who truly constituted it.

For psychoanalysis is nothing more than an artifice, the components of which Freud provided in positing that the whole set of these components encompasses the very notion of these components.

Such that, while the purely formal maintenance of these components suffices for their overall structure to be effective, the incompleteness of the analyst's conception of these components tends, depending on how great it is, to be confused with the limit that the analytic process cannot go beyond in the analysand.

The theory currently in favor verifies this with its amazing confession: the analyst's ego, which must be said to be *autonomous* at the very least, is the measure of reality and, for the analysand [*l'analysé*], his own analysis constitutes the testing of that reality.

Nothing of the kind could possibly be at stake within the confines of analysis; what is at stake is, rather, the restoring of a symbolic chain the three dimensions of which indicate the directions in which the author intends to trace out pathways for the training of analysts. Those dimensions are the dimension:

- of history of a life lived as history;
- of subjection to the laws of language, which alone are capable of overdetermination;
- of the intersubjective game by which truth enters reality [*réel*].

VI. The locus described as that of truth serves as a prelude to the truth of the locus described.

While this locus is not the subject, it is not the other (to be written with a lowercase *o*) who, giving soul to the ego's wagers and body to the mirages of
439 perverse desire, brings about coalescences of the signifier with the signified onto which all resistance grabs hold and in which all suggestion finds its pivotal point, without anything being sketched out there by way of some cunning of reason, if not that they are permeable to it.

The cunning of reason that runs through them, violence being banished, is the refined rhetoric on which the unconscious offers us a handle [*prise*], along with a surprise—introducing this Other (to be provided with a capital *O*), faith in whom is invoked by anyone when he addresses an other (with a lowercase *o*), even if only to lie to him.

The analyst leaves room for this Other beyond the other by the neutrality with which he makes himself be *ne-uter*, neither the one nor the other of the two who are there; and if he remains silent, it is in order to let this Other speak.

The unconscious is the Other's discourse in which the subject receives his own forgotten message in the inverted form suitable for promises.

This Other is, nevertheless, only halfway from a quest that the unconscious betrays by its difficult art and whose ever-so-informed ignorance is revealed by the paradoxes of the object in Freud's work. For, if we listen to him, we learn that reality [*réel*] derives its existence from a refusal, that love creates its object from what is lacking in reality [*réel*], and that desire stops at the curtain behind which this lack is figured by reality [*réel*].

The author will discuss one or two of the points outlined in this abstract, which will serve as a reference point for the discussion.

The talk given was couched in the following terms:

Without stopping to wonder whether the text of my abstract was based on an accurate assessment of my audience, I will indicate that in raising the question "how can we teach what psychoanalysis teaches us?" I was not trying to give an illustration of my mode of teaching. This abstract lays out—so that the discussion may use it as a reference point, as I mentioned at the end of it—theses concerning the order that institutes psychoanalysis as a science, and then extracts from them the principles by which we can maintain the program of its teaching in this order. Were such a statement applied to modern physics, no one would, I think, qualify the discreet use of an algebraic formula, in order to indicate the order of abstraction that it constitutes, as sibylline. Why then would we consider ourselves to be deprived of a more succulent experience here?

Need I indicate that such a statement assumes that the moment is now behind 440
us at which it was important to get the existence of psychoanalysis recognized and, as it were, to produce certificates of good conduct on its behalf?

I take for granted that psychoanalysis' existence as a qualified discipline is more than adequately accepted by all legitimate thinkers.

No one undergoing analysis today is taxed with being unbalanced when it comes to judging his social or legal competence. Rather, and despite the extravagance of this viewpoint, recourse to analysis is taken to involve a praiseworthy attempt at self-criticism and self-control. At the same time, the very people who applaud such recourse are likely to prove far more reserved regarding its use on themselves or their loved ones. The fact remains that the psychoanalyst is considered—rather thoughtlessly, in truth—to know a lot, and the least credulous of his psychiatric colleagues, for example, are quite happy to refer all kinds of cases to him that they themselves do not know how to handle.

Nevertheless, I assume that the specialists in the widely varied disciplines to whom I am speaking today have come here, given the venue, in their capacity as philosophers in a large enough measure for me to begin my discussion by raising the following question: What, in their view, does analysis teach us that is proper to analysis, or the most proper, truly proper, truly the most, the most truly?

I would hardly be going out on a limb were I to presume that the answers I would receive here would be more varied than at the time of the challenge that analysis at first presented the world.

The revolution constituted by the categorical predominance given to the sexual tendencies in human motivations became obscured due to the expansion of the theme of interpersonal relations, and even of social-psychological "dynamics."

Although the libidinal instances could not altogether escape characterization, they could, it was thought upon closer examination, be broken down into existential relations whose regularity and normativeness show them to have reached a truly remarkable state of domestication.

Beyond that, we would supposedly see sketched out a sort of positivistic analogism between morals and instincts. While its conformist aspects no 441 longer offend our sense of propriety, they can still provoke shame, by which I mean the shame that is sensitive to ridicule, and would bring down the curtain—to rely here on the evidence provided by anthropological studies.

Here psychoanalysis' contributions would seem to be imposing, although perhaps all the more subject to caution the more directly they are imposed. This can be gauged by comparing the massive renewal that occurred in the analysis of mythologies, owing to psychoanalytic inspiration, with the formation of a concept like that of "basic personality structure,"* with which the American Procrusteans torment with their yardstick the mystery of supposedly primitive souls.

Nevertheless, one of us would be justified in standing up and underscoring here just how much of what our culture propagates has Freud's name written on it, and in affirming that, regardless of its value, its order of magnitude is comparable to what our culture disseminates that, for better or for worse, has Marx's name written on it.

But we would also have to place in the scales a more militant Freud, a Freud committed to relieving forms of servitude that are more confused than those addressed by his paragon.

Then you would turn to practitioners to ask them to determine the substance of Freud's message on the basis of their own experience. But were you to simply peruse the clearly abundant literature in which they address their problems of technique, you would be surprised to find no surer line, no more decided path of progress in it, than his.

It would become clear to you, rather, that if a certain degree of wear and tear were not foreign to the acceptance of psychoanalysis in educated circles, a sort of strange side effect would meet it head-on, as if some mimesis [*mimétisme*], subverting the effort to convince, had conquered the interpreters in their own compromises.

And you would then have the malaise of wondering whether this "we" [*on*]—in which you would find yourself thrown in with technicians, leading you to recognize in the simple existence of this "we" what it is that would thus like to evade your question—is not itself too questionable in its indetermination not to cast doubt on the very fact of this recognition, assuming that the recognition requires that one base oneself on a firmer alterity, even if only for an intellectual leader.

442 It should be clear that I assume responsibility for this casting of doubt in raising my question and, in this respect, as an analyst, I distinguish myself from those who believe that the behind-closed-doors [*huis clos*] nature of our technique and our tightly sealed lips regarding our knowledge are adequate expedients by which to deal with this failing alterity. But how can one remind

analysts that error finds safety in the rules with which the worries it engenders protect themselves, and to the very degree to which people consider those rules to be transparent?

Let me pose my question again now so that we can marvel at the fact that no one dreams any longer of answering with the simple word "unconscious," because this word has not raised any questions for anyone for a long time. It has not raised any questions because people have endeavored to ensure that its use in Freud's work appears only drowned in the midst of homonymous conceptions to which it owes nothing, even though they preceded it.

These conceptions, far from overlapping, have the following feature in common: they constitute a dualism in psychical functions, in which unconscious is opposed to conscious like instinctual to intellectual, automatic to controlled, intuitive to discursive, passionate to rationalized, and elementary to integrated. Such conceptions created by psychologists were, nevertheless, relatively impermeable to the accents of a natural harmony that the romantic notion of the soul had promoted regarding the same themes; for they preserved in the background an image of levels which, situating their object in the lower one, took it to be confined there and even contained by the upper agency, and which, in any case, imposed upon its effects—if they were to be accepted at the level of this agency—a filtering in which what they lost in energy they gained in "synthesis."

The history of these presuppositions deserves attention in more than one respect, beginning with the political biases on which they are based and which accompany them; the latter refer us to nothing less than a social organicism, an organicism which—since the time of the unsurpassable simplicity with which it was articulated in the fable that earned the consul Menenius Agrippa an ovation—has hardly enriched its metaphor except on the basis of the conscious role granted to the brain in the activities of psychological command in order to arrive at the now assured myth of the virtues of a "brain trust."*

It would be no less curious to observe how the values masked here obliterate the notion of "automatism" in medical anthropology and pre-Freudian psychology, compared to its use by Aristotle, which is far more amenable to everything that has already been restored to it in the contemporary revolution in machines. 443

The use of the term "liberation," to designate the functions that are revealed in neurological disintegrations, clearly marks the values of conflict which preserve here—in other words, in a place where it has no business being—a truth of a different provenance. Is it this authentic provenance that Freud found anew in the conflict that he placed at the heart of the psychical dynamic that constitutes his discovery?

First, let us observe the locus in which the conflict is denoted, and then its function in reality [*réel*]. As for the first, we find it in symptoms that we approach only at the level at which we must not simply say that they are expressed but at which the subject articulates them in words—assuming it is important not to forget that this is the crux of the constant "chatting" to which analysis limits its means of action and even its modes of examination, a position which would render the entire technique inconceivable, including that applied to children, if it were not constitutive and instead merely manifest in the analysis of adults.

This conflict is read and interpreted in the text [of this "chatting"], which must be enriched through the procedure of free association. In this sense, it is thus neither simply the obtuse pressure nor the static-like noise of the unconscious tendency that makes itself heard in this discourse, but the interferences of its voice, if I may introduce in this manner what I will have to elaborate on at length.

What can we really say about this voice? Do we find anew here the imaginary sources whose prestige romanticism incarnated in the *Volksgeist*, the spirit of the race? If that were the import of the symbolism by means of which Freud made headway in the analysis of symptoms while simultaneously defining their psychoanalytic meaning, we would be unable to see why Freud excommunicated Jung, or what authorizes Freud's followers to continue to anathematize Jung's followers. In fact, there is nothing more different than the reading that these two schools apply to the same object. What is funny here is that the Freudians proved unable to formulate such a clear difference in a satisfactory
444 manner. Reveling in the words "scientific" and even "biological," which, like all words, can be spoken by all mouths, did not allow them to score any points along this pathway, even in the eyes of psychiatrists—their heart of hearts does not fail to warn them about the import of the use they themselves make of these words in such uncertain procedures.

Here, however, the path was not simply traced out for us by Freud: he paved the whole road for us with the most sweeping, unvarying, and unmistakable assertions. Read his work, open his texts to any page, and you will rediscover the foundational stonework of this royal road.

If the unconscious can be the object of a kind of reading that has shed light on so many mythical, poetic, religious, and ideological themes, it is not because it provides their genesis with the intermediary link of a sort of "significantness" [*significativité*] of nature in man, or even of a more universal *signatura rerum* that would be at the core of their possible resurgence in each individual. Psychoanalyzable symptoms, whether normal or pathological, can be distinguished not only from diagnostic indices but from all graspable forms of pure expressiveness insofar as they are sustained by a structure that is identical to the structure of language. By this I do not mean a structure that can be situated in some sort of supposedly generalized semiology which can be drawn from its limbo regions, but rather the structure of language as it manifests itself in what I will call "natural languages," those that are effectively spoken by human groups.

This refers to the foundation of the structure, namely, to the duplicity that subjects the two registers that are bound together in it to different laws: the registers of the signifier and the signified. The word "register" here designates two chains taken in their entirety; and the primary fact that they are distinct aprioristically obviates any possibility of establishing a term-by-term equivalence between these registers, regardless of the size of the chains we examine. (In fact, such an equivalence turns out to be infinitely more complex than any one-to-one correspondence, the model of which is only conceivable between one signifying system and another signifying system, according to its definition as given in the mathematical theory of groups.)

Thus, if symptoms can be read, it is because they themselves are already 445
inscribed in a writing process. As particular unconscious formations, symptoms are not significations, but their relation to a signifying structure that determines them. If you will allow me this play on words, I would say that what is always at stake is the agreement between the subject and the verb.

Indeed, what Freud's discovery brings us back to is the enormity of the order into which we have entered—into which we are, as it were, born a second time, in leaving behind the state which is rightly known as the *infans* state, for it is without speech—namely, the symbolic order constituted by language, and the moment of the concrete universal discourse and of all the furrows opened up by it at this time, in which we had to find lodging.

For the main notion articulated here by my remarks goes well beyond the functional and even notional apprenticeship to which the narrow-minded horizon of pedagogues tried to reduce the relations between the individual and language.

If man must truly find lodging in a "milieu" that has just as much a right to our consideration as the edges of reality [*réel*], wrongly presumed to be the only ones that generate experience, Freud's discovery shows us that the milieu of symbolism is consistent enough to even render inadequate the locution that would say of the lodging in question that it does not happen [*va*] all by itself, for what is serious is that it does happen all by itself, even when things are going [*va*] badly.

In other words, the alienation that had been accurately described to us for some time, although on a somewhat panoramic level, as constitutive of the

relations among men on the basis of the relations between their labor and the forms assumed by their production—this alienation, as I was saying, now appears in some sense redoubled because it manifests itself in a particularity that joins with being in forms that must truly be qualified as unprogressive. However, this does not suffice to characterize this discovery as reactionary, regardless of the complicit uses to which it may have been put. One would do better to explain in this way the enraged sullenness of petit-bourgeois mores that seem to accompany a form of social progress that misrecognizes its mainspring in all cases: for presently, it is insofar as this progress is endured that it legitimates psychoanalysis, and it is insofar as it is put into action that it proscribes psychoanalysis. The result is that the effects of Freud's discovery have
446 not yet gone beyond those that Diogenes expected from his lantern.

There is nothing here, however, that contradicts the vast dialectic that makes us serfs of history by superimposing its waves on the brewing of our grand migrations, in what attaches each of us to a scrap of discourse that is more alive than his very life, if it is true that, as Goethe said, when "that which is without life is alive, it can also produce life."[1]

For it is also true that, having been unable to proffer this scrap of discourse from our throats, each of us is condemned to make himself into its living alphabet to trace out its fatal line. In other words, at every level of its marionette's game, it borrows some element so that the sequence of elements suffices to attest to a text without which the desire that is borne in it would not be indestructible.

But this already overstates what we bring this attestation, whereas in its deportment it quite neglects us, transmitting, without our approval, its transformed cipher in our filial lineage. For even if there were no one to read it for as many centuries as was true of the hieroglyphics in the desert, it would remain as irreducible in its absolute nature as a signifier as the hieroglyphics would have remained amid the shifting sands and silence of the stars if no human being had come along to restore their signification.

The following share in this irreducibility: the fragile smoke of dreams, like rebuses at the bottom of one's dish (dreams and rebuses being considered by Freud to be similar in their elaboration); bungled actions, like typographical errors (both of which are successful in their signifierness rather than failed significations); and the frivolity of jokes—the specific joy of which, as Freud shows us on the basis of his technique, stems from the fact that they make us share in the dominance of the signifier over the significations of our fate that are the hardest to bear.

Aren't these, in fact, the three registers that are taken up in the three primordial works in which Freud discovered the laws of the unconscious? If you read them or reread them with this key, you will be surprised to note that Freud,

in enunciating these laws in detail, merely anticipated the laws that Ferdinand de Saussure was to bring to light several years later when he paved the way 447
for modern linguistics.

I would not dream of establishing a table of concordances here whose overly rapid construction would rightly be open to objection. I have indicated elsewhere what condensation, displacement, considerations of representability, and sequences (in which, interestingly enough, Freud at first sought the equivalent of a syntax) correspond to in the fundamental relation between the signified and the signifier.

I simply want to indicate that the function of the signifier proves to predominate in both the simplest and most complex symptoms, having an effect already at the level of puns. We see this, for example, in Freud's extraordinary analysis of the crux of the mechanism of forgetting (1898), in which the relation between the symptom and the signifier seems to emerge fully armed from an unprecedented thought.

Recall the broken tip of the memory's sword: the *signor* of the name Signorelli that Freud could not recall, Signorelli being the author of the famous fresco of the Antichrist in the Cathedral at Orvieto, even though the details of the fresco and the very self-portrait of the painter that is included in it seemed to present themselves all the more clearly to his mind. This is because *signor*, along with *Herr*, the absolute Master, is aspirated and repressed by the apocalyptic breeze that blows in Freud's unconscious in the echoes of the conversation he is in the process of carrying on: It is the disturbance, as he insists there, of a theme which has just emerged, by the preceding theme—which is, in fact, that of death for which one has assumed responsibility.

Thus we find again here the constitutive condition that Freud imposes on a symptom in order for it to deserve to be called a "symptom" in the analytic sense of the term, which is that a memory element from a special, earlier situation be taken up anew in order to articulate the current situation—in other words, that this memory element be unconsciously employed in it as a signifying element, with the effect of shaping the indeterminacy of the lived experience into a tendentious signification. Doesn't that say it all?

I will thus consider it sufficient to underscore the relationship between the effects of the unconscious and the twofold construction of synchrony and diachrony—which, as necessary as it is, it would be pedantic of me to elaborate on in such company—by providing a fable to bring out, through a sort of stereoscopy, both the style of the unconscious and the response that it is suitable to give it.

If the unconscious indeed seems to give new support to the Biblical proverb 448
which says that "The fathers have eaten sour grapes, and the children's teeth

are set on edge," it is on the basis of a readjustment that perhaps satisfies the nullity with which Jeremiah strikes it in citing it.

For I will say that it is because it was said that "the sour grapes that were eaten by the fathers set the children's teeth on edge," that the child—for whom these grapes are indeed far too sour [*verts*], being those of the disappointment all too often brought him, as everyone knows, by the stork—dons anew his fox mask face.

Of course, the lessons dispensed by a woman of genius who revolutionized our knowledge of the child's imaginary formations—the themes of which the initiated will recognize if I entertain the fanciful notion of calling her the tripe butcher—teach us to tell the child that he would like to rip those bad-object grapes out of the stork's guts and that this is why he is afraid of the fox. I am not saying no. But I have more confidence in La Fontaine's fable to introduce us to the structures of myth, that is, to what necessitates the intervention of the frightening fourth party whose role, as a signifier in phobia, seems to be far more of a motor force to me.

Leave this mechanism to our study and retain but the moral that this apologue finds in my wish that this reference to the holy text, *Jeremiah* 31.29, if it is not altogether inconceivable to encounter it in the unconscious, would not automatically (a serendipitous term here) make the analyst wonder about the person in the patient's "environment," as people have been putting it for some time now, whose telephone number it would be.

Whether this joke* be good or bad, you will realize that I am not haphazardly taking the risk of tying it so desperately to the letter, for it is through the mark of arbitrariness characteristic of the letter that the extraordinary contingency of accidents that give the unconscious its true face can be explained.

This is why a slap—being passed down for several generations, born first of the violence of passion, but then becoming more and more enigmatic, being repeated in compulsive scenarios (the construction of which it seems to determine in the manner of a story by Raymond Roussel) until it is no longer anything but an impulse punctuating with its syncopation an almost paranoiac
449 distrust of women—will tell us more when it is inserted as a signifier into a context in which, to an eye glued to a peephole, figures who are less characterized by their real psychology than by profiles comparable to those of Tartaglia and Pantalone in the commedia dell'arte are found anew from one age to the next in a transformed framework, forming the figures of the tarot from which the choices (that were decisive in his destiny) of objects that are now charged for him with the most disconcerting of valences have really stemmed, albeit unbeknown to him.

I will add that it is only in this way that these affinities, which are sources of disorders that cannot be mastered as long as they remain latent, can be recognized; and that a more or less decorative reduction of their paradox to object relations—prefabricated in the brains of twits who are better educated in heartfelt letters to Dear Abby than in the law of the heart—can have no more effect on them than to attempt to subject them to the technique of providing corrective experiences for the emotions that are presumed to be their cause.

For that is certainly what psychoanalysts came up with by the sole pathway of the shame that overcame them when—seeking recognition for their experience, which is so completely spun, right from its very origins, from this so very veridical, fictional structure—they heard each other object, with the overblown gravity of the praetor, that it was not usual to impute such serious consequences to such minimal causes, and that even if one found general frameworks for them, one would all the more completely lose sight of the reason why only some suffer from them and not everyone.

It is owing to their failure to explore the nature of the unconscious (even though the work was already prepared by Freud, simply by his having said that it is overdetermined, but who considers this term long enough to realize that it pertains only to the order of language?) that—the false shame of analysts regarding the object of their activity begetting their aversion, this aversion begetting pretension, and pretension begetting both hypocrisy and impudence, whose proliferating lineage I will put a stop to here—they ended up confusing the apple of genital copulation with the orange of the oblative gift, and promoting the analyst's ego as the elective means by which to reduce the subject's straying from reality. This [reduction is supposed to be accomplished] by no other means than through identification with an ego whose virtue can thus derive only from identification with another ego; but the latter, if it is that of another psychoanalyst, requires recurrence to some paragonized rela- 450
tionship to reality [*réel*]. For nothing and no one, up until recently, it must be said, has ever emphasized or dreamt, regarding the selection of analysts and their training, of concerning himself with the glaringly obvious, conscious biases they have about the world they live in, or with their ignorance (which is manifest in this game of love [*déduit*]) of the rudiments of the classics that are required to orient them in the reality of their own operations.

For the classics [*humanités*] sketch out the experience of man's relation to the signifier, and it is in this relation that the situations that generate what we call humanity are instituted. This is attested to by the fact that Freud, in the midst of full-scale scientism, was led not only to reconceptualize the Oedipus myth, but to promote in our time a myth of origin in the guise of a killing of the father that the primordial law is supposed to have perpetuated, according to the formula with which I have connoted the entrance of symbolism into reality [*réel*]: "in giving it another meaning."

With all the contingency that the instance of the signifier stamps in the unconscious, that instance merely sets out before us all the more surely the dimension that no imaginable experience could enable us to deduce from the datum of a living immanence—namely, the question of being or, better stated, the question *tout court*, "why is one here?," by which the subject casts his sex and his existence as an enigma.

This is what made me pen the following passage (on the same page on which I emphasized, "in the moving drama of neurosis [. . .], the absurd aspects of a disconcerted symbolization whose case of mistaken identity seems more derisory the more one delves into it"), restoring the import of paternal authority such as Jeremiah and Ezekiel in the above-cited passage show it to be at the core of the signifying pact, conjoining it as one must—in the Biblical terms used by the female author[2] of the American "Battle Hymn of the Republic"—with the curse of the mother:

> For the sour grape of speech by which the child received the authentication of the nothingness of existence from a father too early, and the grapes of wrath that responded to the words of false hope with which his mother lured him in feeding him with the milk of her true despair,
> 451 set his teeth on edge more than if he had been weaned from an imaginary jouissance or even deprived of some real attentions.

Indeed, we will not be surprised to realize that both hysterical neurosis and obsessive neurosis presuppose in their structure the terms without which the subject cannot accede to the notion of his facticity with regard to his sex in the one and with regard to his existence in the other. Each of these structures constitutes a sort of response to this facticity.

Responses which are subject, no doubt, to the condition that they be concretized in a behavior on the part of the subject that is a pantomime of it, but which do not, for all that, have any less right to the title "formed and articulated thoughts" that Freud gives to the following shorter-lasting unconscious formations: symptoms, dreams, and parapraxes.

This is why it is a mistake to consider these responses to be simply illusory. They are imaginary only inasmuch as the truth brings out its fictional structure in them.

Asking why the neurotic "is deceived" [*se trompe*], even though the question is better oriented, all too often shows the flat-footed sliding in which analysts, in drifting toward the stupidity of some sort of reality [*réel*] function, have tumbled, along with Freud's predecessors, on a path that is designed instead for the hoof of a divine goat.

Since, moreover, there is more wit in the written form of a word than in the use made of it by a pedant, the "*se*" in "*se trompe*"—which one would be wrong to isolate as representing the neurotic in a logical analysis of the verb that gives his passion a deponent form—warrants our stressing the fact that it indicates the path Freud did not back away from. It suffices to turn the question back on him by converting it into the following terms: "Who is the neurotic deceiving?"

Let me repeat that this places us ten thousand leagues above the question "Who is the neurotic making fun of?" (a question whose target the impenitent neurologist cannot help but make himself).

It must still be articulated that the other who is the partner of an intimate strategy here is not necessarily encountered among the individuals [in the neurotic's entourage], the only points currently accepted, since they are united by relational vectors on the maps onto which modern social psychology projects its schemas.

This other can be the image that is more essential to the desire of the living being than the living being whom he must clutch [*étreindre*] in order to 452
survive through struggle or love. For animal ethology confirms for us the order of lures by which nature proceeds in order to force its creatures into its pathways. The fact that puppets, facsimiles, and mirrors can easily be substituted for the phenotype in order to catch desire in the trap of their emptiness speaks volumes about the function that can be played in man by this generic other, if one knows, moreover, that it is by subordinating his tendencies to it that man learns what it means to be what he calls their master.

But whether a man or a woman, he may have nothing else to present to the real other than this imaginary other in which he has not recognized his being. How then can he attain his object(ive)? Through an exchange of places between his knights [*cavaliers*], I will say, therefore giving the queen [*dame*] responsibility for demonstrating the hysteric's step.

For she can find this real other only in someone of her own sex, because it is in this beyond that she calls for what can incarnate her [*lui donner corps*], because she has not been able to take on a tangible form [*prendre corps*] anywhere shy of it. In the absence of a response from this other, she will notify her of imprisonment for debt [*contrainte par corps*] by having her seized through the services of a straw man, the latter being a substitute for the imaginary other in whom she has not so much alienated herself as she has remained in abeyance before him.

This is how the hysteric comes to know herself [*s'éprouve*] in the homage paid to another woman, and offers up the woman in whom she adores her own mystery to the man whose role she takes without being able to enjoy it [*en jouir*]. In quest, without respite, of what it means to be a woman, she can but stave off [*tromper*] her desire, since this desire is the other's desire, never having achieved [*satisfait à*] the narcissistic identification that would have prepared her to satisfy the one and the other in the position of the object.

Leaving the lady [*dame*] there now, I will return to the masculine as regards the subject of the obsessive strategy. Let me point out to you in passing that this game, which is so palpable in experience and that analysis makes manifest, has never before been articulated in the terms I will use.

Here it is death that one must stave off [*tromper*] using a thousand ruses, and the other who is the subject's ego enters into the game as a prop for the challenge of the thousand feats which alone assure him of the success of his ruses.

The assurance that the ruse derives from the feat turns against itself because of the confidence that the feat derives from the ruse. And this ruse—which is sustained by a supreme reason on the basis of a field outside of the
453 subject that is called the unconscious—is also the ruse whose means and end escape him. For it is the ruse that holds the subject back, and even steals him away from the combat, as Venus did to Paris, making him always be elsewhere than where risks are run, and making him leave in his place but a shadow of himself; for he annuls in advance both gain and loss, by first abdicating the desire that is at stake.

But the jouissance of which the subject is thus deprived is transferred to the imaginary other who assumes [*assume*] it like the jouissance of a spectacle: namely, the spectacle offered by the subject in the cage in which—with the participation of a few wild animals from reality [*réel*], that participation being obtained most often at their expense—he pursues the prowess of the classical equitation exercises by which he proves that he is alive.

The fact that the point is nevertheless merely to prove himself, furtively conjures away death due to the challenge issued to it. But all the pleasure accrues to the other whom one cannot kick out of his place without death being let loose, all the while waiting for death to get the better of him.

This is how death comes to take on the semblance of the imaginary other and how the real Other is reduced to death: a borderline figure who answers the question about [one's] existence.

The way out of these impasses is unthinkable, as I was saying, by any maneuver involving imaginary exchange, since that is what makes them impasses.

The reintegration of the subject into his ego is certainly conceivable, and all the more so since, as opposed to the idea circulating in contemporary psychoanalysis, this ego is far from weak. We see this, moreover, in the assistance that the neurotic, whether hysteric or obsessive, obtains from his semblables who are presumed to be normal in these two tragedies—which are opposite in many respects, even though the second does not, it must be noted, exclude the first, since, even when elided, desire remains sexual (please excuse me for providing but these few indications here).

But the path that this reintegration suggests we take is a mistake, since it can only lead the subject to an increased alienation from his desire, that is, to some form of inversion, insofar as his sex is in question. And insofar as his existence is in question, it can only lead the subject not to a destruction of the tendency (endlessly invoked in psychoanalysis since the author of the word "aphanisis" introduced its analytic nonsense, which was already palpable in its shamelessly scholarly form), but to a sort of *stalemate* of desire, which is 454
not what people refer to as "ambivalence," but an impossibility to maneuver that stems from the very status of the strategy adopted.

The result can be catastrophic here, even as it gives satisfaction. To illustrate it, let us simply imagine what would happen if we treated a man with a limp by making him one-legged. In a society in which the rule is declared that one must hop everywhere, unless one has oneself carried by someone else's legs, that might be appropriate and would leave the subject a good chance of winning group competitions like the human pyramid and centipede.

But the solution must be sought elsewhere, that is, in the Other with a capital *O*, by which I designate a place that is essential to the structure of the symbolic. This Other is required in order to situate the question of the unconscious *in truth*, that is, in order to give it the structural term that makes the entire sequence of neurosis into a question and not a lure—a distinction which is highlighted in the fact that the subject uses his lures only in order to "skirt the question."

As I have often said, this Other is merely the guarantor of Good Faith who is necessarily evoked, even by the Deceiver, as soon as what is at stake is no longer the ploys of struggle or desire but rather the pact of speech.

It is only owing to the place of the Other that the analyst can receive the investiture of the transference that qualifies him to play his legitimate role in the subject's unconscious and to speak up there in interventions that are suited to a dialectic whose essential particularity is defined by the private realm.

Any other place for the analyst leads him back to the dyadic relation, which has no other outcome than the dialectic of misrecognition, negation, and narcissistic alienation that Freud repeatedly indicates throughout his work to be the ego's doing.

Now, contemporary psychoanalysis claims to inscribe its effects in the project of strengthening the ego through a complete misunderstanding of the mainspring by which Freud introduced the study of the ego into his doctrine—namely, on the basis of narcissism and in order to expose therein the sum total of the subject's imaginary identifications.

In a conception that is as diametrically opposed to this as it is retrograde, the ego is considered [by contemporary analysts] to constitute the apparatus of a relationship to reality, the static notion of which no longer bears any rela-
455 tion to the reality principle that Freud instituted in a dialectical relationship with the pleasure principle.

On that basis, people now aim only to eliminate the imaginary strayings [from reality] that are given rise to in the subject by the analytic situation, in the real terms of this situation which is considered to be "so simple." The fact that it provokes these strayings could make us doubt this simplicity, but it seems we must accept the idea that, from the real point of view, it is in effect simple—simple enough, indeed, to appear somewhat closed, since there are no sacrifices that the analyst does not prove to be ready to make in order to keep it that way.

Fortunately, these sacrifices are purely imaginary, but they run the gamut from offering oneself up as fodder to an imaginary *fellatio*—strange substitute for symbolic *filiatio*—to the abolition of the unfortunate distance from the object which creates all of the neurotic's problems. They go on to the pompous avowal of propitious complicities recognized in the countertransference, on the basis of bemired erring concerning the conditions for the righting of dependency and the best pathway by which to compensate the patient for his frustration (a term that is not found in Freud's work). And let us not forget those still stranger excursions among the lost children, including a reference to fear for example, which, in order to render any signifying elaboration of phobia null and void, would make do with an ideal anthropoid for its therapeutic distillation, if only the missing link of an adrenal discharge that strengthens the ego apparatus could manage to give it some verisimilitude. At this extreme of absurdity, the truth ordinarily manifests itself in a grimace—this is what, in fact, happens when one hears, in the same vein, a tearful appeal to goodness, oh my goodness!

This frenzy in the theory manifests, in any case, analysis' resistance to the analyst, which one can merely advise the latter to take into account in order to make room for his own resistance in his analysands' experience. This, in praying heaven that he will be more clement toward them than toward analysis; for regarding the latter, he can say even today, like Anthony said of his mistress, she resisted me and so I assassinated her.

His actual practice is, fortunately, not so somber. No one before whom the

phenomenon of the writing on the wall of the words "Mene, Tekel, Parsin" is 456
constantly repeated at just the right moment, even if they are traced out in cuneiform characters, can indefinitely see in them but festoons and astragals. Even if he reads the phenomenon like one reads coffee grinds, what he reads will never be all that stupid, provided that he reads, even if he does so like Monsieur Jourdain, without knowing what reading is.

For here there is no dearth of Mariette stones with which to rectify his reading, were it only in the "defenses," which are obvious, without seeking any further than the subject's verbalizations. Perhaps he will not know which way to turn in his attempt to account for these defenses; and he may get confused in his conception of the subtle bond that links the text of the palimpsest to the text which, underneath it, staining the ground, alters [*reprend*] its forms and shades. But he cannot stop a singular life of intentions from emerging from this exercise of discernment. He will thus be thrown, his reservations about it notwithstanding, into the heart of the perplexities of spiritual direction which have been elaborated over the centuries along the path of a demand for truth—a demand linked to a no doubt cruel personification of this Other, but which did a fairly good job of sounding the folds in striving to clear out every other affection from people's loins and hearts. This suffices to force the psychoanalyst to evolve in a region that academic psychology has never considered except through a spy-glass.

This is what makes it all the more enigmatic—and let us consider ourselves spared the effort—to question further, in the name of I know not what parody of social critique, a substructure that people take to be analogous to production but nonetheless natural; all the more enigmatic too that people then give themselves the task of bringing it all back into the fold of that psychology, qualified for the occasion as "general psychology," with the result of paralyzing all research by reducing its problems to discordant terms, and even disfiguring analytic experience so thoroughly as to render it unutilizable.

Psychoanalysis' responsibility for the sort of cancer constituted by the recurrent alibis of psychologism is probably not very great, in a society that covers over its irresponsibility with what the word "liberal" once signified.

The real point is not that this sterilizing diversion of research and this degrading complicity of action are encouraged and sustained by chain reaction abdications of responsibility by critics in our culture. It is that they are 457
maintained and protected in psychoanalysis, fed by the very institution which distinguishes, let us not forget, through Freud's express intention, the community of analysts from a scientific society founded upon a common practice. I mean: the very international institution that Freud founded in order to preserve the transmission of his discovery and method.

Did he thus simply miss his target here?

To answer that question, let me first point out that none of the "institutes" currently sponsored by this institution around the world has yet even tried to put together the curriculum of studies whose intention and extension Freud so often and in such detail defined as allowing for no substitute, even if it were tactically motivated—allowing for no integration into the official medical teaching, such as he could see it at his time, for example.

The teaching in these institutes is merely professional teaching and, as such, fails to demonstrate in its programs either a plan or an aim that goes beyond those of a dental school, which are no doubt praiseworthy (this reference was not simply accepted but proffered by the interested parties themselves). Regarding the subject matter in question, however, this goes no further than the training of a qualified nurse or of a social worker, and those who offer training that is ordinarily and fortunately of a higher caliber, at least in Europe, always acquired it from a different origin.

This much is undeniable. But the institutes are not the institution, and we should examine the history of the latter in order to grasp the authoritarian implications by which the extraordinary subjection to which Freud doomed his posterity is maintained—a posterity one hardly dares in this case to qualify as "spiritual."

I have mentioned elsewhere the biographical documents that allow us to conclude that Freud deliberately wanted things to be this way; so much so that he approved in writing the structure by which those whom he charged with the highest responsibilities, by the mere fact of bequeathing his technique to them, would be censured by a *secret* college.

It is not difficult to show how contemptuous Freud was of men whenever his mind confronted them with this task, which was considered by him to be beyond their capabilities. But his contempt was, at that time, consolidated by the fact that his first supporters repeatedly abandoned his views—a gauge in
458 his eyes of their mental and moral inadequacies. Still, their minds and characters clearly far surpassed the best of the crowd that, since then, has spread throughout the world with his doctrine. Lack of faith, moreover, does not receive any sanction from this latter fact, since it necessarily occurs in the direction of the effects that it presumes.

Thus I believe that Freud got what he wanted here: a purely formal preservation of his message, which is manifest in the spirit of reverential authority in which the most obvious changes of that message are made. Indeed, even the slightest idiocy proffered in the insipid garbage constituted by the analytic literature takes the trouble to base itself on a reference to Freud's work, such that, in many cases, if the author were not, in addition, an affiliated member of the institution, one could not find any other mark of analytic qualification in his work.

It is thanks to this—and we must not doubt it, given the conditions of our historical era—that Freud's fundamental concepts have remained unshakable. They owe their value as non-present signifiers to the fact of having remained largely misunderstood.

I think that Freud wanted it to be this way until the day these concepts—whose considerable lead over the other human sciences I have already indicated—could finally be recognized in their ordering, which is flexible but impossible to destroy without detaching them from each other.

This made inevitable both the repression that occurred of the truth they carried and the extraordinary cacophony that currently constitutes the discourses of the deaf to which groups give themselves over in one and the same institution, and to which individuals give themselves over in one and the same group. They do not agree among themselves about the meaning of a single one of the terms that they religiously apply to both the communication and direction of their experience. Their discourses nevertheless harbor those sorts of shameful manifestations of the truth that Freud referred to as the return of the repressed.

A return to Freud, which provides the material for a teaching worthy of the name, can only be produced by the pathway by which the most hidden truth manifests itself in the revolutions of culture. This pathway is the only training that I can claim to transmit to those who follow me. It is called: a style.

Notes

1. Goethe, *Wilhelm Meister* (Hamburg: Christian Wegner Verlag), vol. 2, *Wilhelm Meisters Wanderjahre* [Wilhelm Meister's Travels], I, 2, p. 15.

2. Julia Ward Howe.

459 # The Situation of Psychoanalysis and the Training of Psychoanalysts in 1956

For some . . . and "to others."

We rarely celebrate the hundred-year anniversary of someone's birth. To do so assumes that the work provides a continuation of the man, suggesting his survival. I will have to point to [*dénoncer*] the appearances of this in my twofold subject here.

Being a psychoanalyst myself and having long been confined to practicing analysis, I have seen that the latter can be elucidated by using the terms with which Freud defined it not as precepts but as concepts that are appropriate to these terms.

Being thus engaged as much as possible, and certainly more than I planned, in psychoanalysis' history in action, I will say things here that will only appear daring if one confuses bias with perspective.

My title is also, as I know, such as to put off people whom these things might touch, stopping them from reading on any further. Please excuse this malice: What I have become accustomed to discussing with these terms is the true situation and valid training. Here [on the other hand] it is the real situation and the training actually provided that I would like to account for to a broader audience.

Oh, how universally people would agree if I were to collapse psychoanalysis and training into each other in order to study the situation of the psychoanalyst himself! And how edifying it would be to extend that study to his very lifestyle! I will simply touch on his relation to the world for an instant in order to introduce my topic.

We are aware of the question "How can anyone be a psychoanalyst?"—that still occasionally, when spoken by people of the world, makes us seem like Persians—to which are soon added the words "I wouldn't like to live with a 460
psychoanalyst," the dear pensive woman reassuring us with them of what fate spares us.

This ambiguous reverence is not as far removed as it may seem from the credence, which is no doubt more serious, that science lends us. For although scientists willingly note the relevance of certain facts that are supposed to concern us, it is *from the outside* and with a caveat related to the foreignness of our mental customs that they are willing to allow us.

How could we not but be satisfied with this intellectual segregation, which is the fruit of the distance that we ourselves maintain on the basis of the incommunicability of our experience?

Too bad that such segregation stymies a need for reinforcements, which is all too manifest in that it looks more or less anywhere; one can gauge in our discouraging literature the crumbs with which it contents itself. It will suffice here for me to mention the shudder of ease that went through the ranks of my elders when a disciple of the School,[1] having anointed himself with Pavlovism for the occasion, came to give them his *licet*. The prestige of the conditioned reflex and even of animal neurosis has not ceased since that time to wreak havoc in our reveries . . . Should some of them come to hear about what are known as the "human sciences," they will take to shouting and zealots on the stage conform to the commandments of intelligent figuration.

Assuredly, this gesture—holding out one's hand but never shaking hands—can only have an internal reason, by which I mean that the explanation for it must be sought out in the situation of psychoanalysis rather than of psychoanalysts. For if I have ironically defined psychoanalysis as the treatment one expects from a psychoanalyst, it is nevertheless certainly psychoanalysis that determines the quality of the psychoanalyst.

As I have said, there is in analysis a real situation that can be indicated if we relate the most common cliché that is produced in it—namely, that no new notion has been introduced in psychoanalysis since Freud—to the fact that one is so utterly obliged to resort to the notion of "frustration" as an explanation for everything that it has now become trivial. Yet one would be hard pressed to find the slightest trace of this term in all of Freud's work: for one only finds therein an opportunity to rectify it with the term *Versagung*, which 461
implies renunciation. *Versagung* is thus distinguished from "frustration" by the entire difference between the symbolic and reality [*réel*], a difference which I will assume I can take for granted with my readers. Freud's work can be understood as giving it the weight of a new instance.

It is central here to point out this protruding sign of a diffuse discordance, which is in fact such that since Freud's terms are—so to speak, and we will see that this is not insignificant—left in place, each person designates something different by them when he uses them.

Indeed, there is nothing that better satisfies the requirements of the concept than Freud's terms—in other words, that is more identical to the structure of a relationship, namely, the analytic relationship, and to the thing that is grasped therein, namely, the signifier. This means that these concepts, which are powerfully interrelated, do not correspond to anything that is immediately given to our intuition. Now this is precisely what is substituted for them point for point through an approximation which can only be gross, and which is such that one can compare that approximation to what the idea of force or waves means to someone who has no knowledge of physics.

This is why "transference"—regardless of one's reservations about it and of what each person professes about it—remains, with the sticking power of common consent, identified with a feeling or a constellation of feelings felt by the patient, whereas by simply defining it as the kind of reproduction that occurs in analysis, it becomes clear that the greater part of it must remain unnoticed by the subject.

Similarly, and more insidiously still, "resistance" is associated with the oppositional attitude that the word connotes in its ordinary usage, whereas Freud does not allow for equivocation here, qualifying, as he does, the most accidental events of the subject's life as resistance inasmuch as they pose obstacles to the analysis, if only by obviating his physical presence at his sessions.

Of course, these trivial reminders remain opaque in this form. To know what transference is, one must know what happens in analysis. To know what happens in analysis, one must know where speech comes from. To know what resistance is, one must know what blocks the advent of speech, and it is not some individual disposition, but rather an imaginary interposition which goes
462 beyond the subject's individuality, in that it structures his individualization as specified in the dyadic relation.

Please excuse such an abstract formulation designed to orient our thinking. It merely indicates, thus, like the general formula for gravitation in a text on the history of science, the foundations of our research. One cannot require psychoanalytic popularization to abstain from all such references.

It is not, in fact, that conceptual rigor and developments in technique are lacking in psychoanalytic works. If they remain so sporadic and even inefficient, it is because of a more profound problem that is due to a singular confusion in the precepts of practice.

We know the asystematic attitude that is laid down as the crux of both the so-called fundamental rule of psychoanalysis, which requires the patient not to omit to mention anything that comes to mind—and, in order to do so, to give up all criticism and selection [of what comes to mind]—and of so-called free-floating attention, which Freud expressly recommends to the psychoanalyst as the attitude that simply corresponds to the fundamental rule.

These two precepts, between which the fabric of psychoanalytic experience is, as it were, stretched taut, bring out, it seems, clearly enough the fundamental role of the subject's discourse and of its being listened to [*son écoute*].

This is what psychoanalysts devoted themselves to in the golden age of psychoanalysis, and it bore fruit. It was no accident that the crop they harvested—both from the ravings never before so permitted to roll off the tongue and from the slips never so offered up to an open ear—was so bountiful.

But this very abundance of data, which were sources of knowledge, quickly led them to a knot that they managed to turn into an impasse. Having acquired these data, could they stop themselves from taking their bearings from them in navigating what they heard thereafter? In fact, the problem only arose for them once patients, who soon became just as familiar with this knowledge as they themselves were, served up to them pre-prepared interpretations that it was the analysts' task to provide—which is, it must be admitted, certainly the worst trick one can play on a soothsayer.

No longer believing their two ears, they wanted to find anew the beyond that discourse had, in fact, always had, but they did not know what it was. This is why they invented for themselves a third ear, supposedly designed to perceive that beyond without intermediary. And to designate this immediacy of 463
the transcendent, all the metaphors involving something compact were invoked—affect, lived experience, attitude, discharge, need for love, latent aggressiveness, character armor, and the system of defenses, let us leave aside the magician's shaker and engage in sleight of hand—the recognition of which was no longer accessible henceforth except to this je-ne-sais-quoi of which a clicking of the tongue is the last probation and which introduces into teaching an utterly new requirement: that of the inarticulate.

After that, psychological fancies could be given free rein. This is not the place to write the history of the vagaries of fashion in psychoanalysis. They are hardly noticed by their supporters who are always captivated by the latest one: exhaustion of fantasies, instinctual regression, outwitting of defense, mopping up of anxiety, freeing up of aggression, identification with the analyst's strong ego, imaginary incorporation of his attributes, the dynamic, oh!, the dynamic in which the object-relation is reconstructed, and—according to the most recent echoes, the objective in which a discipline grounded in the subject's history culminates—the *hic et nunc* couple. The latter's twin croaking is ironic not simply because it makes us consult anew the pages of our forgotten Latin, but because it touches on a better brand of humanism by resuscitating the crows we are once again wasting our time gawking at [*les corneilles auxquelles nous revoilà bayant*], no longer having anything but the itchings of our countertransference with which to deduce our auspices from the defiance of their oblique fluttering and the mocking shutter of their winks.

This domain of our erring is not, however, pure smoke and mirrors: Its labyrinth is clearly the one whose thread we were given, but through a fluke this lost thread has dissipated the labyrinth's walls into reflections and—making us skip twenty centuries of mythology in breaking—has changed the corridors of Daedalus into Ariosto's palace in which everything in your beloved or in the rival who defies you is but a lure.

Freud is crystal clear here as he is everywhere else: All his efforts from 1897 to 1914[2] were designed to distinguish between the imaginary and reality [*réel*] in the mechanisms of the unconscious. It is odd that this led psychoanalysts, at two different stages, first to make the imaginary into another reality [*réel*] and then, in our times, to find in the imaginary the norm of reality [*réel*].

464 Of course, the imaginary is not illusion and it gives food for thought. But what allowed Freud to track down the treasure in it, treasure that made his followers rich, is the symbolic determination to which the imaginary function is subordinated and which in Freud's work is always powerfully recalled, whether in discussions of the mechanism of forgetting a word or the structure of fetishism.

By insisting that the analysis of neurosis always be brought back to the knot of the Oedipus complex, it can be said that Freud was precisely aiming to assure the imaginary in its symbolic concatenation, for the symbolic order requires at least three terms, and this forces the analyst not to forget the Other that is present between the two who, since they are there, do not envelop the one who speaks.

But despite what Freud adds to this warning with his theory of the narcissistic mirage, psychoanalysts keep going ever further into the dyadic relation without being struck by the extravagance of the "introjection of the good object," by which they offer themselves up as a new kind of pelican, fortunately in a fantasmatic form, to the appetite of the consumer; nor are they stopped, in their texts celebrating this conception of analysis, by the doubts our nephews will form when wondering about the obscenities proffered by the Obscurantin brothers who found favor and faith in our *novecento*.

In truth, the very notion of preoedipal analysis summarizes the disbanding of the necklace whereby one casts one's swine before pearls. Curiously enough, as the objectives of analysis lose their importance, ritual forms of technique become more highly valued. The coherence of this twofold movement in the new psychoanalysis is sensed by its zealots. And one of them—who, in pages by Michelet where the commode [*chaise percée*] is considered to be the centerpiece of the mores of the seventeenth century, found grist for his mill and material about which to wax strident right up to the no-holds-barred profession that beauty is either scatophagous or is not at all—mustered no less courage when he announced that the conditions in which Freud's final truth was produced were miraculous, and that we must not change one line of them: hence the counting of the minutes that the analyst spends in his seat, to which the subject's unconscious can adjust its habits.

One could have foreseen the results, in which the imaginary, in order to rejoin reality [*réel*], must find the no man's land* that provides access to it by effacing the border between them. Nonspatializing sensoriums indicate them, in which hallucination itself leads to difficulties at its limit. But an inventive 465
emergence always anticipates man's calculations, and it was to everyone's pleasant surprise that a novice once recounted to us, in several modest and unembellished pages that were a great success for him, the elegant solution he had found to a recalcitrant case: "After so many years of analysis, my patient still could not smell me; one day my no-less-patient insistence prevailed: he perceived my odor. The cure lay there."

We would be wrong to steer clear of such audacious moves, since they have their letters patent of nobility. "The Ingenious Dr. Swift" would not withhold his patronage here. By way of proof, consider *The Grand Mystery, or Art of Meditating over an House of Office, Restor'd and Unveil'd*, of which I will cite a passage on pages 5 and 6, not altering anything in it, where he praises the enlightenment one can draw from

> fecal Matter [which] (while the Excrement remains fresh) [provides] an exhalation of like Particles, which ascending through the *Optic* and *Olfactory* Nerves of any Person standing over it, excite by Sympathy, the like Affections in him, and inform him (if first duly instructed, in these profound Mysteries) of all that he can desire to know, concerning the Temper, Thoughts, nay Actions and Fortunes, of the *Author* of the Excrement.

Swift continues, "I hope therefore, it will be no Offence to my Superiors," and we learn on page 10 that these are the "*Doctors* and *Fellows* of the *Royal Society*" who try to make this science a secret,

> that I propose, at the end of this little Treatise, to lodge the supreme Inspection of *Necessary Houses*, in Persons of more Learning and bet-

ter Judgment, than those who are now in possession of that Office. The Dignity of it is evident, [. . .] but it will be in much higher esteem, when occupied by Philosophers and Statesmen, who will be able, from the Taste, Smell, Tincture and Substance of the *issue* of our Body's Natural, to guess at the Constitution of the Body Politic, and to inform and warn the Government of all Plots, design'd Revolutions, and intestine Grumblings of restless and aspiring Men.

It would be vain of me to indulge in the Dean's cynical humor toward the end of his life, if not of his thought. But I would like to recall in passing, in a way that will be perceptible even to olfactory minds, the difference between
466 a naturalist materialism and Freudian materialism; the latter, far from stripping us of our history, assures us of its permanence in its symbolic form, independently of the whims of our assent.

This is not insignificant assuming it suitably represents the traits of the unconscious, which Freud asserted ever more strongly instead of softening them. Then why avoid the questions that the unconscious raises?

If so-called free association gives us access to the unconscious, is it through a liberation that can be compared to a liberation from neurological automatisms?

If the drives that are discovered there are located at the diencephalic level, or even at the rhinencephalic level, how can we understand the fact that they are structured in terms of language?

For while their effects made themselves known in language from the outset, their ruses, which we have since learned to recognize, nonetheless denote a linguistic procedure, in both their triviality and their finesse.

The drives, which in dreams are acted out in almanac-type puns, also exude an air of *Witz* which touches even the most naive readers of the *Traumdeutung* [*The Interpretation of Dreams*]. For they are the same drives whose presence separates witticisms from comedy, asserting themselves in them in a loftier alterity [*altière altérité*].[3]

But defense itself, whose negation suffices to indicate unconscious ambiguity, makes use of forms that are no less rhetorical. Its modes are hard to conceptualize without resorting to the tropes and figures, those of speech or words that are as true as in Quintilian,[4] and which run the gamut from accismus and metonymy to catachresis and antiphrasis, and on to hypallage and even understatement (recognizable in what Fenichel describes); the more the defense seems to us to be unconscious, the clearer this is.

This obliges us to conclude that there is no stylistic form, however elabo-
467 rate (and the unconscious abounds in such forms)—not excepting erudite, con-

cettist, and precious forms—that is disdained by the unconscious, any more than by the author of these lines: the Gongora of psychoanalysis, as people call him, at your service.

Should this be such as to discourage us from rediscovering the unconscious in the peristalsis of a dog, however "Pavlovized" we may assume it to be, it is not designed to require analysts to immerse themselves in macaronic poetry or lessons in tablature for the courtly arts, even though it would make their debates far more pleasant. Still we could require them to be trained in a linguistic problematic, enough to allow them to distinguish symbolism from natural analogy, with which they habitually confuse it.

Such training would cover the distinction between the signifier and the signified, rightly credited to Ferdinand de Saussure, because it is thanks to his teaching that it is now included in the foundations of the human sciences. Let us simply note that, apart from precursors like Baudouin de Courtenay, this distinction was perfectly clear to the ancients, and was attested to in the works of Quintilian and St. Augustine.

In their texts, the primacy of the signifier over the signified already seems inescapable in any discourse on language, even if this idea is so utterly disconcerting that it has not been braved by linguists in our own times.

Only psychoanalysis is capable of *forcing* us to recognize this primacy in *our thinking*, by demonstrating that the signifier does without any cogitation, even the least reflexive, in creating indubitable groupings in the significations that enslave the subject and, furthermore, in manifesting itself in him in this alienating intrusion through which the notion of "symptom" in analysis takes on an emergent meaning: the meaning of the signifier that connotes the subject's relation to the signifier.

Thus I will say that Freud's discovery is the truth that the truth never loses its rights, and that, although it may hide its claims even in the domain destined to the immediacy of instincts, its register alone allows us to conceptualize the inextinguishable duration of desire, a feature of the unconscious which is hardly the least paradoxical, even though Freud never gives it up.

But in order to obviate any misunderstanding, let me make it clear that this register of truth must be followed *to the letter* [à la lettre]; in other words, symbolic determination, which Freud calls overdetermination, must be consid- 468
ered first as a product of syntax, if one wishes to grasp its analogical effects. For these effects occur from the text to meaning, rather than imposing their meaning on the text. This can be seen in the truly senseless desires that are the least twisted of these effects.

Combinatory logic gives us the most radical form of this symbolic determination, and we must learn how to give up the naive requirement that would have us locate its origin in the vicissitudes of the cerebral organization that occasionally reflects it.

This is a healthy rectification, however offensive it may be to psychological bias. And to defend it, it does not seem excessive to recall all the loci in which the symbolic order finds its vehicle, were it only in the peopled silence of the universe that has arisen from physics. Human industry, which the symbolic order determines far more than it serves, exists not merely to preserve it but already visibly extends it beyond that part of it that man masters; and the two kilos of language whose presence I can point to here on the table seem less inert when we find them carried on the crisscrossing airwaves of our broadcasts—to open the very ears of the deaf to the truth that Rabelais was able to encompass in his apologue of the frozen words.

A psychoanalyst should find assurance in the obvious fact that man is, prior to his birth and beyond his death, caught up in the symbolic chain, a chain that founded his lineage before his history was embroidered upon it. He must work at the idea that it is in his very being—in his "total personality," as it is comically put—that man is in fact considered to be a whole, but like a pawn, in the play of the signifier, and this is so even before its rules are transmitted to him, insofar as he ends up discovering them; this order of priorities must be understood as a logical order, that is, as forever current.

No prehistory allows us to efface the cut brought about by the heteronomy of the symbolic. On the contrary, everything it gives us merely deepens the cut: tools whose serial form directs our attention more toward the ritual of their fabrication than toward the uses to which they were put; piles that show nothing other than the symbol anticipating the symbolic's entry into the world; and graves which, beyond any explanation that we can dream up for them, are edifices unknown to nature.

469 The fact that the symbolic is located outside of man is the very notion of the unconscious. And Freud constantly proved that he stuck to it as if it were the very crux of his experience.

This is witnessed by the point at which he made a clean break with Jung, in other words, when the latter published his *Study of the Transformations and Symbolisms of the Libido*. For the archetype makes the symbol into the blossoming of the soul, and that is that; the fact that the unconscious may be both individual and collective had little importance to the man who, explicitly in his *Moses and Monotheism*, and implicitly in his *Totem and Taboo*, admits that a forgotten drama comes down through the ages in the unconscious. But what we must say, following Aristotle's lead, is that it is not the soul that speaks but man who speaks with his soul, on the condition that we add that he receives the language he speaks and that, in order to bear it, he sinks more into it than his soul: he sinks into it his very instincts whose ground resonates in the depths only to throw back the signifier's echo. And when this echo comes back to the surface, the speaker marvels at it and raises up the praise of eternal romanticism. "*Spricht die Seele, so spricht* . . ." "The soul speaks, listen to it . . ." "*ach! schon die Seele nicht mehr* . . ."[5] You can listen to it; the illusion will not last long. You can ask Ernest Jones about it instead, one of the rare disciples who attempted to articulate something about symbolism that held water: he will tell you the fate of the special Commission instituted to give body to his study at the 1910 Congress.[6]

If, moreover, we consider Freud's enduring preference for his *Totem and Taboo* and the fact that he obstinately opposed every attempt to relativize the killing of the father, which he considered to be the inaugural drama of humanity, we can see that what he maintained thereby was the primordial nature of the signifier that is represented by paternity beyond the attributes that it accumulates, the link of generation being but one part of it. Its import as a signifier appears unequivocally in the assertion produced in this way that the true father—that is, the symbolic father—is the dead father. And the connection between paternity and death, which Freud explicitly highlights in many case discussions, allows us to see from whence this signifier garners its primordial rank.

Hammering away like this in order to reestablish a perspective will not, 470
however, give the psychoanalyst the mental means with which to operate in the field this perspective delimits. Of course, it is not a question of mental level, but rather of the fact that the symbolic order can be approached only through its own apparatus. Just as you cannot do algebra without knowing how to write, you cannot handle or parry even the slightest signifying effect without at least suspecting what is implied by writing.

Must it be the case that the views of those that the *Traumdeutung*[7] led to analysis were so short-sighted, or that the hair on the Medusa's head that it presented to them was too long? What is this new interpretation of dreams if not an attempt to redirect the oneiromancer to the sole but irrefutable foundation of all mantic—namely, the battery of its material? I do not mean the matter of the said battery, but rather its ordinal finity. Sticks thrown on the ground or the illustrious swords of the Tarot, the simple game of odds or evens or the supreme kouas of the *I Ching*—in you every possible fate, every conceivable debt, can be summarized, for nothing in you is worthwhile except the combinatory in which the giant of language takes on anew his stature by being suddenly delivered from the Gulliverian bonds of signification. If dreams are still more suitable to it, it is because the elaboration produced by your games is at work in their development: "Only the dream's elaboration interests us,"

Freud says, and again, "A dream is a rebus." What would he have had to add so that we would stop expecting dreams to deliver up the words of the soul? Have the sentences of a rebus ever had the slightest meaning, and does its interest—that is, the interest we take in its deciphering—not derive from the fact that the signification manifest in its images falls away, having no other scope than that of conveying the signifier that is disguised in it?

This would even warrant that I shed psychoanalysis' reflected light back onto the sources that have illuminated my discussion here, by inciting linguists to strike from their papers the illusory locution which makes them speak, pleonastically moreover, of "ideographic" writing. Writing, like dreams, can be figurative, but, like language, it is always symbolically articulated—namely, just like language, it is phonemic, and indeed phonetic as soon as it is read.

Will, lastly, slips of the tongue, when they are stripped bare, make us grasp
471 what is meant by the fact that they allow themselves to be summed up in the following formulation: that in slips discourse manages to overcome feigned significations?

Will we manage thereby to rip the soothsayer away from his desire for entrails and bring him back to the goal of free-floating attention? Even after analysts have spent some fifty million hours finding both their ease and disease in it, it seems that no one has wondered what free-floating attention is.

For although Freud proposed this sort of attention as the counterpart[8] (*Gegenstück*) of free association, the term "free-floating" does not imply fluctuation, but rather evenness of level—this is emphasized by the German term, "*gleichschwebende*."

Let us note, moreover, that the third ear, which I used to deny the existence of the uncertain beyonds of an occult sense, is nevertheless in fact the invention of an author, Theodor Reik, who is rather sensible in his tendency to adapt himself to a realm that is shy of speech.

But what need can an analyst have for an extra ear, when it sometimes seems that two are already too many, since he runs headlong into the fundamental misunderstanding brought on by the relationship of understanding? I repeatedly tell my students: "Don't try to understand!" and leave this nauseating category to Karl Jaspers and his consorts. May one of your ears become as deaf as the other one must be acute. And that is the one that you should lend to listen for sounds and phonemes, words, locutions, and sentences, not forgetting pauses, scansions, cuts, periods, and parallelisms, for it is in these that the word-for-word transcription can be prepared, without which analytic intuition has no basis or object.

It is in this way that the speech that offers itself up to your agreement—as the commonplace belief would have it and with an obviousness that is as fallacious as its truth is attractive, delivering itself up only at a second moment in the following form, "the number two rejoices in being odd" (and it is quite right to rejoice in it, but it can be faulted for not being able to say why)[9]—finds at the unconscious level its most signifying import, purified of its equivocations, when it is translated as: "the two numbers that have no equal are waiting for Godot." 472

I think I have gotten my point across, and it should be clear that the interest I am showing here in mantic is not designed to approve of the fortune-teller style that sets the tone in the theory of instincts.

On the contrary, the study of symbolic determination would allow us to reduce, if not simultaneously isolate, what psychoanalytic experience provides in the way of positive data: and this is not insignificant.

The theory of narcissism and that of the ego, in the way in which Freud oriented the latter in his second topography, are data that extend the most modern research in natural ethology (under the very heading of the theory of instincts).

But even their solidarity, in which they are grounded, is misrecognized, and the theory of the ego is no longer anything but an enormous error: a return to what intuitive psychology itself rejected.

For the lack of theoretical sophistication that I am pointing to in analytic doctrine brings us to the chink in our teaching—which reciprocally corresponds to that lack of theoretical sophistication—namely, to the second topic of my talk to which I shifted a moment ago.

Because psychoanalytic technique concerns the subject's relation to the signifier, the knowledge it has conquered can only be situated as organized [*s'ordonner*] around that.

This gives it its place in the grouping that is asserting itself as the order of the conjectural sciences.

For conjecture is not the improbable: strategy can order it into certainty. Similarly, the subjective is not the value of feeling with which it is often confused: the laws of intersubjectivity are mathematical.

It is in this order that the notions of structure are edified, failing which the view from the inside of the neuroses and the attempt to deal with the psychoses remain fruitless.

The perspective of such research requires training that reserves a very substantial role for language. This is what Freud expressly formulated in his program for an ideal Institute. After what I have been saying here, one should not be surprised that this program includes the whole set of philological studies.[10] 473

Here, as earlier, we can begin with a brutal contrast, by noting that nothing in any of the Institutes affiliated with his name has ever even been sketched out in this direction.

Since our agenda here is to discuss Freud's legacy, let me turn to what has become of it in the present state of affairs.

History shows us the concern that guided Freud in organizing the IPA, or International Psychoanalytical Association, especially starting in 1912, as he supported the form of authority that was to prevail in it, when, in spelling out the details of the institutions, he determined how powers would be exercised and transmitted. It was the concern, which is clearly avowed in his correspondence, to ensure that his thought would be maintained in its completeness when he himself would no longer be there to defend it. Jung's defection, which was more painful to Freud than all the others it followed, posed an anxiety-provoking problem related to such maintenance. In order to deal with it, Freud accepted what was offered to him at that moment: namely, the idea, which came to a sort of young guard who aspired to veteran status, of overseeing the said maintenance of Freud's thought at the heart of the IPA not only through a secret solidarity but through an unknown action.

The *carte blanche* that Freud granted this project,[11] and the security he found
474 in it that calmed him,[12] are attested to in documents by his biographer, himself the last survivor of this secret Committee called the Committee of the Seven Rings, whose existence had been announced by the late Hanns Sachs. Their theoretical import and their actual consequences cannot be veiled by the amused qualification of romanticism[13] with which Freud sweetens the pill of one of these consequences, and the striking incident that Jones rushes to pin on the others, namely, the letter written behind Jones' back to Freud by Ferenczi, which read as follows: Jones, not being Jewish, will never be liberated enough to be sure in this game; "you must keep Jones constantly under your eye and cut off his line of retreat."[14]

The secret history of the IPA has not been written nor should it be. Its effects are of no interest to those who are in on history's secret. And history's secret must not be confused with the conflicts, violence, and aberrations that constitute its fable. The question that Freud raised, whether analysts as a whole live up to the standard of normality that they demand of their patients, is regularly cited in this context and gives analysts an opportunity to show their bravery. It is surprising that the authors of these jibes do not see the ruse in it themselves: anecdote, here as elsewhere, dissimulates structure.

The clearest characteristics of [the IPA's] structure are the very ones that make it invisible, and not only to those who are immersed in it: This is true of the initiation which marks one's access to it, and which, being in our time "rather unique," as they say, is actually flaunted; it is also true of the "Cominternism" whose features are shown by its internal style and whose more ordinary prestige is not disavowed there.

And the steering wheel, which is more or less weighed down with worldly goods that determine its direction, is a fact of reality which does not in itself have to find a remedy; only the spiritual extraterritoriality it embodies deserves sanction. The paradox of the idea that came to me on this point is better kept until later.[15]

Given my aim, we must begin with the remark, which has never before been made, to the best of my knowledge, that Freud started the IPA along its path ten years before he became interested, as we see in *Group Psychology and the Analysis of the* Ego, in the mechanisms that make an organic group, such 475
as the Church or the army, like a crowd. The clear partiality of his exploration there is justified by his fundamental discovery of the identification of each individual's ego with the same ideal image, the mirage of which is borne by the personality of the leader. A sensational discovery, which slightly anticipated the fascistic organizations that rendered it obvious.

Had he become attentive to these effects earlier on,[16] Freud would no doubt have wondered about the field left to the dominance of the function of the boss*, in an organization which, in order to sustain his very speech, certainly could, as in the models he studied, strike a balance by resorting to a symbolic link—that is, to a tradition and a discipline—but not in the same manner, since the objective of tradition and discipline in psychoanalysis is to call into question their very crux, along with man's relation to speech.

Indeed, what is at stake here is nothing less than the problem of the ego's relations to truth. For this effect of imaginary identification (by which can be gauged, in passing, the distance at which the outmoded usages remain from it in which the notion of the ego is debased in psychoanalysis) boils down to the structure of the ego in its greatest generality. Here Freud provides us with the positive mainspring of the moment of consciousness whose dialectical structure Hegel deduced as a phenomenon of infatuation.

This is why I will give the name "Sufficiency" [*Suffisance*] to the sole [*unique*] rank in the psychoanalytic hierarchy. For, as opposed to what a foolish people imagines on the basis of appearances, this hierarchy has only one rank and it is in this respect that it can legitimately call itself democratic—at least if we refer to the meaning this term took on in Antiquity's city states, in which democracy included only the masters.

Sufficiency thus is in itself beyond all proof. It need not suffice for anything since it suffices unto itself.

In order to be passed on—and not having at its disposal the law of blood that implies generation or the law of adoption that presupposes marriage—it

has at its disposal only the pathway of imaginary reproduction which, through
476 a form of facsimile analogous to printing, allows it to print, as it were, a certain number of copies whereby the one [*unique*] becomes plural.

This form of multiplication finds favorable affinities in this situation. For let us not forget that entry into the community of analysts is subjected to the condition of undergoing a training analysis; and there surely must be some reason why the theory of the end of analysis as identification with the analyst's ego first saw the light of day in the circle of training analysts.

But once the Sufficiencies have constituted an analytic Society, and new members are chosen through nomination by the existing members, the notion of class forces itself upon us; it can only appear in the class from which their choice of new members is made by defining it in opposition to their own class.

The opposition of insufficiency, which is suggested by a pure formalism, is dialectically untenable. The slightest taking on [*assomption*] of sufficiency ejects insufficiency from its field, but the thought of insufficiency as a category of being thus radically excludes Sufficiency from all the others. It is the one *or* the other, incompatibly.

We need a category that, while not implying a lack of dignity, indicates that its place is outside of sufficiency, and that one becomes qualified to occupy it by staying there. The name "Little Shoes," for those who situate themselves there, thus seems appropriate to me; for, apart from the fact that it provides enough of an image so that one can distinguish them easily in an assembly, it defines them by this very staying: they are always in their little shoes and they manifest a sufficiency veiled in its opposition to Sufficiency in the very fact that they make do with this.

There nevertheless remains a hiatus between the position thus designated and Sufficiency that no transition can fill. And the rank that simulates it in the hierarchy is nothing but trompe l'oeil there.

For however little we think about it, we will see that there are not lesser or greater degrees of Sufficiency. Either one suffices or one does not; this is already true when it is a question of sufficing for this or that, but is even truer when one must suffice for sufficiency. Thus Sufficiency cannot be attained, either *de facto* or *de jure*, without one having already attained it. But one must nevertheless get there, and that itself supplies us with the intermediate category.

477 Yet it is a category that remains empty. Indeed, it cannot be filled but merely inhabited: it is a station in which one sometimes does what one has to, and about which one can even say that on the whole one does what needs to be done—but these very locutions betray the irreducible limit to which one's approach to it is doomed. I will label this approximation by calling those who occupy it, not the necessary, but the "Truly Necessary" [*Bien-Nécessaires*].

What is the purpose of the Truly Necessary in the organization? To highlight the use of speech, about which, as you can see, I have not yet spoken. Indeed, I have thus far left aside the paradox—which is difficult to understand in a community whose responsibility it is to maintain a certain discourse—that in the community's core classes, including Sufficiencies and Little Shoes, silence is the true master and its temple rests on two taciturn columns.

What could the Little Shoes in fact say? Ask questions? They do not ask them for three reasons, two of which they are aware of.

The first reason is that they are in analysis and a good analysand [*analysé*] does not ask questions—a formulation which must be understood at the same preemptory level at which the proverb "a penny saved is a penny earned" ends the reply to a demand for an accounting considered to be importunate in a famous pastiche by Claudel.

The second reason is that it is strictly impossible to pose a sensible question in the language that has currency in this community, and one would have to have the shamelessness of the Huron or the monstrous gumption of the child to whom the Emperor is naked to point this out; this would, nevertheless, be the only way to open things up for discussion there.

The Little Shoes are unaware of the third reason, under ordinary conditions, and I will only present it at the end of my paper.

Of what use could it be to the Sufficiencies to speak? Sufficing unto themselves, they have nothing to say to each other, and faced with the silence of the Little Shoes, they have no one to answer.

This is why it is left to the Truly Necessary to lodge an appeal against this silence by filling it with their discourse. They do not fail to do so, still less because virtually nothing can impede this discourse once it is set in motion.
Freed, as I have said, from its own logic, what is found there does not shock 478
anyone, what is encountered does not offend anyone, and what is excluded is not done so conclusively. "Yes" has a compatibility with "no" there which is not that of balance but of superfluousness. We might as well say that the two go hand in hand, or, on the other hand, since that goes without saying, we might as well not say it.

This dialectic is of the same ilk as the prose by the would-be gentleman—it is a dialectic unknown to itself—but it answers to an aspiration, that of the prestidigitator who becomes worried when he is applauded for having pulled a rabbit out of his hat, for he himself was surprised to find the rabbit in it. He wonders *why* [*pourquoi*] he succeeded in his trick, and, looking for the answer in the possible reasons that could be given for the rabbit's presence, he finds them equally worthy explanations and lets them all stand, in an indifference born of the presentiment he has that they do not get at what concerns him, which is to determine *in what way* [*en quoi*] his trick was successful.

Thus the Truly Necessary discourse does not suffice to render questions superfluous, but proves to be superfluous in being sufficient for the task.

The superfluousness that translates this [station] shy of sufficiency cannot go to the crux of its chink if Sufficiency itself does not answer it with the superfluousness of its excess.

This is the function of the members of the organization whom I will call "Beatitudes," borrowing this name from the Stoic and Epicurean sects that, as we know, strove to attain the satisfaction of sufficiency.

The Beatitudes are the spokesmen for the Sufficiencies, and this very delegation of power suggests that it is important for us to reconsider the silence of the Sufficiencies, having considered we were done with them a bit hastily.

The Sufficiencies, as I said without insisting, have nothing to say to each other. This is worth explaining.

The ideal of sufficiency, in associations that are commanded by this ideal, hardly encourages speech, but it imposes on them a constraint [*sujétion*] whose effects are uniform.[17] Contrary to what people imagine, in collective identification it is by an individual thread that subjects are informed; this information is shared only because it comes from the same source. Freud emphasized
479 that what is at stake is the identity that narcissistic idealization carries in itself, and allows us thus to complete the image that serves the function of the object there with a schematic trait.

But one can foresee the kind of relations on which such a group will rest in the effects produced by narcissistic identification in couples, whether fraternal jealousy or conjugal acrimony. Regarding the conquest of power, ample use has been made of the *Schadenfreude* garnered by the oppressed party through identification with the *Führer*. In a quest for knowledge, a certain refusal on the scale of being, beyond the object, is the feeling that most solidly ties the troop together: this feeling is knowledge in a pathetic form; people commune in it without communicating, and it is called hatred.

Of course, a "good object," as they put it, can be promoted to such subjection functions, but this image, which makes dogs faithful, makes men tyrannical—for it is Eros, whose true face Plato showed in the phasmid that extends its wings over the destroyed polis, by which the hounded soul is panic-stricken.

To bring this talk back to its present proportions, I will take the hand that Valéry holds out to Freud when, speaking of these "uniques" who people what he calls the "delusional professions,"[18] Valéry spins a metaphor of two electrons whose edifying music he hears buzzing in the atom of their unicity: the one who sings, "There is only me, me, me," and the other who shouts, "But there is this one, that one . . . and this Other too." For, as the author adds, "the name changes often enough."

This is why the "number ones"* that proliferate here turn out, to an expert gaze, to be so many number twos.

Which is to say that the trap [*godant*] they fall into as such, the strangeness of which I mentioned earlier, is carried to a degree of exultation here which is not rendered any more convincing just because it is general, but which will perhaps be clarified by its repercussion.

Where will the fact that the number two rejoices in being odd lead it in this 480
meeting [*réunion*]—that we can legitimately arrange in a single [*unique*] row on the sole condition of connecting each of them in single file to the one that precedes it?

It is plain to see that the number three must descend like God from the machine in order to engender the alternation that will give birth to the odd, before the latter can exercise its seductive powers on the number two.

This remark already indicates the crux of the matter, but we will see it more clearly in a developed form.

In the series thus constituted, we can in fact say that an odd place is occupied by half of the number twos, but since the series has no head, closing on itself instead like a crown, nothing and no one can designate which half it is. Thus the number twos, every man for himself and God for us all, can rightfully claim to be odd, although everyone is sure that half of them cannot be odd. But is this necessarily true? No, it is not, for if half *plus one* of the number twos can say they are of odd rank, that suffices for, having gone too far, there to be no more limits, and for all the number twos, no matter which one we use to begin the series, to be indisputably caught in the counted odd [*impair dénombré*].

Here we see the function of the "One Extra" [*Un En Plus*], but we also see that it must be "Just a One" [*Un Sans Plus*], for every "One More" [*Un Encore*] would be "One Too Many" [*Un De Trop*], making all the number twos fall back into a presumption that remains without remission, it being known to be irremediable.

This One Extra was already in the number three, as a preliminary condition of the series in which it got us to see it more clearly. And this demonstrates that the joy of Sufficiency's number two requires that its duality exceed itself in this One Extra, and that Beatitude, being the excess of Sufficiency, thus has its place outside of it.

But this One Extra that each of the Beatitudes thus is, only being able to be Just a One, is doomed by its position to monologue. And that is why, unlike the Sufficiencies who have nothing to say to each other, the Beatitudes *speak to each other*, but not in order to say more about it to each other.

For this One Extra, with which the number three joins [*se réunit*], is assuredly the mediation of Speech, but by maintaining itself in the Other from
481 which it should detach itself in order to return to the Same, it does not form in its mouth anything but this form which trumpets: the O of an Oracle, that only the appetite of the Truly Necessary can eat away at so as to make of it the U of a Verdict.

But the two superfluities that are conjugated here—by the connivance of the chink in the Inconsistent Discourse with the excess of the Unexplained Discourse—still do not correspond to each other. No more than can as many marbles as one might posit make a strainer that is apt for serving soup.

This is why analytic teaching has been able to retain almost nothing in its sieve of the enormous quantity of experience that has traversed psychoanalysis (for here we cannot say that people have gotten nothing out of its milk billy goat).[19] An observation that anyone who knows anything about analysis will agree with, deep down inside, even if he feels the need, when confronted with my diatribe, to seek the refuge taken by one of those natures whose spinelessness teaches and leads him in equal measures, when in my company he came out one day with the following conclusion: "There is no field in which one *exposes oneself* more totally than in speaking about psychoanalysis."

Such is the organization that constrains Speech to wind its way between two walls of silence, in order to conclude a marriage between confusion and arbitrariness. Speech adapts to this for reasons of advancement: the Sufficiencies regulate the entrance of the Little Shoes into their periphery, and the Beatitudes tell them which of the Little Shoes will become the Truly Necessary; conversely, it is by addressing the Beatitudes that the Truly Necessary will arrive at Sufficiency, and the Sufficiencies respond to them by drawing new Beatitudes from their bosom.

An attentive observer here would count all the forms of indirect fire or of this type of winding one's way known as zigzagging, I might as well say those that provoke the assailant to act invisible.

This is the flaw in the system as a means of selecting subjects, and people should not be surprised that this flaw, when combined with the muzzle it
482 imposes on speech, leads to a few paradoxical results, only two of which I will mention, the one having a permanent effect, the other being based on singular cases.

1. The fact that the curriculum imposed in the lecture courses essentially covers what I call "fictional matters," there being nothing positive taught there but medicine, which is superfluous since it covers the same ground as the public medical schools do—indeed, the fact that it is tolerated warrants admiration.

2. The fact that, since a policy of tenacious silence has to find its way toward Beatitude, illiteracy in its congenital state actually has some chance of succeeding.[20]

But we must still indicate what the conjunction of these two effects can produce in this case, for we will see in it the way in which this system, by limiting itself to this, finds a way to gain strength from it.

It so happened that a Beatitude of type 2 believed he was required by circumstances to prove himself in a teaching of type 1, the promotion to which should have been a great boon to him.

And a fine mess it was, indeed. Certain people clamored for a license to teach, meaning a degree in psychology, the exam for which the Beatitude in question could not have passed, according to them.

But those who were better informed were able to learn something from the great lesson that was thus offered up to them, in which they could suddenly read the supreme Law, an unwritten Law, on which the association was founded—a Law by which each of us finds in his heart his intellectual base and usual morals already laid down, a Law that the long-term observation to which he has been subjected should have, above all, shown he is apt for, a Law whose simple and sure commandment he will hear in himself at grave moments: one must not bother the Beatitudes.

This is the reason—which the Little Shoes are unaware of, even though they have a presentiment of it—for their own silence, and a new generation, having seen the veil ripped away, left the place all the stronger for it, and they rallied around the person who had revealed that reason to them.

But, in all of that, who thinks about the fate of the Beatitudes themselves? 483
Can we imagine the disgrace of a solitary Beatitude when he realizes that, whereas the remarks of the Truly Necessary are mostly superfluous, those of the Truly Fortunate [*Bienheureux*] are usually unfortunate . . . and what his Beatific Solitude can, in this misfortune, become? Will his just barely achieved Sufficiency whisper in his ear that it itself is nothing but a Necessary Evil?

Oh! May the Little Shoes be spared this anxiety! At least, let them be prepared for these dangers. But people do prepare them. As a Beatitude myself, for years I have, in the ceremony referred to as the Second Little Tour, heard from the very lips of the Little Shoes how much good their personal analysis did them; I will indicate here the most frequent, major benefit they mentioned in the homage they paid their training analyst—it can be summarized in one word: disintellectualization.

Oh! How these dear children finally felt free, almost all of whom attributed their decision to study psychiatry to the endless torments of that accursed year which the academic course of French studies inflicts upon you in the company of ideas! No, that was not, as they now knew, what had guided them: What a relief and what a boon to be free of it at so little cost, for once this mistake was cleared up and replaced with the conviction that this damned intellectualism was, in fact, a kind of pruritus, how straight the pathway finally seemed, how easily thought found its way towards nature—aren't our gut feelings designed to assure us of this?

This is what allows a good analytic student of this type to be distinguished at first glance by anyone who has seen one even just once before: by the inner and even posterior air that makes him look as if he were leaning on the macerated fetus of his resistances.

Disintellectualization—this word does not indicate that anyone becomes stupid for all that: unlike ordinary fears and even hopes, analysis is truly incapable of changing anything in this department.

The study of intelligence, the level of which behaviorist psychology thought it could superimpose onto the measure of what the animal knows how to encompass in detour behavior, has often seemed to me capable of improve-
484 ment, at least for man, through a broader reference—namely, through what I would call trace behavior.

I have always been struck, while taking my little dog for a walk so he could attend to his needs, by what we could glean from his activities that would help us analyze the capacities that make for man's success in society, as well as the virtues that Antiquity's thinkers meditated upon under the heading of Means-to-an-End [*Moyen-de-Parvenir*]. I hope that this digression will, at the very least, dispel the misunderstanding I may have given rise to in certain people's minds: the misunderstanding of attributing to me the doctrine of a discontinuity between animal psychology and human psychology, which is truly foreign to my way of thinking.

I simply wanted to maintain that, in order to correctly work on what psychoanalysis classifies in mankind as symptoms—which, being so directly involved in his destiny, not to mention his vocation, seem to fall with these latter under the same heading, that of language—it is preferable, no doubt, not to remain completely illiterate. More modestly stated, the possible risk of making a mistake should not prevent us from making an effort to become literate.

But other needs no doubt take precedence over this, and the burden borne by the Beatitudes, like that borne by the white man, cannot be within a single man's purview.

I heard it, and everyone could have heard it, from the lips of a Sufficiency at a fertile moment of the psychoanalytic institution in France: "We want there to be," this mouth declared, "a hundred mediocre psychoanalysts." He was not affirming in this statement the modesty of a program, but rather the ambitious demand for the qualitative change that Marx's formidable thinking forever showed to be rooted in quantitative change.

And the statistics published to date show that the undertaking, superbly[21] overcoming all obstacles, is in the process of achieving a success in which it exceeds its own standards.

Assuredly, we are still far from what is achieved in other countries, the 13 two-columned quarto pages that barely suffice to list the analysts in the Amer- 485
ican Psychoanalytic Association dwarfing the scant two and a half pages on which the French and British practitioners fit.

The German Diaspora must bear much of the responsibility for this, having given America the highest executives of Beatitude; and we must realize what is represented by the responsibility it takes for all these "dentists," to borrow the term used by these supreme Beatitudes to designate the rank and file*, a term which is imbued with the traditional affectionate paternalism.

It is not difficult to understand why it was among these Beatitudes that the theory of the "autonomous ego" first appeared.[22] How could we but admire the strength of those who initiated the grand project of disintellectualization, which, extending little by little, represents one of the most fertile challenges* by which a civilization can assert its strength, those challenges that it forges within itself? However do they find the time to oversee the project, when all year long they devote themselves to humbling the strong egos and raising up the weak egos [*mois*]?—no doubt during the months [*mois*] that do not include an r.

Assuredly, a civilized state will, in the long run, find something to criticize in the fact that the prebends, on the scale of the considerable investments mobilized by such a community, are left to the discretion of a spiritual power whose odd extraterritoriality I have noted.

But the solution would be easy to find: a small territory, on the scale of philatelic States (Ellis Island, to give a concrete idea), could be ceded by the U.S. Congress—through a vote by the states most involved in this business—to the IPA so that the latter could locate its departments there, including its Congregations of the Index, Missions, and Propaganda; the situation would be better defined, diplomatically speaking, because the decrees that the IPA would hand down to the entire world would be dated and promulgated from this territory; one would clearly know, moreover, whether the function of the autonomous ego is, for example, an article of the ecumenical doctrine's symbolism or simply an article to be given to the Little Shoes for Christmas.

Let me stop here in order to end on an energizing note. Since I was not 486
afraid to show the forces of dissociation to which Freud's heritage is being

subjected, let me point out the remarkable persistence the psychoanalytic institution has demonstrated.

I will deserve little credit for doing so since nowhere else have I found greater confirmation of the virtue that I grant to the pure signifier. For in the use that is made in the psychoanalytic institution of Freud's concepts, how can we fail to see that their signification is in no way taken into account? And yet it is to nothing but their presence that one can attribute the fact that the association has not yet fallen apart and been dispersed into the confusion of Babel.

Thus the coherence maintained in this large body reminds me of the odd imaginings that Poe's genius proposes to us in the extraordinary story of "The Facts in the Case of M. Valdemar."

It is the story of a man who passes away, but since he was under hypnosis during his death throes, his cadaver remains intact, due to the action of the hypnotizer, in a state involving not only an apparent immunity to physical dissolution but also the ability to attest in speech to his atrocious condition.

This is how the association created by Freud metaphorically lives on in its collective being, but here it is a voice that sustains it, the voice of a dead man.

Of course, Freud went so far as to make us recognize the Eros by which life finds a way to prolong its jouissance in the reprieve of its rotting.

In such a case, however, the operation of waking that association up—using the Master's words in a return to life of his Speech—can be confused with the care involved in providing a decent burial.

Pommersfelden-Guitrancourt, September–October 1956

Notes

1. I mean a Thomist.

2. From the letter to Fliess dated September 21, 1897, to the writing of the "Wolf Man" case (see the introductory note to the case history).

3. It should be understood that this is not an *aria di bravura*, but a remark about technique that the reading of Freud's *Witz* makes accessible to one and all. It is true that few psychoanalysts read this book, a fact that I am no longer keeping quiet about after one of the most dignified among them admitted to me as a simple lacuna that he had never opened Freud's *Psychopathology of Everyday Life*.

4. *Sententiarum aut verborum*. See Quintilian, *Institutio Oratoria*, Book IX, Chapters 2 and 3. [The Loeb Classical Library, *Quintilian* III, trans. H. E. Butler (Cambridge, MA: Harvard University Press, 1955)].

5. This is the second verse of Schiller's famous distich, the first verse of which questions as follows, "Warum kann der lebendige Geist dem Geist nicht erscheinen?," to which the second verse is the response. The title of this distich is "Sprache."

6. See Ernest Jones, *Sigmund Freud: Life and Work* (New York: Basic Books, 1955), vol. II, 76.

7. This is known in French as *The Science of Dreams* [in English as *The Interpretation of Dreams*], which Freud designated as his capital work.

8. And not the "pendant," as it is expressed

in a translation that the upper part of an ideal clock no doubt inspired.

9. "Dic cur hic" (the other School)," the epigraph of a *Traité de la contingence* ("Treatise on Contingency") which came out in 1895 (Paris: Librairie de l'Art Indépendant), in which the dialectic of this example is discussed (page 41). It was written by a young man named André Gide and we can only regret that he was diverted so early on from logical problems at which this essay shows him to be so adept. The nonsense* about which I'm speculating here in his footsteps, takes up, if it must be recalled to mind, the burlesque translation given to school children of the Latin phrase: *numero Deus impare gaudet*.

10. See Freud, *GW* XIV, 281 and 283 ["The Question of Lay Analysis," *SE* XX, 246 and 248].

11. In effect, it was from Freud that the actions of the "Committee" received their character and their orders. "This committee would have to be *strictly secret* [italicized in the text provided by Jones] *in its existence and its action* [italicized by me]." From the letter by Freud to Jones dated August 1, 1912, which was to be followed by a trip Freud was to make to London to lay the groundwork of this "plan" with Jones, Ferenczi, and Rank; in Ernest Jones, *Sigmund Freud, Life and Work*, II, 153.

12. "The secret of this Committee is that it has taken from me my most burdensome care for the future, so that I can calmly follow my path to the end," and "Since then I have felt more light-hearted and carefree about how long my life will last." From letters sent by Freud to Eitingon dated October 22, 1919, and November 23, 1919, that is, seven years later (during which the existence of the Committee thus remained unknown even to someone at Eitingon's level), the first of them written to propose that he become a member of the Committee. Jones, *Sigmund Freud*, II, 154.

13. "I know there is a boyish and perhaps romantic element too in this conception . . ." Letter by Freud to Jones cited in Jones, *Sigmund Freud*, II, 153.

14. Jones, *Sigmund Freud*, II, 153.

15. [Added in 1966:] The two preceding paragraphs were not included in the paper published in *Les Études Philosophiques*, the present version having been reserved for a separate printing.

16. [Added in 1966:] The version published [in 1956] was different starting with this paragraph. I have included that version in the appendix to this text.

17. This is what the *euphuism that is customary* in the milieu for describing what affects it designates exquisitely by "the narcissism of minor differences."

18. I cited this passage in its entirety in my thesis, *De la psychose paranoïaque dans ses rapports avec la personnalité* (Paris: Le François, 1932), pages 283 (footnote 1) and 284. It is thus clear that my interest in this subject was not born in the last decade.

19. For those who might not be familiar with the metaphor of the sieve used in milking a billy goat, see Kant's *Critique of Pure Reason*, the section entitled "Transcendental Logic, Part III: Of the Division of General Logic into Analytic and Dialectic." Freud reminds us of it in his text on Schreber. It is not superfluous to note that Freud took it up at the precise point at which Kant submits the following question to his critique: "What is truth?" [See F. Max Müller's translation of Kant's *Critique of Pure Reason* (New York: Doubleday, 1966), 48.]

20. It may also succeed on its own merits. This is witnessed by the inventor of the smelling technique mentioned earlier who, because of this find, was promoted, without any probational stage, from the Truly Necessary, where he would clearly have done marvelous things, to the ranks of the Sufficiencies, and was soon whisked away to the heavens of the Beatitudes.

21. (Added in 1966:) This is the very term that was used by Ernest Jones, and reproduced in the official journal of the English-speaking Psychoanalytic Association, to pay homage to the success of the abovementioned undertaking.

22. See the footnote on page 490 of the appendix to this article.

487

Appendix

The version that was originally published in 1956, starting from the paragraph designated in the footnote on page 485 [in *Écrits* 1966], *read as follows:*

Had he been more attentive to these effects earlier on, Freud would have given more serious thought to the specific pathways required of the institution designed to ensure the transmission of his doctrine. The mere organization of a community would not have seemed to him to insure this transmission against the insufficiency of the very team* of the faithful; several things he apparently said in confidence show that he harbored hard feelings toward them.[1]

He would have realized the root of the affinity between ever psychologizing simplifications, against which analytic experience warned him, and the function of misrecognition characteristic of an individual's ego as such.

He would have perceived the slippery slope that the particularity of the test that this community must impose at its threshold offers up to this misrecognition: namely, analysis, which is customarily referred to as "training analysis." The slightest deflecting of the meaning of what it seeks turns it into an experience of dyadic identification.

I am not the one who is making a judgment here, for it was in the circles of training analysts that the theory of the end of analysis as identification with the analyst's ego was avowed and is still professed.

Now, no matter how closely we assume an ego has managed to conform to the reality it is supposed to gauge, the psychological subjection with which such analysts thus align the completion of an analysis is, if one reads my work correctly, what is most opposed to the truth that analysis must bring out—that truth being the foreignness of unconscious effects, which cut down to size
488 the pretension to autonomy that the ego takes as its ideal. Nor is there anything more contrary to the boon we expect from an analysis: namely, restitution to the analysand of the signifier that explains these unconscious effects, involving a mediation that in fact reveals the aspect of repetition that is precipitated in the model.

The fact that the dyadic pathway, which these analysts choose instead as the aim of analysis, fails to bring about normalization—which might have served as a minimal justification for it—is, as I have said, commonly recognized, but no one draws the obvious inference that there must be a mistake in the premises, people being content to attribute its result to the reflected weaknesses whose accident is, in effect, only too visible.

At any rate, the very fact that the goals of training are asserted in the form of psychological postulates introduces a form of authority into the group that has no counterpart anywhere in science, a form that the term "sufficiency" alone allows us to qualify.

Indeed, only the Hegelian dialectic of infatuation may possibly account for the phenomenon. Failing which, we would have to resort to satire—if its savor did not repulse those who are not part of this milieu—in order to give a fair idea of the way people try to stand out in it.

One can only highlight apparent results here.

Consider, first, the curious position of scientific extraterritoriality with which I began my remarks, and the magisterial tone with which analysts maintain it as soon as they have to respond to the interest their discipline generates among those in neighboring fields.

If, second, the variations that I have pointed out in the different theoretical approaches to psychoanalysis give outsiders the impression that analysis is engaged in an ever conquering progression at the forefront of new fields, it is all the more striking to note just how static the formulations teachable to insiders are compared to the enormous quantity of experience which has, as it were, passed through their hands.

This has resulted in something that is diametrically opposed to the opening-up for which Freud formulated the university project, as I have indicated—namely, in the establishment of a routinized theoretical program, the content of which I could designate quite well with the coined term "fictional matters."

Nevertheless, given the state of neglect in which psychoanalytic method 489
(which was nonetheless revolutionizing in its approach to the phenomena) left psychiatric nosography, it is hard to say whether one should be more surprised that its teaching in this field confines itself to elaborating on the classical symptomatology, or that it manages in this way to cover the same ground as the official courses in psychiatry.

Lastly, however little one forces oneself to keep up with a literature which is, it must be admitted, hardly enticing, one sees the role played in it by ignorance, by which I do not mean to designate learned ignorance or trained ignorance, but rather crass ignorance: the kind of ignorance whose surface has never even been scratched by the plow of a critique of its sources.

These sterilizing phenomena, which are even more blatant when seen from the inside, must be related to the effects of imaginary identification whose fundamental instance Freud revealed in groups and associations. At the very least, we can say that these effects do not foster discussion, which is at the root of all scientific progress. Identification with the image that gives the group its ideal—which is here the image of sufficiency incarnate—certainly founds, as Freud showed in a decisive schema, the communion of the group, but it is precisely at the expense of all articulate communication. Hostile tension is even constitutive of individual-to-individual relations in it. This is what the euphuism that is customary in the milieu quite validly recognizes with the expression "the narcissism of minor differences," which I will translate in more direct terms as "conformist terror."

Those who are familiar with the itinerary of *The Phenomenology of Mind* will find their way around better at this critical juncture, and will be less surprised by the patience that seems to defer any and every questioning excursion in this milieu. Yet the reluctance to call things into question does not concern candidates alone, and it was not a novice who was learning from his courage who explained it as follows: "There is no field in which one *exposes oneself* more totally than in speaking about analysis."

Of course, a "good object," as they put it, can preside over this collective subjection, but this image, which makes dogs faithful, makes men tyrannical—
490 for it is Eros itself, whose phasmid, extending itself over the destroyed polis, by which the hounded soul is panic-stricken, Plato showed us.

This experience thus comes to give rise to its own ideology, but in the form of misrecognition characteristic of the ego's presumption, by resuscitating a theory of the "autonomous ego" that is weighed down with all the question begging which psychology had refuted, without waiting for psychoanalysis, but that unambiguously delivers up the figure of its promoters' ideals.[2]

Assuredly, this analytic psychologism does not fail to encounter resistance. What is interesting is that in treating it as resistance, this psychologism proves to be favored by the many confusions that have appeared in the lifestyles of large cultural regions, insofar as a demand for patterns* manifests itself in them, patterns that it is not inept at furnishing.[3]

We find here the point at which psychoanalysis is deflected toward a form of behaviorism, which is ever more dominant in psychoanalysis' "current tendencies." This movement is supported, as we see, by sociological conditions that go far beyond analytic knowledge as such. What one cannot fail to say here is that Freud, in foreseeing this collusion with behaviorism, denounced it in advance as diametrically opposed to his pathway.[4]

Whatever the outcome must be of the odd spiritual direction in which psychoanalysis thus seems to be heading, its promoters must retain full responsibility for the subjects they take into their charge. And it is here that one cannot but be alarmed by certain ideals that seem to prevail in their training, such as the one that is sufficiently denounced by the term "disintellectualization," which has gained full acceptance.

As if it were not already dreadful that the success of the analytic profession
has attracted so many uneducated enthusiasts to it, is it fitting to consider as
a major and beneficial result of training analysis that even the slightest hint of 491
a thought is proscribed among those for whom all of human reflection would
not suffice to thwart the intempestive actions of all sorts to which their best
intentions expose them?

Thus the plan to produce, for this country alone, "a hundred mediocre psychoanalysts" was proffered in notorious circumstances, and not as the remark of a well-informed modesty, but as the ambitious promise of the shift from quantity to quality illustrated by Marx. The promoters of this plan have even announced, according to the latest news, that they are in the process of exceeding their own standards.

No one doubts, in fact, the importance of the number of workers for the advancement of a science. Yet discordance must not break out on all sides regarding the meaning to be attributed to the experience that founds it. That is, as I have said, the situation of psychoanalysis.

At least this situation seems to me exemplary in that it provides additional proof of the preeminence that I attribute, based on Freud's discovery, to the signifier in the structure of the intersubjective relationship.

The more the analytic community lets Freud's inspiration dissipate, what, if not the letter of his doctrine, will allow it to continue to constitute a body?

Notes

1. Consider what Freud said to Binswanger after one of the weekly meetings held at his house at the beginning of 1907: "So, haben Sie jetzt diese Bande gesehen?" See *Ludwig Binswanger: Erinnerungen an Sigmund Freud* (Bern: Francke Verlag, 1956).

2. This is, as we know, the theory to the yardstick of which Heinz Hartmann, Ernst Kris, and Rudolf Loewenstein intend to reduce the practice of psychoanalysis and to "synchronize" (that is their term) Freud's thought, no doubt a little too vacillating for their taste, if not in their eyes.

(Added in 1966:) This is the yardstick by which one's entry into the New York association is measured.

3. [Added in 1966:] What is demanded of us so greatly dominates our profession at present that it no longer has anything to do with psychoanalysis (this remark was made to me by a psychoanalyst at the end of my recent stay in the United States in 1966).

4. See Freud, *GW* XIV, 78–79 ["An Autobiographical Study," *SE* XX, 52–53].

493 The Instance of the Letter in the Unconscious

or Reason Since Freud

> "Of Children Who Are Wrapped in Swaddling Bands"
>
> O cities of the sea, I behold in you your citizens, women as well as men, tightly bound with stout bonds around their arms and legs by folk who will have no understanding of [y]our speech; and you will only be able to give vent to your griefs and sense of loss of liberty by making tearful complaints, and sighs, and lamentation one to another; for those who bind you will not have understanding of your speech nor will you understand them.[1]
>
> —Leonardo Da Vinci

While the theme of the third volume of *La Psychanalyse*[2] commissioned this contribution by me, I owe this deference to what will be discovered here by introducing it in situating it between writing and speech—it will be halfway between the two.

Writing is in fact distinguished by a prevalence of the *text* in the sense that we will see this factor of discourse take on here—which allows for the kind of tightening up that must, to my taste, leave the reader no other way out than the way in, which I prefer to be difficult. This, then, will not be a writing in my sense of the term.

The fact that I contribute something wholly new at each class of my seminar has heretofore prevented me from providing such a text, except in one class, which has nothing particularly outstanding about it in terms of the series, and is only worth referring to for an idea of its overall level.

For the urgency that I am now taking as a pretext for leaving that aim behind merely covers over the problem that, in maintaining it at the level at which I must present my teachings here, it might stray too far from speech, whose
494 very different measures are essential to the training I seek to effect.

This is why I took the opportunity presented to me at that time by an invitation to meet with the philosophy group of the Fédération des étudiants ès lettres[3] to make an appropriate adjustment to my exposé—its necessary generality matching the extraordinary character of their interest, but its sole object encountering the connivance of their common background, a literary background, to which my title pays homage.

Indeed, how could we forget that Freud constantly, and right until the end, maintained that such a background was the prime requisite in the training of analysts, and that he designated the age-old *universitas litterarum* as the ideal place for its institution?[4]

Thus this reference to the real-life context of my lecture, by showing whom I tailored it for, also marked those to whom it is not addressed.

I mean: none of those who, for whatever reason in psychoanalysis, allow their discipline to take advantage of some false identity.

This is a vice of habit and its effect on the mind is such that its true identity may appear among them as just one more diversion, whose refined redoubling one hopes will not escape the notice of subtler minds.

It is thus that we observe with curiosity the beginnings of a new tack concerning symbolization and language in the *International Journal of Psycho-Analysis*, a great many wetted fingers leafing through works by Sapir and Jespersen. These exercises are still green around the edges, but it is above all the tone that is missing. A certain seriousness always raises a smile when it enters the domain of veracity.

And how could a contemporary psychoanalyst not sense, in coming upon speech, that he had reached this domain, when it is from speech that analytic experience receives its instrument, its frame, its material, and even the background noise of its uncertainties?

I. The Meaning of the Letter 495

My title conveys the fact that, beyond this speech, it is the whole structure of language that psychoanalytic experience discovers in the unconscious. This is to alert prejudiced minds from the outset that the idea that the unconscious is merely the seat of the instincts may have to be reconsidered.

But how are we to take the letter here? Quite simply, literally [*à la lettre*].

By "letter" I designate the material medium [*support*] that concrete discourse borrows from language.

This simple definition assumes that language is not to be confused with the various psychical and somatic functions that serve it in the speaking subject.

The primary reason for this is that language, with its structure, exists prior to each subject's entry into it at a certain moment in his mental development.

Let us note that, although the deficits of aphasia are caused by purely anatomical lesions in the cerebral systems that provide the mental center for these functions, they prove, on the whole, to be distributed between the two aspects of the signifying effect of what I am calling here "the letter" in the creation of signification.[5] This point will become clearer in what follows.

And the subject, while he may appear to be the slave of language, is still more the slave of a discourse in the universal movement of which his place is already inscribed at his birth, if only in the form of his proper name.

Reference to the experience of the community as the substance of this dis-
496 course resolves nothing. For this experience takes on its essential dimension in the tradition established by this discourse. This tradition, long before the drama of history is inscribed in it, grounds the elementary structures of culture. And these very structures display an ordering of exchanges which, even if unconscious, is inconceivable apart from the permutations authorized by language.

With the result that the ethnographic duality of nature and culture is giving way to a ternary conception of the human condition—nature, society, and culture—the last term of which may well be reduced to language, that is, to what essentially distinguishes human society from natural societies.

But I shall neither take sides here nor take this as a point of departure, leaving to their own obscurity the original relations between the signifier and labor. To settle accounts with the general function of *praxis* in the genesis of history by way of a quip, I will confine myself to mentioning that the very society that wished to restore the hierarchy responsible for the relations between production and ideological superstructures to its rightful political place, alongside the privilege of the producers, has nevertheless failed to give birth to an Esperanto whose relations to socialist reality [*réel*] would have ruled out from the start any possibility of literary formalism.[6]

For my part, I will put my faith in only those premises whose value has already been proven, in that they have allowed language to attain the status in experience of a scientific object.

This is what permits linguistics[7] to present itself in the pilot position in this domain, around which a reclassification of the sciences is signaling, as is usu-
497 ally the case, a revolution in knowledge; only the necessities of communication have made me term this domain, in the theme of this volume of *La Psychanalyse*, "the sciences of man"—despite the confusion that may hide behind it.

To pinpoint the emergence of the discipline of linguistics, I will say that, as in the case of every science in the modern sense, it consists in the constitutive moment of an algorithm that grounds it. This algorithm is the following:

$$\frac{S}{s}$$

It is read as follows: signifier over signified, "over" corresponding to the bar separating the two levels.

The sign written in this way should be attributed to Ferdinand de Saussure, although it is not reduced to this exact form in any of the numerous schemas in which it appears in the printed version of the various lectures from the three courses he gave in 1906–7, 1908–9, and 1910–11, which a group of his devoted disciples collected under the title, *Cours de linguistique générale*—a publication of prime importance for the transmission of a teaching worthy of the name, that is, that one can stop only on its own movement.

This is why it is legitimate for us to credit him for the formalization $\frac{S}{s}$, which characterizes the modern stage of linguistics, despite the diversity between schools of linguistics.

The major theme of this science is thus based, in effect, on the primordial position of the signifier and the signified as distinct orders initially separated by a barrier resisting signification.

This is what makes possible an exact study of the connections characteristic of the signifier, and of the magnitude of their function in generating the signified.

For this primordial distinction goes well beyond the debate over the arbitrariness of the sign, such as it has been elaborated since the reflections of Antiquity, and even beyond the impasse, already sensed at that time, which opposed the one-to-one correspondence between word and thing, even in the act of naming—despite the appearances suggested by the role imputed to the index finger pointing to an object as an infant learns its mother tongue, or in
the use of so-called concrete academic methods in the study of foreign lan- 498
guages [*langues*].

We can take things no further along this path than to demonstrate that no signification can be sustained except by reference to another signification.[8] This ultimately leads us to the remark that there is no existing language [*langue*] whose ability to cover the field of the signified can be called into question, one of the effects of its existence as a language [*langue*] being that it fulfills all needs there. Were we to try to grasp the constitution of the object in language, we could but note that this constitution is found only at the level of the concept—which is very different from any nominative—and that the *thing* [*chose*], when quite obviously reduced to the noun, splits into the double, divergent ray of the cause in which the thing has taken shelter in French, and of the nothing [*rien*] to which the thing has abandoned its Latin dress *(rem)*.

These considerations, as existent as they may be to philosophers, divert us from the locus whence language questions us about its very nature. And we will fail to sustain this question as long as we have not jettisoned the illusion that the signifier serves [*répond à*] the function of representing the signified, or better, that the signifier has to justify [*répondre de*] its existence in terms of any signification whatsoever.

For even if it is reduced to this latter formulation, the heresy is the same—the heresy that leads logical positivism in search of the "meaning of meaning,"* as its objective is called in the language [*langue*] in which its devotees snort. It can be seen here how this sort of analysis can reduce the text the most highly charged with meaning to insignificant trifles. Only mathematical algorithms resist this process; they are considered to be devoid of meaning, as they should be.[9]

499 The fact remains that if we were able to subtract solely the notion of the parallelism of its upper and lower terms from the algorithm $\frac{S}{s}$, each term only being taken globally, it would remain the enigmatic sign of a total mystery. Which, of course, is not the case.

In order to grasp its function, I will begin by reproducing the faulty illustration by which its usage is classically introduced:

We can see here how it lends itself to the kind of direction indicated above as erroneous.

In my lecture, I replaced this illustration with another, which can be considered more correct only because it exaggerates in the incongruous dimension psychoanalysts have not yet altogether given up, because of their justified sense that their conformism derives its value from it alone. Here is the other illustration:

GENTLEMEN LADIES

Here we see that, without greatly extending the scope of the signifier involved in the experiment—that is, by simply doubling the nominal type

500 through the mere juxtaposition of two terms whose complementary meanings would seem to have to reinforce each other—surprise is produced by

the precipitation of an unexpected meaning: the image of two twin doors that symbolize, with the private stall offered Western man for the satisfaction of his natural needs when away from home, the imperative he seems to share with the vast majority of primitive communities that subjects his public life to the laws of urinary segregation.

The point is not merely to silence the nominalist debate with a low blow, but to show how the signifier in fact enters the signified—namely, in a form which, since it is not immaterial, raises the question of its place in reality. For in having to move closer to the little enamel plaques that bear it, the squinting gaze of a nearsighted person might be justified in wondering whether it is indeed here that we must see the signifier, whose signified would in this case be paid its last respects by the solemn procession in two lines from the upper nave.

But no contrived example can be as telling as what is encountered in the lived experience of truth. Thus I have no reason to be unhappy I invented the above, since it awoke in the person the most worthy of my trust a childhood memory which, having come serendipitously to my attention, is best placed here.

A train arrives at a station. A little boy and a little girl, brother and sister, are seated across from each other in a compartment next to the outside window that provides a view of the station platform buildings going by as the train comes to a stop. "Look," says the brother, "we're at Ladies!" "Imbecile!" replies his sister, "Don't you see we're at Gentlemen."

Aside from the fact that the rails in this story materialize the bar in the Saussurian algorithm in a form designed to suggest that its resistance may be other than dialectical, one would have to be half-blind to be confused as to the respective places of the signifier and the signified here, and not to follow from what radiant center the signifier reflects its light into the darkness of incomplete significations.

For the signifier will raise Dissension that is merely animal in kind, and destined to the natural fog of forgetfulness, to the immeasurable power of ideological warfare, which is merciless to families and a torment to the gods. To 501
these children, Gentlemen and Ladies will henceforth be two homelands toward which each of their souls will take flight on divergent wings, and regarding which it will be all the more impossible for them to reach an agreement since, being in fact the same homeland, neither can give ground regarding the one's unsurpassed excellence without detracting from the other's glory.

Let us stop there. It sounds like the history of France. Which it is more humane to recall here, and rightly so, than that of England, destined to flip from the Large to the Small End of Dean Swift's egg.

It remains to be grasped up what steps and down what corridor the S of the signifier, visible here in the plurals [*hommes* and *dames*] by which it focuses its welcome beyond the train window, must pass to impress its curves upon the ducts by which—like hot air and cold air—indignation and scorn hiss on this side.

One thing is certain: this access must not, in any case, carry any signification with it if the algorithm, $\frac{S}{s}$, with its bar is appropriate to it. For insofar as the algorithm itself is but a pure function of the signifier, it can reveal only a signifying structure in this transfer.

Now the structure of the signifier is, as is commonly said of language, that it is articulated.

This means that its units—no matter where one begins in tracing out their reciprocal encroachments and expanding inclusions—are subject to the twofold condition of being reduced to ultimate differential elements and of combining the latter according to the laws of a closed order.

These elements, the decisive discovery of linguistics, are *phonemes*; we must not look for any *phonetic* constancy in the modulatory variability to which this term applies, but rather for the synchronic system of differential couplings that are necessary to discern vocables in a given language [*langue*]. This allows us to see that an essential element in speech itself was predestined to flow into moveable type which, in Didots or Garamonds squeezing into lower-cases, renders validly present what I call the "letter"—namely, the essentially localized structure of the signifier.

The second property of the signifier, that of combining according to the
502 laws of a closed order, affirms the necessity of the topological substratum, of which the term I ordinarily use, "signifying chain," gives an approximate idea: links by which a necklace firmly hooks onto a link of another necklace made of links.

Such are the structural conditions that define the order of the signifier's constitutive encroachments up to the unit immediately above the sentence as grammar, and the order of the signifier's constitutive inclusions up to the verbal locution as the lexicon.

In the limits within which these two approaches to understanding linguistic usage are confined, it is easy to see that only signifier-to-signifier correlations provide the standard for any and every search for signification; this is indicated by the notion of "usage" of a taxeme or semanteme, which refers to contexts just one degree above that of the units in question.

But it is not because grammatical and lexical approaches are exhausted at a certain point that we must think that signification rules unreservedly beyond it. That would be a mistake.

For the signifier, by its very nature, always anticipates meaning by deploying its dimension in some sense before it. As is seen at the level of the sentence when the latter is interrupted before the significant term: "I'll never . . .," "The fact remains . . .," "Still perhaps . . ." Such sentences nevertheless make sense, and that sense is all the more oppressive in that it is content to make us wait for it.[10]

But the phenomenon is no different, which—making her appear, with the sole postponement of a "but," as comely as the Shulamite, as honest as a virtuous maiden—adorns and readies the Negress for the wedding and the poor woman for the auction block.

Whence we can say that it is in the chain of the signifier that meaning *insists*, but that none of the chain's elements *consists* in the signification it can provide at that very moment.

The notion of an incessant sliding of the signified under the signifier thus comes to the fore—which Ferdinand de Saussure illustrates with an image resembling the wavy lines of the upper and lower Waters in miniatures from manuscripts of Genesis. It is a twofold flood in which the landmarks—fine streaks of rain traced by vertical dotted lines that supposedly delimit corre- 503
sponding segments—seem insubstantial.

All our experience runs counter to this, which made me speak at one point in my seminar on the psychoses of the "button ties" [*points de capiton*] required by this schema to account for the dominance of the letter in the dramatic transformation that dialogue can effect in the subject.[11]

But while the linearity that Saussure considers to be constitutive of the chain of discourse—in accordance with its emission by a single voice and with the horizontal axis along which it is situated in our writing—is in fact necessary, it is not sufficient. It applies to the chain of discourse only in the direction in which it is oriented in time, even being taken up therein as a signifying factor in all languages [*langues*] in which the time of "Peter hits Paul" is reversed when the terms are inverted.

But it suffices to listen to poetry, which Saussure was certainly in the habit of doing,[12] for a polyphony to be heard and for it to become clear that all discourse is aligned along the several staves of a musical score.

Indeed, there is no signifying chain that does not sustain—as if attached to the punctuation of each of its units—all attested contexts that are, so to speak, "vertically" linked to that point.

Thus, if we take up the word *arbre* (tree) again, this time not in its nominal isolation, but at the endpoint of one of these punctuations, we see that it is not simply because the word *barre* (bar) is its anagram that it crosses the bar of the Saussurian algorithm.

504 For broken down into the double specter of its vowels and consonants, it calls up—with the robur-oak [*robre*] and the plane tree [*platane*]—the significations of strength and majesty that it takes on in our flora. Tapping all the symbolic contexts in which it is used in the Hebrew of the Bible, it erects on a barren hill the shadow of the cross. Next it reduces to a capital Y, the sign of dichotomy—which, without the illustration that historiates armorials, would owe nothing to the tree, however genealogical it claims to be. Circulatory tree, arbor vitae of the cerebellum, lead tree or silver amalgam [*arbre de Diane*], crystals precipitated into a tree that conducts lightning, is it your countenance that traces our destiny for us in the fire-scorched tortoiseshell, or your flash that brings forth from an infinite night that slow change in being in the Ἕν Πάντα of language:

> *No! says the Tree, it says No! in the scintillating*
> *Of its superb head*

verses that I consider to be as legitimately heard in the harmonics of the tree as their reverse:

> *Which the storm treats universally*
> *As it does a blade of grass.*

For this modern verse is organized according to the same law of the parallelism of the signifier, whose concert governs both primitive Slavic epic poetry and the most refined Chinese poetry.

This can be seen in the common mode of beings [*l'étant*] from which the tree and the blade of grass are chosen, so that the signs of contradiction—saying "No!" and "treat as"—can come into being here, and so that, through the categorical contrast between the particularity of "superb" and the "universally" of its reduction, the indiscernible scintillating of the eternal instant may be accomplished in the condensation of *tête* (head) and *tempête* (storm).

But all this signifier can only operate, it may be objected, if it is present in the subject. I answer this objection by assuming that he has shifted to the level of the signified.

For what is important is not whether the subject know more or less about it. (If GENTLEMEN and LADIES were written in a language [*langue*] with which the little boy and girl were unfamiliar, their quarrel would simply be more exclusively a quarrel over words, but it would be no less ready to take on signification for all that.)

505 What this structure of the signifying chain discloses is the possibility I

have—precisely insofar as I share its language [*langue*] with other subjects, that is, insofar as this language [*langue*] exists—to use it to signify *something altogether different* from what it says. This is a function of speech that is more worthy of being pointed out than that of disguising the subject's thought (which is usually indefinable)—namely, the function of indicating the place of this subject in the search for truth.

I need but plant my tree in a locution, *grimper à l'arbre*, or even project onto it the derisive light that a descriptive context gives the word, *arborer*, to not let myself be imprisoned in some sort of *communiqué* of the facts, however official it may be, and if I know the truth, convey it, despite all the censors, *between-the-lines* using nothing but the signifier that can be constituted by my acrobatics through the branches of the tree. These acrobatics may be provocative to the point of burlesque or perceptible only to the trained eye, depending on whether I wish to be understood by the many or the few.

The properly signifying function thus depicted in language has a name. We learned this name in our childhood grammar book on the last page, where the shade of Quintilian, relegated to some phantom chapter to convey final considerations on style, seemed suddenly to hasten its voice due to the threat of being cut off.

It is among the figures of style, or tropes—from which the verb "to find" [*trouver*] comes to us—that this name is, in fact, found. This name is *metonymy*.

I shall refer only to the example of it given there: "thirty sails." For the worry I felt, over the fact that the word "ship" [*bâteau*] that was hiding therein seemed to split its presence there in two by having been able to borrow its figurative sense from the very rehashing of this example, veiled [*voilait*] not so much those illustrious sails [*voiles*] as the definition they were supposed to illustrate.

The part taken for the whole—I said to myself, if the thing is supposed to be based on reality [*réel*]—leaves us with hardly any idea what we are to conclude about the size of the fleet these thirty sails are nevertheless supposed to gauge: for a ship to have but one sail is very rare indeed.

This shows that the connection between ship and sail is nowhere other than 506
in the signifier, and that metonymy is based on the *word-to-word* nature of this connection.[13]

I shall designate as metonymy the first aspect of the actual field the signifier constitutes, so that meaning may assume a place there.

The other aspect is *metaphor*. Let me illustrate it immediately; Quillet's dictionary seemed appropriate to me to provide a sample that would not be suspected of being deliberately selected, and I didn't pursue the farce any farther than Victor Hugo's well-known verse, "His sheaf was neither miserly nor hateful . . . ," with which I presented metaphor, when the time came for it, in my seminar on the psychoses.

Let us say that modern poetry and the Surrealist school led us to take a major step forward here by showing that any conjunction of two signifiers could just as easily constitute a metaphor, if an additional condition—that of the greatest disparity of the images signified—weren't required for the pro-
507 duction of the poetic spark, in other words, for metaphoric creation to occur.

Of course, this radical position is based on the so-called "automatic writing" experiment, which would not have been attempted without the assurance its pioneers drew from Freud's discovery. But it remains marked by confusion because the doctrine behind it is false.

Metaphor's creative spark does not spring forth from the juxtaposition of two images, that is, of two equally actualized signifiers. It flashes between two signifiers, one of which has replaced the other by taking the other's place in the signifying chain, the occulted signifier remaining present by virtue of its (metonymic) connection to the rest of the chain.

One word for another: this is the formula for metaphor, and if you are a poet you will make it into a game and produce a continuous stream, nay, a dazzling weave of metaphors. You will, moreover, obtain the intoxicating effect of Jean Tardieu's dialogue that goes by this title, due solely to the demonstration it provides of the radical superfluousness of all signification to a perfectly convincing representation of bourgeois comedy.

In Hugo's verse, it is obvious that not the slightest light emanates from the assertion that a sheaf is neither miserly nor hateful, because it is clear that the sheaf has no more the merit than the demerit of these attributes, since miserliness and hatred, along with the sheaf, are properties of Booz, who exercises them when he uses the sheaf as he sees fit, without making his feelings known to it.

If "his sheaf" refers back to Booz, as is clearly the case nevertheless, it is because it replaces him in the signifying chain—at the very place that awaited him, because it had been raised up a step by the clearing away of miserliness and hatred. But the sheaf has thus cleared this place of Booz, ejected as he now is into the outer darkness where miserliness and hatred harbor him in the hollow of their negation.

But once *his* sheaf has thus usurped his place, Booz cannot go back to it, the slender thread of the little "his" that attaches him to it being an additional obstacle thereto, because it binds this return with a title of ownership that would detain him in the heart of miserliness and hatred. His asserted generosity is thus reduced to *less than nothing* by the munificence of the sheaf which, being drawn from nature, knows neither our reserve nor our rejections, and even in its accumulation remains prodigal by our standards. 508

But if, in this profusion, the giver disappears with the gift, it is only to reemerge in what surrounds the figure of speech in which he was annihilated. For it is the radiance of fecundity—which announces the surprise the poem celebrates, namely, the promise of acceding to paternity that the old man receives in a sacred context.

Thus it is between a man's proper name qua signifier and the signifier that metaphorically abolishes it that the poetic spark is produced, and it is all the more effective here in bringing about the signification of paternity in that it reproduces the mythical event through which Freud reconstructed the path along which the mystery of paternity advances in the unconscious of every man.

The structure of modern metaphor is no different. Hence the jaculation, "Love is a pebble laughing in the sun," recreates love in a dimension that I have said strikes me as tenable, as opposed to its ever imminent slippage into the mirage of some narcissistic altruism.

We see that metaphor is situated at the precise point at which meaning is produced in nonmeaning—that is, at the passage which, as Freud discovered, when crossed in the opposite direction, gives rise to the word that is "the word" ["*le mot*"] par excellence in French, the word that has no other patronage there than the signifier *esprit* [14]—and at which it becomes palpable that, in deriding the signifier, man defies his very destiny.

But to return to metonymy now, what does man find in it, if it must be more than the power to skirt the obstacles of social censure? Doesn't this form, which gives oppressed truth its field, manifest a certain servitude that is inherent in its presentation?

It's worth taking the time to read a book in which Leo Strauss, from the land that has traditionally offered asylum to those who have chosen freedom, 509 reflects on the relations between the art of writing and persecution.[15] By honing in on the sort of connaturality that ties this art to this condition, he allows us to glimpse something that imposes its form here, in the effect of truth on desire.

But haven't we been feeling for a while now that, in following the paths of the letter to reach the Freudian truth, we are getting hot, its flames spreading all around us?

Of course, as it is said, the letter kills while the spirit gives life. I don't disagree, having had to pay homage somewhere here to a noble victim of the error of seeking in the letter, but I also ask how the spirit could live without the letter. The spirit's pretensions would nevertheless remain indisputable if the letter hadn't proven that it produces all its truth effects in man without the spirit having to intervene at all.

This revelation came to Freud, and he called his discovery the unconscious.

II. The Letter in the Unconscious

In Freud's complete works, one out of three pages presents us with philological references, one out of two pages with logical inferences, and everywhere we see a dialectical apprehension of experience, linguistic analysis becoming still more prevalent the more directly the unconscious is involved.

Thus what is at stake on every page in *The Interpretation of Dreams* is what I call the letter of discourse, in its texture, uses, and immanence in the matter in question. For this book inaugurates both Freud's work and his royal road to the unconscious. And we are informed of this by Freud, whose confession in letters to Fliess that have since been made public, when he launches this book toward us in the early days of this century,[16] merely confirms what he continued to proclaim to the end: that the whole of his discovery lies in this no-holds-barred expression of his message.

510 The first clause, articulated already in the introductory chapter because its exposition cannot be postponed, is that the dream is a rebus. And Freud stipulates that it must be understood quite literally [*à la lettre*], as I said earlier. This is related to the instance in the dream of the same "literating" (in other words, phonemic) structure in which the signifier is articulated and analyzed in discourse. Like the unnatural figures of the boat on the roof, or the man with a comma for a head, which are expressly mentioned by Freud, dream images are to be taken up only on the basis of their value as signifiers, that is, only insofar as they allow us to spell out the "proverb" presented by the oneiric rebus. The linguistic structure that enables us to read dreams is at the crux of the "signifierness of dreams," at the crux of the *Traumdeutung*.

Freud shows us in every possible way that the image's value as a signifier has nothing to do with its signification, giving as an example Egyptian hieroglyphics in which it would be ridiculous to deduce from the frequency in a text of a vulture (which is an aleph) or a chick (which is a vau) indicating a form of the verb "to be" and plurals, that the text has anything whatsoever to do with these ornithological specimens. Freud takes his bearings from certain uses of the signifier in this writing that are effaced in ours, such as the use of determinatives, where a categorical figure is added as an exponent to the literal figuration of a verbal term; but this is only to bring us back to the fact that we are dealing with writing where even the supposed "ideogram" is a letter.

But psychoanalysts who have no training in linguistics don't need the current confusion regarding the term "ideogram" to believe in a symbolism deriving from natural analogy, or even from instinct's coaptational image. This is so true that, apart from the French school, which attends to this, it is with a statement like "reading coffee grounds is not the same as reading hieroglyphics" that I must recall to its own principles a technique whose pathways cannot be justified unless they aim at the unconscious.

It must be said that this is admitted only reluctantly, and that the mental vice denounced above enjoys such favor that the contemporary psychoanalyst can be expected to say that he decodes before resolving to take the journey with Freud (turn at the statue of Champollion, says the guide) that is necessary for him to understand that he deciphers—the latter differing in that a cryptogram 511
only takes on its full dimensions when it is in a lost language [*langue*].

Taking this journey simply amounts to going further in the *Traumdeutung*.

Entstellung, translated as "transposition"—which Freud shows to be the general precondition for the functioning of the dream—is what I designated earlier, with Saussure, as the sliding of the signified under the signifier, which is always happening (unconsciously, let us note) in discourse.

But the two aspects of the signifier's impact on the signified are also found here:

Verdichtung, "condensation," is the superimposed structure of signifiers in which metaphor finds its field; its name, condensing in itself the word *Dichtung*, shows the mechanism's connaturality with poetry, to the extent that it envelops poetry's own properly traditional function.

Verschiebung or "displacement"—this transfer of signification that metonymy displays is closer to the German term; it is presented, right from its first appearance in Freud's work, as the unconscious' best means by which to foil censorship.

What distinguishes these two mechanisms, which play a privileged role in the dream-work, *Traumarbeit*, from their homologous function in discourse? Nothing, except a condition imposed upon the signifying material, called *Rücksicht auf Darstellbarkeit*, which must be translated as "consideration of the means of staging" (the translation by "role of the possibility of representation" being overly approximate here). But this condition constitutes a limitation operating within the system of writing, rather than dissolving the system into a figurative semiology in which it would intersect the phenomena of natural expression. This would probably allow us to shed light on problems with certain types of pictography, which we are not justified in regarding as evolutionary stages simply because they were abandoned in writing as imperfect. Let us say, then, that dreams are like the parlor game in which each person, in

turn, is supposed to get the spectators to guess some well-known saying or variant of it solely by silent gestures. The fact that dreams have speech at their
512 disposal makes no difference since, for the unconscious, speech is but one staging element among others. It is precisely when games and dreams alike run up against the lack of taxemic material by which to represent logical relationships such as causality, contradiction, hypothesis, and so on that they prove they have to do with writing, not mime. The subtle procedures dreams end up using to represent these logical connections—in a much less artificial way than games usually employ—are taken up specifically in Freud's work, where it is once again confirmed that the dream-work proceeds in accordance with the laws of the signifier.

The rest of the dream revision is termed "secondary" by Freud, taking on its value from what is at stake: they are fantasies or daydreams, *Tagtraum*, to use the term Freud prefers to use to situate them in their wish-fulfilling function (*Wunscherfüllung*). Given that these fantasies may remain unconscious, their distinctive feature is clearly their signification. Now, Freud tells us that their role in dreams is either to serve as signifying elements for the statement of the unconscious thought (*Traumgedanke*), or to be used in the secondary revision that occurs—that is, in a function not to be distinguished, he says, from our waking thought (*von unserem wachen Denken nicht zu unterscheiden*). No better idea of this function's effects can be given than by comparing it to patches of colorwash which, when applied here and there on a stencil, can make stick figures—which are rather unprepossessing in themselves—in a rebus or hieroglyphics look more like a painting of people.

I apologize for seeming to spell out Freud's text myself; it is not merely to show how much is to be gained by not lopping off parts of it. It is to be able to situate what has happened in psychoanalysis in terms of its earliest reference points, which are fundamental and have never been revoked.

Right from the outset, people failed to recognize the constitutive role of the signifier in the status Freud immediately assigned to the unconscious in the most precise and explicit ways.

The reason for this was twofold, the least perceived being, naturally, that this formalization was not sufficient by itself to bring people to recognize the
513 instance of the signifier, because when the *Traumdeutung* was published it was way ahead of the formalizations of linguistics for which one could no doubt show that it paved the way by the sheer weight of its truth.

The second reason is merely the flip side of the first, for if psychoanalysts were fascinated exclusively by the significations highlighted in the unconscious, it was because these significations derived their most secret attraction from the dialectic that seemed to be immanent in them.

I demonstrated to those who attend my seminar that the apparent changes of direction or rather changes in tack along the way—that Freud, in his primary concern to ensure the survival of his discovery along with the basic revisions it imposed upon our knowledge, felt it necessary to apply to his doctrine—were due to the need to counteract the ever-accelerating effects of this partiality.

For, I repeat, given the situation he found himself in, where he had nothing corresponding to the object of his discovery that was at the same level of scientific maturity, he at least never failed to maintain this object at the level of its ontological dignity.

The rest was the work of the gods and took such a course that analysis today finds its bearings in the imaginary forms I have just shown to be sketched out through inverse printing on the text they mutilate. It is to them that the analyst's aim now adapts, confusing them, in the interpretation of dreams, with the visionary liberation of the hieroglyphic aviary, and seeking more generally to verify the exhaustion of the analysis in a sort of "scanning"[*][17] of these forms wherever they appear—with the idea that they bear witness both to the exhaustion of the regressions and to the remodeling of "the object-relation" that is supposed to typify the subject.[18]

The technique that is based on such positions can give rise to many varied
effects, which are quite difficult to criticize behind their therapeutic aegis. But 514
an internal critique can emerge from the flagrant discordance between the mode of operation by which the technique legitimates itself—namely, the fundamental rule of psychoanalysis, all the instruments of which, starting with "free association," derive their justification from its inventor's conception of the unconscious—and the complete ignorance reigning there of this very conception of the unconscious. The most trenchant supporters of this technique let themselves off the hook here with a mere flourish: the fundamental rule must, they say, be observed all the more religiously since it is only the fruit of a lucky accident. In other words, Freud never really knew what he was doing.

A return to Freud's texts shows, on the contrary, the absolute coherence between his technique and his discovery, and this coherence allows us to situate his procedures at their proper level.

This is why any rectification of psychoanalysis requires a return to the truth of that discovery, which is impossible to obscure in its original moment.

For in the analysis of dreams, Freud intends to give us nothing other than the laws of the unconscious in their broadest extension. One of the reasons why dreams were the most propitious here is, Freud tells us, that they reveal these laws no less in normal subjects than in neurotics.

In neither, however, does the efficacy of the unconscious cease upon awakening. Psychoanalytic experience consists in nothing other than establishing that the unconscious leaves none of our actions outside its field. The presence of the unconscious in the psychological order—in other words, in the individual's relational functions—nevertheless deserves to be more precisely defined. It is not coextensive with that order, for we know that, while unconscious motivation manifests itself just as much in conscious psychical effects as in unconscious ones, conversely it is elementary to note that a large number of psychical effects that are legitimately designated as unconscious, in the sense of excluding the characteristic of consciousness, nevertheless bear no relation whatsoever, by their nature, to the unconscious in the Freudian sense. It is thus only due to an incorrect use of the term that "psychical" and "unconscious" in this sense are confused, and that people thus term psychical what is actually an effect of the unconscious on the soma, for example.

515 The point is, therefore, to define the topography of this unconscious. I say that it is the very topography defined by the algorithm:

$$\frac{S}{s}$$

What it has permitted me to elaborate concerning the impact of the signifier on the signified allows for its transformation into:

$$f(S)\frac{1}{s}$$

It is on the basis of the copresence in the signified not only of the elements of the horizontal signifying chain but also of its vertical dependencies, that I have demonstrated the effects, distributed in accordance with two fundamental structures, in metonymy and metaphor. We can symbolize them by:

$$f(S \ldots S')\, S \cong S\, (—)\, s$$

that is, metonymic structure, indicating that it is the signifier-to-signifier connection that allows for the elision by which the signifier instates lack of being [*le manque de l'être*] in the object-relation, using signification's referral [*renvoi*] value to invest it with the desire aiming at the lack that it supports. The — sign placed in ( ) manifests here the maintenance of the bar — which, in the first algorithm, denotes the irreducible nature of the resistance of signification as constituted in the relations between signifier and signified.[19]

Now we turn to

$$f\left(\frac{S'}{S}\right)S \cong S\,(+)\,s$$

metaphoric structure, indicating that it is in the substitution of signifier for signifier that a signification effect is produced that is poetic or creative, in other words, that brings the signification in question into existence.[20] The + sign in ( ) manifests here the crossing of the bar, —, and the constitutive value of this crossing for the emergence of signification.

This crossing expresses the condition for the passage of the signifier into the signified, whose moment I pointed out above by provisionally conflating it with the place of the subject. 516

It is the function of the subject, thus introduced, on which we must now dwell since it lies at the crux of our problem.

"I am thinking, therefore I am" (*cogito ergo sum*) is not simply the formulation in which the link between the transparency of the transcendental subject and his existential affirmation is constituted, at the historical apex of reflection on the conditions of science.

Perhaps I am only object and mechanism (and so nothing more than phenomenon), but assuredly, insofar as I think so, I am—absolutely. Philosophers certainly made important corrections here—namely, that in that which is thinking *(cogitans),* I am never doing anything but constituting myself as an object (*cogitatum*). The fact remains that through this extreme purification of the transcendental subject, my existential link to its project seems irrefutable, at least in the form of its actuality, and that *"cogito ergo sum" ubi cogito, ibi sum*, overcomes this objection.

Of course, this limits me to being there in my being only insofar as I think that I am in my thought; to what extent I really think this concerns me alone and, if I say it, interests no one.[21]

Yet to avoid it on the pretext of its philosophical semblances is simply to demonstrate one's inhibition. For the notion of the subject is indispensable even to the workings of a science such as strategy in the modern sense, whose calculations exclude all "subjectivism."

It is also to deny oneself access to what might be called the Freudian universe—in the sense in which we speak of the Copernican universe. Indeed, Freud himself compared his discovery to the so-called Copernican revolution, emphasizing that what was at stake was once again the place man assigns himself at the center of a universe.

Is the place that I occupy as subject of the signifier concentric or eccen-
517 tric in relation to the place I occupy as subject of the signified? That is the question.

The point is not to know whether I speak of myself in a way that conforms to what I am, but rather to know whether, when I speak of myself, I am the same as the self of whom I speak. And there is no reason not to bring in the term "thought" here. For Freud uses the term to designate the elements at stake in the unconscious, that is, in the signifying mechanisms I just pointed to there.

It is nonetheless true that the philosophical *cogito* is at the center of the mirage that renders modern man so sure of being himself in his uncertainties about himself, and even in the distrust he has long since learned to exercise regarding the pitfalls of pride.

Now if, turning the weapon of metonymy against the nostalgia that it serves, I stop myself from seeking any meaning beyond tautology, and if, in the name of "war is war" and "a penny's a penny," I resolve to be only what I am, how can I escape here from the obvious fact that I am in this very act?

And how—in going to the other, metaphoric, pole of the signifying quest, and dedicating myself to becoming what I am, to coming into being—can I doubt that, even if I were to lose myself there, I am there?

Now it is on these very points, where the obvious is subverted by the empirical, that the trick of the Freudian conversion lies.

This signifying game of metonymy and metaphor—up to and including its active tip [*pointe*] that "cotter-pins" my desire to a refusal of the signifier or to a lack of being, and links my fate to the question of my destiny—this game is played, in its inexorable subtlety, until the match is over, where I am not because I cannot situate myself there.

That is, it wasn't going very far to say the words with which I momentarily dumbfounded my audience: I am thinking where I am not, therefore I am where I am not thinking. These words render palpable to an attentive ear with what elusive ambiguity the ring of meaning flees from our grasp along the verbal string.

What we must say is: I am not, where I am the plaything of my thought; I think about what I am where I do not think I am thinking.

This two-sided mystery can be seen to intersect the fact that truth is evoked only in that dimension of ruse whereby all "realism" in creation derives its
518 virtue from metonymy, as well as this other fact that access to meaning is granted only to the double elbow of metaphor, when we hold in our hand their one and only key: namely, the fact that the S and *s* of the Saussurian algorithm

are not in the same plane, and man was deluding himself in believing he was situated in their common axis, which is nowhere.

At least until Freud made this discovery. For if what Freud discovered isn't precisely that, it is nothing.

The contents of the unconscious, in their deceptive ambiguity, supply us no reality in the subject more consistent than the immediate; it is from truth that they derive their virtue in the dimension of being: *Kern unseres Wesen* is Freud's own expression.

Metaphor's two-stage mechanism is the very mechanism by which symptoms, in the analytic sense, are determined. Between the enigmatic signifier of sexual trauma and the term it comes to replace in a current signifying chain, a spark flies that fixes in a symptom—a metaphor in which flesh or function is taken as a signifying element—the signification, that is inaccessible to the conscious subject, by which the symptom may be dissolved.

And the enigmas that desire—with its frenzy mimicking the gulf of the infinite and the secret collusion whereby it envelops the pleasure of knowing and of dominating in jouissance—poses for any sort of "natural philosophy" are based on no other derangement of instinct than the fact that it is caught in the rails of metonymy, eternally extending toward the *desire for something else*. Hence its "perverse" fixation at the very point of suspension of the signifying chain at which the screen-memory is immobilized and the fascinating image of the fetish becomes frozen.

There is no other way to conceive of the indestructibility of unconscious desire—given that there is no need which, when its satiation is prohibited, does not wither, in extreme cases through the very wasting away of the organism itself. It is in a kind of memory, comparable to what goes by that name in our modern thinking-machines (which are based on an electronic realization of signifying composition), that the chain is found which *insists* by reproducing itself in the transference, and which is the chain of a dead desire.

It is the truth of what this desire has been in his history that the subject cries out through his symptom, as Christ said that stones themselves would have cried out, had the children of Israel not lent them their voices.

And this is also why psychoanalysis alone allows us to differentiate in mem- 519
ory the function of remembering. The latter, rooted in the signifier, resolves the Platonic aporias of reminiscence through the ascendancy of history in man.

One need but read *Three Essays on the Theory of Sexuality*—which is covered over for the masses by so many pseudo-biological glosses—to note that Freud has all accession to the object derive from a dialectic of return.

Having thus begun with Holderlin's νόστος, Freud arrives less than twenty years later at Kierkegaard's repetition; that is, his thought, in submitting at the outset to the humble but inflexible consequences of the talking cure* alone, was never able to let go of the living servitudes that, starting from the royal principle of the Logos, led him to rethink the deadly Empedoclean antinomies.

And how, if not on the "other scene" Freud speaks of as the locus of the dream, are we to understand his recourse as a man of science to a *Deus ex machina* that is less derisory in that here it is revealed to the spectator that the machine directs the director himself? How can we fathom the fact that a scientist of the nineteenth century valued more highly than all his other works his *Totem and Taboo*—with its obscene, ferocious figure of the primordial father, who is inexhaustibly redeemed in the eternal blinding of Oedipus—before which contemporary ethnologists bow as before the development of an authentic myth, unless we realize that he had to bow to a force of evidence that went beyond his prejudices?

Similarly, the imperious proliferation of particular symbolic creations—such as what are called the sexual theories of children—which account for even the smallest details of the neurotic's compulsions, answer to the same necessities as do myths.

This is why, to bring you to the precise point of the commentary on Freud's work I am developing in my seminar, little Hans, left in the lurch at the age of five by the failings of his symbolic entourage, and faced with the suddenly actualized enigma to him of his sex and his existence, develops—under the direction of Freud and his father, who is Freud's disciple—all the possible permutations of a limited number of signifiers in the form of a myth, around the signifying crystal of his phobia.

520 We see here that, even at the individual level, man can find a solution to the impossible by exhausting all possible forms of the impossibilities that are encountered when the solution is put into the form of a signifying equation. This is a striking demonstration that illuminates the labyrinth of a case study which thus far has been used only as a scrap heap. It also makes us grasp that the nature of neurosis is revealed in the fact that a symptom's development is coextensive with its elimination in the treatment: whether phobic, hysterical, or obsessive, neurosis is a question that being raises for the subject "from where he was before the subject came into the world" (this subordinate clause is the very expression Freud uses in explaining the Oedipus complex to little Hans).

At stake here is the being that appears in a split second in the emptiness of the verb "to be" and, as I said, this being raises its question for the subject. What does that mean? It does not raise it *before* the subject, since the subject cannot come to the place where being raises it, but being raises it *in* the subject's *place*—in other words, being raises the question in that place *with* the subject, just as one raises a problem *with* a pen and as antiquity's man thought *with* his soul.

Freud brought the ego into his doctrine in this way, defining it by the resistances that are specific to it.[22] I have tried to get people to understand that these resistances are imaginary in nature, like the coaptational lures that ethology shows us in display or combat in animal behavior, these lures being reduced in man to the narcissistic relation introduced by Freud and elaborated by me in "The Mirror Stage." While Freud—by situating in this ego the synthesis of the perceptual functions in which the sensorimotor selections are integrated—seems to agree with the tradition that delegates to the ego the task of answering for reality, this reality is simply all the more included in the suspension of the ego.

For this ego, distinguished first for the imaginary inertias it concentrates against the message of the unconscious, operates only by covering over the displacement the subject is with a resistance that is essential to discourse as such.

This is why an exhaustion of the defense mechanisms, as palpable as 521
Fenichel renders it in his *Problems of Psychoanalytic Technique* because he is a practitioner (whereas his whole theoretical reduction of the neuroses and psychoses to genetic anomalies in libidinal development is pure platitude), turns out to be the other side of unconscious mechanisms, without Fenichel accounting for or even realizing it. Periphrasis, hyperbaton, ellipsis, suspension, anticipation, retraction, negation, digression, and irony, these are the figures of style (Quintilian's *figurae sententiarum*), just as catachresis, litotes, antonomasia, and hypotyposis are the tropes, whose names strike me as the most appropriate ones with which to label these mechanisms. Can one see here mere manners of speaking, when it is the figures themselves that are at work in the rhetoric of the discourse the analysand actually utters?

By obstinately characterizing resistance as having an emotional permanence, thereby making it foreign to discourse, contemporary psychoanalysts simply show that they have succumbed to one of the fundamental truths Freud rediscovered through psychoanalysis. Which is that we cannot confine ourselves to giving a new truth its rightful place, for the point is to take up our place in it. The truth requires us to go out of our way. We cannot do so by simply getting used to it. We get used to reality [*réel*]. The truth we repress.

Now it is especially necessary to the scholar, the sage, and even the quack, to be the only one who knows. The idea that deep within the simplest of souls—and, what's more, in the sickest—there is something ready to blossom is one thing. But that there may be someone who seems to know as much as them about what we ought to make of it . . . come to our rescue yon categories of primitive, pre-logical, and archaic thought—nay, of magical thought, so convenient to attribute to others! It is not fitting that these country bumpkins should keep us breathless by posing enigmas to us that prove overly clever.

To interpret the unconscious as Freud did, one would have to be, as he was, an encyclopedia of the arts and muses, as well as an assiduous reader of
522 the *Fliegende Blätter*. And the task would become no easier were we to put ourselves at the mercy of a thread spun of allusions and quotations, puns and equivocations. Must we make a career out of "antidoted fanfreluches"?

Indeed, we must resolve to do so. The unconscious is neither the primordial nor the instinctual, and what it knows of the elemental is no more than the elements of the signifier.

The three books that one might call canonical with regard to the unconscious—the *Traumdeutung*, *The Psychopathology of Everyday Life*, and *Jokes (Witz) and their Relation to the Unconscious*—are but a web of examples whose development is inscribed in formulas for connection and substitution (though multiplied tenfold by their particular complexity, diagrams of them sometimes being provided by Freud outside the main body of the text), which are the formulas I give for the signifier in its *transference* function. For in the *Traumdeutung* it is in terms of such a function that the term *Übertragung*, or transference, which later gave its name to the mainspring of the intersubjective link between analysand and analyst, is introduced.

Such diagrams are not solely constitutive in neurosis of each of the symptoms, but they alone allow us to encompass the thematic of its course and resolution—as the major case histories provided by Freud demonstrate admirably.

To fall back on a more limited fact, but one that is more manageable as it provides a final seal with which to close these remarks, I will cite the 1927 article on fetishism and the case Freud reports there of a patient for whom sexual satisfaction required a certain shine on the nose (*Glanz auf der Nase*).[23] The analysis showed that he owed it to the fact that his early English-speaking years had displaced the burning curiosity that attached him to his mother's phallus—that is, to that eminent want-to-be, whose privileged signifier Freud revealed—into a "glance at the nose,"* rather than a "shine on the nose"* in the forgotten language [*langue*] of his childhood.

It was the abyss, open to the thought that a thought might make itself heard in the abyss, that gave rise to resistance to psychoanalysis from the outset—
523 not the emphasis on man's sexuality, as is commonly said. The latter is the object that has clearly predominated in literature throughout the ages. And the evolution of psychoanalysis has succeeded by a comical stroke of magic in turning it into a moral instance, the cradle and waiting area of oblativity

and attraction. The soul's Platonic steed, now blessed and enlightened, goes straight to heaven.

The intolerable scandal when Freudian sexuality was not yet holy was that it was so "intellectual." It was in this respect that it showed itself to be the worthy stooge of all those terrorists whose plots were going to ruin society.

At a time when psychoanalysts are busy refashioning a right-thinking psychoanalysis, whose crowning achievement is the sociological poem of the "autonomous ego," I would like to say, to those who are listening to me, how they can recognize bad psychoanalysts: by the word they use to deprecate all research on technique and theory that furthers the Freudian experience in its authentic direction. That word is "intellectualization"—execrable to all those who, living in fear of putting themselves to the test by drinking the wine of truth, spit on men's bread, even though their spittle can never again have any effect but that of leavening.

III. The Letter, being, and the other

Is what thinks in my place, then, another ego? Does Freud's discovery represent the confirmation, at the level of psychological experience, of Manichaeism?[24]

There can, in fact, be no confusion on this point: what Freud's research introduced us to was not some more or less curious cases of dual personality. Even at the heroic era I have been describing—when, like animals in the age of fairy tales, sexuality spoke—the diabolical atmosphere that such an orientation might have given rise to never materialized.[25]

The goal Freud's discovery proposes to man was defined by Freud at the 524
height of his thought in these moving terms: *Wo Es war, soll Ich werden*. Where it was, I must come into being.

This goal is one of reintegration and harmony, I might even say of reconciliation [*Versöhnung*].

But if we ignore the self's radical eccentricity with respect to itself that man is faced with—in other words, the very truth Freud discovered—we will renege on both the order and pathways of psychoanalytic mediation; we will make of it the compromise operation that it has, in effect, become—precisely what both the spirit and letter of Freud's work most repudiate. For, since he constantly points out that compromise is behind all the miseries his analysis assuages, we can say that resorting to compromise, whether explicit or implicit, disorients all psychoanalytic action and plunges it into darkness.

But neither does it suffice to rub shoulders with the moralistic tartufferies of our time or to be forever spouting forth about the "total personality" in order to have said anything articulate about the possibility of mediation.

The radical heteronomy that Freud's discovery shows gaping within man can no longer be covered over without whatever tries to hide it being fundamentally dishonest.

Which other is this, then, to whom I am more attached than to myself [*moi*], since, at the most assented to heart of my identity to myself, he pulls the strings?

His presence can only be understood in an alterity raised to the second power, which already situates him in a mediating position in relation to my own splitting from myself, as if from a semblable.

If I have said that the unconscious is the Other's discourse (with a capital O), it is in order to indicate the beyond in which the recognition of desire is tied to the desire for recognition.

In other words, this other is the Other that even my lie invokes as a guarantor of the truth in which my lie subsists.

Here we see that the dimension of truth emerges with the appearance of language.

Prior to this point, we have to admit the existence—in the psychological relation, which can be precisely isolated in the observation of animal behav-
525 ior—of subjects, not because of some projective mirage, it being the psychologist's vacuous watchword to hack this phantom to pieces, but because of the manifested presence of intersubjectivity. In the animal hidden in his lookout, in the well-laid trap, in the straggler ruse by which a runaway separated from the flock throws a raptor off the scent, something more emerges than in the fascinating erection of display or combat. Yet there is nothing here that transcends the function of a lure in the service of a need, or that affirms a presence in that beyond-the-veil where the whole of Nature can be questioned about its design.

For the question to even arise (and we know that it arose for Freud in *Beyond the Pleasure Principle*), there must be language.

For I can lure my adversary with a movement that runs counter to my battle plan, and yet this movement has its deceptive effect only insofar as I actually make it for my adversary.

But in the proposals by which I initiate peace negotiations with him, what my negotiations propose is situated in a third locus which is neither my speech nor my interlocutor.

This locus is nothing but the locus of signifying convention, as is seen in the comedy of the distressed complaint of the Jew to his pal: "Why are you telling me you are going to Cracow so I'll believe you are going to Lemberg, when you really are going to Cracow?"

Of course the aforementioned flock-movement can be understood in the conventional register of a game's strategy, where it is on the basis of a rule that I deceive my adversary; but here my success is assessed as connoting betrayal—that is, it is assessed in the relationship to the Other who is the guarantor of Good Faith.

Here the problems are of an order whose heteronomy is simply ignored if it is reduced to some "awareness of others," or whatever people choose to call it. For the "existence of the other" having, not long ago, reached the ears of Midas, the psychoanalyst, through the partition that separates him from the phenomenologists' confabs, the news is now being whispered through the reeds: "Midas, King Midas, is the other of his patient. He himself said so." 526

What sort of breakthrough is that? The other—which other?

Which other was the young André Gide aiming at when he defied the landlady, in whose care his mother had placed him, to treat him as a responsible being by unlocking right in front of her—with a key that was fake only insofar as it opened all locks of the same kind—the lock that she herself considered to be the worthy signifier of her educational intentions? Was it she who would later intervene and to whom the child would laughingly say: "Do you really think a lousy padlock can ensure my obedience?" But by simply remaining out of sight and waiting until that evening before lecturing the kid, after giving him a suitably cold reception upon his return home, it was not simply a female other whose angry face she showed him, but another André Gide, one who was no longer really sure, either then or even later when he thought back on it, what he had wanted to do—who had been changed right down to his very truth by the doubt cast on his good faith.

Perhaps it would be worth dwelling on this realm of confusion—which is simply that in which the whole human *opera buffa* is played out—to understand the pathways by which analysis proceeds, not only to restore order here but also to instate the conditions for the possibility of its restoration.

Kern unseres Wesen, "the core of our being"—it is not so much that Freud commands us to target this, as so many others before him have done with the futile adage "Know thyself," as that he asks us to reconsider the pathways that lead to it.

Or, rather, the "this" which he proposes we attain is not a this which can be the object of knowledge, but a this—doesn't he say as much?—which constitutes my being and to which, as he teaches us, I bear witness as much and more in my whims, aberrations, phobias, and fetishes, than in my more or less civilized personage.

Madness, you are no longer the object of the ambiguous praise with which the sage furnished the impregnable burrow of his fear. And if he is, after all, not so badly ensconced there, it is because the supreme agent at work since time immemorial, digging its tunnels and maze, is reason itself, the same Logos he serves.

Then how do you explain the fact that a scholar like Erasmus, with so little talent for the "commitments" that solicited him in his age, as in any other,
527 could hold such an eminent place in the revolution brought about by a Reformation in which man has as much of a stake in each man as in all men?

It is by touching, however lightly, on man's relation to the signifier—in this case, by changing the procedures of exegesis—that one changes the course of his history by modifying the moorings of his being.

It is precisely in this respect that anyone capable of glimpsing the changes we have lived through in our own lives can see that Freudianism, however misunderstood it has been and however nebulous its consequences have been, constitutes an intangible but radical revolution. There is no need to go seeking witnesses to the fact:[26] everything that concerns not just the human sciences, but the destiny of man, politics, metaphysics, literature, the arts, advertising, propaganda—and thus, no doubt, economics—has been affected by it.

But is this anything more than the dissonant effects of an immense truth where Freud has traced a pure path? It must be said here that a technique that takes advantage of the psychological categorization alone of its object is not following this path, as is the case of contemporary psychoanalysis apart from a return to the Freudian discovery.

Thus the vulgarity of the concepts by which its practice shows its mettle, the embroidery of Freudery [*fofreudisme*] which is now mere decoration, and what must be called the discredit in which it prospers, together bear witness to the fundamental repudiation of that discovery.

Through his discovery, Freud brought the border between object and being that seemed to mark the limits of science within its ambit.

This is the symptom of and prelude to a reexamination of man's situation
528 in the midst of beings [*dans l'étant*], as all the postulates of knowledge have heretofore assumed it to be—but please don't be content to classify the fact that I am saying so as a case of Heideggerianism, even prefixed by a "neo-" that adds nothing to the trashy style by which it is common to spare oneself any reflection with the quip, "Separate that out for me from its mental jetsam."

When I speak of Heidegger, or rather when I translate him, I strive to preserve the sovereign signifierness of the speech he proffers.

If I speak of the letter and being, if I distinguish the other from the Other, it is because Freud suggests them to me as the terms to which resistance and transference effects refer—effects against which I have had to wage unequal battle in the twenty years that I have been engaged in the practice that we all, repeating after Freud, call impossible: that of psychoanalysis. It is also because I must help others avoid losing their way there.

It is to prevent the field they have inherited from falling fallow, and to that end to convey that if the symptom is a metaphor, it is not a metaphor to say so, any more than it is to say that man's desire is a metonymy. For the symptom *is* a metaphor, whether one likes to admit it or not, just as desire *is* a metonymy, even if man scoffs at the idea.

Thus, if I am to rouse you to indignation over the fact that, after so many centuries of religious hypocrisy and philosophical posturing, no one has yet validly articulated what links metaphor to the question of being and metonymy to its lack, something of the object of this indignation must still be there—something that, as both instigator and victim, corresponds to it: namely, the man of humanism and the irremediably contested debt he has incurred against his intentions.

T.t.y.e.m.u.p.t.
May 14–26, 1957

Related to this article is a presentation I made on April 23, 1960, to the Philosophical Society regarding the paper Chaim Perelman gave there on his theory of metaphor as a rhetorical function—found in his *Traité de l'argumentation*.

My presentation is included as an appendix (Appendix II) in this volume [*Écrits* 1966].

Notes

1. *Codice Atlantico*, 145. r. a., trans. Louise Servicen (Paris: Gallimard), vol. II, 400.

2. The theme was "Psychoanalysis and the sciences of man."

3. The talk took place on May 9, 1957, in the Descartes Amphitheater at the Sorbonne, and discussion continued afterward over drinks.

4. "Die Frage der Laienanalyse," *GW* XIV, 281–83.

5. This point—so useful in overturning the concept of "psychological function," which obscures everything related to the matter—becomes clear as day in the purely linguistic analysis of the two major forms of aphasia classified by one of the leaders of modern linguistics, Roman Jakobson. See the most accessible of his works (coauthored by Morris Halle), *Fundamentals of Language* ('s Gravenhage and New York: Mouton, 1956), part II, chapters 1 to 4; see too the collection of translations into French of his works that we owe to Nicolas Ruwet, *Essais de linguistique générale* (Paris: Minuit, 1963).

6. Recall that discussion about the need for a new language in communist society really did take place, and that Stalin, much to the relief of those who lent credence to his philosophy, put an end to it as follows: language is not a superstructure.

7. By "linguistics" I mean the study of existing languages [*langues*] as regards their structure and the laws they reveal; this does not include the theory of abstract codes (incorrectly placed under the heading of communication theory), so-called information theory (originating in physics), or any more

or less hypothetically generalized semiology.

8. Cf. St. Augustine's *De Magistro*; I analyzed the chapter "De significatione locutionis" in my seminar on June 23, 1954.

9. Thus I. A. Richards, author of a book about procedures appropriate for reaching this objective, shows us their application in another book. He selects for his purposes a page from Meng Tzu (Mencius, to the Jesuits) and calls the piece *Mencius on the Mind*, given its object. The guarantees provided of the purity of the experiment are nothing compared to the luxury of the approaches employed. And the man of letters, an expert on the traditional Canon that contains the text, is met right on the spot in Peking where our demonstration-model wringer has been transported, regardless of the cost.

But we will be no less transported, though less expensively, upon witnessing the transformation of a bronze, which gives off bell-tones at the slightest contact with thought, into a rag with which to wipe clean the slate of the most depressing British psychologism. And not, alas, without quickly identifying it with the author's own brain—all that remains of his object or of him after he has exhausted the meaning [*sens*] of the one and the common sense of the other.

10. It is in this respect that verbal hallucination, when it takes this form, sometimes opens a door that communicates with the Freudian structure of psychosis—a door which was hitherto missed since it went unnoticed (see my Seminar from 1955–1956).

11. I did so on June 6, 1956, taking as an example the first scene of *Athaliah*, incited, I confess, by an allusion—made in passing by a highbrow* critic in *The New Statesman and Nation*—to the "supreme bitchery" of Racine's heroines, designed to dissuade us from making reference to Shakespeare's savage tragedies, which has become compulsory in analytic circles where such references serve to whitewash the vulgarity of Philistinism.

12. (Added in 1966:) The publication by Jean Starobinski, in *Le Mercure de France* (February 1964), of the notes left by Saussure on anagrams and their hypogrammatical use, from the Saturnine verses to the writings of Cicero, provide the corroboration I didn't have at the time.

13. I pay homage here to what this formulation owes to Roman Jakobson, that is, to his written work, in which a psychoanalyst can always find something to structure his own experience, and which renders superfluous the "personal communications" that I could tout as much as anyone else.

Indeed, one can recognize in such oblique forms of allegiance the style of that immortal couple, Rosencrantz and Guildenstern, who are a set that cannot be broken up, not even by the imperfection of their destiny, for it lasts by the same method as Jeannot's knife, and for the very reason for which Goethe praised Shakespeare for presenting the character in their doublet: all by themselves they are the whole *Gesellschaft*, Society in a nutshell (*Wilhelm Meisters Lehrjahre*, Vol. 5, ed. Trunz [Hamburg: Christian Wegner Verlag], 299)—I mean the International Psychoanalytical Association.

> (We should extract the whole passage from Goethe: Dieses leise Auftreten, dieses Schmiegen und Biegen, dies Jasagen, Streicheln und Schmeicheln, dieses Behendigkeit, dies Schwänzein, diese Allheit und Leerheit, diese rechtliche Schurkerei, diese Unfähigleit, wie kann sie durch einen Menschen ausgedruckt werden? Es sollten ihrer wenigstens ein Dutzend sein, wenn man sie haben könnte; denn sie bloss in Gesellschaft etwas, sie sind die Gesellschaft.)

Let us be grateful, in this context, to the author of "Some Remarks on the Role of Speech in Psycho-Analytic Technique" (*IJP* XXXVII, 6 [1956]: 467) for taking the trouble to point out that his remarks are "based on" work by him that dates back to 1952. This no doubt explains why he has assimilated nothing of the work published since then, but which he is nevertheless aware of since he cites me as its publisher (*sic.* I know what "editor"* means).

14. *Esprit* is clearly the equivalent of the German *Witz* with which Freud marked the aim of his third fundamental book on the unconscious. The far greater difficulty of finding an equivalent in English is instructive: "wit," weighed down by a discussion running from

Davenant and Hobbes to Pope and Addison, left its essential virtues to "humor," which is something else. The only other choice is "pun," but its meaning is too narrow.

15. Leo Strauss, *Persecution and the Art of Writing* (Glencoe, Illinois: The Free Press, 1957).

16. See the correspondence, in particular, letters 107 and 119 selected by its editors.

17. This is the procedure by which a study ensures results through a mechanical exploration of the entire extent of its object's field.

18. (Added in 1966:) By referring only to the development of the organism, the typology neglects the structure in which the subject is caught up in fantasy, the drive, and sublimation, respectively. I am currently developing the theory of this structure.

19. The sign $\cong$ designates congruence.

20. Since S′ designates, in this context, the term that produces the signifying effect (or signifierness), one can see that the term is latent in metonymy and patent in metaphor.

21. Things are altogether different if—in raising a question like "Why are there philosophers?"—I become more candid than usual, since I am raising not only a question that philosophers have been asking themselves since time immemorial, but also the one in which they are perhaps the most interested.

22. (Added in December 1968:) This and the next paragraph were rewritten solely to achieve greater clarity of expression.

23. "Fetischismus," *GW* XIV, 311.

24. One of my colleagues went as far as this thought in wondering if the id (*Es*) of Freud's last doctrine wasn't in fact the "bad ego." (Added in 1966:) You see the kind of people I had to work with.

25. Note, nevertheless, the tone with which people spoke in that period of the impish pranks of the unconscious: *Der Zufall und die Koboldstreiche des Unbewussten* ("Chance and the Impish Pranks of the Unconscious"), one of Silberer's titles, which would be absolutely anachronistic in the present context of soul-managers.

26. I'll highlight the most recent in what flowed quite smoothly from François Mauriac's pen, in the *Figaro littéraire* on May 25, by way of an apology for refusing "to tell us his life story." If one can no longer undertake to do this with the old enthusiasm, the reason, he tells us, is that, "for half a century, Freud, whatever we may think of him," has left his mark there. And after briefly yielding to the received idea that it would be to submit to the "history of our body," Mauriac quickly returns to what his writer's sensibility could not help but let slip out: our discourse, in endeavoring to be complete, would publish the deepest confessions of the souls of all our loved ones.

V

On a Question Prior to Any Possible Treatment of Psychosis 531

This article contains the most important material from the seminar I gave during the first two terms of the 1955–1956 academic year, the material from the third term thus having been excluded. It was published in volume 4 of La Psychanalyse.

Hoc quod triginta tres per annos in ipso loco studui, et Sanctae Annae Genio loci, et dilectae juventuti, quae eo me sectata est, diligenter dedico.

I. Toward Freud

1. Half a century of Freudianism applied to psychosis has left the latter still to be reconceptualized, in other words, *in statu quo ante*.

We might say that, prior to Freud, discussion of psychosis was unable to move beyond a theoretical framework that presented itself as psychology and was merely a "laicized" residue of what I will call the long metaphysical coction of science in the School (with the capital S our reverence owes it).

Now if our science, concerning the *phusis*, in its ever purer mathematization, retains from this cuisine no more than a stench so subtle that one may legitimately wonder whether a substitution of person has not occurred, the same cannot be said concerning the *antiphusis* (that is, the living apparatus that one hopes is capable of taking the measure of the said *phusis*), whose smell of burnt fat indubitably betrays the age-old practice of preparing brains in that cuisine.

Thus the theory of abstraction, necessary to account for knowledge, has become fixed in an abstract theory of the subject's faculties, which the most radical sensationalist question begging has been unable to render more functional with regard to subjective effects.

The ever-renewed attempts to correct its results by the various counter-
weights of affect must, in fact, remain futile as long as one neglects to ask 532
whether or not it is indeed the same subject that is affected.

2. This is the question one learns to avoid once and for all on one's school (with a lowercase s) bench: for even if alternations in the identity of the *percipiens* are accepted, the latter's function in constituting the unity of the *perceptum* is not challenged. Thus diversity of structure in the *perceptum* affects only a diversity of register in the *percipiens*—in the final analysis, that of the *sensoriums*. This diversity is always surmountable, in principle, provided the *percipiens* remains at a level commensurate with reality.

This is why those whose task it is to answer the question raised by the existence of the madman have been unable to stop themselves from interposing between it and them those same school benches, which they find, in this case, to be a convenient wall behind which to take shelter.

Indeed, I would dare to lump together, so to speak, all positions on the matter, whether mechanistic or dynamic, whether they see the genesis of madness as based on the organism or the psyche, and its structure as based on disintegration or conflict. Yes, all of them, however ingenious they may be, insofar as, in the name of the obvious fact that a hallucination is a *perceptum* without an object, they confine themselves to asking the *percipiens* to account for this *perceptum*, without realizing that, in doing so, they skip a step—that of inquiring whether the *perceptum* itself bequeaths a univocal meaning to the *percipiens* who is asked here to explain it.

This step should nevertheless seem legitimate in any unbiased examination of verbal hallucination, in that the latter is not reducible, as we shall see, to any particular *sensorium*, and especially not to any *percipiens* insofar as the *percipiens* would give it its unity.

Indeed, it is a mistake to take verbal hallucination to be auditory in nature, when it is theoretically conceivable that it not be auditory at all (in the case of a deaf-mute, for example, or of some nonauditory register of hallucinatory spelling out of words), but above all if we consider that the act of hearing is not the same when it aims at the coherence of the verbal chain—namely, its overdetermination at each instant by the deferred action [*après-coup*] of its sequence, and the suspension at each instant of its value upon the advent of a meaning that is always susceptible to postponement [*renvoi*]—and when it
533 adjusts to sound modulation in speech, for the purpose of acoustic analysis, whether tonal or phonetic, or even of musical power.

These highly abbreviated remarks would seem to suffice to bring out the different subjectivities we must consider when investigating the *perceptum* (and the extent to which they are misunderstood in patient interviews and the nosology of "voices").

But it might be claimed that we can reduce these differences in subjectivity to levels of objectification in the *percipiens*.

This is not so, however. For it is at the level at which subjective "synthesis" confers upon speech its full meaning that the subject manifests all the paradoxes to which he falls victim in this singular perception. The fact that these paradoxes already appear when it is the other who proffers speech is sufficiently manifested in the subject by the possibility of obeying the other insofar as the latter's speech orders him to listen and to be on guard; for by simply listening in, the subject falls under the sway of a suggestion from which he can only escape by reducing the other to being no more than the mouthpiece of a discourse that is not his own or of an intention that he sets aside in his discourse.

But more striking still is the subject's relation to his own speech, in which what is important is somewhat masked by the purely acoustic fact that he cannot speak without hearing himself. Nor is there anything special in the behavior of consciousness about the fact that he cannot listen to himself without becoming divided. Clinicians did better when they figured out that verbal motor hallucinations are often accompanied by the subject's own partial phonatory movements. Yet they did not articulate the crucial point, which is that, since the *sensorium* is indifferent in the production of a signifying chain:

(a) the signifying chain imposes itself, by itself, on the subject in its dimension as voice;
(b) it takes on, as such, a reality proportionate to the time, which is perfectly observable in experience, involved in its subjective attribution;
(c) and its own structure, qua signifier, is determinant in this attribution, which is distributive as a rule—that is, it has several voices and thus renders equivocal the supposedly unifying *percipiens*.

3. I will illustrate what I have just said with a phenomenon taken from one of my clinical presentations from 1955–1956, the very year of the seminar whose work I am presenting here. Let us say that such a find can only be the reward for complete, albeit enlightened, submission to the patient's properly subjective positions, positions which are all too often forced by being reduced in the doctor/patient dialogue to the morbid process, thus increasing the difficulty of fathoming them due to a not unjustified reticence on the subject's part. 534

It was a case of one of those shared delusions [*délires à deux*]—the typical case of which is the mother/daughter couple, as I showed long ago—in which a feeling of being intruded upon, that had developed into a delusion of being watched, was but the development of the defense characteristic of an affective binary relation, open as such to every alienation.

It was the daughter who, during my examination, presented me—as proof of the insults to which she and her mother were subjected by their neighbors—a fact concerning the boyfriend of their female neighbor who was supposedly harassing them with her onslaughts, after they had had to break off an intimate friendship with her that was at first kindly received. This man—who was thus an indirect party to the situation and, moreover, a rather secondary figure in the patient's allegations—had, according to her, flung at her the offensive term "Sow!" as he passed her in the hallway of their apartment building.

On hearing this, and being hardly inclined to see in it a retort to "Pig!" that would be too easy to extrapolate in the name of a projection which in such cases is never anything more than the psychiatrist's own projection, I asked her straight out what in herself had been proffered the moment before. Not in vain, for she conceded with a smile that, upon seeing the man, she had murmured the following words which, if she is to be believed here, gave no cause for offense: "I've just been to the pork butcher's . . ."

At whom were these words aimed? She was hard pressed to say, giving me the right to help her. For their literal meaning, we cannot neglect the fact, among others, that the patient had suddenly taken leave of her husband and her in-laws—and thus given a marriage her mother disapproved of a conclu-
535 sion that had not changed in the interim—due to the conviction she had formed that these country bumpkins were planning nothing less, in order to finish off this good-for-nothing city girl, than to carve her up piece by piece.

But what difference does it make whether or not one has to resort to the fantasy of the fragmented body in order to understand how the patient, a prisoner of the dyadic relationship, was responding once again here to a situation that was beyond her?

For our present purposes, it is enough that the patient admitted that the sentence was allusive, even though she was unable for all that to demonstrate anything other than perplexity over which of the two people present or the one person absent was targeted by the allusion. For it thus appears that the "I," as subject of the sentence in direct speech, left in abeyance—in accordance with its function as a "shifter," as it is called in linguistics[1]—the designation of the speaking subject for as long as the allusion, in its conjuratory intention no doubt, itself remained oscillating. After a pause, this uncertainty came to an end with the apposition of the word "sow," itself too loaded with invective to follow the oscillation isochronously. This is how the discourse managed to realize its rejecting intention in the hallucination. In the locus where the unspeakable object was rejected into the real, a word made itself heard because, in coming to the place of what has no name, it was unable to follow the subject's intention without detaching itself from it by the dash that introduces the reply—opposing its disparaging antistrophe to the grumbling of the strophe that was thus restored to the patient with the index of the I, resembling in its opacity the exclamations of love, when, running short of signifiers to call the object of its epithalamion, it employs the crudest imaginary means:

"I'll eat you up . . ."

"My sweetie! [*Chou!*]"

"You'll love it . . ."

"You dog, you! [*Rat!*]"

4. I mention this example here only to show in a real-life case that the function of unrealization is not entirely located in the symbol. For in order for its irruption in the real to be incontrovertible, the symbol need but present itself, as it commonly does, in the form of a broken chain.[2] 536

We also see here the effect every signifier has, once it is perceived, of arousing in the *percipiens* an assent composed of the awakening of the *percipiens'* hidden duplicity by the signifier's manifest ambiguity.

Of course, all of this can be considered to be a mirage from the classic perspective of the unifying subject.

But it is striking that this perspective, reduced to itself, offers only such impoverished views regarding hallucination, for example, that the work of a madman, as remarkable as Judge Schreber proves to be in his *Memoirs of My Nervous Illness*,[3] after being well received, even before Freud, by psychiatrists, can be regarded, even after Freud, as a text worth reading as an introduction to the phenomenology of psychosis, and not simply for beginners.[4]

This work provided me with the basis for a structural analysis in my 1955–1956 seminar on Freudian structures in the psychoses when, following Freud's advice, I reexamined it.

The relation between the signifier and the subject that this analysis uncovers can be found—as is apparent in this preamble—in the very appearance of the phenomena, provided that, coming back to it from Freud's experience, one knows where it leads.

But, if properly carried out, an approach that starts from the phenomenon leads back to this point, as was the case for me when my initial study of paranoia thirty years ago brought me to the threshold of psychoanalysis.[5]

Nowhere, in fact, is the fallacious conception of a psychical process in Jaspers' sense—in which a symptom is merely an index—more irrelevant than in dealing with psychosis, because nowhere is the symptom more clearly articulated in the structure itself, assuming one knows how to read it. 537

This makes it incumbent upon us to define this process by the most radical determinants of man's relation to the signifier.

5. But we need not have reached this stage to be interested in the variety of forms verbal hallucinations assume in Schreber's *Memoirs*, or to recognize in them differences quite other than those by which they are "classically" classified, according to the way they involve the *percipiens* (the degree of his "belief") or the latter's reality ("auditivation"): namely, differences that stem instead from their speech structure, insofar as this structure is already in the *perceptum*.

If we consider the text of the hallucinations alone, a distinction immediately arises for the linguist between code phenomena and message phenomena.

Belonging to the code phenomena, in this approach, are the voices that use the *Grundsprache*, which I translate as "basic language" [*langue-de-fond*], and which Schreber describes (S. 13)[6] as "a vigorous though somewhat antiquated German, which is especially characterized by its great wealth of euphemisms." Elsewhere (S. 167) he ruefully refers to "its form, which is authentic on account of its characteristics of noble distinction and simplicity."

These code phenomena are specified in locutions that are neological in both their form (new compound words, though the compounding here takes place in accordance with the rules of the patient's mother tongue) and usage. Hallucinations inform the subject of the forms and usages that constitute the neo-code: the subject owes to them, for example, first and foremost, the term *Grundsprache* that designates this neo-code.

We are dealing here with something fairly akin to the messages that linguists call "autonymous," insofar as it is the signifier itself (and not what it signifies)
538 that is the object of the communication. However, this peculiar but normal relation of the message to itself is redoubled here, in that these messages are taken to be borne by beings whose relations are enunciated by the messages themselves, in modes that prove to be quite analogous to the connections between signifiers. The term *Nervenanhang*, which I translate as "nerve-annexation," and which also comes from these messages, illustrates this remark insofar as passion and action between these beings are reduced to those annexed or disannexed nerves, but also insofar as these nerves, just like the divine rays *(Gottesstrahlen)* with which they are homogeneous, are nothing but the entification of the spoken words they bear (S. 130, which the voices formulate as: "Do not forget that the nature of the rays is that they must speak").

This is the system's relation to its own constitution as signifier, which should be filed under the question of metalanguage and which, in my opinion, demonstrates the impropriety of this notion if it is intended to define elements differentiated within language.

Let us note, on the other hand, that we are presented here with phenomena that have mistakenly been called intuitive due to the fact that the effect of signification anticipates the development of signification therein. What is actually involved is an effect of the signifier, insofar as its degree of certainty (second degree: signification of signification) takes on a weight proportional to the enigmatic void that first presents itself in the place of signification itself.

What is amusing in this case is that it is precisely to the extent that the signifier's high tension drops for the subject—that is, that the hallucinations turn into refrains, mere repetitions whose emptiness is imputed to beings devoid of intelligence and personality, or who are even altogether effaced from the register of being—it is to this very extent, as I was saying, that the voices highlight the *Seelenauffassung*, the "soul-conception" (in the basic language); this conception is manifested in a catalog of thoughts that is not unworthy of a book of classical psychology. This catalog is tied to a pedantic intention on the part of the voices, which does not stop the subject from making highly relevant comments on it. Note that the source of terms is always carefully referenced in these comments; for example, when the subject uses the word *Instanz* (S. 30 note; see also notes on pages 11 to 21), he emphasizes in a note: "this 539
expression . . . is mine."

This is why the primordial importance of memory-thoughts *(Erinnerungsgedanken)* in the psychical economy does not escape him, and he immediately offers proof of this in the poetic and musical use of modulating reprise.

Our patient, who provides the priceless description of this "soul-conception" as "a somewhat idealized representation which souls had formed of human life and thought" (S. 164), thinks that he has "gained insight into the nature of human thought processes and human feelings for which many a psychologist might envy me" (S. 167).

I would agree all the more readily in that, unlike them, he does not imagine that he has wrested this knowledge, whose scope he assesses so humorously, from the nature of things, and in that, while he thinks that he must make use of it, it is, as I have just indicated, on the basis of a semantic analysis![7]

But to return to the thread of my argument, let us turn to the phenomena that I will contrast with the preceding ones as message phenomena.

The latter are interrupted messages, by means of which a relationship is sustained between the subject and his divine interlocutor, a relationship to which the messages give the form of a challenge* or an endurance test.

Indeed, his partner's voice limits the messages in question to the beginning of a sentence whose complement of meaning poses, moreover, no problem to the subject, except for its harassing, offensive character, which is usually so idiotic as to discourage him. The valiance he displays by not faltering in his reply, and even in eluding the traps he is led into, is not the least important aspect for our analysis of the phenomenon.

But I will dwell here again on the very text of what might be called the hallucinatory provocation (or better, protasis). The subject gives us the following examples of such a structure (S. 217),

1. *Nun will ich mich* . . . ("Now I shall . . ."),
2. *Sie sollen nämlich* . . . ("You were to . . ."),
3. *Das will ich mir* . . . ("I shall . . ."),

540 to take only these three—to which he must reply with their significant supplement, which to him is not open to doubt, namely:

1. "resign myself to being stupid,"
2. "be exposed (a word of the basic language) as denying God, as given to voluptuous excesses," not to mention other things,
3. "think about that first."

One might note that each sentence is interrupted at the point at which the group of words that one might call "index-terms" ends, the latter being those designated by their function in the signifier, according to the terminology employed above, as shifters*—that is, the terms in the code that indicate the subject's position on the basis of the message itself.

After which, the properly lexical part of the sentence—in other words, the part that includes the words the code defines by their use, whether it is the shared code or the delusional code—remains elided.

Aren't we struck by the predominance of the signifier's function in these two orders of phenomena, and even incited to seek what lies at the root of the association they constitute: that of a code constituted by messages about the code and of a message reduced to what, in the code, indicates the message?

All this would have to be carefully transcribed onto a graph,[8] the graph with which I have tried this year to represent the signifier's internal connections, insofar as they structure the subject.

For there is a topology here that is altogether different from the topology we might be led to imagine by the requirement of an immediate parallelism between the form of the phenomena and their pathways in the central nervous system.

But this topology—which follows the lines laid down by Freud when, after opening up the field of the unconscious with dreams, he set out to describe the dynamics of the unconscious, without feeling bound by any concern for cortical localization—is precisely what may best prepare the questions we should ask when investigating the surface of the cerebral cortex.

For it is only after linguistic analysis of the phenomenon of language that one can legitimately establish the relation it constitutes in the subject and at the same time delimit the order of "machines" (in the purely associative sense this term takes on in network theory in mathematics) that can bring about this phenomenon. 541

It is no less remarkable that it was the Freudian experience that led the author of these lines in the direction presented here. Let us examine, then, what this experience contributes to our question.

II. After Freud

1. What did Freud contribute here? I began by stating that, regarding the problem of psychosis, his contribution led to backsliding.

This is immediately apparent in the simplistic character of the mainsprings invoked in conceptions that all boil down to the following fundamental schema: how can the inside be shifted outside? Indeed, even though the subject here encompasses an opaque id, it is nevertheless as an ego—that is, and this is clearly expressed in the current psychoanalytic orientation, as the same inexhaustible *percipiens*—that he is invoked in explaining psychosis. This *percipiens* has total power over its no less unchanged correlate, reality, and the model for this power is derived from a fact accessible to everyday experience, that of affective projection.

For what is noteworthy about current theories is the absolutely uncritical way in which the mechanism of projection is put to use in them. Everything objects to it, yet nothing stops them, least of all the obvious clinical fact that there is no relation between affective projection and its supposed delusional effects—between, for example, the jealousy of the unfaithful spouse and the jealousy of the alcoholic.

Freud, in the essay in which he interprets the Schreber case, which is read badly when it is reduced to the rehashings that followed it, uses the form of a grammatical deduction in order to present the switching involved in the relation to the other in psychosis. He employs the different ways of negating the proposition, "I love him," from which it follows that the negative judgment is structured in two stages: the first is a reversal of the value of the verb ("I hate him") or inversion of the gender of the agent or object ("It is not me—or It is not him—but her," or vice versa); the second is a reversal of subjects ("He 542
hates me," "It is her that he loves," "It is she who loves me"). But no one pays any attention to the logical problems formally involved in this deduction.

Furthermore, while Freud in this text expressly dismisses the mechanism of projection as insufficient to account for the problem—entering at this point into a very long, detailed, and subtle discussion of repression, which offers us, all the same, some toothing stones for our problem—suffice it to say that these toothing stones continue to stand out inviolate above the clouds of dust raised on the psychoanalytic construction site.

2. After that, Freud contributed "On Narcissism." It was put to the same use, namely, to a sort of pumping—a sucking in and spewing out, depending on the stages of the theorem—of libido by the *percipiens*, which is thereby capable of inflating and deflating a windbag reality.

Freud provided the first theory of the way in which the ego is constituted on the model of the other in the new subjective economy determined by the unconscious; the response was to acclaim the rediscovery in this ego of the good old reliable *percipiens* and of the synthesizing function.

Is it surprising that the only use made of it regarding psychosis was to definitively foreground the notion of "loss of reality"?

That's not all. In 1924 Freud wrote an incisive article, "The Loss of Reality in Neurosis and Psychosis," in which he directs our attention back to the fact that the problem is not that of the loss of reality, but of the mainspring of what takes its place. His words fell on deaf ears, since the problem had already been resolved: the prop room is inside and the props are taken out as the need arises.

Such is, in fact, the schema with which even Katan remains satisfied—in his studies in which he examines so attentively the stages of Schreber's psychosis, guided by his concern to penetrate the prepsychotic phase—when he highlights the defense against instinctual temptation, against masturbation and homosexuality in this case, in order to justify the upsurge of hallucinatory phantasmagoria, which he considers to be a curtain interposed by the operation of the *percipiens* between the tendency and its real stimulus.

543 What a relief this simplicity would have been to me at one time, if I had thought it sufficed to explain the problem of literary creation in psychosis!

3. Yet can any problem still constitute an obstacle to the discourse of psychoanalysis, when the fact that a tendency gets expressed in reality is considered indicative of regression in the couple they form? What could possibly tire minds that let people talk to them of regression, without distinguishing between regression in structure, regression in history, and regression in development (which Freud always differentiates as topographical, temporal, or genetic)?

I shall refrain from spending time here taking inventory of the confusion. It is old hat to those whom I train and would be of no interest to others. I will confine myself to pointing out, for their common meditation, the sense of unfamiliarity that is produced—in those whose speculation has condemned itself to go around in circles between development and entourage—by the simple mention of characteristics that are nevertheless the very framework of the Freudian edifice: namely, the equivalence Freud maintains of the imaginary function of the phallus in the two sexes (long the despair of fans of false "biological," that is naturalist, windows); the castration complex considered to be a normative phase of the subject's assumption [*assomption*] of his own sex; the myth of the killing of the father rendered necessary by the constitutive presence of the Oedipus complex in every personal history; and, "last but not . . . ,"* the splitting brought about in love life by the instance, indeed the repetitive instance, of the object that is always to be refound as unique. Must we again recall the fundamentally dissident nature of Freud's notion of the drive, the theoretical disjunction between the tendency, its direction, and its object, and not only its original "perversion" but its involvement in a conceptual systematic, a systematic whose place Freud indicated, from the very beginning of his work, under the heading of the sexual theories of children?

Is it not clear that we have been far from all that for a long time now, in an educational naturism that no longer has any other principle than the notion of gratification and its counterpart, frustration, which is nowhere mentioned in Freud's work?

The structures revealed by Freud no doubt continue to sustain—not only in 544
their plausibility, but also in the way they are handled—the vague dynamisms with which contemporary psychoanalysis claims to orient its flow. A forsaken technique would merely be more capable still of performing "miracles"—were it not for the extra dose of conformism that reduces its effects to those of an ambiguous combination of social suggestion and psychological superstition.

4. It is even striking that a demand for rigor is found only in those people whom the course of things keeps out of the mainstream in some respect, such as Ida Macalpine, who gives us cause to marvel, encountering, as we do in reading her work, a sound thinker.

Her critique of the cliché that confines itself to the factor of the suppression of a homosexual drive—which is, moreover, altogether undefined—to explain psychosis is brilliant, and she demonstrates it amply in the Schreber case itself. Homosexuality, which is supposedly the determining factor in paranoiac psychosis, is actually a symptom articulated in the psychotic process.

This process had begun long before the first sign of it appeared in Schreber in the form of one of those hypnopompic ideas—which, in their fragility, present us with tomographies (as it were) of the ego—an idea whose imaginary function is sufficiently indicated to us by its form: that it would "be *beautiful* to be a woman submitting to the act of copulation" [S. 36].

Macalpine, to introduce a valid criticism here, nevertheless seems to neglect the fact that, although Freud places considerable stress on the homosexual question, it is in order to show, first of all, that it conditions the idea of grandeur in delusion; but, more essentially, he indicates in it the mode of alterity by which the subject's metamorphosis occurs—in other words, the place where his successive delusional "transferences" occur. She would have done better to put her trust in the reason why Freud here again stubbornly insists on a reference to the Oedipus complex, which she does not accept.

This difficulty would have led her to discoveries that would certainly have been illuminating to us, for everything still remains to be said about the function of what is known as the inverted Oedipus complex. Macalpine prefers to
545 reject all recourse to Oedipus here, making up for it with a procreation fantasy found in children of both sexes in the form of pregnancy fantasies—which, moreover, she considers to be related to the structure of hypochondria.[9]

This fantasy is, indeed, essential, and I will even add that in the first case in which I obtained this fantasy in a man, it was by a means that marked an important milestone in my career, and he was neither a hypochondriac nor a hysteric.

Macalpine feels—rather subtly, indeed surprisingly so given the way things are today—a need to tie this fantasy to a symbolic structure. But in order to find a structure independent of the Oedipus complex, she goes off in search of ethnographic references, her assimilation of which is hard to gauge in her text. This involves the "heliolithic" theme, which has been championed by one of the most eminent supporters of the English diffusionist school. I am aware of the merit of these conceptions, but they do not seem to me to even remotely corroborate Macalpine's idea that asexual procreation is a "primitive" conception.[10]

Macalpine's error is seen elsewhere, in the fact that she arrives at a result that is diametrically opposed to the result she is seeking.

By isolating a fantasy in a dynamic that she terms intrapsychic, in accordance with the conception of transference she introduces, she ends up designating the psychotic's uncertainty about his own sex as the sensitive spot where
546 the analyst must intervene, contrasting the felicitous effects of intervening there with the catastrophic effect—which is, in fact, constantly found in work with psychotics—of any suggestion that goes in the direction of getting the subject to recognize his latent homosexuality.

Now, uncertainty about one's own sex is a common feature in hysteria, whose diagnostic encroachments Macalpine points out.

The fact is that no imaginary formation is specific[11] or determinant in either the structure or dynamics of a process. And this is why one condemns oneself to missing both of them when, in the hope of grasping them better, one flouts the symbolic articulation that Freud discovered at the same time as the unconscious that is, in effect, consubstantial with the unconscious. The necessity of this articulation is what he indicates to us in his methodical reference to the Oedipus complex.

5. How can we hold Macalpine responsible for such neglect when, rather than being remedied, it has continued to grow in psychoanalysis?

That is why, in order to define the minimal split, which is certainly called for, between neurosis and psychosis, psychoanalysts are reduced to deferring to the ego's responsibility regarding reality: this is what I call leaving the problem of psychosis *in statu quo ante*.

One point was, however, very precisely designated as the bridge across the border between the two domains.

Analysts have even emphasized it in the most inordinate way concerning the question of transference in psychosis. It would be uncharitable to repeat 547
here what has been said on the subject. I shall simply take the opportunity of paying homage to Macalpine's intelligence, when she sums up a position in line with the genius deployed in psychoanalysis today in these terms: in short, psychoanalysts claim to be able to cure psychosis in all cases in which psychosis is not involved.[12]

It is on this point that Midas, laying down the law one day regarding the cases in which psychoanalysis is indicated, expressed himself thus: "It is clear that psychoanalysis is possible only with a subject for whom there is an other!" And Midas crossed the bridge back and forth thinking it to be a wasteland. How could he have done otherwise, since he was unaware that the river lay there?

The term "other," never before heard by the psychoanalytic people, had no other meaning for them than the whispering of the reeds.

III. With Freud

1. It is rather striking that a dimension that is felt to be that of something-Other [*Autre-chose*] in so many of the experiences men have—not at all without thinking about them, rather in thinking about them, but without thinking that they are thinking, and like Telemachus thinking of the expense—has never been thought out to the point of being suitably stated by those whom the idea of thought assures that they are thinking.

Desire, boredom, confinement, revolt, prayer, wakefulness (I would like us to pause here, since Freud explicitly refers to the latter by mentioning, in the middle of his text on Schreber, a passage from Nietzsche's *Zarathustra*),[13] and panic are evidence of the dimension of this Elsewhere and draw our attention to it, not as mere moods that deadpan thinkers can put in their place, but much more so as permanent principles of collective organizations, without which it does not seem human life can maintain itself for long.

548 It is probably not out of the question that the most thinkable one who thinks-about-thinking, thinking that he himself is this Other-thing [*Autre-chose*], may have always been unable to tolerate this possible competition.

But this aversion becomes perfectly clear once the conceptual connection, which nobody had yet thought of, was made between this Elsewhere and the locus, present for all of us and closed to each of us, in which Freud discovered that, without us thinking about it, and thus without anyone being able to think he thinks about it better than anyone else, it [*ça*] thinks. It thinks rather badly, but it thinks steadily. It is in these very terms that Freud announces the unconscious to us: thoughts that, while their laws are not exactly the same as those of our everyday thoughts, whether noble or vulgar, are certainly articulated.

There is no longer any way, therefore, to reduce this Elsewhere to the imaginary form of a nostalgia for some lost or future Paradise; what one finds there is the paradise of the child's loves, where—baudelaire de Dieu!—scandalous things happen.

Moreover, if any doubt still remained in our minds, Freud called the locus of the unconscious *ein anderer Schauplatz*, another scene, borrowing a term that had struck him in a text by Fechner (who, in his experimentalism, is not at all the realist our textbooks suggest he is); Freud repeats it some twenty times in his early works.

This spray of cold water having hopefully sharpened our wits, let us move on to the scientific formulation of the subject's relation to this Other.

2. "In order to set down our ideas" and orient the souls who are lost here, I shall apply the said relation to the previously introduced L schema, which I will simplify as follows:

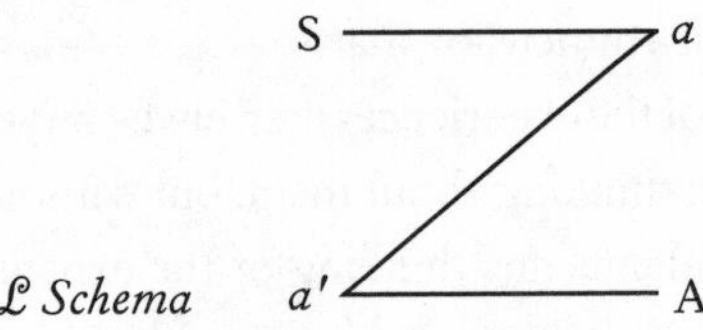

ℒ Schema

549 This schema signifies that the condition of the subject, S (neurosis or psychosis), depends on what unfolds in the Other, A. What unfolds there is articulated like

a discourse (the unconscious is the Other's discourse [*discours de l'Autre*]), whose syntax Freud first sought to define for those fragments of it that reach us in certain privileged moments, such as dreams, slips, and witticisms.

Why would the subject be interested in this discourse if he were not a party to it? He is, indeed, insofar as he is drawn to the four corners of the schema: namely, S, his ineffable and stupid existence; *a*, his objects; *a*′, his ego, that is, his form as reflected in his objects; and A, the locus from which the question of his existence may arise for him.

For it is an experiential truth for psychoanalysis that the question of the subject's existence arises for him, not in the kind of anxiety it provokes at the level of the ego, which is only one element of his cortege, but as an articulated question—"What am I there?"—about his sex and his contingency in being: namely, that on the one hand he is a man or a woman, and on the other that he might not be, the two conjugating their mystery and knotting it in symbols of procreation and death. The fact that the question of his existence envelops the subject, props him up, invades him, and even tears him apart from every angle, is revealed to the analyst by the tensions, suspense, and fantasies that he encounters. It should be added that this question is articulated in the Other in the form of elements of a particular discourse. It is because these phenomena are organized in accordance with the figures of this discourse that they have the fixity of symptoms and that they are legible and dissolve when deciphered.

3. I must therefore emphasize the fact that this question is not presented in the unconscious as ineffable and that this question is a calling into question there—that is, that prior to any analysis this question is articulated there in discrete elements. This is of capital importance, for these elements are the ones that linguistic analysis obliges us to isolate as signifiers, and they are grasped here functioning in their purest form at what is simultaneously the most unlikely and likely point:

- the most unlikely, since their chain is found to subsist in an alterity with
  respect to the subject, which is as radical as that of the still indecipherable 550
  hieroglyphics in the desert's solitude;
- the most likely, because only here can their function—that of inducing signification into the signified by imposing their structure on it—appear quite unambiguously.

For the furrows opened up by the signifier in the real world will certainly seek out the gaps—in order to widen them—that the real world as an entity [*étant*] offers the signifier, so much so that an ambiguity may well persist as to whether the signifier does not, in fact, follow the law of the signified here.

But this is not the case at the level of the calling into question, not of the subject's place in the world, but of his existence as a subject, a calling into question which, starting with him, will extend to his within-the-world relation to objects, and to the existence of the world, insofar as its existence, too, can be called into question beyond its order.

4. It is of the utmost importance to observe—in the experience of the unconscious Other where Freud is our guide—that the question does not find its outlines in protomorphic proliferations of the image, in vegetative intumescences, or in animastic halos radiating from the palpitations of life.

This is the whole difference between Freud's orientation and that of Jung's school, which latches onto such forms: *Wandlungen der libido*. These forms may be brought to the fore in a mantic, for they can be produced using the proper techniques (promoting imaginary creations such as reveries, drawings, etc.) in a situable site. This site can be seen on my schema stretched between *a* and *a′*—that is, in the veil of the narcissistic mirage, which is eminently suited to sustaining whatever is reflected in it through its effects of seduction and capture.

If Freud rejected this mantic, it was at the point at which it neglects the guiding function of a signifying articulation, which operates on the basis of its internal law and of material subjected to the poverty that is essential to it.

Similarly, it is precisely to the extent that this style of articulation has been maintained, by virtue of the Freudian Word [*verbe*], even if it has been dismembered, in the community that claims to be orthodox, that such a profound
551 difference persists between the two schools—although, given where things now stand, neither school is in a position to say why. As a result, the level of their practice will soon seem to be reduced to the distance between the forms of reverie found in the Alps and the Atlantic.

To borrow a formulation that delighted Freud when he heard it from Charcot, "That doesn't stop it from existing," it here being the Other, in its place, A.

For if the Other is removed from its place, man can no longer even sustain himself in the position of Narcissus. The *anima*, like a rubber band, snaps back to the *animus* and the *animus* to the animal, who between S and *a* maintains considerably closer "foreign relations" with its *Umwelt* than our own, without our being able to say, moreover, that its relation with the Other is nil, but simply that we only ever see it in sporadic sketches of neurosis.

5. The **L** of the calling-into-question of the subject in his existence has a combinatory structure that must not be confused with its spatial aspect. In this

respect, it is the signifier itself that must be articulated in the Other, especially in its quaternary topology.

To support this structure, we find here the three signifiers where the Other may be identified in the Oedipus complex. They suffice to symbolize the significations of sexual reproduction, under the relational signifiers of love and procreation.

The fourth term is given by the subject in his reality, foreclosed as such in the system and entering into the play of signifiers only in the form of the dummy [*mort*], but becoming the true subject as this play of signifiers makes him signify.

Indeed, this play of signifiers is not inert, since it is animated in each particular case [*partie*] by the whole ancestral history of real others that the denomination of signifying Others involves in the Subject's contemporaneity. Furthermore, insofar as this play is properly instituted above and beyond each case, it already structures the three instances in the subject—(ideal) ego, reality, and superego—which were determined by Freud's second topography.

Moreover, the subject enters the game as the dummy [*mort*], but it is as a 552
living being that he plays it; it is in his life that he must play the suit he calls trump at some point. He will do so by using a set* of imaginary figures, selected from among the innumerable forms of animastic relations, the choice of which involves a certain arbitrariness, since, in order to cover the symbolic ternary homologically, it must be numerically reduced.

To do so, the polar relation—by which the specular image (of the narcissistic relationship) is linked, as unifying, to the set of imaginary elements of the so-called fragmented body—provides a couple that is not merely readied by a natural fit between development and structure to serve as a homologue for the symbolic Mother/Child relation. While the imaginary couple of the mirror stage, through the counter-natural features it manifests, must be related to a specific prematurity of birth in man, it proves appropriate for providing the imaginary triangle with the base that the symbolic relation may, in some sense, overlap (see the R schema).

Indeed, it is by means of the gap in the imaginary opened up by this prematurity, and in which the effects of the mirror stage proliferate, that the human animal is *capable* of imagining himself mortal—which does not mean that he could do so without his symbiosis with the symbolic, but rather that, without the gap that alienates him from his own image, this symbiosis with the symbolic, in which he constitutes himself as subject to death, could not have occurred.

6. The third term of the imaginary ternary—the one where the subject is identified, on the contrary, with his living being—is nothing but the phallic image,

whose unveiling in this function is not the least scandalous facet of the Freudian discovery.

I will now inscribe here, as a conceptual visualization of this double ternary, what I shall henceforth call the R schema, which represents the lines that condition the *perceptum*—in other words, the object—insofar as these lines circumscribe the field of reality rather than merely depending on it.

Thus, in considering the vertices of the symbolic triangle—I as the ego-
553 ideal, M as the signifier of the primordial object, and P [for *père*] as the position in A of the Name-of-the-Father—we can see how the homologous pinning of the signification of the subject S under the signifier of the phallus may have repercussions on the support of the field of reality delimited by the quadrangle M*im*I. The other two vertices of this quadrangle, *i* and *m*, represent the two imaginary terms of the narcissistic relation: the ego [*m* for *moi*] and the specular image.

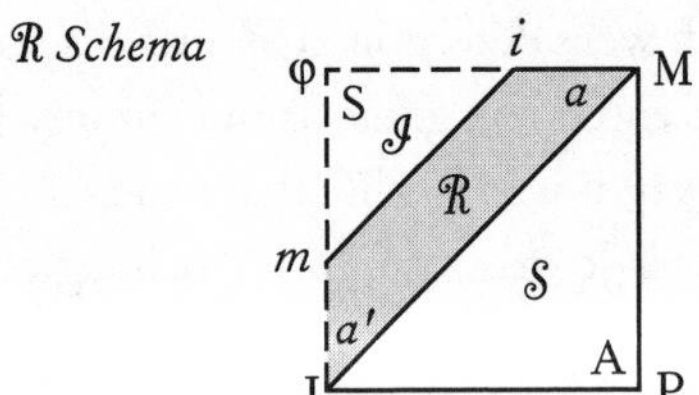

ℛ Schema

We can thus situate between *i* and M—that is, in *a*—the extremities of the segments S*i*, Sa^1, Sa^2, Sa^n, and SM, where we place figures of the imaginary other in the relationships of erotic aggression where they are realized. Similarly, we can situate between *m* and I, that is in *a*′, the extremities of segments S*m*, Sa'^1, Sa'^2, Sa'^n, and SI, where the ego is identified, from its specular *Urbild* to the paternal identification involved in the ego-ideal.[14]

554 Those who attended my 1956–1957 seminar know the use I made of the imaginary ternary laid out here—whose vertex, I, is really constituted by the child, qua desired—in order to restore to the notion of the Object Relation,[15] somewhat discredited by the mass of nonsense that the term has been used to validate in recent years, the capital of experience that legitimately belongs to it.

In effect, this schema allows us to show the relations that refer not to preoedipal stages—which are not, of course, nonexistent, but are analytically unthinkable (as is sufficiently obvious in Melanie Klein's faltering but not altogether misguided work)—but to the pregenital stages insofar as they are organized by the retroactive effect of the Oedipus complex.

The whole problem of the perversions consists in conceiving how the child, in its relationship with its mother—a relationship that is constituted in analysis not by the child's biological dependence, but by its dependence on her love, that is, by its desire for her desire—identifies with the imaginary object of her desire insofar as the mother herself symbolizes it in the phallus.

The phallocentrism produced by this dialectic is all that need concern us here. It is, of course, entirely conditioned by the intrusion of the signifier in 555
man's psyche and strictly impossible to deduce from any preestablished harmony between this psyche and the nature it expresses.

This imaginary effect, which can be felt as a discordance only on the basis of a belief in a normativity proper to instinct, nevertheless gave rise to the long quarrel—which is now dead, but not without leaving wreckage in its wake—concerning the primary or secondary nature of the phallic phase. Even apart from the extreme importance of the question, this quarrel would warrant our interest due to the dialectical exploits it imposed on Ernest Jones in order to maintain, with the claim that he was in complete agreement with Freud, a position that was diametrically opposed to Freud's—namely, a position that made him, with certain minor qualifications no doubt, the champion of the British feminists, enamored of their "to each his own" principle: boys have the dick, girls have the c . . .

7. Freud thus unveiled the imaginary function of the phallus as the pivotal point in the symbolic process that completes, *in both sexes*, the calling into question of one's sex by the castration complex.

The current obscuring of this function of the phallus (reduced to the role of a part-object) in the analytic chorus is simply the continuation of the profound mystification in which culture maintains its symbol—in the sense in which paganism itself presented it only at the culmination of its most secret mysteries.

In the subjective economy, commanded as it is by the unconscious, it is, in effect, a signification that is evoked only by what I call a metaphor—to be precise, the paternal metaphor.

And this brings us back, since it is with Macalpine that I have chosen to dialogue, to her need to refer to a "heliolithism," by which she claims to see procreation codified in a preoedipal culture, where the father's procreative function is eluded.

Anything that can be put forward along these lines, in whatever form, will only better highlight the signifying function that conditions paternity.

For in another debate dating back to the time when psychoanalysts still puzzled over doctrine, Ernest Jones, with a remark that was more relevant than 556
his aforementioned one, contributed a no less inappropriate argument.

Indeed, concerning the state of beliefs in some Australian tribe, he refused to admit that any collectivity of men could overlook the fact of experience that—except in the case of an enigmatic exception—no woman gives birth without having engaged in coitus, or even be ignorant of the requisite lapse of time between the two events. Now the credit that seems to me to be quite legitimately granted to human capacities to observe reality [*réel*] is precisely what has not the slightest importance in the matter.

For, if the symbolic context requires it, paternity will nevertheless be attributed to the woman's encounter with a spirit at such and such a fountain or at a certain rock in which he is supposed to dwell.

This is clearly what demonstrates that the attribution of procreation to the father can only be the effect of a pure signifier, of a recognition, not of the real father, but of what religion has taught us to invoke as the Name-of-the-Father.

Of course, there is no need of a signifier to be a father, any more than there is to be dead, but without a signifier, no one will ever know anything about either of these states of being.

Let me remind those who cannot be persuaded to seek in Freud's texts something to complement the wisdom that their coaches dispense to them, how insistently Freud stresses the affinity of the two signifying relations I just mentioned, whenever the neurotic subject (especially the obsessive) manifests this affinity through the conjunction of their themes.

How, indeed, could Freud fail to recognize such an affinity, when the necessity of his reflection led him to tie the appearance of the signifier of the Father, as author of the Law, to death—indeed, to the killing of the Father—thus showing that, if this murder is the fertile moment of the debt by which the subject binds himself for life to the Law, the symbolic Father, insofar as he signifies this Law, is truly the dead Father.

557 *IV. Schreber's Way*

1. We can now enter into the subjectivity of Schreber's delusion.

The signification of the phallus, as I said, must be evoked in the subject's imaginary by the paternal metaphor.

This has a precise meaning in the economy of the signifier, whose formalization I can only recall to mind here, but which is familiar to those who attend the seminar I am giving this year on unconscious formations. Namely, *the formula for metaphor*, or *for signifying substitution*:

$$\frac{S}{\not{S}'} \cdot \frac{\not{S}'}{x} \rightarrow S\left(\frac{1}{s}\right)$$

Here the capital Ss are signifiers, x is the unknown signification, and s is the signified induced by the metaphor, which consists in the substitution in the signifying chain of S for S′. The elision of S′, represented in the formula by the fact that it is crossed out, is the condition of the metaphor's success.

This applies thus to the metaphor of the Name-of-the-Father, that is, the metaphor that puts this Name in the place that was first symbolized by the operation of the mother's absence.

$$\frac{\text{Name-of-the-Father}}{\text{Mother's Desire}} \cdot \frac{\text{Mother's Desire}}{\text{Signified to the Subject}} \rightarrow \text{Name-of-the-Father}\left(\frac{\text{A}}{\text{Phallus}}\right)$$

Let us now try to conceive of a circumstance of the subjective position in which what responds to the appeal to the Name-of-the-Father is not the absence of the real father, for this absence is more than compatible with the presence of the signifier, but the lack of the signifier itself.

This is not a conception for which nothing has prepared us. The signifier's presence in the Other is, in effect, a presence that is usually closed off to the subject, because it usually persists there in a repressed *(verdrängt)* state, and insists from that place so as to be represented in the signified by means of its repetition automatism *(Wiederholungszwang)*.

Let us extract from several of Freud's texts a term that is sufficiently artic- 558
ulated in them to render them unjustifiable if it does not designate in them a function of the unconscious that is distinct from the repressed. Let us take as demonstrated what constituted the crux of my seminar on the psychoses—namely, that this term, *Verwerfung*, refers to the most necessary implication of Freud's thought when it grapples with the phenomenon of psychosis.

It is articulated in this register as the absence of *Bejahung*—the judgment of attribution—which Freud posits as a necessary precedent for any possible application of *Verneinung* [negation], the latter, in contrast with *Bejahung*, being the judgment of existence; meanwhile, the whole article in which he separates out this *Verneinung* as an element of analytic experience demonstrates in *Verneinung* the owning [*aveu*] of the very signifier that *Verneinung* annuls.

The primordial *Bejahung* thus also bears on the signifier, and other texts allow us to recognize this, in particular, Letter 52 of Freud's correspondence with Fliess, in which it is expressly isolated as the term for an original perception by the name "sign," *Zeichen*.

I will thus take *Verwerfung* to be "foreclosure" of the signifier. At the point at which the Name-of-the-Father is summoned—and we shall see how—a pure and simple hole may thus answer in the Other; due to the lack of the metaphoric effect, this hole will give rise to a corresponding hole in the place of phallic signification.

This is the only form in which it is possible for us to conceptualize something whose outcome Schreber presents to us as that of an injury which he is in a position to reveal only in part, and in which, he says, the term "soul murder" (*Seelenmord*, S. 22), along with the names Flechsig and Schreber, plays an essential role.[16]

It is clear that what we are presented with here is a disturbance that occurred at the inmost juncture of the subject's sense of life. The censorship, which mutilated the text of his *Memoirs* before the addition announced by Schreber to the rather roundabout explanations that he tried to give of the disturbance's process, inclines me to think that he associated facts that could not be pub-
559 lished due to the conventions of the time with the names of people who were still alive. The following chapter [chapter 3] is thus missing in its entirety and, to exercise his perspicacity, Freud had to confine himself to the allusion to *Faust*, *Der Freischütz*, and Byron's *Manfred*, the latter work (from which he assumes Ahriman, the name of one of the manifestations of God in Schreber's delusion, was borrowed) seeming to him to derive its full value in this reference from its theme: the hero dies from the curse borne in him by the death of the object of fraternal incest.

For my part—since like Freud I have chosen to trust in a text which, except for these mutilations, regrettable as they are, remains a document whose guarantees of credibility place it among the finest—it is in the most highly developed form of the delusion, with which the book coincides, that I will try to demonstrate a structure that will prove to be similar to the psychotic process itself.

2. Following this line of approach, I will observe—with the hint of surprise that Freud sees as the subjective connotation of the unconscious when recognized—that the delusion deploys its whole tapestry around the power of creation attributed to the words of which the divine rays *(Gottesstrahlen)* are the hypostasis.

This begins as a leitmotiv in the first chapter, where the author first dwells on what is shocking to thought about the act of bringing something into existence out of nothing, flying, as it does, in the face of the evidence that experience provides to thought of the transformations of matter in which reality finds its substance.

He emphasizes this paradox by contrasting it with ideas that are more familiar to the man he assures us he is, as if there were any need for it: a *gebildet*

German of the Wilhelmine era, raised on Haeckelian metascientism, to support which he provides a list of readings, an occasion for us to fill out, by reading them, what Gavarni somewhere calls a courageous idea of Man.[17]

It is in this very paradox, reflected by the intrusion of a thought, for him hitherto unthinkable, that Schreber sees the proof that something must have 560
happened that did not proceed from his own mind: a proof which, it seems, only the question begging highlighted above in the psychiatrist's position gives us the right to resist.

3. Having said this, let us for our part confine our attention to a sequence of phenomena that Schreber establishes in chapter 15 (S. 204–15).

At this point in the book we know that the support for his side in the forced game of thought *(Denkzwang)*, which God's words constrain him to play (see section I.5 above), has a dramatic stake. God, whose powers of ignorance become apparent later, considering the subject to have been annihilated, leaves him in the lurch *(liegen lassen)*—a threat to which we will return further on.

The fact that the effort to reply—which the subject is thus stuck on, so to speak, in this way in his being as a subject—eventually fails at a moment of "thinking nothing" (*Nichtsdenken* [S. 205]), which certainly seems to be the most humanly merited of rests (Schreber says [S. 47]), leads, according to him, to:

(a) What he calls the bellowing-miracle *(Brüllenwunder)*, a cry torn from his breast that surprises him beyond all warning, whether he is alone or with others who are horrified by the image he offers them of his mouth suddenly agape before the unspeakable void, abandoned by the cigar that was stuck there a moment before;
(b) The cries of "help" *("Hülfe" rufen)*, made by "those of God's nerves separated from the total mass," whose woeful tone is explained by the greater distance to which God withdraws [S. 206];

(two phenomena in which the subjective rending is indistinguishable enough from its signifying mode for me not to belabor the point);

(c) The imminent appearance—in the occult zone of the perceptual field, in the hallway, or in the next room—of manifestations which, though not extraordinary, strike the subject as produced for him;
(d) The appearance, at the next stage, from afar—in other words, out of the

> range of the senses, in the park, *in the real*—of miraculous creations, that is, newly created beings, which, as Macalpine perspicaciously notes, always belong to flying species: birds or insects.

561 Don't these latter meteors of the delusion appear as the trace of a furrow, or as a halo effect, showing the two moments at which, from out of its darkness, the signifier—which has fallen silent in the subject—first makes a glimmer of signification spring forth at the surface of the real, and then causes the real to become illuminated with a flash projected from below its underpinning of nothingness?

Thus, at the height of these hallucinatory effects, these creatures—which are the only ones that deserve to be called "hallucinations" if we rigorously apply the criterion that the phenomenon appear *in reality*—advise us to reconsider in their symbolic solidarity the trio of Creator, Creature, and Created that separates out here.

4. Indeed, it is from the position of the Creator that we will arrive at that of the Created, which subjectively creates the former.

Unique in his Multiplicity, Multiple in his Unity (these are the attributes by which Schreber, like Heraclitus, defines him), this God—broken down, in effect, into a hierarchy of realms, which warrants a separate study of its own—degrades into beings that pilfer disannexed identities.

Immanent in these beings, whose capture by their inclusion in Schreber's being threatens his integrity, God is not without the intuitive prop of a hyperspace, in which Schreber sees even signifying transmissions being conducted along filaments *(Fäden)* that materialize the parabolic trajectory by which they enter his cranium through the occiput (S. 315).

Yet, as time goes by, God, in his manifestations, allows the field of beings devoid of intelligence to expand ever further, beings who do not know what they are saying, inane beings, such as those "miracled birds," those "talking birds," those "forecourts of heaven" (*Vorhöfe des Himmels* [S. 19]), in which Freud's misogyny detected at first glance the silly geese that young girls were considered to be in the ideals of his time, finding his view confirmed by the
562 proper names[18] the subject later gives them. Suffice it to say that, in my view, they are far more representative by virtue of their surprise at the similarity of vocables and the purely homophonic equivalences on which they rely in using them (Santiago = Carthago, Chinesenthum = Jesum Christum, etc., S. 210).

Similarly, God's being in its essence withdraws ever further into the space that conditions it, a withdrawal that can be intuited in the increasing slowness of his speech, which even goes as far as a halting, stammered articulation of every letter of a word (S. 223). Indeed, were we to follow solely what this process indicates, we would regard this unique Other—with which the subject's existence is linked—as suited above all for emptying the places (S. 196 note) in which the murmuring of words unfolds, were Schreber not careful to inform us, in addition, that this God is foreclosed from every other aspect of the exchange. He apologizes for doing so, but however sorry he may be about it, he nevertheless has to observe it: God is not simply impermeable to experience; he is incapable of understanding a living man; he grasps him only from the outside (which certainly seems to be his essential mode); all interiority is closed off to him. A "writing-down-system" (*Aufschreibesystem* [S. 126])—in which acts and thoughts are preserved—recalls, of course, in a displaced way, the notebook kept by the guardian angel from our catechized childhood, but beyond that we should note the absence of any trace of the sounding of loins or hearts (S. 20).

Again, in the same way, after the purification of souls *(Laüterung)* has abolished every remnant of their personal identity in them, everything will be reduced to the eternal subsistence of this verbiage, which is the sole means God has for knowing the very works that men's ingenuity has constructed (S. 300).

How could I fail to note here that the grandnephew of the author of *Novae species insectorum* (Johann Christian Daniel von Schreber) points out that none of the miracled creatures is of a new species, or to add—in opposition to Macalpine, who sees in them the Dove that conveys the fruitful tidings of the Logos from the Father's lap to the Virgin—that they remind me, rather, of the species a magician produces from out of the opening of his waistcoat or sleeve in great numbers?

This leads me at last to the surprising conclusion that the subject who has
fallen prey to these mysteries does not hesitate, Created being though he be, 563
to use words to deal with the dismayingly silly traps set by his Lord, or to stand his ground in the face of the destruction he believes his Lord capable of initiating against him or anyone else, by virtue of a right that legitimates his doing so in the name of the Order of Things *(Weltordnung)*. The fact that this right is on his side is the reason for this unique victory of a creature whom a chain of disturbances has made succumb to his creator's "perfidy" (this word, which he lets slip out not without reservations, is in French in the original: S. 226).

Isn't this recalcitrant created being, who holds out against his fall owing to the sole support of his Word and to his faith in speech, a strange counterpart to Malebranche's continuous creation?

This would warrant another look at the authors covered on the Baccalaureate exam in philosophy, for we have perhaps been overly dismissive of those who did not help pave the way for *homo psychologicus*, in which our era finds the measure of a humanism that is—don't you think?—perhaps somewhat pedestrian.

Between Malebranche and Locke the cleverer is the crazier . . .

Yes, but which one is it? There's the rub, my dear colleague. Come on, drop that stiff manner. When will you feel at ease, then, here where you are on your home turf?

5. Let us now try to locate the subject's position, as it is constituted here in the symbolic order, on the ternary that maps it in my R schema.

It seems to me, then, that if the Created, I, takes the place here of the Law in P, which is left vacant, the place of the Creator is designated here by this *liegen lassen*, this fundamental leaving in the lurch, in which the absence that allowed the primordial symbolization, M, of the mother to be constructed appears to be unveiled, by virtue of the foreclosure of the Father.

Between the two, a line—which would culminate in the Creatures of speech occupying the place of the child who doesn't come, dashing the subject's hopes (see my postscript further on)—would thus be conceived as skirting the hole excavated in the field of the signifier by the foreclosure of the Name-of-the-Father (see the I schema, page 571 below).

564 It is around this hole, where the subject lacks the support of the signifying chain, and which need not, as can be observed, be ineffable to induce panic, that the whole struggle in which the subject reconstructed himself took place. He conducted this struggle honorably, and the "vaginas of heaven" (another meaning of the word *Vorhöfe* mentioned above)—the cohort of miracled young girls who laid siege to the edges of the hole—commented on it in the clucks of admiration wrung from their harpies' throats: "*Verfluchter Kerl!* One hell of a fellow!" In other words: What a great guy! Alas! It was by way of antiphrasis.

6. For in the field of the imaginary, a gap had already recently opened up for him in response to the absence of the symbolic metaphor, a gap that could only find a way to be eliminated in the carrying out of *Entmannung* (emasculation).

This was at first horrifying to the subject, then it was accepted as a reasonable compromise (*vernünftig*, S. 177), and thereafter as an irremissible resolve (S. 179 note) and a future motive for a redemption concerning the entire world.

Although we still are not off the hook regarding the term *Entmannung*, it will surely be less of a hindrance to us than it is to Macalpine, given her standpoint, as I have described it. No doubt she thought she was clarifying things by substituting the word "unmanning"* for "emasculation,"* which the translator of volume III of the *Collected Papers* had innocently believed to suffice to render it; she even went so far as to try to ensure that the translation was altered in the authorized version then being prepared. Perhaps she was struck by some imperceptible etymological suggestion that differentiated the two terms, despite their identical usage.[19]

But to what avail? When she rejects as impropère[20] the calling into question of an organ which, in referring to the *Memoirs*, she considers to be destined only to a peaceful reabsorption into the subject's entrails, does she mean by this to depict the timorous slyness in which it takes refuge close to the body when he shivers with cold, or the conscientious objection the description of which the author of *The Satyricon* maliciously lingers over? 565

Or could it perhaps be that she erroneously believes that the castration complex has always had something to do with real castration?

She is no doubt justified in noticing the ambiguity there is in regarding as equivalent the subject's transformation into a woman *(Verweiblichung)* and castration [*éviration*] (for this is certainly the meaning of *Entmannung*). But she does not see that this ambiguity is that of the very subjective structure which produces it here: the latter implies that what borders, at the imaginary level, on the subject's transformation into a woman is precisely what makes him forfeit any inheritance from which he may legitimately expect the allotment of a penis to his person. This because, whereas being and having are mutually exclusive in theory, they overlap, at least as far as the result is concerned, when a lack is at stake. Which does not prevent the distinction between them from being decisive in what follows.

As we can perceive if we note that the patient is destined to become a woman not because he is foreclosed from the penis, but because he has to be the phallus.

The symbolic parity *Mädchen = Phallus*—or, in English, the equation Girl = Phallus, in the words of Fenichel,[21] this equation providing him the theme of a worthy, albeit somewhat confused, essay—finds its root in the imaginary paths by which the child's desire manages to identify with the mother's want-to-be, into which she herself was, of course, inducted by the symbolic law in which this want is constituted.

It is as a result of the same mainspring that, whether they like it or not, women in reality [*réel*] serve as objects for exchanges ordained by the elementary structures of kinship, which are sometimes perpetuated in the imaginary, while what is simultaneously transmitted in the symbolic order is the phallus.

7. Here the identification, whatever it may be, by which the subject assumed [*assumé*] his mother's desire, triggers, as a result of being shaken up, the dis-
566 solution of the imaginary tripod (note that it was in his mother's apartment, where he had taken refuge, that the subject had his first attack of anxious confusion with suicidal raptus: S. 39–40).

Divination by the unconscious no doubt warned the subject very early on that, unable to be the phallus the mother is missing, there remained the solution of being the woman that men are missing.

This is the meaning of his fantasy, his account of which has often been commented on and which I quoted above from the incubation period of his second illness—namely, the idea "that it would be beautiful to be a woman submitting to the act of copulation" [S. 36]. This is precisely the *pons asinorum* of the Schreberian literature.

Yet this solution was premature at the time because, regarding the *Menschenspielerei* (a term that appeared in the basic language, meaning, in our contemporary idiom, brawling among men) that normally would have ensued, any attempt by Schreber to call upon real men was bound to fall flat, as it were, since they became as improbable as Schreber himself—that is, as devoid as he was of any phallus. This is because a stroke was omitted in the subject's imaginary—no less for them than for him—the stroke, parallel to the outline of their figure, that can be seen in a drawing by little Hans, which is familiar to connoisseurs of children's drawings. It was because others were, from then on, no more than "images of men cobbled together 1, 2, 3" [*"images d'hommes torchées à la six-quatre-deux"*]—to combine, in this translation of *flüchtig hingemachte Männer*, Niederland's remarks on the uses of *hinmachen* and Édouard Pichon's inspired translation of the expression into French.[22]

The upshot being that matters might have stagnated in a rather dishonorable fashion, had the subject not succeeded in brilliantly saving the day.

He himself articulated the way out (in November 1895, that is, two years after the beginning of his illness) with the term *Versöhnung*. The word has the meaning of expiation or propitiation and, given the characteristics of the basic language, must be drawn even more toward the primitive meaning of *Sühne*,
567 that is, sacrifice; instead, people have emphasized its meaning as compromise (reasonable compromise, with which the subject explains the accepting of his destiny; see page 564 above).

Here Freud, going well beyond the subject's own rationalization, admits paradoxically that the "reconciliation" (since this flat meaning of the term *Versöhnung* is the one that was chosen in the French translation) highlighted by the subject finds its mainspring in the underhanded dealings of the partner involved in this reconciliation—namely, in the consideration that God's wife contracts, in any case, an alliance that would satisfy the most pernickety pride.

I think we can say that Freud failed to live up to his own standards here, and in the most contradictory way, in that he accepts as a turning point of the delusion what he refused in his general conception—namely, to make the homosexual theme depend on the idea of grandeur (I will assume that my readers are familiar with his text).

The reason for this failure is found in necessity, that is, in the fact that Freud had not yet formulated "On Narcissism: an Introduction" [1914].

8. Three years after 1911 he probably would not have missed the true reason for the reversal in Schreber's sense of indignation—initially aroused in him by the idea of *Entmannung*—which was precisely the fact that in the interval *the subject had died*.

This, at least, was the event that the voices—always informed by the right sources and ever constant in their information service—made known to him after the fact, complete with the date and name of the newspaper in which the event was announced in the obituaries (S. 81).

We, on the other hand, can make do with the evidence provided by the medical certificates, which depict the patient to us as sunk in a catatonic stupor at the relevant time.

As is commonly the case, his memories of this time are plentiful. Thus we know that, modifying the custom according to which one departs this life feet first, our patient, so as to do it only in transit, took pleasure in keeping his feet out of it—that is, stuck out the window, under the tendentious pretext of exposing them to the cold (S. 172)—thus reviving perhaps (I will leave this to be gauged by those who will only be interested here in the imaginary avatar) the 568
direction of his birth.

But this is not a career that one takes up at a full fifty years of age without becoming disoriented to some degree. Hence the faithful portrait that the voices, annalists I would say, gave him of himself as a "leper corpse leading another leper corpse" (S. 92), a truly brilliant description, it must be admitted, of an identity reduced to a confrontation with its psychical double, but which, moreover, renders patent the subject's regression—a topographical, not a genetic, regression—to the mirror stage, insofar as the relationship to the specular other is reduced here to its mortal impact.

This was also the time at which his body was merely an aggregate of colonies of foreign "nerves," a sort of dump for detached fragments of his persecutors' identities (S. chapter XIV).

It seems to me that the relation of all this to homosexuality, which is certainly manifest in the delusion, requires a more advanced set of rules regarding the theoretical use that can be made of this reference.

It holds great interest, since it is certain that the use of this term in interpretation may cause serious damage if it is not informed by the symbolic relations that I consider determinant here.

9. I believe that this symbolic determination is demonstrated in the form in which the imaginary structure comes to be restored. At this stage, the imaginary structure presents two facets that Freud himself distinguished.

The first is that of a transsexualist practice, not at all unworthy of being related to "perversion," the features of which have been presented in many case histories since that time.[23]

Furthermore, I must point out how the structure I am isolating here may shed light on the highly unusual insistence displayed by the subjects of these case histories on obtaining their father's authorization for, one might even say his hands-on assistance with, their demands for the most radical rectifications.

Be that as it may, we see our subject give himself over to an erotic activity
569 which, he emphasizes, is strictly reserved for solitude, but whose satisfactions he nevertheless admits to—satisfactions his image in the mirror gives him, when, dressed in the cheap adornments of feminine finery, nothing in the upper part of his body, he says, seems to him incapable of convincing any possible aficionado of the female bust (S. 280).

To which we must link, I believe, the development, alleged to be an endosomatic perception, of the so-called nerves of female pleasure in his own integument, particularly in those zones where they are supposed to be erogenous in women [S. 274].

One remark he makes—the remark that if he were to incessantly contemplate woman's image, and never detach his thoughts from the prop of something feminine, God's sensuality would be all the better served—turns our attention to the other facet of his libidinal fantasies.

This facet links the subject's feminization to the coordinate of divine copulation.

Freud very clearly saw in this the sense of mortification, when he stressed everything that links "soul-voluptuousness" *(Seelenwollust)*, which is included in it, to "bliss" [*béatitude*] *(Seligkeit)*, insofar as the latter is the state of deceased souls *(abschiedenen Wesen)*.

The fact that the now blessed voluptuousness should become the soul's bliss is, indeed, an essential turning point, and Freud, it should be noted, stresses its linguistic motivation when he suggests that the history of his language [*langue*] might shed some light on it.[24]

This is simply to make a mistake regarding the dimension in which the letter manifests itself in the unconscious, and which, in accordance with its own literal instance, is far less etymological (or diachronic, to be precise) than homophonic (synchronic). Indeed, there is nothing in the history of the German language [*langue*] that would allow us to relate *selig* to *Seele*, or to relate the happiness that transports lovers to "heaven"—insofar as it is this happiness to which Freud refers in the aria he quotes from *Don Giovanni*—to the happiness promised to the so-called "blessed" souls by their stay in heaven. The dead are *selig* in German only by virtue of a borrowing from Latin, and because of the 570
Latin phrase "of blessed memory" *(beatae memoriae, seliger Gedächtnis)*. Their *Seelen* have more to do with the lakes *(Seen)* in which they sojourned at one time than with anything like their bliss. The fact is that the unconscious is concerned more with the signifier than with the signified, and that the phrase, "*feu mon père*" ("my late father"), may mean there that my father was the fire of God [*le feu de Dieu*], or even give the order for him to be shot: Fire!

But this digression aside, the fact remains that we are, here, in a beyond of the world, which easily accommodates an indefinite postponement of the realization of its goal.

Once Schreber has completed his transformation into a woman, the act of divine fecundation will assuredly take place, although it is clear that God could not compromise himself by taking an obscure journey through the organs (S. 3). (Let us not forget God's aversion to the living being.) It is thus through a spiritual operation that Schreber will feel awakening in him the embryonic germ, whose stirrings he already experienced in the early stages of his illness.

The new spiritual humanity of the Schreberian creatures will be entirely engendered through his womb, of course, so that the rotten and condemned humanity of the present age may be reborn. This is clearly a sort of redemption—since this is how the delusion has been cataloged—but it aims only at the creature of the future, for the creature of the present is struck by a decadence that is correlative to the captation of the divine rays by the voluptuousness that rivets them to Schreber (S. 51–52).

In this, the mirage dimension becomes visible. It is further highlighted by the indefinite amount of time for which the promise is postponed, and is profoundly conditioned by the absence of mediation to which the fantasy bears witness. For we can see that this fantasy parodies the situation of the last surviving couple who, following some human catastrophe, would find themselves confronted with what is total in the act of animal reproduction, holding as they would the power to repopulate the earth.

Here again one can place under the sign of the creature the turning point from which the line flees along its two branches, that of narcissistic jouissance and that of ideal identification—but in the sense in which its image is the decoy of the imaginary capture in which the two branches are rooted. And here, too, the line revolves around a hole, the very hole in which "soul-murder" has installed death.

571 Was this other gulf formed by the simple effect in the imaginary of the futile appeal made in the symbolic to the paternal metaphor? Or must we conceive of it as produced at one remove by the elision of the phallus, which the subject would like to reduce, in order to resolve it, to the lethal gap of the mirror stage? The link, which this time is a genetic one, between this stage and the symbolization of the Mother insofar as she is primordial would certainly have to be evoked to explain this solution.

Can we locate the geometrical points of the R schema on a schema of the subject's structure at the end of the psychotic process? I shall try to do so in the I schema below.

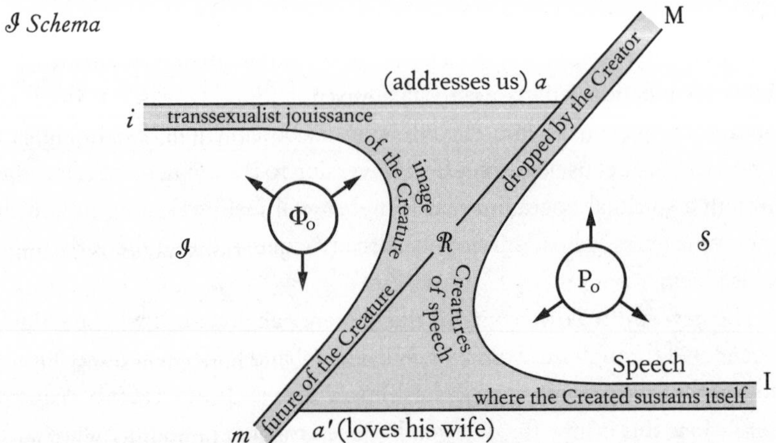

This schema no doubt suffers from the excess endemic to any formalization that is presented in the intuitive realm.

In other words, the distortion that it manifests between the functions identified here by the letters transferred to it from the R schema can only be gauged on the basis of its use in restarting the dialectic.

Let me simply point out here—in the double curve that resembles a hyperbola except for the slippage of the two curves along one of the guiding lines
572 of their asymptote—the link made palpable, in the double asymptote that unites

the delusional ego to the divine other, of their imaginary divergence in space and time to the ideal convergence of their conjunction. And let us not overlook the fact that Freud himself had an intuition of such a form, since he himself introduced the term *asymptotisch* in this context.[25]

The entire width of the real creature, on the other hand, is interposed for the subject between the narcissistic jouissance of his image and the alienation of speech in which the ego-ideal has taken the place of the Other.

The schema shows that the final state of the psychosis does not represent the frozen chaos encountered in the aftermath of an earthquake, but rather the bringing to light of lines of efficiency that makes people talk when it is a problem with an elegant solution.

It materializes in a signifying way what lies at the crux of the true fruitfulness of Freud's research. For it is a fact that without any other support or prop than a written document—which is not only a testimony to, but also a product of, this final state of the psychosis—Freud shed the first light on the very evolution of the psychotic process, allowing us to elucidate its proper determination, by which I mean the only organicity that is essentially involved in this process: the organicity that motivates the structure of signification.

Condensed in the form of this schema, the relations emerge by which the signifier's induction effects, impacting the imaginary, bring about the upheaval in the subject that clinicians refer to as the "twilight of the world," necessitating new signifying effects in response.

In my seminar I showed that the symbolic succession of the anterior realms, and then the posterior realms of God, the lower and the upper, Ahriman and Ormuzd, and their shifts in "policy" (a word of the basic language) with respect to the subject, provide these very responses at the various stages of the imaginary dissolution—which, moreover, the patient's memories and the medical certificates connote sufficiently—in order to restore order in the subject there.

Regarding the question that I am foregrounding here concerning the signifier's alienating impact, I will refer to the low point that came on a night in 573
July of 1894 when Ahriman, the lower God, revealing himself to Schreber in the most impressive trappings of his power, addressed him with a simple and, according to the subject, common word of the basic language: *Luder!*[26]

To translate the word we must do more than simply look it up in the Sachs-Villatte dictionary, to which the French translator confined his efforts. Niederland's reference to "lewd" in English, meaning whore, does not seem acceptable to me as an attempt to convey the sense of spineless or slut, which is what it means when used as an obscene insult.

But if we take into account the archaism indicated as characteristic of the basic language, I believe we can justifiably link this term to the root of the

French *leurre*, and of the English "lure,"* which is certainly the best *ad hominem* address to be expected coming from the symbolic: the Other with a capital *O* can be awfully impertinent.

There remains the disposition of the field **R** in the schema, inasmuch as this disposition represents the conditions in which reality was restored for the subject: for him a sort of island, the consistency of which is imposed on him after proving its constancy,[27] which, to my mind, is linked to what makes it inhabitable for him, but which also distorts it—namely, eccentric reshapings of the imaginary, **I**, and of the symbolic, **S**, which reduce reality to the field of the skew between them.

The subordinate conception that we must have of the function of reality in the process, in both its cause and effects, is what is important here.

I cannot elaborate here on the question, which is nevertheless crucial, of what we are for the subject, we whom he addresses as readers, nor on the question of what remains of his relationship with his wife, for whom his book was initially intended, whose visits during his illness were always greeted by him
574 with the most intense emotion, and for whom, he asserts, alongside the most decisive admission of his delusional vocation, "I retain my former love in full" (S. 179 note).

The maintenance of the trajectory, *Saa′A*, in the I schema symbolizes there the opinion I have formed, on the basis of my examination of this case, that the relation to the other qua relation to one's semblable, and even a relation as elevated as that of friendship in the sense in which Aristotle makes it the essence of the conjugal link, are perfectly compatible with the skewing of the relation to the Other with a capital *O* and all the radical anomalies it brings with it—qualified, improperly but not without some relevance as a first approximation, in the old clinical jargon as a "partial delusion."

Nonetheless, it would be better to consign this schema to the garbage heap, if, like so many others, it prompted anyone to forget, because of an intuitive image, the analysis on which this image is based.

Indeed, one need but think about it to realize how satisfied Macalpine—my interlocutor here whose authentic reflection I will praise now one last time—would be with it, by simply misrecognizing what made me construct it.

What I am asserting here is that, in recognizing the drama of madness, reason is doing what it likes best, *sua res agitur*, because it is in man's relation to the signifier that this drama is situated.

The danger people mention of becoming as mad as the patient no more intimidates me than it did Freud.

Like Freud, I hold that we must listen to the speaker, when what is at stake is a message that does not come from a subject beyond language, but from speech beyond the subject. For it is then that we will hear this speech, which Schreber picked up in the Other, when from Ahriman to Ormuzd, from the evil God to the absent God, it carries the summons in which the very law of the signifier is articulated: *"Aller Unsinn hebt sich auf!"* "All nonsense cancels itself out!" (S. 182–83 and 312).

Here we encounter anew (leaving to those who will concern themselves with me later the task of figuring out why I have left it in abeyance for ten years) what I said in my dialogue with Henri Ey: "Not only can man's being not be understood without madness, but it would not be man's being if it did 575
not bear madness within itself as the limit of his freedom."[28]

V. Postscript

Following in Freud's footsteps, I teach that the Other is the locus of the kind of memory he discovered by the name "unconscious," memory that he regards as the object of a question that has remained unanswered, insofar as it conditions the indestructibility of certain desires. I will answer this question with the conception of the signifying chain, inasmuch as—once this chain has been inaugurated by primordial symbolization (made manifest in the *Fort! Da!* game, which Freud elucidated as lying at the origin of repetition automatism)—it develops in accordance with logical connections whose hold on that which is to be signified, namely, the being of entities, is exerted through the signifying effects I describe as metaphor and metonymy.

It is an accident in this register and in what occurs in it—namely, the foreclosure of the Name-of-the-Father in the place of the Other—and the failure of the paternal metaphor that I designate as the defect that gives psychosis its essential condition, along with the structure that separates it from neurosis.

This thesis, which I am contributing here as a question prior to any possible treatment of psychosis, has a dialectic that can be pursued beyond this point: but I shall stop it here and say why.

First, because it is worth indicating what can be discovered by my halting here.

A perspective that does not distinguish Schreber's relationship with God on the basis of its subjective impact marks this relationship with negative features which make it appear as a mixture rather than as a union of being with being, and which—in the voracity that accommodates disgust there and in the complicity that tolerates its exaction—show nothing, to call things by their rightful names, of the Presence and Joy that illuminate mystical experience. This opposition is not only demonstrated but founded by the astonishing absence in this relationship of the *Du*, in French of the *Tu*—certain languages 576 [*langues*] reserving a vocable (e.g., Thou*) for God's appeal and for the appeal to God—which is the signifier of the Other in speech.

We are familiar with the false modesties that are considered proper in science in this regard; they accompany pedantry's false thoughts when it invokes the ineffability of lived experience, or even "morbid consciousness," in order to disarm the effort it spares itself—namely, the effort that is required at the point at which it is not ineffable precisely because it [*ça*] speaks; at which lived experience, far from separating us, is communicated; and at which subjectivity surrenders its true structure, that structure in which what can be analyzed is identical to what can be articulated.

Thus from the same vantage point to which delusional subjectivity has brought us, I will turn to scientific subjectivity: I mean the subjectivity that the scientist at work in science shares with the man of the civilization that supports it. I will not deny that I have seen enough on this score in our time to wonder about the criteria by which this man—with a discourse on freedom that must certainly be called delusional (I devoted one of my seminars to it), with a concept of the real in which determinism is no more than an alibi that quickly becomes anxiety provoking when one tries to extend its field to chance (I had my audience experience this in a preliminary experiment), and with a belief that unites men, half the universe at least, under the symbol of Father Christmas (which no one can overlook)—would stop me from situating him, by legitimate analogy, in the category of social psychosis which, if I am not mistaken, Pascal established before me.

There is no doubt but that such a psychosis may turn out to be compatible with what is called an orderly state of affairs, but that does not authorize the psychiatrist, even if he is a psychoanalyst, to trust in his own compatibility with this orderly state to believe that he is in possession of an adequate idea of the *reality* to which his patient supposedly proves to be unequal.

Under these conditions, he would perhaps do better to jettison this idea from his assessment of the foundations of psychosis: which brings us back to the objective of its treatment.

To gauge the length of the path that separates us from it, suffice it to mention the mass of delays with which its pilgrims have marked it. Everyone knows
577 that no discussion of the mechanism of transference, however learned it may be, has succeeded in stopping it from being conceived in practice as a relationship whose terms are purely dyadic and whose substratum is utterly confused.

If we simply consider transference on the basis of its fundamental nature as a repetition phenomenon, let me raise the question of what it is repeating in the persecuting persons Freud designates as its effect here.

I can just imagine the lame reply: "Following your approach, a paternal failing no doubt." In this vein, there has been no shortage of accounts of every kind: and the psychotic's "entourage" has been minutely scrutinized for all the so-called biographical and characterological tidbits the anamnesis enabled people to extract from the *dramatis personae*, even from their "interpersonal relations."[29]

Let us nevertheless proceed according to the structural terms I have outlined.

For psychosis to be triggered, the Name-of-the-Father—*verworfen*, foreclosed, that is, never having come to the place of the Other—must be summoned to that place in symbolic opposition to the subject.

It is the lack of the Name-of-the-Father in that place which, by the hole that it opens up in the signified, sets off a cascade of reworkings of the signifier from which the growing disaster of the imaginary proceeds, until the level is reached at which signifier and signified stabilize in a delusional metaphor.

But how can the Name-of-the-Father be summoned by the subject to the only place from which it could have come into being for him and in which it has never been? By nothing other than a real father, not at all necessarily by the subject's own father, but by One-father [*Un-père*].

Yet this One-father must still come to that place to which the subject could not summon him before. For this, the One-father need but situate himself in a tertiary position in any relationship that has as its base the imaginary couple *a-a′*—that is, ego-object or ideal-reality—involving the subject in the field of eroticized aggression that it induces. 578

We should try to detect this dramatic conjuncture at the beginning of each case of psychosis. Whether the conjuncture presents itself to a woman who has just given birth, in her husband's face, to a penitent confessing her sins in the person of her confessor, or to a girl in love in her encounter with "the young man's father," it will always be found, and it will be found more easily if one allows oneself to be guided by "situations" in the novelistic sense of the term. It should be noted in passing that these situations are the novelist's true resource—namely, the resource that brings out the "depth psychology" to which no psychological perspective can give him access.[30]

To move on now to the principle of foreclosure *(Verwerfung)* of the Name-of-the-Father, it must be admitted that the Name-of-the-Father redoubles in the Other's place the very signifier of the symbolic ternary, insofar as it constitutes the law of the signifier.

Provisionally admitting this can cost nothing, it seems, to those who—in their quest for the "environmental" coordinates of psychosis—wander like lost souls from the frustrating mother to the overfeeding mother, feeling nevertheless that in directing their attention to the father's situation, they are burning, as one says in the game of hide-the-thimble.

Even so, in this groping search for a paternal failing—the range of which is unsettling, including as it does the thundering father, the easy-going father, the all-powerful father, the humiliated father, the rigid father, the pathetic father, the stay-at-home father, and the father on the loose—it would probably be excessive to expect the following remark to provide a jolt of any kind: The effects of prestige that are at stake in all of this—and in which (thank heaven!) the ternary relation of the Oedipus complex is not entirely omitted, since the mother's reverence is regarded as decisive in it—boil down to the rivalry between the two parents in the subject's imaginary. In other words, they boil down to what is articulated in the question that regularly, not to say obligatorily, seems to be raised in any self-respecting childhood: "Whom do you love more, daddy or mommy?"

My aim in drawing this parallel is not to reduce anything; quite the contrary, for this question—in which the child never fails to concretize the dis-
579 gust he feels at his parents' childishness—is precisely the question with which the real children, who are the parents (in this sense, there are no other children in the family but the parents), try to mask the mystery of their union, or disunion as the case may be: namely, the mystery of what their kid clearly knows to be the real problem and poses to himself as such.

People will say that they are emphasizing the bond of love and respect by which the mother does or does not situate the father in his ideal place. It is curious, I would reply first, that they do not make much of the same bonds in the opposite direction, proving that the theory is complicit in the veil thrown over the parents' coitus by childhood amnesia.

But what I want to stress is that we should concern ourselves not only with the way the mother accommodates the father as a person, but also with the importance she attributes to his speech—in a word, to his authority—in other words, with the place she reserves for the Name-of-the-Father in the promotion of the law.

Further still, the father's relation to this law must be considered in its own right, for one will find in it the reason for the paradox whereby devastating effects of the paternal figure are found with particular frequency in cases where the father really functions as a legislator or boasts that he does—whether he is, in fact, one of the people who makes the laws or presents himself as a pillar of faith, as a paragon of integrity or devotion, as virtuous or a virtuoso, as serving a charitable cause whatever the object or lack thereof that is at stake, as serving the nation or birth rate, safety or salubrity, legacy or law, the pure, the lowest of the low, or the empire. These are all ideals that provide him with all too many opportunities to seem to be at fault, to fall short, and even to be fraudulent—in short, to exclude the Name-of-the-Father from its position in the signifier.

This result can be obtained with still less, and no one who practices child analysis will deny that children see right through hypocritical behavior, so much so that it can be devastating to them. But who articulates that the lie thus perceived implies a reference to the constitutive function of speech?

It thus turns out that a little severity is not excessive if we are to give the most accessible experience its true meaning. The consequences that may be 580
expected of it in clinical examination and analytic technique can be gauged elsewhere.

I am giving here only what is needed to perceive the clumsiness with which the best inspired authors handle what they find most valuable in following Freud on the ground of the preeminence that he grants to the transference of the relation to the father in the genesis of psychosis.

Niederland provides a remarkable example of this when he draws attention to the delusional genealogy Schreber attributes to Flechsig. This genealogy is constructed with the names of Schreber's own ancestors, Gottfried, Gottlieb, Fürchtegott, and, above all, Daniel, which is handed down from father to son and whose meaning in Hebrew he gives in order to show—in their convergence on the name of God *(Gott)*—a symbolic chain that is important in that it manifests the function of the father in the delusion.[31]

But failing to distinguish in it the instance of the Name-of-the-Father—and to recognize it, it obviously does not suffice that it be visible here to the naked eye—Niederland misses the opportunity to grasp the chain in which the erotic aggressions experienced by the subject are woven together, and thereby to contribute to putting what must properly be termed "delusional homosexuality" in its place.

How, then, could he have dwelt on what is concealed in the statement quoted above from the first lines of Schreber's second chapter[32]—one of those statements so obviously made in order not to be heard that they must catch our ear. What, to take it literally, is the meaning of the fact that the author equally links the names Flechsig and Schreber to soul murder in his bid to take us to the crux of the abuse of which he is the victim? We must leave something for future commentators to elucidate.

Just as uncertain is the attempt, made by Niederland in the same article, to specify—starting with the subject this time, no longer with the signifier (these terms are, of course, foreign to him)—the role of the paternal function in triggering the delusion.

Indeed, if Niederland claims that what occasioned the psychosis was the 581 mere assumption [*assomption*] of paternity by the subject, which is the theme of his essay, then it is contradictory on his part to regard as equivalent the disappointment Schreber mentions of his hopes of becoming a father and his appointment to the High Court, his title as *Senätspräsident* emphasizing the quality of (conscripted) Father that it assigns him—this being the sole reason Niederland gives for his second illness, the first being explained analogously by our author by the failure of his candidacy for the Reichstag.

Whereas reference to the tertiary position, to which the signifier of paternity is summoned in all such cases, would be correct and would eliminate this contradiction.

But from the standpoint of my thesis, it is the primordial foreclosure *(Verwerfung)* that dominates everything with its problem, and the preceding considerations do not leave me unprepared.

For if we refer to the work of Daniel Gottlob Moritz Schreber—the founder of an Institute of Orthopedics at the University of Leipzig, an educator, or, better still, an "educationalist"* as they say in English, a social reformer "with an apostle-like mission to bring health, happiness and bliss to the masses" (sic, *Memoirs*, 1)[33] through physical culture, the initiator of those allotment gardens, intended to preserve in the employee a vegetable garden idealism, which in Germany are still known as *Schrebergärten*, not to mention the forty editions of *Medical Indoor Gymnastics*, of which the little "men cobbled together 1, 2, 3" that illustrate it are more or less explicitly mentioned by Schreber (S. 166)—we will be able to consider as having been exceeded the limits at which the native and the natal give way to nature, the natural, naturism, and even naturalization; at which virtue turns into vertigo, legacy into league, and salvation into saltation; at which the pure verges on the evil realm; and at which we will not be surprised if the child, like the apprentice sailor of Prévert's famous catch, sends packing *(verwerfe)* the whale of imposture, after having, according to the wit of this immortal piece, seen right through the pop [*percé la trame de père en part*].

582 There can be no doubt that the figure of Professor Flechsig, with his researcher's gravity (Macalpine's book contains a photograph that shows him profiled against a colossal enlargement of a cerebral hemisphere), did not succeed in supplementing the suddenly perceived void constituted by the inaugural *Verwerfung* (*"Kleiner Flechsig!"* "Little Flechsig!" proclaim the voices).

At least, this is Freud's conception, insofar as it designates the transference the subject developed to Flechsig as the factor that precipitated the subject into psychosis.

Thanks to which, a few months later, the divine jaculations make their concert heard in the subject in order to tell the Name-of-the-Father to go fuck itself, with the Name of God[34] right behind it, and to found the Son in his certainty that at the end of his trials, he could do no better than to "go"[35] on the whole world (S. 226).

The last word with which our century's "inner experience" has yielded us its computation was thus articulated fifty years ahead of its time by the theod- 583
icy to which Schreber was exposed: "God is a whore."[36]

This is the term in which the process by which the signifier was "unleashed" in the real culminates, after the Name-of-the-Father began to collapse—the latter being the signifier which, in the Other, qua locus of the signifier, is the signifier of the Other qua locus of the law.

I will leave this question prior to any possible treatment of the psychoses at that for the time being. It is a question that introduces, as we see, the conception to be formed of the handling of the transference in such treatment.

To say what we can do in this area would be premature, because it would now be to go "beyond Freud," and it is out of the question to go beyond Freud when psychoanalysis after Freud has, as I have said, returned to a pre-Freudian stage.

At least this is what keeps me from any other objective than that of restoring access to the experience Freud discovered.

For to use the technique he instituted outside the experience to which it applies is as stupid as to toil at the oars when one's ship is stuck in the sand.

December 1957–January 1958

Notes

1. Roman Jakobson borrows this term from Jespersen to designate those words in the code that take on meaning only from the coordinates (attribution, date, and place of emission) of the message. According to Pierce's classification, they are "index-symbols." Personal pronouns are the best example: the difficulties involved in their acquisition and their functional deficiencies illustrate the problematic generated by these signifiers in the subject. (Roman Jakobson, "Shifters, Verbal Categories, and the Russian Verb," Russian Language Project, Department of Slavic Languages and Literatures, Harvard University, 1957.)

2. See the seminar held February 8, 1956, in which I discussed the example of the "normal" vocalization of "la paix du soir."

3. *Denkwürdigkeiten eines Nervenkranken, von Dr. jur. Daniel Paul Schreber, Senätspräsident beim kgl. Oberlandesgericht Dresden a-D.* (Leipzig: Oswald Mutze, 1903), a French translation of which I prepared for the use of my group.

4. This is, notably, the opinion expressed by the authors of the English translation of these *Memoirs*, which was published the year of my seminar (see *Memoirs of My Nervous Illness*, trans. Ida Macalpine and Richard Hunter, London: W. M. Dawson & Sons), in their introduction, p. 25. They also give an account of the book's success on pages 6–10.

5. This was my doctoral thesis in medicine, entitled *De la psychose paranoïaque dans ses rapports avec la personnalité*, which Professor Heuyer, in a letter to me, judged very pertinently in these terms: "One swallow does not make a summer," adding, in connection with my bibliography, "If you've read all that, I pity you." In fact, I had read it all.

6. The parentheses including the letter S followed by numbers will be used here to refer to the corresponding page of the original edition of the *Denkwürdigkeiten*, the original pagination being fortunately provided in the margins of the English translation.

7. Note that my homage here is merely an extension of that of Freud, who did not shy away from recognizing in Schreber's delusion itself a foreshadowing of the theory of the libido (*GW* VIII, 315).

8. See *Écrits* 1966, 808.

9. He who wishes to prove too much goes astray. Thus Macalpine—who, by the way, advisedly dwells on the nature, said by the patient himself to be far too persuasive (S. 39), of the suggestive enthusiasm in which Professor Flechsig indulges (everything indicates that he was usually calmer) with Schreber regarding the benefits of a sleep-cure that he proposes to him—Macalpine, as I was saying, interprets at length the themes of procreation, which she considers to have been suggested by this discourse (see *Memoirs*, "Translators' Analysis of the Case," page 396, lines 12 and 21). She bases her case on the use of the verb "to deliver,"* to designate the effect on his problems to be expected from the treatment, and on that of the adjective "prolific,"* with which she translates, extremely loosely I might add, the German term, *ausgiebig*, applied to the sleep in question.

Now the term "to deliver"* is indisputable considering what it translates, for the simple reason that there is nothing here to translate. I scoured the German text searching for it. The verb was simply forgotten by either the author or the typesetter, and Macalpine, in her work of translation, restored it for us unbeknown to herself. The happiness she must later have felt upon finding that it fit the bill so well was surely well deserved!

10. *Memoirs*, 361, 379–80.

11. I would ask Macalpine (see *Memoirs*, 391–92) whether the number nine, insofar as it is involved in such diverse durations as nine hours, nine days, nine months, and nine years, which she underscores at every point in the patient's anamnesis—finding it again in the time on the clock up until which his anxiety postponed the beginning of the aforementioned sleep-cure, and even in the hesitation between four and five days that recurs several times in one and the same period of his personal recollection—must be conceived as forming part as such (that is, as a symbol) of the imaginary relation she isolates as a procreation fantasy.

The question is of concern to everyone, for it differs from the use Freud, in the Wolf Man case, makes of the form of the Roman numeral V, presumably recalled as having been seen at the end of the clock hand during a scene the Wolf Man witnessed at age one and a half, finding it anew in the opening and shutting of a butterfly's wings, in a girl's spread legs, etc.

12. See *Memoirs*, 13–19.

13. "Before Sunrise," "Vor Sonnenaufgang," in *Also sprach Zarathustra*, Part III. It is the fourth song in this third part.

14. It is interesting to situate object *a* in the R schema so as to shed light on what it contributes regarding the field of reality (a field that bars it).

However much emphasis I have placed on developing it since I wrote this article—by stating that this field functions only when obturated by the screen of fantasy—it still requires a great deal of attention.

There may be some point in indicating that—while it was enigmatic at the time, even though it is perfectly legible to anyone who knows what came later, as is the case if one claims to be basing oneself on it—what the R schema lays flat is a cross-cap.

In particular, the points and I did not choose the letters that correspond to them at random (or for fun)—*m* M and *i* I, which are those by which the only valid cut in this schema (the cut $\overrightarrow{mi}$, $\overrightarrow{\mathrm{MI}}$) is framed, suffice to indicate that this cut isolates a Möbius strip in the field.

This says it all, since this field will henceforth be the mere placeholder of the fantasy whose entire structure is provided by this cut.

I mean that only the cut reveals the structure of the entire surface, because it is able to detach from it the following two heterogeneous elements (noted in my algorithm ($\$\lozenge a$) of fantasy): $\$$—the barred S of the strip to be expected here where it in fact turns up, that is, covering the field **R** of reality—and *a*, which corresponds to the fields **I** and **S**.

It is thus as representation's representative in fantasy—that is, as the originally repressed subject—that $\$$, the barred S of desire, props up the field of reality here; and this field is sustained only by the extraction of object *a*, which nevertheless gives it its frame.

Measuring in increments [*échelons*] that are all vectorialized by an intrusion into the field **R** of the field **I** alone, which is articulated clearly in my text only as the effect of narcissism, shows that it is obviously out of the question that I wanted to bring back in, through some back door, the notion that these effects ("system of identifications," as we read) can theoretically ground reality in any way whatsoever.

Those who have attended my topological presentations (which are justified by nothing but the structure, that remains to be articulated, of fantasy) must surely know that there is nothing measurable that need be preserved in the structure of the Möbius strip, and that this structure boils down—like the real with which we are concerned here—to the cut itself.

This note indicates the current stage of my topological work (July 1966).

15. The title of that seminar.

16. Here is the text: *Einleitend habe ich dazu zu bemerken, dass bei der Genesis der betreffenden Entwicklung deren erste Anfänge weit, vielleicht bis zum* 18. *Jahrhundert zurückreichen, einertheils* die Namen Flechsig und Schreber (my emphasis) *(wahrscheinlich nicht in der Beschränkung auf je ein Individuum der betreffenden Familien) und anderntheils der Begriff des* Seelenmords (in "*Sperrdruck*" [emphasized] in the original) *eine Hauptrolle spielen.*

17. See, in particular, Ernst Haeckel's *Natürliche Schöpfungsgeschichte* (Berlin, 1872) and Otto Casari's *Urgeschichte der Menschheit* (Leipzig: Brockhaus, 1877).

18. The relationship between the proper name and the voice must be situated in language's two-axis structure of message and code, to which I have already referred. See section I.5 above. It is this structure that makes puns on proper names into witticisms.

19. *Memoirs*, 398.

20. This is the spelling of the English word currently in use in Hugues Salel's admirable verse translation of the first ten songs of the *Iliad*; it should suffice to ensure that this spelling survives in French.

21. "Die symbolische Gleichung Mädchen = Phallus," *Int. Zeitschrift für Psychoanalyse* XXII (1936), since translated into English as "The Symbolic Equation: Girl = Phallus" and published in *PQ* XX, 3 (1949): 303–24. French allows us to translate the term more appropriately as *pucelle* ["maid," "maiden," or "virgin"].

22. See W. G. Niederland, "Three Notes on the Schreber Case," *PQ* XX, 4 (1951): 579–91. Édouard Pichon is the author of the translation into French of these terms as "Shadows of men thrown together 1, 2, 3."

23. See Jean-Marc Alby's highly remarkable thesis, "Contribution à l'étude du transsexualisme," Paris, 1956.

24. See Freud, *Psychoanalytische Bemerkungen über einem autobiographisch beschriebenen Fall von Paranoia*, *GW* VIII, 264, fn1.

25. Freud, *GW* VIII, 284 and note.

26. S. 136.

27. At the acme of imaginary dissolution, the subject showed, in his delusional apperception, odd recourse to the following criterion of reality, which is to always return to the same place, and why the stars eminently represent it: this is the theme designated by his voices as "tying-to-the-planets" (*Anbinden an Erden*, S. 125).

28. "Remarks on Psychical Causality" (Paper given on September 28, 1946, at the Journées de Bonneval); see *Écrits* 1966, 151–93.

29. See André Green's thesis, *Le milieu familial des schizophrènes* (Paris, 1957), a work whose clear merit would not have suffered if surer landmarks had guided him toward greater success—in particular, in approaching what he bizarrely terms "psychotic fracture."

30. I wish the best of luck to the student of mine who followed up this remark, wherein lit-

erary criticism can rest assured it holds a thread that will not lead it astray.

31. Niederland, "Three Notes."

32. This sentence is quoted in the footnote on page 558 above.

33. In a note on the same page, Macalpine quotes the title of one of this author's books, *Glückseligkeitslehre für das physische Leben des Menschen*, namely, "Course in Blessed Felicity for the Physical Life of Men."

34. S. 194. *Die Redensart "Ei verflucht"... war noch ein Uberbleibsel der Grundsprache, in welcher die Worte "Ei verflucht, das sagt sich schwer" jedesmal gebraucht werden, wenn irgend ein mit der Weltordnung unerträgliche Erscheinung in das Bewusstsein der Seelen trat, z. B. "Ei verflucht, das sagt sich schwer, dass der liebe Gott sich f... lässt."*

35. I think I can borrow this euphemism from the *Grundsprache*'s own register, which the voices and Schreber himself nevertheless uncharacteristically dispense with here.

I think I can better fulfill the duties of scientific rigor by pointing out the hypocrisy which, in this detour as in others, reduces what Freudian experience demonstrates to something benign, nay, inane. I mean the indefinable use ordinarily made of references like the following: "At this moment in his analysis, the patient regressed to the anal phase." I'd like to see the analyst's face if the patient started "straining," or even just slobbering, on his couch.

All this is but a concealed return to the sublimation that finds shelter in the *inter urinas et faeces nascimur*, implying here that this sordid origin concerns only our bodies.

What analysis uncovers is something altogether different. It is not man's rags, but his very being that takes up its position among the scraps in which his first frolics found their cortege—inasmuch as the law of symbolization, in which his desire must become engaged, catches him in its net by the position as part-object in which he offers himself up on coming into the world, into a world where the Other's desire lays down the law.

This relationship is, of course, clearly articulated by Schreber in what he relates—to put it in such a way as to leave no room for ambiguity—to the act of shitting: namely, the fact of feeling the elements of his being, whose dispersal into the infinitude of his delusion constitutes his suffering, coming together in it.

36. In the form: *Die Sonne ist eine Hure* (S. 384). For Schreber, the sun is God's central aspect. The inner experience I am speaking of here is a reference to Georges Bataille's work. In *Madame Edwarda*, he describes the odd extremity of this experience.

The Direction of the Treatment and the Principles of Its Power 585

Paper given at the Royaumont Colloquium held July 10–13, 1958[1]

I. Who Analyzes Today?

1. People say that an analysis bears the marks of the analysand as a person as if it were self-evident. But they think they are being audacious if they take an interest in the effects that the analyst as a person may have on an analysis. This, at least, explains the shudder that runs through us when trendy remarks are made about countertransference, which contribute, no doubt, to masking its conceptual impropriety: just think of the highmindedness we display when we show that we ourselves are made of the same clay as those we shape!

That was a nasty thing to say. Yet it barely suffices for those it targets, given that people now go about proclaiming, under the aegis of psychoanalysis, that they are working toward "the patient's emotional reeducation" [22].[2]

Situating the analyst's action at this level implies a position based on a principle, with respect to which anything that might be said about countertransference, even if it were not futile, would merely serve as a diversion. For the imposture that I wish to dislodge here now lies beyond this.[3]

I am not, for all that, denouncing the anti-Freudian aspects of contemporary psychoanalysis. Indeed, we should be grateful to the partisans of the latter for throwing down their mask in this regard, priding themselves, as they do, on going beyond what they, in fact, know nothing about, having retained 586
just enough of Freud's doctrine to sense how significantly what they are led to enunciate about their experience diverges from it.

I intend to show how the inability to authentically sustain a praxis results, as is common in the history of mankind, in the exercise of power.

2. Assuredly, a psychoanalyst directs the treatment. The first principle of this treatment, the one that is spelled out to him before all else, and which he finds throughout his training, so much so that he becomes utterly imbued with it, is that he must not direct the patient. The direction of conscience, in the sense of the moral guidance a faithful Catholic might find in it, is radically excluded here. If psychoanalysis raises problems for moral theology, they are not those of the direction of conscience—which, let me remind you, also raises problems.

The direction of the treatment is something else altogether. It consists, first of all, in getting the subject to apply the fundamental rule of psychoanalysis, that is, the directives whose presence at the heart of what is called "the analytic situation" cannot be neglected, under the pretext that the subject would best apply them without thinking about it.

These directives are initially laid out to the patient in the form of instructions which, however little the analyst comments on them, convey, even in the very inflections of his statement of them, the doctrine the analyst himself has arrived at. Which does not mean that the analyst remains unscathed by the mass of prejudices that await him in the patient, based on the idea the latter has been allowed to form of the procedures and aim of the psychoanalytic enterprise by the spreading of notions about analysis in his culture.

This is already enough to show us that, from the initial directives on, the problem of direction cannot be formulated along the lines of univocal communication—a fact that forces us to go no further in our discussion of this stage and to shed light on it by what follows it.

Let me simply state that, if we reduce it to its truth, this stage consists in getting the patient to forget that it is merely a matter of words, but that this does not excuse the analyst for forgetting it himself [16].

3. In any case, I announced that I intended to approach the topic from the analyst's vantage point.

587 Let us say that in the capital outlay involved in the common enterprise, the patient is not alone in finding it difficult to pay his share. The analyst too must pay:

- pay with words no doubt, if the transmutation they undergo due to the analytic operation raises them to the level of their effect as interpretation;
- but also pay with his person, in that, whether he likes it or not, he lends it as a prop for the singular phenomena analysis discovered in transference;

- can anyone forget that he must pay for becoming enmeshed in an action that goes right to the core of being (*Kern unseres Wesens*, as Freud put it [6]) with what is essential in his most intimate judgment: could he alone remain on the sidelines?

Let those who support my cause not be concerned at the thought that I am exposing myself here once again to adversaries who are always only too happy to dismiss me for my metaphysics.

For it is at the heart of their claim to be satisfied with effectiveness that a statement like "the analyst cures not so much by what he says and does as by what he is" [22] can be made. Nobody, apparently, demands an explanation from the author for such a remark, any more than one appeals to his sense of modesty when, with a tired smile directed at the ridicule he incurs, he puts his trust in goodness, his own goodness (we must be good, there being no transcendence in this context), to put an end to a dead-end debate about transference neurosis.[4] But who would be so cruel as to question someone buckling under the weight of his luggage, when his posture clearly indicates that it is full of bricks?

Yet being is being, regardless of who invokes it, and we have the right to ask what it is doing here.

4. So I shall cross-examine the analyst again, insofar as I myself am one, in order to note that the more his being is involved, the less sure he is of his action.

As an interpreter of what is presented to me in words or deeds, I choose my own oracle and articulate it as I please, sole master of my ship after God; and 588
while, of course, I am far from able to weigh the whole effect of my words, I am well aware of the fact and strive to attend to it. In other words, I am always free in the timing and frequency, as well as in the choice of my interventions, so much so that it seems that the rule has been entirely designed so as not to interfere in any way with my activity as an executor—to which corresponds the aspect of "material," which is how my action here takes up what it produces.

5. In handling transference, on the other hand, my freedom is alienated by the splitting my person undergoes in it, and everyone knows that it is here that the secret of analysis must be sought. This does not prevent people from believing they are making progress with the following learned remark: that psychoanalysis must be studied as a situation involving two persons. To be sure, conditions are placed on it that restrict its movements, but the situation thus conceived nevertheless serves to articulate (and with no more artifice than the aforementioned "emotional reeducation") the principles for training the so-

called "weak" ego, by an ego that one likes to believe capable of carrying out such a project because it is strong. That such a view is not expressed without a certain embarrassment is shown by the strikingly clumsy repentances that are offered, like that of the author who specifies that he does not compromise on the need for a "cure from the inside" [22].[5] But it is all the more significant to observe that the subject's assent, referred to in this passage, comes only secondarily, from an effect that was at first imposed.

It is not for my own pleasure that I point out these deviations, but rather to use their pitfalls as markers for our route.

In fact, every analyst (even those who wander off course in this way) always experiences the transference in wonder at this least expected effect of a relationship between two people that would seem to be like any other. He tells himself that he is dealing here with a phenomenon for which he is not responsible, and we know with what insistence Freud stressed the spontaneity of its appearance in the patient.

589 For some time now, analysts—in the heartrending revisions they treat us to—have willingly insinuated that this insistence, with which they for so long built a wall around themselves, expressed a flight on Freud's part from the commitment that the notion of situation presupposes. "We are, you see, up to date," they seem to say.

But it is rather the facile excitement of their gesture in dumping feelings, which they class under the heading of their countertransference, onto one side of the scales—the situation balancing out due to the weight of those feelings—that to me is evidence of a troubled conscience corresponding to a failure to conceptualize the true nature of transference.

One cannot reason from the fantasies the analysand gets propped up to the analyst's person in the same way as an ideal player guesses his opponent's intentions. There is probably always an element of strategy, but one should not be deceived by the metaphor of the mirror, appropriate as it may be to the smooth surface the analyst presents to the patient. An impassive face and sealed lips do not have the same purpose here as in bridge. Instead, the analyst enlists the aid of what in bridge is called the dummy [*le mort*], but he does so in order to bring out the fourth player who is to be the analysand's partner here, and whose hand the analyst, by his maneuvers, strives to get the analysand to guess: such is the restraint—of abnegation, as it were—that is imposed on the analyst by the stakes of the game in analysis.

One might pursue the metaphor by deducing his game therefrom according to whether he places himself "to the right" or "to the left" of the patient—in other words, in a position to play his cards after or before the fourth player, that is, before or after the latter by using the dummy.

But what is certain is that the analyst's feelings have only one possible place in the game, that of the dummy; and that if the dummy is revived the game will proceed without anyone knowing who is leading it.

This is why the analyst is less free in his strategy than in his tactics.

6. Let us go further. The analyst is even less free in what dominates both his strategy and tactics—namely, his politics, where he would do better to take his bearings from his want-to-be than from his being.

To put it another way: his action concerning the patient will escape him along with the idea he forms of his action, as long as he does not reconsider its point of departure in terms of what makes his action possible and does not preserve the paradox of its quadripartition, in order to revise at the core the 590
structure by which all action intervenes in reality.

For contemporary psychoanalysts, this relationship to reality is self-evident. They gauge the patient's defections from it using the authoritarian principle that has been employed by educators since time immemorial. They simply rely on training analysis to ensure its maintenance at a sufficient rate among analysts, about whom one can't help feeling that, in facing the problems of humanity that are addressed to them, their views are sometimes a bit parochial. This is merely to push the problem back to an individual level.

And it is hardly reassuring—when they describe the procedure of analysis as the reduction in the subject of deviations, attributed to his transference and his resistances, but mapped in relation to reality—to hear them gush about the "perfectly simple situation" that is provided by analysis as a means of assessing those deviations. Come now! The educator is hardly ready to be educated if he can judge so superficially an experience that he, too, must nevertheless have undergone.

From such an assessment, one assumes that these analysts would have provided this experience with other means if they had had to depend on their own sense of reality to invent it themselves: a priority shocking to imagine. They half-suspect as much, and that is why they are so punctilious about preserving its forms.

One understands why, in order to prop up so obviously precarious a conception, certain individuals on the other side of the Atlantic felt the need to introduce a stable value here, a standard by which to measure reality [*réel*]: the autonomous ego*. It is the supposedly organized set of the most disparate functions that lend their support to the subject's feeling of innateness. It is regarded as autonomous because it is supposed to be sheltered from the person's internal conflicts ("nonconflictual sphere"*) [14].

One recognizes here a worn-out mirage that the most academic introspective psychology had already rejected as untenable. Yet this regression is celebrated as a return to the fold of "general psychology."

Be that as it may, it solves the problem of the analyst's being.[6] A team of egos*, no doubt less equal than autonomous (but by what stamp of origin do
591 they recognize each other in the sufficiency of their autonomy?), offers itself to Americans to guide them toward happiness*, without upsetting the autonomies, whether egoistic or not, that pave with their nonconflictual spheres the American way* of getting there.

7. Let me summarize. If an analyst dealt only with resistances, he would look twice before hazarding an interpretation, which he in fact does, but this prudence would suffice.

However, this interpretation, if he gives it, will be received as coming from the person the transference imputes him to be. Will he agree to take advantage of this error concerning who he is? Psychoanalytic morals do not forbid it, on the condition that he interpret this effect, failing which the analysis would remain at the level of crude suggestion.

This is an indisputable position, except that the analyst's speech is still heard as coming from the transferential Other, and the subject's exit from the transference is thus postponed *ad infinitum*.

It is therefore because of what the subject imputes the analyst to be (his being being elsewhere) that an interpretation may come back to the place from which it can bear upon the distribution of responses.

But who will say what the analyst is there, and what remains of him when he is up against the wall of the task of interpreting? Let him dare say it himself if the fact that he is a man is all he has by way of an answer. Whether he has any or not would then be all there is to it: yet it is here that he beats a retreat, not only on account of the impudence of the mystery, but because in this having, it is being that is at stake, and how! We shall see later that this "how" is no easy matter.

Thus he prefers to fall back on his ego, and on the reality about which he knows a thing or two. But here he is, then, at the level of "I" and "me" with his patient. How can he manage it if they're at each other's throats? It is here that we astutely count on the secret contacts we must have on the inside—named, in this case, the healthy part *of the ego*, the part that thinks like us.

We might conclude that this brings us back to our initial problem—namely, how to reinvent analysis.

592 Or to recast it: by treating transference as a particular form of resistance.

Many profess to do so. It is to them that I would ask the question that forms the title of this chapter: Who is the analyst? He who interprets by taking advantage of the transference? He who analyzes transference as resistance? Or he who imposes his idea of reality?

It is a question that may pinch a bit harder those to whom it is addressed, and be less easy to sidestep than the question, "Who is speaking?" which one of my students blared into their ears regarding the patient. For their impatient answer—"An animal of our species"—to a changed question would be more annoyingly tautological, to have to say: "Me [*moi*]."

And that's all there is to it.

II. What Is the Place of Interpretation?

1. The preceding does not answer all the questions that occur to a novice. But in gathering together the problems currently raised concerning the direction of an analysis, insofar as this currency reflects contemporary practice, I think I have kept everything in proportion.

Which is to say, the smaller place occupied by interpretation in present-day psychoanalysis—not that people no longer know the meaning of interpretation, but they seem to be embarrassed when they approach it. No author tackles interpretation without first distinguishing it from every other form of verbal intervention that does not constitute interpretation: explanations, gratifications, responses to demands, and so on. This process becomes revealing when it gets close to the center of interest. It stipulates that even something said to lead the subject to an insight* into one of his behaviors, especially its signification as resistance, may be given any other name, "confrontation," for example, if only confrontation of the subject with his own words, without deserving the name "interpretation," simply because it is a clarifying statement.

It is touching to see an author attempt to storm Gestalt theory to find in it a metaphor that would allow him to express what interpretation brings by way of resolution to an ambiguity of intention, and by way of closure to an incompleteness that is nevertheless achieved only after the fact [2]. 593

2. One senses that what is slippery here is the nature of the transmutation that occurs in the subject; this is all the more painful for thought in that it eludes thought at the very moment thought shifts into action. Indeed, no index suffices to show where interpretation operates, unless one accepts in all its radical implications a concept of the function of the signifier, which grasps where it is that the subject subordinates himself to the signifier to so great an extent that he is suborned by it.

In order to decipher the diachrony of unconscious repetitions, interpretation must introduce into the synchrony of signifiers that come together there something that suddenly makes translation possible—this is precisely what is allowed by the function of the Other in the possession of the code, it being in relation to that Other that the missing element appears.

This importance of the signifier in the localization of analytic truth appears implicitly when an author holds firmly to the internal coherence of analytic experience in defining aporias. One should read Edward Glover to gauge the price he pays for not having the term "signifier" at his disposal. In articulating the most relevant views, he finds interpretation everywhere, even in the banality of a medical prescription, being unable to set any limits to it. He even goes so far as to say, quite simply—without our being sure he knows what he is saying—that symptom formation is an inexact interpretation on the subject's part [13].

Conceived of in this way, interpretation becomes a sort of phlogiston: it is manifest in everything that is understood rightly or wrongly, as long as it feeds the flame of the imaginary, of that pure display which, going by the name of aggressiveness, flourishes in the technique of that period (1931—new enough to still be current today [13]).

It is only insofar as interpretation culminates in the here and now of this game that it can be distinguished from the reading of the *signatura rerum*, regarding which Jung tries to outdo Böhme. To follow it there would hardly suit the being of our analysts.

But to keep time with Freud requires a very different tablature, one for which it is useful to know how to take the clock apart.

594 3. My doctrine of the signifier is first of all a discipline, in which those I train have to familiarize themselves with the ways the signifier effects the advent of the signified, which is the only way of conceiving how it is that interpretation, by inscribing itself therein, can produce anything new.

For interpretation is not grounded in some assumption of divine archetypes, but in the fact that the unconscious has the radical structure of language and that a material operates in the unconscious according to certain laws, which are the same laws as those discovered in the study of natural languages [*langues*]—that is, languages [*langues*] that are or were actually spoken.

The phlogiston metaphor, which was suggested to me a moment ago by Glover, derives its appropriateness from the error it evokes: signification no more emanates from life than phlogiston escapes from bodies in combustion. We should speak of signification rather as of the combination of life with the O atom of the sign[7]—the sign insofar as it first of all connotes presence *or* absence, by essentially introducing the *and* that links them, since in connoting presence or absence, it institutes presence against a background of absence, just as it constitutes absence in presence.

One will recall that with characteristic sureness of step in his field, Freud, seeking a model of repetition automatism, stopped at the crossroads formed by a game of occultation and an alternating scansion of two phonemes, whose conjugation by a child made a striking impression on him.

At the same time, we also see in the game that the value of the object is insignificant (the object the child causes to appear and disappear), and that phonetic perfection is less important than phonemic distinction—no one would dispute that Freud was right to translate it immediately by the *Fort! Da!* of the German he as an adult spoke [9].

This is the point of insemination for a symbolic order that preexists the infantile subject and in accordance with which he has to structure himself.

4. I will spare myself the task of providing the rules of interpretation. It is not
that they cannot be formulated, but their formulations presuppose develop- 595
ments that I cannot presume to be known, since I cannot give a condensed account of them here.

I will confine myself to remarking that, in reading the classical commentaries on interpretation, I always regret how little is made of the very facts people supply.

To give an example, everyone acknowledges in his own way that to confirm that an interpretation is well founded, it is not the conviction with which it is received by the subject that counts, its well-foundedness instead being gauged by the material that emerges afterward.

But psychologizing superstition has such a powerful grip on our minds that people always seek out the phenomenon of well-foundedness in the subject's assent, entirely overlooking the consequences of what Freud says about *Verneinung* [negation] as a form of avowal—to say the least, negation by the subject cannot be treated as equivalent to drawing a blank.

This is how theory translates the way in which resistance is engendered in practice. It is also what I am trying to convey when I say that there is no other resistance to analysis than that of the analyst himself.

5. The problem is that contemporary authors seem to have gotten the sequence of analytic effects backward. According to them, interpretation is but hesitant stammering compared to the opening up of a broader relationship in which, at last, we understand each other ("from the inside," no doubt).

Interpretation becomes necessary here because the subject's weakness requires our assistance. It is also something that is very difficult to get his weakness to swallow without rejecting it. It is both at once—in other words, a very awkward means.

But what we have here is only the effect of the analyst's passions: his fear, which is not of making a mistake but of displaying his ignorance; his taste, which is not to satisfy but not to disappoint; his need, which is not to govern but to keep the upper hand. It has nothing to do with countertransference on the part of this or that analyst; it has to do with the consequences of the dyadic relation, if the therapist does not overcome it, and how could he overcome it when he views it as the ideal of his action?

Primum vivere, no doubt: a break must be avoided. That the practice of
596 common decency should be classified as a technique to be taught so that breaks are avoided is one thing. But to confuse this physical necessity, the patient's presence at his appointment, with an analytic relationship is a mistaken notion that will mislead the novice for a long time.

6. From this point of view, transference becomes the analyst's security, and the subject's relation to reality [*réel*] becomes the terrain on which the outcome of the battle is determined. Interpretation, which was postponed until the transference was consolidated, now becomes subordinate to its liquidation.

As a result, interpretation is absorbed into a kind of "working through"*—that one can quite simply translate by "work of transference" [*travail du transfert*]—which serves as an alibi for a sort of revenge the analyst takes for his initial timidity, that is, for an insistence that opens the door to all kinds of forcing, placed under the banner of "strengthening the ego" [21–22].

7. But has anyone observed, in criticizing Freud's approach, as presented for example in the case of the Rat Man, that what surprises us as a preliminary indoctrination is due simply to the fact that Freud proceeds in exactly the opposite order? For he begins by introducing the patient to an initial situating of his position in reality [*réel*], even if this situating leads to a precipitation—I would even go so far as to say a systematization—of symptoms [8].

Another well-known example: Freud brings Dora to realize that she has done more than merely participate in the great disorder of her father's world, whose damaging consequences she complains of—she has made herself its linchpin, and it could not have continued without her connivance [7].

I have long stressed the Hegelian procedure at work in this reversal of positions of the beautiful soul in relation to the reality he accuses. The point is not to adapt him to it, but to show him that he is only too well adapted to it, since he assists in its very fabrication.

But the path to be followed with the other ends here. For the transference has already done its job, demonstrating that what is at stake is something altogether different than relations between the ego and the world.

Freud does not always seem to find his way about very well in the transference in the cases he describes. And that is why they are so precious. 597

For he immediately recognized that the crux [*principe*] of his power lay in the transference—in which respect it did not differ from suggestion—but also that this power only gave him a way out of the problem on the condition that he not use it, for it was then that it took on its whole transferential development.

From then on he no longer addressed the person who was in his proximity, which is why he refused to work face to face with him.

Interpretation in Freud's work is so bold that, in popularizing it, we no longer recognize its import as mantic. When Freud exposes a tendency—what he calls *Trieb*, which is altogether different from an instinct—the freshness of the discovery prevents us from seeing the advent of a signifier that the *Trieb* in itself implies. But when Freud brings to light what can only be called the subject's lines of fate, what we ponder is Tiresias' face confronting the ambiguity where his verdict operates.

For the lines that are divined here have so little to do with the subject's ego, or with anything he may make present here and now in the dyadic relation, that in the case of the Rat Man, it is by a direct hit on the pact that presided over his parents' marriage (that is, on something that occurred well before the Rat Man was born) that Freud finds several conditions intermingled in it—honor just barely saved, emotional betrayal, social compromise, and prescribed debt, of which the great compulsive scenario that led the patient to him seems to be the cryptographic copy—and finally manages to explain the impasses in which the Rat Man's moral life and desire go astray.

But the most striking thing about it is that access to this material was rendered possible only by an interpretation in which Freud relies too heavily on the idea that the Rat Man's father had prohibited his son from marrying the girl to whom he was sublimely devoted, in order to explain the impossibility that seems to have blocked this relationship for him in every way. An interpretation which, to say the least, is inexact, since it is contradicted by the reality it presumes, but which is nevertheless true in the sense that, in it, Freud evinces an intuition that anticipates my own contribution regarding the function of the Other in obsessive neurosis. I have demonstrated that this function may be served, in obsessive neurosis, by a dead man [*un mort*], and that in this 598
case it could not be better served than by the father, insofar as the Rat Man's father had, by his death, acceded to the position Freud recognized as that of the absolute Father.

8. I will ask those who have read my work and who have attended my seminar to forgive me for citing examples with which they are already familiar.

I am doing so not only because I cannot make use of my own analyses to demonstrate the level interpretation reaches—when the interpretation, proving to be coextensive with the subject's history, cannot be communicated in the communicating milieu in which many of my analyses take place without the risk of betraying the subject's identity. For I have succeeded at times in saying enough about a case without saying too much, that is, in conveying my example without anyone, except the person in question, recognizing it.

Nor is it because I regard the Rat Man as a case that Freud cured—for if I were to add that I do not think that the analysis is entirely unconnected with the tragic conclusion of his story by death on the battlefield, what an opportunity for contempt I would be offering to those who wish to find fault!

What I am saying is that it is in a direction of the treatment, ordered, as I have just shown, in accordance with a process that begins with rectification of the subject's relations with reality [*réel*], and proceeds to development of the transference and then to interpretation, that is situated the horizon at which the fundamental discoveries, which we are still living off, surrendered themselves to Freud concerning the dynamics and structure of obsessive neurosis. Nothing more, but nothing less either.

The question now is whether we have lost this horizon by reversing this order.

9. What we can say is that the new pathways by which the approach laid out by the discoverer has supposedly been authenticated are proof of terminological confusion that can only be exposed in particular cases. I will thus take an example that has already contributed to my teaching; it has, of course, been chosen from a first-rate author who, by virtue of his background, is particularly attuned to the dimension of interpretation. I am referring to Ernst Kris and to a case which—he does not hide the fact—he took over from Melitta Schmideberg [15].

599 It concerns a subject inhibited in his intellectual life and particularly incapable of publishing his research on account of an impulse to plagiarize, which, it seems, he was unable to control. Such was the subjective drama.

Melitta Schmideberg had understood it as the recurrence of an adolescent delinquency [25]; the subject stole sweets and books, and it was from this angle that she had undertaken the analysis of the unconscious conflict.

Ernst Kris gently approaches the case anew in accordance with a more methodical interpretation, one that proceeds from the surface to the depths, he says. The fact that he credits this interpretation to "ego* psychology" à la

Hartmann, whose supporter he felt he had to become, is incidental to an assessment of what takes place. Ernst Kris changes perspective on the case and claims to give the subject insight* for a new departure on the basis of a fact that is merely a repetition of his compulsion, but regarding which Kris quite commendably does not content himself with what the patient says. And when the patient claims to have taken, in spite of himself, the ideas for a piece that he has just completed from a book which, on being remembered, enabled him to check it after the fact, Kris looks at the evidence and discovers that nothing has apparently gone beyond what is implied by a shared field of research. In short, having assured himself that his patient is not a plagiarist when he thinks he is, he sets out to show him that he wants to be one in order to prevent himself from really being one—which is what we call analyzing the defense before the drive, the latter being manifested here in an attraction to others' ideas.

This intervention may be presumed to be erroneous, owing simply to the fact that it presupposes that defense and drive are concentric, the one being molded, as it were, around the other.

What proves that it is, in fact, erroneous is the very thing Kris thinks confirms his intervention—namely, that just when he feels he can ask the patient what he thinks of the tables being turned in this way, the patient, daydreaming for a moment, replies that for some time, on leaving his sessions, he has wandered along a street full of attractive little restaurants, scrutinizing their menus in search of his favorite dish: fresh brains.

An admission which, rather than sanctioning the felicity of the intervention by way of the material it contributes, seems to me to have the corrective value of an acting out* in the very report he gives of it. 600

The post-session condiment the patient sniffs out seems to me rather to tell the dinner host that the condiment had been sorely lacking during the meal. However compulsive he may be about smelling it, it is a hint*; being a transitory symptom, no doubt, it warns the analyst that he is barking up the wrong tree.

Indeed, you are barking up the wrong tree, I would continue, addressing the late Ernst Kris, as I remember him at the Marienbad Congress where, the day after my address on the mirror stage, I took my leave, anxious as I was to get a feeling for the spirit of the time—a time full of promises—at the Olympics in Berlin. He kindly objected, "Ça ne se fait pas!" ("That isn't done!"), having already acquired that penchant for the respectable that perhaps influenced his approach here.

Was this what misled you, Ernst Kris, or was it simply that while your intentions may have been upright, and your judgment indubitably so as well, things themselves were askew?

It's not the fact that your patient doesn't steal that is important here. It's that he doesn't . . . Not "doesn't": it's that he steals *nothing*. And that's what you should have conveyed to him.

Contrary to what you believe, it's not his defense against the idea of stealing that makes him believe he is stealing. It's that he may have an idea of his own which never occurs to him or barely crosses his mind.

It is thus useless to engage him in a process of separating out what more or less original ideas his friend filches from him when they chew the fat together, which God himself could not determine.

Couldn't this craving for fresh brains refresh your own concepts, and remind you of the function of metonymy in Roman Jakobson's work? I shall return to this later.

You speak of Melitta Schmideberg as if she had confused delinquency with the id. I am not so sure, and the wording of the title of the article in which she discusses this case suggests a metaphor to me.

You treat the patient as if he were obsessed, but he throws you a line with his food fantasy, giving you the opportunity to be a quarter-of-an-hour ahead
601 of the nosology of your time by providing a diagnosis of anorexia nervosa [*anorexie mentale*]. You would simultaneously refresh, by giving them back their true meaning, this couple of terms which current usage has reduced to the dubious status of an etiological indication.

Anorexia, in this case, concerns the mental realm, concerns the desire on which the idea lives, and this leads us to the scurvy that rages on the raft on which I embark him with the skinny virgins.

Their symbolically motivated refusal seems to me to have a good deal to do with the patient's aversion to what he thinks. His daddy, you tell us, was not very resourceful when it came to ideas. Could it be that the grandfather, who was celebrated for his ideas, disgusted him of them? How can we know? You are surely right to make the signifier "grand," included in the kinship term ["grandfather"], nothing less than the origin of the rivalry played out with the father over who could catch the biggest [*le plus grand*] fish. But this purely formal challenge* seems to me rather to mean: nothing doing.

Your progress, supposedly from the surface, thus has nothing in common with subjective rectification, highlighted above in Freud's method, where, moreover, it isn't motivated by any kind of topographical priority.

The fact is that this rectification is also dialectical in Freud's work. It takes off from the subject's own words in order to come back to them, which means that an interpretation can be exact only by being . . . an interpretation.

To side here with the objective situation is going too far, if only because plagiarism is relative to the customs in force.[8]

But the idea that the surface is the level of the superficial is itself dangerous.

Another topology is necessary if we are not to be mistaken as to the place of desire.

To wipe desire off the map [*carte*] when it is already covered over in the patient's landscape is not the best way of following Freud's teaching. 602

Nor is it a way of getting rid of depth, for it is on the surface that depth is seen, as when one's face breaks out in pimples on holidays.

III. Where Do We Stand Regarding Transference?

1. We must look to the work of my colleague, Daniel Lagache, for an accurate history of the writings devoted—around Freud while he was pursuing his work and since he bequeathed it to us—to transference, which Freud discovered [18]. Lagache's work aims to go much further, by introducing structural distinctions into the phenomenon's function that are essential for its critique. Suffice it to recall the highly relevant alternative he presents—regarding the ultimate nature of transference—between the need for repetition and the repetition of need.

Such work, whose consequences I believe I have been able to draw out in my teaching, shows very clearly, by means of the ordering it introduces, to what extent the aspects on which discussion focuses are often partial, and particularly to what extent the ordinary use of the term "transference," even in psychoanalysis, cannot free itself from its most questionable approach, which is also its crudest: to make transference into the succession or sum total of positive or negative feelings the patient has for his analyst.

To assess where we stand regarding transference in our scientific community, it could be said that there has been no agreement nor light shed on the following points where they would, nevertheless, seem necessary: Is it the same effect of the relation with the analyst that is manifested in the initial infatuation observed at the beginning of treatment and in the web of satisfactions that make this relation so difficult to break off when transference neurosis seems to go beyond strictly analytic means? And is it the relation with the analyst and its fundamental frustration which, in the second phase of analysis, sustains the scansion—frustration, aggression, and regression—in which the most fruitful effects of analysis are supposed to occur? How is the subordination of phenomena to be conceptualized when their movement is traversed by fantasies that openly involve the figure of the analyst? 603

The reason for these persistent obscurities has been formulated in an exceptionally perspicacious study: at each of the stages at which an attempt has been made to reappraise the problems of transference, the divergences in technique that made this task so urgent have not given way to a true critique of the notion itself [20].

2. The notion I want to get at here is so central to analytic action that it may serve as a gauge of the partiality of the theories that have taken the time to conceptualize it. That is, we will not be misled if we judge their partiality on the basis of the handling of transference these theories imply. This pragmatism is justified. For the handling of transference and one's notion of it are one and the same, and however little this notion is elaborated in practice, it cannot but align itself with the partialities of the theory.

On the other hand, the simultaneous existence of these partialities does not necessarily mean that they complete each other. This confirms the fact that they suffer from a central defect.

In order to introduce a little order here already, I will reduce these partialities of the theory to three, even if it means giving in to taking sides to some degree, less serious as it is only for the purposes of exposition.

3. I will link geneticism—in the sense that it tends to ground analytic phenomena in the developmental moments involved in those phenomena and to feed on the so-called direct observation of the child—to a specific technique, one that centers this procedure on the analysis of the defenses.

This link is obvious from a historical perspective. One might even say that it has no other foundation, since it is constituted only on the basis of the failure of the solidarity it presupposes.

One can locate its beginnings in the legitimate credence lent to the notion of an unconscious ego with which Freud reoriented his doctrine. To move from that notion to the hypothesis that the defense mechanisms that were grouped under ego functioning ought themselves to be able to reveal a comparable law of appearance—one that even corresponds to the succession of phases by which Freud had attempted to connect the emergence of the drives with physiology—
604 was the step Anna Freud, in her book *The Ego and the Mechanisms of Defense* [4], proposed to take in order to put it to the test of experience.

It could have occasioned a fruitful critique of the relations between development and the obviously more complex structures Freud introduced into psychology. But the sights were lowered; it was so much more tempting to try to insert the defense mechanisms into the observable stages of sensorimotor development and progressive abilities of intelligent behavior—those mechanisms supposedly separating out in the course of their progress.

One might say that the hopes Anna Freud placed in such an exploration were dashed: nothing emerged from this line of approach that could inform technique, even though the details gleaned from a type of child observation informed by analysis were sometimes very suggestive.

The notion of pattern*, which serves here as an alibi for the failed typology, sponsors a technique which, in seeking to detect a pattern* that isn't current, willingly judges it on the basis of its deviation from a pattern* that finds in its conformism the guarantees of its conformity. One cannot recall without a sense of shame the criteria of success in which this trumped-up work culminates: the achievement of a higher income and the safety valve of an affair with one's secretary, regulating the release of forces that are strictly under wraps in marriage, career, and political community. These do not seem to me to be of sufficient dignity to require an appeal—articulated in the analyst's planning* and even in his interpretation—to the Discord of the life and death instincts, even if only to decorate one's words with the pretentious term "economic," and to pursue it, in an utter and complete misunderstanding of Freud's thought, as the play of a couple of forces that are homologous in their opposition.

4. The second trend where we see what slips away from transference seems less degraded in its analytic relief—namely, that based on object relations.

This theory, however much it has degenerated in France in recent years, has, like geneticism, a noble origin. It was Karl Abraham who opened up this field and the notion of the part-object is his original contribution. This is not the place to demonstrate its value. I am more interested in indicating its connection with the partiality of that aspect of transference which Abraham iso- 605
lates, promoting it in its opacity as the ability to love—as if that were a constitutional facet of the patient in which one could read the degree of his curability, and, in particular, the only aspect concerning which the treatment of psychosis would fail.

In fact, we have two equations here: the so-called sexual transference *(Sexualübertragung)* is at the heart of the love that in French has been called *amour objectal*, object love *(Objektliebe);* and the capacity for transference is a measure of the patient's access to reality [*réel*]. I cannot stress too strongly that this merely begs the question.

In contradistinction to the presuppositions of geneticism, which is supposed to be based on an order of formal emergences in the subject, Abraham's perspective can be explained by a finality that is authorized because it is instinctual, in that it is embellished by the maturation of an ineffable object, the Object with a capital O, that governs the phase of "objectality" (significantly distinguished from objectivity by its affective substance).

This ectoplasmic conception of the object quickly revealed its dangers when it degenerated into the crude dichotomy expressed in the opposition between pregenital character and genital character.

This elementary theme was summarily developed by attributing to pregenital character a slew of features—projective unrealism, greater or lesser degrees of autism, restriction of satisfactions by the defenses, and the wrapping of the object in doubly protective insulation when it comes to the destructive effects that connote it—in other words, an amalgamation of all the defects in the object-relation with a view to showing the reasons for the extreme dependence of the subject that results therefrom. A picture that would be useful, despite its tendency to be confused, if it did not seem designed to serve as a negative for the puerility of the following: "the passage from the pregenital form to the genital form," in which the drives "are no longer characterized by an uncontrollable, unlimited, unconditional need for possession, involving a destructive element. They are truly tender and loving, and if the subject still does not prove to be 'oblative'—that is, disinterested—and if these objects" (here the author recalls my remarks) "are just as profoundly narcissistic objects as they were before, he is now capable of comprehension and adapta-
606 tion to the other. Moreover, the intimate structure of these object relations shows that the object's own pleasure is indispensable to the subject's happiness. The object's preferences, desires, and needs (what a hodgepodge!)[9] are taken into consideration to the highest degree."

However, this does not prevent the ego from having "a stability that runs no risk of being compromised by the loss of a significant Object. It remains independent of its objects."

"Its organization is such that the mode of thought it employs is essentially logical. It does not spontaneously present regression to an archaic mode of apprehending reality, affective thinking and magical belief playing only an absolutely secondary role here; symbolization does not go beyond the extent and importance it has in normal life (!!).[10] The style of relations between subject and object is one of the most highly evolved *(sic)*."[11]

This is the promise held out to those who "at the end of a successful analysis . . . realize the enormous difference between what they used to believe sexual joy to be and what they now experience" [21, page 55].

One is led to understand that for those who have this joy from the outset, "genital relations are, in short, untroubled" [21].

Untroubled except for conjugating themselves irresistibly in the verb "to bang your behind on the chandelier," which marks a place here for the future scholiast to find his eternal opportunity.

5. Although we must agree with Abraham when he suggests that the typical object-relation is manifested in the activity of the collector, perhaps the rule of that relation is not given in this edifying antinomy, but is to be sought, rather, in some impasse that is constitutive of desire as such.

What makes it such that the object presents itself as broken and decomposed is perhaps something other than a pathological factor. And what does this absurd hymn to the harmony of genital relations have to do with reality [*réel*]?

Must we erase the Oedipal drama from our experience when it had to be forged by Freud precisely to explain the barriers and debasements *(Erniedrigungen)* 607 so common in the sphere of love, even the most fulfilled?

Is it our job to disguise Eros, the black God, as the Good Shepherd's curly-haired sheep?

Sublimation may be at work in the "oblation" that radiates from love, but we should try to go a little further into the structure of the sublime and not confuse it with the perfect orgasm—an equation Freud, in any case, opposed.

The worst thing is that the souls who overflow with the most natural tenderness are led to wonder whether they satisfy the delusional normalism of the genital relation—an unheralded burden which we have loaded onto the shoulders of the innocent, like those cursed by the Evangelist.

Yet in reading our work, should any of it survive into a time when people will no longer know what these effervescent words corresponded to in practice, people might imagine that our art was designed to revive sexual hunger in those afflicted with retardation of the sexual gland—to the physiology of which we have, nevertheless, made no contribution, and of which we need know very little indeed.

6. At least three sides are needed to make a pyramid, even a heretical one. The side that closes the dihedron I have described here in the gap left in the conception of transference, strives, one might say, to join the edges together.

If transference derives its power from being brought back to the reality of which the analyst is the representative, and if the goal is to ripen the Object in the hothouse of a confined situation, the analysand is left with only one object to sink his teeth into, if you will allow me the expression, and that is the analyst.

Hence the third mistake on my list—the notion of intersubjective introjection—because it is unfortunately installed in a dyadic relation.

For we are certainly dealing with a unitive pathway, concerning which the various theoretical sauces that accompany it, depending on the topography they refer to, can but retain the metaphor, varying it according to the level of the operation regarded as serious: introjection for Ferenczi, identification with the analyst's superego for Strachey, and terminal narcissistic trance for Balint.

608 I am trying to draw attention to the substance of this mystical consummation and if, once again, I must criticize what is happening right in front of my nose, it is because analytic experience is known to draw its strength from the particular.

The importance given in treatment to the fantasy of phallic devouring, the brunt of which is borne by the image of the analyst, seems worthy of note to me because it tallies so well with a conception of the direction of the treatment that is entirely based on setting the distance between the patient and the analyst, the latter as the object of the dyadic relation.

For, however deficient the theory with which an author systematizes his technique, the fact remains that he really does analyze people, and that the coherence revealed in the error is the guarantor here of the wrong turn practice has taken.

It is the privileged function of the signifier "phallus" in the subject's way of being present in desire that is illustrated here, but in an experience that might be called blind—failing any orientation regarding the true relations in the analytic situation, which, like any other situation involving speech, can only be crushed if one tries to inscribe it in a dyadic relation.

Since the nature of symbolic incorporation is not recognized, for good reason, and since it is ruled out that anything real should be consummated in analysis, it is clear—from the elementary landmarks of my teaching—that anything that occurs that is not imaginary can no longer be recognized. For it is not necessary to know the floor plan of a house to bang one's head against its walls: indeed, one can do so very well without it.

I myself suggested to this author, at a time when we used to discuss things, that if one confines oneself to an imaginary relation between objects there remains nothing but the dimension of distance to order it. I wasn't expecting him to agree with me.

To make distance the sole dimension in which the neurotic's relations with the object are played out generates insurmountable contradictions that can be seen clearly enough both in the system and in the opposite directions different authors derive from the same metaphor to organize their impressions. Too much and too little distance from the object sometimes appear to be confounded
609 so thoroughly as to become confused. And it was not distance from the object, but rather its excessive intimacy with the subject that seemed to Ferenczi to characterize the neurotic.

What determines what each author means is his technique, and the technique of "bringing-together" [*rapprocher*], however priceless an effect the untranslated French term may have in a paper written in English, reveals in practice a tendency that verges on obsession.

It is hard to believe that the ideal prescribed by this author of reducing this distance to zero ("nil" in English) stops him from seeing that his theoretical paradox converges here.

Be that as it may, there is no doubt that this distance is taken as a universal parameter, regulating variations in the technique (however incomprehensible the debate on their magnitude may seem) for dismantling neurosis.

What such a conception owes to the specific conditions of obsessive neurosis is not to be ascribed entirely to the object.

It does not even seem to have to its credit any notable privilege regarding the results it obtains in the treatment of obsessive neurosis. For if I can, as Kris did, mention an analysis which I took over from another analyst, I can attest that such a technique, in the hands of an analyst of indisputable talent, succeeded in producing—in a clinical case of pure obsession in a man—the irruption of an infatuation which, while Platonic, was no less unbridled, and which proved no less irreducible even though it was directed at the first object of the same sex that happened to be at hand in his circle.

To speak of transitory perversion here may satisfy a militant optimist, but only at the cost of failing to recognize, in this atypical restoration of the overly neglected third party to the relation, that one should not pull too hard on the strings of proximity in the object-relation.

7. There is no limit to the eroding of analytic technique through its deconceptualization. I have already referred to what was found in a "wild" analysis, about which, to my pained astonishment, no supervisor had become alarmed. To be able to smell one's analyst seemed in one work to be an achievement to be taken literally, as an indication of the felicitous outcome of the transference.

One can perceive here a sort of involuntary humor, which is what makes the example so valuable. It would have delighted Jarry. It is, in fact, merely
the consequence one can expect from comprehending the development of the 610
analytic situation in terms of reality [*réel*]: and it is true that, taste apart, the olfactory is the only dimension that allows one to reduce distance to zero (nil*), this time in reality [*réel*]. Whether it provides a guide for the direction of the treatment and the principles of its power is more dubious.

But that a stale smell should waft into a technique that is conducted largely by "following one's nose," as they say, is not simply ridiculous. The students who attend my seminar will recall the smell of urine that marked the turning point in a case of transitory perversion, which I dwelt on in order to criticize this technique. It cannot be said that the turning point was unconnected with the incident that motivated the case study, since it was in looking through a crack in the wall of a water* closet to spy on a woman pissing that the patient suddenly transposed his libido, without anything, it seems, predestining it for this—infantile emotions bound up with the fantasy of the phallic mother having until then taken the form of a phobia [23].

It is not a direct connection, however, no more than it would be correct to see in this voyeurism an inversion of the exhibition involved in the atypia of the phobia—which was the correct diagnosis—underlying the patient's anxiety at being teased for being too tall.

As I said, the analyst to whom we owe this remarkable publication proves her rare perspicacity by returning again and again, to the point of tormenting the patient, to the interpretation she made of a certain suit of armor—which appeared in a dream chasing him and armed, moreover, with a syringe containing insecticide—as a symbol of the phallic mother.

"Should I have talked about his father instead?" she wondered. She justified not doing so by the fact that the real father had been deficient [*carence*] in the patient's history.

My students can deplore here the fact that the teaching of my seminar was unable to help her at the time, since they know by what principles I have taught them to distinguish between the phobic object as an all-purpose signifier to make up for [*suppléer*] the Other's lack and the fundamental fetish in every perversion as an object perceived in the signifier's cut.

Failing that, shouldn't this gifted novice have recalled the dialogue between
611 the suits of armor in André Breton's "Discours sur le peu de réalité"? That would have put her on the right track.

But how could we hope for such a thing when this analysis was, in supervision, given a direction that inclined her to constantly harass the patient to bring him back to the real situation? How can we be surprised that, unlike the Queen of Spain, the analyst has legs, when she herself emphasizes it in the harshness of her calls to order, that is, to the present?

Naturally, this procedure played a part in the benign outcome of the acting out* under examination here: since the analyst—who was, moreover, aware of the fact—was thus constantly intervening in a castrating manner.

But why, then, attribute this role to the mother, when everything in the anamnesis of this case indicates that she always acted, rather, as a go-between?

The faltering Oedipus complex was compensated for, but always in the form, which is disarming here in its naïveté, of an entirely forced, if not arbitrary, reference to the analyst's husband—a situation encouraged here by the fact that it was he, himself a psychiatrist, who provided the analyst with this particular patient.

This is not a common situation. In any case, it is to be impugned as lying outside the analytic situation.

My reservations about its outcome are not entirely due to the graceless detours of the treatment, and the patient's joke—probably not devoid of malice—about the fee for the last session being misappropriated to pay for debauchery is not a bad omen for the future.

The question that can be raised is that of the boundary between analysis and reeducation when the very process of analysis is guided by a predominant solicitation of its real effects. This can be seen by comparing the biographical facts in this case with the transference formations: the contribution made by the deciphering of the unconscious is truly minimal. So minimal that one wonders whether the lion's share of the unconscious does not remain intact in the encystment of the enigma which—labeled transitory perversion here—is the subject of this instructive paper.

8. Lest the lay reader be misled, let me say that I wish in no way to disparage a work to which Virgil's epithet *improbus* can rightly be applied.

My only purpose is to warn analysts of the decline their technique suffers 612
when they misrecognize the true place in which its effects are produced.

While they are tireless in their attempts to define it, one cannot say that in falling back on positions of modesty, or even taking fictions as their guide, the analytic experience they develop is always unfruitful.

Geneticism-based research and direct observation are far from having cut themselves off from a properly analytic spirit. When I discussed object-relation themes one year in my seminar, I showed the value of a conception in which child observation is nourished by the most accurate reconsideration of the function of mothering in the genesis of the object: I mean the notion of the transitional object, introduced by D. W. Winnicott, which is key in explaining the genesis of fetishism [27].

The fact remains that flagrant uncertainties in the reading of the major Freudian concepts correspond to weaknesses that plague analytic practice.

What I want to convey is that the more impasses researchers and groups encounter in conceptualizing their action in its authenticity, the more they end up forcing their action into the direction of the exercise of power.

They substitute this power for the relation to being where their action takes place, making its means—especially those of speech—fall from their veridical eminence. This is why it is a sort of return of the repressed, however strange it may be, which—owing to pretensions hardly disposed to encumber themselves with the dignity of these means—occasions the linguistic error of referring to being as though it were a fact of reality, when the discourse that reigns there rejects any questioning that a fine platitude would not have already recognized.

IV. How to Act with One's Being

1. The question of the analyst's being arose very early in the history of analysis. And it should come as no surprise that it was introduced by the analyst
613 most tormented by the problem of analytic action. Indeed, it can be said that Ferenczi's article, "Introjection and Transference," dating back to 1909 [3], was inaugural here and that it anticipated by many years all the themes later developed on the basis of the second topography.

Although Ferenczi conceives of transference as the introjection of the doctor's person into the patient's subjective economy, it is not introjection of this person as a prop for a repetitive compulsion or ill-adapted behavior, or as a fantasy figure. What he means is the absorption into the subject's economy of everything the psychoanalyst makes present in the duo as the here and now of an incarnated problematic. Doesn't Ferenczi reach the extreme conclusion that the treatment can only be complete if the doctor avows to the patient the sense of abandonment the doctor himself is liable to suffer?[12]

2. Must one pay this comical price for the subject's want-to-be to simply be recognized as the heart of analytic experience, as the very field in which the neurotic's passion is deployed?

Apart from the Hungarian school, whose embers are now dispersed and soon to be mere ashes, only the English, with their cold objectivity, have been able to articulate this gap—to which the neurotic, in wanting to justify his existence, attests—and hence to implicitly distinguish the relation to the Other, in which being finds its status, from the interpersonal relation, with its warmth and lures.

It should suffice to cite Ella Sharpe and her pertinent remarks in following the neurotic's true concerns [24]. The strength of her remarks lies in a sort of naïveté reflected in the justly famous brusqueness of her style as both therapist and writer. She is quite out of the ordinary in going as far as vainglory when she requires the analyst to be omniscient if he is to read the intentions of the analysand's discourse correctly.

We must credit her for having given a literary background pride of place in training institutes, even if she does not seem to realize that, in the minimal
614 reading list she proposes, there is a predominance of imaginative works in which the phallus as a signifier plays a central role beneath a transparent veil.

This simply proves that her choice is no less guided by analytic experience than her recommendation is felicitous.

3. It is again by the British, whether by birth or by adoption, that the end of analysis has been most categorically defined as the subject's identification with the analyst. Certainly, opinion varies as to whether it is his ego or superego that is involved. It is not that easy to master the structure Freud isolated in the subject, unless you distinguish therein the symbolic from the imaginary and the real.

Let us simply say that statements made with such a view to affront are not forged without some pressure on those who proffer them. The dialectic of fantasy objects promoted in practice by Melanie Klein tends to be translated in the theory in terms of identification.

For these objects, whether part-objects or not, but certainly signifying objects—the breast, excrement, and the phallus—are no doubt won or lost by the subject; he is destroyed by them or preserves them, but above all he *is* these objects, according to the place where they function in his fundamental fantasy. This form of identification merely demonstrates the pathology of the path down which the subject is pushed in a world where his needs are reduced to exchange values—this path itself finding its radical possibility only in the mortification the signifier imposes on his life by numbering it.

4. It would seem that the psychoanalyst, if he is simply to help the subject, must be spared this pathology, which, as we see, depends on nothing less than an iron-clad law.

This is why people imagine that a psychoanalyst should be a happy man. Indeed, is it not happiness that people ask him for, and how could he give it, commonsense asks, if he does not have a bit of it himself?

It is a fact that we do not proclaim our incompetence to promise happiness in an era in which the question of how to gauge it has become so complicated—in the first place, because happiness, as Saint-Just said, has become a political factor.

To be fair, humanist progress from Aristotle to St. Francis (de Sales) did 615
not fill the aporias of happiness.

It is a waste of time, as we know, to look for a happy man's shirt, and what is called a happy shade is to be avoided for the ills it propagates.

It is certainly in the relation to being that the analyst has to find his operating level, and the opportunities training analysis offers him for this purpose are not only to be calculated as a function of the problem which is supposedly already resolved for the analyst who is guiding him.

There are misfortunes of being that the prudence of colleges and the false shame that ensures domination dare not excise from one.

An ethics must be formulated that integrates Freud's conquests concerning desire: one that would place at the forefront the question of the analyst's desire.

5. If one is attuned to the resonance of earlier work, one cannot fail to be struck by the decline in analytic speculation, especially in this area.

Because they understand a lot of things, analysts on the whole imagine that to understand is an end in itself, and that it can only be a happy end.* The example of physical science may show them, however, that the most impressive successes do not require that one know where one is going.

To think, it is often better not to understand; and one can gallop along, understanding for miles and miles, without the slightest thought being produced.

This, indeed, was how the behaviorists began: "give up understanding." But since they had no other thoughts concerning our particular subject matter, which is *antiphusis*, they adopted the course of using, without understanding it, what we understand—a source of renewed pride for us.

A sample of the kind of morality we are capable of producing is provided by the notion of oblativity. It is an obsessive's fantasy misunderstood by oneself: "everything for the other, my semblable," one propounds with this notion, without recognizing here the anxiety that the Other (with a capital *O*) inspires by not being a semblable.

616 6. I don't claim to teach psychoanalysts what thinking is. They know. But it is not as if they came to understand it by themselves. They learned their lesson from psychologists. Thought is a first try at action, they dutifully repeat. (Freud himself falls into this trap, which does not stop him from being a doughty thinker, whose action culminates in thought.)

In truth, to analysts thought is an action that undoes itself. This leaves some hope that, if one makes them think about it by taking it up again, they will come to rethink it.

7. The analyst is the man to whom one speaks and to whom one speaks freely. That is what he is there for. What does this mean?

Everything that can be said about the association of ideas is mere dressing up in psychologistic clothing. Induced plays on words are far removed from it; because of their protocol, moreover, nothing could be less free.

The subject invited to speak in analysis does not really display a great deal of freedom in what he says. Not that he is bound by the rigor of his associations: they no doubt oppress him, but it is rather that they lead to a free speech, a full speech that would be painful to him.

Nothing is to be feared more than saying something that might be true. For it would become entirely true if it were said, and Lord knows what happens when something can no longer be cast into doubt because it is true.

Is that the procedure used in analysis—a progress of truth? I can already hear the philistines whispering about my intellectualistic analyses: whereas I, to the best of my knowledge, am at the very forefront in preserving what is unsayable there.

I know better than anyone that we listen for what lies beyond discourse, if only I take the path of hearing, not that of auscultating. Yes, certainly not the path of auscultating resistance, blood pressure, opisthotonos, pallor, and adrenal discharge (*sic*) by which a stronger (*resic*) ego should be reformed: what I listen to is based on hearing [*ce que j'écoute est d'entendement*].

Hearing does not force me to understand. The fact remains that what I hear is a discourse, even if it is as seemingly nondiscursive as an interjection. For an interjection is linguistic in nature and not an expressive cry. It is a part of speech that is just as important as any other in its syntactic effects in a given language [*langue*].

In what I indubitably hear, I have nothing to find fault with if I understand 617
none of it, or if I do understand something I am sure to be mistaken. This need not stop me from responding to it. That's what happens outside analysis in such cases. Instead I keep quiet. Everybody agrees that I frustrate the speaker—him first, but me too. Why?

If I frustrate him it is because he is asking [*demande*] me for something. To answer him, in fact. But he knows very well that it would be but words. And he can get those from whomever he likes. It's not even certain that he'd be grateful to me if they were fine words, let alone if they were lousy. It's not these words he's asking for [*demande*]. He is simply demanding of me . . ., by the very fact that he is speaking: his demand is intransitive—it brings no object with it.

Of course, his demand is deployed against the backdrop of an implicit demand, the one for which he is here: the demand for me to cure him, to reveal him to himself, to introduce him to psychoanalysis, to help him qualify as an analyst. But, as he knows, this demand can wait. His present demand has nothing to do with that—it is not even his own, for after all I am the one who offered to let him speak. (Only the subject is transitive here.)

In short, I have succeeded in doing what in the field of ordinary commerce people would like to be able to do with such ease: out of supply [*offre*] I have created demand.

8. But it is, one might say, a radical demand.

Ida Macalpine is no doubt right in wanting to seek the motor force of transference in the fundamental rule of psychoanalysis alone. But she errs in attributing the unobstructed path toward infantile regression to the absence of all objects [20]. This would rather seem to be an obstacle thereto, for, as everyone knows—child analysts more than anyone—it takes a lot of little objects to keep up a relationship with a child.

By means of demand, the whole past begins to open up, right down to earliest infancy. The subject has never done anything but demand, he could not have survived otherwise, and we take it from there.

This is the way that analytic regression can occur and does in fact present itself. People talk about it as if the subject began acting like a child. That no doubt happens, and such playacting does not bode very well. It differs, in any case, from what is usually observed in what passes for regression. For regres-
618 sion displays nothing other than a return to the present of signifiers used in demands that have exceeded their statute of limitations.

9. To return to our point of departure, this situation explains primary transference and the love by which it is sometimes declared.

For if love is giving what you don't have, it is certainly true that the subject can wait to be given it, since the psychoanalyst has nothing else to give him. But he does not even give him this nothing, and it is better that way—which is why he is paid for this nothing, preferably well paid, in order to show that otherwise it would not be worth much.

Although primary transference most often remains little more than a shadow, that doesn't stop this shadow from dreaming and reproducing its demand when there is nothing left to demand. This demand will simply be all the purer since it is empty.

It may be objected that the analyst nevertheless gives his presence, but I believe that his presence is initially implied simply by his listening, and that this listening is simply the condition of speech. Why would analytic technique require that he make his presence so discreet if this were not, in fact, the case? It is later that his presence will be noticed.

In any case, the most acute sense of his presence is tied to a moment at which the subject can only remain silent—that is, when he backs away from even the shadow of demand.

Thus the analyst is he who sustains demand, not, as people say, to frustrate the subject, but in order to allow the signifiers with which the latter's frustration is bound up to reappear.

10. It is worth recalling that it is in the oldest demand that primary identification is produced, the one that occurs on the basis of the mother's omnipotence—namely, the one that not only makes the satisfaction of needs dependent upon the signifying apparatus, but also that fragments, filters, and models those needs in the defiles of the signifier's structure.

Needs become subordinate to the same conventional conditions as does the signifier in its double register: the synchronic register of opposition between irreducible elements, and the diachronic register of substitution and combination, through which language, while it does not fulfill all functions, struc- 619
tures everything in interpersonal relations.

Hence the oscillation found in Freud's statements concerning relations between the superego and reality. The superego is not, of course, the source of reality, as he says somewhere, but it lays down its pathways, before refinding in the unconscious the first ideal marks in which the tendencies are constituted as repressed in the substitution of the signifier for needs.

11. There is thus no need to look any further for the mainspring of identification with the analyst. That identification may assume very different forms, but it will always be an identification with signifiers.

As an analysis proceeds, the analyst deals in turn with all the articulations of the subject's demand. But, as I will explain later, he must respond to them only from his position in the transference.

Who, in fact, doesn't emphasize the importance of what might be called analysis' permissive hypothesis? But we need no particular political regime for that which is not forbidden to become obligatory.

Analysts who might be said to be fascinated by the consequences of frustration merely maintain a position of suggestion that reduces the subject to going back through his demand. That must be what they mean by emotional reeducation.

Goodness is no doubt more necessary there than it is elsewhere, but it cannot cure the evil it engenders. The analyst who wants what is good for the subject repeats what he was trained in and sometimes even twisted by. The most aberrant education has never had any other motive than the subject's own good.

A theory of analysis is conceived, which—unlike the delicate articulation of Freudian analysis—reduces the mainspring of symptoms to fear. It engenders a practice on which what I have elsewhere called the obscene, ferocious figure of the superego is stamped, and in which there is no other way out of transference neurosis than to sit the patient down by the window and point out the bright side of things to him, adding: "Go for it. You're a good kid now" [22].

620 *V. Desire Must Be Taken Literally*

1. A dream, after all, is but a dream, we hear people say these days [22]. Does it mean nothing that Freud recognized desire in dreams?

Desire, not tendencies. For we must read the *Traumdeutung* [*The Interpretation of Dreams*] to know what is meant by what Freud calls "desire" there.

We must pause at the vocable *Wunsch*, and its English translation, "wish,"* to distinguish them from the French *désir* [desire], given that the sound of damp firecrackers with which the German and English words fizzle out suggests anything but concupiscence. Their French equivalent is *voeu*.

These *voeux* may be pious, nostalgic, annoying, or mischievous. A lady may have a dream that is motivated by no other desire than to provide Freud, who has explained to her his theory that dreams are desires, with proof that they are nothing of the kind. What we must keep in mind here is that this desire is articulated in a very cunning discourse. But in order to understand what desire means in Freud's thought, it is just as important to perceive the consequences of the fact that he was satisfied to recognize the dream's desire and the confirmation of his law in that cunning discourse.

For he takes its eccentricity still further, since a dream of being punished may, if it likes, signify a desire for what the punishment suppresses.

But let us not stop at the labels on the drawers, although many people confuse them with the fruits of science. Let us read the texts; let us follow Freud's thinking in the twists and turns it imposes on us, and not forget that, in deploring them himself compared with an ideal of scientific discourse, he claims that he was forced into them by his object of study.[13]

We see then that this object is identical to those twists and turns, since at the first turning point of his book, when dealing with an hysteric's dream, he stumbles upon the fact that, by displacement, in this case specifically by allusion to another woman's desire, a desire from the day before is satisfied in the dream—a desire that is sustained in its eminent position by a desire that is of
621 quite a different order, since Freud characterizes it as the desire to have an unsatisfied desire [7].[14]

One should try and count the number of referrals [*renvois*] made here to bring desire to a geometrically higher power. A single index would not suffice to characterize the exponent. For it would be necessary to distinguish two dimensions in these referrals: a desire for desire, in other words, a desire signified by a desire (the hysteric's desire to have an unsatisfied desire is signified by her desire for caviar: the desire for caviar is its signifier), is inscribed in the different register of a desire substituted for a desire (in the dream, the desire for smoked salmon, characteristic of the patient's female friend, is substituted for the patient's own desire for caviar, which constitutes the substitution of a signifier for a signifier).[15]

2. What we thus find is in no way microscopic, no more than there is any need of special instruments to recognize that a leaf has the structural features of the plant from which it has been detached. Even if one had never seen a plant with its leaves, one would realize at once that a leaf is more likely to be part of a plant than a piece of skin.

The desire in the hysteric's dream, but also any other bit of nothing in its place in this text by Freud, summarizes what the whole book explains about mechanisms said to be unconscious—condensation, sliding, etc.—by attesting to their common structure: namely, desire's relation to the mark of language that specifies the Freudian unconscious and decenters our conception of the subject.

I think that my students will appreciate the kind of access I provide here to the fundamental opposition between the signifier and the signified, language's powers stemming from that opposition, as I show them. While conceptualizing the exercise of those powers, I nevertheless leave them with their work cut out for them.

Let me recall to mind here the automatic functioning of the laws by which 622
the following are articulated in the signifying chain:

(a) the substitution of one term for another to produce a metaphorical effect;
(b) the combination of one term with another to produce a metonymical effect [17].

If we apply them here, we see that, insofar as in our patient's dream smoked salmon—the object of her friend's desire—is all the patient has to offer, Freud, in positing that smoked salmon has been substituted here for caviar, which he takes to be the signifier of the patient's desire, proposes that the dream be viewed as a metaphor of desire.

But what is metaphor if not a positive meaning effect, that is, a certain access gained by the subject to the meaning of her desire?

The subject's desire being presented here as what is implied by her (conscious) discourse, thus, as preconscious—which is obvious since her husband is willing to satisfy her desire, though it is important to the patient, who has persuaded him that she has such a desire, that he not do so, but you still have to be Freud to articulate this as the desire to have an unsatisfied desire—one still must go further to figure out what such a desire means in the unconscious.

For a dream is not the unconscious but, as Freud tells us, the royal road to it. This confirms that the unconscious proceeds on the basis of metaphorical effects. Dreams lay bare such effects. To whom? I shall return to that shortly.

Let us note for the moment that the desire in question, while signified as unsatisfied, is signified thusly by the signifier "caviar," insofar as the signifier symbolizes this desire as inaccessible; note too, however, that as soon as this desire slides, qua desire, into the caviar, the desire for caviar becomes this desire's metonymy—rendered necessary by the want-to-be in which this desire sustains itself.

Metonymy is, as I have been teaching you, an effect which is rendered possible by the fact that there is no signification that does not refer to another signification; the most common denominator of those significations is produced in it—namely, the scant meaning (commonly confused with what is meaningless), I repeat, the scant meaning that turns out to be at the root of this desire, conferring upon it the hint of perversion one is tempted to point to in the present case of hysteria.

623 The truth of this appearance is that desire is the metonymy of the want-to-be.

3. Let us now return to the book known in French as *The Science of Dreams (Traumdeutung)*, though "Mantic" or, better still, "Signifierness" would be more suitable translations than "Science."

Freud in no way claims here to solve all the psychological problems dreams pose. Read it and you will note that Freud does not touch on such rarely explored questions (studies on space and time in dreams, on the sensory stuff of dreams, and on color or atonal dreams are rare or at least contribute little; are smell, taste, and the graininess of touch present like dizziness, turgidity, and heaviness are?). To say that Freud's doctrine is a psychology is a crude equivocation.

Freud can hardly be said to leave himself open to such an equivocation. He tells us, on the contrary, that he is only interested in the dream's "elaboration." What does that mean? Exactly what I translate as the dream's "linguistic structure." How could Freud have become aware of that structure when it was only later articulated by Ferdinand de Saussure? It is all the more striking that Freud anticipated it as that structure overlaps Freud's own terms. But where did he discover it? In a signifying flow whose mystery lies in the fact that the subject doesn't even know where to pretend to be its organizer.

To get him to refind himself therein as desiring is the opposite of getting him to recognize himself therein as a subject, for the brook of desire runs as if along a branch line of the signifying chain, and the subject must take advantage of a crossover in order to catch hold of his own feedback*.

Desire merely subjugates what analysis subjectivizes.

4. This brings me back to the question left unanswered above: "To whom does the dream reveal its meaning before the analyst comes on the scene?"

This meaning exists prior both to its being read and to the science of its deciphering.

Both show that the dream is designed for the recognition—but my voice falters before finishing—of desire. For desire, assuming that Freud is right about the unconscious and that analysis is necessary, can only be grasped in interpretation.

But to return to what I was saying before, the elaboration of the dream is nourished by the desire . . . why does my voice fail to complete the thought?—
for recognition—as if the second word ["recognition"] were extinguished 624
which, when it was the first earlier, resorbed the other ["desire"] in its light. For it is not by sleeping that one gets oneself recognized. And the dream, Freud tells us, without seeming to see the slightest contradiction therein, serves above all the desire to go on sleeping. It involves the narcissistic withdrawal of libido into oneself and the decathexis of reality.

It is, in any case, a fact of experience that when my dream begins to coincide with my demand (not with reality, as is improperly said, which can safeguard my sleep)—or with what proves to be equivalent to it here, the other's demand—I wake up.

5. A dream, after all, is but a dream. Those who now disdain it as a tool in analysis have found, as we have seen, surer and more direct roads by which to bring the patient back to sound principles and normal desires, those that satisfy true needs. Which needs? Why, everyone's needs, my friend. If that is what frightens you, have faith in your psychoanalyst and climb the Eiffel Tower to see how beautiful Paris is. Too bad some people jump over the railing on the first deck, precisely those whose needs have all been restored to their proper proportions. A negative therapeutic reaction, I would call it.

Thank God not everyone takes refusal that far! Nevertheless, the symptom grows back like a weed: repetition compulsion.

But that, of course, is no more than a misconception: one does not get better because one remembers. One remembers because one gets better. Since this formulation was found, there has no longer been any question regarding the reproduction of symptoms, but only regarding the reproduction of analysts; the reproduction of patients has been resolved.

6. Thus a dream is but a dream. A certain psychoanalyst who has the nerve to teach has even gone so far as to write that dreams are produced by the ego. This proves that we run no great risk in wanting to wake men from their dreams: the latter are pursued in broad daylight and by those who rarely indulge in dreaming.

But even these men, if they are psychoanalysts, must read Freud on dreams,
625 because otherwise it is not possible either to understand what he means by the neurotic's desire, repression, the unconscious, interpretation, or analysis itself, or to close in on anything whatsoever related to his technique or doctrine. We shall see how much is contained in the short dream I borrowed above for the purposes of this discussion.

For the desire of our witty hysteric (Freud is the one who characterizes her as such)—I mean her waking desire, that is, her desire for caviar—is the desire of a woman who is fulfilled and yet does not want to be. For her butcher of a husband never neglects to dot the i's and cross the t's when it comes to providing her the kinds of satisfaction everyone needs; nor does he mince words with a painter who flatters him, God knows with what obscure intent, regarding his interesting mug, saying, "Nothing doing! A nice piece of ass is what you need, and if you expect me to get it for you, you can stick it you know where."

Here's a man a woman should have nothing to complain about, a genital character, who must appropriately ensure that when he fucks his wife, she has no need to jerk off afterward. Moreover, Freud does not hide from us the fact that she is very taken with him and teases him all the time.

But there it is: she does not want to be satisfied regarding her true needs alone. She wants other needs that are gratuitous and, in order to be quite sure that they are gratuitous, not to satisfy them. This is why the question "What does the witty butcher's wife desire?" can be answered as follows: "Caviar." But this answer is hopeless because she also does not want any.

7. This is not the whole of her mystery. Far from being imprisoned by this impasse, she finds the key to her freedom in it, the key to the field of the desires of all the witty hysterics in the world, whether butchers' wives or not.

This is what Freud perceives in one of those sidelong glances by which he discovers the truth, shattering in passing the abstractions with which positivist thinkers willingly explain everything: in this case, imitation, a concept so dear to Tarde. We must bring to bear in this particular case the linchpin Freud provides here of hysterical identification. If our patient identifies with her friend, it is insofar as she is inimitable in her unsatisfied desire for that salmon—may
626 God damn it if it is not He himself who smokes it!

Thus the patient's dream is a response to her friend's request [*demande*], which is to come dine at the patient's house. And what could possibly make her friend want to do so, apart from the fine dinners served there, if not the fact—not overlooked by the butcher's wife—that her husband always praises her friend? Now, as her friend is thin, her figure is not likely to attract him, relishing only curves as he does.

Couldn't it be that he too has a desire that remains awry when all in him is satisfied? It is the same mechanism that, in the dream, thwarts her own request [*demande*] due to her friend's desire.

For despite the precision with which the request [*demande*] is symbolized by the newborn accessory, the telephone, it is all for naught. The patient's call does not go through; a fine thing it would be, indeed, for the other [her friend] to fatten up so that her husband could feast on her!

But how can another woman be loved (doesn't the mere fact that her husband holds her friend in high regard suffice to give the patient pause for thought?) by a man who cannot be satisfied with her (he being an "ass man" [*l'homme à la tranche de postérieur*])? This is the precise formulation of the question that is, generally speaking, the question involved in hysterical identification.

8. The subject becomes this question here. In this respect, the woman identifies with the man and the slice [*tranche*] of smoked salmon comes to occupy the place of the Other's desire.

This desire not sufficing for anything (how can all the people be served with this single slice of smoked salmon?), "I must, in the end (and at the end of the dream), give up my desire to throw a dinner party (that is, give up my search for the Other's desire, which is the secret of my own). Everything goes wrong, and you say that a dream is the fulfillment of a desire! How do you explain that one, professor?"

Challenged in this way, psychoanalysts stopped responding a long time ago, having themselves given up pondering their patients' desires; analysts reduce their patients' desires to demands, which simplifies the task of converting them into the analysts' own demands. "Isn't that the reasonable road to take?"—so they adopted it.

But sometimes desire cannot be conjured away quite so easily, being all too visible, smack in the middle of the scene on the banquet table as we see it here, in the form of a salmon, which happens to be a pretty fish; it suffices to present it, as they do in restaurants, under a thin cloth for the unveiling to equal 627
that carried out at the culmination of the mysteries of Antiquity.

To be the phallus, even a somewhat skinny one—isn't that the final identification with the signifier of desire?

That doesn't seem self-evident in the case of a woman, and there are those among us who prefer to have nothing further to do with this obscure discourse. Are we going to have to spell out the role of the signifier only to find ourselves saddled with the castration complex and—God spare us!—penis envy, when Freud, having come to this crossing, no longer knew which way to turn, perceiving only the desert of analysis beyond it?

Yes, but he led them to that crossing, and the place was less infested than transference neurosis, which reduces you to chasing the patient away, begging him to go slowly so as to take his flies with him.

9. Let us nevertheless articulate what structures desire.

Desire is what manifests itself in the interval demand excavates just shy of itself, insofar as the subject, articulating the signifying chain, brings to light his lack of being [*manque à être*] with his call to receive the complement of this lack from the Other—assuming that the Other, the locus of speech, is also the locus of this lack.

What it is thus the Other's job to provide—and, indeed, it is what he does not have, since he too lacks being—is what is called love, but it is also hate and ignorance.

Those passions for being are, moreover, evoked by any demand beyond the need articulated in that demand, and the more the need articulated in that demand is satisfied, the more the subject remains deprived of those passions.

Furthermore, the satisfaction of need appears here only as a lure in which the demand for love is crushed, throwing the subject back into a kind of sleep in which he haunts the limbo realm of being, letting it speak in him. For the being of language is the nonbeing of objects, and the fact that desire was discovered by Freud in its place in dreams—which have always been the bane of all attempts by thought to situate itself in reality—suffices to instruct us.

To be or not to be, to sleep, perchance to dream—even the supposedly simplest dreams of the child (as "simple" as the analytic situation, no doubt) sim-
628 ply display miraculous or forbidden objects.

10. But the child does not always fall asleep in this way in the bosom of being, especially if the Other, which has its own ideas about his needs, interferes and, instead of what it does not have, stuffs him with the smothering baby food it does have, that is, confuses the care it provides with the gift of its love.

It is the child who is the most lovingly fed who refuses food and employs his refusal as if it were a desire (anorexia nervosa).

This is an extreme case where one grasps as nowhere else that hate is the payback for love, but where it is ignorance that is not pardoned.

Ultimately, by refusing to satisfy the mother's demand, isn't the child requiring the mother to have a desire outside of him, because that is the pathway toward desire that he lacks?

11. Indeed, one of the principles that follows from these premises is that:

- if desire is an effect in the subject of the condition—which is imposed on him by the existence of discourse—that his need pass through the defiles of the signifier;
- and if, as I intimated above, by opening up the dialectic of transference, we must establish the notion of the Other with a capital O as being the locus of speech's deployment (the other scene, *ein anderer Schauplatz*, of which Freud speaks in the *Traumdeutung*);

then it must be posited that, as a characteristic of an animal at the mercy of language, man's desire is the Other's desire.

This concerns a totally different function than that of primary identification mentioned above, for it does not involve the assumption by the subject of the other's insignia, but rather the condition that the subject find the constitutive structure of his desire in the same gap opened up by the effect of signifiers in those who come to represent the Other for him, insofar as his demand is subjected to them.

Perhaps we can catch a glimpse in passing of the reason for this effect of
occultation that caught our attention regarding the recognition of desire in the 629
dream. The desire in the dream is not owned [*assumé*] by the subject who says "I" in his speech. Articulated, nevertheless, in the locus of the Other, it is discourse—a discourse whose grammar Freud began to enunciate as such. This is why the wishes it constitutes have no optative inflection to alter the indicative in which they are formulated.

A linguistic point of view would allow us to see that what is called the aspect of the verb is here that of the perfective [*accompli*] (the true meaning of *Wunscherfüllung* [wish-fulfillment]).

It is this ex-sistence (*Entstellung*)[16] of desire in the dream that explains how the dream's signifierness masks its desire, whereas its motive vanishes as being simply problematic.

12. Desire is produced in the beyond of demand, because in linking the subject's life to its conditions, demand prunes it of need. But desire is also excavated in the [area] shy of demand in that, as an unconditional demand for presence and absence, demand evokes the want-to-be in the three figures of the nothing that constitutes the ground for the demand for love, for the hatred that goes so far as to negate the other's being, and for the unspeakableness of what is not known [*s'ignore*] in its request. In this aporia incarnate—of which one might metaphorically say that demand borrows its heavy soul from the hardy offshoots of the wounded tendency, and its subtle body from death as it is actualized in the signifying sequence—desire asserts itself as an absolute condition.

Less still than the nothing that circulates in the round of significations that stir men up, desire is the wake left behind by its trajectory and like the signifier's brand on the speaking subject's shoulder. It is not so much a pure passion of the signified as a pure action of the signifier, which stops at the moment when the living being, having become a sign, renders this action meaningless [*insignifiante*].

This moment of cutting is haunted by the form of a bloody scrap: the pound
630 of flesh that life pays in order to turn it into the signifier of signifiers, which it is impossible to restore, as such, to the imaginary body; it is the lost phallus of embalmed Osiris.

13. The function of this signifier as such in desire's quest is, as Freud detected, the key to what we need to know in order to terminate our analyses—and no artifice can make up for it if we are to achieve this end.

To give some idea of this function, I will describe an incident that occurred at the end of the analysis of an obsessive, that is, after a great deal of work in which I did not confine myself to "analyzing the subject's aggressiveness" (in other words, to pounding away at his imaginary aggressions), but in which he was made to recognize the part he had played in the destructive game foisted by one of his parents on the other parent's desire. He surmised his powerlessness to desire without destroying the Other, thus destroying his own desire insofar as it was the Other's desire.

To arrive at this stage, he was shown how at every moment he manipulated the situation so as to protect the Other, by our exhausting in the transference work [*travail de transfert*] *(Durcharbeitung)* all the artifices of a verbalization that distinguished the other from the Other (with a lowercase *o* and a capital *O*), and that, from the spectator's box reserved for the Other's (with a capital *O*) boredom, made him arrange the circus games between the two others (little *a* and the ego, its shadow).

Of course, it was not enough to go around in circles in some well-explored area of obsessive neurosis to bring him to this traffic circle, or to know this traffic circle in order to lead him to it by a route that is never the most direct. One does not simply need the blueprints to a reconstructed labyrinth, nor even a pile of blueprints that have already been worked up. What is needed above all is the general combinatory that no doubt governs their variety, but that also, even more usefully, accounts for the illusions or, better, shifts in the labyrinth that take place right before one's very eyes. For there is no shortage of either in obsessive neurosis, which is an architecture of contrasts that have not yet been sufficiently noticed and that cannot simply be attributed to differing facades. Amid so many seductive, insurgent, and impassive attitudes, we must grasp the anxieties that are bound up with performance, the grudges that do not prevent generosity (imagine claiming that obsessives are lacking 631 in oblativity!), and the mental infidelities that sustain infrangible loyalties. All this moves as a unit in an analysis, though not without local wilting; the great mass of it nevertheless remains.

Here my subject was at the end of his rope, having reached the point of playing a game of three-card monte with me that was of a rather peculiar kind, in that it revealed a structure of desire.

Let's say that being of mature years, as the comical expression goes, and of a disillusioned turn of mind, he would have willingly misled me into thinking his menopause was the cause of the impotence that struck him, and accused me of the same.

In fact, redistributions of libido are not brought about without certain objects losing their position, even if the position itself is permanent.

In short, he was impotent with his mistress and, having gotten it into his head to use his discoveries about the function of the potential third party in the couple, he suggested that she sleep with another man to see.

Now, if she remained in the place assigned to her by his neurosis, and if his analysis affected her in that position, it was because of the peace she had no doubt made long ago with the patient's desires, but even more so with the unconscious postulates maintained by those desires.

It will thus come as no surprise that, without wasting any time—indeed, that very night—she had a dream, which she recounted to our crestfallen patient hot off the presses.

In the dream she had a phallus—she sensed its shape under her clothing—which did not prevent her from having a vagina as well, nor, especially, from wanting this phallus to enter it.

On hearing this, my patient's powers were immediately restored and he demonstrated this brilliantly to his shrewd paramour.

What interpretation is indicated here?

You will have guessed from the request [*demande*] my patient had made of his mistress that he had been trying for a long time to get me to ratify his repressed homosexuality.

This was an effect of Freud's discovery of the unconscious, one that he was very quick to anticipate: among the regressive demands, the demand for fables will be sated with the truths spread by analysis itself. Analysis, upon its return from America, exceeded his expectations.

But I remained, as you may well have expected, rather off-putting on that 632
point.

Note that the dreamer was no more indulgent in this regard, since her scenario excluded any coadjutor. This would guide even a novice to trust only in the text, if he is trained according to my principles.

Yet I am not analyzing her dream, but rather its effect on my patient.

It would run counter to my practice to get him to see in the dream a truth that is less widely known in analytic history as it is one of my own contributions: that the refusal of castration, if there is any such thing, is first and foremost a refusal of the Other's castration (of the mother's, first of all).

True opinion is not science, and conscience without science is but complicity with ignorance. Our science is transmitted only by articulating what is particular in the situation.

Here the situation is unique in showing the figure that I state in these terms: unconscious desire is the Other's desire—since the dream was designed to satisfy the patient's desire beyond his request [*demande*], as is suggested by the fact that it succeeds in doing so. Although it is not one of the patient's dreams, it may be no less valuable to us since, while it was not addressed to me as it was to the analysand, it addressed the analysand just as well as the analyst could have.

It was an opportunity to get the patient to grasp the function the phallus as a signifier serves in his desire. For it is as a signifier that the phallus operates in the dream in order to enable him to recover the use of the organ it represents, as I will show by the place the dream aims at in the structure in which his desire is caught up.

Apart from what the woman dreamt, there is the fact that she talked to him about it. Was the fact that she presented herself, in this discourse, as having a phallus the only way in which her erotic value was restored to her? Having a phallus was not, in effect, enough to restore to her an object position that allowed her to fit a fantasy on the basis of which my patient, as an obsessive, could maintain his desire in an impossibility that preserved its metonymic conditions. The latter governed a game of escape in his choices that analysis had disturbed, but which the woman restored here by a ruse, the crudeness of which concealed a subtlety that perfectly illustrates the science included in the unconscious.

For, to my patient, it was of no use to have this phallus, since his desire was to be it. And the woman's desire yields to his desire here, by showing him what she does not have.

633 Undiscriminating case studies always make much of any sign of a castrating mother, however small the role the anamnesis gives her. She looms large here, as expected.

People think that their job is then done. But it's of no value in interpretation, where to invoke it would not have taken us very far, except to bring the patient back to the very point where he wound his way between a desire and contempt for that desire: certainly, his ill-tempered mother's contempt for the overly ardent desire whose image his father bequeathed him.

But this would have taught him less about it than what his mistress *said* to him: that having this phallus in her dream didn't stop her from desiring it. Which is why his own want-to-be was touched.

That lack results from an exodus: his being is always elsewhere. He has "tucked it away," one might say. Am I saying this to explain the difficulty of his desire? No, rather to say that his desire is for difficulty.

Let us not, therefore, be misled by the guarantee the subject received from the fact that the dreamer had a phallus and would not have to take it from him—even if to point out, learnedly, that such a guarantee is too strong not to be fragile.

For that would be precisely to fail to recognize that this guarantee would not require so much weight if it did not have to be (im)printed in a sign, and that it is by displaying this sign as such, by making it appear where it cannot be, that this guarantee has its effect.

The condition of desire that especially grabs the obsessive is the very mark by which he finds desire spoiled, the mark of origin of its object—contraband.

A singular mode of grace which is figured only on the basis of a disavowal of nature. A favor is hidden here that is always kept waiting in our subject. And it is by dismissing this favor that one day he will let it enter.

14. The importance of preserving the place of desire in the direction of the treatment requires one to position this place in relation to the effects of demand, the only effects that are currently considered to be at the crux of the power of the treatment.

Indeed, the fact that the genital act must find its place in desire's unconscious articulation is the discovery of analysis, and it is precisely why no one has ever thought of giving in to the patient's illusion that to facilitate his demand 634
for the satisfaction of need would be of any help to him. (Still less to authorize it with the classic *coïtus normalis dosim repetatur.*)

Why do people think differently in believing it to be more essential for the progress of the treatment to work in any way whatsoever on other demands, under the pretext that they are regressive?

Let us begin once again with the notion that the subject's own speech is a message to him, first of all, because it is produced in the Other's locus. It originates in that locus and is worded as such not only because his demand is submitted to the Other's code, but because his demand is dated by this Other's locus (and even time).

This can be clearly read in the subject's most freely given speech. He invokes his wife or his master, so that they have his word with a *tu es* . . ., "you are . . ." (the one or the other), without declaring what he himself is otherwise than by murmuring an order of murder against himself that the equivocation of the French brings to one 's ear.

Although it always shows through in demand, as we see here, desire is nevertheless beyond demand. It is also shy of another demand in which the subject, echoing in the other's locus, would like not so much to efface his dependence by a payback agreement as to fix the very being he proposes there.

This means that it is only from a kind of speech [*une parole*] that would remove the mark the subject receives from what he says that he might obtain the absolution that would return him to his desire.

But desire is nothing but the impossibility of such speech, which, in replying to the first speech can merely redouble its mark by consummating the split *(Spaltung)* the subject undergoes by virtue of being a subject only insofar as he speaks.

(This is symbolized by the slanted bar of noble bastardy, which I assign to the S of the subject in order to indicate that it is this specific subject: $.)[17]

635 The regression people foreground in analysis (temporal regression, no doubt, providing one specifies that it has to do with the time of remembering) concerns only the (oral, anal, etc.) signifiers of demand, and involves the corresponding drive only through them.

Reducing this demand to its place may produce the appearance of a reduction of desire owing to the mitigation of need.

But this is really only the effect of the analyst's heavy-handedness. For if demand's signifiers have sustained the frustrations on which desire is fixated (Freud's *Fixierung*), it is only in their place that desire is exacting [*assujetissant*].

Whether it intends to frustrate or to gratify, any response to demand in analysis reduces transference to suggestion.

There is a relation between transference and suggestion, as Freud discovered: transference is also a suggestion, but a suggestion that operates only on the basis of the demand for love, which is not a demand based on any need. The fact that this demand is constituted as such only insofar as the subject is the subject of the signifier is what allows it to be misused by reducing it to the needs from which these signifiers have been borrowed—which is what psychoanalysts, as we see, do not fail to do.

But identification with demand's omnipotent signifier, of which I have already spoken, must not be confused with identification with the object of the demand for love. The demand for love is also a regression, as Freud insists, when he makes it into the second form of identification, which he distinguished in his second topography when he wrote *Group Psychology and the Analysis of the Ego*. But it is another kind of regression.

Here is the exit* that allows us to leave suggestion behind. Identification with the object as a regression, because it begins with the demand for love, opens up the sequence of transference (opens it up, not closes it)—that is, the pathway by which the identifications that punctuate this regression by stopping it can be exposed.

But this regression is no more dependent on the need in demand than sadistic desire is explained by anal demand, for to believe that a turd is in itself a noxious object is but an ordinary lure of understanding. ("Understanding" in the harmful sense the word takes on in Jaspers' work. "You understand . . ." 636
is an introductory phrase by which someone who has nothing to convey thinks he can impress someone who understands nothing.) But the demand to be a shit—now there's something that it is preferable to view from a different angle when the subject reveals himself there. It's the "misfortune of being" I referred to above.

Whoever cannot carry his training analyses to this turning point—at which it is revealed, with trembling, that all the demands that have been articulated in the analysis (and more than any other the one that was at its core, the demand to become an analyst, which now comes to maturity) were merely transferences designed to keep in place a desire that was unstable or dubious in its problematic—such a person knows nothing of what must be obtained from the subject if he is to be able to ensure the direction of an analysis, or merely offer a well-advised interpretation in it.

These considerations confirm that it is natural to analyze transference. For transference is already, in itself, an analysis of suggestion, insofar as transference places the subject, with regard to his demand, in a position he occupies only because of his desire.

It is only in order to maintain this transference framework that frustration must prevail over gratification.

The subject's resistance, when it opposes suggestion, is but a desire to maintain his desire. As such, his resistance should be considered positive transference, since it is desire that maintains the direction of the analysis, quite apart from the effects of demand.

As you can see, these propositions are rather different from the received opinions on the matter. If they lead people to think that something has gone awry somewhere, I will have succeeded in my aim.

15. This is the place for a few remarks on symptom formation.

Freud—starting with his demonstrative study of such subjective phenom-

ena as dreams, slips, and jokes, which, he says quite categorically, are structurally identical to symptoms (but, of course, to our scientists, all this is clearly inadequate for the experience they have acquired—and by what pathways!—for them to even dream of returning to it)—Freud, as I was saying, stressed again and again that symptoms are overdetermined. To the foolish acolyte engaged in the daily drumbeating that promises the imminent reduction of
637 analysis to its biological bases, this is obvious enough; it is so easy to say that he does not even hear it. "Is that all you've got?" he asks.

Let us leave aside my remarks on the fact that overdetermination is only conceivable, strictly speaking, within the structure of language. What does this mean, as far as neurotic symptoms are concerned?

It means that interference will occur in the effects that correspond in a subject to a particular demand from the effects of a position that he maintains as a subject in relation to the other (here, his semblable).

"That he maintains as a subject" means that language allows him to regard himself as the stagehand, or even the director, of the entire imaginary capture of which he would otherwise be nothing more than the living marionette.

Fantasy is the very illustration of this original possibility. This is why any temptation to reduce fantasy to imagination, that doesn't admit to its failure, is a permanent misconception, a misconception from which the Kleinian school, which has certainly carried things very far here, is not free, having failed to even glimpse the category of the signifier.

However, the notion of unconscious fantasy no longer presents any difficulty once it is defined as an image set to work in the signifying structure.

Let us say that, in its fundamental use, fantasy is the means by which the subject maintains himself at the level of his vanishing desire, vanishing inasmuch as the very satisfaction of demand deprives him of his object.

"Oh, these neurotics are so fussy! What is to be done with them? These people are incomprehensible, upon my word," as one family man put it.

But this is precisely what has been said for a long time—indeed, what has always been said—and analysts haven't gotten any further. The simple-minded call it the irrational, since they haven't even realized that Freud's discovery is ratified by the fact that it first takes it as certain that the real is rational—which, in itself, is enough to cut the ground out from under our exegetes—and then by noting that the rational is real. As a result, Freud can articulate that what presents itself as not very reasonable in desire is an effect of the passage of the rational qua real—that is, of language—into the real, insofar as the rational has already traced its circumvallation there.

For the paradox of desire is not the neurotic's privilege; it is rather that he

takes the existence of this paradox into account in his way of dealing with
desire. This does not give him such a bad ranking in the order of human dig- 638
nity, and it does no honor to mediocre analysts (this is not an assessment, but an ideal formulated in a definite wish made by the interested parties) who, on this point, fail to achieve the same dignity: a surprising distance that analysts have always noted in veiled terms by talking about "other analysts," without our knowing how the latter can be distinguished, since they would never have thought of doing so themselves, if they hadn't first had to oppose the deviation of the former.

16. It is, then, the neurotic's position with respect to desire—let us say, to abbreviate, fantasy—that marks with its presence the subject's response to demand, in other words, the signification of his need.

But this fantasy has nothing to do with the signification in which it interferes. Indeed, this signification comes from the Other, insofar as it depends on the Other whether or not demand is met. But fantasy comes in here only to find itself on the return path of a broader circuit, a circuit that, in carrying demand to the limits of being, makes the subject wonder about the lack in which he appears to himself as desire.

It is incredible that certain features of man's action as such, which have always been obvious enough, have not been highlighted here by analysis. I am talking about what makes man's action the deed that finds support in his epic poem. The analyst reduces this dimension of exploit, performance, and solution strangled by the symbol, what thus makes it symbolic (but not in the alienating sense this term commonly denotes)—the very reason why people speak of *passage à l'acte* [acting out], that Rubicon whose characteristic desire is always camouflaged in history in favor of its success, everything to which the experience of what the analyst calls "acting out"* gives him a quasi-experimental access, since he holds its entire artifice in his hands—the analyst reduces it at best to a relapse on the subject's part, at worst to a mistake on the therapist's part.

One is stupefied by the analyst's false shame in the face of action—a shame that no doubt conceals true shame, the shame he has regarding an action, his own action, one of the highest of actions, when it stoops to abjection.

For what else, in fact, is it, when by intervening the analyst degrades the 639
transference message he is there to interpret into a fallacious signification of reality [*réel*] that is nothing but mystification?

For the point at which the contemporary analyst claims to grasp transference is the distance he defines between fantasy and the so-called "well-adapted response." Well-adapted to what if not to the Other's demand? And why would this demand have any more or less consistency than the response obtained, if the analyst didn't believe he was authorized to deny [*dénier*] all value to fantasy in using the yardstick he takes from his own reality?

Here the very pathway by which he proceeds betrays him, when it is necessary for him to insert himself into fantasy by this pathway and offer himself up as an imaginary Host [*hostie*] to fictions in which an idiotic desire proliferates—an unexpected Ulysses who offers himself up as fodder so that Circe's pigsty may prosper.

Let it not be said that I am defaming anyone here, for it is the precise point at which those who cannot articulate their practice in any other way are themselves sufficiently concerned to question what they are doing: "Aren't fantasies the area in which we provide the subject with the gratification in which the analysis becomes bogged down?" This is the question they keep repeating to themselves with the inescapable insistence of an unconscious torment.

17. Thus, at best, the contemporary analyst leaves his patient at the point of purely imaginary identification—of which the hysteric remains captive, because her fantasy implies ensnarement in it.

This is the very point from which Freud, throughout the first part of his career, wished to extricate the hysteric too quickly by forcing the call for love onto the object of identification (for Elisabeth von R., her brother-in-law [5]; for Dora, Herr K.; for the young homosexual woman in the case of female homosexuality, he sees the problem more clearly, but errs when he regards himself as the object aimed at in reality [*réel*] by the negative transference).

It was not until the chapter on identification in *Group Psychology and the Analysis of the Ego* that Freud clearly distinguished the third form of identification, which is conditioned by its function of sustaining desire and is therefore specified by the indifference of its object.

But our psychoanalysts insist: this indifferent object is the substance of the object—eat of my body, drink of my blood (this profane evocation flows from their pens). The mystery of the analysand's redemption lies in this imaginary
640 effusion, of which the analyst is the sacrificial object [*l'oblat*].

How can the ego, whose aid they claim to enlist here, not suffer, in effect, from the blows of the further alienation they induce in the subject? Long before Freud came on the scene, psychologists knew, even if they did not express it in these terms, that while desire is the metonymy of the want-to-be, the ego is the metonymy of desire.

This is how the terminal identification occurs, in which analysts take such pride.

Whether the identification involves their patient's ego or superego, they aren't sure, or rather, they couldn't care less, but what the patient identifies with is their strong ego.

Freud foresaw this result very clearly in the text I just mentioned, when he showed that the most insignificant object may play the role of an ideal in the genesis of a leader.

It is not in vain that analytic psychology is increasingly turning toward group psychology and even group psychotherapy.

Let us observe its effects in the analytic group itself. It is not true that analysands undergoing training analysis model themselves on the image of their analyst, regardless of the level at which one wishes to detect that image. It is rather that analysands of the same analyst are linked to each other by a feature that may be quite secondary in the psychical economy of each of them, but upon which the analyst's inadequacy in his work is clearly stamped.

Thus the analyst according to whom the problem of desire can be reduced to lifting the veil off of fear, leaves all those he has guided wrapped in this shroud.

18. Thus we have now reached the tricky crux of this power that is ever open to a blind direction. It is the power to do good—no power has any other end—and that is why power has no end. But something else is at stake here: truth, the only truth, the truth about the effects of truth. Once Oedipus set off down this path, he had already given up power.

Where, then, is the direction of the treatment headed? Perhaps we need but question its means to define it in its soundness.

Let us note: 641

(1) that speech possesses all the powers here, the specific powers of the treatment;
(2) that, with the fundamental rule of psychoanalysis, the analyst is far from directing the subject toward full speech, or toward a coherent discourse—rather, the analyst leaves the subject free to have a go at it;
(3) that this freedom is what the subject tolerates least easily;
(4) that demand is exactly what is bracketed in analysis, it being ruled out that the analyst satisfy any of the subject's demands;
(5) that since no obstacle is put in the way of the subject's owning [*aveu*] of his desire, it is toward this owning that he is directed and even channeled;
(6) that resistance to this owning can, in the final analysis, be related here to nothing but desire's incompatibility with speech.

There may still be a few people, even in my usual audience, who are surprised to find such propositions in my discourse.

One senses here the terrible temptation the analyst must face to respond to demand, however minimally.

How, moreover, is the analyst to prevent the subject from attributing this response to him, in the form of a demand to get better, and in accordance with the horizon of a discourse that the subject has all the more reason to impute to him given that our authority has wrongly adopted this discourse?

Who will now relieve us of this tunic of Nessus we have spun for ourselves in maintaining that analysis responds to all the desiderata of demand, and by widely circulated norms? Who will sweep this enormous pile of dung out of the Augean Stables of analytic literature?

What silence must the analyst now impose upon himself if he is to make out, rising above this bog, the raised finger of Leonardo's "St. John the Baptist," if interpretation is to find anew the forsaken horizon of being in which its allusive virtue must be deployed?

19. Since the point is to take desire, and since it can only be taken literally [*à la lettre*], since it is the letter's snare that determines, nay overdetermines, its place as a heavenly bird, how can we fail to require the bird catcher to first be a man of letters?

Who among us has attempted to articulate the importance of the "literary"
642 element in Freud's work, apart from a professor of literature in Zurich who has begun to spell it out?

This is merely an indication. Let us go further. Let us question how things should stand with the analyst (with the analyst's "being"), as far as his own desire is concerned.

Who would still be so naive as to see Freud as the conventional Viennese bourgeois who so astonished André Breton by not manifesting any obsession with the Bacchanalian? Now that we have nothing but his works, will we not recognize in them a river of fire, which owes nothing to François Mauriac's artificial river?

Who was more able than him, when avowing his dreams, to spin the thread on which the ring that unites us with being slides, and make its brief shine glow in closed hands, passing it from the one to the other in the swiftly shifting game of human passion?

Who has inveighed as much as this scholar against the monopolization of jouissance by those who load the burdens of need onto others' shoulders?

Who, as fearlessly as this clinician, so firmly rooted in the everydayness of human suffering, has questioned life as to its meaning—not to say that it has none, which is a convenient way of washing one's hands of the matter, but to say that it has only one, that in which desire is borne by death?

A man of desire, a desire he followed against his will down pathways where it is reflected in feeling, dominating, and knowing, but whose unparalleled signifier he and he alone—like an initiate at the defunct mysteries—succeeded in unveiling: the phallus, the receiving and giving of which are equally impossible for the neurotic, whether he knows that the Other does not have it, or that the Other does have it, because in both cases the neurotic's desire is elsewhere—to be it. And whether male or female, man must accept to have and not have it, on the basis of the discovery that he isn't it.

It is here that is inscribed the final *Spaltung* by which the subject is linked to Logos, and about which Freud was beginning to write [12], giving us, at the final point of an oeuvre that has the dimensions of being, the solution to "infinite" analysis, when his death applied to it the word "Nothing."

Note and References 643

This paper represents a selection from my ongoing seminar. My talk at the colloquium and the responses it received resituated the paper in the context of my teaching.

During the talk I presented a graph that precisely articulates the directions proposed here for the field of analysis and its handling.

Below, the reader will find, in alphabetical order by author, the references indicated in my text by numbers in brackets.

I have used the following abbreviations:

GW: *Gesammelte Werke*, by Freud, published by Imago Publishing, London. The Roman numerals that follow refer to the volume.

SE: *The Standard Edition of the Complete Psychological Works of Sigmund Freud*, the English translation of Freud's works, published by Hogarth Press, London. Again, the Roman numerals refer to the volume.

IJP: *International Journal of Psycho-Analysis*.

PQ: *The Psychoanalytic Quarterly*.

RFP: *Revue Française de Psychanalyse*.

PDA: A work entitled *La Psychanalyse d'aujourd'hui* ["Contemporary Psychoanalysis"] (Paris: PUF, 1956), which I refer to only because of the naive simplicity with which the tendency to degrade the direction of the treatment and the principles of its power in psychoanalysis is presented in it. Designed, no doubt, to circulate outside the psychoanalytic community, it serves as an obstacle inside it. Thus I don't mention its authors, who make no properly scientific contribution in it.

[1] Abraham, Karl, "Die psychosexuellen Differenzen der Hysterie und der Dementia praecox" (1st International Congress of Psychoanalysis, Salzburg, April 26, 1908), *Centralblatt für Nervenheilkunde und Psychiatrie*, number 2, July 1908, Neue folge, Bd. 19: 521–33, and in *Klinische Beiträge zur Psychoanalyse* (Leipzig, Vienna, Zurich: Int. Psych. Verlag, 1921); "The Psycho-Sexual Differences between Hysteria and Dementia Praecox," *Selected Papers* (London: Hogarth Press, 1927): 64–79.

[2] Devereux, Georges, "Some Criteria for the Timing of Confrontations and Interpretations," *IJP* XXXII, 1 (1951): 19–24.

[3] Ferenczi, Sandor, "Introjektion und Übertragung," 1909, *Jahrbuch für psychoanalytische Forschungen* I: 422–57; "Introjection and Transference," *Sex in Psycho-Analysis* (New York: Basic Books, 1952): 35–93.

[4] Freud, Anna, *Das Ich und die Abwehrmechanismen*, Chapter IV, "Die Abwehrmechanismen." See *Versuch einer Chronologie*, 60–63 (Vienna: Intern. psychoanal. Verlag, 1936); *The Ego and the Mechanisms of Defence* (London: Hogarth Press, 1937); (New York: International Universities Press, 1946).

[5] Freud, Sigmund, *Studien über Hysterie* (1895), *GW* I; for the case of Elisabeth von R., see pages 196–251 and especially 125–27; *Studies on Hysteria*, *SE* II, 158–60.

[6] Freud, Sigmund, *Die Traumdeutung* (1900), *GW* II–III. See, in Chap. IV, "Die Traumentstellung," pages 152–56, 157, and 163–68; "Kern unseres Wesens," 609; *The Interpretation of Dreams*, *SE* IV, Chap. IV, "Distortion in Dreams," 146–50, 151, 157–62, and Chap. VII, 603.

644 [7] Freud, Sigmund, "Bruchstück einer Hysterie-Analyse (Dora)," finished on January 24, 1901 (see letter 140 in *Aus den Anfängen*, the correspondence with Fliess originally published in London): *GW* V, 194–95 [*The Origins of Psychoanalysis* (New York: Basic Books, 1954), 325–26]; "Fragment of an Analysis of a Case of Hysteria," *SE* VII, 35–36.

[8] Freud, Sigmund, "Bemerkungen über einen Fall von Zwangsneurose" (1909), *GW* VII. See, in section 1.d, "Die Einführung ins Verständnis der Kur," pages 402–4, and the footnote on pages 404–5; in section 1.f, "Die

Krankheitsveranlassung," namely, Freud's decisive interpretation concerning what I would translate as the subject of the illness; and 1.g, "Der Vaterkomplex und die Lösung der Rattenidee," 417–38; "Notes upon a Case of Obsessional Neurosis," *SE* X. See, section 1.d, "Initiation into the Nature of the Treatment," 178–81 and the footnote on 181; and sections 1.f, "The Precipitating Cause of the Illness," and 1.g, "The Father Complex and the Solution of the Rat Idea," 195–220.

[9] Freud, Sigmund, *Jenseits des Lustprinzips* (1920), *GW* XIII; see, if it is still necessary, pages 11–14 of Chapter II; *Beyond the Pleasure Principle*, *SE* XVIII, 14–16.

[10] Freud, Sigmund, *Massenpsychologie und Ich-Analyse* (1921), *GW* XIII, Chapter VII, "Die Identifizierung," especially pages 116–18; *Group Psychology and the Analysis of the Ego*, *SE* XVIII, 106–8.

[11] Freud, Sigmund, "Die endliche und die unendliche Analyse" (1937), *GW* XVI, 59–99, translated into French as "Terminated (!) analysis and interminable (!!) analysis" (my exclamation marks concern the standards employed in the translation into French of Freud's works. I am mentioning this translation because, according to the sixteenth volume of the *GW* that came out in 1950, it doesn't exist; see page 280), in *RFP* XI, 1 (1939): 3–38.

[12] Freud, Sigmund, "Die Ichspaltung im Abwehrvorgang," *GW* XVII, "Schriften aus dem Nachlass," 58–62. Manuscript dated January 2, 1938 [280] (unfinished); "Splitting of the Ego in the Defensive Process," *Collected Papers* V, 372–75. [*SE* XXIII, 275–78.]

[13] Glover, Edward, "The Therapeutic Effect of Inexact Interpretation: A Contribution to the Theory of Suggestion," *IJP* XII, 4 (1931): 397–411.

[14] Hartmann, Kris, and Loewenstein, various team* contributions in *The Psychoanalytic Study of the Child* since 1946.

[15] Kris, Ernst, "Ego Psychology and Interpretation in Psychoanalytic Therapy," *PQ* XX, 1 (1951): 21–25. [Reprinted, with modifications, in *Selected Papers of Ernst Kris* (New Haven: Yale University Press, 1975), 237–51.]

[16] Lacan, Jacques, my paper for the Rome Congress (September 26–27, 1953), "Fonction et champ de la parole et du langage en psychanalyse" ["The Function and Field of Speech and Language in Psychoanalysis"], *La Psychanalyse* 1 (1956); *Écrits* 1966, 237–322.

[17] Lacan, Jacques, "L'instance de la lettre dans l'inconscient ou la raison depuis Freud" ["The Instance of the Letter in the Unconscious or Reason Since Freud"] (May 9, 1957), *La Psychanalyse* 3 (1957), 47–81; *Écrits* 1966, 493–528.

[18] Lagache, Daniel, "Le problème du transfert" ["The Problem of Transference"] (Paper given at the 14th Conference of French-speaking Psychoanalysts on November 1, 1951), *RFP* XVI, 1–2 (1952): 5–115.

[19] Leclaire, Serge, "À la recherche des principes d'une psychothérapie des psychoses" ["Search for Principles Guiding Psychotherapy with Psychotics"] (Bonneval Congress, April 15, 1957), *L'Évolution psychiatrique* 2 (1958): 377–419.

[20] Macalpine, Ida, "The Development of the Transference," *PQ* XIX, 4 (1950): 500–39, especially 502–8 and 522–28.

645 [21] *PDA*: see pages 51–52 (on "pregenital" and "genital"), passim (on the strengthening of the ego and the method for doing so), and 102 (on distance from the object as the principle of a method of treatment) [Maurice Bouvet, "La clinique psychanalytique. La relation d'objet"].

[22] *PDA*: see pages 133 (on emotional reeducation and the *PDA*'s opposition to Freud regarding the primordial importance of the two-person relation), 132 (on the cure "from the inside"), 135 (what is important . . . is not so much what the analyst says or does as what he is), 136, etc., passim, and 162 (on dismissing [the patient] at the end of the treatment), and 149 (on dreams) [Sacha Nacht, "La thérapeutique psychanalytique"].

[23] R.L. [Ruth Lebovici], "Perversion sexuelle transitoire au cours d'un traitement psychanalytique" ["Transitory Sexual Perversion in the Course of a Psychoanalytic Treatment"], *Bulletin d'activités de l'Association des Psychanalystes de Belgique* 25 (1956): 1–15 (118, rue Froissart, Brussels).

[24] Sharpe, Ella, "The Technique of Psychoanalysis," *Collected Papers on Psychoanalysis* (London: Hogarth Press, 1950). See pages 81 (on the need to

justify one's existence) and 12–14 (on the background and techniques required of the analyst).

[25] Schmideberg, Melitta, "Intellektuelle Hemmung und Ess-störung," *Zeitschrift für psa. Pädagogik* VIII (1934). ["Intellectual Inhibition and Disturbances in Eating," *IJP* XIX (1938): 17–22.]

[26] Williams, J. D., *The Compleat Strategyst*, The Rand Series (New York, Toronto, London: McGraw Hill, 1966). [More recently: (New York: Dover, 1986).]

[27] Winnicott, D. W., "Transitional Objects and Transitional Phenomena," in *IJP* XXXIV, 2 (1953): 29–97.

Notes

1. This is the first of two papers I gave at the International Colloquium at the invitation of the Société Française de Psychanalyse; it was published in *La Psychanalyse* 6 (1961): 149–206.

2. Numbers in square brackets correspond to the references provided at the end of this paper.

3. To turn the term "dislodge" against the spirit of a society, a term that allows us to assess this spirit, for it translates the sentence in which Freud proved himself the equal of the pre-Socratics—*Wo Es war, soll Ich werden*—into French quite simply as *Le Moi doit déloger le ça*, "the ego must dislodge the id."

4. "Comment terminer le traitement analytique," *Revue Française de Psychanalyse* XVIII, 4 (1954): 519 and passim. To gauge the influence of such training, read: Charles-Henri Nodet, "Le psychanalyste," *L'Évolution Psychiatrique* 4 (1957): 689–91.

5. I promise not to tire my readers any further with such stupid formulations, which really only serve here to show what has become of analytic discourse. I apologized to the foreigners in the audience who no doubt had just as many stupid formulations available in their own language [*langue*], if not of quite the same platitudinous level.

6. In France the doctrinaire of being, quoted above, went straight to the following solution: the psychoanalyst's being is innate [22 (page 136)].

7. Rather than being vocalized as the letter symbolizing oxygen, evoked by the metaphor being played out, the "O" may be read as zero, insofar as this number symbolizes the essential function of place in the signifier's structure.

8. For example: in the United States, where Kris has achieved success, publication means title of ownership, and a seminar like mine would have to stake its claim to priority every week against the pillage it couldn't fail to occasion. In France, my ideas penetrate by way of infiltration into a group, in which people obey orders that prohibit my teachings. In being cursed there, ideas can only serve as decorations for a few dandies. Never mind: the void the ideas cause to resound, whether I am cited or not, makes another voice heard.

9. My parentheses.

10. My parentheses.

11. My parentheses.

12. (Added in 1966:) The penultimate sentence of this paragraph and the first line of the next paragraph have been rectified.

13. See letter 118 (September 11, 1899) to Fliess in *Sigmund Freud, Aus den Anfängen der Psychoanalyse* (London: Imago Publishing Company, 1950).

14. Here is the dream as it is presented in the patient's account on page 152 of *GW* II–III: "I

want to throw a dinner party. But I only have a little smoked salmon left. I think of going out shopping, when I remember that it is Sunday afternoon and all the shops are closed. I tell myself that I'll call a few caterers on the phone. But the phone is out of order. Thus I have to give up my desire to throw a dinner party."

15. This is the reason Freud gives for the hysterical identification, specifying that smoked salmon plays for the friend the same role caviar plays for the patient.

16. It must not be forgotten that the term is used for the first time in the *Traumdeutung* on the subject of dreams, and that this use provides its meaning and, simultaneously, that of the term "distortion," which translates it when British analysts apply it to the ego. This remark allows us to evaluate the use made in France of the term "ego distortion" [*distortion du Moi*], which supporters of ego strengthening—insufficiently alerted to the "false cognates" English words constitute (words have so little importance, don't they?)—understand simply as . . . a twisted ego.

17. See ($\$\lozenge$D) and ($\$\lozenge a$) on my graph, reproduced in "Subversion of the Subject," page 817 below. The sign $\lozenge$ registers the relations envelopment-development-conjunction-disjunction. The links it signifies in these two parentheses allow us to read the barred S as "S fading* in demand's cut," and "S fading* before the object of desire"—that is, drive and fantasy.

Remarks on Daniel Lagache's Presentation: "Psychoanalysis and Personality Structure" 647

This text was written up on the basis of a tape recording of a presentation I gave whose introduction was lost due to a malfunction of the recording equipment. I used this as an opportunity to reshape the talk in a way that substantially modifies the improvised version. I should indicate that my intention in doing so was to tighten up my initial articulation of a position that is still essential to my thinking.

This led me to shorten it and, in particular, to cut what, in the heat of the moment, anticipated what was only to be developed later. This is why I resisted my predilection as an author and decided not to include the fable of the mustard jar, which is not, for all that, of merely anecdotal interest, as I have since developed it quite fully.[1]

Except for the fact that I am providing it with its birth certificate here and am indicating that the motive of its birth lay in the feasts which, at least apparently, furnished me with it, I am leaving it to my audience to rediscover the mustard jar implicit in the figures that my readers will find rather more accessible, since they are less subdued by the signifiers of presence.

A text that has never before been communicated in any documentary form whatsoever attests only to the moment of its definitive composition, in this case Easter 1960.

I. Structure and the Subject

The term "structure," which serves as the key word in Daniel Lagache's paper,[2] is at the crux of many contemporary trends in research on mankind, 648
if, as I think, this is the broad meaning that Lagache gives the term "anthropology." A reference to sociology would have seemed to me to better situate structuralism currently.

For it is the topic of a debate that is lively enough that even Claude Lévi-Strauss has not escaped structuralists' attacks on each other, the notion of structure cherished by one of them seeming to be a total aberration to another.

Since I myself use the term "structure" in a way that I believe I can legitimate on the basis of Claude Lévi-Strauss' usage, it is of personal concern to me—and this is certainly the place to say it—not to consider this use to be generally confusing. I am thus all the more interested in putting it to the test of Lagache's elaboration of it.

I accept the category "set" with which he introduces it, insofar as it avoids the implications of totality or purifies them. But this does not mean that its elements are neither isolated nor summable [as Lagache claims]—at least, if we are looking, in the notion of set, for some guarantee of the rigor it has in mathematical theory. The fact that its "parts are themselves structured" thus means that they themselves are capable of symbolizing all the relations definable for the set, which go far beyond their separation and union, the latter being relations that are nevertheless inaugural. Indeed, elements are defined therein by the possibility of being posited as subsets covering any relation defined for the set, this possibility having as its essential characteristic that it is not limited by any *natural* hierarchy.

This is why it seems advisable to me to discard from the outset the term "part" and, *a fortiori*, every datum in the field that includes such formidable unknowns as an organism; for by organizing the entourage (with the notorious "situation" that he has in store for us), such a field already brings to every structural consideration the minimal limitation that Lagache immediately and relevantly qualifies as "geometrical."[3]

649 Now, as I have stressed elsewhere,[4] structure is not form, and we need to learn to think in terms of a topology that is necessitated by structure alone.

I maintain that transcendental aesthetics has to be recast in our times, for linguistics has introduced into science its indisputable status, structure being defined by signifying articulation as such.

When Lagache thus starts from a choice he proposes to us between a structure that is in some sense apparent (which would imply a critique of what is natural in descriptive characteristics) and a structure that he says is located at some distance from experience (since it is a question of the "theoretical model" [page 12] that he recognizes in psychoanalytic metapsychology), this antinomy neglects a mode of structure which, although it is tertiary, cannot be excluded—namely, the effects that the pure and simple combinatory of the signifier determines in the reality in which it is produced. For is it not structuralism that allows us to posit our experience as the field in which it [*ça*] speaks? If the answer is yes, structure's "distance from experience" vanishes, since it operates there not as a theoretical model, but as the original machine that directs [*met en scène*] the subject there.

What Lagache attributes to the economic/dynamic point of view—what he calls the material and its interpretation—is precisely where we see the impact of structure begin in analytic experience, and structuralist research must pursue its effects starting from there. Their economic/dynamic import can be illustrated by a comparison that is equivalent to its own reason: what a turbine, a machine that operates according to a chain of equations, brings to a natural waterfall in order to produce energy.

How could we be astonished, then, that the genetic criterion has resulted in a failure to put the Freudian topographies to the test, to the very extent that their systems are structural?

And perhaps we have to reject the criterion of adaptation until things change considerably—that is, until changes have occurred which psychoanalysis itself will have introduced (unless we enter the impasse of the so-called post-revolutionary problem).

Indeed, the systems whose interrelations (I would suggest the term "para- 650
nomies") Lagache so delicately highlights in each of Freud's two topographies, by distinguishing them on the basis of their functions, are not, for all that, structure in the strict sense of the term. This can be seen in the sort of chiasmus he does not explain whereby the primary process (unfolding in the unconscious) is governed by the identity of thoughts, and the secondary process (insofar as it makes the primary process fall in with reality) finds its criterion in the identity of perceptions [page 20]—whereas perception is more primary in the structure as Lagache understands it, and closer to the pleasure principle, which ensures the reign of the primary process, than everything that seems to be reflected back by an enlightened consciousness as thought.

It is thus worth recalling that, from the outset, Freud did not attribute *the slightest reality* as a differentiated apparatus in the organism to any of the systems in either of his topographies. For people forget to draw therefrom the corollary that, by the same token, he forbade us to force any of these systems back into the fantasized reality of any sort of "totality" of the organism. In short, the structure of which I am speaking has nothing to do with the idea of the "structure of the organism," as supported by the most soundly based facts in *Gestalt* theory. Not that structure, in the strict sense of the term, does not take advantage of gaps in the organic *Gestalt* to submit it to itself. But on the basis of their conjunctions, whether they prove to be based on fission or fissures, a heterogeneity between two orders appears, which we will be less tempted to mask if we grasp its principle. If it is less neglected, the topographical distribution of consciousness, so striking in its dispersion that one might even say it has exploded, will force us to reconsider a fact that Lagache is right to underscore, which is that we have hardly made any progress regarding the nature of consciousness since Freud, by the revision of it that he made necessary, returned to it only in order to complain that he had gotten bogged down in it.

In any case, it is clear that the organism does not escape unscathed. In other words, it surrenders one of its more or less detachable tentacles as collateral to such a structure, due to a social prohibition, for example, in which it, as an individual, may be caught up.

To enter into the heart of the subject with Lagache, we should credit him

651 for denouncing, in passing [page 9], the simple falsification Heinz Hartmann tried to impose on history when he overlooked the fact that, at the time Freud wrote "On Narcissism," he was truly interested in the ego as an agency, the only agency, the same agency he continued to promote afterward. As to the warning Hartmann and his acolytes, Kris and Loewenstein, feel they need to give us to be on guard against a so-called anthropomorphic conception of the second topography, I agree with Lagache that its object has about as much consistency as the foolishness, which is pure sham, that they attribute to us. But it is not in order to accept the impertinence of the other foolishness they attribute to us, a real foolishness, counting on our vainglory at being among those who are not susceptible to being deluded, in order to give us Hobson's choice of a so-called causal conception[5] of the ego. Will Lagache still deny the nefarious influence that Jaspers' antinomy has had, in this three-card monte trick with which they were hoping to dazzle us, by projecting the splendor of physiology onto the closet door out of which they bring, to explain Freud's ego, this dummy [*mannequin*], the rejection of which is the *pons asinorum* of all psychological experience, this verbal subject used as a prop for the synthesis of the most disparate functions? Lagache challenges this thirty-six-legged calf further on, this monster whose fictive seams evoke a collage devoid of artistry, but which quite suits this cabinet of curios where charlatans do not stick out like a sore thumb. What could this baroque conception possibly have to do with psychoanalysis, other than to debase its technique to the point of exploiting the most obscure biases?

As Lagache so forcefully remarks, the fact remains that the very existence of "animistic enclaves," even of alternations experienced as personal in our assent, does not in the least hinder our understanding of the second topography as a theoretical model. For what is important is not "that one can differentiate the systems by their functions," but to recognize, as he does, that "the concept of function is not exclusively physiological" [page 13].

652 My contribution to this debate may incline you to believe that I think he could not have put it any better.

However, my objections to Lagache's attempt will be clear, insofar as what he calls the "structuration of the personality" (indeed, that is part of the title of section IV of his article) refers, in his view, to its formation in intersubjectivity. In my view, his method is not radical enough, and I will say why.

But first let me say that this is not because I disagree with his critique of the exorbitant idealism that strives to make the genesis of the personal world derive from personal consciousness [page 14]—namely, the modern vogue of a form of psychoanalysis that would like to be based exclusively on the observation of children. But he seems to me to be optimistic in assuming that we are free from this bias: Has he forgotten that Piaget has accustomed us to studying the genesis of the shared world in individual consciousness, going so far as to include the categories of scientific thought in it?

I am no less delighted by his remark that "before existing in himself, through himself, and for himself, the child exists for and through other people; he is already a pole of expectations, projects, and attributes" [page 14]. But this would amount to no more than a truism, did he not emphasize the means by which so many expectations and projects make themselves felt in the child's unconscious when he comes into the world. For is it not by means of these "attributes" (a rather odd term in this apposition that slips in at the end of his sentence)? "Attributes": let me stop Lagache at this little word. Did he hope I would not notice it? Otherwise, why did he not himself give it its full import? "A pole of attributes" is what the subject is before he is born (and perhaps it is under their mass that he will suffocate once born). "Of attributes," that is, of signifiers more or less linked in a discourse—we shall have to recall this later when we broach the topic of the id's structure.

But for the time being, isn't Lagache professing the same thing I teach when I define the unconscious as the Other's discourse? For in order for Lagache to be able to give this existence "for and through other people," if not prece- 653
dence, then at least logical antecedence, with respect to the existence of the child "in himself, though himself, and for himself," his future relationship with the entourage of semblables that awaits him and consigns him to the place he occupies in their projects is not sufficient. For in the imaginary dimension that is deployed there, this existence relationship remains inverse, insofar as what is unborn remains utterly hidden from its view. But none of the following—the place the child occupies in the line of descent, according to the convention of kinship structures, the forename [*pré-nom*] that already identifies it at times with its grandfather, the blanks to be filled in on civil status forms, and even what will denote its sex on them—none of those are concerned with what the child is in itself. Let it turn out to be a hermaphrodite and see what happens!

This, as we know, goes much farther, as far as law covers language and truth covers speech: His existence is already pleaded innocent or guilty before he comes into the world, and the thin thread of his truth cannot help but have him already weave a fabric of lies. This is precisely why there will, roughly speaking, be a case of mistaken identity—that is, a mistake regarding the merits of his parents—in his ego-ideal; while, in the old trial of self-justification before God's tribunal, the new little tyke will be saddled with a file that predates his grandparents, in the form of their superego. Freud noted this, and Lagache repeats it; there is nothing to be sought in it except the effect and field of speech and language with the optima that could be indicated on a topological schema, assuming we also see that they only enter reality statistically.

The parents' desire resonates still more deeply here, as we surely know from experience. But this is precisely the question I myself have raised, as some of you here know, regarding the determination of desire by the signifier's effects on the subject.

If Lagache himself were not echoing my promotion of the Word, would he be so sure his pretty reference to incarnation would strike his audience, when he says that "in the course of prenatal existence, being for other people is modified and enriched by *incarnation*" [page 15]?

Yes, "being for other people"—he does not say "being in itself"—and he continues, "toward the middle of gestation." Is it not that by "his first manifestations of activity, the fetus" . . . begins to make people talk about him? Yes, the fact that people talk about him is what defines what Lagache calls here "the
654 rudiments of an existence" (I would say ex-sistence), and all the more strikingly in that he qualifies it as "autonomous" [page 15].

Why not then relate the anteriority of the relation to the Other's discourse to all *primal differentiation*,[6] in which he admits that the subject functions "without existing as a cognitive structure"? Seven lines earlier, however, he argues that "to claim that the newborn has no conscious experiences is to deny the obvious, since he alternates between sleeping and waking." Does this observable wakefulness suffice to assure him of the existence of a subject without any "cognitive structure"?

To my mind, the fact of primal differentiation leaves in abeyance its properly signifying use, on which the advent of the subject depends. To define this primal differentiation in itself, I would say that it is an object-relation *in the real*, thinking that I can prove thereby the robust yet simple nature of the tripartition I use to situate analytic experience in the symbolic, imaginary, and real.

Demand must be added to the need that sustains this primal differentiation for the subject (prior to any "cognitive structure") to make his entrance into the real, while need becomes drive, insofar as its reality is obliterated in becoming the symbol of a love satisfaction.

These categorial requirements, if you will allow me to highlight them, have the following advantages, among others: they banish certain loathsome metaphors such as the child's "symbiotic relationship" [page 16] with the mother (do they constitute a lichen?); they leave us rather dissatisfied with a casual reference to "the interplay of maturation and learning" to account for "an identification in the intersubjective conflict," even if we agree that "the predominance of his passivity means that he receives his temporary person-
655 age from the situation" [page 16]; and they do not allow us to think we have

explained the differentiation between the body and objects by defining that differentiation as syncretic, because that would gloss over the essential dissymmetry between projection and introjection.

Here Lagache's point of view remains classical. But it seems to me that he cannot emphasize, as he does here, the symbolic prematuration through which the child is inscribed in being for other people (in my terms, in the Other's discourse), and at the same time hold that the formal delay which its learning of syntax exhibits (the moment when the child speaks of itself as another speaks to it) is decisive of anything whatsoever "in the conjunction that occurs between being for other people and being for oneself." For, rather than this instant being representative of it, I would say that, since it is a question of discourse, this conjunction has always obtained, since discourse was there from the beginning, even if only in its impersonal presence.

The drama of the subject in the Word is that he experiences his want-to-be there, and the psychoanalyst would do well to define certain moments of it; for the psychologist cannot do anything about it with his questionnaires, and even his recordings, where these moments will not show up so fast—not until a film has managed to capture the structure of lack [*faute*] as constitutive of the game of chess.

It is because it wards off this moment of lack [*manque*] that an image assumes the role of bearing the full brunt of desire: projection, an imaginary function.

Contrary to this, an index is instated at the heart of being to designate the hole in it: introjection, a relation to the symbolic.

The observed progress in objectification during its early stages seems to have no other interest, as Lagache hints, than to mask from us the unconscious moments of the projections and introjections in the course [*suite*] of their development.

I will stop at the same point Lagache did, to take stock of where our perspectives differ. They differ regarding the very function he attributes to intersubjectivity. For the latter is defined, in his view, in a relationship with the other as a semblable, a relationship which is fundamentally symmetrical, as can be seen in the fact that Lagache formulates that the subject learns to treat himself as an object from the other. In my view, the subject has to arise from the given state of the signifiers that cover him [*le recouvrent*] in an Other which 656
is their transcendental locus; he thus constitutes himself in an existence in which the manifestly constitutive vector of the Freudian field of experience—that is, what is known as desire—is possible.

Thus it is hardly necessary for the "subject-ego" to push back the "object-ego" in order to make it "transcendent" for himself [page 17]; rather, the true, if not the good subject, the subject of desire—seen in the light of fantasy and in its hiding place beyond his ken—is nothing other than the Thing,[7] which in and of itself is what is closest to him while escaping him more than anything else.

This is why those who keep abreast of my work know that the noetic equivocation by means of which Lagache causes the subject-ego to vanish [page 18] from what is thought in it, is not what I call the fading* of the subject. For such fading occurs when desire is in abeyance, because the subject is eclipsed in the signifier of demand, and when fantasy becomes fixated, because the subject himself becomes the cut that makes the part-object shine in its unspeakable vacillation.

II. Where Is Id?

The reconstruction that Lagache nevertheless achieves should be examined without considering the preceding objections; for although he takes his bearings from his postulate of personal structure, this postulate can, as usual, only be clarified by its use.

At first sight this use seems to be heuristic, as if Lagache were, in some sense, asking each of the "systems" (this is his term)—id, ego, and superego—to account for what it is missing in order to be a person. One cannot but note here that Lagache discards the term "agency," even though it would seem to favor what he calls his personalist style since it is part and parcel of Freud's formulation of the so-called second topography.

657 From limited heteronomies into relative autonomies (I would suggest: in their paranomy), these systems come together before our eyes by means of this method, without anything preconceived forcing them to combine into a complete person. For—and why not if that is its aim?—the investigation also leads to technique, and Lagache assigns one of these systems, the ego, which is actively brought to the fore [*dégagement*] here, the task of bringing out a unity of being, of course, but in a practical ideality that patently proves to be more selective than structural. The postulate seems to fall here to the level of a dialectical deviation concerning which one would like to know to what extent it meets with Lagache's approval.

The section in which Lagache studies the structure of the id does not disappoint me, and I would endorse many of his formulations verbatim. He seems to me to excel especially in his attempt to situate the subject in the structure here.

Dare I indicate what he would have had to do to avoid the impasse he encounters so brilliantly in his formulations on structure itself, insofar as he considers it to be that of the id? He would have had to face the full force of the paradoxes with which Freud here, as is so often the case, shows us the way.

Three statements, which seem to be rather incompatible, would have to be made to hang together, and this would have to be accomplished on the basis of the very scandal that each of them causes.

The first is that the id is unorganized. The surprising nature of this assertion can but give us pause for thought, given the advent of this agency in the German *Es*, which is supposed to encompass both the indestructibility, affirmed early on (and maintained), of the repressed that is refound in it, and the automatic nature, studied much later, of the repetition that must result from the repressed (the concept of *Wiederholungszwang*, posited on the threshold of *Beyond the Pleasure Principle*).

This statement is linked to another one, which Freud reiterated whenever the occasion presented itself. It concerns the very elements whose laws in the unconscious he first articulated—later constructing their structure, strictly speaking, in the drives—and can be put as follows: these elements do not know negation.

This foreclosure of negation was, of course, corrected, already in *The Interpretation of Dreams*, by the analysis of the detours that prop up something equivalent to negation: deferral, inhibition, and representation by means of an opposite. But in reading Freud's texts closely, one notices that this foreclosure 658
is maintained in the stricter formulation that there is no contradiction that holds up—that is, that has the effect of logical exclusion—between the drives inhabiting the id.

The third statement stems from the aphorisms in the half-light of which *The Ego and the Id* (*Das Ich und das Es*) comes to a close, emerging in the term "silence"—the silence that the death drives are supposed to make reign in the id.

Any attempt to link a structure thus described to any differentiation whatsoever of primal needs in the organism can only multiply its apparent contradictions by ever increasing their weight. Lagache is unable to avoid this problem in following this pathway.

It seems to me that the very difficulties everyone runs up against here confirm my belief that it is impossible to dispense with the function of the signifier.

Let us consider the signifier quite simply in the irreducible materiality that structure entails, insofar as this materiality is its own, and let us conjure the signifier up in the form of a lottery. It will be clear then that the signifier is the only thing in the world that can underpin the coexistence—constituted by disorder (synchronically)—of elements among which the most indestructible order ever to be deployed subsists (diachronically). The associative rigor of which the signifier is capable, in the diachronic dimension, is based on the very commutativity it exhibits by being interchangeable in the synchronic dimension.

Its subsistence as connotation cannot be suspended by being assigned contradictory signs, for an exclusion originating in those signs as such can occur only as a condition of the consistency of the chain that will be constituted. We must add to this the fact that the dimension in which this condition is verified is simply the translation that such a chain lends itself to.

Let us dwell a moment longer on this lottery. We find that it is because the numbers are randomly mixed together ordinally [in the lottery wheel], without any real organization, that we can place bets on which number will come out; whereas it is their structural organization that—allowing them, as they are selected, to be read as an oracle—allows me, in continuing to extract numbers, to affirm that some are missing cardinally.

659 Freud's propositions thus direct us to the medium of the signifier, and right from the first proposition. Need it be stressed that the repercussions in which the second becomes entangled, indicate, by the grammatical reference points Freud always gives in his reconsiderations of it, that it is truly a question of an order of discourse?

This is why we cannot but be struck by the combinatorial indifference with which Freud breaks the drive down into its source, direction, aim, and object. Does it mean that all of this is signifiers? Certainly not, but it is structure. Thus I shall leave aside here its energetic status.

This nevertheless is enough to allow me to respond to Lagache's criterion from the geometrical angle by which he intends to approach it.

The confused image of the id as the "reservoir of the drives," which so rightly disgusts him because it meets with the approval of a crude organicism, is, in fact, rectified by the meaning it receives in my perspective.

Let us think of a mailbox and of the inner cavity of some Baal-like idol; let us now think of the *bocca di leone* which, in combining them, acquired its fearsome function in Venice. A reservoir, yes, as it were, that is what the id is, and even a reserve; but what is produced in it, missives of prayer or denunciation, comes from the outside, and if it accumulates inside, it is in order to sleep there. The opacity of the text stating that silence reigns in the id is thereby dispelled: The silence is not metaphorical, but relates to an antithesis that must be pursued in the subject's relation to the signifier, which is expressly designated to us as the death drive.

But let us return to Lagache and the crux of the question concerning the person. I grant him that Freud posits that there is "no negation, no doubt, [and] no degrees of certainty" in the unconscious system. But Freud does not do so in order to have us imagine that it allows of complete certainty, or of a zero degree of certainty. How could it be otherwise when I have long said that only action gives rise to certainty in the subject?

I think, however, that Lagache's error here is to confuse assertion with certainty. Having thus eliminated the latter, he believes he can square accounts with the former by means of the same procedure, even though it is of unsure 660
repute—the image of the baby being thrown out with the bath water seems appropriate here.

How could this be, though, when from assertion to certainty a link, if not of precedence, at least of logical precession, is established, a link in which the uncertainties that action engenders in its wake of verification assume their place?

Does this not imply disparaging the care, as usual extraordinary in the presence of mind to which it attests, with which Freud dotted the i's and crossed the t's here in expressly articulating *Bejahung* as the first moment of unconscious enunciation, the one presupposed by the fact that it is maintained in *Verneinung* as the second moment? You are familiar with the luster I tried to give to the discussion of *Verneinung* in the early years of my seminar.

I will reach once more into my lottery wheel, and this time I draw out the number 58 . . . This number contains in itself its assertive import, which I would even go so far as to call provocative. Do not object that the vigilance of a subject is necessary here, for the subject is found here simply by virtue of the fact of having slipped into this number by the decimal presence that sums up in two columns what merely constitutes its cipher, the number remaining indifferent, being, among other things, the double of a prime number.

Moreover, to appreciate what this figure can effectively convey about the subject, one need but consult, on the subject of the exploratory function in psychoanalysis of numbers chosen at random, an all too forgotten chapter in Freud's *Psychopathology of Everyday Life*.

Such is the example, taken as the least favorable because of its abstract nature, with which I intend to show that it is in the signifier's foundational duplicity that the subject first finds the hidden stream in which he flows before seeping out—we shall see through which crack.

But if you will allow me, by contrast, to resort to the warm vitality of *Witz*, I will illustrate it in its greatest opacity with the genius that guided Jarry in his find: the condensation of a simple supplementary phoneme in the illustrious interjection "*merdre*." This is the kind of refined triviality we see in slips of the tongue, flights of fancy, and poetry—a single letter was enough to give the most vulgar French exclamation [*merde*: shit] the ejaculatory value, verging on the sublime, of the place it occupies in the epic of Ubu: that of the Word from before the beginning.

661 Imagine what we could do with two letters! For the spelling, *Meirdre*, gematrially offers us everything promising man will ever hear in his history, and *Mairdre* is an anagram of the verb on which "admirable" is based.

Please do not read into this departure from the seriousness of my discussion anything other than my concern to recall that down through the centuries, both in life and in letters, fate reserved for the fool*, oh Shakespeare, the task of keeping accessible the place of truth that Freud brought to light.

Let us now recall the problems the status of interrogative sentences pose for the linguist, in order to gauge all the problems that Lagache raises with a single formulation, striking in the felicity of expression that never fails him in the whole of this text: this "interrogation that calls the ego into question, or even puts it 'to the question'" [page 22]. I clearly perceive the subtlety involved in designating "the agitation that represents the drive in the ego" as its instrument of torture. I approve his prudence all the more in that it is only too obvious that the question cannot come from the id, but rather responds to the id. We have known, however, since *Hemmung, Symptom und Angst* [*Inhibitions, Symptoms and Anxiety*] that the most characteristic agitation in the ego is but a warning sign that brings into play the defenses . . . against the id's assertiveness, not its question.

In truth, Lagache takes such pains here because he wants the function of judgment to be the ego's privilege [page 22].

May I tell him that I believe the whole thrust of Freudian experience contradicts that? When will I be able to show him, text in hand, that the famous *Entwurf* ["Project for a Scientific Psychology"], dedicated to Fliess, has the far from secondary aim of establishing that a fundamental form of judgment, which Freud rightly calls "primal judgment," is already constituted[8] at the level of the system of the first breaches [*frayages*] of pleasure.

I myself cannot fathom otherwise Freud's formulation that drives Lagache to his wits' end: that the drives exist [page 22].

Indeed, it is not a total waste to never hold one's tongue [*donne . . . sa langue*
662 *au chat*] when it is a spoken tongue. For the whole point is perhaps that the drives ex-sist in the sense that they are not in their place, that they present themselves in this *Entstellung*, in this de-position, so to speak, or, as it were, in this crowd of displaced persons. Does this not also give the subject his chance to exist some day? For the true being, however, this chance seems at the very least compromised. For the way things are going—as we know only too well—when language gets in on the act, the drives must multiply instead, and the question (were there anyone to pose it) would rather be how the subject will find any place there at all.

The answer fortunately comes first, in the hole the subject makes for himself there.

We can only hope to make headway in a new critique of judgment, which I take to be initiated in Freud's text, "Negation," if we take up anew what Freud broached in this article and connect it with linguistics. Up until now, apart from the publication of the dialogue [between Hyppolite and myself] that I mentioned earlier, this initiative, as sometimes happens, has no more benefited from any sort of commentary than if it concerned the drunkenness of Noah.

We are willing to let father Freud fool around with a judgment of attribution and a judgment of existence, and even grant the former the privilege [*pas*] of logical antecedence over the negation on which the latter is based. But we analysts are not keen to expose ourselves to the derision of logicians, much less take our chances studying Brentano, even though we know he flourished in Vienna and that Freud even attended his classes.

He conceived of the judgment of attribution, then, as instated on the basis of *Bejahung* alone. Its chain develops a first condensation or syncretism in which a combinatory structure is already found that I myself have illustrated.[9] Given this sort of affirmation by juxtaposition, what can ever be refuted if not by an effect of obstruction?

It is here that the problem of the origin of negation should be taken up anew, assuming we do not mean by that any sort of puerile psychological genesis, 663
but rather a problem of structure that has to be broached in the material of structure.

The particles that express shades of negation are, as we know, highly differentiated in each language; they provide formal logic with opportunities for oddities which prove quite clearly that they involve an essential distortion—that is, another translation of *Entstellung*—that is valid if one relates it to the topology of the subject in the signifying structure.

The proof thereof appears when formal logic, in having to break its bonds with the grammatical forms that carry this distortion, simultaneously tears itself away from linguistics, as if it were a threat to the partiality in which it is tenable, but which can nevertheless refer only to a field of language that must be distinguished as the field of the enunciated.

Hence we can understand one of the reasons why the study of these particles cannot be genetic, when psychology proves to always bring the same logic to it—either the logic of classes or of relations—which we must go beyond. We can see an example of what has to be removed in order for truly structural research to be sustained at its level, when we see the obstacle created for it by even such a small stumbling block as the *ne* whose usage in French in a sentence like "*je crains qu'il ne vienne*" [I'm afraid he may come] is qualified by grammarians as the "expressive *ne*," without anybody ever—no matter how good his glasses—having been able to make out *what* it could be expressive of. Thanks to which grammarians as well-informed and on their guard against any authority other than usage as Brunot and Bruneau, in their *Précis de grammaire historique* (Paris: Masson, 1933), conclude that the headache this *ne* has given everyone is of but "precious little interest," on the pretext "that the rules that have been established for it are variable and contradictory" (page 587).

I would like to see a graph of the zones in which these particles subsist, in some sense, in suspension. I am concocting one of my own making this year,[10] and with it I believe I can designate the bed in which these particles oscillate between a chain of enunciation, insofar as the latter marks the place in which
664 the subject is implicit in pure discourse (imperative, echoing voice, epithalamion, or yelling "fire"), and a chain of statements, insofar as the subject is designated in them by shifters* (namely, "I," all the particles and inflections fixing his presence as the subject of discourse, and with that presence the present of chronology).

In the turn of phrase, *Je crains qu'il ne vienne*, the most elementary analytic art can sense the desire that constitutes the ambivalence characteristic of the unconscious (which a certain kind of abjection rampant in the analytic community confuses with the ambivalence of feelings, an ambivalence in which that community tends to bog down). Is the subject of this desire designated by the "I" of discourse? Certainly not, since the latter is simply the subject of the statement, which merely articulates the fear and its object, "I" here obviously being an index of the presence that enunciates it here and now—that is, being a shifter*. The subject of enunciation, insofar as his desire breaks through, lies nowhere else than in this *ne* whose value can be found in a form of haste in logic—"haste" being the name I give the function to which its use is tied in the phrase, *avant qu'il* ne *vienne* [before he comes]. So-called structure is not without a correlate in energetics, insofar as what I can define as the subject's fatigue manifests itself in neurosis as distinct from muscle fatigue.

A pest might object here that the unconscious cannot be involved, since, as everyone knows, it does not know time. He should go back to grammar class to learn to distinguish the time of chronology—the "aspect forms" that envision what the subject becomes there on the basis of the enunciation—from the forms that situate the statement on a timeline of events. Then he will stop confusing the subject of the perfective with the presence of the past, and will perhaps wake up to the idea that tension involves time and that identification occurs at a scansion's pace [*pas*].

In its uncertain obsolescence, however, this *ne* suggests the idea of a trace that is effaced along the path of a migration or, more precisely, of a puddle that brings out its outline. Couldn't the earliest signifier of negation have been the elision of a signifier? And isn't its vestige found in a form of phonemic censorship, of which we find, as usual, a memorable example in Freud's work—in the Wolf Man's *Espe* ([*W*]*espe*)? But there are many other linguistic forms that can be grouped together in analytic experience, beginning with the elision of the first syllable of the family name, by which the noble bastardy in which 665
a line originates is perpetuated in Russian—namely, in the socio-linguistic structures in force at the Wolf Man's birth.

Here is a suggestion for further research: Do the prefixes of negation merely indicate the place of this signifying ablation by occupying it anew?

The *tu* [silenced or shut up] of the unsaid would then be seen, in French's homophony, to give its form to the *tu* [you] one calls, by which the subject will send himself his own summonses.

I am risking a great deal here in a field in which I am not intimidated by any specialist allegiance. I am fully aware of what I am doing, and my goal here is to convey a structure in which I risk nothing, because it concerns the seriousness of analytic experience—namely, the link between defense and drive.

Lagache clearly indicates the tiresome cacophony of the whirling merry-go-round on which authors butt heads, or even asses, as they scramble in search of its mainsprings. Only psychoanalysts can appreciate the experience that sustains this literature, and seek out the feature that truly stands out in a certain impasse of this discourse. What Lagache points out, regarding the contradiction involved in attributing its success to a defense, leaves in abeyance the question of what it can succeed in.

To outline the relations between the subject and structure—structure being understood here as the structure of the signifier—is to restore the very possibility of the effects of defense. I am accused of claiming that language has magical power. But I profess, on the contrary, that to relate the power of language to some supposedly primitive aberration of the psyche is to render it obscure, and that to thus give it the consistency of an unthinkable fact renders us complicit in it. There is no greater betrayal of our own praxis than the one analysts stoop to thereby.

What I say, therefore, is that no suppression of the signifier—whatever effect of displacement it causes, and even if it were to go so far as to produce the form of sublimation that the term "*Aufhebung*" describes in German—can do any more than free from the drive a reality which, however slight the importance of need may be in it, will merely be all the more resistant because it is a remainder.

Defense creates its effect by another pathway, modifying not the tendency
666 but the subject. The earliest mode of signifying elision, which I am trying to conceptualize here as the matrix of *Verneinung* [negation], asserts the subject negatively, by preparing the void in which he finds his place. Strictly speaking, it is merely an enlargement of the cut in the signifying chain where he could be said to reside, insofar as it is the most radical element in the discontinuous sequence of the chain and, as such, the locus from which the subject assures its subsistence as chain.

It does not suffice for Lagache to tell us the subject "is not distinguished from the drive, from its aim and object." He has to choose, in what he distinguishes, in not wanting to distinguish it from the subject, and the proof thereof is that he immediately tells us that this subject is "dispersed among these different object-relations or *their groupings*" [page 21]. I have italicized this to again distinguish it from the further possibility of a multiplicity without grouping: a pure shimmering of Whole-Ones [*Tout-Uns*] which, while each of them counts an alternation, are not yet fixed in any range.

Be that as it may, we can recognize this union between the subject and the object: It is the ideal that has served since time immemorial as the basis of a classical theory of knowledge that is based on the connaturality with which the knower [*connaissant*], in the course of his knowing, comes to be born along with the known [*co-naître* au *connu*]. How can we fail to see that the whole of analytic experience runs counter to this? This is evinced in the fragmentation that analysis reveals to be there from the outset in the combinatory of the unconscious, and to be structuring in the breakdown of the drive into its component parts.

In short, when Lagache comes closest by saying that "this absence of a coherent subject best characterizes the organization of the id" [page 21], I would say that the absence of the subject, which is produced somewhere in the unorganized id, is the defense that one might call "natural"—however artificial the circle may be that is cleared by burning the brush of the drives—because it offers the other agencies a place to camp in order to organize their defenses.

This is the very place to which each and every thing is called to be washed of sin [*faute*], sin that this place makes possible since it is the place of an absence: for everything might not exist in the first place. It is not enough to note, with this very simple matrix of the first contradiction—to be or not to be—that the judgment of existence founds reality; we must articulate that the judgment
667 of existence can only found reality by raising reality up [*relever*] from the precarious status it has when this judgment receives it from a previously made judgment of attribution.

It is the structure of this place which demands that the nothing [*le rien*] be at the core of creation and which—elevating the subject's ignorance of the real that assigns him his condition to the role of something essential to our experience—forces psychoanalytic thought to be creationist, by which I mean, not content with some evolutionist reference. For the experience of desire in which that thought has to be deployed is the very experience of the want-to-be by which every being [*étant*] could not be at all, or could be other—in other words, by which every being is created as existent. It could be demonstrated that this faith lies at the core of Galileo's development of science.

Let us simply say that this place does not require any supreme being, because, since it is the place of *Plus-Personne* (No One Anymore), it can only be from elsewhere that the "it" of the impersonal is heard, an impersonal about which I myself formulated the question regarding the id at the appropriate time.[11] This question, with which the subject punctuates the signifier, does not encounter any other echo than the silence of the death drive, a drive that had to be involved at some point to provoke the backdrop of depression Melanie Klein reconstituted with the genius that guides her in following the thread of fantasies.

Otherwise the question intensifies in the horror of the answer given by an Odysseus who is more cunning than the legendary one: a divine Odysseus who plays tricks on another Polyphemus (a fine name for the unconscious) with superior derision, by getting him to demand to be nothing at the same time as he proclaims he is a person [*personne*], before blinding him by giving him an eye.

III. On the Ideals of the Person

The ego is this eye, I would say, to stop beating around the bush, unlike Lagache who admirably brings out perplexities in his article on the autonomy of the ego, which he takes to be intrasystemic, and which is never so manifest 668
as when it is serving another's law, being subjected to that law in the very act of defending against it, by first misrecognizing it.

This is the labyrinth through which I have always tried to guide my students by providing them with a bird's-eye view.

Let us say that, thanks to Lagache's suggestions, I will have added something to it here.

For my distinction between the space cleared out for the subject without him occupying it and the ego that finds lodging in that space, resolves the majority of the aporias outlined by Lagache, and even explains certain equivocations—as, for example, the strangeness Lagache attributes to the unconscious, that he knows only occurs when the subject encounters his narcissistic image. In light of what I have just said, I will add: when the subject encounters this image under conditions that make it appear to him to be usurping his place.

At the crux of the true resistances we have to deal with in psychoanalysts' convoluted theoretical discussions of the ego lies the simple refusal to admit that the ego's rightful status in analytic theory is the same as its stains in practice: a function of misrecognition.

This resistance is based on the fact that we clearly have to know something about reality in order to survive in it, and that it is obvious in practice that the experience that accumulates in the ego, especially in the preconscious, provides us landmarks that prove to be the surest for survival. But we forget—and shouldn't we be surprised that it is analysts who forget it?—that this argument founders when what is at stake is . . . the effects of the unconscious. Now these effects extend their influence to the ego itself; indeed, Freud introduced his theory of the relations between the ego and the id expressly to assert this—thus, to extend the field of our ignorance, not of our knowledge. The power of the ego that he later revalidated has to do with an entirely different question.

It is because and insofar as the ego comes to serve in the place left empty for the subject, that it cannot help causing there the distortion [*distorsion*] which (translating into English the foundational *Entstellung* in every drive) has now become the basis in our vocabulary for another error: that of believing that
669 the task of psychoanalysis is to straighten out some sort of curvature of the ego. But the distortions [*déformations*] that impede our progress are not due to the greater or lesser thickness of the lens. There always has to be a lens, in effect, since the naked eye contains one. It is because the lens comes to occupy the place from which the subject can look, and alights on the object-holder that is in fact focused on there when the subject looks from elsewhere, that he superimposes himself, to the great detriment of the whole, on what can come to be ogled there.

Since it is the exemplary fate of diagrams—insofar as they are geometrical, that is—to lend themselves to intuitions based on ego-like errors, let us begin with what is ineradicably sustained by Freud's rash figuration of the relations between the ego and the id,[12] the figuration that I will call the egg with an eye. It is famous for cramming skulls, to which it appeals by condensing, in a signifier suggestive of some sort of lecithin doping for nutritional purposes, the metaphor of the embryonic spot in the very bump that is supposed to represent differentiation in it ("superficial differentiation," people rejoice to think), brought there from the outside world. A geneticism—in which Antiquity's lures concerning the knowledge of love are extended for the use of primates—is thus flattered by the pathways of surprise (in all senses of the word) characteristic of the unconscious.

We need not utterly disdain these lures, however untenable they may be in a rigorous science. For they retain their value at the artisanal and folkloric levels, so to speak. They may even be of considerable use in a bed. They need some focusing, however, analytic technique leaving little to be hoped for from some sort of natural access to them—Longus' pastoral, *Daphnis and Chloe*, gives some hints in this direction, as do more generally the apprenticeships by which the notorious habituses of scholastic psychology are formed.

Let us finish off this Cyclopean egg. It is but a shell—and the double bar that branches off from its curve suffices to indicate its vacuity, along with the image of the slit that makes it resemble a piggy-bank, with which I identified it earlier. As for the magnifying glass [*loupe*], evocative of the lavaterian tumescence, let us say that it most often strolls around on the inside like a little bell, 670
allowing for a musical use, generally illustrated by the historical development of both literary and scientific psychology. All that is missing is a handle and a few frills for us to have the rattle of confirmed madmen, the antidote to humanism, recognized since Erasmus' time as giving humanism its savor.

It is common in our teaching to distinguish what the function of the ego imposes on the world in its imaginary projections, from the defense effects those projections have by filling the place where judgment is made.

And after all, hasn't all that been known and repeated since time immemorial? Why would Freud need to add to this indication that a judgment must assume the position of repression, if not because repression already occupies the position of judgment? When people contest the function I define, following Freud, as *Verwerfung* (foreclosure), do they think they have refuted me by noting that the verb, of which this is the nominal form, is applied to judgment in more than one of Freud's texts? It is only the structural locus in which the exclusion of a signifier occurs that varies between these proceedings of a faculty of judgment that is unified by analytic experience. Here it is in the very symphysis of the code with the locus of the Other that lies the chink in existence that all the judgments about reality in which psychosis develops are unable to fix.

Let me take the opportunity offered by Lagache's review of the relations between the unconscious and the preconscious, to recall—only to those who try to take issue with me on the basis of the link Freud establishes between the preconscious system and verbal memories—that we must not confuse the recollecting of statements with the structures of enunciation, or Gestalt-based links, however invigorated, with the connections [*trames*] of remembering. Recall too that if the conditions of representability inflect the unconscious according to their imaginary forms, there must be a common structure in order for a symbolism, however primitive we assume it to be in the unconscious, to be able *to be translated*—this is its essential feature—into a preconscious discourse (see Freud's letter 52 to Fliess, to which I have repeatedly referred).

671 I must now, finally, turn to the masterly distinction Lagache makes between the functions of the ideal ego and the ego-ideal.[13] Is it not here that we must gauge the well-foundedness of the thesis that guides his study in a personalist direction?

If, indeed, psychoanalysis did not in some way transform the problem of the "person," why would people try to accommodate its data within a perspective that, after all, has hardly proved its mettle in the real world?

To point out that the *persona* is a mask is not to indulge in a simple etymological game; it is to evoke the ambiguity of the process by which this notion has managed to assume the value of incarnating a unity that is supposedly affirmed in being.

Now, the first datum of our experience shows us that the figure of the mask, being split, is not symmetrical. To express this in an image, the figure joins together two profiles whose unity is tenable only if the mask remains closed, its discordance nevertheless instructing us to open it. But what about being, if there is nothing behind it? And if there is only a face, what about the *persona*?

Let me note here that in order to differentiate the ideal ego from the ego-ideal functionally, if not structurally, Lagache adopts a path he at first rejected, that of providing a description of what is "directly observable" in a clinical analysis [page 6]. I believe I am staying faithful to the letter of his text, formulated with an engaging finesse, in paraphrasing him as follows: In a subject's relation to the other as an authority, the ego-ideal, obeying the law to please, leads the subject to displease himself as the price of obeying the commandment; the ideal ego, at the risk of displeasing, triumphs only by pleasing in spite of the commandment.

At this point we might expect Lagache to return to what he says about a structure "at some distance from experience." For, if we remain at the level of the phenomenon, nowhere is the risk of trusting in mirages greater, since one can say that, in at least one respect, these agencies present themselves as mirages
672 in lived experience: the ego-ideal as a model, and the ideal ego as an aspiration (and to such a significant extent), not to say as a dream. This is certainly an occasion to turn for help to what analytic experimentation allows us to construct by way of a metapsychology.

If, although Freud distinguishes the terms ego-ideal and ideal ego in an unmistakable fashion, since the inversion [of adjective and noun] occurs in one and the same text, we still cannot distinguish their use in that text, this should worry us, for, to the best of our knowledge, Freud was never even slightly sloppy in his use of signifiers. Or must we conclude that his topography is not personalist?

I will skip here what is more or less structural or personalist in the insights of Nunberg and Fromm, as well as Fenichel's arbitration—finding what they have to say, as is usual in such debates, rather glib, too much so for my taste, as you know.

Instead, I will risk exposing my own insufficiency by informing Lagache of something that the excessive demands of our work has prevented from coming to his attention—namely, the "model" (strictly speaking) with which I myself tried, the first year of my seminar at Saint Anne Hospital, to illustrate the functioning in the structure of the relations between the ideal ego and the ego-ideal.

It is an optical model that is, of course, sanctioned by Freud's example, and my interest in it can be explained by its affinity with the refractive effects conditioned by the split between the symbolic and the imaginary.

Let me begin by introducing a somewhat complicated device, the use value of which as a model will depend on analogy, as is the rule in such cases.

As we know, when an object is placed at the center of curvature of a spherical mirror, an image is produced that is symmetrical to the object; but what is crucial here is that it is a real image. Under certain conditions—like those of experiments whose only value lay in a still innocent interest in mastering the phenomenon, and which are now relegated to the status of recreational physics—this image can be captured by the eye in its reality, without the commonly used medium of a screen. This is the case in the so-called inverted bouquet illusion, a description of which (to give a serious reference) can be found in *Optique et photométrie dites géométriques* (geometry resurfacing 673
here) by Bouasse, who is a rather curious figure in the history of the field. See page 86 of his book for our object; I will leave for others the gadgets described in the same work that are equally thought provoking since they are less trivial (4th edition, Delagrave, 1947). You will find below a reproduction of the figure provided on page 87 (Figure 1). I will limit my commentary to saying that the real bouquet concealed in the box, S, "to add" as Bouasse puts it "to one's surprise," seems, to an eye focused on the vase, V, that stands on top of the box, to emerge from the neck, A´, of the said vase where the image, B´, appears quite clearly, despite some distortion that the irregular shape of the original object should make quite tolerable.

FIGURE 1

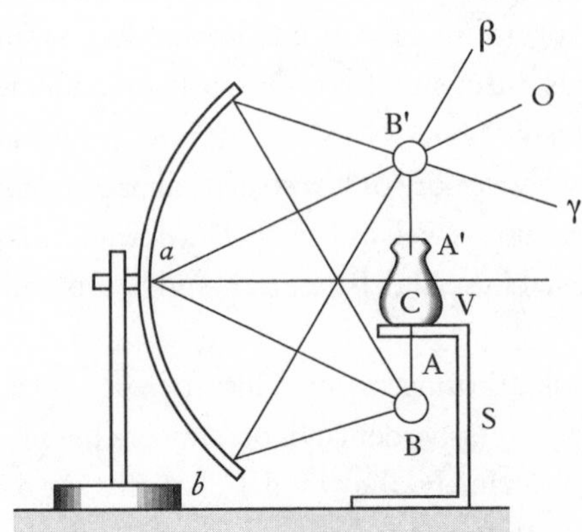

It should be kept in mind, however, that the illusion only occurs if the eye is situated inside the cone, βB´γ, formed by a generatrix joining each point of the image, B´, to the circumference of the spherical mirror; and that, since the cone of converging rays captured by the eye for each point of the image is very small, the image will be more clearly situated in its position the greater its distance from the eye. For this distance gives the eye more room for the linear displacement that is more useful to it than focusing for locating that position, provided the image does not waver too much with the displacement.

The care I am taking in presenting this device is intended to give consis-
674 tency to the elements with which I am going to complete it so that it can function as a theoretical model.

With this model and even its optical nature, I am merely following Freud's example, except that my model includes nothing to prevent it from being confused with a schema of anatomical conduction pathways.

For, as we shall see, the links that will analogically appear here clearly relate to (intra)subjective structures as such, representing the relation to the other here, and making it possible to distinguish here the twofold impact of the imaginary and the symbolic. I have stressed the importance of this distinction for the construction of the subject, once we are forced to conceptualize the subject as the subject in which it [*ça*] can speak, without him knowing anything about it (and even about whom we must say that he knows nothing about it insofar as he speaks).

To do so we have to imagine, in accordance with Figure 2, firstly, that the vase is inside the box and that its real image comes to enclose with its neck the bouquet of flowers that is already mounted on top of the box; the bouquet will play the role of a prop for a possible eye to focus on, a prop that is, as I just indicated, necessary to produce the illusion, which should now be called the inverted vase illusion. We have to imagine, secondly, that an observer—placed somewhere in the device, say, among the flowers themselves or, for the sake of clarity, on the edge of the spherical mirror, but in any case outside of the cone in which the real image can be seen (this is why the real image is not represented in Figure 2)—tries to bring about the illusion by placing a plane mirror in position A; for this plane mirror can provide a virtual image of the real image, without bending the laws of optics. 675

FIGURE 2

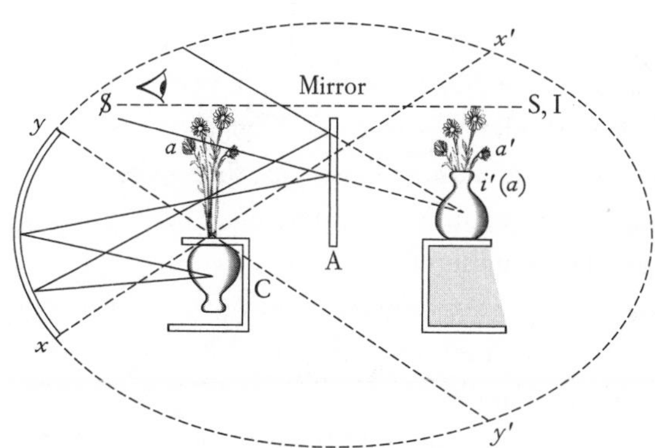

Now in order for the subject, S̸, to see this image in mirror A, it suffices to have his own image (in the virtual space engendered by the mirror, and without it being necessary that he see his image, for he might be outside the field orthogonal to the mirror's surface; see Figure 2 and the dotted line, S̸S) come, in real space (to which the virtual space engendered by a plane mirror corresponds point for point), to be situated inside the cone that delimits the possibility of the illusion (the field x´y´ in Figure 2).

The play of this model partly overlaps the function of misrecognition that my conception of the mirror stage locates at the crux of ego formation. It allows us to state it in what might be termed a generalized form by better linking to the structure the effects of the child's assumption of his specular image—as I considered it justified to interpret those effects in the jubilatory moment in which that assumption electively occurs, between the ages of 6 and 18 months, basing them on a perceptual prematuration inscribed in a discordance in neurological development.

The relations between the images, *i´(a)* and *i(a)*, in my model are not to be taken literally in their optical subordination, but as propping up an analogous imaginary subordination.

For in *i′(a)*, there is not simply what the subject of the model expects to find there, but already a form of the other whose power, no less than the play of bearing relations that begin there, inserts it as a principle of false mastery and fundamental alienation into a synthesis that requires a very different adequation.

It is in order to represent the conditions of this latter, in their theoretical anteriority, that I have placed the illusion of the image, *i(a)*, at the beginning of my model.

676 If this image in fact involves a subjectification, it is, in the first place, through the pathways of autoconduction figured in the model by the reflection in the spherical mirror (which can be taken roughly as depicting some global cortical function). And what the model also indicates with the vase hidden in the box is the scant access the subject has to the reality of this body, which he loses inside himself, at the limit where—a fold of layers that coalesce with his envelope, stitching themselves around the orifice rings—he imagines it to be like a glove that can be turned inside out. There are body techniques where the subject tries to awaken in his consciousness a configuration of this obscure intimacy. The analytic process, being far removed from such techniques, scands the libidinal progress with accents that bear on the body as a container and on its orifices.

Contemporary analysis, more particularly, links the maturation of this progress to something that it designates as object-relations; I emphasize their guiding function when I represent them by the flowers, *a*, in my model—that is, by the very objects the subject focuses on in order to perceive the image, *i(a)*.

But such a model can also help us avoid the biases toward which the most common conceptions of these relations tend. For, acting as a parable, it allows us to indicate the dearth of naturalness involved in a vase-neck's grasp (imaginary, moreover) on elements—flower stems—the bundle of which is completely indeterminate in both its link and its diversity.

The notion of part-object seems to me to be the most accurate discovery analysis has made here, but it made it at the cost of postulating an ideal totalization of this object, thereby losing the benefit of the discovery.

It does not thus seem self-evident to me that the fragmentation of relational functions, which I have articulated as primordial in the mirror stage, is a guarantee that synthesis will continue to grow as the tendencies evolve. Menenius Agrippa's fable has always seemed to me to show—whatever the success of his sweet-talk—that a harmony that is presumed to be organic, in ordering desires, has sold well in all eras. I do not believe Freud emancipated our views on sexuality and its aims so that analysis could add its own mumbo

jumbo to moralists' secular efforts to bring man's desires back to the norms 677
of his needs.

At any rate, the antinomy of the images, *i(a)* and *i′(a)*, being situated for the subject in the imaginary, resolves into a constant transitivism. A sort of ego-ideal-ego is thus produced, whose boundaries (in Federn's sense) are to be taken as propping up uncertainty and allowing for rectification, as perpetuating the equivocation of different circumscriptions that vary according to their status, and even as accepting free zones and isolated fiefs into their complex.

What is striking to me is that psychoanalysis, which operates in the symbolic—and this is indisputable if it proceeds by conquering the unconscious, bringing history into being, and reconstructing the signifier, assuming one does not simply deny that its medium is speech—is able to reshape an ego that is thus constituted in its imaginary status.

Although the phenomenon of vanishing (I call it "fading"*) that Lagache attributes to the subject-ego [page 17] seems noteworthy to me here, I do not confine my attention, as he does, to refinding therein the direction of an abstract noesis; rather, I connote the phenomenon by the structural effect with which I try to constitute the subject's place in the elision of a signifier.

The ego-ideal is a formation that comes to this symbolic place. This is why it is based on the ego's unconscious coordinates. Freud developed his second topography to explain this, as is perfectly clear from reading it, as is the fact that he did not develop it to pave the way for a return of the autonomous ego.

For the question he raises in *Group Psychology and the Analysis of the Ego* is how an object, reduced to its stupidest reality, but functioning for a certain number of subjects as a common denominator (confirming what I will say momentarily about its function as an insignia), can bring about an identification of the ideal ego with the very moronic power of misadventure that the ideal ego turns out to be at its core. Need I mention, to convey the scope of the question, the figure of the Führer and the collective phenomena that have given Freud's text its value of clairvoyance into the very heart of civilization? Indeed I need do so, since, in a comedic reversal of what Freud
wanted to contribute by way of a remedy to civilization's discontents, the 678
very community to which he bequeathed this remedial task has proclaimed the synthesis of a strong ego as a watchword, at the heart of a technique in which the practitioner believes that he obtains results by incarnating this ideal himself.

Be that as it may, these two examples are not designed to banish the function of speech from the determinants we are seeking for the higher jurisdiction [*ressort*] of subjectification.

As you know, I designate this jurisdiction of speech in my topology as the

Other (connoted by a capital *A*). Corresponding to this locus in my model is the real space on which are superimposed the virtual images "behind the mirror"—that is, mirror A (whether we adopt the convention of having the subject accede to this space by free displacement, or, if the mirror is unsilvered and thus transparent to his gaze, by adjusting his position there to some I).

It would be a mistake to think that the Other (with a capital *O*) of discourse can be absent from any distance that the subject achieves in his relationship with the other, the other (with a lowercase *o*) of the imaginary dyad. Lagache's attempt to provide a personalist translation of Freud's second topography, while it certainly cannot be exhaustive in my view, is still less equal to the task because it is content to take the distance between two reciprocal terms as the medium of intersubjectivity on which its principle is based.

For the Other where discourse is situated, which is always latent in the triangulation that consecrates this distance, is not latent as long as it extends all the way to the purest moment of the specular relation: to the gesture by which the child at the mirror turns toward the person who is carrying him and appeals with a look to this witness; the latter decants the child's recognition of the image, by verifying it, from the jubilant assumption in which *it* [elle] certainly *already was*.

But this "already" should not mislead us as to the structure of the presence evoked as a third party here: it owes nothing to the anecdotal personage who incarnates it.

All that subsists here is the being whose advent can only be grasped by no longer being. This is how the most ambiguous tense in the morphology of French verbs, the imperfect, encounters that being. *Il était là* [He was to be there] contains the same duplicity we find in *Un moment plus tard, la bombe éclatait* [The bomb was to explode a moment later], where, without any context, we cannot know whether the event occurred or not.

679 This being is nevertheless posited with the grounding anteriority that it is assured by discourse, in that reserve of attributes in which I say that the subject must make room for himself.

If our contemporary analysts misrecognize, along with this dimension, the experience they inherited from Freud—finding nothing in it but a pretext for renewing a form of geneticism that is always and inescapably the same, since it is erroneous—their sin is revealed by the sole resurgence in their theories of old stigmata, such as the notorious cenesthesia, in which we see the lack of the third point in what is never anything but lame recourse to noesis. But it seems that they can never learn anything when they even fail to acknowledge the blow dealt to their idea of development by what is known as "hospitalism," in which mothering attentions are clearly seen to have no other deficiency than the *anonymity* with which they are meted out.

But how can the earliest subject refind this place in the elision that constitutes it as absence? How can he recognize this void as the Thing that is closest to him, even if he were to deepen it again in the Other's bosom by making *his* cry resound there? He will prefer, rather, to refind there the marks of response that had the power to turn his cry into a call. These marks, in which the all-powerfulness of the response are inscribed, are thus circled in reality with the signifier's line [*trait*]. It is not without reason that these realities are called "insignias." The term is nominative here. It is the constellation of these insignias that constitutes the subject's ego-ideal.

My model shows that it is by situating himself at I that he can tilt mirror A to obtain, among other effects, a certain mirage of the ideal ego.

This is precisely how the neurotic handles the Other in order to constantly renew his sketchy identifications in the wild transference that legitimates our use of the term "transference neuroses."

This is not the whole of the neurotic's subjective mainspring, and I will say why. But we can use my model to question him regarding what becomes of this handling of the Other in psychoanalysis itself.

Without harboring any illusions as to the import of an exercise that carries
weight only by virtue of a crude analogy to the phenomena it allows us to 680
evoke, I propose in Figure 3 an idea of what happens when the Other is an analyst, the subject making him into the locus of his speech.

Since analysis is based on what the subject gains from assuming [*assumer*] his unconscious discourse as his own, its trajectory corresponds in the model to a translation of $\$$ to the signifiers of the space "behind the mirror." The function of the model is then to depict how mirror relations—that is, the imaginary relation to the other and the [visual] capture involved in the ideal ego—drag the subject into the field where he hypostasizes himself in the ego-ideal.

Without entering into a degree of detail that might seem exaggerated, one could say that by progressively effacing itself until it is at a 90-degree angle from where it started, the Other, as mirror A, can, through an almost double rotation, lead the subject from $\$_1$ to occupy position $\$_2$ at I, a position which gave him only virtual access to the inverted vase illusion in Figure 2. In this movement, however, the illusion fades along with the quest that it guides, confirming that the effects of depersonalization observed in analysis, in more or less discrete forms, should be considered less as signs of a limit than of a breakthrough [*franchissement*].

FIGURE 3

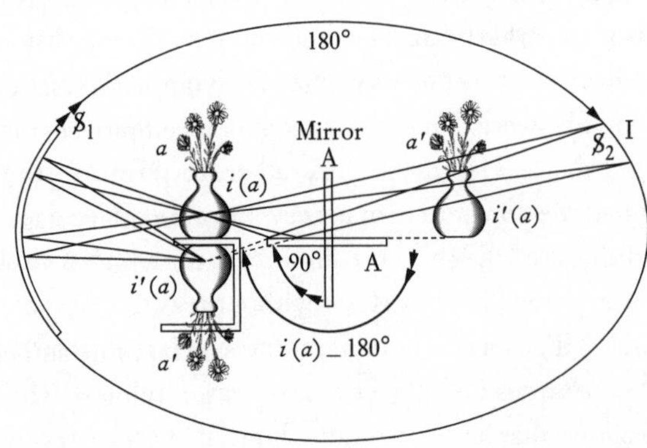

681 For the model again shows that, once the eye, S̸, has reached position I, from which it directly perceives the inverted vase illusion, it also sees, in the now horizontal mirror A, a virtual image of the same vase, *i´(a)*, inverting the real image anew, as it were, and opposing it, like its reflection in water (whether still or moving) gives dream roots to a tree.

We have here the interplay of bank and waters that, let us note, delighted pre-classical mannerism, from Tristan l'Hermite to Cyrano, not without unconscious motives, for poetry was merely anticipating the revolution of the subject, which was signaled in philosophy by the raising of existence to the function of first attribute, not without producing its effects on the basis of a new science, politics, and society.

Can't the artistic indulgences that accompanied it be explained by the value given in the same era to the artifices of anamorphosis?—that is, of the existential divorce in which the body vanishes in spatiality, those artifices that instate in the very prop of perspective a hidden image, reevoking the substance that was lost there. Were my model realizable, it would be amusing to note that the real jar in its box (where the reflection from mirror A alights) contains the imaginary flowers, *a´*, whereas it is the inverted jar illusion (made of a realer image) that contains the true flowers, *a*.

What the model thus depicts is a state Michael Balint describes as the narcissistic effusion that, in his opinion, signals the end of an analysis. His description of it would have been better had he noted an analogous crisscrossing in it: one in which the individual's very specular presence to the other, although it covers his reality, uncovers his ego-related illusion regarding a consciousness of the body as frozen, while the power of object *a*—which, at the end of all these machinations, centers this consciousness—reduces his reflection in the objects *a´* of omnivalent competition to the status of vanities.

According to Michael Balint, in the state of elation that results, the patient believes he has exchanged his ego for his analyst's ego. Let us hope, for his sake, that nothing of the kind has happened.

For even if it is the terminus of the analysis, it is not analysis' end, and even if we see here the end of the means the analysis has employed, they are not the means by which to reach its end.

Which is to say that my model dates back to a preliminary stage of my teaching at which I needed to clear away the imaginary which was overvalued in analytic technique. We are no longer at that stage. 682

I draw people's attention back to desire, which, far more authentically than any ideal-based quest, regulates the neurotic's signifying repetition as well as his metonymy, as people tend to forget. This is not the place for me to say how he has to maintain this desire as unsatisfied (the hysteric) or as impossible (the obsessive).

For my model fails to shed light on object *a*. In depicting a play of images, it cannot describe the function this object receives from the symbolic.

This function gives it the role of an arm at the phobic outpost, an arm against the threat of desire's disappearance, and the role of a fetish in perverse structure, as the absolute condition of desire.

At the point of departure where my model situates it, *a*, the object of desire, is from the moment it begins to function there . . . the object of desire. This means that, while it is a partial object, it is not merely a part, or a spare part [*pièce détachée*] of the device that depicts the body here, but an element of the structure from the outset, and, so to speak, in the initial deal of the cards for the game that is then played out. Being selected as the index of desire from among the body's appendages, object *a* is already the exponent of a function, a function that sublimates it even before it exercises the function; this function is that of the index raised toward an absence about which the "it" [*est-ce*] has nothing to say, if not that this absence comes from where it speaks [*ça parle*].

This is why, when reflected in the mirror, it not only gives us *a*′, the standard of exchange, the currency with which the other's desire enters the circuit of the ideal ego's transitivisms. It is also restored to the field of the Other, serving the function of desire's exponent in the Other.

This is what allows it to take on its elective value at the true terminus of analysis, by figuring, in the fundamental fantasy, that before which the subject sees himself being abolished when he realizes himself as desire.

In order for the subject to accede to this point beyond the reduction of the ideals of the person, it is as desire's object *a*, as what he was to the Other in his erection as a living being, as *wanted** or *unwanted** when he came into the world, that he is called to be reborn in order to know if he wants what he desires . . . This is the kind of truth Freud brought to light with the invention of analysis.

683 It is a field in which the subject has, above all, to do a lot personally to pay the steep ransom for his desire. This is why psychoanalysis calls for an overhauling of ethics.

It is clear, on the contrary, that to flee this task, analysts are prepared to abandon virtually everything, and even to treat problems the subject has assuming his sex in terms of sex roles, as we now see being done in Freudian circles.

The Φ function of the lost signifier, to which the subject sacrifices his phallus, the form $\Phi(a)$ of male desire and $\not{A}\varphi$ of woman's desire, lead us to the end of analysis, the aporia of which Freud bequeathed us with [the concept of] castration. The fact that Lagache does not include the latter's effect in his field suffices to demonstrate the limits of what we can comprehend of the subject of the unconscious in personalist terms.[14]

IV. Toward an Ethics

I saved the structure of the superego for my conclusion. This is because we can only discuss it by examining the Freudian discovery more broadly, namely, from the vantage point of existence. We must realize the extent to which the advent of the subject who speaks banishes the subject of knowledge—whose status as a person was called into question long ago, as the notion of the agent intellect suffices to remind us. I am not, I might remark, the one who is responsible for bringing people back to the crossroads of practical reason.

If Kant's proposition—that there are but two instances in which the subject can see the heteronomy of his being figured, provided he contemplates them "with wonder and respect," which are "the starry sky above him and the moral law within him"—is confirmed here, the conditions under which this contemplation is possible have nevertheless changed.

The infinite spaces have paled behind little letters that more surely prop up the equation of the universe; and the only beings we are willing to grant any say in the matter, apart from our scientists, are other inhabitants who might
684 send us signs of intelligence—which is why the silence of these spaces no longer frightens us in any way.

It is also why we have begun dumping our garbage in them, intending to make these spaces into the landfills that have been the very hallmark of our "hominization" of the planet since prehistoric times—oh, Teilhard the paleontologist, had you forgotten this?

The same goes for the moral law, and for the same reason that makes us shift from language to speech. It also makes us discover that the superego, in its intimate imperative, is indeed "the voice of conscience," that is, a voice first and foremost, a vocal one at that, and without any authority other than that of being a loud voice: the voice that at least one text in the Bible tells us was heard by the people parked around Mount Sinai. This artifice even suggests that its enunciation echoed back to them their own murmur, the Tables of the Law being nonetheless necessary in order for them to know what it enunciated.

Now, for those who know how to read, what is written on those tables is nothing but the laws of Speech itself. In other words, the person truly begins with the *per-sona*, but where does personality begin? An ethics arises, which is converted to silence, not by way of fear, but of desire; and the question is how analysis' pathway of chatter leads to it.

I will remain silent here regarding its practical direction.

But, theoretically speaking, can its goal be to bring the ego to the fore [*dégagement du Moi*]? And what can be expected of it, if its possibilities, to use Lagache's term, only offer the subject the overly indeterminate exit that diverts him from an overly difficult pathway, the one from which we might think it has always been the political secret of moralists to incite the subject to remove [*dégager*] something—his stakes from the game of desire? In this game, humanism is no longer anything but a dilettante's profession.

Does *noscit*, he knows, come from an elision of *ignoscit*, which etymology shows us to have but a false prefix, and which, moreover, does not mean a non-knowledge, but rather the forgetting that consummates forgiveness?

Would *nescit*, to alter but a single letter in it, lead us to suspect that the only negation it contains is retroactively (*nachträglich*) feigned? What does it matter, since, like the negations whose constancy we found laughable in metaphysical objects, this one is but a mask—a mask of first persons.

Notes

1. Especially in my seminar this academic year, 1959–1960, on the ethics of psychoanalysis [Seminar VII, 145–46/120–21].

2. [Added in 1966:] "Today, anthropology is structuralist. One of its major characteristics is the promotion of the category of 'set,' of *unitas multiplex* [. . .]. We begin with the idea that we are not dealing with isolated elements or with sums of elements, but rather with sets whose parts are themselves structured." Daniel Lagache, "La psychanalyse et la structure de la personnalité" (paper given at the Royaumont Colloquium, July 10–13, 1958), published in *La Psychanalyse* 6 (1961): 5.

3. [Added in 1966:] "*The psychological field* is the set of relations between the organism and its entourage. [. . .] There is no organism that is not in a situation, nor is there a situation except for an organism. This necessity is, in the final analysis, geometrical." In Lagache, "La psychanalyse et la structure de la personnalité," 5.

4. At a symposium on structure, held under the auspices of Mr. Bastide.

5. [Added in 1966:] If we are to believe these authors, Freud, in his second model of the psyche, "took as his criterion the *function* of systems or substructures in conflict, and the model

which inspired him was physiology; the role of structural concepts was to favor causal explanations, and if they are among our most valuable tools, it is because they are situated within a genetic context."

6. [Added in 1966:] "The notion of primal differentiation is preferable to that of non-differentiation. [It] is demonstrated by the existence of systems that assure the subject a minimum of autonomy: perceptual, motor, and memory systems, and discharge thresholds for needs and affects. [W]ithout existing as a cognitive structure, the subject functions and actualizes himself successively in the needs that awaken and motivate him. [. . .] These functional object relations are not structured, in the sense that the subject and the object are not differentiated." Lagache, "La psychanalyse et la structure de la personnalité," 15–16.

7. The Thing (*das Ding*) here is antedated, having been introduced only in my seminar this past year, 1959–1960. But this is why the mustard jar offered all the guarantees of incomprehension I needed in order to have it out with it.

8. It is with this question that I initiated my examination of the ethics of psychoanalysis this year, 1959–1960.

9. See *Écrits* 1966, 708.

10. See *Écrits* 1966, 793–827.

11. In a talk in memory of the centennial of Freud's birth, published as "The Freudian Thing"; see *Écrits* 1966, 401–36 [especially 417].

12. The illustration is found in *GW* XIII, 252 [*SE* XIX, 24]. Examined carefully, it confirms my view of Freud's aims in attending to the ego in the second topography.

13. "[T]he antinomy between the ideal ego and the superego/ego-ideal, between narcissistic identification with omnipotence and submission to omnipotence," in Lagache, "La psychanalyse et la structure de la personnalité," 46.

14. [Added in 1966:] See "Position of the Unconscious" in *Écrits* 1966, 830–50.

The Signification of the Phallus 685
Die Bedeutung des Phallus

The following is the unaltered text of a lecture I gave in German on May 9, 1958, at the Max Planck Society in Munich, having been invited to speak there by Professor Paul Matussek.

If one has any notion of the mentality then prevalent in not otherwise uninformed circles, one can imagine how my use of terms that I was the first to extract from Freud's work, such as "the other scene" (to cite one mentioned here), must have resounded.

If deferred action (*Nachtrag*), to take back another of these terms from the domain of the highbrow literati where they now circulate, makes this effort impracticable, it should be realized that they were unheard of at that time.

We know that the unconscious castration complex functions as a knot:

(1) in the dynamic structuring of symptoms, in the analytic sense of the term, in other words, in the dynamic structuring of what is analyzable in the neuroses, perversions, and psychoses;

(2) in regulating the development that gives its *ratio* to this first role: namely, the instating in the subject of an unconscious position without which he could not identify with the ideal type of his sex or even answer the needs of his partner in sexual relations without grave risk, much less appropriately meet the needs of the child who may be produced thereby.

There is an antinomy here that is internal to the assumption [*assomption*] by man *(Mensch)* of his sex: why must he assume the attributes of that sex only through a threat or even in the guise of a deprivation? In *Civilization and Its Discontents,* Freud, as we know, went so far as to suggest not a contingent but an essential disturbance of human sexuality, and one of his last articles concerns the irreducibility—in any finite *(endliche)* analysis—of the aftermath of the castration complex in the masculine unconscious and of *Penisneid* [penis envy] in woman's unconscious.

This is not the only aporia, but it is the first that Freudian experience and the metapsychology that resulted from it introduced into our experience of man. It cannot be solved by reducing things to biological data; the very neces- 686 sity of the myth underlying the structuring brought on by the Oedipus complex demonstrates this sufficiently.

It would be mere artifice to invoke in this case some inherited forgotten experience, not only because such an experience is in itself debatable, but because it leaves the problem unsolved: what is the link between killing the father and the pact of the primordial law, if we include here the fact that castration is the punishment for incest?

It is only on the basis of clinical facts that the discussion can be fruitful. These facts reveal a relation between the subject and the phallus that forms without regard to the anatomical distinction between the sexes and that is thus especially difficult to interpret in the case of women and with respect to women, particularly as concerns the following four points:

(1) why a little girl considers herself, even for a moment, to be castrated, in the sense of deprived of a phallus, by someone whom she at first identifies as her mother—an important point—and then as her father, but in such a way that one must recognize therein a transference in the analytic sense of the term;

(2) why, more primordially, both sexes consider the mother to be endowed with a phallus, that is, to be a phallic mother;

(3) why, correlatively, the signification of castration in fact takes on its (clinically manifest) full weight in the formation of symptoms only on the basis of its discovery as the mother's castration;

(4) these three problems lead, finally, to the why and wherefore of the "phallic phase" in development. Freud, as we know, uses this term to refer to the first genital maturation insofar as, on the one hand, it would seem to be characterized by the imaginary dominance of the phallic attribute and by masturbatory jouissance and, on the other, he localizes this jouissance in the case of women in the clitoris, which is thus raised to the function of the phallus. He thus seems to exclude in both sexes any instinctual map-
687 ping of the vagina as the site of genital penetration until the end of this phase, that is, until the dissolution of the Oedipus complex.

This ignorance smacks of misrecognition in the technical sense of the term—all the more so in that it is sometimes fabricated. Could it correspond to anything other than the fable in which Longus depicts Daphnis and Chloe's initiation as dependent upon the explanations of an old woman?

This is what has led certain authors to regard the phallic phase as the effect of a repression, and the function assumed in it by the phallic object as a symptom. The problem begins when one asks, *which* symptom? Phobia, says one, perversion, says another, and sometimes the same person says both. In the latter case, the quandary is evident: not that interesting transmutations of the object of a phobia into a fetish do not occur, but if they are interesting it is precisely owing to their different places in the structure. It would be pointless to ask these authors to formulate this difference from the perspectives currently in favor that go by the name of "object relations." For on this subject they have no other reference than the approximate notion of part-object, which has never been subjected to criticism since Karl Abraham introduced it. This is unfortunate given the comfort it offers analysts today.

The fact remains that the now abandoned discussion of the phallic phase, if one rereads the surviving texts from 1928–32, is refreshing for the example it sets of doctrinal passion—making one nostalgic, given psychoanalysis' decline following its American transplantation.

Were one to merely summarize the debate, one could but distort the authentic diversity of positions taken up by Helene Deutsch, Karen Horney, and Ernest Jones, to mention only the most eminent.

The series of three articles Jones devoted to the subject is especially suggestive—if only for the first sighting on which he built, which is signaled by the term he introduced: "aphanisis." For in raising, quite rightly, the problem of the relation between castration and desire, he demonstrates his inability to recognize what he nevertheless closes in on so nearly that the term, which will soon provide us with the key, seems to emerge in his work due to its very absence.

Particularly amusing is the way he manages to extract from the very letter
of Freud's text a position that is strictly contrary to it: a true model in a diffi- 688
cult genre.

Yet the question refuses to let itself be dodged, seeming to scoff at Jones' plea to reestablish the equality of natural rights (doesn't it push him to the point where he closes with the Biblical "Male and female created He them"?). What does he, in fact, gain by normalizing the function of the phallus as a part-object if he has to invoke its presence in the mother's body as an "internal object," a term based on fantasies revealed by Melanie Klein, and if he becomes still more unable to separate himself from her views, relating these fantasies to the recurrence, as far back as earliest infancy, of the Oedipal formation?

We will not be led astray if we reexamine the question by asking what could have led Freud to his obviously paradoxical position. For one has to admit that he was better guided than anyone in his recognition of the order of unconscious phenomena, of which he was the inventor, and that, in the absence of an adequate articulation of the nature of these phenomena, his followers were destined to lose their way to a greater or lesser degree.

It is on the basis of this wager—which I place at the crux of the commentary on Freud's work I have been pursuing for seven years—that I have been led to certain results: first and foremost, to promote the notion of the signifier as necessary to any articulation of the analytic phenomenon, insofar as it is opposed to that of the signified in modern linguistic analysis. Freud could not have taken into account modern linguistics, which postdates him, but I would maintain that Freud's discovery stands out precisely because, in setting out from a domain in which one could not have expected to encounter linguistics' reign, it had to anticipate its formulations. Conversely, it is Freud's discovery that gives the signifier/signified opposition its full scope: for the signifier plays an active role in determining the effects by which the signifiable appears to succumb to its mark, becoming, through that passion, the signified.

This passion of the signifier thus becomes a new dimension of the human condition in that it is not only man who speaks, but in man and through man
689 that it [*ça*] speaks; in that his nature becomes woven by effects in which the structure of the language of which he becomes the material can be refound; and in that the relation of speech thus resonates in him, beyond anything that could have been conceived of by the psychology of ideas.

In this sense one can say that the consequences of the discovery of the unconscious have not yet been so much as glimpsed in analytic theory, although its impact has been felt in analytic praxis more than we realize, even if only in the form of people beating a retreat from it.

Let me make it clear that my emphasis on man's relation to the signifier as such has nothing to do with a "culturalist" position, in the ordinary sense of the term—the position Karen Horney, for example, anticipated in the debate over the phallus, a position Freud described as feminist. It is not man's relationship to language as a social phenomenon that is at issue, nor even anything resembling the ideological psychogenesis we are familiar with which is not superseded by peremptory recourse to the thoroughly metaphysical notion—with its question-begging appeal to the concrete—that derisively goes by the name of affect.

What is at issue is to refind—in the laws that govern this other scene (*ein anderer Schauplatz*), which Freud, on the subject of dreams, designates as the scene of the unconscious—the effects that are discovered at the level of the chain of materially unstable elements that constitutes language: effects that are determined by the double play of combination and substitution in the signifier, according to the two axes for generating the signified, metonymy and metaphor; effects that are determinant in instituting the subject. In the process, a topology, in the mathematical sense of the term, appears, without which one soon realizes that it is impossible to even note the structure of a symptom in the analytic sense of the term.

It speaks in the Other, I say, designating by "Other" the very locus evoked by recourse to speech in any relation in which such recourse plays a part. If it speaks in the Other, whether or not the subject hears it with his ear, it is because it is there that the subject finds his signifying place in a way that is logically prior to any awakening of the signified. The discovery of what it articulates in that place, that is, in the unconscious, enables us to grasp at the price of what splitting (*Spaltung*) he has thus been constituted.

The phallus can be better understood on the basis of its function here. In 690
Freudian doctrine, the phallus is not a fantasy, if we are to view fantasy as an imaginary effect. Nor is it as such an object (part-, internal, good, bad, etc.) inasmuch as "object" tends to gauge the reality involved in a relationship. Still less is it the organ—penis or clitoris—that it symbolizes. And it is no accident that Freud adopted as a reference the simulacrum it represented to the Ancients.

For the phallus is a signifier, a signifier whose function, in the intrasubjective economy of analysis, may lift the veil from the function it served in the mysteries. For it is the signifier that is destined to designate meaning effects as a whole, insofar as the signifier conditions them by its presence as signifier.

Let us thus examine the effects of this presence. They include, first, a deviation of man's needs due to the fact that he speaks: to the extent that his needs are subjected to demand, they come back to him in an alienated form. This is not the effect of his real dependence (one should not expect to find here the parasitic conception represented by the notion of dependency in the theory of neurosis), but rather of their being put into signifying form as such and of the fact that it is from the Other's locus that his message is emitted.

What is thus alienated in needs constitutes an *Urverdrängung* [primal repression], as it cannot, hypothetically, be articulated in demand; it nevertheless appears in an offshoot that presents itself in man as desire (*das Begehren*). The phenomenology that emerges from analytic experience is certainly of a kind to demonstrate the paradoxical, deviant, erratic, eccentric, and even scandalous nature of desire that distinguishes it from need. This fact is all too clear not to have been obvious to moralists worthy of the name since time immemorial, and the Freudianism of earlier days seemed obliged to give it its full status. Paradoxically, however, psychoanalysis now finds itself at the head of an age-old obscurantism that is even more boring as it denies this fact due to its ideal of theoretically and practically reducing desire to need.

That is why I must articulate this status here, beginning with demand, the specific characteristics of which are eluded in the notion of frustration (a notion Freud never used).

Demand in itself bears on something other than the satisfactions it calls for.
It is demand for a presence or an absence. This is what the primordial rela- 691

tionship with the mother manifests, replete as it is with that Other who must be situated *shy of* the needs that Other can fulfill. Demand already constitutes the Other as having the "privilege" of satisfying needs, that is, the power to deprive them of what alone can satisfy them. The Other's privilege here thus outlines the radical form of the gift of what the Other does not have—namely, what is known as its love.

In this way, demand annuls (*aufhebt*) the particularity of everything that can be granted, by transmuting it into a proof of love, and the very satisfactions demand obtains for need are debased (*sich erniedrigt*) to the point of being no more than the crushing brought on by the demand for love (all of which is perfectly apparent in the psychology of early child-care, which our analyst/nannies have latched on to).

It is necessary, then, that the particularity thus abolished reappear *beyond* demand. And in fact it does reappear there, but it preserves the structure concealed in the unconditionality of the demand for love. By a reversal that is not simply a negation of the negation, the power of pure loss emerges from the residue of an obliteration. For the unconditionality of demand, desire substitutes the "absolute" condition: this condition in fact dissolves the element in the proof of love that rebels against the satisfaction of need. This is why desire is neither the appetite for satisfaction nor the demand for love, but the difference that results from the subtraction of the first from the second, the very phenomenon of their splitting (*Spaltung*).

One can see how a sexual relationship occupies this closed field of desire and plays out its fate there. This is because it is the field designed for the production of the enigma that this relationship gives rise to in the subject by doubly "signifying" it to him: the return of the demand it gives rise to, in the form of a demand concerning the subject of need; and the ambiguity presented concerning the Other in question in the proof of love that is demanded. The gap constituted by this enigma avers what determines it, namely, to put it as simply and clearly as possible, that for each of the partners in the relationship, both the subject and the Other, it is not enough to be subjects of need or objects of love—they must hold the place of the cause of desire.

This truth lies at the heart of all the defects found in the psychoanalytic field regarding sexual life. It also constitutes the condition of the subject's hap-
692 piness there; and to disguise its gap by assuming that the virtue of the "genital" will resolve it through the maturation of tenderness (that is to say, solely by recourse to the Other as reality), however pious the intent may be, is nonetheless fraudulent. It should be pointed out here that French analysts, with their hypocritical notion of genital oblativity, set a moralizing tone which, to the strains of Salvation Army bands, is pervading the entire landscape.

In any case, man cannot aim at being whole (at the "total personality," another premise with which modern psychotherapy veers off course), once the play of displacement and condensation to which he is destined in the exercise of his functions marks his relation, as a subject, to the signifier.

The phallus is the privileged signifier of this mark in which the role [*part*] of Logos is wedded to the advent of desire.

One could say that this signifier is chosen as the most salient of what can be grasped in sexual intercourse [*copulation*] as real, as well as the most symbolic, in the literal (typographical) sense of the term, since it is equivalent in intercourse to the (logical) copula. One could also say that, by virtue of its turgidity, it is the image of the vital flow as it is transmitted in generation.

All of these remarks still merely veil the fact that it can play its role only when veiled, that is, as itself a sign of the latency with which any signifiable is struck, once it is raised (*aufgehoben*) to the function of signifier.

The phallus is the signifier of this very *Aufhebung*, which it inaugurates (initiates) by its disappearance. That is why the demon of Αἰδως (*Scham*)[1] springs forth at the very moment the phallus is unveiled in the ancient mysteries (see the famous painting in the Villa of the Mysteries in Pompeii).

It then becomes the bar with which the demon's hand strikes the signified, marking it as the bastard offspring of its signifying concatenation.

A condition of complementarity is thus produced in the instating of the subject by the signifier, which explains his *Spaltung* and the interventionist movement in which it is completed.

Namely: 693

(1) that the subject designates his being only by barring everything it signifies, as is seen in the fact that he wants to be loved for himself, a mirage that is not dispelled by simply pointing out that it is grammatical (since it abolishes discourse);

(2) that the part of this being that is alive in the *urverdrängt* [primally repressed] finds its signifier by receiving the mark of the phallus's *Verdrängung* [repression] (owing to which the unconscious is language).

The phallus as a signifier provides the ratio [*raison*] of desire (in the sense in which the term is used in "mean and extreme ratio" of harmonic division).

I shall thus be using the phallus as an algorithm and I cannot, without endlessly inflating my talk, do otherwise than rely on the echoes of the experience that unites us to get you to grasp this usage.

The fact that the phallus is a signifier requires that it be in the place of the Other that the subject have access to it. But since this signifier is there only as veiled and as ratio [*raison*] of the Other's desire, it is the Other's desire as such that the subject is required to recognize—in other words, the other insofar as he himself is a subject divided by the signifying *Spaltung*.

The developments that appear in psychological genesis confirm the phallus' signifying function.

This allows us, first of all, to more correctly formulate Klein's finding that the child apprehends from the outset that the mother "contains" the phallus.

But development is ordained by the dialectic of the demand for love and the test constituted by desire.

The demand for love can only suffer from a desire whose signifier is foreign to it. If the mother's desire *is* for the phallus, the child wants to be the phallus in order to satisfy her desire. Thus the division immanent in desire already makes itself felt by virtue of being experienced in the Other's desire, in that this division already stands in the way of the subject being satisfied with presenting to the Other the real [organ] he may *have* that corresponds to the phallus; for what he has is no better than what he does not have, from the point of view of his demand for love, which would like him to be the phallus.

Clinical work shows us that the test constituted by the Other's desire is decisive, not in the sense that the subject learns by it whether or not he has a real phallus, but in the sense that he learns that his mother does not have one. This
694 is the moment in experience without which no symptomatic consequence (phobia) or structural consequence *(Penisneid)* related to the castration complex can take effect. This seals the conjunction of desire, insofar as the phallic signifier is its mark, with the threat of or nostalgia based on not-having [*manque à avoir*].

Of course, its future depends on the law introduced by the father in this sequence.

But one can indicate the structures that govern the relations between the sexes by referring simply to the phallus' function.

These relations revolve around a being and a having which, since they refer to a signifier, the phallus, have contradictory effects: they give the subject reality in this signifier, on the one hand, but render unreal the relations to be signified, on the other.

This is brought about by the intervention of a seeming [*paraître*] that replaces the having in order to protect it, in one case, and to mask the lack thereof, in the other, and whose effect is to completely project the ideal or typical manifestations of each of the sexes' behavior, including the act of copulation itself, into the realm of comedy.

These ideals are strengthened by the demand they are capable of satisfying, which is always a demand for love, with the reduction of desire to demand as its complement.

Paradoxical as this formulation may seem, I am saying that it is in order to be the phallus—that is, the signifier of the Other's desire—that a woman rejects an essential part of femininity, namely, all its attributes, in the masquerade. It is for what she is not that she expects to be desired as well as loved. But she finds the signifier of her own desire in the body of the person to whom her demand for love is addressed. It should not be forgotten, of course, that the organ that is endowed with this signifying function takes on the value of a fetish thereby. But the result for a woman remains that two things converge on the same object: an experience of love that, as such (see above), ideally deprives her of what the object gives, and a desire that finds its signifier in this object. This is why one may find that a lack of satisfaction of sexual needs, in other words, frigidity, is relatively well tolerated by women, whereas the *Verdrängung* inherent in desire is less in them than in men.

In the case of men, on the other hand, the dialectic of demand and desire engenders effects regarding which one must once again admire Freud's sureness in situating them, in the precise articulations on which they depend, under 695
the heading of a specific debasement *(Erniedrigung)* in the sphere of love.

If, indeed, man is able to satisfy his demand for love in his relationship with a woman, inasmuch as the phallic signifier clearly constitutes her as giving in love what she does not have, conversely, his own desire for the phallus will make its signifier emerge in its residual divergence toward "another woman" who may signify this phallus in various ways, either as a virgin or as a prostitute. There results from this a centrifugal tendency of the genital drive in the sphere of love, which makes impotence much harder for him to bear, while the *Verdrängung* inherent in his desire is greater.

Still it should not be thought that the sort of infidelity that might appear to be constitutive of the masculine function is characteristic of him alone. For if one looks closely, the same split can be found in women, with the proviso that the Loving Other [*l'Autre de l'Amour*] as such—that is, the Other insofar as he is deprived of what he gives—is difficult to see in the backcourt where he replaces the being of the very man whose attributes she cherishes.

One might add here that male homosexuality, in accordance with the phallic mark that constitutes desire, is constituted along the axis of desire, while female homosexuality, on the contrary, as observation shows, is oriented by a disappointment that strengthens the axis of the demand for love. These remarks should be refined through a reexamination of the function of the mask, insofar as it dominates the identifications in which refusals of demand are resolved.

The fact that femininity finds refuge in this mask, by virtue of the *Verdrängung* inherent in desire's phallic mark, has the curious consequence of making virile display in human beings seem feminine.

Correlatively, one can glimpse the reason for a characteristic that has never been elucidated and that shows once again the depth of Freud's intuition: namely, why Freud claims there is only one libido, his text showing that he conceives of it as masculine in nature. The function of the phallic signifier touches here on its most profound relation: that by which the Ancients embodied therein the Nous and the Logos.

Note

1. The demon of Shame.

In Memory of Ernest Jones: 697
On His Theory of Symbolism

> And bring him out that is but woman's son
> Can trace me in the tedious ways of art,
> And hold me pace in deep experiments.
> —Shakespeare, *Henry IV,* Part I, Act 3, Scene 1, 45–47

Far from the funeral pomp with which our departed colleague was honored in accordance with his rank, here I will devote to him a memorial of our solidarity in psychoanalytic work.

While it is homage that suits the position of our group, I will not leave out the emotion that wells up in me from the memory of more personal relations.

I will punctuate three moments of the latter. Their contingency reflects a man who was very diverse in his vivacity: his unmitigated imperiousness toward the newcomer I was in Marienbad, that is, at the last of our council assemblies before a vacuum struck the Viennese sphere, a superficial interaction whose sting can still be seen after the war in one of my writings; the familiarity between us during a visit to the Plat in Elsted, where, among the letters by Freud spread out on an immense table for the first volume of the biography he was writing, I saw him anxious to share with me the seductions of his labor, until the hour of an appointment with a female patient, kept even in his retreat, put an end to it, the haste of which, in its compulsive tone, led me to see the mark of an indelible yoke; and lastly, the grandeur of his July 1957 letter to me in which his apology for not coming to see me at my house in the country invoked the pretext of stoically explored suffering only to accept it as the signal of a lofty competition, death hot at the heels of the work to be completed.

The organ that is the *International Journal of Psychoanalysis*, and which owes
everything to Ernest Jones, from its duration to its quality, allowed to show 698
between some of its lines in the September–October 1958 issue the shadow with

which a long-exercised power always seems to darken when nightfall catches up with it: ink quick to accuse his edifice for the light it obliterated.

This edifice solicits us. For, however metaphorical it may be, it is designed to remind us of what distinguishes the architecture from the building: namely, a logical power that governs [*ordonne*] the architecture beyond what the building allows for by way of possible utilization. Thus no building, unless reduced to the merest of barracks, can do without this order that makes it akin to discourse. This logic harmonizes with efficiency only by dominating it, and their discord is not a simply possible fact in the art of construction.

We can thus gauge how much more essential this discord is in the art of psychoanalysis, where an experience of truth determines the field—that of memory and signification—whereas the phenomena that are found to be most signifying in it remain scandalous compared to the ends of utility with which all power is legitimated.

This is why no consideration of power, even the most legitimate since it involves the professional building,[1] can intervene in the analyst's discourse without affecting the very purpose of his practice at the same time as its medium.

While Jones is the one who did the most to ensure analytic values a certain official standing, and even a status recognized by the public authorities, can we not propose to question the immense apology his theoretical work constitutes in order to assess its dignity?

This can only be done using a sample of his work, and I will select the article published in the *British Journal of Psychology* (IX, 2 [October 1916]: 181–229) on the theory of symbolism, reproduced since then in each of the
699 editions—which are known to be quite different from one another—that followed of his *Papers on Psycho-Analysis*.

This article is uncompromising. Its grasp of the problem sustains it at its proper level, and while it does not resolve the difficulty, it highlights it.

The malice falls flat of those who would like us to see this youngest of the faithful, who was linked not only by the talisman of the seven rings but by the implications of an executive secret,[2] as sorely tried by the Master.

The fact that he, the only *goy* in a circle imbued with its Jewish specificity,[3] was awarded the prize of erecting this monument [his biography] to the Master will no doubt be attributed to the fact that this monument toes the line that the man who opened up a new field of avowal for the world did not want to see crossed into his private life.

One should not fail to reflect upon the resistance of biographical discourse to the analysis of the principal case constituted not so much by the inventor but by the invention of psychoanalysis itself.

Be that as it may, Jones' references to Rank and Sachs in the article I will examine, due to the criteria they put forward of analytic symbolism, are edifying.

The criteria that they place at the top of the list, especially the criterion [that something must have] a constant meaning and be independent from individual interventions[4] [to be considered a symbol], lead to contradictions that Jones points out in the facts; and the reverence he maintains for these autodidacts of the depths does not stop us from sensing the advantage he derives from a rationalism that is rather sure of its method, since it is also exclusive in its principles.

Jones begins,

> The progress of the human mind, when considered genetically, is seen to consist, not—as is commonly thought—merely of a number of accretions added from without, but of the following two processes: on the one hand the extension or transference of interest and understand- 700
> ing from earlier, simpler, and more primitive ideas, etc., to more difficult and complex ones, which in a certain sense are continuations of and symbolise the former; and on the other hand the constant unmasking of previous symbolisms, the recognition that these, though previously thought to be literally true, were really only aspects or representations of the truth, the only ones of which our minds were—for either affective or intellectual reasons—at the time capable.[5]

Such is the tone with which things begin and they advance by ever more closely closing in on the ambiguity this departure opens up.

Many, in our time, will no doubt consider what follows of but historical, nay prehistoric, interest. We should fear that this disdain hides an impasse in which we are presently stuck.

Jones' concern is to point out Jung's fundamental divergence regarding symbolism, which Freud realized already in 1911, breaking with Jung in 1912,[6] and publishing his update on the situation in his "History of the Psychoanalytic Movement" in 1914.

The two different manners of utilizing symbolism in interpretation are decisive as to the direction they give analysis; and they will be illustrated here by an example that may well be considered the earliest one, but that is not out of date, insofar as the snake is not simply a figure that art and fables preserve from an abandoned mythology or folklore. The ancient enemy is not so far from our mirages, for it is still associated with the traits of temptation and the deceit of promises, but also with the prestige of the circle that must be crossed toward wisdom in the turning inward, the closing of the head on the tail, with which it attempts to encircle the world.

Captive head under the Virgin's foot, what will we see of the head that repeats you at the other end of the body of the amphisbaena? A mountain gnosis, whose local hereditary characteristics we would be wrong to neglect, grabbed it anew from the lacustrine retreat where it is still curled up, as Jung put it when he spoke to me of his canton's secrets.

701 A figuration of the libido—that is how a disciple of Jung's will interpret the appearance of a snake in a dream, vision, or drawing, manifesting, unbeknown to himself, that while its seductive power is eternal, it is also always the same. For here we see the subject about to be captured by an autistic eros which, however revamped its [theoretical] apparatus may be, seems like an Old Acquaintance.

In other words, the soul, which is a lucid blind man, reads its own nature in the archetypes that the world echoes back to him: How could he not end up believing he is the world soul?

What is strange is that in their haste to take this soul into account, Calvinist pastors were fooled.[7]

It must be said that having thrown the beautiful soul a line from his Helvetian refuge, it is a rather ironic success for a disciple of Brücke, the offspring of Helmholtz and Du Bois-Reymond.

But it is also the proof that there is no compromise possible with psychology, and that if we admit that the soul knows [*connaisse*] its own structure, with the kind of knowledge [*connaissance*] the soul has, that is, immediate knowledge—even if it were in the moment of falling asleep where Silberer asks us to recognize the "functional symbolism" of the layers of the psyche in a cake knife cutting through a puff pastry—nothing can any longer separate thought from the reverie of a "chymical wedding."

Still it is not easy to grasp the cut so boldly traced by Freud in the theory of the revision [*élaboration*] of dreams, unless we purely and simply refuse the psychological ingenuity of the phenomena brought out by Silberer's observational talent; this is the sorry solution Freud adopts in his discussion of it in the 1914 edition of the *Traumdeutung* [*The Interpretation of Dreams*] when he proffers that the said phenomena apply only to "philosophical minds, [prone] to endopsychic perception [and even] to delusions of observation,"[8] to metaphysicians in the soul, no doubt, that would be the word for it—Jones one-upping Freud here, in effect, by indicating with a somewhat more strident tone the aversion he allows himself to show to this.

702 Let us be glad that spiritual hierarchies—along with the materials, pneumatics, psychics, and all the rest—did not return through this door, but we see here the source of the infatuation of those who consider themselves to be "natural born psychoanalysts."

Nevertheless, this is not a usable argument in this context and Jones does not dream of using it.

Regarding the snake, Jones rectifies [Jung's position by asserting] that it is the symbol not of libido—an energetic notion which, as an idea, can only be brought out at a high degree of abstraction—but of the phallus, insofar as the latter seems to him to be characteristic of a "more concrete idea," even concrete through and through.

For this is the pathway Jones chooses with which to ward off the dangerous return to a kind of mysticism that symbolism seems to allow for, mysticism which seems to him, once unmasked, to exclude itself by itself from any and all scientific consideration.

The symbol is displaced from a more concrete idea (at least that is how he expresses himself on the subject), to which it primarily applies, to a more abstract idea, to which it relates secondarily, which means that this displacement can only take place in a single direction.

Let us stop here for an instant:

To agree that if a waking hallucination makes analysis' first hysteric[9]—her arm having fallen asleep under the weight of her head on her shoulder, pressed onto the back of the chair from which it extended, when she slumped down, toward her father who she was watching over in his death throes—extend this arm with a snake, and even with as many snakes as she had fingers, this snake is the symbol of the phallus and of nothing else. But to whom this phallus belongs "concretely" is what is less easy to determine in the register of contemporary psychoanalysis that is so nicely labeled by Raymond Queneau as the *liquette ninque*. The fact that this phallus is, in effect, recognized as a belonging coveted by the subject [*qui fasse l'envie du sujet*], woman though she be, does not explain anything if one realizes that it emerges so importunately only to be clearly there in the present—namely, in the aforementioned *liquette*—or simply in the bed [*lit*] where it dies with the dying man.

This is the very problem about which Jones, eleven years later, provides a 703
piece worthy of his anthology, owing to the dialectical figure skating he demonstrates in it by developing positions that are the opposite of those adopted by Freud regarding the phallic phase simply by repeatedly asserting that he completely agrees with Freud. But whatever one must think of this unfortunately abandoned debate [on the phallic phase], the question may be asked of Jones: does the phallus—if it is truly the object of phobia or of perversion, which he relates, first the one and then the other, to the phallic phase—remain in the state of a "concrete idea"?

In any case, he is forced to recognize that the phallus takes on a "secondary" application here. This is clearly what he says when he quite dexterously distinguishes between the proto- and deutero-phallic phases. And the phallus, as a concrete idea of the symbols that will be substituted for it in the one and then in the other of these phases, can only be linked to itself by a similitude which is as concrete as this idea is; for otherwise this concrete idea would be nothing but the classic abstraction of the general idea or of the generic object, which would leave our symbols a field of regression that is the one that Jones seeks to refute. In short, I am getting ahead of myself, as you see, regarding the only notion that allows us to conceive of the symbolism of the phallus: the particularity of its function as a signifier.[10]

In truth, there is some pathos in the sort of skirting of this function that its deduction imposes upon Jones. For he immediately realized that analytic symbolism is only conceivable if it is related to the linguistic fact of metaphor, which serves him as a handrail from one end of his discussion to the other.

He quite apparently fails to find his way in it at two moments at which his defective point of departure is related, to my mind, to a very insidious inversion in his thought by which his need for seriousness in analysis prevails, without him analyzing this, over the seriousness of need.

704 This can be seen in a sentence from his debate with Silberer:[11] "[I]f there is any truth at all in psycho-analysis, or, indeed, in any genetic psychology, then the primordial complexes displayed in symbolism *must be*[12] the permanent sources of mental life and the very reverse of mere figures of speech." This remark aims at a certain contingency that Silberer notes quite aptly both in the application of symbols and in the repetitions to which they give consistency,[13] in order to oppose to it the constancy of primordial needs in development (oral needs, for example, whose growing importance Jones supports).

It is in order to return to these early facts that Jones turns to metaphor, by which he intends to understand symbolism.

It is, in a sense, by backing up and for the needs of his polemic that he took up linguistics, but the latter is so tightly linked to his object that it suffices to rectify his aim.

We must credit him with proving himself wrong when he provides his list of primary ideas, about which he rightly remarks that they are few in number and constant, unlike symbols, which can always be added to, piling up on these ideas. These primary ideas are, according to him, "ideas of self and the immediate blood relatives, or of the phenomena of birth, love, and death" [102]. All of these are "ideas," the most concrete of which is the network of the signifier in which the subject must already be caught up in order to be able to constitute himself there as self, as part of a lineage, as existing, as the representative of a sex, and even as dead, for these ideas can only be passed off as primary if all parallelism with the development of needs is abandoned.

The fact that this is not realized can only be explained by flight in the face of the anxiety of origins, and owes nothing to the kind of haste whose con- 705
clusive virtue I have shown when it is grounded in logic.[14]

Isn't it the least one can demand of an analyst that he maintain his logical rigor in [the face of] this anxiety, in other words, that he not spare anxiety to those he teaches, even to ensure his power over them?

This is where Jones seeks his pathway, but where his best recourse fails him, for rhetoricians over the ages have balked at metaphor, obviating his chance to use it to rectify his own approach to symbols. This appears in the fact that he posits that comparison ("simile" in English) lies at the origin of metaphor, taking "John is as brave as a lion" as the logical model for "John is a lion."

We are astonished that his so very lively sense of analytic experience did not alert him to the far greater signifying density of the second enunciation; while recognizing it to be more concrete, he did not render it its primacy.

Absent this step, he did not manage to formulate what analytic interpretation nevertheless makes almost obvious, which is that the relationship between reality [*réel*] and what is thought is not that between the signified and the signifier, and that the primacy reality [*réel*] has over thought is reversed from the signifier to the signified. This overlaps what happens, in truth, in language where meaning effects are created by permutations of signifiers.

Thus while Jones perceives that it is, in some sense, the memory of a metaphor that constitutes analytic symbolism, the so-called decline of metaphor hides its reason from him. He does not see that it is the lion as a signifier that has been abraded right to the yon, and even to the yon-yon, whose meek growl serves as an index of the self-satisfied ideals of Metro-Goldwyn—its roar, still horrible to those lost in the jungle, attesting better to the origins of its use for purposes of meaning.

Jones believes, on the contrary, that the signified has become more porous, that it has become what grammarians call a figurative meaning.

He thus misses its function, sometimes so palpable in symbols and analytic symptoms, of being a sort of regeneration of the signifier.

He loses his way, instead, when he repeats a false law of displacement of 706
the semanteme according to which it is supposed to always go from a particular signification to a more general one, from a concrete to an abstract one, from a material to a more subtle one called figurative or even moral. As if the first example we come across in the daily news did not show its nullity, the word "heavy" [*lourd*], since that is the one that presents itself to me, known to have first signified *le lourdaud* [clumsy oaf], or even *l'étourdi*[15] [lightheaded or scatterbrained] (in the thirteenth century), thus having had a moral mean-

ing before applying, not much earlier than the eighteenth century, as Bloch and von Wartburg teach us, to a property of matter—about which it must be noted, so as not to stop while the getting is so good, that it is misleading insofar as, in opposition to light, it leads to the Aristotelian topic of a qualitative gravity. To save the theory, will we go so far as to credit the common use of words with a presentiment of the scant reality of such a physics?

But what can we say about the application that gave us this word, *lourd*—namely, the new unit of French monetary reform? What vertiginous or grave perspective will we open up, what trance of thickness will we resort to, to situate this new flapping of wings from the literal to the figurative? Would it not be simpler to accept here the obvious material fact that there is no other mainspring of metaphorical effect than the substitution of one signifier for another as such? At least we would then not be *lourd* [dense] (in Franc-Comptois dialect, they say *lourdeau*) in grasping this example, in which the so-called *franc lourd* [new franc], for no stale meaning, can be *lourd* . . . only due to its consequences: for the latter can be inscribed here in accounting terms—namely, purely signifying terms.

Nevertheless, we must not neglect that a meaning effect—which appears, here as elsewhere, extrapolated in the substitution of signifiers—should be foreseen and, indeed, expected: by which every Frenchman will feel he carries a heavier [*plus lourd*] wallet when he has equally weighty bill denominations [*poids des coupures*], although he will feel less lightheaded in the manipulation of their cash currency when he spends the same amount. And who can say how weighted [*pondération*] his spending will become in his tourist peregrinations, but also the unforeseeable effects that the metaphorical slid-
707 ing of his metal coin-related likings toward heavy [*lourde*] industry and heavy machinery will have on the El Dorados of his investments or his luxury utensils?[16] Question: If a comedy is disparaged when it is called heavy-handed [*lourd*], why can't divine Grace be so characterized?

This error regarding the function of language is worth emphasizing, for it is primordial in the difficulties related to symbolism that Jones does not manage to overcome.

Indeed, everything in this debate revolves around whether or not a knowledge-value [*valeur de connaissance*] should be granted to symbolism. The interference of symbols in actions that are more explicit and better adapted to perception has the import of informing us about a more primitive activity in being.

What Silberer calls the negative conditioning of symbolism—namely, the dimming of the most advanced discriminating functions for adapting to reality [*réel*]—takes on a positive value because it allows access to occur. But we would fall into the sin of circular reasoning were we to deduce from it that a more profound reality, even if qualified as psychical, is manifested in it.

All of Jones' efforts are devoted to denying that an archaic symbolism can retain any value compared to a scientific apprehension of reality. But since he continues to refer symbols to ideas, understanding by ideas the concrete props that development is supposed to give symbols, he himself cannot help but maintain the notion of a negative conditioning of symbolism right to the bitter end, which stops him from grasping its structural function.

And yet he provides us with ample proof of the aptness of his orientation in the felicitous encounters he makes along the way: for example, when he pauses at the fact that a child assigns the "quack" he isolates as the signifier of the duck's call not only to ducks, whose natural attribute it is, but to a series of objects, including flies, wine, and even a penny, this time using the signifier as a metaphor [107].

Why must he see here but a new attribution based on the apperception of
a volatile similarity, even if the authority he appeals to in his borrowing—who 708
is no less than Darwin—considers it sufficient that a penny be stamped with an eagle in the corner to include it in it? For however obliging the notion of analogy may be in extending the range of the volatile to the dilution of a fluid, perhaps the function of metonymy, as propped up by the signifying chain, better accounts for the bird's contiguity with the liquid in which it wades.

How can we but regret here that the interest directed to the child by developmentalistic analysis does not pause at this moment, at the very dawn of the use of speech, where the child, who designates with a "bow-wow" what in certain cases we strove in front of him to call only by the name of "dog," assigns this "bow-wow" to just about anything; or at this later moment when the child declares that the cat goes "bow-wow" and the dog goes "meow," showing by his sobs, should we try to correct his game, that in any case the game is not gratuitous?

Were Jones to take these moments, which are always manifest, into account, he would not fall into the eminent error by which he concludes that "it was not the duck as a whole that was named 'quack' [by the child], but only certain abstracted attributes, which then continued to be called by the same word."[17]

It would then become clear to him that what he is seeking—namely, the effect of signifying substitution—is precisely what the child first *finds* [*trouve*], the word to be taken literally in the Romance languages in which *trouver* comes from "trope," for it is by the play of signifying substitution that the child rips things from their ingenuousness in subjecting them to his metaphors.

As an aside, the myth of the child's ingenuousness seems clearly reestablished by this, still to be refuted here.

We must define metaphor by the implantation in a signifying chain of another signifier, by which the one it supplants falls to the rank of the signified, and as a latent signifier perpetuates there the interval by which another signifying chain can be grafted onto it. We thus refind the very dimensions by which Jones strives to establish analytic symbolism.

709 For these dimensions govern the structure that Freud attributes to symptoms and repression. And without them it is impossible to repair the deviation the unconscious, in Freud's sense of the term, underwent due to the symbol's mystification, Jones' goal being to repair it.

Certain erroneous approaches must be cleared away to do so, such as his remark—which is fallacious, fascinating us with its reference to the object—that while a church bell tower can symbolize the phallus, the phallus will never symbolize a bell tower.

For it is no less true that in a dream, even in an ironic forgery of a dream by Cocteau, one can quite legitimately, if the context allows, interpret the image of a Negro who, with sword drawn, comes straight at a female dreamer, as the signifier of her forgetting to take her umbrella with her after her last analytic session. This is even what the most classical analysts called interpretation "toward the exit" [*vers la sortie*], if you'll allow me to translate thus a term introduced in English as "reconstruction upward."*[18]

To put it explicitly, the quality of concreteness in an idea no more determines its unconscious effect than the quality of heaviness [*lourd*] in a heavy body determines the speed at which it falls.

It must be posited that it is the signifier's concrete impact in submitting need to demand which, in repressing desire into the position of that which is misrecognized, provides the unconscious with its order.

Regarding the list of symbols—which is already considerable, as Jones stresses—he notes, opposing an approximation which is not the crudest given by Rank and Sachs (namely, the third characteristic of the symbol: its independence from individual determinations), that this list remains, on the contrary, open to individual invention, adding simply that once put forward, a symbol no longer changes destination. This is a very enlightening remark, assuming we return to the catalog of primary ideas in symbolism commendably prepared by Jones, since it allows us to complete it.

For these primary ideas designate the points at which the subject disappears under the being of the signifier; whether it is a question, indeed, of being oneself, being a father, being born, being loved, or being dead, how can we fail to see that the subject, assuming he is the subject who speaks, sustains himself there only on the basis of discourse?

710 It is thus clear that analysis reveals that the phallus serves the function of

signifying the lack of being [*manque à être*] that is wrought in the subject by his relation to the signifier. This gives its full import to the fact that all the symbols Jones' study highlights are phallic symbols.

Regarding the magnetic points of signification that his remarks suggest, I will thus say that they are points of the subject's umbilication in the cuts made by the signifier, the most fundamental of them being the *Urverdrängung* [primal repression] that Freud always emphasized—namely, the subject's reduplication brought on by discourse, though that reduplication remains masked by the multiplication of what it evokes as entities [*étant*].

Analysis has shown us that it is with images that captivate his eros as a living individual that the subject manages to ensure his implication in the signifying sequence.

Of course, the human individual is not without presenting some indulgence toward this fragmentation of his images; and the bipolarity of corporal autism favored by the privilege of the specular image,[19] a biological fact, lends itself singularly to the fact that his desire's implication in the signifier takes a narcissistic form.

But it is not the connections of need, from which these images are detached, that sustain their perpetuated impact; rather, it is the articulated sequence in which they are inscribed that structures their insistence as signifying.

This is why sexual demand, assuming it need but present itself orally, "ectopizes" images of introjection into the field of "genital" desire. The notion of the oral object that the partner would perhaps become in it, although it has become ever more established at the heart of analytic theory, is nevertheless an elision that is a source of error.

For what happens in the extreme case is that desire finds its fantasmatic prop in what is called a defense on the part of the subject when he is confronted with a partner who is taken as a signifier of completed devouring. (Weigh my terms carefully here.)

It is in the subject's reduplication by the signifier that we find the main- 711
spring of the positive conditioning whose quest Jones pursues because of what he calls "true symbolism," the symbolism that analysis discovered in its constancy and rediscovers, articulating itself ever anew, in the unconscious.

A minimum composition of the battery of signifiers suffices to institute in the signifying chain a duplicity that re-covers his reduplication as a subject, and it is in this redoubling of the subject of speech that the unconscious as such finds a way to become articulated—namely, in a medium that is only apperceived by being perceived as just as stupid as a cryptography without a cipher.

Here lies the heterogeneity of the "true symbolism" that Jones seeks in vain to grasp, and which escapes him precisely to the extent to which he maintains the mirage of negative conditioning, which falsely leaves symbolism confronted with reality [*réel*] at all the "levels" of its regression.

If, as I say, man finds himself open to desiring as many others in himself as his members have names outside of himself, and if he must recognize as many members that are separate from his unit [*unité*], lost without ever having been, as there are entities that are metaphors of these members, we see too that the question of what knowledge-value symbols have is answered, since it is these very members that come back to him after having wandered around the world in an alienated form. This value, which is considerable when it comes to praxis, is nil when it comes to reality [*réel*].

It is very striking to see how much effort it takes Jones to establish this conclusion, which his position requires right from the outset, by the pathways he has chosen. He articulates it with a distinction between "true symbolism," which he conceives of in short as the producer of symbols, and the "symbolic equivalents" that it produces, whose efficacy can only be measured by the objective verification of their grip upon reality [*réel*].

One might note that this amounts to asking analytic experience to grant science its status, thus getting very far away from it. At the very least it should be noted that I am not the one who takes it upon himself to lead our practitioners astray in this way, but rather Jones who has never been reproached for being a metaphysician.

712 But I believe that he is mistaken. For the history of science alone can settle this matter and it brilliantly demonstrates, in the birth of the theory of gravitation, that it was only on the basis of the extermination of all symbolism of the heavens that the terrestrial foundations of modern physics could be established—namely, that as long as some requirement to ascribe to the heavenly orbits a "perfect" shape was maintained (insofar as it implied, for example, the circle's preeminence over the ellipse) from Giordano Bruno to Kepler and from Kepler to Newton, it thwarted the development of the theory's key equations.[20]

But there is no reason to object to the fact that the Cabalistic notion of a God who had consciously withdrawn from matter to leave it to its own movement may have enhanced our confidence in natural experience as necessarily rediscovering the traces of logical creation. For this is the usual detour of all sublimation and one can say that, with the exception of physics, this detour has not been completed. The question for us is whether the completion of this detour can occur in any other way than by being eliminated.

Here again, despite this error we must admire how in his labor—if I allow myself to use this word with the same metaphorical effect as that found in the terms "working through" and *Durcharbeiten* in use in psychoanalysis—our author tills his field with a plowshare that is truly worthy of what analytic work in effect owes to the signifier.

For, to take a final step in his discussion of symbols, he envisions what results from the hypothesis, supposedly accepted by certain authors regarding linguistic and mythological reference points, that agriculture was originally the transposition of a fecundatory coitus into the realm of technics. Can one legitimately say of agriculture at that ideal era that it symbolized copulation?

It is quite clear that the question is not a *de facto* one, no one here having to take sides regarding the real existence in the past of such a stage—which is, in any case, worth adding to the file of pastoral fiction from which the psychoanalyst (not to mention the Marxist) has much to learn about his mental horizons.

The question is merely that of the suitability of applying the notion of sym- 713
bolism here, and Jones answers, without seeming to worry whether or not anyone might agree with him, in the negative,[21] meaning that agriculture thus represents an adequate thought (or a concrete idea), nay a satisfying mode, of coitus!

But if we are truly to follow our author's intentions, we realize that the result is that it is only inasmuch as a certain operation in the realm of technics turns out to be prohibited—because it is incompatible with a certain effect of the laws of marriage and kinship, insofar as that effect concerns, for example, the use [*jouissance*] of the earth—that the operation substituted for the former operation becomes truly symbolic of a sexual satisfaction (except that, from this point on, it is repressed), at the same time as it offers itself up as a prop for naturalist conceptions of a kind that obviates scientific recognition of the union of the gametes as the crux of sexual reproduction.

This is strictly correct insofar as symbolism is considered to be intimately related to repression.

We see that, given this degree of rigor in paradoxical precision, we can legitimately wonder if Jones' work did not accomplish the essential part of what he could do at that time, although he did not go as far as he could have in the direction he found indicated in Freud's work, quoting it from the *Traumdeutung*: "What to-day is symbolically connected was probably in primaeval times united in conceptual and linguistic identity. The symbolic relationship seems to be the remains and sign of an identity that once existed."[22]

And yet he would have gained much in his quest to grasp the true place of symbolism had he remembered that it was granted no room at all in the first edition of the *Traumdeutung*, which means that analysis, in the case of dreams but of symptoms too, need highlight symbolism only as subordinate to the major mainsprings of the processes [*élaboration*] that structure the uncon-

scious—namely, condensation and displacement first and foremost. I am confining myself to these two mechanisms insofar as they would have suf-
714 ficed to make up for Jones' inadequate information regarding metaphor and metonymy as primary effects of the signifier.

Perhaps he would thus have avoided formulating something that contradicts his own perspective, whose major lines I believe I have traced out here (and that contradicts Freud's own explicit warning): that what is repressed in symbolism's metaphorical retreat is affect.[23] This is a formulation that we might like to consider to be but a slip, if it hadn't later been developed into an extraordinarily ambiguous exploration of the whole panoply of affects, insofar as they supposedly substitute for each other as such.[24]

For Freud's conception—developed and published in 1915 in the *Internationale Zeitschrift*, in the three articles on drives and their avatars, repression, and the unconscious—leaves no room for ambiguity on this point: it is the signifier that is repressed, there being no other meaning that can be given in these texts to the word *Vorstellungsrepräsentanz*. As for affects, Freud expressly formulates that they are not repressed; they can only be said to be repressed by indulgence. As simple *Ansätze* or appendices of the repressed, signals equivalent to hysterical fits [*accès*] established in the species, Freud articulates that affects are simply displaced, as is evidenced by the fundamental fact—and it can be seen that someone is an analyst if he realizes this fact—by which the subject is bound to "understand" his affects all the more the less they are really justified.

We can conclude with the example Jones took as his point of departure, which he deployed with his characteristic erudition: the symbolism of
715 Punchinello [*Polichinelle*]. How can one fail to see the dominance of the signifier here, manifest in its most materially phonemic form? For beyond the falsetto and the morphological anomalies of this personage, who descends directly from the Satyr and the Devil, it is clearly homophonies which, condensing in double exposures, like witticisms and slips, most surely give us away—it is the phallus that he symbolizes. The Neapolitan *polecenella*, little turkey, *pulcinella*, little chicken, and *pullus*, a tender term bequeathed by Roman pederasty to the modest outpourings of romantic schoolgirls in my youth, are recovered here by the English "punch," in order, having become *punchinello*, to find anew the dagger, stake, or blunt instrument he dissimulates, which paves the way for him by which to descend, little man, to the dreadful drawer, where the movers, deftly handling the modesty of the Henriettas, will pretend, will pretend to see nothing before he comes back up, resuscitated in his valiance.

Winged phallus, Parapilla,[25] unconscious fantasy of the impossibilities of male desire, treasure in which woman's infinite impotence is exhausted, this member forever lost of all those—Osiris, Adonis, and Orpheus—whose fragmented body must be reassembled by the ambiguous tenderness of the Mother-Goddess, indicates to us, in being found anew in every illustration of this long study on symbolism, not only the eminent function it plays there but how it clarifies it.

For the phallus, as I have shown elsewhere, is the signifier of the very loss the subject suffers due to the fragmentation brought on by the signifier, and nowhere does the counterpart function—by which an object is led into the subordination of desire to the symbolic dialectic—appear in a more decisive manner.

Here we come again upon the sequence indicated above, by which Jones essentially contributed to the elaboration of the phallic phase by resorting a bit more to development. Isn't this the dawn of the maze in which clinical work 716
itself has gotten bogged down and of the return to a greater misrecognition of the essential import of desire, illustrated by a form of treatment involving imaginary immobilization, which is based on the delusional moralism of the ideals of the supposed object-relation? The extraordinary elegance of the point of departure Freud gave us—that is, the conjugation in girls of complaints about their mothers and phallus envy—remains our bedrock in the matter, and it should be understandable that I used it as the point of departure for the dialectic in which I show how demand and desire become separate.

But I will not present any further my own contributions in a study that can but bow—in confining itself to the sole text it concerns—before the obstinate dialectical demands, the loftiness of perspective, the feeling for analytic experience, the grasp of the whole of it, the immense information, the inflexibility regarding goals, the faultless erudition, and, lastly, the weight [*poids*] that give Jones' work its exceptional place.

Is it a less worthy homage because this discussion of symbolism led us so close to this destiny of man to go toward being since he cannot become one? Shepherd of being, proffers the philosopher of our time, while he accuses philosophy of having been its bad shepherd. Answering him with another refrain [*lai*], Freud makes the good subject of philosophical knowledge definitively disappear, the subject who found in the object a sure status, before the bad subject of desire and its impostures.

Isn't it this bad subject that Jones, showing yet another sign of his talent, proves to advocate when he concludes, conjugating metaphor with symbolism: "The circumstance that the same image can be employed for both of these functions should not blind us to the important differences between them. Of these the principal one is that with metaphor the feeling to be expressed is over-sublimated, whereas with symbolism it is under-sublimated (*sic*); the one relates to an effort that has attempted something beyond its strength, the other to an effort that is prevented from accomplishing what it would."

These lines reminded me, with a feeling of returning to the light of day, of the immortal division of human functions that Kierkegaard promulgated for
717 all posterity a division that is, as we know, tripartite, including only officers, maids, and chimney-sweeps. If it surprised certain people with their new being, it already has the enlightened merit here of mentioning the building in which it is obviously inscribed.

For, more than by recalling Jones' Welsh origins, his small stature, his dark cast, and his skill, it is surely because I have followed him, and even conjured him up, in this discussion [*cheminement*] like a chimney in a wall, that in this reexiting in a dazzling pursuit, I suddenly felt assured—regardless of what may be owed to him by the representatives of the two highest offices in the international community of analysts, and particularly in the British Psychoanalytic Institute—to see him permanently take his place in the heavens of chimney-sweeps, of which he is surely the finest example to my mind.

Which, asks the *Talmud*, of two men who exit one after the other from a chimney in the living room will have the idea to dust himself off, when they look at each other? Wisdom settles the question here regarding all the subtleties that could be deduced from the darkness of the faces they present each other and the reflections which, in each of them, diverge, when it expressly concludes: when two men meet coming out of a chimney, they both have dirty faces.

Guitrancourt, January–March 1959

Notes

1. Power as an aim is articulated as a factor that degrades analytic training* in an article by Thomas S. Szasz, "Psychoanalytic Training: A Socio-Psychological Analysis of Its History and Present Status," *IJP* XXXIX (1958): 598–613.

This is the same aim whose impact on the direction of the treatment I denounced in the paper ["Direction of the Treatment"] I gave at the Royaumont Congress last July.

Szasz traces its effects in the external organization of training*, in particular, in the selection of candidates, without getting to the bottom of its incompatibility with psychoanalytic treatment itself, that is, with the first stage of the training*.

2. The extraordinary history of this Committee is revealed to us in Jones' *The Life and Works of Sigmund Freud*, vol. II, chapter 6, 172–88.

3. See Ferenczi's letter dated August 6, 1912, in *Sigmund Freud*, vol. II, 173.

4. I am forcing the meaning of *Bedingungen* here.

5. Jones, *Papers on Psycho-Analysis*, 87–88.

6. At stake were the positions adopted by Jung in the two parts of *Wandlungen und Symbole der Libido*, which came out in 1911 and 1912, respectively. [*Transformations and Symbols of the Libido* was first published in English as *Psychology of the Unconscious* (1916); it was rewritten in 1952 and republished as *Symbols*

of Transformation; it was later translated by Beatrice M. Hinkle as *Psychology of the Unconscious: A Study of the Transformations and Symbolisms of the Libido* (Princeton, NJ: Princeton University Press, 1991), as part of *The Collected Works of C. G. Jung*.]

7. The author of these lines holds that only the Roman Prostitute can, with indemnity, have close relations with what she rejects.

8. See *GW* II–III, 510 [in English, see *SE* V, 505–6].

9. See the case of Anna O., not included in *GW* because it was Breuer's case. The passage evoked here can be found in *SE* II, 38 (*Studies on Hysteria*) or on page 30 of the original edition of *Studien über Hysterie*.

10. This excursion is not gratuitous. For after his 1927 "Precocious Development of Feminine Sexuality" and his 1932 "Phallic Phase," Jones concludes with a monumental declaration in 1935 before the Vienna Psychoanalytic Society, indicating his complete endorsement of the geneticism of fantasies which Melanie Klein makes the linchpin of her doctrine, and in which all reflection on symbolism in psychoanalysis remained closed until my paper in 1953 ["Function and Field"].

11. *Papers on Psycho-Analysis*, 125.

12. My emphasis.

13. Jones goes so far here as to use analysis as a weapon when he suggests [on page 125] that Silberer's use of the term "ephemeral"—which is, nevertheless, logically justified in Silberer's text—is symptomatic.

14. See "Logical Time and the Assertion of Anticipated Certainty," *Écrits* 1966, 197–213.

15. Earlier, no doubt: *le sale* (that which is dirty).

16. It would be nice to know what fears about these metaphorical effects ruled out, in the most recent policy decisions, the initially announced term "heavy franc" [*franc lourd*], substituting "the new franc" for it.

17. Jones, *Papers on Psycho-Analysis*, 107.

18. See Rudolf M. Loewenstein, "Some Thoughts on Interpretation in the Theory and Practice of Psychoanalysis," in *The Psychoanalytic Study of the Child*, vol. XII (New York: International Universities Press, 1957), 143, and "The Problem of Interpretation," *PQ* XX, 1 (1951): 1–14.

19. See my conception of the mirror stage and the biological foundation I gave it in the prematurity of birth [of human beings].

20. See Alexandre Koyré, *From the Closed World to the Infinite Universe* (Baltimore: Johns Hopkins University Press, 1957), where he summarizes his luminous work on the subject.

21. Jones, *Papers on Psycho-Analysis*, 136.

22. Jones, *Papers on Psycho-Analysis*, 105.

23. Jones, were he to apply analytic suspicion to himself, would have to be tipped off by the feeling of strangeness with which he himself is affected ("a curious statement," he says, on pages 123–24 of his *Papers on Psycho-Analysis*) in reading Silberer's nevertheless grounded remark "that the universality, or the general validity and intelligibility of a symbol, varies inversely with respect to the part played in its determination by affective factors."

In short, the points of misrecognition Jones cannot let go of instructively prove to be related to the metaphor of the *weight* [*poids*] he intends to give to true symbolism. He thereby winds up arguing against his own meaning, as, for example, resorting to the subject's conviction to distinguish the unconscious effect—that is, the properly symbolic effect—that a common figure of speech can have on him (page 128).

24. See Jones, "Fear, Guilt and Hate," a paper delivered at the Second International Congress of Psychoanalysis in Oxford in July 1929, published in *Papers on Psycho-Analysis*, 304–19.

25. This is the title of an obscene poem in five cantos, supposedly translated from the Italian, copiously illustrated and published in London in 1782 without any indication of who the publisher was. This word makes emerge there, in a form that assists all the women who pronounce it, the object to whose glory these cantos are devoted, an object I could no better designate than by calling it the universal phallus (as one says, *clef universelle* [skeleton or master key that fits all locks]).

On an Ex Post Facto Syllabary

The note that one might have expected me to append in passing in the preceding text to the name of Silberer is not really missing: it can be found in the text in a dissolved form. I have done this in response to the fact that Jones devotes a whole chapter, the fourth one interpolated before his conclusion, to the discussion of Silberer's invention.

718 This results in a redoubling of the whole of his argumentation in this part of the text, creating a lame equivalence which strikes me as one symptom (among others) of the problem found in the theory that Jones presents us.

The note that must be made regarding Silberer can take on its value by clarifying why, if it may be said of a text, I have been unable to do anything more than redouble its problem.

Silberer intends to trace what becomes of the symbol's (historic) impact, which he qualifies (quite pertinently) as a "material phenomenon," when it accedes to the *function* of determining a psychical state, or even of establishing the so-called constitution of a rhythm or penchant.

The "functional phenomenon" that he makes of it is a function recovered from what is material, from which it results that what it "symbolizes" henceforth is an elaborate structure, and all the more rightfully so since it is, in fact, one of its consequences.

I am forcing his notorious illustration of it in which he qualifies as a layer cake the cake into which he seems to have had a hard time inserting an adequate knife, in the transition to sleep in which his struggle with this cake replaced his efforts to bring his thought back to the level of arousal necessary for it to be equal to his existence as a subject.

Psychical strata are evoked here, displacing the phenomenon by suggesting a possible endoscopy of depths that verge on the sublime.

The phenomenon is indisputable. This is why Freud made room for it in a note he added to the *Traumdeutung* [*The Interpretation of Dreams*] in 1914, and particularly in the most striking form of it that Silberer provided in 1911, as the symbolism of the threshold (*Schwellensymbolik*), which is possibly enriched by the addition of a guardian at that threshold.

But the phenomenon seduces us from another angle. One might say that it springs off the still green trampoline of Freud's discovery to conquer anew the psychology that one would need but resuscitate from its dust.

Now, it is here that the brakes that Jones intends to slam on by championing Freud take on the value that interests us here, since he confirms *ab ovo*, I mean, at the germination stage of psychoanalysis, the position I adopt in my teaching.

Jones explicitly goes so far here as to enunciate the principle with which Jung excluded himself from psychoanalysis.

It can be summarized in a word, which is relevant in recalling that the 719
thing is still there, regardless of where its label comes from: what Jones intends to ward off is the "hermeneuticization" of psychoanalysis.

The symbol that he calls true, because it designates the one that Freud isolated, does not "symbolize" in the sense in which the figures of the Old Testament symbolize on the basis of what becomes of them in the New Testament, which remains the commonsense meaning of symbolism.

This is why it is easy for him to point out the slippage that occurs in Silberer's work, slippage which aligns him with Jung. The symbol allows itself to be surpassed by what it figures once it comes to be no more than a figurative meaning.

Now, what it allows to surpass it are the invisible realities that return behind a veil which they have perhaps not always had but which they have had for quite a while; and our memory of this veil must be effaced.

Let us not be mistaken here. The role Freud grants to the "functional phenomenon" is granted due to the secondary revision of the dream, which says it all, in my view, since Freud explicitly defines secondary revision as the scrambling of the code [*chiffre*] of the dream that occurs by means of a camouflaging which he no less explicitly designates as imaginary.

It does not exclude the absurdity (which must be still more absurd than it lets on, and devoid of any form when it is intimately inscribed) that leads Jones in 1916 to relate it to "a personal communication" he had with Freud, when it is found, however unrelated it may seem, in the lines that tie the "functional phenomenon" to the 1914 edition of the *Traumdeutung*.[1]

One can read there, regarding the functional phenomenon that it concerns, above all, no doubt, about minds "of an especially philosophical and introspective type."

Which is laughable and can be made fun of (as you have seen, I do not deprive myself of doing so) because the question is echoed here whether philosophy suffices to subtract such minds from the effects of the unconscious, when the very discussion shows that, at the time when what Freud said was still taken seriously, the functional phenomenon makes his analysis of the dream come up short since it is not an effect of desire (that is, of *libido*, of desire as sexual).

720 In this case, with the exception being as real as the norm and requiring that we account for its encroachment, the question means: Are there two different laws of sleep?

Now, it is its ridiculousness that is instructive. This is due to the following which can be demonstrated: that a certain rejection of the experience to which Freud gave himself over here is justified insofar as it is the inaugural step of science.

It is the step that I have introduced in psychoanalysis by distinguishing the symbolic from the imaginary in their relationship to the real. This distinction is forced upon us since it derives from psychoanalytic practice through the critique of its intervention and proves to be eristic for the theoretical edifice.

It is a methodological distinction, therefore, which does not constitute for all that—let me indicate this since the term is offered up to me—any sort of threshold in reality [*réel*]. Indeed, if symbolic structuration finds its material in disjoining the imaginary from the real, it becomes all the more effective in disjoining the real itself by being reduced to the signifier's relation to the subject—namely, to a schematism whose value is, at first glance, determined by the degree to which it forces the imaginary to decline.

Although the rigor of this approach is required for access to the second retreat where object *a* traces itself out on the basis of another knot,

I will confine my attention here to the fact that we sense that Jones, failing here, simply highlights how badly he needs my categories.

It is up to me to demonstrate that Freud uses them, given the never failing sureness with which he settles matters in his field, giving himself the last word when scientificity is at stake.

But is that so surprising when his attachment to science explains the aversion with which he supports his adventure, and that the symbolic, the imaginary, and the real are nothing but a *vade mecum* which we use in emergencies, in this field which is ever suspended above those who find it comfortable, being forewarned when they wallow in it?

Thus we can articulate that it is not because the threshold as a symbol, or better stated, as a signifier marking the place where it begins to be called by another name—the house, the naos, and even the outside in what is unpronounceable about it—is materially a flat field stone, which is laid down or put in place, that one can in any way (based on the metaphor of the threshold, employed to note, on a curve coordinating objectified variables, the point at which a state manifests itself, even if it were itself objectified on the basis of apperception or simply the qualitative difference of a sensation) imagine a graspable ledge anywhere in the real, *a fortiori* any layer whatsoever, which constitutes the psychical 721
field (and even the field of simple representation) in it as stratified—that is, as unitary.

It would thus be perfectly futile to qualify the thresholds, which nevertheless are possible to register [*inscrire*], as "functional phenomena" on the basis of the feeling in every field of a heavy and a light, both of which are equally heavy with symbolism, as we shall see further on—if we think we can thereby give them the slightest value in the theory of gravitation, which only took form by borrowing signifiers from an entirely different realm.

Jones, like me, considers this point to be relevant to the matter, which is why he discusses it and settles it as he does. Doesn't he realize to what extent it ultimately involves giving up Antiquity's fantasy about knowledge [*connaissance*]? We need but note here his recourse to the decency of psychoanalytic thought.

But we should also note that this recourse is weakened by him when he articulates it only on the basis of the fact that what is figurative in metaphor must yield to what is concrete in symbolism.

For the entire fiction—which, by attributing the characteristics of primitiveness, archaism, lack of differentiation, and even neurological disintegration to symbolism, contributes to our seeing in it only the virtuality of synthetic functions—acquires the force of argument on the basis of this concrete. Adding to it their potentiality merely crowns the error by wrapping it in mystique.

Brandishing the sword on this terrain which is thus secondary in 1916, Jones no doubt triumphs. We will excuse him for failing to ward off the danger that will arise shy of it: precisely from the *psychologization* with which psychoanalytic practice will ever more weigh itself down in opposition to Freud's discovery.

For no sense of shame can prevail against an effect at the level of the profession, that of enrolling the practitioner in services in which psychologization is a perfect pathway for all sorts of well specified necessities in the social world: How can one refuse to speak the language of those for whom one serves as a prop? When the question is framed in this way, one cannot even see any harm in it. Psychoanalysis has withered to such an extent that it thus forgets that its first responsibility is to language.

This is why Jones proves to be "too weak"* (as it was repeated to me) to politically master Anafreudianism. I have coined this term to designate a form of Freudianism that is reduced for use in an *ana*, and which is supported by Freud Anna.

722 The fact that Jones furthered the cause of the Kleinians against this clan suffices to demonstrate that he opposed it. The fact that he indicated in Vienna his total agreement with Melanie Klein, however weak her conceptualizations must have seemed to him with respect to his own requirements, also suffices to demonstrate his faithfulness to a truly psychoanalytic approach.

And since this agreement proclaimed in Vienna concerned the discussion that he dominated about the phallic phase in women, let me provide a commentary to help those who, as I have seen, show little finesse in understanding my meaning here.

In the preceding text, I highlighted the astonishing fact that Jones remains deaf to the import of his own catalog of "primary ideas" that group symbols in the unconscious. For if we extend this catalog on the basis of his statement that the concrete grounds the true symbol, he merely brings out more clearly the counter-truth of this statement. For every one of these ideas is lacking in the concrete, since they stand up in the real only thanks to the signifier, so much so that one could say that they only ground a reality by having it raise itself up on a base of unreality [*irréel*]: death, desire, and the name of the father.

It would thus be hopeless to expect Jones to realize that the symbolic function allows the nodal point to appear here at which a symbol comes to the place of lack constituted by the "missing from its place" that is necessary for the dimension of displacement, from which the whole play of symbols stems, to arise.

I immediately suggested the symbol of the snake in the very modulation of the sentence [in the preceding text] in which I evoked the fantasy by which Anna O . . . falls asleep in the *Studies on Hysteria*, the snake which is not a symbol of libido, of course, no more than the bronze serpent is a symbol of redemption—nor is this snake the symbol of the penis, as Jones professes, but rather the symbol of the place where the penis is missing.

If I thus did not take the logical structure any further [in that text], it was no doubt because I was dealing with an audience that had been rendered unprepared for the rudiments of its articulation.

All of my rhetoric aims at bolstering the training effect that I must nevertheless provide that audience.

It must be added here that those who seemed the best prepared to anticipate its implications preferred to beat their heads against the form of this sentence.

A little game, of Chinese origin if one is to believe the instructions,
nicely illustrates the function of place in symbolism, for it requires the 723
player to simply slide pieces of unequal sizes over a surface, where they leave empty a modest square, in order to arrive at a predetermined position. The same is no doubt also true of the resistances that it demonstrates in the practice of the combinatory. The game is called Red Donkey [*l'Âne Rouge*].

The resistance I am referring to is in the imaginary. And it is because, in my very first steps in psychoanalysis, I gave it its status in the mirror stage that I was later able to give symbolism its proper place.

Indeed, confusions in the symbolic stem from the imaginary—this has been known forever. But the error, which is no less longstanding, is to try to remedy this through a critique of representation, when the imaginary remains prevalent in it. Jones remains dependent upon this conception, for when he defines the symbol as an "idea" of the concrete, he already consents to it being but a figure.

His bias is Baconian. We are marked by this in school where we are taught that the decisive axis of science lies in its recourse to the *sensorium*, which is qualified as experimental.

The imaginary is not in any sense the illusory, in my view. On the contrary, I grant it its function as real by basing it on biology—that is, as we saw earlier in the IRM, on the innate effect of the imago, which is manifest in all forms of display.

In this respect, we are faithful in psychoanalysis to an affiliation that we feel the need to distinguish quite foolishly from the term "biological" in order to oppose it to a culturalism to which we claim to contribute in no regard.

We simply do not indulge in those forms of delusion that we have sufficiently designated. To biologize in our field is to bring back into it everything that is useful to us in the science known as biology, and not simply to call upon something real that is alive.

To speak of urethral or anal instinct, or even to mix them together, has no more biological meaning than to tickle one's semblable or to be an undertaker. To highlight animal ethology or the subjective impact of neonatal prematurity in *Hominoidea* does have biological meaning.

Symbolic thought must be situated, as I try to do, in relation to scientific thought, but we will find nothing in it if we seek out this relationship in the virtual or potential.

724 This relationship is found in the actual.

There has never been any other thought than symbolic thought, and scientific thought is the kind of thought that reduces symbolism by grounding the subject in it—this is called mathematics in everyday language.

It is thus not at all with respect to a depreciation of thought, a retardation of the subject, an archaism of development, or even a dissolution of mental function—or more absurdly still, the metaphor of being freed from automatisms that supposedly register its results—that symbolism can be situated, even if it perpetuates the impact related to these states in the real.

Conversely, one cannot say that symbolic thought has always been ripe with scientific thought, if one intends to include no knowledge in it. This merely provides material for historical casuistry.

Psychoanalysis has the privilege that symbolism is reduced in it to the truth effect that, whether it is extracted or not from its pathetic forms, it isolates in its knot as the counterpart without which nothing can be conceived of by way of knowledge.

"Knot" here means the division that the signifier engenders in the subject, and it is a true knot in that it cannot be flattened out.

The knot of the functional phenomenon is merely a false knot according to this criterion, and this is why Jones pretends that it redoubles the first knot. But flattening out the second one does not make the first one easier to deal with.

The structure of the symbol is that of a knot that one cannot flatten out; this structure is such that one cannot found an identification unless something serves as the support to cut it.

1966

Note

1. See *La Science des rêves* (Paris: Alcan, 1939), 308–9 and 450–52 [in English, see *SE* V, 214, footnote 4, and 503–6].

725

Guiding Remarks for a Convention on Female Sexuality

I. Historical Introduction[1]

If we consider the experience of psychoanalysis in the course of its sixty-year development, no one will be surprised to hear that, while it conceived of itself at first as grounding the castration complex—the first offspring of its origins—in repression brought on by the father, it has progressively turned its interest toward frustrations coming from the mother, an interest by which this complex has not been better elucidated, although its forms have been distorted.

A notion of affective deficiency, directly linking developmental problems to real defects in mothering, is paralleled by a dialectic of fantasies whose imaginary field is the maternal body.

What is at stake here is obviously the conceptual promulgation of woman's sexuality and it allows us to note a striking negligence.

II. Definition of the Subject

This negligence concerns the very point to which people would like to draw attention at this juncture: namely, the female part [*partie*], if this term has any meaning, in what is at stake in genital relations where the act of coitus occupies at least a local place.

Or, so as not to lower ourselves from the lofty biological landmarks with which we continue to be content: What libidinal pathways are assigned to women by the anatomically visible signs of sexual differentiation among higher organisms? 726

III. Review of the Facts

Such a project requires us to first review:

(a) the phenomena attested to by women under the conditions of psychoanalytic experience regarding the avenues and act of coitus, insofar as these phenomena confirm or fail to confirm the nosological bases of our medical point of departure;
(b) the subordination of these phenomena to the mainsprings that our analytic activity recognizes as desires, and especially to their unconscious offshoots—with the effects on the psychical economy that result therefrom, whether they are afferent or efferent with respect to the act—among which those of love can be regarded separately, not to mention the transition of their consequences to children;
(c) the never recanted implications of a psychical bisexuality related first to anatomical duplications, but which have been progressively transferred to "personological" identifications.

*IV. The Shine [*Éclat*] of Absences*

From such a summary, certain absences can be isolated whose interest cannot be avoided by withdrawing the case [*non-lieu*]:

1. While we must always be reserved when it comes to the clinical interpretation of the new findings of physiology (for example, the facts of chromosomal sex and its genetic correlates, its distinction from hormonal sex, and their proportional share in anatomical determination—or simply what has been found regarding the libidinal privilege of the male hormone, and even the ordering of estrogen metabolism in the menstrual phenomenon), they nevertheless give us pause for thought since they have been ignored by a practice in which people readily base their case on a messianic access to decisive chemisms.

The distance from reality [*réel*] that is maintained here may, indeed, raise the question of the dividing line [*coupure*] involved—which, if it is not to be
drawn between the somatic and the psychical that are consubstantial, must be 727
drawn between organism and subject, on condition that we repudiate for the latter the affective valuation with which the theory of error has burdened it,

in order to articulate it instead as the subject of a combinatory, the latter alone giving the unconscious its meaning.

2. Inversely, a paradox that originates in the psychoanalytic approach—the key position of the phallus in libidinal development—is of interest due to the insistence with which it is repeated in the facts.

It is here that the question of the phallic phase in women becomes still more problematic, in that after having created an uproar from 1927 to 1935, it has since been left tacitly intact, interpreted by everyone however he likes.

It is by investigating the reasons for this that we can put an end to this suspension [of the question].

Imaginary, real, or symbolic: as concerns the impact of the phallus in the subjective structure to which development adapts, these are not terms from an individual's teaching but the very terms by which, in writings by certain authors, the conceptual slippage is indicated that has led, since it was not checked, to the lifelessness of analytic experience after the stagnation of debate.

V. The Darkness Cast upon the Vaginal Organ

The apperception of a prohibition, however oblique the preceding may have been, may serve us as a prelude.

Is it confirmed by the fact that our discipline—which, justifying its field in terms of sexuality, seemed to promise to bring the whole secret of sexuality to light—has left what is recognized about feminine jouissance at the exact point at which a hardly zealous physiology threw in the towel?

The rather trivial opposition between clitoral jouissance and vaginal satisfaction has been so greatly reinforced by the theory that it has worried many subjects, and the theory has even taken this worry up as a theme, if not as a demand—though we cannot say, for all that, that the opposition between them has been elucidated any more correctly.

This is true because the nature of vaginal orgasm has kept its obscurity inviolate.

728 For the massotherapeutic notion of the sensitivity of the cervix and the surgical notion of a *noli tangere* regarding the posterior wall of the vagina prove in fact (in hysterectomies of course, but also in vaginal aplasias!) to be contingent.

Representatives of the fairer sex, however loud their voices among analysts, do not seem to have given their all to remove the seal of secrecy.

Apart from the famous "taken on lease" of rectal dependence on which

Lou Andreas-Salomé took a personal stand, they have generally confined themselves to metaphors whose loftiness in the ideal signifies nothing preferable to what the hoi polloi give us by a way of a less intentional poetry.

A convention on female sexuality is not about to cause to weigh upon us the threat of Tiresias' fate.

VI. The Imaginary Complex and Questions of Development

If this state of affairs betrays a scientific impasse in approaching reality [*réel*], the least one can nevertheless expect from psychoanalysts, meeting at a convention, is that they not forget that their method was born of a similar impasse.

If symbols here have only an imaginary hold, this is probably because images are already subjected to an unconscious symbolism, in other words, to a complex. This is an opportune moment to recall that images and symbols *in* women cannot be isolated from images and symbols *of* women.

The representation (*Vorstellung* in the sense in which Freud uses the term when he notes that it is what is repressed) of female sexuality, whether it is repressed or not, conditions its implementation, and its displaced emergences (in which the therapist's doctrine may turn out to be an interested party) seal the fate of the tendencies, however naturally refined [*dégrossies*] one assumes them to be.

It should be recalled that Jones—in his address to the Vienna Psychoanalytic Society, which seems to have scorched the earth for all contributions since—already found nothing to offer but a pure and simple rallying cry to Kleinian concepts in the perfectly brutal form in which Klein presents them: I am referring to Melanie Klein's lack of concern for the fact that the earliest Oedipal fantasies, which she includes in the maternal body, actually derive 729
from the reality presupposed by the Name-of-the-Father.

When we consider that this is all Jones comes up with in his attempt to dispel Freud's paradox, which instates women in a primal ignorance of their sexual organ but which is also tempered by the educated admission of our own ignorance—his attempt being motivated to such a degree by his belief in the dominance of the natural order that he finds it pleasing to assure it with a quote from *Genesis*—it is difficult to see what has been gained.

For since it is a question of the wrong that has been done to the female sex ("is a woman born or made?" Jones cries) by the equivocal function of the phallic phase in the two sexes, it does not seem that femininity is any better specified when the phallus' function becomes still more equivocal by being taken all the way back to oral aggression.

So much noise will not have been in vain, however, if it allows us to modulate the following questions on the lyre of development, since that is its music.

1. Is the bad object of a fantastic phallophagy, which extracts it from the bosom [*sein*] of the maternal body, a paternal attribute?

2. In the case of the same object, raised to the ranks of the good object and desired as a more manageable (*sic*) and more satisfying (in what respect?) nipple, the question becomes more precise: Is it from the same third party that it is borrowed? For it does not suffice to adopt the notion of the "combined parent"—we still must know whether it is as an image or a symbol that this hybrid is constituted.

3. How does the clitoris, as autistic as its solicitations may be, imposing itself nevertheless in reality [*réel*], come to be compared with the preceding fantasies?

If it is independently that it places the little girl's sexual organ under the sign of an organic minus-value, the aspect of proliferating duplication that fantasies take on from it renders them suspect by falling under the heading of "legendary" fabulation.

If it (too) combines with both the bad and the good object, then we need a theory that explains the equivalence function [*fonction d'équivalence*] served by the phallus in the advent of any object of desire, the simple mention of its "partial" character not sufficing.

4. In any case, the question rearises of the structure Freud's approach
730 introduced: namely, the fact that the relation of deprivation or not-being [*manque à être*] symbolized by the phallus is established as a diversion [*dérivation*] from the not-having [*manque à avoir*] engendered by any particular or global frustration of demand; and that it is on the basis of this substitute—which, in the final analysis, the clitoris puts in its place before succumbing in the competition—that the field of desire precipitates its new objects (at the top of the list, the future child [of her own]) by reclaiming [*récupération*] the sexual metaphor in which all the other needs were already taken up.

This remark assigns a limit to questions about development, requiring that they be subordinated to a fundamental synchrony.

VII. Misrecognitions and Biases

At this same point, it is appropriate to investigate whether phallic mediation exhaustively accounts for everything drive-related that can manifest itself in women, especially the whole current of maternal instinct. Why not posit here that the fact that everything that is analyzable is sexual does not mean that everything that is sexual is accessible to analysis?

1. Regarding the [girl's] supposed ignorance [*méconnaissance*] of the vagina: If, on the one hand, it is difficult not to attribute to repression its frequent persistence for an implausibly long period of time, the fact remains that—apart from several case studies (by Josine Müller) that I will set aside due to the very traumas to which they attest—the proponents of "normal" knowledge [*connaissance*] of the vagina are reduced to basing this knowledge on the primacy of a displacement downward of the mouth's experiences, that is, to seriously aggravating the discordance they claim to palliate.

2. Next there is the problem of female masochism which already appears in the promotion of a partial drive—that is, a drive that is regressive in its condition, whether or not it is characterized as pregenital—to the status of a pole of genital maturity.

Indeed, such a characterization cannot be considered to be simply a homonym for "passivity," which is already metaphorical; and its idealizing function, the inverse of its regressive aspect, shines through clearly in the fact that
it is not discussed, unlike the accumulation—which is perhaps forced in mod- 731
ern analytic genesis—of castrating and devouring, dislocating and stupefying effects in feminine activity.

Can we rely on what masochistic perversion owes to male invention and conclude that female masochism is a fantasy of male desire?

3. In any case, I will denounce the irresponsible mental retardation that claims to deduce fantasies of the breaking of corporal boundaries from an organic constant whose prototype would be the rupture of the ovular membrane—a crude analogy that shows clearly enough how far such people are from Freud's way of thinking in this domain when he elucidates the taboo of virginity.

4. For we verge here on the mainspring by which *vaginismus* is distinguished from neurotic symptoms even when they coexist, which explains why the former yields to a suggestive procedure whose success is well known in painless childbirth.

If analysis has, in effect, degenerated to the point of swallowing its own vomit by tolerating that people in its circle confuse anxiety and fear, it is perhaps time to distinguish between unconscious and bias regarding the signifier's effects.

And to recognize, simultaneously, that the analyst is just as liable as anyone else to have a bias regarding sex, above and beyond [*passé*] what the unconscious reveals to him.

Do we recall Freud's oft-repeated advice not to reduce the supplement of the feminine with respect to the masculine to the complement of the passive with respect to the active?

VIII. Frigidity and Subjective Structure

1. Frigidity—however broad its realm may be, and it is almost generic if one takes into account its transitory form—presupposes the entire unconscious structure that determines neurosis, even if it appears outside of the context of symptoms. This accounts, on the one hand, for the fact that it is refractory to all somatic treatments and, on the other hand, for the usual failure of the dedicated efforts [*bons offices*] of the most desired partner.

732 Analysis alone mobilizes it, at times incidentally, but always in a transference that cannot be contained in the infantilizing dialectic of frustration, or even deprivation, but clearly such that it brings symbolic castration into play. This amounts here to the recalling to mind of a principle.

2. This principle is easy to lay out: Castration cannot be deduced from development alone, since it presupposes the subjectivity of the Other as the locus of its law. The difference between the sexes [*L'altérité du sexe*] is denatured by this alienation. A man serves here as a relay so that a woman becomes this Other to herself, as she is to him.

It is in this respect that an unveiling of the Other involved in the transference can modify a symbolically commanded defense.

I mean that the defense here can be conceptualized, firstly, in the dimension of mascarade that the presence of the Other liberates in the sexual role.

If one begins anew from this veil effect to relate the object's position to it, one will divine how the monstrous conceptualization, whose analytic asset was investigated above, may deflate. Perhaps this conceptualization simply means that everything can be attributed to a woman insofar as she represents the absolute Other in the phallocentric dialectic.

We must thus return to penis envy (*Penisneid*) in order to observe that at two different times, and with a certainty equally lessened at each of them by the memory of the other, Jones makes of it a perversion and then a phobia.

The two assessments are equally false and dangerous. The one marks the effacement of the function of structure before that of development, toward which analysis has slipped ever further—to be contrasted here with Freud's emphasis on phobia as the cornerstone of neurosis. The other inaugurates the rise of the maze to which the study of the perversions has found itself condemned in attempting to account for the function of the object in perversion.

At the last detour of this palace of mirages, people arrive at the splitting* of the object, not having known how to discern, in Freud's admirable interrupted note on the splitting* of the ego*, the fading* of the subject that accompanies it.

"Fading" is perhaps also the term that can dissipate the illusion of the splitting* in which analysis has gotten bogged down by making good and bad into attributes of the object. 733

If the sexes have different positions with respect to the object, it is owing to the distance that separates the fetishistic form of love from the erotomaniacal form of love. We should find its salient features in the most ordinary lived experience.

3. If one begins with a man in order to assess the reciprocal position of the sexes, one sees that phallus-girls, this equation having been posited by Fenichel in a meritorious yet groping manner, proliferate in a Venusberg to be situated beyond the "You are my wife" by which he constitutes his partner; it is confirmed thereby that what reemerges in the subject's unconscious is the Other's desire [*le désir de l'Autre*], that is, [a desire for] the phallus that was desired by the Mother.

After which, the question arises of knowing whether the real penis, because it belongs to her sexual partner, destines a woman to an attachment devoid of duplicity, although it does not effect the elimination of the incestuous desire which supposedly occurs naturally here.

One would be approaching the problem from the wrong angle were one to consider it to be resolved.

4. Why not admit, in fact, that if there is no virility that castration does not consecrate, it is a castrated lover or a dead man (or the two in one) who, for woman, hides behind the veil in order to call her adoration to it—that is, [he calls] from the same locus beyond the maternal semblable from which the threat came to her of a castration that does not really concern her.

Thus it is because of this ideal incubus that an embrace-like receptivity must be displaced in a sheath-like sensitivity onto the penis.

This is thwarted by any imaginary identification a woman may have (in her stature as an object offered up to desire) with the phallic standard [*étalon*] that props up fantasy.

In the either/or position in which the subject finds herself caught between a pure absence and a pure sensitivity, we should not be surprised that the narcissism of desire immediately latches onto the narcissism of the ego* that is its prototype.

The fact that insignificant beings may be inhabited by such a subtle dialectic is what analysis accustoms us to, and it is explained by the fact that banality is the ego's* least significant shortcoming.

5. The figure of Christ, which is evocative in this respect of other older
figures, plays a more extensive role [*instance*] here than the subject's religious 734
allegiance would imply. And it is worth noting that the unveiling of the most hidden signifier, that of the Mysteries, was reserved for women.

At a more down-to-earth level we thus account for: a) the fact that the duplicity of the subject is masked in women, all the more so in that the partner's servitude makes him especially apt to represent the victim of castration; b) the true reason why the demand that the Other be faithful takes on its particular character in women; c) the fact that she justifies this demand all the more readily with the supposed argument of her own faithfulness.

6. This review of the problem of frigidity is traced out in terms in which analysis' classical instances can easily be reaccommodated. Its broad outlines attempt to help avoid the pitfall owing to which analytic writings are becoming ever more denatured: namely, their resemblance to the reassembly of a bicycle by a savage who has never seen one, using spare parts [*organes détachés*] from models that are far enough apart historically that they do not bear any relation to each other, their use for two different purposes thus not being ruled out.

At the very least, let some elegance renew the comic side of the trophies thus obtained.

IX. Female Homosexuality and Ideal Love

1. Studying the framework of perversion in women introduces another perspective.

Given that it has been largely demonstrated for most of the male perversions that their imaginary motive is the desire to preserve a phallus—the one that interested the subject in his mother—the absence in women of fetishism, which represents the virtually blatant case of this desire, leads us to suspect that this desire has a different fate in the perversions women present.

For to suppose that a woman herself assumes the role of the fetish merely introduces the question of her different position with respect to desire and the object.

Jones—in his article, "The Early Development of Female Sexuality," which inaugurated a series—begins from his exceptional experience of
735 homosexuality in women and takes things up in a middle register [*médium*] that he might perhaps have done better to sustain. He has the subject's desire bifurcate in the choice she is supposedly forced to make between her incestuous object, her father here, and her own sex. The resulting light that Jones sheds on the matter would be greater if he did not stop short due to his reliance upon the overly convenient prop of identification.

Better armed observation would show, it seems, that what is at stake is, instead, a sublation [*relève*] of the object: one might say a challenge that is accepted [*défi relevé*]. Freud's original case study, inexhaustible as usual, allows us to grasp that this challenge finds its point of departure in a demand [*exigence*] for love which is held up to ridicule in reality [*réel*] and that it leads to nothing less than artificially making a virtue of [*se donner les gants de*] courtly love.

If courtly love, more than any other form of love, prides itself on being the love that gives what it does not have, this is certainly what the female homosexual excels in doing regarding what she is missing.

It is not really the incestuous object that she chooses at the expense of her own sex; what she does not accept is that this object only assumes [*assume*] his sex at the cost of castration.

This is not to say that she renounces hers for all that: on the contrary, in all the forms of female homosexuality, even unconscious, the supreme interest is in femininity and Jones clearly detected the link here between the fantasy of man, the invisible witness, and the care taken by the subject in giving her partner jouissance.

2. We must still learn something from the natural ease with which such women invoke their quality as men, in order to contrast it with the delusional style of the male transsexualist.

Perhaps we see thereby the doorway that leads from female sexuality to desire itself.

The passivity of the act does not at all correspond to this desire; female sexuality appears, instead, as the effort of a jouissance enveloped in its own contiguity (of which any circumcision perhaps indicates the symbolic break) in order to be *realized in competition* with the desire that castration liberates in the male in giving him the phallus as its signifier.

Is it then this signifying privilege that Freud is aiming at when he suggests that there is perhaps but one libido and that it is marked with the male sign? If some chemical configuration supported it beyond, could we fail to see the exalting conjunction of the dissymmetry of the molecules employed by the 736
living construction with the lack in the subject orchestrated by language, which is such that desire's supporters and the appellants of the fairer sex (the partiality of the term *sexe* always being the same here) act there as rivals?

X. Female Sexuality and Society

Several questions remain to be raised regarding the social impact of female sexuality.

1. Why does the analytic myth come up short concerning the prohibition of incest between father and daughter?

2. How are we to situate the social effects of female homosexuality, in rela-

tion to those that Freud attributes—regarding presuppositions that diverge radically from the allegory to which they have since been reduced—to male homosexuality: namely, a sort of entropy moving in the direction of a degrading of the community?

Without going so far as to contrast it with the antisocial effects that earned Catharism, as well as the Love it inspired, its disappearance, could we not, if we consider the eros of female sexuality in the more accessible movement of the Précieuses, grasp what it conveys by way of information as running counter to social entropy?

3. Lastly, why does the social instance of women remain transcendent to the contractual order propagated by labor? And, in particular, is the status of marriage maintained by its effect, despite the decline of paternalism?

These are all questions that cannot be reduced to an orderly field of needs.

Written two years before the Convention.

Note

1. This convention, known as the International Colloquium of Psychoanalysis, took place September 5–9, 1960, at the city university of Amsterdam. My text was published in the last issue of the journal *La Psychanalyse* to which I directly contributed [VII (1962): 3–14].

VI

The Youth of Gide, or the Letter and Desire 739

On a book by Jean Delay and another by Jean Schlumberger[1]

> Σκαιοῖσι μὲν γὰρ καινὰ προσφέρων σοφὰ
> δόξεις ἀχρεῖος κοὐ σοφὸς πεφυκέναι
> τῶν δ᾽ αὐ δοκούντων εἰδέναι τι ποικίλον
> κρείσσων νομισθεὶς λυπρὸς ἐν πόλει φανεῖ.
> —Euripides, *Medea*, 298–301

> And whether it is a metaphor or not, what I am saying here is perfectly true.
> —André Gide, *La Tentative amoureuse*

The work that Jean Delay devoted to the youth of André Gide, which came out in two volumes, one a year after the other, has already met with considerable success.[2] Literary critics have, without any notable discordance, acclaimed it and appreciated the wide variety of its merits.

I would like to show here the conjunction whereby a work, which is scientifically grounded in the fact that its author is eminently qualified to approach it from a general perspective, manages, in the particularity of its object, to lay out a problem in which the usual generalities change: it is to these most topical works that history promises a long life.

The problem, that of *man's relationship to the letter*, calls history itself into question, and thus it will be understood that contemporary thought grasps it only by enveloping it through a convergence effect of a geometrical kind, or, since we recognize that a strategy is found in the unconscious, by proceeding with an envelopment maneuver that can be discerned in our so-called human sciences—which are already no longer overly human.

Relating Delay's work to this problem does not excuse me from promising the reader—and in order to introduce the most inexperienced to the matters that will be discussed here—a pleasure that will captivate him in the book's very first pages, without him having to resist, and that will carry him, 740
effortlessly, it will seem to him, right to the last of its 1,300 pages.

The sureness of the writing is the instrument of the pleasure in which he will be, in some sense, absorbed. The word "masterful" can be applied here first to the art of a form of composition—whose folds are dissimulated by an alternation of perspectives, documents, analysis, commentary, and reconstructions—that only comes to one's attention by appearing each time to offer it respite.

It is upon closing the book that the reader realizes that nothing in it was motivated by anything other than a concern with providing an exact, delicate assessment. The touch of humor with which the author tempers its execution at moderate intervals is merely the room he makes for the comedy that structures things: assuming that the tone he adopts in it surprises the reader in remaining devoid of affectation while running parallel to the modulation, which is one-of-a-kind, that his model brought out in his work.

This is the threshold of the performance we are about to witness, for it denotes the author's disposition, which is that of what in Gidian terms I would call the most tender attention. For this is clearly the kind of attention that leads him to revive somewhere the archaic genitive of the "Gide childhoods." And it is also the one that Gide was able to distinguish in their friendship, which developed late in his life.

Thus we see why Delay, who has already proven his talent as a writer in sensitive work that future generations will return to, only employs his art in proportion to the *artifex* to whom he devotes it. This is confirmed by the astonishing uniformity, throughout this long work, of the qualities I have just mentioned, and justifies my changing as I please the Buffonesque aphorism, enunciating it as follows: the style is the object.

In so doing, Delay claims to isolate a genre: psychobiography. Regardless of the law to which he wishes to submit it, the fact that he simultaneously provides its chef-d'oeuvre cannot be without importance in grasping its limit. This limit seems to me to be singularly revealed in the fate that befalls the work, and regarding which the old sacred monster wagered, I would swear to it, in giving his partner the material for an exceptional test, certain as he was that in taking it up, he could but complete it.

741 Delay's very success shows what his lot was: the greater the rigor he applied to the subject of such an author, the more likely he would be to produce the most necessary complement to the author's work. The psychobiographical "postface" to the writer aimed at here turns out, once completed, to have become a preface to his works, not being doomed to simply follow them on the bookshelves, like a neighbor bearing witness, like Boswell for Johnson, and like Eckermann with Goethe, but beating the very drum to which their message will continue to march.

The reader will excuse me for theorizing here about the turning point that Sainte-Beuve constitutes, in order to shift it from literary criticism to a literary condition. Let us say, so as not to beat around the bush, that Sainte-Beuve grants the critic the power to make the writer's private life intrude into the literary work to the degree of his own vanity. Allow me to define this private life in relation to the work itself, of which it becomes in some sense the negative, being everything about himself that the writer did not publish.

We are well aware of the project Sainte-Beuve used to justify this, which is a natural history of minds. But withholding our judgment regarding such an aim, and without otherwise taking a stand on the naturalness that it qualifies, we can separate out the obvious effects it has had on the condition it places on the work of writing.

I am thus adopting a stance of objective neutrality regarding Proust's position "against Sainte-Beuve," regardless of the relevance it derives from the poet's authority to speak about his creation, and more expressly from an analysis of the poetic message, which leaves no doubt but that approaching it requires a method suited to its nature.

Proust's own writings indisputably show that the poet finds the material of his message in his own life. But the operation carried out by this message reduces his life events to their use as material. And this is true even though the message claims to articulate the experience that furnished these events, for at the very most the message can manage to be seen in this experience.

We must not hesitate to go so far as to say that the signifierness of the message makes do with all the falsifications brought to what the experience supplies, the latter including at times the writer's very flesh. Indeed, the only thing that is of importance is a truth that is based on the fact that the message
condenses in its unveiling. There is so little opposition between this *Dichtung* 742
and *Wahrheit* in its nakedness that the fact of the poetic operation must make us notice, instead, the following feature which we forget in every truth: truth shows itself [*s'avère*] in a fictional structure.[3]

As for insights into the published work, what literary critics have produced by resorting to the writer's private life has remained rather evasive to date, with respect to their naturalness. But this practice—protests against which in the name of some kind of decency merely miss the point—has instead engendered a revolution in literary values. It has done so by introducing into a market, whose effects have been regulated by printing techniques for the past four centuries, a new sign of value: what we call short(er) writings [*petits papiers*]. The manuscripts that print had relegated to the function of the unpublished reappear as an integral part of the work with a function that deserves examination.

This is clearly the material offered up in the present work: personal notes taken by Gide for his memoirs, published as *Si le grain ne meurt*; unpublished passages from his journal; notes he took on his readings between the ages of 20 and 24, significantly designated by him as his "subjective"; the enormous correspondence with his mother up until her death when he was 26; and a pile of unpublished letters collected by those around him, which increases the size of the edifice by the square of its mass when added to the published letters.

In this mass we must include the hole left by the correspondence with his
743 cousin, Madeleine Rondeaux, who became his wife, a hole whose place, importance, and cause I will discuss later.

Things told to Delay in confidence and seen by him in person take up only a discreet amount of room here, which is fortunately less exiguous than he tells us he would have liked, but which he seems rather to have effaced.

Neither Gide's work nor the content of these intimate writings leaves any doubt as to the aim of the consummate *homo litterarius* Delay sees in him. The short(er) writings are, right from the outset and still more when they are tied together in bundles with string, planned with an eye to the body they must constitute, if not in the work itself, at least in relation to it. One might wonder what such an aim could offer of interest to Sainte-Beuve if it were truly naturalness he had in mind.

In this aim, indeed, Gide does not simply redouble his message by adding his private thoughts to them—he cannot help but have his actions oriented by them. Let us note that his actions do not defer, as has always been the case, solely to his concern with glory, but also, and we find this term in his own writing, to his concern with his biography.

To suspect on that basis that his entire life was insincere would be absurd, even if one were to argue that his biography recounts nothing base, no betrayal, no jealousy, no sordid motivation, and still less ordinary stupidity. One might note here that a psychoanalysis, while it is going on, constrains the subject's actions more than he thinks, and that this changes nothing in the problems raised by his behavior. We sense clearly enough that when Gide explains his loaning of capital to an esteemed friend in need[4] by expressly indicating that he is "looking after [his] biography," he is staking his confidence on this wager, in which pride has other outlets than to broadcast his good deed.

The soul is always permeable to an element of discourse. What we are looking for, in the place in which the soul is constituted by the history of a word, are the effects to which many other words have contributed and from which the dialogue with God tries to take its bearings. These remarks are not
744 irrelevant to Gide's soliloquy as a beautiful soul.

This soliloquy is conveyed in his literary work; aren't the short(er) writings distinguished from that work simply by their deferred communication?

It is here that Delay's book enlightens us with its appearance: the short(er) writings differ not in their content but in the audience to whom they are addressed.

They are addressed to the biographer, and not to just any biographer. Reading Goethe's memoirs, Gide wrote to his mother that he was "learning more by reading how Goethe blew his nose than [he] would by reading about how a *concièrge* received Holy Communion." And he added: "Moreover, these memoirs are of very little interest regarding what they recount . . . If they were not *written* by Goethe, if Goethe had had Eckermann write in his stead, there would remain merely their slight interest as documents."[5]

Let us say that, in allowing Delay to *write in his stead* about his short(er) writings, Gide was not unaware that Delay knew how to write nor that he was not Eckermann. But he also knew that Delay was an eminent psychiatrist, and that, in the final analysis, the eternal destination of these short(er) writings was the psychobiographer.

Let us consider what leads people to say that the psychoanalyst in our times has taken the place of God. This reflection of omnipotence (which, moreover, the analyst greets with the pedantic-like detour of challenging this omnipotence at the core of his patient's thinking) must come to him from somewhere.

It comes from the fact that, in order to live with his soul, man in our times needs the catechism's answer that gave him consistency.

Gide knew how to do what it was appropriate to do with God and thus expected something else. Delay does not pointlessly mention Montaigne here and his way of addressing another who is yet to come regarding his private life, in which he gives up trying to discern what the signifier will be for this other. A similar form of address allows us to understand why the ambiguity with which Gide develops his message is found again in his short(er) writings.

The miracle, which is how we should designate the present situation, is
that in applying his role as consultant to the letter of the short(er) writings, 745
Delay relays this ambiguity, finding anew in this soul the very effect in which the message formed. In Narcissus' water, the grassy depths have the same wavelength as the reflection of the foliage.

Through Delay's work, psychology has a unique confrontation with literary criticism. The lesson is gripping, for we see the subject's composition become organized in all its rigor therein.

Allow me to say how this can be instructive. First, I will not consider following in Delay's footsteps, however much one may forget that one is following him in seeing him so beautifully take up where Gide left off. A bloodhound on a hunter's track, he is not the one who will efface it. He stops and points it out to us with his shadow. He isolates, as if from himself, the very absence that caused it.

Regarding the family that was Gide's own and not a social abstraction, Delay begins with a chronicle.

He shows us how the tree of the bourgeoisie that arose under Louis XIV grew from a farmer, Nicolas Rondeaux, who acquired wealth by trading staples from the colonies, already no doubt Arnolphe imagining himself to be Monsieur de la Souche. His son married into the family of a certain Father D'Incarville, his grandson was granted the name de Sétry, and his great-grandson was Charles Rondeaux de Montbray, who was fascinated by the Enlightenment and even by illuminism—since F therefore M therefore—and suffered several misfortunes due to the French Revolution. This hardy tree—which was constantly grafted with high quality branches, and was not lacking in the crowning jewel of scholarly distinction granted for research in the natural sciences—left, after the storm, a seedling that was still vigorous.

Édouard Rondeaux [Charles's son] could rival in deal making with the Turelures, who in those new times offered up as an ideal their practice—"get rich"—thanks to which they supposedly elevated the grandeur of France. If, however, their political preeminence never led to a clear title to this elevation, it is perhaps because the only virtue that accounted for their existence, self-abnegation, was a little too exposed in those times to the suspicion of hypocrisy. Fortunately, they delegated the tradition of this virtue, along with its privileges, to their wives, which explains the comedy to which their memory has been consigned.

This comedy, which is especially immanent in a surprising dialogue found in the correspondence between Gide and his mother, is preserved throughout
746 the book from the tragedy of the relation to the maternal figure wrought by psychologizing pedantry. This is clear right from this section of the book in the sketch of the blossoming of men's paunches, which is juxtaposed with the striking fact that, in two generations of Protestant affiliation, the women turn this family into a stronghold of Protestantism and a playpen of moral mothering—to which we owe the boon, after reduction of the penultimate males in the family to an insignificant status, of an illustrious specimen of humanity.

His father's bourgeois background suggests another extraction, that of lawyers and academics, whom Delay credits with Florentine ancestry. The grandfather's close supervision of Paul Gide's preparations for his aggregation examination, Paul being André's father, is told movingly in order to introduce both the lightning-fast advancement of this original professor of law, and the loss felt by André for a sensitive father who only extricated himself from an unfulfilling marriage through an untimely death.

The heartrending image of this father appears in the veiled confession of a maxim tucked away in one of Paul's diaries, and in the tone of his filial devotion as retransmitted by Gide—one of Delay's rare references to his own memories.

But further on a letter written by Uncle Charles rouses heightened emotions in us, regarding which we turn in vain to psychology for answers when we set out to reduce them to the supposed norms of comprehension. Responding to something told him in confidence by his nephew concerning the loss of his virginity to Meriem, the charming Oulad, this cultured man violently opposed an act about which the least one can say is that the context of customary, nay ritual, prostitution in which it was situated would require him to temper his moralizing about it; nevertheless, Uncle Charles finds nothing better with which to depict its stigma than the stain of the act, impossible to undo once committed, of parricide that Lady Macbeth attempts in vain to efface.[6]

So it is that at the first stirrings of his explorations, the very thing dissipates 747
that Gide believed he had to retain by way of Tainean reverence for the incompatibilities of the inheritance turning sour in his blood. Myths give way to a method that recreates every being in his discourse, to repay each for his speech.

A marriage of psychology and the letter—I would like to echo here a title by William Blake that was dear to Gide, in order to designate what happens when the letter, being educated by psychology, refinds in it its own instance in a position to direct it.

If Delay notes in passing that Janet's description of psychasthenia is confirmed here, it is to show that the description Gide provides of his own states of mind coincides with it, except for the fact that Gide's description is written in stricter language.[7] We see here how we can wonder whether the scientific functions used to articulate the theory—reality function and psychological tension—are not simple metaphors of the symptom, and whether a symptom which is poetically so fruitful is not itself constructed like a metaphor, which would not for all that reduce it to a *flatus vocis*, the subject here paying the price of the signifying operation with the elements of his personality.

This suggests, in my view, the ultimate mainspring of the psychoanalytic discovery. None of these avenues is foreign to Delay; he tries them out here, one after the other, without being able to do any better than to refer to fragments of theory into which analytic doctrine is currently disintegrating. Yet he is able to turn everything to advantage assuming he brings each stone to the right place, so much so that one can say that this book would not be the same without psychoanalysis.

It did not even for a minute run the risk of resembling what the analytic world calls a work of "applied psychoanalysis." Delay immediately rejects what this absurd qualification translates by way of confusion on the part of analysts. Psychoanalysis is applied, strictly speaking, only as a treatment and thus to a subject who speaks and hears.

In the absence of such circumstances it can only be a question of psycho-
748 analytic method, the method that proceeds with the deciphering of signifiers without concern for any form of presumed existence of the signified.

What Delay's work shows brilliantly is that a study, to the extent to which it observes this principle, and owing solely to its honest espousal of the proper method for reading literary material, encounters the very structure of the subject that psychoanalysis sketches out in the organization of its own exposition.

Psychoanalysts will no doubt consider that this once again proves just how important their doctrine is. They would do better to be concerned at the fact that no work that has come out under the rubric of applied psychoanalysis is preferable to this one as regards the purity of the method employed and the well-foundedness of its results.

Delay always begins with the material his subject offers him: in this case, the road paved by Gide himself, who was, as we know, interested in psychoanalysis.

It was Jacques Rivière's circle that first brought Freud's message to the forefront [in France] after World War I, the medical circle in which the astonishing Hesnard had discussed Freud starting in 1910, although he had to be begged to do so. Gide attempted to undergo analysis with Mrs. Sokolnicka who had come at that time to France as a *missa dominica* for the Viennese orthodoxy. He was a bit too much not to have escaped the holds—lacking, no doubt, in a bit of penetrating strength—of the likable pioneer. It is surprising that he was so little concerned with looking at the texts and judged Freud in a way whose repercussions cannot spare even someone of his stature.[8]

It is nevertheless in light of the explanations given by Sokolnicka, presented in an undisguised manner in his novel *The Counterfeiters*, that he sheds light on a childhood tragedy which befalls the character, little Boris, and which is taken up by Delay for what it is—namely, an elaboration of Gide's own drama.

Little Boris, consigned to his grandfather's care, is nevertheless not submitted to the same conditions as he who, from the time of the death of his
749 father when he was 11, tells us that he felt "suddenly enveloped completely by a love that, from that time forward, closed in" on him, that of his mother.[9]

On the other hand, we have the pleasure of seeing what we already understand, apt to bring knowing nods from the initiated, which can be easily obtained by recalling the overriding importance of the relationship with the mother in the affective life of homosexuals. Beyond that, we have the Oedipus complex, which has become a common term, people speaking about it as they might speak of a dresser—after having been the illness whose destructive effects Gide met with sarcasm that was less costly to him than the earlier instance.[10]

Delay certainly does not limit himself to such a vague articulation.

Who was his mother for this child, and this voice by which love was identified with the commandments of duty? We are aware that there is more than one way to overly cherish a child, and this is true for the mothers of homosexuals as well.

Delay does not give us the map of the labyrinth of identifications with which psychoanalysts cheat in their writings in order not to lose their way. But he has the advantage of finding his way because he does not let go of the thread of his case.

He finds his way by unforgettably unfolding the components of the mother's discourse wherein we can glimpse the composition of her personality.

He dwells on what others might push aside in a vain attempt to look behind it. Regarding Gide's mother as a young girl—who is as unattractive to her suitors as to the graces, and who, her wedding being slow to come, whiles away the time by developing a passion for her governess [Anna Shackleton]—Delay impassively makes her letters speak: jealousy and despotism are not excluded from this passion, even if they are not openly shown, nor are the embraces of an innocent joy, as anchored as they may be in the habits of vestal virgins. Surely we must find another depth to this attachment, behind these unassailable manifestations, for it to have resisted the prejudices of those around her, in a rebellion designed to vanquish them, who objected to it in the name of their difference in social rank.

Just as the antics of the chambermaids correspond to the pathos of the sublime characters in Marivaux's plays, a memory of Gide's as a child corresponds to this: straining to hear in nocturnal space the modulated sobs coming from the garret, where the servants, Marie and Delphine, the latter to 750
be married the next day, were breaking up.

The psychoanalyst can but stop and pause before a screen, which is certainly all the more piquant here as Marie was to become one of the "dragons" who would watch out for what it was that the child was not supposed to be prodigal at.

The silence he was able to maintain at the time, except deep within himself, shows one small facet of an extensive taciturn reign in which darker powers constitute virtue.

In this hallway filled with white-on-black medallions, Delay does not stand still. He knows to what pace he must match his stride, and what shadow, never more than glimpsed in a doorway, designates the female walker, who is formidable in that she always leaves empty the room ahead that she stays in their race around the apartment.

It was this emptiness that the child filled with monsters, the fauna of which we know, since an haruspex, with childlike eyes, an inspired tripe butcher, catalogued them for us, seeing them in the entrails of the nourishing mother.

Because of this, we have attributed these fantasies to the imagination of the child, with its black instincts, without having yet progressed so far as to realize that the mother too had the same fantasies as a child, and that to broach the question by asking what route fantasies take to pass from mother to child would perhaps place us on the very path from which they derive their true impact.

A nightmare, which is part of this series,[11] haunts Gide's sleep right up until the end, except that, starting at one point, he finds the *Crique* that eats him "funny." But what never ceases to fill him with anguish is the appearance on the scene of a shape, that of a woman whose veil has fallen, allowing him to see but a black hole,[12] or who slips away like sand between his fingers when he touches her.[13]

Another abyss corresponds to this in him, the one that opens up in his pri-
751 mal jouissance: the destruction of a beloved toy, the noisy breaking of dishes when the servant carrying them is suddenly tickled, and the strange metamorphosis of Gribouille drifting with the current of a river, sprouting branches and leaves—all these lead him to orgasm.[14]

Jolts, slips, and grimacing shapes—when the actors, the number of whom corresponds to that in Antiquity's plays, come in the front door to populate the stage with their masks, death has already come in the backdoor. For its place to be marked there, that place need no longer even be empty—it is enough for it to be numbered. Or, better put, isn't death itself the number assigned to the places? That is why it is so quick to change places.

The child hears the pure voice of death three times. It is not greeted with anguish, but with a trembling that rises up from the very depths of his being, a sea [*mer*] that submerges everything, a *Schaudern*, the allophonic signifierness of which Delay trusts in to confirm its signification of allogeneity—teaching us its semiology, especially that of the relation to the "second reality" and of the feeling of being cut off from relations with his semblables, by which this state is distinguished from anxious temptation.[15]

This is an example of clinical finesse, and further increases our chagrin at the mindless repetition of stupidities that we hear as psychiatrists, when everything remains to be articulated.

I will not here go into why four corners are necessary in the relation of the ego to the other, and then to the Other, where the subject is constituted as signified.

I will simply refer the reader to the chapters that situate them very simply through the sole progression, which is exemplary to my mind, of Delay's study.

This progression begins with the fact that the earlier constructions, which were more necessary for the child, are redoubled in the writer's creations, having to occupy the four places which were rendered more uncertain due to the lack that dwelled there.

This is why the constitution of the "Persona," which is the title of the chapter with which the fourth book of Delay's biography culminates, refers us back to the analysis of the *Voyage d'Urien*—a work which is interpreted by Delay, without leaving itself open to dispute any more than the deciphering 752
of a rebus does, as the *Voyage du Rien* [Voyage of the Nothing]—which is the highlight of the third book.

Similarly, "The Creation of a Double," which, in bringing the second book to a close, is the pivotal point of the two parts of the work, refers back to "A Divided Child" in the first book.

This *Spaltung* or splitting of the ego, with which Freud's pen stopped *in articulo mortis*, clearly seems to me to be the specific phenomenon here. It affords me the opportunity to express anew my astonishment at the common sense of psychoanalysts, which banishes that splitting from all considered reflection, isolating itself instead in a notion like the weakness of the ego, whose relevance can be gauged once more in the case of Gide by the assertion he could make without his behavior belying it: "It rarely happens that I give up on something; adversity wrings from me nothing more than a postponement."[16]

Must I, in order to awaken their attention, show them how to handle a mask that unmasks the face it represents only by splitting in two and that represents this face only by remasking it? And then explain to them that it is when the mask is closed that it composes this face, and when it is open that it splits it?[17]

When Gide declares to Robert de Bonnières that "We must all represent,"[18] and when in his ironic *Paludes*[19] he speculates about being and appearing, those who, because they have a rented mask, persuade themselves that they have a face underneath it, think "Literature!"—without suspecting that Gide is expressing here a problem which is so personal that it is the very problem of the person.

Freud's ego-ideal is painted on this complex mask, and it forms, along with the repression of one of the subject's desires, by the unconscious adoption of the very image of the Other who has the usufruct [*jouissance*] of this desire and both the right to enjoy it and the means with which to do so.

Gide as a child, between death and masturbatory eroticism, receives, as far
753 as love is concerned, only the kind of speech that protects and the kind that prohibits; in taking his father, death took away the speech that humanizes desire. This is why desire is limited to the clandestine for him.

As he tells us, one evening was for him his rendezvous with fate, the illumination of his night, and his engagement in vows—vows in the name of which he was to make his cousin Madeleine Rondeaux his wife and which initiated for him what he maintained right up until the end to have been his only love.

How can we conceptualize what happened in that instant which "determined the course of his life" and that he cannot "recall without anguish," as he says in *La Porte étroite*? What is this state of being "drunk with love, with pity, with an indistinguishable mixture of enthusiasm, self-abnegation, and virtue," where he calls upon God to "offer [himself] up to Him, unable to conceive that existence could have any other object than to shelter this child from fear, from evil, from life."[20]

Were we to consider this event, as Delay is inclined to, as a mythical memory formation, it would simply be all the more significant. For in his position as a 13-year-old boy at the mercy of the "reddest torments" of childhood in the presence of a 15-year-old girl, this vocation to protect her signals the intervention of an adult. This adult is all the more certainly identifiable with the very person from whom he seeks to protect her—since it is this person's presence, at that very moment on the floor that the young André passed in a bound up the stairs, that drew him into the house with all of the charm of the clandestine, if she was not, in fact, the object of his visit—namely, his amiable aunt who was in the process of dissipating the heat of passion, whoever it was who brought it out in her (Gide gives two different versions of this episode).

Now this aunt—if we are to believe *La Porte étroite*, which in any case bears the truth of fiction—played the role of seductress with the young boy, and we cannot fail to note that her maneuvers bear an astonishing resemblance to the torturous delights,[21] whose confession by Gide in *Et nunc manet in te*, taken to be scandalous, whether they occurred during his honeymoon
754 or not, clearly corresponds to his most feverish fascinations, fascinations that he hardly sought to hide.

It thus seems here that the subject finds himself transformed into a woman as desiring. Potiphar hides behind Pasiphaë, whom he tells us he becomes, bellowing when opening himself up to be penetrated by nature, just as the model of his aunt can be divined where Delay points to it, behind the "mimodrama" of his childhood hysteria.

By this means in the imaginary, he becomes the desired child—in other words, he becomes what he missed out on, in the unfathomable relationship that unites the child with the thoughts that surrounded his conception—and a little of that grace returns to him whose absolute absence in his childhood photo stirred up in François Mauriac a kind of theologal horror.[22]

But this transformation comes only as a residue of a symbolic subtraction which occurred in the place where the child, faced with his mother, could only reproduce the self-abnegation of her jouissance and the envelopment of her love. Desire left nothing here but its negative impact, giving form to the ideal of an angel that impure contact cannot touch.

To convince ourselves that this love, "embalmed so as not to suffer the ravages of time"[23]—about which Gide says, "No one can imagine the love of an Uranist"[24]—is truly love, why limit ourselves to his testimony? Because it is not consistent with the "Dear Abby"-like understanding of love on which psychoanalysts, with their chimerical belief in oblative/genital relations, insist?

As Delay rightly emphasizes, everything here is supported by a very old tradition, justifying his mention of the mystical bonds of courtly love. Gide himself was not afraid to relate his union, despite its bourgeois trappings, to Dante's mystical union with Beatrice. And if psychoanalysts were capable of understanding what their master said about the death instinct, they would be able to recognize that self-realization can become bound up with the wish to end one's life.

In fact, Gide's feeling for his cousin was truly the height of love, if love 755
means giving what one does not have and if he gave her immortality.

This love, which took form in a Manichean meditation, had to be born at the point at which death had already overtaken [*doublé*] the missing object. Let us recognize death's passage in the supposed sister [Lucie] Gide gives himself in his *Cahiers d'André Walter*, in order to make his heroine [Emmanuèle] the one who subtly substitutes her image for that of the dead sister.[25] He has this imaginary sister die in 1885, that is, at the age Madeleine was when his love laid hold of her, in order to have her be born with him. And despite what Jean Schlumberger says,[26] there is no reason to discredit what Gide writes about her to Valéry, in his final struggle to convince Madeleine to marry him: "She's Morella."[27] Woman of the beyond, disowned in her daughter, who dies when Poe calls her by her name which should never have been pronounced . . . The cryptogram of the position of the beloved object in relation to desire is there, in the duplication reapplied to itself. The second mother, the desiring mother, is lethal and this explains the ease with which the ingrate form of the first, the loving mother, manages to replace her, in order to superimpose herself[28]—without the spell being broken—on the form of the ideal woman.

It remains to be seen why desire and its violence—the latter, being the violence of the intruder, was not devoid of repercussions on the young subject (Delay rightly emphasizes this)—did not break this mortal spell after having given shape to it.

Here I think Delay is on the right track when he sees in Madeleine the ultimate reason why this love had to remain unrealized, except that when he dwells on the glass wall that separated the two beings who he animates for us, he perhaps deludes himself into thinking that it is fragile because of its thinness.

The book leaves no doubt that Madeleine wanted an unconsummated marriage. But she wanted it for unconscious reasons that happened to be the most appropriate for leaving André's impasse intact.

756 This happens to appear, as is often the case with things that are difficult to see, in a form which becomes the most obvious form once designated. The abolition in the girl of any acknowledgment of her mother, after the latter had left the family, is the indicator which guarantees that the salutary desire—to which the disgraced child attributed a man's face—could no longer come back in from the outside.

There is, thus, no need to be a genius to find this in Madeleine's writings: She remains for a very long time, after the drama and well beyond the beginning of her marriage, fixated on her love for her father. In noting her emotional penchants, on the third line she evokes his figure (let us try to understand this in the strict sense of the term) as if it were from the beyond.[29]

What would have happened if Madeleine had turned toward André the face of Mathilde (her mother, whom she resembled) that a womanly flush [*la couleur du sexe*] had revived?

In my view, in order to embrace this Ariadne he would have had to kill a Minotaur that would have sprung forth between his arms.

Gide, of course, dreamt of being Theseus. But even if the fate of the checkmated Ariadne had been shorter, Theseus' vicissitudes would have been no different.

It is not merely because it veers to the right rather than to the left that desire creates difficulties for human beings.

The privilege of a desire that lays siege to the subject cannot become obsolete unless this particular turn in the labyrinth, where the fire of an encounter has etched his coat of arms, has been taken a hundred times.

Of course the cipher of this encounter is not simply a print, but a hieroglyph, and may be transferred from one text to others.

But all the metaphors in the world cannot exhaust its meaning, which is not to have any, since it is the mark of the iron with which death brands the flesh when the Word has disentangled flesh from love.

757 This mark, which perhaps is no different than what the Apostle calls "a

thorn in the flesh," has always seemed horrific to wisdom, which has done everything to disregard it.

Let us note that wisdom has been punished for this with the air of slavery it has conserved throughout the ages, an air it probably owes to being encumbered by carrying this branding iron under its robes, acting as if nothing were the matter.

And we could, were we to give it some more thought, take up anew the question of the Master in a new light, indicating that it is not so much his jouissance that concerns him but his desire that he does not disregard.

It seems remarkable that, as time went by, it was around a calling into question of desire by wisdom that a drama was reborn in which the Word is involved.

This is why Gide is of importance. However slight his singularity may be, after all, he is interested in it, and the world that he sets in motion for it is concerned by it, because a chance depends upon it that one might call that of the aristocracy. Indeed, it is the last and only chance the aristocracy has not to be thrown out with the weeds.

Let us say that the weeds appeal on the basis of what they have already furnished to culture, and that psychoanalysis, designed to bring to the bench the most amazing deposition in this debate, is expected to appear there when the fog, in which the weight of its responsibility has plunged it, will have cleared.

On this ground Delay was able to perceive in Gide's construction the essential piece, the one by which the fabrication of the mask—which is exposed to a splitting whose infinite repercussions exhaust the image of André Walter (in the first of the two volumes)—finds the dimension of the persona who becomes André Gide, in order that he convey to us that it is nowhere but in this mask that the secret of desire is revealed to us and, with it, the secret of all nobility.

This piece is Goethe's message, and Delay indicates when it intervenes (plus or minus a few days) as well as the articulation that it constitutes.[30]

Prior to Delay, only Gide's mother recognized the decisive effect of 758
Goethe's message at that time. This demonstrates that the passion of a woman with no special gifts can reach the truth that psychoanalytic method reconstructs, when it is coupled with finesse, whereas commonsense, represented here by Charles Gide, remains utterly blind.[31]

Delay nevertheless makes clear the weight of the missing piece, the one represented by the loss of virtually all of Gide's letters to Madeleine, a correspondence that covered the span of his adult life up until 1918.

It is to their destruction by Madeleine in 1918 that we owe the projection by Gide onto his love of a testimony that was considered scandalous by some and remains a problem for all; here Delay's analysis sheds light by gauging its gravity, his analysis sealing it, in short, with objective confirmation.[32]

This testimony, which Gide entitled *Et nunc manet in te*, was written after his wife's death. The title, if one restores the full citation, indicates the meaning of the text, if it were not already clear: it evokes the punishment that weighs on Orpheus beyond the grave due to Eurydice's resentment at the fact that Orpheus, by turning around to see her as they climbed out of hell, condemned her to return there.[33]

Thus, it is not the beloved object that this title invokes as dwelling inside of he who offers up a confession under its sign, but rather an eternal punishment: "Poenaque respectus et nunc manet, Orpheus, in te."[34]

Shall I take things so far as to highlight the extraordinarily ironic meaning this choice takes on by indicating that the poem, "The Gnat," from which it is taken (which is attributed to Virgil) revolves around the death this insect
759 receives at the hands of the very shepherd whose salvation it ensured when it woke him up by stinging him, and that the news of hell that the mosquito gives the shepherd in a dream merits him the cenotaph that makes his memory live on for all posterity?

In truth, one hardly wonders about the limits of good taste in reading these lines by Gide. They are quite simply atrocious due to the conjunction in them of a kind of mourning that insists on renewing its vows—I loved her and I will love her forever—and the misery of a disabused look at what the other's fate was, which no longer has anything to retain itself but the ravages of an inhuman deprivation, which arose in his memory with the offended specter of his most tender need.

I am not setting myself the task of applying here what I teach about desire, insofar as desire reins in this need in each of us. For there is no truth here which serves to dispense justice.

Nothing about desire, which is lack, can either be weighed or placed in scale pans, unless they are those of logic.

I would like this book by Gide to keep its cutting edge for those men whose destiny in life is to pass on the furrow of a lack, in other words, all men, and for those who lament it, in other words, many of them.

This suffices to indicate that I am not one of those to whom the figure of Madeleine, however wounded she appears here, comes out of it diminished, as some claim.

Whatever shadow may be cast on her face by the tragic footlights, her face is not disfigured. The light that Gide projects here emanates from the same point at which Delay's work places its projectors and from which I myself direct the psychoanalytic lighting.

A different feeling proves that when it is inspired by respectability, that lighting can have a less respectful effect.

Jean Schlumberger reproaches Gide for having obscured his wife's face with the blackness of the shadows in which he moved toward her. Does he think he can dissipate these shadows with his fair-skinned memories?

It is hard not to consider a reparative pretension to be detrimental when it futilely works against a voice that is now extinguished to convince it to give up its pretensions.

The challenge that inspires it, in producing for us a defender of patrician 760
virtues (*sic*),[35] is not easily taken up when it is pursued to laud bourgeois well-being, and the evidence is weakened by an admitted inattention to what was happening in reality behind the art of appearances.[36]

In truth, the honor rendered to these virtues would incline me to observe instead that the courtly lists gain nothing by being adorned with Courteline, and that the remark that Gide had, after all, "happiness that was tailor-made for him,"[37] while it brings peace to one's home in this context, may seem out of place.

Schlumberger's testimony would, in short, limit its own import to the susceptibilities of a distinguished fervor, did it not try to convince us that Madeleine was a bird-brain and that the ideas of her late-nineteenth-century world equated homosexuality with cannibalism, with the bestiality found in myths, and with human sacrifices,[38] all of which assumes an ignorance of the classics that Madeleine, at any rate, cannot be taxed with.

Yet Schlumberger's efforts were not in vain since they furnished us with more pertinent evidence. For it turns out that Madeleine, refined, cultured, and gifted, but highly secretive, knew how not to see what she did not want to know; that her influence beyond a small circle of friends could be tempered enough not to be noticed, especially by a personality who was more adept at affecting others; and that the crystal clarity of her judgment, which Gide exalted, could allow the opaque angle of its refraction to appear in the form of a certain harshness.[39]

Nevertheless, Schlumberger's offer to evaluate someone's class on the basis of class traits perhaps deserves the image—which Bernard Frank's true acid wit would have been capable of providing—of throwing a thick cement tome to someone who is drowning [*pavé du lion*].

Why not realize that Madeleine, who was no doubt completely absorbed in the mystery of the destiny that united her with André Gide, escapes just as surely any worldly approach as she withdrew, with icy determination, from a
messenger who was sure enough that he was bearing divine speech to inter- 761
fere in her bedroom affairs.[40]

To what extent she managed to become what Gide made her into[41] remains impenetrable, but the sole act in which she clearly showed that she was separate from it was the act of a woman, a true woman, in her uncompromising nature as woman [*entièreté de femme*].

The act was that of burning Gide's letters, which are what she had that was "most precious." The fact that she gives no other reason for it than having "had to do something"[42] adds the sign of an unleashing provoked by the only intolerable betrayal.

Love, the first love to which this man accedes beyond her, his face having betrayed its fleeting convulsion a hundred times—she recognizes it in what she sees in his face: less nobility, she says simply.[43]

Hence André Gide's groan—that of a female primate[44] struck in the stomach, wailing over the ripping away of these letters that were a doubling of himself, which is why he calls them his child—can but seem precisely to fill the very gap that the woman's act wished to open up in his being, deepening it slowly as one after the other of the letters was thrown onto the fire of his blazing soul.

Turning over and over in his heart the redemptive intention he attributes to Madeleine's gaze, which he depicts as ignoring his poignant sighs, to this passerby who goes through her demise without meeting him, André Gide is mistaken. Poor Jason who has gone off to conquer the Golden Fleece of happiness—he does not recognize Medea!

Nevertheless, the question I would like to raise here lies elsewhere. And it involves the laughter, variously modulated by the laws of decorum, that
762 greets the news innocently spread by Gide of his tragedy, for this laughter is a response to the loss that he proclaims to be that of the most precious legacy he was bequeathing to posterity.

This laughter reduced Gide himself to smiling at having written: "Perhaps there never was a more beautiful correspondence."[45] But the fact that he cried over it as such and testified to the blow this bereavement dealt to his being, in terms equaled only by those he used in speaking of his loss of Madeleine herself, after the years had strangely reestablished her confidence in him and her proximity to him, isn't that worth weighing in the balance? And how can we weigh it?

We must recognize that this laughter does not bear the meaning of indifference with which the author of the book that I have just added to this file says he greeted Gide's plaintive cry in the back of a theater box in the rue du Vieux-Colombier. And it would be pointless to attribute it to the obscenity befitting fraternal mobs.

Rather, I intend to bring out in this laughter the human meaning awakened by high comedy. And I shall not muffle the echo it receives from the inimitable imbroglio Molière depicts for us, when he has Harpagon sing the praises of his treasure box [*cassette*], confusing it with his own daughter when someone who is in love with her speaks to him of her.

In other words, I am not aiming here at humanity's loss, or the humanities' loss, of Gide's correspondence, but rather at the fateful exchange by which the letter comes to take the very place from which desire has withdrawn.

On the last page of the edition of *Et nunc manet in te*,[46] which includes the pages that complete the *Journal* regarding relations between Gide and Madeleine, we find the following phrase at the end of lines that make our head spin: "which offers nothing more, in the ardent place of the heart, than a hole." It seems to us to pin the lover's plaintive cry to the place in the living heart that has been emptied of the beloved being.

However, we have incorrectly read this: What is at stake is the void left in the text of the *Journal* for the reader by the suppression of the pages that are restored in this new edition. But it is in reading incorrectly that we have nevertheless read correctly.

It is thus here that Gide's irony, which would be almost unique were it not 763
for Heine, breaks down when he evokes the deadly touch with which love was marked for him, this "No, we will not be true lovers, my dear," whose tone Delay highlights in Gide's notebook entry from January 3, 1891, following its path and aftermath in his papers and works.[47]

It is here that his courage failed him, he who incurred derision and even risked misfortune in order to have his desire recognized, and here that his intuition—which "made more than a tract"[48] of his Corydon, providing an astonishing glimpse of the libido theory—abandoned him.

It is here that gave way the humor of a man whose wealth assured his independence, but who was placed in the position of Master beyond his bourgeois background because he raised the question of his particularity.

The letters in which he placed his soul . . . had no carbon copy [*double*]. When their fetishistic nature appeared it gave rise to the kind of laughter that greets subjectivity caught off guard.

It all ends with comedy, but who will put a stop to the laughter?

Is it the Gide who contents himself in his final days with writing down on paper silly stories, childhood memories, and lucky deeds all mixed together, which take on a strange glow in his *Ainsi soit-il*?[49]

"Are you almost done, Signora Velcha?"—where did this incantation come from which was repeated by his cousins, little girls like any others, this incantation that was irrevocable for them if they risked saying it, and that they revealed to him once in the attic retreat where it scanded their dance?

From the same fateful trio of female magicians who reappeared in his destiny.

And the hand that transcribed that incantation, was it still his, when he
764 already at times believed he was dead? Immobile, was it the hand of the adolescent caught in the polar ice of the *Voyage d'Urien*, which held out the words that one could read: *Hic desperatus*?[50] Stirring, did this hand imitate the piano-playing-like movements made by his moribund mother, which made Gide associate his mother's death with the music of a disappointed striving toward beauty? *Haec desperata*?[51]

The movement of this hand is not in itself, but in its lines, my lines, which here continue those Gide traced out, your lines, which will be those of the forthcoming book on Nietzsche that you, Delay, have announced.

This movement will only stop when it reaches the appointed place of which you are already aware, since you are on your way to it, when it reaches the question on the face offered up by the Word beyond comedy, at the moment at which comedy turns, of its own accord, into farce: How can we know which of the jugglers holds the real Punchinello?[52]

Notes

1. This article first came out in *Critique* 131 (April 1958): 291–315.

2. Jean Delay, *La jeunesse d'André Gide* (Paris: Gallimard, 1956–1957), 2 volumes. [In English, see *The Youth of André Gide*, abridged and translated by June Guicharnaud (Chicago and London: University of Chicago Press, 1963).]

3. The appropriateness of this reminder here would be sufficiently proven, were this necessary, by one of the many unpublished texts that Delay brings us, shedding the most suitable light on them. I will cite here from the unpublished journal referred to as Brévine since Gide resided in the village known as La Brévine in October of 1894 (see *Jeunesse de Gide*, vol. II, 667, footnote [not included in *The Youth of Gide*]):

> The novel will prove that it can depict something other than reality—emotion and thought directly. It will show just how far it can be deduced *prior to the experience of things*—that is, just how far it can be composed—that is to say, be a work of art. It will show that it can be a work of art, composed from scratch, based on a realism not of little facts and contingencies, but a superior realism.

A reference to the mathematical triangle follows, and then Gide continues,

> In their very relations, each part of a work must prove the truth of each of the other parts—there is no other proof necessary. Nothing is more irritating than the proof de Goncourt gives for everything he says: He saw it! He heard it! As if proof by reality were necessary.

Obviously, no poet has ever thought otherwise . . . but no one follows up on this thought.

4. See *Jeunesse de Gide*, vol. II, 387–88. The friend in question is Maurice Quillot and Gide mentions the loan in a letter to his mother dated October 17, 1894.

5. *Jeunesse de Gide*, vol. II, 491. [In English, *The Youth of Gide*, 410 (abridged).]

6. I am leaving aside here the impact for the censor [Uncle Charles] of the fact that the incident is presented to him as an experiment by his student. The singularity of his judgment is no less palpable. See, in *Jeunesse de Gide*, vol. II, 442, the letter by Uncle Charles starting with the words "One cannot deny that this incident is the mark of an absolute derailing of the moral sense" up to page 445, where the rebuke ends with the words, the "stain that nothing can

efface." [Not included in *The Youth of Gide.*]

7. See *Jeunesse de Gide*, vol. I, 240: "feelings of incompleteness, or as Gide says, of 'lack'; of strangeness, or as Gide says, of 'estrangement'; of splitting, or as Gide says, of a 'second reality' (which is far more appropriate; my comment); of inconsistency, or as Gide says, of 'deconsistency' (which is more exact; my comment)." [*The Youth of Gide*, 110, translation modified.]

8. See his *Journal, 1889–1939* (Paris: Gallimard, 1948), 785–86 [June 19, 1924], cited in *Jeunesse de Gide*, vol. I, 248. Gide's formulation "Freud, [that] brilliant imbecile," is proffered perpendicularly, as it were, to objections that are, strangely enough, not very strong. [In English, see *The Journals of André Gide, 1889–1949* (New York: Alfred A. Knopf, 1947–1951), 4 vol., trans. Justin O'Brien, reprinted more recently (Urbana & Chicago: University of Illinois Press, 2000).]

9. *Jeunesse de Gide*, vol. I, 165 [*The Youth of Gide*, 79, translation modified].

10. See Gide's bantering remark to Delay regarding the "spreading oedipemic" in *Jeunesse de Gide*, vol. I, 265 [*The Youth of Gide*, 125].

11. *Ainsi soit-il*, 98, cited in *Jeunesse de Gide*, vol. I, 138 [in English, see *So Be It, or the Chips Are Down*, trans. Justin O'Brien (London: Chatto and Windus, 1960), and *The Youth of Gide*, 65].

12. *Jeunesse de Gide*, vol. I, 525, citing Gide's *Cahiers d'André Walter* in Gide, *Oeuvres complètes* (Paris: Gallimard, 1933–1939), vol. I [*The Youth of Gide*, 225, abridged].

13. *Jeunesse de Gide*, vol. II, 104, citing *Et nunc manet in te*, 35 [not included in *The Youth of Gide*; in English, *Et nunc manet in te* can be found in *Madeleine*, trans. Justin O'Brien (Chicago: Ivan R. Dee, 1989)].

14. *Jeunesse de Gide*, vol. I, 249–50 [*The Youth of Gide*, 115–16, abridged].

15. See *Jeunesse de Gide*, vol. I, 171–76, and 321–29. *Si le grain ne meurt*, vol. I, 135, 136, and 195 [*The Youth of Gide*, 80–83, 153–54].

16. Cited in *Jeunesse de Gide*, vol. II, 479 [*The Youth of Gide*, 404, translation modified], from *Si le grain ne meurt*, vol. II, 357, which can be associated with another citation, "Too bad, I will act otherwise" (*Jeunesse de Gide*, vol. II, 18 [not included in *The Youth of Gide*]), which was written in his notebook on January 1, 1891, after the major refusal he received from Madeleine.

17. They can find this mask in the chapter entitled "Split Representation in the Art of Asia and America," in *Structural Anthropology* [New York: Basic Books, 1963], by my friend Claude Lévi-Strauss, especially plates IV–VII.

18. *Jeunesse de Gide*, vol. II, 70 [not included in *The Life of Gide*], citing the scene from *Si le grain ne meurt*, vol. I, 274–75, and reminding us that Gide indicates that this formulation is the "pure secret" of his life.

19. And in his *Journal, 1889–1939*, 25 [August 7, 1891], cited in *Jeunesse de Gide*, vol. II, 52 [*The Youth of Gide*, 263]. [*Paludes* can be found in English in *Marshlands & Prometheus Misbound*, trans. George D. Painter (New York and Toronto: McGraw-Hill, 1965).]

20. See *Jeunesse de Gide*, vol. I, 299–302 [*The Youth of Gide*, 144–46] and *La Porte étroite*, 26–28 [*Straight Is the Gate*, 13–15].

21. See *Et nunc manet in te* (Neuchâtel and Paris: Ides et Calendes, 1947), 41 [*Souvenirs et Voyages*, 948].

22. See *Jeunesse de Gide*, vol. I, 225 note [not included in *The Youth of Gide*].

23. Reported by Roger Martin du Gard; see Jean Schlumberger's *Madeleine et André Gide* (Paris: Gallimard, 1956), 193. [In English, see *Madeleine and André Gide*, trans. Richard H. Akeroyd (New Orleans: Portals Press, 1980); Lacan takes considerable liberties in quoting from this text.]

24. *Madeleine et André Gide*, 186 and 193.

25. See *Jeunesse de Gide*, vol. I, 494 and note [not included in *The Youth of Gide*], and *Cahiers d'André Walter* (*Oeuvres complètes*, vol. I, 40–41).

26. To him this connection seems "truly absurd"; see *Madeleine et André Gide*, 80.

27. See *Jeunesse de Gide*, vol. II, 98 and 173, and vol. I, 300 [*The Youth of Gide*, 144 and 278].

28. Delay's book is full of evidence of such a banal phenomenon, but the latter takes on its importance here because of its devastating context. See *Ainsi soit-il*, 128.

29. See, for example, *Jeunesse de Gide*, vol. II, 187 [*The Youth of Gide*, 305, translation modified]: "Perhaps I really only know two feelings in life: anxiety regarding the future and sadness

over missing Daddy . . ." This is from the letter written by Madeleine Rondeaux to her aunt Juliette Gide in October 1892. See also *Jeunesse de Gide*, vol. II, 25, the quote from Madeleine's diary that footnote 3 situates in February 1891 [not included in *The Youth of Gide*].

30. See *Jeunesse de Gide*, vol. II, 155–59, 177, 245ff (see the chapter entitled "Premeditations"), 266 (the myth of Lynceus), and 277 [*The Youth of Gide*, 297–98 abridged, 303 abridged, 322ff, 329, 334].

31. See Charles Gide's unpublished letter to Mrs. Paul Gide dated April 16, 1895, in *Jeunesse de Gide*, vol. II, 496–97 [*The Youth of Gide*, 413].

32. See *Jeunesse de Gide*, vol. I, "De l'angélisme," 492–519; vol. II, "Le mariage blanc," 557–92, and the masterful pages in "La consultation," 516–56 [*The Youth of Gide*, "Angelism and Its Other Side," 215–24, "The Unconsummated Marriage," 443–57, and "Medical Advice," 423–42, all abridged].

33. A remark from Gide's *Journal, 1889–1939*, 840, can be related to this.

34. My edition, published by Aldes, places a comma after *respectus*, which contemporary annotated editions leave out, as I think they should, given the meaning.

35. *Madeleine et André Gide*, 18.

36. *Madeleine et André Gide*, 184.

37. *Madeleine et André Gide*, 169.

38. *Madeleine et André Gide*, 94.

39. As attested to by Mrs. Van Rysselberghe, in *Madeleine et André Gide*, 143–44. This is in contrast to what Gide says in *Et nunc manet in te*, 69.

40. See the correspondence between Claudel and Gide collected by Robert Mallet, entitled *Correspondance, 1899–1926* (Paris: Gallimard, 1949), [especially the] letter from Madeleine Gide to Paul Claudel, dated August 27, 1925, in response to a note from Paul Claudel, which is also provided.

41. "Alissa [. . .] she wasn't, but she became her," is André Gide's reply to a question posed to him by Delay. See *Jeunesse de Gide*, vol. I, 502–3, and vol. II, 32. [*The Youth of Gide*, 218; second reference not included].

42. *Madeleine et André Gide*, 197.

43. *Madeleine et André Gide*, 199.

44. We must credit Jean Schlumberger for having perceived the female character of Gide's long cries. He deduces from it what a more virile attitude should have inspired in him: "To open his wife's bedroom door." Why? To give her a little kiss, of course, to make it all better. See *Madeleine et André Gide*, 213.

45. See the note on page 83 of the supplement to the *Journal*, provided in *Et nunc manet in te* (Neuchâtel's edition) [*Souvenirs et Voyages*, 962 note].

46. The Neuchâtel edition.

47. This almost parodic irony of the works, from the *Poésies* to *Paludes*, is commented upon by Delay in the following terms, in which the tone of his own irony can be seen when, regarding the precious *Tentative amoureuse*, he concludes, "In short, Luc, enchanted at the prospect of realizing his desire, becomes disenchanted when he realizes it and becomes sorrowful, whereas Gide, by expressing the desire of this double instead of living it, also becomes disenchanted but in a very different sense: he breaks the spell and becomes joyful, such that the disenchantment in the sense of a charm is a re-enchantment in the sense of chant" [*Jeunesse de Gide*, vol. II, 241; not included in *The Youth of Gide; La Tentative amoureuse* (1893) was translated into English as "The Lovers' Attempt" in *The Return of the Prodigal Son*, trans. Aldyth Thain (Logan, UT: Utah State University Press, 1960)].

48. This is François Porché's view, as expressed in the volume of the *Nouvelle Revue Française*.

49. See *Jeunesse de Gide*, vol. I, 184 [not included in *The Youth of Gide*], and *Ainsi soit-il*, 95–96 [*Souvenirs et Voyages*, 1027–28].

50. *Jeunesse de Gide*, vol. II, 211 [*The Youth of Gide*, 311].

51. *Jeunesse de Gide*, vol. II, 501 [*The Youth of Gide*, 416].

52. [Noted added in 1966:] *Ecco, ecco, il vero Pulcinella*: I would appreciate it if whoever recalls where Nietzsche evokes this cry from the podium in Naples by a monk brandishing a crucifix, would be so kind as to provide me with the reference here that I cannot seem to find.

Kant with Sade

This essay was to have served as a preface to *Philosophy in the Bedroom*. It was published in the journal *Critique* (CXCI, April 1963) as a review of the edition of Sade's works for which it was intended: the 15-volume set brought out in 1963 by Éditions du Cercle du livre précieux.[1]

The notion that Sade's work anticipated Freud's—if nothing else, as a catalogue of the perversions—is a stupidity repeated in works of literary criticism, the blame for which goes, as usual, to the specialists.

I, on the contrary, maintain that the Sadean bedroom is of the same stature as those places from which the schools of ancient philosophy borrowed their names: Academy, Lyceum, and Stoa. Here as there, one paves the way for science by rectifying one's ethical position. In this respect, Sade did indeed begin the groundwork that was to progress for a hundred years in the depths of taste in order for Freud's path to be passable. Add to that another sixty years before one could say why.

If Freud was able to enunciate *his* pleasure principle without even having to worry about indicating what distinguishes it from the function of pleasure in traditional ethics—without risking that it be understood, by echoing a bias uncontested for two thousand years, as reminiscent of the attractive notion that a creature is preordained for its good and of the psychology inscribed in different myths of benevolence—we can only credit this to the insinuating rise in the nineteenth century of the theme of "delight in evil" [*bonheur dans le mal*].

Sade represents here the first step of a subversion of which Kant, as piquant as this may seem in light of the coldness of the man himself, represents the turning point—something that has never been pointed out as such, to the best of my knowledge.

Philosophy in the Bedroom came eight years after the *Critique of Practical Reason*. If, after showing that the former is consistent with the latter, I can
766 demonstrate that the former completes the latter, I shall be able to claim that it yields the truth of the *Critique*.

As a result, the postulates with which the *Critique* concludes—the alibi of immortality in the name of which it suppresses progress, holiness, and even love (everything satisfying that could come from the law), and its need for a will to which the object that the law concerns is intelligible—losing even the lifeless support of the function of utility to which Kant confined them, reduce the work to its subversive core. This explains the incredible exaltation that anyone not prepared by academic piety feels upon reading it—a reaction that will not be spoiled by my having explained it.

One might say that the shift involved in the notion that it feels good to do evil [*qu'on soit bien dans le mal*]—or, if you will, that the eternal feminine does not elevate us—was made on the basis of a philological remark: namely, that the idea that had been accepted up until then, which is that it feels good to do good [*qu'on est bien dans le bien*], is based on a homonymy not found in German: *Man fühlt sich wohl im Guten*. This is how Kant introduces us to his *Critique of Practical Reason*.

The pleasure principle is the law of feeling good [*bien*], which is *wohl* in German and might be rendered as "well-being" [*bien-être*]. In practice, this principle would submit the subject to the same phenomenal sequence that determines his objects. The objection that Kant raises against this is, in accordance with his rigorous style, intrinsic. No phenomenon can lay claim to a constant relationship to pleasure. No law of feeling good can thus be enunciated that would define the subject who puts it into practice as "will."

The quest to feel good would thus be a dead end were it not reborn in the form of *das Gute*, the good that is the object of the moral law. Experience tells us that we make ourselves hear commandments inside of ourselves, the imperative nature of which is presented as categorical, in other words, unconditional.

Note that this good [*bien*] is assumed to be the Good [*Bien*] only if it presents itself, as I just said, in spite of all objects that would place conditions upon it—that is, only if it opposes any and every uncertain good that these objects might bring one according to some theoretical equivalence, such that it impresses us as superior owing to its universal value. Thus the weight of the Good appears only by excluding everything the subject may suffer from due to his interest in an object, whether drive or feeling—what Kant designates, for that reason, as "pathological."

We would thus find anew here the Sovereign Good of the Greeks by induction from this effect, if Kant, as is his wont, did not specify once more that this Good does not act as a counterweight but rather, so to speak, as an anti-weight—that is, as subtracting weight from the pride [*amour-propre*] (*Selbstsucht*) the subject experiences as contentment (*arrogantia*) in his pleasures, insofar as a look at this Good renders these pleasures less respectable.[2] This is both precisely what the text says and quite suggestive. 767

Let us consider the paradox that it is at the very moment at which the subject no longer has any object before him that he encounters a law that has no other phenomenon than something that is already signifying; the latter is obtained from a voice in conscience, which, articulating in the form of a maxim in conscience, proposes the order of a purely practical reason or will there.

For this maxim to constitute a law, it is necessary and sufficient that, being put to the test of such reason, the maxim may be considered universal as far as logic is concerned. This does not mean—let us recall what "logic" entails—that it forces itself on everyone, but rather that it is valid in every case or, better stated, that it is not valid in any case if it is not valid in every case.

But this test, which must be based on pure, though practical, reason, can only be passed by maxims of the type that allows for analytic deduction.

This type is illustrated by the faithfulness required in returning a deposit:[3] we can get some shut-eye after making a deposit knowing that the depositary must remain blind to any condition that would oppose this faithfulness. In other words, there is no deposit without a depositary worthy of his task.

One can sense the need for a more synthetic foundation, even in such an obvious case. At the risk of some irreverence, let me, in turn, illustrate the flaw in it with a maxim by Father Ubu that I have modified slightly: "Long live Poland, for if there were no Poland, there would be no Poles."

Let no one, out of some slowness of wit or emotivity, doubt my attachment to a freedom without which the people mourn. But while the analytic explanation of it here is irrefutable, its indefectibility is tempered by the observation that the Poles have always been known for their remarkable resistance to the eclipses of Poland, and even to the lamentation that ensued. 768

We encounter anew here what led Kant to express his regret that no intuition offers up a phenomenal object in the experience of the moral law.

I agree that this object slips away throughout the *Critique*. But it can be surmised in the trace left by the implacable suite Kant provides to demonstrate its slipping away, from which the work derives an eroticism that is no doubt innocent, but perceptible, the well-foundedness of which I shall show through the nature of the said object.

This is why I will ask those of my readers who are still virgins with respect to the *Critique*, never having read it, to stop reading my text here and to return to it after perusing Kant's. Let them see if it does, indeed, have the effect I say it does. In any case, I promise them the pleasure that is brought by the feat itself.

The other readers will follow me now into *Philosophy in the Bedroom*, at least into the reading thereof.

It proves to be a pamphlet, but a dramatic one, in which the stage lighting allows the dialogue and the action to be taken to the very limits of what is imaginable. The lights go dark for a moment to make room for a diatribe—a sort of pamphlet within the pamphlet—entitled "Yet Another Effort, Frenchmen, If You Would Become Republicans."

What is enunciated in it is ordinarily understood, if not appreciated, as a mystification. One need not be alerted to the fact that a dream within a dream points to a closer relationship to the real to see an indication of the same kind in the text's deriding of the historical situation. It is blatant and one would do well to look twice at the text.

The crux of the diatribe is, let us say, found in the maxim that proposes a rule for jouissance, which is odd in that it defers to Kant's mode in being laid down as a universal rule. Let us enunciate the maxim:

769 "I have the right to enjoy your body," anyone can say to me, "and I will exercise this right without any limit to the capriciousness of the exactions I may wish to satiate with your body."

Such is the rule to which everyone's will would be submitted, assuming a society were to forcibly implement the rule.

To any reasonable being, both the maxim and the consent assumed to be given it are at best an instance of black humor.

But aside from the fact that if the deductions in the *Critique* prepared us for anything, it is for distinguishing the rational from the sort of reasonable that is no more than resorting in a confused fashion to the pathological, we now know that humor betrays the very function of the "superego" in comedy. A fact that—to bring this psychoanalytic agency to life by instantiating it and to wrest it from the renewed obscurantism of our contemporaries' use of it—can also spice up [*relever*] the Kantian test of the universal rule with the grain of salt it is missing.

Are we not thus incited to take more seriously what is presented to us as not entirely serious? As you may well suspect, I will not ask if it is necessary or sufficient that a society sanction a right to jouissance, by permitting everyone to lay claim to it, for its maxim to thus be legitimated by the imperative of moral law.

No *de facto* legality can decide if this maxim can assume the rank of a universal rule, since this rank may also possibly oppose it to all *de facto* legalities.

This is not a question that can be settled simply by imagining it, and the extension of the right that the maxim invokes to everyone is not what is at issue here.

At best one could demonstrate here the mere possibility of generalizability, which is not universalizability; the latter considers things as they are grounded and not as they happen to work out.

I cannot pass up the opportunity to point out the exorbitant nature of the role people grant to the moment of reciprocity in structures, especially subjective ones, that are intrinsically incompatible with reciprocity.

Reciprocity—a relation that is reversible since it is established along a simple line that unites two subjects who, due to their "reciprocal" position, consider this relation to be equivalent—is difficult to situate as the logical time of any sort of breakthrough [*franchissement*] on the subject's part in his relation to the signifier, and far less still as a step in any sort of development, whether or not it can be considered psychical (in which it is always so con- 770
venient to blame the child when providing veneers with a pedagogical intent).

Be that as it may, we can already credit our maxim with serving as a paradigm for a statement that as such excludes reciprocity (reciprocity and not "my turn next time").

Any judgment regarding the odious social order that would enthrone our maxim is, thus, of no import here, for the question is whether to grant or refuse to grant this maxim the characteristic of a rule acceptable as universal in moral philosophy—moral philosophy being recognized, since Kant's time, as involving the unconditional practice of reason.

We must obviously acknowledge this characteristic in the maxim for the simple reason that its sole proclamation (its *kerygma*) has the virtue of instating both the radical rejection of the pathological (that is, of every preoccupation with goods, passion, or even compassion—in other words, the rejection by which Kant cleared the field of moral law) and the form of this law, which is also its only substance, insofar as the will becomes bound to the law only by eliminating from its practice every reason that is not based on the maxim itself.

Of course, these two imperatives—between which moral life can be stretched, even if it snaps our very life—are imposed on us, according to the Sadean paradox, as if upon the Other, and not upon ourselves.

But this only differs from Kant's view at first blush, for the moral imperative latently does no less, since its commandment requisitions us as Other.

We perceive quite nakedly here what the aforementioned parody of the obvious universality of the depositary's duty was designed to introduce us to—namely, that the bipolarity upon which the moral law is founded is nothing but the split [*refente*] in the subject brought about by any and every intervention of the signifier: the split between the enunciating subject [*sujet de l'énonciation*] and the subject of the statement [*sujet de l'énoncé*].

The moral law has no other principle. Yet it must be blatant, for otherwise it lends itself to the mystification we sense in the gag* "Long live Poland!"

In coming out of the Other's mouth, Sade's maxim is more honest than Kant's appeal to the voice within, since it unmasks the split in the subject that is usually covered up.

The enunciating subject stands out here as clearly as in "Long live
771 Poland," where the only thing that sticks out is what its manifestation amusingly evokes.

To confirm this view, one need but consider the doctrine with which Sade himself establishes the reign of his principle: the doctrine of human rights. He cannot use the notion that no man can be the property, or in any way the prerogative, of another man as a pretext for suspending everyone's right to enjoy him, each in his own way.[4] The constraint he endures here is not so much one of violence as of principle, the problem for the person who makes it into a sentence not being so much to make another man consent to it as to pronounce it in his place.

Thus the discourse of the right to jouissance clearly posits the Other qua free—the Other's freedom—as its enunciating subject, in a way that does not differ from the *Tu es* which is evoked out of the lethal depths [*fonds tuant*] of every imperative.

But this discourse is no less determinant for the subject of the statement, giving rise to him with each addressing of its equivocal content: since jouissance, shamelessly avowed in its very purpose, becomes one pole in a couple, the other pole being in the hole that jouissance already drills in the Other's locus in order to erect the cross of Sadean experience in it.

Leaving off my discussion of its mainspring here, let me recall instead that pain, which projects its promise of ignominy here, merely intersects the express mention of it made by Kant among the connotations of moral experience. What pain is worth in Sadean experience will be seen better by approaching it via what might be disconcerting in the artifice the Stoics used with regard to it: scorn.

Imagine a revival of Epictetus in Sadean experience: "You see, you broke it," he says, pointing to his leg. To reduce jouissance to the misery of an effect in which one's quest stumbles—doesn't this transform it into disgust?

This shows that jouissance is that by which Sadean experience is modified. For it only proposes to monopolize a will after having already traversed it in order to instate itself at the inmost core of the subject whom it provokes beyond that by offending his sense of modesty [*pudeur*].

For modesty is an amboceptor with respect to the circumstances of being: 772
between the two, the one's immodesty by itself violating the other's modesty. A connection that could justify, were such justification necessary, what I said before regarding the subject's assertion in the Other's place.

Let us question this jouissance, which is precarious because it depends on an echo that it sets off in the Other, only to abolish it little by little by attaching the intolerable to it. In the end, doesn't it seem to us to be thrilled only by itself, like another horrible freedom?

Thus we will see appear the third term that, according to Kant, is lacking in moral experience—namely, the object that Kant, in order to guarantee it to the will in the implementation of the Law, is constrained to relegate to the unthinkability of the thing in itself. But is this not the very object we find in Sadean experience, which is no longer inaccessible and is instead revealed as the being-in-the-world, the *Dasein*, of the tormenting agent?

Yet it retains the opacity of that which is transcendent. For this object is strangely separated from the subject. Let us observe that the herald of the maxim need be no more here than a point of broadcast. It could be a voice on the radio recalling the right promoted by the supplemental effort the French would have consented to make in response to Sade's appeal, the maxim having become an organic Law of their regenerated Republic.

Such voice-related phenomena, especially those found in psychosis, truly have this object-like appearance. And in its early days, psychoanalysis was not very far from relating the voice of conscience to psychosis.

Here we see why Kant views this object as evading every determination of transcendental aesthetics, even though it does not fail to appear in a certain bulge in the phenomenal veil, being not without hearth or home, time in intuition, modality situated in the unreal [*irréel*], or effect in reality. It is not simply that Kant's phenomenology is lacking here, but that the voice—even if insane—forces [upon us] the idea of the subject, and that the object of the law must not suggest malignancy on the part of the real God.

Christianity has assuredly taught men to pay little attention to God's jouissance, and this is how Kant makes palatable his voluntarism of Law-for-Law's-sake, which is something that exaggerates, one might say, the *ataraxia*

of the Stoics. One might be tempted to think that Kant feels pressured here
773 by what he hears too close by, not from Sade but from some nearby mystic, in the sigh that muffles what he glimpses beyond, having seen that his God is faceless: *Grimmigkeit*? Sade says: supremely-evil-being.

But humph! *Schwärmereien*, black swarms—I chase you away in order to return to the function of presence in the Sadean fantasy.

This fantasy has a structure that we will see again further on; in it the object is but one of the terms in which the quest it figures can die out [*s'éteindre*]. When jouissance petrifies in the object, it becomes the black fetish, in which can be recognized the form that was verily and truly offered up at a certain time and place, and still is in our own time, so that one can adore the god therein.

This is what becomes of the executioner in sadism when, in the most extreme case, his presence is reduced to being no more than the instrument.

But the fact that the executioner's jouissance becomes fixated there does not spare his jouissance the humility of an act in which he cannot help but become a being of flesh and, to the very marrow, a slave to pleasure.

This duplication neither reflects nor reciprocates (why wouldn't it "mutualize"?) the duplication that took place in the Other owing to the subject's two alterities.

Desire—which is the henchman of the subject's split—would no doubt be willing to call itself "will to jouissance." But this appellation would not make desire any more worthy of the will it invokes in the Other, in tempting that will [to go right] to the extreme of its division from its pathos; for when it does so, desire departs [*part*] beaten down, doomed to impotence.

For desire disappears [*part*] under pleasure's sway, pleasure's law being such as to make it always fall short of its aim: the homeostasis of the living being, always too quickly reestablished at the lowest threshold of tension at which he scrapes by, the ever early fall of the wing, with which desire is able to sign the reproduction of its form—a wing which here must nevertheless rise to the function of representing the link between sex and death. Let us lay that wing to rest behind its Eleusinian veil.

Pleasure, a rival of the will in Kant's system that provides a stimulus, is thus in Sade's work no more than a flagging [*défaillant*] accomplice. At the moment of climax [*jouissance*], it would simply be out of the picture if fantasy did not intervene to sustain it with the very discord to which it succumbs.

Stated differently, fantasy provides the pleasure that is characteristic of
774 desire. Let us recall that desire is not the subject, for it cannot be indicated

anywhere in a signifier of any demand whatsoever, for it cannot be articulated in the signifier even though it is articulated there.

Taking pleasure in fantasy is easy to grasp here.

Physiology shows that pain has a longer cycle than pleasure in every respect, since a stimulation provokes pain at the point at which pleasure stops. However prolonged one assumes it to be, pain, like pleasure, nevertheless comes to an end—when the subject passes out.

Such is the vital datum that fantasy takes advantage of in order to fixate—in the sensory aspect of Sadean experience—the desire that appears in its agent.

Fantasy is defined by the most general form it receives in an algebra I have constructed for this purpose—namely, the formula ($\$ \lozenge a$), in which the lozenge $\lozenge$ is to be read as "desire for," being read right to left in the same way, introducing an identity that is based on an absolute non-reciprocity. (This relation is coextensive with the subject's formations.)

Be that as it may, this form turns out to be particularly easy to animate in the present case. Indeed, it relates the pleasure that has been replaced by an instrument (object *a* in the formula) here to the kind of sustained division of the subject that experience orders.

This only occurs when its apparent agent freezes with the rigidity of an object, in view of having his division as a subject entirely reflected in the Other.

From the vantage point of the unconscious, a quadripartite structure can always be required in the construction of a subjective ordering. My didactic schemas take this into account.

Let us modulate the Sadean fantasy with a new schema of this kind:

SCHEMA 1

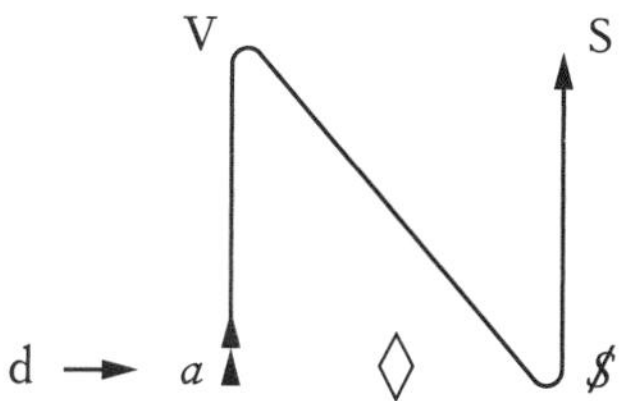

The lower line accounts for the order of fantasy insofar as it props up the 775
utopia of desire.

The curvy line depicts the chain that allows for a calculus of the subject. It is oriented, and its orientation constitutes here an order in which the appearance of object *a* in the place of the cause is explained by the universality of its relationship to the category of causality; forcing its way into Kant's transcendental deduction, this universality would base a new Critique of Reason on the linchpin [*cheville*] of impurity.

Next there is the V which, occupying the place of honor here, seems to impose the will [*volonté*] that dominates the whole business, but its shape also evokes the union [*réunion*] of what it divides by holding it together with a *vel*—namely, by offering up to choice what will create the $\$$ of practical reason from S, the brute subject of pleasure (the "pathological" subject).

Thus it is clearly Kant's will that is encountered in the place of this will that can only be said to be a will to jouissance if we explain that it is the subject reconstituted through alienation at the cost of being nothing but the instrument of jouissance. Thus Kant, being interrogated "with Sade"—that is, Sade serving here, in our thinking as in his sadism, as an instrument—avows what is obvious in the question "What does he want?" which henceforth arises for everyone.

Let us now make use of this graph in its succinct form to find our way around in the forest of the fantasy that Sade develops according to a systematic plan in his work.

We will see that there is a statics of the fantasy, whereby the point of aphanisis, assumed to lie in $\$$, must in one's imagination be indefinitely pushed back. This explains the hardly believable survival that Sade grants to the victims of the abuse and tribulations he inflicts in his fable. The moment of their death seems to be motivated there merely by the need to replace them in a combinatory, which alone requires their multiplicity. Whether unique (Justine) or multiple, the victim is characterized by the monotony of the subject's relation to the signifier, in which, if we rely on our graph, she consists. The troupe of tormentors (see *Juliette*), being object *a* in the fantasy and situating themselves in the real, can have more variety.

The requirement that the victims' faces always be of incomparable (and, moreover, unalterable, as I just said) beauty is another matter, which we cannot account for with a few banal and quickly fabricated postulates about sex appeal. Rather, we should see here the grimace of what I have shown regard-
776 ing the function of beauty in tragedy: the ultimate barrier that forbids access to a fundamental horror. Consider Sophocles' *Antigone* and the moment when the words Ερως ἀνιχατε μάκαν ring out.[5]

This excursus would be of no value here did it not introduce what one might call the discordance between the two deaths, introduced by the existence of the condemnation. The between-two-deaths of the shy of [*l'en-deçà*] is essential to show us that it is no other than the one by which the beyond [*l'au-delà*] is sustained.

This can be clearly seen in the paradox constituted in Sade's work by his position regarding hell. The idea of hell, refuted a hundred times by him and cursed as religious tyranny's way of constraining people, curiously returns to explain the gestures of one of his heroes who is, nevertheless, among the most taken with libertine subversion in its reasonable form: the hideous Saint-Fond.[6] The practices, whose final agony he imposes on his victims, are based on his belief that he can render their torment eternal in the hereafter [*l'au-delà*]. He highlights the authenticity of this behavior by concealing it from his accomplices and the authenticity of this credence by the difficulty he has explaining himself. Thus we hear him, a few pages later, try to make his behavior and credence sound plausible in his discourse with the myth of an attraction tending to gather together the "particles of evil."

This incoherence in Sade's work, overlooked by sadists (they, too, are a bit hagiographic), could be explained by noting in his writings the formally expressed term "the second death." The assurance he expects from it against the awful routine of nature (which crime, as he tells us elsewhere, serves to disrupt) would require that it go to an extreme in which the vanishing [*évanouissement*] of the subject is redoubled. He symbolizes this in his wish that the very decomposed elements of our body be destroyed so that they can never again be assembled.

The fact that Freud nevertheless recognizes the dynamism of this wish[7] in certain of his clinical cases, and that he very clearly, perhaps too clearly, reduces its function to something analogous to the pleasure principle by 777
relating it to a "death drive" (demand [*demande*] for death)—this will not be accepted by those who have been unable to learn from the technique they owe Freud, or from his teachings, that language has effects that are not simply utilitarian or, at the very most, for purposes of display. Freud is [only] of use to them at conventions.

In the eyes of such puppets, the millions of men for whom the pain of existence is the original reason for the practices of salvation that they base on their faith in Buddha, are undoubtedly underdeveloped; or, rather, they think like Buloz, the director of *La Revue des Deux Mondes*, who told Renan[8] straight out when he turned down his article on Buddhism (this according to Burnouf) at some point during the eighteen-fifties, that it is "impossible that there are people that dumb."

If they believe that they have better ears than other psychiatrists, have they somehow escaped hearing such pain in a pure state model the song of certain patients referred to as melancholic?

Have they not heard one of those dreams by which the dreamer remains overwhelmed, having, in the felt condition of an inexhaustible rebirth, plumbed the depths of the pain of existence?

Or, in order to put hell's torments back in their place, torments which could never be imagined beyond what men traditionally inflict in this world, shall we implore them to think of our everyday life as having to be eternal?

We must hope for nothing, not even hopelessness, to combat such stupidity, which is, in the end, sociological; I am mentioning it here only so that people on the outside will not expect too much, concerning Sade, from the circles of those who have a surer experience of forms of sadism.

Especially regarding a certain equivocal notion that has been gaining ground about the relation of reversion that supposedly unites sadism with a certain idea of masochism—it is difficult for those outside such circles to imagine the muddle this notion creates. We would do better to learn from it the lesson contained in a fine little tale told about the exploitation of one man by another, which is the definition of capitalism, as we know. And socialism, then? It is the opposite.

Unintended humor—this is the tone with which a certain circulation of psychoanalysis occurs. It fascinates people because it goes, moreover, unnoticed.

778 But there are doctrinaires who strive for tidier appearances. One acts the part of a do-good existentialist, another, more soberly, that of a ready-made* personalist. This results in the claim that the sadist "denies the Other's existence." Which is precisely, one must admit, what has just come out in my analysis.

To pursue my analysis, is it not the case, rather, that the sadist discharges the pain of existence into [*rejette dans*] the Other, but without seeing that he himself thereby turns into an "eternal object," if Whitehead is willing to let us have this term back.

But why wouldn't it belong to both of us? Isn't this—redemption and immortal soul—the status of the Christian? Let us not proceed too quickly, so as not to go too far either.

Let us note, instead, that Sade is not duped by his fantasy, insofar as the rigor of his thinking is integrated into the logic of his life.

Let me give my readers an assignment here.

The fact that Sade delegates a right to jouissance to everyone in his Republic is not translated in my graph by any symmetrical reversal [*réversion*] along an axis or around some central point, but only by a 90-degree rotation of the graph, as follows:

SCHEMA 2

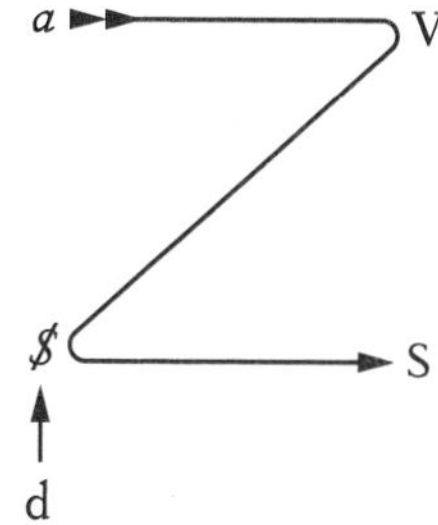

V, the will to jouissance, leaves no further doubt as to its nature, because it appears in the moral force implacably exercised by the President of Montreuil [Sade's mother-in-law] on the subject; it can be seen that the subject's division does not have to be pinned together [*réunie*] in a single body.

(Let us note that it is only the First Consul who seals this division with its effect of administratively confirmed alienation.)

This division here pins together [*réunit*] as S the brute subject incarnating
the heroism characteristic of the pathological in the form of faithfulness to 779
Sade manifested by those who at first tolerated his excesses—his wife, his sister-in-law, and why not his manservant too?[9]—and others who have been effaced from his history.

For Sade, $ (barred S), we finally see that, as a subject, it is through his disappearance that he makes his mark, things having come to their term. Incredibly, Sade disappears without anything—even less than for Shakespeare—of his image remaining to us, after he gave orders in his will to have a thicket efface the very last trace on stone of a name that sealed his fate.

Μὴ φῦναι,[10] "not to be born"—Sade's curse is less holy than Oedipus', and does not carry him toward the Gods, but is immortalized in his work, whose unsinkable buoyancy Jules Janin backhandedly shows us, saluting it behind the books that hide it, if we are to believe him, in every worthy library, like the writings of St. John Chrysostom or Pascal's *Pensées*.

But Sade's work is annoying, according to you—yes, like thieves at a fair—your honor and member of the Académie Française; but his work always suffices to bother you, one of you by the other, both one and the other, and one in the other.[11]

A fantasy is, in effect, quite bothersome, since we do not know where to situate it due to the fact that it just sits there, complete in its nature as a fantasy, whose only reality is as [*de*] discourse and which expects nothing of your powers, asking you, rather, to square accounts with your own desires.

The reader should now reverentially approach those exemplary figures who, in the Sadean boudoir, assemble and disassemble in a carnival-act-like rite: "Change of positions."

It is a ceremonial pause, a sacred scansion.

780 Let us salute here the objects of the law, of which you will know nothing unless you know how to find your way around in the desires those objects cause.

It is good to be charitable
But to whom? That is the question.

A certain Monsieur Verdoux answered this question every day by putting women in an oven until he himself got the electric chair. He thought that his family wanted to live in greater comfort. More enlightened, the Buddha offered himself up to be devoured by those who did not know the way. Despite this eminent patronage, which might well be based solely on a misunderstanding (it is not clear that a tigress enjoys eating Buddha), Verdoux's abnegation stemmed from an error that deserves to be dealt with severely, since a little lesson from the *Critique*, which does not cost much, would have helped him avoid it. No one doubts but that the practice of Reason would have been both more economical and more legal, even if his family would have had to go hungry now and then.

"But what's with all these metaphors," you will say, "and why . . . ?"

The molecules that are monstrous insofar as they assemble here for an obscene jouissance, awaken us to the existence of other more ordinary jouissances encountered in life, whose ambiguities I have just mentioned. They are suddenly more respectable than these latter, appearing purer in their valences.

Desires . . . here are the only things that bind them, and they are exalted in making it clear that desire is the Other's desire.

If you have read my work up to this point, you know that, more accurately stated, desire is propped up by a fantasy, at least one foot [*pied*] of which is in the Other, and precisely the one that counts, even and above all if it happens to limp.

The object, as I have shown in Freudian experience—the object of desire, where we see it in its nakedness—is but the slag of a fantasy in which the subject does not come to after blacking out [*syncope*]. It is a case of necrophilia.

The object generally vacillates in a manner that is complementary to the subject['s vacillation].

This is what makes it as ungraspable as is the object of the Law according to Kant. But here we suspect that a rapprochement is necessary: Doesn't the moral law represent desire in the case in which it is no longer the subject, but rather the object that is missing [*fait défaut*]?

Doesn't the subject—alone remaining present, in the form of the voice 781
within, speaking nonsensically most of the time—seem to be adequately signified by the bar with which the signifier $\$$ bastardizes him, that signifier being released from the fantasy ($\$ \lozenge a$) from which it *dérive*, in the two senses of the term [*dérive* meaning both derives and drifts]?

Although this symbol returns the commandment from within at which Kant marvels to its rightful place, it opens our eyes to the encounter which, from Law to desire, goes further than the slipping away of their object, for both the Law and desire.

It is the encounter in which the ambiguity of the word "freedom" plays a part; the moralist, by grabbing freedom for himself, always strikes me as more impudent still than imprudent.

But let us listen to Kant himself illustrate it once more:

> Suppose someone alleges that his lustful inclination is quite irresistible to him when he encounters the favored object and the opportunity. [Ask him] whether, if in front of the house where he finds this opportunity a gallows were erected on which he would be strung up immediately after gratifying his lust, he would not then conquer his inclination. One does not have to guess long what he would reply. But ask him whether, if his prince demanded, on the threat of the same prompt penalty of death,[12] that he give false testimony against an honest man whom the prince would like to ruin under specious pretenses, he might consider it possible to overcome his love of life, however great it may be. He will perhaps not venture to assure us whether or not he would overcome that love, but he must concede without hesitation that doing so would be possible for him. He judges, therefore, that he can do something because he is conscious that he ought to do it, and he cognizes freedom within himself—the freedom with which otherwise, without the moral law, he would have remained unacquainted.[13]

The first response that is presumed to be given here by a subject, about whom we are first told that a great deal transpires by means of words, gives me the impression that we are not being given the letter [of what he said]

when that is the crux of the matter. For the fact is that, in order to express it, Kant prefers to rely on someone whose sense of shame we would, in any case,
782 risk offending, for in no case would he stoop so low: namely, the ideal bourgeois to whom Kant elsewhere declares that he takes his hat off, no doubt in order to counter Fontenelle, the overly gallant centenarian.[14]

We will excuse the hoodlum, then, from having to testify under oath. But it is possible that a partisan of passion, who would be blind enough to combine it with questions of honor, would make trouble for Kant by forcing him to recognize that no occasion precipitates certain people more surely toward their goal than one that involves defiance of or even contempt for the gallows.

For the gallows is not the Law, nor can the gallows be wheeled in by the Law here. Only the police have the necessary trucks, and while the police can be the State, as Hegel says, the Law is something else, as we have known since Antigone.

Kant, besides, does not contradict this with his apologue. The gallows is brought in merely so that he can attach to it, along with the subject, his love of life.

Now, this is what the desire in the maxim *Et non propter vitam vivendi perdere causas* can become in a moral being, rising, precisely because he is moral, to the rank of a categorical imperative, assuming he has his back to the wall [*au pied du mur*]—which is precisely where he is forced here.

Desire, what is called desire, suffices to make life meaningless if it turns someone into a coward. And when law is truly present, desire does not stand up, but that is because law and repressed desire are one and the same thing—which is precisely what Freud discovered. We are ahead at half-time, professor.

Let us chalk up our success to the infantry, the key to the game, as we know. For we have not brought in either our knight—which would have been easy, since it would be Sade, whom we believe to be qualified enough here—our bishop, our rook (human rights, freedom of thought, your body is your property), or our queen, an appropriate figure with which to designate the daring deeds of courtly love.

This would have involved moving too many people for a less certain result.

For if I claim that for a few bantering remarks, Sade risked—knowing full well what he was doing (consider what he did with his "outings," whether
783 licit or illicit)—imprisonment in the Bastille for a third of his lifetime (it was rather well-aimed banter, no doubt, but all the more demonstrative with

respect to its recompense), I'll have Pinel and his Pinelopies taking aim at me. Moral madness, the latter opine. In any case, a fine affair it is! I am reminded to show respect for Pinel, to whom we owe one of the noblest steps of humanity. "Thirteen years in Charenton for Sade were, however, part of this step," [I retort]. "But he should not have been sent there," [I am told]. "That's the whole point," [I continue]. It was Pinel's step that led him there. His place, and all thinkers agree on this point, was elsewhere. But there you have it: those who think clearly [*qui pensent bien*] think that his place was outside, and the right-thinking [*les bien-pensants*], starting with Royer-Collard, who demanded it at the time, wanted him condemned to hard-labor, if not to the scaffold. This is precisely why Pinel was an important moment in the history of thought. Willy-nilly, he supported the destruction, on the right and the left, by thought of freedoms that the Revolution had just promulgated in the very name of thought.

For if we consider human rights from the vantage point of philosophy, we see what, in any case, everyone now knows about their truth. They boil down to the freedom to desire in vain.

A lot of good that does us [*Belle jambe*]! But it gives us an opportunity to recognize in it the impulsive [*de prime-saut*] freedom we saw earlier, and to confirm that it is clearly the freedom to die.

But it also gives us the opportunity to be frowned upon by those who find it low in nutritional value. They are plentiful in our time. We see here the renewed conflict between needs and desires in which, as if by chance, it is the Law that empties the shell [*qui vide l'écaille*].

To counter Kant's apologue, courtly love offers us a no less tempting path, but it requires us to be erudite. To be erudite by one's position is to bring on the attack of the erudites, and in this field that is tantamount to the entrance of the clowns.

Kant could very easily make us lose our serious demeanor here already since he hasn't the slightest sense of comedy (this is proved by what he says about it when he discusses it).

But someone who has no sense of comedy whatsoever is Sade, as has been pointed out. This topic could perhaps be fatal to him, but a preface is not designed to do the author a disservice.[15]

Let us thus turn to the second stage of Kant's apologue. It no more proves his point than the first stage did. For assuming that Kant's helot here has the slightest presence of mind, he will ask Kant if perchance it would be his duty to bear true witness were this the means by which the tyrant could satisfy his desire. 784

Should he say that the innocent man is a Jew, for example, if he truly is one, before a tribunal (we have seen such situations) that considers this a punishable offense? Or that he is an atheist, when it is quite possible that he himself has a better grasp on the import of the accusation than a consistory that simply wants to establish a file? And in the case of some deviation from "the party line," will he plead that this deviation is not guilty at a time and a place where the name of the game is autocritique? Why wouldn't he? After all, is an innocent man ever completely spotless? Will he say what he knows?

We could make the maxim that one must counter a tyrant's desire into a duty, if a tyrant is someone who appropriates the power to enslave the Other's desire.

Thus with regard to the two examples (and the precarious mediation between them) that Kant uses as a lever to show that the Law weighs in the scales not only pleasure but also pain, happiness and even the burden of abject poverty, not to mention the love of life—in short, everything pathological—it turns out that desire can have not only the same success but can obtain it more legitimately.

But if the credence we lent the *Critique* due to the alacrity of its argumentation owed something to our desire to know where it was heading, can't the ambiguity of this success turn the movement back toward a revising of the concessions we unwittingly made?

For example, the disgrace that rather quickly befell all objects that were proposed as goods [*biens*] because they were incapable of achieving a harmony of wills: simply because they introduce competition. Such was the case of Milan, about which both Charles V and François I knew what it cost them for each to see the same good in it.

For that is clearly to misrecognize the status of the object of desire.

I can introduce its status here only by reminding you what I teach about desire, which must be formulated as the Other's desire [*désir de l'Autre*] since it is originally desire for what the Other desires [*désir de son désir*]. This is what makes the harmony of desires conceivable, but not devoid of danger. For when desires line up in a chain that resembles the procession of Breughel's blind
785 men, each one, no doubt, has his hand in the hand of the one in front of him, but no one knows where they are all going.

Now, in retracing their steps, they all clearly experience a universal rule, but this is because they do not know any more about it.

Would the solution in keeping with practical reason be that they go around in circles?

Even when lacking, the gaze is clearly the object that presents each desire with its universal rule, by materializing its cause, in binding to it the subject's division "between center and absence."

Let us therefore confine ourselves to saying that a practice like psychoanalysis, which takes desire as the subject's truth, cannot misrecognize what follows without demonstrating what it represses.

In psychoanalysis, displeasure is understood to provide a pretext for repressing desire, displeasure arising, as it does, along the pathway of desire's satisfaction; but displeasure is also understood to provide the form this very satisfaction takes in the return of the repressed.

Similarly, pleasure redoubles its aversion when it recognizes the law, by supporting the desire to comply with it that constitutes defense.

If happiness means that the subject finds uninterrupted pleasure in his life, as the *Critique of Practical Reason* defines it quite classically,[16] it is clear that happiness is denied to whomever does not renounce the pathway of desire. This renunciation can be willed, but at the cost of man's truth, which is quite clear from the disapproval of those who upheld the common ideal that the Epicureans, and even the Stoics, met with. Their *ataraxia* deposed their wisdom. We fail to realize that they degraded desire; and not only do we not consider the Law to be commensurably exalted by them, but it is precisely because of this degrading of desire that, whether we know it or not, we sense that they cast down the Law.

Sade, the former aristocrat, takes up Saint-Just right where one should. The proposition that happiness has become a political factor is incorrect. It has always been a political factor and will bring back the scepter and the censer that make do with it very well. Rather, it is the freedom to desire that is a new factor, not because it has inspired a revolution—people have always fought and died for a desire—but because this revolution wants its struggle to be for the freedom of desire.

Consequently, the revolution also wants the law to be free, so free that it 786
must be a widow, the Widow *par excellence,* the one that sends your head to the basket if it so much as balks regarding the matter at hand. Had Saint-Just's head remained full of the fantasies in *Organt*, Thermidor might have been a triumph for him.

Were the right to jouissance recognized, it would consign the domination of the pleasure principle to an obsolete era. In enunciating this right, Sade imperceptibly displaces for each of us the ancient axis of ethics, which is but the egoism of happiness.

One cannot say that every reference to it is eliminated in Kant's work, given the very familiarity with which it accompanies him, and still more given the offshoots of it seen in the exigencies that make him argue both for some retribution in the hereafter and progress in this world.

Should another happiness be glimpsed whose name I first uttered, the status of desire would change, demanding a reexamination of it.

But it is here that something must be gauged. How far does Sade lead us in the experience of this jouissance, or simply of its truth?

For the human pyramids he describes, which are fabulous insofar as they demonstrate the cascading nature of jouissance, these water buffets of desire built so that jouissance makes the Villa d'Este Gardens sparkle with a baroque voluptuousness—the higher they try to make jouissance spurt up into the heavens, the more insistently the question "What is it that is flowing here?" demands to be answered.

Unpredictable quanta by which the love/hate atom glistens in the vicinity of the Thing from which man emerges through a cry, what is experienced, beyond certain limits, has nothing to do with what desire is propped up by in fantasy, which is in fact constituted on the basis of these limits.

We know that Sade went beyond these limits in real life.

Otherwise, he probably would not have given us this blueprint of his fantasy in his work.

Perhaps I will surprise people when I call into question what his work also tries to convey of this real experience.

Confining our attention to the bedroom, for a rather lively glimpse of a girl's feelings about her mother, the fact remains that wickedness [*méchanceté*],
787 so suitably situated by Sade in its transcendence, does not teach us much that is new here about her changes of heart.

A work that wishes to be bad [*méchant*] cannot allow itself to be a bad piece of work, and one has to admit that *Philosophy in the Bedroom* leaves itself open to this ironic remark by a whole strain of good works found in it.

It's a little too preachy.

Of course, it is a treatise on the education of girls[17] and it is subject, as such, to the laws of a genre. Despite its merit of bringing to light the "anal sadism" that obsessively permeated this subject for the two preceding centuries, it remains a treatise on education. The victim is bored to death by the preaching and the teacher is full of himself.

The historical or, better, erudite information here is dreary and makes us miss someone like La Mothe-le-Vayer. The physiology contained in it is made up of wet nurses' notions, and as for what might pass for sex education, one has the impression that one is reading a modern medical treatise on the subject, which says it all.

More coherence in his scandal would help him see, in the usual impotence of educational intentions, the very impotence against which fantasy here fights—whence arises the obstacle to every valid account of the effects of education, since what brought about the results cannot be admitted to in discussing the intention.

This remark [*trait*] would have been priceless, due to the praiseworthy effects of sadistic impotence. The fact that Sade failed to make it gives us pause for thought.

His failure here is confirmed by another that is no less remarkable: The work never presents us with a successful seduction in which his fantasy would nevertheless find its crowning glory—that is, a seduction in which the victim, even if she were at her last gasp, would consent to her tormentor's intention, or even join his side in the fervor of her consent.

This demonstrates from another vantage point that desire is the flip side of the law. In the Sadean fantasy, we see how they support each other. For Sade, one is always on the same side, the good or the bad; no wrongdoing can change that. It is thus the triumph of virtue: This paradox merely comes down to the derision characteristic of edifying books, the kind *Justine* aims at too much not to have adopted it.

Apart from the nose that twitches, which we find at the end of *The Dia- 788
logue of a Priest with a Dying Man*, a posthumous work (admit that this is a subject hardly suited to other graces than divine grace), a lack of witticisms—and, one might say, more broadly, of the wit*, the need for which Alexander Pope had, over a century before, already indicated—makes itself felt at times in Sade's work.

This is obviously forgotten owing to the invasion of pedantry that has weighed on French letters since W.W. II.*

But if you need a strong stomach to follow Sade when he recommends calumny, the first article of morality that he would institute in his republic, one might prefer that he add the spice of someone like Renan. "Let us be thankful," the latter writes, "that Jesus encountered no law against insulting a whole class of citizens. For the Pharisees would have been inviolable."[18] Renan continues:

> His exquisite mockery and magic provocations always hit home. The Nessus-tunic of ridicule that the Jew, the son of the Pharisees, has been dragging in tatters behind him for eighteen centuries, was woven by Jesus with divine skill. A masterpiece of high-level mockery, his scathing

> remarks have become burned into the flesh of the hypocrite and of the falsely devout. Incomparable remarks, worthy of a Son of God! Only a God knows how to kill in this fashion. Socrates and Molière merely graze the skin. Jesus carries fire and rage into the very depths of one's bones.[19]

For these remarks derive their value from the sequel that we know, I mean his vocation as an Apostle from the rank of the Pharisees and the universal triumph of Pharisaic virtues. This, you will agree, lends itself to an argument that is more relevant than the rather sorry excuse that Sade is content with in his apology for calumny—namely, that an honest man will always triumph over it.

This platitude does not encumber the somber beauty that radiates from this monument of challenges. This beauty evinces the experience that I am seeking behind the make-believe quality [*fabulation*] of the fantasy: it is a tragic experience, insofar as it projects its condition here in a light [that comes] from beyond all fear and pity.

789 Bewilderment and shadows, such is the conjunction, unlike that found in jokes,[20] that fascinates us in these scenes with its ember-like brilliance.

This tragedy is of the kind that becomes clearer later on in the century in more than one work, whether erotic novel or religious drama. I would call it senile tragedy; until I said so, no one realized, except schoolboys in their jokes, that it is but a stone's throw from noble tragedy. To see what I mean, read Claudel's trilogy, *Le Père humilié*. (To see what I mean, one should also know that I have shown that this trilogy contains the characteristics of the most authentic tragedy. It is Melpomene who, along with Clio, is decrepit, without our knowing which one will bury the other.)

We are now finally enjoined to examine *Sade, My Neighbor,* the invocation of which we owe to the perspicacity of Pierre Klossowski. Being extreme, his perspicacity has no need to resort to the same things as the highbrow literati.[21]

It is undoubtedly Klossowski's discretion that makes him justify his formulation with a reference to Saint Labre. I do not, however, feel inclined to give it the same justification.

My structural reference points make it easy to grasp that the Sadean fantasy is better situated among the stays of Christian ethics than elsewhere.

But what must be kept in mind is that Sade himself refuses to be my neighbor, not so that I can refuse to be his neighbor in turn but so as to recognize the meaning of his refusal here.

In my view, Sade does not have neighborly enough relations with his own malice [*méchanceté*] to encounter his neighbor in it, a characteristic he shares with many people and with Freud, in particular. For this is indeed the only reason why beings, who are sometimes experienced, back away from the Christian commandment.

We see what is, to my mind, the crucial test of this in Sade's rejection of the death penalty, the history of which would suffice to prove, if not its logic, at least that it is one of the correlates of Charity.

Sade thus stopped at the point where desire and the law become bound up with each other [*se noue*].

If something in him let itself remain tied to the law in order to take the
opportunity, mentioned by Saint Paul, to become inordinately sinful, who 790
would cast the first stone? But Sade went no further.

It is not simply that his flesh is weak, as it is for each of us; it is that the spirit is too willing not to be deluded. His apology for crime merely impels him to an oblique acceptance of the Law. The Supreme Being is restored in Evil Action [*le Maléfice*].

Listen to him praise his technique of immediately implementing whatever comes into his head, thinking too that by replacing repentance with reiteration he can be done with the law within. To encourage us to follow his example, he comes up with nothing better than the promise that nature, woman that she is, will magically give us ever more.

We would be foolish to have faith in this typical dream of potency.

It indicates to us clearly enough, in any case, that it cannot be true that Sade, as Klossowski suggests—all the while noting that he does not believe it—achieved the sort of apathy that involves having "returned to nature's bosom, in the waking state, in our world"[22] inhabited by language.

I have forbidden myself to say a word about what Sade is missing here. Let it be sensed in the climax of *Philosophy in the Bedroom*, it being the curved needle, dear to Buñuel's heroes, which is finally called upon to resolve in the girl a *penisneid* [penis envy] that is posited to some degree in it.

In any case, it appears that nothing has been gained by replacing Diotima here with Dolmancé, a person whom the usual orifice seems to frighten more than is fitting, and who—did Sade see this?—concludes the whole business with a sort of *Noli tangere matrem*. Syphilized and sewn shut—the mother remains prohibited. My verdict is confirmed regarding Sade's submission to the Law.

There is thus precious little here—in fact, nothing—by way of a treatise that is truly on desire.

What is announced about desire here, in this mistake based on an encounter, is at most but a tone of reason.

R. G., September 1962

Notes

1. [Added in 1971:] This essay was commissioned from me for the abovementioned edition [but was not included in it]. I will add here, for the fun of it, that it was recommissioned from me when the success of my *Écrits* rendered it plausible (. . . to the person who had replaced me?). [It was included as a postface in the same publisher's 1966 edition of Sade's *Oeuvres complètes*.]

2. I refer the reader to Barni's very acceptable French translation published in 1848, p. 247 and following here, and to the Vorländer edition (published by Meiner) for the German text, p. 86 here.

3. See the Comment on Theorem III of the first chapter of the "Analytic of Pure Practical Reason," Barni, 163; Vorländer, 31. [In English, *Critique of Practical Reason,* 40–41.]

4. See Sade, *Philosophie dans le boudoir* in *Oeuvres complètes*, vol. III (Paris: Cercle du livre précieux, 1963), 501–2. [In English, see *Philosophy in the Bedroom* in *The Complete Justine, Philosophy in the Bedroom, and Other Writings,* trans. R. Seaver and A. Wainhouse (New York: Grove Press, 1965), 318–19.]

5. *Antigone*, v. 781.

6. See *Histoire de Juliette* (Sceaux: Pauvert, 1954), vol. II, 196–97. [In English, *Juliette*, 369–70].

7. It is a subjective dynamism: physical death is the object of the wish for a second death.

8. See Renan's preface to his *Nouvelles études d'histoire religieuse* (Paris: Calmann-Lévy, 1884). [In English, see Ernest Renan, *Studies in Religious History* (New York: Scribner and Welford, 1887), 1–2.]

9. It should not be thought that I am lending credence here to the legend that he personally intervened in Sade's imprisonment. See Gilbert Lély, *Vie du Marquis de Sade* (Paris: Gallimard, 1952–1957), vol. II, pp. 577–80, and p. 580, note 1. [In English, see *The Marquis de Sade: A Biography,* trans. A. Brown (New York: Grove Press, 1962), 415–16.]

10. This is the chorus of *Oedipus at Colonus*, v. 1225.

11. See Maurice Garçon's *L'affaire Sade* (Paris: Pauvert, 1957). He cites J. Janin from *La Revue de Paris* in 1834, in his plea, pp. 84–90. A second reference is found on page 62: J. Cocteau, as a witness, wrote that Sade is annoying, but did not fail to recognize him as a philosopher and a moralizer.

12. The original German text reads: threatening to put him to death immediately.

13. Barni, p. 173. This is found in the Comment on Problem II (*Aufgabe*) of Theorem III in the first chapter of the "Analytic of Pure Practical Reason," ed. Vorländer, p. 35.

14. See p. 253 of Barni's translation, p. 90 in the Vorländer edition.

15. [Added in 1971:] What would I have written by way of a postface?

16. Theorem II of the first chapter of the "Analytic of Pure Practical Reason," p. 25 in the Vorländer edition, altogether incorrectly translated by Barni, p. 159.

17. Sade expressly indicates this in his complete title.

18. See Renan's *Vie de Jésus*, 17th edition, p. 339 [(Paris: Calmann-Lévy, [1863])]. [In English, see *The Life of Jesus*, trans. J. H. Holmes (New York: Modern Library, 1927), 299 (translation modified).]

19. Renan, *Vie de Jésus*, 346. [In English, see *The Life of Jesus*, 304 (translation modified).]

20. Freud, as we know, takes Heymans' *Sidération et lumière* (bewilderment and light) as a starting point. [See *SE* VIII, 12–13, where the German *Verblüffung und Erleuchtung* is rendered as "bewilderment and illumination."]

21. [Added in 1971:] This last sentence was addressed to a future academician, himself an expert in malicious comments; I see that he recognized himself in the one that opens this article. [Deleted in 1971:] *Sade, mon prochain* is the title of Klossowski's work that was published by Seuil in 1947. It is the only contemporary contribution to the Sadean question that does not strike me as marred by the tics of the highbrow literati. (This sentence, too laudatory for others, was at first included in my text for a future academician, himself an expert in malicious comments). [In English, see *Sade, My Neighbor,* trans. A. Lingis (Evanston, Ill.: Northwestern University Press, 1991).]

22. See Klossowski's *Sade, mon prochain*, p. 94, note.

VII

The Subversion of the Subject and the Dialectic of Desire in the Freudian Unconscious 793

This text represents my contribution to a conference on "La Dialectique," held at Royaumont from September 19 to 23, 1960. The conference was organized by the "Colloques philosophiques internationaux," and I was invited to participate by Jean Wahl.

It is the date of this text—which predates the Bonneval Colloquium from which the text that follows stemmed ["Position of the Unconscious" follows this one in *Écrits* 1966]—that leads me to publish it, in order to give the reader an idea how far my teaching has always been ahead of what I could make more widely available.

(The graph presented here was constructed for my seminar on unconscious formations. It was worked out particularly in relation to the structure of jokes, which I took as a point of departure, before a surprised audience. That was in the first term of the seminar, which was the last term of 1957. An account of the seminar, along with the graph provided here, was published at the time in the *Bulletin de psychologie*.)

A structure is constitutive of the praxis known as psychoanalysis. This structure cannot be immaterial to an audience like the one here today, which is supposed to be philosophically sophisticated.

The thesis that being a philosopher means being interested in what everyone is interested in without knowing it has the interesting peculiarity that its relevance does not imply that it can be settled either way. For it can only be settled if everyone becomes a philosopher.

I am talking about its philosophical relevance, for that is, in the end, the schema Hegel gave us of History in *The Phenomenology of Mind*.

Summarizing it in this way has the advantage of providing us with a mediation that is convenient for situating the subject: on the basis of a relationship to knowledge.

It is also convenient for demonstrating the ambiguity of such a relation- 794
ship.

This same ambiguity is manifested by the effects of science in the contemporary universe.

The scientist himself is a subject, one who is particularly qualified in his constitution, as is shown by the fact that science did not come into the world all by itself (its birth was not without vicissitudes, and was preceded by a number of failures—abortion or prematurity).

Now this subject who must know what he is doing, or so we presume, does not know what is already, in fact, of interest to everyone regarding the effects of science. Or so it would appear in the contemporary universe, where everyone finds himself at the same level as the scientist as far as this point of ignorance is concerned.

In and of itself, this warrants our speaking of a subject of science—a notion to which an epistemology that can be said to display more pretension than success would like to measure up.

Hence—let it be noted here—the entirely didactic reference I have made to Hegel in order to convey, for my analytic training purposes, where things stand regarding the question of the subject such as psychoanalysis properly subverts it.

What qualifies me to proceed along this path is obviously my experience of this praxis. What made me decide to do so—those who follow my work will attest to this—is a failure of theory coupled with abuses in its transmission, which, while presenting no danger to the praxis itself, result, in both cases, in a total absence of scientific status. To raise the question of the minimal conditions required for such a status was not perhaps an impertinent point of departure. It has turned out to lead a long way.

I am not referring here to anything as broad in scope as a challenging of different societies' practices—in particular, to the stockpile of conclusions I have been forced to draw in order to counter the notorious deviations in analytic praxis that claim to be genuinely psychoanalytic in England and America.

What I will specifically try to define is subversion, and I apologize to this assembly, whose qualifications I mentioned earlier, for being unable to do more in its presence than elsewhere—namely, to take this assembly as such as the pivot of my demonstration, the onus being on me to justify taking such liberties with regard to it.

795 Nevertheless, I shall take advantage of your kindness in assuming we agree that a science cannot be conditioned upon empiricism.

Secondly, we encounter what has already been constituted, with a scientific label, by the name of psychology.

Which I challenge—precisely because, as I will show, the function of the subject, as inaugurated by Freudian experience, disqualifies from the outset what, going by the name "psychology," merely perpetuates an academic framework, no matter how one dresses up its premises.

Its criterion is the unity of the subject, which is one of the presuppositions of this sort of psychology; it should even be taken as symptomatic that this theme is ever more emphatically isolated, as if the return of a certain subject of consciousness [*connaissance*] were at stake, or as if the psychical had to obtain recognition as doubling the organism.

Here we must take as exemplary the idea in which a whole body of traditional thought comes together in accrediting a term, "state of consciousness," that is not without basis. Whether we're dealing with the states of enthusiasm described by Plato, the degrees of samadhi in Buddhism, or the experience (*Erlebnis*) one has under the influence of hallucinogens, it is important to know how much of this is authenticated by any theory.

Authenticated in the register of what consciousness includes by way of connaturality.

It is clear that Hegelian knowledge, in the logicizing *Aufhebung* [sublation] on which it is based, puts as little stock in these states as such as does modern science, which may recognize in them an object of experience, in the sense of an opportunity to define certain coordinates, but in no way an ascesis that could, so to speak, be "epistemogenic" or "noophoric."

It is in this respect that reference to them is relevant to us.

For I assume you are sufficiently informed about Freudian practice to realize that such states play no part in it; but what is not fully appreciated is the fact that this supposed "depth psychology" does not dream of using these states to obtain illumination, for example, or even assign any value to them along the path it sketches out.

For that is why—though it is not stressed—Freud steers clear of hypnoid states, even when it comes to explaining the phenomena of hysteria. That is the amazing thing: Freud prefers the hysteric's discourse to hypnoid
states. What I have called "fertile moments" in my mapping of paranoiac 796
knowledge [*connaissance*] is not a Freudian reference.

I have some difficulty in getting across—in a circle infatuated with the most incredible illogicality—what it means to interrogate the unconscious as I do, that is, to the point at which it gives a reply that is not some sort of ravishment or takedown, but is rather a "saying why."

If we conduct the subject anywhere, it is to a deciphering which assumes that a sort of logic is already operative in the unconscious, a logic in which, for example, an interrogative voice or even the development of an argument can be recognized.

The whole psychoanalytic tradition supports the view that the analyst's voice can intervene only if it enters at the right place, and that if it comes too early it merely produces a closing up.

In other words, a strain of psychoanalysis that is sustained by its allegiance to Freud cannot under any circumstances pass itself off as a rite of passage to some archetypal, or in any sense ineffable, experience. The day someone who is not simply a moron obtains a hearing for a view of this kind will be the day all limits will have been abolished. We are still a long way from that.[1]

Thus far we have merely broached our subject. For we must home in more precisely on what Freud himself articulates in his doctrine as constituting a "Copernican" step.

For such a step to be constituted, is it enough that a privilege should be revoked—in this case, the one that put the earth in the central place? Man's subsequent destitution from an analogous place due to the triumph of the idea of evolution gives one the sense that such revocation implies an advantage that is confirmed by its constancy.

But can we be so sure this is an advantage or real progress? Does any-
797 thing make it seem that the other truth, if we may so term revealed truth, has seriously suffered as a result? Don't we realize that, by exalting the center, heliocentrism is no less of a lure than seeing the earth as the center, and that the existence of the ecliptic probably provided a more stimulating model of our relations with truth, before it lost much of its interest when it was reduced to being no more than the earth bowing assent?

In any case, it is not because of Darwin that men believe themselves to be any the less the best among the creatures, for it is precisely of this that he convinces them.

The use of Copernicus' name as a reference has more hidden resources that touch specifically on what has already just slipped from my pen regarding our relation to the true—namely, the emergence of the ellipse as being not unworthy of the locus from which the so-called higher truths take their name. The revolution is no less important even though it concerns only "celestial revolutions."

From that point on, to dwell on it no longer means simply revoking some idiotic notion stemming from the religious tradition, which, as can be seen well enough, is none the worse for it, but rather of tying more closely together the regime of knowledge and the regime of truth.

For if Copernicus' work, as others have remarked before me, is not as Copernican as we think it is, it is because the doctrine of double truth continues to offer shelter to a knowledge that, up until then, it must be said, appeared to be quite content with that shelter.

So here we are at the palpable border between truth and knowledge; and it might be said, after all, that at first sight our science certainly seems to have readopted the solution of closing the border.

Yet if the history of Science's birth is still a sufficiently burning question for us to be aware that at that border something shifted at that time, it is perhaps here that psychoanalysis distinguishes itself by representing a new seism that occurred there.

For let us reexamine from this angle the service we expect from Hegel's phenomenology: that of marking out an ideal solution—one that involves a permanent revisionism, so to speak, in which what is disturbing about truth is constantly being reabsorbed, truth being in itself but what is lacking in the realization of knowledge. The antinomy the Scholastic tradition posited 798
as principial is here taken to be resolved by virtue of being imaginary. Truth is nothing but what knowledge can learn that it knows merely by putting its ignorance to work. This is a real crisis, in which the imaginary is eliminated in engendering a new symbolic form, to use my own categories. This dialectic is convergent and proceeds to the conjuncture defined as absolute knowledge. As it is deduced, this conjuncture can only be the conjunction of the symbolic with a real from which nothing more can be expected. What is this, if not a subject finalized in his self-identity? From which one can conclude that this subject is already perfect(ed) here and is the fundamental hypothesis of the entire process. He is named, in effect, as the substratum of this process; he is called *Selbstbewusstsein*, the being of the conscious, wholly conscious self.

Would that it were so! But the history of science itself—I mean of our science, since its inception, assuming we situate its first birth in Greek mathematics—presents itself, rather, in the form of detours that comply very little with this immanentism. And scientific theories—let us not be misled on this score by any resorption of the special theory of relativity into the general theory—do not, in any way, fit together according to the thesis/antithesis/synthesis dialectic.

Indeed, a number of creaks—confusedly given voice to by the great minds responsible for some of the cardinal changes in physics—remind us that, after all, it is elsewhere that the moment of truth must sound for this field of knowledge as for others.

Why wouldn't we think that the astonishing indulgence science is showing toward psychoanalytic hype may be due to the theoretical hope psychoanalysis offers—a hope that is not merely the result of the prevailing confusion?

I am not, of course, referring to the extraordinary lateral transference by which psychology reimmerses its categories in psychoanalysis to reinvigorate its lowly purposes of social exploitation. For the reason already stated, I regard the fate of psychology as irremediably sealed.

In any case, my two-pronged reference to Hegel's absolute subject and to science's abolished subject sheds the light necessary to accurately formulate
799 Freud's dramatism: the return of truth to the field of science at the same time as it comes to the fore in the field of its praxis—repressed, it reappears there.

Who cannot see the distance that separates the unhappiness of consciousness—which, however deeply ingrained it may be in Hegel's work, can still be said to be but the suspension of knowing—from civilization's discontents in Freud's work, even if it is only in the inspiration of a sentence which is, as it were, disavowed, that Freud marks for us what, on reading it, cannot be articulated otherwise than the skewed relation that separates the subject from sex?

There is nothing, then, in my approach to situating Freud that owes anything to the judicial astrology in which the psychologist is immersed. Nothing that proceeds on the basis of quality, much less of intensity, or of any phenomenology from which idealism may draw reassurance. In the Freudian field, the words notwithstanding, consciousness is a characteristic that is as obsolete to us in grounding the unconscious—for we cannot ground it on the negation of consciousness (that unconscious dates back to Saint Thomas Aquinas)—as affect is unsuited to play the role of the protopathic subject, since it is a function without a functionary.

Starting with Freud, the unconscious becomes a chain of signifiers that repeats and insists somewhere (on another stage or in a different scene, as he wrote), interfering in the cuts offered it by actual discourse and the cogitation it informs.

In this formulation, which is mine only in the sense that it conforms as closely to Freud's texts as to the experience they opened up, the crucial term is the signifier, revived from ancient rhetoric by modern linguistics, in a doctrine whose various stages I cannot trace here, but of which the names Ferdinand de Saussure and Roman Jakobson stand for its dawn and its present-day culmination, not forgetting that the pilot science of structuralism in the West has its roots in Russia, where formalism first flourished. Geneva 1910 and Petrograd 1920 suffice to explain why Freud did not have this particular instrument at his disposal. But this historically motivated lacuna makes all the more instructive the fact that the mechanisms described by Freud as those of the primary process, by which the unconscious is gov-

erned, correspond exactly to the functions this school of linguistics believes determine the most radical axes of the effects of language, namely metaphor and metonymy—in other words, the effects of the substitution and combination of signifiers in the synchronic and diachronic dimensions, respectively, 800
in which they appear in discourse.

Once the structure of language is recognized in the unconscious, what sort of subject can we conceive of for it?

In a concern for method, we can try to begin here with the strictly linguistic definition of *I* as signifier, where it is nothing but the shifter* or indicative that, qua grammatical subject of the statement, designates the subject insofar as he is currently speaking.

That is to say, it designates the enunciating subject, but does not signify him. This is obvious from the fact that there may be no signifier of the enunciating subject in the statement—not to mention that there are signifiers that differ from *I*, and not only those that are inadequately called cases of the first person singular, even if we add that it can be lodged in the plural invocation or even in the Self [*Soi*] of auto-suggestion.

I believe, for example, that I have detected the enunciating subject in the French signifier *ne*, said by grammarians to be "expletive," a term that already prefigures the incredible opinion of those among the best who regard its form as subject to sheer whimsy. Would that the weight I give it make them think twice, before it not but become obvious they have missed the point [*avant qu'il* ne *soit averé qu'ils n'y comprennent rien*]—take out that "not but" [*ne*] and my enunciation loses its force as an attack, *I* eliding me in the impersonal. Yet I fear that in this way they could not but come to vilify me [*Mais je crains ainsi qu'ils* n'*en viennent à me honnir*]—skip that "not but" [*n'*] and its absence, toning down my alleged fear to declare my repugnance to a timid assertion, reduces the emphasis of my enunciation by situating me in the statement.

But if I say "*tue*" (kill), because they are killing me, where am I situating myself if not in the *tu* on the basis of which I glare at them [*toise*]?

Don't sulk—I am merely referring obliquely to what I am reluctant to cover over with the inevitable map of clinical work.

Namely, the right way to answer the question "Who is speaking?" when the subject of the unconscious is at stake. For the answer cannot come from him if he doesn't know what he is saying, or even that he is speaking, as all of analytic experience teaches us.

Hence the place of the "inter-said" [*inter-dit*], constituted by the "intra-said" [*intra-dit*] of a between-two-subjects, is the very place at which the

transparency of the classical subject divides, undergoing, as it does, the effects of fading* that specify the Freudian subject due to its occultation by
801 an ever purer signifier; may these effects lead us to the frontiers where slips of the tongue and jokes become indistinguishable in their collusion, or even where elision is so much more allusive in driving presence back to its lair, that we are astonished the hunt for Dasein hasn't made any more of it.

Lest our hunt be in vain, we analysts must bring everything back to the cut qua function in discourse, the most significant being the cut that constitutes a bar between the signifier and the signified. Here we come upon the subject who interests us since, being bound up in signification, he seems to be lodging in the preconscious. This would lead us to the paradox of conceiving that discourse in an analytic session is worthwhile only insofar as it stumbles or even interrupts itself—were not the session itself instituted as a break in a false discourse, that is, in what discourse realizes when it becomes empty as speech, when it is no more than the worn coinage Mallarmé speaks of that is passed from hand to hand "in silence."

The cut made by the signifying chain is the only cut that verifies the structure of the subject as a discontinuity in the real. If linguistics enables us to see the signifier as the determinant of the signified, analysis reveals the truth of this relationship by making holes in meaning the determinants of its discourse.

This is the path by which an imperative can be fulfilled, the imperative Freud raised to the sublime stature of a pre-Socratic gnome in his formulation, "Wo Es war, soll Ich werden," which I have commented upon more than once, and which I am now going to inflect differently.

I will limit myself to examining one step in its grammar: "where it was . . ." [*là où ce fut* . . .]—what does that mean? If it were but this [*ça*] that might have been (to use the aoristic form), how to come to the same place in order to make myself be there, by stating it now?

But the French translation says: "*Là où c'était* . . ." Let us take advantage of the distinct imperfect it provides. Where it was just now, where it was for a short while, between an extinction that is still glowing and an opening up that stumbles, *I* can [*peut*] come into being by disappearing from my statement [*dit*].

An enunciation that denounces itself, a statement that renounces itself, an ignorance that sweeps itself away, an opportunity that self-destructs—what remains here if not the trace of what really must be in order to fall away from being?

A dream related by Freud in his article, "Formulations on the Two Prin-
802 ciples of Mental Functioning," gives us a sentence, related to the pathos

with which the figure of a dead father returning as a ghost would be invested: "He did not know he was dead."[2]

I have already used this sentence to illustrate the subject's relation to the signifier—through an enunciation that makes a human being tremble due to the vacillation that comes back to him from his own statement.

If this figure of the dead father subsists only by virtue of the fact that one does not tell him the truth of which he is unaware, what then is the status of the *I* on which this subsistence depends?

He did not know . . . He was to know a bit later. Oh! may that never happen! May *I* die rather than have him know. Yes, that's how I get there, where it was (to be): who knew, thus, that *I* was dead?

Being of non-being, that is how *I* comes on the scene as a subject who is conjugated with the double aporia of a veritable subsistence that is abolished by his knowledge, and by a discourse in which it is death that sustains existence.

Will we weigh this being against the being Hegel as subject forged—Hegel being the subject who, regarding history, adopts the discourse of absolute knowledge? We recall that Hegel admitted to having experienced the temptation of madness. Isn't our path the one that overcomes that, by going right to the truth of the vanity of this discourse?

I will not expound my doctrine on madness here. For I have included this eschatological excursion only to designate the gap that separates the two relations—Freudian and Hegelian—between the subject and knowledge.

And to show that there is no surer root of these relations than the different ways in which the dialectic of desire is distinguished in them.

For in Hegel's work it is desire (*Begierde*) that is given responsibility for the minimal link the subject must retain to Antiquity's knowledge [*connaissance*] if truth is to be immanent in the realization of knowledge. The "cunning of reason" means that, from the outset and right to the end, the subject knows what he wants.

It is here that Freud reopens the junction between truth and knowledge to the mobility out of which revolutions arise.

In this respect: that desire becomes bound up at that junction with the Other's desire, but that the desire to know lies in this loop.

Freud's biologism has nothing to do with the preachy abjection that 803
wafts up to us from psychoanalytic headquarters.

And you had to be made to experience the death instinct, which is held in such abomination there, to get on the true wavelength of Freud's biology. For to evade the death instinct in his doctrine is not to know his doctrine at all.

On the basis of the approach I have prepared for you, you should recognize in the metaphor of the return to the inanimate—which Freud ascribes to every living body—the margin beyond life that language assures the human being of due to the fact that he speaks, and which is precisely the margin where this being places in signifying position, not only those parts of his body that lend themselves to this because they are exchangeable, but the body itself. Thus it becomes apparent that the object's relation to the body can in no way be defined as based on a partial identification that would have to be totalized there, since, on the contrary, this object is the prototype of the body's signifierness as the human being's ante.

Here I will take up the challenge made to me when people translate as "instinct" what Freud calls *Trieb*—which "drive" would seem to translate quite well into English, but which is avoided in the *Standard Edition*. In French, my last resort would be *dérive* [drift], if I were unable to give the bastardized term *pulsion* [drive or urge] its point of impact.

And so I insist on promoting the idea that, whether grounded or not in biological observation, instinct—among the modes of knowledge [*connaissance*] required by nature of living beings so that they satisfy its needs—is defined as a kind of [experiential] knowledge [*connaissance*] we admire because it cannot become [articulated] knowledge [*un savoir*]. But in Freud's work something quite different is at stake, which is a *savoir* certainly, but one that doesn't involve the slightest *connaissance*, in that it is inscribed in a discourse of which the subject—who, like the messenger-slave of Antiquity, carries under his hair the codicil that condemns him to death—knows neither the meaning nor the text, nor in what language [*langue*] it is written, nor even that it was tattooed on his shaven scalp while he was sleeping.

This apologue barely exaggerates just how little the unconscious has to do with physiology.

This can be gauged by crosschecking the contribution made by psychoanalysis to physiology since its inception: its contribution has been nil, even as far as the sexual organs are concerned. No amount of fabulation will prevail against this balance sheet.

804 For, of course, psychoanalysis concerns the reality [*réel*] of the body and of its imaginary mental schema. But to recognize their import in the perspective authorized by "development," we must first realize that the more or less fragmented integrations that seem to account for the order of development, function first and foremost like elements of a heraldry, a heraldry of the body. This is confirmed by the use that is made of them in reading children's drawings.

This is the crux—to which I shall return later—of the paradoxical privilege the phallus continues to have in the unconscious dialectic, the theory of the part-object not sufficing to explain it.

Need I now say—if one understands the kind of support I have sought in Hegel's work by which to criticize a degradation of psychoanalysis that is so inept that it has no other claim to fame than that of being contemporary—that it is inadmissible that I should be accused of having been lured by a purely dialectical exhaustion of being, and that I can but hold a particular philosopher[3] responsible for authorizing this misunderstanding?

For far from giving myself over to some logicizing reduction where desire is at stake, I detect in desire's irreducibility to demand the very mainspring of what also prevents it from being reduced to need. To put it elliptically: it is precisely because desire is articulated that it is not articulable—by which I mean in the discourse that suits it, an ethical, not a psychological discourse.

I must now lay out for you in much greater detail the topology that I have developed in my teaching over the past few years, that is, introduce a certain graph, which, I should indicate, also serves purposes other than the one I have in mind here, having been constructed and perfected quite explicitly in order to map out on its different levels the most broadly practical structure of the data of analytic experience. It will serve here to show 805
where desire is situated in relation to a subject defined on the basis of his articulation by the signifier.

GRAPH 1

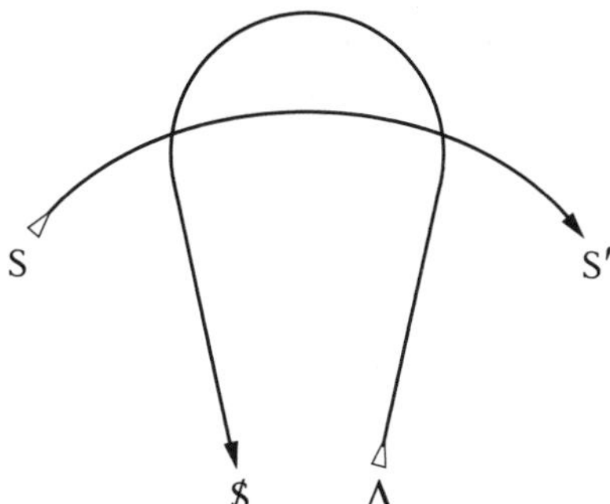

This is what might be called its elementary cell (see Graph 1). In it is articulated what I have called the "button tie" [*point de capiton*], by which the signifier stops the otherwise indefinite sliding of signification. The signifying chain is assumed to be borne by the vector $\overrightarrow{S.S'}$. Without even going into the subtleties of the negatively oriented direction in which its double intersection with the vector $\overrightarrow{\Delta.\$}$ occurs—only in this latter vector does one see the fish it hooks, a fish less suitable for representing what it withdraws from our grasp in its vigorous swimming than the intention that tries to drown it in the flood-tide of pre-text, namely, the reality that is imagined in the ethological schema of the return of need.

The diachronic function of this button tie can be found in a sentence, insofar as a sentence closes its signification only with its last term, each term being anticipated in the construction constituted by the other terms and, inversely, sealing their meaning by its retroactive effect.

But the synchronic structure is more hidden, and it is this structure that brings us to the beginning. It is metaphor insofar as the first attribution is constituted in it—the attribution that promulgates "the dog goes meow, the cat goes woof-woof," by which, in one fell swoop, the child, by disconnecting the thing from its cry, raises the sign to the function of the signifier and reality to the sophistics of signification, and in his contempt for verisimilitude, makes necessary the verification of multiple objectifications of the same thing.

806 Does this possibility require the topology of a four-corners game? This sort of question seems innocent enough, but it may give us some trouble if the subsequent construction must depend on it.

I will spare you the stages by revealing directly the function of the two points of intersection in this elementary graph [see Graph 2]. The first, labeled A, is the locus of the treasure trove of signifiers, which does not mean of the code, for the one-to-one correspondence between a sign and a thing is not preserved here, the signifier being constituted on the basis of a synchronic and countable collection in which none of the elements is sustained except through its opposition to each of the others. The second, labeled *s*(A), is what may be called the punctuation, in which signification ends as a finished product.

Let us observe the dissymmetry between the one, which is a locus (a place, rather than a space), and the other, which is a moment (a scansion, rather than a duration).

Both are related to the offer to the signifier that is constituted by the hole in the real, the one as a hollow for concealment, the other as drilling toward a way out.

The subject's submission to the signifier, which occurs in the circuit that goes from *s*(A) to A and back from A to *s*(A), is truly a circle, inasmuch as the assertion that is established in it—being unable to close on anything but its own scansion, in other words, failing an act in which it would find its certainty—refers back only to its own anticipation in the composition of the signifier, which is in itself meaningless [*insignifiante*].

To be possible, the squaring of this circle only requires the completeness of the signifying battery installed in A, henceforth symbolizing the Other's locus. This allows us to see that this Other is but the pure subject of modern game strategy, and is as such perfectly accessible to the calculation of conjecture—in the sense that the real subject, in making his own calculations, need not take into account any so-called subjective (in the usual, that is, psychological, sense of the term) aberration, but only the inscription of a combinatory whose combinations may be exhaustively enumerated.

This squaring of the circle is nevertheless impossible, but solely because the subject constitutes himself only by subtracting himself from it and by decompleting it essentially, such that he must, at one and the same time, 807
count himself here and function only as a lack here.

The Other, as preliminary site of the pure subject of the signifier, occupies the key [*maîtresse*] position here, even before coming into existence here as absolute Master—to use Hegel's term with and against him. For what is omitted in the platitude of modern information theory is the fact that one cannot even speak of a code without it already being the Other's code; something quite different is at stake in the message, since the subject constitutes himself on the basis of the message, such that he receives from the Other even the message he himself sends. Thus the notations A and *s*(A) are justified.

Code messages and message codes separate out into pure forms in the psychotic subject, the subject who makes do with this preliminary Other alone.

Observe, as an aside, that this Other, distinguished as the locus of Speech, nevertheless emerges as Truth's witness. Without the dimension it constitutes, the deceptiveness of Speech would be indistinguishable from the feint, which, in fighting or sexual display, is nevertheless quite different. Deployed in imaginary capture, the feint is integrated into the play of approach and retreat that constituted the first dance, in which these two vital situations find their scansion, and the partners who fall into step with it find what I will dare to write as their "dancity." Moreover, animals show that they are capable of such behavior when they are being hunted down; they manage to throw their pursuers off the scent by briefly going in one direction as a lure and then changing direction. This can go so far as to suggest on the part of game animals the nobility of honoring the parrying found in the hunt. But an animal does not feign feigning. It does not make tracks whose deceptiveness lies in getting them to be taken as false, when in fact they are true—that is, tracks that indicate the right trail. No more than it effaces its tracks, which would already be tantamount to making itself the subject of the signifier.

All this has been articulated only in a confused way by philosophers who are nevertheless professional. But it is clear that Speech begins only with the passage from the feint to the order of the signifier, and that the signifier requires another locus—the locus of the Other, the Other as witness, the witness who is Other than any of the partners—for the Speech borne by the signifier to be able to lie, that is, to posit itself as Truth.

808 Thus Truth draws its guarantee from somewhere other than the Reality it concerns: it draws it from Speech. Just as it is from Speech that Truth receives the mark that instates it in a fictional structure.

The first words spoken decree, legislate, aphorize, and are an oracle; they give the real other its obscure authority.

Take just one signifier as an insignia of this omnipotence, that is, of this wholly potential power, of this birth of possibility, and you have the unary trait which—filling in the invisible mark the subject receives from the signifier—alienates this subject in the first identification that forms the ego-ideal.

This is inscribed by the notation I(A), which I must substitute, at this stage, for $, the barred S of the negatively oriented vector, moving $ from the vector's endpoint to its starting point (see Graph 2).

GRAPH 2

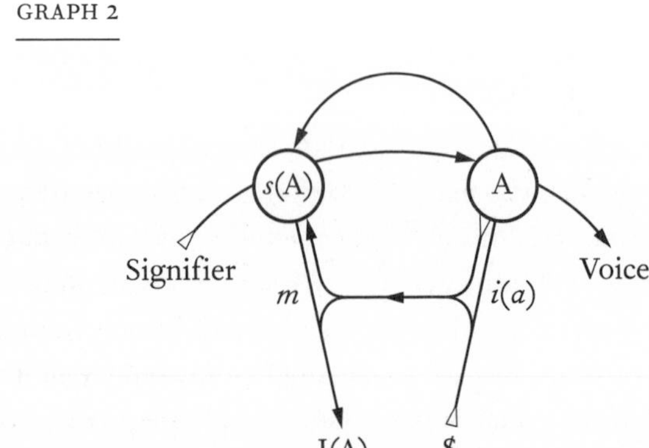

This is a retroversion effect by which the subject, at each stage, becomes what he was (to be) [*était*] before that, and "he will have been" is only announced in the future perfect tense.

Here arises the ambiguity of a misrecognizing that is essential to knowing myself [*un méconnaître essentiel au me connaître*]. For, in this "rear view," all the subject can be sure of is the anticipated image—which he had caught of himself in his mirror—coming to meet him. I won't go back over the function of my "mirror stage" here, the first strategic point I developed as an objection to the supposedly "autonomous ego" in favor in psychoanalytic theory, whose academic restoration justified the mistaken proposal to strengthen the ego in a type of treatment diverted thereafter toward successful adaptation—a phenomenon of mental abdication tied to the aging of the psychoanalytic group in the Diaspora owing to the war, and the reduction of an eminent practice to a *Good Housekeeping* seal of approval attesting to its suitability to the "American way of life."*[4] 809

Be that as it may, what the subject finds in this altered image of his body is the paradigm of all the forms of resemblance that will cast a shade of hostility onto the world of objects, by projecting onto them the avatar of his narcissistic image, which, from the jubilation derived from encountering it in the mirror, becomes—in confronting his semblables—the outlet for his most intimate aggressiveness.

It is this image that becomes fixed—this is the ideal ego—from the point at which the subject fixates as ego-ideal. The ego is thus a function of mastery, a game of bearing, and constituted rivalry. In the capture it undergoes due to its imaginary nature, the ego masks its duplicity; that is, consciousness, in which the ego assures itself an indisputable existence (a naïveté that is displayed in Fénelon's work), is in no way immanent in the ego, but rather transcendent, since consciousness is based on the ego-ideal as unary trait (the Cartesian cogito does not fail to recognize this).[5] As a result, the transcendental ego itself is relativized, implicated as it is in the misrecognition in which the ego's identifications originate.

This imaginary process, which goes from the specular image to the constitution of the ego along the path of subjectification by the signifier, is signified in my graph by the $\overrightarrow{i(a).m}$ vector, which is one-way but doubly articulated, first as a short circuit of the $\overrightarrow{\$.\mathrm{I}(\mathrm{A})}$ vector, and second as a return route of the $\overrightarrow{\mathrm{A}.s(\mathrm{A})}$ vector. This shows that the ego is only completed by being articulated not as the *I* of discourse, but as a metonymy of its signification (what Damourette and Pichon take as the "filled out" person, as opposed to the "ethereal" person, the latter being no other than the function I designated earlier as that of the shifter*).

The promotion of consciousness as essential to the subject in the historical aftermath of the Cartesian cogito is indicative, to my mind, of a misleading emphasis on the transparency of the *I* in action at the expense of the opacity of the signifier that determines it; and the slippage by which *Bewusstsein*
serves to cover over the confusion of the *Selbst* actually reveals, in *The Phe-* 810
nomenology of Mind, that the reason for Hegel's error lies in his rigor.

The very movement that shifts the axis of the phenomenon of mind toward the imaginary relation to the other (that is, to the semblable connoted by a lowercase *a*), brings its effect to light: namely, the aggressiveness that becomes the balance arm of the scales around which the equilibrium of semblable to semblable decomposes in the relationship between Master and Slave, a relationship that is replete with all the cunning tricks by which reason advances its impersonal reign.

Regarding this slavery that inaugurates the roads to freedom—a myth rather than an actual genesis, no doubt—I can point here to what it hides precisely because I have revealed what it hides as no one had before.

The struggle that gives rise to this slavery is rightly called a struggle of pure prestige, and what is at stake—life itself—is well suited to echo the danger of the generic prematurity of birth, which Hegel was unaware of, and which I have situated as the dynamic mainspring of specular capture.

But death—precisely because it is dragged into the stakes (making this a more honest wager than Pascal's, though Hegel's too is a poker game, since limits are placed on how high the bid can be raised)—simultaneously shows what is elided by a preliminary rule as well as by the final settlement. For, in the final analysis, the loser must not perish if he is to become a slave. In other words, a pact always precedes violence before perpetuating it, and what I call the symbolic dominates the imaginary, allowing us to wonder whether or not murder really is the absolute Master.

For it is not enough to decide the question on the basis of its effect: Death. We need to know which death,[6] the one that life brings or the one that brings life.

Without criticizing the Hegelian dialectic for what it leaves out—the lack of a bond that would keep the society of masters together was pointed out long ago—I simply wish to stress what, on the basis of my own experience, strikes me as blatantly symptomatic in it, that is, as indicative of repression.
811 This is clearly the theme of the cunning of reason, whose seductiveness is in no wise lessened by the error I pointed out above. The work, Hegel tells us, to which the slave submits in giving up jouissance out of fear of death, is precisely the path by which he achieves freedom. There can be no more obvious lure than this, politically or psychologically. Jouissance comes easily to the slave, and it leaves work in serfdom.

The cunning of reason is a seductive notion because it echoes a well-known individual myth characteristic of obsessives, obsessive structure being known to be common among the intelligentsia. But even if someone in this category avoids the professor's bad faith, he cannot easily deceive himself that his work will grant him access to jouissance. Paying truly unconscious homage to the story as written by Hegel, he often finds his alibi in the death of the Master. But what of this death? He quite simply waits for it.

In fact, it is from the Other's locus where he situates himself that he follows the game, thus eliminating all risk to himself—especially the risk of a joust—in a "self-consciousness" for which death is but a joke.

I say this so that philosophers will not believe they can minimize the importance of the irruption constituted by what Freud said about desire.

And this on the pretext that demand, along with the effects of frustration, has buried everything that trickles down to them from a practice which has degenerated into an educative banality that is no longer even redeemed by its laziness.

Yes, the enigmatic traumas of the Freudian discovery are now considered to be merely suppressed cravings. Psychoanalysis is nourished by the observation of children and by the childishness of the observations. Let us skip the reports thus generated, edifying as they all are.

And devoid, as they all are now, of the slightest hint of humor.

Their authors are now far too concerned with obtaining a respectable position to leave any room for the irremediable ludicrousness the unconscious owes to its roots in language.

Yet it is impossible, for those who claim that discordance is introduced into the needs assumed to exist at the subject's origins by the way demand is received, to neglect the fact that there is no demand that does not in some respect pass through the defiles of the signifier.

And while the somatic *ananke* of man's inability to move, much less be
self-sufficient, for some time after birth provides grounds for a psychology 812
of dependence, how can that psychology elide the fact that this dependence is maintained by a universe of language? Indeed, needs have been diversified and geared down by and through language to such an extent that their import appears to be of a quite different order, whether we are dealing with the subject or politics. In other words, to such an extent that these needs have passed over into the register of desire, with everything it forces us to face in this new experience of ours: the age-old paradoxes desire has created for moralists and the mark of the infinite that theologians find in it, not to mention the precariousness of its status, as expressed in its most recent form by Sartre—desire, a useless passion.

What psychoanalysis shows us about desire in what might be called its most natural function, since the survival of the species depends on it, is not only that it is subjected, in its agency, its appropriation, and even its very normality, to the accidents of the subject's history (the notion of trauma as contingency), but also that all this requires the assistance of structural elements —which, in order to intervene, can do very well without these accidents. The inharmonious, unexpected, and recalcitrant impact of these elements certainly seems to leave to the experience [of desire in its most natural function] a residue that drove Freud to admit that sexuality had to bear the mark of some hardly natural flaw.

We would be mistaken if we thought that the Freudian Oedipus myth puts an end to theology on the matter. For the myth does not confine itself to working the puppet of sexual rivalry. It would be better to read in it what Freud requires us to contemplate using his coordinates; for they boil down to the question with which he himself began: What is a Father?

"It is the dead Father," Freud replies, but no one hears him; and it is regrettable that, due to the mere fact that Lacan takes it up again under the heading of the "Name-of-the-Father," a situation that is hardly scientific should still deprive him of his normal audience.[7]

813 Yet analytic reflection has vaguely revolved around the problematic misrecognition of the function of the sire among certain primitive peoples, and psychoanalysts—rallying round the contraband flag of "culturalism"—have even argued about the forms of an authority about which it cannot even be said that any branch of anthropology has provided a definition of any importance.

Will we wait until we are confronted with a practice, which may in the course of time become standard practice, of artificially inseminating women who are at odds with phallicism with the sperm of some great man, before we deign to pronounce a verdict on the paternal function?

Yet the Oedipal show cannot run indefinitely in forms of society that are losing the sense of tragedy to an ever greater extent.

Let us begin with the conception of the Other as the locus of the signifier. No authoritative statement has any other guarantee here than its very enunciation, since it would be pointless for the statement to seek it in another signifier, which could in no way appear outside that locus. I formulate this by saying that there is no metalanguage that can be spoken, or, more aphoristically, that there is no Other of the Other. And when the Legislator (he who claims to lay down the Law) comes forward to make up for this, he does so as an impostor.

But the Law itself is not an impostor, nor is he who authorizes his actions on its basis.

The fact that the Father may be regarded as the original representative of the Law's authority requires us to specify by what privileged mode of presence he sustains himself beyond the subject who is led to really occupy the place of the Other, namely, the Mother. The question is thus pushed back a step.

It will seem strange that—in opening up here the incommensurate space all demand implies, since it is a request for love—I didn't allow for more "making" and debating on this point.

And that instead I focused it on what closes shy of it, due to the same effect of demand, to truly create the place of desire.

Indeed, it is quite simply, and I am going to say in what sense, as the Other's desire that man's desire takes shape, though at first only retaining a subjective opacity in order to represent need in it.

I will now explain in what way this opacity in some sense constitutes the substance of desire.

Desire begins to take shape in the margin in which demand rips away from 814
need, this margin being the one that demand—whose appeal can be unconditional only with respect to the Other—opens up in the guise of the possible gap need may give rise to here, because it has no universal satisfaction (this is called "anxiety"). A margin which, as linear as it may be, allows its vertiginous character to appear, provided it is not trampled by the elephantine feet of the Other's whimsy. Nevertheless, it is this whimsy that introduces the phantom of Omnipotence—not of the subject, but of the Other in which the subject's demand is instated (it's about time this idiotic cliché was, once and for all, and for all parties, put in its place)—and with this phantom, the necessity that the Other be bridled by the Law.

But I will stop here again in order to return to the status of desire, which presents itself as independent of the Law's mediation, because Law originates in desire—owing to the fact that, by an odd symmetry, desire reverses the unconditionality of the demand for love, in which the subject remains subjected to the Other, in order to raise it to the power of an absolute condition (in which "absolute" also implies "detachment").

Given the advantage won over the anxiety related to need, this detachment is successful right from its humblest mode—that in which it was glimpsed by a certain psychoanalyst in his work with children, which he called the "transitional object," in other words, the shred of blanket or beloved shard the child's lips or hands never stop touching.

This is, frankly, no more than an emblem; representation's representative in the absolute condition is in its proper place in the unconscious, where it causes desire in accordance with the structure of fantasy I will extract from it.

For it is clear here that man's continued nescience of his desire is not so much nescience of what he demands, which may after all be isolated, as nescience of whence he desires.

This is where my formulation that the unconscious is (the) discourse about the Other [*discours de l'Autre*] fits in, in which the *de* should be understood in the sense of the Latin *de* (objective determination): *de Alio in oratione* (you complete it: *tua res agitur*).

But we must also add that man's desire is the Other's desire [*le désir de l'homme est le désir de l'Autre*] in which the *de* provides what grammarians call a "subjective determination"—namely, that it is qua Other that man desires (this is what provides the true scope of human passion).

815 This is why the Other's question [*la question* de *l'Autre*]—that comes back to the subject from the place from which he expects an oracular reply—which takes some such form as *"Chè vuoi?,"* "What do you want?," is the question that best leads the subject to the path of his own desire, assuming that, thanks to the know-how of a partner known as a psychoanalyst, he takes up that question, even without knowing it, in the following form: "What does he want from me?"

GRAPH 3

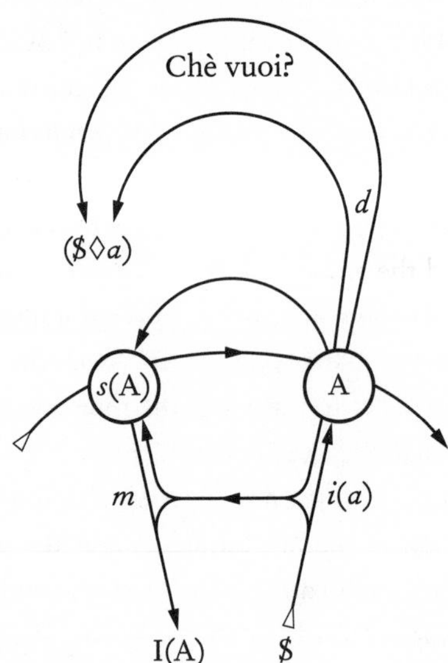

It is this superimposed level of structure that will nudge my graph (see Graph 3) toward its completed form, inserting itself there first like the outline of a question mark planted in the circle of the capital A, for Other, symbolizing the question it signifies with a disconcerting collineation.

Of what bottle is this the opener? Of what answer is it the signifier, the master key?

It should be noted that a clue may be found in the clear alienation that leaves it up to the subject to butt up against the question of his essence, in that he may not misrecognize that what he desires presents itself to him as what he does not want—a form assumed by negation in which misrecognition is inserted in a very odd way, the misrecognition, of which he himself is unaware, by which he transfers the permanence of his desire to an ego that is nevertheless obviously intermittent, and, inversely, protects himself from his desire by attributing to it these very intermittences.

Of course, one may be surprised by the extent of what is accessible to self-consciousness, on the condition that one has learnt it through another channel. Which is certainly the case here.

For if we are to rediscover the pertinence of all this, a sufficiently sophisticated study, that can only be situated in the context of analytic experience, must enable us to complete the structure of fantasy by essentially linking here, regardless of its occasional elisions, the moment of a fading* or eclipse of the sub- 816
ject—which is closely tied to the *Spaltung* or splitting he undergoes due to his subordination to the signifier—to the condition of an object (whose privilege I have done no more than touch on above in reference to diachrony).

This is what is symbolized by the abbreviation ($\$\lozenge a$), which I have introduced as an algorithm; and it is no accident that it breaks the phonemic element constituted by the signifying unit right down to its literal atom. For it is designed to allow for a hundred and one different readings, a multiplicity that is acceptable as long as what is said about it remains grounded in its algebra.

This algorithm and the analogs of it used in the graph in no way contradict what I said earlier about the impossibility of a metalanguage. They are not transcendent signifiers; they are indices of an absolute signification, a notion which will, I hope, seem appropriate to the condition of fantasy without further commentary.

The graph shows that desire adjusts to fantasy as posited in this way—like the ego does in relation to the body image—but the graph also shows the inversion of the misrecognitions on which the one and the other are based, respectively. Thus closes the imaginary path, by which I must come into being in analysis, where the unconscious was (to be) *itself.*

Let us say—borrowing the metaphor used by Damourette and Pichon about the grammatical ego and applying it to a subject to which it is better suited—that fantasy is really the "stuff" of the *I* that is primally repressed, because it can be indicated only in the fading* of enunciation.

Indeed, our attention is now drawn to the subjective status of the signifying chain in the unconscious or, better, in primal repression (*Urverdrängung*).

In my deduction, it is easier to understand why it was necessary to investigate the function on which the subject of the unconscious is based, because we realize that it is difficult to designate that subject anywhere as subject of a statement—and therefore as articulating it—when he does not even know he is speaking. Hence the concept of the drive, in which the subject is designated on the basis of a pinpointing that is organic, oral, anal, and so on, which satisfies the requirement that the more he speaks, the further he is from speaking.

817 COMPLETE GRAPH

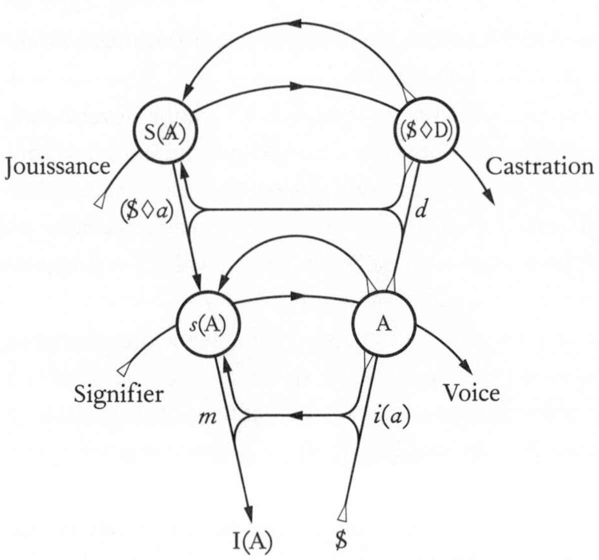

But while my complete graph allows us to situate the drive as the treasure trove of signifiers, its notation, ($◇D), maintains its structure by linking it to diachrony. The drive is what becomes of demand when the subject vanishes from it. It goes without saying that demand also disappears, except that the cut remains, for the latter remains present in what distinguishes the drive from the organic function it inhabits: namely, its grammatical artifice, so manifest in the reversals of its articulation with respect to both source and object. (Freud is a veritable wellspring on this point.)

The very delimitation of the "erogenous zone" that the drive isolates from the function's metabolism (the act of devouring involves organs other than the mouth—just ask Pavlov's dog) is the result of a cut that takes advantage of the anatomical characteristic of a margin or border: the lips, "the enclosure of the teeth," the rim of the anus, the penile groove, the vagina, and the slit formed by the eyelids, not to mention the hollow of the ear (I am avoiding going into embryological detail here). Respiratory erogeneity has been little studied, but it is obviously through spasms that it comes into play.

Let us note that this characteristic of the cut is no less obviously prevalent in the object described by analytic theory: the mamilla, the feces, the phallus (as an imaginary object), and the urinary flow. (An unthinkable list, unless we add, as I do, the phoneme, the gaze, the voice . . . and the nothing.) For isn't it plain to see that the characteristic of being partial, rightly emphasized in objects, is applicable not because these objects are part of a total object, which the body is assumed to be, but because they only partially represent the function that produces them?

A common characteristic of these objects as I formulate them is that they 818
have no specular image, in other words, no alterity.[8] This is what allows them to be the "stuff" or, better put, the lining—without, nevertheless, being the flip side—of the very subject people take to be the subject of consciousness. For this subject, who thinks he can accede to himself by designating himself in the statement, is nothing but such an object. Ask someone with writer's block about the anxiety he experiences and he will tell you who the turd *is* in his fantasy.

It is to this object that cannot be grasped in the mirror that the specular image lends its clothes. A substance caught in the net of shadow, and which, robbed of its shadow-swelling volume, holds out once again the tired lure of the shadow as if it were substance.

What the graph now offers us is situated at the point at which every signifying chain takes pride in closing its signification. If we are to expect such an effect from unconscious enunciation, it is here in S(Ⱥ) and read as: signifier of a lack in the Other, a lack inherent in the Other's very function as the treasure trove of signifiers. And this is so insofar as the Other is called upon (*chè vuoi*) to answer for the value of this treasure, that is, to answer for its place in the lower chain certainly, but with the signifiers constitutive of the upper chain—in other words, in terms of the drive.

The lack at stake is one I have already formulated: that there is no Other of the Other. But is this characteristic of truth's Faithlessness really the last word worth giving in answer to the question, "What does the Other want from me?" when we analysts are its mouthpiece? Surely not, and precisely because there is nothing doctrinal about our role. We need not answer for any ultimate truth, and certainly not for or against any particular religion.

It is already significant that I had to situate here [in S(Ⱥ)] the dead Father in the Freudian myth. But a myth is nothing if it props up no rites, and psychoanalysis is not the Oedipal rite—a point to be expanded on later.

No doubt a corpse is a signifier, but Moses' tomb is as empty for Freud as Christ's was for Hegel. Abraham revealed his mystery to neither of them.

For my part, I will begin with what the abbreviation S(Ⱥ) articulates, 819
being first of all a signifier. My definition of the signifier (there is no other)

is as follows: a signifier is what represents the subject to another signifier. This latter signifier is therefore the signifier to which all the other signifiers represent the subject—which means that if this signifier is missing, all the other signifiers represent nothing. For something is only represented to.

Now insofar as the battery of signifiers is, it is complete, and this signifier can only be a line that is drawn from its circle without being able to be counted in it. This can be symbolized by the inherence of a (−1) in the set of signifiers.

It is, as such, unpronounceable, but its operation is not, for the latter is what occurs whenever a proper name is pronounced. Its statement is equal to its signification.

Hence, by calculating this signification according to the algebra I use, namely:

$$\frac{\text{S (signifier)}}{\text{s (signified)}} = \text{s (the statement)},$$

$$\text{with S} = (-1)\text{, we find: s} = \sqrt{-1}$$

This is what the subject is missing in thinking he is exhaustively accounted for by his cogito—he is missing what is unthinkable about him. But where does this being, who appears in some way missing from the sea of proper names, come from?

We cannot ask this question of the subject qua *I*. He is missing everything he needs in order to know the answer, since if this subject, *I*, was dead [*moi J'étais mort*], he would not know it, as I said earlier. Thus he does not know I'm alive. How, therefore, will *I* prove it to myself?

For I can, at most, prove to the Other that he exists, not, of course, with the proofs of the existence of God with which the centuries have killed him, but by loving him, a solution introduced by the Christian kerygma.

It is, in any case, too precarious a solution for us to even think of using it to circumvent our problem, namely: What am *I*?

I am in the place from which "the universe is a flaw in the purity of Non-Being" is vociferated.

And not without reason for, by protecting itself, this place makes Being itself languish. This place is called Jouissance, and it is Jouissance whose absence would render the universe vain.

Am I responsible for it, then? Yes, of course. Is this Jouissance, the lack of
820 which makes the Other inconsistent, mine, then? Experience proves that it is usually forbidden me, not only, as certain fools would have it, due to bad

societal arrangements, but, I would say, because the Other is to blame—if he was to exist [*existait*], that is. But since he doesn't exist, all that's left for me is to place the blame on *I*, that is, to believe in what experience leads us all to, Freud at the head of the list: original sin. For even if we did not have Freud's express and sorrowful avowal, the fact remains that the myth we owe to him—the most recent in history—is of no more use than the myth of the forbidden fruit, except for the fact (and this is not one of its assets as a myth) that, being more succinct, it is considerably less stultifying.

But what is not a myth, although Freud formulated it just as early on as he formulated the Oedipus myth, is the castration complex.

In the castration complex we find the mainspring of the very subversion I am trying to articulate here by means of its dialectic. For this complex, which was unknown as such until Freud introduced it into the formation of desire, can no longer be ignored in any reflection on the subject.

In psychoanalysis it seems that, rather than attempting to carry its articulation further, people have deliberately avoided providing any explanation of it. Which is why this great Samson-like body has been reduced to providing grist for the mill of the Philistines of general psychology.

Certainly there is a bone(r) [*os*] here. Since it is precisely what I am claiming—namely, what structures the subject—it essentially constitutes in the subject the gap that all thought has avoided, skipped over, circumvented, or stopped up whenever thought apparently succeeds in sustaining itself circularly, whether the thought be dialectical or mathematical.

This is why I am given to guiding my students to the places where logic is disconcerted by the disjunction that breaks through from the imaginary to the symbolic, not in order to indulge in the paradoxes that are thus generated, or in some supposed crisis in thought, but, on the contrary, to redirect their fake shine to the gap they designate—which I always find quite simply edifying—and above all to try to create a method from a sort of calculus whose very inappropriateness would flush out the secret.

Such is the phantom known as the cause, which I have pursued in the purest symbolization of the imaginary through the alternation from the sim- 821
ilar to the dissimilar.[9]

Let us observe carefully, therefore, what it is that objects to conferring on my signifier S(Ⱥ) the meaning of mana or of any such term. It is the fact that we cannot be satisfied to explain it on the basis of the poverty of the social fact, even if the latter were traced back to some supposedly total fact.

Claude Lévi-Strauss, commenting on Mauss' work, no doubt wished to see in mana the effect of a zero symbol. But it seems that what we are dealing with in our case is rather the signifier of the lack of this zero symbol. This is why, at the risk of incurring a certain amount of opprobrium, I have indicated how far I have gone in distorting mathematical algorithms in my own use of them: for example, my use of the symbol, $\sqrt{-1}$, also written *i* in the theory of complex numbers, can obviously be justified only if I give up any claim to its being able to be used automatically in subsequent operations.

We must keep in mind that jouissance is prohibited [*interdite*] to whoever speaks, as such—or, put differently, it can only be said [*dite*] between the lines by whoever is a subject of the Law, since the Law is founded on that very prohibition.

Indeed, were the Law to give the order, "*Jouis*!" ["Enjoy!" or "Come!"], the subject could only reply "*J'ouïs*" ["I hear"], in which the jouissance would no longer be anything but understood [*sous-entendue*].

But it is not the Law itself that bars the subject's access to jouissance—it simply makes a barred subject out of an almost natural barrier. For it is pleasure that sets limits to jouissance, pleasure as what binds incoherent life together, until another prohibition—this one being unchallengeable—arises from the regulation that Freud discovered as the primary process and relevant law of pleasure.

It has been said that in this discovery Freud merely followed the course already being pursued by the science of his time—nay, a long-standing tradition. To appreciate the true audacity of his step, we have only to consider his reward, which was not long in coming: the stalemate regarding the heteroclite nature of the castration complex.

822 The latter is the sole indication of this jouissance in its infinitude, which brings with it the mark of its prohibition, and which requires a sacrifice in order to constitute this mark: the sacrifice implied in the same act as that of chosing its symbol, the phallus.

This choice is allowed because the phallus—that is, the image of the penis—is negativized where it is situated in the specular image. That is what predestines the phallus to give body to jouissance in the dialectic of desire.

We must distinguish, therefore, between the principle of sacrifice, which is symbolic, and the imaginary function which is devoted to it, but which veils the principle at the same time that it gives it its instrument.

The imaginary function is the one Freud formulated as governing object cathexis as narcissistic. I came back to this myself when I showed that the specular image is the channel taken by the transfusion of the body's libido toward the object. But insofar as a part remains preserved from this immersion, concentrating in itself the most intimate aspect of autoeroticism, its position as a "pointy extremity" in the form predisposes it to the fantasy of it falling off—in which its exclusion from the specular image is completed as is the prototype it constitutes for the world of objects.

It is thus that the erectile organ—not as itself, or even as an image, but as a part that is missing in the desired image—comes to symbolize the place of jouissance; this is why the erectile organ can be equated with the $\sqrt{-1}$, the symbol of the signification produced above, of the jouissance it restores—by the coefficient of its statement—to the function of a missing signifier: (-1).

If it serves to tie together in this way the prohibition of jouissance, it is nevertheless not for reasons of form, but because the supersession of these reasons signifies what reduces all coveted jouissance to the brevity of autoeroticism. The pathways that are altogether traced out by the anatomical conformation of speaking beings—namely, the further perfected hand of the monkey—have not, in effect, been disdained in a certain philosophical ascesis as pathways of a wisdom that has incorrectly been termed cynical. Certain individuals[10] in our times, obsessed no doubt by this memory, have suggested to me that Freud himself belongs to the tradition of "bodily techniques," as Mauss calls it. The fact remains that analytic experience demonstrates the original character of the guilt generated by such practices. 823

Guilt that is related to the reminder of the jouissance that is not found in the service rendered to the real organ, and consecration of the signifier's imaginary function of prohibiting objects.

Indeed, this is the radical function for which a wilder analytic era found more accidental causes (due to education), just as it reinterpreted the other forms—in which it took an interest, to its credit—of sanctification of the organ (circumcision) as traumas.

The shift of $(-\varphi)$ (lowercase phi) as phallic image from one side to the other of the equation between the imaginary and the symbolic renders it positive in any case, even if it fills a lack. Although it props up (-1), it becomes Φ (capital phi) there, the symbolic phallus that cannot be negativized, the signifier of jouissance. And it is this characteristic of Φ that explains both the particularities of women's approach to sexuality, and what makes the male sex the weaker sex with regard to perversion.

I will not take up perversion here, inasmuch as it barely accentuates the function of desire in man, insofar as desire institutes the dominance—in the privileged place of jouissance—of object *a* in fantasy, which desire substitutes for Ⱥ. Perversion adds to that a recuperation of φ that would scarcely seem original if it did not concern the Other as such in a very particular way. Only my formula for fantasy allows us to bring out the fact that the subject here makes himself the instrument of the Other's jouissance.

It is of more concern to philosophers to grasp the relevance of this formula in the case of the neurotic, precisely because the neurotic skews it.

Indeed, the neurotic, whether hysteric, obsessive, or, more radically, phobic, is the one who identifies the Other's lack with the Other's demand, Φ with D.

Consequently, the Other's demand takes on the function of the object in the neurotic's fantasy—that is, his fantasy (my formulas make it possible to realize this immediately) is reduced to the drive: $(\$ \lozenge D)$. This is why it was possible to catalog all the neurotic's drives.

But the prevalence given by the neurotic to demand—which, in an analytic movement opting for facility, shifted the whole treatment toward the
824 handling of frustration—hides the anxiety induced in him by the Other's desire, anxiety that cannot be misrecognized when it is covered over by the phobic object alone, but which is more difficult to understand in the case of the other two neuroses when one is not in possession of the thread that makes it possible to posit fantasy as the Other's desire. Once we posit this, we find fantasy's two terms split apart, as it were: the first, in the case of the obsessive, inasmuch as he negates the Other's desire, forming his fantasy in such a way as to accentuate the impossibility of the subject vanishing, the second, in the case of the hysteric, inasmuch as desire is sustained in fantasy only by the lack of satisfaction the hysteric brings desire by slipping away as its object.

These features are confirmed by the obsessive's fundamental need to be the Other's guarantor, and by the Faithlessness of hysterical intrigue.

In fact, the image of the ideal Father is a neurotic's fantasy. Beyond the Mother—demand's real Other, whose desire (that is, her desire) we wish she would tone down—stands out the image of a father who would turn a blind eye to desires. This marks—more than it reveals—the true function of the Father, which is fundamentally to unite (and not to oppose) a desire to the Law.

The Father the neurotic wishes for is clearly the dead Father—that is plain to see. But he is also a Father who would be the perfect master of his desire—which would be just as good, as far as the subject is concerned.

This is one of the stumbling blocks the analyst must avoid, and the crux of the interminable aspect of transference.

It is why a calculated vacillation of the analyst's "neutrality" may be more valuable to a hysteric than any number of interpretations—provided, of course, that the fright this risks bringing about in the patient does not lead to a breaking off of the analysis, and that the analysand is convinced by what follows that the analyst's desire was in no way involved in the matter. This, of course, is not a recommendation regarding technique, but a perspective on the question of the analyst's desire for those who could not otherwise have any notion of it: how the analyst must safeguard the imaginary dimension of his nonmastery and necessary imperfection for the other, is as important a matter to deal with as the deliberate reinforcement in the analyst of his nescience regarding each subject who comes to him for analysis, of an ever renewed ignorance so that no one is considered a typical case.

To return to fantasy, let us say that the pervert imagines he is the Other in order to ensure his own jouissance, and that this is what the neurotic reveals 825
when he imagines he is a pervert—in his case, to ensure control over the Other.

This explains the supposed perversion at the crux of neurosis. Perversion is in the neurotic's unconscious in the guise of the Other's fantasy. But this does not mean that the pervert's unconscious is right out in the open. He, too, defends himself in his desire in his own way. For desire is a defense, a defense against going beyond a limit in jouissance.

In its structure as I have defined it, fantasy contains (−φ), the imaginary function of castration, in a hidden form that can switch from one of its terms to the other. That is to say, like a complex number, it alternatively imaginarizes (if you will allow me this term) one of these terms in relation to the other.

Included in object *a* is *agalma*, the inestimable treasure that Alcibiades declares is contained in the rustic box the figure of Socrates is to him. But let us note that a minus sign (−) is attributed to it. It is because Alcibiades has not seen Socrates' prick—permit me to follow Plato here, who does not spare us the details—that Alcibiades the seducer exalts in Socrates the *agalma*, the marvel that he would have liked Socrates to cede to him by avowing his desire. Alcibiades' subjective division, which he carries within him, shines through quite clearly on this occasion.

Such is woman concealed behind her veil: it is the absence of the penis that makes her the phallus, the object of desire. Evoke this absence in a more precise way by having her wear a cute fake one under a fancy dress, and you, or rather she, will have plenty to tell us about: the effect is 100 percent guaranteed, for men who don't beat around the bush, that is.

Thus by exhibiting his own object as castrated, Alcibiades flaunts the fact that he is imbued with desire—a fact that does not escape Socrates' attention—for someone else who is present, Agathon. Socrates, as the precursor of psychoanalysis, and confident of his position at this fashionable gathering, does not hesitate to name Agathon as the transference object, bringing to light through an interpretation a fact that many analysts are still unaware of: that the love-hate effect in the psychoanalytic situation is found outside of it.

But Alcibiades is by no means a neurotic. In fact, it is because he is the

826 epitome of desirousness, and a man who pursues jouissance as far as possible, that he can thus (though with the help of an instrumental drunkenness) produce before everyone's eyes the central articulation of the transference, when in the presence of the object adorned with its sparkle.

The fact remains that he projected onto Socrates the ideal of the perfect Master—that he completely imaginarized Socrates through the action of $(-\varphi)$.

In the case of the neurotic, $(-\varphi)$ slips under the $\$$ in fantasy, favoring the imagination that is characteristic of him, that of the ego. For the neurotic underwent imaginary castration at the outset; it sustains the strong ego that is his, so strong, one might say, that his proper name bothers him, so strong that deep down the neurotic is Nameless.

Yes, it is behind this ego, which certain analysts choose to strengthen still more, that the neurotic hides the castration he denies.

But, contrary to appearances, he cleaves to this castration.

What the neurotic does not want, and what he strenuously refuses to do until the end of his analysis, is to sacrifice his castration to the Other's jouissance, by allowing it to serve the Other.

And, of course, he is not wrong, for—although, deep down, he feels he is the most vain thing in existence, a Want-To-Be or a One-Too-Many—why would he sacrifice his difference (anything but that) to the jouissance of an Other, which, let us not forget, does not exist. Yes, but if by chance it was to exist [*existait*], it would enjoy it [*il en jouirait*]. And that is what the neurotic does not want. For he figures that the Other demands his castration.

What analytic experience attests to is that castration is what regulates desire, in both normal and abnormal cases.

Providing it oscillates by alternating between $\$$ and *a* in fantasy, castration makes of fantasy a chain that is both supple and inextensible by which the fixation of object cathexis, which can hardly go beyond certain natural limits, takes on the transcendental function of ensuring the jouissance of the Other that passes this chain on to me in the Law.

Anyone who really wants to come to terms with this Other has open to him the path of experiencing not the Other's demand, but its will. And then: to either realize himself as an object, turning himself into the mummy of some Buddhist initiation, or satisfy the will to castrate inscribed in the Other, which leads to the supreme narcissism of the Lost Cause (the latter
827 being the path of Greek tragedy, which Claudel rediscovers in a Christianity of despair).

Castration means that jouissance has to be refused in order to be attained on the inverse scale of the Law of desire.

I won't go any further here.

[Endnote]

This article is coming out here for the first time: an unexpected shortage of the funds that are usually provided in ample quantity to publish the complete proceedings of such colloquia having left it in abeyance, along with all the fine things that adorned it.

I should mention, for the record, that the "Copernican" discussion was added later, and that the end of the article on castration was not delivered at the colloquium due to lack of time, and was in fact replaced by a few words on the machine, in the modern sense of the word, by which the subject's relation to the signifier can be materialized.

From the fellow feeling natural in any discussion, let us not exclude the fellow feeling aroused in me by a particular disagreement. The term "a-human," which someone wanted to attribute to what I had said, did not bother me in the least; I was flattered, rather, as I had helped occasion the birth of the new element it brings to the category. I noted with no less interest the sizzling, that followed soon afterward, of the word "hell," since the voice that pronounced it gave it a certain distinctive piquancy owing to the speaker's declared allegiance to Marxism. I must admit that I appreciate humanism when it comes from a camp where, although employed with no less cunning than elsewhere, it at least has a certain candor about it: "When the miner comes home, his wife rubs him down . . ." That leaves me defenseless.

In a private conversation, someone close to me asked me (this was the form his question took) whether talking to a brick wall implied faith in an eternal scribe. Such faith is not necessary, was the reply, to whoever knows that every discourse derives its effects from the unconscious.

Notes

1. (Added in 1966:) Even in attempting to interest people in telepathy, under the heading of psychological phenomena—or in the whole Gothic psychology that can be resuscitated on the basis of Myers' work—the crudest adventurer will be unable to break out of the field in which Freud has already confined him, by presenting what he accepts of these phenomena as requiring translation, in the strict sense of the term, in the corroborative effects of contemporary discourses.

Even when prostituted, psychoanalytic theory remains sanctimonious (a well-known characteristic of the brothel). As we say since Sartre, she's a respectable girl: she won't walk the street on just any side.

2. *GW* VIII, 237–38.

3. I am referring here to the friend who invited me to this conference, after having, some months before, revealed in print his reservations—based on his personal ontology—about "psychoanalysts" who were too "Hegelian" for his liking, as if anyone in this group but me could even be associated with Hegel.

This in the hodgepodge text of pages from his diary cast to the four winds (of chance, no doubt), from which a journal (*La Nouvelle*

Revue française) had nevertheless benefited.

Regarding which I pointed out to him that in the, even entertaining, terms in which he dressed up this ontology of his in his informal notes, I found its "certainly not, but perhaps" procedure designed to mislead.

4. I have left this paragraph in the text only as a monument to an outdated battle (added in 1962: What was I thinking? {1966. 1957. 1968 . . . ha, ha!}).

5. (Added in 1962:) The words in parentheses here have been added with a view to pinpointing later developments regarding identification.

6. This, too, is a reference to what I proffered in my seminar, *L'Éthique de la psychanalyse* (1959–1960, forthcoming), on the second death. I agree with Dylan Thomas that there aren't two. But is the absolute Master, then, the only one that remains?

7. [Added in 1966:] The very fact that I said this at the time at this point in my paper, even if I didn't put it more forcefully, suggests an appointment with fate since, three years later, it was precisely regarding the theme of the Name-of-the-Father that I adopted the sanction of laying to rest the theses I had promised in my seminar, due to the permanence of this situation.

8. (Added in 1962:) I have since justified this by means of a topological model borrowed from surface theory in an *analysis situs*.

9. (Added in 1962:) More recently, in the opposite direction, in the attempt to correlate topologically defined surfaces with the terms I employ here in the subjective articulation. Not to mention in the simple refutation of the supposed paradox, "I am lying."

10. (Added in 1971:) This plural covers an eminent contemporary philosopher.

Position of the Unconscious 829

Remarks made at the 1960 Bonneval Colloquium, rewritten in 1964

Henri Ey—thanks to his authority which has made him the most influential figure in French psychiatric circles—brought together in his ward at Bonneval Hospital a very broad spectrum of specialists around the theme of the Freudian unconscious (October 30 to November 2, 1960).

The talk given by my students Laplanche and Leclaire promoted at the colloquium a conception of my work which, since the talk was published in *Les temps modernes,* has become definitive, despite the divergence between their positions that was manifested therein.

Interventions made at a colloquium, when there is something at stake in the debate, sometimes require a good deal of commentary to be situated.

And once all the papers given there have been thoroughly rewritten, the task becomes an arduous one.

Its interest wanes, moreover, with the time it takes to rewrite them, for one would have to replace it with what takes place during that time considered as logical time.

In short, three and a half years later, though barely having had the leisure to monitor the interval, I made a decision that Henri Ey, in a book on the colloquium to be published by Desclée de Brouwer, introduces in the following way:

> This text summarizes Jacques Lacan's interventions which, due to their importance, formed the axis of all the discussions. The transcripts of these interventions have been condensed by Jacques Lacan in these pages written at my request in March 1964.

I hope the reader will allow that for me this logical time has been able to reduce the circumstances, in a text extracted from a more intimate gathering, to this mention of them. (1966)

Remarks made at a colloquium such as this, inviting philosophers, psychia- 830
trists, psychologists, and psychoanalysts on the basis of their respective expertise, fail to agree on the level of truth of Freud's texts.

Concerning the unconscious, one must go straight to the crux of Freud's experience.

The unconscious *is* a concept founded on the trail [*trace*] left by that which operates to constitute the subject.

The unconscious *is not* a species defining the circle of that part of psychical reality which does not have the attribute (or the virtue) of consciousness.

There may be phenomena that are subsumed by the unconscious according to both of these acceptations; the latter remain no less foreign to each other. The only relation between them is one of homonymy.

The importance I attribute to language as the cause of the subject requires that I be more specific: aberrations abound when the concept "unconscious" is depreciated by being applied *ad libitum* to phenomena that can be classified under the homonymous species. It is unthinkable that the concept might be restored on the basis of these phenomena.

Let me specify my own position concerning the equivocation to which the "is" and "is not" of my initial positions might give rise.

The unconscious *is* what I say it is, assuming we are willing to hear what Freud puts forward in his theses.

Saying that for Freud the unconscious *is not* what goes by that name in other contexts would be of little value if what I meant were not grasped: the unconscious, prior to Freud, *is not* purely and simply. This is because it names nothing [prior to Freud] that counts any more as an object—nor warrants being granted any more existence—than what would be defined by situating it in the "un-black" [*l'in-noir*].

The unconscious before Freud has no more consistency than this un-black—namely, the set of what could be classified according to the various meanings of the word "black," by dint of its refusal of the attribute (or virtue) of blackness (whether physical or moral).

What, indeed, could the following possibly have in common—to take the eight definitions collated by Dwelshauvers in a book that is old (1916), but not so far out-of-date that, were such a catalogue to be prepared anew today, its heterogeneity would not be diminished: the sensory unconscious (implied
831 by the so-called optical effects of contrast and illusion); the automatic unconscious developed by habit; the co-consciousness (?) of split personalities; ideational emergences of a latent activity that appears in creative thought as if it were oriented, and telepathy which certain people would like to relate to such thought; the learned and even integrated reserves of memory; the passions in our character which get the better of us; the heredity that is recognized in our natural gifts; and finally the rational or metaphysical unconscious that is implied by "mental acts"?

(None of them can be grouped together, except confusedly, because of what psychoanalysts have added by way of obscurantism in failing to distinguish the unconscious from instinct, or, as they say, from the instinctual—the archaic or primordial, succumbing thereby to an illusion decisively dispelled by Claude Lévi-Strauss—and even from the genetic character of a supposed "development.")

My claim is that they have nothing in common if one grounds oneself in psychological objectivity, even if the latter is derived by extension from the schemas of psychopathology, and that this chaos merely reflects psychology's central error. This error consists in taking the very phenomenon of consciousness to be unitary, speaking of the same consciousness—believed to be a synthetic faculty—in the illuminated area of a sensory field, in the attention that transforms it, in the dialectic of judgment, and in ordinary daydreaming.

This error is based on the undue transfer to these phenomena of the value of a thought experiment that uses them as examples.

The Cartesian *cogito* is the major, and perhaps terminal, feat of this experiment in that it attains knowledge certainty. But it merely indicates all the more clearly just how privileged the moment upon which it is based is, and how fraudulent it is to extend its privilege to phenomena endowed with consciousness, in order to grant them a status.

For science, the *cogito* marks, on the contrary, the break with every assurance conditioned by intuition.

And the much sought-after [*recherchée*] latency of this founding moment, as *Selbstbewusstsein* [self-consciousness], in the dialectical sequence of Hegel's phenomenology of mind, is based upon the presupposition of absolute knowledge.

Everything, on the contrary, points to the distribution of consciousness in psychical reality—however the latter's texture is ordered—that distribution being heterotopic in terms of levels and erratic at each level.

The only homogeneous function of consciousness is found in the ego's 832
imaginary capture by its specular reflection, and in the function of misrecognition that remains tied to it.

The negation inherent in psychology in this regard should rather, following Hegel, be chalked up to the law of the heart and the frenzy of self-conceit.

The credit granted to this perpetuated presumption, to consider only what it receives by way of scientific honors, raises the question of where its value is situated; it cannot come down to the mere publication of more or less copious treatises.

Psychology transmits ideals: the psyche therein no longer represents anything but the sponsorship that makes it qualify as academic. Ideals are society's slaves.

A certain kind of progress in our own society illustrates this, when psychology not only furnishes the means, but even defers to the wishes of market research.

When a market study had concluded upon the proper means by which to sustain consumption in the U.S.A., psychology enlisted, enlisting Freud along with it, to remind the half of the population most exposed to business' goal that women only realize their potential through gender ideals (see Betty Friedan on the concerted effort to create a "feminine mystique" in that post-war decade).

Perhaps psychology reveals, through this ironic channel, why it has always subsisted. But scientists may recall that the ethics implicit in their training commands them to refuse all such blatant ideology. The unconscious as understood by psychologists is thus debilitating for thought, due to the very credence thought must lend it in order to argue against it.

Now the debates that have taken place during this colloquium have been remarkable in that they have constantly turned to the Freudian concept in all its difficulty, and have derived their very strength from this difficulty.

This is remarkable inasmuch as psychoanalysts' only endeavor, in today's world, is to enter psychology's ranks. The aversion everything coming from Freud meets with in their community has been plainly avowed, especially by a subset of the psychoanalysts present.

This fact cannot be excluded from the examination of the issue at hand.
833 No more than can another fact: that it is due to my teaching that this colloquium has reversed the trend. I am saying this not merely to make mention of the fact—many have done so—but also to note that this obliges me to account for the paths I have followed.

What psychoanalysis finds itself enjoined to do when it returns to the fold of "general psychology" is to sustain what deserves to be exposed—right here and not in the far-off realms of our former colonies—as primitive mentality. For the kind of interest that psychology comes to serve in our present society, of which I have given an idea, finds therein its advantage.

Psychoanalysis thus underwrites it by furnishing an astrology that is more decent than the one to which our society continues to surreptitiously sacrifice.

I thus consider justified the prejudice psychoanalysis encounters in Eastern Europe. It was up to psychoanalysis not to deserve that prejudice, as it was possible that, presented with the test of different social exigencies, psychoanalysis might have proved less tractable had it received harsher treatment. I gauge that on the basis of my own position in psychoanalysis.

Psychoanalysis would have done better to examine its ethics and learn from the study of theology, following a path indicated by Freud as unavoidable. At the very least, its deontology in science should make it realize that it is responsible for the presence of the unconscious in this field.

This function was served by my students at this colloquium, and I contributed thereto in accordance with the method that I have constantly adopted on such occasions, situating each in his position in relation to the subject. The main axis is indicated clearly enough in the written responses.

It would be of some interest, if only to the historian, to have the transcripts of the talks actually given, even if they were cut where blanks appeared due to defects in the recording devices. They underscore the absence of he whose services designated him as the person who could highlight with the greatest tact and accuracy the detours of a moment of combat in a place where ideas were exchanged—his connections, his culture, and even his social savvy allowing him to understand better than anyone else the recordings with their intonations. His failure already ensconced him in the good graces of defection.

I will stop deploring the opportunity that was missed, everyone having since taken ample advantage of a time-worn practice, carefully reworking his 834
presentation. I will take the opportunity to explain my present doctrine of the unconscious, all the more legitimately as the resistances of a peculiar allocation of roles impeded me from saying more about it at the colloquium.

This consideration is not political, but technical. It is related to the following condition, established by my doctrine: psychoanalysts are part and parcel of the concept of the unconscious, as they constitute that to which the unconscious is addressed. I thus cannot but include my discourse on the unconscious in the very thesis it enunciates: the presence of the unconscious, being situated in the locus of the Other, can be found in every discourse, in its enunciation.

The very subject of he who would propose to sustain this presence—the analyst—must, according to this hypothesis, in the same movement be given form [*informé*] and "called into question," in other words, be put to the test of his own splitting by the signifier.

This explains the sense of an arrested spiral one has in reading the work presented by my students, Serge Leclaire and Jean Laplanche. For they limited him to the kind of testing one does on a spare part.

Which is the very sign that my statements are, in all their rigor, made first of all for the function they only *serve* in their stead.

In the introductory phase, one can illustrate the effect of enunciation by asking a student if he can imagine the unconscious existing in animals, unless they have some degree of language—human language. If he indeed agrees that this is the condition that would allow him to at least consider the possibility, you have verified that he distinguishes between "unconscious" and "instinct."

Propitious initial omen, for if we were to call upon each analyst as well, regardless of the doctrine he was most trained in, and ask him whether, in fulfilling his role (fostering the patient's discourse, restoring its meaning effect, putting himself on the line [*s'y mettre en cause*] by responding, as well as by remaining silent), he ever had the feeling he was dealing with anything like an instinct—could he say yes?

Reading analytic writings and official translations of works by Freud (who never wrote the word "official") that use the term "instinct" right and left, it is perhaps worth obviating a rhetoric that obturates the concept's effectiveness. The style appropriate for a paper on analytic experience does
835 not constitute the whole of theory. But it guarantees that the statements by which analytic experience operates preserve within themselves the backward movement [*recul*] of enunciation in which metaphorical and metonymical effects are constituted—namely, in accordance with my theses, the very mechanisms Freud described as those of the unconscious.

But here the question is legitimately raised: are they effects of language or of speech? Let us assume that the question here only assumes the outlines of Saussure's dichotomy. Directed at what interests Saussure—effects on language [*la langue*]—it supplies warp and woof to what is woven between synchrony and diachrony.

When it is directed back at what calls us into question (as much as at he who questions us, if he is not already lost in the stays of his question)—namely, the subject—the alternative [language or speech] proposes itself as a disjunction. Now it is this very disjunction that provides us with the answer, or, rather, it is in leading the Other to constitute itself as the locus of our answer—the Other furnishing the answer in a form that inverts the question into a message—that we introduce the effective disjunction on the basis of which the question has meaning.

The effect of language is to introduce the cause into the subject. Through this effect, he is not the cause of himself; he bears within himself the worm of the cause that splits him. For his cause is the signifier, without which there would be no subject in the real. But this subject is what the signifier represents, and the latter cannot represent anything except to another signifier: to which the subject who listens is thus reduced.

One therefore does not speak to the subject. It speaks of him, and this is how he apprehends himself; he does so all the more necessarily in that, before he disappears as a subject beneath the signifier he becomes, due to the simple fact that it addresses him, he is absolutely nothing. But this nothing is sustained by his advent, now produced by the appeal made in the Other to the second signifier.

As an effect of language, in that he is born of this early split, the subject translates a signifying synchrony into the primordial temporal pulsation that is the constitutive fading* of his identification. This is the first movement.

But in the second, desire—bedding down in the signifying cut in which metonymy occurs, the diachrony (called "history") that was inscribed in fading—returns to the kind of fixity Freud grants unconscious wishes (see the last sentence of the *Traumdeutung* [*The Interpretation of Dreams*]).

This secondary subornation not only closes the effect of the first by pro- 836
jecting the topology of the subject into the instant of fantasy; it seals it, refusing to allow the subject of desire to realize that he is an effect of speech, to realize, in other words, what he is in being but the Other's desire.

This is why any discourse is within its rights to consider itself not responsible for this effect. Any discourse except that of the teacher when he addresses psychoanalysts.

I have always considered myself accountable for such an effect, and, while unequal to the task of guarding against it [*d'y parer*], it was the secret prowess of each of my "seminars."

For the people who come to hear me are not the first communicants Plato exposed to Socrates' questioning.

The fact that the "secondary" they come out of must be doubled with a preparatory, says enough about its shortcomings and superfluities. Of their "philosophy [classes]," most have retained but a grab-bag of phrases—a catechism gone haywire—which anaesthetizes them from being surprised by truth.

They are thus even more easily preyed upon by prestige operations, and by the ideals of high personalism by which civilization presses them to live beyond their means.

Intellectual means, that is.

The ideal of authority with which the analytic candidate who is a physician falls in; the public opinion poll with which the mediator of relational impasses lets himself off the hook; the meaning of meaning* in which every quest finds its alibi; phenomenology, a lap that awaits whatever may fall into it—the range is vast and the dispersion great at the outset of an ordered obtuseness.

Resistance, equal in its denial effect despite Hegel and Freud, unhappy consciousness and discontent in civilization.

A κοινή of subjectification underpins resistance, which objectifies the false evidence of the ego and routes every proof away from certainty and towards endless procrastination. (Should I be opposed by an appeal to Marxists, Catholics, or even Freudians, I promise to request a roll call.)

This is why only the kind of teaching that grinds up this κοινή can trace out the path of what is known as "training analysis" [*analyse didactique*], for the results of analytic experience are distorted by the very fact of being inscribed in this κοινή.

837 This doctrinal contribution has a name—it is, quite simply, "scientific spirit"; that spirit is altogether lacking in the places where psychoanalysts are recruited.

My teaching is anathema in that it is inscribed in this truth.

The objection that has been raised, concerning the impact of my teaching on the transference of analysts in training, will make future analysts laugh, if, thanks to me, there are still analysts for whom Freud exists. But what it proves is the absence of any doctrine of training analysis that includes the latter's relations with the affirmation of the unconscious.

It will thus be understood that my use of Hegel's phenomenology bore no allegiance to his system, but was intended as an example with which to counter the obvious fact of identification. It is in the way in which one conducts an examination of a patient and draws one's conclusions that a critique of intellectual fables is proposed. It is by not avoiding the ethical implications of our praxis for deontology and scientific debate that the beautiful soul will be unmasked. The law of the heart, as I have said, is a bigger nuisance than paranoia. It is the law of a ruse which, in the cunning [*ruse*] of reason, traces out a meander whose current is seriously slowed.

Beyond that, the statements Hegel makes, even if one sticks to the text, provide the opportunity to always say something Other. Something Other which corrects their fantasmatic link with synthesis, while preserving the effect they have of exposing the lures of identification.

That is my *Aufhebung* [sublation], which transforms Hegel's (his own lure) into an occasion to point out—in lieu and place of the leaps of an "ideal progress"—the avatars of a lack.

To confirm the function of this point of lack, nothing is better, after that, than Plato's dialogue, insofar as it comes under the genre of comedy, does not shy away from indicating the point at which one can do nothing but oppose the "marionette's mask to wooden insults," and remains stone-faced through the centuries, rooted to a hoax, waiting for someone to find a better hold than the one it clings to in its judo match with the truth.

This is why Freud is a guest one can risk inviting impromptu to the *Symposium*, if only on the basis of the short note in which he indicates what he owes to its clear-sightedness concerning love, and perhaps to the tranquillity
838 of its view of transference. He is probably the kind of man who would revive its bacchant lines, which no one remembers having said after the drunkenness.

My seminar was not "where it speaks" [*là où ça parle*], as people happened to say jokingly. It brought forth *the place* from which it could speak, opening more than one ear to hear things that would have been passed over indifferently since they would not have been recognized. One of my auditors put this naively, announcing the marvelous fact that, that very evening, or perhaps just the day before, he had come across in a session with a patient what I had said in my seminar—verbatim.

The place in question is the entrance to the cave, towards the exit of which Plato guides us, while one imagines seeing the psychoanalyst entering there. But things are not that easy, as it is an entrance one can only reach just as it closes (the place will never be popular with tourists), and the only way for it to open up a bit is by calling from the inside.

This is not unsolvable—assuming the "open sesame" of the unconscious consists in having speech effects, since it is linguistic in structure—but requires that the analyst reexamine the way in which it closes.

What we have to account for is a gap, beat, or alternating suction, to follow some of Freud's indications, and that is what I have proceeded to do in grounding the unconscious in a topology.

The structure of what closes [*se ferme*] is, indeed, inscribed in a geometry in which space is reduced to a combinatory: it is what is called an "edge" in topology.

By formally studying the consequences of the irreducibility of the cut it makes, one could rework some of the most interesting functions between aesthetics and logic.

One notices here that it is the closing of the unconscious which provides the key to its space—namely, the impropriety of trying to turn it into an inside.

This closing also demonstrates the core of a reversion time, quite necessarily introduced [if we are to explain] the efficiency of discourse. It is rather easily perceived in something I have been emphasizing for a long time: the retroactive effect of meaning in sentences, meaning requiring the last word of a sentence to be sealed [*se boucler*].

Nachträglichkeit (remember that I was the first to extract it from Freud's 839
texts) or deferred action [*après-coup*], by which trauma becomes involved in symptoms, reveals a temporal structure of a higher order.

But above all, experience with this closing shows that it would not be gratuitous on the part of psychoanalysts to reopen the debate over the *cause*, a phantom that cannot be banished from thought, whether critical or not. For the cause is not, as is said of being as well, a lure of forms of discourse—otherwise it would have already been dispelled. It perpetuates the reason that subordinates the subject to the signifier's effect.

It is only as instance of the unconscious, the Freudian unconscious, that one grasps the cause at the level at which someone like Hume attempts to flush it out, which is precisely the level at which it takes on consistency: the retroaction of the signifier in its efficiency, which must be rigorously distinguished from the final cause.

Were we to demonstrate that it is the only true first cause, the apparent discordance of Aristotle's four causes would, in fact, dissipate; from their terrain, analysts could contribute to this reformulation.

They would have the benefit of being able to use the Freudian term "overdetermination" as something other than an evasive answer. What follows introduces the feature that commands the functioning relationship between these forms: their circular, albeit nonreciprocal, articulation.

While there is closing and entry, they do not necessarily separate: they provide two domains with a mode of conjunction. They are the subject and the Other, respectively, and these domains are to be substantified here only on the basis of my theses concerning the unconscious.

The subject, the Cartesian subject, is what is presupposed by the unconscious—I have shown that elsewhere.

The Other is the dimension required by the fact that speech affirms itself as truth.

The unconscious is, between the two of them, their cut in action.

This cut is seen to command the two fundamental operations with which the
840 subject's causation should be formulated. These operations are ordered in a
circular, yet nonreciprocal, relationship.

The first, alienation, constitutes the subject as such. In a field of objects, no relationship is conceivable that engenders alienation apart from the relationship with the signifier. Let us take as our point of departure the fact that no subject has any reason to appear in the real unless there are speaking beings in it. A physics is conceivable that accounts for everything in the world, including its animate part; a subject intervenes only inasmuch as there are, in this world, signifiers that mean nothing and must be deciphered.

To grant priority to the signifier over the subject is, in my book, to take into account the experience Freud opened up for us: the signifier plays and wins, if I may say so, before the subject is aware of it, to such an extent that in the play of *Witz* (in witticisms, for example) it may surprise the subject. What it lights up with its flash is the subject's division from himself.

But the fact that the signifier reveals to the subject his own division should not make us forget that this division stems from nothing other than that very same play, the play of signifiers—signifiers, not signs.

Signs are polyvalent: they no doubt represent something to someone, but the status of that someone is uncertain, as is that of the supposed language of certain animals, a sign language which neither allows for metaphor nor engenders metonymy.

This someone could, by some stretch of the imagination, be the universe, insofar as information, so we are told, circulates in it. Any center in which information is total(iz)ed can be taken for a someone, but not for a subject.

The register of the signifier is instituted on the basis of the fact that a signifier represents a subject to another signifier. This is the structure of all unconscious formations: dreams, slips of the tongue, and witticisms. The same structure explains the subject's original division. Produced in the locus of the yet-to-be-situated Other, the signifier brings forth a subject from a being that cannot yet speak, but at the cost of freezing him. The ready-to-speak that *was to be* there—in both senses of the French imperfect "*il y avait*," placing the ready-to-speak an instant before (it was there but is no longer), but also an instant after (a few moments more and it would have been there because it could have been there)—disappears, no longer being anything but a signifier.

It is thus not the fact that this operation begins in the Other that leads me 841
to call it "alienation." The fact that the Other is, for the subject, the locus of his signifying cause merely explains why no subject can be his own cause [*cause de soi*]. This is clear not only from the fact that he is not God, but from the fact that God himself cannot be his own cause if we think of him as a subject; Saint Augustine saw this very clearly when he refused to refer to the personal God as "self-caused" [*cause de soi*].

Alienation resides in the subject's division, the cause of which I just designated. Let us proceed to discuss its logical structure. This structure is a *vel*, which shows its originality here for the first time. In order to do so, it must be derived from what is known, in so-called mathematical logic, as union (which has already been acknowledged to define a certain kind of *vel*).

This union is such that the *vel* of alienation, as I call it, imposes a choice between its terms only to eliminate one of them—always the same one regardless of one's choice. The stakes are thus apparently limited to the preservation or loss of the other term, when the union involves two terms.

This disjunction is incarnated in a highly illustratable, if not dramatic, way as soon as the signifier is incarnated at a more personalized level in demand or supply: in "your money or your life" or "liberty or death."

It is merely a question of knowing whether or not (*sic aut non*) you want to keep life or refuse death, because, regarding the other term in the alternative, money or liberty, your choice will in any case be disappointing.

You should be aware that what remains is, in any case, diminished: it will be life without money and, having refused death, a life somewhat inconvenienced by the cost of freedom.

This is the stigma of the fact that the *vel* here, functioning dialectically, clearly operates on the *vel* of logical union, which is known to be equivalent to an "and" (*sic et non*). This is illustrated by the fact that, in the long run, you will have to give up your life after your money, and in the end the only thing left will be your freedom to die.

Similarly, our subject is subjected to the *vel* of a certain meaning he must receive or petrification. But should he retain the meaning, the nonmeaning
842 produced by his change into a signifier will encroach on this field (of meaning). This nonmeaning clearly falls within the Other's field, although it is produced as an eclipse of the subject.

This [*la chose*] is worth saying, for it qualifies the field of the unconscious to take a seat, I would say, in the place of the analyst—let us take that literally—in his armchair. We have arrived at such a pass that we should leave him this armchair in a "symbolic gesture." The latter is an expression commonly used to say "a gesture of protest," and its import would be to challenge the order—so prettily avowed by its crude motto in "Francglaire" (to coin a term), directly issuing from the ἀμαθία a princess perpetrated upon French psychoanalysis by replacing the pre-Socratic tone of Freud's precept, "Wo Es war, soll Ich werden," with the croaking strains of—"the ego" (the analyst's, no doubt) "must dislodge the id" (the patient's, of course).

The fact that people have objected to Serge Leclaire's claim that the unicorn sequence is unconscious, by pointing out that Leclaire himself is conscious of it, means that they do not see that the unconscious only has meaning in the Other's field; still less do they see the consequence thereof: that it is not the effect of meaning that is operative in interpretation, but rather the articulation in the symptom of signifiers (without any meaning at all) that have gotten caught up in it.[1]

Let us turn now to the second operation, in which the subject's causation closes, to test the structure of the edge in its function as a limit, but also in the twist that motivates the encroachment of the unconscious. I call this operation "separation." We will see that it is what Freud called "*Ichspaltung*" or the splitting of the subject, and grasp why Freud, in the text in which he introduces it ["The Splitting of the Ego"], grounds it in a splitting, not of the subject, but of the object (namely, the phallic object).

The logical form dialectically modified by the second operation is called "intersection" in symbolic logic; it is also the product formulated by a

belonging *to* __ and *to* __. This function is modified here by a part taken
from a lack situated within another lack, through which the subject finds 843
anew in the Other's desire the equivalent of what he is *qua* subject of the unconscious.

In this way, the subject is actualized in the loss in which he surged forth as unconscious, through the lack he produces in the Other, following the course Freud considered to constitute the most radical drive: the "death drive," as he called it. A belonging *neither to* __ is called upon here to fill a *nor to* __. Empedocles' act, responding thereto, shows that a will [*vouloir*] is involved. The *vel* returns in the form of a *velle*. That is the end of the operation. Now for the process.

Separare, separating, ends here in *se parere*, engendering oneself. Let us dispense with the obvious gems we find in the works of Latin etymologists concerning the slippage in meaning from one verb to the other. One should simply realize that this slippage is grounded in the fact that they are both paired with the function of the *pars*.

The part is not the whole, as they say, though usually without thinking. For it should be emphasized that the part has nothing to do with the whole. One has to come to terms with it [*en prendre son parti*]; it plays its game [*sa partie*] all by itself. Here the subject proceeds from his partition to his parturition. This does not imply the grotesque metaphor of giving birth to himself anew. Indeed, language would be hard pressed to express that with an original term, at least in Indo-European climes where all the words used for this purpose are of juridical or social origin. "*Parere*" was first of all to procure (a child for one's husband). This is why the subject can procure for himself what interests him here—a status I will qualify as "civil." Nothing in anyone's life unleashes more determination to succeed in obtaining it. In order to be *pars*, he would easily sacrifice the better part of his interests, though not in order to become part of the whole, which, moreover, is in no way constituted by others' interests, still less by the general interest which is distinguished therefrom in an entirely different manner.

Separare, *se parare*: in order to attribute to himself [*se parer*] the signifier to which he succumbs, the subject attacks the chain—that I have reduced to a binary, at its most elementary level—at its interval. The repeating interval, the most radical structure of the signifying chain, is the locus haunted by metonymy, the latter being the vehicle of desire (at least that is what I teach).

It is, in any case, through the impact whereby the subject experiences in
this interval something that motivates him Other [*Autre chose*] than the meaning effects by which a discourse solicits him, that he in fact encounters the 844
Other's desire, before he can even call it desire, much less imagine its object.

What he will place there is his own lack, in the form of the lack he would (like to) produce in the Other through his own disappearance—the disappearance (which he has at hand, so to speak) of the part of himself he receives from his initial alienation.

But what he thus fills is not the lack [*faille*] he encounters in the Other, but rather, first of all, the lack that results from the constitutive loss of one of his parts, by which he turns out to be made of two parts. Therein lies the twist whereby separation represents the return of alienation. For the subject operates *with* his own loss, which brings him back to his point of departure.

His "can he lose me?" is, no doubt, the recourse he has against the opacity of the desire he encounters in the Other's locus, but it merely brings the subject back to the opacity of the being he receives through his advent as a subject, such as he was first produced by the other's summoning.

It is an operation whose fundamental outlines are found in psychoanalytic technique. For it is insofar as the analyst intervenes by scanding the patient's discourse that an adjustment occurs in the pulsation of the rim through which the being that resides just shy of it must flow.

The true and final mainspring of what constitutes transference is the expectation of this being's advent in relation to what I call "the analyst's desire," insofar as something about the analyst's own position has remained unnoticed therein, at least up until now.

This is why transference is a relationship that is essentially tied to time and its handling. But what is the being that responds to us, operating in the field of speech and language, from shy of the cave's entrance? I would go so far as to embody it in the form of the very walls of the cave that would (like to) live, or rather come alive with palpitations whose living movement must be grasped now—that is, now that I have articulated the function and field of speech and language in their conditioning.

I do not see how anyone can rightfully claim that I neglect dynamics in my topology; I orient it, which is better than to make a commonplace of it (the most verbal is not where people are willing to say it is).

845 As for sexuality, which people would like to remind me is the force we deal with and that it is biological, I retort that analysts perhaps have not shed as much light as people at one time hoped on sexuality's mainsprings, recommending only that we be natural, repeatedly trotting out the same themes of billing and cooing. I will try to contribute something newer by resorting to a genre that Freud himself never claimed to have superseded in this area: myth.

To compete with Aristophanes on his own turf in the above-mentioned *Symposium*, let us recall his primitive double-backed creatures in which two halves are fused together as firmly as those of a Magdeburg sphere; the halves, separated later by a surgical operation arising from Zeus' jealousy, represent the beings we have become in love, starving for our unfindable complement.

In considering the sphericity of primordial Man as much as his division, it is the egg that comes to mind and that has thus perhaps been repressed since Plato, given the preeminence granted for centuries to the sphere in a hierarchy of forms sanctioned by the natural sciences.

Consider the egg in a viviparous womb where it has no need for a shell, and recall that, whenever the membranes burst, a part of the egg is harmed, for the membranes of the fertilized egg are offspring [*filles*] just as much as the living being brought into the world by their perforation. Consequently, upon cutting the cord, what the newborn loses is not, as analysts think, its mother, but rather its anatomical complement. Midwives call it the "afterbirth" [*délivre*].

Now imagine that every time the membranes burst, a phantom—an infinitely more primal form of life, in no wise willing to settle for a duplicate role in some microcosmic world within a world—takes flight through the same passage.

Man [*l'Homme*] is made by breaking an egg, but so is the "Manlet" [*l'Hommelette*].

Let us assume the latter to be a large crêpe that moves like an amoeba, so utterly flat that it can slip under doors, omniscient as it is guided by the pure life instinct, and immortal as it is fissiparous. It is certainly something that would not be good to feel dripping down your face, noiselessly while you sleep, in order to seal it.

If we are willing to allow the digestive process to begin at this point, we 846
realize that the Manlet has ample sustenance for a long time to come (remember that there are organisms, which are quite differentiated, that have no digestive tract).

It goes without saying that a struggle would soon ensue with such a fearsome being, and that the struggle would be fierce. For it can be assumed that, since the Manlet has no sensory system, it has for guidance but the pure real; it thus has an advantage over us men who must always provide ourselves with a homunculus in our heads in order to turn that real into a reality.

Indeed, it would not be easy to obviate the paths of its attacks, which would, moreover, be impossible to predict, as it would also know no obstacles. It would be impossible to educate and just as impossible to trap.

As for destroying the Manlet, one had best avoid letting it proliferate, for to cut it up would help it reproduce, and the least of its cuttings to survive—even after having been set afire—would preserve all of its destructive powers. Apart from killing it with a lethal ray that has yet to be tested, the only solution would be to lock it up, placing it in the jaws of a Magdeburg sphere, for example, which turns up again here, as if by chance, as the only appropriate tool for the job.

But the *whole* Manlet would have to slip into the sphere, and would have to do so by itself. Even the bravest person would be justified in thinking twice before touching it in order to shove a negligible overflowing amount [*un rien*] back in, for fear that it would slip between his fingers and take up its abode who knows where?

Except for its name, that I will now change to a more decent one, "lamella" (of which the word "*omelette*" is, in fact, but a metastasis),[2] this image and this myth seem to me apt for both illustrating and situating what I call "libido."

This image shows "libido" to be what it is—namely, an organ, to which its habits make it far more akin than to a force field. Let us say that it is *qua* surface that it organizes this force field. This conception can be tested by realizing that Freud considered the drive to be structured like a montage, and by relating it to that.

847 Referring to electromagnetic theory, and, in particular, to a theorem known as Stokes' theorem, would allow me to situate the reason for the constancy of the drive's pressure, which Freud emphasizes so greatly,[3] in the fact that this surface is based on a closed rim, which is the erogenous zone.

It is also clear that what Freud calls the *Schub* or flow [*coulée*] of the drive is not its discharge, but should rather be described as the turning inside out and outside in of an organ whose function should be situated in relation to the preceding subjective coordinates.

This organ must be called "unreal," in the sense in which the unreal is not the imaginary and precedes the subjective realm it conditions, being in direct contact with the real.

That is what my myth, like any other myth, strives to provide a symbolic articulation for, rather than an image.

My lamella represents here the part of a living being that is lost when that being is produced through the straits of sex.

This part is certainly indicated in the media that microscopic anatomy materializes in the globules expulsed at the two stages of the phenomena organized around chromosome reduction and in the maturation of a sexed gonad.

Represented here by a deadly being, it marks the relationship—in which the subject plays a part—between sexuality, specified in the individual, and his death.

Regarding what is represented thereof in the subject, what is striking is the type of anatomical cut (breathing new life into the etymological meaning of the word "anatomy") by which the function of certain objects—which should not be called partial, but which stand apart from the others—is determined.

The breast, to take an example of the problems to which these objects give 848
rise, is not merely a source of "regressive" nostalgia, having been a source of highly prized nourishment. It is, I am told, related to the mother's body, to its warmth, and even to tender loving care. But that does not sufficiently explain its erotic value, which a painting (in Berlin) by Tiepolo, in the exalted horror with which it presents Saint Agatha after her ordeal, illustrates far better.

In fact, it is not a question of the breast [*sein*], in the sense of the mother's womb [*matrice*; *sein* also means womb], even though people mix as they like resonances in which the signifier relies heavily on metaphor. It is a question of the breast specified in the function of weaning which prefigures castration.

Weaning has been too extensively situated, since Klein's investigations, in the fantasy of the partition of the mother's body for us not to suspect that the plane of separation, which makes the breast the lost object involved [*en cause*] in desire, passes between the breast and the mother.

For if we recall that mammalian organization places the young, from the embryo right up to the newborn, in a parasitical relation to the mother's body, the breast appears as the same kind of organ—to be understood as the ectopia of one individual onto another—as that constituted by the placenta at the beginning of the growth of a certain type of organism which remains specified by this intersection.

Libido is this lamella that the organism's being takes to its true limit, which goes further than the body's limit. Its radical function in animals is materialized in a certain ethology by the sudden decline [*chute*] in an animal's ability to intimidate other animals at the boundaries of its "territory."

This lamella is an organ, since it is the instrument of an organism. It is sometimes almost palpable [*comme sensible*], as when an hysteric plays at testing its elasticity to the hilt.

Speaking subjects have the privilege of revealing the deadly meaning of this organ, and thereby its relation to sexuality. This is because the signifier as such, whose first purpose is to bar the subject, has brought into him the meaning of death. (The letter kills, but we learn this from the letter itself.) This is why every drive is virtually a death drive.

849 It is important to grasp how the organism is taken up in the dialectic of the subject. The organ of what is incorporeal in the sexed being is the aspect of the organism that the subject manages to invest [*placer*] when his separation occurs. It is through this organ that he can really make his death the object of the Other's desire.

In this way, the object he naturally loses, excrement, and the props he finds in the Other's desire—the Other's gaze or voice—come to this place.

The activity in the subject I call "drive" (*Trieb*) consists in dealing with these objects in such a way as to recover from them, to restore to himself, his earliest loss.

There is no other pathway by which the impact of sexuality is manifested in the subject. A drive, insofar as it represents sexuality in the unconscious, is never anything but a partial drive. This is the essential failing [*carence*]—namely, the absence [*carence*] of anything that could represent in the subject the mode of what is male or female in his being.

The vacillation that psychoanalytic experience reveals in the subject regarding his masculine or feminine being is not so much related to his biological bisexuality, as to the fact that there is nothing in his dialectic that represents the bipolarity of sex apart from activity and passivity, that is, a drive versus outside-action polarity, which is altogether unfit to represent the true basis of that bipolarity.

That is the point I would like to make here—sexuality is distributed on one side or the other of our *rim* as a threshold of the unconscious in the following manner:

On the side of the living being as a being that will be taken up in speech—never able in the end to come to be altogether in speech, remaining shy of the threshold which, notwithstanding, is neither inside nor out—there is no access to the opposite sex as Other except via the so-called partial drives wherein the subject seeks an object to take the place of the loss of life he has sustained due to the fact that he is sexed.

On the side of the Other—the locus in which speech is verified as it encounters the exchange of signifiers, the ideals they prop up, the elementary structures of kinship, the metaphor of the father considered as a principle of separation, and the ever reopened division in the subject owing to his initial alienation—on this side alone and by the pathways I have just enumerated, order and norms must be instituted which tell the subject what a man or a woman must do.

850 It is not true that God made them male and female, even if the couple Adam and Eve imply that; such a notion is also explicitly contradicted by the

highly condensed myth found in the same text regarding the creation of Adam's companion.

No doubt Lilith was there from before, but that does not explain anything.

Breaking off here, I leave to the past the debates [at the Bonneval colloquium] in which, concerning the Freudian unconscious, irresponsible interventions were quite welcome, precisely because those responsible for them only came there halfheartedly, not to say from a certain side [*bord*].

One of the results was, nevertheless, that the order issued by this side to pass over my teaching in silence was not respected.

The fact that, regarding the Oedipus complex, the last act—or rather the role of warm-up band—went to a hermeneutic feat, confirms my assessment of this colloquium and has since revealed its consequences.

At my own risk, I indicate here the means [*l'appareil*] by which accuracy could return.[4]

Notes

1. Abbreviated version of my answer to an ineffective objection.

2. I hear that those who espouse the virtues of mother's milk laugh at my references to . . . metastasis and metonymy (*sic*). But the one whose face is perfect for illustrating the slogan that I would make its brand name, rarely makes people laugh: laughing cow dung [*la bouse de vache qui rit*].

3. It is well known what this theorem states about curl flux. It assumes a continuously differentiable vector field. In such a field, since the curl of a vector is based on the derivatives of the vector's components, it can be shown that the circulation of this vector along a closed curve is equal to the curl flux calculated for the surface whose boundary is defined by this curve. In other words, by positing this flux as invariable, the theorem establishes the notion of a flux "through" an orificial circuit, that is, such that the original surface need no longer be taken into account.

For topologists: $\int \overrightarrow{dl}.\ \overrightarrow{V} = \iint \overrightarrow{dS}.\ \text{Curl}\ \overrightarrow{V}.$

4. Let it be pointed out, nevertheless, that in restoring here, in an ironic way, the function of the "partial" object, without making the reference to regression in which it is usually shrouded (let it be understood that this reference can only be operative on the basis of the structure defining the object that I call object *a*), I have not been able to extend it to the point that constitutes its crucial interest—namely, the object (−φ) as "cause" of the castration complex.

This object is discussed in the next paper in this volume.

But the castration complex, which is at the crux [*noeud*] of my current work, exceeds the limits assigned to the theory by tendencies in psychoanalysis that were claiming to be new shortly before the war and by which it is still affected as a whole.

The size of the obstacle I must overcome here can be gauged by the time it took me to provide this sequel to my Rome discourse and by the fact that, even now as I correct the proofs [for the 1966 Seuil edition], the original collection that is to include it still has not been published.

851 # On Freud's "Trieb" and the Psychoanalyst's Desire[1]

The drive, as it is constructed by Freud on the basis of the experience of the unconscious, prohibits psychologizing thought from resorting to "instinct," with which it masks its ignorance by assuming the existence of morals in nature.

It can never be often enough repeated, given the obstinacy of psychologists who, as a group and *per se*, are in the service of technocratic exploitation, that the drive—the Freudian drive—has nothing to do with instinct (none of Freud's expressions allows for confusion here).

Libido is not sexual instinct. Its reduction, when taken to an extreme, to male desire, indicated by Freud, should suffice to alert us to this fact.

Libido, in Freud's work, is an energy that can be subjected to a kind of quantification which is all the easier to introduce in theory as it is useless, since only certain *quanta* of constancy are recognized therein.

Its sexual coloring, so categorically maintained by Freud as its most central feature, is the color of emptiness: suspended in the light of a gap.

This gap is the gap desire encounters at the limits imposed upon it by the principle ironically referred to as the "pleasure principle," the latter being
852 relegated to a reality which, indeed, is but the field of praxis here.

It is from this very field that Freudianism hews a desire, the crux of which is essentially found in impossibilities.

Such are the outlines moralists could have discerned therein were our times not so prodigiously tormented by idyllic exigencies.

This is what is meant by Freud's constant reference to *Wunschgedanken* (wishful thinking*) and the omnipotence of thought: it is not megalomania that he points to with them, but rather the reconciliation of opposites.

This might mean that Venus is proscribed from our world, implying theological decline.

But Freud reveals to us that it is thanks to the Name-of-the-Father that man does not remain bound [*attaché*] to the sexual service of his mother, that aggression toward the Father is at the very heart of the Law, and that the Law is at the service of the desire that Law institutes through the prohibition of incest.

For the unconscious demonstrates that desire is tied to prohibition and that the Oedipal crisis is determinant in sexual maturation itself.

Psychologists immediately turned this discovery into its opposite in order to draw from it the moral of the importance of being gratified by one's mother—a form of psychotherapy that infantilizes adults, without recognizing children any better.

All too often, the psychoanalyst toes the same line. What is eluded thereby?

If the fear of castration is at the crux of sexual normalization, let us not forget that, since it no doubt bears upon the transgression it prohibits in the Oedipus complex, it nevertheless seeks to bring about obedience thereto in it, by stopping its slippage in a homosexual direction.

Thus it is, rather, the assumption [*assomption*] of castration that creates the lack on the basis of which desire is instituted. Desire is desire for desire, the Other's desire, as I have said, in other words, subjected to the Law.

(It is the fact that a woman must go through the same dialectic, whereas nothing seems to oblige her to do so—she must lose what she does not have—which tips us off, allowing us to articulate that it is the phallus by
default that constitutes the amount of the symbolic debt: a debit account 853
when one has it, a disputed credit when one does not.)

Castration is the altogether new mainspring Freud introduced into desire, giving desire's lack the meaning that remained enigmatic in Socrates' dialectic, although it was preserved in the recounting of the *Symposium*.

The ἄγαλμα in the ἐρῶν proves to be the motor force [*principe*] by which desire changes the nature of the lover. In his quest, Alcibiades spills the beans regarding love's deception and its baseness (to love is to want to be loved) to which he was willing to consent.

The discussion at the colloquium did not permit me to go so far as to demonstrate that the concept of the drive represents the drive as a montage.

The drives are our myths, said Freud. This must not be understood as a reference to the unreal. For it is the real that the drives mythify, as myths usually do: here it is the real which creates [*fait*] desire by reproducing in it the relationship between the subject and the lost object.

There is no lack of objects involving profits and losses to occupy its place. But only a limited number of them can play the role best symbolized by the lizard's self-mutilation, its tail being jettisoned when in distress. Misadventure of desire at the hedges of jouissance, watched out for by an evil god.

This drama is not as accidental as it is believed to be. It is essential: for desire comes from the Other, and jouissance is located on the side of the Thing.

Freud's second topography concerns the pluralizing quartering of the subject that results therefrom—yet another opportunity not to see what should strike us, which is that identifications are determined by desire there without satisfying the drive.

This occurs because the drive divides the subject and desire, the latter sustaining itself only by the relation it misrecognizes between this division and an object that causes it. Such is the structure of fantasy.

What then can the analyst's desire be? What can the treatment to which the analyst devotes himself be?

Will he fall into the kind of preaching that discredits the preacher whose noble feelings have replaced faith, and adopt, like him, an unwarranted "direction"?

One cannot but note here that, apart from the libertine who was the great
854 writer of comedies in the century of genius, no one, not even during the Enlightenment, has challenged the physician's privilege, although it is no less religious than others.

Can the analyst take cover behind this ancient investiture when it is moving in a secularized form towards a kind of socialization that can avoid neither eugenics nor the political segregation of anomalies?

Will the psychoanalyst take up the torch, not of an eschatology, but of the rights of a primary aim [*fin première*]?

What then is the aim [*fin*] of analysis beyond therapeutics? It is impossible not to distinguish the two when the point is to create an analyst.

For, as I have said, without going into the mainspring of transference, it is ultimately the analyst's desire that operates in psychoanalysis.

The style of a philosophical conference inclines everyone, so it seems, to highlight instead his own impermeability.

I am no more unable to do so than the next person, but in the field of psychoanalytic training, the displacement process makes teaching cacophonous.

Let us say that, in teaching, I relate technique to the primary aim [*fin première*].

I regretted in concluding that, on the whole, Enrico Castelli's profound question was left aside.

Blame it on nihilism here (and the reproach of nihilism) for keeping me from confronting the demonic, or anxiety, whichever one prefers.

Note

1. This is a summary of the comments I made at a remarkable colloquium organized in Rome by Professor Enrico Castelli, the second in a series on ethical problems posed by the effects of science, which Enrico Castelli admirably knows how to turn into questioning aporias.

This colloquium, entitled "Technique and Casuistry," was held at the University of Rome on January 7 to 12, 1964.

I avoided spelling out too quickly, in a way that would not have been controllable, what I later articulated concerning the drive in my lectures [Seminar XI] at the *École Normale Supérieure*, which began several days later.

This text was given to the *Atti* of the colloquium to serve as a summary of my paper and my remarks.

855

Science and Truth

This is the typescript of the opening class of the seminar I gave during the 1965–1966 school year at the École Normale Supérieure on *The Object of Psychoanalysis* [Seminar XIII], as a lecturer for the École Pratique des Hautes Études (Section 6).

The text of this class came out in the first issue of *Cahiers Pour l'Analyse,* published by the "Epistemology Circle" at the École Normale Supérieure, in January of 1966.

Shall I say that I established the status of the *subject* in psychoanalysis last year? I went so far as to develop a structure that accounts for the state of splitting [*refente*] or *Spaltung* where the psychoanalyst detects it in his praxis.

He detects it on a more or less daily basis. He accepts it as a given, since the mere recognition of the unconscious suffices to ground it and since it also submerges him, so to speak, by its constant manifestation.

But for him to know the status of his praxis, or to simply direct it in keeping with what is accessible to him, it is not enough for him to take this division as an empirical fact, or even for the empirical fact to become a paradox. A certain reduction is necessary that is sometimes long in completion, but always decisive in the birth of a science; such a reduction truly constitutes its object. Epistemology takes upon itself the job of defining this in each and every case, without having proven, at least to my mind, equal to the task.

For I do not believe that epistemology has fully accounted in this manner for the decisive change that, with physics paving the way, founded Science in the modern sense, a sense that is posited as absolute. Science's position is justified by a radical change in the *tempo* of its progress, by the galloping form
856 of its interference in our world, and by the chain reactions that characterize what one might call the expansions of its energetics. In this situation, what seems radical to me is the modification that has occurred in our subject position [*position de sujet*], in the sense that it is inaugural therein and that science continues to strengthen it ever further.

Koyré is my guide here and, as we know, he is still unrecognized [*méconnu*].

I did not thus just make an immediate pronouncement concerning psychoanalysis' vocation as a science. But it might have been noticed that I took my lead last year from a certain moment of the subject that I consider to be an essential correlate of science, a historically defined moment, the strict repeatability in experience of which perhaps remains to be determined: the moment Descartes inaugurates that goes by the name of *cogito*.

This correlate, as a moment, is the defile of a rejection of all knowledge, but is nevertheless claimed to establish for the subject a certain anchoring in being; I sustain that this anchoring constitutes the definition of the subject of science, "definition" to be understood in the sense of a narrow doorway.

This lead did not guide me in vain, for it led me at year end to formulate our experienced division as subjects as a division between knowledge and truth, and to accompany it with a topological model, the Möbius strip; this strip conveys the fact that the division in which these two terms come together is not to be derived from a difference in origin.

Whoever lends credence to the technique for reading Freud that I had to impose when the task at hand was simply one of synchronically resituating each of his terms, will be able to proceed in reverse chronological order from the *Ichspaltung* (to which death put an end), to the articles on fetishism (1927) and the loss of reality (1924), to observe that the doctrinal revamping known as the second topography introduced the terms *Ich*, *Über-Ich*, and even *Es* without certifying them as apparatuses, introducing instead a reworking of analytic experience in accordance with a dialectic best defined as what structuralism has since allowed us to elaborate logically: namely, the subject—the subject caught up in a constituting division.

After that, the reality principle loses the discordance that supposedly characterizes it in Freud's work when, on the basis of a comparison of texts, it is thought to be split between a notion of reality that includes psychical reality and another that makes it the correlate of the perception-consciousness system.

The reality principle must be read as it is in fact designated: as the strain of 857
experience sanctioned by the subject of science.

It suffices to give this some thought for the following ideas, which are disallowed as overly obvious, to assume their proper place.

For example, that it is unthinkable that psychoanalysis as a practice and the *Freudian* unconscious as a discovery could have taken on their roles before the birth—in the century that has been called the century of genius, that is, the seventeenth century—of science. "Science" should be taken here in the absolute sense just indicated, a sense which does not efface what formerly went by the same name, but which, rather than harking back to its archaic roots, draws to itself the latter's lead in such a way as to better demonstrate its difference from any other science.

One thing is certain: If the subject is truly there, at the nexus [*noeud*] of that difference, all humanist references become superfluous in science, the subject cutting them short.

In saying this about psychoanalysis and Freud's discovery, I am not concerned with the incidental fact that it was because his patients came to him in the name of science, and because of the prestige science conferred upon its servants—even its lowly ones—at the end of the nineteenth century, that Freud was able to found psychoanalysis by discovering the unconscious.

I am saying, contrary to what has been trumped up about a supposed break on Freud's part with the scientism of his time, that it was this very scientism—which one might designate by its allegiance to the ideals of Brücke, themselves passed down from Helmholtz and Du Bois-Reymond's pact to reduce physiology, and the mental functions considered to be included therein, to the mathematically determined terms of thermodynamics (the latter having attained virtual completion during their lifetimes)—that led Freud, as his writings show, to pave the way that shall forever bear his name.

I am saying that this way never shed the ideals of this scientism, as it is called, and that the mark it bears of the latter is not contingent but, rather, remains essential to it.

Its credit is preserved by this mark, despite the deviations to which it gave rise, Freud having opposed these deviations with timely sureness and inflexible rigor.

858 Witness his break with the most prestigious of his followers, Jung, as soon as the latter slipped into something whose function can only be defined as an attempt to reinstate a subject endowed with depths (with an "s"), that is, a subject constituted by a relationship—said to be archetypal—to knowledge. The said relationship was not reduced to that exclusively allowed by modern science, the latter being no other than the one I defined last year as punctual and vanishing: that relationship to knowledge which, since its historically inaugural moment, has retained the name "*cogito*."

It is due to this indubitable origin, blatant in all of Freud's work, and to the lesson he left us as head of a school, that Marxism is unable—and I do not believe any Marxist has seriously contested this point—to attack his ideas on the basis of their historical extraction.

I have in mind here his affiliation with the society of the dual monarchy, Freud remaining confined within Judaizing limits in his spiritual aversions; and with the capitalist order that conditioned his political agnosticism (who among you will write an essay worthy of Lamennais on indifference in political matters?); and, I would add, with bourgeois ethics, for which the dignity of his life inspires in us a respect that has prevented his work from attaining a stature—otherwise than in our misunderstanding of it and confusions about it—comparable to that of the only men of truth we still have: revolutionary agitators, writers whose style leaves its mark on language (I'm thinking of someone in particular), and the precursor of the thought that renews being.

You sense my haste here to put behind me the many precautions taken to remind psychoanalysts of their least debatable certainties.

I will nevertheless have to rehash them, even if it entails a certain heavy-handedness.

To say that the subject upon which we operate in psychoanalysis can only be the subject of science may seem paradoxical. It is nevertheless here that a demarcation must be made, failing which everything gets mixed up and a type of dishonesty sets in that is elsewhere called objective; but it is people's lack of audacity and failure to locate the object that backfires. One is always responsible for one's position as a subject. Those who would like to may call
that terrorism. I have the right to be amused, for it is not in a setting where 859
doctrine is fair game for bargaining that I should fear obfuscating anyone by formulating that guileless errors are the most unforgivable of all errors.

The psychoanalyst's position leaves no escape, excluding as it does the tenderness of the beautiful soul. If it is a paradox even just to say so, it is perhaps once again the same paradox.

Be that as it may, I posit that every attempt, or even temptation, in which current theory persists in being a relapse, further incarnating the subject, amounts to errancy—ever fruitful in error, but as such faulty [*fautive*]. For example, when the subject is incarnated in man, himself nothing in such theories but a child.

For man is then taken to be a primitive, distorting the whole primary process, just as children are taken to be underdeveloped men, masking the truth about what originally happens during childhood. In short, what Claude Lévi-Strauss has denounced as the archaic illusion is inevitable in psychoanalysis if one is not steadfast in one's theory regarding the principle I just mentioned: only one subject is accepted as such in psychoanalysis, the one that can make it scientific.

Which suffices to indicate that I do not believe that, in this respect, psychoanalysis lays claim to any special privileges.

There is no such thing as a science of man, and this should be understood along the lines of "there's no such thing as an insignificant savings." There is no such thing as a science of man because science's man does not exist, only its subject does.

My lifelong repugnance for the appellation "human sciences" is well known; it strikes me as the very call of servitude.

But the fact is that the term is also incorrect, except in the case of psychology which has discovered ways to outlive itself by providing services to the technocracy—sliding, as it were (as a sensational article by Canguilhem concludes, with truly Swiftian humor), like a toboggan from the Pantheon to the Prefecture of Police. Psychology will thus meet with failure at the level of the selection of creators in science, and of the encouragement and backing of research.

It is easy to see that none of the other sciences in this class constitutes an anthropology. Consider Lévy-Bruhl and Piaget. Their concepts—so-called
860 prelogical mentality and supposedly egocentric thought or discourse—refer only to the assumed mentality, presumed thought, and actual discourse of science's subject (not science's man). The upshot being that too many people now think that limits (mental, certainly), weakness of thought (presumable), and actual discourse (a bit tricky in the case of the man of science, for he is someone rather different) lend weight to these constructions, whereas the latter, while probably not devoid of objectivity, are relevant to science only insofar as they contribute nothing about the magician, for example, and little about magic; and if they contribute something about the traces of these latter, the traces are of but the magician or magic, as it was not Lévy-Bruhl who traced them. The reckoning in Piaget's case is still more unfavorable: He contributes nothing about children and little about their development, missing as he does what is essential therein; and, as concerns the logic he displays (Piaget's child, that is) in his responses to statements whose series constitutes the test he undergoes, Piaget comes up with nothing other than the very same logic that governs the enunciation of the statements that make up the test—that is, the logic of the man of science, in which the logician, I will not deny it, in this case maintains his importance.

In sciences that are far more valuable, although their status stands in need of reevaluation, one finds that proscription of the archaic illusion—an illusion we can generalize with the expression "psychologization of the subject"—in no way fetters fecundity.

A case in point is game theory, better called strategy, which takes advantage of the thoroughly calculable character of a subject strictly reduced to the formula for a matrix of signifying combinations.

The case of linguistics is subtler as it must take into account the difference between the enunciated and enunciation, that is, the impact of the subject who speaks as such (and not of the subject of science). This is why linguistics revolves around something else—namely, the battery of signifiers, whose prevalence over signification effects must be ensured. Here too antinomies appear, scaled to the extremism of the position adopted in object selection. What is clear is that one can go very far in the elaboration of the effects of language, since one can construct a poetics that owes no more to references to the mind of the poet than to its incarnation.

It is in the realm of logic that the theory's various refractive indices appear 861
in relation to the subject of science. They differ as regards the lexicon, syntactic morphemes, and sentential syntax.

Hence the theoretical differences between linguists such as Jakobson, Hjelmslev, and Chomsky.

It is logic that serves here as the subject's navel, logic insofar as it is in no way linked to the contingencies of a grammar.

The formalization of grammar must literally circumvent this logic if it is to be successfully carried out, but the circumventing movement is inscribed in this very operation.

I will indicate further along how modern logic is situated (see the third example below). It is indisputably the strictly determined consequence of an attempt to suture the subject of science, and Gödel's last theorem shows that the attempt fails there, meaning that the subject in question remains the correlate of science, but an antinomic correlate since science turns out to be defined by the deadlocked endeavor to suture the subject.

One should descry therein the crucially important mark of structuralism. It ushers into every "human science" it conquers a very particular mode of the subject for which the only index I have found is topological: the generating sign of the Möbius strip that I call the "inner eight."

The subject is, as it were, internally excluded from its object [*en exclusion interne à son objet*].

The allegiance to such a structuralism manifested in Claude Lévi-Strauss' work can be accredited to my thesis, assuming I confine myself for the moment to its periphery. It is clear, notwithstanding, that he highlights the scope of the natural classifications savages invent—especially their knowledge of fauna and flora, Lévi-Strauss emphasizing the fact that it surpasses our own—precisely because he can argue for a certain recuperation occurring in chemistry, owing to a physics of sapid and odorous qualities, otherwise stated, to a correlation between perceptual values and molecular architecture arrived at by means of combinatorial analysis, that is, by the mathematics of the signifier, as has been the case in every science to date.

862 Knowledge is thus clearly separated here from the subject along the correct lines, entailing no postulation of insufficient development, which, incidentally, would not be easy to substantiate.

What's more, when Lévi-Strauss, after having extracted the combinatory latent in the elementary structures of kinship, reports that a certain "informer," to use the ethnologist's term, is himself fully capable of drawing the Lévi-Straussian graph, what is he telling us if not that, here again, he extracts the subject from the combinatory in question—the subject who on the graph has no other existence than the denotation *ego*?

In demonstrating the power of the apparatus constituted by the mytheme in analyzing mythogenic transformations, which at this stage seem to become established in a synchrony simplified by their reversibility, Lévi-Strauss does not presume to deliver up to us the nature of the myth-maker. He simply knows here that his informer, while able to write *The Raw and the Cooked*—though lacking the genius whose mark has been left there—cannot do it, however, without checking at the cloakroom, that is, at the Museum of Man, a certain number of operative instruments, otherwise known as rituals, that consecrate his subject existence as a myth-maker; in checking them, what in another grammar would be called his assent is rejected from the field of structure. (See Newman's *Grammar of Assent*, somewhat powerful, albeit written for execrable purposes—I will perhaps be led to mention it again.)

The object of mythogeny thus is not linked to any development or stasis of the responsible subject. It is not concerned with this latter subject but rather with the subject of science. And the closer the informer himself is to reducing his presence to that of the subject of science, the more correctly is the collecting [of myth versions] carried out.

I believe, however, that Lévi-Strauss would have reservations about the introduction, during the collection of documents, of a psychoanalytically inspired approach, a sustained collection of dreams for example, with all that would entail by way of transferential relationships. But why would he, when I maintain to him that our praxis, far from altering the subject of science—the only one about which he can or wants to know anything—is entitled to intervene only when it tends toward this subject's satisfactory realization in the very field that interests Lévi-Strauss?

863 Is this to say that a nonsaturated but calculable subject would be the object that, in accordance with the forms of classical epistemology, subsumes the body of sciences that one might call "conjectural"—which I myself have opposed to the term "human sciences"?

I believe it to be all the less indicated as this subject is part of the conjuncture constituting science as a whole.

The opposition between exact sciences and conjectural sciences is no longer sustainable once conjecture is subject to exact calculation (using probability) and exactness is merely grounded in a formalism separating axioms and compounding laws from symbols.

We cannot, however, be satisfied with the simple observation that a particular formalism is more or less successful, for in the final analysis we must explain its trappings—trappings that have not arisen miraculously, but that have instead undergone renewal after crises which, since a certain unswerving direction seems to have been taken in science, have been terribly effective.

Let me reiterate that there is something in the status of science's object that seems to me to have remained unelucidated since the birth of science.

And let me remind you that while, certainly, to now pose the question of psychoanalysis' object is to reraise a question I broached upon first mounting this rostrum—that of psychoanalysis' position inside or outside of science—I have also indicated that the question probably cannot be answered without the object's status in science as such being thereby modified.

The object of psychoanalysis (I am laying down my cards now—you may have already guessed my hand, given this talk of the object) is no other than what I have already proposed about the function played in analysis by object *a*. Is knowledge of object *a* thus the science of psychoanalysis?

This is precisely the equation that must be avoided, since object *a* must be inserted, as we already know, into the division of the subject by which the psychoanalytic field is quite specifically structured—this is the point with which I resumed my seminar today.

This is why it was important to promote firstly, and as a fact to be distinguished from the question of knowing whether psychoanalysis is a science (that is, whether its field is scientific), the fact that its praxis implies no other subject than that of science.

What you will be so kind as to permit me to conjure up, with an image like 864
that of the opening up of the subject in psychoanalysis, must be reduced to this great an extent if we are to grasp what the subject receives therein by way of truth.

One senses that this is a tortuously circuitous process akin to taming. Object *a* is not peaceful, or rather one should say, could it be that it does not leave you in peace? least of all those of you who have the most to do with it: psychoanalysts, who are thus those I electively try to target with my discourse. It's true. The scheduled starting point of our meeting today, being the one at which I left you last year—that of the subject's division between truth and knowledge—is a familiar point to them. It is the one to which Freud urges them with his call "Wo Es war, soll Ich werden," which I retranslate, once again, to accentuate it here, as "Where it was, there must I come to be as a subject."

Now I demonstrate to analysts the strangeness of this point by taking it from behind, which consists here rather in bringing them back to its front. How could the obscure being, who was [*était*] forever awaiting me, come to be totalized by a line that can only be drawn by dividing this being still more clearly from what I can know of it?

It is not only in theory that the question of double inscription arises, having given rise to a perplexity whereupon my students Laplanche and Leclaire could have read its solution in their own split over how to approach the problem. The solution is not, in any case, of the Gestaltist type, nor is it to be sought on the plate where Napoleon's head is inscribed in a tree. It is quite simply to be found in the fact that an inscription does not etch into the same side of the parchment when it comes from the printing-plate of truth and when it comes from that of knowledge.

The fact that these inscriptions commingle could have been simply accounted for by topology, there being at hand's reach a surface in which front and back are situated so as to join up at all points.

This goes much further than an intuitive schema, for it is in so to speak wrapping around the analyst in his being that this topology can grasp him.

This is why, although the analyst shifts topology to another plane, it can only be in a breaking up of a puzzle which must, in any case, be reduced to this basis.

Which is why it is worth restating that in the test of writing *I am thinking:*
865 *"therefore I am,"* with quotes around the second clause, it is legible that thought only grounds being by knotting itself in speech where every operation goes right to the essence of language.

While Heidegger gives us the expression "*cogito sum*" somewhere, serving his own purposes, it should be noted that he algebrizes the phrase, and we can justifiably highlight its remainder: "*cogito ergo*"; it is evident therein that nothing gets spoken without leaning on the cause.

Now this cause is what is covered (over) by the "*soll Ich,*" the "must I" of Freud's formulation, which, in inverting its meaning [*sens*], brings forth the paradox of an imperative that presses me to assume [*assumer*] my own causality.

Yet I am not the cause of myself, though not because I am the creature. The case is precisely the same for the Creator. I refer you on this point to Augustine and the prologue of his *De Trinitate* [*On the Trinity*].

The Spinozian self-cause can take on the name of God. It is some-Thing Else [*Autre Chose*]. But let us leave that to the two words I will only play on by stipulating that the Spinozian self-cause is also some-Thing other [*Chose autre*] than the Whole, and that this God, being other in this way, is nevertheless not the God of pantheism.

In the *ego* that Descartes accentuates by virtue of the superfluousness of its function in certain of his Latin texts (a subject of exegesis that I leave here to the specialists), one must grasp the point at which it continues to be what it presents itself as: dependent on the god of religion. A curious scrap of *ergo*, the *ego* is bound up with this God. Descartes' approach is, singularly, one of safeguarding the *ego* from the deceitful God, and thereby safeguarding the *ego*'s partner—going so far as to endow the latter with the exorbitant privilege of guaranteeing the eternal truths only insofar as he is their creator.

The lot shared by the *ego* and God that is emphasized here is the same as that rendingly proffered by Descartes' contemporary, Angelus Silesius, in his mystical adjurations, upon which he imposes the form of distichs.

Those who keep up with my work would do well to recall here the use I made of the cherubinic wanderer's jaculatory prayers, taking them up within the trajectory of the introduction to narcissism I was working on, following my own bent, the year of my commentary on President Schreber.

Now one can be a bit shaky at this junction, that is how beauty walks [*c'est le pas de la beauté*], but one has to shake it just right [*il faut y boiter juste*].

And first of all by realizing that the two sides do not fit together there [*ne s'y emboîtent pas*].

This is why I will take the liberty of letting it go a moment, so as to begin 866
anew with the audacity I adopted at one time, but which I will only repeat insofar as I recall it to mind. For otherwise I would be repeating it twice, whereupon one could call it *bis repetita*, in the true sense of this expression, which does not mean simple repetition.

I'm referring to "The Freudian Thing," a talk the text of which is that of a second talk, deriving as it does from the occasion upon which I repeated it. It was pronounced the first time (may this insistence, in its very triviality, make you sense the temporal opposition [*contrepied*] repetition engenders) in a Vienna where my biographer will situate my first encounter with what must be called the lowest depths of the psychoanalytic world, and above all with a bigwig whose level of culture and responsibility corresponded to that required of a body guard[1]—but it did not much matter to me: it was idle chatter. I had simply wanted it to be in Vienna that my voice be heard in homage for the centennial of Freud's birth—not so as to mark the site of a deserted locus, but to mark that other site my discourse is now closing in on.

It is well known that I already took for granted at that time, as others do now, that the way opened up by Freud has no other meaning than the one I have taken up—namely, that the unconscious is language. Thus did the inspiration strike me, seeing in Freud's way an allegorical figure strangely come alive, and the nudity donned by she who arises from the well quivering with a new skin, to lend her a voice—this gesture in a sense playfully echoing Saint-Just's challenge whereby he sent forth to heaven an avowal, enshrined by the assembled audience, of being no more than that which turns to dust, "and which speaks to you," he added.

"I, truth, speak . . ." and the prosopopeia continues. Think about the unnamable thing that, by virtue of its ability to pronounce these words, would go right to the being of language—if we are to hear them as they must be pronounced: in horror.

But everyone reads into the unveiling what he can. To its credit let us
867 chalk up the muffled—though no less derisory—dramatism of the *tempo* at the end of this text, which you will find in *Évolution Psychiatrique* 1 (1956), by the title "*La Chose Freudienne*."[2]

I do not believe I owed the rather cool reception my audience gave me, upon the repeated delivery of the talk this text reproduces, to that same horror people felt. While willing to acknowledge what they considered to be its oblative value, their deafness proved to be quite peculiar.

It is not that the thing (the "Thing" in the title) shocked them, at any rate not as much as it shocked some of my fellow helmsmen back then, piloting the raft upon which, through their doing, I patiently bed-fellowed ten long years—for the narcissistic sustenance of our shipwrecked companions—with Jaspersian understanding and vacuous personalism, working like mad to keep us all from being tainted by the liberal heart-to-heart. "Thing is not a pretty word," someone told me verbatim; "doesn't it simply ruin our quest for the ultimate in psychology's unity where one obviously would not dream of 'thingifying'—tush! who can you trust? We thought you were in the avant-garde of progress, comrade."

One does not see oneself as one is, and even less so when one approaches oneself wearing philosophical masks.

But let us leave that aside. To gauge the full extent of the misunderstanding, as it arose in my audience at that time, over an issue of some consequence, I will take up a point that came to light at more or less the same moment, and that one might find touching because of the enthusiasm it supposes: "Why," someone set the question rolling, and the concern is still in the air, "doesn't he say the truth about truth?" [*le vrai sur le vrai*].

This proves just how futile my apologue and its prosopopeia were.

To lend my voice to support these intolerable words, "I, truth, speak . . . ," goes beyond allegory. Which quite simply means everything that can be said

of truth, of the only truth—namely, that there is no such thing as a metalanguage (an assertion made so as to situate all of logical positivism), no language being able to say the truth about truth, since truth is grounded in the fact that 868
truth speaks, and that it has no other means by which to become grounded.

This is precisely why the unconscious, which tells the truth about truth, is structured like a language, and why I, in so teaching, tell the truth about Freud who knew how to let the truth—going by the name of the unconscious—speak.

This lack of truth about truth—necessitating as it does all the traps that metalanguage, as sham and logic, falls into—is the rightful place of *Urverdrängung*, that is, of primal repression which draws toward itself all the other repressions—not to mention other rhetorical effects that we can recognize only by means of the subject of science.

And this is why we use other means to get to the bottom of it. But it is of the utmost importance that these means be unable to release [*élargir*] this subject. They have the advantage of no doubt touching on what is hidden from him. But there is no other truth about truth that can cover over this sore point than proper names, Freud's or my own, unless one stoops to old wives' tales with which to degrade henceforth ineffaceable testimony: a truth whose horrible face everyone is fated to refuse, or even crush—when it cannot be refused, that is, when one is a psychoanalyst—under the millstone that I have occasionally used as a metaphor to remind people, via another mouthpiece, that stones too know how to scream when need be.

People will thus perhaps consider me justified in not having found the question "Why doesn't he say . . . ?" terribly touching, coming as it did from someone whose workaday role in a truth agency's offices made his naïveté doubtful, and in having henceforth preferred to do without the services he provided in mine, which has no need of cantors who dream of sacristy . . .

Must it be stated that we have to know [*connaître*] other bodies of knowledge [*savoirs*] than that of science when it comes to dealing with the epistemological drive?

Returning again to what is at issue: Is this to admit that we must give up the notion in psychoanalysis that a body of knowledge corresponds to every truth? This is the breaking point whereby we depend upon the advent of science. We no longer have anything with which to join knowledge and truth together but the subject of science.

At least this subject allows us to do so, and I will now go further into 869
how—leaving my Thing to sort things out by itself with noumena, in short order I suspect: for a truth that speaks has no-thing much [*peu de chose*] in common with a noumenon that, for as long as pure reason can remember, has always kept its mouth shut.

This reminder is not irrelevant since the medium that will serve us at this point is one I brought up earlier. It is the cause: not the cause as logical category, but as causing the whole effect. Will you psychoanalysts refuse to take on the question of truth as cause when your very careers are built upon it? If there are any practitioners for whom truth as such is supposed to act, are you not them?

Make no mistake about it, in any case: It is because this point is veiled in science that you have kept an astonishingly well-preserved place in what plays the role of collective hope in the vagabond conscience that accompanies revolutions in thought.

In writing that "Marx's theory is omnipotent because it is true," Lenin says nothing of the enormity of the question his speech raises: If one assumes the truth of materialism in its two guises—dialectic and history, which are, in fact, one and the same—to be mute, how could theorizing this increase its power? To answer with proletarian consciousness and the action of Marxist politicos seems inadequate to me.

The separation of powers is at least announced in Marxism, the truth as cause being distinguished from knowledge put into operation.

An economic science inspired by *Capital* does not necessarily lead to its utilization as a revolutionary power, and history seems to require help from something other than a predicative dialectic. Aside from this singular point, which I shall not elaborate on here, the fact is that science, if one looks at it closely, has no memory. Once constituted, it forgets the circuitous path by which it came into being; otherwise stated, it forgets a dimension of truth that psychoanalysis seriously puts to work.

I must, however, be more precise. It is widely known that theoretical physics and mathematics—after every crisis that is resolved in a form for which the term "generalized theory" can in no way be taken to mean "a shift to generality"—often maintain what they generalize in its position in the pre-
870 ceding structure. That is not my point here. My concern is the toll [*drame*], the subjective toll that each of these crises takes on the learned. The tragedy [*drame*] has its victims, and nothing allows us to say that their destiny can be inscribed in the Oedipal myth. Let us say that the subject has not been studied to any great extent. J. R. Mayer, Cantor—well I am not going to furnish a list of first-rate tragedies, leading at times to the point of madness; the names of certain of our contemporaries, in whose cases I consider exemplary the tragedy of what is happening in psychoanalysis, would soon have to be added to the list. I posit, moreover, that this tragedy cannot itself be brought within Oedipus without throwing the latter into question.

You see the program that is being sketched out here. It is not about to be realized. I even consider it to be rather blocked.

I am broaching it prudently, and for today I ask you to see yourselves in the reflected light of such an approach.

Which is to say that we are going to bring this light to bear on other fields than psychoanalysis that lay claim to truth.

It must be said that, to the subject of science, magic and religion—two such fields that are distinct from science, so much so that people have situated them in relation to science, as a false or lesser science in the case of magic, and as going beyond its limits, or even in a truth-conflict with science in the case of religion—are mere will-o'-the-wisps, but not to the suffering subject with whom we deal.

Will it be said: "He's coming to it now—what is the suffering subject if not the one from whom our privileges stem? And what right do your intellectualizations give you to him?"

In response, I will start off with something I came across in the work of a philosopher recently awarded full academic honors. According to him, "The truth of pain is pain itself." Leaving this matter for today to the realm he explores, I will come back to it [later in the year] to explain how phenomenology serves as a pretext for the counter-truth and to explain the latter's status.

I will take it up now only to ask you analysts a question: Does or doesn't what you do imply that the truth of neurotic suffering lies in having the truth as cause?

I propose the following:

Concerning magic, I begin with a viewpoint that allows for no confusion as to my scientific allegiance, but is confined to a structuralist definition. This viewpoint assumes that signifiers answer as such to signifiers. Signifiers 871
in nature are called up by incantatory signifiers. They are metaphorically mobilized. The Thing, insofar as it speaks, answers our insistent prayers.

This is why the order of natural classifications I invoked from Lévi-Strauss's studies permits us, through its structural definition, to glimpse the bridge of correspondences by which the effective operation is conceivable, in the same way in which the operation was conceived.

This is, nevertheless, a reduction that neglects the subject here.

Everyone knows that the readying [*mise en état*] of the subject—the shamanizing subject—is essential here. Let us observe that the shaman, in the flesh, is part of nature, and that the operation's correlative subject must hew himself from this corporeal medium. This mode of hewing [*recoupement*] is debarred from the subject of science. Only his structural correlatives in the operation are situable for him, but they are exactly situable.

It is in the form of signifiers that what must be mobilized in nature appears: thunder and rain, meteors and miracles.

Everything is organized here in accordance with the antinomic relationships by which language is structured.

I must thus investigate the effect of demand in magic, with the idea of testing whether the relationship to desire defined by my graph can be detected in it.

Only in this way, to be described later on, using an approach which does not involve coarse recourse to analogy, can psychoanalysts consider themselves qualified to say anything about magic.

Their comment that magic is always sexual has its value here, but does not suffice to authorize them to do so.

I will conclude with two points worthy of your attention: Magic involves the truth as cause in its guise as efficient cause.

Knowledge is characterized in magic not only as remaining veiled for the subject of science, but as dissimulating itself as such, as much in the operative tradition as in its action. This is one of magic's conditions.

As for religion, I will simply indicate the same structural approach and, just
872 as summarily, that this outline is grounded in an opposition between structural traits.

Is it possible to hope that religion will take on a more straightforward status in science? I ask this because for some time now strange philosophers have been giving the flimsiest definition of the relations between science and religion, primarily taking them to be deployed in the same world, religion having the more encompassing position therein.

On this delicate point, about which certain people would want me to adopt analytic neutrality, I promote the principle that befriending everyone is an inadequate policy for maintaining intact the position from which one must operate.

In religion, the putting into play of truth as cause by the subject—the religious subject, that is—described earlier is taken up in a completely different operation. An analysis on the basis of the subject of science necessarily leads one to bring out in religion mechanisms that are familiar to us from obsessive neurosis. Freud perceived them in a flash that gives them an import surpassing all traditional criticism. The intent to measure religion against obsessive neurosis is in no way incommensurate.

If one cannot begin with remarks such as this—that the role played by revelation in religion translates as a negation [*dénégation*] of truth as cause, that is, revelation negates [*dénie*] what grounds the subject in considering himself to be a party to the cause [*partie prenante*]—then there is little chance of giving the so-called history of religions any limits, in other words, any rigor.

Let us say that a religious man leaves responsibility for the cause to God, but thereby bars his own access to truth. Thus he is led to place the cause of his desire in God's hands, and that is the true object of his sacrifice. His demand is subordinated to his presumed desire for a God who must then be seduced. The game of love starts in this way.

Religious people thus confer upon truth the status of guilt. The upshot being a distrust of knowledge, most evident in the cases of those Church Fathers who proved to be the best reasoners.

Truth in religion is relegated to so-called "eschatological" ends, which is to say that truth appears only as final cause, in the sense that it is deferred to an end-of-the-world judgment.

Hence the obscurantist stench that permeates all scientific uses of finality.

I have noted in passing how much we have to learn about the structure of 873
the subject's relationship to truth as cause from the writings of the Church Fathers, and even from the first conciliar decisions. The rationalism organizing theological thought is in no way a matter of fancy, as the platitude would have it.

If there is fantasy therein, it is in the most rigorous sense of the institution of a real that covers (over) the truth.

The fact that Christian truth had to formulate the untenable notion of a Three and One God does not strike me as inaccessible to scientific investigation. On this point, ecclesiastical power makes do very well with a certain discouragement of thought.

Before accentuating the impasses of such a mystery, it is worthwhile reflecting upon the necessity of this mystery's articulation; thought must be measured against this necessity.

The questions must be broached at the level at which dogma lapses into heresy—and the question of the *Filioque* seems to me to allow of explanation in topological terms.

Structural apprehension must be primary therein; it alone permits an accurate assessment of the function of images. *De Trinitate* here has all the marks of a theoretical work and we can take it as a model.

Were this not the case, I would advise my students to encounter a sixteenth century tapestry awaiting them in the foyer of the Mobilier National, on display for another month or two, that forces itself upon one's gaze.

The Three People, who are all represented identically, perfectly at ease talking among themselves on the fresh banks of Creation, are quite simply anxiety-provoking.

And what is hidden by such a well-made machine, when it confronts the couple, Adam and Eve, in the flower of their sin, is certainly of the sort to be proposed as a mental exercise on human relationships, ordinarily imagined to never exceed duality.

But my audience should first become versed in Augustine . . .

I seem to have thus only defined characteristics of religions from the Jewish tradition. They are obviously designed to show us why the latter is of inter-
874 est—and I am inconsolable at having had to drop my project of relating the function of the Name-of-the-Father to the study of the Bible.[3]

The key nevertheless lies in a definition of the relation of the subject to truth.

I believe I can say that insofar as Claude Lévi-Strauss conceives of Buddhism as a religion of the generalized subject, that is, as involving an infinitely variable stopping down of truth as cause, he flatters this utopia by believing that it concords with the universal reign of Marxism in society.

Which is perhaps to make too little of the exigencies of the subject of science, and to lend too much credence to the emergence in theory of a doctrine of the transcendence of matter.

Ecumenism only seems to have a chance if it is grounded in an appeal to the feebleminded.

As for science, I cannot today say what seems to me to be the structure of its relations to the truth as cause, since our progress this year shall contribute to an understanding of this point.

I will broach the topic with the strange remark that our science's prodigious fecundity must be examined in relation to the fact, sustaining science, that science does-not-want-to-know-anything about the truth as cause.

You may recognize therein my formulation of *Verwerfung* or "foreclosure," which forms a closed series here with *Verdrängung*, "repression," and *Verneinung*, "negation," whose function in magic and religion I have indicated in passing.

What I have said of the relationship between *Verwerfung* and psychosis, especially as *Verwerfung* of the Name-of-the-Father, is apparently at odds here with this attempt at structural situation.

If one remarks, however, that a successful paranoia might just as well seem to constitute the closure of science—assuming psychoanalysis were called

upon to represent this function—and if, moreover, one acknowledges that psychoanalysis is essentially what brings the Name-of-the-Father back into 875
scientific examination, one comes upon the same apparent deadlock; but one has the feeling that this very deadlock spurs on progress, and that one can see the chiasmus that seemed to create an obstacle therein coming undone.

The current state of the drama of psychoanalysis' birth, and the ruse that hides therein by beguiling writers' conscious ruses, should perhaps be taken into account here, for I was not the one who came up with the expression "successful paranoia."

I shall certainly have to indicate that the impact of truth as cause in science must be recognized in its guise as formal cause.

But that will be so as to clarify that psychoanalysis instead emphasizes its guise as material cause, a fact that qualifies psychoanalysis' originality in science.

This material cause is truly the form of impact of the signifier that I define therein.

The signifier is defined by psychoanalysis as acting first of all as if it were separate from its signification. Here we see the literal character trait that specifies the copulatory signifier, the phallus, when—arising outside of the limits of the subject's biological maturation—it is effectively (im)printed; it is unable, however, to be the sign representing sex, the partner's sex—that is, the partner's biological sign; recall, in this connection, my formulations differentiating the signifier from the sign.

It suffices to say in passing that in psychoanalysis, history constitutes a different dimension than development—and it is an aberration to try to reduce it to the latter. History unfolds only in going against the rhythm of development—a point from which history as a science should perhaps learn a lesson, if it expects to escape the ever-present clutches of a providential conception of its course.

In short, we once again come upon the subject of the signifier as I articulated it last year. Conveyed by a signifier in its relation to another signifier, the subject must be as rigorously distinguished from the biological individual as from any psychological evolution subsumable under the subject of understanding.

In minimal terms, this is the function I grant language in theory. It seems 876
to me compatible with historical materialism, the latter having left this point unaddressed. Perhaps the theory of object *a* will also find its place therein.

As we shall see, this theory is necessary to a correct integration of the function—from the standpoint of knowledge and the subject—of truth as cause.

In passing, you might have glimpsed, in the four modes of the cause's refraction just surveyed here, an analogous nominal schema and the same number of modes as in Aristotle's physics.

It is no accident, since his physics is marked by a logicism that still retains the savor and sapience of an original grammaticism:

Τοσαῦτα τόν ἀριθμὸν τὸ διὰ τί περιείληφεν.

Will it seem valid to us that the cause remains exactly as many-sided in polymerizing?

It is not the sole goal of this exploration to afford you an elegant take on frameworks that, in and of themselves, fall outside of our jurisdiction: magic, religion, and even science itself.

My primary concern is to remind you that, as subjects of psychoanalytic science, you must resist the temptation of each of these relations to truth as cause.

But not in the way in which you are at first likely to understand this.

Magic tempts you only insofar as you project its characteristics onto the subject with which you are dealing—in order to psychologize it, that is, misrecognize it.

So-called "magical thinking"—always attributed to someone else—is not a stigma with which you can label the other. It is just as valid for your fellow man as for yourself within the most common limits, being at the root of even the slightest of commandment's effects.

To be more explicit, recourse to magical thinking explains nothing. What must be explained is its efficiency.

As for religion, it should rather serve us as a model not to be followed, instituting as it does a social hierarchy in which the tradition of a certain relation to truth as cause is preserved.

877 Simulation of the Catholic Church, reproduced whenever the relation to truth as cause reaches the social realm, is particularly grotesque in a certain Psychoanalytic International, owing to the condition it imposes upon communication.

Need it be said that in science, as opposed to magic and religion, knowledge is communicated?

It must be stressed that this is not merely because it is usually done, but because the logical form given this knowledge includes a mode of communication which sutures the subject it implies.

Such is the main problem raised by communication in psychoanalysis. The first obstacle to its scientific value is that the relation to truth as cause, in its material guises, has remained neglected by the circle of its elaborators.

Shall I conclude by returning to the point with which I began today: the division of the subject? This point constitutes a knot.

Let us recall that Freud unties the knot in his discussion of the lack of the mother's penis, where the nature of the phallus is revealed. He tells us that the subject divides here regarding reality, seeing an abyss opening up here against which he protects himself with a phobia, and which he at the same time covers over with a surface upon which he erects a fetish—that is, the existence of the penis as maintained albeit displaced.

Let us, on the one hand, extract the (no) [*pas-de*] from the (no-penis) [*pas-de-pénis*], to be bracketed out, and transfer it to the no-knowledge [*pas-de-savoir*] that is the hesitation step [*pas-hésitation*] of neurosis.

Let us, on the other hand, recognize the subject's efficacy in the *gnomon* he erects, a *gnomon* that constantly indicates truth's site to him.

Revealing that the phallus itself is nothing but the site of lack it indicates in the subject.

This is the same index that directs me to the path along which I want to proceed this year, that is, the path you yourselves shy away from, as you are called forth as analysts in that lack.

December 1, 1965

Notes

1. Later an executant in the operation of destroying my teaching; the outcome, of which the audience present was aware, is of interest to the reader only as concerns the disappearance of the journal *La Psychanalyse* and my promotion to the rostrum at which I gave the present lecture.

2. See the last lines of "The Freudian Thing," *Écrits* 1966, 436.

3. I put on hold the Seminar that I had announced in 1963–1964 on the Name-of-the-Father, after having closed its opening lesson (in November of 1963) with my resignation from the public forum of Saint Anne Hospital at which my seminars had been held for ten years.

879 Appendix I: A Spoken Commentary on Freud's "Verneinung" by Jean Hyppolite

To start off with, I must thank Dr. Lacan for insisting that I present this article by Freud to you, because it gave me the opportunity to do a night's work and to bring you the child of this labor.[1] I hope that it will prove worthy in your eyes. Dr. Lacan was kind enough to send me the German text along with the French. It was a wise thing to do, because I don't think I would have understood anything in the French text if I hadn't had the German.[2]

I wasn't familiar with this text. It has an absolutely extraordinary structure, and deep down it is extremely enigmatic. Its construction is not at all like that of a professor. The text's construction is, I don't want to say dialectical, so as not to overuse the word, but extremely subtle. And it obliged me to come up with a real interpretation using both the German text and the French text (in which the translation is not very accurate but is, on the whole, honest enough when compared with others). This is the interpretation I am going to offer you. I think it is valid, but it is not the only possible one and it is certainly worth discussing.

Freud begins by presenting his title, "Die Verneinung." And I realized, making the same discovery Dr. Lacan had already made, that it would be better to translate it into French as "La dénégation."

Similarly, further on you will find "etwas im Urteil verneinen," which is not "the negation of something in the judgment," but a sort of "revocation of
880 a judgment" [*déjugement*].[3] Throughout the text, I think one must distinguish

between the negation [*négation*] within judgment and the attitude of negation [*négation*]; otherwise it does not seem possible to understand it.

The French text does not bring out the extremely concrete, almost amusing style of the examples of negation with which Freud begins. Consider the first one, which contains a projection whose role you can easily situate given the work you've done in this seminar, in which the patient, let us call him the psychoanalyzed person [*psychanalysé*], says to his analyst: "Now you'll think I mean to say something insulting, but really I've no such intention." "We realize," Freud says, "that this is a rejection, by projection, of an idea that has just come to mind" [*SE* XIX, 235].

"I realized in everyday life that when, as frequently happens, we hear someone say 'I certainly don't mean to offend you by saying what I am about to say,' we must translate this as 'I mean to offend you.' Such an intention is never lacking."

But this remark leads Freud to a very bold generalization, in which he raises the problem of negation insofar as it might be at the very origin of intelligence. This is how I understand the article, in all its philosophical density.

Similarly, he gives an example of someone saying: "You ask who this person in the dream can be. It's *not* my mother." In which case, the question is settled, we can be sure that it is indeed her.

He goes on to cite a technique which is useful to the psychoanalyst but, in addition, we could say, to anyone, for shedding light on what has been repressed in a given situation. "What would you consider the most unlikely imaginable thing in that situation? What do you think was furthest from your mind at that time?" If the patient, or whomever you happen to be talking to at a party or over dinner, lets himself fall into your trap and tells you what he considers to be the most unbelievable thing, then that is what you have to believe.

Thus we have here an analysis of concrete techniques which is generalized until its foundation is encountered in a mode of presenting what one is in the mode of not being it. Because that is exactly how it is constituted: "I am going to tell you what I am not; pay attention, this is precisely what I am." This is how Freud takes up the function of negation and, in order to do so, he uses a word which I could not but feel at home with, the word *Aufhebung*, which, as you know, has had a variety of fates; it is not for me to say it . . .

Dr. Lacan: Indeed, it is. If not you, then whose responsibility would it be?

Prof. Hyppolite: It is Hegel's dialectical word, which means simultaneously 881
to deny, to suppress, and to conserve, and fundamentally to lift [*soulever*]. In

reality, it might be the *Aufhebung* of a stone, or equally the cancellation of my subscription to a newspaper. Freud tells us here: "negation is an *Aufhebung* of the repression, though not, of course, an acceptance of what is repressed" [*SE* XIX, 235–36].

Something truly extraordinary begins here in Freud's analysis; something emerges from these anecdotes, which we might well have taken for nothing more than anecdotes, that is of prodigious philosophical import and that I will attempt to summarize shortly.

Presenting one's being in the mode of not being it is truly what is at stake in this *Aufhebung* of the repression, which is not an acceptance of that which is repressed. The person who is speaking says, "This is what I am not." There would no longer be any repression here, if repression signified unconsciousness, since it is conscious. But the crux of the repression persists[4] in the form of unacceptance.

Freud now leads us through an argument of extreme philosophical subtlety. It would be a gross oversight were we to let a remark Freud makes slip by, simply on account of its unreflective use in everyday speech: "in this the intellectual function is separated from the affective process" [*SE* XIX, 236].

For there is truly a profound discovery in the manner in which he goes on to deal with it.

To present my hypothesis, I will say that, in order to carry out an analysis of the intellectual function, he does not show how the intellectual separates from the affective, but how the intellectual is that sort of suspension of content for which the somewhat barbaric term "sublimation"[5] would not be inappropriate. Perhaps what is born here is thought as such, but not before the content has been affected by a negation.

Let me recall to mind a philosophical text (I once again apologize for doing so, although Dr. Lacan can guarantee you that it is necessary). At the end of one of Hegel's chapters, the point is to substitute true negativity for the appetite for destruction that takes hold of desire and that is conceptualized there in a profoundly mythical rather than a psychological manner—to substitute, as I was saying, an ideal negation [*négation*] for the appetite for destruction that takes hold of desire and that is such that, in the final outcome of the primordial struggle in which the two combatants face off, there is no one left to determine who won and who lost.

882 The negation that Freud talks about here, insofar as it is different from the ideal negation [*négation*] in which the intellectual is constituted, shows us the sort of genesis whose vestiges Freud points to, at the moment of concluding his text, in the negativism characteristic of certain psychotics.[6]

And Freud goes on to explain, mythically speaking still, what differentiates this moment [of ideal negation] from negativity.

In my view, this is what has to be acknowledged in order to understand what is truly being spoken of as "negation" in this article, even though it is not immediately obvious. Similarly, a dissymmetry expressed by two different words in Freud's text—which have been translated by the same word in French—must be noted between the movement toward affirmation based on the unifying tendency of love, and the genesis, based on the destructive tendency, of the kind of negation whose true function is to engender intelligence and the very position of thought.

But let us proceed more slowly.

We have seen that Freud posits the intellectual as separate from the affective. Even if the desired modification, "the acceptance of what is repressed," occurs during the analysis, the repression is not, for all that, eliminated. Let us try to conceptualize the situation.

First stage: here is what I am not. What I am is deduced therefrom. The repression still persists in the guise of negation.

Second stage: the psychoanalyst obliges me to accept intellectually what I formerly denied [*niais*], and Freud adds, after a dash and without any explanation—"the repressive process itself is not yet removed (*aufgehoben*) by this" [*SE* XIX, 236].

This seems very profound to me. If the psychoanalyzed person accepts this, he goes back on his negation and yet the repression is still there! I conclude from this that one must give what happens here a philosophical name, a name Freud did not pronounce: negation of the negation. Literally, what transpires here is intellectual, but only intellectual, affirmation qua negation of the negation. These terms are not to be found in Freud's text, but I think that all we are doing is extending his thought by formulating it in this way. That is what he really means.

At this point (and let us be vigilant in working with a difficult text!), Freud
finds himself in a position to be able to show how the intellectual separates 883
<in action>[7] from the affective, and to give a formulation of a sort of gene-
sis of judgment, that is, in short, a genesis of thought.

I apologize to the psychologists here, but I am not very fond of positive psychology in itself. One might take this genesis for positive psychology, but its import seems more profound to me, being historical and mythical in nature. And given the role that Freud has this primordial affectivity play, insofar as it gives rise to intelligence, I think that it should be understood in the way that Dr. Lacan teaches, which is that the primal form of relation known psychologically as the affective is itself situated within the distinctive field of the human situation, and that, while it gives rise to intelligence, it is because, from the outset, it already brings with it a fundamental historicity. There is no pure affect on the one hand, entirely engaged in the real, and pure intellect on the other, which detaches itself from it in order to grasp it anew. In the genesis described here, I see a sort of grand myth. And behind the appearance of positivity in Freud's text, there is a grand myth sustaining it.

What does this mean? What is there behind affirmation[8]? There is *Vereinigung*, which is Eros. And what is there behind negation (careful—intellectual negation will be something more)? The appearance here of a fundamental, dissymmetrical symbol. Primordial affirmation is nothing more than affirming: but to negate [*nier*] is more than to wish to destroy.

The process that leads to this point, which has been translated into French as *rejet* [rejection], even though Freud did not use the term *Verwerfung* here, is still more strongly stressed, since he uses *Ausstossung*,[9] which means expulsion.

We have here, in some sense, <the formal couple of> two primary forces—the force of attraction[10] and the force of expulsion—both of which seem to be under the sway of the pleasure principle, which cannot but strike one in this text.[11]

This is, thus, the earliest [*première*] history of judgment. Freud now distinguishes between two different types of judgment.

In accordance with what everyone learns about the elements of philosophy, there is a judgment of attribution and a judgment of existence: "The
884 function of judgment . . . affirms or disaffirms the possession by a thing of a particular attribute; and it asserts or disputes that a representation [*Vorstellung*] has an existence in reality" [*SE* XIX, 236].

Freud now shows what lies behind the judgment of attribution and behind the judgment of existence. It seems to me that in order to understand his article, one must consider both the negation [*négation*] of the attributive judgment and the negation [*négation*] of the judgment of existence as falling short of negation [*négation*] when it appears in its symbolic function. In the final analysis, judgment does not yet exist in this moment of emergence; rather, there is an early [*premier*] myth of the outside and the inside, and that is what we have to figure out.

You can sense the import of this myth of the formation of the outside and the inside, for alienation is grounded in these two terms. What is translated in their formal opposition becomes, beyond that, alienation and hostility between the two.

What makes these four or five pages so dense is that, as you see, they call everything into question, and move from concrete remarks, seemingly so minor and yet so profound in their generality, to something which brings with it an entire philosophy, an entire structure of thought.

What is there behind the judgment of attribution? There is the "I should like to take in (to myself) [*(m')approprier*], introject" or the "I should like to expel."

At the outset, Freud seems to be saying, but "at the outset" means nothing more than in the myth "once upon a time . . ." In this story, once upon a time there was an ego [*moi*] (by which we should understand here a subject) for whom nothing was as yet foreign.

The distinction between the foreign and himself involves an operation, an expulsion. This renders comprehensible a proposition which, appearing rather abruptly, seems for a moment to be contradictory:

"Das Schlechte," what is bad, "das dem Ich Fremde," what is foreign to the ego [*moi*], "das Aussenbefindliche," and what is found outside, "ist ihm zunächst identisch," are, at first, identical for him.

Now, just before this, Freud says that one introjects and one expels, and that there is therefore an operation which is the operation of expulsion <without which> the operation of introjection <would have no meaning>. This is the primordial operation that is the <basis for> the judgment of attribution.

But what lies at the origin of the judgment of existence is the relationship between representation and perception. It is very difficult here not to miss the sense in which Freud deepens this relationship. What is important is that, "at the outset," it is indifferent whether one knows if there is [*il y a*] or
there is not. There is: the subject reproduces his representation of things 885
based on the initial perception he had of them. When he says now that this exists, the question is <not>[12] whether this representation still has the same status in reality but whether he can or cannot refind it. This is the relationship between the representation and reality that Freud emphasizes <as testing; he bases this relationship> on the possibility of refinding its object once again. Repetition as the emphasized mainspring proves that Freud is operating in a more profound dimension than Jung, the latter's dimension being more properly that of memory.[13] We must not lose the thread of Freud's analysis here. (But it is so difficult and detailed that I am afraid of making you lose it.)

What was at stake in the judgment of attribution was expelling or introjecting. In the judgment of existence, it is a question of attributing to the ego, or rather to the subject (it is more comprehensive), a representation that no longer has an object that corresponds to it, although an object had corresponded to it at an earlier stage. What is at stake here is the genesis "of the outside and of the inside."

Hence this offers us, as Freud says, "an insight into the birth" of judgment, "from the interplay of primary drive-impulses." So here there is a sort of "continuation, along lines of expediency, of the original process by which the ego took things into itself [*appropriation au moi*] or expelled them from itself, according to the pleasure principle" [*SE* XIX, 239].

"Die Bejahung," affirmation, Freud tells us, "als Ersatz der Vereinigung," insofar as it is simply the equivalent of unification, "gehört dem Eros an," is due to Eros, which is what lies at the source of affirmation. For example, in the judgment of attribution, there is the fact of introjecting, of taking into oneself [*approprier*] instead of expelling outside.

He doesn't use the word *Ersatz* regarding negation [*négation*], but rather the word *Nachfolge*. But the French translator renders it by the same word as *Ersatz*. The German text gives: affirmation is the *Ersatz* of *Vereinigung*, and negation [*négation*] is the *Nachfolge* of expulsion or, more precisely, of the destructive drive (*Destruktionstrieb*).

This thus becomes entirely mythical. There are two instincts, which are, as it were, tangled together in this myth which bears the subject: one instinct of unification, the other of destruction. A grand myth, as you see, and one which repeats others. But the little nuance—whereby affirmation in some sense
886 merely substitutes for unification, whereas negation [*négation*] results (afterward) from expulsion—alone seems to me capable of explaining the sentence that follows regarding only negativism and the destructive instinct. For this explains how there can be a pleasure in negating [*dénier*], a negativism that results straightforwardly from the suppression[14] of the libidinal components; in other words, what has disappeared in this pleasure in negating [*nier*] (disappeared = repressed) are the libidinal components.

Does the destructive instinct also depend consequently upon <the> pleasure <principle>? I think this is very important, crucial for technique.[15]

However, Freud tells us that "the performance of the function of judgment is only made possible by *the creation of the symbol of negation*."[16]

Why doesn't Freud say that the functioning of judgment is made possible by affirmation? Because negation [*négation*] has a role to play, not as a tendency toward destruction, nor within a form of judgment, but insofar as it is the fundamental attitude of symbolicity rendered explicit.

"The creation of the symbol of negation permitted an initial degree of independence from repression and its consequences and, thereby, also from the compulsion (*Zwang*) of the pleasure principle" [*SE* XIX, 239].

A sentence whose meaning would not have created any problem for me, if I had not first linked the tendency toward destruction to the pleasure principle.

Because there is a difficulty here. What does the dissymmetry between affirmation and negation [*négation*] thus signify? It signifies that all of the repressed can once again be taken up and reutilized in a sort of suspension, and that, in some sense, instead of being dominated by the instincts of attraction and expulsion, a margin for thought can be generated, an appearance of being so in the guise of not being so, which is generated with negation—that is, where the symbol of negation [*négation*] is linked to the concrete attitude of negation.

For this is how one must understand the text, if one accepts its conclusion, which at first struck me as a bit strange:

"This view of negation fits in very well with the fact that in analysis we 887
never discover a 'no' in the unconscious . . ." [*SE* XIX, 239].

But we certainly find destruction there. We must thus clearly distinguish between the destructive instinct and the form of destruction, otherwise we will not understand what Freud meant. In negation, we must see a concrete attitude at the origin of the explicit symbol of negation [*négation*]; this explicit symbol alone makes possible something like the use of the unconscious, all the while maintaining the repression.

This is what seems to me to be the meaning of the end of the concluding sentence: "recognition of the unconscious on the part of the ego is expressed in a negative formula" [*SE* XIX, 239].

That's it in a nutshell: in analysis there is no "no" to be found in the unconscious, but recognition of the unconscious by the ego demonstrates that the ego is always misrecognition; even in knowledge [*connaissance*], one always finds in the ego, in a negative formulation, the hallmark of the possibility of having the unconscious at one's disposal even as one refuses it.

"There is no stronger evidence that we have been successful in our effort to uncover the unconscious than when the patient reacts to it with the words 'I didn't think that,' or 'I didn't (ever) think of that'" [*SE* XIX, 239].

Thus, in these four or five pages of Freud's—and I apologize if I myself have demonstrated some difficulty in finding in them what I believe to be their thread—there is, on the one hand, an analysis of the sort of concrete attitude that emerges from the very observation of negation; on the other hand, the possibility of seeing the intellectual dissociate <in action> from the affective; finally, and above all, a genesis of everything that leads up to the primal level, and consequently the origin of judgment and of thought itself (in the form of thought as such, since thought is already there before, in the primal [state], but it is not there as thought of), which is grasped by means of negation.

Notes

1. (Lacan's note:) "Je t'apporte l'enfant d'une nuit d'Idumée!"

2. The French translation of Freud's *Verneinung* was published as "La Négation" in the official organ of the Société Psychanalytique de Paris, *RFP* VII, 2 (1934): 174–77. The German text first came out in *Imago* IX in 1925 and has since been reproduced in several collections of Freud's works. It can be found in *GW* XIV, as the second article, pages 11–15. [In English, see "Negation" in *SE* XIX, 235–39; the newer German edition is *Studienausgabe* III (Frankfurt: Fischer Verlag, 1982), 373–77, abbreviated here as *Stud.*]

3. (Lacan's note:) This is indicated by the sentence that follows beginning with *Verurteilung*, that is, the condemnation that it designates as equivalent to (*Ersatz* [*SE* XIX, 236: "substitute for"]) repression, whose very "no" must be taken as a hallmark, as a certificate of origin comparable to "Made in Germany"* stamped on an object.

4. "Bei Fortbestand des Wesentlichen an der Verdrängung" (*GW* XIV, 12; *Stud* III, 374). ["What is essential to the repression persists" (*SE* XIX, 236).]

5. (Lacan's note in 1955:) I intend some day to establish a strict definition of this term in psychoanalysis—something which has not yet been done. (Lacan's note in 1966:) A promise since kept.

6. "Die allgemeine Verneinungslust, der Negativismus mancher Psychotiker ist wahrscheinlich als Anzeichen der Triebentmischung durch Abzug der libidinösen Komponenten zu verstehen" (*GW* XIV, 15). ["The general pleasure in negation, the negativism displayed by many psychotics, is probably to be understood as a sign of a defusion of drives that has taken place through a withdrawal of the libidinal components" (*Stud* III, 376–77; *SE* XIX, 239, translation modified).]

7. (Lacan's note:) All words in such brackets* have been added.

8. *Bejahung*.

9. *GW* XIV, 15.

10. *Einbeziehung*.

11. The seminar in which Lacan gave a commentary on *Beyond the Pleasure Principle* did not take place until 1954–1955.

12. (Lacan's note:) Words added by the editor in accordance with Freud's text: "Der erste und nächste Zweck der Realitätsprüfung ist also nicht, ein dem Vorgestellten entsprechendes Objekt in der realen Wahrnehmung zufinden, sondern es *wiederzufinden*, sich zu überzeugen, dass es noch vorhanden ist" (*GW* XIV, 14). ["The first and immediate aim, therefore, of reality-testing is, not to find an object in real perception which corresponds to the one presented, but to refind such an object, to convince oneself that it is still there" (*SE* XIX, 237–38, *Stud* III, 375).]

13. (Lacan's note:) Is the author referring here to Platonic reminiscence?

14. The German here is *Abzug*: deduction, discount, withholding; "what is withheld in the pleasure in negating are the libidinal components." Its possibility is related to the *Triebentmischung*, which is a sort of return to a pure state, a decanting of the drives that is usually, and poorly, translated as *désintrication des instincts* ["defusion of instincts" (*SE* XIX, 239)].

15. (Lacan's note:) The admirable way in which Prof. Hyppolite's exposé at this point closes in on the difficulty seems all the more significant to me in that I had not as yet produced the theses, which I was to develop the following year in my commentary on *Beyond the Pleasure Principle*, on the death instinct, which is so thoroughly evaded and yet so present in this text.

16. Underlined by Freud.

Appendix II: Metaphor of the Subject[1] 889

This is the text, rewritten in June 1961, of remarks I made on June 23, 1960, in response to a talk by Chaim Perelman, in which he invoked "the idea of rationality and the rule of law" before the French Philosophical Society.

It anticipates, to some degree, as concerns metaphor, what I have since been formulating by way of a logic of the unconscious.

I am indebted to François Regnault for having reminded me of this text in time to add it to the second edition of this volume.

Procedures of argumentation interest Mr. Perelman because they are scorned [*mépris*] by the scientific tradition. He is thus led to plead, before a Philosophical Society, that they have been misunderstood [*méprise*].

He would do better to go beyond defense if he would win us over to his side. This is the sense in which the remark that I will bring to his attention is intended: it is on the basis of the unconscious' manifestations, which I deal with as an analyst, that I have developed a theory of the effects of the signifier that intersects rhetoric. This is attested to by the fact that my students, in reading works of rhetoric, recognize it to be their daily fare at my seminar.

Thus I shall be led to question him less about what he has argued here, perhaps too cautiously, than about a point at which his written work takes us right to the crux of thought.

Metaphor, for example, which I link up, as is well known, with one of the two fundamental facets of the play of the unconscious.

It cannot be said that I disagree with the way Perelman deals with metaphor, detecting therein a four-term operation, or even with the fact that he defends his decisively separating it from images on such grounds.

I do not, however, believe that he is justified in thinking he has reduced it to the function of analogy.[2]

If we take it for granted that, in the case of analogy, the specific effect of
the relations A/B and D/C is sustained by the very heterogeneity by which 890
they divide up into theme and phoros, this formalism is no longer valid for

metaphor, and the best proof thereof is that the formalism becomes confused in the very illustrations Perelman provides of it.

There are, as it were, four terms in metaphor, but their heterogeneity involves a dividing line—three against one—and is tantamount to the dividing line between the signifier and the signified.

To expand on a formula I gave for metaphor in my article entitled "The Instance of the Letter in the Unconscious,"[3] I will rewrite it as follows:

$$\frac{S}{S'_1} \cdot \frac{S'_2}{x} \longrightarrow S\left(\frac{1}{s''}\right)$$

Metaphor is, quite radically speaking, the effect of the substitution of one signifier for another in a chain, nothing natural predestining the signifier for this function of phoros apart from the fact that two signifiers are involved, which can, as such, be reduced to a phonemic opposition.

To demonstrate this using one of Perelman's own examples, the one he has judiciously chosen from Berkeley's third dialogue,[4] "An ocean of false science" will be written as follows (since it is better to restore what the French translation already tends to "make dormant" [*endormir*], to do justice, along with Perelman, to a metaphor so felicitously found by rhetoricians):

$$\frac{\text{an ocean}}{\text{learning}} \text{ of } \frac{\text{false}}{x} \longrightarrow \text{an ocean}\left(\frac{1}{?}\right)$$

Learning—*enseignement*—indeed, is not science, and one senses even more clearly in the former that the term has no more to do with the ocean than a fish with a bicycle.

The sunken cathedral of what had been previously taught [*enseigné*] concerning this matter is still likely to ring fruitfully in our ears when it is reduced to the alternation of a muffled and sonorous bell by which the phrase penetrates us—lear-ning, lear-ning—not from the depths of a liquid layer, but due to the fallacy of its own arguments.

The ocean is one of those arguments and nothing else. I mean literature, which must be understood in its historical context, by which it bears the meaning that the cosmos can, at its outermost bounds, become a locus of deception. A signified thus, you may retort, with which the metaphor begins. Perhaps, but within the range of its effect it goes beyond mere recurrence,
891 being based on the nonmeaning of what is just one term among others of the same learning.

What is produced, however, at the place of the question mark in the second part of my formula is a new species in signification: a falseness that disputation cannot fathom, for it is unsoundable—the wave and depth of the imaginary's ἄπειρος in which any vessel is swallowed up should it seek to draw forth something.

By being "awakened" in its freshness, this metaphor, like every other, shows its true colors in the work of the surrealists.

The radical nature of metaphor is seen in the fit of rage, related by Freud, that his Rat Man flew into as a child, when he had yet to be armed with foul language, before becoming a full-fledged obsessive neurotic. Upon being thwarted by his father, the boy yelled at him, "*Du Lampe, du Handtuch, du Teller" usw* ("You lamp! You towel! You plate!" and so on), his father being unsure whether to consider this criminal or genius on his son's part [*SE* X, 205].

I myself intend not to lose sight here of the dimension of insult [*injure*] in which metaphor originates—insult that is more serious than we imagine when we reduce it to wartime invective. For the injustice that is gratuitously done to every subject by use of an attribute with which any other subject is inclined to take a dig at him stems from such insults. "The cat goes bow-wow, the dog goes meow, meow." This is how the child spells out the powers of discourse and inaugurates thought.

One might be surprised that I feel the need to take things so far concerning metaphor. But Perelman will grant me that in invoking, to satisfy his analogical theory, the coupled terms swimmer and scholar, and then terra firma and truth, and in admitting that one can thus multiply them *ad infinitum,* what he formulates evidently manifests that they are all equally irrelevant and come down to what I say: no extant signification has anything to do with the question.

Of course, speaking of the constitutive disorganization of every enunciation does not say it all, and the example Perelman revives from Aristotle,[5] "the evening of life" to speak of old age, is quite telling in that it does not even point out the repression of the most unpleasant facet of the metaphorized term in order to bring out a sense of peacefulness that old age in no way implies in real life [*le réel*].

For if we question the peacefulness of the evening [*la paix du soir*], we realize that it involves no other dimension than the muting of vocal exercises: whether the jabbering of harvesters or the chirping of birds.

Considering which, we might remember that while language is essentially 892
blah blah blah, it is nevertheless from language that having and being derive.

This is what the metaphor I chose in the abovementioned article[6]—namely, Victor Hugo's "His sheaf was neither miserly nor spiteful," from "Booz Sleeping" (*Booz endormi*)—plays on, and it does not idly evoke the link that, in rich people, unites the position of having with the refusal inscribed in their being. For this is the impasse of love. And its very negation would do no more here, as we know, than posit it, if the metaphor introduced by the substitution of "his sheaf" for the subject did not bring forth the only object the having of which necessitates the failure to be it—the phallus—around which the whole poem revolves right down to its last twist.

This means that the most serious reality, and even the sole serious reality for man, if one considers its role in sustaining the metonymy of his desire, can only be retained in metaphor.

What am I trying to get at, if not to convince you that what the unconscious brings back to our attention is the law by which enunciation can never be reduced to what is enunciated in any discourse?

Let us not say that I choose my terms in it, regardless of what I have to say—although it is not pointless to recall here that the discourse of science, insofar as it commends itself by its objectivity, neutrality, and dreariness, even of the Sulpician variety, is just as dishonest and ill-intentioned as any other rhetoric.

What must be said is that the I of this choice is born somewhere other than in the place where the discourse is enunciated—namely, in the person who listens to it.

Doesn't this provide the status of rhetorical effects, in showing that they extend to all signification? Let people object that they stop at mathematical discourse—I will agree all the more in that I place the highest value on that discourse precisely because it signifies nothing.

The only absolute statement was made by the competent authority—namely, that no roll of the dice in the signifier will ever abolish chance. This is so because chance exists only within a linguistic determination, no matter how we consider it, whether in combination with automatism or encounter.

Notes

1. See *Écrits* 1966, 528, fn1.

2. See the pages I would go so far as to qualify as "admirable" in the *Traité de l'argumentation*, Vol. II (Paris: PUF, 1958), 497–534 [in English: Chaim Perelman and Lucie Olbrechts-Tyteca, *The New Rhetoric: A Treatise on Argumentation* (Notre Dame and London: University of Notre Dame Press, 1969)].

3. See *Écrits* 1966, 493–528.

4. See *Traité de l'argumentation*, 537.

5. See *Traité de l'argumentation*, 535 [see Aristotle's *Poetics*, 1457b].

6. See *Écrits* 1966, 506.

Translator's Endnotes

General Notes

Many of the terms used in this translation could be explained at length, but I will limit myself here to some that may be particularly confusing.

Assumer

Assumer corresponds to the English "to assume" in the sense of to take on (as in "to assume a responsibility"), but also implies taking in, adopting, incorporating, owning, dealing with, and coming to terms with. I generally translate *assumer* as "to assume" and *assomption* as "assumption," and include the French in brackets when the usage seems somewhat foreign (e.g., "the subject assumes an image" and "the subject's assumption of his own sex").

De

This is, in my experience, the most difficult word to translate in *Écrits*. Among its meanings: of, from, with, by, because of, thanks to, based on, by means of, constituted by, due to, by virtue of, since, by way of, in the form of, through, regarding, about, involved in, insofar as, and as. Lacan's use of *de* seems to me to be highly unusual among French authors, especially in "Subversion of the Subject."

Certain uses of *de* are particularly open to multiple interpretations, due to its function as either a subjective genitive or an objective genitive (or intentionally designed by Lacan to suggest both). Consider, in particular, formulations like *le désir de l'Autre* (see below) and *la jouissance de l'Autre* (is it the jouissance the Other has or the subject's jouissance of the Other?).

Demande

The French term here can be as strong as the English "demand" or as weak as "request." I have translated it as both, depending on the context, but provide the French in brackets when I render it as the latter.

Le désir de l'Autre

Apart from the usual meanings, "desire for the Other" and "the Other's desire" (only the latter of which is captured by the formula "the desire of the Other," since we say "desire for" not "desire of" something), it should be kept in mind that Lacan often uses the French here as a shorthand for saying "what the Other desires" or "the object of the Other's desire." For example, in the sentence, *Le désir de l'homme, c'est le désir de l'Autre,* one of the obvious meanings is that man desires what the Other desires. It is also implied that, as a man, I want the Other to desire me.

Le donné

Le donné (the French equivalent, first used by Henri Bergson, of the German *Gegeben*), is a phenomenological term denoting what is immediately present to the mind before the mind acts upon it—that is, what is not constructed, inferred, or hypothetical. It is often rendered in English as "given," but in order to bring out its connection with *la donnée*, usually translated as "datum" or "given" (as in the "the givens of the problem"), I reserve "pregiven" for *le donné* and "given" for *la donnée*. As *le donné* does not necessarily imply that subsequent intellection or construction will take place, the "pre" of "pregiven" should not be thought to necessarily indicate temporal antecedence. David Carr, in his translation of Husserl's *The Crisis of the European Sciences and Transcendental Phenomenology: An Introduction to Phenomenological Philosophy* (Evanston: Northwestern University Press, 1970), translates *Gegeben* as "pregiven."

Duel or Duelle (for example, *relation duelle*)

I have avoided the obvious translation "dual" here because, in contemporary American psychology, "dual relations" are when a patient's therapist is also his or her teacher, for example, the therapist playing two different roles in relation to the patient. In Lacan's usage, *la relation duelle* is the imaginary relation between ego *(a')* and alter ego *(a)*, as opposed to the symbolic relation. I have systematically translated the adjective as "dyadic."

Entendre

Entendre means both to hear and to understand, and readers should keep in mind that both meanings may be germane when they come across either of these English verbs in the translation.

Expérience

The French term here is often used by itself, without any predicate (e.g., *dans l'expérience*). Psychoanalytic experience is usually what is at issue, but not always. The term also means experiment, as in a scientific experiment, and it is not always clear which is intended.

Instance

Lacan's *instance*, like Freud's *Instanz*, is often translated here as "agency," especially when Lacan is talking about the various Freudian agencies (id, ego, and superego). However, *instance* also implies a power or authority (as when we speak of a Court of the First Instance), and an *insistent*, urgent force, activity, or intervention. "Agency" in no way conveys the *insistence* so important to Lacan's use of the term in such contexts. *Instance* also means a particular example or case of something (cf. *enstasis*, the obstacle one raises to an adversary's argument or the exception to a universal predicate, hence an instance or counterinstance that refutes a general claim), as Lacan indicates in Seminar XX, 65.

Jouissance

I have assumed that the kind of enjoyment beyond the pleasure principle (including orgasm) denoted by the French *jouissance* is well enough known by now to the English-reading public to require no translation.

Langue and *Langage*

I have consistently translated both *langage* and *langue* as "language," but I always include the French in brackets after *langue* to allow the English reader to distinguish them.

Manque-à-être

Lacan himself apparently selected the English translation "want-to-be," no doubt at least in part due to its polyvalence. I have generally adopted that translation, though in certain instances I have preferred other renderings, such as "lack of being" and "failure to be."

Méconnaissance

This term is very common in French, and in certain contexts is best translated as "ignorance," "neglect," or "oversight"; similarly, the verb form, *méconnaître*, is often best translated as "to overlook," "to misunderstand," "to be unaware of," "to omit," "to ignore," "to neglect," or "to disregard." Lacan sometimes uses this term to refer to an almost deliberate misrecognition or misunderstanding of something (e.g., an idea or a wish), a knowledge (or knowing) that is missed or botched almost on purpose; in those cases, I render it as "misrecognition" or "misrecognize."

Négation and *Dénégation*

The importance of negation and the different forms it can take is at least as crucial to Lacan's work as it is to Freud's. Many of the terms Lacan uses to talk about it are either accepted translations or his own translations of Freud's terms, each of which has certain technical and/or idiomatic uses in German, which do not necessarily coincide with idiomatic uses in French—all of which is compounded in translating these terms into English.

The rarest, *Verwerfung*, is the easiest from a translator's standpoint; Lacan translates it first as *rejet* (rejection) and *retranchement* (excision, suppression, subtraction, deduction, retrenchment, or entrenchment; see *Écrits* 1966, 386), and then more consistently as *forclusion* (foreclosure). The verb form in French is *forclore*, translated here as "to foreclose." Freud's clearest statement about foreclosure is found in "The Neuro-Psychoses of Defence" (*GW* I, 72, and *SE* III, 58); there Strachey translates the verb form *verwirft* as "rejects."

Verneinung (negation) is rendered in French in two different ways: *négation* and *dénégation*. I render both as either "negation" or "denial," depending on the context. I translate the corresponding French verb, *nier*, as either "to negate" or "to deny," depending on the context.

Verleugnung (disavowal) is rendered in French in two different ways: *déni* and *désaveu*. *Dénier* (the verb form) is very close in French usage to *nier*, but I always translate the former as "to disavow" (except when I include the French in brackets).

Objectivation

The French here means objectification, in the two related senses of the term: turning something into an object and, perhaps more usually, rendering something objective (not necessarily in the absolute sense, but in the sense of putting something "outside" in such a way that others can observe or study it).

Oblativité

A supposed tendency to give to others selflessly or disinterestedly, discussed in French analytic texts of the 1950s, translated here as "oblativity" (the adjectival form being "oblative"). The term was introduced by Laforgue in 1926 and was rendered as "self-sacrifice" in Lacan's "Some Reflections on the Ego," *IJP* XXXIV, 1 (1953): 17.

Réel

This term is often used by French authors as an alternate term for *réalité* (reality), without any reference whatsoever to the Lacanian category of the real. Lacan himself often uses the term in this way, and always does so *prior* to developing his formulation of the real in juxtaposition to the imaginary and the symbolic in the early 1950s. It is not always obvious whether it should be translated as "real" or "reality" after that time, and so I provide the French in brackets whenever I translate it as "reality" in texts written after the 1940s.

Savoir and *Connaissance*

French generally distinguishes between *savoir*, as a factual, explicit, articulated kind of knowledge (e.g., knowing the date of a particular historical event), and *connaissance* as a more experiential kind of knowing (e.g., knowing a person or how to speak a language), though there are numerous exceptions to this rough and ready categorization. See, in particular, Lacan's discussion in "Subversion of the Subject" (*Écrits* 1966, 803). I have translated both *savoir* and *connaissance* as "knowledge," though I provide *savoir* in brackets after the word "knowledge" when it appears in texts before 1950 and *connaissance* in brackets after the word "knowledge" when it appears in texts after 1950, 1950 marking a kind of tipping of the scales in Lacan's usage of the terms from *connaissance* to *savoir*. Note that *connaissance* can also mean consciousness and is thus rendered accordingly when the context seems to call for it.

Semblable

This term is often translated as "fellow man" or "counterpart," but in Lacan's usage it refers specifically to the mirroring of two imaginary others (*a* and *a*′) who *resemble* each other (or at least see themselves in each other). "Fellow man" corresponds well to the French *prochain*, points to man (not woman), the adult (not the child), and suggests fellowship, whereas in Lacan's work *semblable* evokes rivalry and jealousy first and foremost. "Counterpart" suggests parallel hierarchical structures within which the two people take on similar roles, that is, symbolic roles, as in "The Chief Financial Officer's counterpart in his company's foreign acquisition target was Mr. Juppé, the *Directeur financier*." Jacques-Alain Miller has suggested that we translate *semblable* as "alter ego," but since "alter ego" is also occasionally used independently by Lacan and since it has a number of inapposite connotations in English ("a trusted friend" and "the opposite side of one's personality"), I have preferred to revive the somewhat obsolete English "semblable" found, for example, in *Hamlet*, Act V, Scene II, line 124: "his semblable is his mirror; and who else would trace him, his umbrage, nothing more." It was still used by Virginia Woolf in *Between the Acts* (New York: Harcourt, Brace and Company, 1941).

Sens and *Signification*

These two terms are often synonymous and are translated as "meaning" in most contexts. In linguistics, however, a distinction is generally made between *signification* as a psychological process and *sens* as a static term for the mental image resulting from that psychological process. Given the linguistic horizon of so much of Lacan's work, I have translated *sens* as "meaning" and *signification* as "signification," except when indicated. *Sens,* of course, also means direction and sense. See Lacan's later comments on *sens* and *signification* in "L'étourdit" in *Autres Écrits* (Paris: Seuil, 2001), 479–80.

Signifiance

This French term, which I generally translate as "signifierness," might also be translated as "significance," "signifyingness," or "meaningfulness." According to André Lalande's *Vocabulaire technique et critique de la philosophie* (Paris: PUF, 1976), the term was introduced into French linguistics in the 1960s, deriving from the English "significance," and is related to the English "connotation." According to the *Dictionnaire historique de la langue française* (Paris: Robert, 1994), "The word, which until recently was no longer in use, was taken up anew in the vocabulary of semiology and semiotics, designating (probably modeled on the English "significance") the fact of having meaning, opposed to *non signifiance*." Lacan uses it to translate the *deutung* of Freud's *Traumdeutung* (*Écrits* 1966, 623), which Strachey renders as "interpretation." In the course of Lacan's work, it takes on the meaning of "signifierness" or the "signifying nature" of signifiers—in other words, the sense in which the signifier dominates the signified. See, in particular, Lacan's "Instance of the

Letter" (1957) where he equates it with *l'effet signifiant,* the signifying effect or signifier effect (*Écrits* 1966, 515, fn2).

Le signifiant
The French here, generally translated as "the signifier," is subject to the same translation headaches as many other singular French nouns: the French tend to use singulars where in American English we would be more likely to use plurals. (In speaking of women, for example, the French would be likely to talk about *la femme* not *les femmes.*) In certain contexts, I have preferred to translate *le signifiant* as "signifiers" (providing the French in brackets), but it should be kept in mind that Lacan also conceives of "the signifier" as forming a system and as collectivizable and unquantifiable in certain respects (see, for example, Seminar XX on this point).

Sujet
Like *réel, sujet* (subject) is often used by French authors, and by Lacan himself—at all periods of his work—to refer simply to the subject of a study or experiment, to a patient, or to a person without any reference whatsoever to the Lacanian distinction between the ego and the subject (however the Lacanian subject is conceived of). While I always translate *sujet* as "subject," it should be kept in mind that the technical Lacanian sense often is not intended (indeed, sometimes the meaning of "the topic at hand" is primary). Grammatically, *sujet* is masculine, but it can obviously refer to a man or a woman.

Subjectivation
The French here means either subjectification—turning someone (or something) into a subject—or the fact of rendering something subjective, which I have translated here as "subjectivization." Similarly, *subjectiver* (the verb form) can mean either to subjectify or to subjectivize. It is often unclear which term should be used.

Notes on Texts

In these notes, the numbers in parentheses refer first to the page numbers of the original French edition, *Écrits* 1966—which are provided in the margins of the present translation—and then, after a comma, to the paragraph number (partial and short paragraphs are counted, as well as section titles and epigraphs) or footnote number (abbreviated "fn"; "367,fn1" refers, for example, to the first footnote that appears on French page 367 and not to the actual number of the footnote in the text as a whole, the English edition's footnotes being consecutively numbered, unlike the French edition's). References to Lacan's Seminars are to the volume number and the original French pagination, and then (after a slash) to that of the published English edition, when available (in the case of Seminars III and XX, I provide only the French pagination since it is included in the margins of the English editions). In these notes, words found in parentheses after French text indicate the corresponding text in the English translation.

Notes to "Overture to this Collection"

(9,2) "*Le style est l'homme même*" (The style is the man himself) is from George-Louis Leclerc Buffon (1707–1788) in his discourse to the *Académie Française* upon his election as a member of that prestigious literary association on August 25, 1753. See *Discours sur le style* (Paris: Hachette, 1843). It can be found in English in *The Portable Enlightenment Reader*, ed. Isaac Kramnick (New York: Viking, 1995), 319–22. Regarding the *linge parant Buffon en train d'écrire* (the cloth that adorned Buffon while he wrote), Séchelles' *Voyage à Montbard* indicates that Buffon wore a grey silk bonnet and a red dressing gown with white stripes while he wrote. The *linge* here perhaps alludes to the role of pieces of cloth as transitional objects—tickle blankets, blankies, or nappies—associated by Lacan with object *a* (see *Écrits* 1966, 814). Here it is perhaps object *a* that obscures or replaces "man." Séchelles also indicates that Buffon considered man inseparable from his clothing and could not write unless he was dressed in accordance with the solemnity of his subject matter. Cf. Lacan's comments on Picasso and his parakeet and the expression *l'habit ne fait pas le moine* in Seminar XX, 12.

(9,3) See Marie-Jean Hérault de Séchelles (1759–1794), *Voyage à Montbar* (Paris: Solvet, 1785). The book was published anonymously, perhaps not at Séchelles' bidding, in 1785 as *Visite à Buffon*, and contains details about Buffon's character and writings based on Séchelles' discussions with Buffon at the latter's home. The year IX in the revolutionary calendar corresponds to 1801. The text can be found in a more recent edition, entitled *Buffon: Biographie Imaginaire et Réelle*, by Yann Gaillard, followed by the "Voyage à Montbard" by Hérault de Séchelles (Paris: Hermann, 1977). *Le propos* (the saying) here is "the style is the man himself."

(9,4) *Un fantasme du grand homme* (a fantasy of the great man) could also be rendered as "one of the great man's fantasies." It is not entirely clear who *qui* (which I have rendered by Buffon) refers to here: it could be Séchelles, Buffon, or possibly even the fantasy itself, in which case we would have to read: "the fantasy organizes him in a scenario . . ." See Voltaire's *Candide*.

(9,6) See *Écrits* 1966, 298. The interlocutor was Claude Lévi-Strauss.

(10,1) See the end of the "Seminar on 'The Purloined Letter,' " *Écrits* 1966, 41.

(10,2) The *maître à penser* (intellectual master) in question seems quite clearly to be Poe's Dupin.

(10,4) This is a likely reference to the "inner eight" found in Seminar XI, 143/156. It could perhaps refer instead to the Möbius strip (see Seminar IX).

(10,5) The idea here is presumably that one can thus *already* find in Lacan's 1956 "Seminar on 'The Purloined Letter'" ideas that were not fully developed until the 1960s.

(10,6) *Petit a* (little *a*) also sounds like *petit tas*, little pile.

(10,7) On style and the object, see *Écrits* 1966, 740. *Que leur adresse commande* (which the audience to whom they were addressed required) can also be rendered as "which their skill required." *Mettre du sien* (pay the price with elbow grease) has a number of different meanings: provide some good will, work hard at it, and contribute something of one's own. For a discussion of this "Overture," see Judith

Miller's illuminating essay, "Style Is the Man Himself" in *Lacan and the Subject of Language*, ed. Mark Bracher (New York & London: Routledge, 1991), 143–51.

NOTES TO "SEMINAR ON 'THE PURLOINED LETTER'"

(11,2) The epigraph is from Goethe's *Faust*, Part I; in Walter Kaufmann's translation: "And if we score hits / And everything fits, / It's thoughts that we feel." The reader who compares the French and English will note that I have sometimes placed words in quotes that Lacan does not put in quotes; this is either because they come directly from Baudelaire's translation of Poe's story or because they seem to be Lacan's own rendition of parts of Poe's story.

(11,3) *Automatisme de répétition* (repetition automatism): Lacan does not employ here the more usual French translation of Freud's *Wiederholungszwang* (usually translated into English as "repetition compulsion"), which is *compulsion de répétition*.

Lacan uses a term here, *ex-sistence*, which was first introduced into French in translations of Heidegger's work (e.g., *Being and Time*), as a translation for the Greek *ekstasis* and the German *Ekstase*. The root meaning of the term in Greek is standing outside of or standing apart from something. In Greek, it was generally used for the "removal" or "displacement" of something, but it also came to be applied to states of mind which we would now call "ecstatic." (Thus a derivative meaning of the word is "ecstasy.") Heidegger often played on the root meaning of the word, "standing outside" or "stepping outside oneself," but also on its close connection in Greek with the root of the word for "existence." Lacan uses it to talk about "an existence which stands apart from," which insists as it were from the outside, to talk about something not included on the inside, something which, rather than being intimate, is "extimate."

(11,5) *Prägung* is also sometimes translated as "imprinting"; cf. *Écrits* 1966, 431. *Imprégnation* (impregnation) has many meanings in French, including fecundation of the ovum and the passing on of hereditary influences; penetration of a substance into the matter of a body (absorption) or the trace left by such a substance; the coloration of tissues; diffuse and profound penetration into the mind of ideas or feelings that are slowly assimilated; the action and influence of external stimuli on the "subconscious"; and the phase of development in which an animal becomes attached to the first being or object it sees (imprinting).

I have been unable to find *partialisations* (partializations) in any dictionary, but *partialiser* can be found in Cotgrave's 1611 *Dictionarie of French and English*, where it is defined as "to partialize, side, be partial, or take sides." In the seventeenth century, *partialité* meant division or faction. The *Oxford English Dictionary* provides the following meanings for "partialize": 1) to take a part or side, favor one side unduly or unjustly; 2) to render partial or one-sided, to divide into parties; 3) to concern oneself with a part and not the whole; and 4) to make partial as opposed to universal.

Allure (appearance) can also mean speed, pace, gait, cadence, distinction, style, class, and trim (as in sailing). It is essentially a false cognate of the English "allure."

(12,3) See Seminar II, chapter 15 and the beginning of chapter 16.

(13,1) Lacan cites Baudelaire's translation here—"retournée, la souscription en dessus" (turned over, the address facing up)—whereas Poe writes, "The address, however, was uppermost, and, the contents thus unexposed . . ."

(13,4) See endnote to *Écrits* 1966, 16, paragraph 7, regarding this "second time." Reading *trois* (three) for *dix-huit* (eighteen): Lacan seems to confuse the length of time he himself spent working on the combinatory analysis found in the "Suite" to "The Seminar on 'The Purloined Letter' "—eighteen months, as he tells us later (*Écrits* 1966, 39)—with the figure Poe provides when he has the Prefect say, "For three months a night has not passed . . ."

(14,5) "So fatal a scheme, / If not worthy of Atreus, is worthy of Thyestes." These lines are from Atreus' monologue in Act V, Scene V, lines 13–15, of Prosper-Jolyot de Crébillon's play, *Atrée et Thyeste* (1707). They refer to Atreus' plan to take revenge on his brother Thyestes (who had stolen his wife from him some twenty years earlier) by serving him his own son's blood to drink.

(15,8) *Autruiche* condenses *autruche* (ostrich), *Autriche* (Austria), *autrui* (other people), *tricher* (to trick), and perhaps other words as well. *Politique* means politics or policy.

(16,1) See Seminar II, chapters 13 and 14. On other possible translations of *discours de l'Autre* (the Other's discourse), see *Écrits* 1966, 814, where it is translated as "discourse about the Other."

(16,7) This is actually the third "Dupin tale"; the first two were "The Murders in the Rue Morgue" and "The Mystery of Marie Rogêt."

(17,6) *Ordonnance de fiction* (fictional ordering) could also be rendered as "fictional order," "order as fiction," or "fictional prescription." Cf. *Écrits* 1966, 808, where Lacan says that "it is from Speech that Truth receives the mark that instates it in a fictional structure."

(19,6) See Freud's *Group Psychology and the Analysis of the Ego*, especially *SE* XVII, 116.

(20,1) A probable reference to "Function and Field."

(20,2) See *SE* VIII, 115, where the text is somewhat different: "What a liar you are!" broke out the other. "If you say you're going to Cracow, you want me to believe you're going to Lemberg. But I know that in fact you're going to Cracow. So why are you lying to me?"

(21,2) See Sébastien-Roch Nicolas Chamfort's *Maximes et pensées*, Part 2, 42.

(21,3) *Maîtres-mots* (magic words) refers to words imbued with special powers or with a specific energy or efficacy, sometimes also rendered as "key words."

(21,5) The Greek here literally means the unconcealed.

(21,fn1) The original note must have been written for the first edition in 1966, for I have been unable to find it in any other edition.

(22,4) The Latin here is rendered by Baudelaire as "false distribution of the middle term"; in English it is rendered as "fallacy of the undistributed middle," and refers to the failure to realize that if all A's are B's, all B's are not necessarily A's.

(22,5) *Mauvaises querelles* (unprovoked arguments) can be translated in a number of ways, including "quarrels for quarreling's sake," "quarreling for no reason," and "trumped-up quarrels," all suggesting some kind of bad faith on the part of the person who starts the argument. *Raison raisonnante* (reasoning reason) means reason that proceeds by reasoning; it is often used pejoratively.

(24,1) See 2 *Corinthians* 3.6.

(24,2) *Partitive* (partitive) is a grammatical term meaning "which considers a part in relation to a whole that cannot be counted" (*Le Petit Robert*). *Du rififi chez les hommes* (brawling among men) is a book by Auguste Le Breton (Paris: Gallimard, [1953] 1992) that was made into a film by Dassin. Cf. *Écrits* 1966, 566.

(25,4) *Pour revenir à nos policiers* (to return to our policemen) echoes Rabelais' *pour revenir à nos moutons* (to return to our sheep) in *Gargantua*. The sheep make an appearance a few pages further on.

(25,fn1) This is a collection of critical articles on Joyce's *Finnegans Wake* by Samuel Beckett, Marcel Brion, Frank Budgen, Stuart Gilbert, Eugene Jolas, Victor Llona, Robert McAlmon, Thomas McGreevy, Elliot Paul, John Rodker, Robert Sage, and William Carlos Williams, with Letters of Protest by G.V.L. Slingsby and Vladimir Dixon.

(26,3) *Les fêtes de l'amour* (Cupid's festivities) may be a reference to *Les fêtes de l'amour et de Bacchus* (The Festivities of Cupid and Bacchus), a pastoral in a prologue and three acts by Jean-Baptiste Lully, first performed in 1672.

(26,5) Father Ubu is a character in Alfred Jarry's play *Ubu Roi ou les polonais* (Paris: Eugène Fasquelle, [1888] 1922); in English see *King Turd*, trans. B. Keith and G. Legman (New York: Boar's Head Books, 1953).

(27,1) *Féconde* (enriches) also means fertilizes, makes fertile or fruitful, impregnates, inseminates, and pollinates. *Transferts* (transfers) also means transferences.

(27,2) Lacan has combined at least three different expressions in the first sentence here, leaving some uncertainty as to how it should be translated: "Les écrits emportent au vent les traites en blanc d'une cavalerie folle." *Traites (ou chèques) de cavalerie* are checks, drafts, or bills of exchange written out of politeness, even though both parties to the transaction are aware that they cannot be cashed or paid; *traites en blanc* implies that they are blank checks; *une cavalerie folle* might be rendered as "an insane charge of the cavalry." In the second sentence, "loose sheets" corresponds to *feuilles volantes* and "purloined letters" to *lettres volées.*

(27,3) Charles de Beaumont, Chevalier d'Eon (1728–1810), was a French officer and secret agent for Louis XV who was stationed at the courts of Russia and London. He first disguised himself as a woman in Russia in order to gain access to the Empress and subsequently "disguised" himself as a man. When the French government recalled him later from London, where his gallantries risked compromising the English court, he was instructed to maintain his female disguise and surrender certain compromising papers. He had maintained a confidential correspondence with Louis XV on political matters and left behind thirteen volumes of the *Loisirs du Chevalier d'Eon* (1775). Lacan may be referring here to the correspondence he published in Paris in 1778 entitled "Pièces relatives aux démêlés entre Mademoiselle d'Eon de Beaumont, chevalier de l'Ordre roial & militaire de Saint Louis & ministre plénipotentiare de France, &c. &c. &c. et le Sieur Caron, dit de Beaumarchais &c. &c. &c." After his death a physical examination proved he was in fact a man.

(27,6) *Lettre sommatoire* (demanding letter): *sommatoire* seems to be used primarily in mathematics in the term *fonction sommatoire* (summation function); that does not, however, seem to be the context implied here.

(28,1) *Foi jurée* (pledge of loyalty) can be rendered in many ways, including "her word" (i.e., she has given him her word), "pledged word," "pledge of faith," "sworn pledge," and "sworn oath." In the pages that follow here I translate *foi* in isolation as "loyalty." See Georges Davy, *La Foi jurée: Étude Sociologique du Problème du Contrat* (Paris: Félix Alcan, 1922), reprinted in *European Sociology* (New York: Arno Press, 1975).

(28,6) Figuratively, *nous ne l'avons pas volé* (I have not stolen it) means I deserve it or I earned it.

(29,3) *Souffrance* alone (i.e., not in the expression *en souffrance*) means suffering. Outside of the postal realm, *en souffrance* usually means pending or in abeyance.

(30,2) *Comme armes et bagages* (like weapons and baggage) evokes the expression to do something *avec armes et bagages*, meaning completely or with all of one's equipment, but it is not clear that this is the intended meaning here.

(30,3) *A tomber en possession de la lettre* (By coming into the letter's possession) is taken by Lacan to mean both coming to possess the letter and to be possessed by it.

(30,4) *Rapt* (theft) is more commonly used to refer to kidnapping or abduction, but the Latin root and context here suggest "theft."

(31,3) *Provigner* (multiply . . . by layering) refers to a technique for propagating plants, but is also structured like *pro-loigner.* Thus Lacan is purloining, prolonging, and propagating his own "monster" here.

(31,5) Lacan modifies the usual expression here, *lâcher la proie pour l'ombre* (literally, "to drop one's prey for a shadow," figuratively, "to forego an assured benefit for a futile hope" or "to give up what one already has to go chasing after shadows"). In his version, we find "les miroitements dont l'ombre se sert pour ne pas lâcher sa proie" (the shimmering that shadows exploit in order not to release their prey).

(31,7) Lacan comments in Seminar XVIII (May 18, 1971) that *signe* (sign) here should be understood as "letter." *En position de signifiant, voire de fétiche* (in a position as signifier, nay, as fetish) could also be rendered as "in the position of signifier (or in signifying position), or even of fetish."

(31,9) See *John* 20:17 (cf. *Écrits* 1966, 790) and Plato's *Meno,* 80a.

(32,4) A Chambre Ardente was an extraordinary legal commission under the Old Regime which had the authority to apply the punishment of fire to the condemned party. Henri II first created the Chambre Ardente in 1547 to try heretics.

(32,6) *Passer à l'acte* (become actual) would more typically mean to act out. Here the juxtaposition seems to be between a potential power and an actual (almost kinetic) power.

(34,1) *Charge* (burden) can mean weight, burden, responsibility, accusation, and even exaggerated portrait designed to ridicule someone (i.e., caricature).

(34,fn1) Poe's story actually came out (in an abridged form) in *Chambers' Edinburgh Journal* in November 1844, following its 1844 publication in the American annual, *The Gift*. See also Marcel Mauss, *The Gift: Forms and Functions of Exchange in Archaic Societies* (New York: W. W. Norton, [1925] 1967).

(36,2) *Château Saint-Ange* (Sant'Angelo's Castle) seems to be a reference to the famous castle in Rome.

(36,3) See "The Effectiveness of Symbols" in Claude Lévi-Strauss, *Structural Anthropology* (New York: Basic Books, 1963).

(36,5) Dupin was presented as a "virtual pauper taking refuge in ethereal pursuits" in "The Murders in the Rue Morgue."

(36,fn1) This seems to be a reference to Marie Bonaparte who pointed out Baudelaire's mistake in translating Poe's "beneath" the mantlepiece as *au-dessus* (above). See her *Life and Works of Edgar Allan Poe: A Psycho-Analytic Interpretation*, trans. John Rodker (New York: Humanities Press, 1971), a short selection of which can be found in *The Purloined Poe*, eds. John Muller and William Richardson (Baltimore: Johns Hopkins University Press, 1988).

(37,4) Cf. Corneille, *Le Cid*, Act 2, Scene 2, line 434: "*A vaincre sans péril, on triomphe sans gloire,*" literally, "To vanquish without peril is to triumph without glory"; in Samuel Solomon's translation, "Who conquers without danger wins dishonor"; see *Pierre Corneille: Seven Plays* (New York: Random House, 1969).

(38,4) The Latin here literally means king and soothsayer.

(38,5) *Sacré* (sacred) is also often used to mean damn or bloody, as in damn (or bloody) fool; *un sacré imbécile* would be a hell of an idiot.

(38,6) *Peu soucieux d'essuyer ses penchants indiscrets* (not very interested in enduring their indiscreet tendencies) could instead be understood as "not very concerned with mopping up (or eliminating) their indiscreet tendencies." The Latin here has been translated in a number of ways, including "Cobbler, stick to thy last" and "The shoemaker should not go beyond his last." It is the Latin version of a rebuke said to have been addressed by the artist, Apelles, to a shoemaker who began by criticizing the artist's rendition of a slipper in one of his works and then went on to criticize other aspects of the work as well. The artist's point was that the cobbler should confine his remarks to what he knows something about.

(39,7) *Il est* (he is) sounds like *il hait* (he hates) in French.

(40,1) *Monstrum horrendum*, terrifying monster, is from Virgil's *Aeneid*, Book 3, line 658.

(40,4) In quoting these lines a second time, Lacan (inadvertently?) replaces *dessein* (scheme, plan) with *destin* (destiny, fate); I have let this stand in the text owing to the context.

(40,5) *Noue* (weave) also means bind, tie up, and knot. *L'invité de pierre* (the stone guest) evokes the statue of the dead commander in the Don Juan story; see, for example, Molière's version entitled *Dom Juan ou le festin de pierre*, known in English as *Don Juan or the Stone Guest*.

(40,6) Cf. Seminar II, 240/205.

(41,5) When Lacan's "Seminar on 'The Purloined Letter' " was first published (in *La Psychanalyse* 2 (1956): 1–44), the "Introduction," which begins a couple of pages further on, preceded the main body of the "Seminar." "This text" thus seems to refer to the "Seminar" here. This prefatory "Presentation of the Suite" was added in 1966.

(41,6) *Qui de cet air, sortaient d'en prendre* (who were leaving, having gotten a feel for it) plays on the expression *prendre l'air* (to go out for a breath of fresh air) and harks back to *prendre un air* (to get a feel) in the preceding sentence, which usually means to take on an air (or airs).

(42,5) The "four pages" Lacan mentions here were, presumably, from the bottom of page 3 to the bottom of page 7 in the first edition, corresponding to pages 47–51 in *Écrits* 1966.

(42,6) *Mémoration* (remembering) is quite a rare term in French. According to the *Trésor de la Langue Française*, it means "evocation of a memory [*souvenir*] fixed (in one's mind) a longer or shorter period of time before"; it stems from the Latin *memoratio*, meaning "the action of recalling, remembering."

(42,11) See "Notiz über den 'Wunderblock,'" *GW* XIV, 3–8, and "A Note upon the 'Mystic Writing-Pad,'" *SE* XIX, 227–32.

(43,8) The imperfect *était* could suggest an alternate reading: "what was not to be."

(43,9) *Se faire valoir* (to get itself noticed) is a possible formulation of the drive.

(44,1) "Level of aspiration" seems to be a term developed by the Gestalt psychologist Kurt Lewin.

(44,2) *Planche* (blackboard) seems to refer to school slang in which the term refers either to the blackboard itself or to the fact of being called up to the blackboard by one's teacher to answer a question in writing in front of the whole class.

(44,9) See Seminar II, chapter 15.

(45,3) See, for example, Heinz Hartmann, "Technical Implications of Ego Psychology"; Hartmann affirms that "analysis is gradually and unavoidably, though hesitantly, becoming a general psychology . . ." (*PQ* XX, 1 [1951]: 35). In "The Development of the Ego Concept in Freud's Work," Hartmann also writes that "the trend toward a general psychology has been inherent in psycho-analysis from its inception" (*IJP* XXVII, 6 [1956]: 434).

(46,1) See Soren Kierkegaard's *Repetition* in *Fear and Trembling/Repetition: Kierkegaard's Writings*, Vol. 6 (Princeton, NJ: Princeton University Press, 1983).

(46,2) *Remémoration* (remembering) is defined, in the *Trésor de la Langue Française*, as "the reactivation of a memory; the action of putting something back into one's memory; the process by which the subject evokes in his consciousness events preserved in his unconscious." It is sometimes translated into English as "recalling" or "recollection."

(46,7) *Appel* is usually translated as call, appeal, or cry, and could possibly refer here to a roll call. However, in conjunction with the verb *prendre*, a sports metaphor is evoked here: in the long jump, for example, one runs a certain distance and then *prend son appel*, one "takes off" on a certain foot, *le pied d'appel* or "take-off foot." *Appel* is here the jumping-off point, so to speak, the point from which one's impulsion originates.

(47,fn1) As I have indicated at length in Appendix I of my *Lacanian Subject* (Princeton: Princeton University Press, 1995), Lacan clearly has *overlapping* series of symbols in mind here, such that the 1 in his example refers to the first three symbols found in the top line (+ + +), the first 2 to the second, third, and fourth symbols in the top line (+ + –), the first 3 to the third, fourth, and fifth symbols in the top line (+ – +), and so on.

(48,5) Since it is clear in the 1–3 Network that one cannot move from a 1 to a 3 without an intervening 2, the dash Lacan provides between the Arabic numerals must stand for one intervening symbol. Indeed, the complete set of triplets each Greek letter refers to can be represented as follows:

α	β	γ	δ
111, 123	112, 122	212, 232	221, 211
333, 321	332, 322	222	223, 233

Note that, although γ only refers to three triplets, one of them (222) has twice as high a probability of turning up as the others, establishing Lacan's point in the next paragraph.

(49,2) In other words, while any one letter may follow *directly* upon any other, any one letter may not follow *indirectly* upon any other. The case Lacan considers here, to begin with, is the determination of or limitation imposed upon the *third* position. If we begin with the letter α at Time 1, the letter at Time 2 can be α, β, γ, or δ, but we always get an α or a β at Time 3. This is because the four possible α combinations (111, 123, 333, and 321) all end in either 1 or 3 (see the table in the preceding note). As the last number of these triplets will become the first number of the Time 3 triplets, and as α and β are the only letters to comprise combinations beginning with 1 and 3, only α and β can appear at Time 3. This whole reasoning process can be repeated if, instead of α, we begin with the letter δ, for all δ combinations also end in 1 or 3. These two syntactic rules are shown on the top line of the AΔ Distribution.

On the other hand, all γ and β combinations end in 2, and since only γ and δ combinations begin with 2, only they can appear at Time 3 if there is a γ or a β at Time 1. These two syntactic rules are shown on the bottom line of the AΔ Distribution.

(50,2) The arrows in Tables Ω and O present all 16 combinations of the four letters paired up two by two (the short arrows in Table Ω give six pairs, αδ, δδ, δγ, γβ, ββ, and βα, while the long arrows give αγ and γα, for a total of eight; the other eight are found in Table O), where the first letter in each pair is situated at Time 1 and the second at Time 4. The second line in each table shows which letter is excluded at both Times 2 and 3 from each of the four pairs found in the line directly above it (e.g., δ is excluded at Times 2 and 3 from αδ, δδ, δγ, and αγ), while the third line in each table shows which letter is excluded at Time 2 and which at Time 3 from each of the four pairs found above it in the top line of the table (e.g., α is excluded at Time 2 and γ is excluded at Time 3 from αδ, δδ, δγ, and αγ).

(50,4) *Actualité* (actuality) also refers in French to that which is current or in the present. *Il* (it), often repeated here, grammatically refers to *parcours subjectif* (subjective trajectory), but might better be rendered as "the subject." Given the date of the text, one might be inclined to translate *réel* as "reality" here instead of as "real." However, a comparison of the *Écrits* 1966 text with the original published in 1956 shows that this section of the text was completely rewritten for the 1966 publication.

(50,fn1) The only place where I have been able to find the verb *quadrer* (situates in quadrants) is in Cotgrave's 1611 *Dictionarie of French and English*, where it is defined as "to square, suit, be fit, agree, or stand well with." Nevertheless, these do not seem to correspond to the likely meaning intended here, which is that of framing or placing in quadrants.

(51,6) Lacan seems to be referring to the fact that the excluded letters in lines 2 and 3 line up "directly" under the same letters in line 1 of Table Ω, whereas they line up in a "crossed" manner in Table O (the ones to the left in lines 2 and 3 corresponding to the ones to the right in line 1 and vice versa).

(52,2) *Échauffements* (excitations) also has older medical meanings, including irritations, inflammations, and slight constipations.

(52,6) *Dépasse de beaucoup en étendue* (extends far beyond) also evokes Descartes' extension, given the appearance of *matière* (matter) at the beginning of the same sentence.

(53,2) On defiles, cf. Freud's "defile of consciousness" in *SE* II, 291.

(54,2) See the general note on "oblativity" at the beginning of the translator's endnotes.

(54,9) Note that the usual French typographic convention for quotes is « and ».

(55,10) *Es* in German means it; *das Es* is the id. *Disjoint* (disjoint) could also be rendered as "disjunctive" or "disjoined."

(55,11) *Gril* (grill) has other possible meanings as well, including an openwork fence upstream of a sluice gate, an openwork floor above the loft of a theater stage, and an openwork fairing (or filleting) worksite.

(56,4) The "attempt" here seems to be to reformulate the L schema as the L chain.

(56,fn1) See Abbé de Choisy, *Mémoires de l'Abbé de Choisy habillé en femme* (Paris: Mercure de France, 1979); in English, see *The Transvestite Memoirs of the Abbé de Choisy and the Story of the Marquise-Marquis de Banneville* (London: Peter Owen, 1994).

(56,fn2) The "convention" Lacan adds here functions as follows: the periods function as blanks to be filled by either symbol, 1 or 0. 1.1 is thus to be read as 111 or 101, 1.0 as 110 or 100, and so on. I have changed the 1–3 Network so that the order in which terms are added corresponds to that of the α, β, γ, δ Network.

(58,4) *Frisure* (folds) usually refers to curls, as in curly hair. Here it seems to refer to the sulci of the brain.

(59,1) The "general narrator" says, "It is merely . . . an identification of the reasoner's intellect with that of his opponent." Lacan seems to equate intellect with reasoning here.

(60,6) In addition to meaning die (the singular of dice) and thimble, *dé* is also, in the words of *Le Robert: Dictionnaire Historique de la Langue Française*, "one of the most productive prefixes in the French language, indicating that an action takes place in reverse or is annulled."

(61,1) See Goethe's *Faust*.

Notes to "On My Antecedents"

(65,4) *Évolution Psychiatrique* was also the name of a journal which published a number of Lacan's early works.

(65,7) *Raisonnants* (related to rationality) can mean rational, accessible to reason, reasonable, logical, or affirming the primacy of reason.

(65,fn2) Lacan may have Paulette Houdyer in mind; see her *L'affaire des soeurs Papin: Le diable dans la peau* (Paris: Julliard, 1966).

(66,4) See Paul Éluard, *Poésie involontaire et poésie intentionnelle* (Paris: Seghers); cf. *Écrits* 1966, 168.

(69,5) See the last paragraph of "Beyond the 'Reality Principle,'" *Écrits* 1966, 92.

(69,9) *Causalisme* is the doctrine that science seeks causes and not merely regular antecedents.

(70,5) Lacan develops this aspect of the mirror stage at length in Seminar VIII, chapters 23–24.

(70,7) It seems possible to also read Lacan's French here, *Quoi que couvre l'image pourtant* (Regardless of what covers the image, nevertheless), as "Regardless of what the image nevertheless covers." Lacan seems to deliberately change the usual terminology later in the sentence by inverting the adjectives, saying "the depressive return of the second phase" instead of "the second return of the depressive phase."

(71,1) Reading *personne ne saurait* (no one knows) for *personne se saurait*.

(72,1) *La psychanalyse, didactique (une virgule entre)*, rendered here simply as "Training Analysis," literally means "Psychoanalysis, training (with a comma in between)."

Notes to "Beyond the 'Reality Principle'"

(73,4) As Lacan indicates (*Écrits* 1966, 69, 88, 90, and 92), this article was intended to have two parts, but the second part was never written.

(76,3) The Latin here goes back to the Scholastic philosophers, and can be rendered more or less as "Nothing is found in the intellect that was not before in the senses." Hobbes and Locke both quote it, and Leibniz gave it the proviso, *nisi intellectus ipse*, meaning "except the intellect itself."

(77,1) See Taine's *De l'intelligence* (1870), which also contains the term "polypary of images" cited on the next page.

(80,2) *Pithiatisme* (pithiatism) was the term used to designate a set of non-organic problems that could be cured or reproduced by suggestion and that were considered to be an integral part of hysteria. Joseph Babinsky introduced it in 1901.

(83,1) *Ne rien vouloir dire* idiomatically means not to mean anything. See Charles Blondel, *La conscience morbide* (Paris: F. Alcan, 1914).

(84,2) *Les corse* (gives them consistency) could also be rendered as "strengthens them," "complicates them," or "makes them more interesting." *Hors du sujet* (outside the subject) evokes *hors sujet*, which means off the topic, not relevant to the subject at hand.

(86,3) See Plutarch's chapter on Caesar in his *Lives*.

(86,5) See Ignace Meyerson, "Les images," *Journal de psychologie normale et pathologique* XVI (1929): 625–709.

(88,1) See Freud's use of the term "hominization" in *SE* XXIII, 75 and 153; it refers there to the process of becoming human.

Notes to "The Mirror Stage"

(93,1) *La fonction du Je* (*I* function) could also be rendered as "the function of the *I*" throughout this article.

(93,4) See Wolfgang Köhler, *The Mentality of Apes*, trans. Ella Winter (London: Routledge & Kegan Paul, 1927); the first German edition was published in 1917, the first English edition in 1925.

(93,6) A reference to the work of James Mark Baldwin (1861–1934), the American philosopher and psychologist.

(94,1) *Le fixer* (fix it in his mind) can mean

a number of things, including to stare at it, pin it down, and fix it in the sense in which a photographer uses fixer to develop a picture.

(94,3) See general note above on *assumer* and *assomption.*

(95,1) *Un relief de stature* (the contour of his stature) could instead be understood as "the contour of the stature." In gestalt theory, *prégnance* refers to the power forms have to impose themselves upon perception or force themselves upon us.

(95,2) *Disposition en miroir* (mirrored disposition) implies the right-left reversal characteristic of mirror images.

(95,3) On the sexual maturation of pigeons, see L. Harrison Matthews, "Visual Stimulation and Ovulation in Pigeons" in the *Proceedings of the Royal Society*, Series B, 126 (1939): 557–560. On the development of the migratory locust, see R. Chauvin's work in *Annales de la Société entomologique de France* (1941, third quarter): 133, 272. These and other references are provided in Lacan's paper "Some Reflections on the Ego," *IJP* XXXIV, 1 (1953): 11–17, and in "Remarks on Psychical Causality" in *Écrits* 1966, 189 and 190–91.

(95,fn1) In English, see "The Effectiveness of Symbols" in *Structural Anthropology*, trans. Claire Jacobson and Brooke Grundfest Schoepf (New York: Basic Books, 1963).

(96,2) See Roger Caillois, "Mimétisme et psychasthénie légendaire," *Le minotaure* VII (1935); in English, see "Mimicry and Legendary Psychasthenia," *October* XXXI (1984): 17–32.

(96,3) *Détermine* (limits) could also be translated as "specifies," "defines," "decides," or "fixes." André Breton introduced the term *peu de réalité* (scant reality) in his 1924 "Introduction au discours sur le peu de réalité"; see *Point du Jour* (Paris: Gallimard, 1970); in English, see "Introduction to the Discourse on the Paucity of Reality" in *Break of Day*, trans. Mark Polizzotti and Mary Ann Caws (Lincoln: University of Nebraska Press, 1999), 3–20.

(96,4) See Jakob von Uexküll, *Umwelt und Innenwelt der Tiere* (Berlin: Julius Springer, 1909).

(97,1) The term "fetalization" (also spelled "foetalization") was introduced by Louis Bolk; see *Das Problem der Menschwerdung* (Jena: Gustav Fischer, 1926).

(97,2) *Poussée* (pressure) is the usual translation of Freud's *Drang*, one of the components of the drive; see *SE* XIV, 122. *Quadrature* (squaring) is the French term for what is referred to in English as "the squaring of the circle" (*la quadrature du cercle*). *Récolement* (audit) is a legal term designating the operation of reading a witness' deposition back to him or her to see if he or she approves of it. In financial contexts it can also be translated as "audit," "checking," "reexamination," or "verification" (of accounts or inventory); this could lead to the following possible translation: "the inexhaustible squaring (or settling) of the ego's accounts."

(97,3) *Corps morcelé* (fragmented body) is sometimes rendered as "body in pieces."

(98,1) *Annulation* (undoing what has been done) might ordinarily be translated as cancellation, rendering null and void, or invalidation. Here, however, it seems that Lacan is directly referring to the mechanism of "undoing" (something that has been done) found in obsessive neurosis. See, in particular, *SE* X, 235–36 and 243, and *SE* XX, 119–20; in the latter, Strachey indicates that he is translating Freud's *ungeschehenmachen*, which literally means "making unhappened."

(98,4) See Charlotte Bühler, *From Birth to Maturity: An Outline of the Psychological Development of the Child* (London: Kegan Paul, Trench & Trubner, 1935).

(98,6) The French term *primaire* (rendered in the standard English translation of *narcissisme primaire* by "primary") also has the connotation of primal or primordial.

(99,1) See Jean-Paul Sartre's *Being and Nothingness*.

(99,2) Lacan's creation here, *self-suffisance* (self*-sufficiency), also suggests a note of self-complacency, self-conceit, and smugness.

(99,3) *Concentrationnaire* (concentration-camp) is an adjective that was coined after World War II to describe life in concentration camps. In the hands of certain writers it became, by extension, applicable to many aspects of life. In "Paris Alive: The Republic of Silence" Sartre wrote "Never were we [the French] freer than under the German occupation" (*Atlantic Monthly* [December 1944]: 39–40).

(99,6) See "The Passions of the Soul," in *The Philosophical Works of Descartes* (Cambridge: Cambridge University Press, 1967), 331–427.

Notes to "Aggressiveness in Psychoanalysis"

(103,2) Lacan's use of "bipolar" here is *not* a reference to the contemporary psychiatric label.

(105,3) *Angustiae* anguishes or narrow straits (of birth).

(106,3) *The Republic*, Book I, 336 ff.

(107,2) *Amour-propre*: self-love, self-regard, self-esteem, vanity, or pride.

(108,3) *Le redan et la chicane* (stepping and staggering technique) was a technique employed in military fortifications at the time of Louis XIV. *Fortifications à la Vauban* (military fortification) were unassailable fortifications designed by Sébastien le Prestre de Vauban, 1633–1707.

(109,1) *Préjudicielle* (prior) is a legal term, describing questions and costs associated with a legal judgment that must be handed down *prior* to the principal suit. It could also be translated as "preliminary" or "prerequisite." See Freud, "Negation" (*Die Verneinung*), *SE* XIX, 235.

(109,2) *Complaisance* (self-indulgence) could also be translated as "complacency."

(109,6) *Une surface sans accidents* (a smooth surface) has no topographical relief or accidental attributes.

(110,6) See Lacan's 1932 doctoral dissertation published as *De la psychose paranoïaque dans ses rapports avec la personnalité* (Paris: Seuil, 1980).

(110,7) *Kakon:* "bad (object)" in Greek.

(111,3) See Pierre Janet, "Les sentiments dans le délire de persécution," *Journal de Psychologie* XXIX (1932): 161–240 and 401–60.

(112,2) The French original of this text and *Écrits* 1966 both read *spectaculaire* (spectacular) instead of *spéculaire* three times in this article, whereas Lacan's other texts almost always read *spéculaire* (specular); *spectaculaire* should probably be understood here in the sense of "relating to or constituting a spectacle."

(112,3) See H. Wallon, *Les origines du caractère chez l'enfant: Les Préludes du sentiment de personnalité* (Paris: PUF, [1934] 1954).

(113,3) *Einfühlung* is usually rendered as "empathy," "understanding," or "sensitivity."

(113,4) *Se fixe à* (fixates on) could also be translated as "latches onto," "attaches himself to," or "freezes himself in."

(114,4) See Freud's discussion of the three possible contradictions of the single proposition, "I love him" (*SE* XII, 63–64). The three principal forms of paranoia Freud discusses there are jealousy, erotomania, and persecution. See Lacan's discussion of this in his "Discours de Rome" in *Autres écrits* (Paris: Seuil, 2001), 156–57. *Désordre* (disorder) can also be rendered as "chaos" or "mess"; it is not a reference to the eponymous psychiatric notion. On the "beautiful soul," see Hegel's *Phenomenology of Spirit*, trans. A. V. Miller (Oxford: Oxford University Press, 1977), 383.

(114,5) *The Confessions of St. Augustine*, trans. J. G. Pilkington (New York: The Heritage Press, 1963), 7. To translate the French rendition of the Latin Lacan provides (perhaps taken from a published French translation): "I saw with my own eyes and knew very well an infant in the grip of jealousy: he could not yet speak, and already he observed his foster brother, pale and with an envenomed look."

(116,2) *Désarroi* here means distress, confusion, helplessness, complete disorganization, and disarray.

(116,3) Here as elsewhere, Lacan uses *répression* (now usually reserved in French for "repression" in the political sense) instead of the more usual *refoulement* (now reserved in French for "repression" in the psychoanalytic sense).

(117,2) See, in particular, *SE* XIII, 141–43.

(117,4) See K. von den Steinen, *Unter der Natürvölker Zentralbräsiliens* (Berlin: Dietrich Reiner, 1894), 305–6, and L. Lévy-Bruhl, *Les fonctions mentales dans les sociétés inférieures* (Paris: Alcan, 1910), 77–78.

(118,1) On identity, cf. *Écrits* 1966, 213. "Je est un autre" ("I is an other") is from Rimbaud's letter to Georges Izambard dated May 13, 1871. See Arthur Rimbaud, *Oeuvres complètes* (Paris: Gallimard, 1954), 268.

(118,5) On *oblativité* (oblativity), see general note above.

(119,1) *En libérer l'altruisme* (free altruism from it) could also be translated as "free up its altruism" or "free up the altruism therein." See Maxim 113, "Il y a de bons mariages, mais il n'y en a point de délicieux," in La Rochefoucauld, *Maximes* (Paris: Garnier Frères, 1967).

(119,3) Cf. Seminar III, 287, and Seminar XX, 70, where Lacan refers to Pierre Rousselot, *Pour l'histoire du problème de l'amour au moyen âge* (Münster: Aschendorffsche Buchhandlung, 1907). Rousselot explains that "physical love" was not understood in the Middle Ages as corporal or bodily, but rather as natural love—the kind of love one finds in nature between mother bear and cub, for example (see page 3). In the translation of Saint Thomas Aquinas' *Summa Theologica* prepared by the Fathers of the English Dominican Province, it is rendered as "natural love" (Chicago: Encyclopedia Britannica, 1952) (Question 60).

(119,5) On the climacteric, see *SE* XII, 46.

(120,3) Note that *Malaise dans la civilisation* is the standard French title of Freud's *Das Unbehagen in der Kultur*, known in English as *Civilization and its Discontents*.

(120,4) *Yang* here is likely intended in the sense of "face," referring thus to the importance of saving face.

(121,2) I have assumed that where the French text reads *ces* (these), it should, in fact, read *ses* (its): "revealing in its crises . . ."

(121,4) Spartacism: the views adopted by the Spartacists in the Spartacus League, which took its inspiration from the revolt of the Roman gladiators.

(122,1) "Great winged drone" is a reference to Plato's *Republic*, 572e–573a.

(123,5) The two philosophies Lacan just mentioned are those of Darwin and Hegel.

(124,2) The French term *irresponsable* is often used like the English "irresponsible" (qualifying, for example, someone who does not think before he or she acts), but the longer-standing meaning of the French term qualifies someone who does not have to answer for his or her acts (for example, the King in certain monarchies is answerable to no one); hence my translation here: "innocent." *En rupture du ban qui voue l'homme moderne* (who has thrown off the shackles that condemn modern man) is quite ambiguous, since being *en rupture de ban* means two rather different things—being someone who has "illegally returned to a country from which he or she has been exiled" (that is, a certain kind of outlaw) and someone who has been "emancipated from the constraints of his or her condition or state"—and since it could be the *rupture* or the *ban* that "condemns modern man to the most formidable social hell."

Notes to "A Theoretical Introduction to the Functions of Psychoanalysis in Criminology"

(126,4) See Saint Paul's Epistle to the Romans 7:7, for example: "I can only know sin by means of the Law. Indeed, I would never have thought to covet had the Law not said 'Thou shalt not covet.'"

(126,5) According to the *Trésor de la Langue française*, *loi positive* (positive law) designates written law as opposed to natural or unwritten law; given what follows in the text, however, Lacan would seem to be referring either to what is known in English as positive law (existing law created by legally valid procedures)—although in French that is usually signified by *droit positif*—or to substantive law (the positive law that creates, defines, and regulates the rights and duties of parties and that may give rise to a cause of action, as distinguished from "adjective law" which pertains to the practice and procedure or legal machinery by which substantive law is determined or made effective).

(126,7) See Bronislaw Malinowski, *Crime and Custom in Savage Society* (New York: Harcourt, Brace & Company; London: K. Paul, Trench, Trubner & Co., 1926); this work is still in print by other publishers.

(127,4) "Holy Office" refers to the Catholic congregation charged with maintaining purity of faith, formerly known as the Inquisition; its name was changed in 1965 from Holy Office to Congregation for the Doctrine of the Faith. "People's Court" here probably refers to local courts in the former Soviet Union, or to Nazi Germany.

(128,1) *Scande* (scand) is the verb form of "scansion," and the infinitive *scander* is usually translated as "to scan" or "scanning" (as in scanning verse, or dividing verse into metrical feet). I have opted here to introduce a neologism—to scand, scanding—so as to distinguish the far more common contemporary uses of scanning (looking over rapidly, quickly running through a list, taking ultra-thin pictures of the body with a scanner, or "feeding" text and images in digital form into a computer) from Lacan's idea here of cutting, punctuating, or interrupting something.

(128,2) The subtitle of the *Gorgias* is "On Rhetoric; Refutative."

(128,3) *L'infatuation du Maître* (infatuation with the Master) might instead be rendered as "the Master's infatuation." On the meaning of punishment, see, for example, *Gorgias* 525B.

(128,4) See *SE* XXI, 53, and *Gorgias* 482A (sometimes rendered as "philosophy is always true")

(129,1) *Irréalise* (Unrealizes) does not seem to suggest that psychoanalysis undoes the *reality* of crime, but rather highlights its imaginary and symbolic motives or components. The *Trésor de la Langue française* gives the following meanings for *irréaliser*: to not accomplish; to render unreal by thought or imagination; to lose one's identity or personality by identifying with or projecting oneself into a different world; or to lose one's real character by taking on an enchanting or fanciful form.

(130,2) See Harald Schultz-Henke's *Der Gehemmte Mensch: Entwurf eines Lehrbuches der Neo-Psychoanalyse* (Stuttgart: Thieme, 1947).

(130,5) In American English, the more typical formulation would be "ignorance of the law is no excuse."

(130,6) Here and in the next paragraph, Lacan juxtaposes *délits* (offenses) and crimes; *délit* could be understood as an intentional crime or as a misdemeanor.

(131,1) See Franz Alexander and Hugo Staub, *Der Verbrecher und seine Richter: Ein psychoanalytischer Einblick in die Welt der Paragraphen* (Vienna: Internationaler Psychoanalytischer Verlag, 1929), translated into English by Gregory Zilboorg as *The Criminal, the Judge and the Public: A Psychological Analysis* (New York: Macmillan, 1931). The French edition also included an article by Alexander entitled "Un possédé du voyage en auto" (the man obsessed with car trips). Marie Bonaparte's text can be found in French in the *Revue Française de Psychanalyse* I, 1 (1927).

(132,1) Reading *faisaient* (place) for *faisait*.

(132,5) *Oedipisme* (Oedipalism) is a term created by Charles Blondel to designate self-mutilation of one or both eyes; see his book, *Les Auto-Mutilateurs* (1906). Although this is the only definition I have been able to find in any dictionary, Lacan seems to use it in a far more general manner in this article (cf. *Écrits* 1966, 606).

(133,1) *Puissance captatrice* (power to captivate): as an adjective, *captatrice* qualifies something that holds one's attention, something that is captivating.

(133,4) See August Aichhorn's *Verwahrloste Jugend: Die Psychoanalyse in der Fürsorgeerziehung* (Leipzig, Vienna, & Zurich: Internationaler Psychoanalytischer Verlag, 1925), translated into English as *Wayward Youth* (New York: The Viking Press, 1935). See also Kate Friedlander's *The Psycho-Analytical Approach to Juvenile Delinquency: Theory, Case-Studies, Treatment* (London: Routledge & Kegan Paul, 1947). Freud wrote a preface to Aichhorn's book that can be found in *SE* XIX, 273–78.

(134,1) See Lagache's "Contribution to the Psychology of Criminal Behaviour: Psychoanalytic Commentary on an Expert's Report," in *The Work of Daniel Lagache: Selected Writings 1938–1964*, trans. E. Holder (London: Karnac Books, 1993), 33–65, where *conduite imaginaire* (imaginary behavior) is translated as "imaginary conduct" on page 64. In French, see "Contribution à la psychologie de la conduite criminelle" in *RFP* XII (1948): 541–70.

(134,4) See Bernardino Alimena's *La premeditazione in rapporto alla psicologia, al diritto, alla legislazione comparata* ("Premeditation in Relation to Psychology, Law, and Comparative Legislation") (Torino: Bocca, 1887).

(134,5) Cesare Lombroso (1835–1909) was an Italian criminologist.

(135,2) See William Healy's *The Individual Delinquent: A Text-Book of Diagnosis and Prognosis for All Concerned in Understanding Offenders* (Boston: Little, Brown, and Co., 1915), reprinted by Patterson Smith in 1969, and partially reprinted in Joseph Jacoby's *Classics of*

Criminology (Prospect Heights, Ill.: Waveland Press, 1994).

(135,5) *Névrosique* (neurotic) is an alternate spelling for *névrotique*. See G. M. Gilbert's *Nuremberg Diary*.

(135,6) Catamnesis is the follow-up medical history of a patient. Lacan is likely alluding to Schmideberg's "The Analytic Treatment of Major Criminals: Therapeutic Results and Technical Problems" in the volume referenced in the next endnote.

(135,8–136,1) See *Searchlights on Delinquency: New Psychoanalytic Studies Dedicated to Professor August Aichhorn, on the Occasion of his Seventieth Birthday, July 27, 1948*, ed. K. R. Eissler (New York: International Universities Press, 1949). *Probation* (probation) here refers primarily to proving that a particular individual committed a crime, that is, demonstrating that individual's guilt. Older meanings include test and trial.

(137,2) See Angelo Hesnard's *L'univers morbide de la faute* (Paris: PUF, 1949).

(137,3) There is a likely reference here to Sartre's *Being and Nothingness*.

(137,5) One of the meanings of *responsabilité* (responsibility) is "obligation to endure punishment" for one's acts.

(137,6) *Fait la loi* (lays down the law) literally means makes the law, but also implies commands or is in command.

(138,4) The University of Bologna, created in the eleventh century, was an extension of the Roman law school that had been in existence there since the fifth century. The 1288 "Statutes of Bologna" regulated the use of torture in criminal proceedings. *Droit des gens* (Law of Nations) is the French term for the Latin *jus gentium*, which refers to natural law and public international law.

(139,1) See Gabriel Tarde's *La philosophie pénale*, originally published in 1890, reprinted by Éditions Cujas in Paris in 1972.

(139,3) Lacan is presumably referring here to the essay by Roger Grenier entitled "Le Rôle d'accusé" ("The Role of the Accused") published in *Les Temps Modernes* in 1947 (and republished as a separate work by Gallimard in 1948). It is perhaps worth noting what Grenier says there about "*le fait divers*" (random news item) Lacan mentioned earlier in this article: "Le fait divers se place ainsi au cœur de l'un ou l'autre des deux problèmes essentiels: ce que l'homme est dans le monde, et ce qu'il est lui-même. Rien ne saurait être plus intéressant" ("The random news item is thus situated at the heart of one or the other of two essential problems: what man is in the world and what he is himself. Nothing could be more interesting").

Irresponsabilité (*non compos mentis*) does not refer here to someone who does not take his or her responsibilities seriously, but to someone who is mentally deficient (not in his or her right mind) and thus cannot be held accountable for his or her acts.

(140,4) Joseph-Arthur Gobineau (1816–1882) was a French diplomat and writer. He discussed the concept of ketman in *Les Religions et les Philosophies dans l'Asie Centrale* (Paris: G. Crés, 1923). "Ketman" seems to refer to the deliberate dissimulation or concealment of beliefs and opinions, especially religious ones, for self-protection or for the good of the faith. *Jang* (Yang) likely refers here to the importance of saving face.

(140,5) See Georges Politzer's *Critique des fondements de la psychologie* (Paris: PUF, [1928] 2003).

(141,2) See Fritz Wittels' "The Ego of the Adolescent" in *Searchlights on Delinquency*, 256–62.

(141,4) Jeffrey Gray describes one such experiment as follows: "In a famous experiment by Shenger-Krestovnika, published in 1921, a dog was trained to salivate to a circle but not to an ellipse. The ellipse was then made progressively more like a circle. When the ratio of the axes of the ellipse was reduced to 9:8, the dog could discriminate it from a circle only with great difficulty. It showed some signs of success on this problem for about three weeks, but then its behavior was disrupted. It was unable to respond correctly not only on this difficult task, but also when presented with obvious ellipses and circles that had given it no trouble in the earlier part of the experiment. What is more, instead of coming to stand quietly in the apparatus of the past, the animal now showed extreme excitement, struggling and howling." See Gray's *Ivan Pavlov* (New York: Viking, 1980), 119–20.

(141,6) Clotho, Lachesis, and Atropos are the three Fates.

(142,6) The reference here ("genetic" psychology) is to Jean Piaget. Cf. Lacan's critique of Piaget in *Écrits* 1966, 860.

(143,1) *Vive la mort* ("Long live death") likely refers to the Francoists' "Viva la muerte!"

(143,2) *Inanisation* means "insufficient nourishment which can lead to inanition."

(143,5) Jacqueline Boutonier, "Réflexions sur l'autobiographie d'un criminel" in *RFP* XXIII (1950): 182–214. The adolescent boy she discusses in this article kills an older woman (somewhat intentionally, hoping to rob her) in her apartment, and when he feels her blood splattering on him, he runs to the sink to wash off the blood. There, he says, "I found myself facing a mirror and I looked awful. That's when I completely lost my head. I made up the story of having been attacked myself. I laid down at the entrance to the building and called out 'help'" (206). Boutonier comments that he encountered "a blood-covered 'double' in the mirror who made tangible for him the presence of an assassin" (207), and that "the assassin he had become could no longer coincide with the image [he had of himself as] a child loved by his mother" (208).

(144,1) Lacan seems to be referring here to the use of "truth serums"; cf. his comments on them in *Écrits* 1966, 258.

(144,5) That is, the subject may be led, if he has a psychotic structure, to invent something—to foment a delusion—when required to "confess to something he does not know" while drugged.

(144,6) Paulus (or Paolo) Zacchias (or Zacchia) (1584–1659) was the physician of Pope Innocent X. In his main work, *Quaestiones medico-legales* ("Questions of Legal Medicine" or "Questions of Medical Jurisprudence") (Rome, 1621–1625, republished in Amsterdam in 1651), he provided answers to hundreds of questions related to medical practice.

(145,4) The Western Electric Company undertook a large-scale study of worker productivity between 1924 and 1933 at its Electrical Works Plant in Hawthorne, Illinois, initially in partnership with the National Research Council and later with Harvard Business School.

(145,5) See Charlie Chaplin's *Monsieur Verdoux* (1947).

(146,1) *La servitude du travail* (wage slave) is quite obscure; it literally means the slavery (or constraint) of labor, and could perhaps be understood as slavery to one's job or slave labor.

(146,2) Sun Yat-sen (1866–1925) was the leader of the Chinese Kuomintang (Nationalist Party) and is known as the father of modern China; he traveled extensively in Europe and North America. See Plato's *Republic* 542C–580C.

(146,5) On "the law of the heart," see Hegel's *Phenomenology of Mind* (New York: Harper & Row, 1967), 391 ff.

(147,2) The Latin phrase *homo homini lupus*, "man is a wolf to man," was a popular Roman proverb found in Plautus' play *Asinaria*. Thomas Hobbes later used it in his work. Freud cites it in *SE* XXI, 111.

(147,5) "Organ, direction, and object" is a reference to the component parts of the drive as Freud defines it. See *SE* XIV, 122. *Couteau de Jeannot* (Jeannot knife) refers to something that retains its name even though everything about it changes; Jeannot changed the blade and the handle of his knife three times, but to him it was still the same knife. Freud refers to something similar with the term "Lichtenberg knife" in *SE* VIII, 60, fn1, and *SE* XIV, 66.

(148,1) *Intègrent* (incorporate) could also be rendered as "become one with," "join," or "enter into."

(148,4) *Grivèleries* (bill dodging) refers to cases in which someone eats a meal in a restaurant, for example, and slips out without paying the bill.

(148,8) *Un terme de constante situationnelle* (A situational constant) literally means a term of (a) situational constant (or permanent feature); it might possibly be understood as a "limit-term invariant." Cf. Lacan's discussion of the "constancy" of the drives in *Écrits* 1966, 846–47, including the footnote on 847.

(148,9) *Fatales* (fateful) also means inevitable or fatal.

(149,4) "Strife and Love" is a reference to Empedocles' *Philia* and *Neikos*. Cf. Freud, *SE* XXIII, 246.

Notes to "Presentation on Psychical Causality"

(151,5) The reference here is to Bernard le Boyer de Fontenelle (1657-1757), a poet, playwright, moralist, and philosopher (cf. *Écrits* 1966, 782), who reputedly said, "If my hand were full of truths, I certainly wouldn't open it for men to see them."

(152,1) Reading *Je vous laisse juger de* (I'll let you be the judge of) instead of *Je vous laisse de juger*.

(152,4) For a later account of some of the same material in English, see "Hughlings Jackson's Principles and the Organo-dynamic Concept of Psychiatry," *American Journal of Psychiatry*, 118 (1962): 673–82.

(152,5) *L'étendue* (material substance) is the term for Descartes' *res extensa* (extended or material substance, a material thing), as opposed to *res cogitans* (thinking substance, a thinking thing). It is sometimes rendered simply as "extension."

(153,fn1) Reading "1946" for "1945."

(154,2) Benedict de Spinoza, *A Spinoza Reader*, trans. Edwin Curley (Princeton: Princeton University Press, 1994), 86.

(154,4) *Omnitudo realitatis* (literally, "the sum total of reality") is Kant's definition of God in *The Critique of Pure Reason*.

(154,6) In psychiatry, "agnosia" is the partial or total inability to recognize objects by use of the senses. The adjectival form is "agnostic."

(155,1) Gelb and Goldstein discuss this patient, Schneider, in numerous works, including "Zur Psychologie des optischen Wahrenhmungs- und Erkennungsvorganges (Psychologische Analyse hirnpathologischer Fälle auf Grund von Untersuchungen Hirnverletzter, l.") in *Zeitschrift für die gesamte Neurologie und Physiologie* 41 (1918): 1–143, part of which can be found in English in *A Source Book of Gestalt Psychology* (London: Routledge & Kegan Paul, 1938), 315–25. References to other discussions of Schneider by Gelb and Goldstein and by Bénary and Hochheimer can be found in Maurice Merleau-Ponty's detailed discussion of this case in *Phenomenology of Perception*, trans. Colin Smith (London: Routledge & Kegan Paul, [1945] 1962), 103–147.

(157,4) The reference here is to Hippolyte Taine (1828–1893), the French philosopher, historian, and literary critic.

(158,2) *Était resté lettre morte* (remained a dead letter) could also be rendered "went unheeded."

(159,2) *Amour-propre* (pride) can also be rendered as "self-love," "self-regard," "self-esteem," or "vanity."

(160,2) Polyxena was the daughter of Priam and Hecuba.

(160,4) Reading *C'est qu'il* (This is because it), as in the original version of the text, for *C'est qu'l* (obvious typographical error).

(161,2) Reading *que partout ailleurs* (than anywhere else), as in the original version of the text, for *partout ailleurs* (leading to a non-grammatical phrase).

(161,5) Politzer, who advocated the foundation of a "concrete psychology," failed to write the majority of the works he announced (his *Critique des fondements de la psychologie* was to be the first of three parts of a larger work entitled *Matériaux pour la critique des fondements de la psychologie*, which itself was announced as preliminary to a projected *Essai critique sur les fondements de la psychologie*). In 1929 he became a member of the Communist Party and abandoned psychology.

(161,6) Deucalion was the son of Prometheus who survived a deluge with Pyrrha, his wife. Setting sail from Thessalia, Hermes told him to throw the bones of their mothers overboard to repopulate the earth, which he did knowing that they were but stones. From the stones men and women were born.

(161,7) *Menée* (ploy) usually means plotting, intrigue, or maneuver in the plural; in the singular, however, it also means the path taken by a deer in fleeing from a hunter (an escape route) and the small movement of a gear in a clock's mechanism as one tooth takes the place of the next.

(162,5) Lacan is parodying Molière's line in *The Imaginary Invalid*, "Dignus, dignus est intrare in nostro docto corpore" (third interlude).

(163,1) *Lumières* (enlightened intellects) literally means lights, and *leur en aura assez fait voir* (has given [them] a hard enough time) literally means "has given [them] enough to see."

(163,4) See Descartes, *Discourse on Method and Meditations on First Philosophy*, trans. Donald A. Cress (Indianapolis & Cambridge: Hackett, 1998), "First Meditation," 60.

(163,6) *Dans le coup* (involved) more colloquially means "in on the action (or deal or secret)," "hip," or "in the know."

(166,3) "Healthy minds in healthy bodies" (*mens sana in corpore sano*) is from Juvenal's *Satires* X, 356. Charles Blondel, *La conscience morbide* (Paris: F. Alcan, 1914).

(166,5) The Latin *flatus vocis* means a mere name, word, or sound without a corresponding objective reality, and was used by nominalists to qualify universals. On the soul and its passions, see "The Passions of the Soul," in *The Philosophical Works of Descartes* (Cambridge: Cambridge University Press, 1967), 331–427.

(166,7) I have not been able to find *abîmes de l'existence* (abysses of existence) in Pascal's work, but one finds *abîme de l'existence* in Chateaubriand's work.

(166,8) *Noeud* also means knot, and I translated it earlier in this text as "noose."

(167,1) A reference to Stendhal's novel, *Lucien Leuwen*. On Polonius, see *Hamlet*, Act III, Scene 4.

(167,3) *L'insensé* (nonsense) also means that which is insane (as an adjective) and the insane (as a noun).

(167,4) *Figement* (fixation) also refers in linguistics to the process by which the elements of a syntagm lose their autonomy.

(168,2) Diafoirus comes from Monsieur Diafoirus, the name given to a charlatan physician by Molière in *Le malade imaginaire*, best known in English as *The Imaginary Invalid*. According to the Pléiade edition of Molière's *Oeuvres complètes*, vol. II (Paris: Gallimard, 1971), this word, with a pedantic Latin ending, is made up of *dia*, from the Greek "to cross," and *foire*, meaning market, but also meaning "the course (or flow) of the stomach" in the medicine of the time.

(169,10) *Moments féconds* (fertile moments) may be related to Freud's term, "productive stage" of hysteria (see *SE* II, 17). Cf. Seminar III, 26, and *Écrits* 1966, 180.

(170,6) Descartes, *Discourse on Method and Meditations on First Philosophy*, 60, translation modified. See Jules de Gaultier, *Le Bovarysme* (Paris: Mercure de France, 1902).

(170,8) Louis II of Bavaria is also known as Mad King Ludwig (1845–1886).

(171,3) See Las Cases, *Mémorial de Sainte-Hélène* (1823).

(171,5) On "the law of the heart," see Hegel's *Phenomenology of Mind* (New York: Harper & Row, 1967), 391 ff.

(172,4) The paragraph begins with a paraphrase of Molière's well known "Ah! Qu'en termes galants ces choses-là sont mises!" from *Le Misanthrope*, Act I, Scene 2.

(172,fn2) Hyppolite's thesis was published as *Genèse et structure de la Phénomenologie de l'esprit*, and translated into English as *Genesis and Structure of Hegel's Phenomenology of Spirit*, trans. S. Cherniak and J. Heckman (Evanston: Northwestern University Press, 1974). Alexandre Kojève's notes were edited by Raymond Queneau and published as *Introduction à la lecture de Hegel: Leçons sur la Phénoménologie de l'Esprit professées de 1933 à 1939 à l'École des Hautes Études* (Paris: Gallimard, 1947). They were abridged and translated into English by James H. Nichols, Jr., and published as *Introduction to the Reading of Hegel: Lectures on the Phenomenology of Spirit* (New York: Basic Books, 1969).

(173,1) Shlomo Avineri, in his *Hegel's Theory of the Modern State* (Cambridge: Cambridge University Press, 1973), cites a passage from a letter by Hegel to Niethammer: "This morning I saw the Emperor [Napoleon]—this world-soul (*diese Weltseele*)—ride through town [. . .]. It is a marvelous feeling to see such a personality, concentrated in one point, dominating the entire world from horseback [. . .]. It is impossible not to admire him" (October 13, 1806). Kojève discussed Hegel's admiration for Napoleon in his *Lectures*.

(173,6) *Foyer* (focal point) also means fire, *rayonnant* (radiating) also means radiant, and *feux* (passions) also means lights and fires.

(174,2) This and all the other lines from Molière's *Le Misanthrope* are from Richard Wilbur's translation in *The Misanthrope and Tartuffe* (New York: Harcourt, Brace & World, 1965), which I have slightly modified. The first two quotes are from Act I, Scene 1; the third is from Act IV, Scene 3.

(174,8) "J'aime mieux ma mie, au gué" is apparently a line from an old song; it means roughly "I love my beloved better." See Act I, Scene 2.

(175,3) *Kakon* means "bad (object)" in Greek.

(175,7) Regarding "Secret Note," Lacan seems to be referring to Descartes' notebooks, which were published in Latin as *Cogitationes Privatae* by Adam and Tannery in volume X of their complete works of Descartes entitled *Oeuvres*. Regarding "advances behind a mask," cf. Descartes' "larvatus pro deo," literally "I advance masked before God." Cf. Lacan's "Radiophonie" in *Autres écrits* (Paris: Seuil, 2001), 437.

(176,9) A reference to Flaubert's *Madame Bovary*.

(177,6) The Greek here is Pindar's phrase "Become such as you are"; see, for example, *Pindar: Olympian Odes, Pythian Odes*, trans. William H. Race (Cambridge, Mass.: Harvard University Press, 1997), 239.

(180,3) The term "paranoiac knowledge" had already appeared in print by the time Lacan published this article, although it had not yet at the time he gave this talk. See "The Mirror Stage," *Écrits* 1966, 94, and "Aggressiveness in Psychoanalysis," *Écrits* 1966, 111.

(181,1) *Écrits* 1966 reads *spectaculaire* (spectacular) here instead of *spéculaire* (specular) as most of Lacan's later texts do; *spectaculaire* should probably be understood here in the sense of "relating to or constituting a spectacle." On Augustine, see *Écrits* 1966, 114.

(182,4) *Du complexe* (of the [Oedipus] complex) could, instead, be rendered as "of complexes."

(182,7) *Où l'expérience les a faits d'abord apercevoir* (for it was the latter that first allowed these effects to be perceived by analysis) could, alternatively, be rendered as "for it was the latter that analysis first exposed."

(185,1) This article was most recently reprinted, under the title "Les complexes familiaux dans la formation de l'individu," in *Autres écrits* (Paris: Seuil, 2001), 23–84. See especially pages 36–45.

(185,6) See Jean Lhermittes, *L'image de notre corps* (Paris: Nouvelle Revue Critique, 1939).

(186,1) Aristotle's illusion is that with one's fingers crossed, one touch stimulus feels like two.

(187,8) The age of reason is usually considered to be seven by the French. However, in the text Lacan cites here (*un enfant n'est pas un homme*), "Discours sur les passions de l'amour" (attributed to Pascal), the author suggests that the age of reason rarely begins before the age of twenty.

(188,2) See Descartes, "The Passions of the Soul," in *The Philosophical Works of Descartes*, 331–427.

(188,4) Here is an alternate rendition: "When man, seeking the emptiness of thought, advances in the faint gleam of imaginary space that casts no shadow, expecting nought from what might emerge from it, a mirror without lustre shows him a surface in which nothing is reflected."

Notes to "Logical Time and the Assertion of Anticipated Certainty"

(199,1) Cf. Sartre's *Huis Clos* (*No Exit*) and his comment in "Paris Alive: The Republic of Silence": "Never were we [the French] freer than under the German occupation" (*Atlantic Monthly* [December 1944]: 39–40).

(199,3) "Resolution" should probably be understood here in the sense in which it is used at times in physics: the act of breaking down or transforming something into its component parts (for example, the resolution of a beam of white light into its various constituent wavelengths). "Forms" here refers to the different types of reasoning catalogued and examined in classical logic; at certain other points in the text, it designates modes of reasoning in general.

(200,4) Reading *leur* (to the others), as in the original version of the text, instead of *lui* (to him).

(202,4) *Expérience* (experience) also means experimentation.

(203,1) *Temps d'arrêt* (interruption) literally means "stopping time," or "time of immobility," emphasizing the length or duration of the halt, standstill, or stop as well as the stopping, suspending, or interrupting itself. "Interruption" should thus be understood here as the *duration* of a disruption, as an *intermission* lasting a certain (though unspecified) amount of time. Other possible translations of *temps d'arrêt* in technical contexts include "dwell time," "holding time," "downtime," "fault time," "outage," "waiting time," and "time drop."

(204,2) *Fuite* (slipping away) also means flight, leaking away, or fading.

(204,5) *Saisir* (discern) means to grasp, seize, understand, realize, or appropriate.

(204,7) Unlike the original version, *Écrits* 1966 has two colons between "two blacks" and "one white" here, but only one colon two paragraphs further on. I have reduced that to one colon in both places.

(205,2) *Creuse l'intervalle* (widens the interval) can be understood in the sense in which one says *creuse l'écart* between two racers or competitors, meaning extends or increases the distance or time gap between the two. *Creuser* also means to dig, excavate, or hollow out.

(206,4) While with *temps de battement* Lacan accentuates an *action*, a sort of blinking or beat(ing) of time itself, on page 208 (paragraph 1) Lacan uses the expression *battement de temps*, emphasizing the temporal component, the *duration*.

(207,1) *Scander* (scand) is the verb form of "scansion," and is usually translated as "to scan" or "scanning" (as in scanning verse, or dividing verse into metrical feet). I have opted here to introduce a neologism—to scand, scanding—so as to distinguish the far more common contemporary uses of scanning (looking over rapidly, quickly running through a list, taking ultra-thin pictures of the body with a scanner, or "feeding" text and images in digital form into a computer) from Lacan's idea here of cutting, punctuating, or interrupting something.

(212,2) Here are some possible alternate translations: "if in this race to the truth one is alone, not accompanied by everyone, in reaching the truth, still . . ." or "whether, in this race to the truth, it is but one or all who get there, nevertheless . . ."

(212,5) *Tres faciunt collegium* is a hackneyed Latin expression for "three people constitute a (decision-making) body."

(213,fn2) In the original version of the paper, Lacan indicated here that this paper was a "fragment of an *Essai d'une logique collective*" (An Attempt at a Collective Logic).

Notes to "Presentation on Transference"

(215,2) "The person" in question here was Maurice Bénassy.

(215,3) See Daniel Lagache, "Le problème du transfert" ["The Problem of Transference"], *RFP* XVI, 1–2 (1952): 5–115; a sample of Lagache's work on transference can be found in English in "Some Aspects of Transference," *IJP* XXXIV, 1 (1953): 1–10.

(215,fn1) See Bluma Zeigarnik, "Das Behalten erledigter und unerledigter Handlungen," *Psychologische Forschung* IX (1927): 1–85. In English, see "On Finished and Unfinished Tasks" in *A Source Book of Gestalt Psychology*, ed. Willis D. Ellis (New York: Harcourt-Brace 1938).

(218,5) *Son père ferme les yeux* (her father turns a blind eye) may be a reference to one of Freud's dreams, recounted in *The Interpretation of Dreams*, that includes the line "You are requested to close the eyes" (*SE* IV, 317–18).

(219,1) *"Que voulez-vous y changer?"* ("What's to be done about it?") literally means "What do you want to change therein?" but figuratively is a fatalistic, rhetorical statement akin to "That's the way it is" or "What can you do?"

(220,1) The German here means ability,

potency, capacity, power, or means.

(221,3) *Automatismes de répétition* (repetition automatisms): Lacan does not employ here the more usual French translation of Freud's *Wiederholungszwang* (usually translated into English as "repetition compulsion"), which is *compulsion de répétition.*

(222,3) The "homage" in question is presumably Herr K's lakeside proposition.

(223,8) See Madame de Lafayette, *La Princesse de Clèves* (Paris: Claude Barbin, 1678); in English, see *The Princesse de Clèves*, translated by Nancy Mitford and revised by Leonard Tancock (New York: Penguin Books, 1978).

(224,1) See *SE* IV, ix, and *SE* V, 608.

(225,1) *Une affirmation du moi* (an affirmation of the ego) could also be understood as "an affirmation by (or on the part of) the ego."

(226,2) *Sa particularité* (its particularity) could, alternatively, be rendered as "his own particularity."

Notes to "On the Subject Who Is Finally in Question"

(230,2) It might be worth recalling that in the early years of psychoanalysis especially, training analyses were very often shorter than "personal analyses," trainees leaving their home cities and countries for only a few months to undergo analysis with Freud or one of the other early pioneers. The tradition of short training analyses seems to have persisted well beyond that early stage.

(230,4) *Emporte* (leads to) could also be understood as sweeps away, carries off, wins, steals, or even kills. *La* in *la négliger* (neglecting that "personal analysis") could, instead, refer to the proposal (hence: "neglecting that proposal").

(230,8) *On noie le poisson sous l'opération de sa pêche* (we obscure the picture in the very process of painting it) literally means we drown the fish (figuratively, we divert people's attention from the topic at hand) in the very operation of fishing it out.

(232,2) *Effusion unitive* (feeling of unity) is a likely reference to Wilhelm Reich; cf. *Écrits* 1966, 342.

(232,3) Jones used the Greek term "aphanisis" to refer to the "total, and of course permanent, extinction of the capacity (including opportunity) for sexual enjoyment"; see "Early Development of Female Sexuality" (1927), in *Papers on Psycho-Analysis*, 5th edition (Boston: Beacon, 1961), 440. According to Jones, the fear of aphanisis is more fundamental than that of castration in both sexes, castration being only a "special case" of aphanisis in boys. Cf. *Écrits* 1966, 687. Ferenczi introduced the term "amphimixis" to refer to "the synthesis of two or more eroticisms into a higher unity"; see his *Thalassa: A Theory of Genitality*, trans. H. Bunker (London: Karnac Books, [1924] 1989).

(233,3) Lacan discusses Heinrich Heine's condensation "famillionaire" (including familiar and millionaire) at length in Seminar V. See Freud, *SE* VIII, 12–13.

(234,5) *Défaut* (failure) also means lack or defect.

(234,6) Lacan discusses Marx in some detail in Seminar XVI.

(234,9) It is not clear whether Lacan is referring to the "two senses of the term" *symptôme* (symptom), *propre* (proper)—which could be rendered as "own," "characteristic," or even "clean"—or *opération* (operation), which also means opening up.

(234,10) Lacan is referring to the expression *il n'y a pas de fumée sans feu*, where there's smoke there's fire.

(235,4) *Être stupide au critère* (to be dumbfounded by the criterion) could be rendered instead as "to be numb to the criterion); *critère* can also mean proof or reason.

(236,4) Lacan is presumably referring here to Anthony Wildens' early translation of Lacan's "The Function and Field of Speech and Language in Psychoanalysis," published in *The Language of the Self* (Baltimore: Johns Hopkins University Press, 1975); Wilden also helped Lacan translate a talk he gave at Johns Hopkins in 1966, entitled "Of Structure as an Inmixing of an Otherness Prerequisite to Any Subject Whatever," published in *The Structuralist Controversy* (Baltimore and London: Johns

Hopkins University Press, 1970), 186–201. The second student is probably Jan Miel who translated "L'instance de la lettre dans l'inconscient" as "The Insistence of the Letter in the Unconscious" in *Yale French Studies* 36/37 (1966): 112–47.

(236,5) Du *psychanalyste* (*some* psychoanalyst) is a rather oddly formed expression, but deliberately so here: Lacan seems to want to indicate with this syntagm that while it is perhaps too much to hope for to be able to point to some people who are *fully* psychoanalysts, we can hope that there will be people who are psychoanalysts in at least some respect, that is, who are imbued with the analyst's desire at least at some level.

Notes to "Function and Field"

(239,5) *Soutenance* (claims) literally means a thesis defense; it could, perhaps, also be translated here by "justifications."

(241,9) "Them" (*les*) at the end of the sentence presumably refers to "the side" and "the disorder."

(242,5) A probable reference to Michael Balint's "Changing Therapeutic Aims and Techniques in Psycho-Analysis" (1949) in *Primary Love and Psychoanalytic Technique* (London: Hogarth Press, 1952).

(243,2) On the analyst's being, see "Direction of the Treatment."

(243,3) *Pédagogie maternelle* (child's education by its mother) may be a reference to Anna Freud's "maternal education."

(244,2) *Égarement* (confusion) here could also be translated as "madness."

(244,5) See "Obsessive Actions and Religious Practices," *SE* IX, 117.

(245,1) Lacan presumably means that it is futile "to explain a symptom" to a patient "by its meaning as long as the latter is not recognized" by the patient, and that "in the absence of such recognition, analytic action can only be experienced as aggressive" by the patient.

(245,2) *Annulation* (undoing what has been done) might ordinarily be translated as cancellation, rendering null and void, or invalidation. Here, however, it seems that Lacan is directly referring to the mechanism of "undoing" (something that has been done) found in obsessive neurosis. See, in particular, *SE* X, 235–36 and 243, and *SE* XX, 119–20; in the latter, Strachey indicates that he is translating Freud's *ungeschehenmachen*, which literally means "making unhappened."

(245,4) See Lacan's "Intervention au Premier Congrès mondial de psychiatrie," republished in *Ornicar?* 30 (1984): 7–10 and in Jacques Lacan, *Autres écrits* (Paris: Seuil, 2001), 127–30.

(246,4) A *magistère* is a grand master of a military order, such as the Order of Malta, or a doctrinal, moral, or intellectual authority that is imposed in an absolute fashion.

(246,5) The "frontier fields" are those enumerated in *Écrits* 1966, 242–43.

(247,1) The reference here is to Rimbaud's "Les chercheuses de poux." See, for example, Arthur Rimbaud, *Oeuvres complètes* (Paris: Gallimard, 1972), 65–66; in English, see "The Ladies Who Look for Lice," in *Arthur Rimbaud: Complete Works*, trans. Paul Schmidt (New York and London: Harper & Row, 1967), 76–77. The "author" in question in the passage is the French analyst, Maurice Benassy.

(247,3) "Donne en ma bouche parole vraie et estable et fay de moy langue caulte." *L'Internele Consolacion*, Chapter XLV: "Qu'on ne doit pas chascun croire et du legier trebuchement de paroles." See *L'Internele Consolacion: Texte du manuscrit d'Amiens* (Paris: Éditions d'art Édouard Pelletan, 1926).

(247,4) *Cause toujours* usually implies that the person who says it couldn't care less about or doesn't believe what the other person is saying, and might in fact prefer the latter shut up. *Causer* means to talk or chat, and *cause toujours* could be literally rendered as "keep talking," "talk anyway," or "go on," even though the context indicates that the speaker means the opposite of what he or she is saying (as when we say "go on" ironically or in exasperation). Agrammatically it might be construed to mean "Always a cause." *Causalisme* is the doctrine that science seeks causes and not merely regular antecedents.

(247,5) Note that *réponse* (response) can also be translated as "answer" or "reply."

(248,1) *Appel* means call, appeal, or summons, and is related to *appeler*, which I translate variously as "to call (for)," "to (make an) appeal," or "to summon." *Le vide* (emptiness) can also be translated as "the void," "vacuum" ("nature abhors a vacuum" is, in French, *la nature a horreur du vide*), or "vacuousness"; the latter would be a particularly appropriate alternative in this sentence and again two paragraphs further on. *Parole vide* is translated here as "empty speech."

(248,2) It is not entirely clear from the grammar who begins speaking here, but I have assumed that, since it was the analyst who responded to the patient's speech with silence (two paragraphs back), it is the analyst who now speaks up.

(248,3) It is not clear here if the subject manifests self-indulgence (*complaisance*) or indulgence toward the analyst.

(248,4) A *prud'homme* (bombastic, smug fellow) is a legal magistrate—an elected member of a council or tribunal—whose job it is to rule on employer/employee disputes. However, the term has also come to refer to "a mediocre, conceited bourgeois who likes making emphatic and empty declarations."

(249,2) Boileau, "L'Art Poétique," chant I: "Hâtez-vous lentement, et sans perdre courage,/ Vingt fois sur le métier remettez votre ouvrage" (Paris: Gallimard, 1966), 161. In Pope's translation: "Gently make haste, of labour not afraid/ A hundred times consider what you've said." Somewhat more literally translated: "Hurry slowly, and without lapsing into gloom/ Rework what you've made twenty times on the loom." Cf. *Boileau: Selected Criticism*, trans. E. Dilworth (New York: Bobbs-Merrill, 1965), 16.

(250,2) *La frustration de son travail* (being frustrated in his labor) could also be translated as "his work being frustrated" or "his work being frustrating." *Désir de mort* could also be rendered as "desire for death."

(251,7) A tessera is a small tablet or die used by the ancient Romans as a ticket, tally, voucher, means of identification, or password. The tessera was used in the early mystery religions, where fitting together again the two halves of a broken piece of pottery was used as a means of recognition by the initiates, and in Greece the tessera was called the *sum bolon*. A central concept involved in the symbol is that of a link. The reference to Mallarmé is to a passage in his preface to René Ghil's *Traité du Verbe* (1866); see Stéphane Mallarmé, *Oeuvres complètes* (Paris: Gallimard, 1945), 368 and 857.

(252,2) A *partie du discours* is a part of speech; here Lacan writes *"partie" de ce discours* ("part" of this discourse). A *soupir* is a sigh, but is also a rest in music—hence "rest of a silence."

(252,4) Regarding *trébuchements si légers* (stumblings so slight), see the epigraph to this section.

(252,5) Molière uses *tarte à la crème* (vacuous buzzword) to qualify a meaningless and pretentious formulation by means of which one claims to have an answer for everything.

(253,5) Reference is made here to the Biblical phrase, "for they have ears in order not to hear," but the French *pour ne point entendre* means both in order not to hear and in order not to understand. I have assumed that Lacan is playing off the two meanings, but their order could be reversed to read as follows: "having ears *in order not to understand*, in other words, in order to detect what is to be heard." The next reference is to Reik's *Listening with the Third Ear* (New York: Garden City Books, 1949), published in Great Britain as *The Inner Experience of a Psychoanalyst* (London: George Allen & Unwin, 1949).

(254,3) It should be noted that *anamnèse* (anamnesis) means the history (or story) the *patient* provides of his or her life and illness; "anamnesis" in English does not necessarily imply that it is the patient who recounts the (hi)story, but I use it throughout this article as if it did.

(255,1) The Latin *flatus vocis* means a mere name, word, or sound without a corresponding objective reality, and was used by nominalists to qualify universals.

(255,2) *Verbaliser* (verbalize), in its legal sense, means to book (or report) someone, but it also means to talk too much or too long. *Pan-*

dore (Pandora), in addition to referring to the woman of Greek mythology, is a somewhat old slang term for a policeman. Like "the Word," *le Verbe* is a translation for the Greek "Logos." Hereafter, *le verbe* is always translated as "the Word." The Greek *epos* means word, speech, tale, song, promise, saying, message, or, in the plural, epic poetry or lines of verse.

(256,fn1) See *SE* XVII, 44. The French translation by Marie Bonaparte and Rudolph M. Loewenstein renders it as *après-coup*.

(256,fn2) See *SE* XVII, 45, fn1.

(257,fn2) See *SE* III, 143–56.

(258,1) The order or instruction Lacan usually refers to as a *consigne* is to "say whatever comes to mind" or "say anything and everything that comes to mind" (*tout dire*).

(258,4) The unconscious here is "a third term" between speaker and addressee.

(259,1) *Sit venia verbo*, which might be rendered "if you will pardon the expression," is found in *GW* XII on page 116, where Freud uses it to qualify his syntagma *einen unbewussten Begriff*, rendered by Strachey as "unconscious concept" (*SE* XVII, 84), but which Lacan renders here by *pensée inconsciente* (unconscious thought). *Verbo* literally means word.

Court comme le furet (darts) is a reference to a game in which a group of people sit in a circle and quickly pass a small object—referred to as *le furet*, though a *furet* is literally a ferret—from hand to hand, while a player standing in the middle of the circle tries to guess which hand holds the *furet*.

(259,2) The Italian here is Galileo's famous "And yet it moves!" (referring to the earth's movement around the sun). The Latin could be rendered as a "thought experiment."

(260,2) Cf. *Écrits* 1966, 511, where Lacan associates metaphor with condensation and metonymy with displacement.

(261,3) *Elles* (they) after the dash presumably refers to two different riots (or "riot" as understood at two different moments in time); it could also possibly refer to "victory" and "defeat."

(262,1) *Annuler* (undoes) also means to void, invalidate, annul, and cancel out.

(262,5–263,1) *Aucun ne répugne plus à l'esprit de notre discipline* (No course is more repugnant to the spirit of our discipline) could also be translated as "No one finds the spirit of our discipline more repugnant."

(263,3) *Non liquet*: it is not clear. Cf. *SE* XVII, 57–60 and *SE* XXII, 54.

(263,4) Matthew, 23.4; I have provided this and other translations of the New Testament from *The New Oxford Annotated Bible* (Oxford: Oxford University Press, 1973).

(263,fn1) Pascal's wager is discussed in Pensée 233 of the Brunschvicg edition, 451 of the Pléiade edition. Lacan discussed Pascal's wager at length in Seminars XIII and XVI.

(264,2) "Il y a des gens qui n'auraient jamais été amoureux s'ils n'avaient jamais entendu parler de l'amour" (Maxim 136), in La Rochefoucauld, *Maximes* (Paris: Garnier Frères, 1967), 36. In English, see *The Maxims of La Rochefoucauld* (New York: Random House, 1959), 57.

(264,3) On the Wolf Man, see *SE* XVII, 106–19, especially 110–11.

(264,5) "Une vérité de La Palice" is a self-evident truth, a truism.

(265,1) "No need to close your eyes" may be a reference to one of Freud's dreams, recounted in *The Interpretation of Dreams*, that includes the line "You are requested to close the eyes" (*SE* IV, 317–18).

There may be a reference here to the "bouche de la vérité" or "mouth of truth" in Rome.

Rollet (script) is an old term for a small role (a "bit part") or a small scroll or sheet of paper on which words were written.

(265,2) See, in particular, Freud's discussion in *SE* XXII, 47–56; on page 56 of that text, Freud mentions an example from Dorothy Burlingham's "Child Analysis and the Mother," *PQ* IV (1935): 69.

(266,2) There are several extant translations of Jesus' reply to the question "Who are you?": "Even what I have told you from the beginning," "What I have told you all along," "What I have told you from the outset," "Why do I talk to you at all."

(266,4) There is a possible reference here to Aristotle's notion that philosophy begins with wonder.

(266,6) *Des points faibles de sa chaire*, rendered in context here as "which parts of his body are sensitive," might also suggest "weaknesses of the flesh."

(267,1) See Plato, *The Sophist*, 246. *Dignus est intrare* is the phrase used by the chorus in the macaronic Latin of the burlesque ceremony with which Molière's *Le Malade imaginaire* ends. See, for example, *Molière: Le Malade imaginaire* (Oxford: Oxford University Press, 1965), 145, and *The Would-Be Invalid*, trans. Morris Bishop (New York: Appleton-Century-Crofts, 1950), 75. On being smelled by one's analysand, see Seminar IV, 79.

(267,4) See *SE* XIII, 177.

(268,1) *Version* (version) can also mean translation. *Élaboration* (telling) also means revision, as in "secondary revision."

(268,5) See *The Psychopathology of Everyday Life*, *SE* VI (1901).

(269,1) On numbers, see *SE* VI, chapter 12, 239–79. The next reference seems to be to *GW* IV, 276; in Strachey's rendition, "the existence of highly composite thought processes which are yet quite unknown to consciousness" (*SE* VI, 247).

(269,4) See, above all, *SE* VI, 243–48.

(270,3) See *SE* VIII (1905). Regarding the problems translating important terms found in that book from German into English, see the "Editor's Preface," pages 7–8. Similar problems present themselves here since, while *esprit* translates Freud's *Witz* quite nicely, neither corresponds very well to "wit" or "jokes" in English.

(270,5) See *SE* VIII, 55, 61–65, and 105–8. In Strachey's translation (*SE* VIII, 106): "Anyone who has allowed the truth to slip out in an unguarded moment is in fact glad to be free of pretence."

(271,1) In Strachey's translation (*SE* VIII, 105): "Thus jokes can also have a subjective determinant of this kind . . . It declares that only what I allow to be a joke *is* a joke."

(271,2) The third person is the person who hears the joke (the first person being the one who tells the joke, the second the one the joke is about). See *SE* VIII, 100, 148–58, and elsewhere. An amboceptor is something that brings things together with its two receptors.

(271,5) The reference here is to I. A. Richards and C. K. Ogden's book, *The Meaning of Meaning* (New York: Harcourt, Brace, 1945 [1923]).

(272,1) The French here, *Argonautes pacifiques*, suggests the title of Malinowski's book, *Argonauts of the Western Pacific* (New York: E. P. Dutton, 1953).

(273,5) See C. V. Hudgkins, "Conditioning and the Voluntary Control of the Pupillary Light Reflex," *Journal of General Psychology* 8 (1933): 3. Hudgkins' work was based on preliminary work by H. Cason, "The Conditioned Eyelid Reaction," *Journal of Experimental Psychology* 5 (1933): 153.

(274,2) *Contre-épreuve* (control test) could also be translated by "countertest" or "test of the contrary hypothesis." Reducing "contract" to its first syllable, con, and pronouncing it *à la française*, evokes the meanings idiot, stupid, and asshole, among others.

(275,3) Jacques Prévert, "Inventaire," *Oeuvres Complètes*, vol. I (Paris: Gallimard, 1966), 131. The producing of sterile monsters is an image borrowed from Goya.

(276,1) Anatole France, *L'île des pingouins* (Paris: Calmann-Lévy, 1908); *Penguin Island*, trans. A. W. Evans (New York: Dodd, Mead & Co., 1925).

(276,3) The reference here is to the Fort! Da! game discussed in *Beyond the Pleasure Principle* (1920), *SE* XVIII, 14–17.

(276,5) The Greek here can be rendered as "A possession for all time." Thucydides, *The Peloponnesian War*, I, xxiii. In Crawley's translation: "I have written my work, not as an essay which is to win the applause of the moment, but as a possession for all time"; see, for example, *The Complete Writings of Thucydides* (New York: Modern Library, 1951), 14–15. *Place partout* (ubiquity) is similar in structure and sound to the more usual *passe partout* (skeleton key or master key).

(276,6) This ŠiRonga proverb is the epigraph to Claude Lévi-Strauss, *Elementary Structures of Kinship* (Boston: Beacon Press, 1969), found on page 1. I have followed the published translation, which—perhaps erroneously—translates *cuisse* (thigh, or leg when it comes to food) as "hip."

(278,3) The phrase including *inadéquates* (fail to correspond to) could alternatively be rendered as "that are always more or less incommensurate with."

(278,5) Rabelais' Panurge says that he's always believed debts to be "a sort of connecting-link between Heaven and earth, a unique interrelationship of the human race—I mean without which all humans would soon perish—peradventure to be that great soul of the universe, which, according to the Academics, gives life to all things"; if we imagine a world without debts, "There, among the stars, there will be no regular course whatever. All will be in disarray. Jupiter, not thinking himself a debtor to Saturn, will dispossess him of his sphere . . . The moon will remain bloody and dark: on what ground will the sun impart his light to her? He was in no way bound to. The sun will not shine on their earth, the stars will exert no good influence there, for the earth was desisting from lending them nourishment by vapors and exhalations, by which (. . .) the stars were fed." See *The Complete Works of François Rabelais*, trans. Donald M. Frame (Berkeley: University of California Press, 1991), 267–73 (*Tiers livre*, chapters 3 and 4).

(279,1) On "substantific," cf. Rabelais' *substantifique moëlle* (the very substance, "the real stuff").

(279,2) See, for example, Lévi-Strauss' *Introduction à l'oeuvre de Marcel Mauss* (Paris: PUF, 1950), where he compares the notion of mana to the concept of the zero-phoneme introduced into phonology by Roman Jakobson. In English, see *Introduction to the Work of Marcel Mauss*, trans. Felicity Baker (London: Routledge & Kegan Paul, 1987), 63–64 and 72.

(279,3) "By bone and flesh" is an allusion to an opposition brought out by Claude Lévi-Strauss in *The Elementary Structures of Kinship* (Boston: Beacon, 1969), especially in chapter 24.

(279,6) *Se fait reconnaître* (gains recognition) literally means gets itself recognized; less literally, it means to achieve, garner, or gain recognition (and even to be recognized as a legitimate child, not a bastard).

(280,5) *Qui fait de la maladie l'introduction du vivant à l'existence du sujet* (which makes illness what institutes the existence of the subject in the living being) could also be translated as "which makes illness that which thrusts the living being into existence as a subject."

(281,2) *Chiffre* (cipher) also means number.

(281,4) A palimpsest is a piece of parchment or other writing material from which the writing has been erased to make way for a new text. See Freud's discussion of recollection and memory in "A Note on the Mystic Writing Pad" (1925), *SE* XIX, 227–32.

(281,7) *Désordre* (disorder) can also be rendered as "chaos" or "mess"; it is not a reference to the eponymous psychiatric notion.

(282,4) *L'aire des circonvolutions* (the region of the brain) literally means the area (the language) is wound or coiled around. But *circonvolutions cérébrales* refer to the folds of the brain, gyrus, or circumvolutio. Cf. Seminar I (303/274), where Lacan uses *circonvolutions* alone to refer to gray matter, translated there as "circumvolutions" (convolutions of the surface of the brain). Metaphorically, *circonvolutions* can mean circumlocutions.

(282,5) From T. S. Eliot, *The Hollow Men* (1925); see *T. S. Eliot: Collected Poems 1909–1962* (New York: Harcourt, Brace & World, 1970), 77–82.

(283,1) On "the philosophy of the skull," see Hegel's *Phenomenology of Spirit*, trans. A. V. Miller (Oxford: Oxford University Press, 1977), sections 327–40. Pascal: "Les hommes sont si nécessairement fous, que ce serait être fou, par un autre tour de folie, de n'être pas fou," *Pensées* (Brunschvicg ed. 414, Pléiade ed. 184).

(283,3) On the Church and the army, see in particular chapter V of *Group Psychology and the Analysis of the Ego* (1921), *SE* XVIII.

(283,4) "Direction," that is, "guidance," as in the religious sense of *direction de consciences*.

(284,8) Cf., for example, Claude Lévi-Strauss, *Structural Anthropology*, trans. C. Jacobson and B. G. Schoepf (New York: Basic Books, 1963), 31 ff.

(285,fn1) An English translation of a later version of the article can be found in Claude Lévi-Strauss, *Structural Anthropology*, 55–66.

(286,1) *Front d'airain* (brazen face) seems to be an allusion to Lassalle's *loi d'airain*, the "iron law of wages."

(286,2) This is discussed by Lacan at length in Seminar II.

(286,5) ". . . that [August] Voice / Who knows itself when it sings / To be no longer the voice of anyone / As much as [the voice] of the waves and woods." Paul Valéry, "La Pythie," in *Poésies* (Paris: Gallimard, 1942).

(287,3) See Lacan's "Logical Time and the Assertion of Anticipated Certainty" in *Écrits* 1966.

(288,1) *Relève* (continuation) can also be translated as "sublation."

(288,2) See Lacan's "The Neurotic's Individual Myth," trans. M. N. Evans, *PQ* XLVIII, 3 (1979): 405–25, originally published in French in 1953.

(288,3) See "The Question of Lay Analysis" (1926), *SE* XX, 246; Strachey renders the last two items in the list as "the science of literature."

(288,4) The "triangle" may be that composed of history, mathematics (or ethnology), and linguistics.

(289,5) See Lacan's later comments on this poem in Seminar XIX, January 6, 1972.

(289,6) "For I have seen with my own eyes the Cumean Sibyll hanging inside a jar, and whenever boys would ask her: 'What do you wish, O Sibyll,' she would reply: 'I wish to die.'" This is the epigraph to T. S. Eliot's *The Waste Land* (1922); see *T. S. Eliot: Collected Poems 1909–1962* (New York: Harcourt, Brace & World, 1970), 51–76.

(290,6) See *SE* X, 166–67. In Strachey's translation, the passage reads as follows: "his face took on a very strange, composite expression I could only interpret as one of *horror at pleasure of his own of which he himself was unaware*."

(291,4) For Freud's first definition of resistance, see "The Psychotherapy of Hysteria" (1895), *SE* II, 290 ff.

(293,2) *Scopie* (vision) comes from the Greek, *skopia*, the act of observing. Socrates and his desire were discussed at length by Lacan in Seminar VIII; Kierkegaard on repetition was taken up in Seminar XI.

(293,3) *Fasse justice de leur puissance* (turns their power into justice) could alternatively mean refutes or challenges their power. *Maîtres-mots* (magic words) refers to words imbued with special powers or with a specific energy or efficacy. On Humpty Dumpty, see Lewis Carroll, *Through the Looking Glass* in *The Annotated Alice*, ed. Martin Gardner (New York: Clarkson N. Potter, 1960), 269.

(295,3) See "Analysis Terminable and Interminable" (1937), *SE* XXIII, 219.

(295,5) See *Shakespear's dramatische Werke*, trans. Ludwig Tieck and August Wilhelm von Schlegel (Berlin: Reimer, 1843).

(296,2) The French rendered here as "*summoning*" reads "intimation" in italics, which could be either the English term or the French (meaning summoning) with emphasis added. Cf. *Écrits* 1966, 305 and 319, where it appears without italics.

(296,fn1) Kris' article is reprinted in *Selected Papers of Ernst Kris* (New Haven: Yale University Press, 1975), 237–51; see especially 250–51.

(297,4) See, for example, Karl von Frisch, *Bees: Their Vision, Chemical Senses, and Language* (Ithaca: Cornell University Press, 1950 and 1971), chapter 3, above all, pages 89 ff. See also Frisch, *The Dancing Bees: An Account of the Life and Senses of the Honey Bee* (London: Methuen & Co., 1954), especially chapter 11.

(298,4) Pascal: "Tu ne me chercherais pas, si tu ne m'avais trouvé," the words of Christ in "Le mystère de Jesus," *Pensées* (Brunschvicg ed. 553, Pléiade ed. 736).

(298,5) *Vous vous rencontrez avec lui* (you encounter each other) can also mean you share the same views or you meet.

(298,fn1) See Emile Littré, *Dictionnaire de la langue française*, 7 volumes (Paris: Hachette, 1885), under *parabole*: "action de mettre à côté."

(300,fn1) Lacan discusses this paper again in "Direction of the Treatment."

(301,2) *Corps subtil* (subtle body) is a reference to the matter ("aether" or "ether") formerly believed to surround the earth.

(301,3) See *SE* XVII, 89–97, 107–8, 112–13 (and note); the *Wespe* incident is reported on page 94.

(301,4) See *SE* X, 225, 260, 280–81, 294–95.

(302,1) *Mettre à l'index* (exclude) can also be translated as "to boycott," "to condemn," "to exclude," and "to put on a list of prohibited books." I translate it again as "exclude" a few pages further on.

(302,5) See *SE* X, 198.

(303,3) This is a possible reference to *SE* X, 199–200. Strachey translates Freud as follows here: "He dreamt that *he saw my daughter in front of him; she had two patches of dung instead of eyes.*" Nevertheless, the exact reference is not clear, even in the "Original Record of the Case" (see *SE* X, 293) and the more complete French edition: *L'homme aux rats: Journal d'une analyse* (Paris: PUF, 1974).

(303,4) In Strachey's rendition (*SE* X, 249): "Like so many other young men of value and promise, he perished in the Great War."

(304,1) *Mortelles* (deadly) can be translated as "mortal," "lethal," "fatal," or "deadly boring." *Se voir* could also be translated as "see himself."

(304,2) The Latin here could be rendered as "To each his own jouissance" or "Everyone is led by his own pleasure (or passion)."

(304,3) Cf. Seminar IV, 27, and *Écrits* 1966, 630.

(305,3) See R. Sterba, "The Fate of the Ego in Analytic Therapy," *IJP* XV, 2–3 (1934): 117–26.

(305,5) "Fragment of an Analysis of a Case of Hysteria" (1905), *SE* VII, 7–122. See Lacan's extensive discussion of the Dora case in "Presentation on Transference" (1951), *Écrits* 1966, 215–26.

(306,1) See *SE* VII, 120–22.

(306,2) *SE* VII, 120, fn1. The account itself was published four years after the breaking off of the analysis in 1901.

(306,3) See Pierre Janet, *The Mental State of Hystericals*, trans. C. R. Corson (Washington, D.C.: University Publications of America, 1977), originally published in French in 1892 and in English in 1901.

(307,6) *Mettre bille-en-tête* (jumping to conclusions) means to run headlong or headfirst. "Shuttling back and forth": presumably from one side of the wall to the other, from the unsaid to the said. I have been unable to determine the meaning of *donne la marque* (starts the ball rolling); it may have to do with starting a race, "pointing the finger," or setting the rhythm. *Aller au trou* (going to prison) also has other slang meanings and it is not entirely clear to me what Lacan is getting at here.

(308,3) "Indication of reality" (*indice de réalité*) here seems to refer to Freud's *Realitätszeichen;* see "Project for a Scientific Psychology" (1895), *SE* I, 325–28 and elsewhere.

(308,4) This may be a reference to "Observations on Transference Love" (1915), *SE* XII, 167–68.

(308,fn1) See Lacan's discussion of bundling in Seminar IV, 87 ff.

(309,1) *Contre-effet* (counter) could alternatively be translated as "side effect."

(310,2) "Lay" in the sense of a simple narrative poem, ballad, or song.

(310,8) *Échéance* (due date) can be translated as "deadline," "maturity date," "payment date," "expiration date," "term," and so on.

(311,2) In the case of the Wolf Man (*SE* XVII, 11); the Latin here could be translated as "out of modesty."

(311,fn1) The usual French translation of "*Die endliche und die unendliche Analyse*" (1937) is "*Analyse terminée et analyse interminable*"; the usual English is "Analysis Terminable and Interminable" (*SE* XXIII, 216–53). Lacan renders it here by "*analyse finie ou indéfinie.*"

(311,fn2) Here is the Loeb Classical Library translation, prepared by John C. Rolfe (New York: Putnam, 1927): "When inquiry is made about the choice of a prosecutor, and judgement is rendered on the question to which of two or more persons the prosecution of a defendant, or a share in the prosecution, is to be entrusted, this process and examination by jurors is called *divinatio* . . . But some others think that the *divinatio* is so called because, while prosecutor and defendant are two things that are, as it were, related and connected, so that neither can exist without the other, yet in this form of trial, while there is already a defendant, there is as yet no prosecutor, and therefore the factor which is still lacking and unknown—namely, what man is to be the prosecutor—must be supplied by divination" (131–33).

(312,2) *Un prytanée* (analytic academy) is a kind of educational establishment in France that is free for the sons of military personnel.

(312,3) See Ruth Mack Brunswick, "A Supplement to Freud's 'History of an Infantile Neurosis,'" *IJP* IX (1928), republished in *The Wolf-Man* (New York: Basic Books, 1971), 263–307. For further details and references, see Ernest Jones, *The Life and Work of Sigmund*

Freud (New York: Basic Books, 1953), vol. 2, 306–12.

(312,4) Lacan discussed the Wolf Man case at length in his early 1952 seminar at which no stenographer was present.

(313,1) On "the fall of heavy bodies," see Charles François, "La théorie de la chute des graves. Évolution historique du problème," *Ciel et Terre* 34 (1913): 135–37, 167–69, 261–73. See *Lichtenberg: Aphorisms & Letters*, trans. Franz Mautner and Henry Hatfield (London: Jonathan Cape, 1969), 49.

(313,4) See Leenhardt, "La parole qui dure" (Tradition, mythe, statut), *Do Kamo* (1947): 173 ff.

(314,2) The French here, "*la coupure du* timing," literally means "cutting [the session] based on timing." Given the context, it seems clear that Lacan is referring to the "standard" practice of timing sessions, that is, ending them based on a specified clock time. Hence: "after a fixed number of minutes has elapsed."

(315,8) Note that *défendre* means both to defend and to prohibit.

(316,7) Wilhelm Reich, *Character Analysis* (New York: Simon & Schuster, 1972), trans. V. R. Carfagno. The schema Lacan refers to here seems to be that found on page 392, "the most general form of this movement of sexual superimposition."

(317,3) See *Beyond the Pleasure Principle*, *SE* XVIII.

(317,5) See Ernest Jones, *The Life and Work of Sigmund Freud* (New York: Basic Books, 1953), vol. 1, 27–29.

(318,1) See *SE* XXIII, 244–47.

(318,2) *SE* XVIII, 57–58.

(318,3) Martin Heidegger, *Being and Time*, trans. John Macquarrie and Edward Robinson (Oxford: Basil Blackwell, 1962): 294. I have followed the translation Lacan gives in the text; the English translation cited here reads: "that possibility which is one's ownmost, which is nonrelational, and which is not to be outstripped."

(318,5) *Le mort* (the dead person) can also be translated as "the dummy" in the context of bridge (the card game). Cf. "Direction of the Treatment," *Écrits* 1966, 551.

(319,1) See *SE* XVIII, 14–17.

(319,2) *Son action* (his action) could also possibly be translated as "language's action" or "his desire's action." *Elle* (His action) at the beginning of the next sentence would then be "Language's action" or "Desire's action."

(319,4) The French at the end of the paragraph, *intimation bannissante*, could also be rendered as "formal notification of banishment." "His" in this paragraph seems always to refer back to the child, except the last instance, which seems to refer to the partner.

(319,6) *Truchement* (means) has a number of older meanings, including interpreter, spokesperson, and representative, and newer meanings, including mediation, intermediary, and medium (that which expresses or conveys ideas or feelings, for example, music). Here Lacan seems to be suggesting that death serves as a *means* to an end for the subject (the paragraphs that follow illustrate this).

Vient à la vie de son histoire (is born into the life of his history) could alternatively be rendered as "comes to life through his history."

(320,4) *Jeu de furet* (darting game): see earlier note on *le furet* (corresponding to *Écrits* 1966, 259). It could perhaps be translated here as "guessing game," "shifting game," or "musical chairs."

(320,6) Leenhardt, for example, uses this spatial representation in his *Do Kamo* to represent the native's existence as a locus of relationships with others.

(321,3) *Souci* (care-ridden) is the usual French translation of Heidegger's *Sorge*, and *savoir* (knowledge) of Hegel's *Wissen*.

(321,4) There is a possible reference to *Numbers*, 21.9, at the end of this paragraph.

(321,fn1) See, above all, Seminar IX, *Identification* (1961–1962).

(322,8) "*Soumission, don, grâce*." The three Sanskrit nouns (*damah, danam, daya'*) are also rendered "self-control," "giving," "compassion" (*Rhadhakrishnan*); the three verbs, "control," "give," "sympathize" (T. S. Eliot, *The Waste Land*, Part V; "What the thunder said"). For a more recent translation, see *The Brihadaranyaka Upanishad*, trans. Swami Sivanada (India: Divine Life Society, 1985), 487–88.

(322,fn2) In his *Pour un Malherbe*. "Resound" is *résonner* in French; *réson* is a homonym of *raison* (reason). See Lacan's later comments on Ponge's *réson* in Seminar XIX, January 6, 1972.

Notes to "Variations on the Standard Treatment"

(323,5) Lacan's text, included in the 1955 edition, was not included in the 1960 or any later editions.

(324,2) The *étiquette* (label) presented here is probably the word *cure-type* (standard treatment).

(324,6) On assessments as cursory as "improved," "much improved," and "cured," see H. E. Eysenck, *The Scientific Study of Personality* (London: Routledge and Kegan Paul, 1952), cited by E. Glover in "Therapeutic Criteria of Psycho-Analysis," *IJP* XXXV, 2 (1954): 96.

(324,7) See especially "Recommendations to Physicians Practising Psycho-Analysis," *SE* XII, 111–20. *Furor sanandi* can be understood as "passion for healing" or "desire to cure"; Freud refers in his article to "therapeutic ambition" (119). See also *SE* XII, 171.

(325,4) This is a reference to Aesop's fable, "The Bat, the Birds, and the Beasts."

(325,6) *De toutes plumes* (all analytic writers) literally means from all pens, or all feathers (quills)—the latter harking back to the birds in Aesop's fable.

(326,1) The brackets in this quote are Lacan's.

(327,4[6]) I have been unable to find the English in Glover's text that corresponds here to *y perd la mesure de ses limites* (loses any measure of its "therapeutic applicability") and have thus adapted it to what seemed to be the closest passage in his paper.

(328,8) In other texts, Lacan does not seem to think that Freud's concept of transference has managed to weather the storm so well. See, for example, *Écrits* 1966, 461.

(329,1) *Ananke* means necessity.

(329,3) The "misunderstanding" Lacan is referring to here is the one mentioned on page 325, paragraph 5.

(330,4) *Joué* (duped) and *qu'il ne la joue* (than he performs it) are extremely polyvalent, given the many meanings of *jouer*: to play, act, perform, risk, stake, fool, and back.

(331,1) *Recueille* (records) also means collects, gathers, wins, inherits, or reaps. *Ce qu'il "veut dire"* would usually be translated simply as "what it 'means'"; it literally means what it "wants to say." "The other [. . .] deliver[ed] to the listener as constituted" is the speaker's ego, the ego being constituted like an other; see, in particular, *Écrits* 1966, 178–82 and 344–46.

(331,2) *Propos* (topic) also means intention.

(331,4) Cf. *Écrits* 1966, 592–93.

(332,3) See Lacan's extensive discussion of those training methods in "The Situation of Psychoanalysis in 1956."

(332,4) The expression, "analysis of resistances," is used by Richard Sterba in "The Fate of the Ego in Analytic Therapy," *IJP* XV, 2–3 (1934): 117, a text Lacan cites further on. Sterba also uses the expression "analytic situation" in the same text, a term already found in Freud's work (*SE* XII, 161, and *SE* XIX, 274).

(332,5) Lacan may be referring to Freud's "Lines of Advance in Psycho-Analytic Therapy," *SE* XVII, 159–68, or to *Beyond the Pleasure Principle* (1920), *SE* XVIII.

(334,1) *Faisceau* (array) also means beam, bundle, stack, and fasciculus. See *SE* II, 289. See also "Repression," *SE* XIV, 149; the translation there, however, is less telling than the earlier version (*Collected Papers* V, 88) which reads: "It is as though the resistance of consciousness against them [the derivatives of what was primally repressed] was in inverse proportion to their remoteness from what was originally repressed."

(334,6) *Matériel* (material) also means equipment, hardware, supplies, stock, tools, and set of facts. *En matériel* (like material) might also be rendered as "out of material."

(335,2) Reading *un effet faux* (a false effect) for *en effet faux*. Lacan is referring here to Franz Alexander's *Psychoanalysis of the Total Personality: The Application of Freud's Theory of the Ego to the Neuroses* (New York: Nervous and Mental Disease Publishing Company, [1927] 1930).

(335,4) The lines quoted here are from Anna Freud's *The Ego and the Mechanisms of Defense*, revised edition (New York: International Universities Press, 1966), 3. The book was originally published in German in 1936. Lacan provides his own translation here rather than using Anne Berman's in *Le moi et les mécanismes de défense* (Paris: PUF, 1949).

(336,1) See Freud's 1894 paper, "The Neuro-Psychoses of Defence," *SE* III, 45–61.

(337,3) On smelling each other, see *Écrits* 1966, 267, 465, and 609–10, and Seminar IV, 79.

(338,fn2) On page 120, Sterba refers to a "*dissociation* within the ego" which results in a "double consciousness." Lacan's term here, *dédoublement* (dissociation), would usually be translated as "splitting." Sterba also indicates that in order for his interpretations to "have a more profound effect, it is necessary constantly to repeat them" (123), and refers in several places to the analyst's attempt to bring about "intellectual contemplation" (122) in the analysand.

(341,1) *Menschenkenntnis*, *Menschenforschung*: knowledge of human nature, research on human nature.

(345,1) *En la totalité de sa Gestalt* (as a unified whole) literally means in the totality of its (or his) gestalt.

(345,2) See H. Nunberg, "The Synthetic Function of the Ego" (1930), in *Practice and Theory of Psychoanalysis* (New York: International Universities Press, 1960). Sterba mentions Nunberg's concept of the ego in the paper Lacan cites here.

(345,3) *Faute heureuse* (happy fault): Lacan uses here the usual French translation of the Latin *felix culpa*.

(346,1) There seems to be a problem with the French here, which reads *révèle sa signification mortelle, et de mort du même temps: qu'il existe*; the version of the text published in 1955 reads *révèle sa signification mortelle, et en même temps qu'il existe* (reveal its mortal signification and, at the same time, that he exists). The 1966 version might be understood to distinguish between *signification mortelle*, the signification that kills, and *signification de mort*, the signification of death, but *du même temps* seems erroneous; I have thus followed the 1955 version.

(346,2) *Doubler* (to stand in for) has many other meanings, including to double, overtake, line, dub, and double-cross.

(346,3) *Sympathie* (sympathy) also means friendliness.

(346,4) *Prégnance* (visual power) refers to the power forms have to impose themselves upon perception or force themselves upon us. It can also take on the more general meaning of being full of implicit meanings or consequences.

(347,3) *Prestiges* (illusions), in the plural, usually means illusions (created by magic or optics) or diabolical (or seductive) artifices; it can also mean enchantment, charm, or appeal. In the singular, it can usually be rendered as "prestige" in English, though I have sometimes translated it as "illusion" here; when I do so, I include the French in brackets.

(349,4) Glover, "Therapeutic Criteria," 95, 98, and 99.

(350,3) Reading *accorde* (has) for *accordé*, as in the original version of the text.

(350,5) *Portée* (weight) here also means import, reach, scope, range, and impact.

(350,6) Porte *la parole* (*supports* speech) evokes *porte-parole*, spokesperson or mouthpiece. *Porter* here also suggests that the analyst carries and transmits the analysand's speech and even *la fait porter*: makes it hit home or makes it have an impact.

(351,3) "The concept of concept" is a likely reference to Hegel's *Science of Logic* (Atlantic Highlands, New Jersey: Humanities Press, 1969), Vol. II. Note that the translator of this edition, A. V. Miller, uses the term "notion" rather than "concept." It might be more idiomatic here to say "action" instead of "act," but the *analytic act* later becomes a specific Lacanian concept. On the meaning of meaning, see I. A. Richards and C. K. Ogden's book, *The Meaning of Meaning* (New York: Harcourt, Brace, [1923] 1945).

(351,5) *Foi donnée* (promise made) can also mean oath sworn, sworn faith, or commitment made. On "You are my wife," see *Écrits* 1966, 298.

(351,6) *Une parole* (an instance of speech) can also mean a promise. The second half of *intér-essés*, *essés*, recalls the Latin *esse*, "being," while the first part recalls "intersubjectivity."

(352,3) Con-vince: "vince" comes from *vaincre*, meaning to vanquish.

(352,4) *Per-suadé* (per-suaded): *per* denotes completion and *suadere* to advise or urge.

(353,1) *En elle* (in truth) might alternatively be rendered "in this key."

(353,2) *Sa vérité* (its truth) might alternatively be rendered as "his truth."

(353,4) I have been unable to find the French term, *révélante*, that I have translated here as "revelatory," in any dictionary.

(353,5) On the question of his choice of a wife, see *SE* X, 198.

(354,1) *Chaîne de paroles* (word chain) is a probable reference to the term *Wortbrücke* (*GW* VII, 433), rendered by Strachey as "verbal bridge" (*SE* X, 213–14); *Brücke* can, however, also be translated as "link."

(354,3) *S'y croise avec* (crossbreeds with) implies a kind of crossbreeding of different species. See Lacan's paper, "The Neurotic's Individual Myth," trans. M. N. Evans, *PQ* XLVIII, 3 (1979): 405–25; it was originally printed in French in 1953.

(355,1) Lacan is referring here to Siegfried Bernfeld's "An Unknown Autobiographical Fragment by Freud," *American Imago* IV (1946): 3–19.

(355,5) Cf. "For they have ears in order not to hear."

(356,1) See Lacan's long quote from *Attic Nights* in *Écrits* 1966, 311.

(359,4) *Conscience*: Lacan is playing here off the fact that the French means both conscience and consciousness.

(360,3) See the myth of Amphitryon and the eponymous plays by Plautus, Molière, Giraudoux, and many other authors. See, also, Lacan's discussion in Seminar II, chapter 21.

(360,5) The physician/grammarian here is Édouard Pichon; see Jacques Damourette and Édouard Pichon, *Des mots à la pensée: Essai de grammaire de la langue française*, 7 volumes (Paris: Bibliothèque du français moderne, 1932–51). Their work contains important discussions of the notion of "discordance" that Lacan refers to elsewhere (in Seminar XX, for example).

(362,2) *Subornement* (subornation) is an old, alternate form of *subornation*, meaning subornation, in the juridical sense, or the seduction, corruption (through bribery), perversion, depraving, or leading astray of someone.

Notes to "On a Purpose"

(363,1) Lacan's choice of the word *dessein* (purpose) here may well be related to the lines by Crébillon included in the "Seminar on 'The Purloined Letter'": Un dessein si funeste/ S'il n'est digne d'Atrée, est digne de Thyeste (*Écrits* 1966, 14).

(363,4) On the repression of "signor," see *Écrits* 1966, 379.

(364,3) *Poubellication* is a condensation of *poubelle*, garbage can (or dustbin), and *publication*, publication. It can perhaps also be seen to contain *embellir*, to beautify, and other words as well. Cf. Seminar XIII (December 15, 1965) and Seminar XX, chapter 3.

(365,2) Benveniste's article (which discusses Freud's text, "The Antithetical Meaning of Primal Words," *SE* XI, 155–61) can be found in *La Psychanalyse* 1 (1956): 5–16, and in English in Émile Benveniste, *Problems in General Linguistics*, 65–75. Lacan's translation of Heidegger's "Logos" can also be found in *La Psychanalyse* 1 (1956): 59–79; Heidegger's text can be found in English in *Early Greek Thinking* (New York: Harper & Row, 1975).

(365,5) On resistance and repression, see *SE* II, 289, and *SE* XIV, 149. *De fonctionner en retour* (by functioning in the opposite direction): Lacan seems to imply here that if we can say "the greater the resistance, the greater the repression," we can also say "the greater the repression, the greater the resistance" (or possibly "the less the resistance, the less the repression").

(366,1) *Il se montre à l'épreuve* (it [i.e., being] shows itself in the process) might also be rendered as "it is seen in the test" or "it delivers itself up in the trying."

(366,8) *Tour* (twist back) has many meanings, including turn, tour, trip, twist, and trick. Lacan may be alluding here to the inner eight discussed in Seminar XI, 143/156; cf. *Écrits* 1966, 861. *Renverser* (reverse) can also mean invert and overturn. In the next paragraph, Lacan may be alluding to the cross-cap.

(367,2) See *SE* XIX, 168. *Pied-plat* (rabble) literally means flatfooted; figuratively, it means a coarse, ignorant, or servile person of low extraction.

(367,5) *De notre index le commandement de sa boucle* (my index would command it to continue) strikes me as quite obscure; there seems to be a play on *bout* and *boucle*.

Notes to "Introduction to Jean Hyppolite's Commentary on Freud's 'Verneinung'"

(370,2) Monsieur Jourdain is a character in Molière's play, *Le bourgeois gentilhomme*, best known in English as *The Would-Be Gentleman* (see especially Act II, Scene 4). Cf. *Écrits* 1966, 456 and 478. *Imageant* (imaginative) is a philosophical term found in Sartre's *L'imaginaire* (Paris: Gallimard, 1940) meaning productive of images; it is translated in *The Psychology of Imagination* (New York: Rider and Company, 1950) as "imaginative."

(372,1) See *SE* II, 289, and *SE* XIV, 149.

(373,3) See *SE* XII, 101.

(373,fn1) See Seminar III, 181–82, where Lacan indicates that he had made the same comment in an earlier seminar.

(375,5) *La belle affaire!* (Big deal!) could also be translated as "Isn't that just great!"

(375,6) Carl von Clausewitz (1780–1831) was a Prussian general and a military theorist who wrote *On War* (*Vom Kriege*).

(376,3) See *SE* XII, 104, footnote 1.

(377,1) Purgons is a doctor from Molière's play *The Imaginary Invalid* (see especially Act III, Scene 5).

(377,2) See Lacan's exchange with "Dr. Z*" in Seminar I, 34–37/26–28.

(377,3) See endnote to *Écrits* 1966, 80, paragraph 2.

(378,4) *Élaboration* (elaboration) could also be translated as "revision," in which case *se poursuit* (is carried out) might better be rendered as "continues." As we see (*SE* V, 518 fn2), the one step (*pas*) from the sublime to the ridiculous is the *Pas de Calais*, the English Channel.

(379,1) Lacan had just discussed Freud's forgetting of the name Signorelli a week earlier in Seminar I, 57–59/46–48. Actually, Freud's traveling companion is not a medical colleague, but he discussed with this traveling companion a part of a conversation he had had earlier with a fellow physician. *Retrancher* (Lacan's translation for Freud's *Verwerfung*, as we shall see in his "Response to Jean Hyppolite's Commentary") means to suppress, cut off a part, prune, remove, amputate, excise, and eliminate. "The broken half of the sword of speech" may be a reference to the tale of Tristan and Isolde, in which a part of Tristan's sword remains stuck in the head of the giant, Morholt, whom he slays. Cf. *Écrits* 1966, 447.

(379,2) For a different gloss on *discours de l'Autre,* see *Écrits* 1966, 814, where it is translated as "discourse about the Other."

(380,2) A tessera is a small tablet or die used by the ancient Romans as a ticket, tally, voucher, means of identification, or password. The tessera was used in the early mystery religions, where fitting together again the two halves of a broken piece of pottery was used as a means of recognition by the initiates, and in Greece the tessera was called the *sum bolon*. A central concept involved in the symbol is that of a link.

Notes to "Response to Jean Hyppolite's Commentary on Freud's 'Verneinung'"

(382,7) The Heideggerian terminology here, *l'être dans l'étant*, could alternatively be translated as "Being (with)in the existent."

(383,2) The French at the end of the paragraph, *d'aloi peu relevé* (that hardly seems promising), is more ironic than the English suggests in that *aloi* also used to refer to the legal status of a currency or of a goldsmith's work, and *relevé* can also mean spicy or strong (for tastes and odors). This may be a reference to the idea of being smelled by one's analysand mentioned in *Écrits* 1966, 267 and 337, and Seminar IV, 79. Cf. *Écrits* 1966, 610.

(383,3) The first sentence here could, alternatively, be rendered as: "In this text by Freud, the affective is conceived of as that which, of a primordial symbolization, preserves its effects right down to the discursive structuration" or "In this text by Freud, the affective is conceived of as that part of a primal symbolization that preserves its effects right down to the discursive structuration."

(383,7) The first example will be seen to concern hallucination in Freud's case of the Wolf Man, whereas the second example concerns acting out in Kris' case of the man who loved fresh brains.

(384,fn1) See Raymond de Saussure, "Present Trends in Psychoanalysis," in *Actes du Congrès International de Psychiatrie* V (1950): 95–166.

(384,3) Maurice Merleau-Ponty, *Phénoménology de la perception* (Paris: Gallimard, 1945); *The Phenomenology of Perception*, trans. Colin Smith (New York: Humanities Press, 1962).

(385,5) One of the "neopractitioners" Lacan seems to have in mind here is Ernst Kris, discussed further on. The topic of "planning" is explicitly addressed in the last section of his article, "Ego Psychology and Interpretation in Psychoanalytic Therapy," *PQ* XX, 1 (1951): 15–29. "Planning" seems to imply the establishment of regular patterns in analyses, allowing the analyst to predict the course of a specific analytic case and plan his or her interventions accordingly. Lacan may also have Anna Freud in mind; see *Écrits* 1966, 604.

(386,3) *Est restée lettre morte* (went unheeded) literally means remained a dead letter.

(386,fn1) No stenographer was present at the seminars Lacan gave in 1951–1952 and 1952–1953, nor were they tape-recorded.

(386,fn2) Strachey renders the German phrase here as "he would have nothing to do with it, in the sense of having repressed it." *Verwerfung* is translated as "condemning judgement" in *SE* XVII, 80, and the verb form as "to reject" in *SE* XVII, 79 and 84. *Retrancher* means to suppress, cut off a part, prune, remove, amputate, excise, and eliminate. Freud's clearest statement about foreclosure is found in "The Neuro-Psychoses of Defence" (*SE* III, 58), where the verb form *verwirft* is translated by Strachey as "rejects": "In both the instances [of defence] considered so far, defence against the incompatible idea was effected by separating it from its affect; the idea itself remained in consciousness, even though weakened and isolated. There is, however, a much more energetic and successful kind of defence. Here, the ego rejects the incompatible idea together with its affect and behaves as if the idea had never occurred to the ego at all. *But from the moment at which this has been successfully done the subject is in a psychosis, which can only be classified as 'hallucinatory confusion.'*"

(387,5) The usual French for what is known in English as Freud's "primary process" is *processus primaire*; here Lacan gives *procès primaire* (primal process).

(388,1) *Comme étant* (as existent) could, alternatively, be rendered as "in the guise of a being."

(388,3) *Au jour de la symbolisation primordiale* (to light in the primordial symbolization) could also be rendered as "into the light of primordial symbolization"; *au jour du symbolique* (to light in the symbolic) could also be rendered as "into the light of the symbolic."

(388,4) See *SE* XIX, 239, which reads "the ego took things into itself or expelled them from itself." Lacan referred to punctuation in his introduction to Hyppolite's presentation.

(389,2) Freud's sentence is from *SE* XIX, 237 (translation modified). *Cause tout seul* (talks all by itself) could also be rendered as "talks to itself" or "causes all by itself."

(389,3) *SE* XVII, 85, reads, "When I was five years old, I was playing in the garden near my nurse, and was carving with my pocket-knife in the bark of one of the walnut trees that come into my dream as well. Suddenly, to my unspeakable terror, I noticed that I had cut through the little finger of my (right or left?) hand, so that it was hanging on by its skin. I felt no pain, but great fear. I did not venture to say anything to my nurse, who was only a few paces distant, but I sank down on the nearest seat and sat there incapable of casting another glance at my finger. At last I calmed down, took a look at the finger, and saw that it was entirely uninjured."

(390,4) *Moufte* (balk) could also be rendered as "open his trap" or "flinch."

(392,1) *Déclic* (click) is a notoriously difficult term to translate, signifying as it does something that happens or gives way ("snaps"), which then constitutes a breakthrough or turning point of some kind (in comprehension, in speaking a language, in one's psychical state, etc.).

(392,3) Lacan here uses a term, *ek-sistence* (which he later spells *ex-sistence*), which was first introduced into French in translations of Heidegger's work (e.g., *Being and Time*), as a translation for the Greek *ekstasis* and the German *Ekstase*. The root meaning of the term in Greek is standing outside of or standing apart from something. In Greek, it was generally used for the "removal" or "displacement" of something, but it also came to be applied to states of mind which we would now call "ecstatic." (Thus a derivative meaning of the word is "ecstasy.") Heidegger often played on the root meaning of the word, "standing outside" or "stepping outside oneself," but also on its close connection in Greek with the root of the word for "existence." Lacan uses it to talk about "an existence which stands apart from," which insists as it were from the outside, to talk about something not included on the inside, something which, rather than being intimate, is "extimate."

(394,4) Lacan's interpretation of the English account of the case leaves something to be desired; here, for example, the English reads as follows: "[O]ne day the patient reported he had just discovered in the library a treatise published years ago in which the same basic idea was developed. It was a treatise with which he had been familiar, since he had glanced at it some time ago" (page 22).

(394,5) Again, Lacan's interpretation of the English is open to question. Kris writes: "His paradoxical tone of satisfaction and excitement [about finding his idea in the treatise in the library] led me to inquire in very great detail about the text he was afraid to plagiarize. In a process of extended scrutiny it turned out that the old publication contained useful support of his thesis but no hint of the thesis itself" (Ibid., 22).

(395,3) *Désordre* (disorder) can also be rendered as "chaos," "havoc," or "mess."

(396,1) Lacan inserts "(*sic*)" after the word he proposes to translate Kris' "exploratory": *préparatoire* (preparatory). His French rendition of Kris' text is highly abbreviated.

(397,2) Reading *patrie* (homeland) for *partie* (part).

(397,3) Lacan provides a comment here (which I have omitted) on the English term "engineering," suggesting that it is related to the famous American "how to," or, if not, to the notion of planning (discussed in the last section of Kris' article). He seems, however, not to understand the meaning of the verb form, "to engineer," as used here, for the translation he provides is "s'en emparer est une question de savoir s'y prendre" (taking it is a matter of knowing how to go about it).

(397,4) Lacan perhaps confuses "attractive" with "attentive" here, because he suggests in his translation that these are restaurants where one is well looked after, or well attended to (*où l'on est bien soigné*).

(398,6) On "introjection of the analyst's ego," see, for example, R. Sterba, "The Fate of the Ego in Analytic Therapy," *IJP* XV, 2–3 (1934): 117–26.

Notes to "The Freudian Thing"

(401,6) *Il se consommait* (it occurred) can also be rendered as "it came to an end" or "it was at its height."

(402,2) It should be kept in mind throughout this article that *sens* (meaning) also means both direction and sense.

(406,2) Lacan makes a pun here on the French pronunciation of *Bondy* and *bandits*. The Bondy Forest, to the north of Paris, was long famous as a haunt of bandits.

(406,3) *Gros sabots* (big clodhoppers) figuratively means all-too-obvious allusions or intentions visible from a mile away.

(407,1) The *Pays du Tendre* was an allegorical country in which love was the sole preoccupation. It was the creation of Mademoiselle de Scudéry and other novelists of the seventeenth century, described in *La carte du tendre* (map of Tendre).

(407,2) *Cornes-au-cul* (all that other crap) is an expression found in Alfred Jarry's "La Chanson du Décervelage," in *Ubu Roi ou les Polonais* (Paris: Eugène Fasquelle, 1922), 183–86. It is an exclamation (like "wow," "damn," or "shiver me timbers"), which literally means horns on (or in) the ass (it is found, in the singular, with this meaning in Rabelais' *Gargantua*, chapter 16); here it seems to suggest something like "etcetera" or "and all the rest." *Cornes* (horns) by itself commonly refers to cuckoldry.

(407,3) *Mic-mac* (mess) can, alternatively, be rendered as "intrigue." *New-look* ("new-look") was a term introduced by Christian Dior in 1947 to describe a new style in clothing; it was later applied to politics as well.

(408,3) The unusual *s'il faut dire* (if it must be said) may be a play on the homophony between *faut* (must) and *faux* (false). The *écrin* (jewelry box) at the end of the paragraph may be a reference to the "jewel-case" in Dora's dream, which Freud associates with the female genitals (*SE* VII, 64 and 69–70). In old French, *écrin* is occasionally used to refer to a box for precious items of any kind, including the bones of a king, which would perhaps allow it to be rendered as "casket."

(408,4) *La chose parle d'elle-même* (The Thing Speaks of Itself) is an idiomatic expression meaning it is self-explanatory; it could also be translated as "The Thing Speaks All by Itself."

(409,1) *Moi la vérité, je parle* (I, truth, speak) could also be rendered as "I, truth, am speaking." Later on, *je parle* (I speak) could be translated as "I am speaking."

(409,2) *Pigeon-vole* (certain games) refers to a children's game in which one player pronounces the name of an object followed by "vole" (flies), and the other players must raise their hands *only if* the object can, in fact, fly.

(410,1) *Caute* (cunning) is an old French term with a number of different meanings, running the gamut from crafty, subtle, wily, cunning, and sly to circumspect, cautious, prudent, and wary. Cf. Pascal's "Cleopatra's nose: had it been shorter, the whole face of the earth would have changed," *Pensées* (Brunschvicg ed. 162).

(410,2) *SE* IV, 277–78.

(411,1) *Égarement* (deviation) has a number of meanings, including going astray, deviating from the straight and narrow (of a religious or other doctrine), mental distraction, and error (of one's ways).

(411,2) *Flair* (smell) could also be translated as "sixth sense" or "intuition." Cf. Carl Jung, "On the Psychology of the Trickster-Figure" (1954), *Collected Works*, vol. 9. *Je me défends* (I am being defensive) could also be rendered as "I am defending myself" or "I defend myself."

(411,3) *Parade* (parade) is a fencing term that can be translated as "parry" or "parade"; it also means (ceremonial) display.

(411,4) *Les bijoux indiscrets* (*The Indiscreet Jewels*) is a book by Denis Diderot, written in 1748.

(412,1) A golem, in Jewish folklore, is a man-made figure constructed in the form of a human being and endowed with life, an automaton.

(412,3) *Boursouflure* (budding) could also be rendered as "swelling."

(412,4) See Giordano Bruno, *De gli eroici furori* in *Opere italiane* (Bari: Gius, Laterza & Figli, 1923–27), translated by Paul Eugene Memmo, Jr. as *The Heroic Frenzies* (Chapel Hill: University of North Carolina Press, 1966). In the myth, Actaeon, coming upon Diana during her bath, is turned by her into a stag and then chased and killed by his own dogs.

(413,1) *Aigle* (eagle) is also slang for "genius." Lacan seems to be making fun here of those who would situate the role of language at this level (where the fact that an airplane in the sky looks like the analyst—or like the eagle that represents the analyst's "genius"—is considered to be an articulate response from the gods).

(413,2) *Fonds ni forme* (content nor form): *le fond et la forme* is usually translated as "content and form" or "substance and form"; note, however, that Lacan uses *fonds* here, which has certain meanings that differ from those of *fond* (such as fund, collection, land, business, assets, reserve, ground, and even constitution, as in *fonds mental*). Note, too, that *fond* and *fonds* overlap in meaning so much in certain cases that many authors use them interchangeably; Littré suggests they should be considered the same word.

(414,1) On Stalin's pronouncement, see *Écrits* 1966, 496, fn1.

(414,3) *Ordre de la chose* (The Thing's Order) could also be understood as "How the Thing is Ordered (or Organized)."

(414,6) *Unité* (unity) can also be rendered as "unit."

(414,7) *S'assure ordinairement de* (usually secures) can also be rendered as "usually ensures" or "is usually ensured by."

(415,2) *Désordre* (disorder) can also be rendered as "chaos" or "mess"; it is not a reference to the eponymous psychiatric notion.

(415,8) Regarding the "total social fact," see Marcel Mauss, *The Gift*.

(416,1) *Conscience commune* (collective consciousness) seems to be a sociological term introduced by Durkheim.

(416,4) "They will never know anything about it, even in the way implied by repression": This seems to be a paraphrase of Freud's comment about the Wolf Man's *Verwerfung* of castration (*SE* XVII, 84).

(416,6) The German is from *GW* XV, 86; see *SE* XXII, 80.

(416,fn1) See Lacan's "Science and Truth" in *Écrits* 1966.

(417,1) Actually, there seems to be no such published English translation. The early translation of the *New Introductory Lectures on Psycho-Analysis* by W. J. H. Sprott (New York: W. W. Norton, 1933) provides "Where id was, there shall ego be"; the *Standard Edition* provides "Where id was, there ego shall be" (1964). The fact remains that both translations take *Es* and *Ich* here to be the Freudian agencies, id and ego.

(417,fn1) In the *Standard Edition*, the following translation is provided: "It is a work of culture—not unlike the draining of the Zuider Zee" (*SE* XXII, 80).

(418,fn1) Marie Bonaparte was the author of that translation.

(419,3) See Lacan's "Variations on the Standard Treatment" (1955) in *Écrits* 1966, written as a counterweight to an article that appeared in the same *Encyclopédie médico-chirurgicale, Psychiatrie* describing the "standard treatment."

(420,1) *Retourner* (re-turn) means to turn around, turn over, turn upside down, invert, reverse, return, and send back.

(420,2) The Latin here refers to the correspondence theory of truth whereby truth lies in the correspondence (*adæquatio*) between a thing (*rei*) and our conception of it (*intellectus*). French uses the term *adéquation* where English uses "correspondence." In the next sentence, Points reads *qui nous parle, voire qui parle à nous* (instead of *en nous*), which might be translated as "that speaks us, nay, that speaks to us."

(420,5) *Chosisme* (literally "thingism") here is likely a reference to the *nouveau roman* (or antinovel), characterized by the novelist's concern with things in themselves, not things as human symbols or metaphors. It simultaneously refers to a philosophical doctrine in which concepts are taken as concrete things. Note that Lacan refers to Anna Freud's language in *The Ego and the Mechanisms of Defense* as "*chosiste*" (Seminar I, 76/63).

(421,2) Heinz Hartmann's "The Development of the Ego Concept in Freud's Work," *IJP* XXVII, 6 (1956): 425–38, includes much of this terminology about the ego being autonomous. Later in the paragraph we find another reference to Heinz Hartmann who, in his "Technical Implications of Ego Psychology," writes that "analysis is gradually and unavoidably, though hesitantly, becoming a general psychology . . ." (*PQ* XX, 1 [1951]: 35), and who, in "The Development of the Ego Concept in Freud's Work," writes that "the trend toward a general psychology has been inherent in psycho-analysis from its inception" (*IJP* XXVII, 6 [1956]: 434). In Seminar I (33/25) Lacan seems to suggest that Kris also refers to it in that way. Cf. R. M. Loewenstein's "Conflict and Autonomous Ego Development During the Phallic Phase" in *The Psychoanalytic Study of the Child*, V (New York: International Universities Press, 1950).

(421,4) Lacan here and in the next sentence shortens the usual *opération* (operation) to *o-pé*, leaving out *ration*; pronounced in a certain way, *c't o-pé* sounds like *stopper* (to stop).

(421,6) Regarding the "pulpit of quarrelsome memory," see Nicolas Boileau's poem, "Le lutrin." A *table à la Tronchin* is a writing table whose top can be raised and tilted as much as one likes. Introduced in the fifteenth century, it was popularized in the eighteenth century by

Théodore Tronchin, a Swiss doctor (1709–1781).

(422,2) Speculation, faulty banking policy, and political intrigue (in which John Law played an important role) centering around the rue Quincampoix in Paris led to the bankruptcy of the French financial system in 1720. A well-known hunchback in that street let people sign agreements on his hump as if it were a desk or lectern, a service for which he is reported to have received 150,000 pounds (the "hefty rent"). *Cote* (standing) also happens to mean furniture tax!

(422,3) *Intersigne* (index) is a mark or index, or the mysterious relationship that appears (by telepathy or second sight) between two facts.

(423,2) A *motion nègre-blanc* (ambiguous mollifying motion) is a (parliamentary) motion written in ambiguous terms designed to appease a number of different parties.

(423,3) Cf. Pascal's reference to man as "un roseau pensant" ("a thinking reed"), *Pensées* (Brunschvicg ed. 347–48).

(424,2) Or "some supposedly internal progress . . . as sporadic as the purely external arrangements that condition it." This is a possible reference to the mirrors placed on opposite walls in the entrance halls of thousands of Parisian apartment buildings.

(424,5) *Elles* (they) seems to refer back to "technical analyses" here.

(425,3) *À sa mesure* (measured against) suggests that reality is considered to correspond to the ego, fit the ego, or be proportionate to the ego (as when we say "on a human scale"). But it also evokes the saying that "man is the measure of all things," evoked again a few lines down.

(426,2) *Moi* also means ego. Giving a "t" to *doit* makes it a third person singular.

(426,5) The pleonasm seems to be the addition of the "personally" to the "you" in "interest you personally" (in the French, "you" and "personally" are separated by the clause between the dashes in the English).

(428,2) In France, a notary has considerable legal training and exercises many of the functions of a lawyer. *Attelage* (team) evokes a team of oxen or horses, or the harness or yoke that keeps them working as a team. It can also mean coupling or attachment. In military parlance, *Rassemblement!* (Regroup!) would normally be translated as "Fall in!" But it literally means assembling, gathering, union, rallying, and rounding up.

(429,1) "So are you": or "Takes one to know one" (said when someone accuses you of being a pig, for example); cf. *SE* XII, 52.

(429,2) Although I have been unable to find the adjective *recollectif* (recollective) anywhere, it seems to be related to *rassemblement* (regroup). The series of three here (intuitive illumination, recollective command, and the retorting aggressiveness of verbal echo) thus corresponds to the three situations Lacan described above: the "Aha!" moment, "Regroup!" and the "So are you" of the transitivist quarrel. On "retorting aggressiveness," cf. *Écrits* 1966, 199 where we find the expression "aggressive retortions."

(429,4) See John Rickman, *Selected Contributions to Psycho-Analysis* (New York: Basic Books, 1957 and Glasgow: The University Press, 1957), above all chapters 19, 21, and 22. *Insoutenable* (untenable) also means unbearable.

(429,6–430,1 and 3) Note that, while in the text I translate *l'Autre* as the Other with a capital *O*, and *l'autre* as the other with a lowercase *o*, in Lacan's schemas and mathemes the former is designated by A and the latter by *a* and *a*′. *Réunion* (union) is a term used in set theory and is an early reference to the different "vels" Lacan discusses in Seminar XI.

(430,2) *Dégager*, in *qui dégage formellement la mort* (which formally brings out death), has many different meanings, including to redeem, release, radiate, separate out, isolate, set off, highlight, define, elucidate, relieve, and liberate.

(430,7) Points erroneously reads *contraires* (contraries) instead of *contraintes* (constraints) in the first sentence.

(431,1) *Ajustées à* (worked out at) could alternatively be translated as "adjusted to" or "adapted to."

(432,1) See Lacan's discussion of the plus/minus (+/–) series in Seminar II and his development of the 1,2,3, and α,β,γ,δ series in the "Suite" to the "Seminar on 'The Purloined Letter'" in *Écrits* 1966.

The last sentence of the paragraph is Lacan's

way of saying that the nth term in the series is determined by the several terms that precede it in the series; the nth term can be *any* of the possible letters (α,β,γ,δ) only if the n–1st, n–2nd, and n–3rd terms are not fixed in advance (i.e., the "compensations demanded by" the n–4th term are satisfied by the nth term).

(432,2) *Motifs* (motives) can also be rendered as "themes" or "leitmotivs."

(432,3) Points erroneously reads *conversation* (conversation) here instead of *conservation* (preservation).

(433,6) *L'invité de pierre* (the stone guest) evokes the statue of the dead commander in the Don Juan story; see, for example, Molière's version entitled *Dom Juan ou le festin de pierre*, known in English as *Don Juan or the Stone Guest.*

(433,7) The use of *raisin* (grape) at the beginning of the sentence and *grappe de la colère* (literally, bunch or bundle of anger) evoke *les raisins de la colère*, "the grapes of wrath" from "The Battle Hymn of the Republic" by Julia Ward Howe. *Raisin vert* (sour grape) also evokes the "sour grapes" referred to in *Jeremiah* 31.29; cf. *Écrits* 1966, 448 and 450.

(434,5) *Quiproquo* (case of mistaken identity) also means misunderstanding.

(436,3) On Freud's three challenges or "'impossible' professions," see, for example, *SE* XXIII, 248. On certain points made in "The Freudian Thing," see Lacan's later comments in Seminar XIX, March 8, 1972.

Notes to "Psychoanalysis and Its Teaching"

(437,9) *Suppôt* (basis) can often be translated as "servant" or "henchman" (as in *suppôt du diable* or *suppôt de Satan*), but it was also used, up until the seventeenth century (in the literature of which Lacan was very well versed), to mean "that which serves as a basis for something" and in philosophy to mean "substance with its accidents."

(437,10) *Les psychanalystes d'aujourd'hui* (contemporary psychoanalysts) is a probable reference to the collective publication, *La psychanalyse d'aujourd'hui* ("Contemporary Psychoanalysis") (Paris: PUF, 1956), discussed extensively by Lacan in "Direction of the Treatment." The reference is even clearer further on in the article: *Écrits* 1966, 453 and 454.

(439,3) *Il se fait n'être* (he makes himself be) also evokes the homonym *naître*, to be born. *Ne-uter* emphasizes the components of the Latin *neuter*, meaning neither the one nor the other. The *n'* in *n'être* is simply part of the usual French construction leading up to *ni l'un ni l'autre*.

(441,7) *Tête pensante* (intellectual leader) designates a person who occupies a central place in an organization or project ("the brains").

(442,2) See *Écrits* 1966, 514 and 830–31.

(442,4) Menenius Agrippa, faced with an uprising by the plebeians, told the latter a parable about how the stomach and the limbs cannot do without each other, forming one body as they do, just like the rulers and the people. The story was taken up by Quintilian, Plutarch, and Rabelais (*Tiers livre*, chapters 3 and 4), among others.

(444,3) See Jakob Böhme's *De Signatura Rerum* (1651); in English see *The Signature of All Things and Other Writings* (Cambridge and London: James Clarke, 1969).

(445,1) *Verbe* (verb) also means word or language.

(445,4) Lacan juxtaposes "*milieu*" here (meaning environment but also middle) with *arêtes* (edges). *Consistant* (consistent) also means substantial.

(446,1) It is said that Diogenes, the Cynic, searched for an honest man in broad daylight with a lighted lantern.

(446,5) *Le trébuchement de la conduite* (bungled actions) literally means the stumbling of behavior.

(447,2) *Séquences* (sequences) presumably refers to the order of scenes in a dream which can express logical relations (such as if/then and either/or) according to Freud; see *The Interpretation of Dreams*, chapter 6, section C, "The Means of Representation in Dreams." See also "Instance of the Letter."

(447,3) See "The Psychical Mechanism of Forgetfulness" (1898), *SE* III, 289–97.

(447,4) This may be a reference to the tale of Tristan and Isolde, in which a part of Tristan's sword remains stuck in the head of the giant, Morholt, whom he slays. Cf. *Écrits* 1966, 379.

(448,2) *Verts* (sour) also means green, unripe, sprightly, sharp, stiff, and severe. The grammar here also allows us to read "far too sour to be those . . ." Given the number of references in this text to Jean de la Fontaine's fables, note that "The Fox and the Grapes" also refers to grapes that are too green.

(448,3) See Jean de la Fontaine's fable, "The Fox and the Stork." *Mouvant* (motor force) usually means shifting, undulating, unstable, or fluid, but its older use implies a motor or driving force.

(448,4) Phone numbers in France were at first expressed as a name (usually of a town) followed by four numbers, as in Passy 22.15. "Jeremiah 31.29" *could* thus be read in the same way.

(448,6) Raymond Roussel (1877–1933) was a French writer who has been claimed as a precursor by numerous authors associated with surrealism and poststructuralism.

(449,1) *Chattière* (peephole) also means cat-flap (a door that allows a cat to go in and out of a room or house) or roof vent, and is perhaps more often written *chatière*. There seem to be at least two grammatical problems with this sentence; I have assumed that a comma should be inserted before *un oeil appliqué* (to an eye glued) and that we should read *d'où seront sortis . . . les choix* instead of *d'où sera sorti . . . les choix*.

(449,2) Dear Abby corresponds roughly to agony aunt in the United Kingdom. On "the law of the heart," see Hegel's *Phenomenology of Mind* (New York: Harper & Row, 1967), 391 ff. Lacan is likely referring, after that, to Franz Alexander and Theodore French's term "corrective emotional experience" found in their *Psychoanalytic Therapy: Principles and Application* (New York: Ronald Press, 1946).

(449,4) *Ils en sont venus à baptiser carpe du don oblatif le lapin de la copulation génitale* (they ended up confusing the apple of genital copulation with the orange of the oblative gift) plays on the French expression *le mariage de la carpe et du lapin* (the marriage of the carp to the rabbit), which is considered to be a bizarre alliance of two incompatible beings; Lacan would thus seem to be saying that analysts have confused genital copulation with the oblative gift, two things that are fundamentally irreconcilable. The carp and the gift may also be a reference to the story of "The Heron and the Turtle" from Sumerian literature. Cf. Freud, *SE* XXIII, 262.

(450,4) The passage parenthetically cited is from *Écrits* 1966, 434.

(450,5–451,1) *Écrits* 1966, 433–34.

(452,1) *Étreindre* (clutch) means both hug or embrace and clasp or constrain. On lures, see *Écrits* 1966, 95–96 and 188–91. *Simile* (facsimiles): I have been unable to find this term in any dictionary. It might also be rendered by "simulacra" here; given the context, it does not seem to be a term of rhetoric, though it is probably related to the Latin *similis*.

(452,2) This is a possible reference to the way knights (*cavaliers*) in the game of chess move in a zigzagging fashion, somewhat like the L schema. However, *cavaliers* can also be translated as "dance partners" and *dame* as "lady," the "hysteric's step" then clearly referring to a sort of dance. Note that Freud refers to the "Knight's Move" in *Studies on Hysteria*, *SE* II, 289.

(452,3) *Lui donner corps* (incarnate her) means to fill her out, give her strength, or give her body. *Prendre corps* (take form) means to take on a real, tangible form, to become concrete or precise. *Contrainte par corps*, which literally means bodily constraint, also means attachment of property in legal proceedings; *corps* by itself means body. *Le* (her) after *contrainte par corps* could, instead, refer to "this body." The whole paragraph is ambiguously formulated and is open to multiple interpretations.

(452,4) Lacan seems to be saying that, had a certain narcissistic identification occurred, she could satisfy both her desire and the other's desire by situating herself as an object.

(453,1) Venus (or Aphrodite) rescued Paris from single combat with Menelaus during the Trojan War.

(453,6) Reading *d'autant plus que* (all the more so since), as in the original version of the text, for *d'autant que plus*.

(453,7) Ernest Jones introduced the Greek term "aphanisis" to refer to the "total, and of course permanent, extinction of the capacity (including opportunity) for sexual enjoyment"; see "Early Development of Female Sexuality"

(1927), in *Papers on Psycho-Analysis*, 5th edition (Boston: Beacon, 1961), 440.

(454,2) *Pyramide et mille-pattes* (human pyramid and centipede) are children's games.

(454,8) *Appareil* (apparatus) also means stonework or set of elements working toward the same end that form a whole (i.e., a system).

(455,3) While the term "frustration" is found in the English version of Freud's discussion of the Schreber case (*SE* XII, 57 and 62), the German there reads *Versagung* (*GW* VIII, 293 and 298), which Lacan says implies renunciation, not frustration (*Écrits* 1966, 460–61). See also *SE* XVI, 300, and *GW* XI, 310. Cf. *Écrits* 1966, 543.

(455,5) The writing on the wall of the words Mene, Tekel, Parsin is from *Daniel* 5.25.

(456,1) Reading *lit* (reads) instead of *dit* (says). Monsieur Jourdain is a character in Molière's play, *Le bourgeois gentilhomme*, best known in English as *The Would-Be Gentleman* (see especially Act II, Scene 4), who speaks in prose without realizing it. Cf. *Écrits* 1966, 370 and 478.

(456,2) Auguste Mariette (1821–1881) was a French archeologist who worked extensively in Egypt. *Reprend* (alters) could also be translated as "repeats," "reassumes," or "picks up." *Psychologie de faculté* (academic psychology) may also be a reference to the old school of "faculty psychology" that attempted to account for human behavior by positing various mental powers or agencies on an a priori basis. It may, too, refer to the Faculty of Medicine, often referred to ironically as simply *la faculté* when writers wanted to ridicule the ineptitude of physicians.

(457,6) See "The Situation of Psychoanalysis and the Training of Psychoanalysts in 1956," above all *Écrits* 1966, 473–75. Note that this text written in 1956 should precede "Psychoanalysis and Its Teaching" (1957) in *Écrits*.

Notes to "The Situation of Psychoanalysis and the Training of Psychoanalysts in 1956"

(459,4) *Confiné dans* (confined to): Lacan had not been allowed a *teaching* role in the Société Psychanalytique de Paris.

(459,8) This is an allusion to Montesquieu's *Persian Letters* in which he writes, "Ah! ah! Monsieur est Persan? C'est une chose bien extraordinaire! Comment peut-on être Persan?" See Montesquieu, *Oeuvres complètes* (Paris: Gallimard, [1721] 1949), vol. I, 176–77. John Ozell rendered it, in 1722, as "Ha, ha! The Gentleman a *Persian!* Strange! That any body shou'd be a *Persian!*" in his translation entitled *Persian Letters* (New York & London: Garland, [1722] 1972), vol. I, 108.

(460,4) *Ils courent à la voix* (they take to shouting) could instead mean they resort to voting.

(460,5) Lacan defined psychoanalysis as "the treatment one expects from a psychoanalyst" in "Variations on the Standard Treatment," *Écrits* 1966, 329.

(462,4) Alternate for "free-floating attention": "evenly hovering (or evenly suspended) attention."

(462,8) See Theodor Reik's *Listening with the Third Ear* (New York: Garden City Books, 1949), published in Great Britain as *The Inner Experience of a Psychoanalyst* (London: George Allen & Unwin, 1949).

(463,1) *Gobelet* (shaker) seems here to refer to a prestidigitator's instrument for tricks involving sleight of hand, which takes the form of a goblet.

(463,2) *Hic et nunc* is the Latin for here and now. *Les corneilles auxquelles nous revoilà bayant* (the crows we are once again wasting our time gawking at) is based on the expression, *bayer aux corneilles*, meaning to waste one's time stupidly staring at the sky; *corneilles* means crows.

(464,2) *Noeud* (knot) also means nodal point.

(464,3) The pelican is considered by the French to be a symbol of a father's love for his children. Various Medieval notions about the pelican's behavior, including the belief that it feeds or revives its young with blood pecked from its own breast, led to the pelican becoming a symbol for Christ.

(464,4) *Siège* (seat) may possibly refer back to *chaise percée* (commode).

(465,1) *Mon patient ne pouvait toujours pas*

me sentir (my patient still could not smell me) also means my patient still could not stand me.

(465,2) According to *The Bibliographer's Manual of English Literature*, by W. T. Lowndes (London: Henry G. Bohn, 1863), the author of this text attributed to Swift is unknown; the original English title continues as follows "after the manner of the ingenious Dr. S—ft" (London: J. Roberts, 1726).

(466,7) I have been unable to find *accisme* (accismus) in any French dictionary, but it seems quite clearly to come from the Greek *akkismos*, meaning coyness or affectation. The *OED* defines accismus as "A feigned refusal of that which is earnestly desired."

(467,3) Jan Niecislaw Baudouin de Courtenay was a Polish linguist (1845–1929) who introduced the linguistic term "phoneme" and anticipated facets of structural linguistics.

(468,1) *Retors* (twisted) also means devious, wily, or crafty.

(468,3) See Rabelais' *Le quart livre*, chapters 55 and 56. In English, see *The Complete Works of François Rabelais*, trans. Donald M. Frame (Berkeley: University of California Press, 1991). According to Louis Moland, the editor of a complete edition of Rabelais' work, the notion of "words that freeze" (*des paroles qui gèlent*) is borrowed from Plutarch, who attributes it to Antiphanes, one of Plato's disciples. Plutarch says, "Antiphanes, one of Plato's acquaintances, playfully said that there was a city where words froze in the air as soon as they were pronounced, and when they melted in the summer, the city's inhabitants could hear what they had spoken about during the winter." See *François Rabelais: Tout ce qui existe de ses oeuvres* (Paris: Garnier Frères, 1880), 699.

(468,5) *Coupure* (cut) also evokes Gaston Bachelard's *coupure* (or *rupture*) *epistémologique*, "epistemological break," referred to by Thomas Kuhn as "paradigm shift."

(469,2) Lacan is referring here to Jung's *Wandlungen und Symbole der Libido* (Leipzig and Vienna: 1912). *Transformations and Symbols of the Libido* was first published in English as *Psychology of the Unconscious* (1916); it was rewritten in 1952 and republished as *Symbols of Transformation*; it was later translated by Beatrice M. Hinkle as *Psychology of the Unconscious: A Study of the Transformations and Symbolisms of the Libido* (Princeton, New Jersey: Princeton University Press, 1991), as part of *The Collected Works of C. G. Jung*.

(470,2) *Orinomante* (oneiromancer): I have assumed that an inversion has occurred in the spelling of this word, which should read *oniromante*, referring thus to someone who reads the future, or engages in divination, by means of dreams (from the Greek *oneiromantis*; another English equivalent is oneiromantist; the closest French equivalent I have actually found is *oniromancie*). Otherwise Lacan may be gallicizing a Greek term here, or possibly even forging one. *Mante* corresponds to the Greek *mantis* and the English mantic. If the original spelling is correct, *orino* could be based on the Greek *orinein*, meaning to stir up or excite, but is more likely a misspelled version of *orneo*, as in the Greek *orneomantis*, referring to the reading of portents in the flights of birds (or in the entrails of sacrificial victims) by an augur, and more generally to those who foretell the future (prophet or soothsayer). One further possibility might stem from the old French term *orine*, meaning origin.

The dream's "elaboration" is probably the "first revision" of the dream by displacement and condensation, prior to the secondary revision (known in French as *l'élaboration secondaire*); it could also possibly be the recounting of the dream by the dreamer. Lacan does not provide any page reference here; note that the term "rebus" seems to initially appear on the first page of chapter 6, "The Dream-Work," in *The Interpretation of Dreams* (*SE* IV, 277).

(471,4) *Un en-deçà de la parole* (a realm that is shy of speech) seems to refer here to the realm that involves speech and not something beyond it.

(471,6 & fn2) *Numero Deus impare gaudet* ("The God delights in odd numbers" or "Uneven numbers are the god's delight") comes from Virgil's *Eclogues*, 8, 75. The burlesque translation (the number two rejoices in being odd) can be found in Gide's *Paludes*.

(472,1) This might possibly be understood as saying that the analyst and the analysand, like Vladimir and Estragon in Samuel Beckett's play, *Waiting for Godot* (New York: Grove Press, 1954), are waiting for the third party, the Other or Godot, to appear.

(472,5) *Se fondent* (are grounded) is ambiguous, since both *fonder* and *fondre* are written *fondent* in the third person plural. The first might suggest the translation "are grounded," the second "fuse," "combine," or "melt together."

(474,4) *Volant* (steering wheel) also means reserve fund, shuttlecock, and safety margin.

(475,4) *Suffisance* (Sufficiency) also means self-importance, arrogance, self-satisfaction, self-complacency, and smugness. Lacan plays on a number of these meanings in the pages that follow.

(476,5) *Petits Souliers* (Little Shoes) literally means small shoes, but to be in one's *petits souliers* means to feel uncomfortable, be in an awkward or difficult situation, or be in a quandary. *Ce maintien* (this very staying) seems to hark back to *s'y tenir* (staying there) in the previous sentence. However, *maintien* also means deportment.

(477,4) *Il n'y a pas de petites économies* (a penny saved is a penny earned) is an expression akin to "every little bit helps" in English, and literally means "there's no such thing as small savings." The French expression is often completed by the following: "Il n'y a que de grandes pertes" ("There are only big losses").

(477,5) See Hans Christian Andersen's "The Emperor's New Clothes."

(478,2) *Le bourgeois gentilhomme* is the title of a play by Molière, best known in English as *The Would-Be Gentleman* (see especially Act II, Scene 4). Its main character, Monsieur Jourdain, speaks in prose without realizing it. Cf. *Écrits* 1966, 370 and 456.

(479,1) See *SE* XVIII, 116.

(479,6) *Godant* (trap) is derived from the old French verb *goder* (to rejoice or to rail someone), and is a variant of *gaudir*, itself related to the Latin *gaudere* (to enjoy: *jouir*, in contemporary French), which is evoked in the next sentence where Lacan refers anew to the Latin phrase: *numero Deus impare gaudet*. *Godant* can also mean hearsay, rumor, lie, or deception.

(479,fn1) This corresponds to pages 278–79 in the newer Points edition (Paris: Seuil, 1980). Lacan modifies here the passage as it appears there and adds a capital A to *autre*. See Paul Valéry, "Lettre à un ami," in *M. Teste* (Paris: l'Intelligence, 1927), 59–61.

(480,1) *Réunion* (meeting) also means union in set theory.

(480,2) On the number three, see Aristotle's *On the Heavens*, 268a: "For, as the Pythagoreans say, the world and all that is in it is determined by the number three, since beginning and middle and end give the number of an 'all,' and the number they give is the triad. And so, having taken these three from nature as (so to speak) laws of it, we make further use of the number three in the worship of the Gods. Further, we use the terms in practice in this way. Of two things, or men, we say 'both,' but not 'all': three is the first number to which the term 'all' has been appropriated."

(480,4) *Passée la borne* (having gone too far) literally means having gone beyond the mile marker; Lacan attributes the expression to Fenouillard here.

(481,5) *Chicane* (zigzagging) also means chicane and deception.

(482,6) *Licence* (license and then degree) can mean an authorization to teach or a bachelor's degree. *Certains crièrent à la licence* (Certain people clamored for a license) also means that certain people got into an uproar over licentiousness.

(483,3) *Prurit* (pruritus) also means irrepressible desire.

(485,3) The months without an r in them are May, June, July, and August, corresponding more or less to summer vacation in the northern hemisphere.

(485,5) "Index" is a probable reference to the catalog of books prohibited by the Roman Catholic Church.

(486,7) *Les soins d'une sépulture décente* (the care involved in providing a decent burial) is vaguely worded and could instead be rendered as "the care required to maintain a decent grave site."

(489,3) Freud's "decisive schema" can be found in *SE* XVIII, 116. The expression, "narcissism of minor differences," is found in *SE* XXI, 114.

(489,4) *Débucher* (critical juncture) refers to the moment at which an animal being hunted suddenly emerges from the woods.

(490,fn1) See Heinz Hartmann, Ernst Kris, and Rudolf Loewenstein, "Notes on the Theory of Aggression," in *The Psychoanalytic Study of the Child*, Vol. 3/4 (New York: International Universities Press, 1949), 14.

Notes to "The Instance of the Letter"

(493,1) *Instance* (Instance) can take on virtually all of the meanings of "instance" in English (urgent or earnest solicitation, entreaty or instigation, insistence, lawsuit or prosecution, argument, example or case, and exception); in addition, it can mean authority as well as agency (it is used, for example, to refer to Freud's agencies, *Instanzen*, the ego, id, and superego).

(493,3) *Commandait* (commissioned) can also mean commanded, obliged, imposed, forced, necessitated, ordered, exacted, required, called for, and enjoined. The first two occurrences of "writing" in this text translate *l'écrit* and the third occurrence *un écrit*, not *écriture*; the first two could also be translated as "the written" and the third as "a written text."

(493,4) It should be kept in mind throughout this essay that *sens* (rendered in this instance as "sense") can also be translated as "meaning" or "direction." *Facteur* (factor) can also mean postman, mailman, or purveyor.

(493,5) The exceptional class may be an allusion to Seminar III, chapter 19, "Freud in the Century."

(493,fn1) See *The Notebooks of Leonardo Da Vinci* II, trans. Edward MacCurdy (New York: Reynal & Hitchcock, 1938), 499. Cf. Seminar IV, 337.

(494,7) *Le véridique* (veracity) could, perhaps, also be rendered as "the veridical." See, in particular, the December 1956 issue of the *IJP*, mentioned in Seminar IV, 188.

(494,fn2) See "The Question of Lay Analysis," *SE* XX, 245–48.

(495,fn1) In English, see "Two Aspects of Language and Two Types of Aphasic Disturbances," in *Selected Writings*, vol. II (The Hague: Mouton, 1971), 239–59.

(496,1) *Le drame historique* (the drama of history) could, alternatively, be rendered as "historical drama."

(497,2) As J.-A. Miller points out (in his 1993–1994 seminar entitled "Donc," May 11, 1994), the French here should read *étages* ("floors" or "levels," as it is rendered here), as in the originally published version of the paper, instead of *étapes* (stages).

(497,3) Saussure's text was originally published in French in 1915; a critical edition was prepared by Tullio de Mauro (Paris: Payot, 1972). In English, see Saussure, *Course in General Linguistics*, trans. Wade Baskin (New York: McGraw-Hill, 1959) and, more recently, trans. Roy Harris (Chicago: Open Court, 1983). Page references here to Saussure are first to the critical French edition and then to Baskin's translation.

(498,2) *Nom* (noun) could alternatively be translated as "name." *Rayon* (ray) also means beam, radius, spoke, shelf, and department.

(498,fn1) June 23, 1954, corresponds to chapter 20 of Seminar I.

(498,fn2) The first book mentioned here is Ivor Armstrong Richards and C. K. Ogden, *The Meaning of Meaning* (New York: Harcourt, Brace, [1923] 1945). The full reference for the second book is *Mencius on the Mind: Experiments in Multiple Definition* (London: Kegan Paul, Trench, Trubner & Co., 1932).

(500,1) *Isoloir* (private stall) literally means polling or voting booth; in the nineteenth century, it was used to refer to a place where one is off by oneself, isolated, apart from others.

(500,2) The last few words of the paragraph could, alternatively, be rendered as "in two lines down the main aisle."

(500,5) *Il faudrait n'avoir pas les yeux en face des trous* (one would have to be half-blind) literally means one must not have one's eyes in front of holes or lined up with the holes (sockets); figuratively it means one must be half-asleep, half-blind, or not seeing clearly. Lacan adds here that "it is a fitting image."

(501,2) See Swift's *Gulliver's Travels* (part I, chapter 4), in which the prolonged war between the two kingdoms of Lilliput and Blefuscu originated in a dispute over whether eggs should be broken at the large or small end.

(501,3) The S is not, unfortunately, visible in the English here, the plural of "gentleman" being indicated otherwise than by the addition of an "s." *Coudes* (curves) also means elbow joints and bends. Cf. *Écrits* 1966, 518.

(501,4) The "access" in question here is presumably from one side to the other, that is, from the outside of the train to the inside.

(501,7) Didot and Garamond are names of different typefaces.

(502,1) *Anneaux* (links) is often translated as "rings," but in the context of a *chain*, it means links. The term translated here by "necklace," *collier*, can also be translated as "chain." Saussure introduces the term "chain" in his *Course in General Linguistics*, 103/70.

(502,2) *Locution verbale* (verbal locution) could, alternatively, be translated as "verb phrase."

(502,6) The allusions are to the "I am very dark, but comely" of the Song of Solomon 1.5, and to the nineteenth-century cliché of the "poor, but honest" woman.

(502,fn1) The reference here is to Seminar III, *The Psychoses*. See also *Écrits* 1966, 539–40.

(503,1) See Saussure, *Course in General Linguistics*, 156/112.

(503,2) A "button tie" is a stitch used by an upholsterer to secure a button to fabric and stuffing, for example, to prevent the stuffing from moving; it is, I think, the closest English term to the upholsterer's term Lacan uses: *point de capiton*. Russell Grigg, in his translation of Lacan's Seminar, Book III, *The Psychoses* (New York: W. W. Norton, 1993), renders *capitonnage* as "quilting" and *point de capiton* as "quilting point"; see 293–305.

(503,3) As in "Paul is hit by Peter." Cf. Seminar III, 256. *Temps* (time) also means tense, in the grammatical sense.

(503,fn1) See Seminar III, 297–304 and 326; see also *The New Statesman and Nation*, May 19, 1956.

(504,1) In French, *arbre de la croix*, "tree of the cross," refers to the cross to which Jesus was attached (see the second sentence in the paragraph). I have forged a verb, "to historiate," from the adjective "historiated," meaning decorated with figures of people, animals, or flowers, as illuminated or ornamental initial letters, for example.

On Heraclitus' Ἓν Πάντα, see Lacan's translation of Heidegger's "Logos" in *La Psychanalyse* 1 (1956): 59–79. "Fire-scorched tortoiseshell" refers to early forms of divination (leading up to the *I Ching*) in which tortoiseshell was heated in a fire, causing cracks to appear in it; the cracks were then interpreted.

The verses, in French, are "Non! dit l'Arbre, il dit: Non! dans l'étincellement / De sa tête superbe / Que la tempête traite universellement / Comme elle fait une herbe." This is the last stanza of Paul Valéry's, "Au Platane" in *Charmes* (Paris: Gallimard, 1952), 43; note that according to the edition cited here, the first line reads: "—Non! dit l'Arbre. Il dit: Non! par l'étincellement."

(504,5) I have assumed that the original version, reading *sache* (know) should be preferred here to *cache* (hide) found in *Écrits* 1966.

(504,7) *Étage* (level) also means floor; cf. *Écrits* 1966, 497.

(505,1) A probable reference to Stendhal's "La parole a été donnée à l'homme pour cacher sa pensée" ("Speech was given to man to disguise his thought").

(505,2) *Grimper à l'arbre* literally means to climb the tree, but figuratively means to be fooled, to be a dupe, to be taken in. *Arborer*, meaning to raise (a flag or banner, for example), has come to mean to display or wear ostentatiously.

(505,4) According to Bloch and Von Wartburg, *trouver* probably comes from *tropare*, a derivative of *tropus*, meaning figure of rhetoric.

(505,5) *Bateau* can also take on the figurative sense of an old saw or hackneyed theme.

(506,3) The verse here, "Sa gerbe n'était point avare ni haineuse," is from the poem "Booz endormi." In French and English, see *The Penguin Book of French Verse*, 3 (Baltimore: Penguin Books, 1957), 69–73; the prose translation given there is: "His sheaves of corn were not mean or hateful." Note that *Écrits* 1966 erroneously reads *pas* instead of *point*. On metaphor, see Seminar III, chapters 17 and 18.

(506,fn1) Rudolf M. Loewenstein, the author of the paper mentioned in the third paragraph, refers in it to a "personal communication" with Roman Jakobson.

Jeannot's knife is an allusion to something that retains its name even though everything about it changes; Jeannot changed the blade and the handle of his knife three times, but to him it was still the same knife.

The passage by Goethe can be found in English in *Wilhelm Meister's Apprenticeship*, trans. Eric A. Blackall (New York: Suhrkamp, 1989), 180: "The creepiness, the bowing and scraping, the approving, flattering and insinuating, their adroitness and strutting, wholeness and emptiness, their utter roguery, their ineptness—how could all this be portrayed by one person? There should be at least a dozen of them, if that were feasible. For they are not just something in society, they are society."

(507,4) See Tardieu's play, *Un mot pour un autre* ("One Word for Another"), in *Le professeur Froeppel: nouvelle édition revue et augmentée de Un mot pour un autre* (Paris: Gallimard, 1978). Cf. Seminar III, 257–58.

(508,1) *Aune* (standards) also means alder (a type of tree).

(508,2) First sentence, alternate rendering: "But if, in this profusion, the giver disappears with the giving of the gift . . ."

(508,4) See Seminar III, 257.

(508,5) *Mot* has a number of different meanings, including word, solution, and witticism. In the latter context, *esprit* means wit, though a few paragraphs down, Lacan plays off the fact that *esprit* also means spirit and mind. See Strachey's remarks on *Witz* in his preface to *Der Witz und seine Beziehung zum Unbewussten*, known in English as *Jokes and their Relation to the Unconscious*, *SE* VIII, 6–8.

(509,3) The "noble victim" may well be Loewenstein, whose letter ("personal communication" with Jakobson) is alluded to in Lacan's footnote on page 506.

(509,fn2) See Sigmund Freud, *The Origins of Psychoanalysis: Letters to Wilhelm Fliess* (New York: Basic Books, 1954).

(510,1) The term "rebus" seems to initially appear on the first page of chapter 6, "The Dream-Work" (*SE* IV, 277). Lacan seems to have coined a new adjective here, *littérant* ("literating"), in order to avoid saying "literal." See the general note above on *signifiance* (signifierness).

(510,2) The French *déterminatif* is a bit narrower in meaning than "determinative," and refers to "a sign that is not pronounced, which is placed before an ideogram to complete its meaning" (J.-F. Phelizon, *Vocabulaire de la linguistique* [Paris: Roudil, 1976]).

(510,4) Jean-François Champollion (1790–1832), the first scholar to decipher the Egyptian hieroglyphics. *Stations* (journey) recalls the "stations of the cross."

(511,3) *Entstellung* is usually translated into French as *déformation* and into English as "distortion."

(511,7) *Rücksicht auf Darstellbarkeit* is translated as "Considerations of representability" in *SE* V, 339. The "parlor game" here is known in English as "charades."

(512,1) On the dream-work, see *SE* IV, 326 ff.

(512,2) *Von unserem wachen Denken nicht zu unterscheiden* is from *GW* II/III, 493, and is translated as a psychical function "which is indistinguishable from our waking thoughts" in *SE* V, 489.

(514,5) See *Écrits* 1966, 442 and 830–31.

(515,2) *Le manque de l'être* could alternatively be translated as "being's lack."

(516,1) See *Écrits* 1966, 504.

(516,4) *Sous la forme de son actualité* (in the form of its actuality) might, alternatively, be rendered "in its instantaneousness" or "instantaneously." *"Cogito ergo sum" ubi cogito, ibi sum* can be rendered as "Where I am thinking 'I am thinking, therefore I am,' there I am."

(516,fn1) See *Pourquoi des philosophes* (1957), the title of a book by Jean-François Revel; it can be found in a recent edition of his works, *Jean-François Revel* (Paris: Robert Laffont, 1997).

(517,6) *Tour* (trick) has many meanings, including turn, tour, trip, twist, and trick.

(517,8) *Ambiguïté de furet* (elusive ambiguity) literally means "ferret-like ambiguity" and is one of Lacan's many references to the game involving the *furet*.

(518,1) *Double coude* (double elbow) also means double curve, bend, elbow joint, or knee. It harks back to the *coudes* (curves) the S of the signifier impresses upon the ducts (*Écrits* 1966, 501).

(518,3) *Décevante* (deceptive) could alternatively be rendered as "disappointing." *Kern unseres Wesen* (the core of our being) is found in *SE* V, 603, and *SE* XXIII, 197.

(518,4) *Mécanisme à double détente* (two-stage mechanism) could also be translated as two-cycle, double-trigger, or double-reduction mechanism. *Fixe* (fixes) does not mean repairs, but rather freezes or renders fixed in place.

(518,6) The French *composition* (in the phrase "signifying composition") could also be translated as "structure," "configuration," or "combination."

(519,3) See Holderlin's poem "Homecoming/To the Kinsmen." The end of the paragraph could alternatively read: "that led him from the royal principle of the Logos to rethink the deadly Empedoclean antinomies."

(519,4) Regarding the "other scene," see *SE* IV, 48, and *SE* V, 536.

(520,1) In Strachey's rendition, Freud's passage reads as follows: "Long before he was in the world, I went on, I had known that a little Hans would come who would be so fond of his mother that he would be bound to feel afraid of his father because of it" (*SE* X, 42).

(520,2) Alternate for "being raises it *in* the subject's *place*": "being raises it *in* the subject's *stead*." The original version of the French text read "Aristotle's man" instead of "antiquity's man."

(521,1) See Otto Fenichel, *Problems of Psychoanalytic Technique* (New York: The Psychoanalytic Quarterly, 1941).

(521,4) The *Fliegende Blätter* was a comic weekly of the late nineteenth and early twentieth centuries. *Fanfreluches antidotés* (antidoted fanfreluches) is from Rabelais' *Gargantua*, chapter 2; it literally means something like "remedied frills," but constitutes here a consummately obscure literary reference. There could also be a play here on *métier* (career), which also means loom (*métier à tisser*); thus "Must we serve as a loom for 'antidoted fanfreluches?' "

(522,3) *Transfert* (transference) also means transfer, conveyance, and even translation, in certain contexts. Cf. *SE* IV, 277, where *Übertragung* is rendered as "transcript."

(522,5) Alternate for "with which to close [*sceller*] these remarks": "with which to put a stamp of approval on." Alternate for "that attached him [*l'attachait*] to": "that made him attached to."

(522,fn1) See *SE* XXI, 152.

(523,3) Cf. Seminar III, 258.

(524,1) *Wo Es war, soll Ich werden* is from *GW* XV, 86, and corresponds to *SE* XXII, 80.

(524,3) See, for example, *SE* XXII, 15 and 222.

(524,8) See, for example, "Direction of the Treatment," *Écrits* 1966, 623–24.

(525,4) *Parole* (speech) can also be understood here as word, in the sense in which one says, "I give you my word (i.e., I promise) that I'll do it."

(525,5) See *SE* VIII, 115. Strachey renders the joke as follows: "Two Jews met in a railway carriage at a station in Galicia.

"'Where are you going?' asked one.

"'To Cracow,' was the answer.

"'What a liar you are!' broke out the other. 'If you say you're going to Cracow, you want me to believe you're going to Lemberg. But I know that in fact you're going to Cracow. So why are you lying to me?'"

(525,7) On Midas, cf. *Écrits* 1966, 547.

(526,4) Alternate for "confusion": "embarrassment."

(526,5) *Reviser* (reconsider) is an alternate spelling of *réviser.*

(526,6) *Fait mon être* (constitutes my being) could also be translated as "creates my being" or "plays the part of my being."

(527,4) A reference to the collective publication, *La psychanalyse d'aujourd'hui* ("Contemporary Psychoanalysis") (Paris: PUF, 1956), discussed in "Direction of the Treatment."

(528,2) See Lacan's aforementioned translation of Heidegger's "Logos."

(528,5) End of paragraph, presumably, "against the collateral of his intentions."

(528,6) This obscure abbreviation was explained by Lacan (in a note to his Spanish translator, Tomás Segovia, dated October 15, 1970) as "*Tu t'y es mis un peu tard,*" loosely translated as "You got down to it a bit late." The "e." for *"es"* is missing in all editions.

(528,7) The text, *La nouvelle rhétorique: Traité de l'argumentation* (Paris: PUF, 1958), is by Charles Perelman and Lucie Olbrechts-Tyteca; in English see *The New Rhetoric: A Treatise on Argumentation* (Notre Dame and London: University of Notre Dame Press, 1969). *Écrits* 1966 here erroneously reads *Théorie* instead of *Traité*, and on page 889 provides the date of Lacan's presentation as June 23, 1960.

Notes to "On a Question"

(531,2) *La Psychanalyse* 4 (1959): 1–50.

(532,2) *Percipiens:* one that perceives. *Perceptum*: object perceived, sense-datum. *Sensoriums*: senses, sensory apparatuses, seats or organs of sensation.

(533,1) *Renvoi* has a large number of meanings, including referral, deferment, suspension, discharge, sending back, return, and cross-reference.

(534,1) See Seminar III, chapter 4.

(535,3) *Intention de rejet* (rejecting intention) includes Lacan's first translation *(rejet)* of Freud's *Verwerfung*, which he renders further on as "foreclosure." In French, a dash is often provided in a written text before a quoted reply. Lacan provides dashes before *Chou!* and *Rat!*

(535,fn1) See Roman Jakobson, *Selected Writings*, vol. 2 (The Hague: Mouton, 1971), 130–47.

(535,fn2) February 8, 1956, corresponds to chapter 10 in Seminar III.

(536,fn2) The translation has been reissued with an introduction by Samuel M. Weber (Cambridge, Mass.: Harvard University Press, 1988).

(536,fn3) In English, see Jacques Lacan, "The Case of Aimée," in eds. John Cutting and M. Shepherd, *The Clinical Roots of the Schizophrenia Concept* (Cambridge: Cambridge University Press, 1987).

(537,5) For passages from the *Memoirs* quoted by Freud in his commentary, I provide Strachey's translation; otherwise I use the previously referenced English version, changing the text at times to better render Lacan's own translation. Here that version reads, "In contrast the genuine basic language . . . excelled in form also by its dignity and simplicity."

(538,1) Strachey translates *Nervenanhang* as "nerve-connection" (*SE* XII, 39, fn1) and Macalpine and Hunter as "nerve-contact" (S. 82).

(539,2) *Erinnerungsgedanken* is translated by Macalpine and Hunter as "human-thoughts-of-recollection" (S. 165).

(541,5) *Increvable* (inexhaustible) also means tireless and unburstable.

(541,7) See *SE* XII, 63–64.

(542,6) This seems to be a reference to the last paragraph of Freud's paper, "prop room" corr7esponding to what Strachey renders as "store-house" (*SE* XIX, 187).

(543,4) This might seem to be blatantly contradicted in the Schreber case itself, where the word "frustration" is found in Freud's discussion of the Schreber case (*SE* XII, 57 and 62). But the German reads *Versagung* in both cases (*GW* VIII, 293 and 298), which Lacan says implies renunciation, not frustration (*Écrits* 1966, 460–61).

(544,4) The English reads "rather pleasant" (S. 36) where Lacan reads *beau* (beautiful).

(544,6) Strachey tends to translate this as the "negative" Oedipus complex, but occasionally renders it as "inverted" (e.g., *SE* XVII, 6), the translation used systematically in *Memoirs*.

(545,2) Cf. *Écrits* 1966, 315.

(545,4) Reading *ailleurs* (as in the original version of the text, rendered here as "elsewhere") instead of *d'ailleurs* (moreover).

(545,fn1) See Seminar III, 347.

(546,1) See *Memoirs*, 23 and 410–11.

(546,fn1) See *SE* XVII, 89–91.

(547,2) On Midas, cf. *Écrits* 1966, 525.

(547,5) *Pensant à la dépense* ("thinking of the expense") is borrowed from Paul-Jean Toulet's *Contrerimes* (Paris: Gallimard, [1921] 1979), 45.

(547,6) *Le pense-sans-rire* (deadpan thinkers) is a pun on *pince-sans-rire*, "deadpan."

(547,fn2) See *SE* XII, 54 and *Thus Spoke Zarathustra* in *The Portable Nietzsche*, trans. Walter Kaufmann (New York: Viking, 1968).

(548,1) *Le pense-à-penser le plus pensable* (the most thinkable one who thinks-about-thinking) would seem to be a reference to the ego.

(548,2) Cf. Lichtenberg's comment: "We should say *it thinks*, just as we say *it lightens*. To say *cogito* is already to say too much as soon as we translate it *I think*. *To* assume, to postulate the *I* is a practical requirement." G. C. Lichtenberg, *Aphorisms*, trans. R. J. Hollingdale (London: Penguin, 1990).

(548,3) A pun on "Baudelaire" and the oath *bordel de Dieu*. Cf. Baudelaire's phrase, "le vert paradis des amours enfantines."

(548,4) The original version and *Écrits* 1966 both read *le réaliste* (the realist), whereas Points reads *l'organiciste* (the organicist). On the *anderer Schauplatz*, see, for example, *SE* IV, 48, and *SE* V, 536.

(548,6) The complete L schema was introduced on page 53 of *Écrits* 1966 in a text not included in this Selection: the "Suite" to the "Seminar on 'The Purloined Letter.' "

(549,1) For a different gloss on *discours de l'Autre*, see *Écrits* 1966, 814, where it is translated as "discourse about the Other."

(550,4) *Intra-mondaine* (within-the-world) seems to be a translation of Heidegger's *innerweltlich*.

(550,8) *Verbe* (Word): like "the Word," *le Verbe* is a translation for the Greek "Logos." Hereafter, *le verbe* is always translated as "the Word."

(551,5) *Où peut s'identifier l'Autre* (where the Other may be identified) could possibly—assuming an unusual use of *où*—be rendered as "with which the Other may be identified."

(551,6) *Jeu* (play) can also be translated as "game" and is so translated below. *Le mort* can be translated as "the dead person" or "the dummy" as in bridge. Cf. *Écrits* 1966, 589.

(552,1) *En tant que mort* (as the dummy) could also be rendered by "as dead," and *comme vivant* (as a living being) by "as alive."

Il lui faut prendre la couleur qu'il annonce (he must play the suit he calls trump) evokes the expression *annoncer la couleur*, meaning to lay one's cards on the table or say where one stands; literally, it means to propose, in a card game (such as bridge), what suit will be trump.

(552,2) Instead of "it proves appropriate for providing," one could read "it finds itself appropriated to provide."

(552,4) *Où le sujet s'identifie . . . avec* (where the subject is identified . . . with) could possibly—assuming an unusual use of *où*—be rendered as "where the subject identifies . . . with."

(553,3) Instead of "where the ego identifies itself," one could read "with which the ego is identical" or "where the ego is identified."

(554,fn1) *Représentant de la représentation* (representation's representative) is Lacan's translation for Freud's *Vorstellungsrepräsentanz*, rendered in the *Standard Edition* by "ideational representative," and generally designates that which stands in for (or represents) the drive at the "ideational" level (i.e., at the level of representation); it could also be translated as "the representative of representation." In Seminar VII, Lacan equates Freud's *Vorstellungsrepräsentanz* with the signifier (page 75–76/61).

(555,2) Raymond Queneau employs the slang term *phalle* (dick) in a passage from *Les Enfants du limon* (Paris: Gallimard, [1938] 1987): "détailler les phalles de messieurs et les mottes de dames, qui ni d'Adam ni d'»ve elle ne connaissait."

(557,6) Instead of "Mother's Desire," one could read "Desire for the Mother." Note that the formula "Desire of the Mother" does not, in fact, capture both of these meanings, but only the former.

(557,7) *Carence* (lack) also means deficiency.

(558,2) See *SE* XIX, 235–39. *Aveu* (owning) means avowal, confession, owning up, and admission.

(558,4) Or "At the point to which the Name-of-the-Father is summoned." An alternative reading for the first part of the sentence: "A pure and simple hole in the Other may thus correspond to the point to which the Name-of-the-Father is called upon [to come]—we shall see how."

(558,6) *Désordre* (disturbance) can also be rendered as "disorder," "chaos," or "mess"; it is not a reference to the eponymous psychiatric notion. I translate it again as "disturbance" on *Écrits* 1966, 563.

(558,fn1) The English translation reads as follows: "I want to say by way of introduction that the leading roles in the genesis of the development, the first beginnings of which go back perhaps as far as the eighteenth century, were played on the one hand by the names of Flechsig and Schreber (probably not specifying any individual member of these families), and on the other by the concept of *soul murder*."

(559,1) Lacan uses a very uncommon term here, *apophanies* (manifestations). Note that Kraus Conrad uses the term to refer to an experience of delusional certainty sometimes described by schizophrenics; after having been uncertain and having felt threatened by an imminent catastrophe, the *apophanie* seems to involve an overflowing of significance. The term may possibly be related to the English "apophany," which is a kind of rhyme in which two single-syllable words share opening and closing consonants but not the intervening vowel; in that case, Ahriman would be one of the rhyming forms of the name of God in Schreber's delusion.

(560,3) Strachey translates *Denkzwang* as "enforced thinking" (*SE* XII, 25), and Macalpine and Hunter render it as "compulsive thinking." *Liegen lassen* is translated in *Memoirs* as "forsakes him" and "forsaken," depending on the context (S. 56 and 94, and *Memoirs*, 362).

(561,1) *Météores* (meteors) could also be rendered here as "flashes."

(561,4) For the first part of the first sentence here, Macalpine and Hunter provide "Many in One or One in Many" (S. 196n).

(562,4) This seems to be a reference to *Memoirs*, 379n.

(563,4) *De Malebranche ou de Locke / Plus malin le plus loufoque . . .*

(564,1) Strachey translates *Verfluchter Kerl* as "The deuce of a fellow," *SE* XII, 36.

(564,5) "Conscientious objection" would seem to refer here to male impotence. Cf. Lacan's comment: "Analytic discourse demonstrates—allow me to put it this way—that the phallus is the conscientious objection made by one of the two sexed beings to the service to be rendered to the other" (Seminar XX, 13).

(564,fn1) See also *Memoirs*, 24, 27, and 361; note that Strachey did not change "emasculation" to "unmanning" in the *Standard Edition.*

(565,2) "Real castration": castration of the biological organ, as opposed to symbolic castration.

(565,5) *Manque-à-être*: see general note above.

(566,1) *Manque à* (is missing) means both does not have (lacks) and pines for.

(566,4) *Du rififi chez les hommes* (brawling among men) is a book by Auguste Le Breton (Paris: Gallimard, [1953] 1992) that was made into a film by Dassin. See *SE* X, 13, where we find Hans' addition to the giraffe drawn by his father; see also Seminar IV, 264.

(566,fn1) Strachey translates this as "cursorily improvised men" and Macalpine as "fleeting-improvised-men." Pichon's translation, *ombres d'hommes bâclés à la six-quatre-deux* (shadows of men thrown together 1, 2, 3), may also contain a reference to a technique for very quickly sketching a human profile by drawing the numbers 6, 4, and 2 in a certain arrangement.

(567,5) *La personne du sujet* (him) literally means the person of the subject, and less literally means the subject's personality or the subject as a person.

(568,8) "Radical rectifications": presumably, sex-change operations.

(569,1) "Psycho-Analytic Notes on an Autobiographical Account of a Case of Paranoia," *SE* XII, 30, fn2.

(571,1) In "the symbolization of the Mother insofar as she . . . ," *elle* (she) could alternatively be translated as "it," referring back to symbolization.

(572,fn1) See *SE* XII, 48.

(573,2) Niederland does not claim that "lewd" means whore, nor does it seem to be borne out etymologically.

(573,4) *Décalage* (skew) could also be translated as "gap" or "discrepancy."

(575,3) See the "Suite" to the "Seminar on 'The Purloined Letter,'" especially *Écrits* 1966, 42, 52, and 56. *L'être de l'étant* (the being of entities) could also be translated as "the Being of beings."

(575,7) *Isole . . . de* (distinguish . . . on the basis of) could, alternatively, be rendered "distinguish . . . from." Further on, I read *montrent* (show, after the second dash) for *montre* (shows). Note that all three French editions of this text read *pour* ("for" or "because of") instead of *par* found in the usual expression "appeler les choses par leur nom" (to call things by their rightful names).

(576,3) On Pascal, see *Écrits* 1966, 283.

(577,7) *Un-père* could alternatively be rendered as "A-father."

(578,3) *Redouble* (redoubles) could also be translated as "relines," "increases," "intensifies," "duplicates," or "reduplicates."

(578,4) Hide-the-thimble is the "hot and cold" game in which one player hides an object and another player searches for it, the first player giving clues like "cold" (when the second is not at all close to the object), "warm" (when closer), and "hot," "boiling," or "burning" (when right in front of it).

(578,5) On "Whom do you love more, daddy or mommy?" see *SE* X, 238.

(579,4) *Pire* (lowest of the low) could also be translated as "worst elements."

(581,1) In Ancient Rome, the members of the Senate were referred to as *patres conscripti*, *pères conscrits*, conscripted (or conscribed) fathers.

(581,4) The usual expression, *de part en part* (through and through), has been changed here, at the end of the paragraph, to *de père en part*. The latter might even evoke *de père en fils*, "from father to son." *Trame* means plot, web, or warp.

(581,fn1) Macalpine renders it as "How to Achieve Happiness and Bliss by Physical Culture."

(582,3) *Jaculation* (jaculation), which literally means pitching, throwing, or hurling, has in French taken on the figurative sense of *élan d'enthousiasme*, passionate impulse or enthusiastic surge.

(582,4) *Comput* (computation) refers to the set of rules allowing one to determine the date of a holiday, for example, in the context of the establishment of a calendar.

(582,fn1) In the English translation, we find the following: "The phrase 'O damn' in particular was a remnant of the basic language, in which the words 'O damn, that is hard to say' were used whenever the souls became aware of a happening inconsistent with the Order of the World, for instance 'Oh damn, it is extremely hard to say that God allows himself to be f......'" (179).

(583,fn1) I have followed the slightly modified Points text here.

Notes to "The Direction of the Treatment"

(585,3) *La personne de l'analysé* (the analysand as a person) and *la personne de l'analyste* (the analyst as a person) could alternatively be translated as "the analysand's (or analyst's) person" or "the analysand's (or analyst's) personality."

(585,4) *Rééducation émotionnelle* (emotional reeducation) was likely the French translation adopted for Franz Alexander and Theodore French's term "corrective emotional experience" found in their *Psychoanalytic Therapy: Principles and Application* (New York: Ronald Press, 1946). See also *Écrits* 1966, 619.

(585,fn3) See Anne Berman's translation, *Nouvelles conférences sur la psychanalyse* (Paris: Gallimard, 1936).

(586,7) It should be kept in mind that *paroles* (words) can also be translated as "speech."

(589,2) *Malheur de la conscience* (troubled conscience) seems to be a reference to *conscience malheureuse* (unhappy consciousness), the usual French translation of Hegel's *unglückliches Bewusstsein*. See Jean Wahl, *Le Malheur de la conscience dans la philosophie de Hegel* (Paris: PUF, 1951).

(589,3) *Le mort* (the dummy) also means the dead man. *Lien* (restraint) also means link, bond, tie, and shackle.

(590,6) This is a reference to Heinz Hartmann who, in his "Technical Implications of Ego Psychology," writes that "analysis is gradually and unavoidably, though hesitantly, becoming a general psychology . . ." (*PQ* XX, 1 [1951]: 35), and who, in "The Development of the Ego Concept in Freud's Work," writes that "the trend toward a general psychology has been inherent in psycho-analysis from its inception" (*IJP* XXVII, 6 [1956]: 434). In Seminar I (33/25), Lacan suggests that Kris also refers to analysis as a "general psychology." The idea of a "nonconflictual sphere" was first introduced by Hartmann in "Ich-Psychologie und Anpassungsproblem," *Internationale Zeitschrift für Psychoanalyse und Imago* XXIV (1939), published in English as *Ego Psychology and the Problem of Adaptation*, trans. D. Rapaport (New York: International Universities Press, 1958).

(590,7) The French pronunciations of *égaux* (equal) and *egos* are usually identical.

(590,fn1) "The doctrinaire of being" is Sacha Nacht.

(592,3) *Moi* means both me and ego.

(593,2) *Elle* (the last "thought" in the first sentence) could, alternatively, refer back to "the transmutation" and *passer au fait* could, alternatively, be understood as "gets to the point" or "gets down to brass tacks." Alternate reading for the end of the paragraph: "where the subject is subordinated (or subordinate) to the signifier to so great an extent that he is seduced by it."

(593,3) *Recel* (possession) also means receiving or harboring (usually of stolen goods).

(593,6) See Jakob Böhme's *De Signatura Rerum* (1651); in English see *The Signature of All Things and Other Writings* (Cambridge and London: James Clarke, 1969).

(593,7) *Être à l'heure de Freud* (to keep time with Freud) literally means to be at the same time or hour as Freud (to be in the same time zone or register, to keep in step with him, or to synchronize watches with him).

(594,1) Alternate reading for end of paragraph: "through being inscribed there, can produce anything new."

(594,4) Regarding "repetition automatism": Lacan does not employ here the more usual French translation of Freud's *Wiederholungszwang* (usually translated into English as "repetition compulsion"), which is *compulsion de répétition*. But he does employ it later in this article.

(596,3) Lacan provides here his own translation, *travail du transfert* (work of transference), of Freud's *Durcharbeitung*, which is usually translated into French as *perlaboration*. Later in the text he provides *travail de transfert*.

(596,5) *Désordre* (disorder) can also be rendered as "havoc," "chaos" or "mess"; it is not a reference to the eponymous psychiatric notion.

(596,6) See "Presentation on Transference" (1951) in *Écrits* 1966.

(597,2) *Principe* (crux) also means principle and recalls the title of the present article. "Crux" always translates *principe* in this article.

(597,4) Lacan uses *tendance* (tendency) instead of *pulsion* (drive) almost exclusively in this paper.

(597,5) Presumably "prescribed" in the legal sense of a debt not paid off in the stipulated time frame and that is no longer claimable by the creditor.

(598,4) Regarding "what an opportunity for contempt I would be offering to those who wish to find fault": the French, *que n'offrirais-je à honnir à ceux qui mal y pensent*, is based on a phrase usually attributed to François I, "honni soit qui mal y pense" (evil be to him who evil thinks), but for which Edward III, King of England, should perhaps be credited; see Georges Minois, *Du Guesclin* (Paris: Fayard, 1993), 85, who dates the expression to April 23, 1348.

(598,5) Regarding "rectification of the subject's relations with reality": this is a probable reference to Freud's remarks to the Rat Man in their very first sessions (*SE* X, 169 and 173) regarding the "errors of memory" and "displacements" involved in the pince-nez matter, and to Freud's remarks to Dora, mentioned earlier in the text (*SE* VII, 35–36).

(598,7) See Lacan's commentary on this case in Seminar I, 71–72/59–61; Seminar III, 92–93; and *Écrits* 1966, 393–99.

(599,2) The French here reads *infantile*, instead of "adolescent," but the case history (see reference 15) twice mentions "puberty," as does Lacan himself elsewhere (*Écrits* 1966, 394 and 396).

(599,3) On "analyzing the defense before the drive," see H. Hartmann and E. Kris, "The Genetic Approach in Psychoanalysis," *The Psychoanalytic Study of the Child*, vol. 1 (New York: International Universities Press, 1945), 15: "interpretation should start as close as possible to the experience of the patient—'from the higher layers'—and elucidate the structure of the 'defenses' before they proceed to what stems from the id."

(600,2) *Moutarde après dîner* (post-session condiment) is most often seen in the expression "c'est (comme) de la moutarde après dîner" (literally, "it's like an after-dinner mustard"), meaning it's something that came too late, only after it was no longer of any use (presumably, one would have wanted to have the mustard as a condiment *during* dinner).

(600,5) The original text plays on the two-part negation in French: "Ce n'est pas que votre patient ne vole pas, qui ici importe. C'est qu'il ne . . . Pas de ne: c'est qu'il vole *rien*."

(601,2) "The mental realm" as opposed to the realm of food.

(601,3) *Rien à frire* (nothing doing) literally means nothing to fry, and is preferred here to the more usual *rien à faire*, due to the reference to fish in the previous sentence.

(602,1) *Carte* (map) also evokes the menus Kris' patient studied (thus: "To take desire off the menu . . .").

(602,4) Cf. Lacan's comments on the distinction between the need for repetition and the repetition of need in Seminar VIII, 207. Cf. *Écrits* 1966, 328.

(602,5) See, above all, *Écrits* 1966, 647–84.

(603,5) *Écrits* 1966 reads *particularités* (particularities), but the earlier version in *La Psychanalyse* 6 reads *partialités* (partialities), which makes more sense here.

(604,2) See "The Genetic Approach in Psychoanalysis," 24.

(604,4) On such patterns, see "The Genetic Approach in Psychoanalysis," 12.

(605,3) *Objectalité* (objectality) might also be rendered as "object relatedness," but its contrast with "objectivity" would then be diminished.

(605,5) "Negative" here in the sense of the photographic negative of an image. This quote and a number of those that follow are from Maurice Bouvet, "La clinique psychanalytique. La relation d'objet," in *La psychanalyse d'aujourd'hui* (Paris: PUF, 1956); Lacan also discusses Bouvet's article in Seminar IV, chapters 1 and 2.

(606,7) The antinomy: pregenital versus genital.

(607,1) See, for example, "On the Universal Tendency to Debasement in the Sphere of Love," *SE* XI, 179–90.

(607,4) See Matthew, 23.4, and *Écrits* 1966, 263.

(607,6) The French *hérésie* (heretical) is a quasi-homonym of R.S.I. (the title of Lacan's Seminar XXII, 1974–1975), which stands for real, symbolic, imaginary, and may be an early play on that homophony. The three sides here are the three theories: geneticism, object relations, and intersubjective introjection.

(608,2) See, for example, Bouvet, "La clinique psychanalytique," 102–3. All of page 608 can be understood as a commentary on Bouvet's work as found in his *Oeuvres Psychanalytiques*, vols. I–II (Paris: Payot, 1967–1968); Lacan comments on Bouvet at length in Seminar V, 387–92.

(609,6) On this "case of pure obsession in a man," cf. Seminar V, 447.

(609,8) Cf. "Function and Field," 267.

(610,2) *Pif* means nose, and to do something *au pif* or *au pif(f)omètre* (following one's nose) is to do it by guesswork, without calculating, "to play it by ear." Lacan discusses the case mentioned here at length in Seminar IV, 88–92.

(610,6) *Pour suppléer à* (to make up for [the Other's lack]) might be better rendered as "to hold the place of" or "to stand in for."

(611,1) See André Breton's 1924 "Introduction au discours sur le peu de réalité" in *Point du Jour* (Paris: Gallimard, 1970); in English, see "Introduction to the Discourse on the Paucity of Reality" in *Break of Day* (Lincoln: University of Nebraska Press, 1999), 3–20.

(611,9) A probable reference to Virgil's *labor improbus* in *Georgica* 1, 146, translated as "remorseless toil" by James Rhoades in *Great Books of the Western World*, XIII (Chicago: Britannica, 1952), 41.

(612,3) Lacan discussed object-relation themes in Seminar IV, 1956–1957.

(612,6) *Pataquès* (linguistic error) most commonly means a mistake in pronunciation, but can also mean any big linguistic error.

(613,1) The second topography is that of the id, ego, and superego.

(614,3) *Heurter* (affront) also means to hurt, offend, clash, oppose, and even buck the trend.

(614,4) "Won or lost": see *Écrits* 1966, 853.

(615,2) This is a reference to a story about a rich man who is told he can become happy by wearing a happy man's shirt; he searches far and wide until he finds a happy man, but the latter is so poor he has no shirt to give the rich man. "Happy shade" is a reference to Chateaubriand's *Mémoires d'Outre-tombe.*

(615,4) *Malheurs de l'être* (misfortunes of being): cf. *Écrits* 1966, 589 (where *malheur* is translated as "troubled") and 636.

(616,1) *Essai de l'action* could also be rendered as "experimental action." Cf. *SE* XII, 221, and *SE* V, 599–600.

(618,1) *Prescription* (statute of limitations) is a legal term implying a certain time limit; the idea thus seems to be that signifiers used in the demands in question are not supposed to be used beyond a certain age, that they are out of date.

(618,8) See Seminar IV, 69. On defiles, cf.

Freud's "defile of consciousness" in *SE* II, 291.

(619,1) *S'il ne remplit certes pas tout* (while it does not fulfill all functions) could also be translated as "even if it doesn't fill everything."

(620,4) *Fusent* (fizzle out) could also be translated as "sizzle" or "burn out," since in the context of pyrotechnics, *fuser* means to burn without exploding.

(620,fn1) In English, see *The Origins of Psychoanalysis* (New York: Basic Books, 1954), 296–97, and *The Complete Letters of Sigmund Freud to Wilhelm Fliess, 1887–1904* (Cambridge, Mass.: Harvard University Press, 1985), 370–71.

(621,4) *Glissement* (sliding) can be translated as sliding, slippage, or shifting and is used here by Lacan to translate Freud's *Verschiebung*, usually translated as "displacement" (*déplacement* in French). See, in particular, "Instance of the Letter," *Écrits* 1966, 511.

(621,fn1) Strachey provides the following translation of the dream recounted by the "butcher's witty wife" (*SE* IV, 147): "I wanted to give a supper-party, but I had nothing in the house but a little smoked salmon. I thought I would go out and buy something, but remembered then that it was Sunday afternoon and all the shops would be shut. Next I tried to ring up some caterers, but the telephone was out of order. So I had to abandon my wish to give a supper-party." The dream is also discussed by Lacan in Seminar V, chapter 20, and Seminar XVII, 84–85.

(622,3) On metaphor as a positive meaning effect, see *Écrits* 1966, 515. The French at the end of the sentence, *un certain passage du sujet au sens du désir*, allows for a number of other possible readings: "a certain movement of the subject in terms of desire," "a certain movement of the subject toward the meaning of desire," "a certain movement of the subject in the direction of desire," "a certain shift by the subject in relation to desire," "a certain shift by the subject as regards her desire," and "a certain shift of the subject as desiring subject."

(622,4) Regarding "the desire to have an unsatisfied desire," see Freud's various formulations in *GW* IV, 153, and *SE* IV, 148–49.

(622,5) On the "royal road," see *SE* V, 608. The French translation is *voie royale; voie* is used again in Lacan's text, *Écrits* 1966, 624 and 626.

(622,7) Regarding *peu de sens* (scant meaning), cf. Breton's expression "peu de réalité" (scant reality) from "Introduction au discours sur le peu de réalité."

(623,2) *Signifiance*, rendered in this translation as "signifierness," might also be translated here as "significance" or "meaningfulness."

(623,4) The dream's "elaboration" is probably the "first revision" of the dream by displacement and condensation, prior to the secondary revision (known in French as *l'élaboration secondaire*); it could also possibly be the recounting of the dream by the dreamer. On "linguistic structure," see Saussure's *Course in General Linguistics* (New York: McGraw-Hill, 1959).

(623,5) Desire is associated with metonymy, while the subject is associated with metaphor; see *Écrits* 1966, Appendix II, "Metaphor of the Subject." Lacan is surely referring in this passage to his "Graph of Desire" (*Écrits* 1966, 805 and 817). *Dérivation* (branch line) could also be translated as "branch circuit." Cf. *SE* VII, 72.

(623,6) *Le désir ne fait qu'assujettir ce que l'analyse subjective. Assujettir* could also be translated as "to subject" (e.g., to subject someone to something); *subjective* could also be translated as "renders subjective," "renders subject," or "subjectifies." Desire subjugates the drives (the id) whereas analysis brings the subject into being there; see, for example, *Écrits* 1966, 524: "Where it (or id) was, it is necessary for me to come into being" ("*Là où fut ça, il me faut advenir*"). Cf. "On Freud's 'Trieb' and the Psychoanalyst's Desire," *Écrits* 1966, 851–54.

(623,8) In the next paragraph, Lacan plays on the "fire" (*feu*) in the expression *faire long feu* (falters) in this paragraph: it was extinguished or went out (*s'éteignait*) and cast light. The expression itself derives from early firearms terminology; when the fuse on a gun cartridge burned too slowly, the gun would go off at the wrong time and *one would miss one's mark*. The expression is more often used nowadays in its negative form (*ne pas faire long feu*) to indicate that something has not lasted very long. In the present context, one could also translate the phrase as, "but my voice drawls interminably before finishing."

(624,1) In the preceding paragraph, Lacan

mentioned that dreams are designed for the "recognition of desire"; here it is the "desire for recognition" that is at stake.

(624,5) This entire paragraph seems to be ironic, Lacan clearly agreeing with Freud that one gets better because one remembers.

(625,2) In Strachey's rendition of Freud's account, the husband is said to have replied that "he was sure the painter would prefer a piece of a pretty young girl's behind to the whole of his face." In Lacan's account, he is characterized as replying, "une tranche du train de derrière d'une belle garce, voilà ce qu'il vous faut," literally, "a slice of a pretty bitch's rear end is what you need" (*garce* can also mean "prostitute," and *une belle garce* can mean "hot stuff").

(625,6) Jean-Gabriel de Tarde, the French sociologist (1843–1904), believed that social phenomena were based on the repetition of individual psychical processes (such as invention and creation, on the one hand, and imitation, diffusion, and tradition, on the other). See, in particular, his book, *Les Lois de l'imitation*, published in 1890; in English, *The Laws of Imitation*, trans. E. C. Parsons (Gloucester, Mass.: P. Smith, 1962).

(626,3) The French at the end of the paragraph, *qui va du désir de son amie faire l'échec de sa demande*, is quite vague, and could also be rendered as "makes use of her friend's desire to thwart her own demand." The only request (*demande*) in question thus far in Lacan's discussion seems to be the friend's request "to come dine at the patient's house," but in the next sentence Lacan characterizes the patient's phone calls to caterers in her dream as a request as well. The desire most recently mentioned is the husband's presumed desire for his wife's friend, but the way it is expressed it could also be understood as the friend's desire for the patient's husband. Thus the patient "thwarts her own request due to her friend's desire for the husband or her husband's desire for her friend." Thanks to her "hysterical identification" with her friend, however, by thwarting her own request she also thwarts her friend's request to dine at the patient's home. *Sa demande* can thus imply "her own request" as well as "her friend's request," just as *le désir de son amie* can imply "her husband's desire for her friend," "her friend's desire for her husband," and even "her own desire for her friend," for (as we shall see) her husband's desire becomes her own.

(626,6) Recall that *le désir de l'Autre* (the Other's desire) is also a shorthand, at times, for "the object of the Other's desire" or "what the Other desires."

(627,1) What was revealed in the mysteries is a matter of much debate. Part of the Orphic ritual is thought to have involved the mimed or actual dismemberment of an individual representing the god Dionysus. Cf. Lacan's reference to the pound of flesh and the lost phallus of Osiris embalmed two pages further on, his reference to Freud's unveiling of the phallus at the end of this article, and his further reference to the mysteries in *Écrits* 1966, 555 and 688. As Jacques-Alain Miller has pointed out, here as elsewhere in *Écrits* the fish seems to have to do with a kind of ultimate meaning or truth: a phallic signification. See, in particular, *Écrits* 1966, 805.

(627,3) Figuratively speaking, *logogriphe* (obscure discourse) can mean an obscure, unintelligible discourse or language; literally, it means a word game or enigma in which one must guess the word whose letters allow one to form several other words—given "sire" and "deer," for example, one has to find "desire." On Freud's later considerations on the castration complex and penis envy, see *SE* XXIII, 252–53.

(627,9) Alternate reading for "limbo realm": "purgatory." Regarding the "it" that speaks in him: there are too many masculine nouns in this passage (need, being, love, and lure) to be absolutely sure which one Lacan has in mind, though "need" seems quite likely. In the next sentence, *à sa place* (in its place) could refer to being's place, need's place, nonbeing's place, or even desire in its place or desire where it is situated.

(628,7) Reading *un* (an), as in the original version of the text, instead of *en*.

(628,8) Regarding *ein anderer Schauplatz*, see *SE* IV, 48, and *SE* V, 536. *Écrits* 1966 erroneously reads *eine* instead of *ein* and *andere* instead of *anderer*.

(629,1) See *Écrits* 1966, 623.

(629,2) *Accompli* is a synonym of *perfectif*

(perfective) in this context. See J.-F. Phelizon, *Vocabulaire de la linguistique* (Paris: Roudil, 1976).

(629,4) The grammar of the second sentence allows of a different reading: "demand evokes the want-to-be in the following three figures: the nothing that constitutes the heritage of the demand for love, the hatred that goes so far as to negate the other's being, and the unspeakable in what is not known in its request." *Fonds* (ground) could also be rendered as "fund" or "reserve" here. *Corps subtil* (subtle body) is a reference to the matter ("aether" or "ether") formerly believed to surround the earth.

(629,5) *Insignifiante* could, alternatively, be rendered as "insignificant" or "nonsignifying."

(630,2) Alternative for "in desire's quest": "in the quest for desire."

(630,3) *Colin-tampon* (pounding away) is a name given to a former battery of drummers in Swiss regiments. The more usual expression, *se soucier de quelque chose comme de colin-tampon*, means to not make anything of something, not concern oneself with it. The grammar at the end of this paragraph also allows us to read "thus surmising his desire itself insofar as it was the Other's desire."

(630,4) *Arranger* (arrange) can mean to organize or even stage something, "stage" in the sense of fixing the outcome of a match in advance. Note that, while in the text I translate *l'Autre* as the Other with a capital *O*, and *l'autre* as the other with a lowercase *o*, in Lacan's schemas and mathemes the former is designated by A and the latter by *a* and *a'*.

(630,5) Alternate term for "traffic circle": "roundabout."

(631,3) *D'âge mûr* (of mature years) probably strikes Lacan as comical because it contains the word *mûr* (ripe), which English only includes in the contraindicated "ripe old age."

(631,4) *Inamovible* (permanent) also means fixed (in place).

(631,9) *Commère* (shrewd paramour) formerly meant godmother, but has taken on several more recent meanings: gossip; cunning woman; bold and energetic woman; and a music hall emcee.

(632,4) Cf. Rabelais' "science without conscience is but the demise of the soul."

(632,8) *Le cède au sien* (yields to his desire) could also be rendered as "is inferior to," but my sense is that that is not the intended meaning.

(633,2) *Le mépris de sa mère acariâtre à décrier* (his ill-tempered mother's contempt for) could also be translated as "his contempt for his ill-tempered mother for disparaging."

(633,4) *Mettre à gauche* (tuck it away) is usually used in reference to money: "to put money aside," "to tuck (or sock) some money away." Alternative reading for "his desire is for difficulty": "his desire is based on difficulty."

(633,6) *S'imprimer* (rendered here as "(im)printed") could also be translated as "etched," "stamped," "published," "communicated," or "transferred." Cf. Lacan's discussion of the sign and the phallus in Seminar VIII, chapter 18 (April 26, 1961).

(633,7) The "mark of origin" may be an allusion to Freud's "Negation," *SE* XIX, 236.

(634,1) On *coïtus normalis dosim repetatur*, cf. *SE* XIV, 14–15.

(634,4) *Foi* (word) literally means faith. *Tu es* (you are) is similar in pronunciation to *tuez* (kill).

(634,8) This is a heraldic reference to the slanted bar one finds on certain coats of arms, said in a number of works of fiction (in error, apparently) to represent the fact that their bearers are bastards of noble birth.

(635,6) The "object of the demand for love" would seem to be the person to whom one's demand for love is addressed.

(635,7) *Scandent* (punctuate) comes from *scander*, to scan verse; cf. "scansion."

(636,8) A *palotin* (foolish acolyte) is an acolyte, associate, or henchman of Father Ubu's in Alfred Jarry's play *Ubu Roi ou les polonais* (Paris: Eugène Fasquelle, [1888] 1922); in English see *King Turd*, trans. B. Keith and G. Legman (New York: Boar's Head Books, 1953). Alternate reading for "Is that all you've got?": "What else is new?"

(637,6) *Mise en fonction* (set to work) could, alternatively, be rendered as "put into operation."

(638,3) This is, once again, a commentary on the Graph of Desire.

(638,4) The French here evokes the *chanson de geste*, a set of medieval French epic poems relating the deeds of one and the same hero. *Passage à l'acte* is the French translation of the

German *Agieren* (translated into English as "acting out") that was usual in the 1950s. Lacan confirms that here; see also Daniel Lagache's translation of Melitta Schmideberg's "Note sur le transfert" ("Note on Transference") in *RFP* XVI, 1–2 (1952): 263–67, especially page 265, and the *Robert* dictionary under "acte." Nevertheless, Lacan begins to distinguish *passage à l'acte* from acting out later (see, for example, Seminar XIV, February 22, 1967).

(639,3) *Hostie* (Host) is the eucharistic wafer; between the fourteenth and seventeenth centuries it meant a victim offered up in sacrifice. Alternative reading for "idiotic desire": "dulled desire."

(639,6) On the young homosexual woman and Dora, see, in particular, Seminar IV, chapters 7 and 8.

(639,7) See *SE* XVIII, 107.

(640,1) *Oblat* (sacrificial object) has a number of meanings: a child given to the Church and dedicated to God, a member of a religious order who gives up his or her possessions but takes no vows, a person who sacrifices him- or herself, or the eucharistic wafer.

(640,4) *Ils n'en ont cure* (they couldn't care less) is a play on words here, for it literally means "they have no cure for it."

(640,8) Cf. Seminar IV, 246.

(641,6 and 7) *Aveu* (owning) means avowal, confession, owning up, and admission.

(641,10) The French here contains a *ne pas* (not) before "attributing" that I have left out, believing that it was included in error.

(641,11) The "tunic of Nessus" is the poisoned tunic that caused Hercules' death.

(642,3) See Mauriac's *Le Fleuve de feu* (Paris: Bernard Grasset, 1923); in English, *The River of Fire*, trans. G. Hopkins (London: Eyre & Spottiswoode, 1954).

(642,4) The *jeu du furet* (swiftly shifting game) is a game in which a group of people sit in a circle and quickly pass a small object—referred to as *le furet*, though a *furet* is literally a ferret—from hand to hand, while a player standing in the middle of the circle tries to guess which hand holds the *furet*. Cf. *Écrits* 1966, 259.

(642,8) *S'articule au* (linked to) could also be translated as "is articulated in (or with)" or "links up with." See Lacan's comments on Freud's "Splitting of the Ego in the Defensive Process" in chapter 22 of Seminar VII.

(644,ref.18) A sample of Lagache's work on transference can be found in English in "Some Aspects of Transference," *IJP* XXXIV, 1 (1953): 1–10.

Notes to "Remarks on Daniel Lagache's Presentation: 'Psychoanalysis and Personality Structure'"

(648,4) *Distinction et réunion* (separation and union): Lacan is presumably referring here to specific axioms in set theory; the former goes by a number of different names, including comprehension axiom, axiom of comprehension, separation axiom, axiom of separation, specification, specification axiom, axiom of specification, and *Aussonderungsaxiom*.

(649,fn1) The symposium was entitled "Colloque sur le mot 'structure'" (Colloquium on the Word "Structure") and was held in Paris on January 10–12, 1958. An echo of it can be found in Roger Bastide's "Colloque sur le mot 'structure,'" *Les Annales* XIV, 2 (1959): 351-52. Bastide included certain of the talks given at the colloquium in his *Sens et usage du terme structure dans les sciences sociales* (The Hague: Mouton, 1962).

(650,1) *Paranomies* (paranomies): I have found this term in Italian and English dictionaries (not in French) where it signifies a form of aphasia that involves the inability to attribute the correct name to a recognized object; in German it seems to refer to the use of the wrong designations for things. It may also generally signify "incompatibilities." Lacan, however, seems to use it here and on page 657 to refer to something that goes beyond heteronomies and autonomies.

(651,1) See Heinz Hartmann, "The Development of the Ego Concept in Freud's Work," *IJP* XXXVII, 6 (1956): 425–38. A *carte forcée* (Hobson's choice) is a card that an illusionist forces you to choose, all the while making it seem as though you are choosing it freely. *Représentées* (fictive) is an adjective here meaning cerebral, fictional, or imaginary—that is, all in the mind. Reading *détonne* (stick out like a sore thumb), later in the same sentence, meaning to be inharmonious or sing off key, instead of *détone* (detonate, explode, make a loud noise, or happen quickly).

(651,fn1) Lacan is actually quoting part of Lagache's summary (on page 11 of his text) of the article by Hartmann, Kris, and Loewenstein entitled "Comments on the Formation of Psychic Structure," *The Psychoanalytic Study of the Child*, II (1946): 11–38. A discussion of anthropomorphism is found on page 16 of this latter text, and the "distance from experience" that Lacan repeatedly attributes to Lagache (starting on *Écrits* 1966, 649) is actually first quoted by Lagache from this same article on page 17.

(653,1) *Précession* (antecedence) means precession in astronomy and physics, but by extension it also means the fact of preceding something else. Giving a male child the same name as his grandfather was, for example, a Carolingian tradition.

(653,2) On the ego-ideal (or superego) as including elements from our grandparents and great-grandparents, see, for example, *SE* XXII, 67.

(653,5) I have changed the last quote from Lagache to correspond to Lagache's text. Lacan provides *premiers moments* where Lagache provides *rudiments*.

(655,3) *Faute* (lack) has many meanings, including error, mistake, misdemeanor, wrong, and lack. *Film* (film) earlier in the sentence also means sequence, course, or unfolding (of events).

(656,fn1) *Pour qu'ait eu lieu l'explication avec* (in order to have it out with it) could alternatively be rendered as "to explain it alongside it."

(657,1) *Subornement* (deviation) is an old, alternate form of *subornation*, meaning subornation, in the juridical sense, or the seduction, corruption (through bribery), perversion, depraving, or leading astray of someone.

(657,7) See *SE* IV, 326 and 337 (chapter 6, section C).

(658,5) *Elle* (corresponding to the second instance of "materiality" in the first sentence) could, alternatively, refer back to "structure" here.

(659,4) Note that Freud describes "the id as the great reservoir of libido" in *The Ego and the Id, SE* XIX, 30, fn1. See also *SE* VII, 218.

(659,5) The *bocca di leone* was a secret complaint box (used to anonymously report crimes such as tax evasion) located in the Sala del Bussola in the Palazzo Ducale (or Doge's Palace) in Venice. Interestingly, a sculpture entitled the "Drunkenness of Noah" (mentioned by Lacan further on) is also found on the corner of the Doge's Palace.

(659,6) The Freud quote is from *SE* XIV, 186. On action and certainty, see "Logical Time."

(660,3) *Bejahung* means affirmation, approval, or admission. For Lacan's discussions of *Verneinung*, see Seminar I, "Introduction to Jean Hyppolite's Commentary on Freud's '*Verneinung*,' " "Response to Jean Hyppolite's Commentary," and Hyppolite's "Spoken Commentary on Freud's '*Verneinung*.' "

(660,4) *Chiffre* (cipher) also means number, code, figure, total, and combination. Lacan does very little with the number 58 here; does it refer to 1958, when this paper was first presented? Or to the fact that, having been born April 13, 1901, Lacan was finishing out his 58th year when he wrote up the final version of this paper, during Easter vacation of 1960 (Easter fell on April 7 that year)? The number does not seem to correspond to numbers assigned to letters in *merdre* . . .

(660,7) Reading *jaculatoire* (ejaculatory) instead of *joculatoire*, which seems to be nonexistent, although it may be related to the English "jocular." On *merdre*, see Alfred Jarry's *Ubu Roi ou les Polonais* (Paris: Eugène Fasquelle, 1922); in English see *King Turd*, trans. B. Keith and G. Legman (New York: Boar's Head Books, 1953). The word can be seen to contain, at a minimum, *merde* (shit), *meurtre* (murder), and *mère* (mother).

(661,1) "Gematry" is, according to the *OED*, "a cabalistic method of interpreting the Hebrew Scriptures by interchanging words whose letters have the same numerical value when added." The French *gematrie* can also more generally mean cryptogram.

(661,3) To put someone to the question is a

euphemism for torture. *Tenaille* (instrument of torture) is a kind of pliers or pincers designed to break bones as part of torture.

(661,5) *Frayages* (breaches) is Lacan's translation for Freud's term *Bahnungen*, translated in *The Origins of Psychoanalysis* (New York: Basic Books, 1954) as "facilitations."

(661,7) *Donner sa langue au chat* (hold one's tongue) implies giving up or throwing in the towel; literally, it means giving one's tongue to the cat.

(663,4) There may well be an error in the French here, as Pichon and Damourette, to whom Lacan generally refers regarding the French *ne*, refer to it as an "expletive," not an "expressive" (cf. *Écrits* 1966, 800). I have argued in my *Lacanian Subject* (Princeton: Princeton University Press, 1995) that we may have something equivalent to this *ne* in English with the word "but," especially in expressions like "I can't help but think that . . . ," "I can't but not wonder at his complacency," and "I can't but not suspect him of having done it."

(664,3) *Formes d'aspect* (aspect forms) refers to a set of inflectional forms of a verb that indicate the nature of the action or the manner in which the action is regarded, especially with reference to its beginning, duration, completion, or repetition and without reference to its position in time; these forms include the completive, imperfective, inchoative, iterative, and perfective. *Accompli* (perfective) is a synonym of *perfectif* in this context. See J.-F. Phelizon, *Vocabulaire de la linguistique* (Paris: Roudil, 1976). *Pas* (pace) is also the second half of the most common two-part form of negation in French: *ne pas*.

(664,4) See *SE* XVII, 94.

(665,3) The first *tu* here is from *taire*, to be silent or to shut up. *Creuser sa forme au tu d'appel* (to give its form to the *tu* one calls) is quite polyvalent, as *creuser* can mean widen, deepen, accentuate, render concave, dig out, or sound, and *au* here could be understood as either in or with. I have interpreted Lacan's French here on the model of the colloquialism *creuser une faim à quelqu'un* (to make someone hungry).

(666,1) *Sous l'aspect de négatif* (negatively) literally means in the negative aspect (or in a negative manner) and may be a technical term in linguistics. *Sa* (its) at the end of the paragraph could, alternatively, be translated as "his."

(666,3) The French here, *co-naître au connu*, also evokes the idea of awakening to the known and of coming to know what is known.

(666,5) *Faute* (sin) is not the most common French term for sin, which is *péché*. *Faute* enters into many expressions as indicative of a lack or absence of something—for example, *faute de x*, meaning "failing *x*" or "in the absence of *x*."

(667,1) *Relever* (raise . . . up) is also the French for sublating.

(667,3) *Plus-Personne* also literally means Plus No One; idiomatically, it can mean there is nothing there anymore. *Est-ce* ("it," which literally means "is it") sounds like the German for "id": *Es*.

(667,4) *Personne* (person) also means no one.

(668,7) *Entstellung* is usually translated into French as *déformation*.

(669,4) *Cyclope* (Cyclopean) can also mean Herculean, as in a Herculean task. *Tirelire* (piggy-bank) also means head and Lacan mentioned *caboches* (skulls) two paragraphs back. *Loupe* (magnifying glass) also means burr and cyst. There is a likely reference here to Johann Kaspar Lavater (a friend of Goethe's), author of the *Physiognomische Fragmente* (1775–1778), a study of physiognomics (a theory suggesting that emotions and long-lasting character traits become inscribed on the body surface and that it is thus possible to read the state of one's soul in one's outer appearance), and of the *Secret Journal of a Self Observer* ([1772–1773] 1795).

(670,1) *Fanfreluches . . . antidote* (frills . . . antidote) evokes Rabelais' *fanfreluches antidotées*, which literally means something like "remedied frills." See Rabelais' *Gargantua*, chapter 2. Lacan is alluding here to Erasmus' *In Praise of Folly*.

(670,3) *Une judiciaire* (faculty of judgment): the nominal form here is not directly related to juridical matters; in the seventeenth and eighteenth centuries, it was used as an elliptical form of *rhétorique judiciaire* to designate the part of rhetoric that concerns judgment, the faculty of distinguishing truth from falsehood. It could also be rendered simply as "judgment."

(670,4) Freud's letter to Fliess is dated December 6, 1896; see *The Origins of Psycho-*

analysis, 173–81, and *The Complete Letters of Sigmund Freud to Wilhelm Fliess* (Cambridge, Mass.: Belknap, 1985), 207–14, especially 208.

(671,2) *Dans le siècle* (in the real world) literally means in the century and has a religious connotation of living in the world as opposed to cut off from it in a convent or monastery.

(671,4) *Dimidiée* (split) has certain scientific meanings—in medicine it is used to refer to what concerns one of the two sides of the body (as in *anesthésie dimidiée*) and in botany to a situation in which only one of two sides of a plant or plant feature is developed—and can, more generally, be understood as "split," each side being treated or behaving differently. Lacan is clearly referring in this passage to Claude Lévi-Strauss' article "Split Representation in the Art of Asia and America" in *Structural Anthropology* (New York: Basic Books, 1963); see also Lévi-Strauss' preface to *La Voie des Masques* (Paris: Plon, 1975) where he cites at length his own 1943 article, "The Art of the Northwest Coast at the American Museum of Natural History," *Gazette des Beaux-Arts* (1943): 175–82. Cf. Lacan's discussion of masks in *Écrits* 1966, 752.

(672,5) See, for example, Freud's comments on the ego as "a mental projection of the surface of the body" in *The Ego and the Id* (*SE* XIX, 26) and his likening of the "mental apparatus" to a microscope, telescope, or camera in *The Interpretation of Dreams* (*SE* V, 536 and 611).

(673,1) See Henri Pierre Maxime Bouasse, *Optique et photométrie, dites géométriques* (Paris: Delagrave, [1934] 1947).

(675,4) For the placement of *i(a)*, see Figure 3, further on.

(675,5) In gestalt theory, *prégnance* (power) refers to the power forms have to impose themselves upon perception or force themselves upon us. It can also take on the more general meaning of being full of implicit meanings or consequences.

(676,3) *Parabole* (parable) also means parabola. *Faisceau* (bundle) also means beam (as in light beam) and fasciculus.

(676,5) Menenius Agrippa, faced with an uprising by the plebeians, told the latter a parable about how the stomach and the limbs cannot do without each other, forming one body as they do, just like the rulers and the people. The story was taken up by Quintilian, Plutarch (in the life of Coriolanus), and Rabelais (*Tiers livre*, chapters 3 and 4), among others.

(677,2) See Paul Federn, *Ego Psychology and the Psychoses* (New York: International Universities Press, 1952).

(677,6) *Méchef* (ill-doing), a term from the Middle Ages that has rarely been used in French since the seventeenth century, means misfortune, unfortunate event, or evil act. The whole sentence here is open to different readings, for *est capable de précipiter l'identification du Moi Idéal jusqu'à ce pouvoir de méchef* can be understood in several different ways, such as "can even bring about an identification, on the part of the ideal ego, with the feeble power of mischief."

(678,2) *Ressort* (jurisdiction), here and in the next sentence, could also mean mainspring.

(678,5) *Elle* (it [at the end of the paragraph]) could, grammatically, refer to *image*, *reconnaissance*, or *assomption*. *Reconnaissance* strikes me as most likely.

(679,1) *Antériorité de borne* (grounding anteriority) is quite polyvalent, a *borne* being a limit, a mile marker, a terminal, and a ground (in electricity).

(679,2) Cenesthesia is mentioned by Lagache on page 8 of his text. On "hospitalism," see René A. Spitz's paper entitled "Hospitalism," in *The Psychoanalytic Study of the Child*, I (New York: International Universities Press, 1945), 53–74.

(679,3) I have assumed that Lacan is referring here to the three stages of the advent of the signifier, outlined more fully in Seminar IX, *Identification*: 1) there is a trace; 2) the trace is effaced; 3) a line or circle is drawn around the place where the trace was effaced.

(681,1) *Morte ou vive* (still or moving) literally means dead or alive.

(681,2) See Tristan l'Hermite's poem "Le promenoir des deux amants," in *Plaintes d'Acante* (1633).

(682,5) *Objet partiel* (partial object) is more usually translated as "part-object." *Exposant* (exponent) also means exhibitor (at a fair or gallery). There is a possible reference here to Thomas, the "doubter," at the Last Supper with his raised finger.

(682,8) *Le sujet est appelé à renaître* (he is called to be reborn) could also be understood as "he has (or is given) the chance to be reborn," "he comes to be reborn," "he is invited (or enjoined or incited) to be reborn," or even "he is destined to be reborn."

(683,1) *De sa personne . . . payer* (to do a lot personally to pay) literally means to pay with one's person (body or personality) and figuratively means to pay dearly, suffer, or work hard to pay.

(683,3) See *SE* XXIII, 250–53.

(683,5) The notion of the "agent intellect" is attributed to Aristotle (see *On the Soul*, or *De Anima*, 3.5) and is extensively discussed by Saint Thomas Aquinas in his *Summa Theologica*.

(683,6) Lacan gives a rendition here of Kant's words, "der bestirnte Himmel über mir und das moralische Gesetz in mir," from the conclusion of his second *Critique*. In English, see Werner S. Pluhar's translation of the *Critique of Practical Reason* (Indianapolis and Cambridge: Hackett, 2002), 203.

(684,2) Freud uses the term "hominization" in *SE* XXIII, 75 and 153, where it means the process of becoming human. Lacan is also referring here to Pierre Teilhard de Chardin (1881–1955). Cf. *Écrits* 1966, 88.

(684,3) Lagache mentions the "voice of conscience" on page 12 of his article.

(684,8) *Nescit*: he does not know.

Notes to "The Signification of the Phallus"

(685,1) The title of this article, *La signification du phallus*, could also be translated as "The Phallus' Signification," "What the Phallus Signifies," "The Phallus as Signification," or "The Signification That the Phallus Is." See Lacan's discussion of the title as involving a subjective genitive or an objective genitive in Seminar XIX (January 19, 1972).

(685,8) See *SE* XXI, 105–7, and Freud's article, "Analysis Terminable and Interminable" (1937), *SE* XXIII, 209–54. In "Variations on the Standard Treatment," Lacan translates the title of this article as "L'analyse finie et l'analyse sans fin," "Finite (or Finished) Analysis and Endless Analysis."

(686,4) Presumably, a "transference" from the mother to the father.

(687,2) Cf. "Guiding Remarks," *Écrits* 1966, 730. For another example of such ignorance, consider the wedding night of Louis the Sixteenth as told by Alexandre Dumas senior in *Joseph Balsamo*, chapter 64.

(687,3) The person who "sometimes . . . says both" seems to be Ernest Jones; see "Guiding Remarks," *Écrits* 1966, 732. On transmutations of the object see, for example, R. von Krafft-Ebing's *Psychopathia Sexualis* (New York: Physicians and Surgeons Book Company, [1900] 1935).

(687,6) Jones used the Greek term "aphanisis" to refer to the "total, and of course permanent, extinction of the capacity (including opportunity) for sexual enjoyment"; see "Early Development of Female Sexuality" (1927), in *Papers on Psycho-Analysis*, 5th edition (Boston: Beacon, 1961), 440. According to Jones, the fear of aphanisis is more fundamental than that of castration in both sexes, castration being only a "special case" of aphanisis in boys. The other two articles in the series Lacan mentions are "The Phallic Phase" and "Early Female Sexuality," both of which are included in *Papers on Psycho-Analysis*. The key mentioned at the end of the paragraph would seem to be the term "signifier."

(688,2) Lacan plays, at the very beginning of the paragraph, on the expression *noyer le poisson* (to throw someone off track, create confusion, or mix things up, in order to dodge a question), saying "le poisson ne se laisse pas noyer." The phallus is often associated by Lacan with a fish; see, for example, *Écrits* 1966, 626–27 and 805. "Male and female created He them" is found on page 484 of Jones' paper, "The Phallic Phase."

(689,4) Regarding *ein anderer Schauplatz*, see *SE* IV, 48 and *SE* V, 536. *Écrits* 1966 erroneously reads *eine* here instead of *ein* and *andere* instead of *anderer*; this is corrected in Points. *Versants* (axes) is Lacan's translation into French of Jakobson's term, "aspects," in his article "Two Aspects of Language and Two

Types of Aphasic Disturbances," in *Selected Writings*, vol. II (The Hague: Mouton, 1971), 239–59.

(689,5) Or "The discovery of what he articulates . . ."

(690,5) This might seem to be contradicted in Freud's discussion of the Schreber case (*SE* XII, 57 and 62), for example, but the German there reads *Versagung* (*GW* VIII, 293 and 298), which Lacan says implies renunciation, not frustration (see *Écrits* 1966, 460–61).

(691,1) Love as "giving what you don't have" is a major theme in Seminar VIII (see, for example, pages 46 and 157), but was introduced by him a number of years earlier.

(691,2) *Aufhebt* is a verb form of *Aufhebung*, an Hegelian term now often translated into English as "sublation," the infinitive verb form being "to sublate." Alternate reading for "the crushing brought on by the demand for love": "the crushing (or annihilation) of the demand for love."

(691,4) Note that *signifier* (signifying) also means to legally notify or serve a notice.

(692,2) A reference to Franz Alexander's *The Psychoanalysis of the Total Personality: The Application of Freud's Theory of the Ego to the Neuroses* (New York: Nervous and Mental Disease Publishing Company, [1927] 1930).

(692,4) *Attraper* (grasped) could also be rendered here as "grabbed."

(692,fn1) Note that *Pudeur* (Shame) is better translated as "modesty" in most contexts.

(693,4) *Raison du désir* also means the "reason for desire" and "desire's reason."

(693,9) *L'épreuve du désir* (the test constituted by desire) can be understood as "the test (or testing) of desire," "desire as a test," "desire's acid-test," or "the ordeal, trial, or test (the subject undergoes) due to desire." *L'épreuve du désir de l'Autre* (the test constituted by the Other's desire) two paragraphs further on can be understood along the same lines.

(694,1) *Manque à avoir* could also be translated as "want-to-have" or "lack-in-having."

(694,5) *Paraître* could also be translated as "appearing." There seems to be a problem in the French here, given the parallel structure Lacan sets up here: ". . . in one case, . . . in the other" (the French reads *dans l'autre* instead of *de l'autre*). In any case, it seems clear that the protecting has to do with men and the masking with women.

(695,1) See Freud's article, "On the Universal Tendency to Debasement in the Sphere of Love" (1912), *SE* XI, 177–90.

(695,3) *L'Autre de l'Amour* (Loving Other) could also be rendered as "the Other of Love," "the Other who gives Love," or "the Other involved in Love." *Recul* (backcourt) can also mean recoil, backward movement, stepping back, distance, distancing, and background.

(695,6) See *SE* XXII, 131. Cf. *Écrits* 1966, 735 and 851.

NOTES TO "IN MEMORY OF ERNEST JONES: ON HIS THEORY OF SYMBOLISM"

(697,5) Marienbad was the site of the Fourteenth International Psychoanalytic Congress in August 1936 and was presided over by Jones; Lacan first presented his work on the mirror stage there. See *Écrits* 1966, 67 and 184–85.

(699,1) See, for example, Ernest Jones, *Papers on Psycho-Analysis*, 5th edition (Boston: Beacon, 1961).

(701,5) "Chymical wedding" is a reference to Christian Rosenkreuz's *The Chymical Wedding*; for a recent poetic version in English, see *The Chymical Wedding of Christian Rosenkreuz*, translated by Jon Valentine (Spring Valley, NY: Saint George Publications, 1981). Cf. *SE* V, 344–45.

(701,6) *Métaphysiciens dans l'âme* (metaphysicians in the soul) might be more idiomatically rendered as "dyed-in-the-wool metaphysicians."

(702,7) *Liquette* is a slang term for shirt, and at a certain point referred, in the vocabulary of fashion, to a woman's shirt that was cut like a man's. *Ninque* may possibly refer to the color white or to a white flower. *Liquette ninque* could then possibly be understood as a white shirt or a flowery (woman's) shirt.

(705,6) Lacan reduces the pronunciation of "lion" to the last syllable, which could be written "yon." Repeating it in "yon-yon" strikes him as a particularly weak sound (or "meek growl") compared to "lion."

(706,1) See Lacan's favorite etymological dictionary: *Dictionnaire étymologique de la langue française* by Oscar Bloch and Walther von Wartburg (Paris: PUF, 1932).

(706,2) André Breton introduced the term *peu de réalité* (scant reality) in his 1924 "Introduction au discours sur le peu de réalité"; see *Point du Jour* (Paris: Gallimard, 1970); in English, see "Introduction to the Discourse on the Paucity of Reality" in *Break of Day*, trans. Mark Polizzotti and Mary Ann Caws (Lincoln: University of Nebraska Press, 1999), 3–20.

(706,2–3) Lacan is likely referring here to the monetary reform that equated 100 old French francs with 1 new French franc.

(707,1) *Ferraille* (metal coin) literally means scrap metal, but it can also take on the meaning of loose change.

(708,1) *Barbote* (wades) also means bubbles a gas through a liquid.

(715,1) Lacan is playing here on the old vernacular expression *avoir un polichinelle dans le tiroir* (literally, to have a Punch in the drawer) for indicating that a woman is pregnant (akin to the English expression "to have a bun in the oven").

(715,fnl) "Parapilla" was likely published in 1776 by Charles Borde; see Jean-Jacques Pauvert's *Anthologie historique des lectures érotiques*, vol. 1, *De Gilgamesh à Saint-Just* (Paris: Stock/Spengler, 1995), 974–76.

(716,4) Jones, *Papers on Psycho-Analysis*, 144. Lacan adds the parenthetical *sic.*

(717,2) *Évocation* (conjured him up) literally means evocation and also refers to the right of a higher court to summon for review a case pending before a lower court. One might consider reading *suie* (soot) instead of *suite* (pursuit), as in the original version of the article.

(717,3) Regarding the present paper, see also Seminar V, chapter 15.

Notes to "On an Ex Post Facto Syllabary"

(717,5) *Après coup* (Ex Post Facto) is also used to translate Freud's *Nachträglichkeit* (deferred action).

(718,5) A *millefeuille* (layer cake) is known in American English as a "Napoleon"; Lacan seems to be concerned here with the notion of the many layers in the cake's crust, which is usually a *pâte feuilleté* (puff pastry), or of the successive layers of crust and pastry cream and/or custard.

(719,2) *De ce qui prend avènement du Nouveau* (on the basis of what becomes of them in the New Testament) strikes me as quite opaque, but is perhaps shed light on by the next paragraph in the text.

(721,8) Lacan plays here on the similar French pronunciation of *anas* (ana, that is, a collection of miscellaneous information, anecdotes, or sayings about a particular subject or person) and Anna.

(722,5) The *serpent d'airain* (bronze serpent) is a reference to the bronze snake with which Moses saved the Hebrews from God's punishment of the fiery serpents; see *Numbers* 21:4–9.

(722,8) Lacan is perhaps referring to the end of the third to last paragraph before this one.

(723,1) Something quite similar to this can be found in the game known as "Fifteen."

(723,5) Lacan is likely referring here to Konrad Lorenz's "innate releasing mechanism"—a term he never uses anywhere else in *Écrits*—but he merely writes I.R.M. In Seminar VIII, he mentions releasing mechanisms, but does not cite Lorenz.

(724,2) *Réduit le symbolisme à y fonder le sujet* (reduces symbolism to grounding the subject in it) could, alternatively, be rendered as "reduces symbolism when it grounds (or to grounding) the subject in it."

Notes to "Guiding Remarks for a Convention on Female Sexuality"

(726,8) *Non-lieu* literally means a non-place or non-locus (a no place), and in legal contexts means nonsuit or withdrawal of case.

(727,1) *La théorie de l'erreur* (the theory of error) seems to refer to Spinoza's (or possibly William James') attempt to understand human error.

(727,8) *Ce qui s'avoue* (what is recognized)

could also be understood as "what is acknowledged" or "what can be avowed."

(728,3) See Lou Andreas-Salomé's "'Anal' und 'Sexual'" in *Imago* 4 (1916): 249. Freud mentions this in *SE* VII, 187, and *SE* XXII, 101. The vagina here supposedly borrows, rents, or leases its sensitivity from the anus.

(728,8) *Dégrossies* (refined) comes from *dégrossir*, meaning to give the rudiments of education (to someone), carve away the biggest pieces before proceeding with the finish work (as in preparing to finish a statue made of stone), whittle down, or slim down.

(728,9) See Ernest Jones, "Early Female Sexuality" (1935) in Jones's *Papers on Psycho-Analysis* (Boston: Beacon, 1961).

(729,2) Jones' quote from *Genesis*, "In the beginning . . . male and female He created them," is the last line of his paper, "The Phallic Phase," in *Papers on Psycho-Analysis*, 484.

(729,3) Jones, *Papers on Psycho-Analysis*, 495.

(729,6) Klein's notion of the "combined parent" is introduced by Klein in *The Psycho-Analysis of Children* (London: Hogarth Press, 1959 [1949]), chapters 8 and 11.

(729,9) The French here literally means function of equivalence, and refers to the way in which the phallus makes objects equivalent or equates them; see, in particular, Seminar VIII, 295–99.

(730,1) *De la récupération de la métaphore sexuelle* (by reclaiming the sexual metaphor) is especially open to interpretation, due to the two *de*'s and the fact that *récupération* has a number of different meanings: salvaging, reclaiming, recovering, co-opting, and appropriating. On having and being, cf. *SE* XVIII, 106.

(730,5) See Josine Müller, "A Contribution to the Problem of Libidinal Development of the Genital Phase in Girls," *IJP* XIII (1932): 361–68. Cf. Ernest Jones, "The Phallic Phase," 456, and Karen Horney, "The Dread of Women," *IJP* XIII (1932): 348–60.

(731,3) See "The Taboo of Virginity," *SE* XI, 193–208.

(731,9) Cf. *SE* XI, 201: ". . . the cheerless phenomenon of permanent and obstinate frigidity which no tender efforts on the part of the husband can overcome."

(732,2) *L'altérité du sexe* (The difference between the sexes) could instead be rendered as "Sexual difference," "Sexual alterity," or even "The alterity of the fairer sex."

(732,3) The "symbolically commanded defense" here seems to be frigidity.

(733,3) Venusberg is the magical mountain abode of Venus, with certain brothel-like characteristics, which figures prominently in Wagner's opera, *Tannhäuser*. Freud refers to it in his *Introductory Lectures on Psycho-Analysis*, *SE* XVI, 321. See Otto Fenichel's article, "The Symbolic Equation: Girl = Phallus," in *The Collected Papers of Otto Fenichel* (New York: W. W. Norton, 1954). On "You are my wife," cf. *Écrits* 1966, 298, and Seminar III. The end of the paragraph could, alternatively, read: "what reemerges in the subject's unconscious is what the Other desires, that is, the phallus that was desired by the Mother."

(733,4) Lacan seems to be suggesting that a man *is* duplicitous (he has a wife or partner but keeps looking for the phallus—as the object desired by his mother as Other—in a proliferating series of girls who embody the phallus for him), whereas a woman is not duplicitous, apart from the persistence in her of an incestuous desire.

(733,8) *Étalon* (standard) also means stallion and stud (as in a virile man).

(734,9) Jones' 1927 article can be found in *Papers on Psycho-Analysis*, 438–51.

(735,2) *Relève* (sublation) also means replacing, changing, or relaying. *Se donner les gants* (making a virtue) also evokes *jeter le gant*, to defy or challenge (throw down the gauntlet), and *relever le gant*, to accept the challenge or combat. See "The Psychogenesis of a Case of Homosexuality," *SE* XVIII, 147–72, especially 153 where Freud says, "She was probably making a virtue of necessity when she kept insisting on the purity of her love . . ." Lacan comments on the case at length in Seminar IV, chapters 6, 7, and 8.

(735,3) Love as "giving what you do not have" is a major theme in Seminar VIII (see pages 46, 157, and elsewhere).

(735,9) See *SE* XXII, 131; cf. *Écrits* 1966, 695 and 851.

(736,1) Lacan is parenthetically referring to the "partiality" of the term *sexe* in French, which in this and other cases I have rendered by "fairer sex," as it refers to women, not men.

(736,6) Catharism may have inspired the courtly love tradition.

Notes to "The Youth of Gide, or the Letter and Desire"

(739,3) I have slightly modified the Greek Lacan provides to conform to that provided in the Loeb Classical Library edition of *Euripides* (Cambridge, Mass.: Harvard University Press, 1912). The passage from *Medea* can be rendered as follows: "If you bring novel wisdom to fools, you will be regarded as useless, not wise; and if the city regards you as greater than those with a reputation for cleverness, you will be thought vexatious"; see *Euripides*, trans. David Kovacs (Cambridge, Mass.: Harvard University Press, forthcoming).

(740,2) *Replis* (folds) can also refer to military maneuvers by which one withdraws to regroup at another location.

(740,4) *Les enfances Gide* (Gide childhoods) is from *Jeunesse de Gide*, vol. I, 15; in French the construction does not employ a classic genitive (as in *les enfances de Gide*). *The Youth of Gide* simply renders this as "Gide's childhood" (5).

(740,5) *Artifex* is the Latin for one who practices an art or a craft, that is, an artist or artisan. Cf. Buffon's "The style is the man himself" and Lacan's comments on it in *Écrits* 1966, 9–10. *Objet* (object) can also mean objective.

(740,6) The "old sacred monster" is probably Gide, and Delay "his partner"; hence the end of the paragraph can be understood as: "certain as Gide was that in taking it up, Delay could but complete it."

(741,3) See Delay's discussion of Sainte-Beuve in *Jeunesse de Gide*, vol. I, 11; *The Youth of Gide*, 3.

(741,5) *Le message trouve-t-il à se reconnaître* (the message can manage to be seen) can also be rendered as "the message manages to see itself (or: to be recognized)."

(742,1) *S'avère* (shows itself) can also be understood as "is confirmed" and even as "is averred."

(742,3) *Si le grain ne meurt* can be found in André Gide, *Souvenirs et Voyages* (Paris: Gallimard [1955] 2001), 81–330. Delay and Lacan are presumably referring to the edition published in three volumes by Nouvelle Revue Française in 1926. In English, see *If It Die, An Autobiography*, trans. D. Bussy (London: Secker & Warburg, 1951).

(743,fn1) In English, see *The Youth of Gide*: "*Not to have had confidence*, or more precisely, *not to have had faith* in someone—if by chance that someone is Someone—is a stain I don't want to have on my life. That's about it—I'm looking after my biography [*je soigne ma biographie*]" (373).

(744,8) Delay's comments on Montaigne can be found in *Jeunesse de Gide*, vol. I, 15; *The Youth of Gide*, 5–6.

(745,5) Arnolphe is an ambitious bourgeois in Molière's play, *L'Ecole des femmes,* who adopts the name "de la Souche," which he then uses exclusively. *Souche* means stump, stock, and lineage. *Vert* (hardy) literally means green, but also connotes a number of other qualities, such as vigor, leafiness, sourness, youth, immaturity (as of a fruit that has yet to ripen), and unreadiness.

(745,6) Turelures is a likely reference to Paul Claudel's play *Le pain dur. Enrichissez-vous* (get rich) was the advice given to Édouard Rondeaux by a neighbor of his; see *Jeunesse de Gide*, vol. I, 128 (not included in *The Youth of Gide*).

(746,2) The "aggregation examination" is a competitive exam that entitles the successful candidate to teach at the highest educational levels.

(746,3) Lacan is probably referring here to the thoughts Paul Gide jotted down on a piece of paper that Delay found among his class notes and legal studies; see *Jeunesse de Gide*, vol. I, 81–82 (not included in *The Youth of Gide*). Among them we find: "He who must be pitied in our life here below is not the lover without hope, nor the deceived lover, nor even the lover who has lost what he loves—it is the man who has never loved."

(746,5) *Abrupts d'âme* (heightened emotions): Lacan transforms the usual *états d'âme* (emotions, but literally, states of the soul) into *abrupts d'âme, abrupts* meaning cliffs (as a noun); I have assumed that he meant to emphasize dramatic surges of emotion thereby.

(747,1) A reference to the determinist, Hyppolite Adolphe Taine (1828–1893).

(747,2) See William Blake's *The Marriage of Heaven and Hell.*

(747,3) On the relation between symptoms and metaphors, see *Écrits* 1966, 528 and 889–92. The Latin *flatus vocis* means a mere name, word, or sound without a corresponding objective reality, and was used by nominalists to qualify universals.

(748,6) *Les Faux-monnayeurs* was translated into English by Dorothy Bussy as *The Counterfeiters* (New York: Knopf, 1927).

(749,2) *Armoire* (dresser) literally means a wardrobe or cupboard: a large free-standing piece of furniture in which one stores clothing, linens, and other household items. It is one of the most common pieces of furniture in French households (currently being supplanted by the construction of built-in closets), and Lacan perhaps chose it here (as opposed to other static objects) because such wardrobes tend to form part of a room's barely-noticed background. Note that *armoire* can also be used to describe a person who is "built like a tank," and can take on pejorative connotations of brutish insensitivity and cruelty.

(750,1) Anna Marie Leuenberger worked as a maid for Gide's family for over 25 years, and when they lived in the rue de Tournon, she shared a room with Delphine, a young cook. Their room (according to *Jeunesse de Gide*, vol. I, 309; not included in *The Youth of Gide*) was located above the back kitchen or pantry; Lacan refers to their room as a *soupente*, which is usually just temporary quarters or a part of a room (a loft, attic, or space under a flight of stairs). The scene is recounted by Gide in *Si le grain ne meurt*.

(750,5) The "tripe butcher" is a fairly obvious reference to Melanie Klein.

(750,7) The *Crique* is a kind of bogeyman (like Plato's Mormo), who punishes children by cutting them into pieces and eating them.

(751,1) The breaking of dishes may be an allusion to *Le dîner de Mademoiselle Justine* by Madame de Ségur; see her *Oeuvres*, vol. 2, edited by Claudine Beaussant (Paris: Robert Laffont, 1990), 985–1022; the metamorphosis of Gribouille is from George Sand's *Histoire du véritable Gribouille* (1850). The *rameau de verdure* (branches and leaves) may allude to a palm frond. Ségur also mentions Gribouille.

(751,5) Cf. Lacan's L schema, found, for example, in Seminar II, 134/109, and *Écrits* 1966, 53.

(752,1) Gide's *Voyage d'Urien* (1893) was translated into English as *Urien's Voyage* by Wade Baskin (New York: Philosophical Library, 1964).

(752,3) *In articulo mortis* means at death's door(step). See Freud's 1938 article, "Splitting of the Ego in the Process of Defence," *SE* XXIII, 275–78.

(752,4) On masks, see also *Écrits* 1966, 671.

(752,5) *Personne* (person) could also be rendered here as "personality." On "being and appearing" (or seeming), cf. *Écrits* 1966, 694.

(753,3) *La Porte étroite* (Paris: Arthème Fayard, 1937) was translated by D. Bussy as *Straight Is the Gate* (New York: Vintage, 1952).

(753,4) *Chaleurs de Phèdre* (heat of passion) literally means the heat of Phaedrus and may be a reference to Plato's *Phaedrus* (which includes a discussion of love) or to Racine's play, *Phèdre et Hippolyte*; consider, for example, the following lines from the latter: "Et que tes vains secours cessent de rappeler/ Un reste de chaleur, tout prêt à s'exhaler" (Act I, Scene 3, lines 315–16). *Chaleurs* is also an older medical term for a generalized or localized sensation of malaise. The "two different versions of this episode" can be found in *La Porte étroite* and *Si le grain ne meurt*.

(753,5) Lacan seems to be drawing a comparison between the scene in which Madeleine's mother groped Gide, after commenting on how badly he was always dressed (see *La Porte étroite*, 17–18; *Straight Is the Gate*, 10) and the scene in the train from Biskra in which Gide groped a couple of boys in the next compartment to the one he was sharing with Madeleine (*Souvenirs et Voyages*, 947–48).

(754,2) Potiphar is the Egyptian officer whose wife tried to seduce Joseph; see *Genesis* 39:1–20. Pasiphaë is the wife of Minos, mother of Ariadne, and mother of the Minotaur by the Cretan bull.

(754,3) *L'enfant désiré* (desired child) might, more commonly, be rendered as "a child who was wanted" (as opposed to an unwanted child). Lacan stresses this point again in Seminar XIX (February 3, 1972).

(754,5) The term "uranism" was introduced in 1860 (or 1862) in a novel written by a magistrate under the pseudonym Numa Numantius. It comes from the goddess of pure love, uranian (heavenly) Aphrodite. For Lacan's comments on oblative, genital relations, see *Écrits* 1966, 605–7. Dear Abby corresponds roughly to agony aunt in the United Kingdom.

(754,6) *Accomplissement de vie* (self-realization), literally "accomplishing one's life," could also be rendered as "life fulfillment" or "making an accomplishment of one's life." *Se confondre avec* (become bound up with) could also be rendered as "be confounded with," "be confused with," or "merge with." Gide mentions Dante and Beatrice in *Et nunc manet in te*; see *Souvenirs et voyages*, 938.

(754,fn1) I have moved this footnote from the word "embalmed" two paragraphs below to its present position because it refers to a footnote in *Jeunesse de Gide* on François Mauriac's reactions to a book of photos of Gide, entitled *L'Iconographie d'André Gide*. For an idea of Gide's appearance as a child, see *Jeunesse de Gide*, vol. I, 144 (not included in *The Youth of Gide*).

(755,2) "The missing object" here is presumably Gide's father who died when Gide was 11—that is, about two years before his love for Madeleine was born. Regarding Morella, see Edgar Allan Poe's story entitled "Morella" from 1850. *La mère . . . du désir* (the desiring mother) could also be rendered as "the mother of desire" or "the desired mother," just as *la mère . . . de l'amour* (the loving mother) could also be rendered as "the mother of love" or "the beloved mother."

(756,2) *L'au-delà* (the beyond) can also be rendered as "the hereafter." Cf. Lacan's comment, "it is a castrated lover or a dead man (or the two in one) who, for woman, hides behind the veil in order to call her adoration to it," in *Écrits* 1966, 733.

(756,5) One of Gide's works was entitled *Thésée* (Theseus); it can be found in English in *Two Legends: Oedipus and Theseus*, trans. John Russell (New York: Vintage, 1958).

(756,6) There is a possible allusion here to the Old Testament injunction to turn neither to the right nor to the left; see, for example, *Joshua* 1:7.

(757,1) "A thorn in the flesh" is from *2 Corinthians* 12:7–11.

(757,7) On "nobility," see *Hegel's Phenomenology of Spirit*, trans. A. V. Miller (Oxford: Oxford University Press, 1977), 311.

(758,5) *Et nunc manet in te* can be understood as "Henceforth she dwells in you" or "And now she lives on in you," but the reference of "she" is ambiguous. See *The Minor Poems of Vergil: Comprising the Culex, Dirae, Lydia, Moretum, Copa, Priapeia, and Catalepton*, trans. J. J. Mooney (Birmingham: Cornish Brothers, 1916), where the fuller line is rendered as "'Twas Orpheus looked behind and now on thee the punishment remains," the translator having thought, like Lacan, that it is the punishment that remains or lives on.

(759,5) *Faire passer le sillon d'un manque* (pass on the furrow of a lack) could also be understood as "transmit (or convey) the furrow of a lack" or "get the furrow of a lack accepted."

(760,1) *Sur le laus de* (to laud) is based on the old French *laus* (borrowed from the Latin *laus*), meaning to laud, praise, or honor.

(760,5) *Pavé du lion* seems to condense a number of ideas and expressions: a *pavé* is a big, fat book that is difficult or boring; *le pavé de l'ours* (literally "the bear's cobblestone") refers to something that is more of a hindrance than a help. *Un lion* can be a lion or a celebrity. If Schlumberger is the celebrity, his book is more of a hindrance than a help? Cf. *la part du lion*, the lion's share.

(761,2) Apart from the usual meanings of *entier* (the root of *entièreté*)—whole, total, and complete—the word can also connote purity, truth, and the uncastrated state (e.g., an unneutered horse); faithful and loyal are still earlier meanings.

(761,3) Gide quotes Madeleine as saying "C'était ce que j'avais de plus précieux au monde" ("It was what I had that was most precious to me"), and "J'ai brûlé tes lettres pour faire quelque chose" ("I burnt your letters to do something"), *Souvenirs et Voyages*, 961.

(761,5) Cf. Gide's remark, "I am suffering as if she had killed our child," in *Souvenirs et Voyages*, 961.

(762,2) Gide describes the circumstances of this belated reconciliation in *Souvenirs et Voyages*, 954–57.

(762,3) *Loge* (theater box) could refer either to the Masonic Lodge in the former Couvent de la Miséricorde in the rue du Vieux Colombier in Paris, or to a box of seats in the theater located in the same street. While *tourbes confraternelles* (fraternal mobs) in the next sentence would incline me to choose the former, Gide's journal entry of December 15, 1921, mentions both Jean Schlumberger and the theater in the rue du Vieux-Colombier (*Journal, 1889–1939*, 707). Lacan may well be playing off the reader's knowledge of the existence of both in the same street.

(762,4) See Molière's *L'Avare* (*The Miser*), Act V, Scene 3. The dialogue in that scene plays off the fact that *cassette* is a feminine noun; thus both the *cassette* and the daughter can be referred to as *elle*.

(762,6) The words cited are from *Souvenirs et Voyages*, 977.

(763,fn2) See, in English, *Corydon*, trans. anonymous (New York: Noonday, 1961).

(764,1) The words were actually written on the coffin; in the cadaver's hand was a blank piece of paper.

(764,2) Delay had announced that he was working on a "Psychobiography of Nietzsche," but never completed it.

(764,3) See *Jeunesse de Gide*, vol. I, 75.

Notes to "Kant with Sade"

(766,2) Kant's postulates presumably lose "even the lifeless support of the function of utility to which Kant confined them" in Sade's *Philosophy in the Bedroom*.

(766,3) On "the eternal feminine does not elevate us," cf. Goethe's "the eternal feminine elevates us" in *Faust* II, v. 12104–12111. *Bien* is used both as an adverb ("well," as in *je me sens bien*, "I feel well") and as a noun ("good," as in *le bien et le mal*, "good and evil") in French. I have tried to retain some of Lacan's wordplay here by juxtaposing "the good" with "feeling good." Cf. Kant, *Critique of Practical Reason*, trans. Werner S. Pluhar (Indianapolis and Cambridge: Hackett, 2002), 80–81.

(767,1) See *Critique of Practical Reason*, 94–100, and especially 96, where *Selbstsucht* is rendered as "selfishness." The term "counterweight" is found on page 99.

(767,5) Lacan plays here off the expressions *dormir sur ses deux oreilles* (to rest easy) and *se boucher les oreilles* (to turn a deaf ear to something).

(767,6) See Alfred Jarry's play *Ubu Roi ou les polonais* (Paris: Eugène Fasquelle, [1888] 1922), Act V, Scene 4; in English see *King Turd*, trans. B. Keith and G. Legman (New York: Boar's Head Books, 1953).

(768,9–769,1) See Seminar VII, 96/79 and 237/202.

(769,4) On the function of the superego in comedy, see *SE* XXI, 165.

(769,6) According to the *Trésor de la Langue française*, in legal contexts the adjective *positive* (*de facto*) designates written law (as opposed to natural or unwritten law)—that is, law that is established by a divine or human authority. Cf. *Écrits* 1966, 126.

(769,8) On the difference between general rules and universal rules, see *Critique of Practical Reason*, 53.

(770,2) *La charge de revanche* ("my turn next time") is an idiomatic expression used, for example, when someone treats you to a meal and you say it will be your treat next time.

(770,3) *La morale* (moral philosophy) also means ethics.

(770,6) *C'est de l'Autre que son commandement nous requiert* (its commandment requisitions us as Other) could also be understood as "it is from the Other that its commandment requisitions us."

(771,3) *Tuant* (lethal) would normally be translated as "exhausting," but Lacan is playing off of *Tu es* (you are) here, which sounds exactly like *Tuer* (to kill). In a Biblical context, *Tu es* might be rendered as "Thou art." *Tuant* might literally be taken here as you-ing.

(772,1) An amboceptor is something that brings things together with its two receptors.

(772,4) The "voice on the radio" may be an allusion to de Gaulle's famous radio address to the French from London during WW II.

(772,6) *Impose l'idée du sujet* (forces [upon us] the idea of the subject) might also be understood as "forces ideas on the subject."

(772,7) Ataraxia designates tranquillity of the soul, apathy, detachment, calm, and serenity.

(773,1) *Grimmigkeit* means wrathfulness; Lacan is referring here to Jakob Böhme (1575–1624). Cf. Seminar VII, 255/215. *L'être suprême en méchanceté* (supremely-evil-being) is from *Juliette*; see Sade, *Oeuvres complètes*, vol. VIII (Paris: Cercle du livre précieux, 1964), 386, and in English, *Juliette*, trans. A. Wainhouse (New York: Grove Press, 1968), 399, where it is translated as "Being Supreme in Wickedness."

(773,2) *Schwärmereien* means fanaticism, mysticism, and enthusiasm; *Schwärme* means swarms, and the French *essaims* (swarms) is pronounced like Lacan's matheme S_1. See *Critique of Practical Reason*, 94, 110, and 204.

(773,3) "The form that was verily and truly offered up in a certain time and place" seems to be a reference to the Greek mysteries. Cf. *Écrits* 1966, 627.

(773,8) *Soumis au plaisir* (under pleasure's sway) literally means in submission to pleasure or subdued by pleasure.

(774,1) Cf. *Écrits* 1966, 804.

(774,4) *Dans le sensible de* (in the sensory aspect of) could also be rendered as "in what is palpable in."

(774,5) *Poinçon* (lozenge) also means diamond or stamp. The lozenge in ($\$\lozenge a$) can apparently be read backwards and forwards: the object desires the subject and the subject desires the object.

(774,7) *Toute entière de l'Autre renvoyée* (entirely reflected in the Other) could, alternatively, be rendered as "entirely repaired for him by the Other."

(774,8) *Depuis l'inconscient* (From the vantage point of the unconscious) could also be understood as "Since the discovery of the unconscious."

(775,2) *Permet un calcul du sujet* (allows for a calculus of the subject) could also be understood as "allows us to calculate the subject [presumably the subject's position]." *Cheville* (linchpin) also means peg, butcher's hook, mainspring, kingpin, ankle, and even superfluous padding (used in a poem to maintain a particular rhyme scheme).

(775,3) *Réunion* (union) is a term used in set theory and is a reference added by Lacan in 1966 to the different "vels" he discusses in Seminar XI, for example. See also *Écrits* 1966, 841–42. *Le sujet brut* (the brute subject) is a raw or unrefined subject, in the sense that it has not yet been treated or processed (that is, alienated).

(776,1) Sophocles' words have been variously translated as, for example, "Love unconquered in (the) fight," "O Love, our conqueror, matchless in might," and "O Love, in every battle victor owned." See Seminar VII, 256/216–17, 279–80/238–39, 303–4/261, 311/267–68, and 327/281.

(776,3) On rendering "torment eternal in the hereafter," cf. Seminar VII, 303/261. On "particles of evil," see *Juliette* in *Oeuvres complètes*, vol. VIII, 386–87; in English, *Juliette*, 399–400.

(776,4) On "the second death," see *Oeuvres complètes*, vol. IX, 175–77, and *Juliette*, 771–72; cf. Seminar VII, 248–50/210–11.

(778,1) "Ready-made personalist" seems to be a reference to Daniel Lagache; see *Écrits* 1966, 656.

(778,2) Reading *sadique* (sadist) instead of *sadisme* (sadism), as in the original version of the article. See Alfred North Whitehead, *Process and Reality*, ed. D. R. Griffin and D. W. Sherburne (New York: Free Press, [1929] 1978), 44.

(778,8) Lacan perhaps means that the two "parts" of the divided subject need not be found in one and the same body, S being located in the Other, and $\$$ in the subject. See Seminar X, where Lacan situates the subject on the left-hand side of these schemas and the Other on the right-hand side.

(778,10–779,1) There seems to be a grammatical problem in this sentence which renders its meaning quite unclear: "Cette division ici réunit comme S le sujet brut incarnant l'héroïsme propre au pathologique sous l'espèce de la fidelité à Sade dont vont témoigner ceux qui furent d'abord complaisants à ses excès, sa femme, sa belle-soeur, — son valet, pourquoi pas?—, d'autres dévouements effacés de son histoire." Normally, one would say *réunir quelque chose à quelque chose d'autre*, but Lacan does not seem to do so here. *Réunit* (pins together) is obviously related to *réunion*, which means union in the context of set theory; it can also be rendered as "assembles," "ties together," "gathers," or "unites."

(779,2) There was to be no gravestone at all, according to Sade's will. See *The Marquis de Sade: The Complete Justine, Philosophy in the Bedroom, and Other Writings*, compiled and translated by R. Seaver and A. Wainhouse (New York: Grove Press, 1966), 157.

(779,3) Cf. Seminar VII, 292/250, and Seminar III, 277, where Lacan proposes to translate the Greek as "not to have been born like this." Jules Janin (1804–1874) was a novelist and critic who became a member of the Académie Française in 1870.

(779,4) *Ennuyeuse* (annoying) also means boring.

(779,5) *Qui n'a réalité que de discours* (whose only reality is as discourse) could also be rendered as "whose only reality is based on discourse" or "whose only reality is that of discourse."

(779,6) See *Oeuvres complètes*, vol. III, 475, and *The Marquis de Sade*, 293.

(780,2) Lacan misquotes La Fontaine here, who writes "Il est bon d'être charitable. Mais envers [Lacan writes "avec" instead of "envers"] qui? C'est là [Lacan writes "Voilà" instead of "C'est là"] le point"; see "Le Villageois et le Serpent" in *Fables*.

(780,3) Lacan is referring here to Charlie Chaplin's *Monsieur Verdoux* (1947).

(780,5) *Spinthrienne* (obscene) is an adjective used to qualify medals and engraved stones that depict obscene scenes.

(780,7) *Pied* (foot) is used in certain expressions related to jouissance, such as *prendre son pied* (to get off or climax). *Boîter* (to limp) more figuratively means to not work or hold water. The end of the sentence could also be rendered as "if it begins to limp."

(781,1) Cf. Lacan's reference to the bar in heraldry that, according to some, designates noble bastardy (*Écrits* 1966, 692).

(781,4) See *Critique of Practical Reason*, 44. Cf. Seminar VII, 129–31/108–9 and 222/188–89.

(781,5) *Chez lui beaucoup se passe en paroles* (a great deal transpires by means of words) is quite vague and I have not found any such comment in Kant's text to help clarify it. The idea is perhaps that the "ideal bourgeois" is all talk, no action—that is, is fundamentally not "a man of action."

(782,1) Bernard le Boyer de Fontenelle (1657–1757) was a poet, playwright, moralist, and philosopher. Kant refers to Fontenelle in *Critique of Practical Reason* on page 100, and Barni translates Kant's *niedrigen, bürgerlich-gemeinen Mann* (lowly, plain common man) as *l'humble bourgeois*. Cf. *Écrits* 1966, 151.

(782,5) Lacan intentionally or unintentionally adds the word *non* (not) to Juvenal's *Et propter vitam vivendi perdere causas* here; Kant cites the whole passage of which it is a part in *Critique of Practical Reason*, 198–99, which is rendered, in *The Satires of Juvenal Translated* (New York: AMS Press, 1978), as:

> Be a good soldier, a good guardian, or an impartial judge; if ever you are summoned as a witness in a dubious and uncertain case, though Phalaris himself should command you to be deceitful and, having brought his bull, should dictate perjury, count it the highest crime to prefer life to honor and to lose, for the sake of living, all that makes life worth living (*Satires* VIII, 79–84).

(783,1) *Pinellerie* (Pinelopies) seems to be a made-up word for the followers of Philippe Pinel, the French physician (1745–1826). *Belle affaire* (a fine affair it is!) can also be rendered as "big deal!" Lacan provides here a likely reference to Antoine-Athanase Royer-Collard who wanted Sade moved out of Charenton to "une maison de sûreté ou un château-fort," that is, to "a prison or a fortified castle."

(783,3) Lacan is likely referring here to those who run headlong at the chance to defy the gallows and death, contradicting Kant. *Prime-saut* (impulsive) evokes jumping, and thus plays off *Belle jambe* (A lot of good that does us), which literally means lovely leg.

(783,4) *Vide l'écaille* (empties the shell) is a possible reference to Homer's hymn to Mercury. It could, perhaps, refer instead to the "scales" (although that would usually be the plural *écailles*) that fall from one's eyes (*Acts* 9:18); hence: "it is the Law that removes the scales." *Écaille* has many meanings, running the gamut from a scarlet red to a mollusk shell, possibly allowing for translations as varied as "it is the Law that swallows the oyster," "it is the Law that scales the fish" (although one would usually say *vider le poisson*), and "it is the

Law that empties our mortal shell or coil."

(783,8) The "second stage of Kant's apologue" is the example of being commanded to bear false witness that Lacan cited two pages earlier (*Écrits* 1966, 781).

(784,4) *Longueurs* (examples) literally means lengths, and Lacan seems to be playfully likening Kant's examples to planks or poles used as levers to move something heavy; the French also figuratively refers to a long and boring passage in a book or film, for example.

(784,6) See *Critique of Practical Reason*, 41–42.

(784,8) See the general endnote by the translator regarding *désir de l'Autre* as indicating both desire for the Other to desire us and as desire for *what* the Other desires. The context seems to incline toward the latter here.

(785,4) *Entre centre et absence* (between center and absence) is a reference to Henri Michaux's book of poetry entitled *Entre centre et absence* (Paris: Henri Matarasso, 1936). Cf. Lacan's "Lituraterre" in *Autres Écrits* (Paris: Seuil, 2001), 16.

(785,8) In English: "However, a rational being's consciousness of the agreeableness of life (*von der Annehmlichkeit des Lebens*) as uninterruptedly accompanying his whole existence is *happiness*" (*Critique of Practical Reason*, 34).

(785,9) *Le ci-devant* (the former aristocrat) can also be understood as "the aforementioned." Louis Antoine de Saint-Just (1767–1794) was one of the principal theoreticians of the French Revolution and was executed with Robespierre on July 27, 1794. His comment on happiness, "Le bonheur est une idée neuve en Europe" (Happiness is a new idea in Europe), can be found in Saint-Just, *Oeuvres complètes* (Paris: Gérard Lebovici, 1984), 715. On happiness as having become a political factor, cf. *Écrits* 1966, 614, and Seminar VII, 338/292.

(786,1) *La Veuve* (the Widow) was a nineteenth-century slang term for the guillotine. *Organt* was the title of a satirical poem published anonymously by Saint-Just in 1789, condemning the monarchy and the aristocracy. Thermidor was the eleventh month of the Republican year (July 20–August 18). On 9 Thermidor, Saint-Just was prepared to deliver a speech on behalf of Robespierre but was not permitted to and was subsequently guillotined.

(787,2) *Bonne oeuvre* (good works) is usually given in the plural in French and rendered as "good works" or "good deeds."

(787,5) François de La Mothe-le-Vayer (1585 [or 1588]–1672) was a French critic, grammarian, and philosopher (skeptic), and became a member of the Académie Française in 1639.

(787,fn1) The complete title is *Philosophy in the Bedroom, or the Immoral Teachers, Dialogues Intended for the Education of Young Ladies*. Cf. the book's epigraph: "La mère en prescrira la lecture à sa fille" (Mothers will oblige their daughters to read it).

(788,1) "Le Dialogue entre un prêtre et un moribond" can be found in *Oeuvres complètes*, vol. XIV, 53–64; in English, see *The Marquis de Sade*, 165–75.

(788,3) The "Nessus-tunic" is the poisoned tunic that caused Hercules' death.

(788,4) On calumny, see *Oeuvres complètes*, vol. III, 494–95; in English, see *The Marquis de Sade*, 311–12.

(788,5) Regarding "fear and pity," see Aristotle's *Poetics*, 1449b; cf. Seminar VII, 286–92/243–50 and 372/322–23.

(789,2) *Le père humilié* is actually one part of the Coûfontaine trilogy, which includes *L'otage* (1911), *Le pain dur* (1918), and *Le père humilié* (1920); there seems to be some disagreement about the actual publication dates of the latter two plays. In English, see Paul Claudel, *Three Plays*, trans. John Heard (New York: H. Fertig, [1945] 1991), which includes *The Hostage*, *Crusts*, and *The Humiliation of the Father*. Lacan discusses the trilogy in Seminar VIII. Melpomene is the muse of tragedy, Clio the muse of epic poetry and history.

(789,4) Regarding the "reference to Saint Labre," see the epigraph to the 1947 edition of *Sade, mon prochain*.

(789,7) *Voisin* (neighborly relations) means both close and neighbor. The Christian commandment alluded to in the next sentence is no doubt to "love thy neighbor as thyself." For Freud's comments on the commandment to "Love thy neighbor as thyself," see *SE* XXI, 109–12; cf. Seminar VII, 92/76, 219/186–87, 227–29/193–96, and 233/198.

(790,1) See Saint Paul's *Epistle to the Romans* 7:7–13. Cf. Seminar VII, 101/83, 208/177, and 223/189.

(790,2) Cf. *Matthew* 26:41, "The spirit is willing but the flesh is weak." *Le Maléfice* (Evil Action) is more typically translated as "curse," "charm," or "spell," but also means crime or wicked activities.

(790,5) Lacan misquotes Klossowski here; Klossowski writes "le philosophe de l'apathie affermit sa conviction [. . .] qu'il a cessé d'appartenir au monde unique de tous les hommes, et qu'il est parvenu à l'état de veille, dans son proper monde, au sein de la nature" ("the philosopher of apathy sharpens his conviction that [. . .] he has ceased to belong to the unique world of all men, and that he has arrived in a waking state, in his own world, at the heart of Nature"). In English, see *Sade, My Neighbor*, 94–95.

(790,6) The reference here is to Luis Buñuel's 1952 film entitled *El*. *Qui se pose un peu là* (that is posited to some degree in it) is quite vague and could also be understood as "that lands (or arises) somewhat there."

(790,7) On Diotima, see especially Plato's *Symposium*, 201d–212b. On *Noli tangere matrem*, cf. *John* 20:17. Lacan's text simply reads *V . . . ée*, which I have interpreted as *Vérolée* (Syphilized), following Sade's text and James Swenson's suggestion.

Notes to "The Subversion of the Subject"

(793,3) The proceedings of the Bonneval Colloquium, published six years after the Colloquium was held as *"L'Inconscient". VIe Colloque de Bonneval, 1960* (Paris: Desclée de Brouwer, 1966), did not come out until after *Écrits* was published in 1966.

(793,4) See Jacques Lacan, *Le Séminaire, Livre V, Les Formations de l'inconscient, 1957–1958* (Paris: Seuil, 1998), edited by Jacques-Alain Miller.

(795,4) *Doubler* (doubling) also means to line (as when one lines a coat with another layer of fabric).

(796,fn2) *Respectueuse* (respectable girl) is a reference to Sartre's play, *La putain respectueuse* (Paris: Nagel, 1946).

(797,1) *L'écliptique* could refer to eclipses or to the ecliptic, the plane of the earth's path around the sun; the earth's axis forms an angle of about 23 degrees 27 minutes with respect to the ecliptic, which may be the way in which the earth "bows assent."

(797,3) "Ellipse" derives from the Greek *elleipsis* meaning lack. Regarding "celestial revolutions," cf. the title of Copernicus' work, *De revolutionibus orbium coelestium*.

(797,5) Copernicus seems to come up with a model in which the sun is at the center of the universe *in order to simplify computation* of the positions of the heavenly bodies, and seems to divorce the model from Truth as revealed in Scripture.

(797,8) The French at the end of the first sentence, *ce qui manque à la réalisation du savoir*, could also be translated as follows: "what is missing when knowledge is realized."

(798,1) *Principielle* (principial) means relative to a principle as the first cause of a thing.

(798,3) *À se donner voix fort confuse dans les grandes consciences* (confusedly given voice to by the great minds) could also be translated as "confusing the great minds."

(799,2) "Skew" is included by Lacan in the original as a translation for *de travers* (skewed).

(799,3) "Protopathic" to be understood in the etymological sense of the term: originally feeling, experiencing, or suffering.

(799,4) The parenthetical reference is to the phrase *ein anderer Schauplatz* found in *SE* V, 536, and *SE* VIII, 176.

(799,5) In particular, the mechanisms of condensation and displacement belong to the primary process. See "The Instance of the Letter," above all *Écrits* 1966, 511.

(800,3) I have adopted the following convention in this article: I have rendered je as I, Je as *I*, and *Je* as *I̲*. *Le sujet de l'énoncé* has been rendered here as "the subject of the statement," while *le sujet de l'énonciation* has been rendered as "the enunciating subject." The latter could also be rendered as "subject of (the) enunciation."

(800,5) Under the assumption that "but" or "not but" in English serves a function similar to that of the so-called expletive *ne* in French, I have attempted to provide English sentences here that illustrate the same point as Lacan's French.

(800,6) *Tue* is the first and third person singular of *tuer*, to kill, in the present and present subjunctive tenses, as well as the imperative, "kill." *Ils m'assomment* (they are killing me) also means they are boring me to death or overwhelming me. *Tu* is the informal form of "you," and *toise* also contains *toi* (you).

(800,9) *Interdit* (without the hyphen) means prohibited, interdicted, or forbidden; *inter-dit* may be a French translation of the Greek μη όν (another translation being *dit-que-non*), a kind of no-saying or nay-saying. Cf. Seminar IX, *Identification*. The French text in this paragraph is immensely complicated and my impression is that the third to last *la* should be deleted.

(801,2) See Mallarmé's preface to René Ghil's *Traité du Verbe* (1866) in Stéphane Mallarmé, *Oeuvres complètes* (Paris: Gallimard, 1945), 368 and 857.

(801,3) The first few words of the paragraph, *Cette coupure de la chaîne signifiante*, could also be translated as "The cut [the analyst makes] in the signifying chain," "The signifying chain as cut," or "The signifying chain's cut."

(801,4) The German text is found in *GW* XV, 86; in English, see *SE* XXII, 80.

(801,5) *Fut* (was) is a *passé simple* or historical past tense. *Eût été* (might have been) is a pluperfect subjunctive.

(801,6) The French imperfect *était* allows for at least two different translations: "was" or "was to be" (in the sense of was supposed to be or designed to be, it not being specified if it actually came to be); Lacan refers, in Seminar XV (January 10, 1968), to the French linguist Gustave Guillaume (1883–1960) on this point. *Là où c'était pour un peu* (where it was for a short while) can also be rendered as "where it would have been if not for [something that happened]" or "where it would only have taken a little bit more for it to be." Note that *peut* is the third person singular form of the present verb, *pouvoir*, not the first. *Écrits* 1966 mistakenly reads *peux*; the Points edition corrects this.

(801,7) The reflexive verbs here could be translated differently: "An enunciation that is denounced, a statement that is renounced, an ignorance that is dissipated, an opportunity that is missed . . ."

(802,1) In the English translation, the sentence reads as follows: "his father had really died, only without knowing it" (*SE* XII, 225–26). In *The Interpretation of Dreams*, the same dream is recounted in the following terms: "he had really died, only he did not know it" (*SE* V, 430).

(802,4) The French imperfect in the second sentence, *il savait*, allows for two different translations: "A bit later he knew" and "He was supposed to find out a bit later." I try to suggest a similar ambiguity with the wording I provide here.

(803,3) *En position de signifiant* (in signifying position) could also be translated as "in the position of a signifier." The French at the end of the paragraph, *cet objet est le prototype de la signifiance du corps comme enjeu de l'être*, can be translated in a number of other ways: "this object is the prototype of the body qua signifierness as being's stakes" or "of the body's significance as what is at stake for being (or for human beings)."

(803,6) *Du peu de physiologie que l'inconscient intéresse*, could also be translated as "how little physiology the unconscious involves (or brings into play)."

(804,1) In the first sentence, *le réel du corps et de l'imaginaire de son schéma mental*, is somewhat ambiguous; if the first *de* is simply an error, which seems likely to me, and is removed we could translate as follows: "psychoanalysis concerns the reality (or real) of the body and the imaginary of its mental schema (or its mental schema as imaginary)."

(804,3) *D'aujourd'hui* (contemporary) is a probable reference to the collection entitled *La Psychanalyse d'aujourd'hui* ("Contemporary Psychoanalysis") discussed by Lacan in "Direction of the Treatment."

(805,2) A "button tie" is a stitch used by an upholsterer to secure a button to fabric and stuffing, for example, to prevent the stuffing from moving; it is, I think, the closest English term to the upholsterer's term Lacan uses: *point de capiton*. Russell Grigg, in his translation of Lacan's Seminar, Book III, *The Psychoses* (New York: W. W. Norton, 1993), renders *capitonnage* as "quilting" and *point de capiton* as "quilting point"; see 293–305. *Rétro-*

grade, apart from its usual meaning (retrograde), takes on the specific mathematical meaning of "negatively oriented" in relation to vectors. In the last sentence of the paragraph, Lacan is playing on the French expression, *noyer le poisson*, literally "to drown the fish," figuratively, to bury the subject being discussed or sidestep the issue.

(805,4) *Le chien fait miaou, le chat fait oua oua* (the dog goes meow, the cat goes woof-woof) is a nursery rhyme or song in which various animals are attributed the wrong sound. The French at the end of the paragraph, *ouvre la diversité des objectivations à vérifier, de la même chose* (makes necessary the verification of multiple objectifications of the same thing), is somewhat obscurely phrased but seems to imply that the child's contempt for verisimilitude is such that the same thing (e.g., an animal) can be characterized or objectified in multiple manners (e.g., by different cries), and we have to look to experience to verify which of them is correct.

(806,1) The *jeu des quatre coins* (four-corners game) is a sort of musical chairs game with five players; four players begin in the four corners of a quadrilateral, and have to try to change corners while the fifth player tries to claim one of the corners for him- or herself. The four corners may be a reference to the quadripartite structure of metaphor adumbrated by Lacan in June of 1960 and written up in "Metaphor of the Subject," *Écrits* 1966, 889–92.

(806,2) I have translated *connoté* here, and in the next sentence, by "labeled," as it does not seem to me that Lacan is referring to the connotation/denotation distinction. Saussure uses the term *trésor* (treasure or treasure trove) to describe language *(langue)* in *Cours de linguistique générale*, ed. Tullio de Mauro (Paris: Payot, [1915] 1972), 30. It is translated as "fund" in *Course in General Linguistics*, trans. Roy Harris (Chicago: Open Court, 1983), 13.

(806,5) This passage clearly evokes Lacan's early paper "Logical Time and the Assertion of Anticipated Certainty" found in *Écrits* 1966. *Insignifiante* (meaningless) could, alternatively, be rendered as "insignificant" or "nonsignifying."

(806,6) Presumably "making his own calculations" regarding the Other's strategy.

(807,2) See *Hegel's Phenomenology of Spirit*, trans. A. V. Miller (Oxford: Oxford University Press, 1977), 117. *Préalable* (preliminary) can also be rendered as "prerequisite" or "prior."

(807,4) *Parade* (display) is also a fencing term (as are *feinte*, feint, and *rupture*, retreat) that can be translated as "parry" or "parade"; it also means (ceremonial) display.

(808,2) "The first words spoken": *Le dit premier.*

(808,3) See *SE* XIX, 31.

(809,3) *Trait unaire de l'idéal du moi* (the ego-ideal as unary trait) could also be translated as "the ego-ideal's unary trait."

(809,4) *Écrits* 1966 mistakenly reads $s(A).\overrightarrow{A}$; this is corrected in Points. See Damourette and Pichon, *Des mots à la pensée: Essai de grammaire de la langue française*, 7 vols. (Paris: Bibliothèque du français moderne, 1932–1951). Note that *étoffée* (filled out) can also mean stuffed or enriched, and that *subtile* (ethereal) can also mean subtle or rarefied.

(809,fn2) See, in particular, Seminar IX (1961–1962), *Identification* (unpublished).

(810,2) *Fléau* (balance arm) also means scourge, curse, bane, or plague. Cf. *Écrits* 1966, 99.

(810,fn1) The seminar referred to here was edited by Jacques-Alain Miller and published by Seuil in 1986. It was translated into English by Dennis Porter as *The Seminar of Jacques Lacan, Book VII: The Ethics of Psychoanalysis* (New York: W. W. Norton, 1992).

(811,2) See Lacan's 1953 paper, "Le mythe individuel du névrosé ou poésie et vérité dans la névrose," published in *Ornicar?* 17/18 (1979): 289–307. In English, see "The Neurotic's Individual Myth," *PQ* XLVIII (1979): 405–25. *L'histoire* (the story) could also be translated as "history."

(811,5) Taking *relever* (redeemed) differently here, *que ne relèvent même plus ses mollesses* could also be translated as "that is no longer even highlighted by its lack of verve (or lifelessness)."

(811,8) *Saugrenu* (ludicrousness) means bizarre, unexpected, and somewhat ridiculous.

(812,2) *Fêlure* (flaw) also means crack, fissure, fracture, and split.

(812,3) *Guignol* (puppet) also means someone who is funny or ridiculous without trying to be.

(812,fn1) Lacan had initially entitled the seminar to be held in 1963–1964, "The Names-of-the-Father"; owing to Lacan's exclusion from the Société Française de Psychanalyse, only one class of the intended seminar was given, an English translation of which can be found in *Television: A Challenge to the Psychoanalytic Establishment*, ed. Joan Copjec (New York: W. W. Norton, 1990). The seminar that was given instead was the *Four Fundamental Concepts of Psychoanalysis* (Seminar XI), given under the auspices of the École Normale Supérieure at the invitation of Louis Althusser. I have assumed that there is a negation missing at the beginning of the note, for the French reads *fût-ce en termes plus vigoureux* (even if in stronger terms) instead of *ne fût-ce en termes plus vigoureux*.

(813,3) See Seminar VIII, 121–22.

(813,4) *Le*, which I have translated here as "it" (in "to seek it") would seem to refer back to "guarantee," but in that case it would have to be *la*. The only masculine nouns it could refer to are "the Other" or "locus."

(813,7) Lacan is playing on the expression *ébats amoureux*, which can mean lovemaking, making out, petting, and so on. He splits the expression such that *l'amour* (love) appears before the dash and *d'ébat* (which is usually plural, not singular as it is here) appears after it in a context where *débat* (debate) would usually go. *Ébat* alone also means frolicking.

(813,9) Here as elsewhere, *désir de l'Autre* (the Other's desire) could also be translated as "desire for the Other" or "desire for what the Other desires."

(814,1) *Vertige* is more polyvalent than "vertigo," connoting not only giddiness, but also intoxication, madness, temptation, and confusion.

(814,3) The "shred of blanket" is often referred to as a tickle blanket, blankey, or nappy. On the transitional object, see D. W. Winnicott, "Transitional Objects and Transitional Phenomena," in *IJP* XXXIV (1953), reprinted in D. W. Winnicott, *Through Pediatrics to Psycho-Analysis* (New York: Brunner/Mazel, 1992), 229–42.

(814,4) *Représentant de la représentation* (representation's representative) is Lacan's translation for Freud's *Vorstellungsrepräsentanz*, rendered in the Standard Edition by "ideational representative," and generally concerns something that stands in for (or represents) the drive at the "ideational" level (i.e., at the level of representation); it could also be translated as "the representative of representation." In Seminar VII, Lacan equates Freud's *Vorstellungsrepräsentanz* with the signifier (pages 75–76/61).

(814,6) The French here could also be translated as "discourse on (or concerning) the Other." The deliberately incorrect (forced) Latin, *de Alio in oratione*, could be translated as "concerning the Other in discourse (or the Other who is speaking)," and *tua res agitur* as "it concerns you" or "your interest is at stake." *Tua res agitur* comes from Horace's *Epistles*, Book 1, Epistle 18, where we find "Nam tua res agitur, paries cum proximus ardet, et neglecta solent incendia sumere vires." This has been translated as "'Tis your own safety that's at stake when your neighbor's wall is in flames, and fires neglected are wont to gather strength." Freud modifies the phrase in *SE* V (441) as does Lacan in *Écrits* 1966 (574); cf. "Father, don't you see I'm burning," *SE* V, 509.

(815,1) Lacan borrows this "*Chè vuoi?*" from Jacques Cazotte's *Le diable amoureux* (1772); see, in particular, the annotated French edition by Annalisa Bottacin (Milan: Cisalpino-La Goliardica, 1983), pages 56–57. In English, see *The Devil in Love* (New York: Houghton Mifflin, 1925).

(815,3) *Clé universelle* (master key) is also the technical term for a specific tool, known in English as an adjustable spanner, monkey wrench, or pipe wrench, that resembles Graph 3 in certain respects. Lacan makes it clear in Seminar XV (January 17, 1968) that what he has in mind here is "the key that opens all boxes," that is, "a skeleton key" or "master key."

(816,4) *Se règle sur* (adjusts to) can also be translated as "models itself on," "adapts itself to," or even "targets." Note that while (on Graph 3) desire (d) is on the right and fantasy ($\$\Diamond a$) is on the left, the ego (m) is on the left and the body image, $i(a)$, is on the right. This is, I believe, the "inversion" Lacan is referring to here. The French at the end of the paragraph, *là où* s'*était l'inconscient*, provides a reflexive where Lacan's more usual translation of Freud's *Wo Es war, soll Ich werden* reads *là où c'était. S'était* and *c'était* are homonyms. Cf. "The Freudian Thing."

(816,5) *Étoffe* (stuff) also means fabric, cloth, and material. I translate it in the same way throughout this article.

(816,7) *Repérage* (pinpointing) means position finding, getting one's bearings, finding landmarks helping one get oriented, identification, registration, marking out, and locating. It is sometimes translated as "mapping."

(817,1) See, in particular, "Instincts and Their Vicissitudes," *SE* XIV, 126–35. For early commentary on the Graph, see Seminar V; for later commentary on the Graph, see Seminar XVI, December 11, 1968, and January 8, 1969.

(818,1) See *Écrits* 1966, 54–55, where Lacan uses the same term, *doublure* (lining).

(818,2) In French, *proie* (translated here as "substance") is usually "prey," but is also used in the phrase *lacher la proie pour l'ombre* ("to drop the substance for the shadow" or "to give up what one already has for some uncertain alternative").

(819,2) *Un trait qui se trace de son cercle* (a line that is drawn from its circle) seems to be a direct commentary on the Complete Graph; a few pages back, Lacan tells us that the drive ($\$\lozenge D$) is the treasure trove of signifiers, and S(Ⱥ) is found at the end of a line drawn from the circle that contains ($\$\lozenge D$). Elsewhere, I have translated *trait* as "characteristic." The verb *tracer* could also be interpreted in the sense of "to blaze (a trail)" or "to outline" here.

(819,4) See, for example, *Écrits* 1966, 515.

(819,5) *Ce qu'il est d'impensable* (what is unthinkable about him) literally means "what he is that is unthinkable," i.e., his "unthinkableness." *En défaut* (missing) can take on a number of different meanings: in error, at fault, in the wrong, or failing to fulfill one's commitments.

(819,6) Earlier (*Écrits* 1966, 802) Lacan mentioned the father, in a dream Freud recounts, who "did not know he was dead."

(820,1) *Inconsistant* (inconsistent) can also mean insubstantial or weak.

(820,3) *Avec sa dialectique* (by means of its dialectic) could alternatively be translated as "along with its (or his, i.e., Freud's) dialectic."

(820,5) *Os* (literally "bone") would normally be translated as "hitch" in this context, but given that Lacan is discussing the castration complex here, the slang meaning, "hard-on," should probably be kept in mind.

(820,6) See Edmund Husserl, *The Crisis in the European Sciences and Transcendental Phenomenology*, trans. David Carr (Evanston: Northwestern University Press, 1970).

(821,1) On the alternation from the similar (*semblable*) to the dissimilar, see the "Presentation of the Suite" to the "Seminar on 'The Purloined Letter,' " *Écrits* 1966, 41–61.

(821,3) See Lévi-Strauss' comments on the "zero-phoneme" in *Introduction à l'oeuvre de Marcel Mauss* (Paris: PUF, 1950); in English, see *Introduction to the Work of Marcel Mauss*, trans. Felicity Baker (London: Routledge and Kegan Paul, 1987). "Used automatically": that is, as mathematicians use it.

(821,5) *Sous-entendue* (understood) means the jouissance is implied or hinted at.

(822,4) *Caducité* (falling off) comes from the Latin *caducus* and *cadere*, meaning to fall. Ordinary modern meanings include out-of-date, null and void, and dépassé; in botany, *organes caducs* are parts of a plant that are designed to detach themselves from the plant and fall off. Assuming there were no mistake in the French at the end of the sentence, *où vient s'achever l'exclusion où elle se trouve de l'image spéculaire et du prototype qu'elle constitue pour le monde des objets*, would be translated as follows: "in which is completed its exclusion from the specular image and from the prototype it constitutes for the world of objects." Since the phallus here seems to constitute the prototype of the world of objects, I have assumed that the last *du* in the sentence should in fact be *le*; Lacan could, however, be saying that it constitutes the prototype and yet is excluded therefrom.

(822,6) *Pour ces raisons de forme* (for reasons of form) could also be translated as "for these formal reasons" or "for these reasons of shape," or possibly even "for form's sake."

(823,2) In *la fonction du signifiant imaginaire* (the signifier's imaginary function), the adjective "imaginary" could grammatically qualify either "function" or "signifier," but there doesn't seem to me to be any such thing in Lacan's work as an "imaginary signifier."

(823,4) *D'un côté à l'autre de l'équation de l'imaginaire au symbolique* (from one side to the other of the equation between the imaginary and the symbolic) could alternatively be translated as "from one side of the equation to the other, from the imaginary to the symbolic." The equation in question is, I suspect, the one found on page 819, with $(-\varphi)$ equated with s, as indicated on page 822.

(824,1) Alternate for "to posit fantasy as the Other's desire": "to posit fantasy as what the Other desires."

(824,2) *Se porter caution de l'Autre* (to be the Other's guarantor) could also be translated as "to stand security for the Other" or "to be surety for the Other," both financial metaphors.

(824,3) The parenthetical clarification Lacan provides here, "that is, her desire," remains ambiguous since he says *son désir* (one's desire) instead of *son désir à elle* (her desire). An alternate translation for the text between the dashes, *Autre réel de la demande dont on voudrait qu'elle calme le désir (c'est-à-dire son désir)*, would be: "the real Other of the demand with which we wish she would calm desire (that is, our desire)." *Fermerait les yeux* (would turn a blind eye) may be a reference to one of Freud's dreams, recounted in *The Interpretation of Dreams*, that includes the line "You are requested to close the eyes" (*SE* IV, 317–18).

(824,4) The French at the end of the paragraph, *ce qui vaudrait autant pour le sujet*, could also be translated as "which would amount to the same thing (or more) for the subject."

(825,1) *S'assurer de* (ensure control over) can mean to verify or become sure of, but when it is used in reference to a person it means to maintain control over or keep in one's possession. In reference to God, it could mean to verify or assure oneself of God's existence.

(825,2) *En tant que* (in the guise of) could also be translated as "qua." *À ciel ouvert* (right out in the open) is the expression Lacan uses to describe the unconscious in psychosis. An alternate translation for the sentence would be: "But this does not mean that the pervert wears his unconscious on his sleeve."

(825,4) See Plato's *Symposium* and Lacan's detailed commentary on it in Seminar VIII.

(826,3) *Imagination* (imagination) can also mean chimera, dream, or imagining.

(827,7) *Parler pour le tableau noir* (talking to a brick wall) literally means speaking for the blackboard.

Notes to "Position of the Unconscious"

(829,9) *VIe Colloque de Bonneval: l'Inconscient* (Paris: Desclée de Brouwer, 1966), 159.

(830,4) *Espèce* (species) should no doubt be understood here in terms of Medieval philosophy, where it is distinguished in ontological discussions from "genus"; the genus here would be psychical reality, and the species that which does not have the attribute "consciousness."

(830,8) *L'inconscient* est *ce que nous disons* (The unconscious *is* what I say it is) could be also rendered as "The unconscious *is* what we say."

(830,11) Georges Dwelshauvers, *L'inconscient* (Paris: Flammarion, 1916), especially 14–16.

(831,1) On "co-consciousness," cf. Lecture XIX of Freud's *Introductory Lectures on Psychoanalysis, SE* XVI. In his dissertation, *De la psychose paranoïaque dans ses rapports avec la personnalité* (Paris: Seuil, [1932] 1980), Lacan attributes the term to Morton Prince and includes the words "second personality" in parentheses after it (page 44).

(831,2) Reading *rassemble* (grouped together) for *ressemble*, as in the Desclée de Brouwer version of the text. See the chapter entitled "The Archaic Illusion" in *The Elementary Structures of Kinship* (Boston: Beacon, 1969).

(831,7) *Recherchée* (sought-after) can also mean intended, affected, inventive, or meticulous.

(832,6) See Betty Friedan, *The Feminine Mystique* (New York: W. W. Norton, 1963), especially chapter nine, "The Sexual Sell."

(833,1) Reading *beaucoup l'ont fait* (many have done so) for *beaucoup l'on fait* (meaning unclear).

(833,2) In his "Technical Implications of

Ego Psychology," Heinz Hartmann writes that "analysis is gradually and unavoidably, though hesitantly, becoming a general psychology . . ." (*PQ* XX, 1 [1951]: 35), and in his "Development of the Ego Concept in Freud's Work," he writes that "the trend toward a general psychology has been inherent in psycho-analysis from its inception" (*IJP* XXVII, 6 [1956]: 434). See Lucien Levy-Bruhl's *La mentalité primitive* (Paris: PUF, 1922).

(833,7) Lacan is referring here to Daniel Lagache.

(833,8) *Là gâchée* (missed) is an allusion to Daniel Lagache.

(834,7) *S'y mettre en cause* (putting himself on the line) could also be translated as "calling himself into question" or "situating himself as cause."

(835,1) *Recul* has many other meanings as well: distance, perspective, backing away (from), recoil, kick, postponement, lagging, reverse movement, and switching back. I have interpreted it here as referring to the retroactive effect of enunciation on the enunciated or statement. On metaphor and metonymy, see *Écrits* 1966, 511–18.

(835,5) *Ça* (It) is also the French for "id."

(835,8) *Subornement* (subornation) is an old, alternate form of *subornation*, meaning subornation, in the juridical sense, or the seduction, corruption (through bribery), perversion, or leading astray of someone. *Boucler* (closes) also means to buckle or bring full circle.

(836,5) *Propédeutique* (preparatory) here refers to college prep classes formerly taken by French high school graduates; thus their *secondary* education was followed by *introductory* classes—classes that introduced them into "higher education."

(836,8) See Ivor Armstrong Richards and C. K. Ogden's book, *The Meaning of Meaning* (New York: Harcourt, Brace, [1923] 1945); cf. *Écrits* 1966, 150 and 271.

(836,9) *Malheur de la conscience* (unhappy consciousness) seems to be a reference to *conscience malheureuse*, the usual French translation of Hegel's *unglückliches Bewusstsein*. See Jean Wahl, *Le Malheur de la conscience dans la philosophie de Hegel* (Paris: PUF, 1951).

(836,10) The Greek here means common or shared thing or element.

(837,5) *Autre-chose* (something Other) could also be translated more idiomatically as "something Else."

(837,8) Cf. *SE* XVIII, 58.

(838,1) Reading *tenu* (said) for *stenu* (obvious typographical error).

(838,6) "Edge" and "rim" are the terms I have most often used here to translate *bord*, a term with topological, corporal, and political meanings running the gamut from edge, perimeter, rim (as of a bodily orifice or topological surface which closes upon itself), and limit, to border, side (in the sense of front or back, or political position), and margin.

(838,8) *Fermeture* (closing) also means lock, locking, and shutting; in topology it is translated as "closure," and a set is said to be "closed" if it contains each of its limit points.

(839,2) *Critique* (critical) should, no doubt, be understood here in the sense of Kant's *Critiques*. *Formes du discours* (forms of discourse) seems to be modeled on *parties du discours*—parts of speech. Lacan himself says that there would be no being without the verb "to be": "*il n'y a d'être que de parler; s'il n'y avait pas le verbe être, il n'y aurait pas d'être du tout*" ("there is only being due to speaking; were it not for the verb 'to be,' there would be no being at all") (Seminar XXI, January 15, 1974). It should be kept in mind that *raison* (reason) can also mean ratio or proportion.

(839,3) "In its efficiency": that is, in its capacity as efficient cause.

(839,7) *Est le présupposé de l'inconscient* (is what is presupposed by the unconscious) could also be rendered as "is the presupposition of the unconscious."

(840,2) In French, *est le fait du sujet* (constitutes the subject as such) would most usually mean that it is the subject's doing, that is, that alienation is due to the subject or brought about by the subject, but that makes little sense given what follows. *S'y impose* (intervenes) might also be translated as "imposes itself therein," "intrudes therein," or "forces itself upon the world (or upon physics)." Reading *dans ce monde* (in this world) for *dans de monde* (meaning unclear).

(840,7) *Figer* (freezing) means to fix (like a fixer in photography or a fixative), congeal, clot, or coagulate. The French imperfect functions to some extent like the English "The bomb *was to* go off two minutes later," where the grammar allows one to imagine at least two different temporal contexts: one in which the bomb is set to go off in two minutes, and will go off if we do not manage to defuse it beforehand; and another in which, looking back on the situation, we note that the bomb actually went off two minutes after the moment we are considering (for example, in a documentary, one might hear, "The bomb *was to go off* two minutes later, killing the President and the First Lady"), did not go off at all (e.g., "the documents *were to be* destroyed, but turned up in KGB files rendered public many years later"), or went off, but not at the designated time. Lacan uses this example from Raymond Queneau's *On est toujours trop bon avec les femmes* (Paris: Gallimard, 1971) and refers, in Seminar XV (January 10, 1968), to the French linguist Gustave Guillaume (1883–1960) on the French imperfect.

(841,1) The reference here is to St. Augustine's *De Trinitate*.

(841,2) *Vel* is the Latin for "or," "either/or," or "alternative." *Réunion* (union) is one of a pair of terms from set theory, Venn diagrams, and Euler circles, the other term being "intersection." Sheridan mistakenly translates it as "joining" in Seminar XI.

(841,5) *Sic aut non* means yes or no.

(841,6) *Écorné* (diminished) also means spoiled, marred, abraded, eroded, and chipped away.

(842,1) *Mordre sur* (encroach on) also means to bite into, gnaw into, or make a dent in. *Relève de* (falls within) means comes under, is related to, and has to do with. See the diagrams and discussions provided in Seminar XI, 190–95 /209–215.

(842,2) The Greek here means ignorance, crudeness, inexperience, or blunder.

(842,2) See Marie Bonaparte's French translation of Freud's *New Introductory Lectures on Psycho-Analysis*, the last page of Lecture XXXI. The original German is found in *GW* XV, 86; in English see *SE* XXII, 80.

(842,3) See Leclaire's paper in *L'inconscient*; in English, see *Returning to Freud: Clinical Psychoanalysis in the School of Lacan*, ed. Stuart Schneiderman (New Haven: Yale University Press, 1980); see also Lacan's commentary in Seminar XI, 192/212 and 226/250.

(842,5) Belonging, for example, to both set x and set y.

(843,1) *D'une part prise du manque au manque* (by a part taken from a lack situated within another lack) is highly ambiguous and could be interpreted in a number of ways (e.g., a part taken from one lack into the other, grasped by the lack in lack, grasped in the lack-to-lack lineup, taken from a lack by another lack); considered in terms of the diagrams Lacan provides in Seminar XI, it seems that the part is "taken" from the place where the two circles representing the subject and the Other overlap.

(843,2) *Le sujet se réalise* (the subject is actualized) suggests that the subject comes to be, is constituted, or achieves self-actualization. The Latin *velle*—in French *vouloir*—means to will, to desire, to want, or to wish. Empedocles' act is that of flinging himself into Mount Etna's volcanic crater. *Fin* (end) can be understood here as either terminus or goal.

(843,4) *En prendre son parti* (come to terms with it) could also be rendered as "come to a decision about it" or "make up one's mind about it." *Partition* (partition) also means musical score.

(843,5) *Se parer du signifiant* (to attribute to himself the signifier) literally means to adorn or bedeck himself with the signifier; more figuratively it means to take it upon himself, to assume it (like one assumes a responsibility), or to claim it for himself. The binary Lacan is referring to here is S_1 and S_2.

(844,2) *Placer* (place) is also a financial metaphor for "invest."

(844,3) *Comble* (fills) also means fulfills, makes up for, or fills in (or up). *Faille* has many meanings, running from failing, flaw, defect, weakness, and shortcoming, to rift and fault (in the geological sense).

(844,4) *Peut-il me perdre* (can he lose me?) can also be rendered as "is he willing to lose me?" or "can he afford to lose me?" or "could he bear for me to be gone?"

(844,5) *Scander* is the verb form of "scansion," and is usually translated as "to scan" or "scanning" (as in scanning verse, or dividing verse into metrical feet). I have opted here to introduce a neologism—to scand, scanding—so as to distinguish the far more common contemporary uses of scanning (looking over rapidly, quickly running through a list, taking ultra-thin pictures of the body with a scanner, or "feeding" text and images in digital form into a computer) from Lacan's idea here of cutting, punctuating, or interrupting something (usually the analysand's discourse).

(844,6) *Attente de* (expectation of) also means waiting for.

(844,8) *Verbal* (verbal) could also be understood in the sense of verb-like here, thus word-like; *où l'on veut bien le dire* (where people are willing to say it is) could also mean where people are willing to say it, or put it into words.

(845,6) *Hommelette* is a conflation of *Homme*, Man, and *omelette* (omelet); the ending, "ette," is a diminutive; compare with *femmelette*. Recall the French proverb, "*Pour faire une omelette il faut casser des oeufs*" (To make an omelet, you have to break some eggs). Cf. Seminar XI, 179/197.

(846,5) *Un rien* could also be translated as a mere smidgen or as a trifling, trivial, or insignificant quantity, but the *rien* or nothing is also one of the "objects" associated with Lacan's object *a*.

(846,6) There seems to be a punctuation problem in the French in this paragraph; I have attempted to rectify it by joining the two sentences here.

(847,1) See "Instincts and their Vicissitudes" (1915); the *Standard Edition* gives "pressure" as the translation for *Drang*, while the *Collected Papers*, translated under the supervision of Joan Riviere, give "impetus"; Lacan's French translation is "*poussée*." The "surface" Lacan mentions here is presumably the ultraflat Manlet (or lamella).

(847,2) *Schub* is also translated "thrust"—see "Instincts and their Vicissitudes" (1915)—appearing in that essay in connection with images like "successive eruptions of lava." *Evagination aller et retour* (turning inside out and outside in): the figure provided in Seminar XI of the circuit of the drive might suggest that this be translated somewhat differently—for example, "back and forth evagination" or "insertion in and back out."

(847,5) *Par les voies du sexe* (through the straits of sex) means by sexual passageways (or pathways or means) or via sex.

(847,fn1) "Curl flux" is perhaps more commonly known as "the flux integral of the curl of a vector field," "the surface integral of the normal component of the curl of a vector field," or "the collective measure of rotational tendency taken over the entire surface." Stokes' theorem says that the flux integral of the curl of a vector field over a surface is equal to the line integral of the vector field around its boundary curve. Thus, for a given closed curve, the "curl flux" over any surface whose boundary is exactly this closed curve is the same. The theorem gives the conditions for which the flux remains constant.

(848,1) Saint Agatha was reputed to have had her breasts cut off.

(848,2) *Matrice* can take on a great many meanings, including womb, die, matrix, register, and mold in the sense of a shaping ring or die in which something is cast; note that *sein*, which I have translated here as "breast," can also mean womb, bosom, or uterus.

(848,3) "Plane" to be understood here in the geometrical sense.

(849,7) *L'Autre du sexe opposé* (the opposite sex as Other) could also be translated as "the Other of the opposite sex."

(849,8) See Seminar XX for a continuation of this discussion.

(850,1) *Si c'est le dire du couple d'Adam et Ève* (even if the couple Adam and Eve imply that) could also be rendered as "if this is said of the couple Adam and Eve."

(850,5) Paul Ricoeur spoke last, and soon published his hermeneutic reading of Freud and the Oedipus complex in *Freud and Philosophy: An Essay on Interpretation* (New Haven: Yale University Press, 1970; first published in French in 1965). Cf. Seminar XI, 140–41/153–54. *La vedette américaine* (the role of warm-up band) generally refers to someone who performs the opening act for a bigger star, and often connotes a subpar performer.

Notes to "On Freud's 'Trieb' and the Psychoanalyst's Desire"

(851,4) See *SE* XXII, 131; cf. *Écrits* 1966, 695 and 735.

(851,6) *Couleur-de-vide* (color of emptiness) could also mean devoid of color.

(852,4) See, for example, *SE* XIII, 84–85.

(852,10) *Elle y affecte tout autant l'obéissance*

(it nevertheless seeks to bring about obedience thereto in it) is quite ambiguous: *elle* (it) presumably refers back to "fear of castration"; *affecte* (seeks to bring about) can mean affects, assigns, feigns, seeks, or takes on; and *y* seems to refer to "sexual normalization" or possibly "the Oedipus complex."

(852,12) *Par défaut* (by default), the expression Lacan uses here to qualify the phallus, has a number of meanings: *juger quelqu'un par défaut*, for example, means to judge someone in his or her absence (*in absentia*), or "by default," that person having failed to show up at the hearing or trial. *Un défaut* is a fault, inadequacy, defect, flaw, failing, deficiency, imperfection, shortcoming, or failure.

(853,1) *Compte débiteur* (debit account) means an account that is in the red, overdrawn, or showing a deficit. Further financial definitions include "account receivable" (from the perspective of a person who owes someone else something) and "blank credit." *Créance* (credit) means credit, claim, or debt; it can take on the meaning of "account receivable" from the perspective of a person who claims that someone else owes him or her something.

(853,3) On *agalma* (object *a*) and *eron* (the beloved), see Lacan's commentary on the *Symposium* in Seminar VIII.

(853,5) See *SE* XXII, 95.

(853,6) Cf. *Écrits* 1966, 614.

(853,11) *Direction* (direction) might also be rendered as "guidance" in this context, as in "spiritual guidance."

(854,1) Lacan is likely referring to Molière (1622–1673).

(854,3) Eschatology concerns the *fins dernières*, the last or final matters: death, the Last Judgment, heaven, and hell. By counterpoint here, *fin*, which generally means end or goal, also takes on the meaning of matter or concern. Cf. *Écrits* 1966, 872.

Notes to "Science and Truth"

(855,6) *Ce qu'il en est de son praxis* (the status of his praxis) could also be understood here as "the praxis of that splitting."

(856,1) *Position de sujet* (subject position) could also be translated as "position as subject," and is thus translated at various points in the text.

(856,3) "Last year" here is a reference to Seminar XII, "Problèmes cruciaux pour la psychanalyse" (1964–1965). *Peut-être nous avons à savoir* (perhaps remains to be determined) could instead be rendered as "we perhaps have to be aware of it."

(856,4) *Défilé* (defile) should perhaps be understood in the sense of a narrow, difficult path; since the French also means procession or succession, however, it could perhaps imply consequence or aftermath. Cf. Freud's "defile of consciousness" in *SE* II, 291, and Kant's notion of science as a "narrow gate" in *Critique of Practical Reason*, trans. Werner S. Pluhar (Indianapolis and Cambridge: Hackett, 2002), 205. *Rejet* (rejection) was the first translation Lacan adopted for Freud's *Verwerfung;* he later preferred *forclusion*, "foreclosure." The rejection here seems to be Descartes' rejection of all knowledge through hyperbolic doubt. *Dont* (this anchoring) could alternatively refer back to "a rejection of all knowledge." On anchoring, cf. *Écrits* 1966, 527.

(856,6) See Freud's unfinished article, "Die Ichspaltung im Abwehrvorgang," translated into English as "Splitting of the Ego in the Process of Defence," *SE* XXIII, 275–78, dated January 2, 1938.

(856,7) *Une autre qui en fait* (another that makes it): the *en* here is open to different readings, as it could refer to "reality," "the reality principle," or even "psychical reality."

(858,3) Lamennais was a French writer (1782–1854) on religious and political subjects, known for his *Essai sur l'indifférence en matière religieuse* in four volumes (1817–1823).

(858,6) "To say that the subject upon which": Lacan refers here to the subject as a which (*quoi*), not a whom, an interesting case in point as French most often does not allow us to decide either way, *il* and *elle* referring as easily to a he or a she as to a masculine or feminine noun. He does so again later in the article.

(859,1) Lacan is no doubt referring here to the wheeling and dealing that took place within the *Société Française de Psychanalyse* in 1963—leading to Lacan's marginalization and "excommunication"—that proved to what extent French analysts were prepared to compromise on theoretical issues to obtain IPA affiliation.

(859,3) *Fautive* (faulty) can also mean at fault in the moral sense.

(859,4) See the chapter entitled "The Archaic Illusion" in *The Elementary Structures of Kinship* (Boston: Beacon, 1969).

(859,6) *Il n'y a pas de petites économies* (there's no such thing as an insignificant savings) is an expression akin to "every little bit helps" or "a penny saved is a penny earned" in English, and literally means "there's no such thing as small savings"; the implication here is that regardless of the amount saved, it is already significant, the qualifier "small," or "insignificant" as I've translated it here, thus being inappropriate. The French expression is often completed by the following: *Il n'y a que de grandes pertes* ("There are only big losses").

(859,8) The Pantheon, situated atop the Mont Sainte-Geneviève, is the burial place of some of France's most distinguished writers and thinkers; the rue Saint-Jacques leads, in an uninterrupted downhill stretch, from the Mont Sainte-Geneviève, past the Sorbonne, and on to the Ile-de-la-Cîté, site of Paris' main police station. See Canguilhem's article, "Qu'est-ce que la psychologie," *Revue de Métaphysique et de Morale* 1 (1958), reprinted in *Cahiers Pour l'Analyse* 1–2 (1966), above all page 91, where Canguilhem points out that psychology, in singlemindedly pursuing instrumental goals, has no *independent* criteria or values with which to guide the selection of its own future researchers.

(860,4) See Lévi-Strauss and Jakobson's article on Baudelaire's poem "Les chats," *L'Homme* II, 1 (1962): 5–21; in English, see "Charles Baudelaire's 'Les Chats,' " in *The Structuralists: From Marx to Lévi-Strauss* (Garden City: Doubleday, 1972), 124–46.

(861,1) An "index of refraction" or "refractive index" is the ratio of the velocity of light or other radiation in the first of two media to its velocity in the second, as it passes from the one to the other.

(861,6) See Seminar XI, *The Four Fundamental Concepts of Psychoanalysis*, edited by J.-A. Miller, translated by A. Sheridan (New York: W. W. Norton, 1978), 156 [corresponding to page 143 in the French edition], where it is translated as "interior eight."

(861,7) *En exclusion interne à son objet* (internally excluded from its object) can, it seems to me, be phrased in a number of different ways. Most generally, but cumbersomely: the subject is in a relation of internal exclusion with respect to its object; more precisely, the subject is excluded from within its object—that is, is both within its object and at the same time excluded therefrom. See Lacan's formulations in Seminar VII, *The Ethics of Psychoanalysis*, edited by J.-A. Miller and translated by Dennis Porter (New York: W. W. Norton, 1992), 122/101 and 167/139: "cet intérieur exclu qui . . . est ainsi exclu à l'intérieur" ["this excluded inside (or interior) which . . . is thus excluded from within"] and "cette extériorité intime, cette extimité" ["this intimate exteriority (or externality or outside), this 'extimacy'"].

(862,2) See *The Elementary Structures of Kinship*, 172, 173, 180, and 332.

(862,3) The reference here is to John Henry Newman; the book was published in 1870.

(863,1) In, for example, "The Freudian Thing," *Écrits* 1966, 435. See, too, 285–86.

(863,3) *Séparant axiomes et lois de groupement des symboles* (separating axioms and compounding laws from symbols) could, alternatively, be translated as "separating axioms from laws for grouping symbols."

(863,4) *Apprêt* (trappings) literally means finish (as in an antiskid finish on a floor) or dressing (for leather or fabric).

(863,6) Lacan is referring here to his opening lecture of Seminar XI, "Excommunication."

(864,2) *Se pourrait-il qu'il ne vous laisse pas tranquilles?* (could it be that it does not leave you in peace?) could also be translated as "could it be that it does not leave you alone?" *Qui avec lui ont le plus à faire* (who have the most to do with it) could, alternatively, read "who deal with it most." *Là où c'était, là comme sujet dois-je advenir* (Where it was, there must I come to be as a subject): the original German is found in *GW* XV, 86; in English see *SE* XXII, 80.

(864,3) Lacan may be suggesting that we take Freud's formulation, "Wo Es war, soll Ich werden," backward: "I must come to be (as a subject) where it/id was."

(864,4) See Jean Laplanche's contribution to the joint article with Serge Leclaire, "L'inconscient: une étude psychanalytique," in *L'inconscient, VIe Colloque de Bonneval* (Paris: Desclée de Brouwer, 1966), 95–130 and 170–77. See too Lacan's discussion in Seminar XI and in "Radiophonie" in *Scilicet* 2–3 (1970): 68–69. See Soren Kierkegaard's discussion of the plate Lacan mentions here in *The Concept of Irony*, translated by L. M. Capel (Bloomington: Indiana University Press, 1965), 56: "There is an engraving that portrays the grave of Napoleon. Two large trees overshadow the grave. There is nothing else to be seen in the picture, and the immediate spectator will see no more. Between these two trees, however, is an empty space, and as the eye traces out its contour Napoleon himself suddenly appears out of the nothingness, and now it is impossible to make him disappear. The eye that has once seen him now always sees him with anxious necessity."

(864,8) The perhaps unfamiliar ring to Descartes' phrase is due to the English translation of Descartes' *Philosophical Writings* by J. Cottingham (Cambridge: Cambridge University Press, 1986).

(865,2) Heidegger gives us this expression in *Being and Time*, for example, paragraphs 24, 46, and 211.

(865,3) *Sens* (meaning) also means direction, and Lacan may be referring to reading Freud's formulation, "Wo Es war, soll Ich werden," backward.

(865,6) *Chute* (scrap) might also be considered to have a religious connotation here, *la chute* being the fall (from grace). *Solidaire de* (bound up with) could also be translated as "one with" or even "consubstantial with."

(865,7) Angelus Silesius (otherwise known as Johannes Scheffler) was a German theologian and poet, known especially for *Der cherubinische Wandersmann* (1674), written in the form of distichs, that is, rhymed couplets; see the partial English translation: *Selections from the Cherubinic Wanderer*, translated and introduced by J. E. C. Flitch (London: Allen & Unwin, 1932).

(865,8) *Jaculation* (jaculatory prayers) could also be translated in this context as "ejaculatory prayers" or simply "ejaculations": "short prayers 'darted up' to God" (*OED*). The only reference I have been able to locate to Silesius in Seminar III is on page 361 where Lacan uses the words "ejaculatory speech" (*parole jaculatoire*); he refers to Silesius more directly in Seminar II, 160/131; his intended reference here, however, seems to be to Seminar I, 257–58/231–33, a seminar in which one finds a long discussion of narcissism and a few lines of one of Silesius' prayers.

(865,9) *Boiter* (to be a bit shaky) means both to limp (or wobble) and to be unsound, as in the case of a theory. The *joint* (junction) here seems to be that of God and the *ego* (referred to two paragraphs above); the latter two also seem to be the most likely referents of the "two sides" mentioned in the next paragraph.

(866,3) *Celle* (she) refers to the truth. See Saint-Just, *Oeuvres complètes*, 986: "Je méprise la poussière qui me compose et qui vous parle" ("I scorn the dust of which I am made and which speaks to you").

(866,4) See *Écrits* 1966, 409. *Innomable* (unnamable) also means unspeakably foul.

(867,3) *La gâche* (ruin) is an allusion to Daniel Lagache; "psychology's unity" is an allusion to the title of Lagache's book, *L'unité de la psychologie* (Paris: PUF, 1949). The French *chosifier, fi!, à qui se fier?* ('thingifying'—tush! who can you trust?) is quite playful.

(867,5) The someone here is Jean-Bertrand Pontalis.

(868,3) *Toutes les chutes que constitue le métalangage en ce qu'il a de faux-semblant, et de logique* (all the traps metalanguage, as sham and logic, falls into) is quite complex. *Chutes* (traps) could, alternatively, be understood as scraps, and thus the sentence could read "all the scraps metalanguage, as sham and logic, constitutes." On screaming stones, cf. *SE* III, 192.

(868,4) *Élargir* (release) can mean widen, enlarge, expand, stretch, discharge, or release. On stones that know how to scream, see, for example, *Écrits* 1966, 518.

(868,6) In French one commonly speaks of *un savoir* (literally, "a knowledge") and *des savoirs* (literally, "knowledges"), the sense ranging from some knowledge to a whole field or fields of knowledge.

(869,1) *La ferme* (has always kept its mouth

shut) also means closes it, and thus one could read it as closing or shutting truth in or off.

(869,2) *Causer* (causing) also means to chat, talk, or gab.

(869,4) See "The Three Sources and Three Component Parts of Marxism" (1913) in V. I. Lenin, *Collected Works,* vol. 19 (Moscow: Progress Publishers, 1960), p. 23.

(870,7) "The truth of pain is pain itself": as Jacques-Alain Miller indicated in his class ("From the Symptom to Fantasy and Back") on April 13, 1983, the reference here is to Michel Henry; see his *L'essence de la manifestation* (Paris: PUF, 1963).

(871,1) *Objurgations* (insistent prayers) could alternatively be translated as "objurgations"—harsh or violent reproofs.

(873,5) The *Filioque* is a doctrine according to which the Holy Ghost proceeds both from the Father and from the Son (in Latin, *Filioque* means and from the son).

(874,3) *Diaphragmatisation* (stopping down) indicates the closing of an aperture, like that of a camera.

(875,2) Freud introduced the term "successful paranoia."

(875,6) *Sans pouvoir être le signe à représenter le sexe étant du partenaire* (it is unable, however, to be the sign representing sex, the partner's sex) is quite ambiguous, devoid as it is of punctuation. *Le sexe* could be understood as the "fairer sex"; *le sexe étant du partenaire* could conceivably be construed as "the partner's existent sex"; and *étant du partenaire* could be rendered as "the partner's sign" (instead of "the partner's sex").

(876,5) The reference here is to 198a, lines 15–16, of Aristotle's *Physics*, translated in rather different ways by the various French and English translators, many of whom combine it with the sentence that immediately precedes it in the original. Wicksteed and Cornford, for example, give: "It is clear, then, that there are such things as causes, and that *they can be classified under the four heads that have been enumerated*" (the part in italics corresponding roughly to the Greek text cited). See Aristotle, *The Physics*, translated by P. H. Wicksteed and F. M. Cornford (London: Harvard University Press, 1929). A word seems to be missing from Lacan's quote, as in all of the versions of the Greek I consulted, the first word, Τοσαῦτα, is followed by γαρ.

(876,6) A polymer is a large *aggregate* molecule, that is, it is made up of several smaller molecules; "polymerizing" can thus be understood here in the sense of aggregating, or becoming an aggregate: the cause becomes a composite.

(877,1) Lacan seems to be deliberately distorting the name of the International Psychoanalytical Association, generally known in French as the *Association psychanalytique internationale*; Lacan's name for it here, *Internationale psychanalytique*, evokes the communist Internationals.

(877,7) *Pas* can mean both no (or not) and step; we might also read *pas-de-savoir* as "the no that makes for (or constitutes) knowledge," which might also be written "no-ledge."

(877,8) *Le point de vérité* (truth's site) means the point, place, or position of truth; "site of lack" in the next sentence corresponds to the French *ce point de manque*.

Notes to "A Spoken Commentary on Freud's 'Verneinung' by Jean Hyppolite"

(879,1) Interpolations in less than (<) and greater than (>) signs are Lacan's, whereas interpolations in square brackets are the translator's. The footnotes are Hyppolite's, unless otherwise indicated.

(879,4) In keeping with Strachey's translation of *Verneinung* in the *Standard Edition*, *dénégation* is translated here as "negation" (although it could arguably be better translated as "denial"), and *négation* is translated as "negation" followed by the French in brackets. *Dénier* means to refuse to recognize as one's own; it is the opposite of avow, confirm, and grant. Although Hyppolite admits that *dénégation* is a better translation than *négation* for *Verneinung*, he does not seem to consistently translate it as *dénégation*.

(879,5) Strachey translates "etwas im Urteil

verneinen" as "to negate something in a judgment" (*SE* XIX, 236).

(879,fn1) "I bring you the child of an Idumaean night!" is a line from Stéphane Mallarmé's "Don du poème" ("Gift of a Poem").

(879,fn3) The phrase "Made in Germany" appears in English in the original German (and in the French), highlighting the fact that the hallmark of repression is written in a foreign language. The requirement that German goods display a hallmark of origin (written in English) was imposed on the governments of Germany and Austria following World War I, and although the ruling was intended to facilitate discrimination against German goods, in fact it had the opposite effect, since goods bearing the stamp "Made in Germany" soon became sought after.

(880,3) This passage in quotes seems to be from one of Freud's other texts.

(880,8) Jean Hyppolite translated Hegel's *Phänomenologie des Geistes* (*Phenomenology of Spirit*) into French in 1941 and published a long study of Hegel's text in 1946, translated into English as *Genesis and Structure of Hegel's* Phenomenology of Spirit (Evanston, Ill.: Northwestern University Press, 1974).

(885,3) The term in the German text at this point is "Einbeziehung," earlier rendered as "attraction," whereas the earlier use of "*approprier*" was a rendering of "einführen"; *SE* renders both "Einbeziehung" and "einführen" as "take into."

(885,5) For this sentence, Strachey gives: "Affirmation—as a substitute for uniting—belongs to Eros; negation—the successor to expulsion—belongs to the instinct of destruction" (*SE* XIX, 239).

(886,7) In *une apparition de l'être sous la forme de ne l'être pas* (an appearance of being so in the guise of not being so), *l'être* could, alternatively, be understood as "being repressed" or even "being thought."

(886,fn3) This passage is not actually underlined in the German text, which reads as follows: "Die Leistung der Urteilsfunktion wird aber erst dadurch ermöglicht, dass die Schöpfung des Verneinungssymbols dem Denken einen ersten Grad von Unabhängigkeit von den Erfolgen der Verdrängung und somit auch vom Zwang des Lustprinzips gestattet hat" (*GW* XIV, 15; *Stud* III, 377). "But the performance of the function of judgment is not made possible until the creation of the symbol of negation has endowed thinking with a first measure of freedom from the consequences of repression and, with it, from the compulsion of the pleasure principle" (*SE* XIX, 239).

Notes to "Metaphor of the Subject"

(889,1) The title, *La Métaphore du Sujet*, could also be rendered, "The Metaphor That Is the Subject," "The Subject's Metaphor," or better still "The Subject as Metaphor."

(890,1) Note that Lacan modifies the usual order of the letters in this formulation, which, according to Aristotle and Perelman, is A/B and C/D or A:B::C:D. "Phoros" comes from the Greek *pherein*, meaning to carry or bear; according to Perelman, "theme" refers to the couple A/B, while "phoros" refers to the couple C/D.

(890,6) The expression by Berkeley may be found, for example, in *Berkeley's Philosophical Writings* (New York: Collier Books, 1974), 221; the French translation renders Berkeley's "learning" as "science."

(890,9) *La cathédrale engloutie* (The sunken cathedral) is the title of the Prelude for Piano, Book 1, Number 10 (1910), by Claude Debussy in which Debussy manages to make the piano sound very much like bells ringing. See *The New Grove Dictionary of Music and Musicians*, ed. Stanley Sadie (New York: Macmillan, 1980), Vol. 5, 306a. Someone with a strong French accent in English is likely to emphasize the second syllable in "learning," making a *ringing* sort of sound ('ning, 'ning).

(891,2) The Greek Lacan provides here has many meanings, among which the Doric for ἤπειρος, meaning terra firma, continent, or land; infinite or immense; inextricable or without issue; and ignorance of or lacking in experience of.

(891,5) *Injure* (insult) could also be understood as verbal abuse, but given the example Lacan has just provided, it seems clear that he is referring to the realm of swearing (inventing swear words) and insulting people.

(891,6) Perelman equates "ocean" with A and "learning" with C in the following schema:

$$\frac{A}{B}\ \frac{C}{D}$$

He suggests that B and D can be implicitly assumed to be any of the following pairs: swimmer, scholar; stream, truth; and terra firma, truth.

(891,8) See Lacan's discussion of *la paix du soir* in Seminar III, 156–57. I have been unable to find *jabraille* (jabbering) in any dictionary; it might, alternatively, refer to singsong.

(892,5) *Sulpicien* (Sulpician) qualifies the company of the priests of Saint Sulpice as well as the conventional, drab religious art sold in the Saint Sulpice quarter in Paris.

(892,7) Lacan often refers to Bertrand Russell on this point.

(892,8) See Mallarmé's poem, "Un coup de dés jamais n'abolira le hasard" (No roll of the dice will ever abolish chance). Cf. Lacan's later discussion of automatism and encounter (*automaton* and *tuché*) in Chapter 5 of Seminar XI.

Classified Index of the Major Concepts 893

The reader will find here an index that is intended to serve as a key.

This idea is consistent with a body of work that is devoted less to introducing than to calling into question, and is propitious for a reader who is assumed to come to it from a somewhat firm point.

If this point is from the outside, the key favors, as it should, this position by bringing an internal measure to it, in a topicality that can extend from the psychoanalytic revamping of the theory of the subject to preparing to go through an analysis of one's own, with chord markings in between for a few specialists.

If this point is from the inside—that is, from where psychoanalysis is applied—the mediation is then reversed, although one must nevertheless distinguish between those practitioners who attend my Seminar and those who abstain from doing so. This mediation will provide the former with a likely opportunity to gauge the degree to which my texts go beyond it, being already familiar, as they are, with the experience behind it. It will give the latter the chance to become concerned with it in theirs.

J. L.

Clarification

1. The reader will find in this index, prepared according to an order that I have established, the major concepts of Lacan's theory, keyed to the contexts here that provide their essential definitions, functions, and principal properties.
2. On the pages listed after each term in the index, it is the concept that must be looked for, not the word. I have chosen to designate what is subsumed by the expression that seemed to me most adequate and most comprehensive, usually proceeding retroactively from the latest stage of the theory.
3. It did not escape me that, with such an articulation, I was offering an interpretation. It thus seemed opportune to me to explain it briefly, so that one might, after following my reasoning, deduct it from the sum of the index.
4. I have opted to isolate the concepts which, touching on the theory of the subject, concern the human sciences as a whole, even if it denies them their name, with the effect of punctuating the specificity of analytic experience (in its Lacanian definition: the bringing into play of the reality of 894
the unconscious, the introduction of the subject to the language of his desire).

5. If the signifier is constitutive for the subject (I, A), we may follow, through its defiles, the process of transformation (mutilation) that makes a subject of man by means of narcissism (I, B). The properties of symbolic overdetermination explain why the logical time of this history is not linear (I, C).
6. We must next consider in their simultaneity the elements successively presented (II, A, B, C). We will note that the topology of the subject finds its status only by being related to the geometry of the ego (II, B, 4 and II, C, 3). Then we will be able to grasp the functioning of communication: all the pieces of the game fall into place in its structure (II, D).
7. From the structure of communication, we will deduce the power of the treatment, with what ear to listen to the unconscious, and what training to give analysts (III, A, B). The last part (III, C) is centered on the eminent signifier of desire. The following section (IV) is clinical (its inventory is succinct).
8. As for Lacanian epistemology, it marks, in my sense, psychoanalysis' position *in* the epistemological break, insofar as the subject foreclosed from science returns in the *impossible* of his discourse through the Freudian field. There is, therefore, but one ideology Lacan theorizes: that of the "modern ego," that is, the paranoiac subject of scientific civilization, whose imaginary is theorized by a warped psychology in the service of free enterprise.
9. The density of certain texts makes it pointless to break them down in the index. This includes the "Introduction to the Seminar on 'The Purloined Letter'" (the theory of the chain), "Kant with Sade" (desire and the Law, the structure of fantasy), "Subversion of the Subject and Dialectic of Desire" (the subject and the signifier), and "Position of the Unconscious" (desire and fantasy, alienation and splitting).
10. Let me add here that it is clear that Lacanian discourse is closed to enthusiasm, having recognized in what is known as its "openness" the progress of a systematization whose coherence was definitively established by the Rome Paper ["Function and Field"], and whose closure was assured. This is why, according to my conception of these *Écrits*, it is to our benefit to study them as forming a system, despite the elliptical style, necessary, Lacan says, to the training of analysts. For my own part, not needing to concern myself with the theory's efficacy in that field, I will encourage the reader by proposing that there is no outer limit (that is, not produced by the functioning of thought under the constraint of its structure) to the expansion of formalization in the field of discourse, in that there is no locus where its power fails whose circumference it cannot discern—and

eliminate the hole by changing syntax. We must be prepared to see its negative reform elsewhere. I am referring to Boole, to Carnap, and to Guéroult's studies on Berkeley.

Jacques-Alain Miller

[N.B.: Page numbers correspond to the French pagination in the margins. Italicized page numbers reference the most important passages.]

I. The Symbolic Order 895

A. The Supremacy of the Signifier

B. The Defiles of the Signifier

C. The Signifying Chain

897 *II. The Ego and the Subject*

A. The Body, The Ego, The Subject (The Organism, One's Own Body, The Fragmented Body)

B. The Function of the Ego

C. The Structure of the Subject

D. Intersubjective Communication

III. Desire and Its Interpretation

A. Unconscious Formations

B. Analytic Experience

C. The Phallus

IV. Clinical Practice

A. Freud's Cases

B. Psychiatry's Clinical Categories

V. Epistemology and Theory of Ideology

A. Epistemology

B. The Theory of Ideology

903 # Commentary on the Graphs

If it is true that perception eclipses structure, a schema will infallibly lead the subject "to forget, because of an intuitive image, the analysis on which this image is based" (*Écrits* 1966, 574).

It is the task of symbolism to prohibit imaginary capture—by which its difficulty follows from the theory.

While reading some clarifications about Lacan's schemas, this warning should not be forgotten.

The fact remains that such a precaution reveals the a priori lack of correspondence between a graphic representation and its object (the *object* of psychoanalysis) *in the space of intuition* (defined, if you will, by Kant's aesthetic). Thus all the constructions gathered together here (with the exception of the networks of overdetermination which function in the signifier's order) have only a didactic role: their relation to the structure is one of analogy.

On the other hand, *there is no longer any occultation of the symbolic* in the topology that Lacan establishes, because this space is the very space in which the subject's logical relations are schematized.

The inadequacy of analogies is unequivocally pointed out by Lacan in the optical model of the ideals of the person, precisely in the absence of the symbolic object *a*. From the note added to the **R** schema (*Écrits* 1966, 553–54), one may learn the rules by which to transform intuitive geometry into the topology of the subject.

J.–A. M.

I. The Schema of the Intersubjective Dialectic (“L Schema”; complete schema, 53; simplified schema, 548; representation of the schema by the L chain, 55) 904

The schema shows that the dyadic relation between the ego and its projection *a a′* (indifferently its image and that of the other) constitutes an obstacle to the advent of the subject, S, in the locus of its signifying determination, A. The quaternary is fundamental: “A quadripartite structure can always be required—from the standpoint of the unconscious—in the construction of a subjective ordering” (*Écrits* 1966, 774). Why? Because to restore the imaginary relation in the structure that stages it leads to a duplication of its terms: the other with a lowercase *o* [designated as *a* on the schema] being raised to the power of the Other with a capital *O* [designated as A on the schema], the cancellation of the subject of the signifying chain doubling the ego. Symmetry or reciprocity belongs to the imaginary register, and the position of the Third Party implies that of the fourth, who is given, depending on the levels of analysis, the name of “barred subject” or dummy (*mort*). (See 589, analytic bridge.)

II. The Optical Model of the Ideals of the Person (Figure 1, 673; Figure 2, 674; Figure 3, 680)

Figure 1: “The inverted bouquet illusion” in Bouasse’s work.

The illusion involves the production, by means of a spherical mirror, of a real image (which is inverted and symmetrical) of a hidden bouquet, which comes to be situated in the neck of a real vase, the latter functioning as a focal point.

This illusion retroactively receives its interpretation from the second figure (675–76): the real image, henceforth designated by *i(a)*, represents the subject’s specular image, whereas the real object *a* serves the function of the partial object, precipitating the formation of the body. We find here a phase that precedes (according to an order of logical dependence) the mirror stage—which presupposes the presence of the real Other (678).

Figure 2: A variation on the preceding figure.

In the second figure, the bouquet and the vase exchange roles, while a virtual image is produced through the localization of the observer within the spherical mirror and the introduction of the plane mirror A.

This construction must be interpreted as follows:

905 1. The reality of the vase and its real image *i(a)*, which are invisible to the observer (and absent from the representation), depict the reality of the body and its real image, which are inaccessible to the subject's perception.

2. The only image that is accessible to him is the virtual image *i'(a)* of the illusion, the imaginary reflection in which the development of his body in a definitive alienation is anticipated. Note that the real image and the virtual image are both in the imaginary register, but the second (a perception mediated by the subject's relation to the Other) redoubles the illusion of the first ("direct" perception—which is, as such, fictitious).

3. Lastly, it is the point I (the point of the ego-ideal where the unary trait must be situated) which commands the subject's image of himself (679).

Figure 3: A transformation of the preceding figure.

Figure 3 is obtained from the preceding figure by a 90-degree rotation of the plane mirror and a displacement of the subject to point I. Its objective is to represent the moment of the treatment in which the analyst (whose position is situated by the mirror), neutralizing himself as imaginary other, cancels out the mirage effects produced by the subject, and in which the latter overcomes the dyadic relation and empty speech to perceive his real image: he accedes to the language of his desire. The vanishing of the virtual image is interpreted as the dissolution of the narcissistic image which resituates the subject in the position he held in the first figure, except that he is only led back to it by the effacement of the plane mirror (thus by its mediation), and we must not neglect the residue of the operation: the new virtual image that reforms in the horizontal mirror, signaling that the direct perception is fictitious.

It is in this manner that a form of "psychoanalysis, which operates in the symbolic, [. . .] is able to reshape an ego that is [. . .] constituted in its imaginary status" (677).

The model, which provides the imaginary and real functions of object *a*, says nothing about its symbolic function (682).

III. The Structure of the Subject (The R Schema, 553; Schreber's Schema (I), 571; Sade's Schemas: Schema 1, 774, Schema 2, 778)

*1. Composition of the symbolic, the imaginary, and the real ("**R** Schema")*

The **R** schema is made up of the union of two triangles, the symbolic ternary and the imaginary ternary, by the quadrangle of the real, delimited in a square by the base of each triangle. If the triangle of the symbolic occupies half of the square all by itself, the other two figures sharing the other half, it 906
is because, in structuring them, it must overlap them in the drawing. The dotted line stands for the imaginary.

This construction requires a twofold reading:

1. It may be read as a representation of the statics of the subject. One can thus distinguish: (a) the triangle **I** resting on the dyadic relation between the Ego and the Other (narcissism, projection, capture), with, as its apex, φ, the phallus, the imaginary object, ìthe one where the subject is identified, on the contrary, with his living being" (552), that is, the form in which the subject represents himself to himself; (b) the field **S**, with the three functions of the Ego-ideal, I, in which the subject situates himself in the register of the symbolic (see the optical model), of the signifier of the object, M, of the Name-of-the-Father, P [for *père*], and in the locus of the Other, A. The line I M may be regarded as doubling the relation between the subject and the object of desire through the mediation of the signifying chain, a relation that Lacan's algebra later wrote as $\$\lozenge a$ (but the line immediately proves to be an inadequate representation); (c) the field **R**, framed and maintained by the imaginary relation and the symbolic relation.

2. But it is also the subject's history that is noted here: along the segment *i* M are situated the figures of the imaginary other, which culminate in the figure of the mother, the real Other, inscribed in the symbolic under the signifier of the primordial object, the subject's first outside, which bears in Freud's work the name *das Ding* (cf. *Écrits* 1966, 656); along the segment *m* I follow the imaginary identifications that form the child's ego until he receives his status

in the real from symbolic identification. One thus finds a specified synchrony of the ternary, **S**: the child in I is linked to the mother in M, as desire for her desire; in the tertiary position is the Father, conveyed by the mother's speech.

In his note added in 1966, Lacan shows how to translate this square into his topology. The surface **R** is to be taken as the flattening out of the figure that would be obtained by joining *i* to I and *m* to M, that is, by the twist that characterizes the Möbius strip in complete space: the presentation of the schema in two dimensions is thus related to the cut that spreads the strip out. This explains why the straight line I M cannot refer to the relation between the subject and the object of desire: the subject is merely the cut of the strip, and what falls from it is called object *a*. This verifies and complements Jean-Claude Milner's formulation regarding "$\$\Diamond a$": "the terms are heterogeneous, although there is homogeneity attached to the places" (*Cahiers pour l'analyse* 3 [1966]: 96). Therein lies the power of the symbol.

2. Schreber's schema
"Schema of the subject's structure at the end of the psychotic process."

This schema is a variation of the preceding one: the foreclosure of the Name-of-the-Father (here P_0), which leads to the absence of representation of the subject, S, by the phallic image (Φ_0 here), skews the relation among the three
907 fields: the divergence of the imaginary and the symbolic, the reduction of the real to the slippage between them.

The point *i* of the delusional ego is substituted for the subject, while the ego–ideal, I, takes the place of the Other. The trajectory S *a a*´A is transformed into the trajectory *i a a*´I.

3. Sade's schemas (1 and 2)
Schemas of the Sadean fantasy.

Four terms are involved: *a*, the object of desire in fantasy; $\$$, its correlate (according to $\$\Diamond a$), which is the fading* of the subject; S, the subject characterized as the "brute subject of pleasure," which we can say connotes the organism in the imaginary, from which the barred subject of the chain must be born; and finally V, the will as a will to jouissance, which is detached from pleasure just as the barred subject is detached from the real. Note that the division of the subject "does not have to be located in a single body" (778), since there is no homology between symbolic space and the space of intuition.

The transformation from the first to the second schema, which "is not translated [. . .] by any symmetrical reversal along an axis or around some central point" (778), merely expresses the displacement of the function of the cause, depending on the time of the Sadean fantasy.

IV. The Networks of Overdetermination
(The 1–3 Network, 48; the A Δ Distribution, 49; Tables Ω and O, 50; representation of the 1–3 Network, 56; α, β, γ, δ Network, 57)

The progressive construction of the networks brings out certain properties of overdetermination:

1. The 1–3 Network: the emergence of simple anticipation by a network of dissymmetrical distribution, in which memory appears as the elementary law of repetition (see the related, pseudo-symmetrical graph).

2. The A Δ Distribution and Tables: the emergence, by means of a second dissymmetrical distribution, of a complex form of anticipation completed by retroaction.

3. Representation of the 1–3 Network: transformation of the preceding network into the α, β, γ, δ Network.

V. The Graphs of Desire
(Graph 1, 805; Graph 2, 808; Graph 3, 815; Graph 4, 817)

On Graph 1, one may read the inversion that constitutes the subject in his
traversing of the signifying chain. This inversion takes place by *anticipation*, 908
whose law imposes at the first intersection (on the vector $\overrightarrow{S.S'}$) the last word (also to be understood as the solution [*fin mot*], that is, punctuation), and *retroaction*, enunciated in the formulation of intersubjective communication, which necessitates a second intersection, in which the receiver and his battery are to be situated. Graph 2 combines, starting from the elementary cell, imaginary identification and symbolic identification in subjective synchrony; the signifying chain here receives its specification as speech. It becomes the vector of the drive, between desire and fantasy, in the complete graph—the intermediary graph simply punctuating the subject's question to the Other: "What does he want from me?" which is to be inverted in its return, "What do you want from me?"

917 # Bibliographical References in Chronological Order

The Mirror Stage

An early version of this paper was delivered at the Fourteenth International Congress of Psychoanalysis in Marienbad on August 2–8, 1936, with Ernest Jones presiding. It was part of the second scientific session held on August 3 at 3:40 P.M., and was listed under the title "The Looking-glass Phase" in *IJP* XVIII, 1 (1937): 78.

Beyond the "Reality Principle"

This text was written in Marienbad and Noirmoutier between August and October 1936. It was published in a special issue on Freudian studies of *Évolution Psychiatrique* 3 (1936): 67–86.

Logical Time and the Assertion of Anticipated Certainty

This paper was written in March 1945 and published in a special issue, entitled *1940–1944*, of *Les Cahiers d'Art* (1945): 32–42.

Aggressiveness in Psychoanalysis

This theoretical paper was presented in Brussels in mid-May 1948 at the Eleventh Congress of French-Speaking Psychoanalysts. It was published in *Revue Française de Psychanalyse* XII, 2 (1948): 367–88.

The Mirror Stage as Formative of the I *Function,*
as Revealed in Psychoanalytic Experience

The present version of this paper was delivered on July 17, 1949, in Zurich at the Sixteenth International Congress of Psychoanalysis, and was published in *Revue Française de Psychanalyse* XIII, 4 (1949): 449–55.

A Theoretical Introduction to the Functions of Psychoanalysis in Criminology

This paper was written in collaboration with Michel Cénac and presented at the Thirteenth Conference of French-Speaking Psychoanalysts (May 29, 1950). It was first published in *Revue Française de Psychanalyse* XV, 1 (1951): 7–29.

Presentation on Psychical Causality

This presentation was given on September 28, 1946, at the psychiatric conference held in Bonneval. It was published in [*Évolution Psychiatrique* XII, 1 (1947): 123–65, and in] a volume entitled *Le Problème de la psychogenèse des névroses et des psychoses* ("The Problem of the Psychogenesis of the Neuroses and Psychoses"), by Lucien Bonnafé, Henri Ey, Sven Follin, Jacques Lacan, and Julien Rouart (Paris: Desclée de Brouwer, 1950), 23–54.

Presentation on Transference 918

This paper was given at the 1951 Congress of "Romance Language-Speaking Psychoanalysts." It was published in *Revue Française de Psychanalyse* XVI, 1–2 (1952): 154–63.

The Function and Field of Speech and Language in Psychoanalysis

This paper was presented at the Rome Congress held September 26–27, 1953, at the Institute of Psychology at the University of Rome. It was published in *La Psychanalyse* I (1956): 81–166.

Introduction to Jean Hyppolite's Commentary on Freud's "Verneinung"
Response to Jean Hyppolite's Commentary on Freud's "Verneinung"

This is the text of a class of my seminar on Freudian Technique held February 10, 1954, at the medical school clinic at Saint Anne Hospital. The seminar was devoted, during the 1953–1954 school year, to Freud's writings on technique; the text of this class came out in *La Psychanalyse* I (1956): 17–28 and 41–49.

Variations on the Standard Treatment

This paper was written during Easter vacation of 1955. It was published in the 1955 edition of the *Encyclopédie médico-chirurgicale*, vol. III (insert 37812-C10), and was not included in later editions.

Seminar on "The Purloined Letter"

This presentation was given on April 26, 1955. It was written up (and dated as having been completed in Guitrancourt and San Casciano) between mid-May and mid-August 1956. It was published in *La Psychanalyse* II (1957): 1–44.

The Freudian Thing, or the Meaning of the Return to Freud in Psychoanalysis

This is an expanded version of a lecture given at the Vienna Neuropsychiatric Clinic on November 7, 1955. It came out in *Évolution Psychiatrique* XXI, 1 (1956): 225–52.

The Situation of Psychoanalysis and the Training of Psychoanalysts in 1956

The second version of this paper was published in a special issue of *Les Études Philosophiques* (1956) commemorating the hundred year anniversary of Freud's birth. The first version only came out as an offprint.

Psychoanalysis and Its Teaching

This talk was given at the French Philosophical Society on February 23, 1957. It came out in the *Bulletin de la Société Française de Philosophie* XLIX (1957): 65–85.

The Instance of the Letter in the Unconscious, or Reason Since Freud

This is the text of a lecture given on May 9, 1957, in the Descartes Amphitheater at the Sorbonne, at the request of the philosophy group of the Fédération des étudiants ès Lettres. The lecture was written up May 14–16, 1957, and published in *La Psychanalyse* III (1957): 47–81, the theme of the volume being "Psychoanalysis and the Sciences of Man."

919 *On a Question Prior to Any Possible Treatment of Psychosis*

This article contains the most important material from the first two terms of my 1955–1956 seminar, *The Psychoses*. It was written up in December 1957 and January 1958, and came out in *La Psychanalyse* IV (1959): 1–50.

The Youth of Gide, or the Letter and Desire

This article was published in *Critique* CXXXI (1958): 291–315.

The Signification of the Phallus (Die Bedeutung des Phallus)

This lecture was given in German on May 9, 1958, at the Max Planck Society in Munich, at the invitation of Professor Paul Matussek.

The Direction of the Treatment and the Principles of Its Power

This is the first of two papers I presented at the Royaumont International Colloquium held July 10–13, 1958, at the invitation of the Société Française de Psychanalyse. It was published in *La Psychanalyse* VI (1961): 149–206.

Remarks on Daniel Lagache's Presentation:
"Psychoanalysis and Personality Structure"

This is the second paper I presented at the Royaumont Colloquium held July 10–13, 1958. Final redaction: Easter vacation 1960. Published in *La Psychanalyse* VI (1961): 111–147.

In Memory of Ernest Jones: On His Theory of Symbolism

This essay was written in Guitrancourt, January to March 1959, and was published in *La Psychanalyse* V (1960): 1–20.

Guiding Remarks for a Convention on Female Sexuality

This paper was given at the International Colloquium of Psychoanalysis held September 5–9, 1960, at the city university of Amsterdam. It was written two years before the colloquium and published in *La Psychanalyse* VII (1962): 3–14.

The Subversion of the Subject and the Dialectic of Desire
in the Freudian Unconscious

This was my contribution to a conference on "La Dialectique" held in Royaumont September 19–23, 1960, at the invitation of Jean Wahl. The conference was organized by the "Colloques philosophiques internationaux."

Position of the Unconscious

This paper summarizes the remarks I made at the Colloquium held October 30 to November 2, 1960, at Bonneval Hospital. They were condensed in March 1964 at Henri Ey's request for his collection of the talks given at the colloquium, published as *L'inconscient* (Paris: Desclée de Brouwer, 1966).

Kant with Sade 920

This essay was to have served as a preface to *Philosophy in the Bedroom* (in the 15-volume edition of Sade's work published by Éditions du Cercle du livre précieux in 1963). It was written in R.G. in 1962 and published in *Critique* CXCI (1963): 291–313.

On Freud's "Trieb" and the Psychoanalyst's Desire

This is a summary of the comments I made at a colloquium on "Technique and Casuistry" that was organized by Professor Enrico Castelli at the University of Rome on January 7–12, 1964. It was published in *Tecnica e Casistica: Tecnica, Escatologia e Casistica* (Rome: Instituto di Studi Filosofici, 1964).

Science and Truth

This is the typescript of the opening class (held on December 1, 1965) of the seminar I gave during the 1965–1966 school year at the École Normale Supérieure (in the rue d'Ulm) on *The Object of Psychoanalysis*, as a lecturer for the École Pratique des Hautes Études (Section 6). It came out in the first issue of *Cahiers Pour l'Analyse*, published by the "Epistemology Circle" at the École Normale Supérieure, in January of 1966.

Metaphor of the Subject

This is the text, rewritten in June 1961, of remarks I made on June 23, 1960, in response to a talk by Chaim Perelman, in which he invoked "the idea of rationality and the rule of law" before the French Philosophical Society.

Index of Freud's German Terms

[N.B.: Page numbers correspond to the French pagination in the margins.]

I am including here an index of Freud's terms that are cited in German in this collection. Their meaning is given in the text, when I am not commenting on their meaning or in fact discussing how the term or phrase should be translated. Providing their pages numbers may be useful to those who would like to find them anew after reading the text.

Index of Proper Names

[N.B.: Page numbers correspond to the French pagination in the margins. Freud is not included here since he is mentioned on virtually every page.]